READINGS IN
Hardware/Software Co-Design

The Morgan Kaufmann
Series in Systems on Silicon

SERIES EDITORS:

PETER J. ASHENDEN
Ashenden Designs Pty, Ltd.
University of Adelaide

WAYNE WOLF
Princeton University

The rapid growth of silicon technology and the demands of applications are increasingly forcing electronics designers to take a systems-oriented approach to design. This has lead to new challenges in design methodology, design automation, manufacturing, and testing. The main challenges are to enhance designer productivity and to achieve correctness on the first pass. The Morgan Kaufmann Series in Systems on Silicon presents high-quality, peer-reviewed books authored by leading experts in the field who are uniquely qualified to address these issues.

UPCOMING TITLES INCLUDE

The Designer's Guide to VHDL, 2nd Edition
Peter J. Ashenden

**The System Designer's Guide to VHDL-AMS:
Analog, Mixed-Signal and Mixed-Technology Modeling**
Peter J. Ashenden
Gregory D. Peterson
Darrell A. Teegarden

Rosetta User's Guide: Model-Based Systems Design
Perry Alexander, Peter J. Ashenden, David L. Barton

Rosetta Developer's Guide: Semantics for Systems Design
Perry Alexander
Peter J. Ashenden
David L. Barton

READINGS IN
Hardware/Software Co-Design

Giovanni De Micheli
Stanford University

Rolf Ernst
Technical University of Braunschweig

Wayne Wolf
Princeton University

MORGAN KAUFMANN PUBLISHERS
AN IMPRINT OF ACADEMIC PRESS
A Harcourt Science and Technology Company
SAN FRANCISCO   SAN DIEGO   NEW YORK   BOSTON
LONDON   SYDNEY   TOKYO

Senior Editor Denise E. M. Pendrose
Publishing Services Manager Scott Norton
Assistant Development Editor Marilyn Alan
Production Coordinator Mei Levenson
Editorial Assistant Courtney Garnaas
Series Art Direction, Cover Design, and Photography Chen Design Associates, SF
Text Design and Composition Susan M. Sheldrake, ShelDragon Graphic Design
Copyeditor Erin Milnes
Proofreader Mei Levenson
Printer Victor Graphics

Designations used by companies to distinguish their products are often claimed as trademarks or registered trademarks. In all instances in which Morgan Kaufmann Publishers is aware of a claim, the product names appear in initial capital or all capital letters. Readers, however, should contact the appropriate companies for more complete information regarding trademarks and registration.

Morgan Kaufmann Publishers
340 Pine Street, Sixth Floor, San Francisco, CA 94104-3205, USA

ACADEMIC PRESS
A Harcourt Science and Technology Company
525 B Street, Suite 1900, San Diego, CA 92101-4495, USA
http://www.academicpress.com

Academic Press
Harcourt Place, 32 Jamestown Road, London, NW1 7BY, United Kingdom
http://www.academicpress.com

© 2002 by Academic Press
All rights reserved
Printed in the United States of America

05 04 03 02 01   5 4 3 2 1

No part of this publication may be reproduced, stored in a retrieval system, or transmitted in any form, by any means—electronic, mechanical, photocopying, or otherwise—without the prior written permission of the publisher.

Library of Congress Cataloging-in-Publication Data

De Micheli, Giovanni.
    Readings in hardware/software co-design / Giovanni De Micheli, Rolf Ernst, Wayne Wolf.
      p. cm.
    Includes bibliographical references and index.
    ISBN 1-55860-702-1
    1. Embedded computer systems. 2. Microprocessors. 3. Computer software. I. Ernst, Rolf. II. Wolf, Wayne Hendrix. III. Title
TK7895.E42 D46 2001
004.16—dc21   2001029289

This book is printed on acid-free paper.

CONTENTS

PREFACE ix

ACKNOWLEDGMENTS xi

CHAPTER 1: **Introduction** 1

Hardware-Software Cosynthesis for Digital Systems 5
R. K. Gupta and G. De Micheli

Hardware-Software Cosynthesis for Microcontrollers 18
R. Ernst, J. Henkel, and T. Benner

Hardware-Software Co-Design 30
G. De Micheli and R. K. Gupta

Codesign of Embedded Systems: Status and Trends 45
R. Ernst

CHAPTER 2: **Modeling** 55

Dataflow Process Networks 59
E. A. Lee and T. M. Parks

Design of Embedded Systems: Formal Models, Validation, and Synthesis 86
S. Edwards, L. Lavagno, E. A. Lee, and A. Sangiovanni-Vincentelli

SpecSyn: An Environment Supporting the Specify-Explore-Refine Paradigm for
Hardware/Software System Design 108
D. D. Gajski, F. Vahid, S. Narayan, and J. Gong

VHDL Generation from SDL Specifications 125
J.-M. Daveau, G. Fernandes Marchioro, C. Alberto Valderrama, and A. Amine Jerraya

STATEMATE: A Working Environment for the Development of
Complex Reactive Systems 135
*D. Harel, H. Lachover, A. Naamad, A. Pnyeli, M. Politi, R. Sherman,
A. Shtull-Trauring, and M. Trakhtenbrot*

The Synchronous Approach to Reactive and Real-Time Systems 147
A. Benveniste and G. Berry

CHAPTER 3: **Analysis and Estimation** 161

Performance Estimation of Embedded Software with Instruction Cache Modeling 167
Y.-T. S. Li, S. Malik, and A. Wolfe

Scheduling Algorithms for Multiprogramming in a Hard-Real-Time Environment 179
C. L. Liu and J. W. Layland

Performance Estimation for Real-Time Distributed Embedded Systems .195
    T.-Y. Yen and W. Wolf

Rate Analysis for Embedded Systems 207
    A. Mathur, A. Dasdan, and R. K. Gupta

Power Analysis of Embedded Software: A First Step Towards Software Power Minimization . . .222
    V. Tiwari, S. Malik, and A. Wolfe

A Survey of Design Techniques for System-Level Dynamic Power Management 231
    L. Benini, A. Bogliolo, and G. De Micheli

Power Estimation of Embedded Systems: A Hardware/Software Codesign Approach 249
    W. Fornaciari, P. Gubian, D. Sciuto, and C. Silvano

A Framework for Estimating and Minimizing Energy Dissipation of
Embedded HW/SW Systems 259
    Y. Li and J. Henkel

Hardware/Software Co-Synthesis with Memory Hierarchies 265
    Y. Li and W. Wolf

System Level Memory Optimization for Hardware-Software Co-design 278
    K. Danckaert, F. Catthoor, and H. De Man

A Path-Based Technique for Estimating Hardware Runtime in HW/SW-Cosynthesis 283
    J. Henkel and R. Ernst

CHAPTER 4: System-Level Partitioning, Synthesis, and Interfacing 289

The Extended Partitioning Problem: Hardware/Software Mapping, Scheduling, and
Implementation-bin Selection 293
    A. Kalavade and E. A. Lee

Hardware-Software Codesign of Embedded Systems 313
    M. Chiodo, P. Giusto, A. Jurecska, H. C. Hsieh, A. Sangiovanni-Vincentelli,
    and L. Lavagno

SOS: Synthesis of Application-Specific Heterogeneous Multiprocessor Systems 324
    S. Prakash and A. C. Parker

An Architectural Co-Synthesis Algorithm for Distributed, Embedded Computing Systems 338
    W. Wolf

Control Generation for Embedded Systems on Composition of Modal Processes 350
    P. Chou, K. Hines, K. Partridge, and G. Borriello

Interface Co-Synthesis Techniques for Embedded Systems 358
    P. Chou, R. B. Ortega, and G. Borriello

Protocol Selection and Interface Generation for HW-SW Codesign 366
    J.-M. Daveau, G. Fernandes Marchioro, T. Ben-Ismail, and A. Amine Jerraya

Clairvoyant: A Synthesis System for Production-Based Specification 375
    A. Seawright and F. Brewer

Real-Time Multi-Tasking in Software Synthesis for Information Processing Systems 389
    F. Thoen, M. Cornero, G. Goossens, and H. De Man

Co-Synthesis and Co-Simulation of Control-Dominated Embedded Systems 395
    A. Balboni, W. Fornaciari, and D. Sciuto

CoWare—A Design Environment for Heterogeneous Hardware/Software Systems 412
    D. Verkest, K. Van Rompaey, I. Bolsens, and H. De Man

CHAPTER 5: Implementation Generation   427

Embedded Software in Real-Time Signal Processing Systems: Design Technologies 433
    G. Goossens, J. Van Praet, D. Lanneer, W. Geurts, A. Kifli, C. Liem, and P. G. Paulin

Generating Compact Code from Dataflow Specifications of Multirate
Signal Processing Algorithms 452
    S. S. Bhattacharyya, J. T. Buck, S. Ha, and E. A. Lee

Memory Management for Embedded Network Applications 465
    S. Wuytack, J. L. da Silva, Jr., F. Catthoor, G. de Jong, and C. Ykman-Couvreur

Lower Bound on Latency for VLIW ASIP Datapaths 477
    M. F. Jacome and G. de Veciana

Constraint Analysis for DSP Code Generation 485
    B. Mesman, A. H. Timmer, J. L. van Meerbergen, and J. A. G. Jess

Instruction Selection Using Binate Covering for Code Size Optimization 499
    S. Liao, S. Devadas, K. Keutzer, and S. Tijang

A Retargetable Compilation Methodology for Embedded Digital Signal Processors
Using a Machine-Dependent Code Optimization Library 506
    A. Sudarsanam, S. Malik, and M. Fujita

Incremental Hardware Estimation During Hardware/Software Functional Partitioning 516
    F. Vahid and D. D. Gajski

CHAPTER 6: Co-Simulation and Emulation   523

Ptolemy: A Framework for Simulating and Prototyping Heterogeneous Systems 527
    J. Buck, S. Ha, E. A. Lee, and D. G. Messerschmitt

Synthesis and Simulation of Digital Systems Containing Interacting
Hardware and Software Components 544
    R. K. Gupta, C. N. Coelho, Jr., and G. De Micheli

An Engineering Environment for Hardware/Software Co-simulation 550
    D. Becker, R. K. Singh, and S. G. Tell

A Hardware-Software Codesign Methodology for DSP Applications 556
    A. Kalavade and E. A. Lee

A Hardware-Software Co-simulator for Embedded System Design and Debugging 569
    A. Ghosh, M. Bershteyn, R. Casley, C. Chien, A. Jain, M. Lipsie, D. Tarrodaychik, and O. Yamamoto

A Unified Model for Co-simulation and Co-synthesis of Mixed Hardware/Software Systems . . .579
    C. A. Valderrama, A. Changuel, P. V. Raghavan, M. Abid, T. Ben Ismail, and A. A. Jerraya

Compiled HW/SW Co-simulation 584
    V. Živojnović and H. Meyr

Hardware-Software Prototyping from LOTOS 590
   L. Sánchez Fernández, Gernot Koch, N. Martínez Madrid, M. L. Lopéz Vallejo,
   C. Delgado Kloos, and W. Rosenstiel

CHAPTER 7: **Reconfigurable Computing Platforms** 607

Programmable Active Memories: Reconfigurable Systems Come of Age 611
   J. Vuillemin, P. Bertin, D. Roncin, M. Shand, H. H. Touati, and P. Boucard

Logic Emulation with Virtual Wires 625
   J. Babb, R. Tessier, M. Dahl, S. Zimi Hanono, D. M. Hoki, and A. Agarwal

Embryonics: A New Methodology for Designing Field-Programmable
Gate Arrays with Self-Repair and Self-Replicating Properties 643
   D. Mange, E. Sanchez, A. Stauffer, G. Tempesti, P. Marchal, and C. Piguet

CHAPTER 8: **Case Studies** 657

Electronic and Firmware Design of the HP DesignJet Drafting Plotter 661
   A. H. Mebane IV, J. R. Schmedake, I.-S. Chen, and A. P. Kadonaga

Design and Implementation of a Robot Control System Using a Unified
Hardware-Software Rapid-Prototyping Framework 669
   M. B. Srivastava, T. I. Blumenau, and R. W. Brodersen

The Infopad Multimedia Terminal: A Portable Device for Wireless Information Access 673
   T. E. Truman, T. Pering, R. Doering, and R. W. Brodersen

A Processor-Coprocessor Architecture for High End Video Applications 688
   E. Maas, D. Hermann, R. Ernst, P. Rüffer, S. Hasenzahl, and M. Seitz

AUTHOR INDEX   693

SUBJECT INDEX   695

ABOUT THE AUTHORS   697

PREFACE

The explosion in demand for devices powered by embedded computing systems in the 1990s created the impetus for a new field in computer engineering—hardware/software co-design. This field considers the design of embedded computing systems that include programmable CPUs, as well as other types of hardware units. Some of the functionality will be implemented as software running on the embedded CPUs; while other functions may be implemented in hardwired or reconfigurable logic. Hardware/software co-design explicitly considers the trade-offs between implementation technologies and the interactions between components of various types.

An *embedded computing system*, often called simply an *embedded system*, is any device that uses a programmable CPU to implement part of its functionality but is not a general-purpose computer. A driving force in the adoption of embedded computing has been the desire to implement complex functions that are too hard or expensive to build in hardwired logic, mechanical linkages, or other traditional means. In automobiles, for example, microprocessors have allowed much more sophisticated control algorithms to be used in engines to provide lower emissions and better gas mileage. In printers, microprocessors have made it possible to print complex page designs.

Historically, the early 4-bit and 8-bit microprocessors of the 1970s could do little more than perform simple control functions for I/O devices. By the mid-1980s, sophisticated 16-bit and 32-bit microprocessors appeared on the market allowing system designers to build much more complex functionality into systems. Such complex devices were cheap enough that they could be considered for use in a variety of applications.

However, as powerful microprocessors came into use, it became increasingly clear that the design methods used for 8-bit microprocessor–based systems of the 1970s did not scale well to more complex systems using larger microprocessors. Projects that put tens of thousands of lines of code onto an embedded processor resembled in some respects traditional, mainframe-based software development projects. But embedded systems often also had to meet real-time performance requirements and stringent constraints on total system cost. The hand-crafted techniques used for small microprocessors couldn't handle the system complexity. Traditional software development models didn't sufficiently take into account the interdependencies between hardware and software design when creating an embedded system.

As a result, a variety of groups started to think about new techniques and methodologies for joint hardware and software design of embedded computing systems. Of course, good designers had long considered the design of hardware and software together. Today, the term *hardware/software co-design* has become much more specific and generally conveys the tool-based design of hardware/software systems.

This book is intended to serve as an introduction to this discipline by collecting the most important papers on this topic and organizing them in a way that emphasizes its basic principles. The field, while still young and extremely active, has matured enough for these basic principles to become apparent. A collection of key papers in the area can be helpful to several audiences, including practicing engineers who wish to quickly gain a basic understanding of the field, graduate students and engineers who are just entering the field and who wish to learn essential lessons from the top researchers and designers who created the field, and experienced designers who will appreciate a reference that contains all the important papers in a single volume.

This book should be particularly helpful to researchers and designers of embedded systems-on-silicon because their work will necessarily build on many of the principles that underlie hardware/software co-design. Although hardware/software co-design is important for board-level design, it is essential for VLSI implementation. The size and complexity of systems-on-silicon that include hundreds of millions of transistors demands the use of embedded processors. Changes are very costly in both time and money for systems-on-silicon, and it is important that the system designers select the right architecture from the start.

We have created a companion website for this book

at *http://www.ee.princeton.edu/~wolf/embedded-readings*. This site includes a list of additional important papers in the field. We will update this site at least once a year to include what we believe are the most significant recent contributions to the field.

We hope this collection is of use to you, the reader. We'd like to hear your comments on the book and the website.

Giovanni De Micheli, Stanford
Rolf Ernst, Braunschweig
Wayne Wolf, Princeton

RESOURCES

The principal conferences and workshops that publish papers in hardware/software co-design are:
- Design Automation Conference (DAC)
- International Conference on Computer-Aided Design (ICCAD)
- Design Automation and Test in Europe (DATE)
- Asia-South Pacific Design Automation Conference (ASP-DAC)
- International Workshop on Hardware/Software Co-Design (CODES)
- IEEEE International Symposium on System-Level Synthesis (ISSS)

Refereed journals and magazines that publish articles on hardware/software co-design computing include
- *IEEE Transactions on Computer-Aided Design of Integrated Circuits and Systems*
- *ACM Transactions on Design Automation of Electronic Systems*
- *Design Automation of Embedded Systems*
- *IEEE Computer*
- *IEEE Micro*
- *IEEE Design & Test of Computers*

INTRODUCTORY REFERENCES

[Pro97] *Proceedings of the IEEE* 85, no. 3 (March 1997). *This special issue is devoted to hardware/software co-design. The article by De Micheli and Gupta reproduced in this book opens the issue.*

[Wol94] W. H. Wolf, "Hardware-software co-design of embedded systems," *Proceedings of the IEEE* 82, no. 7 (July, 1994): 967–989. *This early survey article surveys the major problems in co-design.*

ACKNOWLEDGMENTS

We wish to thank the many people who have contributed ideas, comments, and criticism to this collection, especially Jason Cong, UCLA; Raul Camposano, Synopsys; Rajesh Gupta, UC Irvine; Randy Harr, Synopsys; Martyn Edwards, University of Manchester; Margarida F. Jacome, University of Texas-Austin; Ahmed Amine Jerraya, TIMA Laboratory; Luciano Lavagno, Politecnico di Torino; and Frank Vahid, UC Riverside.

We also thank the following publishers for permission to reprint the articles found in this book:

Chapter 1: Introduction

[Gup93] R. K. Gupta and G. De Micheli, "Hardware-software cosynthesis for digital systems." Copyright © 1993 IEEE. Reprinted with permission from *IEEE Design & Test of Computers* 10, no. 3 (Sept. 1993): 29–41.

[Ern93] R. Ernst, J. Henkel, and T. Benner, "Hardware-software cosynthesis for microcontrollers." Copyright © 1993 IEEE. Reprinted with permission from *IEEE Design & Test of Computers* 10, no. 4 (Dec. 1993): 64–75.

[DeM97] G. De Micheli and R. K. Gupta, "Hardware-software co-design." Copyright © 1997 IEEE. Reprinted with permission from Proceedings of the *IEEE* 85, no. 3, (March 1997): 349–65.

[Ern98] R. Ernst, "Codesign of embedded systems: Status and trends." Copyright © 1998 IEEE. Reprinted with permission from *IEEE Design and Test of Computers* 15, no. 2 (April–June 1998): 45–54.

Chapter 2: Modeling

[Lee95] E. A. Lee and T. M. Parks, "Dataflow process networks." Copyright © 1995 IEEE. Reprinted with permission from Proceedings of the *IEEE* 83, no. 5 (May 1995): 773–99.

[Edw97] S. Edwards, L. Lavagno, E. A. Lee, and A. Sangiovanni-Vincentelli, "Design of embedded systems: formal models, validation, and synthesis." Copyright © 1997 IEEE. Reprinted with permission from Proceedings of the *IEEE* 85, no.3 (March 1997): 366–90.

[Gaj98] D. D. Gajski, F. Vahid, S. Narayan, and J. Gong, "SpecSyn: An environment supporting the specify-explore-refine paradigm for hardware/software system design." Copyright © 1998 IEEE. Reprinted with permission from *IEEE Transactions on VLSI Systems* 6, no. 1 (1998): 84–100.

[Dav96] J.- M. Daveau, G. Frenandes Marchioro, C. Alberto Valderrama, and A. A. Jerraya, "VHDL Generation from SDL Specifications." XIII IFIP Conference on CHDL, Toledo, Spain, April 20–25, 1997. Published in Carlos Delgado Kloos and Eduard Cerny, eds., *Hardware Description Languages and Their Applications, Specification, Modelling, Verification, and Synthesis of Microelectronic Systems*, Chapman & Hall, Dordrecht, 1997, 1–20. Copyright © IFIP 1996.

[Har90] D. Harel, H. Lachover, A. Naamad, A. Pnueli, M. Politi, R. Sherman, A. Shtull-Trauring, and M. Trakhtenbrot, "STATEMATE: A working environment for the development of complex reactive systems." Copyright © 1990 IEEE. Reprinted with permission from *IEEE Transactions on Software Engineering* 16, no. 4 (April 1990): 403–14.

[Ben91] A. Benveniste and G. Berry, "The synchronous approach to reactive real-time systems." Copyright © 1991 IEEE. Reprinted with permission from Proceedings of the *IEEE* 79, no. 9 (Sept. 1991): 1270–82.

Chapter 3: Analysis and Estimation

[Li99a] Y.-T. S. Li, S. Malik, and A. Wolfe, "Performance estimation of embedded software with instruction cache modeling," *ACM Transactions on Design Automation of Electronic Systems* 4, no. 3 (July 1999): 257–79. Copyright © 1999, Association for Computing Machinery, Inc.

[Liu73] C. L. Liu and J. W. Layland, "Scheduling algorithms for multiprogramming in a hard-real-time environment," *Journal of the ACM* 20, no. 1 (Jan. 1973): 46–61. Copyright © 1973, Association for Computing Machinery, Inc.

[Yen98] T.-Y. Yen and W. Wolf, "Performance estimation for real-time distributed embedded systems." Copyright © 1998 IEEE. Reprinted with permission from *IEEE Transactions on Parallel and Distributed Systems* 9, no. 11 (Nov. 1998): 1125–36.

[Mat98] A. Mathur, A. Dasdan, and R. K. Gupta, "Rate analysis for embedded systems," *ACM Transactions on Design Automation of Electronic Systems* 3, no. 3 (July 1998): 408–36. Copyright © 1998, Association for Computing Machinery, Inc.

[Tiw94] V. Tiwari, S. Malik, and A. Wolfe, "Power analysis of embedded software: A first step towards software power minimization." Copyright © 1994 IEEE. Reprinted with permission from *IEEE Transactions on VLSI Systems* 2, no.4 (Dec. 1994): 437–45.

[Ben00] L. Benini, A. Bogliolo, and G. De Micheli, "A survey of design techniques for system-level dynamic power management." Copyright © 2000 IEEE. Reprinted with permission from *IEEE Transactions on VLSI Systems* 8, no. 3 (June 2000): 299–316.

[For98] W. Fornaciari, P. Gubian, D. Sciuto, and C. Silvano, "Power estimation of embedded systems: A hardware/software codesign approach." Copyright © 1998 IEEE. Reprinted with permission from *IEEE Transactions on VLSI Systems* 6, no. 2 (June 1998): 266–75.

[Li98] Y. Li and J. Henkel, "A framework for estimating and minimizing energy dissipation of embedded HW/SW systems," in *Proceedings, 35th Design Automation Conference*, ACM Press, New York, 1998, 188–94. Copyright © 1998, Association for Computing Machinery, Inc.

[Li99c] Y. Li and W. Wolf, "Hardware/software co-synthesis with memory hierarchies." Copyright © 1999 IEEE. Reprinted with permission from *IEEE Transactions on CAD of Integrated Circuits and Systems* 18, no. 10 (Oct. 1999): 1405–17.

[Dan97] K. Danckaert, F. Catthoor, and H. De Man, "System level memory optimization for hardware-software co-design." Copyright © 1997 IEEE. Reprinted with permission from Proceedings, *Fifth International Workshop on Hardware/Software Co-design*, IEEE Computer Society Press, Los Alamitos, 1997, 55–59.

[Hen95] J. Henkel and R. Ernst, "A path-based technique for estimating hardware runtime in HW/SW-cosynthesis." Copyright © 1995 IEEE. Reprinted with permission from *Proceedings, Eighth IEEE International Symposium on System-Level Synthesis*, 1995, 116–21.

Chapter 4: System Level Partitioning, Synthesis and Interfacing

[Kal97] A. Kalavade and E. A. Lee, "The extended partitioning problem: Hardware/software mapping, scheduling, and implementation-bin selection," *Design Automation for Embedded Systems* 2, no. 2 (March 1997): 125–63. Copyright © 1997, Kluwer Academic Publishers.

[Chi94] M. Chiodo, P. Giusto, A. Jurecska, H. C. Hsieh, A. Sangiovanni-Vincentelli, and L. Lavagno, "Hardware-software codesign of embedded systems." Copyright © 1994 IEEE. Reprinted with permission from *IEEE Micro* 14, no. 4 (Aug. 1994): 26–36.

[Pra92] S. Prakash and A. C. Parker, "SOS: Synthesis of application-specific heterogeneous multiprocessor systems," *Journal of Parallel and Distributed Computing* 16 (1992): 338–51. Copyright © 1992 Academic Press.

[Wol97] W. Wolf, "An architectural co-synthesis algorithm for distributed, embedded computing systems." Copyright © 1997 IEEE. Reprinted with permission from *IEEE Transactions on VLSI Systems* 5, no. 2 (June 1997): 218–29.

[Cho98] P. Chou, K. Hines, K. Partridge, and G. Borriello, "Control generation for embedded systems on composition of modal processes." Copyright © 1998 IEEE. Reprinted with permission from Proceedings, *ICCAD 98*, IEEE Computer Society Press, Los Alamitos, 1998, 46–53.

[Cho95] P. Chou, R. B. Ortega, and G. Borriello, "Interface co-synthesis techniques for embedded systems." Copyright © 1995 IEEE. Reprinted with permission from Proceedings, *ICCAD 95*, IEEE Computer Society Press, Los Alamitos, 1995, 280–87.

[Dav97] J. M. Daveau, G. Frenades Marchioro, T. Ben-Ismail, and A. A. Jerraya, "Protocol selection and interface generation for HW-SW codesign." Copyright © 1997 IEEE. Reprinted with permission from *IEEE Transactions on VLSI Systems* 5, no.1 (March, 1997): 136–44.

[Sea94] A. Seawright and F. Brewer, "Clairvoyant: A synthesis system for production-based specifications." Copyright © 1994 IEEE. Reprinted with permission from *IEEE Transactions on VLSI Systems* 2, no. 2 (June 1994): 172–85.

[Tho95] F. Thoen, M. Cornero, G. Goossens, and H. De Man, "Real-time multi-tasking in software synthesis for information processing systems." Copyright © 1995 IEEE. Reprinted with permission from *Proceedings, Eighth International Symposium on System-Level Synthesis*, IEEE Computer Society Press, Los Alamitos, 1995, 45–53.

[Bal96] A. Balboni, W. Fornaciari, and D. Sciuto, "Co-synthesis and co-simulation of control-dominated embedded systems," *Design Automation for Embedded Systems* 1, no. 3 (July 1996): 257–89. Copyright © 1996 Kluwer Academic Press.

[Ver96] D. Verkest, K. Van Rompaey, I. Bolshens, and H. De Man, "CoWare—A design environment for heterogeneous hardware/software systems," *Design Automation for Embedded Systems* 1, no. 4 (Oct. 1996): 357–86. Copyright © 1996 Kluwer Academic Press.

Chapter 5: Implementation Generation

[Pau97] G. Goossens, J. Van Praet, D. Lanneer, W. Geurts, A. Kifli, C. Liem, and P. G. Paulin, "Embedded software in real-time signal processing systems: Design technologies." Copyright © 1997 IEEE. Reprinted with permission from *Proceedings of the IEEE* 85, no. 3 (March 1997): 419–35.

[Bat95] S. S. Battacharyya, J. T. Buck, S. Ha, and E. A. Lee, "Generating compact code from data-flow specifications of multirate signal processing algorithms." Copyright © 1995 IEEE. Reprinted with permission from *IEEE Transactions on Circuits and Systems I: Fundamental Theory and Applications* 42, no. 3 (March 1995): 138–50.

[Wuy99] S. Wuytack, J. L. da Silva, Jr., F. Catthoor, G. de Jong, and C. Ykman-Couvreur, "Memory management for embedded network applications." Copyright © 1999 IEEE. Reprinted with permission from *IEEE Transactions on CAD of Integrated Circuits and Systems* 18, no. 5 (May 1999): 533–44.

[Jac99] M. F. Jacome and G. de Veciana, "Lower bound on latency for VLIW ASIP datapaths." Copyright © 1999 IEEE. Reprinted with permission from Proceedings, *ICCAD 99*, IEEE Computer Society Press, Los Alamitos, 1999, 261–68.

[Mes99] B. Mesman, A. Timmer, J. van Meerbergen, and J. A. G. Jess, "Constraint analysis for DSP code generation." Copyright © 1999 IEEE. Reprinted with permission from *IEEE Transactions on CAD of Integrated Circuits and Systems* 18, no. 1 (Jan. 1999): 44–57.

[Lia95] S. Liao, S. Devadas, K. Keutzer, and S. Tijang, "Instruction selection using binate covering for code size optimization." Copyright © 1999 IEEE. Reprinted with permission from Proceedings, *ICCAD 95*, IEEE Computer Society Press, Los Alamitos, 1995, 393–99.

[Sud99] A. Sudarsanam, S. Malik, and M. Fujita, "A retargetable compilation methodology for embedded digital signal processors using a machine dependent code optimization library," *Design Automation for Embedded Systems* (March, 1999): 187–206. Copyright © 1999 Kluwer Academic Press.

[Vah95] F. Vahid and D. D. Gajski, "Incremental hardware estimation during hardware/software functional partitioning." Copyright © 1999 IEEE. Reprinted with permission from *IEEE Transactions on VLSI Systems* 3, no. 3 (Sept. 1995): 459–64.

Chapter 6: Co-Simulation and Emulation

[Buc94] J. Buck, S. Ha, E. A. Lee, and D. G. Messerschmitt, "Ptolemy: A framework for simulating and prototyping heterogeneous systems," *International Journal of Computer Simulation* 4 (April 1994): 155–82. Copyright © 1991 Swets &Zeitlinger Publishers,Heereweg. Used with permission.

[Gup92] R. K. Gupta, C. N. Coelho, Jr., and G. De Micheli, "Synthesis and simulation of digital systems containing interacting hardware and software components." Copyright © 1992 IEEE. Reprinted with permission from *Proceedings, 29th Design Automation Conference*, IEEE Computer Society Press, Los Alamitos, 1992, 225–30.

[Bec92] D. Becker, R. K. Singh, and S. G. Tell, "An engineering environment for hardware/software co-simulation." Copyright © 1992 IEEE. Reprinted with permission from *Proceedings, 29th Design Automation Conference*, IEEE Computer Society Press, Los Alamitos, 1992, 129–34.

[Kal93] A. Kalavade and E. A. Lee, "A hardware-software codesign methodology for DSP applications." Copyright © 1993 IEEE. Reprinted with permission from *IEEE Design & Test of Computers* 10, no. 3 (Sept. 1993): 16–28.

[Gho95] A. Ghosh, M. Bershteyn, R. Casley, C. Chien, A. Jain, M. Lipsie, D. Tarrodaychik, and O. Yamamoto, "A hardware-software co-simulator for embedded system design and debugging," in *Proceedings, ASP-DAC 95*, ACM Press, New York, A-3B.3. Copyright © 1995, Association for Computing Machinery, Inc.

[Val95] C. A. Valderrama, A. Changuel, P. V. Raghavan, M. Abid, T. Ben Ismail, and A. A. Jerraya, "A unified model for co-simulation and co-synthesis of mixed hardware/software systems," in Proceedings, *ED&TC 95*, ACM Press, New York, 1995, session 4B, 180–84. Copyright © 1995, Association for Computing Machinery, Inc.

[Ziv96] V. Živojnović and H. Meyr, "Compiled HW/SW

co-simulation," in *Proceedings, 33rd Design Automation Conference*, ACM Press, New York, 1996, 690–95. Copyright © 1996, Association for Computing Machinery, Inc.

[Fer98] L. Sánchez Fernández, Gernot Koch, N. Martínez Madrid, M. Lusia López Vallejo, C. Delgado Kloos, and W. Rosenstiel, "Hardware-software prototyping from LOTOS," *Design Automation for Embedded Systems* 3, no. 2/3 (March 1998): 117–48. Copyright © 1998 Kluwer Academic Press.

Chapter 7: Reconfigurable Computing Platforms

[Vui96] J. E. Vuillemin, P. Bertin, D. Roncin, M. Shand, H. H. Touati, and P. Boucard, "Programmable Active Memories: Reconfigurable Systems Come of Age." Copyright © 1996 IEEE. Reprinted with permission from *IEEE Transactions on VLSI Systems* 4, no. 2 (March 1996): 56–69.

[Bab97] J. Babb, R. Tessier, M. Dahl, S. Z. Hanono, D. M. Hoki, and A. Agarwal, "Logic emulation with virtual wires." Copyright © 1997 IEEE. Reprinted with permission from *IEEE Transactions on CAD of Integrated Circuits and Systems* 16, no. 6 (June 1997): 609–29.

[Man98] D. Mange, E. Sanchez, A. Stauffer, G. Tempesti, P. Marchal, and C. Piguet, "Embryonics: A new methodology for designing field-programmable gate arrays with self-repair and self-replicating properties." Copyright © 1998 IEEE. Reprinted with permission from *IEEE Transactions on VLSI Systems* 6, no. 3 (Sept. 1998): 387–99.

Chapter 8: Case Studies

[Meb92] A. H. Mebane IV, J. R. Schmedake, I.-S. Chen, and A. P. Kadonaga, "Electronic and firm-ware design of the HP DesignJet drafting plotter," *Hewlett-Packard Journal* 43, no. 6 (Dec. 1992): 16–23. Copyright © 1992 Hewlett-Packard Journal.

[Sri92] M. B. Srivastava, T. I. Blumenau, and R. W. Brodersen, "Design and implementation of a robot control system using a unified hardware-software rapid-prototyping framework." Copyright © 1992 IEEE. Reprinted with permission from *Proceedings, ICCAD '92*, IEEE Computer Society Press, Los Alamitos, 1992, 124–27.

[Tru98] T. E. Truman, T. Pering, R. Doering, and R. W. Brodersen, "The InfoPad multimedia terminal: A portable device for wireless information access." Copyright © 1998 IEEE. Reprinted with permission from *IEEE Transactions on Computers* 47, no. 10 (Oct. 1998): 1073–87.

[Maa97] E. Maas, D. Hermann, R. Ernst, P. Rüffer, S. Hasenzahl, and M. Seitz, "A processor-coprocessor architecture for high-end video applications." Copyright © 1997 IEEE. Reprinted with permission from Proceedings, *ICASSP 97*, IEEE, New York, 1997, 595–98.

CHAPTER ONE

Introduction

Hardware-Software Cosynthesis for Digital Systems 5
    R. K. Gupta and D. De Micheli

Hardware-Software Cosynthesis for Microcontrollers 18
    R. Ernst, J. Henkel, and T. Benner

Hardware-Software Co-design 30
    G. De Micheli and R. K. Gupta

Codesign of Embedded Systems: Status and Trends 45
    R. Ernst

Hardware/software co-design is the study of the design of embedded computing systems. It encompasses several problems:
- *Co-specification.* Creating specifications that describe both hardware and software elements (and the relationships between them);
- *Co-synthesis.* Automatic or semi-automatic design of hardware and software to meet a specification;
- *Co-simulation.* Simultaneous simulation of hardware and software elements, often at different levels of abstraction.

The co-synthesis problem can be broken up into four principal phases [Wol94]: (1) scheduling: choosing times at which computations occur; (2) allocation: determining the processing elements (PEs) on which computations occur; (3) partitioning: dividing up the functionality into units of computation; and (4) mapping: choosing particular component types for the allocated units.

These phases are, of course, related. However, as in many design problems, it is often desirable to separate these problems to some extent to make the problem more tractable.

EARLY WORK

Many of these new methods for hardware/software co-design were first discussed at the International Workshop on Hardware-Software Co-Design (known as the CODES workshop), held in the fall of 1992. No proceedings were made of that workshop. Given the very early state of the field, the presentations described a number of different approaches to co-design.

The presentations described a number of approaches to co-design: a simulation- and modeling-driven methodology; a requirements-driven methodology; Petri nets; behavioral modeling; formal semantics; interface synthesis; architectural description languages; object-oriented design; protocol design; software-oriented co-specification; and hardware/software partitioning.

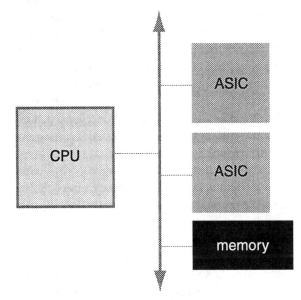

Figure 1: An architectural template for hardware/software partitioning.

The most durable concept to come out of that workshop was hardware/software partitioning. As shown in Figure 1, hardware/software partitioning targets an architectural template based on a typical microprocessor/

ASIC configuration. A CPU and one (or possibly more) ASICs are interconnected by the CPU bus. The bus is used both for data transfers between the CPU and ASIC and for control of the ASIC. The function to be implemented on this hardware platform is specified in some form, such as a programming language–style description. Any given portion that functionality may be implemented on either the CPU or the ASIC. The type of CPU is given as part of the template and its functionality is fixed; the ASIC, on the other hand, is synthesized on the fly. The decision as to where to implement an element of functionality depends on both performance and cost considerations. The ASIC may be able to perform certain functions much more quickly than the CPU. Other functions, however, may be able to performed about as efficiently as the CPU and without the overhead associated with transferring data to and from the ASIC. Because the CPU is a given, the system's manufacturing cost depends on the cost of the ASIC, which depends on what functions are implemented on it and the hardware requirements (measured in chip area) required to implement them.

Hardware/software partitioning introduces a design methodology that makes use of several techniques that will become important in other styles of co-synthesis as well. (1) The functional specification must be partitioned into processes, each of which denotes a thread of execution. The best way to partition a specification depends in part on the characteristics of the underlying hardware platform, so it may make sense to try different functional partitionings. (2) The performance of the function executing on the platform must be determined. Since exact performance depends on a great number of hardware and software details, we usually rely on approximations. (3) The processes must be allocated onto various processing elements of the platform.

Hardware/software partitioning typically has primary and secondary objectives. The primary objective is to meet a performance requirement. The secondary objective is to minimize hardware cost, which in this case can be measured as the area of the ASIC. Although power consumption has become an important metric for co-synthesis, early systems concentrated on performance and did not directly consider power consumption.

Hardware/software partitioning makes some assumptions that help simplify the solution of the problem:
  We know the type of CPU in advance.
- All communication is performed across a single bus.
- Most hardware/software partitioning algorithms assume that the implementation is single-threaded—the CPU and ASIC do not execute simultaneously.

Two of the papers in this section, "Hardware-Software Cosynthesis for Digital Systems," by Rajesh K. Gupta and Giovanni De Micheli [Gup93] and "Hardware-Software Cosynthesis for Microcontrollers," by Rolf Ernst, Jörg Henkel, and Thomas Benner [Ern93], are expanded versions of presentations at the first CODES workshop. Both these papers describe systems that use the same basic approach outlined above. However, they take quite different approaches to implementing the steps. The Vulcan system of Gupta and De Micheli performed a fairly coarse-grained partitioning of the functional specification into processes. It optimized the system by first putting all the functionality into the ASIC and then moving functions out to the CPU in order to reduce cost. The COSYMA system of Ernst, Henkel, and Benner concentrated on speeding up loop nests by analyzing loops and basic blocks in a program. Its optimization strategy used an approach opposite to that of Vulcan: COSYMA started with all the functionality on the CPU and moved successively larger blocks of operations to the ASIC in order to meet performance requirements.

Hardware/software partitioning has often been used as a synonym for hardware/software co-synthesis. However, in our view, the partitioning problem is best used as a term to describe a special case of the general co-synthesis problem. Hardware/software partitioning resembles a traditional graph partitioning problem because the system architecture is given. We can view the hardware/software partitioning as dividing the graph that represents the functional specification into two partitions, one for the CPU and one for the ASIC. In more general co-design problems, we do not start with an architectural template, and so we cannot view the problem as dividing the functionality among processing elements.

ADVANCES IN THE FIELD

The other two articles in this section, "Hardware/Software Co-Design," by De Micheli and Gupta [DeM97] and "Codesign of Embedded Systems: Status and Trends," by Ernst [Ern98], give us a look at the field after it had become more mature.

Ernst reviews the embedded system design process. The requirements phase comes first, in which a natural language description of the customer's needs is captured. The specification phase puts the requirements in more formal terms for use by the design team. Based on the specification, the system architecture development phase—a phase central to co-design—develops the basic hardware and software architectures. Based on that architectural description, hardware, software, and interfaces between hardware and software can be developed. Those hardware and software components are then integrated and tested. This leads to a view of the design exploration process that shows how trade-offs can be made at each level of abstraction: during specification, process transformations, hardware/software allocation and scheduling, synthesis of the hardware and software components, and co-simulation.

Ernst highlights modeling and verification as critical steps in the design methodology. If hardware and software component designs are not properly coordinated, it is quite likely that serious bugs in the interfaces between these components will be discovered too late, during the integration and testing phase that comes at the end of the design cycle. Part of the solution is to use modeling languages to capture intent and to use co-simulation to exercise the models. Co-simulation can help capture bugs early before they propagate into the implementation.

Both articles survey techniques for co-synthesis and give a taxonomy. The four basic steps performed during co-synthesis are very similar to the steps performed in a variety of domains ranging from distributed systems to high-level synthesis:

1. Partitioning the functional description into processes,
2. Allocating processes to processing elements,
3. Scheduling processes on the PEs,
4. Binding processing elements to particular component types.

A distinction is often made between allocating and binding because these decisions are driven by issues at different levels of granularity. Allocation determines the number of processing elements in the hardware platform but does not make detailed decisions about the types of processing elements. Binding chooses exact component types for the processing elements. Basic decisions about the number of processing elements can often be made without choosing exact component types, but choosing component types generally requires a fairly complete architectural model in order to accurately judge the relatively small distinctions between component types.

De Micheli and Gupta consider the range of scheduling techniques used at the hardware, instruction, and process levels of abstraction. Hardware scheduling is usually performed statically at design time, using heuristic methods such as list- or force-directed scheduling. Instruction-level scheduling may be performed statically at compile time or dynamically by the CPU's execution unit. Process-level scheduling may be performed statically or dynamically.

De Micheli and Gupta identify several levels of programmability for digital systems: application, instruction, and hardware. Application-level programming is often directed at user customization. It may be provided by programs that take user input or by programming languages running on the embedded system. Instruction-level programmability is provided by instruction set architectures embodied in CPUs. A digital signal processor (DSP) is a CPU optimized for use in digital signal processing applications. Some embedded systems allow the user to program its CPUs directly, whereas others hide the ISA from the user. Hardware-level programming allows the hardware to be configured after manufacturing. A well-known case is a reconfigurable circuit, which uses either volatile or nonvolatile memory to determine the functions of logic blocks and/or the interconnections between logic elements.

De Micheli and Gupta cite the growing importance of reconfigurable logic in embedded computing. Field-programmable gate arrays (FPGAs), which embody reconfigurable logic, can be used to personalize a system after manufacturing. An evolvable system allows concurrent partial reconfiguration and execution. In order to effectively make use of reconfigurable logic in an embedded system, the designer must be able to partition the functional description based on the characteristics of the reconfigurable platform. This process requires analyzing the application and determining what parts are best suited for reconfigurable logic. Selecting logic to be implemented in a new reconfigurable unit is a difficult problem that, at this writing, still requires some manual intervention. Reconfigurable systems can also be used for computer-aided prototyping. An FPGA can run at much higher speeds than a software simulator in most cases. Such speed allows designers to exercise the system much more thoroughly and may allow the system to be interfaced to its external connections for more realistic execution. If the prototype will be re-implemented before manufacture, partitioning the functional description and allocating it to hardware will become simpler and more amenable to automation.

Another important area of co-design, as described by both articles, is the design of application-specific instruction processors (ASIPs). An ASIP is a CPU whose instruction-set architecture has been optimized for an application or set of applications. An ASIP provides a balance between functionality and flexibility: While specialized instructions and hardware resources in the ASIP allow efficient execution of the basic operations required by the application, the ASIP's programmability allows the specific sequence of steps performed to be changed during design or even after manufacture. Effective use of the architecture, particularly in the case of a synthesized architecture, requires a compiler tuned for the architecture. As a result, ASIP synthesis systems often try to generate a compiler at the same time as the ISA is generated.

GUIDE TO THIS BOOK

The remainder of this book is divided into chapters containing articles that expand on the basic themes described in this introduction:

- *Modeling*. Because parallelism is so important to the design of embedded computing systems, the choice of an appropriate modeling paradigm is very important. A variety of modeling formalisms and methodologies have been developed that capture various aspects of system behavior.
- *Analysis and estimation*. Co-design can be only as good as the information upon which it bases its decisions. Performance estimation is of course critical, given the central nature of performance requirements in most designs. Power analysis has become increasingly important and well understood.
- *System-level partitioning, synthesis, and interfacing*. These are the basic steps of co-synthesis. A range of techniques are available for individual steps and for methodologies that combine the steps in various ways.
- *Implementation generation*. Once the architecture has been generated, the designs for the hardware and software components must be created. Efficient implementation generation generally requires taking into account the nature of the designs created by earlier co-synthesis phases.
- *Co-simulation and emulation*. Co-simulation helps designers evaluate architectures without creating full implementations for all the components.

Emulation makes use of FPGA technology to further speed up execution of system models.
- *Reconfigurable computing platforms*. Reconfigurability helps blur the boundary between traditional fixed hardware and programmable CPUs. Taking best advantage of reconfigurability encourages using a mixture of run-time and design-time techniques.
- *Case studies*. In order to understand hardware/software co-design, it is very important to understand the types of systems that designers want to create and the challenges that these designers face. This section includes descriptions of a range of embedded system designs.

Readers will come to this material with varying backgrounds and expectations. Hardware/software co-design covers a broad range of topics and touches upon background material from a number of disciplines: computer architecture, software engineering, real-time systems, hardware design, and so on. The material can be approached along several different themes:

- *Computer architecture*. Embedded systems designers tend to ask about the implications of the application on the underlying architecture. Embedded systems often target a narrower range of applications than do general-purpose computer systems.
- *Software*. Embedded software design emphasizes real-time performance. Power consumption of software is another important problem that is much more prominent in embedded systems than it is in general-purpose systems.
- *Computer-aided design*. Embedded systems, because they have a great deal of software content, have much larger specifications than do traditional hardware designs. As a result, analysis of performance, power, and other characteristics becomes more complex.

We have tried to order the papers into a logical presentation for the typical reader, taking a top-down approach from specification through implementation.

Hardware-Software Cosynthesis for Digital Systems

RAJESH K. GUPTA
GIOVANNI DE MICHELI
Stanford University

As system design grows increasingly complex, the use of predesigned components, such as general-purpose microprocessors, can simplify synthesized hardware. While the problems in designing systems that contain processors and application-specific integrated circuit chips are not new, computer-aided synthesis of such heterogeneous or mixed systems poses unique challenges. Here, we demonstrate the feasibility of synthesizing heterogeneous systems by using timing constraints to delegate tasks between hardware and software so that performance requirements can be met.

MOST DIGITAL SYSTEMS used for dedicated applications consist of general-purpose processors, memory, and application-specific hardware circuits. Examples of such embedded systems appear in medical instrumentation, process control, automated vehicles, and networking and communication systems. Besides being application specific, such system designs also respect constraints related to the relative timing of their actions. For that reason we call them real-time embedded systems.

Design and analysis of real-time embedded systems pose challenges in performance estimation, selection of appropriate parts for system implementation, and verification of such systems for functional and temporal properties. In practice, designers implement such systems from their specification as a set of loosely defined functionalities by taking a design-oriented approach. For instance, consider the design shown in Figure 1 (next page) of a network processor that is connected to a serial line and memory. This processor receives and sends data over the serial line using a specific communication protocol (such as the protocol for Ethernet links).

The decision to map functionalities into dedicated hardware or implement them as programs on a processor usually depends on estimates of achievable performance and the implementation cost of the respective parts. While this division impacts every stage of the design, it is largely based on the designer's experience and takes place early in the design process. As a consequence, portions of a design often are either under- or over-designed with respect to their required performance. More important, due to the ad hoc nature of the overall design process, we have no guarantee that a given implementation meets required system performance (except possibly by over-designing).

In contrast, we can formulate a methodical approach to system implementation as a synthesis-oriented solution, a tactic that has met with enormous success in individual integrated circuit chip design (chip-level synthesis). A synthesis approach for hardware proceeds with systems described at the behavioral level, by means of an appropriate specification language. While the search for a suitable specification language for digital systems is the subject of ongoing research, use of procedural hardware de-

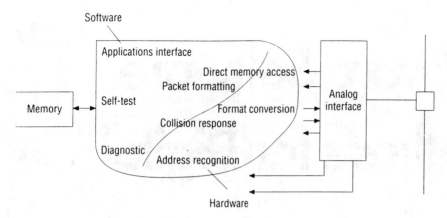

Figure 1. A design-oriented approach to system implementation.

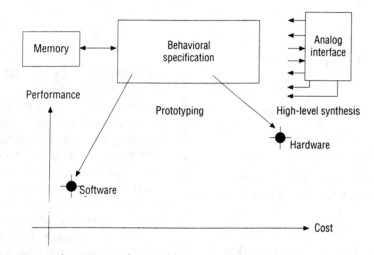

Figure 2. A synthesis-oriented approach to system implementation.

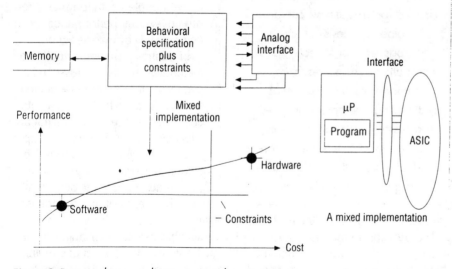

Figure 3. Proposed approach to system implementation.

scription languages (HDLs) to describe integrated circuits has been gaining wide acceptance in recent years.

A synthesis-oriented approach to digital circuit design starts with a behavioral description of circuit functionality. From that, it attempts to generate a gate-level implementation that can be characterized as a purely hardware implementation (Figure 2). Recent strides in high-level synthesis allow us to synthesize digital circuits from high-level specifications; several such systems are available from industry and academia. Gajski[1] and Camposano and Wolf[2] provide surveys of these. Synthesis produces a gate-level or geometric-level description that is implemented as single or multiple chips. As the number of gates (or logic cells) increases, such a solution requires semicustom or custom design technologies, which then leads to associated increases in cost and design turnaround time. For large system designs, synthesized hardware solutions consequently tend to be fairly expensive, depending upon the technology chosen to implement the chip.

On the other end of the system development cost and performance spectrum, one can also create a software prototype, amenable to simulation, of a system using a general-purpose programming language. (See Figure 2.) The Rapide prototyping system[3] is one example. Designers can build such software prototypes rather quickly and often use them for verifying system functionality. However, software prototype performance very often falls short of what time-constrained system designs require.

Practical experience tells us that cost-effective designs use a mixture of hardware and software to accomplish their overall goals (Figure 1). This provides sufficient motivation for attempting a synthesis-oriented approach to achieve system implementations having both hardware and software components. Such an approach would benefit from a systematic analysis of design trade-offs that is com-

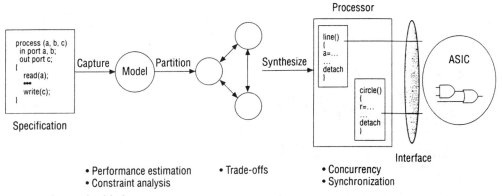

Figure 4. Synthesis approach to embedded systems.

mon in synthesis while also creating cost-effective systems.

One way to accomplish this task is to specify constraints on cost and performance of the resulting implementation (Figure 3). We present an approach to systematic exploration of system designs that is driven by such constraints. Our work builds upon high-level synthesis techniques for digital hardware[4] by extending the concept of a resource needed for implementation.

As shown in Figure 4, this approach captures a behavioral specification into a system model that is partitioned for implementation into hardware and software. We then synthesize the partitioned model into interacting hardware and software components for the target architecture shown in Figure 5. The target architecture uses one processor that is embedded with an application-specific hardware component. The processor uses only one level of memory and address space for its instructions and data. Currently, to simplify the synthesis and performance estimation for the hardware component, we do not pipeline the application-specific hardware. Even with its relative simplicity, the target architecture can apply to a wide class of applications in embedded systems.

Among the related work, Woo, Wolf, and Dunlop[5] investigate implementing hardware or software from a cospecification. Chou, Ortega, and Borriello[6] describe synthesis of hardware or software for interface circuits. Chiodo et al.[7] discuss a methodology for generating hardware and software based on a unified finite-state-machine-based model. Given a system specification as a C-program, Henkel and Ernst[8] identify portions of the program that can be implemented into hardware to achieve a speedup of overall execution times. Srivastava and Brodersen[9] and Buck et al.[10] present frameworks for generating hardware and software components of a system. Investigators have proposed several new architectures that use field-programmable gate arrays to create special-purpose coprocessors to speed up applications (PAM[11], MoM[12]) or to create prototypes (QuickTurn[13]).

Capturing specification of system functionality and constraints

We capture system functionality using a hardware description language, *HardwareC*.[14] The cosynthesis approach formulated here does not depend upon the particular choice of the HDL, and could use other HDLs such as VHDL or Verilog. However, the use of HardwareC leverages the use of Olympus tools developed for chip-level synthesis.[4]

HardwareC follows much of the syntax and semantics of the programming language, with modifications necessary for correct and unambiguous hardware

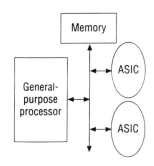

Figure 5. Target architecture.

modeling. HardwareC description consists of a set of interacting processes that are instantiated into blocks using a declarative semantics. A process model executes concurrently with other processes in the system specification. A process restarts itself on completion. Operations within a process body allow for nested concurrent and sequential operations.

Figure 6 shows an example of an HDL functionality specification. This example performs two data input operations, followed by a conditional in which a counter index is generated. The specification uses counter index z to seed a down-counter indicated by the while loop. A graph-based representation as shown captures this HDL specification.

In general, the system model consists of a set of hierarchically related sequencing graphs. Within a graph, vertices represent language-level operations and edges represent dependencies be-

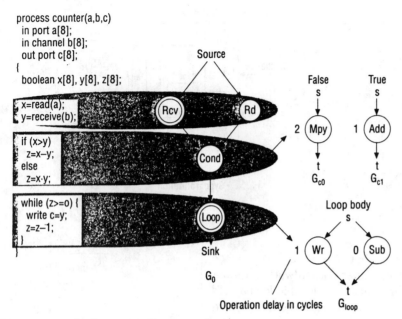

Figure 6. Example of input specification and capture.

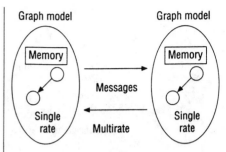

Figure 7. Properties of the graph model.

tween the operations. Such a representation makes explicit the concurrency inherent in the input specification, thus making it easier to reason about properties of the input description. As we shall soon see, it also allows us to analyze timing properties of the input description.

Model properties. The sequencing graph is a polar one with source and sink vertices that represent no-operations. Associated with each graph model is a set of variables that defines the shared memory between operations in the graph model. Source and sink vertices synchronize executions of operations in a graph model across multiple iterations. Thus, polarity of the graph model ensures that there is exactly one execution of an operation with respect to each execution of any other operation. This makes execution of operations within a graph single rate (Figure 7). The set of variables associated with a graph model defines the storage common to the operations; it serves to facilitate communication between operations.

Given the single-rate execution model, it is relatively straightforward to ensure ordering of operations in a graph model that preserves integrity of memory shared between operations. However, operations across graph models follow multirate execution semantics. That is, there may be variable numbers of executions of an operation for an operation in another graph model. Because of this multirate nature of execution, the operations use message-passing primitives like send and receive to implement communications across graph models. Use of these primitives simplifies specification of inter-model communications. A multirate specification is an important feature for modeling heterogeneous systems, because the processor and application-specific hardware may run on different clocks and speeds.

HDL descriptions contain operations to represent synchronization to external events, such as the receive operation, as well as data-dependent loop operations. These operations, called nondeterministic delay (ND) operations, present unknown execution delays. The ability to model ND operations is vital for reactive embedded system descriptions. Figure 6 indicates ND operations with double circles.

A system model may have many possible implementations. Timing constraints are important in defining specific performance requirements of the desired implementation. As shown in Figure 8, timing constraints are of two types:

- **Min/max delay constraints:** These provide bounds on the time interval between initiation of execution of two operations.
- **Execution rate constraints:** These provide bounds on successive initiations of the same operation. Rate constraints on input/output operations are equivalent to constraints on throughput of respective inputs/outputs.

These two types of constraints are sufficient to capture constraints needed by most real-time systems.[15] Our synthesis system captures minimum delay constraints in the graphical representation by providing weights on the edges to indicate delay of the corresponding source operation. Capturing maximum delay constraints requires additional backward edges (Figure 9).

Model analysis. Having captured system functionality and constraints in a graphical model, we can now estimate system performance and verify the consistency of specified constraints. Performance measures require estimation of operation delays. We compute these delays separately for hardware and software implementations based on the type of hardware to be used and the processor used to run the software. A processor cost model captures processor characteristics. It consists of an execution delay function for a basic set of processor operations, a memory address calculation function, a memory access time, and processor interruption response time.

Timing constraint analysis attempts to answer the following question: Can imposed constraints be satisfied for a given implementation? We indicate an implementation of a model by assigning appropriate delays to the operations with known delays (not ND) in the graph model. Constraint satisfiability relates to the structure as well as the actual delay and constraint values on the graph. Some structural properties of the graphs (relating to ND operations and their dependencies) may make a constraint unsatisfiable regardless of the actual delay values of the operations. Further, some constraints may be mutually inconsistent: for example, a maximum delay constraint between two operations that also have a larger minimum delay constraint. No assignment of nonnegative operation delay values can satisfy such constraints.

In the presence of ND operations in a graph model, we consider a timing constraint satisfiable if it is satisfied for all possible (and maybe infinite) delay values of the ND operations. We consider a timing constraint marginally satisfiable if it can be satisfied for all possible values within specified bounds on the delay of the ND operations. Marginal satisfiability analysis is useful because it allows the use of timing constraints that can be satisfied under some implementation assumptions (acceptable bounds on ND operation delays). Without these assumptions the general timing constraint satisfiability analysis would otherwise consider these constraints ill-posed.[16]

We perform timing constraint analysis by graph analysis on the weighted sequencing graphs. Consider first the case where the graph model does not contain any ND operations. Here, we can label every edge in the graph with a finite and known weight. In such a graph, we cannot satisfy a min/max delay constraint if a positive cycle in the graph model exists.[16] Next, in the presence of ND operations, timing constraints are satisfiable if no cycles containing ND operations exist. For a cycle containing an ND operation, it is impossible to determine satisfiability of timing constraints, and only marginal satisfiability can be guaranteed. As we will see, it is possible to break the cycle by graph transformations that preserve the HDL program semantics.

For nonpipelined implementations, we can treat rate constraints as min/max delay constraints between corresponding source and sink operations of the graph model. Thus we can apply the above min/max constraint satisfiability criterion to the analysis of rate constraints.

Note that in some cases system throughput (specified by rate constraints) can be optimized significantly with little or no impact on system latency by using a pipelined execution model and extra resources. Indeed, for deterministic and fixed-rate systems particularly used for digital signal processing applications, researchers have developed extensive transformations that determine and achieve bounds on system throughput.[17] However, as noted earlier, systems modeled by the sequencing graphs generally operate at different rates. In addition, because of the presence of ND operations due to loops, the rate at which a particular operation executes may change over time. While this property is essential for modeling control-dominated embedded systems, it aggravates the problem of determining absolute bounds on achievable system throughput.

We illustrate the issue of rate constraints on graphs containing ND operations in Example A (next page).

In general, consider a process P that contains an ND operation due to an un-

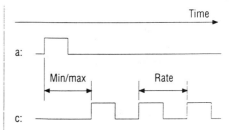

Figure 8. Timing constraints.

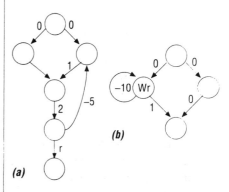

Figure 9. Representation of timing constraints: min/max constraint (a), rate constraint (b).

bounded loop. The ND operation induces a bipartition of the calling process, $P = F \cup B$, such that the set of operations in F (for example, the read operation in process test) must be performed before invoking the loop body. Further, the set of operations in B can only be performed after completing executions of the loop body. We can then use functional pipelining of F, B, and the loop to improve the reaction rate of P. Since we assume nonpipelined hardware, these transformations are used only in the context of the software component.

Constraint analysis and software. The linear execution semantics imposed by the software running on a single-processor target architecture complicates constraint analysis for a software implementation of a graph model. That is, performing delay analysis for software operations requires a complete order of operations in the graph model. In creat-

Example A

Consider the following process fragment

```
process test (p, ...)
    in port p [SIZE];
{
    ...
    v = read p ;
    while (v >= 0)
    {
        < loop-body >
        v = v – 1 ;
    }
}
```

Here, v is a Boolean array that represents an integer. In the presence of rate constraint r on the *read* operation, the constraint graph has a cycle containing an ND operation relating to the unbounded *while* loop operation. Note that the rate constraint corresponds to directed edge from sink t to source s in the graph of Figure A.

The overall execution time of the *while* loop determines the interval between successive executions of the read operation. Due to this variable-delay loop operation, the input rate at port p is variable and cannot always be guaranteed to meet the required rate constraint. In general, determining achievable throughput at port p is difficult. As we explain next, marginal satisfiability of the rate constraint can be ensured by graph transformations and by using a finite-size buffer.

Figure A shows the sequencing graph model P corresponding to process test. Identifier rd refers to the read operation, lp refers to the while loop operation. Symbols P1, P2, and so forth in the execution trace below indicate successive invocations of the process test. L1, L2, L3, and L4 indicate multiple invocations of the lp operation. Depending on the side effects produced by the loop-body, the original graph P can be transformed into fragments Q and R such that executions of Q and R can overlap to improve the throughput of the read operation in Q. Data transfers from Q to R by means of a buffer. See Example B on page 37 for a consideration of a software implementation of P.

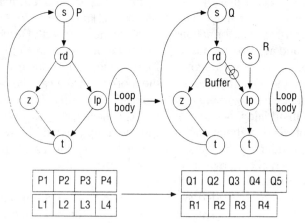

Figure A. *Breaking ND cycle by graph transformation.*

ing a complete order of operations, it is likely that unbounded cycles may be created, which would make constraints unsatisfiable.

As shown in Figure 10, any serialization that puts an ND operation between two operations *op1* and *op2* will make any maximum delay constraint between *op1*

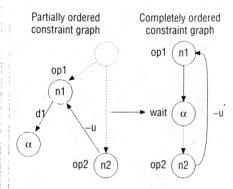

Figure 10. *Linearization in software leads to creation of unsatisfiable timing constraints. Constraint maxtime from op1 to op2 = u cycles.*

and *op2* unsatisfiable. However, note that while all computations must be performed serially in software, communication operations can proceed concurrently. In other words, it is possible to overlap execution of ND operations (wait for synchronization or communication) with some (unrelated) computation. But such an overlap requires the ability to schedule operations dynamically in software since the simultaneously active ND operations may complete in orders that cannot be determined statically.

Typically, dynamic scheduling of operations involves delay overheads due to selection and scheduling of operations. Therefore, a good model of software is to think of software as a set of fixed-latency concurrent threads (Figure 11). We define a thread as a linearized set of operations that may or may not begin by an ND operation indicated by a circle in Figure 11. Other than the beginning ND operation, a thread does not contain any ND operations. We consider the delay of the initial ND operation part of the scheduling delay and, therefore, not included in the latency of the program thread. Use of multiple concurrent program threads instead of a single program to implement the software also avoids the need for complete serialization of all operations that may create un-

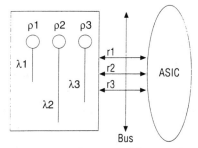

Figure 11. Software model to avoid creation of ND cycles.

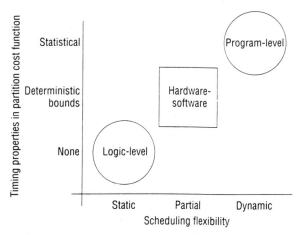

Figure 12. Use of timing properties in partition cost function.

bounded cycles.

In this software model, we can check marginal satisfiability of constraints on operations belonging to different threads, assuming a fixed and known delay of scheduling operations associated with ND operations (context switch delay, for example).

System partitioning

The system-level partitioning problem refers to the assignment of operations to hardware or software. The assignment of an operation to hardware or software determines the delay of the operation. In addition, assignment of operations to a processor and to one or more application-specific hardware circuits involves additional delays due to communication overheads.

Any good partitioning scheme must attempt to minimize this communication. Further, as operations in software are implemented on a single processor, increasing operations in software increases processor utilization. Consequently, overall system performance depends on the effect of hardware-software partition on utilization of the processor and the bandwidth of the bus between the processor and application-specific hardware.

A partitioning scheme thus must attempt to capture and make use of a partition's effect on system performance in making trade-offs between hardware and software implementations of an operation. An efficient way to do this would be to devise a partition cost function that captures these properties. We would then use this function to direct the partitioning algorithm toward a desired solution, where an optimum solution is defined by the minimum value of the partition cost function.

Note that we need to capture not only the effects of sizes of hardware and software parts but also the effect on timing behavior of these portions in our partition cost function. In contrast, most partitioning schemes for hardware have focused on optimizing area and pinout of resulting circuits. Capturing the effect of a partition on timing performance during the partitioning stage is difficult. Part of the problem arises because the timing properties are usually global in nature, thus making it difficult to make incremental computations of the partition cost function as is essential for developing effective partition algorithms. Approximation techniques have been suggested to take into account the effect of a partition on overall latency.[18]

Note, however, that partitioning in the software world does make extensive use of statistical timing properties to drive the partitioning algorithms.[19] We draw the distinction between these two extremes of hardware and software partitioning by the flexibility to schedule operations. Hardware partitioning attempts to divide circuits that implement scheduled operations. Conversely, the program-level partitioning addresses operations that are scheduled at runtime.

Our approach to partitioning for hardware and software takes an intermediate approach. As shown in Figure 12, we use deterministic bounds on timing properties that are incrementally computable in the partition cost function. That is, we can compute the new partition cost function in constant time. We accomplish this by using a software model in terms of a set of program threads as shown in Figure 11 and a partition cost function, f, that is a linear combination of its variables. The following properties characterize this software component:

- **Thread latency** λ_i (seconds) indicates the execution delay of a program thread.
- **Thread reaction rate** ρ_i (per second) is the invocation rate of the program thread.
- **Processor utilization** P is calculated by

$$P = \sum_{i=1}^{n} \lambda_i \cdot \rho_i$$

- **Bus utilization** B (per second) is the total amount of communication taking place between the hardware and software. For a set of m variables to be transferred between hardware and software,

$$B = \sum_{j=1}^{m} r_j$$

r_j is the inverse of the minimum time interval (in seconds) between two consecutive samples for variable j, which is marked for destination to one of the program threads.

Characterization of software using λ, ρ, P, and B parameters makes it possible to calculate static bounds on software performance. Use of these bounds is helpful in selecting an appropriate partition of system functionality between hardware and software. However, it also has the disadvantage of overestimating performance parameters such as processor and bus bandwidth utilization. Typically, there is a distribution of thread invocations and communications based on actual data values being transferred, which is not accounted for in these parameters.

We compute hardware size S_H bottom-up from the size estimates of the resources implementing the individual operations. In addition, we characterize the interface between hardware and software by a set of communication ports (one for each variable) between hardware and software that communicate data over a common bus. The overhead due to communication between hardware and software is manifested by the utilization of bus bandwidth as described earlier.

Given the cost model for software, hardware, and interface, we can informally state the problem of partitioning a specification for implementation into hardware and software as follows:

From a given set of sequencing graph models and timing constraints between operations, create two sets of sequencing graph models such that one can be implemented in hardware and the other in software and the following is true:

- Timing constraints are satisfied for the two sets of graph models.
- Processor utilization, $P \leq 1$.
- Bus utilization, $B \leq \overline{B}$.
- A partition cost function, $f = f(S_H, B, P^{-1}, m)$ is minimized.

An exact solution to the constrained partitioning problem—a solution that minimizes the partition cost function—requires that we examine a large number of solutions. Typically, that number is exponential to the number of operations under partition. As a result, designers often use heuristics to find a "good" solution, with the objective of finding an optimal value of the cost function that is minimal for some local properties.

Most common heuristics to solving partitioning problems start with a constructive initial solution that some iterative procedure can then improve. Iterative improvement can follow, for example, from moving or exchanging operations and paths between partitions. A good heuristic is also relatively insensitive to the initial solution. Typically, exchange of a larger number of operations makes the heuristic more insensitive to the starting solution, at the cost of increasing the time complexity.

In the following, we describe the intuitive features of the partitioning algorithm. We have presented details elsewhere.[20] The procedure identifies operations that can be implemented in software such that the corresponding constraint graph implementation can be satisfied and the resulting software (as a set of program threads) meets required rate constraints on its inputs and outputs. As an initial partition we assume that ND operations related to data-dependent loop operations define the beginning of program threads in software, while all other operations are implemented in hardware. The rate constraints on software inputs/outputs translate into bounds on required reaction rate ρ_i of corresponding program thread T_i. Maximum achievable reaction rate $\overline{\rho}_i$ of a program thread is computed as the inverse of its latency. The latency of a program thread is computed using a processor delay cost model and includes a fixed scheduling overhead delay.

From an initial solution we perform iterative improvement by migrating operations between the partitions. Migration of an operation across a partition affects its execution delay. It also affects the latency and reaction rate of the thread to which this operation is moved. We similarly compute its effect on processor and bus bandwidth utilization. At any step, we select operations for migration so that the move lowers the communication cost, while maintaining timing constraint satisfiability. In addition, we check for communication feasibility by verifying that $\overline{\rho}_i \geq \rho_i$ for each thread, and that processor and bus utilization constraints are satisfied.

System synthesis

From partitioned graph models, our next problem is to synthesize individual hardware and software components. Ku[14] and others[1,2] address in detail the generation of hardware circuits for sequencing graph models. Therefore, we concentrate on generation of software and interface circuitry from partitioned models. The problem of software synthesis is to generate a program from partitioned graph models that correctly implements the original system functionality. We assume that the resulting program is mapped to real memory, so the issues related to memory management are not relevant to this problem. The partitioning discussed previously identified graph models that are to be implemented in hardware and operations (organized as program threads) that are to be implemented in software. See Example B.

The program generation from a thread can either use a coroutine or subroutine scheme. Since, in general, there can be dependencies into and from the program threads, a coroutine model is

> **Example B**
>
> We can implement the process test shown in Example A as following two program threads in software.
>
> | Thread T1 | Thread T2 |
> |---|---|
> | read v | loop_synch |
> | detach | <loop_body> |
> | | v = v − 1 |
> | | detach |
>
> In its software implementation of process test, thread T1 performs the reading operations, and thread T2 consists of operations in the body of the loop. For each execution of thread T1 there are v executions of thread T2.

> **Example C**
>
> Consider the threads T1 and T2 generated from process test mentioned in Example A. The overall execution time of the while loop determines the interval between successive executions of the read operation. Due to this variable-delay loop operation, the input rate at port p is variable so we cannot always guarantee the reaction rate of T1. Since the set of operations in loop-body may alter the contents of memory in process test, thread T1 must be blocked until the completion of T2. Thus the process test can be thought of as consisting of two parallel processes, as shown in Figure B. We need the first operation of thread T2, wait1, to observe the data dependency of operations in thread T2. We need the second wait operation, wait2, to guarantee that any memory side effects of T2 for variables in T1 are correctly reflected. To obtain a deterministic bound on the reaction rate of the calling thread, it is possible to unroll the looping thread by creating a variable number of program threads. However, in this case each iteration of the looping thread would carry scheduling overhead. Dynamic creation of program threads may also lead to violation of processor utilization constraint as described in previous sections.
>
> However, it is possible to overlap execution of loop thread T2 with execution of thread T1, and to ensure marginal timing constraint satisfiability. Note that we can remove operation

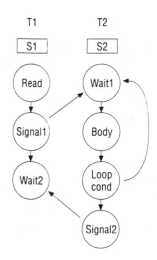

Figure B. Dependence of a program thread on a program thread corresponding to a loop.

wait2 if the looping thread does not produce any side effect on storage S1 of the calling thread. That is, the loop body only reads and does not modify the variables common to S1 and S2. In such cases we can use data buffers between program threads to maintain the reaction rate of a program thread. For implementation details, see Gupta, Coelho, and De Micheli.[1]

Reference

1. R.K. Gupta, C. Coelho, and G. De Micheli, "Program Implementation Schemes for Hardware-Software Systems," *Notes of Int'l Workshop Hardware-Software Codesign*, Oct. 1992, and CSL Tech. Report TR-92-548, Stanford University, Stanford, Calif., 1992.

more appropriate. A dependency between two operations can be either a data or a control dependency. Depending upon predecessor relationships and timing of the operations, we can make some of these redundant by inserting other dependencies such that resulting program threads are convex—all external dependencies are limited to the first and last operations.

For a given subgraph corresponding to a program thread, we can move an incoming data dependency up to its first operation and move an outgoing data dependency down to its last operation. This procedure produces a potential loss of concurrency. However, it makes the task of routine implementation easier since we can implement all the routines as independent programs with statically embedded control dependencies.

Rate constraints and software. In the presence of dependencies on ND operations, we cannot always guarantee that a given software implementation will meet the data rate constraints on its I/O ports. In case of synchronization-related ND operations, we can check for marginal satisfiability of timing constraints by assigning a context-switch delay to the respective wait operations. However, in the case of unbounded loop-related ND operations, the delay due to these operations consists of active computation time. Marginal timing satisfiability analysis therefore requires that we estimate loop index values. We illustrate this in Example C.

Hardware-software interface. Because of the serial execution of the software component, a data transfer from

Example D

Consider the mixed implementation of a graphics controller that contains two threads for generation of line and circle coordinates in software as shown in Figure C. The interface protocol using control FIFO is specified as follows:

```
queue [2] controlFIFO [1];
queue [16] line_queue [1], circle_queue [1];

when ((line_queue.dequeue_rq+ & !line_queue.empty) & !controlFIFO.full) do
controlFIFO enqueue #2;
when ((circle_queue.dequeue_rq+ & !circle_dequeue.empty) & !controlFIFO.full)
do controlFIFO enqueue #1;
when (controlFIFO.dequeue_rq +&!controlFIFO.empty)do controlFIFO de-
queue dlx.0xff000[1:0];
```

In this example, two data queues with 16 bits of width and 1 bit of depth, *line_queue* and *circle_queue*, and one queue with 2 bits of width and 1 bit of depth, *controlFIFO*, are declared. The guarded commands specify the conditions on which the number 1 or the number 2 is enqueued—here, a '+' after a signal name means a positive edge and a '–' after the signal means a negative edge. The first when condition states that when a dequeue request for the queue *line_queue* arrives and this queue is not empty and the queue *controlFIFO* is not full, then enqueue the value 2 (representing identifier for a corresponding program thread that consumes data from the line queue) into the *controlFIFO*.

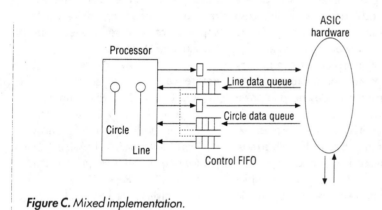

Figure C. *Mixed implementation.*

hardware to software must be explicitly synchronized. By using a polling strategy, we can design the software component to perform premeditated transfers from the hardware components based on its data requirements. This requires static scheduling of the hardware component. Where software functionality is limited by communications—that is, where the processor is busy waiting for an input-output operation most of the time—such a scheme would suffice. Further, in the absence of any unbounded-delay operations, we can simplify the software component in this scheme to a single program thread and a single data channel since all data transfers are serialized. However, this approach would not support any branching nor any reordering of data arrivals, since the design would not support dynamic scheduling of operations in hardware.

To accommodate differing rates of execution among the hardware and software components, and due to unbounded delay operations, we look for a dynamic scheduling of different threads of execution. Availability of data forms the basis for such a scheduling. One mechanism to perform such scheduling is a control FIFO (first in, first out) buffer, which attempts to enforce the policy that data items are consumed in the order in which they are produced. As shown in Example D, the hardware-software interface consists of data queues on each channel and a control FIFO that holds the identifiers for the enabled program threads in the order in which their input data arrives. The control FIFO depth equals the number of threads of execution, since a thread execution stalls pending availability of the requested data.

Note that thread scheduling by means of a control FIFO does not explicitly prioritize the program threads. This is because, for safety reasons, the control FIFO serves program threads strictly in the order in which their identifiers are enqueued. In some systems we may want to invoke a program thread as soon as its needed data becomes available. Such systems would be better served by a preemptive scheduling algorithm based on relative priorities of the threads. However, preemption comes at significant operating system overhead. In contrast, nonpreemptive prioritized scheduling of program threads is possible with relatively minor modifications to control FIFO. Example E describes the actual interconnection schematic between hardware and software for a single data queue.

We can implement the control FIFO and associated control logic either in hardware as a part of the ASIC component or in software. If we implement the control FIFO in software, the system no longer needs the FIFO control logic since the control flow is already in software. In this case, the q_rq lines from data queues connect to processor unvectored interrupt lines, where the system uses respective interruption service routines to enqueue the thread identifier tags into the control FIFO. During the enqueue operations the system disables the interrupts to preserve integrity of the software control flow.

Example

As an experiment in achieving mixed system designs, we attempted synthesis of an Ethernet-based network coprocessor. The coprocessor is modeled as a set of 13 concurrently executing processes that interact with each other by means of 24 send and 40 receive operations. The total description consists of 1,036 lines of HDL code. A hardware-software implementation of the coprocessor takes 8,572 bytes of program and data storage for a DLX processor[21] and 8,394 equivalent gates using an LSI Logic 10K library of gates.

We can thus build the mixed implementation using only one ASIC chip plus an off-the-shelf processor. A complete hardware implementation would require use of a custom chip or two ASIC chips. More importantly, we can guarantee that the mixed solution using a DLX processor running at 10 MHz will meet the imposed performance requirements of a maximum propagation delay of 46.4 µs, a maximum jam time of 4.8 µs, a minimum interframe spacing of 67.2 µs, and an input bit-rate of 10 Mbytes/s.

Example E

Figure D shows schematic connection of the FIFO control signals for a single data queue. In this example, the data queue is memory mapped at address 0xee000 while the data queue request signal is identified by bit 0 of address 0xee004 and enable from the microprocessor (up_en) is generated from bit 0 of address 0xee008. The following describes the FIFO and microprocessor connections. *cntc* refers to a data queue associated with the circle drawing program threads. *mp* refers to a model of the microprocessor. A signal name is prefixed with a period to indicate the associated hardware or software model.

```
cntc.rq_line [0:0] = @ mp.0xee004[0:0];     # request
cntc.en_line [0:0] = mp.0xee008[0:0];       # enable up en
cntc.ab_line [0:0] = mp.0xee000_rd;         # absorb up ack
```

The control logic needed to generate the enqueue is described by a simple state transition diagram shown in Figure E. The control FIFO is ready to enqueue (indicated by $gn = 1$) process id if the corresponding data request (q_rq) is high and the process has enabled the thread for execution (up_en). Signal up_ab indicates completion of a control FIFO read operation by the processor.

In case of multiple in-degree queues, the enqueue_rq is generated by OR-ing the requests of all inputs to the queues. In case of multiple-out-degree queues, the signal dequeue_rq is generated also by OR-ing all dequeue requests from the queue.

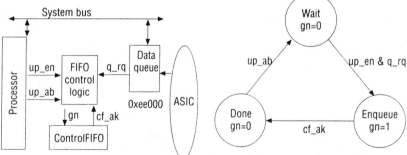

Figure D. Control FIFO schematic.

Figure E. FIFO control state transition diagram.

SYNTHESIS OF EMBEDDED REAL-TIME systems from behavioral specifications constitutes a challenging problem in hardware-software cosynthesis. Due to the relative simplicity of the target architecture compared to general-purpose computing systems, it also affords an opportunity in computer-aided design, by which we can automatically synthesize such systems from a unified specification. Further, the ability to perform constraint and performance analysis for such systems provides a major motivation for using the synthesis approach instead of design-oriented implementation approaches.

Even when manually designed, such systems can benefit greatly from prototypes created by a cosynthesis approach. A cosynthesis approach lets us reduce the size of the chip-synthesis task, while meeting the performance constraints, such that we can use field- or mask-programmable hardware to provide fast turnaround on complex system designs.

For hardware-software synthesis to be

effective, we need specification languages that capture and use capabilities of both hardware and software. The approach presented in this article makes use of an HDL to formulate the problem of cosynthesis as an extension of hardware synthesis. In the process, the approach makes many simplifications for the generated software and leaves room for considerable optimization of the software component.

Currently, we are attempting to develop transformations to simplify control flow in the sequencing graph models, which we can use to minimize interface synchronization requirements. We also plan to investigate extensions to the target architecture to include hierarchical memory schemes and multiple processors. <D&T>

Acknowledgments

We acknowledge discussions and contributions by Claudionor Coelho and David Ku. This research was sponsored by NSF-ARPA, under grant MIP 9115432, and by a fellowship provided by Philips at the Stanford Center for Integrated Systems.

References

1. *Silicon Compilation*, D. Gajski, ed., Addison Wesley, Reading, Mass., 1988.
2. *High-Level VLSI Synthesis*, R. Camposano and W. Wolf, eds., Kluwer Academic Publishers, Norwell, Mass., 1991.
3. D.C. Luckham, "Partial Ordering of Event Sets and Their Application to Prototyping Concurrent Timed Systems," *J. Systems and Software*, July 1993.
4. G. De Micheli et al., "The Olympus Synthesis System for Digital Design," *IEEE Design & Test of Computers*, Vol. 7, No. 5, Oct. 1990, pp. 37-53.
5. N. Woo, W. Wolf, and A. Dunlop, "Compilation of a Single Specification Into Hardware and Software," *Notes of Int'l Workshop Hardware-Software Codesign*, Oct. 1992.
6. P. Chou, R. Ortega, and G. Borriello, "Synthesis of the Hardware/Software Interface in Microcontroller-Based Systems," *Proc. Int'l Conf. Computer-Aided Design*, IEEE Computer Society Press, Los Alamitos, Calif., 1992, pp. 488-495.
7. M. Chiodo et al., "Synthesis of Mixed Hardware-Software Implementations from CFSM Specifications," Memo UCB/ERL M93/49, June 1993, Univ. of California at Berkeley, and *Notes of Int'l Workshop on Hardware-Software Codesign*, Oct. 1992.
8. J. Henkel and R. Ernst, "Ein Softwareorientierter Ansatz zum Hardware-Software CoEntwurf" [A Software-oriented Approach to Hardware-Software Codesign], *Proc. ITG Conf., Recnergestuetzter Entwurf und Architektur mikroelektroninisher Systeme*, Darmstadt, Germany, 1992, pp. 267-268.
9. M.B. Srivastava and R.W. Brodersen, "Rapid-Prototyping of Hardware and Software in a Unified Framework," *Proc. Int'l Conf. Computer-Aided Design*, IEEE CS Press, 1991, pp. 152-155.
10. J. Buck et al., "Ptolemy: A Framework for Simulating and Prototyping Heterogeneous Systems," to be published in *Int'l J. Computer Simulations*.
11. P. Bertin, D. Roncin, and J. Vuillemin, "Introduction to Programmable Active Memories," in *Systolic Array Processors*, J. McCanny, J. McWhirter, and E. Swartzlander, Eds., Prentice Hall, New York, 1989, pp. 300-309.
12. R.W. Hartenstein, A.G. Hirschbiel, and M. Weber, "Mapping Systolic Arrays Onto the Map-Oriented Machine," in *Systolic Array Processors*, J. McCanny, J. McWhirter, and E. Swartzlander, eds., Prentice Hall, New York, 1989, pp. 300-309.
13. S. Walters, "Reprogrammable Hardware Emulation Automates System-Level ASIC Validation," *Wescon/90 Conf. Records*, Electron. Conventions Mgt., Nov. 1990, pp. 140-143.
14. D. Ku and G. De Micheli, *High-Level Synthesis of ASICs Under Timing and Synchronization Constraints*, Kluwer Academic Publishers, Norwell, Mass., 1992.
15. B. Dasarathy, "Timing Constraints of Real-Time Systems: Constructs for Expressing Them, Method for Validating Them," *IEEE Trans. Software Engineering*, Vol. SE-11, No. 6, Jan. 1985, pp. 80-86.
16. D. Ku and G. De Micheli, "Relative Scheduling Under Timing Constraints: Algorithms for High-level Synthesis of Digital Circuits," *IEEE Trans. CAD/ICAS*, Vol. 11., No. 6, June 1992, pp. 696-718.
17. K.K. Parhi, "Algorithm Transform for Concurrent Processors," *Proc. IEEE*, Dec. 1989, IEEE Press, Piscataway, N.J., pp. 1879-1985.
18. R.K. Gupta and G. De Micheli, "Partitioning of Functional Models of Synchronous Digital Systems," *Proc. Int'l Conf. Computer-Aided Design*, IEEE CS Press, 1990, pp. 216-219.
19. V. Sarkar, *Partitioning and Scheduling Parallel Programs for Multiprocessors*, MIT Press, Cambridge, Mass., 1989.
20. R.K. Gupta and G. De Micheli, "System-Level Synthesis Using Re-programmable Components," *Proc. European Design Automation Conf.*, IEEE CS Press, 1992, pp. 2-7.
21. J.L. Hennessy and D.A. Patterson, *Computer Architecture: A Quantitative Approach*, Morgan Kaufman Publishers, Palo Alto, Calif., 1990, pp. 88-137.

Rajesh K. Gupta is a doctoral student in the Department of Electrical Engineering at Stanford University. His primary research interests are the design and synthesis of VLSI circuits and systems. Gupta received an MS in electrical engineering and computer science from the University of California, Berkeley, and a BTech in electrical engineering from the Indian Institute of Technology in Kanpur. Earlier he worked on VLSI design at various levels of abstraction as a member of the design teams for the 80386-SX, 486, and Pentium microprocessor devices at Intel. He is coauthor of a patent on a PLL-based clock circuit, and is currently a Philips fellow at the Center for Integrated Systems at Stanford.

Giovanni De Micheli is an associate professor of electrical engineering and computer science at Stanford University. His research interests include several aspects of the computer-aided design of integrated circuits with particular emphasis on automated synthesis, optimization, and verification of VLSI circuits. He is coeditor of *Design Systems for VLSI Circuits: Logic Synthesis and Silicon Compilation*, and coauthor of *High-Level Synthesis of ASICs Under Timing and Synchronization Constraints*. He graduated from the Politecnico di Milano with a degree in nuclear engineering and received a PhD in electrical engineering and computer science from the University of California, Berkeley. De Micheli is a senior member of the IEEE and is associate editor of the *IEEE Proceedings*, the *IEEE Transactions on VLSI Systems*, and *Integration: The VLSI Journal*.

Send correspondence about this article to the authors at the Center for Integrated Systems, CIS 18, Stanford University, Stanford, CA 94305; rgupta@momus.stanford.edu.

Hardware-Software Cosynthesis for Microcontrollers

ROLF ERNST
JÖRG HENKEL
THOMAS BENNER
Technical University
of Braunschweig

The authors present a software-oriented approach to hardware-software partitioning, which avoids restrictions on the software semantics, and an iterative partitioning process based on "hardware extraction" controlled by a cost function. This process is used in Cosyma, an experimental cosynthesis system for embedded controllers. As an example, the authors demonstrate the extraction of coprocessors for loops. They present results for several benchmark designs.

SMALL EMBEDDED-CONTROL systems consisting of a few integrated circuits are a growing field with a large share of the semiconductor market. Applications include office automation, telecommunications, consumer products, and industrial and automotive control. Embedded control requires reactive systems—that is, systems that react in real time to external asynchronous events, rather than process an input and produce an output after some time, as in classical data processing.

An embedded-control system's architecture is a combination of programmable microprocessor cores with memory and hardwired or field-programmable peripheral devices. Hardware and software together form the control system.

Applications of small embedded-control systems are increasingly complex; examples include 3D signal processing, computer vision, and fuzzy logic. Consequently, the architectures have become more complex, catching up with workstation technology using 32-bit RISC (reduced instruction-set computer) processors.

At the same time, manufacturers have a strong incentive to speed up system design to meet tight time-to-market requirements. Hardware design often must start when the specification is still subject to change. All this makes designing the system increasingly difficult. As a result, small embedded-controller design is changing. At the high end particularly higher level languages (often C) are gradually replacing assembly coding.

For our research work, we selected integrated embedded systems, or microcontrollers, because of their manageable size and economic importance. To minimize customized hardware in microcontrollers, hardware designers are currently developing libraries of standardized peripheral components—for example, in the European OMI (Open Microcontroller Initiative) project. Although this approach allows fast design turnaround and quick modifications, it severely limits design space. At the controller interface, the library approach might be acceptably efficient because most interface functions are relatively simple (counters, timers, serial-parallel conversion), or they are standardized (CAN-Bus, ISDN, Ethernet) or analog (A/D conversion). Much more difficult, however, is deciding which processor core(s) to use, whether to use one or more—possibly different—cores, and how to distribute the work load. Application-specific coprocessors could be very cost effective if they were targeted to those small parts of the software where most of the computation time is spent.

All these decisions require intricate knowledge of the system, which a hardware designer usually does not have, and they must be reevaluated in case of modifications. The library approach covers none of this. So, in general, the designer will stay on the safe side and overdesign processor performance, even in cost-sensitive volume markets.

A microcontroller overdesign can have a high impact on chip area. For example, the difference between a 32-bit RISC and a 16-bit processor may be several hundred thousand transistors, including additional memory for increased instruction and program size. So, for embedded systems, hardware-software codesign potentially has a much higher impact than, for example, logic synthesis.

In the following discussion, we use the term *hardware-software cosynthesis* for codesign systems aiming at automated cost optimization under constraints, mainly timing constraints.

A software-oriented cosynthesis approach

Our hardware-software cosynthesis approach is based on the standard microcontroller architecture, consisting of a processor core, memory, and customized hardware. The processor core is a standard microprocessor, and the customized hardware is synthesized (or user defined).

We implement as many operations as possible in software running on the processor core. The reasons for this choice include the high memory density of standard microprocessors, the availability of optimally adapted compilers, and the careful verification and field testing of standard cores. Moreover, it makes

For embedded systems, hardware-software codesign potentially has a much higher impact than, for example, logic synthesis.

software debugging simpler and overcomes problems of hardware synthesis efficiency for larger functions. Last but not least, it gives us much flexibility in case of modifications.

We generate external hardware only when timing constraints are violated. Exceptions are basic and inexpensive I/O functions—for example, the standard processor interface (address bus, data bus, and control signals), serial and parallel I/O, and user-provided peripheral functions such as an optimized field bus interface selected from a library.

Timing constraints for interface control signals, such as Request and Acknowledge signals, span a small part of the whole control task and thus leave little architectural choice. But other timing constraints are more global, such as control process cycle times, dead times, data-sampling rates, and interprocess communication. These more global constraints concern extended code sections and give much choice as to which part of a function to implement in hardware. If multiple tasks execute concurrently, one might even decide to move part of a noncritical task to a hardware function to save processor time for a critical task.

The problem is to analyze the software and to select an appropriate part of the software for implementation in hardware, to meet timing constraints.

At present, we can handle only coprocessors and user-defined interface modules. Eventually, we would like to use the following circuit types:

- *Primitive structures at the interfaces*: counters, timers, and so on. The user should be able to provide more complex peripheral structures such as bus interfaces.
- *Coprocessors*. Coprocessors should be small so that they can be implemented by high-level synthesis.
- *Second core processor*. If a coprocessor is not appropriate because there is no distinct critical software function or because it is too large, another (possibly different) standard core could be implemented.

In all three cases, the user must be able to define hardware modules. Hardware function selection and circuit type definition constitute a partitioning problem. Because analysis and partitioning occur in the software functions, we call our approach software-oriented hardware-software partitioning.

Related work

Srivastava and Brodersen present a CAD framework for rapid prototyping.[1] The target architecture consists of dedicated and programmable hardware modules, and the system software is generated to run on it. As in the Codes environment,[2] Srivastava and Brodersen emphasize integrated design of hardware and software, specification, and cosimulation. Windirsch et al. describe rapid prototyping in mechatronic system design.[3]

A second group of researchers views hardware-software codesign mainly as a partitioning problem. Barros and Rosenstiel[4] present a clustering approach using closeness criteria (see, for example, Lagnese and Thomas[5]) to control the partitioning process. The designer decides on the clustering. This indirect approach covers part of the design space. Athanas and Silverman use an "instruction set meta-

> *Finer-grain partitioning, using coprocessors and second cores, becomes more and more important as processor performance rises and system software increases.*

morphosis" to speed up a standard processor core (MC68010).[6] Computation-intensive code segments are moved to hardware, but the method is limited to the coarse granularity of the function level. The resulting high speedup values, however, seem unlikely for modern RISC processors. All these approaches work with manual partitioning.

Only one system—besides Cosyma, the system we describe in this article—performs an automatic partitioning process.[7,8] (Woo, Wolf, and Dunlop's work heads in the same direction.[9]) This cosynthesis system, Vulcan, uses a system architecture similar to the one in our approach. The input language is HardwareC, a subset of C defined for hardware description, with integer as the only data type. The cosynthesis starts with a configuration in which all functions, except program constructs with unbounded delay, are implemented as hardware modules. The remaining functions are implemented as software on a standard core processor. Then the design system tries to gradually move hardware functions to software, checking timing constraints and synchronism as it does so. The high-level synthesis system Olympus generates the hardware. This is a hardware-oriented partitioning approach. In contrast to our software-oriented approach, only constructs that initially can be implemented in customized hardware can move to software. That means the input system description has some limitations in dynamic data structures and system complexity.

Microcontroller system modeling

Because C seems to be a preferred language for embedded-control programming, we pragmatically defined C^x, a superset of the ANSI C standard, as the input language. We avoided restrictions when we enhanced the C language, because software development, software efficiency, and verification are becoming dominant problems of embedded-system design, accounting for most of the development costs. Obviously, some C constructs cannot be mapped to hardwired logic, such as dynamic data structures, but in a software-oriented approach, this only means that these constructs must be excluded from implementation in hardware. Our main extensions of C are

- timing: minimum and maximum delays and duration between C labels of a task[10]
- task concept
- task intercommunication

Our approach to user interaction in the selection of hardware and the inclusion of user-defined hardware functions, such as library functions, is similar to the solution in the Olympus synthesis system.[11] The designer must describe the behavior to be implemented in hardware as a C function, which is then moved to hardware and implemented by synthesis or by the user-defined hardware. The same is possible the other way around; that is, the designer can define a C function that must not be implemented in hardware, to allow modifications even after hardware development.

Hardware-software partitioning problem

Partitioning must identify if and where system constraints, in our case timing constraints, are violated. Partitioning can occur at different levels of granularity: task, function, basic block, or even single statement. Partitioning on even lower levels, such as the assembly language level, is not useful because the assembly code is already based on processor details. In the following discussion we use the term *coarse-grain partitioning* for task-level and function-level partitioning and *fine-grain partitioning* for basic-block-level and statement-level partitioning. By these terms, Srivastava and Brodersen,[1] Buchenrieder and Veith,[2] and Athanas and Silverman[6] use coarse-grain manual partitioning approaches. Barros and Rosenstiel[4] use fine-grain manual partitioning, and Gupta and De Micheli[7] use fine-grain automatic partitioning.

Partitioning at the task or subtask levels is typical for manual design. Sometimes, partitioning at this level is almost obvious. An example is a signal-processing task consisting of high-speed filtering of input data exceeding a processor's performance, followed by a more complex algorithm with lower performance requirements.

Finer-grain partitioning, using coprocessors and second cores, becomes more and more important as processor performance rises and system software increases. At finer granularity, however, partitioning is less obvious and more difficult because its side effects have a high impact. The most important side effects are

- *Communication time overhead*: Additional I/O operations of the processor core require additional computation time. Load/store architectures typical of RISC controllers even require an extra instruction for each read and write operation. In an extreme case, the

overall timing might be worse than before partitioning.
- *Communication area overhead*: Besides obvious wiring overhead, communication can require buffers or memories. Buffer or memory size estimation is not always a simple problem.
- *Interlocks:* If variables are allocated to an external hardware register, they might not (yet) be available by the time the processor software can process them. This leads to waiting time in the software.
- *Compiler effects:* When a program is fragmented by the extraction of statements or basic blocks, the efficiency of compiler optimization will change. Also, pipeline efficiency and concurrent unit utilization (superscalar architectures) will be different. These effects are hard to predict.

In addition to the large design space including processor selection, peripheral component and coprocessor definition, and synthesis, which we pointed out earlier, these side effects make it even harder for a system designer to partition at levels of finer granularity. There are a few exceptions such as floating-point or graphics coprocessors.

Nevertheless, fine-grain partitioning offers a high potential for system optimization, as we will show in our examples. The exploitation of fine-grain partitioning is one opportunity provided by hardware-software cosynthesis. Therefore, our approach concentrates on fine-grain partitioning (currently on the basic-block-level only), but we can also use it for coarse-grain partitioning.

The Cosyma system

As a platform for our research, we developed the cosynthesis system Cosyma (cosynthesis for embedded architectures). Figure 1 gives an overview. The system description in C^x is translated into an internal graph representation

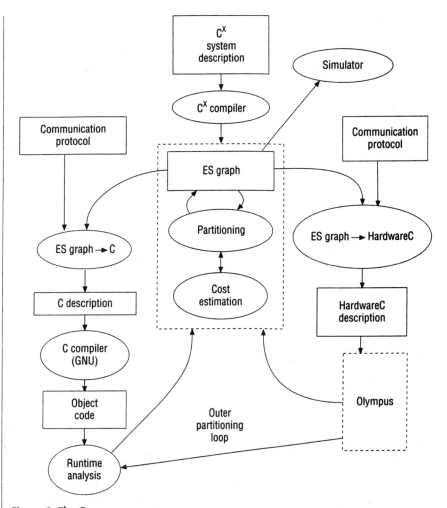

Figure 1. The Cosyma system.

suitable for partitioning. The following are the requirements of this internal representation:

- It should completely represent all input constructs including dynamic data structures, recurrence, parallel processes, and timing.
- The user should have strong influence on the syntactic structure of the software (to maintain good programming style).
- The representation should support partitioning and generation of a hardware description for parts moved to hardware.
- Estimation techniques such as a simple runtime estimation by local scheduling on the graph should be possible.

A control and dataflow graph, typically used in high-level synthesis, does not meet the first and second requirements but is appropriate for the last two. Therefore, we defined an extended syntax graph, or ES graph, which is a syntax graph extended by a symbol table and local data and control dependencies.[12] The ES graph is a directed acyclic graph describing a sequence of declarations, definitions, and statements. Each identifier occurring in the graph is accompanied by a pointer to its definition. Conversely, pointers to all instances extend each definition, building an implic-

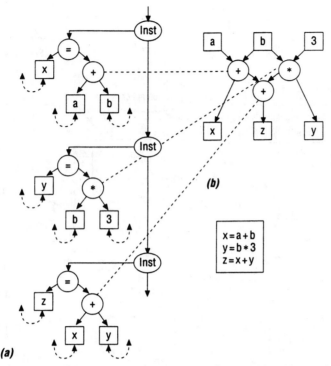

Figure 2. The extended-syntax graph (ES graph): part of the syntax graph (a) and corresponding BSB (b).

it symbol table.

The syntax graph itself allows the description of the whole input language but does not contain any information about the data dependencies occurring in the graph. Therefore, we overlaid the syntax graph with a second graph consisting of cross-linked blocks, called basic scheduling blocks (BSBs). Both graphs share the same operator nodes, thereby enabling a fast transition from the syntax graph to the dataflow graph and vice versa.

Figure 2 illustrates the relationships between the two representations. The dashed lines represent the physical identity of the operator nodes in both graphs. The ES graph is implemented as a C++ class and appears as an overlay of a syntax graph by a control and dataflow graph. Thus, for a given node, the system can easily and quickly switch from one view to the other. A simulator for the ES graph supports verification of the C^x description (including parallel processes) and profiling. Profiling is required for partitioning.

We execute hardware-software partitioning on the ES graph by marking nodes to be moved to hardware. A translator (ES graph → C) generates C functions for the software, reconstructing the structure of the original C^x description preserved in the ES graph. Then, the hardware-software communication protocol is inserted. The communication protocol is generated from a template, and the data to be communicated are determined from a dataflow analysis of the ES graph.

A standard (GNU) C compiler generates the object code, which can then be simulated with an RT- (register-transfer) level simulator.[13] Currently, Cosyma supports only a Sparc processor core. We chose Sparc because it is becoming one of the preferred 32-bit RISC architectures in microcontrollers. We execute a runtime analysis on the object code to check for violations of the timing constraints in the C^x description. This runtime analysis can be an RT-level simulation, but we have also developed a hybrid timing verification approach that is much faster and provides almost the same precision.[13]

For hardware generation, Cosyma currently uses the Olympus high-level synthesis system.[11] Olympus accepts HardwareC as an input language. An important feature in this context is that Olympus allows us to link user-defined hardware modules to the synthesis process, either as HardwareC functions or by overloading the regular HardwareC operators. We overloaded our own library of 32-bit multipliers and ALUs.

Several independent but sequential subgraphs of the ES graph (statements, basic blocks, or functions) can be mapped to a single coprocessor. Therefore, if the coprocessor is activated, a subgraph index must be communicated from the processor to the coprocessor, indicating which subgraph to execute. The HardwareC descriptions for the individual subgraphs are encapsulated in a switch statement controlled by the subgraph index, BSB-Id (see Figure 3).

So far, we have not determined the hardware-software partitioning approach. Cosyma is not restricted to a particular approach; rather it was intended as an experimental platform for hardware-software partitioning approaches. However, there are some reasons to focus on iterative partitioning:

- The results of optimizing compilation and processor pipeline utilization are hard to predict. Thus, software timing estimation is very difficult, particularly if the partitioning approach must be usable for different processor cores and compilers.
- Estimating high-level synthesis results is even more difficult. The effects and applicability of high-level transformations, such as tree height reduction or percolation-based synthesis,[14] and the efficiency of scheduling and allocation are extremely hard to predict.
- Communication time overhead can

be high compared to circuit partitioning and can require up to hundreds of clock cycles for a single coprocessor run. This overhead depends on communication mechanisms, memory organization, variable allocation, and so on. So the overall costs of hardware-software partitioning can be highly nonmonotonic.

We concluded that an iterative partitioning approach would be best suited for cosynthesis with cost optimization. In our case, iteration includes hardware synthesis, compilation, and timing analysis of the resulting hardware-software system with RT-level timing precision. The iteration loop is shown as the outer partitioning loop in Figure 1.

For the partitioning process, we concentrate on stochastic algorithms. Stochastic algorithms let us use arbitrary cost functions and iteration steps to make a trade-off between computation time and result quality. Thus, they are well suited to partitioning experiments, even if the relation of computation time to quality might not be optimal. At present, we use simulated annealing.

Simulated annealing with each move evaluated throughout the design loop, however, would be impractical, considering the computation time for synthesis, compilation, and runtime analysis. Therefore, we introduced a dual-loop approach. We execute simulated annealing on an inner loop, based on a cost function with estimated results. This cost function is adapted to the actual results in the outer loop.

The cost function plays an important role in our partitioning approach. We use it not only to estimate costs but also to control the partitioning process.

Usually, simulated annealing starts with a feasible solution and accepts only moves that lead to another feasible solution. In our software-oriented approach, however, we must start with a nonfeasible solution—that is, a solution that does not meet the time constraints. Instead of

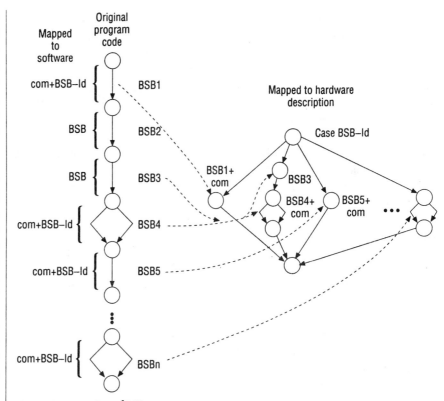

Figure 3. Extraction of BSBs.

trying to enforce a feasible solution as a starting point (as in the hardware-oriented approach), we solve the optimization problem with a high cost penalty for runtimes exceeding the time constraints and a steep decrease of costs for improved timing. This prevents annealing before a feasible solution is reached or further partitioning is not possible.

Currently, all the tools we have presented are operational. Thus, we can achieve one fully automatic partitioning result. The automatic cost function adaptation, however, is not implemented yet. So if a first design does not meet constraints, we must start a new run through the Cosyma system. The user selects new parameters for the second and all further runs.

Cost function and preprocessing

Practical control systems with several thousand lines of description, in which hardware-software partitioning is not obvious (and therefore cannot easily be done manually), may have a large design space. To reduce this design space, one could try employing knowledge of control system characteristics, component libraries, and synthesis tool or compiler properties. One way to do that is an approach known from synthesis as clustering with closeness criteria.[5] Closeness criteria are the use of common variables (data closeness), the probability of common execution of two operations (control closeness), and the similarity of operations that allow sharing of function units (operator closeness). Such global clustering, however, seems difficult here. The success of floating-point coprocessors, for example, would place a high weight on operator closeness. On the other hand, the common use of counters and timers in peripheral devices would place a high weight on data and control closeness.

We decided to use another approach, which we call hardware extraction.

Hardware extraction is the use of a partitioning cost function that favors for implementation in hardware those system parts that can be implemented well in hardware. Such a cost function encodes knowledge of synthesis, compilers, and libraries. Different cost functions can work in parallel or in sequence to extract different types of target hardware.

As an example, we developed a cost function to extract coprocessors for computation-time-intensive system parts, especially loops. As we have already mentioned, such coprocessors could be a valuable alternative to the library approach.

Simulation and profiling identify computation-time-intensive system parts. Given user-defined input patterns, we execute a simulation on the ES graph. We determine the number of times each node (including nodes representing subgraphs, such as function nodes) is executed. Next, we estimate the potential speedup through hardware synthesis and the communication penalty for nodes moved to hardware. Currently, we estimate on the basic-block level only (more precisely, we define a basic scheduling block that considers loops as basic blocks, too). We estimate the potential speedup with

- an operator table, which holds the execution times of the function units used in synthesis, and
- a local scheduling of the operations in the ES graph to estimate the potential concurrency, either using a simple list scheduling for a bounded number of hardware function units (currently a user-defined parameter) or using ASAP (as soon as possible) scheduling.

The estimate of communication time overhead of a basic block includes

- a dataflow analysis providing the number of variables to be communicated if this basic block alone is moved to hardware and the number of variables to be communicated if the adjacent blocks are moved to hardware as well; and
- the number of clock cycles for a variable transfer, given the processor type and communication mechanism.

All these are preprocessing steps and need not be repeated during inner-loop simulated annealing. ES graph basic blocks containing operations that cannot be mapped to hardware are excluded from this procedure.

We define costs incrementally. Currently, we partition only on the basic-block level. When a basic block B is moved to hardware, the cost increment dc is defined as

$$dc(B) = a(T_c, T_s) * [t_{neff}(B) + t_{com}(B) - t_{HW\text{-}SW}(B) - t_{SW}(B)] * lt(B)$$

where:

- $a(T_c, T_s) = \text{sign}(T_c - T_s) * \exp[(T_c - T_s)/T]$, with T_c the given time constraint, T_s the resulting time needed by the hardware-software system between the time labels of T_c, and T a constant factor. This corresponds to an exponential weighting of runtimes above the given constraints. Below the constraints, the sign is changed to avoid increasing the synthesis task by the unnecessary moving of basic blocks to hardware.
- $t_{neff}(B)$ is the effective hardware timing (synthesis result) for n function units, initialized with the local schedule mentioned earlier.
- $t_{com}(B)$, $t_{HW\text{-}SW}(B)$, and $t_{SW}(B)$ are the communication overhead, the hardware-software time overlap (in case of parallel execution; in the experiments $t_{HW\text{-}SW}(B) = 0$), and the runtime when the basic block is implemented in software, all initialized with estimated values.
- $lt(B)$ is the number of times the basic block was executed during profiling.

For the partitioning process we need knowledge of the hardware-software communication overhead. For m BSBs, 2^m-1 hardware partitions are possible; therefore, preprocessing of the exact communication costs is not practical. Instead, we estimate costs only for adjacent BSBs in the control flow. This avoids a global dataflow analysis.[15] Each BSB is attributed with a set (in_a) of variables used inside the block before they are defined and a set (out_a) of variables defined in a. These sets give an upper bound of the communication necessary when the BSB alone is moved to hardware.

Usually, we move several BSBs to hardware, and to avoid redundant variable exchange, we must consider communication between these BSBs. Let us consider BSB a as having been moved to hardware. The additional number of variable transfers from software to hardware is estimated as

$$in'_a = in_a - \bigcap_{b \in \text{predecessors}(a)} (in_b \cup out_b)$$

Estimations for out_a and for moving an operation back to software can be derived similarly.

To keep the coprocessor overhead small, we use a small, fixed shared-memory space. If variable var i will be transmitted to a coprocessor register, it is first moved to the shared memory with load and store operations. Assuming fixed-size data values, the time $t_{com}(a)$ is proportional to the number of elements in the in sets and out sets. When estimating $t_{com}(a)$, we must take memory and register allocation into account. Figure 4 outlines the communication steps for a single variable transfer through shared memory.

In our example, each variable communication requires eight clock cycles corresponding to up to eight instruction executions on the processor. This means that communication overhead minimization is important in fine-grain

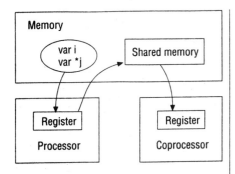

Figure 4. Variable communication path.

hardware-software partitioning. Therefore, the translation from the ES graph to HardwareC uses a more precise communication analysis than an analysis of adjacent blocks.[16] In case of arrays, only pointers are communicated via the shared memory (Figure 4, var *j).

The cost function does not explicitly account for hardware costs. Instead, for our experiments, the user provides the number n of functional units in the coprocessor as a hardware cost parameter, and the system optimizes the timing. In future experiments, we will add hardware costs to the cost function, as provided by the synthesis tool.

Target architecture and communication protocol

The experimental results presented in the next section are based on the target architecture shown in Figure 5. The standard Sparc processor[17] communicates with a synthesized coprocessor via memory communication. At present, software and hardware execute in mutual exclusion, and the Sparc and the coprocessor are coupled by the principle of communicating sequential processes. We are also working on other communication mechanisms.

When the processor writes to a predefined reference address, a Start signal is issued to the coprocessor and a Hold signal to the processor (BHold: Hold signal, AOE: address bus enable, DOE: data bus enable). The data word written to the ref-

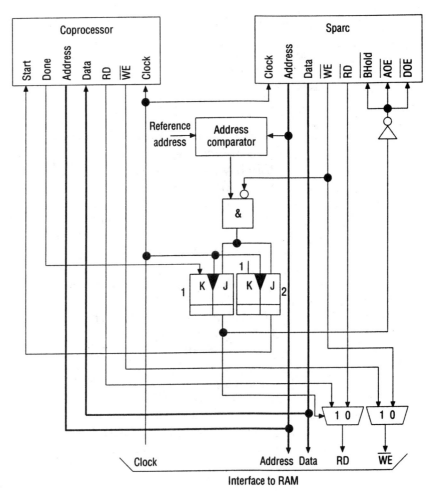

Figure 5. Memory-coupling circuit.

erence address is the BSB-Id (Figure 3), which indicates the hardware function to be executed. The Sparc switches to the Hold state and the coprocessor enables its data and address lines. The coprocessor decodes the BSB-Id and begins executing the corresponding code segment. At the end of the segment, the Done signal is issued, the coprocessor stops, and the Sparc processor leaves the Hold state.

Experiments

For demonstration we start with a manually partitioned example because of the simplicity of the result. The example is a practical algorithm, a chroma-key algorithm for high-definition television studio equipment.[18] The desired response time was 1 second. The algorithm needed 3 seconds on a Sparc1+. The program has 1,400 lines of C code. In the manual experiment, we applied a simplified cost function to partition two loops with 34 lines of code, which are iterated 10,070 times, taking 90% of the computation time. Figure 6 (next page) shows the program section with the two loops, 30c and 30d, shaded. This hardware partition consists of several consecutive BSBs, but it is still fine-grain compared to function- or task-level partitioning. The coprocessor executes the two BSBs (30c and 30d) and is therefore called 10,070 times in each process execution.

We translated the section to HardwareC. The variables cr, $cr1$, $cr2$, and cb are

```
while (cb <= cb2 + key1) {
    if (cb > vtab[cr] ) {
        if (cb >= htab[cr] )
            kt[cr] [cb] = 255 ;
        else {
            iabsv = 512 ;   /* = 256 + 256 */
/* ========================= area 30c ========================= */
            for (i = cr1; i <= cr2; i++) {
                ihilf = labs (cr – i) + labs (cb – vtab [i] ) ;
                if       (ihilf < iabsv) {
                        iabsv = ihilf;
                }
            } /*of for i*/
            iabsh = 512 ;   /* = 256 + 256 */
/* ========================= area 30d ========================= */
            for (i = cr1; i <= cr2; i++) {
                ihilf = labs (cr – i) + labs (cb – htab [i] ) ;
                if       (ihilf < iabsh) {
                        iabsh = ihilf;
                }
            } /*of for i*/
/* ========================= area t1 ========================= */
            kt[cr] [cb] = iabsv * 255 / (iabsv + iabsh) ;
        }    /*of else*/
    }
    FORLIM = min (cr + keyr, cr2) ;

    for (v = max(cr1, cr – key1); v <= FORLIM; v++) {
        FORLIM1 = min (cb + keyr, cb2) ;

        for (u = max(cb1, cr – key1); u <= FORLIM; u++) {
            kt[v] [u] = kt[cr] [cb] ;
        }
    }

    cb += keyf;
}  /*of while cb <= cb2*/
```

Figure 6. *Loops in chroma-key algorithm.*

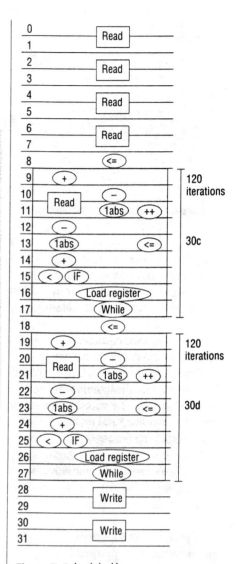

Figure 7. *Scheduled loops.*

read from memory upon activation of the coprocessor, and the values *iabsv* and *iabsh* are written to memory immediately before control returns to the processor. The table values in *vtab* are read during processing. Olympus provided the schedule in Figure 7, which uses two ALUs.

The result was a circuit with 17,300 gate equivalents and a 120-ns clock cycle time using the LSI 1.5-μm library. After manually inserting a few drivers into high-fan-out nets, we reduced the coprocessor cycle time to the processor cycle time of 30 ns with 18,000 gate equivalents. The loop execution time was 65.2 μs per coprocessor call and 0.65 sec. for all 10,070 calls. The total execution time was 1 sec., a speedup of 3, at much less cost than a second Sparc core.

More interesting for synthesis is automatic partitioning. We obtained the results for our next examples with a *fully automatic* partitioning process, excluding the outer loop:

1. System specifications
2. Translation of system specifications to the ES graph representation by the C^x compiler

3. Partitioning by simulated annealing
4. Mapping to software and hardware descriptions by translating tools
5. High-level synthesis and software compilation
6. Runtime analysis

Except for the Olympus system, all tools belong to the Cosyma system.

We selected benchmarks to demonstrate the feasibility of an automatic partitioning process, although its efficiency is not yet optimal. Much work is still needed to exploit the full optimization potential. In the examples, T_c is moderately defined as $T_c = 1/2\ T_s$ (T_s for an all-software solution), so that the HardwareC description is small enough that Olympus can finish within a couple of hours on a Sparc10/41. In all cases, the maximum number n of function units to be implemented in hardware was limited to 1. A function unit is assembled from a 32-bit ALU, which is built from bit-slice components (Texas Instruments 74×181), and a 32-bit nonpipelined multiplier that needs two clock cycles for a multiplication.

Our results, shown in Figures 8 and 9, demonstrate the behavior of simulated annealing for some realistic benchmarks, Simp and Fft. We executed the partitioning 10 times for each benchmark. Each partitioning run started with a different random seed. Two interesting aspects are the selection of the basic blocks and the repeatability of the results for different initial conditions (random seeds) of simulated annealing, suggesting the usefulness of the cost function. Figures 8a and 9a show the number of times each basic block was moved to hardware; Figures 8b and 9b show the number of iterations of a block during profiling. As already mentioned, the desired speedup was set to 2.

Figure 8 shows that two of the three most often extracted blocks correspond to computation-intensive code segments. One of them was extracted in all 10 runs. Here the factor It of the cost function

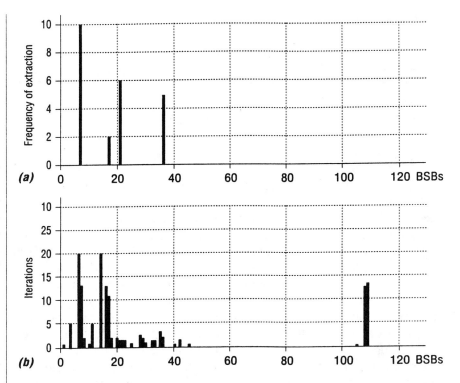

Figure 8. The Simp benchmark: probability of extraction (a) and frequency of iteration (b).

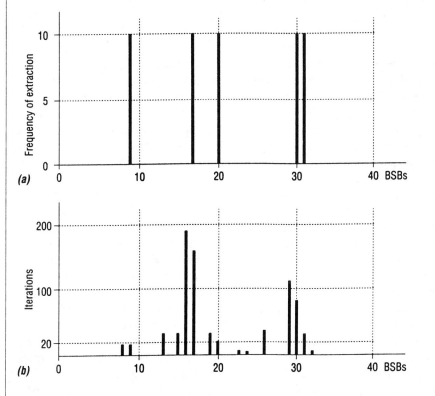

Figure 9. The Fft benchmark: probability of extraction (a) and frequency of iteration (b).

Table 1. Partitioned benchmarks.

Benchmark	Clock cycles used		t_c (%)	Speedup
	SW	HW-SW		
Diesel	22,403	16,394	9.9	1.4
Smooth	1,781,712	1,393,525	49.6	1.3
3d	1,377	1,514	13.8	0.9

dominates. At first glance, it is surprising that the two blocks 108 and 109 with peak execution rates in Figure 8b never move to hardware. A closer look at these code segments shows that the speedup of coprocessor hardware would not have been large enough to compensate for the communication overhead t_{com}. This negative gain is multiplied by the execution rate, making an implementation in hardware very unlikely.

For the benchmark shown in Figure 9, again most extracted basic blocks correspond to computation-intensive code segments. Obviously, all five blocks are extracted in all 10 partitioning runs, reflecting that the blocks are iterated relatively often and that communication overhead is small enough relative to operation speedup. As other experiments showed, these benchmarks are exemplary. In almost all cases, they could reach the required speedup, supporting our approach of driving the annealing process toward a feasible design point using an exponential cost function.

We experimented with three more benchmarks. The results assume that hardware and software use the same instruction cycle (as in the HDTV example). We are not at all limited to this assumption, but it simplifies comparison of system performance before and after partitioning.

The Diesel benchmark (see Table 1) is a real-time algorithm for the digital control of a turbocharged diesel engine. Our timing analysis tool calculated a computation time of T_s = 22,403 cycles on a Sparc1+ processor. An automatically generated hardware-software codesign could reach a speedup of 1.4 (16,394 cycles) under the given constraints.

The second benchmark, Smooth, executing a filter algorithm on a digital image, gave almost the same result.

The third benchmark, 3d, is an interesting example showing that automated hardware-software codesign is not a trivial task. Under the same conditions where Diesel and Smooth resulted in a real speedup, we achieved a "speedup" of 0.9 with 3d. Here the partitioning did not consider the optimizing potential of the GNU C-compiler. An investigation showed that a code segment consisting mainly of two multiplications was extracted to hardware. The partitioning algorithm assumed two cycles per multiplication. Including transfer times, a hardware realization would amount to less than 10 cycles, and software execution would take about 40 cycles (in our experiments, we took the estimated execution times of the Sparc processor from a table). Studying the assembler code produced by the GNU C-compiler revealed, however, that both of the multiplications had one constant factor converted to additions and shifts.

Table 1 also shows the communication overhead for the three benchmarks. An amount of up to 50% is not unusual for the group of benchmarks (real-time applications for small embedded systems) we investigated. Reducing communication overhead seems to be one of the most important factors in gaining a higher speedup.

For a higher speedup we also need a synthesis tool that schedules and optimizes across basic-block boundaries, using some of the techniques mentioned earlier. We are currently working on such an approach.[19]

FINE-GRAIN HARDWARE-SOFTWARE partitioning is feasible and useful in microcontroller design. The results of automated software-oriented partitioning with hardware extraction are promising and are similar for different initial conditions. The examples and the partitions we have presented are not trivial. We expect further improvements from optimized communication mechanisms, and, in particular, from synthesis with high-level transformations, pipelining, and scheduling across basic blocks. Precise estimations of synthesis results and shorter synthesis computation times are very important for the industrial use of cosynthesis systems such as Cosyma.

References

1. M.B. Srivastava and R.W. Brodersen, "Rapid-Prototyping of Hardware and Software in a Unified Framework," *Proc. Int'l Conf. Computer-Aided Design*, IEEE Computer Society Press, Los Alamitos, Calif., 1991, pp. 152-155.
2. K. Buchenrieder and C. Veith, "CODES: A Practical Concurrent Design Environment," handout from Int'l Workshop on Hardware-Software Codesign, Estes Park, Colo., Oct. 1992.
3. P. Windirsch et al., "Application-Specific Microelectronics for Mechatronic Systems," *Proc. Third European Design Automation Conf.*, IEEE CS Press, 1992, pp. 194-199.
4. E. Barros and W. Rosenstiel, "A Method for Hardware/Software Partitioning," *Proc. Compeuro*, IEEE CS Press, 1992.
5. E. Dirkes Lagnese and D.E. Thomas, "Architectural Partitioning for System-Level Design," *Proc. 26th Design Automation Conf.*, IEEE CS Press, 1989, pp. 62-67.

6. P. Athanas and H.F. Silverman, "Processor Reconfiguration Through Instruction-Set Metamorphosis," *Computer*, Vol. 26, No. 3, Mar. 1993, pp. 11-18.
7. R.K. Gupta and G. De Micheli, "System-Level Synthesis Using Re-programmable Components," *Proc. Third European Conf. Design Automation*, IEEE CS Press, 1992, pp. 2-7.
8. R.K. Gupta, C.N. Coelho, Jr., and G. De Micheli, "Synthesis and Simulation of Digital Systems Containing Interacting Hardware and Software Components," *Proc. 29th Design Automation Conf.*, IEEE CS Press, 1992, pp. 225-234.
9. N. Woo, W. Wolf, and A. Dunlop, "Compilation of a Single Specification into Hardware," handout from Int'l Workshop Hardware-Software Codesign, Estes Park, Colo., Oct. 1992.
10. B. Dasarathy, "Timing Constraints of Real-Time Systems: Constructs for Expressing Them, Methods of Validating Them," *IEEE Trans. Software Engineering*, Jan. 1985, pp. 80-86.
11. G. De Micheli et al., "The Olympus Synthesis System," *IEEE Design & Test of Computers*, Vol. 7, No. 5, Oct. 1990, pp. 37-53.
12. T. Benner, J. Henkel, and R. Ernst, "Internal Representation of Embedded Hardware/Software Systems," to be published in *Proc. Second IFIP Int'l Workshop Hardware/Software Codesign*, IFIP, Geneva, 1993.
13. W. Ye et al., "Fast Timing Analysis for Hardware-Software Cosynthesis," *Proc. Int'l Conf. Computer Design*, IEEE CS Press, 1993, pp. 452-457.
14. R. Potasman, "Percolation-Based Synthesis," *Proc. 27th Design Automation Conf.*, IEEE CS Press, 1990, pp. 444-449.
15. A.W. Aho, R. Sethi, and J.D. Ullmann, *Compilers: Principles, Techniques and Tools*, Addison-Wesley, Reading, Mass., 1986.
16. G. Glawe, *Erstellen eines Code-Generators zur Umsetzung eines C-Syntax-Graphen in die Hardwarebeschreibungssprache HardwareC [A Code Generator for the Translation of a C Syntax Graph into the Hardware Description Language HardwareC]*, master's thesis, Technical Univ. of Braunschweig, Germany, May 1993.
17. Cypress Semiconductor, *Data Book*, Cypress Semiconductor, San Jose, Calif., 1992.
18. C. Ricken, *Optimierung der automatischen Einpegelung eines HDTV-Chromakey-Mischers [Optimization of an Automatic Color Level Control for an HDTV Chroma-key Blue Screen System]*, master's thesis, Technical Univ. of Braunschweig, 1992.
19. U. Holtmann and R. Ernst, "Experiments with Low-Level Speculative Computation Based on Multiple Branch Prediction," *IEEE Trans. VLSI Systems*, Sept. 1993.

Rolf Ernst is a professor of electrical engineering at the Technical University of Braunschweig, Germany. His research interests are VLSI CAD and digital circuit design. Previously, he was a member of the technical staff in the CAD and Test Laboratory of AT&T Bell Laboratories and a research assistant at the University of Erlangen, Germany. He holds a diploma in computer science and a PhD in electrical engineering from the University of Erlangen. He is a member of the IEEE, the IEEE Computer Society, and the German GI (Society for Computer Science).

Jörg Henkel is pursuing a PhD in electrical engineering at the Technical University of Braunschweig, where he is involved in the development of Cosyma, the experimental system for hardware-software codesign. In addition, his interests include high-level synthesis and computer architecture. He received a diploma in electrical engineering from the Technical University of Braunschweig.

Thomas Benner is a research assistant at the Technical University of Braunschweig, working on the Cosyma project. His interests are hardware-software codesign, computer architecture, graph theory, and digital circuit design. He holds a diploma in computer science from the Technical University of Braunschweig, where he is pursuing a PhD in electrical engineering. He is a member of the German GI (Society for Computer Science).

Address correspondence to Rolf Ernst, Institut für Datenverarbeitungsanlagen, Technische Universität Braunschweig, Hans-Sommer-Str. 66, D-38106 Braunschweig, Germany; ernst@ida.ing.tu-bs.de.

Hardware/Software Co-Design

GIOVANNI DE MICHELI, FELLOW, IEEE, AND RAJESH K. GUPTA, MEMBER, IEEE

Invited Paper

Most electronic systems, whether self-contained or embedded, have a predominant digital component consisting of a hardware platform which executes software application programs. Hardware/software co-design means meeting system-level objectives by exploiting the synergism of hardware and software through their concurrent design. Co-design problems have different flavors according to the application domain, implementation technology and design methodology.

Digital hardware design has increasingly more similarities to software design. Hardware circuits are often described using modeling or programming languages, and they are validated and implemented by executing software programs, which are sometimes conceived for the specific hardware design. Current integrated circuits can incorporate one (or more) processor core(s) and memory array(s) on a single substrate. These "systems on silicon" exhibit a sizable amount of embedded software, which provides flexibility for product evolution and differentiation purposes. Thus the design of these systems requires designers to be knowledgeable in both hardware and software domains to make good design tradeoffs.

This paper introduces the reader to various aspects of co-design. We highlight the commonalities and point out the differences in various co-design problems in some application areas. Co-design issues and their relationship to classical system implementation tasks are discussed to help the reader develop a perspective on modern digital system design that relies on computer-aided design (CAD) tools and methods.

I. INTRODUCTION

Most engineering designs can be viewed as systems, i.e., as collections of several components whose combined operation provides useful services. Components can be heterogeneous in nature and their interaction may be regulated by some simple or complex means. Most examples of systems today are either electronic in nature (e.g., information processing systems) or contain an electronic subsystem for monitoring and control (e.g., plant control).

Manuscript received February 1, 1996; revised December 2, 1996. This work was supported in part by DARPA, under Contract DABT 63-95-C-0049, and in part by NSF CAREER Award MIP 95-01615.

G. De Micheli is with the Computer Systems Laboratory, Stanford University, Stanford, CA 94305 USA (e-mail: nanni@galileo.stanford.edu).

R. K. Gupta is with the Department of Computer Science, University of California, Irvine, CA 92797 USA (e-mail: rgupta@ics.uci.edu).

Publisher Item Identifier S 0018-9219(97)02017-3.

Moreover, the implementation of electronic systems and subsystems shows often a predominant digital component.

We focus in this paper on the digital component of electronic systems, and refer to them as (digital) systems for brevity. The majority of such systems are programmable, and thus consist of hardware and software components. The value of a system can be measured by some objectives that are specific to its application domain (e.g., performance, design, and manufacturing cost, and ease of programmability) and it depends on both the hardware and the software components. *Hardware/software co-design* means meeting system-level objectives by exploiting the synergism of hardware and software through their concurrent design. Since digital systems have different organizations and applications, there are several co-design problems of interest. Such problems have been tackled by skillful designers for many years, but detailed-level design performed by humans is often a time-consuming and error-prone task. Moreover, the large amount of information involved in co-design problems makes it unlikely that human designers can optimize all objectives, thus leading to products whose value is lower than the potential one.

The recent rise in interest in hardware/software co-design is due to the introduction of *computer-aided design* (CAD) tools for co-design (e.g., commercial simulators) and to the expectation that solutions to other co-design problems will be supported by tools, thus raising the potential quality and shortening the development time of electronic products. Due to the extreme competitiveness in the marketplace, co-design tools are likely to play a key strategic role. The forecast of the worldwide revenues of integrated circuit sales (Fig. 1), and in particular for those used in dedicated applications (Fig. 2), explains the high demand of electronic system-level design tools, whose volume of sales is expected to grow at a compound annual rate of 34% in the 1993–1998 time frame, according to Dataquest.

The evolution of integrated circuit technology is also motivating new approaches to digital circuit design. The trend toward smaller mask-level geometries leads to higher integration and higher cost of fabrication, hence to the need

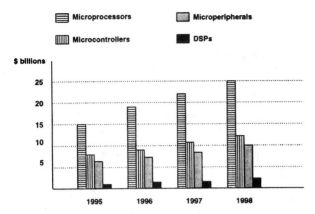

Fig. 1. Forecast of the growth of electronic components. (Source: Dataquest.)

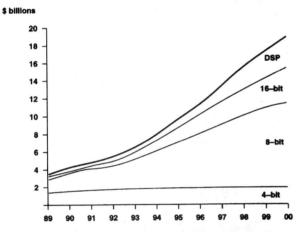

Fig. 2. Worldwide revenues for the sales of microcontrollers and DSP integrated circuits. The bold line shows the total growth. (Source: ICE.)

of amortizing hardware design over large production volumes. This suggests the idea of using software as a means of differentiating products based on the same hardware platform. Due to the complexity of hardware and software, their *reuse* is often key to commercial profitability. Thus complex macrocells implementing *instruction-set processors* (ISP's) are now made available as processor *cores* (Fig. 3 [38]). Standardizing on the use of cores or of specific processors means leveraging available software layers, ranging from operating systems to embedded software for user-oriented applications. As a result, an increasingly larger amount of software is found on semiconductor chips, which are often referred to as *systems on silicon*. Thus hardware (e.g., cores) and software (e.g., microkernels) can be viewed as commodities with large *intellectual property* values. Today both the electronic market expansion and the design of increasingly complex systems is boosted by the availability of these commodities and their reuse as system building blocks.

The recent introduction of *field-programmable gate array* (FPGA) technologies has blurred the distinction between hardware and software. Traditionally a hardware circuit used to be configured at manufacturing time. The functions of a hardware circuit could be chosen by the execution of a program. Whereas the program could be modified even at run-time, the structure of the hardware was invariant. With field-programmable technology it is possible to configure the gate-level interconnection of hardware circuits after manufacturing. This flexibility opens new applications of digital circuits, and new hardware/software co-design problems arise. For example, one (or more) FPGA circuits may be configured on-the-fly to implement a specific software function with better performances than executing the corresponding code on a microprocessor. Subsequently, the FPGA can be *re*programmed to perform another specific function without changing the underlying hardware. Thus from a user perspective, a reprogrammable hardware board can perform a function indistinguishable from that of a processor. Nevertheless the programming mechanisms and the programmer's view of the hardware is very different.

Hardware/software co-design is a complex discipline, that builds upon advances in several areas such as software compilation, computer architecture and *very large scale integration* (VLSI) circuit design. Co-design is perceived as an important problem, but the field is fragmented because most efforts are applied to specific design problems. Thus co-design has a different flavor according to the context in which it is applied. For example, co-design can be seen as a management discipline to achieve complex system products [15].

It is the purpose of this special issue to shed some light on the recent developments of co-design in different application domains. In this paper, we want to put several co-design problem in perspective, to show differences and similarities, as well as to show the cross fertilization in different scientific fields. For this reason, we describe first distinguishing features of electronic systems that are useful to classify co-design problems. We consider next system-level co-design issues for different kinds of electronic systems and components. Eventually, we review the fundamental algorithmic approaches for system-level design and organization of hardware/software systems, that form the foundations for system-level design tools.

II. DISTINGUISHING FEATURES OF ELECTRONIC SYSTEMS

We associate co-design problems with the classes of digital systems they arise from. We attempt to characterize these systems using some general criteria, such as domain of *application*, degree of *programmability*, and *implementation* features.

A. Application Domains

A digital system may be providing a service as a self-contained unit, or as a part of a larger system. A traditional computer (with its peripherals) is an example of the first kind of systems. A digital control system for a manufacturing plant is an example of the latter case. Systems that fall in this second category are commonly referred to as *embedded systems*.

CHAPTER 1: Introduction

Fig. 3. Example of an integrated circuit with programmable cores. The VCP chip has two processors: the VC core, which is based on the MIPS-X processor, is placed in the top right corner, while the VP+ DSP processor occupies the top left part of chip above a memory array. (Courtesy of Integrated Information Technology.)

The term embedded means being part of a larger unit and providing a dedicated service to that unit. Thus a personal computer can be made the embedded control system for manufacturing in an assembly line, by providing dedicated software programs and appropriate interfaces to the assembly line environment. Similarly, a microprocessor can be dedicated to a control function in a computer (e.g., keyboard/mouse input control) and be viewed as an embedded controller.

Digital systems can be classified according to their principal domain of application. Examples of self-contained (i.e., nonembedded) digital systems are information processing systems, ranging from laptop computers to supercomputers, as well as emulation and prototyping systems. Applications of embedded systems are ubiquitous in the manufacturing industry (e.g., plant and robot control), in consumer products (e.g., intelligent home devices), in vehicles (e.g., control and maintenance of cars, planes, ships), in telecommunication applications, and in territorial and environmental defense systems.

Digital systems can be geographically distributed (e.g., telephone network), locally distributed (e.g., aircraft control with different processing units on a local area network), or lumped (e.g., workstations). In this paper, we consider a system to be lumped when it is concentrated in a physical unit, although it may involve more than one processing unit.

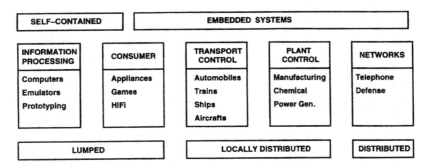

Fig. 4. Some application domains of electronic systems.

B. Degree of Programmability

In most digital systems, the hardware is programmed by some software programs to perform the desired functions. (Nonprogrammable hardwired systems are few and not relevant to this survey.) Hence the abstraction level used for programming models is the means of interaction between hardware and software. There are two important issues related to programming: 1) who has access to programming the system and 2) the technological levels at which programming is performed.

1) Access to Programming: To understand the extent to which system programmability has an effect on system design, we distinguish end-users from application developers, system integrators, and component manufacturers. Historically, each of these groups represents a separate industry or a separate organization. The application developer requires systems to be retargetable so as to port a given application across multiple hardware platforms. The chief use of system programmability for a system integrator is in ensuring compatibility of system components with market standards. Finally, the component manufacturer is concerned with maximizing component or module reuse across its product lines.

Let us take the personal computer as an example. The end-user programming is often limited to application-level programming (such as a spreadsheet) or scripting. An application developer relies on the programming language tools, operating system, and the high-level programming environment for application development. Most of these ingredients have, to a large extent, become off-the-shelf commodity products for the personal computer industry, bringing programming closer to the end-user as well. Component manufacturing for personal computers is driven by interconnection bus and protocol standards. Increasing semiconductor densities have resulted in coalescing system components, even with very diverse functionalities, onto single chips, leading to fewer but more versatile system hardware components.

When considering embedded systems, the end-user has limited access to programming because most software is already provided by the system integrator, who is often also the application developer. For example, the motion-control system of a robot arm for use in manufacturing contains embedded software for coordinating the movement of the different mechanical parts. The user can program only the moves and the actions.

2) Levels of Programming: Digital systems can be programmed at different levels, namely the *application, instruction,* or *hardware* levels. The highest abstraction level is the application level, where the system is running dedicated software programs that allow the user to specify desired functionality options using a specialized language. Examples range from programming a videocassette recorder (VCR) to setting navigation instructions in an automated steering controller of a ship.

Most digital systems use components with an *instruction set architecture* (ISA). Examples of such components are microprocessors, microcontrollers, and programmable *digital signal processors* (DSP's). The instruction set defines the boundary between hardware and software, by providing a programming model of the hardware. Instruction-level programming is achieved by executing on the hardware the instructions supported by the architecture. It is important to note that in some systems the end-user can compile programs to execute on the ISA, as in the case of computers. In other systems, such as in some embedded systems, the ISA is not visible to the user because it runs embedded software. In the former case, the compiler must have user-friendly features (e.g., descriptive diagnostic messages) and adequate speed of compilation, while in the latter case the compiler algorithms can afford to be more computationally expensive in the interest of a better final result [74] (i.e., more compact machine code).

Hardware-level programming means configuring the hardware (after manufacturing) in a desired way. A simple and well-known example is microprogramming, i.e., determining the behavior of the control unit by a microprogram, which can be stored in binary form in a memory. Emulation of other architectures can be achieved by altering the microprogram. Today microprogramming is common for DSP's, but not for general purpose microprocessors using RISC architectures [52] mainly due to performance reasons.

Reconfigurable circuits are the limiting case of hardware-level programming. Field-programmable technology allows us to configure the interconnections among logic blocks and to determine their personality. Reconfiguration can be global or local (i.e., the entire circuit or a portion thereof can be altered), and may be applied more than once. Whereas microprogramming allows us to (re)configure the control unit, reconfigurable systems can be modified in both the data path and controller. Moreover, such circuits need not to be partitioned into data path and control unit, but they can be organized with wide freedom.

Overall, reconfigurabilty increases the usability of a digital system, but it does not increase its performances except on tailored applications. For general-purpose computing, top performance is achieved today by superscalar RISC architectures [52], which are programmed at the instruction level. For dedicated applications, hard-wired (nonprogrammable) *application-specific integrated circuits* (ASIC's) achieve often the best performance and the lowest power consumption. In both cases, hardware design may be expensive, because of *nonrecurrent engineering* (NRE) costs, and not flexible enough to accommodate engineering changes and upgrades. Thus the challenge for reconfigurable design technologies is to arrive at a competitive level of performance, while exploiting the hardware flexibility in addressing other important system-level issues, such as support for engineering changes, self-adaptation to the environment, and fault-tolerance.

C. Implementation Features

System implementation deals with circuit design style, manufacturing technology and integration level. We touch briefly on these issues, because we want to maintain a high-level view of the problem which is fairly independent of the physical implementation.

Digital systems rely on VLSI circuit technology. The circuit design style relates to the selection of circuit primitives (e.g., choice of library in a semicustom technology), clocking strategy (e.g., single/multiple clocks and asynchronous), and circuit operation mode (e.g., static and dynamic).

A system may have components with different scale of integration (e.g., discrete and integrated component) and different fabrication technologies (e.g., bipolar and CMOS). The choice of hardware technology for the system components affects the overall performance and cost, and therefore is of primary importance.

System-level field programmability can be achieved by storing programs in read/write memories and/or exploiting programmable interconnections. In the former case, the software component is programmed, while in the latter the hardware is configured. With field-programmable technologies, circuit configuration is achieved by programming connections using transistors driven by memory arrays [110] or by antifuses [44]. Circuits of the first type are reprogrammable and will be considered in this survey, while the others can be programmed only once.

When considering co-design problems for lumped systems, we can distinguish between systems consisting of components (like ASIC's, processors, and memories) mounted on a board or chip carrier and single-chip systems consisting of an ASIC with one or more processor cores and/or memories. The programmable core is usually a processor provided as a macro-cell in the ASIC

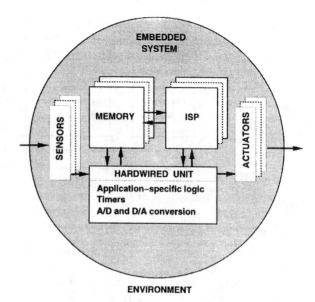

Fig. 5. Scheme of the essential parts of an embedded control system with one (or more) ISP(s).

implementation technology [38, Fig. 3]. Whereas a core may provide the same functionality as the corresponding standard part, cost and performance considerations may bias the choice of integration level. The advantages of higher integration are usually higher reliability, lower power-consumption budget, and increased performance. The last two factors come from the lack of I/O circuitry in the core and its direct connection to the application-specific logic. The disadvantages are larger chip sizes and higher complexity in debugging the system.

III. GENERAL CO-DESIGN PROBLEMS AND DESIGN APPROACHES

We consider now different facets of co-design. Namely, we present first the major objectives in embedded system design. We describe next the design of ISA's and their use in both self-contained information processing systems and embedded systems. Last but not least, we address the major co-design issues for reconfigurable systems.

A. Co-Design of Embedded Systems

Embedded systems are elements of larger systems. Some embedded systems provide monitoring and control functions for the overall system (e.g., vehicular control, manufacturing control), while others perform information-processing functions within a network (e.g., telecommunication systems).

Embedded control systems usually regulate mechanical components via *actuators* and receive input data provided by *sensors*. Single-chip implementation of embedded controllers often integrate on the same chip analog to digital conversion (and vice versa) of some I/O signals and sometimes the sensors themselves (e.g., accelerometer for airbag control). Often embedded control systems have also a data-processing component (Fig. 5).

Control systems are *reactive* systems, because they are meant to react to stimuli provided by the environment. *Real-time* control systems [99] implement functions that must execute within predefined time windows, i.e., satisfy some *hard* or *soft* timing constraint [117], [118]. Timers are thus important components of real-time controllers.

The required functions and size of embedded controllers may vary widely. Standard programmable microcontrollers and microcontroller cores provide usually low-cost and flexible solutions to a wide range of problems. Nevertheless, control systems that are either complex (e.g., avionic controls) or that require high-throughput data processing (e.g., radio navigation) need specific designs that leverage components or cores such as microprocessors or DSP's.

Whereas performance is the most important design criterion for information processing systems, *reliability, availability*, and *safety* are extremely important for control systems. System reliability measures the probability of correct control operation even in presence of failures of some component, whereas availability contemplates the on-line repair of faulty components. Safety measures the probability of avoiding catastrophic failures. For example, the availability of a nuclear steam supply system is the probability (as a function of time) that a nuclear reactor can produce energy under a scheduled maintenance, while its safety is the probability that the system has no failure leading to a hazardous situation for the operators and the environment.

Since control functions can be implemented both in hardware and in software, specific design disciplines must be used to insure reliability, availability, and safety. Some formal verification techniques for embedded controllers are nowadays available to insure design correctness by comparing different representation levels and assessing system properties. System-level testing techniques must be used to check the correctness of operation of the physical system implementation. Functional redundancy may be used to enhance reliability.

Specific co-design problems for embedded systems include modeling, validation, and implementation. These tasks may be complex because the system function may be performed by different components of heterogeneous nature, and because the implementation that optimizes the design objectives may require a specific hardware/software partition. The design of embedded control systems is surveyed in [36].

Embedded systems for telecommunication applications involve data processing, where data can be a digital form of audio and video information. Data compression, decompression, and routing is often performed with the aid of programmable processors of various kinds. Co-design issues in this domain are described in [17], [43], and [88].

B. Co-Design of ISA's

The concept of ISA plays a fundamental role in digital system design [52]. An ISA provides a programmer's view of hardware by supporting a specific programming model. The definition of an instruction set permits the parallel development of the hardware and of the corresponding compiler. Components based on ISA's, i.e., (e.g., microprocessors, DSP's, and programmable microcontrollers) are commonly used in (self-contained) information processing systems and in embedded systems. Therefore a good ISA design is critical to achieving system usability across applications. In addition, increasing applications now demand processor performance that pushes the limits of semiconductor technology. Performance critical design of processors requires combined design of hardware and software elements.

The primary goal of co-design in ISP development is to optimize utilization of the underlying hardware. This is done by customizing the software development ranging from application programs to operating systems. The operating system is the software layer closest to the underlying hardware, and its role is different in computing and embedded systems (see Section IV-B3) The extent of the operating system layer in embedded systems varies from specialized real-time kernels [99] to lightweight run-time schedulers [45], according to the design goals and requirements.

Compiler development should start as early as ISA definition. Indeed, compilers are needed for the evaluation of the instruction-set choices and overall processor organization, in order to verify whether the overall performance goals are met [53]. Whereas retargetable compilers are useful in the architectural development phase, optimizing compilers are key to achieving fast-running code on the final products. In addition, speed of compilation is important for information processing applications (e.g., computers), where the end-user programs the system at the instruction-level (i.e., via programs in programming languages). Such a requirement is less important for applications of ISA's within embedded systems, where the user has limited access to programmability, as mentioned in Section II-B.

The organization of modern general-purpose processors exploits deep pipelines, concurrency, and memory hierarchies. Hardware/software trade-off is possible in pipeline-control [57] and cache-management mechanisms [53]. The selection of an instruction set is usually guided by performance and compatibility goals. This task is generally based on experience and on the evaluation of software simulation runs, although recent efforts have aimed at developing tools for computer-assisted instruction set selection [55].

Let us now consider the use of components based on ISA's for embedded data-processing systems. Such systems often use dedicated software programs with specific instruction profiles. Therefore significant performance improvements may be achieved by selecting particular instruction sets which match the application requirements. In some application domains, such as data processing for telecommunications (see Fig. 4), it has been shown practical to replace standard processors by *application-specific instruction set processors* (ASIP's), which are instruction-level programmable processors with an architecture tuned to a specific application [43], [88]. In an ASIP design, the instruction set and hardware structure are chosen to support efficiently the instruction mix of the embedded software of the specific application. For example, ASIP's feature particular register configurations and specific interconnections among the registers, busses, and other hardware resources.

It is possible to view ASIP's as intermediate solutions between ISP's and ASIC's. ASIP's are more flexible than ASIC's, but less than ISP's. Nevertheless, they can be used for a family of applications in a specific domain. The performance of an ASIP on specific tasks can be higher than an instruction-set processor (because of the tuning of the architecture to the instruction mix) but it is usually lower than an ASIC. Opposite considerations apply to power consumption. The ASIP design time and nonrecurring engineering costs can be amortized over a larger volume than an ASIC, when the ASIP has multiple applications. Moreover, engineering changes and product updates can be handled graciously in ASIP's by reprogramming the software and avoiding hardware redesign. Unfortunately, because an ASIP is a specific architecture, it requires a compiler development which adds to the nonrecurring engineering costs. Such a compiler must also produce high-quality machine code to make the ASIP solution competitive. On the other hand, compilation speed is not a major requirement, since most ASIP-based system programmed (once only) by the manufacturer and not by the end-user.

Differently from general-purpose and digital-signal processors, ASIP's may be designed to support fairly different instruction sets, because compatibility requirements are less important and supporting specific instruction mixes is a desired goal. Unfortunately the price of the flexibility in choosing instruction sets is the need of developing application-specific compilers. Despite the use of *retargetable-compiler* technology [79], the computer-aided development of compilers that produce high-quality code for specific architectures is a difficult problem and solved only in part to date, namely for fixed-point arithmetic operations. Problems and solutions in retargetable compilation are addressed by [43] and [88] in this issue.

C. Co-Design of Reconfigurable Systems

Reconfigurable systems exploit FPGA technology, so that they can be personalized after manufacturing to fit a specific application. The operation of reconfigurable systems can either involve a configuration phase followed by an execution phase or have concurrent (partial) configuration and execution. In the latter case, the systems are called *evolvable*.

We consider first nonevolvable systems and their applications to the acceleration of computation and to prototyping. In both cases, the overall digital systems include a reconfigurable subsystem that emulates the software or the hardware execution, and sometimes a combination of both.

Let us turn our attention to co-design techniques that can accelerate software execution. There are often bottlenecks in software programs that limit their performance (e.g., executing transcendental floating-point operations or inner loops where sequences of operations are iterated). ASIC coprocessors can reduce the software execution time, when they are dedicated to support specific operations (e.g., floating-point or graphic coprocessors) or when they implement the critical loops in hardware while exploiting the local parallelism. Whereas ASIC coprocessors accelerate specific functions, coprocessors based on reconfigurable hardware can be applied to the speedup of arbitrary software programs with some distinctive characteristics (e.g., programs with parallelizable bit-level operations).

One of the first examples of programmable coprocessors is provided by the *programmable active memories* (PAM's) [13], which consist of a board of FPGA's and local memory interfaced to a host computer. Two models of PAM's, named *PeRLe-0* and *PeRLe-1*, were built. They differ in the number and type of FPGA used, as well as operating frequency. The hardware board for *PeRLe-1* is shown in Fig. 6 [112].

To accelerate the execution of a program with a PAM, the performance-critical portion of the program is first extracted and compiled into the patterns that configure the programmable board. Then, the noncritical portion of the program is executed on the host, while the critical portions are emulated by the reconfigurable subsystem. Experimental results show a speedup of one to two orders of magnitude, on selective benchmark programs, as compared to the execution time on the host [13].

The major hardware/software co-design problems consist of identifying the critical segments of the software programs and compiling them efficiently to run on the programmable hardware. The former task is not yet automated for PAM's and is achieved by successive refinement, under constraints of communication bandwidth and load balancing between the host and the programmable hardware. The latter task is based on hardware synthesis algorithms, and it benefits from performance optimization techniques for hardware circuits [13], [30]. Several other systems for software acceleration have been implemented [7], [86].[1]

A different application of reconfigurable systems is in *computer-aided prototyping*. In this case, we are interested in validating a target system yet to be manufactured by configuring and executing a prototype implemented with a reconfigurable medium. Prototypes provide design engineers with more realistic data on correctness and performance than system-level simulation [81], thus reducing the likelihood of an expensive redesign of the target system.

Prototyping of complex digital systems including multiple hardware components and software programs is appealing to designers, because it allows testing software programs on hardware, while retaining the ability to change the hardware (and software) implementation concurrently. Once the hardware configuration has been finalized, it can be mapped onto a "hard" silicon implementation using synthesis systems [30] that accept as inputs hardware models compatible with those used by the emulation systems (e.g., *VHDL* [91] and *Verilog HDL* [107] models).

---

[1] See URL http://www.io.com/~guccione/HW_list.html for a comprehensive list.

Fig. 6. The *PeRLe-1* implementation. (Courtesy of P. Bertin.)

Evolvable systems [97] are digital systems where reconfiguration of one of its parts is concurrent with execution. One of the goals of evolvable systems is to adapt automatically to the environment. As an example, consider a network interface unit, that receives and retransmits data with different formats. Upon sensing the protocol and format of the incoming data, such a unit configures itself to optimize data translation and transmission. Whereas such a unit could be implemented with nonevolvable technology, the ability to reconfigure the hardware may be the key to sustain higher data rates.

Fault tolerance in evolvable systems can be obtained by detecting the malfunctioning unit, and by reconfiguring a part of the system to regenerate a fault-free replacement of the faulty unit. This can be achieved under several assumptions, some of which are typical of fault-tolerant system design, including that of having enough spare reconfigurable circuits to implement the faulty unit on-the-fly.

Evolvable systems are the subject of several research efforts [97]. An interesting application of reconfigurable hardware for fault-tolerance applications is *embryonics* (embryological electronics) [28], [78], a discipline where biological models of organization are used for electronic system design. There are a few implementations of embryonic systems, relying on this general implementation strategy [78]. The underlying hardware is a memory-based field-programmable circuit that uses a decision diagram structure. The hardware is organized as a rectangular matrix of cells, each one addressable by its coordinates and communicating with its neighbors. The overall system function is mapped onto the programmable cells. Circuit configuration is performed by feeding each cell with a compiled software program (bit stream) containing the functionality of the entire system. This parallels the organization of multicellular living beings, where the genome of each cell is a repository of information of the entire being. The program is transmitted from an initial cell to the others. Then each cell extracts the portion of the overall program pertinent to its operation (using the coordinate information) and configures itself. This parallels the synthesis of a living cell from the gene structure.

After a boot phase in which the information is transmitted to all cells and the cells self-configure, the system can start operating. Upon failure of a cell in providing the required function, the neighboring cells readapt their operations so that the faulty cell is replaced by a working clone, and the overall system function is preserved. This reconfiguration, called *cicatrization*, allows the system to recover from failures after a finite delay.

Interesting applications of embryological circuits include embedded system applications with high reliability requirements, such as control of unmanned spacecrafts or of robots operating in hostile environments. Hardware/software co-design problems relate to how software programs are used to configure and program the underlying hardware circuit, as well as to how the reconfigurable circuit is organized.

IV. Design of Hardware/Software Systems

We consider here the high-level (i.e., technology independent) steps in the design of hardware/software systems. We consider the problem in its breadth, rather than in its depth, to highlight similarities and differences in co-design of digital systems of different nature. We also draw parallels among techniques applicable to hardware and software (e.g., scheduling). We refer the interested reader to the other articles in this issue for an in-depth analysis applicable to different domains.

The design of hardware/software systems involves *modeling*, *validation*, and *implementation*. We call modeling the process of conceptualizing and refining the specifications, and producing a hardware and software model. We call validation the process of achieving a reasonable level of confidence that the system will work as designed, and we call implementation the physical realization of the hardware (through synthesis) and of executable software (through compilation).

When considering embedded systems, different modeling paradigms and implementation strategies may be followed [36]. We exclude here pure hardware (e.g., ASIC) and pure software (e.g., embedded software running on an ISA) implementations, because we concentrate on co-design. Therefore, the overall model of an embedded system involves both hardware and software. The modeling style can be *homogeneous* or *heterogeneous*. In the former case, a modeling language (e.g., the C programming language) or a graphical formalism (e.g., Statecharts [51]) is used to represent both the hardware and software portions. A hardware/software *partitioning* problem can then be stated as finding those parts of the model best implemented in hardware and those best implemented in software. Partitioning can be decided by the designer, with a successive refinement and annotation of the initial model, or determined by a CAD tool. We will consider computer-aided partitioning in more detail in Section IV-A.

When using a heterogeneous modeling style, the hardware/software partition is often outlined by the model itself, because hardware and software components may be expressed in the corresponding languages. Nevertheless, system designers may want to explore alternative implementations of some components. For example, the first release of a product may contain a sizable software component (for time to market and flexibility reasons) while later releases may implement part of this software in hardware for performance and/or cost reasons. Tools which support implementation *retargeting* help the designer avoiding manual translation of the models or parts thereof. A few CAD environments for heterogeneous design and retargeting have been realized [8], [24], [26], [29], [64], [114].

ISA's are modeled at different levels. Instruction sets provide the essential information about the architecture, supporting both hardware and software development. The processor organization is usually described in a *hardware description language* (HDL) for hardware synthesis purposes, while processor models (e.g., bus functional models) are often used for cosimulation.

In the case of reconfigurable systems, we need to distinguish between modeling the target application and modeling the host. The first task is pertinent to the system user, while the second to its developer. Thus, these two modeling tasks are very different aspects of co-design.

As systems become more complex, validation is necessary to insure that correct functionality and required performance levels are achieved in the implementation of a system model. Moreover, validation takes different flavors according to the system's application domain. For example, satisfaction of performance objectives (in addition to correctness) is extremely important in processor design. Performance validation is often based on cosimulation of hardware and software [53]. On the other hand, embedded controllers may have less stringent performance requirements to be validated, but their correctness of operation must be verified under all possible environmental conditions, to insure overall system safety levels [36].

The implementation of a hardware/software system may involve several subtasks, the major being hardware synthesis and software compilation. Both topics are complex and several references describe them in depth [2], [30]. We review in Sections IV-A–B techniques affecting the macroscopic system implementation characteristics, and in particular the boundary between hardware and software. Namely, we focus our attention on: 1) partitioning and allocation of system functions to hardware and software and 2) scheduling hardware operations, program instructions and software processes. These two topics address *where* and *when* the system functions are implemented respectively.

A. Hardware/Software Partitioning

The partition of a system into hardware and software is of critical importance because it has a first order impact on the cost/performance characteristics of the final design. Therefore any partitioning decision, performed either by a designer or by a CAD tool, must take into account the properties of the resulting hardware and software blocks.

The formulation of the hardware/software partitioning problem differs according to the co-design problem being confronted with. In the case of embedded systems, a hardware/software partition represents a physical partition of system functionality into application-specific hardware and software executing on one (or more) processor(s). Various formulations to this partitioning problem can be compared on the basis of the architectural assumptions, partitioning goals and solution strategy. We consider each of these issues in detail in the next subsections.

When considering general purpose computing systems, a partition represents a logical division of system functionality, where the underlying hardware is designed to support the software implementation of the complete system functionality. This division is elegantly captured by the instruction set. Thus instruction selection strongly affects the system hardware/software organization.

In the case of reconfigurable systems, the flavor of the partitioning problem depends on the available primitives. For systems consisting of arrays of FPGA chips only, partitioning the system function into the components corresponds to performing technology mapping [16]. On the other hand, for systems consisting of processors and FPGA components, partitioning involves both a physical partition of system functionality (as in the case of embedded systems) and mapping.

1) Architectural Assumptions: Since usually embedded systems are implemented by processors and application-specific hardware, the most common architecture in these systems can be characterized as one of *coprocessing*, i.e., a processor working in conjunction with dedicated hardware to deliver a specific application. The particular implementation of the coprocessing architecture varies in the degree of parallelism supported between hardware and software components. For instance, the coprocessing hardware may be operated under direct control of the processor, which stalls while the dedicated hardware is operational [37], or the coprocessing may be done concurrently with software execution [47]. Similarly, the choice of one (or more than one) processor(s) for the target architecture strongly affects the partitioning formulation [11]. As an example [77], an evaluation of possible coprocessing architectures for a three-dimensional (3-D) computer graphics application leads to an architecture where a processor controls the application-specific coprocessor which maintains its independent data storage. The reported speedup varies from 1.32 to 2.0 across different benchmarks.

The hardware/software interface defines another architectural variable that strongly affects the partitioning problem formulation. It is common to assume that communication operations are conducted using memory-mapped I/O by the processor [26], [49]. However, memory-mapped I/O is often an inefficient mechanism for data transfer [63]. More efficient methods, including dedicated device drivers, have been considered for co-processing architectures [21], but their relation to partitioning has not been articulated yet. Yen and Wolf [119] developed analysis and synthesis methods of bus-oriented communication schemes among processing elements. Other researchers [84] use explicit scheduling of the communication operations in the partitioning loop to improve the quality of the resulting partition in terms its ability to satisfy external timing constraints.

2) Partitioning Objectives: Coprocessing architectures are often chosen to improve the system performance in executing specific algorithms [5], [34]. Accordingly, in some approaches partitioning seeks to maximize the overall speedup for a given application [13], [37], [63], [108]. The speedup estimation is almost always done by a profiling analysis that takes into account typical data sets over which the application behavior is estimated. Due to this data dependence, in some application areas the overall speedup may not be a well-defined metric. Furthermore, in some applications and particularly in those with real-time response requirements, it may not be a useful metric either. In such cases, metrics such as size of implementation and timing constraint satisfaction are used to drive the partitioning subtask. For instance, partitioning is used to improve the hardware utilization by pipelining multiple functions [14].

Constrained partitioning formulations often use capacity constraints, such as size of individual hardware or software portions, to generate a physical division of functionality such that each block can be implemented in a single component. This capacity-constrained partitioning formulation is commonly used in system prototyping applications, where an application is mapped onto multiple FPGA components by a partitioning method [16].

Performance-constrained partitioning formulations focus either on global constraints (such as overall latency) [65], or on the satisfaction of local timing constraints between operations [45]. In this case the partitioning goal is to reduce system cost by migrating part of the system functionality to software, thus reducing the application-specific hardware to implement, while satisfying the performance requirements.

3) Partitioning Strategies: A common misconception in partitioning formulations is that automated methods are the only viable approach to solving partitioning problems when using CAD tools. Often a determination of hardware versus software implementation of a specific functionality is done at levels of abstraction that are not even modeled in system specifications. In the absence of requisite modeling capability, the system partitioning simply can not be carried out using automated tools. Thus there exists a strong relationship between the models used for capturing system functionality and the abstraction level at which the partitioning is carried out. Even when it is possible to create a detailed mathematical model of the partitioning problem, the complexity of the resulting formulation renders it useless for conventional algorithmic methods. Thus we will consider in this section both heuristic approaches and a problem decomposition strategy to handle the complexity of the partitioning problem under some architectural assumptions.

Given a specific architecture, partitioning of a system-level functional description results in a labeling of its tasks as hardware or software operations. The exact solution of such a partitioning problem, even in the simplest cases, requires a solution to computationally intractable problems [41]. In an attempt to mathematically model the variables affecting the partitioning problem, *integer programming* (IP) and *integer linear programming* (ILP) formulations have been proposed recently [11], [42], [84]. Comparison of mathematical programming approaches to hardware/software partitioning is difficult, because the quality of results is often strongly affected by the parametric accuracy of the variables used and by the complexity of the cost/performance model.

Heuristic approaches to partitioning consist primarily of two strategies: *constructive* methods such as clustering techniques [9], [33] and *iterative* methods such as network flow [101], binary-constraint search [111], and dynamic programming [63]. By far, the most used methods are based on variable-depth search methods such as variants of the

Kernighan–Lin (KL) migration heuristics, or probabilistic hill-climbing methods such as simulated-annealing or genetic algorithms. Ernst *et al.* [37] used profiling results on a C-like description to estimate the potential speedup in extracting blocks of code for hardware implementation. The actual selection of code blocks for hardware is done by a simulated annealing algorithm that is used to maximize overall speedup. Reported results indicate speed-up of up to a factor of three on a *chromakey* algorithm for HDTV [37]. Design space search methods, such as using KL's algorithm, are often used following a constructive initial solution to arrive at a feasible solution that meets imposed cost/performance constraints. Reference [45] presents a KL-based algorithm that is used to drive the partition toward meeting timing constraints. Vahid *et al.* [111] use a combination of clustering followed by binary-constraint search that dynamically adjusts the optimization function balance between performance and hardware size as the algorithm progresses to minimize size of hardware while meeting constraints. Another similar approach [65] uses a composite objective function (taking time criticality and local affinity into account) to drive the partition. The results are shown to be qualitatively close to optimal while taking much less computing time.

Let us now examine what makes the problem of partitioning hard. The partitioning and synthesis subtasks are closely interrelated. The cost function of a partitioning problem needs to be evaluated using estimates of the resulting hardware and software. However, the abstraction level at which partitioning is carried out is so high that only rough estimates are available. As an example, consider a hardware/software partitioning problem whose objective is to maximize the application speedup under a constraint on the hardware size. The results of operation scheduling can be used to better estimate the effect of partitioning on the overall latency, and more importantly on the communication cost. This information can be used to select operations for partitioning that results in maximum overall speedup. On the other hand, partitioning a set of scheduled tasks would sacrifice the flexibility of optimizing the communication cost. This dilemma is addressed directly [84] using an integer programming formulation for the partitioning problem that uses an approximate schedule of operations. Solution to this IP programming is followed by a solution to the IP formulation of the scheduling problem that updates the schedule.

The above solution points to a problem decomposition strategy that is a straightforward extension of the decoupling of scheduling and binding in high-level synthesis [30]. In principle, task partitioning, scheduling, and binding to resources should be performed concurrently. Nevertheless, most practical approaches serialize these tasks, while some suggested interactive and iterative approached to partitioning and synthesis [62], [68].

Let us consider first the case where scheduling is followed by concurrent binding/partitioning subtasks. An example of this approach targets pipelined ASIP's [14]. Partitioning is done simultaneously with binding, and the clock cycle constraint of partitioning is derived from pipeline scheduling done prior to partitioning. This approach works well in cases where the objective of partitioning is to minimize hardware resource requirements. A scheduled input identifies the temporally mutually exclusive operations that can be implemented on a common resource. The partitioner can use the schedule information to divide operations into compatible groups such that binding subtask is able to maximize resource utilization. Such designs are typically resource dominated, therefore, an optimal resource utilization results in reduction of overall size.

The approach of applying partitioning prior to scheduling/binding is fairly common. A difficulty with this approach is the loss of parametric accuracy and controllability of the final result since the partitioning decisions are made early on. As a result most methods in this category either rely on extensive profiling or preprocessing of the input in order to make intelligent decisions about the hardware versus software implementations. Eles [35] presents a two-stage partitioning approach where a prepartitioning of VHDL input is followed by a detailed partitioning using simulated annealing. Constructive methods are quite popular to derive initial hardware/software grouping. For instance, different forms of clustering methods based on similarity measures [9] or closeness criteria [4], [8] are used to group together operations into hardware and software parts.

In addition to handling the strong relationship between different implementation subtasks, a partitioning problem formulation faces the classical dilemma of having to choose between accurate performance/cost measures on partition results versus the efficiency of the partitioning algorithm that determines the extent of design space search. While good estimation methods for hardware performance and size exist, the software component is generally characterized by a significant variability in performance parameters primarily due to architectural features such as caches and a very strong dependence of delay on the input data values. Recent research effort in this direction has been directed at accurate modeling of software delay using analysis of control paths [72], [87], [93], and program annotations [82]. Architectural modeling for software uses pipelining [120], instruction caches [73] and bus-activity using DMA [60]. These continuing efforts have successfully improved the estimation accuracy to be within 50–100% of the actual worst-case delay. The need for timing predictability continues to adversely affect the design of tightly constrained systems to such an extent that many systems use distressingly simple architectures (such as turning off cache memories), thus rarely exploiting the peak performance of the underlying hardware in real applications.

B. Scheduling

The *scheduling* problem has many facets. Scheduling algorithms have been developed in both the operation research and computer science community, with different models and objectives. The techniques that are applicable today to the design of hardware and software systems draw ideas from both communities.

Generally speaking, hardware and software scheduling problems differ not just in the formulation but in their overall goals. Nevertheless, some hardware scheduling algorithms are based on techniques used in the software domain, and some recent system-level process scheduling methods have leveraged ideas in hardware sequencing.

Scheduling can be loosely defined as assigning an execution *start time* to each *task* in a set, where tasks are linked by some relations (e.g., dependencies, priorities,...). The tasks can be elementary (like hardware operations or computer instructions) or can be an ensemble of elementary operations (like software programs). When confusion may arise, we will refer to tasks as *operations* in the former case, and to *processes* in the latter. The tasks can be *periodic* or *aperiodic*, and task execution may be subject to *real time* constraints or not. Scheduling under timing constraints is common for hardware circuits, and for software applications in embedded control systems. Tasks execution requires the use of *resources*, which can be limited in number, thus causing the serialization of some task execution. Most scheduling problems are computationally intractable [41], and thus their solutions are often based on heuristic techniques.

We consider next scheduling algorithms as applied to the design of hardware, compilers, and operating systems.

1) Operation Scheduling in Hardware: We consider now the major approaches to hardware scheduling. These techniques have been implemented (to different extent) in CAD tools for the design of ASIC's and DSP's [32], [66], [85], [106], which are modeled with a behavioral-level HDL (e.g., VHDL, Verilog HDL, and DFL [115]). The behavioral model can be abstracted as a set of operations and dependencies. The hardware implementation is assumed to be synchronous, with a given cycle-time. Operations are assumed to take a known, integer number of cycles to execute. (We will consider removing this assumption later). The result of scheduling, i.e., the set of start times of the operations, is just a set of integers. The usual goal is to minimize the overall execution *latency*, i.e., the time required to execute all operations.

Constraints on scheduling usually relate to the number of resources available to implement each operation and to upper/lower bounds on the time distance between start times of operation pairs. Usually, the presence of resource constraints makes the problem intractable [30], [41].

The scheduling problem can be cast as an integer linear program [30], [42], [50], where binary-valued variables determine the assignment of a start time to each operation. Linear constraints require each operation to start once, to satisfy the precedence and the resource constraints. Latency can also be expressed as a linear combination of the decision variables. The scheduling problem has a dual formulation, where latency is bounded from above and the objective function relates to minimizing the resource usage, which can also be expressed as a linear function. Timing and other constraints can be easily incorporated in the ILP model [42].

The appeal of using the ILP model is due to the uniform formulation even in presence of different constraints and to the possibility of using standard solution packages. Its limitation is due to the prohibitive computational cost for medium-large cases. This relegates the ILP formulation to specific cases, where an exact solution is required and where the problem size makes the ILP solution viable.

Most practical implementations of hardware schedulers rely on *list scheduling*, which is a heuristic approach that yields good (but not necessarily optimal) schedules in linear (or overlinear) time. A list scheduler considers the time slots one at a time, and schedules to each slot those operations whose predecessors have been scheduled, if enough resources are available. Otherwise the operation execution is deferred. Ties are broken using a priority list, hence the name.

Another heuristic for scheduling is *force-directed* scheduling [89], which addresses the latency-constrained scheduling problem. Here, operations are scheduled into the time slots one at a time, subject to time-window constraints induced by precedence and latency constraints. Ties among different time slots for each operation are broken using a heuristic based on the concept of *force*, which measures the tendency of the operation to be in a given slot, to minimize overall concurrency. The computational cost of force-directed scheduling is quadratic in the number of operations.

When resource constraints are relaxed, the scheduling problem can sometimes be solved in polynomial time. For example, scheduling with timing constraints on operation time separation can be cast as a longest-path problem [30]. On the other hand, scheduling under release times and deadlines is intractable, unless the operations take a single cycle to execute [41].

There are several generalizations of the scheduling problem. In some cases, operations are not restricted to take an integral number of cycles to execute, and more than one operation can be *chained* into a single time slot. Pipelined circuits require specific constraints on data rates, and additional resource conflicts have to be taken into account due to the concurrent execution of operations in different pipestages. Periodic operation subsets, e.g., iteration construct bodies, may be advantageously scheduled using *loop pipelining* techniques [30], which is an example of a method borrowed from software compilers [116]. Chaining and pipelining can be incorporated in ILP, list, and force-directed schedulers.

The *synchronization* of two (or more) operations or processes is an important issue related to scheduling. Synchronization is needed when some delay is unknown in the model. *Relative scheduling* is an extended scheduling method to cope with operations with unbounded delays [67] called *anchors*. In this case, a static schedule cannot be determined. Nevertheless, in relative scheduling the operations are scheduled with respect to their anchor ancestors. A finite-state machine can be derived that executes the operations in an appropriate sequence, on the basis of the relative schedules and the anchor completion signals. The relative scheduling formulation supports the analysis of timing constraints, and when these are consistent with the model, the resulting schedule satisfies the constraint for any anchor delay value. Scheduling with *templates* [70] is a similar approach, where operations are partitioned into templates that can be seen as single scheduling units. Thus templates are useful for hierarchical scheduling and scheduling multicycle resources (e.g., pipelined multipliers).

2) Instruction Scheduling in Compilers: Compilers are complex software tools, consisting of a front-end, a suite of optimization routines operating on an intermediate form, and a back-end (called also *code generation*) which generates the machine code for the target architecture. In the context of compilation, instruction scheduling on a uniprocessor is the task of obtaining a linear order of the instructions. Thus it differs from hardware scheduling because the resource constraints typically refer to storage elements (e.g., registers) and the hardware functional resource is usually one ALU. In the more general case, scheduling can be viewed as the process of organizing instructions into streams.

Instruction scheduling is related to the choice of instructions, each performing a fragment of the computation, and to register allocation. When considering compilation for general-purpose microprocessors, instruction selection and register allocation are often achieved by dynamic programming algorithms [2], which also generate the order of the instructions. When considering retargetable compilers for ASIP's, the compiler back-end is often more complex, because of irregular structures such as inhomogeneous register sets and connections. As a result, instruction selection, register allocation and scheduling are tightly-coupled phases of code generation [43]. In both cases, scheduling objectives are reducing the code size (which correlates with the latency of execution time) and minimizing *spills*, i.e., overflows of the register file which require memory access.

Optimizing compiler algorithms for ASIP's and general-purpose DSP's has been a subject of recent research activities [79]. Instruction selection, instruction scheduling, and register spilling problems for ASIP's are addressed by Liao *et al.* [71]. The same group formulates the instruction selection problem as a binate covering problem, that is solved using a branch-and-bound algorithm [74]. Scheduling has been modeled by resource and instruction set conflicts and solved by bipartite matching algorithms [109]. Araujo *et al.* [6] considered code generation for basic blocks in heterogeneous memory-register DSP processors and used register-transfer paths to convert basic block graphs into expression trees which are used in code generation.

The co-design of deeply pipelined microprocessors can leverage the coupling between instruction scheduling and hardware organization. Pipeline hazard avoidance can be achieved by hardware means (e.g., stall) or by software means (e.g., instruction reorder and NOP insertion). Recent research [57] has addressed the problem of the concurrent synthesis of the pipeline control hardware and the determination of an appropriate instruction reorder that the corresponding back-end compiler should use to avoid hazards. The same group [59] has also proposed a methodology for synthesizing instruction sets from application benchmarks.

3) Process Scheduling in Different Operating Systems: Process scheduling is the problem of determining when processes execute and includes handling synchronization and mutual exclusion problems. Algorithms for process scheduling are important constituents of operating systems and run-time schedulers [104].

The model of the scheduling problem is more general than the one previously considered. Processes have a coarser granularity and their overall execution time may not be known. Processes may maintain a separate context through local storage and associated control information. Scheduling objectives may also vary. In a *multitasking* operating system, scheduling primarily addresses increasing processor utilization and reducing response time. On the other hand, scheduling in *real-time operating systems* (RTOS) primarily addresses the satisfaction of timing constraints.

We consider first scheduling without real-time constraints. The scheduling objective involves usually a variety of goals, such as maximizing CPU utilization and throughput as well as minimizing response time. Scheduling algorithms may be complex, but they are often rooted on simple procedures such as *shortest-job first* (SJF) or *round robin* (RR) [92]. The SJF is a priority-based algorithm that schedules processes according to their priorities, where the shorter the process length (or, more precisely, its CPU burst length) the higher the priority. This algorithm would give the minimum average time for a given set of processes, if their (CPU-burst) lengths were known exactly. In practice, predictive formulas are used. Processes in a SJF may be allowed to preempt other processes to avoid starvation.

The round-robin scheduling algorithm uses a circular queue and it schedules the processes around the queue for a time interval up to a predefined quantum. The queue is implemented as a *first-in/first-out* (FIFO) queue and new processes are added at the tail of the queue. The scheduler pops the queue and sets a timer. If the popped process terminates before the timer, the scheduler pops the queue again. Otherwise it performs a *context switch* by interrupting the process, saving the state, and starting the next process on the FIFO.

Process scheduling in real-time operating system [100] is characterized by different goals and algorithms. Schedules may or may not exist that satisfy the given timing constraints. In general, the primary goal is to schedule the tasks such that all deadlines are met: in case of success (failure) a secondary goal is maximizing earliness (minimizing tardiness) of task completion. An important issue is predictability of the scheduler, i.e., the level of confidence that the scheduler meets the constraints.

The different paradigms for process scheduling in RTOS can be grouped as static or dynamic [100]. In the former case, a schedulability analysis is performed before run time, even though task execution can be determined at run time based on priorities. In the latter case, feasibility is checked at run time [100]. In either case, processes may be considered periodic or aperiodic. Most algorithms assume periodic tasks and tasks are converted into periodic tasks when they are not originally so.

Rate monotonic (RM) analysis [76] is one of the most celebrated algorithms for scheduling periodic processes on a single processor. RM is a priority-driven preemptive algorithm. Processes are statically scheduled with priorities that are higher for processes with higher invocation rate, hence the name. Liu and Layland showed that this schedule is optimum in the sense that no other fixed-priority scheduler can schedule a set of processes which cannot be scheduled by RM [76]. The optimality of RM is valid under some restrictive assumptions, e.g., neglecting context-switch time. Nevertheless, RM analysis has been the basis for more elaborate scheduling algorithms [21], [27].

Let us consider now hardware/software system implementations obtained by partitioning a system-level specification, as mentioned in Section IV-A. The implementation consists of a set of software fragments executing on a processor in parallel with the execution of other tasks in dedicated hardware. A relevant problem is to determine the execution windows for both the hardware and software tasks. Since the partition depends on the specific application and design objectives, a run-time scheduler for the system is required that fits the hardware/software partition. Conversely, a given partition may be chosen because a run-time scheduler can assign schedule tasks while satisfying given deadline and rate constraints.

We summarize an approach fully described in [45]. Software tasks are represented by *threads*, each thread being a set of operations with known execution, except possibly the head of the thread. Operations within threads are statically scheduled (with respect to the head of the thread), so that timing constraints are *marginally satisfied*, i.e., within the limits of the lack of knowledge of the delay of the thread head operation. Threads execution is then dynamically determined by a nonpreemptive run-time scheduler whose task is to synchronize the execution of hardware and software. Thread-based scheduling can be seen as an application and extension of relative scheduling to the hardware/software domain, thus showing the cross-fertilization of the hardware and software fields.

We briefly describe now process scheduling in *Chinook*, a CAD environment for designing reactive real-time systems [21]. The overall system can have different *modes* of operation, each having a schedule. Timing watchdogs can disable modes and cause mode transitions. Upon changing of mode, the system starts running the corresponding schedule. Timing constraints may be intermodal or intramodal. Each mode has a periodic set of tasks, which is unrolled and scheduled under timing constraints, using an extension of the relative scheduling formulation [21]. With this scheduling technique, Chinook supports the mapping of an embedded system model to one (or more) processor and peripherals while ensuring the satisfaction of timing constraints.

In summary, process scheduling plays an important role in the design of mixed hardware/software systems, because it handles the synchronization of the tasks executing in both the hardware and software components. For this reason, it is currently a subject of intensive research.

V. Accomplishments

We underline here briefly the major accomplishments in this field, and we refer the readers to the other articles of this issue for specific results. Hardware/software co-design has attracted the attention of several research groups worldwide, as documented by books [29], [39], [95], journal articles, and publications in symposia. Some of the research addresses incremental changes to system-level design tools, to cope with software components in predominantly hardware designs. The need for addressing practical problems and for fitting into existing design methodologies where modeling styles and languages are not negotiable, limits significantly the power of these tools to search creatively the co-design solution space. Other research contributions propose paradigm shifts in system-level design, by assuming a wide freedom in the way systems are modeled and designed. While these approaches will probably provide the basis for long-term innovation, they often lead to design tools which are not readily usable by system designers because disconnected from existing design practices.

Several research computer-aided co-design environments have been released, and some of these are used for research and/or product development, e.g., *Castle* [105], *Chinook* [24], *Cosmos* [61], *Cosyma* [37], *Coware* [114], *Polis* [26], *Ptolemy* [64], *Siera* [103], *Specsym* [40], and *Tosca* [8]. (See [29] for additional information on some of these systems.)

Commercial co-design tools are available to address some of the problems mentioned in this survey. Some CAD vendors provide design entry systems and co-simulation environments. Cosimulation is widely applicable to general-purpose and digital-signal processor design, as well as to embedded system design. For the telecommunication domain, specialized environments support the vertical design of systems from design entry to physical realization. System emulators, based on field-programmable technology, have proven to be successful for validating large systems.

Commercial products in the software domain include compilers for general-purpose and dedicated processors with standard and application-specific architectures, as well as real-time operating systems and microkernels. Such products find several applications in embedded systems.

VI. Conclusion

Hardware/software co-design presents an enormous challenge, as well as an opportunity, for system designers. Use and reuse of hardware and software macro blocks can lead to products of superior quality (i.e., performance/cost, flexibility, ...) with a shorter design and development time as compared to traditional integrated circuit design methodologies. The progress in electrical system design will depend, among other factors, on the level of support provided by CAD tools. In particular, digital system products will benefit from concurrent hardware/software design which exploits the synergism of hardware and software in the search for solutions that use at best the current manufacturing technology and the availability of hardware components and software programs.

Scientific and commercial interest in hardware/software co-design methods and tools has risen significantly in the recent years. Product-level use of co-design tools has been reported in some application domains, (e.g., co-simulation, emulation, synthesis for embedded controllers, retargetable compilers). The sector of computer-aided co-design tools is growing at a rapid pace because the potential payoffs make it an attractive area for research as well as an exciting business opportunity.

Overall, hardware/software co-design is a wide field of research, because of the diversity of applications, design styles and implementation technologies. Since this area is still not completely defined, we can expect some evolutionary and some revolutionary changes in the way digital systems are designed. Thus hardware/software co-design is the key design technology for digital systems.

REFERENCES

[1] T. Agerwala, "Microprogramming optimization: A survey," *IEEE Trans. Computers*, vol. C-25, pp. 962–973, Oct. 1976.
[2] A. Aho, R. Sethi, and J. Ullman, *Compilers: Principles, Techniques and Tools*. Reading, MA: Addison-Wesley, 1988.
[3] A. Alomary, T. Nakata, Y. Honma, M. Imai, and N. Hikichi, "An ASIP instruction set optimization algorithm with functional module sharing constraints," in *Proc. ICCAD*, 1993, pp. 526–532.
[4] S. Antoniazzi, A. Balboni, W. Fornaciari, and D. Sciuto, "HW/SW codesign for embedded telecom systems," in *Proc. ICCD*, 1994, pp. 278–281.
[5] R. Amerson, R. Carter, W. B. Culbertson, P. Kuekes, and G. Snider, "Teramac-configurable custom computing," in *FPGA's for Custom Computing Machines*, Apr. 1995.
[6] G. Araujo, S. Malik, and M Lee, "Using register-transfer paths in code generation for heterogeneous memory-register architectures," in *Proc. DAC*, 1996, pp. 591–596.
[7] J. Babb, R. Tessier, and A. Agarwal, "Virtual wires: Overcoming pin limitations in FPGA-based logic emulators," in *Proc. IEEE Workshop on FPGA's for Custom Computing Machines*, Apr. 1993.
[8] A. Balboni, W. Fornaciari, and D. Sciuto, "Cosynthesis and cosimulation of control-dominated embedded systems," *Design Automat. Embedded Syst.*, vol. 1, no. 3, pp. 257–289, July 1996.
[9] E. Barros, W. Rosenstiel, and X. Xiong, "A method for partitioning UNITY language in hardware and software," in *Proc. EURODAC*, 1994, pp. 220–225.
[10] D. Becker, R. Singh, and S. Tell, "An engineering environment for hardware-software co-simulation," in *Proc. DAC*, 1992, pp. 129–134.
[11] A. Bender, "Design of an optimal loosely coupled heterogeneous multiprocessor system," in *Proc. EDTC*, 1996, pp. 275–281.
[12] A. Benveniste and G. Berry, "The synchronous approach to reactive and real-time systems," *Proc. IEEE*, vol. 79, pp. 1270–1282, Sept. 1991.
[13] P. Bertin, D. Roncin, and J. Vuillemin, "Introduction to programmable active memories," in *Systolic Array Processors*, J. McCanny, J. McWhirter, and E. Schwartzlander, Eds. Englewood Cliffs, NJ: Prentice-Hall, 1989.
[14] N. Binh, M. Imai, A. Shiomi, and N. Hickichi, "A HW/SW partitioning algorithm for designing pipelined ASIP's with least gate counts," in *Proc. DAC*, 1996, pp. 527–532.
[15] K. Buchenrieder, A. Sedelmeier, and C. Veith, "Industrial HW/SW codesign," in *Hardware/Software Co-Design*, G. De Micheli and M. Sami, Eds. Amsterdam: Kluwer, 1996, pp. 453–466.
[16] J. Cong and Y. Ding, "Combinational logic synthesis for LUT based field programmable gate arrays," *TODAES, ACM Trans. Design Automat. Electron. Syst.*, vol. 1, no. 2, pp. 145–204, Apr. 1996.
[17] I. Bolsens, H. De Man, B. Lin, K. van Rompaey, S. Vercautern, and D. Verkest, "Hardware-software codesign of digital telecommunication systems," *Proc. IEEE*, this issue, p. 391–418.
[18] J. R. Burch, E. M. Clarke, K. L. McMillan, D. L. Dill, and L. J. Hwang, "Symbolic model checking: 10^{20} states and beyond," *Informat. and Computation*, vol. 98, no. 2, pp. 142–170, June 1992.
[19] J. R. Burch, E. M. Clarke, D. E. Long, K. L. McMillan, and D. L. Dill, "Symbolic model checking for sequential circuit verification," *IEEE Trans. CAD/ICAS*, vol. 13, no. 4, pp. 401–424, Apr. 1994.
[20] D. Bursky, "Microcontroller design exploits reusable cores," *Electron. Design*, vol. 42, no. 6, pp. 53–68, Mar. 1994.
[21] P. Chou, E. Walkup, and G. Borriello, "Scheduling strategies in the co-synthesis of reactive real-time systems," *IEEE Micro*, vol. 14, no. 4, pp. 37–47, Aug. 1994.
[22] P. Chou and G. Borriello, "Software scheduling in co-synthesis of reactive real-time systems," in *Proc. DAC*, 1994, pp. 1–4.
[23] ———, "Interval scheduling: Fine-grained code scheduling for embedded systems," in *Proc. DAC*, 1995.
[24] P. Chou, R. Ortega, and G. Borriello, "The Chinook hardware/software co-design system," in *Proc. ISSS*, Cannes, France, 1995, pp. 22–27.
[25] M. Chiodo, P. Giusto, A. Jurecska, H. Hsieh, L. Lavagno, and A. Sangiovanni, "A formal methodology for hardware/software co-design of embedded systems," *IEEE Micro*, vol. 14, no. 4, pp. 26–36, Aug. 1994.
[26] M. Chiodo, D. Engels, P. Giusto, A. Jurecska, H. Hsieh, L. Lavagno, K. Suzuki, and A. Sangiovanni, "A case study in computer-aided co-design of embedded controllers," *Design Automat. Embedded Syst.*, vol. 1, no. 2, pp. 51–67.
[27] M. Cochran, "Using the rate monotonic analysis to analyze the schedulability of ADARTS real-time software design," in *Int. Workshop on Hardware/Software Co-design*, Sept. 1992.
[28] H. de Garis, "Evolvable hardware," in *Proc. Artificial Neur. Nets and Genetic Algorithms*, Apr. 1993, pp. 441–449.
[29] G. De Micheli and M. Sami, *Hardware/Software Co-Design*. Amsterdam: Kluwer, 1996.
[30] G. De Micheli, *Synthesis and Optimization of Digital Circuits*. New York: McGraw-Hill, 1994.
[31] ———, "Computer-aided hardware/software co-design," *IEEE Micro*, vol. 14, no. 4, pp. 10–16, Aug. 1994.
[32] G. De Micheli, D. Ku, F. Mailhot, and T. Truong, "The olympus synthesis system for digital design," *IEEE Design and Test*, pp. 37–53, Oct. 1990.
[33] E. D. Lagnese and D. Thomas, "Architectural partitioning for system level descriptions," in *Proc. DAC*, 1989, pp. 62–67.
[34] T. Ebisuzaki *et al.*, "GRAPE: Special purpose computer for classical many-body simulations," in *Proc. Advances in Computing Techniques*, 1994, pp. 218–231.
[35] P. Eles, "VHDL system-level specification and partitioning in a hardware/software co-synthesis environment," *Int. Workshop on Hardware/Software Codesign*, Sept. 1994, pp. 22–24.
[36] S. Edward, L. Lavagno, E. Lee, and A. Sangiovanni, "Design of embedded systems: Formal models, validation and synthesis," *Proc. IEEE*, this issue, pp. 366–390.
[37] R. Ernst, J. Henkel, and T. Benner, "Hardware-software co-synthesis for micro-controllers," *IEEE Design and Test*, pp. 64–75, Dec. 1993.
[38] C. Feigel, "Processors aim at desktop video," *Microprocess. Rep.*, vol. 8, no. 2, Feb. 1994.
[39] D. Gajski, S. Narayan, F. Vahid, and J. Gong, *Specification and Design of Embedded Systems*. Englewood Cliffs, NJ: Prentice-Hall, 1994.
[40] D. Gajski, F. Vahid, and S. Narayan, "A system design methodology: Executable specification refinement," in *Proc. EDAC*,

Codesign of Embedded Systems: Status and Trends

ROLF ERNST
Braunschweig University of Technology

New methodologies and CAD tools support an integrated hardware-software codesign process.

EVER-INCREASING EMBEDDED-SYSTEM design complexity combined with a very tight time-to-market window has revolutionized the embedded-system design process. The concurrent design of hardware and software has displaced traditional sequential design. Further, hardware and software design now begins before the system architecture (or even the specification) is finalized. System architects, customers, and marketing departments develop requirement definitions and system specifications together. System architects define a system architecture consisting of cooperating system functions that form the basis of concurrent hardware and software design.

Interface design requires the participation of both hardware and software developers. The next step integrates and tests hardware and software—this phase consists of many individual steps. Reusing components taken from previous designs or acquired from outside the design group is a main design goal to improve productivity and reduce design risk.

Figure 1 shows the structure of a design process, highlighting the hardware and software design tasks. A concurrent design starting with a partially incomplete specification requires close cooperation of all participants in the design process. Hardware and software designers and system architects must synchronize their work progress to optimize and debug a system in a joint effort. The early discovery of design faults, a prerequisite for hitting the market window, is a central requirement to that cooperation.

A heavy burden is placed on the system architect, who must make decisions based on predicted technology data. To this end, reliable design estimates are essential. Today, such estimates are based on experience and reused components.

Reuse depends on libraries. Libraries of system functions have a higher reuse potential than libraries of physical components with a fixed layout (they become obsolete as technology progresses). The challenge is to support the migration of system functions between different technologies and between hardware and software without a redesign.

What I have described thus far is already a hardware-software codesign process to some extent, but it still lacks a unified approach. This unified approach is the aim of computer-aided hardware-software codesign.

Modeling and verification

A major problem in the design process is synchronization and integration of hardware and software design. This requires permanent control of consistency and correctness, which becomes more time consuming with increasing levels of detail. In hardware-software cosimulation, software execution is simulated as running on the target hardware. Since gate- as well as register-transfer-level (RTL) hardware simulations are too slow for

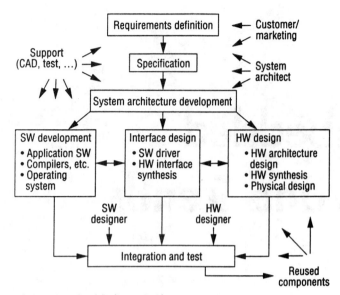

Figure 1. Embedded-system design process.

practical software simulation, abstract execution models are needed.

For that purpose, the processor is modeled at a higher level of abstraction than the implemented hardware part. The cosimulation problem[1] lies in coupling the different models to make the hardware simulation sufficiently accurate. In the worst case, the processor and hardware obtain arbitrated access to the same bus and memory. Accurate timing in this situation requires adapted memory and bus models and new simulation strategies. An example of this approach is the cosimulation tool Seamless CVS from Mentor Graphics. CVS uses a target processor model (an instruction set simulator) and bus models that abstract processor interaction with the memory depending on concurrent access from hardware and software.

The main issue is the availability of a library containing processor and memory models provided by the electronics design automation (EDA) vendor or the core processor provider.[2] Library standardization efforts, such as VSI Alliance, might be able to overcome some of the model compatibility problems.

A more abstract approach reduces the processor execution to the pure functional behavior without timing and only models the interface timing behavior. The software runs on any target platform, preferably the host workstation or PC. Software execution couples to the hardware model via a simulator-specific hardware-software communication protocol that requires a designer to perform software enhancement. Only hardware interface models are necessary, thus alleviating the library problem. On the other hand, while the software function and the interface timing can be analyzed, timing and performance analyses are restricted to the hardware part (for example, the tool Eaglei from Viewlogic).

The current cosimulation approaches work best on larger ratios of internal processor operations to processor I/O operations and hardware activity. In this case, the execution time can be reduced by more than three orders of magnitude compared to complete RTL simulation, up to the full host performance for the more abstract second approach. Designs with application-specific processors (ASIPs) and core processor extensions with special-function coprocessors are harder to deal with, due to the custom hardware's much higher activity. In this case, custom abstract cosimulation models must be developed as part of the design process. When models for these highly active parts become available, the cosimulation process can continue as usual.

A second problem is the early detection of design faults. The design team creates an abstract system model—a cospecification simulated or formally verified for certain system properties. Simulation requires an executable cospecification, also called a virtual prototype. Numerous system design tools from different application domains support cospecification simulation, including STATEMATE, MatrixX, MATLAB, COSSAP, or Bones and SPW.

Rapid prototyping with hardware-in-the-loop emulates the physical behavior of a system and can replace virtual prototyping. This proves necessary when simulation time dominates design time.

Executable specifications face several problems. Depending on the application domain and specification semantics, they are based on different models of computation. Some support modeling and simulations of event-driven reactive systems, while others target dataflow systems. A combination using both domains (for example, telecommunications) implies simulation overhead. The inclusion of reused components and functions that must match the input specification's level of abstraction remains a problem. Finally, virtual prototypes do not cover most of the nonfunctional constraints and objectives, such as power consumption or safety.

Synthesis

Industrial tools for system synthesis are not as developed as modeling and analysis tools. On the software side, we can use real-time operating systems (RTOSs) for load distribution and scheduling. Codesign, however, requires a closer look at processes and communication. The second problem is code generation. Specialized architectures, such as digital signal processors or microcontrollers, dominate the embedded-system market due to their superior cost efficiency—especially compared to modern general-purpose processors.[3] Special processor compilation, however, is in many cases far less efficient than manual code generation. Consequently, a considerable amount of assembly coding in embedded systems is still observed.[4]

Even if compilation improved, there is still the problem of generating efficient compliable code (such as C) from abstract models. This problem can be solved for small reactive systems with finite-state machine behavior and with simple operations on data. However, as soon as more complex data operations are required, the design space grows tremendously and the design, when executed manually, includes target-system-specific transformations. Good examples include memory optimization requiring target-architecture-dependent loop transformations, optimized word length selection, and process restructuring for fine-grain load distribution. For example, C code developed for the TI TMS320C6x is not optimized for running on Philips TriMedia or MPACT processors. The problem is worse here than with parallel compilers because of architecture specialization.[5] Porting functions between hardware and software implementation becomes particularly cumbersome.[6]

Fortunately, given a certain state of circuit technology, the choice of hardware or software implementation is predetermined for many system parts. However, this border moves with technological progress and new constraints. Power minimization and increased flexibility requirements drive this development.

To be competitive, an automated code generator must cover a large design space using transformation rules, and this far exceeds current techniques. Nevertheless, there are many commercial C or VHDL code generators—such as STATEMATE, MATLAB, or MatrixX—suitable for prototyping and acceptable for the final design. They are suitable in cases of simply structured target architectures and low-to-moderate cost efficiency and performance requirements. Other tools restrict the processor types (usually to standard microprocessors) and the language scope (for example, the Cmicro code generator for the SDL tool suite of Telelogic). Guaranteed timing behavior of the generated code is another problem.

One can circumvent the code generation problem with libraries of predefined and parameterized code modules adapted to an application. This of course requires a matching of input to target system modules based on a large module library. User-defined and library parts are then combined with a suitable schedule. This corresponds to a partially automated design for a specific system domain. The COSSAP, SPW, and Bones tools fall under this category, as well as the Mentor Graphics DSP Station.

On the hardware side, we see a growing set of high-level synthesis tools: the Behavioral Compiler of Synopsys, Monet of Menor Graphics, and RapidPath of DASYS. While this is a big step forward for cosynthesis, we still need to look at problems with memory optimization, parallel heterogeneous hardware architectures, programmable hardware synthesis and optimization, and communication optimization, to name just a few. Similar to software synthesis, the design space is still narrow when compared with a manual design. Interface synthesis has been neglected for a long time in commercial tools, and only recently have the first commercial systems appeared. The CoWare system (as an example of an interface synthesis generating both hardware and software parts of a protocol) and the Synopsys Protocol Compiler (as an example of a hardware interface synthesis tool) represent this group.

In summary, there are tools that reach a remarkable degree of automation for specific applications yet do not exploit the design space to obtain an optimized solution. Other tools create competitive designs, but only for very specific problems using hardware or software component libraries, leaving the rest of the design to be created and integrated manually. Besides the integration effort, development of such specific libraries ties up design capacity.

The current synthesis tool landscape leaves the impression of a patchwork of partial solutions that must be mixed and matched by the designer. Portability is rudimentary at best. The situation is certainly better than not having synthesis tools, but parts can hardly be expected to grow together over time into a homogeneous system. Interestingly, the current discussion on reusable intellectual property circuit functions focuses on circuit technology, library, and interface compatibility issues. These logistical problems sometimes seem to block the more fundamental design issues discussed earlier.

Exploration and optimization

An integrated and coherent codesign system should capture the complete design specification, support design space exploration with optimization based on this specification, and, if possible, cosynthesize a selected design point. Research has provided numerous contributions toward this goal, but issues of completeness and design process integration still arise.[7] Even push-button cosynthesis approaches (which have been demonstrated for special applications and architectures) can only solve part of the design problem.

Complete design capture

Some of the languages previously mentioned for executable cospecifications in commercial systems and many others (including VHDL and C)[5,8-10] can serve as input to the codesign process. In general, systems are described as a set of communicating and concurrent entities activated at a given time or upon arrival of events or data. The name "process" denotes such an entity. Upon activation, the process executes a function, thereby changing or generating output data and reading or consuming input data. Depending on the language, these functions can range from very simple, logical operations to very large, high-level programs.

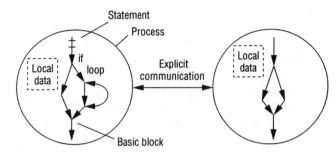

Figure 2. Communication in process partitioning.

To be complete, the input description must contain all design constraints, such as timing requirements. It can also contain information such as preselected components or cost functions to guide the design space exploration process.

At this point, the design might still not be fully captured. Think of a telecommunications system used in a larger network or a video coder optimized for maximum average performance. In these cases, we need additional information about process execution and input/output data (to analyze the internal execution paths of the processes). Current cosynthesis systems expect either profiling data or execution traces. These data are also part of the design description.[11]

Global optimization

The high-level and general views of cospecification as an input to the cosynthesis process sufficiently identify some of the main problems in design space exploration and optimization. First, the activation rules of the processes are modified for implementation. A process, ready for execution upon arrival of an external event, might eventually be executed by interrupt or periodically, polling for the event. The introduction of buffers delays process execution, thus widening the design space; it also supports pipelining. There is a rich variety of solutions originating in real-time software development.[12] Design constraints, mainly the required timing, limit feasible solutions. As a consequence, the input and target models of computation can be quite different, affecting the individual components as well as their interaction. This requires global system optimization.

Global optimization has become more complicated due to the combination of (static) data flow and reactivity in a single application. Take an MPEG2 encoder generating a fixed bit rate signal to be transmitted over a communication channel with a very small receiver buffer, as used in digital video broadcasting.[13] In this application, adaptive video coding that controls the buffer level is useful.[13] We can still describe the system as a dataflow network, but data flow is controlled with a tight feedback loop that limits pipelining, communication, or internal buffering in the encoder.

Secondly, the input process size (granularity) is appropriate for system function description but not necessarily for design space exploration and hardware-software implementation. Also, the designer might want to reuse system parts with processes that were optimized to another design and thus must be retargeted.

Process transformation

Before discussing the optimal process size for design space exploration and optimization, let's review some of the process transformation problems and techniques. With process transformation, we can partition and merge processes, which in turn requires communication transformation. Explicit or implicit communications occur in the abstract system specification used as input (the cospecification). As an example, concurrent finite-state machine variables, by definition, are globally accessible and arbitrarily referenced. Referencing variables implies communication, which is inserted when the concurrent finite-state machines are distributed over several components.

Communication transformation. Figure 2 shows the problem of manual communication transformation. Except for simple finite-state machine processes, a process generally contains one or several threads, each consisting of basic blocks with a sequence of statements. They all work on a set of local data. If communication between processes is restricted to explicitly specified process communication (like send or receive statements), then no process can access another process' data except through communication statements. A cosynthesis system can easily determine the required communication actions if the processes are assigned to different components—the communication statements directly map to physical communication actions. At a finer partitioning granularity, dataflow analysis is required to find the required communication.[13-15] Resolving variable array indices becomes important in breaking up processes, since array accesses often occur in loops with optimization potential.[15] Another approach avoids breaking up processes and asks the user to write several versions of a communicating processes system, but this leads to verbose process descriptions and places the burden of process transformation on the designer.

If the individual process contains concurrent elements, then inserting communication statements is generally insufficient. State charts, for example, assume synchronous operation and broadcasting. If state charts are partitioned and communication is inserted, synchrony must be checked and adapted.[16]

Process merging. This high-level transformation problem is mostly postponed to back-end cosynthesis tasks, namely scheduling, high-level synthesis, and software code generation. The reduction in communication overhead when merging processes is estimated as a preprocessing step to cosynthesis, typically just counting variables to be communicated. This can only be done for a subset of all combinations, such as nearest neighbors in the control or data flow. Also, communication overhead grows with finer partitioning. The overhead declines later by using shared memory and by communicating pointers to blocks of variables rather than communicating all the variables directly;[17] however, the high-level transformation problem remains. To enable maximum memory optimization, partitioning of the local variable set and the larger array variables must complement fine-grain partitioning. This aspect still requires intensive investigation, since it is highly relevant in data signal processor (DSP) loop optimization.

Figure 3 summarizes the granularity dilemma. Approaches at the finest level of granularity (used for ASIPs) do not exploit the full design space.

The bulk of cosynthesis approaches for reactive systems with short process execution times use the input processes without changes,[9,18,19] thus saving the partitioning step. Cosynthesis approaches for systems with higher computation requirements provide most of the contributions to process partitioning. They work mostly on the basic block level;[15,20] other systems select the function level as a compromise, since a function call still exposes the communicated parameters, saving the analysis step.

Because most system designs are not extreme, it is useful to adapt the level of granularity to the application[21] and to the target architecture. So far, little work has been done in granularity adaptation.

High-level transformations are also important to retarget a process (for example, from a RISC to a DSP with a complex memory system). At the current state of research (and probably for some time to come), this transformation step needs designer interaction.

Architecture definition

Many embedded systems consist of a complex, heterogeneous set of standard processors, ASIPs, coprocessors, memories, and peripheral components. The designer typically preselects the architecture to reduce the design space.[10,12] It can also be hard-coded as a cosynthesis template—examples include processor-coprocessors,[9,15,20] VLIW-ASIPs,[22] or single buses with shared memory.[23] There are a few exceptions[24,25] where the search space is controlled by using clustering (for example, according to deadlines or by string encoding in a genetic algorithm).

Design space exploration

At this point, we have defined the architecture, and the input system of processes has been analyzed and adapted. The allocation of processes to components and (complex) vari-

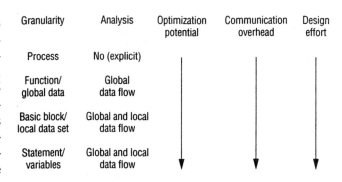

Figure 3. *Granularity effects.*

ables to memory, the mapping of abstract process communication to physical communication, and the scheduling of processes sharing the same resource remain as problems.

Hardware-software partitioning. The architecture determines the cosynthesis approach. The main difference appears between ASIPs (requiring a fine-grain, statement-level approach) and processor-coprocessor systems (working on at least a basic-block level).

ASIPs hold a large market share in markets where the extra design effort is justified. Given an application, the problem of ASIP design is to derive an appropriate processor architecture that can implement application-specific software. For that purpose, one must adapt compilers, libraries, operating system functions (if any), and the simulation and debugging environment. Specialization often leads to irregular register sets and interconnects, which makes compilation and compiler adaptation hard but not infeasible. Most of the work considers hardware design and software generation as separate tasks, just as in quantitative general-purpose processor design.[3]

Approaches combining both tasks are mostly based on standard compilers and try to group three address code statements into complex instructions, thereby adapting the data path[22] and exploring only a part of the overall ASIP design space.[5]

Another ASIP design automation approach with a fixed single-processor template (soft core) uses the instruction word length as a main user-defined parameter to optimize program memory size.[26] In contrast, design space exploration for more complex embedded ASIPs with numerous free parameters, such as multiprocessor DSP architectures, is based on user-driven quantitative exploration.[27]

Standard processors lead to a different set of cosynthesis problems. Here, the software development environments are given, and the application splits into a part implemented on the processor and a part implemented in application-specific hardware (coprocessors). From a tool perspective,

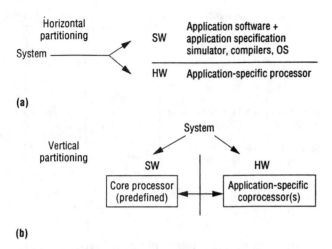

Figure 4. Partitioning types. Application-specific processors (a) and processor and coprocessor (b).

this corresponds to a clear separation in application functions: some are synthesized by hardware synthesis tools and others are handled by software development tools. This was the original meaning of the term hardware-software partitioning. In the case of ASIPs, hardware and software syntheses are applied to the same application functions in sequence, but hardware and software are eventually disjoined. To highlight the differences, we use the terms vertical hardware-software partitioning and horizontal hardware-software partitioning, as shown in Figure 4.

The role of hardware-software partitioning is the optimized distribution of system functions to software and hardware components. There is a general similarity to the scheduling problem in real-time operating systems (RTOSs).[28] Time constraints must be regarded, context switching is required, and we need process communication and synchronization.

However, there are major differences. First, the design space is much larger, since the hardware architecture is not finalized and includes components with vastly different properties that software drivers encapsulate and substitute in RTOSs. In hardware-software partitioning, time constraints can range to less than a microsecond—considerably below typical time constraints in an RTOS, giving high importance to communication and context switch overhead.

Communication synthesis. This step must map communication in the input description to physical communication in the target architecture. Target system hardware and software components can communicate via shared memory, or they can exchange messages. There are many different media: point-to-point, switched channels, buses, or larger networks. The channels can be buffered or nonbuffered. There are many protocols, including packet transfer or split transaction. Cost and bandwidth vary widely. In other words, communication design space resembles the component design space in size.

Given the input and output communication models, we can identify three major tasks: communication channel selection, communication channel allocation, and communication channel scheduling.

Currently, no tool can cover the whole variety of communication mechanisms.[25] Communication channel selection is mostly manual or predefined, with few exceptions. Communication channel allocation is mostly treated as a consequence of process allocation. Tools with static nonpreemptive process scheduling regularly perform communication scheduling. In these cases, static communication scheduling complements process scheduling to obtain an overall fixed schedule.

Hardware-software scheduling. Scheduling enables hardware and software resource sharing. On the process level, there are several scheduling policies derived from RTOSs,[28] for example, static table-driven, priority-based preemptive scheduling, and various other dynamic plan-based policies that have not yet been applied to codesign.

Priority-based preemptive scheduling is the classic approach of commercial RTOSs. Process priorities are determined a priori (static priority) or at runtime (dynamic priority). They are used in reactive as well as dataflow systems with sufficiently coarse process granularity. Dynamic priority assignment requires a runtime scheduler process that assigns priorities according to process deadlines. This increases component utilization, in particular for reactive systems, but makes timing verification harder.

In static (table-driven) scheduling, the order of process execution is determined at design time. It has been used for periodic process scheduling, where a static schedule exists for the least common multiple (LCM) of all process periods.[29] The process sequence can be stored in a schedule table, but the processes can also be merged into a sequence to use the compiler (or the synthesis tool) to minimize context switching overhead,[30] usually at the cost of a larger program. This is the domain of small processes, where context switching times are significant compared with the process execution times. Static scheduling can also combine with preemptive scheduling. Processes communicating with static data flow triggered by the same event can be clustered and scheduled statically, while the process clusters are scheduled preemptively. This allows for local dataflow optimization, including pipelining and buffering.

In recent years, static scheduling has also been used in event-driven reactive systems. A first approach is to adapt the sequence of executions in a static schedule to the input events and data.[17] A second approach is to collect all parts of a process activated by the same event in one static thread of operations,[31] which can then be statically scheduled into a single process. Both scheduling approaches can be combined and used as a basis for process merging in event-driven systems.

Complex embedded architectures require distributed scheduling policies for hardware and software parts such as scheduling, which is optimized for several communicating hardware and software components. Communication, especially in context with processing, has drawn little attention in RTOS research or has been treated pessimistically.[12] This treatment is not acceptable for highly integrated embedded systems, where communication and buffering have a major impact on performance, power consumption, and cost. Global approaches to distributed scheduling of communicating processes have been proposed for preemptive[12] and static scheduling.[29]

Instead of a uniform scheduling policy, components or subsystems may use different policies, especially when combining different but compatible system types; but the policies must be compatible. An example is the TOSCA system.[9] It uses static priority scheduling for software implementation of concurrent finite-state machines, while the hardware side does not share resources, thus avoiding hardware scheduling. In the POLIS system,[8,18] software scheduling is even less constrained. A more complicated approach[32] proposes static priority (rate monotonic)[28] software scheduling combined with interrupt-activated, shared-hardware coprocessors in a robot control system. Notably, out of these global policies, only the static uniform approach supports global buffering between components, which is explained by the complex behavior of preemptive scheduling.

Exploiting process semantics, such as mutually exclusive process execution and conditional communication,[32,33] can improve scheduling efficiency. In static scheduling, this knowledge can optimize utilization,[33] while in preemptive scheduling, it can help to verify timing constraints and to optimize communication.

A major problem of static scheduling is data-dependent process execution found not only in software execution, but also in hardware with conditional control flow. Since nonpreemptive scheduling must assume worst-case behavior, data-dependent timing leads to lower average system performance. One approach is to resort to dynamic scheduling with local buffers, even in purely static dataflow applications.[34]

The variety of process models of computation and scheduling policies (and their possible combinations) is a challenge to design space exploration and cosynthesis. It requires design representations that allow the mixing and matching of different models of computation for scheduling. Software reuse and object-oriented design imply that critical system parts that the designer knows in detail will combine with less familiar legacy code.

Memory optimization. Memory is becoming a dominant cost factor in integrated systems and often bottlenecks system performance. Allocation of data to memory can, in principle, be combined with hardware-software partitioning and process scheduling.[35] Memory optimization, however, drastically increases the number of design parameters beyond the assignment of data variables to memories and accesses to memory ports. Multidimensional data arrays can be rearranged in memory by index transformations to improve memory use or simplify array index generation.[36] Loop transformations can minimize memory accesses and size.

The optimal access pattern is technology dependent. SDRAM, for example, requires efficient burst access to rows. This influences memory allocation and transformations, especially in cases of memory hierarchies. Past research has examined program cache optimization exploiting the program structure and profiling results to minimize cache misses at the cost of extra main memory space.[37] Other work considers optimization for architectures with memories of different types, such as a combination of scratch-pad SRAM and DRAM.[38] Dynamic memory allocation is another problem that we have only recently addressed in hardware-software codesign.[39]

Estimation. All optimization steps discussed must acknowledge final implementation data, such as the execution time of a process when executed on a specific processor or a coprocessor, and the required sizes of program and data memory. At the time of cosynthesis, these data are not yet available, except for reused system parts. All other hardware and software data must be estimated.

One way to obtain such data is to implement each single process with the target synthesis tool or compiler, and then run them on the (simulated) target platform or use formal analysis.[11] Since efficient synthesis tools and compilers are not available for all target architectures, this approach does not cover the whole design space. In practice, tool license problems could arise, since a company might not want to acquire tools for a large range of possible processors just for the sake of design space exploration.

A second approach is to estimate the results using a simplified but generic version of the synthesis tools, such as a list scheduler or a path-based scheduler, in case the data path architecture isn't completely familiar.[17]

Notably, neither of the two approaches is fully accurate, since both, in general, cannot precisely predict the savings in cost and timing when several processes share the same hardware component,[15] which is the standard case in design. Analyzing all potentially useful combinations of processes and resources, however, is prohibitively time consuming except for critical system parts.

Despite these limitations, the current estimation techniques are already much closer to real implementation than

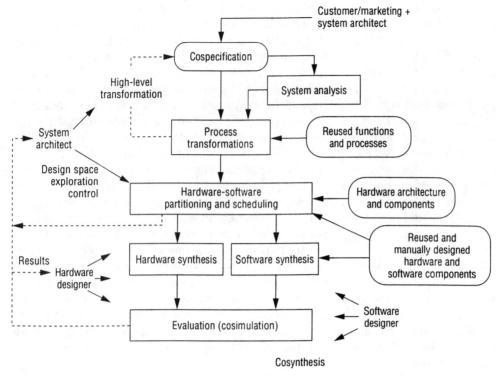

Figure 5. *Design space exploration process.*

simple back-of-the-envelope estimations.

Exploration and cosynthesis process

Now, we can put the pieces together to propose an integrated computer-aided design space exploration and cosynthesis approach. Figure 5 shows that the system architecture development process of Figure 1 has been detailed into the process transformation, hardware-software partitioning, and scheduling steps. System analysis provides system data derived from the executable cospecification (for example, profiling data). Process transformation prepares the specified system for the exploration process by matching the different parts of the cospecification that may be described in different languages and models of computation.

The system architect can apply high-level transformations to this description to better match the process to the intended memory model. Computer support for high-level transformations will improve over time, but there will always be a difficult-to-automate, creative part. For this reason, we should leave the architecture selection to the system architect and the designers, who can then explore different alternatives, possibly iterating over the high-level transformation process.

In the next phase, the system architect or the design team can control the design space exploration process by changing the selected components (processor types, memories, co-processors, peripheral units), communication channels, the scheduling policy, or whatever parameters the cosynthesis system supports. Next, the cosynthesis tools partition and schedule the system and provide feedback on the resulting system data. The design space exploration process should be completed by hardware and software synthesis to validate the estimations.

A fully automated hardware and software synthesis process (including interface synthesis) requires flexible and powerful high-level synthesis tools supporting component reuse as well as compilers with excellent code generators. Since both are not readily available for all architectures, manual design support of these back-end steps will still be necessary to obtain optimized results in a large design space. This sounds like bad news for an automated design process, but design space exploration does not depend on a complete synthesis of all parts. Instead, it can exploit data for those parts of a design in which efficient compilers and synthesis tools or reused hardware and software components are available, and use estimations for the remaining parts. Cosimulation can then evaluate the system timing, where abstract models can be used for the nonimplemented parts.

This approach has many advantages:

- The design space exploration process is split into two loops with increasing turnaround time and accuracy. The first loop ends with partitioning and scheduling; the second one includes part of the hardware and software synthesis. Estimation precision can be increased by manual interaction. Using both loops, precision can gradually be improved in the course of the design process, increasing result reliability and avoiding unnecessary precision requirements in the early design phases. The short iteration time of the first loop allows iteration over the cospecification parameters. Benner and Ernst[40] have demonstrated how the impact of a specified maximum bus throughput on the optimum architecture of a design could be investigated within a few hours.

- Reuse of components is supported at different levels of abstraction.
- The intermediate results of process transformation and hardware-software partitioning and scheduling can be used for the final design, and therefore, there is little overhead.
- The design process can quickly respond to changes in the specification.
- The design process can profit from an increasing set of intellectual property libraries as well as from progress in hardware synthesis and compiler technology, without a change in the overall methodology.

The many interfaces in Figure 5 give an idea of the work required to integrate the research results into an easy-to-use and extendible industrial design environment. I think it's evident that this effort would be well spent.

COMPUTER-AIDED HARDWARE-SOFTWARE CODESIGN has made considerable progress in the past few years. The greatest demand is currently in system analysis, including cosimulation, coverification, and (executable) cospecification, which is obvious when considering the current design process. Cosynthesis and computer-aided design space exploration are only beginning to reach the industrial design practice. Using a possible design space exploration scenario, we have identified the major problems of this emerging EDA field and have reviewed the results of ongoing research. Highly automated and optimizing cosynthesis approaches have been demonstrated, but for a limited class of architectures and applications. We have, however, seen how the results can contribute to an advanced interactive design space exploration process for a much wider range of architectures. Reuse at different levels of the design process and design migration between different implementation technologies can occur without the need for a complete automation of design steps.

References

1. P. Dreike and J. McCoy, "Cosimulating Hardware and Software in Embedded Systems," *Proc. Embedded Systems Programming Europe*, IEEE Computer Soc. Press, Los Alamitos, Calif., Sep. 1997, pp. 12-27.
2. D. Jaggar et al., "ARM Architecture and Systems," *IEEE Micro*, Vol. 17, No. 4, Jul.-Aug. 1997, pp. 9-11.
3. J.L. Hennessy and D.A. Patterson, *Computer Architecture—A Quantitative Approach*, 2nd ed., Morgan-Kaufmann, San Mateo, Calif., 1996.
4. P. Paulin et al.. "Trends in Embedded Systems Technology: An Industrial Perspective," *Hardware-Software Codesign*, G. De Micheli and M. Sami, eds., Kluwer Academic, Boston, Mass.. 1996, pp. 311-337.
5. W. Wolf et al.. *Hardware-Software Codesign: Principles and Practices*. Kluwer Academic, 1997.
6. D. Herrmann et al., "High-Speed Video Board as a Case Study for Hardware-Software Codesign," *Proc. Int'l Conf. Computer Design*, IEEE CS Press, 1996, pp. 185-190.
7. J. van den Hurk and J. Jess, *System-Level Hardware-Software Codesign*, Kluwer Academic, 1998.
8. M. Chiodo et al., "A Case Study in Computer-Aided Codesign of Embedded Controllers," *J. Design Automation Embedded Systems*, Vol. 1, No. 1, 1996, pp. 51-67.
9. A. Balboni, W. Fornaciari, and D. Sciuto, "Cosynthesis and Cosimulation of Control-Dominated Embedded Systems," *J. Design Automation Embedded Systems*, Vol. 1, No. 3, Jun. 1996, pp. 257-288.
10. D.D. Gajski et al., *Specification and Design of Embedded Systems*, Kluwer Academic, 1994.
11. W. Ye and R. Ernst, "Embedded Program Timing Analysis Based on Path Clustering and Architecture Classification," *Proc. Int'l Conf. Computer-Aided Design*, IEEE CS Press, 1997, pp. 598-604.
12. T.-Y. Yen and W. Wolf, *Hardware-Software Cosynthesis of Distributed Embedded Systems*, Kluwer Academic, 1996.
13. M. Zhou, *Optimization of MPEG-2 Video Encoding*, doctoral dissertation, TU Braunschweig/HHI Berlin, 1997.
14. S. Agrawal and R. Gupta, "Dataflow-Assisted Behavioral Partitioning for Embedded Systems," *Proc. Design Automation Conf.*, ACM, N.Y., 1997, pp. 709-712.
15. R. Ernst, J. Henkel, and T. Benner, "Hardware-Software Cosynthesis for Microcontrollers," *IEEE Design & Test*, Vol. 10, No. 4, Dec. 1993, pp. 64-75.
16. P. Chou and G. Borriello, "An Analysis-Based Approach to Composition of Distributed Embedded Systems," *Proc. Int'l Work. Hardware-Software Codesign*, IEEE CS Press, 1998.
17. R. Ernst et al., "The COSYMA Environment for Hardware-Software Cosynthesis of Small Embedded Systems," *J. Microprocessors and Microsystems*, Vol. 20, No. 3, May 1996, pp. 159-166.
18. M. Chiodo et al., "Hardware-Software Codesign of Embedded Systems," *IEEE Micro*, Vol. 14, No. 4, Jul.-Aug. 1994, pp. 26-36.
19. T.D. Ismail, M. Abid, and A. Jerraya, "COSMOS: A Codesign Approach for Communicating Systems," *Proc. Int'l Work. Hardware-Software Codesign*, IEEE CS Press, 1994, pp. 17-24.
20. R.K. Gupta and G. De Micheli, "A Cosynthesis Approach to Embedded System Design Automation," *J. Design Automation Embedded Systems*, Vol. 1, No. 1, Jan. 1996, pp.

69-120.
21. J. Henkel and R. Ernst, "A Hardware-Software Partitioner Using a Dynamically Determined Granularity," *Proc. Design Automation Conf.*, ACM, 1997, pp. 691-696.
22. J. Wilberg and R. Camposano, "VLIW Processor Codesign for Video Processing," *J. Design Automation Embedded Systems*, Vol. 1, No. 1, 1996, pp. 79-119.
23. J. Axelson, *Analyis and Synthesis of Heterogeneous Real-Time Systems*, doctoral thesis, Dept. of Computers and Info. Studies, Linköping Studies in Sci. and Tech., 1997.
24. B.P. Dave and N. Jha, "CASPER: Concurrent Hardware-Software Cosynthesis of Hard Real-Time Aperiodic and Periodic Specifications of System Architectures," *Proc. DATE*, IEEE CS Press, 1998, pp. 118-124.
25. J. Teich, T. Blickle, and L. Thiele, "An Evolutionary Approach to System-Level Synthesis," *Proc. Int'l Work. Hardware-Software Codesign*, IEEE CS Press, 1997, pp. 167-172.
26. B. Shakleford et al., "Memory-CPU Size Optimization for Embedded System Design," *Proc. DATE*, IEEE CS Press, 1997, pp. 246-251.
27. P. Lieverse et al., "A Clustering Approach to Explore Grain Sizes in the Definition of Weakly Programmable Processing Elements," *Proc. Work. Signal Processing Systems*, IEEE CS Press, 1997, pp. 107-120.
28. K. Ramamritham and J. A. Stankovic, "Scheduling Algorithms and Operating Systems Support for Real-Time Systems," *Proc. IEEE*, Piscataway, N.J., Jan. 1994, pp. 55-67.
29. E.A. Lee and D.G. Messerschmitt, "Synchronous Data Flow," *Proc. IEEE*, Sep. 1987, pp. 1235-1245.
30. A. Österling, T. Benner, and R. Ernst, "Code Generation and Context Switching for Static Scheduling of Mixed Control and Data Oriented HW/SW Systems," *Proc. Asia Pacific Conf. Hardware Description Languages*, Tsing Hua Univ., 1997, pp. 131-135.
31. J. Li and R.K. Gupta, "HDL Optimization Using Timed Decision Tables," *Proc. Design Automation Conf.*, IEEE CS Press, 1996, pp. 51-54.
32. V.J. Mooney and G. DeMicheli, "Real-Time Analysis and Priority Scheduler Generation for Hardware-Software Systems with a Synthesized Run-Time System," *Proc. Int'l Work. Hardware-Software Codesign*, IEEE CS Press, 1997, pp. 605-612.
33. P. Eles et al., "Scheduling of Conditional Process Graphs for the Synthesis of Embedded Systems," *Proc. DATE*, IEEE CS Press, 1998, pp. 132-138.
34. J.A. Leijten et al., "Stream Communication between Real-Time Tasks in a High-Performance Multiprocessor," *Proc. DATE*, IEEE CS Press, 1998, pp. 125-131.
35. E. De Greef, F. Catthoor, and H. De Man, "Memory Organization for Video Algorithms in Programmable Signal Processors," *Proc. Int'l Conf. Computer Design*, IEEE CS Press, 1995, pp. 552-557.
36. H. Schmit and D. Thomas, "Address Generation for Memories Containing Multiple Arrays," *Proc. Int'l Conf. Computer-Aided Design*, IEEE CS Press, 1995, pp. 510-514.
37. H. Tomiyama and H. Yasuura, "Optimal Code Placement of Embedded Software for Instruction Caches," *Proc. ED&TC*, IEEE CS Press, 1996, pp. 96-101.
38. P.R. Panda, N.D. Dutt, and A. Nicolau, "Efficient Utilization of Scratch-Pad Memory in Embedded Processor Applications," *Proc. ED&TC*, IEEE CS Press, 1997, pp. 7-11.
39. G. de Jong et al., "Background Memory Management for Dynamic Data Structure Intensive Processing Systems," *Proc. Int'l Conf. Computer-Aided Design*, IEEE CS Press, 1995, pp. 515-520.
40. T. Benner and R. Ernst, "An Approach to Mixed System Cosynthesis," *Proc. Int'l Work. Hardware-Software Codesign*, IEEE CS Press, 1997, pp. 9-14.

Rolf Ernst is a professor at the Institute of Computer Engineering at the Technical University of Braunschweig, Germany. His current interests are in hardware-software codesign, high-level synthesis, rapid prototyping, and embedded-system architecture.

Address questions or comments to Rolf Ernst, Institut fuer Datenverarbeitungsanlagen, Technische Universitaet Braunschweig, Hans-Sommer-Str. 66, D-38106 Braunschweig, Germany; ernst@ida.ing.tu-bs.de.

CHAPTER TWO

Modeling

Dataflow Process Networks 59
   E. A. Lee and T. M. Parks

Design of Embedded Systems: Formal Models, Validation, and Synthesis 86
   S. Edwards, L. Lavagno, E. A. Lee, and A. Sangiovanni-Vincentelli

SpecSyn: An Environment Supporting the Specify-Explore-Refine Paradigm for
Hardware/Software System Design 108
   D. D. Gajski, F. Vahid, S. Narayan, and J. Gong

VHDL Generation from SDL Specification 125
   J.M. Daveau, G. Marchioro, C. Valderrama, and A. Jerraya

Statemate: A Working Environment for the Development of Complex Reactive Systems 135
   D. Harel et al

The Synchronous Approach to Reactive and Real-Time Systems 147
   A. Benveniste and G. Berry

INTRODUCTION

System models are representations that highlight some characteristics while abstracting away some others. Typically, system models that capture all aspects of a design are complex and less useful than feature-specific models. Design of complex systems benefits from the orthogonalization of concerns, that is, from deconstructing the design problem into subproblems that are fairly independent of each other. The utilization of different, sometimes orthogonal, models is useful for capturing a design as well as capturing those features that are most important to its designers.

With these premises in mind, we can say that modeling hardware/software systems is both an art and a science. The art consists of selecting the appropriate model for the system aspect that the designer needs to highlight and matching the model to the desired properties or to the desired transformations. Nevertheless, each model should be founded on a sound mathematical basis. A large body of scientific literature has been dedicated to analyzing models of computation and their properties. It is often the case that modeling languages are confused with models of computation. Modeling languages express computational models in specific text forms. Languages can have different flavors and features, but what really matters is the underlying computational model, which defines the expressive power of the language.

MODELS OF COMPUTATION

Edwards *et al.* [Edw97] reviewed models of computations in the context of modeling embedded systems. They stressed that a comprehensive system-level model should include a functional specification, system properties, performance indexes (*e.g.*, cost, speed, power consumption), and design constraints (on the performance indexes). Specifications of complex systems need by no mean be homogeneous, that is, expressed with a uniform formalism. Indeed, different formalisms may be used to represent different aspects of the design. It is therefore important to understand the properties and expressive power of the different underlying models of computation and their interrelations.

Edwards *et al.* identified four primary models of computation that are relevant to embedded system design: *discrete event*, *data-flow process networks*, (communicating) *finite-state machines* and *synchronous/reactive* models. Discrete-event models are important for understanding circuit and system simulation, as well as those languages that were conceived for simulation, such as VHDL and Verilog HDL.

Lee and Parks [Lee95] reviewed data-flow process networks, which are a special case of Kahn process networks, a model of computation where a number of concurrent processes communicate through unidirectional FIFO channels, where writes to the channel are non-blocking and reads are blocking. In data flow process networks, each process consists of repeated firings of a data-flow actor, which is a quantum of computation. Several variants of dataflow process networks have been used as underlying computational models for commercial design systems, such as SPW (Cadence), COSSAP (Synopsys) and the DSP Station (Mentor Graphics) among others.

LANGUAGES

Models of computations find application in system design by their expression in modeling languages. The variety of system description languages mirrors the variety in mathematical models of computation.

The finite-state machine (FSM) model is the cornerstone for constructing control systems. Because of its simplicity and clear and sound mathematical model, synthesis and verification technologies with FSM models have reached maturity and stability. The SDL language [Dav97b] is one example of a state-oriented modeling language. SDL has been standardized by the ITU and is widely used in the telecommunications industry to describe the behavior of telephone switching systems, protocols, and so forth. SDL allows designers to describe multiple concurrent processes that communicate by signals. Daveau *et al.* [Dav97b] describe techniques for synthesizing VHDL implementations from SDL signals.

Nevertheless, design with FSM models may be cumbersome, because of state explosion. Harel's *StateCharts* [Har90] and further refinements increased enormously the usability of FSMs as a specification model for system design. With StateCharts, a user can decompose a sequential model in a hierarchical fashion, by capturing concurrent and sequential behavior. Such a hierarchical decomposition can reduce state explosion and keep the size of a state-based representation small enough so that it retains its visual appeal. Thus StateCharts can be used in graphic entry systems, where designers can create StateCharts and focus on any specific aspect of sequential behavior. Animation of StateCharts provides immediate visual feedback to designers. Moreover, because of the underlying FSM semantics, synthesis and verification from StateCharts can be effectively achieved.

The synchronous approach to modeling reactive systems has been an area of active research in Europe, especially in France. Synchronous languages are based on the assumption that programs react instantaneously to external events. Thus the notion of physical time is replaced by a simpler concept of order among events: The only relevant notions are the simultaneity and precedence between events.

The Esterel language [Ben91] is a synchronous language with procedural semantics. The language supports concurrent behavior, as a way to reduce the state explosion problem, and considers timing as a first-class citizen. For example, Esterel's construct `do {} watching event` allows designers to specify actions that are bounded by temporal events, such as timeouts. Esterel programs can be compiled into finite-state models, which can be synthesized and formally verified. These features make Esterel very powerful in capturing the needs of real-time reactive systems design, as they often occur within embedded control systems.

Unfortunately, the synchronous languages, like most formalisms based on finite-state models, cannot adequately represent computation flows. The *program state machine* paradigm extends the finite-state machine model by allowing "programs" to be associated with system states. Thus, computation flows can be described within an FSM framework. Gajski's SpecCharts [Gaj98] are a modeling paradigm based on program state machines. Synthesis tools, such as SpecSyn, have shown the usefulness of this model in the context of emebedded system design. Indeed, this modeling style allows designers to highlight the principal modes of operation of a system and the related transitions and to embed the detailed specification of each mode within the overall system control flow.

ADDITIONAL READINGS IN MODELING

[Pau00] J. M. Paul, S. N. Peffers, and D. E. Thomas, "A codesign virtual machine for hierarchical, balanced hardware/software system modeling," in *Proceedings, 37th Design Automation Conference*, ACM Press, New York, 2000, 390–95. *Describes a computational model for system-level design.*

[Des00] D. Desmet, D. Verkest, and H. De Man, "Operating system based software generation for system-on-chip," in *Proceedings, 37th Design Automation Conference*, ACM Press, New York, 2000, 396–401. *Presents C++-based modeling methodology that captures dynamic behavior.*

[Lee98] E. A. Lee and Alberto Sangiovanni-Vincentelli, "A framework for comparing models of computation," *IEEE Transactions on CAD of Integrated Circuits and Systems*, 17, no. 12 (Dec. 1998): 1217–29. *Provides a meta-model for comparing several models of computation.*

[Thi99] L. Thiele, K. Strehl, D. Ziegenbein, R. Ernst, and J. Teich, "FunState—an internal design representation for codesign," in *Proceedings, ICCAD 99*, IEEE, New York, 1999, 558–65. *Describes an internal representation for co-design that uses functions driven by state machines to capture the behavior of the system and of interacting components.*

[Mac99] P. Maciel, E. Barros, and W. Rosenstiel, "A Petri net model for hardware/software codesign," *Design Automation for Embedded Systems* 4, no. 4 (Oct. 1999): 243–310. *Uses Petri nets to reason about properties of an embedded system.*

[Jer99] A. Jerraya and R. Ernst, "Multi-language system design," in *DATE Conference Proceedings,* IEEE Computer Society Press, Los Alamitos, 1999, 696–99. *Describes techniques for using multiple design languages to describe complex systems.*

[All98] A. Allara, W. Fornaciari, F. Salice, and D. Sciuto, "A model for system-level timed analysis and profiling," in *Proceedings, DATE 98*, IEEE Computer Society Press, Los Alamitos, 1998, 204–10. *Presents an OCCAM II–based modeling system and associated simulation environment.*

[You98] J. S. Young, J. MacDonald, M. Shilman, A. Tabbara, P. Hilfinger, and A. R. Newton, "Design and specification of embedded systems in Java using successive, formal refinement," in *Proceedings, 35th Design Automation Conference*, ACM Press, New York, 1998, 70–75. *A specification methodology based on Java for reactive embedded systems.*

[Cho98] P. Chou and G. Borriello, "Modal processes: Toward enhanced retargetability through control composition of distributed embedded systems," in *Proceedings, 35th Design Automation Conference*, ACM Press, New York, 1998, 88–93. *Uses both hierarchical FSMs and process styles to describe embedded system control.*

Dataflow Process Networks

EDWARD A. LEE, FELLOW, IEEE, AND THOMAS M. PARKS

We review a model of computation used in industrial practice in signal processing software environments and experimentally in other contexts. We give this model the name "dataflow process networks," and study its formal properties as well as its utility as a basis for programming language design. Variants of this model are used in commercial visual programming systems such as SPW from the Alta Group of Cadence (formerly Comdisco Systems), COSSAP from Synopsys (formerly Cadis), the DSP Station from Mentor Graphics, and Hypersignal from Hyperception. They are also used in research software such as Khoros from the University of New Mexico and Ptolemy from the University of California at Berkeley, among many others.

Dataflow process networks are shown to be a special case of Kahn process networks, a model of computation where a number of concurrent processes communicate through unidirectional FIFO channels, where writes to the channel are nonblocking, and reads are blocking. In dataflow process networks, each process consists of repeated "firings" of a dataflow "actor." An actor defines a (often functional) quantum of computation. By dividing processes into actor firings, the considerable overhead of context switching incurred in most implementations of Kahn process networks is avoided.

We relate dataflow process networks to other dataflow models, including those used in dataflow machines, such as static dataflow and the tagged-token model. We also relate dataflow process networks to functional languages such as Haskell, and show that modern language concepts such as higher-order functions and polymorphism can be used effectively in dataflow process networks. A number of programming examples using a visual syntax are given.

I. MOTIVATION

This paper concerns programming methodologies commonly called "graphical dataflow programming" that are used extensively for signal processing and experimentally for other applications. In this paper, "graphical" means simply that the program is explicitly specified by a directed graph where the nodes represent computations and the arcs represent streams of data. The graphs are typically hierarchical, in that a node in a graph may represent another directed graph. The nodes in the graph can be either language primitives or subprograms specified in another language, such as C or FORTRAN.

It is common in the signal processing community to use a visual syntax to specify such graphs, in which case the model is often called "visual dataflow programming." But it is by no means essential to use a visual syntax. A few graphical programming environments allow an arbitrary mixture of visual and textual specification, both based on the same language. For example, the Signal [12], [68], Lustre [46], and Silage [50] languages all have a visual and a textual syntax, the latter available in the commercial Mentor Graphics DSP Station as DFL. Other languages with related semantics, such as Sisal [73], are used primarily or exclusively with textual syntax. The language Lucid [92], [96], while primarily used with textual syntax, has experimental visual forms [10].

Hierarchy in graphical program structure can be viewed as an alternative to the more usual abstraction of subprograms via procedures, functions, or objects. It is better suited than any of these to a visual syntax, and also better suited to signal processing.

Some examples of graphical dataflow programming environments intended for signal processing (including image processing) are Khoros, from the University of New Mexico [84] (now distributed by Khoral Research, Inc.), Ptolemy, from the University of California at Berkeley [25], the signal processing worksystem (SPW), from the Alta Group at Cadence (formerly Comdisco Systems), COSSAP, from Synopsys (formerly Cadis), and the DSP Station, from Mentor Graphics (formerly EDC). MATLAB from The MathWorks, which is popular for signal processing and other applications, has a visual interface called SIMULINK. A survey of graphical dataflow languages for other applications is given by Hills [51]. These software environments all claim variants of dataflow semantics, but a word of caution is in order. The term "dataflow" is often used loosely for semantics that bear little resemblance to those outlined by Dennis in 1975 [38] or Davis in 1978 [35]. A major motivation of this paper is to point out a rigorous formal

---

Manuscript received August 29, 1994; revised January 30, 1995. This work is part of the Ptolemy project, which is supported by the Advanced Research Projects Agency and the US Air Force under the RASSP program contract number F33615-93-C-1317, Semiconductor Research Corp. project number 94-DC-008, National Science Foundation contract number MIP-9201605, Office of Naval Technology (via Naval Research Laboratories), the State of California, and the following companies: Bell Northern Research, Dolby, Hitachi, Mentor Graphics, Mitsubishi, NEC, Pacific Bell, Philips, Rockwell, Sony, and Synopsys.

The authors are with the Department of Electrical Engineering and Computer Sciences, The University of California, Berkeley, CA 94720 USA.

IEEE Log Number 9409997.

underpinning for dataflow graphical languages, to establish precisely the relationship between such languages and functional languages, and to show that such languages benefit significantly from such modern programming concepts as polymorphism, strong typing, and higher-order functions. Although it has been rarely exploited in visual dataflow programming, we also show that such languages can make effective use of recursion.

Most graphical signal processing environments do not define a language in any strict sense. In fact, some designers of such environments advocate minimal semantics [76], arguing that the graphical organization by itself is sufficient to be useful. The semantics of a program in such environments is determined by the contents of the graph nodes, either subgraphs or subprograms. Subprograms are usually specified in a conventional programming language such as C. Most such environments, however, including Khoros, SPW, and COSSAP, take a middle ground, permitting the nodes in a graph or subgraph to contain arbitrary subprograms, but defining precise semantics for the interaction between nodes. Following Halbwachs [47], we call the language used to define the subprograms in nodes the *host language*. Following Jagannathan, we call the language defining the interaction between nodes the *coordination language* [56].

Many possibilities have been explored for precise semantics of coordination languages, including for example the computation graphs of Karp and Miller [61], the synchronous dataflow graphs of Lee and Messerschmitt [66], the cyclostatic dataflow of Lauwereins *et al.* [17], [63], the processing graph method (PGM) of Kaplan *et al.* [60], granular lucid [56], and others [3], [28], [33], [56], [94]. Many of these limit expressiveness in exchange for considerable advantages such as compile-time predictability.

Graphical programs can be either interpreted or compiled. It is common in signal processing environments to provide both options. The output of compilation can be a standard procedural language, such as C, assembly code for programmable DSP processors [80], or even specifications of silicon implementations [37]. Often, considerable effort is put into optimized compilation (see for example [15], [41], [81], [88]).

II. FORMAL UNDERPINNINGS

In most graphical programming environments, the nodes of the graph can be viewed as processes that run concurrently and exchange data over the arcs of the graph. However, these processes and their interaction are usually much more constrained than those of CSP [52] or SCCS [74]. A better (and fortunately much simpler) formal underpinning is the Kahn process network [58].

A. Kahn Process Networks

In a process network, concurrent processes communicate only through one-way FIFO channels with unbounded capacity. Each channel carries a possibly infinite *sequence* (a *stream*) that we denote $X = [x_1, x_2, \cdots]$, where each x_i is an atomic data object, or *token* drawn from some set. Each token is written (produced) exactly once, and read (consumed) exactly once. Writes to the channels are *nonblocking* (they always succeed immediately), but reads are *blocking*. This means that a process that attempts to read from an empty input channel stalls until the buffer has sufficient tokens to satisfy the read. Lest the reader protest, we will show that this model of computation does not actually require either multitasking or parallelism, although it is certainly capable of exploiting both. It also usually does not require infinite queues, and indeed can be much more efficient in its use of memory than comparable methods in functional languages, as we will see.

A process in the Kahn model is a mapping from one or more input sequences to one or more output sequences. The process is usually constrained to be *continuous* in a rather technical sense. To develop this idea, we need a little notation.

Consider a *prefix ordering* of sequences, where the sequence X precedes the sequence Y (written $X \sqsubseteq Y$) if X is a prefix of (or is equal to) Y. For example, $[x_1, x_2] \sqsubseteq [x_1, x_2, x_3]$. If $X \sqsubseteq Y$, it is common to say that X approximates Y, since it provides partial information about Y. The empty sequence is denoted $\perp$ (*bottom*), and is obviously a prefix of any other sequence. Consider a (possibly infinite) increasing chain of sequences $\chi = \{X_0, X_1, \cdots\}$, where $X_0 \sqsubseteq X_1 \sqsubseteq \cdots$. Such an increasing chain of sequences has one or more upper bounds Y, where $X_i \sqsubseteq Y$ for all $X_i \in \chi$. The *least upper bound* $\sqcap \chi$ is an upper bound such that for any other upper bound $Y, \sqcap \chi \sqsubseteq Y$. The least upper bound may be an infinite sequence.

Let S denote the set of finite and infinite sequences. This set is a *complete partial order* (*cpo*) with the prefix order defining the ordering. The "complete" simply means that every increasing chain has a least upper bound in S. Let S^p denote the set of p-tuples of sequences as in $\boldsymbol{X} = \{X_1, X_2, \cdots, X_p\} \in S^p$. The set $\perp \in S^p$ is understood to be the set of empty sequences.

Such sets of sequences can be ordered as well; we write $\boldsymbol{X} \sqsubseteq \boldsymbol{X}'$ if $X_i \sqsubseteq X'_i$ for each $i, 1 \leq i \leq p$. A set of p-tuples of sequences $\chi = \{\boldsymbol{X}_0, \boldsymbol{X}_1, \cdots\}$ always has a *greatest lower bound* $\sqcup \chi$ (possibly $\perp$), but it may or may not have a *least upper bound* $\sqcap \chi$. If it is an increasing chain, $\chi = \{\boldsymbol{X}_0, \boldsymbol{X}_1, \cdots\}$, where $\boldsymbol{X}_0 \sqsubseteq \boldsymbol{X}_1 \sqsubseteq \cdots$, then it has a least upper bound, so S^p is a cpo for any integer p.

1) A Functional Process $F: S^p \rightarrow S^q$ maps a set of input sequences into a set of output sequences. Given an increasing chain of sets of sequences χ, it will map this set into another set of sequences Ψ that may or may not be an increasing chain. Let $\sqcap \chi$ denote the least upper bound of the increasing chain χ. Then F is said to be *continuous* if for all such chains $\chi, \sqcap F(\chi)$ exists and

$$F(\sqcap \chi) = \sqcap F(\chi). \qquad (1)$$

This is analogous to the notion of continuity for conventional functions, if the least upper bound is interpreted as a limit, as in

$$\sqcap \chi = \sqcap \{X_0 \sqsubseteq X_1 \sqsubseteq \cdots\} = \lim_{i \to \infty} X_i. \quad (2)$$

Kahn sketches a proof that networks of continuous processes have a more intuitive property called *monotonicity* [58]. A process F is monotonic if $X \sqsubseteq X' \Rightarrow F(X) \sqsubseteq F(X')$. This can be thought of as a form of causality, but one that does not invoke time. Moreover, in signal processing, it provides a useful abstract analog to causality that works for multirate discrete-time systems without requiring the invocation of continuous time. Given an increasing chain χ, a monotonic process will map this set into another increasing chain Ψ.

For completeness, we now prove Kahn's claim that a continuous process is monotonic [58]. To do this, we prove that if a process is not monotonic, then it cannot be continuous. If the process F is not monotonic, then there exist X and X' where $X \sqsubseteq X'$, but $F(X) \not\sqsubseteq F(X')$. Let $\chi = \{X_0 \sqsubseteq X_1 \sqsubseteq \cdots\}$ be any increasing chain such that $X_0 = X$ and $\sqcap \chi = X'$. Then note that $F(\sqcap \chi) = F(X')$. But this cannot be equal to $\sqcap F(\chi)$ because $X \in \chi$ and $F(X) \not\sqsubseteq F(X')$. This concludes the proof.

A key consequence of these properties is that a process can be computed iteratively [70]. This means that given a prefix of the final input sequences, it may be possible to compute part of the output sequences. In other words, a monotonic process is nonstrict (its inputs need not be complete before it can begin computation). In addition, a continuous process will not wait forever before producing an output (i.e., it will not wait for completion of an infinite input sequence).

A network of processes is, in essence, a set of simultaneous relations between sequences. If we let X denote all the sequences in the network, including the outputs, and I the set of input sequences, then a network of functional processes can be represented by a mapping F where

$$X = F(X, I). \quad (3)$$

Any X that forms a solution is called a *fixed point*. Kahn argues in [58] that continuity of F implies that there will be exactly one "minimal" fixed point (where minimal is in the sense of prefix ordering) for any inputs I. Thus we can get an execution of the network by first setting $I = \bot$ and finding the minimal fixed point. Other solutions can then be found from this one by iterative computation, where the inputs are gradually extended; this works because of the monotonic property.

Note that continuity implies monotonicity, but not the other way around. One process that is monotonic but not continuous is $F: S \to S$ given by

$$F(X) = \begin{cases} [0]; & \text{if } X \text{ is a finite sequence} \\ [0, 1]; & \text{otherwise}. \end{cases} \quad (4)$$

Only two outputs are possible, both finite sequences. To show that this is monotonic, note that if the sequence X is infinite and $X \sqsubseteq X'$, then $X = X'$, so

$$Y = F(X) \sqsubseteq Y' = F(X'). \quad (5)$$

If X is finite, then $Y = F(X) = [0]$, which is a prefix of all possible outputs. To show that it is not continuous, consider the increasing chain

$$\chi = \{X_0, X_1, \cdots\}, \quad \text{where} \quad X_0 \sqsubseteq X_1 \sqsubseteq \cdots \quad (6)$$

where each X_i has exactly i elements in it. Then $\sqcap \chi$ is infinite, so

$$F(\sqcap \chi) = [0, 1] \neq \sqcap F(\chi) = [0]. \quad (7)$$

Iterative computation of this function is clearly problematic.

A useful property is that a network of monotonic processes itself defines a monotonic process. This property is valid even for process networks with feedback loops, as is formally proven using induction by Panagaden and Shanbhogue [78]. It should not be surprising given the results so far that one can formally show that networks of monotonic processes are *determinate*.

B. Nondeterminism

A useful property in some modern languages is an ability to express nondeterminism. This can be used to construct programs that respond to unpredictable sequences of events, or to build incomplete programs, deferring portions of the specification until more complete information about the system implementation is available. Although this capability can be extremely valuable, it needs to be balanced against the observation that for the vast majority of programming tasks, programmers need determinism. Unfortunately, by allowing too much freedom in the interaction between nodes, some graphical programming environments can surprise the user with nondeterminate behavior. Nondeterminate operations can be a powerful programming tool, but they should be used only when such a powerful programming tool is necessary. The problems arise because, as shown by Apt and Plotkin [4], nondeterminism leads to failures of continuity.

Taking a Bayesian perspective, a system is random if the information *known* about the system and its inputs is not sufficient to determine its outputs. The semantics of the programming language may determine what is known, since some properties of the execution may be unspecified. However, since most graphical programming environments do not define complete languages, it is easy (and dangerous) to circumvent what semantics there are by using the host language. In fact, the common principle of avoiding over specifying programs leaves aspects of the execution unspecified, and hence opens the door to nondeterminate behavior. Any behavior that depends on these unspecified aspects will be nondeterminate.

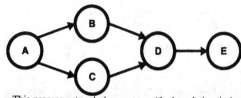

Fig. 1. This process network does not specify the relative timing of the processing in nodes B and C. If D is a nondeterminate merge, it does not specify in which order the results should appear at E.

Nondeterminism can be added to Kahn networks by any of five methods: 1) allowing processes to test inputs for emptiness, 2) allowing processes to be internally nondeterminate, 3) allowing more than one process to write to a channel, 4) allowing more than one process to consume data from a channel, and 5) allowing processes to share variables. Boussinot argues that 3) can implement 1) and 2), and gives the semantics of such extended process networks [19]. Shared variables, however, form a particular pitfall in a coordination language, since they are so easy to implement using the host language.

For example, in the process network shown in Fig. 1, nothing in the graph specifies the relative timing of the processing in nodes B and C. Suppose that nodes B and C each modify a variable that they share. Then the order in which they access this variable could certainly affect the outcome of the program. The problem here is that the process network semantics, which specify a communication mechanism, have been circumvented using a shared variable in the host language. While this may be a powerful and useful capability, it should be used with caution, and in particular, it should not surprise the unwary programmer. Such a capability has been built into the PGM specification [60] in the form of what are called "graph variables." A similar use of shared variables with "peek" and "poke" nodes appears in [79].

If B and C share a variable as described above, then they are potentially nonmonotonic. Knowing that $F(X_0) = Y_0$, $F(X_1) = Y_1$, and $X_0 \sqsubseteq X_1$ is not enough to conclude that $Y_0 \sqsubseteq Y_1$ because the extended inputs might somehow affect the order in which the shared variable is accessed. However, they could be monotonic if, for example, the discipline used to access the shared variable is equivalent to implementing a Kahn channel.

As a rather different example, suppose that actor D in Fig. 1 is a *nondeterminate merge* (any of the three variants discussed by Panagaden and Shanbhogue [78]). Its behavior is that if a data value (a *token*) is available on either input, it can immediately move that token to its output. Now, the output depends on the order in which B and C produce their outputs, and on the timing with which D examines its inputs. It has been shown that a nondeterminate merge must be either unfair or nonmonotonic, and hence not continuous [21]. Although rather involved technically, *unfair* intuitively means that it favors one input or the other.

Arvind and Brock [6] argue that the nondeterminate merge is practically useful for resource management problems. A resource manager accepts requests for a resource (e.g., money in a bank balance), arbitrates between multiple requests, and returns a grant or deny, or some related data value. It is observed that such a resource manager can be used to build a memory cell, precisely the type of resource that functional programming is trying to get away from. Abramsky [2] points out that the functionality of a nondeterminate merge is widely used in practice in time-dependent systems, despite unsatisfactory formal methods for reasoning about it.

A network with a nondeterminate merge clearly might be nondeterminate, but it might also be determinate. For example, suppose that C in Fig. 1 never actually produces any outputs. Then the nondeterminate merge in D will not make the network nondeterminate.

The nondeterminate merge does not satisfy one of Kahn's conditions for a process network, that reads from channels be blocking. This constraint makes it impossible for a process to test an input for the presence of data. Thus if D is a nondeterminate merge, then the graph in Fig. 1 is not, strictly speaking, a Kahn process network.

We have been using the term "determinate" loosely. If we now formally define determinism in the context of process networks, then the main result of this section follows immediately. Define the *history* of a channel to be the sequence of tokens that have traversed the channel (i.e., have been both written and read). A Kahn process network is said to be *determinate* if the histories of all the internal and output channels depend only on the histories of the input channels. A monotonic process is clearly determinate. Since a network of monotonic processes is monotonic [78], then a network of monotonic processes is also determinate.

C. Streams

The graphical programming environments that we are concerned with are most often used to design or simulate real-time signal processing systems. Real-time signal processing systems are reactive, in that they respond to a continual stream of stimuli from an environment with which they cannot synchronize [11]. Skillcorn [92] argues that streams and functions on them are a natural way to model reactive systems. Streams are such a good model for signals that the signal processing community routinely uses them even for nonreal-time systems.

Wendelborn and Garsden [97] observe that there are different ideas in the literature of what a stream is. One camp defines streams recursively, using cons-like list constructors, and usually treats them functionally using lazy semantics. This view is apparently originally due to Landin [62]. Lazy semantics ensure that the entire stream need not be produced before its consumer operates on it. For example, Burge [26] describes streams as the functional analog of coroutines that "may be considered to be a particular method of representing a list in which the creation of each list element is delayed until it is actually needed." As another example, in Scheme, streams are typically implemented as a two-element cell where one element has the value of the head of the stream and the other has the procedure that computes the rest of the stream [1]. Recursive operations on streams require use of a special "delay" operator that defers the recursive call until access to the "cdr" of the stream element is attempted. This *ad hoc* mechanism makes recursive streams possible in a language without lazy semantics. Another mechanism that avoids laziness is the so-called *I-structures* used in some dataflow languages [9].

Another camp sees streams as channels, just like the channels in a Kahn process network. A channel is not functional, because it is modified by appending new elements to it. Kahn and MacQueen outline in [59] a demand-driven multitasking mechanism for implementing such channels. Ida and Tanaka argue for the channel model for streams, observing that it algorithmically transforms programs from a recursive to an iterative form [55]. Dennis, by contrast, argues for the recursive-cons representation of streams in Sisal 2 for program representation, but suggests translating them into nonrecursive dataflow implementations using the channel model [40]. Franco *et al.* also argue in [43] for using the channel model, with a demand-driven execution style, and propose an implementation in Scheme. The channels are implemented using a "call with current continuation" mechanism in Scheme. This mechanism essentially supports process suspension and resumption, although the authors admit that at the time of their writing, no Scheme implementation supported this without the considerable expense of a control-stack copy.

A unique approach implemented in the language Silage [50] blends the benefits of a declarative style with the simplicity of the channel model. In Silage, a symbol "x" represents an infinite stream. The language has the notion of a global cycle, and a simple reference to a symbol "x" can be thought of as referring to the "current value" of the stream x. An implicit infinite iteration surrounds every program. This language is being used successfully for both software and hardware synthesis in the Mentor Graphics DSP Station, the Cathedral project at IMEC [37], and in the Hyper project at University of California at Berkeley [83]. The use of a global cycle in a process network context has also been studied by Boussinot [20], who observes that it permits suspension and interruption of processes in a predictable way.

A more general approach is to associate with each stream a "clock," as done in Lustre [46] and Signal [12]. A clock is a logical signal that defines the alignment of tokens in different streams. For example, one could have a stream y where only every second token in y aligns with a token in another stream x. Although both streams may be infinite, one can view x as having twice as many tokens as y. A powerful algebraic methodology has been developed to reason about relationships between clocks, particularly for the Signal language [12], [68]. Caspi has described a preliminary attempt to abstract the notion of clocks so that it applies to process networks [29]. He has applied this abstraction to the Lucid language to solve certain problems like determining whether the program executes in bounded memory [30]. A different solution to the same problem is given by Buck [22], who uses the so-called balance equations, described below in Section II-E-3.

The difference between the two models for streams need not be important in practice, except that the choice of model may lead to unfortunate choices in language design. We prefer the channel model for a number of reasons. Stylistically, unlike the recursive-cons model, it puts equal emphasis on destruction (consumption of data from the stream) as construction (production of data onto the stream). Moreover, it does not suggest costly lazy evaluation. While a demand-driven style of control is popular among theoreticians, no established signal processing programming environment uses it, partly because of the cost, and partly because the same benefits (avoiding unnecessary computation) can usually be obtained more efficiently through compile-time analysis [22], [66]. The same objectives are addressed by *path analysis*, used to reduce the cost of lazy evaluation in functional languages through compile-time analysis [18].

In the channel model for streams, unlike the streams in the synchronous languages Silage, Lustre, and Signal, there is no concept of simultaneity of tokens (tokens in different streams lining up). Instead, tokens are queued using a FIFO discipline, as done in early dataflow schema [36].

It is especially important in signal processing applications to recognize that streams can carry truly vast amounts of data. A real-time digital audio stream, for instance, might carry 44 100 samples per second per channel, and might run for hours. Video sequences carry much more. Viewing a stream as a conventional data structure, therefore, gets troublesome quickly. It may require storing forever all of the data that ever enters the stream. Any practical implementation must instead store only a sliding window into the stream, preferably a small window. But just by providing a construct for random access of elements of a stream, for example, the language designer can make it difficult or impossible for a compiler to bound the size of the window.

A useful stream model in this context must be as good at losing data (and recycling its memory) as it is at storing data. The prefix-ordered sequences carried by the channels in the Kahn process networks are an excellent model for streams because the blocking reads remove data from the stream. However, special care is still required if the memory requirements of the channels in a network are to remain bounded. This problem will be elaborated below.

In [85]–[87], Reekie *et al.* consider the problem of supporting streams in the functional programming language Haskell [53]. They propose some interesting extensions to the language, and motivate them with a convincing discussion of the information needed by a compiler to efficiently implement streams. To do this, they use the Kahn process network model for Haskell programs, and classify them into *static* and *dynamic*. In static networks, all streams are infinite. In dynamic networks, streams can come and go, and hence the structure of the network can change. Mechanisms for dealing with these two types of networks are different. Static networks are much more common in signal processing, and fortunately much easier to implement efficiently, although we will consider both types below.

For efficiency, Reekie *et al.* wish to evaluate the process networks eagerly, rather than lazily as normally required by Haskell [87]. They propose eager evaluation whenever strictness analysis [54] reveals that a stream is "head strict," meaning that every element in the stream will be evaluated. This is similar to the optimization embodied in the Eazyflow execution model for dataflow graphs, which combines data-driven and demand-driven evaluation of operator nets by partitioning the net into subnets that can be evaluated eagerly without causing any wasteful computation [57]. This, in effect, translates the recursive-cons view of streams into a channel view.

Reekie *et al.* also point out that if analysis reveals that a subgraph is synchronous (in the sense of "synchronous dataflow" [66], [67]), then very efficient evaluation is possible. While this latter observation has been known for some time in signal processing circles, putting it into the context of functional programming has been a valuable contribution. To clarify this point, we can establish a clear relationship between dataflow, functional languages, and Kahn process networks.

Streams can be generalized to higher dimensionality, as done in Lucid [92] and Ptolemy [31], [65]. This, however, is beyond the scope of this paper.

D. Dataflow, Functional Languages, and Process Networks

A dataflow *actor*, when it fires, maps input tokens into output tokens. Thus an actor, applied to one or more streams, will fire repeatedly. A set of *firing rules* specify when an actor can fire. Specifically, these rules dictate precisely what tokens must be available at the inputs for the actor to fire. A firing *consumes* input tokens and *produces* output tokens. A sequence of such firings is a particular type of Kahn process that we call a *dataflow process*. A network of such processes is called a *dataflow process network*.

More specialized dataflow models, such as Dennis' static dataflow [39] or synchronous dataflow [66], [67] can be described in terms of dataflow processes. The models used by most signal processing environments mentioned above can also be described in terms of dataflow processes. The tagged token model of Arvind and Gostelow [7], [8] is related, but not identical, as we will show. Signal [12] and Lustre [46], which are called "synchronous dataflow languages," do not form dataflow processes at all because they lack the FIFO queues of the communication channels. They can, however, be implemented using dataflow process networks, with certain benefits to parallel implementation [69].

A sufficient condition for a dataflow process to be continuous, as defined in (1), is that each actor firing be *functional*, and that the set of firing rules be *sequential*. Here, "functional" means that an actor firing lacks side effects and that the output tokens are purely a function of the input tokens consumed in that firing. This condition is stronger than the Kahn condition that a *process* be functional, meaning that the output *sequences* are a function of the input *sequences* [58]. With Kahn's condition, actors can have and manipulate state. We later relax this constraint so that actors can have and manipulate state as well. "Sequential" means that the firing rules can be tested in a predefined order using only blocking reads. A little notation will help make this rather technical definition precise.

1) Firing Rules: An actor with $p \geq 1$ input streams can have N firing rules

$$\mathcal{R} = \{\mathbf{R}_1, \mathbf{R}_2, \cdots, \mathbf{R}_N\}. \qquad (8)$$

The actor can fire if and only if one or more of the firing rules is satisfied, where each firing rule constitutes a set of *patterns*, one for each of p inputs,

$$\mathbf{R}_i = \{R_{i,1}, R_{i,2}, \cdots, R_{i,p}\}. \qquad (9)$$

A pattern $R_{i,j}$ is a (finite) sequence. For firing rule i to be satisfied, each pattern $R_{i,j}$ must form a prefix of the sequence of unconsumed tokens at input j. An actor with $p = 0$ input streams is always enabled.

For some firing rules, some patterns might be empty lists, $R_{i,j} = \perp$. This means that any available sequence at input j is acceptable, because $\perp \sqsubseteq X$ for any sequence X. In particular, it does *not* mean that input j must be empty.

To accommodate the usual dataflow firing rules, we need a generalization of the prefix ordering algebra. The symbol "*" will denote a token wildcard. Thus the sequence [*] is a prefix of any sequence with at least one token. The sequence [*, *] is a prefix of any sequence with at least two tokens. The only sequence that is a prefix of [*] is $\perp$, however. Notice therefore, that the statement [*] $\sqsubseteq X$ is *not* saying that any one-token sequence is a prefix of X. All it says is that X has at least one token.

Let A_j, for $j = 1, \cdots, p$, denote the sequence of available unconsumed tokens on the jth input. Then the firing rule $\mathbf{R}_i$ is enabled if

$$R_{i,j} \sqsubseteq A_j, \quad \text{for all} \quad j = 1, \cdots, p. \qquad (10)$$

We can write condition (10) using the partial order on sets of sequences

$$\mathbf{R}_i \sqsubseteq \mathbf{A} \qquad (11)$$

where $\mathbf{A} = \{A_1, A_2, \cdots, A_p\}$.

For many actors, the firing rules are very simple. Consider an adder with two inputs. It has only one firing rule, $\mathbf{R}_1 = \{[*], [*]\}$, meaning that each of the two inputs must have at least one token. More generally, synchronous dataflow actors [66], [67], always have a single firing rule, and each pattern in the firing rule is of the form [*, *, ⋯, *], with some fixed number of wildcards. In other words, an

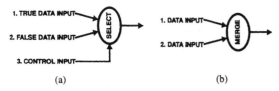

Fig. 2. The select and nondeterminate merge actors each combine two data streams into one, but the select actor uses a Boolean control signal to determine how to accomplish the merge.

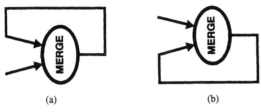

Fig. 3. Illustration that the firing rules of the nondeterminate merge are not sequential. A blocking read of either input will cause one of these two networks to deadlock inappropriately.

SDF actor is enabled by a fixed number of tokens at each input.[1]

A more interesting actor is the *select* actor in Fig. 2(a), which has the firing rules $\{R_1, R_2\}$, where

$$R_1 = \{[*], \bot, [T]\} \quad (12)$$
$$R_2 = \{\bot, [*], [F]\} \quad (13)$$

where T and F match *true* and *false*-valued Booleans, respectively. The behavior of this actor is to read a Boolean control input, then read a token from the specified data input and copy that token to the output. The firing rules are sequential, in that a blocking read of the control input, followed by a blocking read of the appropriate data input, will invoke the appropriate firing rule.

The nondeterminate merge with two inputs, also shown in Fig. 2(b), also has two firing rules

$$R_1 = \{[*], \bot\} \quad (14)$$
$$R_2 = \{\bot, [*]\}. \quad (15)$$

These rules are not sequential. A blocking read of either input fails to produce the desired behavior, as illustrated in Fig. 3. In Fig. 3(a), a blocking read of the top input will never unblock. In Fig. 3(b), a blocking read of the bottom input will never unblock. In both cases, the behavior is incorrect. Note that with any correct implementation of the nondeterminate merge, both networks in Fig. 3 are nondeterminate. It is unspecified how many times a given token will circulate around the feedback loop between arrivals of tokens from the left.

---

[1] An SDF actor also produces a fixed number of tokens when it fires, but this is not captured in the firing rules. An interesting variant, called *cyclo-static dataflow* [17], permits the number of tokens produced and consumed to vary cyclically. Modeling this with firing rules requires a straightforward generalization. We will give this generalization below in Section III-B-2.

2) Identifying Sequential Firing Rules: In general, a set of firing rules is sequential if the following procedure does not fail:[2]

1) Find an input j such that $[*] \sqsubseteq R_{i,j}$ for all $i = 1, \cdots, N$. That is, find an input such that all the firing rules require at least one token from that input. If no such input exists, fail.
2) For the choice of input j, divide the firing rules into subsets, one for each specific token value mentioned in the first position of $R_{i,j}$ for any $i = 1, \cdots, N$. If $R_{i,j} = [*, \cdots]$, then the firing rule R_i should appear in all such subsets.
3) Remove the first element of $R_{i,j}$ for all $i = 1, \cdots, N$.
4) If all subsets have empty firing rules, then succeed. Otherwise, repeat these four steps for any subset with any nonempty firing rules.

The first step identifies an input where a token is required by all firing rules. The idea of the second step is that reading a token from that particular input will often at least partially determine which firing rules apply. Observing its value, therefore, will often reduce the size of the set of applicable firing rules.

Consider the *select* actor in Fig. 2. The above steps become:

1) $j = 3$.
2) The firing rules divide into two sets, $\{R_1\}$ and $\{R_2\}$, each with only one rule.
3) The new firing rules become $R_1 = \{[*], \bot, \bot\}$ in the first subset and $R_2 = \{\bot, [*], \bot\}$ in the second subset.
4) The procedure repeats trivially for each subset, and in step 3, the modified firing rules become empty.

For the nondeterminate merge, the procedure fails immediately, in the first application of step 1.

3) Relationship to Higher-Order Functions: Constraining the actors to be functional makes a dataflow process roughly equivalent to the function "*maps*" used by Burge [26] and Reekie [85]. It is similar to the "*map*" function in Haskell and the "*mapcar*" function in Lisp, except that it introduces the notion of consuming the tokens that match the firing rule, and hence easily deals with infinite streams.

All of these variants of "map" are *higher-order functions*, in that they take functions as arguments and return functions [71]. We define $F = map(f)$, where $f: S^p \to S^q$ is a function, to return a function $F: S^p \to S^q$ that applies f to each element of a stream when one of a set of firing rules

---

[2] In (8), we imply that the number of firing rules is finite. J. Reekie has pointed out in a personal communication that if we relax this constraint, then for some sequential firing rules corresponding to determinate actors, this procedure will not fail, but will also never terminate. Thus as a practical matter, we may need the additional restruction that the procedure terminate. His example is an actor with two inputs, one of which is an integer specifying the number of tokens to consume from the other. The firing rules take the form $\{\{[0], \bot\}, \{[1], [\cdot]\}, \{[2], [\cdot, \cdot]\}, \cdots\}$.

is enabled. More precisely, $F = map(f)$, where

$$F(R\!:\!X) = f(R)\!:\!F(X) \qquad (16)$$

and R is any firing rule of f. The colon ":" indicates concatenation of sequences. That is, if X and Y are each in S^p, then $X\!:\!Y$ is a new set of sequences formed by appending each sequence in Y to the end of the corresponding sequence in X. Following the notation in Haskell, (16) defines the sequences returned by F when the input sequences have R as a prefix.

Notice that definition (16) is recursive. The recursion terminates when the argument to F no longer has any firing rule as a prefix.

The function f will typically require only some finite number of tokens on each input, while the function returned by $map(f)$ can take infinite stream arguments. Thus $F = map(f)$ is a dataflow process, where each firing consists of one application of the dataflow actor function f.

4) A Nondeterminate Example: An example that combines many of the points made so far can be constructed using the nondeterminate operator introduced by McCarthy [72] and used by Hudak [53]:

$$f_1(x, \bot) = x$$
$$f_1(\bot, y) = y$$
$$f_1(x, y) = x \text{ or } y \text{ chosen randomly.}$$

These three declarations define the output of the f_1 function under three firing rules: $R_1 = \{[*], \bot\}$, $R_2 = \{\bot, [*]\}$ and $R_3 = \{[*], [*]\}$. A dataflow process could be constructed by repeatedly firing this function on stream inputs.

McCarthy points out that the expression $f_1(1, 2) + f_1(1, 2)$ could take on the value 3, and uses this to argue that nondeterminism implies a loss of referential transparency.[3] However, when used to create a dataflow process, this example actually mixes two distinct causes for nondeterminism. Random behavior in an actor acting alone is sufficient to lose determinacy and referential transparency. The simpler definition:

$$f_2(x, y) = x \text{ or } y \text{ chosen randomly}$$

is sufficient for $f_2(1, 2) + f_2(1, 2)$ to take on the value 3. If the choice of random number is made using a random number generator, then normally the random number generator has state, initialized by a seed. Perhaps the seed should be shown explicitly as an argument to the function:

$$f_3(x, y, s) = x \text{ or } y \text{ chosen by generating}$$
$$\text{a random number from seed } s.$$

---

[3] A basic notion used in the λ calculus [32], referential transparency means that any two identical expressions have identical values. If $f_1(1,2) + f_1(1,2) = 3$, then clearly the two instances of $f_1(1,2)$ cannot have taken on the same value.

Suddenly, we regain referential transparency and determinacy. It would not be possible for $f_3(1, 2, 3) + f_3(1, 2, 3)$ to equal 3, for example. Without giving the seed as an argument, f_3 is not functional.

Consider the simplified definition:

$$f_4(x, \bot) = x$$
$$f_4(\bot, y) = y$$
$$f_4(x, y) = y.$$

This definition has no random numbers in it, but in a dataflow process network, it is still possible for $f_4(1, 2) + f_4(1, 2)$ to equal 3. The firing rules are not sequential. The output depends on how the choice between firing rules is made, something not specified by the language semantics.

We can show directly that an attempt to construct a dataflow process from the function f_4 yields a process that is not monotonic, and hence is not continuous. Let $F_4 = map(f_4)$ represent the dataflow process made with actor function f_4. It is easy to show that the process is not monotonic. In fact, it is not even a function, since for some inputs, it can take on more than one possible output value. Consider $F_4(X_1, Y_1)$ and $F_4(X_2, Y_2)$ where

$$X_1 = [1], X_2 = [1, 1], \quad \text{and} \quad Y_1 = \bot, Y_2 = [2] \qquad (17)$$

where Y_1 is the empty sequence. Clearly, $X_1 \sqsubseteq X_2$ and $Y_1 \sqsubseteq Y_2$. However,

$$F_4(X_1, Y_1) \not\sqsubseteq F_4(X_2, Y_2). \qquad (18)$$

We get $F_4(X_1, Y_1) = [1]$, while $F_4(X_2, Y_2)$ can take on any of the following possible values: $[2, 1]$, $[1, 2]$, $[1, 2, 1]$, $[1, 1, 2]$, or $[2, 1, 1]$. This is clearly nondeterminate (and nonfunctional). Only three of the five possible outcomes satisfy the monotonicity constraint. And these choose rather arbitrarily from among the firing rules. If we were to make a policy of these choices, it would be easy to construct other example inputs that would violate monotonicity.

One might argue for a different interpretation of the firing rules, in which a $\bot$ in a firing rule pattern matches only an empty input (no tokens available). Under this interpretation, we get $F_4(X_1, Y_1) = [1]$ and $F_4(X_2, Y_2) = [2, 1]$. While not monotonic, this might appear to be determinate (recall that we've only argued that continuity is *sufficient* for determinacy, not that it is *necessary*). But further examination reveals that we have made some implicit assumptions about synchronization between the input streams. To see this, consider the prefix ordered sequences

$$X_1 = [1], X_2 = [1], X_3 = [1, 1], \quad \text{and}$$
$$Y_1 = \bot, Y_2 = [2], Y_3 = [2]. \qquad (19)$$

It would seem reasonable to argue that these are in fact exactly the same sequences as in (17). We are just looking at the value of the sequences more often. However, under

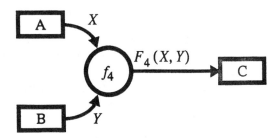

Fig. 4. A variant of McCarthy's ambiguous function embedded in a dataflow process network.

sequential ⇒ continuous ⇒ monotonic	
monotonic	$X \sqsubseteq Y \Rightarrow F(X) \sqsubseteq F(Y)$.
continuous	$\forall \chi = \{X_0, X_1, \ldots\}$ such that $X_0 \sqsubseteq X_1 \sqsubseteq \ldots$, $F(\sqcap \chi) = \sqcap F(\chi)$.
sequential	$\forall X = \{X_1, X_2, \ldots, X_p\}, \exists i, 1 \le i \le p$, such that $\forall Y \sqsupseteq X$ where $Y_i = X_i, F(Y) = F(X)$.

Fig. 5. Summary of function class definitions and their relationships for the function F: $S^p \to S^q$.

the same implicit synchronization assumptions, the output is different:

$$F_4(X_1, Y_1) = [1], F_4(X_2, Y_2) = [2]$$
$$F_4(X_3, Y_3) = [2, 1]. \tag{20}$$

These outputs are not prefix ordered, as they would be for a monotonic process.

This issue becomes much clearer if one considers a more complete dataflow process network, as shown in Fig. 4. The dataflow processes A and B have no inputs, so their firing rule is simple; they are always enabled. They produce at their outputs the streams X and Y. The problems addressed above, in this context, refer to the relative timing of token production at A and B compared to the timing of the firings of the $F_4 = map(f_4)$ process. In dataflow process network semantics, this timing is not specified.

5) Firing Rules and Template Matching: Some functional languages use template matching in function definitions the way we have been using firing rules. Consider the following Haskell example (with slightly simplified syntax):

$$\text{fac } 0 = 1$$
$$\text{fac } n = n \times \text{fac}(n-1).$$

This defines a factorial function. If the argument is 0, the result is 1. If the argument is n, the result is $n \times \text{fac}(n-1)$. These are not ambiguous because the semantics of Haskell gives priority to the first template, removing any ambiguity. The second template is really a shorthand for "any n except 0." These two templates, therefore, viewed as firing rules, are naturally sequential, since each rule consumes one token and implicitly states: "use me if no previously declared firing rule applies and the inputs match my pattern." Of course, this does not remove ambiguities due to function arguments where no data is needed. (Haskell has lazy semantics, deferring the evaluation of function arguments until the data is needed, so a function may be invoked that will decide it does not need data from one its arguments).

Embedding this example, the factorial function, in a dataflow process network introduces new and interesting problems. Consider $F(X)$, where $F = map$ (fac) and X is a stream. Each firing of the actor can trigger the creation of new streams, so this process network is not static. We will consider more interesting recursive examples than this in considerable detail below, so we defer further discussion.

6) Sequential Processes: Vuillemin [95] has given a mathematical definition of sequential functions that is entirely consistent with the notion given here of sequential firing rules. Both our actor functions and the processes made from them are sequential in his sense. The definition and its relationship to continuity and monotonicity is summarized in Fig. 5.

A process F: $S^p \to S^q$ is *sequential* if it is continuous and if for any $\boldsymbol{X} = \{X_1, X_2, \cdots, X_p\}$, there exists an $i, 1 \le i \le p$, such that for any $\boldsymbol{X}'$ where $\boldsymbol{X} \sqsubseteq \boldsymbol{X}'$ and $X_i = X_i', F(\boldsymbol{X}) = F(\boldsymbol{X}')$. This is intuitively easy to understand in the context of process networks if one considers $\boldsymbol{X}'$ to be simply a more evolved state of the input streams than $\boldsymbol{X}$. In other words, $\boldsymbol{X}'$ extends the streams in $\boldsymbol{X}$, except the one stream X_i, which is not extended. The process is sequential because it needs for the stream X_i to be extended before it can extend any output stream. Moreover, for any $\boldsymbol{X}$, there is an i such that the process needs X_i to be extended before it can extend the output. Notice that this definition of sequentiality can be applied just as easily to an actor function f as to a process $F = map(f)$. Given this, the following theorem is obvious.

Theorem: If an actor function f has sequential firing rules, then the process $F = map(f)$ is sequential.

The question naturally arises whether there are nonsequential functions that are continuous (and thus guarantee determinacy). In fact, a rather trivial example of such a function is the identity function with two inputs,

$$f(X_1, X_2) = \{X_1, X_2\}. \tag{21}$$

It is easy to see that it is not sequential (extending either input extends the output). It is also straightforward to prove that it is continuous. In order to define $F = map(f)$, we need a set of firing rules. A reasonable set of firing rules for the identity function is $\boldsymbol{R}_1 = \{[*], \bot\}$ and $\boldsymbol{R}_2 = \{\bot, [*]\}$. Even though these are the same firing rules used earlier for the nondeterminate merge, the identity function is clearly determinate. In this case f is continuous and $F = map(f)$ is also continuous.

The question naturally arises whether the above theorem extends to continuous functions. That is, given that f is continuous, can we conclude that $F = map(f)$ is continuous? The answer is no, as demonstrated by the following counter example. Let Y be some nonempty finite sequence. Define

$$f(X_1, X_2) = \{Y: X_1, Y: X_2\}. \tag{22}$$

The colon ":" again means concatenation of two sequences. This function is similar to the identity function, with the simple difference that it prepends a prefix to each of two input sequences. It is easy to show that this is continuous. However, $F = map(f)$ is not continuous if we use the firing rules we defined for the identity function. In fact, it is not monotonic, nor even functional. That is, for any input sequences X_1 and X_2, there is more than one possible output. This is because the function f produces a copy of the prefix on *both* outputs when it fires. On the output streams there can be any number of copies of the sequence Y inserted between tokens from the corresponding input stream.

Berry [14] has defined a class of functions called *stable functions* that may not be sequential but are always continuous. This class is not as broad as the class of continuous functions, but in certain circumstances, is easier to work with. But this is beyond the scope of this paper.

7) The Relationship to Kahn Process Networks: Dataflow process networks with sequential firing rules and functional actors are a special case of Kahn process networks. They construct a process F as a sequence $map(f)$ of atomic actor invocations f. Instead of suspending a process on a blocking read or nonblocking write, processes can be freely interleaved by a *scheduler*, which determines the sequence of actor firings. Since the actors are functional, no state needs to be stored when one actor terminates and another fires. The biggest advantage, therefore, is that the context switch overhead of process suspension and resumption is entirely avoided.

There is still the cost of scheduling. However, for most programs, this cost can be entirely shifted to the compiler [66], [22]. While it is impossible to always shift all costs to the compiler [22], large clusters within a process network can be scheduled at compile time, greatly reducing the number of dataflow processes that must be dynamically scheduled. As a consequence of this efficiency, much finer granularity is practical, with processes often being as simple as to just add two streams. We will now consider execution models in more detail.

E. Execution Models

Given a dataflow process network, a surprising variety of execution models can be associated with it. This variety is due, in no small part, to the fact that a dataflow process network does not over specify an algorithm the way nondeclarative semantics do. Execution models have different strengths and weaknesses, and there is, to date, no clear winner.

1) Concurrent Processes: Kahn and MacQueen propose an implementation of Kahn process networks using multitasking with a primarily demand-driven style [59]. A single "driver" process (one with no outputs) demands inputs. When it suspends due to an input being unavailable, the input channel is marked "hungry" and the source process is activated. It may in turn suspend, if its inputs are not available. Any process that issues a "put" command to a hungry channel will be suspended and the destination process restarted where it left off, thus injecting also a data-driven phase to the computation. If a "get" operation suspends a process, and the source process is already suspended waiting for an input, then deadlock has been detected.

In the Kahn and MacQueen schema, configuration of the network on the fly is allowed. This allows for recursive definition of processes. Recursive definition of streams (data) is also permitted in the form of directed loops in the process graph.

The repeated task suspension and resumption in this style of execution is relatively expensive, since it requires a context switch. It suggests that the granularity of the processes should be relatively large. For dataflow process networks, the cost can be much lower than in the general case, and hence the granularity can be smaller.

2) Dynamic Scheduling of Dataflow Process Networks: Dataflow process networks have other natural execution models due to the breakdown of a process into a sequence of actor firings. A firing of an actor provides a different quantum of execution than a process that suspends on blocking reads. Using this quantum avoids the complexities of task management (context switching and scheduling) that are implied by Kahn and MacQueen [59] and explicitly described by Franco *et al.* [43]. Instead of context switching, dataflow process networks are executed by scheduling the actor firings. This scheduling can be done at compile time or at run time, and in the latter case, can be done by hardware or by software.

The most widely known execution models for dataflow process networks have emerged from research into computer architectures for executing dataflow graphs [5], [93]. This association may be unfortunate, since the performance of such architectures has yet to prove competitive [49]. In such architectures, actors are fine-grained, and scheduling is done by hardware. Although there have been some attempts to apply these architectures to signal processing [77], the widely used dataflow programming environments for signal processing have nothing to do with dataflow architectures.

Some signal processing environments, for example COSSAP from Cadis (now Synopsys) and the dynamic dataflow domain in Ptolemy, use a run-time scheduler implemented in software. This performs essentially the same function performed in hardware by dataflow machines, but is usually used with actors that have larger granularity. The scheduler tracks the availability of tokens on the inputs to the actors, and fires actors that are enabled.

3) Static Scheduling of Dataflow Process Networks: For many signal processing applications, the firing sequence can be determined statically (at compile-time). The class of dataflow process networks for which this is always possible is called *synchronous dataflow* [61], [66], [67].

In synchronous dataflow, the solution to a set of *balance equations* relating the production and consumption of tokens gives the relative firing rates of the actors. These relative firing rates combined with simple precedence analysis allows for the static construction of periodic schedules. Synchronous dataflow is used in COSSAP (for code generation, not for simulation), in the multirate version of SPW from the Alta Group of Cadence (formerly Comdisco), and in several domains in Ptolemy.

Balance equation methods have recently been extended to cover most dynamic dataflow graphs [22], [64] and have been implement in the Boolean dataflow and CGC (code generation in C) domains in Ptolemy. However, Buck has shown that the addition of only the *select* actor of Fig. 2 and a *switch* actor (which routes input data tokens to one of two outputs under the control of a Boolean input) to the synchronous dataflow model is sufficient to make it Turing complete [22]. This means that one can implement a universal Turing machine using this programming model. It also means that many critical questions become undecidable. For this reason, Buck's methods cannot statically schedule all dynamic dataflow graphs. For Turing complete dataflow models, it is still necessary for some programs to have some responsibilities deferred to a run-time scheduler.

4) Compilation of Dataflow Graphs: The static schedules that emerge from Buck's Boolean dataflow scheduler are finite sequential representations of an infinite execution of a dataflow graph. Given such a schedule, the dataflow graph can be translated into a lean sequential program, a process we normally call compilation. (Parallel implementations are briefly discussed below in Section III-I).

In addition to scheduling, efficient compilation requires that memory allocation be done statically, if possible. Despite the Kahn process network model of infinite FIFO channels, it is usually possible to construct bounded memory implementations with statically allocated memory for the channels [22]. Unfortunately, since the Boolean dataflow model is Turing complete, it is undecidable whether an arbitrary dataflow graph can be executed in bounded memory, so static memory allocation for the channels is not always possible. But for most programs, it is, so the cost of dynamically allocated memory for the channels only needs to be incurred when the static analysis techniques break down.

To address the same problems, Benveniste *et al.*, argue in [13] for the so-called synchronous approach to dataflow, where clocks are associated with tokens carried by the channels. A major part of the motivation is to guarantee bounded memory. There are other compelling advantages to this approach as well. The clocks impose a *total order* on tokens in the system, compared to the *partial order* specified in a process network. This makes it easy to implement, for example, a *determinate* merge operation. Viewed another way, actors can test their inputs for *absence* of data, something that would cause nondeterminism in process networks. However, the synchronous approach alone does not make the critical questions decidable. So further restrictions on a language are required if all programs are to be "executable" [13]. Moreover, one could argue that the total ordering in a synchronous specification is in fact an overspecification, reducing the implementation options. However, this can be at least partially ameliorated by *desynchronizing* the implementation, as explored by Mafeïs and Le Guernic [69].

5) The Tagged-Token Model: An execution model developed by Arvind and Gostelow [7], [8] generalizes the dataflow process network model. In this model, each token has a tag associated with it, and firing of actors is enabled when inputs with matching tags are available. Outputs to a given stream are produced with distinct tags. An immediate consequence is that there is no need for a FIFO discipline in the channels. The tags keep track of the ordering. More importantly, there is no need for the tokens to be produced or consumed in order. The possibility for out-of-order execution allows us to construct dataflow graphs that would deadlock under the FIFO scheme but not under the tagged-token scheme. We will consider a detailed example below, after developing a usable language.

III. Experimenting with Language Design

The dataflow process network model, as defined so far, provides a framework within which we can define a language. To define a complete language, we would need to specify a set of primitive actors. Instead, we will outline a coordination language, leaving the design of the primitives somewhat arbitrary. There are often compelling reasons to leave the primitives unspecified. Many graphical dataflow environments rely on a host language for specification of these primitives, and allow arbitrary granularity and user extensibility. Depending on the design of these primitives, the language may or may not be functional, may or may not be able to express nondeterminism, and may or may not be as expressive other languages.

Granular Lucid, for example, is a coordination language with the semantics of Lucid [56]. Coordination languages with dataflow semantics are described by Suhler *et al.* [94], Gifford and Lucassen [44], Onanian [77], Printz [82], and Rasure and Williams [84]. Contrast these to the approach of Reekie [85] and the DSP Station from Mentor Graphics [41], where new actors are defined in a language with semantics identical to those of the visual language. There are compelling advantages to that approach, in that all compiler optimizations are available down to the level of the host language primitives. But the hybrid approach, in which the host language has imperative semantics, gives the user more flexibility. Since our purpose is to explore the dataflow process network model fully, this flexibility is essential.

A. The Ptolemy System

To make the discussion concrete, we will use the Ptolemy software environment [25] to illustrate some of the tradeoffs. It is well suited for several reasons:

- It has both a visual ("block diagram") and a textual interface; the visual interface is similar in principle to many of those used in other signal processing software environments.
- It does not have any model of computation built into the kernel, and hence can be used to experiment with different models of computation, and interactions between the models.
- Three dataflow process network "domains" have already been built in Ptolemy, precisely to carry out such experiments.
- The set of primitive actors is easily extended (using C++ as the host language). This gives us more than enough freedom to test the limits of the dataflow process network model of computation.

A *domain* in Ptolemy is a user-defined subsystem implementing a particular model of computation. Three Ptolemy domains have been constructed with dataflow semantics, and one with more general process network semantics. The *synchronous dataflow* domain (SDF) [66], [67] is particularly well suited to signal processing [24], where low-overhead execution is imperative. The SDF domain makes all scheduling decisions at compile time. The *dynamic dataflow* domain (DDF) makes all scheduling decisions at run-time, and is therefore much more flexible. The *Boolean dataflow domain* (BDF) attempts to make scheduling decisions for dynamic dataflow graphs at compile time, using the so-called token-flow formalism [22], [64]. It resorts to run-time scheduling only when its analysis techniques break down. The *process network* domain (PN) uses a multitasking kernel to manage process suspension and resumption. It permits nonblocking reads, and hence allows nondeterminism.

Ptolemy supports two distinct execution models, *interpreted* and *compiled*. Compilation can be implemented using a simple code generation mechanism, allowing for quick experimentation, or it can be implemented using more sophisticated transformation and optimization techniques. Such optimization may require more knowledge about the primitives than the simple code generation mechanism, which simply stitches together code fragments defining each actor [80].

B. Visual Hierarchy—The Analog to Procedural Abstraction

In keeping with the majority of signal processing programming environments, we will use a visual syntax for the interconnection of dataflow processes. In fact, in Ptolemy, a program is not entirely visual, since the actors and data structures are defined textually, using C++. Only the gross program structure is described visually. The visual equivalent of an expression, of course, is a subgraph. Subgraphs can be encapsulated into a single node, thus forming a larger dataflow process by composing smaller ones. This is analogous to procedural abstraction in imperative languages and functional abstraction in functional languages.

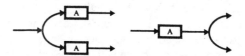

Fig. 6. Referential transparency implies that these two dataflow process networks are equivalent.

1) Determinacy and Referential Transparency: To make the dataflow process network determinate, as discussed above, it is sufficient for the actors to have two properties: Their mappings from input tokens to output tokens should be functional (free from side effects), and the firing rules for each actor should be sequential, in the technical sense given in Section II-D. If our actors have these properties, then our language has referential transparency, meaning that syntactically identical expressions have the same value regardless of their lexical position in the program.

With referential transparency, the two subgraphs shown in Fig. 6 are equivalent. The two inputs to the identical dataflow processes A are identical streams, so the outputs will be identical. If the primitive actors are functional, then hierarchical actors may be functional as well, but there are some complications due to scheduling, directed loops in the graph, and *delays*.

2) Functional Behavior and Hierarchy: In modern languages, it is often considered important that abstractions be semantically little different from language primitives. Thus, if the primitive actors are functional, the hierarchical nodes should be functional. If the primitive actors have firing rules, then the hierarchical nodes should have firing rules. We will find this goal problematic.

A hierarchical node in a dataflow process network has a subnetwork and input/output ports, as shown in the examples in Fig. 7. To reach the above ideal, we should be able to describe the behavior of a hierarchical node by $F = map(f)$, where f constitutes a single, functional firing of the hierarchical node. This is not always possible. Two problems arise: f may not be well defined, and when it is, it may not be functional. Note that no problem arises in defining the hierarchical node to be a mapping F from input sequences to output sequences. F will be functional if the actors in the hierarchial node have functional firings and sequential firing rules.

a) Firing subgraphs—the balance equations: Examples that have more than one actor, such as in Fig. 7(a) and (c), raise the question of how to determine how many firings of the constituent actors make up a "reasonable" firing of a hierarchical node. One approach would be to solve the *balance equations* of [64], [66], [67] to determine how many firings of each actor are needed to return a subsystem to its original state. By "original state" we mean that the number of unconsumed tokens on each internal channel (arc) should be the same before and after the firing.

Consider the example in Fig. 7(a). Following Lee and Messerschmitt [66], the "1" symbol next to the output of A_1 means that it produces one token when it fires. The "1" next to the input of A_2 means that it consumes one token

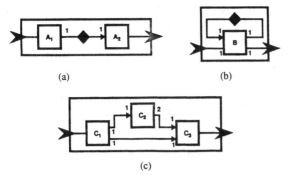

Fig. 7. Hierarchical nodes in a dataflow process network may not be functional even if the primitives they contain are functional. The large arrowheads indicate input and output for the hierarchical node.

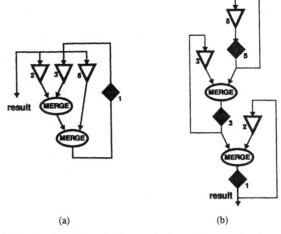

Fig. 8. Two inconsistent dataflow graphs that compute an ordered sequence of integers of the form $2^a 3^b 5^c$. The triangular icons multiply their inputs by the indicated constant. The delay icon (a diamond) represents an initial token with value 1, 3, or 5, as annotated.

when it fires. A "reasonable" firing of the hierarchical node would therefore consist of one firing of A_1 and one of A_2. The single balance equation for this example is

$$r_{A_1} \times 1 = r_{A_2} \times 1 \qquad (23)$$

where r_{A_i} is the number of firings of A_i. This equation simply says that r_{A_i} should be such that the number of tokens produced on the arc should equal the number consumed, thus keeping it "in balance." Any "firing" of the hierarchical node that invokes the ith actor r_{A_i} times (for all i) will therefore return the subsystem to its original state. For dynamic dataflow graphs, these balance equations are a bit more complicated, but often lead to definitive conclusions about the relative number of firings of the actors that are required to maintain balance.

A nonempty set of firings that returns a subsystem to its original state is called a *complete cycle* [64]. Unfortunately, three problems arise. First, some useful systems have balance equations with no solution [22], [23]. Such systems are said to be *inconsistent*, or *unbalanced*, and have no complete cycle, and usually have unbounded memory requirements. A simplified (and probably not useful) example is shown in Fig. 7(c). The balance equations for this subsystem are (one for each arc)

$$r_{C_1} \times 1 = r_{C_2} \times 1 \qquad (24)$$
$$r_{C_1} \times 1 = r_{C_3} \times 1 \qquad (25)$$
$$r_{C_2} \times 2 = r_{C_3} \times 1. \qquad (26)$$

These equations have no solution. Indeed, any set of firings of these actors will leave the subsystem in a new state.

To hint that unbalanced systems are sometimes useful, consider an algorithm that computes an ordered sequence of integers of the form $2^a 3^b 5^c$ for all $a, b, c \geq 0$. This problem has been considered by Dijkstra [42] and Kahn and MacQueen [59]. A dataflow implementation equivalent to the first of two by Kahn and MacQueen is shown in Fig. 8(a). The "merge" block is an ordered merge [64]; given a nondecreasing sequence of input values on two streams, it merges them into a single stream of nondecreasing values, and removes duplicates. A more efficient implementation that does not generate such duplications (and hence does not need to eliminate them) is given in Fig. 8(b). It is also inconsistent. Neither of these can be implemented with bounded memory.

The second, more fundamental problem is that the existence of complete cycles for dynamic dataflow graphs is *undecidable* [22]. Thus no algorithm will be able to identify a complete cycle for all graphs that have one.

A third problem is that the actors in a hierarchical node may not form a *connected* graph without considering as well the graph within which the hierarchical node sits. In this case, the balance equations for the hierarchical node alone will have more than one solution. There is no way to select among these solutions.

When a hierarchical node has a complete cycle that can be identified, then we may be able to define f to be the mapping performed by this complete cycle. In this case, $F = map(f)$ captures the behavior of the hierarchical node. Unfortunately, there are still difficulties.

b) Side effects and state: Even when a hierarchical node has a complete cycle, a second problem arises in our attempt to define its mapping in terms of $F = map(f)$. Even if all actors within the node are functional, the hierarchical node may not be.

Consider the example in Fig. 7(b). A single firing of actor B obviously defines a complete cycle. The feedback loop is used to implement a recurrence, so the feedback channel will store tokens from one firing of the hierarchical node for use in the next firing. With this usage, the hierarchical node has state, and is therefore not functional even if f_B is. In this case, the feedback loop must be initialized with tokens in order to avoid deadlock.

The shaded diamond is called a *delay*, which is typically implemented as an initial token in the channel. It cannot be described by $F = map(f)$, where f is functional, but its behavior is easily defined by $F(X) = i{:}X$, where X is the input sequence, i is the initial token, and ":" is the concatenation operator. The initial token enables the first firing of actor B if it requires a token on the top input. It is called a "delay" because for any channel with a unit delay, the nth token read from the channel is the $(n-1)$th written to it. A feedback loop with delay effectively stores state, making any single firing of the hierarchical node nonfunctional.

The delay shown in Fig. 7(b) is typically implemented using the "cons" operator to initialize streams when streams are based on the recursive-cons model [62]. It is roughly equivalent to the "D" operator in the tagged-token model [8]. It is the visual equivalent of "fby" (followed by) in Lucid [92] and the "pre" operator in Lustre [47]. In the single assignment language Silage, developed for signal processing [50], a delay is written "x@1." This expression refers to the stream "x" delayed by one token, with the initial token value defined by a declaration like "x@@1 = *value*." For example,

$$x = 1 + x@1;$$
$$x@@1 = 0$$

defines a stream consisting of all nonnegative integers, in order.

In functional languages, instead of using a recurrent construct like a delay, state is usually carried in the program using recursion. Consider, for example, the following Haskell program:

$$\text{integrate } xs = \text{scanl } (+) \; 0 \; xs$$

where *scanl* is a higher order function with three arguments, a function, a number, and a list. It is defined as follows (taking certain liberties with Haskell syntax):

$$\text{scanl } f \; q \; \bot = [q]$$
$$\text{scanl } f q \; (x{:}xs) = q{:}\text{scanl } ff(q,x)xs$$

These two definitions use template matching; the first is invoked if the third argument is an empty stream. The q first gives the initial value for the sum, equivalent to the value of the initial token in a delay, and later carries the running summation. The syntax $(x{:}xs)$ divides a list into the first element (x) and the rest (xs). The syntax $q{:}expr$ represents a list where q is the head and $expr$ defines the rest, just as we have done above for sequences. For example,

$$\text{scanl } (+) \; 0 \; [1,2,3,4]$$

produces [0, 1, 3, 6, 10].

The program above uses recursion to carry state, via the higher-order function *scanl*. It has been observed that for efficiency this recursion must be translated into an iterative implementation [40], [43], [55]. For streams this is mandatory, since otherwise the depth of the recursion could become extremely large.

Delays in a hierarchical node can make a single firing of the node nonfunctional even if it is not in a feedback loop. Consider the example in Fig. 7(a). The balance equations tell us that a complete cycle consists of one firing of A_1 and one of A_2. But under this policy, state will have to be preserved between firings on the arc connecting the two actors, making a firing of the hierarchical node nonfunctional.

Some of the problems with state could be solved by requiring all delays to appear only at the top level of the hierarchy, as was done for example in the BOSS system [89]. This is awkward, however, and anyway provides only a partial solution. A better solution is simply to reconcile the desire for functional behavior with the desire to maintain state. This can be done simultaneously for hierarchical nodes and primitives, greatly increasing the flexibility and convenience of the language, while still maintaining the desirable properties of functional behavior.

The basic observation is that internal state in a primitive or a hierarchical node is *syntactic sugar* (a convenient syntactic shorthand) for delays on feedback loops at the top level of the graph. In other words, there is no reason to actually put all such feedback loops at the top level if semantics can be maintained with a more convenient syntax. With this observation, we can now allow actors with state. These become more like *objects* than *functions*, since they represent both data and methods for operating on the data. The (implicit) feedback loop around any actor or hierarchical node with state also establishes a precedence relationship between successive firings of the actor. This precedence serializes the actor firings, thus ensuring proper state updates.

Once we allow actors with state, it is a simple extension to allow actors with other side effects, such as those handling I/O. The inherently sequential nature of an actor that outputs a stream to a file, for example, is simply represented by a feedback loop that does not carry any meaningful data, but establishes precedences between successive firings of the actor.

If actors have state, the notation $F = map(f)$ is no longer directly valid. With a little adaptation, however, we can still use it. If we wish to model an actor with p inputs and q outputs, plus state, we can define $F: F^{p+1} \to S^{q+1}$ based on an actor function $f: S^{p+1} \to S^{q+1}$, where the extra argument carries the state from one firing to the next.

With this device, notice that the firing rules can now depend on the state. For example, in the cyclo-static dataflow model of Lauwereins *et al.* [63], an actor can consume a cyclically varying number of tokens on an input. For instance, a dataflow process with one input and one output might consume one token on its odd-numbered firings and two tokens on even-numbered firings. In this case, a binary-valued state variable will have value zero on even-numbered firings and one on odd-numbered firings. Thus the firing rules become

$$R_1 = \{[0], [*]\} \quad (27)$$
$$R_2 = \{[1], [*, *]\} \quad (28)$$

where the first argument is the state. Any cyclo-static actor can be modeled in this way. In fact, firing rules that change over the course of several firings can be modeled in the same way even if they do not vary cyclically, as long as the firing rules for the nth firing can be determined during the $(n-1)$th firing.

C. Function Arguments—Parameters and Input Streams

In Ptolemy, as in many software environments of this genre, there are three phases to the execution of a program. The *setup* phase makes a pass over the hierarchical program graph initializing delays, initializing state variables, evaluating *parameters*, evaluating whatever portion of the schedule is precomputed, and performing whatever other setup functions the program modules require. The *run* phase involves executing either the precomputed schedule or a dynamic schedule that is computed on-the-fly. If the run is finite (it often is not), there is a *wrapup* phase, in which allocated memory is freed, final results are presented to the user, and any other required cleanup code is executed.

The *parameters* that are evaluated during the setup phase are often related to one another via an expression language. Thus parameters represent the part of the computation that does not operate on streams, in which values that might be used during stream processing are computed. Some simple examples are the gain values associated with the triangular icons in Fig. 8 or the initial values of the delays in the same figure. In principle, these values may be specified as arbitrarily complex expressions.

The gain blocks in Fig. 8 may be viewed as functions with two arguments, the multiplying constant and the input stream. But unlike functional languages, a clear syntactic distinction is made between *parameter arguments* and *stream arguments*. In functional languages, if the distinction is made at all, it is made through the type system. The syntax in Ptolemy is to use a textual expression language to specify the value of the parameters, using a parameter screen like that in Fig. 9. This expression language has some of the trappings of standard programming languages, including types and scoping rules. It could be entirely replaced by a standard programming language, although preferably one with declarative semantics.

Parameters are still formally viewed as arguments to the function represented by the actor. But the syntactic distinction between parameters and stream arguments is especially convenient in visual programming. It avoids cluttering a diagrammatic program representation with a great many arcs representing streams that never change in value. Moreover, it can make the job of a compiler or interpreter simpler, obviating the optimization step of identifying such static streams. In Ptolemy, when compiled mode is used for implementation, code generation occurs

after the parameters have been evaluated, thus allowing highly optimized, application-specific code to be generated. For example, instead of a single telephone channel simulator subroutine capable of simulating any combination of impairments, optimized code that takes advantage of the fact that the third harmonic distortion is set to zero (see Fig. 9) can be synthesized. This becomes particularly important when the implementation is via hardware synthesis, as is becoming increasingly common in signal processing systems.

Sometimes, all of the arguments to a function are parameters, in which case we call the actor a *source*, since it has no dynamic inputs (see, for example, the A and B actors in Fig. 4). Referential transparency for source actors is also preserved, as long as the parameters are considered. Thus the transformation shown in Fig. 6 is now possible only if the actors or subgraphs being consolidated have identical parameters. Thus with these syntactic devices (actors with state, the notation $F = map(f)$, delays, and actors with parameters as well as inputs), referential transparency is still possible. We call such actors *generalized functional actors*.

D. Firing Rules and Strictness

A function is strict if it requires that all its arguments be present before it can begin computation. A dataflow process, viewed as a function applied to a stream, clearly should not be strict, in that the stream should not have to be complete for the process to begin computation. The process is in fact defined as a sequence of firings that consume partial input data and produce partial output data. But in our context, this is a rather trivial form of nonstrictness.

A dataflow process is composed of a sequence of actor firings. The actor firings themselves might be strict or nonstrict. This is determined by the firing rules. For example, an actor formed from the McCarthy f_1 function in Section II-D-4 is clearly nonstrict, since it can fire with only one of the two arguments available. A process made with this actor, however, is not continuous, and the process is nondeterminate.

It is possible to have a determinate process made of nonstrict actors. Recall the *select* actor from Fig. 2(a).

$$\text{select}(x, \perp, T) = x$$
$$\text{select}(\perp, y, F) = y$$

The firing rules implied by this definition are sequential, since a token is always required for the third argument, and the value of that argument determines which firing rule applies. Moreover, *select* is functional, so a process made up of repeated firings of this actor is determinate. The Ptolemy icon for this process is shown in Fig. 10. This function, however, is clearly not strict, since the function does not require that all three arguments be present. Moreover, we will see that this nonstrictness is essential for the most general form of recursion. The fact that nonstrictness is essential for recursion in functional languages has been

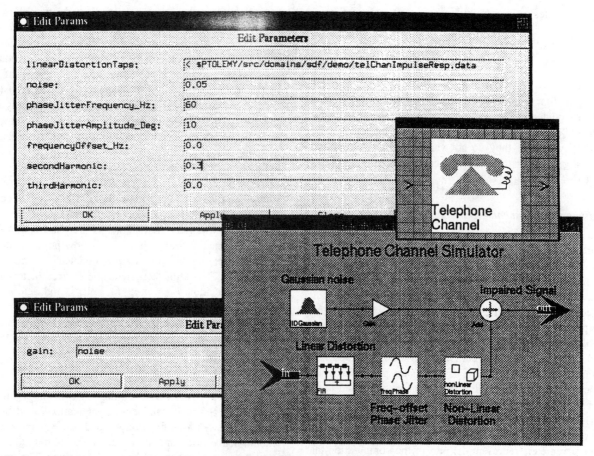

Fig. 9. Top: A typical parameter screen in Ptolemy for a hierarchical node that models a telephone channel. The first parameter is given as a reference to a file. The icon for the node is shown to the right. The next level down in the hierarchy is shown in the lower right window. At the lower left, the parameter screen shows that the parameter for the Gain actor inherits its value from the "noise" parameter above it in the hierarchy. Parameter values can also be expressions.

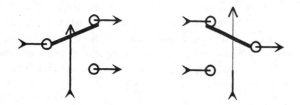

Fig. 10. Switch and Select actors in the dynamic dataflow domains of Ptolemy. These are determinate actors that merge or split streams under the control of a Boolean stream.

observed before, of course [53] (at least the if-then-else must be nonstrict in the consequent and the alternative).

The next natural question is whether hierarchical nodes should be strict. In particular, for those hierarchical nodes for which there exists a well defined firing, should that firing be strict? The example shown in Fig. 11 suggests a definitive "no" for the answer. A hierarchical node A is composed of subprocesses B and C as shown in the figure. A firing of the expanded definition in Fig. 11(b) might consist of a firing of B followed by C. However, when connected as shown in Fig. 11(a), the network deadlocks,

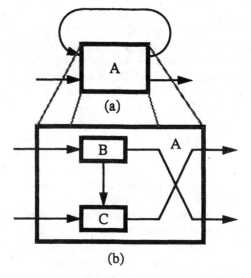

Fig. 11. A hierarchical node A in a simple subnetwork (a) and its expanded definition (b). If the actor A is strict, the subnetwork in (a) deadlocks.

quite unnecessarily, if we insist that the hierarchical node have both inputs available before firing.

All three dataflow domains in Ptolemy have nonstrict hierarchical nodes. To implement this, most schedulers used in these domains take a simple approach: They flatten the hierarchy before constructing a schedule. This approach may be expensive for large programs with repeated use of the same hierarchical nodes, particularly if in-line code is generated. It also precludes incremental compilation of hierarchical nodes. But it appears to be necessary to support graphs like that in Fig. 11. At least one more sophisticated scheduler [16] constructs strict hierarchical nodes (when this is safe) through a clustering process, in order to build more compact schedules. It ignores the user-specified hierarchy in doing this.

E. Recurrences and Recursion

Functional languages such as Haskell commonly use recursion to carry state. The comparable mechanism for dataflow process networks is feedback loops, usually with initial tokens, as shown in Fig. 7(a) and (b). These feedback loops specify recurrence relations, but are not self-referential in the usual sense of recursion. Ida and Tanaka [55] and Abramsky [2] have also noted the advantages of this representation. A consequence of this is that recursion plays a considerably reduced role in dataflow process networks compared to functional languages. But this does not mean that recursion is not useful.

Consider the "sieve of Eratosthenes," an algorithm considered by Kahn and MacQueen [59], among others. It computes prime numbers by constructing a chain of "filters," one for each prime number it has found so far. Each filter removes from the stream any multiple of its prime number. The algorithm starts by creating a single filter for the prime number 2 in the chain and runs each successively larger integer through the chain of filters. Each time a number gets through to the end of the chain, it must be prime, so a new filter is created and added to the chain. A recursive implementation of this algorithm is concise, convenient, and elegant, although of course we can express any recursive algorithm iteratively [53].

A recursive implementation in the dynamic dataflow domain of Ptolemy is shown in Fig. 12. The icon with the concentric squares is actually a higher-order function (explained further below) that invokes a named hierarchical node (*sift*) when it fires. In this case, the named hierarchical node is a recursive reference to the very hierarchical node in which the icon appears. More direct expression of recursion is not yet supported by the Ptolemy graphical interface, although it is supported in the underlying kernel. Ptolemy implements this in a simple, and rather expensive way; it dynamically expands the graph when the recursive block is invoked. More efficient implementations are easy to image, however.

Note that recursion in Fig. 12 expresses a "mutable graph," in that the structure of the graph changes as the program executes. Such dynamics are also permitted by Kahn and MacQueen [59] and in TLDF [94]. Mutability, however, considerably complicates compile-time analysis of the graph. The compile-time scheduling methods in [22] and [66] have yet to be extended to recursive graphs. This raises the interesting question of whether recursion precludes compile-time scheduling. We find, perhaps somewhat surprisingly, that often it does not. To illustrate this point, we will derive a recursive implementation of the fast Fourier transform (FFT) in the synchronous dataflow domain in Ptolemy, and show that it can be completely scheduled at compile time. It can even be statically parallelized, with the recursive description imposing no impediment. The classic derivation of the FFT leads directly to a natural and intuitive recursive representation. For completeness, we repeat this simple derivation here.

The Nth order discrete Fourier transform (DFT) of a sequence $x(n)$ is given by

$$X_k = \sum_{n=0}^{N-1} x(n) e^{-j(2\pi/N)kn} \tag{29}$$

for $0 \leq k < N$. To get the values for other k, simply periodically repeat the values given above, with period N. Define

$$W_N = e^{-j(2\pi/N)} \tag{30}$$

and note the following properties:

$$W_N^2 = W_{N/2} \quad \text{and} \quad W_N^{N+k} = W_N^k. \tag{31}$$

Using this we can write

$$X_k = \sum_{n=0}^{N-1} x(n) W_N^{kn} = \sum_{\substack{n=0 \\ n \text{ even}}}^{N-2} x(n) W_N^{kn} + \sum_{\substack{n=1 \\ n \text{ odd}}}^{N-1} x(n) W_N^{kn}. \tag{32}$$

By change of variables on the summations, this becomes

$$X_k = \sum_{n=0}^{(N/2)-1} x(2n) W_{N/2}^{kn} + \left(\sum_{n=0}^{(N/2)-1} x(2n+1) W_{N/2}^{kn} \right) W_N^k. \tag{33}$$

This is the key step in the derivation of the so-called "decimation-in-time FFT"; the first summation is the $(N/2)$ order DFT of the even samples, while the second is the $(N/2)$ order DFT of odd samples. Thus, in general, we can write

$$DFT_N(x(n)) = DFT_{N/2}(x(2n)) + W_N^k DFT_{N/2}(x(2n+1)). \tag{34}$$

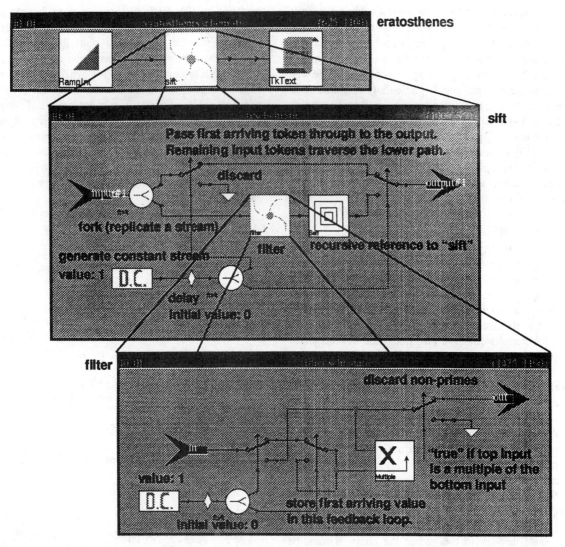

Fig. 12. A recursive implementation of the sieve of Eratosthenes in the dynamic dataflow domain in Ptolemy. The top-level system (with just three actors) produces all the integers greater than 1, filters them for primes, and displays the results. Other icons are explained once each.

Recall that $DFT_N(x(n))$ is periodic with period N, so $DFT_{N/2}(x(2n))$ is periodic with period $N/2$.

From this, we arrive at the recursive specification shown in Fig. 13. The first actor is a *distributor*, which collects two samples each time it fires, routing the first one to the top output and the second one to the lower output. The recursive invocation of this block accomplishes the decimation in time. The outputs of the distributor are connected to two *IfThenElse* blocks, represent one of two possible replacement subsystems. When the *order* parameter is larger than some threshold, the *IfThenElse* block replaces itself with a recursive reference to the galaxy within which it sits, implementing an FFT of half the order. When the *order* parameter gets below some threshold, then the *IfThenElse* block replaces itself with some direct implementation of a small order FFT. The *IfThenElse* block is another example of a higher-order function, and will be discussed in more detail below. The *repeat* block takes into account the periodicity of the DFT's of order $N/2$ without duplicating the computation. The *expgen* block at the bottom simply generates the W_N^k sequence. The sequence might be precomputed, or computed on the fly.

A more traditional visual representation of an FFT is shown in Fig. 14. This representation is extremely inconvenient for programming, however, since it cannot represent FFTs of the size typically used (128–1024 points). Moreover, any such visual representation has the order of the FFT and the granularity of the specification hardwired into the specification. It is better to have both parameterized, as in Fig. 13. Moreover, we argue that the visual representation in Fig. 13 is more intuitive, since it is a more direct representation of the underlying idea.

An interesting generalization of the conditional used in the recursion in Fig. 13 would use templates on the parameter values to select from among the possible implementations for the node. This would make the recursion

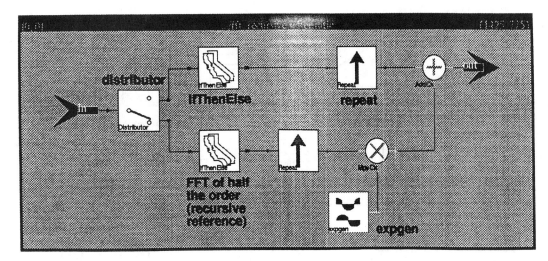

Fig. 13. A recursive specification of an FFT implemented in the SDF domain in Ptolemy. The recursion is unfolded during the setup phase of the execution, so that the graph can be completely scheduled at compile time.

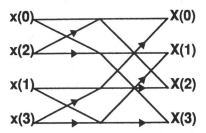

Fig. 14. A fourth-order decimation-in-time FFT shown graphically. The order of the FFT, however, is hard-wired into the representation.

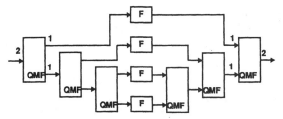

Fig. 15. An analysis/synthesis filter bank under the SDF model. The depth of the filter bank, however, is hard-wired into the representation.

stylistically identical to that found in functional languages like Haskell, albeit with a visual syntax. This can be illustrated with another practical example of an application of recursion.

Consider the system shown in Fig. 15. It shows a multirate signal processing application: an analysis/synthesis filter bank with harmonically spaced subbands. The stream coming in at the left is split by matching highpass and lowpass filters (labeled "QMF" for "quadrature mirror filter"). These are decimating polyphase finite impulse response (FIR) filters, so for every two tokens consumed on the input, one token is produced on each of two outputs. The left-most QMF only is labeled with the number of tokens consumed and produced, but the others behave the same way. The output of the lowpass side is further split by a second QMF, and the lowpass output of that by a third QMF. The boxes labeled "F" represent some function performed on the decimated stream (such as quantization). The QMF boxes to the right of these reconstruct the signal using matching polyphase interpolating FIR filters.

There are four distinct sample rates in Fig. 15 with a ratio of 8:1 between the largest and the smallest. This type of application typically needs to be implemented in real time at low cost, so compile-time scheduling is essential.

The graphical representation in Fig. 15 is useful for developing intuition, and exposes exploitable parallelism, but it is not so useful for programming. The depth of the filter bank is hard-wired into the visual representation, so it cannot be conveniently made into a parameter of a filter-bank module. The representation in Fig. 16 is better. A hierarchical node called "FB," for "filterbank" is defined, and given a parameter D for "*depth*." For $D > 0$ the definition of the block is at the center. It contains a self-reference, with the parameter of the inside reference changed to $D-1$. When $D = 0$, the definition at the bottom is used. The system at the top, consisting of just one block, labeled "FB($D = 3$)," is exactly equivalent to the representation in Fig. 15, except that the visual representation does not now depend on the depth. The visual recursion in Fig. 16 can be unfolded completely at compile time, exposing all exploitable parallelism, and incurring no unnecessary run-time overhead.

F. Higher-Order Functions

In dataflow process networks, all arcs connecting actors represent streams. The icons represent both actors and the processes made up of repeated firings of the actor. Functional languages often represent such processes using

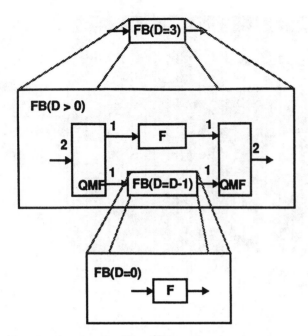

Fig. 16. A recursive representation of the filter bank application. This representation uses template matching.

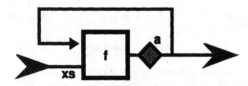

Fig. 17. Visual syntax for the dataflow process network equivalent of the Haskell "scanl f a xs" higher-order function.

higher order functions. For example, in Haskell,

$$\text{map } f \ xs$$

applies the function f to the list xs. Every single-input process in a dataflow process network constitutes an invocation of such a higher order function, applied to a stream rather than a list. In a visual syntax, the function itself is specified simply by the choice of icon. Moreover, Haskell has the variant

$$\text{zipWith } f \ xs \ ys$$

where the function f takes two arguments. This corresponds simply to a dataflow process with two inputs. Similarly, the Haskell function

$$\text{scanl } f \ a \ xs$$

takes a scalar a and a list xs. The function f is applied first to a and the head of xs. The function is then applied to the first returned value and the second element of xs. A corresponding visual syntax for a dataflow process network is given in Fig. 17.

Recall our proposed syntactic sugar for representing feedback loops such as that in Fig. 17 using actors with state. Typically the initial value of the state (a) will be a

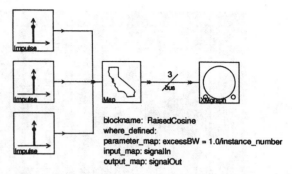

Fig. 18. An example of the use of the *Map* actor to plot three different raised cosine pulses.

Panel 1. Icon for the Map higher-order function in Ptolemy.

parameter of the node. In fact, dataflow processes with state cover many of the commonly used higher-order functions in Haskell.

The most basic use of icons in our visual syntax may therefore be viewed as implementing a small set of built-in higher-order functions. More elaborate higher-order functions will be more immediately recognizable as such, and will prove extremely useful. Pioneering work in the use of higher-order functions in visual languages was done by Hills [51], Najork and Golin [75], and Reekie [85]. We will draw on this work here.

We created an actor in Ptolemy called *Map* that generalizes the Haskell *map*. Its icon is shown in Panel 1.

It has the following parameters:

blockname	The name of the replacement actor.
where_defined	The location of the definition of the actor.
parameter_map	How to set the parameters of the replacement actor.
input_map	How to connect the inputs.
output_map	How to connect the outputs.

Our implementation of *Map* is simple but effective. It creates one or more instances of a the specified actor (which may itself be a hierarchical node) and splices those instance into its own position in the graph. Thus we call the specified actor the *replacement actor*, since it takes the place of the *Map* actor. The *Map* actor then self-destructs. This is done in the setup phase of execution so that no overhead is incurred for the higher order function during the run phase of execution, which for signal processing applications is the most critical. This replacement can be viewed as a form of partial evaluation of the program [34].

Consider the example shown in Fig. 18. The replacement actor is specified to be *RaisedCosine*, a built-in actor in

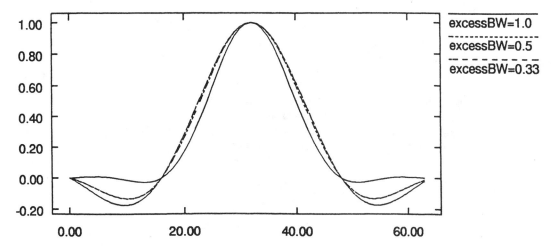

Fig. 19. The plot that results from running the program in Fig. 18.

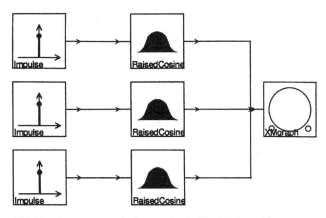

Fig. 20. A program equivalent to that in Fig. 18, but without higher-order functions.

the signal processing environment in Ptolemy. Since this is built-in, there is no need to specify where it is defined, so the *where_defined* parameter is blank. The *RaisedCosine* actor has a single input named *signalIn* and a single output named *signalOut*, so these names are given as the values of the *input_map* and *output_map* parameters. The *parameter_map* parameter specifies the values of the *excessBW* parameter for each instance of the replacement block to be created. This parameter specifies the excess bandwidth of the raised cosine pulse generated by this actor. The value of the *excessBW* parameter will be 1.0 for the first instance of the *RaisedCosine* actor, 0.5 for the second, and 0.33 for the third.

The diagonal slash through the last connection on the right in Fig. 18 is a *Bus*. Its single parameter specifies the number of logical connections that the single visual connection represents. Here, the bus width is three. This must be so because there are three inputs to the *Map* actor, so three instances of the *RaisedCosine* actor will be created. The three outputs from these three instances need somewhere to go. The result of running this system is shown in Fig. 19.

The program in Fig. 18 is equivalent to that in Fig. 20. Indeed, after the setup phase of execution, the topology of the process network will be exactly as in Fig. 20. The *Map* actor itself will not appear in the topology.

In both Figs. 18 and 20, the number of instances of the *RaisedCosine* actor is specified graphically. In Fig. 18, it is specified by implication, through the number of instances of the *Impulse* actor. In Fig. 20 it is specified directly. Neither of these really takes advantage of higher-order functions. The program in Fig. 21 is equivalent to both Figs. 18 and 20, but can be more easily modified to include more or fewer instances of the *RaisedCosine* actor. It is only necessary to modify the parameters of the bus icons, not the visual representation.

The left-most actor in Fig. 21 is a variant of the *Map* actor called *Src*. It has no inputs. In this case, the number of instances of the replacement actor that are created must match the number of *output* streams.

In the visual programming languages ESTL [75] and DataVis [51], higher-order functions use a "function slots" concept, visually representing the replacement function as a box inside the icon for the higher-order function. We have implemented in Ptolemy a conceptually similar visual representation. Variants of the *Map* and *Src* actors, called *MapGr* and *SrcGr*, have the following icons (see Panel 2).

It is important to realize that the above graphic contains only two icons, each representing a single actor. The complicated shape of the icon is intended to be suggestive of its function when it is found in a block diagram. The *MapGr* and *SrcGr* actors work just like the *Map* and *Src* actors, except that the programmer specifies the replacement block visually rather than textually. For example, the system in Fig. 21 can be specified as shown in Fig. 22. Notice that replacement actors *Impulse* and *RaisedCosine* each have one instance shown visually. The *MapGr* and *SrcGr* actors have only a single parameter, called *parameter_map*. The other parameters of *Map* and *Src* are now represented visually (the replacement block and input/output mapping).

Note that the same effect could be accomplished by tricks in the graphical user interface, as done for instance in

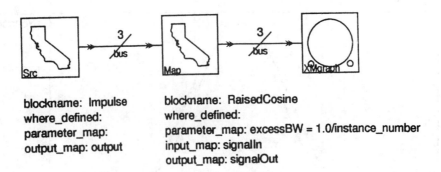

Fig. 21. A program equivalent to that in Figs. 18 and 20, except that the number of instances of the *RaisedCosine* and *Impulse* actors can be specified by a parameter.

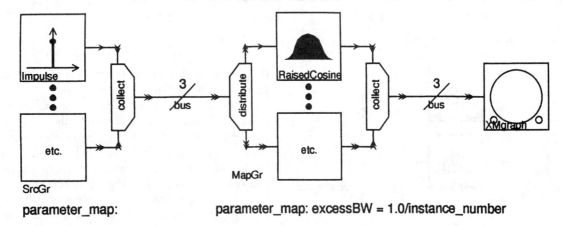

Fig. 22. A program equivalent to that in Fig. 21 except that the replacement actors for the two higher-order actors are specified visually rather than textually.

GRAPE II [63]. However, this then requires modifying the GUI to support new capabilities.

A number of additional variations are possible. First, the replacement actor may have more than one input, in which case the input streams are grouped in appropriately sized groups to provide the arguments for each instance of the specified actor. For example, if the replacement actor has two inputs, and there are 12 input streams, then six instances of the actor will be created. The first instance will process the first two streams, the second the next two streams, etc.

Since the *Map* actor always creates at least one instance of the replacement actor, it cannot be used directly for recursion. Such a recursion would never terminate. A variant of the *Map* actor can be defined that instantiates the replacement actor(s) only at run time. This is (essentially) what we used in Fig. 12 to implement recursion. Using dynamic dataflow, the *dynamic Map* actor fires conditionally. When it fires, it creates an instance of its replacement actor (which may be a hierarchical node recursively referenced), and self-destructs.

The dynamic *Map* was the first higher-order function implemented in Ptolemy (it was implemented under a different name by Soonhoi Ha). Its run-time operation is quite expensive, however, requiring dynamic creation of a dataflow graph. So there is still considerable motivation for recursion that can be statically unrolled, as done in Fig. 13.

In fact, that system is implemented using another higher-order function, *IfThenElse*, which is derived from *Map*. The *IfThenElse* actor takes two replacement actors as parameters plus a predicate. The predicate specifies which of the two replacement actors should be used. That actor is expanded into a graph instance and spliced into the position of the *IfThenElse* actor. The *IfThenElse* actor, like the *Map* actor, then self-destructs. Since the unused replacement actor argument is not evaluated, the semantics are nonstrict, and the *IfThenElse* actor can be used to implement recursion. The recursion is completely evaluated during the setup phase of execution (or at compile time), so the recursion imposes no run-time overhead during the run phase. This is analogous to the unrolling style of partial evaluation [34], and could be called *manifest recursion*.

The higher order functions above have a key restriction: the replacement actor is specified by a parameter, not by an input stream. Thus, we avoid embedding unevaluated closures in streams. In Ptolemy, since tokens that pass through the channels are C^{++} objects, it would not be hard to implement the more general form. It warrants further investigation.

G. The Tagged-Token Execution Model

Recall that the tagged-token execution model developed by Arvind and Gostelow [7], [8] allows out-of-order execution. This allows some dataflow graphs to produce output

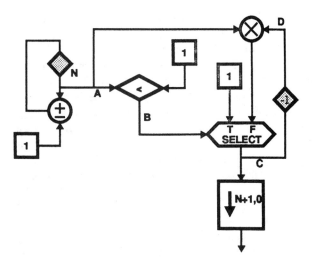

A	B	C	D
N	F	N!	(N-1)!
N-1	F	(N-1)!	(N-2)!
N-2	F	(N-2)!	(N-3)!
...	...	...	...
2	F	2	1
1	T	1	1
0	T	1	

Fig. 23. This factorial program deadlocks without out-of-order execution, as provided for example by the tagged token model.

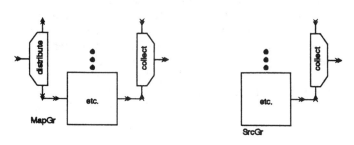

Panel 2. Icons for the *MapGr* and *SrcGr* higher-order functions in Ptolemy.

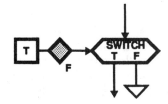

Fig. 24. One way to implement a negative delay, which discards the first token that arrives on the input stream.

that would deadlock under the FIFO channel model. An example is shown in Fig. 23. This graph computes $N!$ if out-of-order execution is allowed, but deadlocks without producing an output under the FIFO model. The sequence of values on the labeled arcs is given in the table in the figure.

The loop at the left counts down from N to 0, since the delay is initialized to N and the value circulating in the loop is decremented by 1 each time around. The test (diamond shape) compares the value at A to 1. When $A < 1$, it outputs a *true*. Until that time, the *select* is not enabled, because there are no tokens on the *false* input. But notice that at that time, the queue at the control input (B) of the select has N *false* tokens followed by one *true* token. The *false* tokens still cannot be consumed. If out-of-order execution is not allowed, then the *select* will never be able to fire. However, since the *select* has no state, there is no reason to prohibit out-of-order execution.

Out-of-order execution requires bookkeeping like that provided by the tagged-token model. The consumption of the *true* token is by the $(N+1)$th firing (logically) of the *select*. Thus the 1 produced at its output is (logically) the $(N+1)$th output produced by the *select*. Hence, at C, we show the 1 output as the *last* entry in the table, even though it is the first one produced temporally. The logical ordering must be preserved.

Recall that a delay is an initial token on a channel. The delay at the left is an ordinary delay, where the initial token is initialized to value N. The delay on the right, however, is something new, a *negative delay*. Instead of an initial token, this delay discards the first token that enters the channel. It can be implemented in a variety of ways, one of which is shown in Fig. 24. The effect of the negative delay is shown in column D: the first token (logically, not temporally) produced by the *select* is discarded by the negative delay. Thus the 1 produced by the $(N+1)$th firing (logically) of the *select* must be consumed by the Nth firing of the multiply at the upper right. The other input of the multiply has a value "1" as its Nth input (A), so the Nth output (logically) or first output (temporally) of the multiply is $1 \times 1 = 1$. This makes available the Nth token (logically) of the *select false* input, which can now be consumed by the Nth firing (logically) of the *select*. The "1" produced here will be multiplied by 2, enabling the $(N-2)$th firing of the *select*. We continue until the first firing (logically) of the *select* produces $N!$. At this point, there are $N+1$ tokens at the *downsampler* input (the icon at the bottom with the downward arrow), enabling it. It consumes these tokens and outputs the first one (logically). Thus the output of the downsampler is $N!$.

Note that although this might appear to be an unduly complicated way to compute a factorial, it nonetheless demonstrates that enabling out-of-order execution does increase the expressiveness in the language. Of course, this has limited value if its only use is to represent obscure and unnecessarily complicated algorithms.

H. Data Types and Polymorphism

A key observation about our dataflow process networks so far is that the only data type represented visually is the stream. The tokens on a stream can have arbitrary type, so this approach is more flexible than it sounds like at first. For instance, we can embed arrays into streams directly by sequencing the elements of the array, or by encapsulating each array into a single token, or by generalizing to multidimensional streams [65], [92]. In Ptolemy, tokens can contain arbitrary C^{++} objects, so the actors can operate on these tokens in rather sophisticated ways, making effective use of data abstraction.

Ptolemy networks are strongly typed. Each actor port (input or output) has a type, and type consistency is statically checked. Polymorphism, in which a single actor can operate on any of a variety of data types, is supported in a natural way.

Hudak distinguishes two types of polymorphism, *parametric* and *ad hoc* (or *overloading*) [53]. In the former, a function behaves the same way regardless of the data type of its arguments. In the latter, the behavior can be different, depending on the type. Although in principle both are supported in Ptolemy, we have made more use of parametric polymorphism in the visual programming syntax. The way that parametric polymorphism is handled is that actors declare their inputs or outputs to be of type "anytype." The actors then operate on the tokens via abstracted type handles.

Polymorphic blocks in Ptolemy include all those that perform control functions on streams, like the *distributor* in Fig. 13. The *Map* actor is also polymorphic, although in a somewhat more complicated way.

I. Parallelism

For functional languages, the dominant view appears to be that parallelism must be explicitly defined by the programmer by annotating the program with the processor allocation [53]. Moreover, as indicated by Harrison [48], the ubiquity of recursion in functional programs sequentializes what would otherwise be parallel algorithms. Harrison proposes using higher-order functions to express parallel algorithms in a functional language, in place of recursion. The parallel implementation is accomplished by mechanized program transformations from the higher-order function description. This is called "transformational parallel programming," and has also been explored by Reekie and Potter [87] in the context of process networks. The transformations could also be interactive, supported by "meta-programming." One transformation methodology is the unfold/fold method of Burstall and Darlington [27], which is based on partial (symbolic) evaluation and substitution of equal expressions.

In the dataflow community, by contrast, parallelism has always been implicit. This is, in part, due to the scarce use of recursion. A dataflow graph typically reveals a great deal of parallelism that can be exploited either by runtime hardware [5] or, if the firing sequence is sufficiently predictable, a compiler [45], [82], [90], [91].

Dataflow process networks can combine the best of these. Parallelism can be implicit, and higher-order functions can be used to simplify the syntax of the graphical specification. The phased execution, in which the static higher-order functions are evaluated during a setup phase, is analogous to the fold/unfold method of Burstall and Darlington [27], but there is no need for a specialized transformation tool that "understands" the semantics of the higher-order functions. Thus parallelism is exploited equally well with user-defined higher-order functions as with those that are built into the language.

Moreover, in a surprising twist, the use of statically evaluated higher-order functions enables the use of recursion *without compromising parallelism*. The recursion is evaluated during the setup phase, before the parallelizing scheduler is invoked. Thus the scheduler sees only the fully expanded graph, not the recursion. It can fully exploit at compile time the parallelism in this graph. Thus we regain much of the elegance that the use of recursion lends to functional languages. An example (a recursive specification of an FFT) is given above in Fig. 13. In situations where the recursion cannot be evaluated during the setup phase, as in the sieve of Eratosthenes in Fig. 12, it is much more difficult to exploit the parallelism at compile time.

IV. Conclusions

Signal processing software environments are domain-specific. Some of the techniques they use, including (and maybe especially) their visual syntax has only been proven in this domain-specific context. Nonetheless, they have (or can have) the best features of the best modern languages, including natural and efficient recursion, higher-order functions, data abstraction, and polymorphism.

This paper presents a theory of design that has been (at least partially) put into practice by the signal processing community. In the words of Milner [74], such a theory "does not stand or fall by experiment in the conventional scientific sense." It is the "pertinence" of a theory that is judged by experiment rather than its "truth."

Acknowledgment

The authors would like to thank the entire Ptolemy team, but especially Joe Buck, Soonhoi Ha, Alan Kamas, and Dave Messerschmitt, for conceiving and building a magnificent infrastructure for the kinds of experiments described here. The authors also gratefully acknowledge helpful comments and suggestions from Albert Benveniste, Gerard Berry, Shuvra Bhattacharyya, John Reekie, Vason Srini, Juergen Teich, and the anonymous reviewers. The inspiration for this paper came originally from Jack Dennis, who pointed out the need to relate the work with dataflow in signal processing with the broader computer science community.

REFERENCES

[1] H. Abelson and G. J. Sussman, *Structure and Interpretation of Computer Programs*. Cambridge, MA: MIT Press, 1985.
[2] S. Abramsky, "Reasoning about concurrent systems," in *Distributed Computing*, F. B. Chambers, D. A. Duce, and G. P. Jones, Eds. London: Academic, 1984.
[3] W. B. Ackerman, "Data flow languages," *Computer*, vol. 15, no. 2, Feb. 1982.
[4] K. R. Apt and G. D. Plotkin, "Countable nondeterminism and random assignment," *J. ACM*, vol. 33, no. 4, pp. 724–767, 1986.
[5] Arvind, L. Bic, and T. Ungerer, "Evolution of data-flow computers," in *Advanced Topics in Data-Flow Computing*, J.-L. Gaudiot and L. Bic, Eds. Englewood Cliffs, NJ: Prentice-Hall, 1991.
[6] Arvind and J. D. Brock, "Resource managers in functional programming," *J. Parallel and Distrib. Computing*, vol. 1, no. 5–21, 1984.
[7] Arvind and K. P. Gostelow, "Some relationships between asynchronous interpreters of a dataflow language," in *Formal Description of Programming Languages*, IFIP Working Group 2.2, 1977.
[8] ———, "The U-interpreter," *Computer*, vol. 15, no. 2, Feb. 1982.
[9] Arvind, R. S. Nikhil, and K. K. Pingali, "I-structures: Data structures for parallel computing," *ACM Trans. Programming Lang. and Syst.*, vol. 11, no. 4, pp. 598–633, Oct. 1989.
[10] E. A. Ashcroft and R. Jagannathan, "Operator nets," in *Proc. IFIP TC-10 Working Conf. on Fifth-Generation Computer Architectures*, North-Holland: The Netherlands, 1985.
[11] A. Benveniste and G. Berry, "The synchronous approach to reactive and real-time systems," *Proc. IEEE*, vol. 79, pp. 1270–1282, Sept. 1991.
[12] A. Benveniste and P. Le Guernic, "Hybrid dynamical systems theory and the SIGNAL language," *IEEE Trans. Autom. Contr.*, vol. 35, pp. 525–546, May 1990.
[13] A. Benveniste, P. Caspi, P. Le Guernic, and N. Halbwachs, "Data-flow synchronous languages," in J. W. de Bakker W.-P. de Roever, and G. Rozenberg, Eds., *A Decade of Concurrency—Reflections and Perspectives, Lecture Notes in Computer Science no. 803*. Berlin: Springer-Verlag, 1994.
[14] G. Berry, "Bottom-up computation of recursive programs," *Revue Française d'Automatique, Informatique et Recherche Opirationnelle*, vol. 10, no. 3, pp. 47–82, Mar. 1976.
[15] S. Bhattacharyya and E. A. Lee, "Memory management for synchronous dataflow programs," to appear in *IEEE Trans. Signal Process.*, May 1995.
[16] ———, "Looped schedules for dataflow descriptions of multirate signal processing algorithms," to appear in *Formal Methods in System Design* (updated from UCB/ERL Tech. Rep., May 21, 1993).
[17] G. Bilsen, M. Engels, R. Lauwereins, and J. A. Peperstraete, "Static scheduling of multi-rate and cyclo-static DSP applications," in *Proc. 1994 Workshop on VLSI Signal Process.*, IEEE Press, 1994.
[18] A. Bloss and P. Hudak, "Path semantics," in *Proc. 3rd Workshop on the Mathematical Foundations of Programming Language Semantics, Lecture Notes in Computer Science*. Berlin: Springer-Verlag, no. 298, pp. 479–489, 1987.
[19] F. Boussinot, "Reseaux de processus avec melange equitable: Une approche du temps reel," Ph.D. dissertation, Université P. et M. Curie, and Université Paris, France, June 1981.
[20] ———, "Reseaux de processus reactifs," Rapport de Recherche no. 12/91, INRIA, Sophia-Antipolis, France, Nov. 1991 (in French).
[21] J. D. Brock and W. B. Ackerman, "Scenarios, a model of nondeterminate computation," in *Proc. Conf. on Formal Definition of Programming Concepts*, LNCS 107. Berlin: Springer-Verlag, 1981, pp. 252–259.
[22] J. T. Buck, *Scheduling Dynamic Dataflow Graphs with Bounded Memory Using the Token Flow Model*, Tech. Rep. UCB/ERL 93/69, Ph.D. Dissertation, Dept. EECS, Univ. Calif., Berkeley, CA, 1993.
[23] J. Buck and E. A. Lee, "The token flow model," presented at Data Flow Workshop, Hamilton Island, Australia, May, 1992. Also in *Advanced Topics in Dataflow Computing and Multithreading*, L. Bic, G. Gao, and J.-L. Gaudiot, Eds. New York: IEEE Computer Soc. Press, 1994.
[24] J. Buck, S. Ha, E. A. Lee, and D. G. Messerschmitt, "Multirate signal processing in Ptolemy," in *Proc. Int. Conf. on Acoust., Speech, and Signal Processing*, Toronto, Canada, Apr. 1991.
[25] ———, "Ptolemy: A framework for simulating and prototyping heterogeneous systems," *Int. J. Computer Simulation*, Apr. 1994.
[26] W. H. Burge, "Stream processing functions," *IBM J. R & D*, vol. 19, no. 1, Jan. 1975.
[27] R. M. Burstall and J. Darlington, "A transformation system for developing recursive programs," *J. ACM*, vol. 24, no. 1, 1977.
[28] N. Carriero and D. Gelernter, "Linda in context," *Comm. ACM*, vol. 32, no. 4, pp. 444–458, Apr. 1989.
[29] P. Caspi, "Clocks in dataflow languages," *Theoretical Computer Sci.*, vol. 94, no. 1, Mar. 1992.
[30] ———, "Lucid synchrone," in *Proc. OPOPAC*, HERMES, Paris, 1993, pp. 79–93.
[31] M. J. Chen, "Developing a multidimensional synchronous dataflow domain in Ptolemy," *MS Rep.*, ERL Tech. Rep. UCB/ERL no. 94/16, Univ. Calif., Berkeley, CA, May 1994.
[32] A. Church, *The Calculi of Lambda-Conversion*. Princeton, NJ: Princeton Univ. Press, 1941.
[33] F. Commoner and A. W. Holt, "Marked directed graphs," *J. Computer and Syst. Sci.*, vol. 5, pp. 511–523, 1971.
[34] C. Consel and O. Danvy, "Tutorial notes on partial evaluation," *20th ACM Symp. on Principles of Programming Languages*, Jan. 1993, pp. 493–501.
[35] A. L. Davis, "Data driven nets: A maximally concurrent, procedural, parallel process representation for distributed control systems," Tech. Rep., Dept. Computer Sci., Univ. Utah, Salt Lake City, Utah, July 1978.
[36] A. L. Davis and R. M. Keller, "Data flow program graphs," *Computer*, vol. 15, no. 2, Feb. 1982.
[37] H. De Man, F. Catthoor, G. Goossens, J. Vanhoof, J. Van Meerbergen, S. Note, and J. Huisken, "Architecture-driven synthesis techniques for mapping digital signal processing algorithms into silicon," *Proc. IEEE*, vol. 78, pp. 319–335, Feb. 1990.
[38] J. B. Dennis, "First version data flow procedure language," Tech. Rep. MAC TM61, May 1975, MIT Lab. Computer Sci.
[39] ———, "Data flow supercomputers," *IEEE Compu.*, vol. COM–13, Nov. 1980.
[40] ———, "Stream data types for signal processing," unpublished memo, Sept 1992.
[41] D. Desmet and D. Genin, "ASSYNT: Efficient assembly code generation for DSP's starting from a data flowgraph," *Trans. ICASSP '93*, Minneapolis, MN, Apr. 1993.
[42] E. W. Dijkstra, *A Discipline of Programming*. Englewood Cliffs, NJ: Prentice Hall, 1976.
[43] J. Franco, D. P. Friedman, and S. D. Johnson, "Multi-way streams in scheme," *Comput. Lang.*, vol. 15, no. 2, pp. 109–125, 1990.
[44] D. K. Gifford and J. M. Lucassen, "Integrating functional and imperative programming," in *Proc. 1986 ACM Conf. on Lisp and Functional Programming*, 1986, pp. 28–38.
[45] S. Ha, "Compile-time scheduling of dataflow program graphs with dynamic constructs," Ph.D. dissertation, EECS Dept., Univ. Calif., Berkeley, CA, Apr. 1992.
[46] N. Halbwachs, P. Caspi, P. Raymond, and D. Pilaud, "The synchronous data flow programming language LUSTRE," *Proc. IEEE*, vol. 79, pp. 1305–1319, Sept. 1991.
[47] N. Halbwachs, *Synchronous Programming of Reactive Systems*. Dordrecht: Kluwer, 1993.
[48] P. G. Harrison, "A higher-order approach to parallel algorithms," *The Computer J.*, vol. 35, no. 6, 1992.
[49] J. Hicks, D. Chiou, B. S. Ang, and Arvind, "Performance studies of id on the monsoon dataflow system," *J. Parallel and Distributed Computing*, vol. 18, no. 3, pp. 273–300, July, 1993.
[50] P. Hilfinger, "A high-level language and silicon compiler for digital signal processing," in *Proc. Custom Integ. Circuits Conf.* Los Alamitos, CA: IEEE Computer Soc., 1985, pp. 213–216.
[51] D. D. Hills, "Visual languages and computing survey: Data flow visual programming languages," *J. Visual Lang. and Computing*, vol. 3, pp. 69–101.
[52] C. A. R. Hoare, "Communicating sequential processes," *Commun. ACM*, vol. 21, no. 8, Aug. 1978.
[53] P. Hudak, "Introduction to Haskell and functional programming," *ACM Compu. Surveys*, Sept. 1989.
[54] J. Hughes, "Compile-time analysis of functional programs," in *Research Topics in Functional Programming*, Turner, Ed. Reading, MA: Addison-Wesley, 1990.
[55] T. Ida and J. Tanaka, "Functional programming with streams," in *Information Processing '83*. Amsterdam: Elsevier, 1993.

[56] R. Jagannathan, "Parallel execution of GLU programs," presented at *2nd Int. Workshop on Dataflow Computing*, Hamilton Island, Queensland, Australia, May 1992.

[57] R. Jagannathan and E. A. Ashcroft, "Eazyflow: A hybrid model for parallel processing," in *Proc. Int. Conf. on Parallel Process.*, IEEE, Aug. 1984, pp. 514–523.

[58] G. Kahn, "The semantics of a simple language for parallel programming," in *Proc. IFIP Cong. '74*, Amsterdam: North-Holland, 1974.

[59] G. Kahn and D. B. MacQueen, "Coroutines and networks of parallel processes," *Information Processing '77*, B. Gilchrist, Ed. Amsterdam: North-Holland, 1977.

[60] D. J. Kaplan *et al.*, "Processing graph method specification version 1.0," unpublished memo, Naval Res. Lab., Washington, DC, Dec. 1987.

[61] R. M. Karp and R. E. Miller, "Properties of a model for parallel computations: Determinacy, termination, queueing," *SIAM J.*, vol. 14, pp. 1390–1411, Nov. 1966.

[62] P. J. Landin, "A correspondence between Algol 60 and Church's lambda notation," *Commun. ACM*, vol. 8, 1965.

[63] R. Lauwereins, P. Wauters, M. Adi, and J. A. Peperstraete, "Geometric parallelism and cyclo-static dataflow in GRAPE-II," in *Proc. 5th Int. Workshop on Rapid System Prototyping*, Grenoble, France, June 1994.

[64] E. A. Lee, "Consistency in dataflow graphs," *IEEE Trans. Parallel and Distib. Syst.*, vol. 2, Apr. 1991.

[65] ——, "Representing and exploiting data parallelism using multidimensional dataflow diagrams," in *Proc. ICASSP '93*, Minneapolis, MN, Apr. 1993.

[66] E. A. Lee and D. G. Messerschmitt, "Static scheduling of synchronous data flow programs for digital signal processing," *IEEE Trans. Computers*, Jan. 1987.

[67] ——, "Synchronous data flow," *Proc. IEEE*, Sept. 1987.

[68] P. Le Guernic, T. Gauthier, M. Le Borgne, and C. Le Maire, "Programming real-time applications with SIGNAL," *Proc. IEEE*, vol. 79, Sept. 1991.

[69] O. Maffeïs and P. Le Guernic, "From signal to fine-grain parallel implementations," in *Int. Conf. Parallel Architectures and Compilation Techn.*, IFIP A-50, North-Holland, Aug. 1994, pp. 237–246.

[70] D. McAllester, P. Panagaden, and V. Shanbhogue, "Nonexpressibility of fairness and signaling," to appear in JCSS, 1993.

[71] J. McCarthy, "Recursive functions of symbolic expressions and the computation by machine, Part I," *Comm. ACM*, vol. 3, no. 4, Apr. 1960.

[72] ——, "A basis for a mathematical theory of computation," in *Computer Programming and Formal Systems*. Amsterdam: North-Holland, 1978, pp. 33–70.

[73] J. McGraw, "Sisal: Streams and iteration in a single assignment language," *Language Ref. Manual*, Lawrence Livermore Nat. Lab., Livermore, CA.

[74] R. Milner, *Communication and Concurrency*. Englewood Cliffs, NJ: Prentice-Hall, 1989.

[75] M. A. Najork and E. Golin, "Enhancing show-and-tell with a polymorphic type system and higher-order functions," in *Proc. IEEE Workshop on Visual Languages*, Skokie, IL, Oct. 1990, pp. 215–220.

[76] T. J. Olson, N. G. Klop, M. R. Hyett, and S. M. Carnell, "MAVIS: A visual environment for active computer vision," in *Proc. IEEE Workshop on Visual Languages*, Seattle, WA, Sept. 1992, IEEE Comput. Soc., 1992, p. 170–176.

[77] J. S. Onanian, "A signal processing language for coarse grain dataflow multiprocessors," Tech Rep. MIT/LCS/TR-449, Cambridge, MA, June 1989.

[78] P. Panagaden and V. Shanbhogue, "The expressive power of indeterminate dataflow primitives," *Inf. and Computation*, vol. 98, no. 1, May 1992.

[79] J. L. Pino, T. M. Parks, and E. A. Lee, "Mapping multiple independent synchronous dataflow graphs onto heterogeneous multiprocessors," in *Proc. IEEE Asilomar Conf. on Signals, Syst., and Computers*, Nov. 1994.

[80] J. L. Pino, S. Ha, E. A. Lee, and J. T. Buck, "Software synthesis for DSP using Ptolemy," *J. VLSI Signal Process.*, vol. 9, no. 1, pp. 7–21, Jan. 1995.

[81] D. G. Powell, E. A. Lee, and W. C. Newman, "Direct synthesis of optimized DSP assembly code from signal flow block diagrams," in *Proc. ICASSP*, San Francisco, Mar. 1992.

[82] H. Printz, "Automatic mapping of large signal processing systems to a parallel machine," Ph.D. dissertation, Memo. CMU-CS-91-101, School of Computer Sci., Carnegie Mellon Univ., May 1991.

[83] J. Rabaey, C. Chu, P. Hoang, and M. Potkonjak, "Fast prototyping of datapath-intensive architectures," *IEEE Design and Test of Computers*, pp. 40–51, June 1991.

[84] J. Rasure and C. S. Williams, "An integrated visual language and software development environment," *J. Visual Lang. and Computing*, vol. 2, pp. 217–246, 1991.

[85] H. J. Reekie, "Toward effective programming for parallel digital signal processing," Res. Rep. 92.1, Univ. of Technology, Sydney, NSW, Australia, May 1992.

[86] ——, "Integrating block-diagram and textual programming for parallel DSP," in *Proc. 3d Int. Symp. on Signal Processing and its Applications*, QLD, Australia, Aug. 1992.

[87] H. J. Reekie and J. Potter, "Transforming process networks," presented at the Massey Functional Programming Workshop, Massey Univ., Parmerston North, New Zealand, Aug. 1992.

[88] ——, "Generating efficient loop code for programmable DSPs," in *Proc. ICASSP '94*, Adelaide, Australia, Apr. 1994.

[89] K. S. Shanmugan, G. J. Minden, E. Komp, T. C. Manning, and E. R. Wiswell, "Block-oriented system simulator (BOSS)," *Telecommun. Lab.*, Univ. Kansas, Internal Memo, 1987.

[90] G. C. Sih and E. A. Lee, "A compile-time scheduling heuristic for interconnection-constrained heterogeneous processor architectures," *IEEE Trans. Parallel and Distrib. Syst.*, vol. 4, Feb. 1993.

[91] ——, "Declustering: A new multiprocessor scheduling technique," *IEEE Trans. Parallel and Distrib. Syst.*, June 1993.

[92] D. B. Skillcorn, "Stream languages and data-flow," in *Advanced Topics in Data-Flow Computing*, J.-L. Gaudiot and L. Bic, Eds. Englewood Cliffs, NJ: Prentice-Hall, 1991.

[93] V. Srini, "An architectural comparison of dataflow systems," *Computer*, vol. 19, no. 3, Mar. 1986.

[94] P. A. Suhler, J. Biswas, K. M. Korner, and J. C. Browne, "TDFL: A task-level dataflow language," *J. Parallel and Distrib. Syst.*, vol. 9, no. 2, June 1990.

[95] J. Vuillemin, "Proof techniques for recursive programs," Ph.D. dissertation, Compu. Sci. Dept., Stanford Univ., 1973.

[96] W. W. Wadge and E. A. Ashcroft, *Lucid, the Dataflow Programming Language*. London: Academic, 1985.

[97] A. L. Wendelborn and H. Garsden, "Exploring the stream data type in SISAL and other languages," in *Advanced Topics in Dataflow Computing and Multithreading*, L. Bic, G. Gao, and J.-L. Gaudiot, Eds. New York: IEEE Compu. Soc., 1994.

Edward A. Lee (Fellow, IEEE) received the B.S. degree from Yale University in 1979, the S.M. degree from MIT in 1981, and the Ph.D. degree from the University of California at Berkeley in 1986.

He is presently a Professor in the Department of Electrical Engineering and Computer Sciences at the University of California at Berkeley. He is Director of the Ptolemy project there, and the former Director of the Gabriel project. From 1979 to 1982 he was a member of the technical staff in the Advanced Data Communications Laboratory at AT&T Bell Laboratories in Holmdel, NJ. He is a founder of Berkeley Design Technology Inc., and has also consulted for a number of other companies. His research interests include real-time software, discrete-event, systems, parallel computation, architecture and software techniques for signal processing, and design methodology for heterogeneous systems. He is a coauthor of *Digital Communication* (Kluwer, 1988 and 1994) and *Digital Signal Processing Experiments* (Prentice Hall, 1989), and the author of numerous technical papers and two patents.

Dr. Lee received the NSF Presidential Young Investigator award.

Thomas M. Parks received the B.S.E. degree in electrical engineering and computer science from Princeton University in 1987. He is now a Ph.D. candidate in the Department of Electrical Engineering and Computer Sciences at the University of California at Berkeley.

He is presently working on real-time dataflow computing as part of the Ptolemy project. From 1987 to 1989 he was an Assistant Staff Member in the Speech Systems Technology Group at MIT Lincoln Laboratory, where he designed and implemented multiprocessor architectures for real-time signal processing. He also contributed to research projects in low-rate speech coding and continuous speech recognition. His research interests include computer music, computer architecture, digital signal processing, real-time systems, and dataflow computing.

Design of Embedded Systems: Formal Models, Validation, and Synthesis

Stephen Edwards, Luciano Lavagno, Edward A. Lee, and Alberto Sangiovanni-Vincentelli

Abstract—This paper addresses the design of reactive real-time embedded systems. Such systems are often heterogeneous in implementation technologies and design styles, for example by combining hardware ASICs with embedded software. The concurrent design process for such embedded systems involves solving the specification, validation, and synthesis problems. We review the variety of approaches to these problems that have been taken.

I. INTRODUCTION

Reactive real-time embedded systems are pervasive in the electronics system industry. Applications include vehicle control, consumer electronics, communication systems, remote sensing, and household appliances. In such applications, specifications may change continuously, and time-to-market strongly affects success. This calls for the use of software programmable components with behavior that can be fairly easily changed. Such systems, which use a computer to perform a specific function, but are neither used nor perceived as a computer, are generically known as embedded systems. More specifically, we are interested in reactive embedded systems. Reactive systems are those that react continuously to their environment at the speed of the environment. They can be contrasted with interactive systems, which react with the environment at their own speed, and transformational systems, which take a body of input data and transform it into a body of output data [1].

A large percentage of the world-wide market for microprocessors is filled by micro-controllers that are the programmable core of embedded systems. In addition to microcontrollers, embedded systems may consist of ASICs and/or field programmable gate arrays as well as other programmable computing units such as Digital Signal Processors (DSPs). Since embedded systems interact continuously with an environment that is analog in nature, there must typically be components that perform A/D and D/A conversions. A significant part of the design problem consists of deciding the software and hardware architecture for the system, as well as deciding which parts should be implemented in software running on the programmable components and which should be implemented in more specialized hardware.

Embedded systems often are used in life critical situations, where reliability and safety are more important criteria than performance. Today, embedded systems are designed with an ad hoc approach that is heavily based on earlier experience with similar products and on manual design. Use of higher level languages such as C helps somewhat, but with increasing complexity, it is not sufficient. Formal verification and automatic synthesis of implementations are the surest ways to guarantee safety. However, both formal verification and synthesis from high levels of abstraction have been demonstrated only for small, specialized languages with restricted semantics. This is at odds with the complexity and heterogeneity found in typical embedded systems.

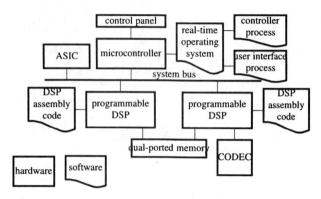

Fig. 1. A typical reactive real-time embedded system architecture.

We believe that the design approach should be based on the use of one or more formal models to describe the behavior of the system at a high level of abstraction, before a decision on its decomposition into hardware and software components is taken. The final implementation of the system should be made as much as possible using automatic synthesis from this high level of abstraction to ensure implementations that are "correct by construction." Validation (through simulation or verification) should be done as much as possible at the higher levels of abstraction.

A typical hardware architecture for an embedded system is illustrated in Figure 1. This type of architecture combines custom hardware with embedded software, lending a certain measure of complexity and heterogeneity to the design. Even within the software or hardware portions themselves, however, there is often heterogeneity. In software, control-oriented processes might be mixed under the supervision of a multitasking real-time kernel running on a microcontroller. In addition, hard-real-time tasks may run cooperatively on one or more programmable DSPs. The design styles used for these two software subsystems are likely to be quite different from one another, and testing the interaction between them is unlikely to be trivial.

The hardware side of the design will frequently contain one or more ASICs, perhaps designed using logic or behavioral synthesis tools. On the other hand, a significant part of the hardware design most likely consists of interconnections of commodity components, such as processors and memories. Again, this time on the hardware side, we find heterogeneity. The design styles used to specify and simulate the ASICs and the interconnected commodity components are likely to be quite different. A typical system, therefore, not only mixes hardware design with software design, but also mixes design styles within each of these categories.

Most often the set of tasks that the system implements are not specified in a rigorous and unambiguous fashion, so the design process requires several iterations to obtain convergence. Moreover, during the design process, the level of abstraction, detail, and specificity in different parts of the design varies. To complicate matters further, the skill sets and design styles used by different engineers on the project are likely to be different. The net result is that during the design process, many different specification and modeling techniques will be used.

Managing the design complexity and heterogeneity is the key problem. We believe that the use of formal models and high-level synthesis for ensuring safe and correct designs depends on understanding the interaction between diverse formal models. Only then can the simplicity of modeling required by verification and synthesis be reconciled with the complexity and heterogeneity of real-world design.

The concurrent design process for mixed hardware/software embedded systems involves solving the following subproblems: specification, validation, and synthesis. Although these problems cannot be entirely separated, we deal with them below in three successive sections.

II. SPECIFICATION AND MODELING

The design process is often viewed as a sequence of steps that transforms a set of specifications described informally into a detailed specification that can be used for manufacturing. All the intermediate steps are characterized by a transformation from a more abstract description to a more detailed one.

A designer can perform one or more steps in this process. For the designer, the "input" description is a *specification*, the final description of the design is an *implementation*. For example, a software designer may see a set of routines written in C as an implementation of her/his design even though several other steps may be taken before the design is ready for manufacturing. During this process, verification of the quality of the design with respect to the demands placed on its performance and functionality has to be carried out. Unfortunately, the descriptions of the design at its various stages are often informal and not logically connected by a set of precise relationships.

We advocate a design process that is based on representations with precise mathematical meaning so that both the verification and the map from the initial description to the various intermediate steps can be carried out with tools of guaranteed performance. Such an approach is standard in certain communities, where languages with strong formal properties are used to ensure robust design. Examples include ML [2], dataflow languages (e.g. Lucid [3], Haskell [4]) and synchronous languages (e.g., Lustre, Signal, Esterel [5]).

There is a broad range of potential formalizations of a design, but most tools and designers describe the behavior of a design as a relation between a set of inputs and a set of outputs. This relation may be informal, even expressed in natural language. It is easy to find examples where informal specifications resulted in unnecessary redesigns. In our opinion, a *formal model of a design* should consist of the following components:

1. A *functional specification*, given as a set of explicit or implicit relations which involve inputs, outputs and possibly internal (state) information.[1]

2. A *set of properties* that the design must satisfy, given as a set of relations over inputs, outputs, and states, that can be checked against the functional specification.
3. A *set of performance indices* that evaluate the quality of the design in terms of cost, reliability, speed, size, etc., given as a set of equations involving, among other things, inputs and outputs.
4. A *set of constraints* on performance indices, specified as a set of inequalities.

The functional specification fully characterizes the operation of a system, while the performance constraints bound the cost (in a broad sense). The set of properties is redundant, in that in a properly constructed design, the functional specification satisfies these properties. However, the properties are listed separately because they are simpler and more abstract (and also incomplete) compared to the functional specification. A property is an assertion about the behavior, rather than a description of the behavior. It is an abstraction of the behavior along a particular axis. For example, when designing a network protocol, we may require that the design never deadlock (this is also called a *liveness* property). Note that liveness does not completely specify the behavior of the protocol; it is instead a property we require our protocol to have. For the same protocol, we may require that any request will eventually be satisfied (this is also called *fairness*). Again this does not completely specify the behavior of the protocol but it is a required property.

Given a formal model of the functional specifications and of the properties, we can classify properties in three groups:

1. Properties that are *inherent* in the model of computation (i.e., they can be shown formally to hold for all specifications described using that model).
2. Properties that can be verified *syntactically* for a given specification (i.e., they can be shown to hold with a simple, usually polynomial-time, analysis of the specification).
3. Properties that must be verified *semantically* for a given specification (i.e., they can be shown to hold by executing, at least implicitly, the specification for all inputs that can occur).

For example, consider the property of *determinate behavior*, i.e., the fact that the output of a system depends only on its inputs and not on some internal, hidden choice. Any design described by a dataflow network (a formal model to be described later) is determinate, and hence this property need not be checked. If the design is represented by a network of FSMs, determinacy can be assessed by inspection of the state transition function. In some discrete event models (for example those embodied in Verilog and VHDL) determinacy is difficult to prove: it must be checked by exhaustive simulation.

The design process takes a model of the design at a level of abstraction and *refines* it to a lower one. In doing so, the designer must ensure that the properties at that level of abstraction are verified, that the constraints are satisfied, and that the performance indices are satisfactory. The refinement process involves also mapping constraints, performance indices and properties to the lower level so that they can be computed for the next level down.[2] Figure 2 shows a key refinement stage in embedded system design. The more abstract specification in this case is an

---
[1] We will define later on what we mean exactly by inputs, outputs and state information. For now, consider them as sequences of values.

[2] The refinement process can be defined formally once the models of the design are formally specified, see McMillan [6].

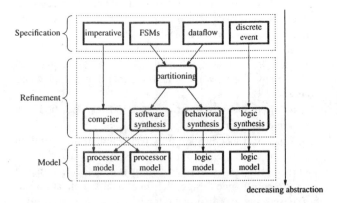

Fig. 2. An example of a design refinement stage, which uses hardware and software synthesis to translate a functional specification into a model of hardware.

executable functional model that is closer to the problem level. The specification undergoes a synthesis process (which may be partly manual) that generates a model of an implementation in hardware. That model itself may still be fairly abstract, capturing for example only timing properties. In this example the model is presumably used for hardware/software partitioning.

While figure 2 suggests a purely top-down process, any real design needs more interaction between specification and implementation. Nonetheless, when a design is complete, the best way to present and document it is top down. This is enough to require that the methodology support top-down design.

A. Elements of a Model of Computation

A *language* is a set of symbols, rules for combining them (its *syntax*), and rules for interpreting combinations of symbols (its *semantics*). Two approaches to semantics have evolved, *denotational* and *operational*. A language can have both (ideally they are consistent with one another, although in practice this can be difficult to achieve). Operational semantics, which dates back to Turing machines, gives meaning of a language in terms of actions taken by some abstract machine, and is typically closer to the implementation. Denotational semantics, first developed by Scott and Strachey [7], gives the meaning of the language in terms of relations.

How the abstract machine in an operational semantics can behave is a feature of what we call the *model of computation* underlying the language. The kinds of relations that are possible in a denotational semantics is also a feature of the model of computation. Other features include communication style, how individual behavior is aggregated to make more complex compositions, and how hierarchy abstracts such compositions.

A design (at all levels of the abstraction hierarchy from functional specification to final implementation) is generally represented as a set of components, which can be considered as isolated monolithic blocks, interacting with each other and with an environment that is not part of the design. The model of computation defines the behavior and interaction of these blocks.

In the sections that follow, we present a framework for comparing elements of different models of computation, called the tagged-signal model, and use it to contrast different styles of sequential behavior, concurrency, and communication. We will give precise definitions for a number of terms, but these definitions will inevitably conflict with standard usage in some communities. We have discovered that, short of abandoning the use of most common terms, no terminology can be consistent with standard usage in all related communities. Thus we attempt to avoid confusion by being precise, even at the risk of being pedantic.

A.1 The Tagged-Signal Model

Two of the authors (Lee and Sangiovanni-Vincentelli) have proposed the tagged-signal model [8], a formalism for describing aspects of models of computation for embedded system specification. It is denotational in the Scott and Strachey [7] sense, and it defines a semantic framework (of signals and processes) within which models of computation can be studied and compared. It is very abstract—describing a particular model of computation involves imposing further constraints that make it more concrete.

The fundamental entity in the Tagged-Signal Model is an event—a value/tag pair. Tags are often used to denote temporal behavior. A set of events (an abstract aggregation) is a signal. Processes are relations on signals, expressed as sets of n-tuples of signals. A particular model of computation is distinguished by the order it imposes on tags and the character of processes in the model.

Given a set of *values* V and a set of *tags* T, an *event* is a member of $T \times V$, i.e., an event has a tag and a value. A *signal* s is a set of events. A signal can be viewed as a subset of $T \times V$. A *functional signal* is a (possibly partial) function from T to V. The set of all signals is denoted S. A *tuple* of n signals is denoted $\mathbf{s}$, and the set of all such tuples is denoted S^n.

The different models of time that have been used to model embedded systems can be translated into different order relations on the set of tags T in the tagged signal model. In particular, in a *timed system* T is totally ordered, i.e., there is a binary relation $<$ on members of T such that if $t_1, t_2 \in T$ and $t_1 \neq t_2$, then either $t_1 < t_2$ or $t_2 < t_1$. In an *untimed system*, T is only partially ordered.

A *process* P with n signals is a subset of the set of all n-tuples of signals, S^n for some n. A particular $\mathbf{s} \in S^n$ is said to *satisfy* the process if $\mathbf{s} \in P$. An $\mathbf{s}$ that satisfies a process is called a *behavior* of the process. Thus a *process* is a set of possible *behaviors*, or a relation between signals.

For many (but not all) applications, it is natural to partition the signals associated with a process into *inputs* and *outputs*. Intuitively, the process does not determine the values of the inputs, and does determine the values of the outputs. If $n = i + o$, then (S^i, S^o) is a partition of S^n. A process with i inputs and o outputs is a subset of $S^i \times S^o$. In other words, a process defines a *relation* between input signals and output signals. A $(i + o)$-tuple $\mathbf{s} \in S^{i+o}$ is said to *satisfy* P if $\mathbf{s} \in P$. It can be written $\mathbf{s} = (\mathbf{s}_1, \mathbf{s}_2)$, where $\mathbf{s}_1 \in S^i$ is an i-tuple of *input signals* for process P and $\mathbf{s}_2 \in S^o$ is an o-tuple of *output signals* for process P. If the input signals are given by $\mathbf{s}_1 \in S^i$, then the set $I = \{(\mathbf{s}_1, \mathbf{s}_2) \mid \mathbf{s}_2 \in S^o\}$ describes the inputs, and $I \cap P$ is the set of behaviors consistent with the input $\mathbf{s}_1$.

A process F is *functional* with respect to a partition if it is a single-valued, possibly partial, mapping from S^i to S^o. That is, if $(\mathbf{s}_1, \mathbf{s}_2) \in F$ and $(\mathbf{s}_1, \mathbf{s}_3) \in F$, then $\mathbf{s}_2 = \mathbf{s}_3$. In this case, we can write $s_2 = F(s_1)$, where $F : S^i \to S^o$ is a (possibly partial) function. Given the input signals, the output signals are determined (or there is unambiguously no behavior).

Consider, as a motivating example introducing these several mechanisms to denote temporal behavior, the problem of modeling a time-invariant dynamical system on a computer. The underlying mathematical model, a set of differential equations over continuous time, is not directly implementable on a digital computer, due to the double quantization of real numbers into finite bit strings, and of time into clock cycles. Hence a first translation is required, by means of an *integration rule*, from the differential equations to a set of *difference equations*, that are used to compute the values of each signal with a given tag from the values of some other signals with previous and/or current tags.

If it is possible to identify several strongly connected components in the dependency graph[3], then the system is *decoupled*. It becomes then possible to go from the total order of tags implicit in physical time to a *partial order* imposed by the depth-first ordering of the components. This partial ordering gives us some freedom in implementing the integration rule on a computer. We could, for example, play with scheduling by embedding the partial order into the total order among clock cycles. It is often convenient, for example, to evaluate a component completely, for all tags, before evaluating components that depend on it. Or it is possible to spread the computation among multiple processors.

In the end, time comes back into the picture, but the *double mapping*, from total to partial order, and back to total order again, is essential to

1. *prove properties* about the implementation (e.g., stability of the integration method, a bound on the maximum execution time, ...),
2. *optimize* the implementation with respect to a given cost function (e.g., size of the buffers required to hold intermediate signals versus execution time, satisfaction of a constraint on the maximum execution time, ...),

A.2 State

Most models of computation include components with state, where behavior is given as a sequence of state transitions. In order to formalize this notion, let us consider a process F that is functional with respect to partition (S^i, S^o). Let us assume for the moment that F belongs to a timed system, in which tags are totally ordered. Then for any tuple of signals s, we can define $s_{>t}$ to be a tuple of the (possibly empty) subset of the events in s with tags greater than t.

Two input signal tuples $r, s \in S^i$ are in relation E_t^F (denoted $(r^i, s^i) \in E_t^F$) if $r_{>t} = s_{>t}$ implies $F(r)_{>t} = F(s)_{>t}$. This definition intuitively means that process F cannot distinguish between the "histories" of r and s prior to time t. Thus, if the inputs are identical after time t, then the outputs will also be identical.

E_t^F is an equivalence relation, partitioning the set of input signal tuples into equivalence classes for each t. Following a long tradition, we call these equivalence classes the *states* of F. In the hardware community, components with only one state for each t are called *combinational*, while components with more than one state for some t are called *sequential*. Note however that the term "sequential" is used in very different ways in other communities.

A.3 Decidability

Components with a *finite* number of states differ significantly from those with an *infinite* number of states. For certain infinite-state models (those that are Turing-complete), many desirable properties are undecidable—they cannot be determined in a finite amount of time for all systems. These properties include whether a system will need more memory than is available, whether a system will halt, and how fast a system will run. Hopcroft and Ullman [9] discuss these issues at length.

Undecidability is not an insurmountable barrier, and decidability is not sufficient to answer all questions in practice (e.g., because the required run-time may be prohibitive). Many successful systems have been designed using undecidable languages (i.e., those in which questions about some programs are undecidable). Although no algorithm can solve an undecidable problem for *all* systems, algorithms exist that can solve them for *most* systems. Buck's Boolean Dataflow scheduler [10], for example, can answer the halting and bounded memory problems for many systems specified in a Turing-complete dataflow model, although it does, necessarily, fail to reach a conclusion for some systems.

The non-terminating nature of embedded systems opens the possibility of using infinite time to solve certain undecidable problems. Parks' [11] scheduler, for example, will execute a potentially infinite-state system forever in bounded memory *if it is possible to do so*. However, it does not answer the question of how much memory is needed or whether the program will eventually halt.

The classical von Neumann model of computation[4] is a familiar model of sequential behavior. A memory stores the state and a processor advances the state through a sequence of memory operations. Most commonly-used programming languages (e.g., C, C++, Lisp, Pascal, FORTRAN) use this model of computation. Often, the memory is viewed as having an unbounded number of finite-valued words, which, when coupled with an appropriate choice of processor instructions, makes the model Turing complete[5]. Modern computer systems make this model practical by simulating unbounded memory with an elaborate hierarchy (registers, cache, RAM, hard disk). Few embedded systems, however, can currently afford such a scheme.

A.4 Concurrency and Communication

While sequential or combinational behavior is related to individual processes, embedded systems will typically contain several coordinated concurrent processes. At the very least, such systems interact with an environment that evolves independently, at its own speed. But it is also common to partition the overall model into tasks that also evolve more or less independently, occasionally (or frequently) interacting with one another.

---

[3] A directed graph with a node for each signal, and an edge between two signals whenever the equation for the latter depends on the former.

[4] It is formalized in the abstract model called random access machine or random access stored program [12].

[5] Turing-completeness can be obtained also with a finite number of infinite-valued words.

Communication between processes can be *explicit* or *implicit*. In explicit communication, a *sender* process informs one or more *receiver* processes about some part of its state. In implicit communication, two or more processes share a common notion of state.

Time plays a larger role in embedded systems than in classical computation. In classical transformational systems, the correct result is the primary concern—when it arrives is less important (although *whether* it arrives, the termination question, *is* important). By contrast, embedded systems are usually real-time systems, where the time at which a computation takes place can be more important than the computation itself.

As we discussed above, different models of time become different order relations on the set of tags T in the tagged signal model. Recall that in a *timed system* T is totally ordered, while in an *untimed system* T is only partially ordered. Implicit communication generally requires totally ordered tags, usually identified with physical time.

The tags in a *metric-time system* have the notion of a "distance" between them, much like physical time. Formally, there exists a partial function $d : T \times T \to \mathbf{R}$ mapping pairs of tags to real numbers such that $d(t_1, t_2) = 0 \Leftrightarrow t_1 = t_2$, $d(t_1, t_2) = d(t_2, t_1)$ and $d(t_1, t_2) + d(t_2, t_3) >= d(t_1, t_3)$.

A *discrete-event system* is a timed system where the tags in each signal are order-isomorphic with the integers (for a *two-sided* system) or the natural numbers (for a *one-sided* system) [8]. Intuitively, this means that any pair of ordered tags has a finite number of intervening tags.

Two events are *synchronous* if they have the same tag. Two signals are synchronous if each event in one signal is synchronous with an event in the other signal and vice versa. A *system* is *synchronous* if every signal in the system is synchronous with every other signal in the system. A *discrete-time system* is a synchronous discrete-event system.

Synchronous/reactive languages (see e.g. [5]) are synchronous in exactly this sense. The set of tags in a behavior of the system denotes a global "clock" for the system. Every signal conceptually has an event at every tag, although in some models this event could have a value denoting the absence of an event (called *bottom*). At each clock tick, each process maps input values to output values. If cyclic communication is allowed, then some mechanism must be provided to resolve or prevent circular dependencies. One possibility is to constrain the output values to have tags corresponding to the next tick. Another possibility (all too common) is to leave the result unspecified, resulting in nondeterminacy (or worse, infinite computation within one tick). A third possibility is to use fixed-point semantics, where the behavior of the system is defined as a set of events that satisfy all processes.

Concurrency in physical implementations of systems occurs through some combination of *parallelism*, having physically distinct computational resources, and *interleaving*, sharing of a common physical resource. Mechanisms for achieving interleaving vary widely, ranging from operating systems that manage context switches to fully-static interleaving in which concurrent processes are converted (compiled) into a single nonconcurrent process. We focus here on the mechanisms used to manage communication between concurrent processes.

Parallel physical systems naturally share a common notion of time, according to the laws of physics. The time at which an event in one subsystem occurs has a natural ordering relationship with the time at which an event occurs in another subsystem. Physically interleaved systems also share a natural common notion of time.

Logical systems, on the other hand, need a mechanism to explicitly share a notion of time. Consider two imperative programs interleaved on a single processor under the control of time-sharing operating system. Interleaving creates a natural ordering between events in the two processes, but this ordering is generally unreliable, because it heavily depends on scheduling policy, system load and so on. Some synchronization mechanism is required if those two programs need to cooperate.

More generally, in logically concurrent systems, maintaining a coherent *global* notion of time as a total order on events, can be extremely expensive. Hence in practice this is replaced whenever possible with an *explicit synchronization*, in which this total order is replaced by a partial order. Returning to the example of two processes running under a time-sharing operating system, we take precautions to ensure an ordering of two events only if the ordering of these two events matters.

A variety of mechanisms for managing the order of events, and hence for communicating information between processes, has arisen. Some of the most common ones are:

- Unsynchronized
  In an unsynchronized communication, a producer of information and a consumer of the information are not coordinated. There is no guarantee that the consumer reads valid information produced by the producer, and there is no guarantee that the producer will not overwrite previously produced data before the consumer reads the data. In the tagged-signal model, the repository for the data is modeled as a process, and the reading and writing events have no enforced ordering relationship between their tags.
- Read-modify-write
  Commonly used for accessing shared data structures, this strategy locks a data structure between a read and write from a process, preventing any other accesses. In other words, the actions of reading, modifying, and writing are atomic (indivisible). In the tagged-signal model, the repository for the data is modeled as a process where events associated with this process are totally ordered (resulting in a globally partially ordered model). The read-modify-write is modeled as a single event.
- Unbounded FIFO buffered
  This is a point-to-point communication strategy, where a producer generates a sequence of data tokens and consumer consumes these tokens, but only after they have been generated. In the tagged-signal model, this is a simple connection where the signal on the connection is constrained to have totally ordered tags. The tags model the ordering imposed by the FIFO model. If the consumer implements blocking reads, then it imposes a total order on events at all its input signals. This model captures essential properties of both Kahn process networks and dataflow [13].
- Bounded FIFO buffered
  In this case, the data repository is modeled as a process that imposes ordering constraints on its inputs (which come from the producer) and the outputs (which go to the consumer).

Each of the input and output signals are internally totally ordered. The simplest case is where the size of the buffer is one, in which case the input and output events must be interleaved so that each output event lies between two input events. Larger buffers impose a maximum difference (often called *synchronic distance*) between the number of input and output events.

Note that some implementations of this communication mechanism may not really block the writing process when the buffer is full, thus requiring some higher level of flow control to ensure that this never happens, or that it does not cause any harm.

- Rendezvous

  In the simplest form of rendezvous, implemented for example in Occam and Lotos, a single writing process and a single reading process must simultaneously be at the point in their control flow where the write and the read occur. It is a convenient communication mechanism, because it has the semantics of a single assignment, in which the writer provides the right-hand side, and the reader provides the left-hand side. In the tagged-signal model, this is imposed by events with identical tags [8]. Lotos offers, in addition, multiple rendezvous, in which one among multiple possible communications is *non-deterministically* selected. Multiple rendezvous is more flexible than single rendezvous, because it allows the designer to specify more easily several "expected" communication ports at any given time, but it is very difficult and expensive to implement correctly.

Of course, various combinations of the above models are possible. For example, in a partially unsynchronized model, a consumer of data may be required to wait until the first time a producer produces data, after which the communication is unsynchronized.

The essential features of the concurrency and communication styles described above are presented in Table I. These are distinguished by the number of transmitters and receivers (e.g., broadcast versus point-to-point communication), the size of the communication buffer, whether the transmitting or receiving process may continue after an unsuccessful communication attempt (blocking reads and writes), and whether the result of each write can be read at most once (single reads).

B. Common Models of Computation

We are now ready to use the scheme developed in the previous Section to classify and analyze several models of computation that have been used to describe embedded systems. We will consider issues such as ease of modeling, efficiency of analysis (simulation or formal verification), automated synthesizability, optimization space versus over-specification, and so on.

B.1 Discrete-Event

Time is an integral part of a discrete-event model of computation. Events usually carry a totally-ordered time stamp indicating the time at which the event occurs. A DE simulator usually maintains a global event queue that sorts events by time stamp.

Digital hardware is often simulated using a discrete-event approach. The Verilog language, for example, was designed as an input language for a discrete-event simulator. The VHDL

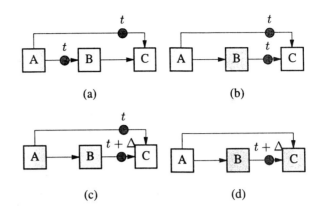

Fig. 3. Simultaneous events in a discrete-event system. (a) Process A produces events with the same time stamp. Should B or C be fired next? (b) Zero-delay process B has fired. How many times should C be fired? (c) Delta-delay process B has fired; C will consume A's output next. (d) C has fired once; it will fire again to consume B's output.

language also has an underlying discrete-event model of computation.

Discrete-event modeling can be expensive—sorting time stamps can be time-consuming. Moreover, ironically, although discrete-event is ideally suited to modeling distributed systems, it is very challenging to build a distributed discrete-event simulator. The global ordering of events requires tight coordination between parts of the simulation, rendering distributed execution difficult.

Discrete-event simulation is most efficient for large systems with large, frequently idle or autonomously operating sections. Under discrete-event simulation, only the changes in the system need to be processed, rather than the whole system. As the activity of a system increases, the discrete-event paradigm becomes less efficient because of the overhead inherent in processing time stamps.

Simultaneous events, especially those arising from zero-delay feedback loops, present a challenge for discrete-event models of computation. In such a situation, events may need to be ordered, but are not.

Consider the discrete-event system shown in Figure 3. Process B has zero delay, meaning that its output has the same time stamp as its input. If process A produces events with the same time stamp on each output, there is ambiguity about whether B or C should be invoked first, as shown in Figure 3(a).

Suppose B is invoked first, as shown in Figure 3(b). Now, depending on the simulator, C might be invoked once, observing both input events in one invocation, or it might be invoked twice, processing the events one at a time. In the latter case, there is no clear way to determine which event should be processed first.

The addition of delta delay makes such nondeterminacy easier to prevent, but does not avoid it completely. It introduces a two-level model of time in which each instant of time is broken into (a potentially infinite number of) totally-ordered delta steps. The simulated time reported to the user, however, does not include delta information. A "zero-delay" process in this model actually has delta delay. For example, Process B would have delta delay, so firing A followed by B would result in the situation in Figure 3(c). The next firing of C will see the event

TABLE I

A COMPARISON OF CONCURRENCY AND COMMUNICATION SCHEMES.

	Transmitters	Receivers	Buffer Size	Blocking Reads	Blocking Writes	Single Reads
Unsynchronized	many	many	one	no	no	no
Read-Modify-Write	many	many	one	yes	yes	no
Unbounded FIFO	one	one	unbounded	yes	no	yes
Bounded FIFO	one	one	bounded	yes	maybe	yes
Single Rendezvous	one	one	one	yes	yes	yes
Multiple Rendezvous	one	one	one	no	no	yes

from A only; the firing after that will see the (delay-delayed) event from B.

Other simulators, including the DE simulator in Ptolemy [14], attempt to statically analyze data precedences within a single time instant. Such precedence analysis is similar to that done in synchronous languages (Esterel, Lustre, and Signal) to ensure that simultaneous events are processed deterministically. It determines a partial ordering of events with the same time stamp by examining data precedences.

Adding a feedback loop from Process C to A in Figure 3 would create a problem if events circulate through the loop without any increment in time stamp. The same problem occurs in synchronous languages, where such loops are called causality loops. No precedence analysis can resolve the ambiguity. In synchronous languages, the compiler may simply fail to compile such a program. Some discrete-event simulators will execute the program nondeterministically, while others support tighter control over the sequencing through graph annotations.

B.2 Communicating Finite State Machines

Finite State Machines (FSMs) are an attractive model for embedded systems. The amount of memory required by such a model is always decidable, and is often an explicit part of its specification. Halting and performance questions are always decidable since each state can, in theory, be examined in finite time. In practice, however, this may be prohibitively expensive.

A traditional FSM consists of:
- a set of input symbols (the Cartesian product of the sets of values of the input signals),
- a set of output signals (the Cartesian product of the sets of values of the output signals),
- a finite set of states with a distinguished initial state,
- an output function mapping inputs and states to outputs, and
- a next-state function mapping inputs and states to (next) states.

The input to such a machine is a sequence of input symbols, and the output is a sequence of output symbols.

Traditional FSMs are good for modeling sequential behavior, but are impractical for modeling concurrency or memory because of the so-called state explosion problem. A single machine mimicking the concurrent execution of a group of machines has a number of states equal to the *product* of the number of states of each machine. A memory has as many states as the number of values that can be stored at each location *raised to the power* of the number of locations. The number of states alone is not always a good indication of complexity, but it often has a strong correlation.

Harel advocated the use of three major mechanisms that reduce the size (and hence the visual complexity) of finite automata for modeling practical systems [15]. The first one is hierarchy, in which a state can represent an enclosed state machine. That is, being in a particular state a has the interpretation that the state machine enclosed by a is active. Equivalently, being in state a means that the machine is in one of the states enclosed by a. Under the latter interpretation, the states of a are called "or states." Or states can exponentially reduce the complexity (the number of states) required to represent a system. They compactly describe the notion of *preemption* (a high-priority event suspending or "killing" a lower priority task), that is fundamental in embedded control applications.

The second mechanism is concurrency. Two or more state machines are viewed as being simultaneously active. Since the system is in one state of each parallel state machine simultaneously, these are sometimes called "and states." They also provide a potential exponential reduction in the size of the system representation.

The third mechanism is non-determinism. While often non-determinism is simply the result of an imprecise (maybe erroneous) specification, it can be an extremely powerful mechanism to reduce the complexity of a system model by *abstraction*. This abstraction can either be due to the fact that the exact functionality must still be defined, or that it is irrelevant to the properties currently considered of interest. E.g., during verification of a given system component, other components can be modeled as non-deterministic entities to compactly constrain the overall behavior. A system component can also be described non-deterministically to permit some optimization during the implementation phase. Non-determinism can also provide an exponential reduction in complexity.

These three mechanisms have been shown in [16] to cooperate synergistically and orthogonally, to provide a potential triple exponential reduction in the size of the representation with respect to a single, flat deterministic FSM[6].

Harel's Statecharts model uses a synchronous concurrency model (also called synchronous composition). The set of tags is a totally ordered countable set that denotes a global "clock" for the system. The events on signals are either produced by state transitions or inputs. Events at a tick of the clock can trigger state transitions in other parallel state machines at the same

---

[6]The exact claim in [16] was that "and" type non-determinism (in which all non-deterministic choices must be successful), rather than hierarchical states, was the third source of exponential reduction together with "or" type non-determinism and concurrency. Hierarchical states, on the other hand, were shown in that paper to be able to simulate "and" non-determinism with only a polynomial increase in size.

clock. Unfortunately, Harel left open some questions about the semantics of causality loops and chains of instantaneous (same tick) events, triggering a flurry of activity in the community that has resulted in at least twenty variants of Statecharts [17].

Most of these twenty variants use the synchronous concurrency model. However, for many applications, the tight coordination implied by the synchronous model is inappropriate. In response to this, a number of more loosely coupled asynchronous FSM models have evolved, including behavioral FSMs [18], SDL process networks [18], and codesign FSMs [19].

A model that is closely related to FSMs is Finite Automata. FAs emphasize the acceptance or rejection of a sequence of inputs rather than the sequence of output symbols produced in response to a sequence of input symbols. Most notions, such as composition and so on, can be naturally extended from one model to the other.

In fact, any of the concurrency models described in this paper can be usefully combined with FSMs. In the Ptolemy project [14], FSMs are hierarchically nested with dataflow, discrete-event, or synchronous/reactive models [20]. The nesting is arbitrarily deep and can mix concurrency models at different levels of the hierarchy. This very flexible model is called "*charts," pronounced "star charts," where the asterisk is meant to suggest a wildcard.

Control Flow Expressions (CFEs, [21]) have been recently proposed to represent the control flow of a set of operations in a cycle-based specification language. CFEs are an algebraic model extending Regular Expressions [9] and can be compiled into FSMs that can be used in the synthesis of a control unit.

B.3 Synchronous/Reactive

In a synchronous model of computation, all events are synchronous, i.e., all signals have events with identical tags. The tags are totally ordered, and globally available. Simultaneous events (those in the same clock tick) may be totally ordered, partially ordered, or unordered, depending on the model of computation. Unlike the discrete-event model, all signals have events at all clock ticks, simplifying the simulator by requiring no sorting. Simulators that exploit this simplification are called cycle-based or cycle-driven simulators. Processing all events at a given clock tick constitutes a cycle. Within a cycle, the order in which events are processed may be determined by data precedences, which define microsteps. These precedences are not allowed to be cyclic, and typically impose a partial order (leaving some arbitrary ordering decisions to the scheduler). Cycle-based models are excellent for clocked synchronous circuits, and have also been applied successfully at the system level in certain signal processing applications.

A cycle-based model is inefficient for modeling systems where events do not occur at the same rate in all signals. While conceptually such systems can be modeled (using, for example, special tokens to indicate the absence of an event), the cost of processing such tokens is considerable. Fortunately, the cycle-based model is easily generalized to multirate systems. In this case, every nth event in one signal aligns with the events in another.

A multirate cycle-based model is still somewhat limited. It is an excellent model for synchronous signal processing systems where sample rates are related by constant rational multiples, but in situations where the alignment of events in different signals is irregular, it can be inefficient.

The more general synchronous/reactive model is embodied in the so-called synchronous languages [22]. Esterel [23] is a textual imperative language with sequential and concurrent statements that describe hierarchically-arranged processes. Lustre [24] is a textual declarative language with a dataflow flavor and a mechanism for multirate clocking. Signal [25] is a textual relational language, also with a dataflow flavor and a more powerful clocking system. Argos [26], a derivative of Harel's Statecharts [27], is a graphical language for describing hierarchical finite state machines. Halbwachs [5] gives a good summary of this group of languages.

The synchronous/reactive languages describe systems as a set of concurrently-executing synchronized modules. These modules communicate through signals that are either present or absent in each clock tick. The presence of a signal is called an event, and often carries a value, such as an integer. The modules are reactive in the sense that they only perform computation and produce output events in instants with at least one input event.

Every signal in these languages is conceptually (or explicitly) accompanied by a clock signal, which has meaning relative to other clock signals and defines the global ordering of events. Thus, when comparing two signals, the associated clock signals indicate which events are simultaneous and which precede or follow others. In the case of Signal and Lustre, clocks have complex interrelationships, and a clock calculus allows a compiler to reason about these ordering relationships and to detect inconsistencies in the definition. Esterel and Argos have simpler clocking schemes and focus instead on finite-state control.

Most of these languages are static in the sense that they cannot request additional storage nor create additional processes while running. This makes them well-suited for bounded and speed-critical embedded applications, since their behavior can be extensively analyzed at compile time. This static property makes a synchronous program finite-state, greatly facilitating formal verification.

Verifying that a synchronous program is causal (non-contradictory and deterministic) is a fundamental challenge with these languages. Since computation in these languages is delay-free and arbitrary interconnection of processes is possible, it is possible to specify a program that has either no interpretation (a contradiction where there is no consistent value for some signal) or multiple interpretations (some signal has more than one consistent value). Both situations are undesirable, and usually indicate a design error. A conservative approach that checks for causality problems structurally flags an unacceptably large number of programs as incorrect because most will manifest themselves only in unreachable program states. The alternative, to check for a causality problem in any reachable state, can be expensive since it requires an exhaustive check of the state space of the program.

In addition to the ability to translate these languages into finite-state descriptions, it is possible to compile these languages directly into hardware. Techniques for translating both Esterel [28] and Lustre [29] into hardware have been proposed. The result is a logic network consisting of gates and flip-flops that can be optimized using traditional logic synthesis tools. To execute such a system in software, the resulting network is simply simulated. The technique is also the basis to perform more efficiently causality checks, by means of implicit state space traversal techniques [30].

B.4 Dataflow Process Networks

In dataflow, a program is specified by a directed graph where the nodes (called *actors*) represent computations and the arcs represent totally ordered sequences (called *streams*) of events (called *tokens*). In figure 4(a), the large circles represent actors, the small circle represents a token and the lines represent streams. The graphs are often represented visually and are typically hierarchical, in that an actor in a graph may represent another directed graph. The nodes in the graph can be either language primitives or subprograms specified in another language, such as C or FORTRAN. In the latter case, we are mixing two of the models of computation from figure 2, where dataflow serves as the coordination language for subprograms written in an imperative host language.

Dataflow is a special case of Kahn process networks [13], [31]. In a Kahn process network, communication is by unbounded FIFO buffering, and processes are constrained to be continuous mappings from input streams to output streams. "Continuous" in this usage is a topological property that ensures that the program is determinate [13]. Intuitively, it implies a form of causality without time; specifically, a process can use partial information about its input streams to produce partial information about its output streams. Adding more tokens to the input stream will never result in having to change or remove tokens on the output stream that have already been produced. One way to ensure continuity is with blocking reads, where any access to an input stream results in suspension of the process if there are no tokens. One consequence of blocking reads is that a process cannot test an input channel for the availability of data and then branch conditionally to a point where it will read a different input.

In dataflow, each process is decomposed into a sequence of *firings*, indivisible quanta of computation. Each firing consumes and produces tokens. Dividing processes into firings avoids the multitasking overhead of context switching in direct implementations of Kahn process networks. In fact, in many of the signal processing environments, a major objective is to statically (at compile time) schedule the actor firings, achieving an interleaved implementation of the concurrent model of computation. The firings are organized into a list (for one processor) or set of lists (for multiple processors). Figure 4(a) shows a dataflow graph, and Figure 4(b) shows a single processor schedule for it. This schedule is a list of firings that can be repeated indefinitely. One cycle through the schedule should return the graph to its original state (here, state is defined as the number of tokens on each arc). This is not always possible, but when it is, considerable simplification results [32]. In many existing environments, what happens within a firing can only be specified in a host language with imperative semantics, such as C or C++. In the Ptolemy system [14], it can also consist of a quantum of computation specified with any of several models of computation, such as FSMs, a synchronous/reactive subsystem, or a discrete-event subsystem [33].

A useful formal device is to constrain the operation of a firing to be functional, i.e., a simple, stateless mapping from input

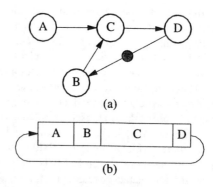

Fig. 4. (a) A dataflow process network (b) A single-processor static schedule for it

values to output values. Note, however, that this does not constrain the process to be stateless, since it can maintain state in a self-loop: an output that is connected back to one of its inputs. An initial token on this self-loop provides the initial value for the state.

Many possibilities have been explored for precise semantics of dataflow coordination languages, including Karp and Miller's computation graphs [34], Lee and Messerschmitt's synchronous dataflow graphs [35], Lauwereins *et al.*'s cyclo-static dataflow model [36], [37], Kaplan *et al.*'s Processing Graph Method (PGM) [38], Granular Lucid [39], and others [40], [41], [42], [43]. Many of these limit expressiveness in exchange for formal properties (e.g., provable liveness and bounded memory).

Synchronous dataflow (SDF) and cyclo-static dataflow require processes to consume and produce a fixed number of tokens for each firing. Both have the useful property that a finite static schedule can always be found that will return the graph to its original state. This allows for extremely efficient implementations [32]. For more general dataflow models, it is undecidable whether such a schedule exists [10].

A looser model of dataflow is the tagged-token model, in which the partial order of tokens is explicitly carried with the tokens [44]. A significant advantage of this model is that while it logically preserves the FIFO semantics of the channels, it permits out-of-order execution.

Some examples of graphical dataflow programming environments intended for signal processing (including image processing) are Khoros [45], and Ptolemy [14].

B.5 Other models

Another commonly used partially ordered concurrency model is based on rendezvous. Two or more concurrent sequential processes proceed autonomously, but at certain points in their control flow, coordinate so that they are simultaneously at specified points. Rendezvous has been developed into elaborate process calculi (e.g., Hoare's CSP [46] and Milner's CCS [47]). It has also been implemented in the Occam and Lotos programming languages. Ada also uses rendezvous, although the implementation is stylistically quite different, using remote procedure calls rather than more elementary synchronization primitives.

Rendezvous-based models of computation are often called *synchronous*. However, by the definition we have given, they are not synchronous. Events are partially ordered, not totally ordered, with rendezvous points imposing the partial ordering constraints.

No discussing of concurrent models of computation would be complete without mentioning Petri nets [48], [49]. Petri nets are, in their basic form, neither Turing complete nor finite state. They are interesting as uninterpreted model for several very different classes of problems, including some relevant to embedded system design (e.g., process control, asynchronous communication, scheduling, ...). Many questions about Petri nets can be answered in finite time. Moreover, a large user community has developed a large body of theoretical results and practical design aids and methods based on them. In particular, partial order-based verification methods (e.g. [50], [51], [6]) are one possible answer to the state explosion problem plaguing FSM-based verification techniques.

C. Languages

The distinction between a language and its underlying model of computation is important. The same model of computation can give rise to fairly different languages (e.g., the imperative Algol-like languages C, C++, Pascal, and FORTRAN). Some languages, such as VHDL and Verilog, support two or more models of computation[7].

The model of computation affects the *expressiveness* of a language — which behaviors can be described in the language, whereas the syntax affects compactness, modularity, and reusability. Thus, for example, object-oriented properties of imperative languages like C++ are more a matter of syntax than a model of computation.

The expressiveness of a language is an important issue. At one extreme, a language that is not expressive enough to specify a particular behavior is clearly unsuitable, but the other extreme also raises problems. A language that is too expressive often raises the complexity of analysis and synthesis. In fact, for very expressive languages, many analysis and synthesis problems become undecidable: no algorithm will solve all problem instances in finite time.

A language in which a desired behavior cannot be represented succinctly is also problematic. The difficulty of solving analysis and synthesis problems is at least linear in the size of the problem description, and can be as bad as several times exponential, so choosing a language in which the desired behavior of the system is compact can be critical.

A language may be very incomplete and/or very abstract. For example, it may specify only the interaction between computational modules, and not the computation performed by the modules. Instead, it provides an interface to a host language that specifies the computation, and is called a coordination language (examples include Linda [41], Granular Lucid [39], and Ptolemy domains [14]). Or the language may specify only the causality constraints of the interactions without detailing the interactions themselves nor providing an interface to a host language. In this case, the language is used as a tool to prove properties of systems, as done, for example, in process calculi [46], [47] and Petri nets [48], [49]. In still more abstract modeling, components in the system are replaced with nondeterminate specifications that give constraints on the behavior, but not the behavior itself. Such abstraction provides useful simplifications that help formal verification.

D. Heterogeneous Models of Computation

The variety of models of computation that have been developed is only partially due to immaturity in the field. It appears that different models fundamentally have different strengths and weaknesses, and that attempts to find their common features result in models that are very low level, difficult to use. These low level models (such as Dijkstra's P/V systems [52]) provide a good theoretical foundation, but not a good basis for design.

Thus we are faced with two alternatives in designing complex, heterogeneous systems. We can either use a single unified approach and suffer the consequences, or we can mix approaches. To use the unified approach today we could choose between VHDL and C for a mixed hardware and software design, doing the entire design in one or the other (i.e. specifying the software in VHDL or the hardware in C). Or worse, we could further bloat the VHDL language by including a subset designed for software specification (e.g. by making Ada a subset of VHDL). In the alternative that we advocate, we mix approaches while keeping them conceptually distinct, for example by using both VHDL *and* C in a mixed hardware/software design.

The key problem in the mixed approach, then, is to define the semantics of the interaction of fundamentally different models of computation. It is not simply a problem of interfacing languages. It is easy, for example, to provide a mechanism for calling C procedures from VHDL. But what does it mean if two concurrent VHDL entities call C procedures that interact? The problem is exacerbated by the lack of agreed-upon semantics for C or VHDL.

Studying the interaction semantics of mixed models of computation is the main objective of the Ptolemy project [14]. There, a hierarchical framework is used, where a specification in one model of computation can contain a primitive that is internally implemented using another model of computation. The object-oriented principle of information hiding is used to isolate the models from one another as much as possible.

III. VALIDATION

Validation loosely refers to the process of determining that a design is correct. Simulation remains the main tool to validate a model, but the importance of formal verification is growing, especially for safety-critical embedded systems. Although still in its infancy, it shows more promise than verification of arbitrary systems, such as generic software programs, because embedded systems are often specified in a more restricted way. For example, they are often finite-state.

Many safety properties (including deadlock detection) can be detected in a time-independent way using existing model checking and language containment methods (see, e.g., Kurshan [53] and Burch et al. [54]). Unfortunately, verifying most temporal properties is much more difficult (Alur and Henzinger [55] provide a good summary). Much more research is needed before this is practical.

---

[7] They directly support the Imperative model within a process, and the Discrete Event model among processes. They can also support Extended Finite State Machines under suitable restrictions known as the "synthesizable subset".

A. Simulation

Simulating embedded systems is challenging because they are heterogeneous. In particular, most contain both software and hardware components that must be simulated at the same time. This is the co-simulation problem.

The basic co-simulation problem is reconciling two apparently conflicting requirements:
- to execute the software as fast as possible, often on a host machine that may be faster than the final embedded CPU, and certainly is very different from it; and
- to keep the hardware and software simulations synchronized, so that they interact just as they will in the target system.

One approach, often taken in practice, is to use a general-purpose software simulator (based, e.g., on VHDL or Verilog) to simulate a model of the target CPU, executing the software program on this simulation model. Different models can be employed, with a tradeoff between accuracy and performance:
- Gate-level models
  These are viable only for small validation problems, where either the processor is a simple one, or very little code needs to be run on it, or both.
- Instruction-set architecture (ISA) models augmented with hardware interfaces
  An ISA model is a standard processor simulator (often written in C) augmented with hardware interface information for coupling to a standard logic simulator.
- Bus-functional models
  These are hardware models only of the processor interface; they cannot run any software. Instead, they are configured (programmed) to make the interface appear as if software were running on the processor. A stochastic model of the processor and of the program can be used to determine the mix of bus transactions.
- Translation-based models
  These convert the code to be executed on a processor into code that can be executed natively on the computer doing the simulation. Preserving timing information and coupling the translated code to a hardware simulator are the major challenges.

When more accuracy is required, and acceptable simulation performance is not achievable on standard computers, designers sometimes resort to *emulation*. In this case, configurable hardware emulates the behavior of the system being designed.

Another problem is the accurate modeling of a controlled electromechanical system, which is generally governed by a set of differential equations. This often requires interfacing to an entirely different kind of simulator.

A.1 Co-simulation Methods

In this section, we present a survey of some of the representative co-simulation methods, summarized in Table II. A unified approach, where the entire system is translated into a form suitable for a single simulator, is conceptually simple, but computationally inefficient. Making better use of computational resources often means distributing the simulation, but synchronization of the processes becomes a challenge.

The method proposed by Gupta *et al.* [56] is typical of the unified approach to co-simulation. It relies on a single custom simulator for hardware and software that uses a single event queue and a high-level, bus-cycle model of the target CPU.

Rowson [57] takes a more distributed approach that loosely links a hardware simulator with a software process, synchronizing them with the standard interprocess communication mechanisms offered by the host operating system. One of the problems with this approach is that the relative clocks of software and hardware simulation are not synchronized. This requires the use of handshaking protocols, which may impose an undue burden on the implementation. This may happen, for example, because hardware and software would not need such handshaking since the hardware part runs in reality much faster than in the simulation.

Wilson [58] describes the use of a commercial hardware simulator. In this approach, the simulator and software compiled on the host processor interact via a bus-cycle emulator inside the hardware simulator. The software and hardware simulator execute in separate processes and the two communicate via UNIX pipes. Thomas *et al.* [59] take a similar approach.

Another approach keeps track of time in software and hardware independently, using various mechanisms to synchronize them periodically. For example, ten Hagen *et al.* [60] describe a two-level co-simulation environment that combines a timed and untimed level. The untimed level is used to verify time-independent properties of the system, such as functional correctness. At this level, software and hardware run independent of each other, passing messages whenever needed. This allows the simulation to run at the maximum speed, while taking full advantage of the native debugging environments both for software and for hardware. The timed level is used to verify time-dependent properties, requiring the definition of time in hardware and software. In hardware, time can be measured either on the basis of clock cycles (cycle-based simulation, assuming synchronous operation) for maximum performance, or on the basis of estimated or extracted timing information for maximum precision. In software, on the other hand, time can be measured either by profiling or clock cycle counting information for maximum performance, or by executing a model of the CPU for maximum precision. The authors propose two basic mechanisms for synchronizing time in hardware and software.

1. Software is the master and hardware is the slave. In this case, software decides when to send a message, tagged with the current software clock cycle, to the hardware simulator. Depending on the relation between software and hardware time, the hardware simulator can either continue simulation until software time or back-up the simulation to software time (this requires checkpointing capabilities, which few hardware simulators currently have).
2. Hardware is the master and software is the slave. In this case, the hardware simulator directly calls communication procedures which, in turn, call user software code.

Kalavade and Lee [61] and Lee and Rabaey [63] take a similar approach. The simulation and design environment Ptolemy [14] is used to provide an interfacing mechanism between different domains. In Ptolemy, objects described at different levels of abstraction and using different semantic models are composed hierarchically. Each abstraction level, with its own semantic model, is a "domain" (e.g., dataflow, discrete-event). Atomic objects (called "stars") are the primitives of the domain (e.g.,

TABLE II
A COMPARISON OF CO-SIMULATION METHODS.

Author	Hardware Simulation	Software Simulation	Synchronization Mechanism
Gupta [56]	logic custom	bus-cycle custom	single simulation
Rowson [57]	logic commercial	host-compiled	handshake
Wilson [58]	logic commercial	host-compiled	handshake
Thomas [59]	logic commercial	host-compiled	handshake
ten Hagen (1) [60]	logic commercial	host-compiled	handshake
ten Hagen (2) [60]	cycle-based	cycle-counting	tagged messages
Kalavade (1) [61]	logic custom	host-compiled	single simulation
Kalavade (2) [61]	logic custom	ISA	single simulation
Lee [61]	logic custom	host-compiled	single simulation
Sutarwala [62]	logic commercial	ISA on HW simulation	single simulation

dataflow operators, logic gates). They can be used either in simulation mode (reacting to events by producing events) or in synthesis mode (producing software or a hardware description). "Galaxies" are collections of instances of stars or other galaxies. An instantiated galaxy can belong to a domain different than the instantiating domain. Each domain includes a scheduler, which decides the order in which stars are executed, both in simulation and in synthesis. For synthesis, it must be possible to construct the schedule statically. Whenever a galaxy instantiates a galaxy belonging to another domain (typical in co-simulation), Ptolemy provides a mechanism called a "wormhole" for the two schedulers to communicate. The simplest form of communication is to pass time-stamped events across the interface between domains, with the appropriate data-type conversion.

Kalavade and Lee [61] perform co-simulation at the specification level by using a dataflow model and at the implementation level by using an ISA processor model augmented with the interfaces within a hardware simulator, both built within Ptolemy.

Lee and Rabaey [63] simulate the specification by using concurrent processes communicating via queues within a timed model (the Ptolemy communicating processes domain). The same message exchanging mechanism is retained in the implementation (using a mix of microprocessor-based boards, DSPs, and ASICs), thus performing co-simulation of one part of the implementation with a simulation model of the rest. For example, the software running on the microprocessor can also be run on a host computer, while the DSP software runs on the DSP itself.

Sutarwala and Paulin [62] describe an environment coupled with a retargetable compiler [64] for cycle-based simulation of a user-definable DSP architecture. The user only provides a description of the DSP structure and functionality, while the environment generates a behavioral bus-cycle VHDL model for it, which can then be used to run the code on a standard hardware simulator.

B. Formal Verification

Formal verification is the process of mathematically checking that the behavior of a system, described using a formal model, satisfies a given property, also described using a formal model. The two models may or may not be the same, but must share a common semantic interpretation. The ability to carry out formal verification is strongly affected by the model of computation, which determines decidability and complexity bounds. Two distinct types of verification arise:

- Specification Verification: checking an abstract property of a high-level model. An example: checking whether a protocol modeled as a network of communicating FSMs can ever deadlock.
- Implementation Verification: checking if a relatively low-level model correctly implements a higher-level model or satisfies some implementation-dependent property. For example: checking whether a piece of hardware correctly implements a given FSM, or whether a given dataflow network implementation on a given DSP completely processes an input sample before the next one arrives.

Implementation verification for hardware is a relatively well-developed area, with the first industrial-strength products beginning to appear. For example, most logic synthesis systems have a mechanism to verify a gate-level implementation against a set of Boolean equations or an FSM, to detect bugs in the synthesis software[8].

While simulation could fall under these definitions (if the property is "the behavior under this stimulus is as expected"), the term formal verification is usually reserved for checking properties of the system that must hold for all or a broad class of inputs. The properties are traditionally broken into two classes:

- Safety properties, which state that no matter what inputs are given, and no matter how non-deterministic choices are resolved inside the system model, the system will not get into a specific undesirable configuration (e.g., deadlock, emission of undesired outputs, etc.)
- Liveness properties, which state that some desired configuration will be visited eventually or infinitely often (e.g., expected response to an input, etc.)

More complex checks, such as the correct implementation of a specification, can usually be done in terms of those basic properties. For example, Dill [65] describes a method to define and check correct implementation for asynchronous logic circuits in an automata-theoretic framework.

In this section we only summarize the major approaches that have been or can be applied to embedded system verification. These can be roughly divided into the following classes:

- Theorem proving methods provide an environment that assists the designer in carrying out a formal proof of specifica-

---

[8]This shows that the need for implementation verification is not eliminated by the introduction of automated synthesis techniques.

tion or implementation correctness. The assistance can be either in the form of checking the correctness of the proof, or in performing some steps of the proof automatically (e.g., Gordon and Melham's HOL [66], the Boyer-Moore system [67] and PVS [68]). The main problems with this approach are the undecidability of some higher order logics and the large size of the search space even for decidable logics.

- Finite automata methods restrict the power of the model in order to automate proofs. A Finite Automaton, in its simplest form, consists of a set of states, connected by a set of edges labeled with symbols from an alphabet. Various criteria can be used to define which finite or infinite sequences of symbols are "accepted" by the automaton. The set of accepted sequences is generally called the *language* of the automaton. The main verification methods used in this case are language containment and model checking.

  - In language containment, both the system and the property to be verified are described as a synchronous composition of automata. The proof is carried out by testing whether the language of one is contained in the language of the other (Kurshan's approach is typical [53]). One particularly simple case occurs when comparing a synchronous FSM with its hardware implementation. Then both automata are on finite strings, and the proof of equivalence can be performed by traversing the state space of their product [69].
  - Simulation relations are an efficient *sufficient* (i.e., conservative) criterion to establish language containment properties between automata, originating from the process algebraic community ([47], [46]). Informally, a simulation relation is a relation R between the states of the two automata such that for each pair of states s, s' in R, for each symbol labeling an edge from s, the pair of next states under that symbol is also in R. This relation can be computed much more quickly than the exact language containment test (that in the case of nondeterministic automata requires an exponential determinization step), and hence can be used as a fast heuristic check. If the same simulation relation holds in both directions (i.e., it is true also for each symbol labeling an edge from s'), then it is called a *bisimulation*. Bisimulation can be used as test for behavioral equivalence that directly supports composition and abstraction (hiding of edge labels). Moreover, self-bisimulation is an equivalence relation among states of an automaton, and hence it can be used to minimize the automaton (the result is called the "quotient" automaton).
  - In model checking (see, e.g., [70], [71], [54], [6]), the system is modeled as a synchronous or asynchronous composition of automata, and the property is described as a formula in some temporal logic [72], [73]. The proof is again carried out by traversing the state space of the automaton and marking the states that satisfy the formula.

- Infinite automata methods can deal with infinite state spaces when some minimization to a finite form is possible. One example of this class are the so-called timed automata ([74]), in which a set of real-valued clocks is used to measure time. Severe restrictions are applied, in order to make this model decidable. Clocks can only be tested, started, and reset as part of the edge labels of a finite automaton. Also, clocks can only be compared against integer values and initialized to integer values. In this case, it is possible to show that only a finite set of equivalence class representatives is sufficient to represent exactly the behavior of the timed automaton ([75], [74]). McManis and Varaiya [76] introduced the notion of suspension, which extends the class of systems that can be modeled with variations of timed automata. It is then possible, in principle, to verify timing constraint satisfaction by using preemptive scheduling, which allows a low-priority process to be stopped in the middle of a computation by a high-priority one.

The main obstacles to the widespread application of finite automata-based methods are the inherent complexity of the problem, and the difficulty for designers, generally accustomed to simulation-based models, to formally model the system or its properties. The synchronous composition of automata, which is the basis of all known automata-based methods, is inherently sensitive to the number of states in the component automata, since the size of the total state space is the product of the sizes of the component state spaces.

Abstraction is the most promising technique to tackle this problem, generally known as state-space explosion. Abstraction replaces (generally requiring extensive user intervention) some system components with simpler versions, exhibiting nondeterministic behavior. Nondeterminism is used to reduce the size of the state space without losing the possibility of verifying the desired property. The basic idea is to build provably conservative approximations of the exact behavior of the system model, such that the complexity of the verification is lower, but no false positive results are possible. I.e., the verification system may say that the approximate model does not satisfy the property, while the original one did, thus requiring a better approximation, but it will never say that the approximate model satisfies the property, while the original one did not [75], [77], [78]. The quotient with respect to bisimulation can also be used in place of every component, thus providing another mechanism (without false negative results) to fight space explosion.

The systematic application of formal verification techniques since the early stages of a design may lead to a new definition of "optimal" size for a module (apart from those currently in use, that are generally related to human understanding, synthesis or compilation). A "good" leaf-level module must be small enough to admit verification, and large enough to possess interesting verifiable properties. The possibility of meaningfully applying abstraction would also determine the appropriate size and contents of modules at the upper levels of the hierarchy.

Another interesting family of formal verification techniques, useful for heterogeneous systems with multiple concurrent agents, is based on the notion of partial ordering between computations in an execution of a process network. Direct use of available concurrency information can be used during the verification process to reduce the number of explicitly explored states ([6], [51], [50]). Some such methods are based on the so-called "Mazurkiewicz traces," in which a "trace" is an equivalence class of sequences of state transitions where concurrent transitions are permuted [79], [80].

Model checking and language containment have been especially useful in verifying the correctness of protocols, which are particularly well-suited to the finite automaton model due to their relative data independence. One may claim that these two (closely related) paradigms represent about the only solutions to the specification verification problem that are currently

close to industrial applicability, thanks to:
- The development of extremely efficient *implicit* representation methods for the state space, based on Binary Decision Diagrams ([81], [69]), that do not require to represent and store every reachable state of the modeled system explicitly.
- The good degree of automation, at least of the property satisfaction or language containment checks themselves (once a suitable abstraction has been found by hand).
- The good match between the underlying semantics (state-transition objects) and the finite-state behavior of digital systems.

The verification problem becomes much more difficult when one must take into account either the actual value of data and the operations performed on them, or the timing properties of the system. The first problem can be tackled by first assuming equality of arithmetic functions with the same name used at different levels of modeling (e.g., specification and implementation, see Burch and Dill [82]) and then separately verifying that a given piece of hardware implements correctly a given arithmetic function (see Bryant [83]). The timing verification problem for sequential systems, on the other hand, still needs to be formulated in a way that permits the solution of practical problems in a reasonable amount of space and time. One possibility, proposed almost simultaneously by [84] and [85], is to incrementally add timing constraints to an initially untimed model, rather than immediately building the full-blown timed automaton. This addition should be done iteratively, to gradually eliminate all "false" violations of the desired properties due to the fact that some timing properties of the model have been ignored. The iteration can be shown to converge, but the speed of convergence still depends heavily on the ingenuity of the designer in providing "hints" to the verification system about the next timing information to consider.

As with many young technologies, optimism about verification techniques initially led to excessive claims about their potential, particularly in the area of software verification, where the term "proving programs" was broadly touted. For many reasons, including the undecidability of many verification problems and the fact that verification can only be as good as the properties the designer specifies, this optimism has been misplaced. Berry has suggested using the term "automatic bug detection" in place of "verification" to underscore that it is too much to hope for a conclusive proof of any nontrivial design. Instead, the goal of verification should be a technology that will help designers preventing problems in deployed systems.

IV. SYNTHESIS

By "synthesis," we mean broadly a stage in the design refinement where a more abstract specification is translated into a less abstract specification, as suggested in Figure 2. For embedded systems, synthesis is a combination of manual and automatic processes, and is often divided into three stages: mapping to architecture, in which the general structure of an implementation is chosen; partitioning, in which the sections of a specification are bound to the architectural units; and hardware and software synthesis, in which the details of the units are filled out.

We informally distinguish between *software synthesis* and *software compilation*, according to the type of input specification. The term software compilation is generally associated with an input specification using C- or Pascal-like imperative, generally non-concurrent, languages. These languages have a syntax and semantics that is very close to that of the implementation (assembly or executable code). In some sense, they already describe, at a fairly detailed level, the desired *implementation* of the software. We will use the term software synthesis to denote an optimized translation process from a high-level specification that describes the *function* that must be performed, rather than the way in which it must be implemented. Examples of software synthesis can be, for example, the C or assembly code generation capabilities of Digital Signal Processing graphical programming environments such as Ptolemy ([86]), of graphical FSM design environments such as StateCharts ([87]), or of synchronous programming environments such as Esterel, Lustre and Signal ([5]).

Recently, higher and higher level synthesis approaches have started to appear. One particularly promising technique for embedded systems is *supervisory control*, pioneered by Ramadge and Wonham ([88]). While most synthesis methods start from an explicit model of *how* the system that is being designed must behave, supervisory control describes *what* it must achieve. It cleverly combines a classical control system view of the world with automata-theoretic techniques, to synthesize a control algorithm that is, in some sense, optimum.

Supervisory control distinguishes between the plant (an abstraction of the physical system that must be controlled) and the controller (the embedded system that must be synthesized). Given a finite-automaton model of the plant (possibly including limitations on what a controller can do) and of the expected behavior of the complete system (plant plus controller), it is possible to determine:
- if a finite-state controller satisfying that specification exists, and
- a "best" finite-state controller, under some cost function (e.g., minimum estimated implementation cost).

Recent papers dealing with variations on this problem are, for example, [89], [90].

A. Mapping from Specification to Architecture

The problem of architecture selection and/or design is one of the key aspects of the design of embedded systems. Supporting the designer in choosing the right mix of components and implementation technologies is essential to the success of the final product, and hence of the methodology that was used to design it. Generally speaking, the mapping problem takes as input a functional specification and produces as output an architecture and an assignment of functions to architectural units.

An architecture is generally composed of:
- hardware components (e.g., microprocessors, microcontrollers, memories, I/O devices, ASICs, and FPGAs),
- software components (e.g., an operating system, device drivers, procedures, and concurrent programs), and
- interconnection media (e.g., abstract channels, busses, and shared memories).

Partitioning determines which parts of the specification will be implemented on these components, while their actual implementation will be created by software and hardware synthesis.

The cost function optimized by the mapping process includes a mixture of time, area, component cost, and power consumption, where the relative importance depends heavily on the type of application. Time cost may be measured either as execution time for an algorithm, or as missed deadlines for a soft real-time system[9]. Area cost may be measured as chip, board, or memory size. The components of the cost function may take the form of a hard constraint or a quantity to be minimized.

Current synthesis-based methods almost invariably impose some restrictions on the target architecture in order to make the mapping problem manageable. For example, the architecture may be limited to a library of pre-defined components due to vendor restrictions or interfacing constraints. Few papers have been published on automating the design of, say, a memory hierarchy or an I/O subsystem based on standard components. Notable exceptions to this rule are papers dealing with retargetable compilation (e.g., Theissinger *et al.* [91]), or with a very abstract formulation of partitioning for co-design (e.g., Kumar *et al.* [92], [93], Prakash and Parker [94], and Vahid and Gajski [95]). The structure of the application-specific hardware components, on the other hand, is generally much less constrained.

Often, the communication mechanisms are also standardized for a given methodology. Few choices, often closely tied to the communication mechanism used at the specification level, are offered to the designer. Nonetheless, some work has been done on the design of interfaces (e.g., Chou *et al.* [96]).

B. Partitioning

Partitioning is a problem with any design using more than one component. It is a particularly interesting problem in embedded systems because of the heterogeneous hardware/software mixture. Partitioning methods can be classified, as shown in Table III, according to four main characteristics:
- the specification model(s) supported,
- the granularity,
- the cost function, and
- the algorithm.

Explored algorithm classes include greedy heuristics, clustering methods, iterative improvement, and mathematical programming.

So far, there seems to be no clear winner among partitioning methods, partly due to the early stage of research in this area, and partly due to the intrinsic complexity of the problem, which seems to preclude an exact formulation with a realistic cost function in the general case.

Ernst *et al.* [110], [111], [97] use a graph-based model, with nodes corresponding to elementary operations (statements in C*, a C-like language extended with concurrency). The cost is derived:
- by profiling, aimed at discovering the bottlenecks that can be eliminated from the initial, all-software partition by moving some operations to hardware;
- by estimating the closeness between operations, including control locality (the distance in number of control nodes between activations of the same operation in the control flow graph), data locality (the number of common variables among operations), and operator closeness (the similarities, e.g., an add and a subtract are close); and
- by estimating the communication overhead incurred when blocks are moved across partitions. This is approximated by the (static) number of data items exchanged among partitions, assuming a simple memory-mapped communication mechanism between hardware and software.

Partitioning is done in two loops. The inner loop uses simulated annealing, with a quick estimation of the gain derived by moving an operation between hardware and software, to improve an initial partition. The outer loop uses synthesis to refine the estimates used in the inner loop.

Olokutun *et al.* [98] perform performance-driven partitioning working on a block-by-block basis. The specification model is a hardware description language. This allows them to use synthesis for hardware cost estimation, and profiling of a compiled-code simulator for software cost estimation. Partitioning is done together with scheduling, since the overall goal is to minimize response time in the context of using emulation to speed up simulation. An initial partition is obtained by classifying blocks according to whether or not they are synthesizable, and whether or not the communication overhead justifies a hardware implementation. This determines some blocks which must either go into software or hardware. Uncommitted blocks are assigned to hardware or software starting from the block which has most to gain from a specific choice. The initial partition is then improved by a Kernighan and Lin-like iterative swapping procedure.

Kumar *et al.* [92], [93], on the other hand, consider partitioning in a very general and abstract form. They use a complex, set-based representation of the system, its various implementation choices and the various costs associated with them. Cost attributes are determined mainly by profiling. The system being designed is represented by four sets: available software functions; hardware resources; communications between the (software and/or hardware) units; and functions to be implemented, each of which can be assigned a set of software functions, hardware resources and communications. This means that the given software runs on the given hardware and uses the given communications to implement the function. The partitioning process is followed by a decomposition of each function into virtual instruction sets, followed by design of an implementation for the set using the available resources, and followed again by an evaluation phase.

D'Ambrosio *et al.* [112], [99] tackle the problem of choosing a set of processors on which a set of cooperating tasks can be executed while meeting real-time constraints. They also use a mathematical formulation, but provide an optimal solution procedure by using branch-and-bound. The cost of a software partition is estimated as a lower and an upper bound on processor utilization. The upper bound is obtained by rate-monotonic analysis (see Liu and Layland [113]), while the lower bound is obtained by various refinements of the sum of task computation times divided by task periods. The branch-and-bound procedure uses the bounds to prune the search space, while looking for optimal assignments of functions to components, and satisfying the timing constraints. Other optimization criteria can be included beside schedulability, such as response times to tasks with soft deadlines, hardware costs, and expandability, which

---

[9] Real-time systems, and individual timing constraints within such systems, are classified as soft or hard according to whether missing a deadline just degrades the system performance or causes a catastrophic failure.

TABLE III
A COMPARISON OF PARTITIONING METHODS.

Author	Model	Granularity	Cost Function	Algorithm
Henkel [97]	CDFG (C*)	operation	profiling (SW) synthesis and similarity (HW) communication cost	hand (outer) simulated annealing (inner)
Olokutun [98]	HDL	task	profiling (SW) synthesis (HW)	Kernighan and Lin
Kumar [93]	set-based	task	profiling	mathematical programming
Hu [99]	task list	task	profiling schedule analysis	branch and bound
Vahid [95]	acyclic DFG	operation	profiling (SW) processor cost (HW) communication cost	mixed integer-linear programming
Barros (1) [100]	Unity (HDL)	operation	similarity concurruency/sequencing	clustering
Barros (2) [101]	Occam	operation hierarchy	similarity concurrenency/sequencing hierarchy	clustering
Kalavade [102]	acyclic DFG	operation	schedulability	heuristic with look-ahead
Adams [103]	HDL (?)	task	profiling (SW) synthesis (HW)	hand
Eles [104]	VHDL	task	profiling	simulated annealing
Luk [105]	Ruby (HDL)	operation hierarchy	rate matching	hand
Steinhausen [106]	CDFG (HDL, C)	operation	profiling	hand
Ben Ismail [107]	communicating processes	task	?	hand
Antoniazzi [108]	FSMs	task	?	hand
Chou [96]	timing diagram	operation	time (SW) area (HW)	min-cut
Gupta [56], [109]	CDFG (HDL)	operation	time	heuristic

favors software solutions.

Barros *et al.* [100] use a graph-based fine-grained representation, with each unit corresponding to a simple statement in the Unity specification language. They cluster units according to a variety of sometimes vague criteria: similarity between units, based on concurrency (control and data independence), sequencing (control or data dependence), mutual exclusion, and vectorization of a sequence of related assignments. They cluster the units to minimize the cost of cuts in the clustering tree, and then improve the clustering by considering pipelining opportunities, allocations done at the previous stage, and cost savings due to resource sharing.

Kalavade and Lee [102] use an acyclic dependency graph derived from a dataflow graph to simultaneously map each node (task) to software or hardware and schedule the execution of the tasks. The approach is heuristic, and can give an approximate solution to very large problem instances. To guide the search process, it uses both critical path information and the suitability of a node to hardware or software. For example, bit manipulations are better suited to hardware while random accesses to a data structure are better suited to software.

Vahid, Gajski *et al.* [95], [114] perform graph-based partitioning of a variable-grained specification. The specification language is SpecCharts, a hierarchical model in which the leaves are "states" of a hierarchical Statecharts-like finite state machine. These "states" can contain arbitrarily complex behavioral VHDL processes, written in a high-level specification style. Cost function estimation is done at the leaf level. Each level is assigned an estimated number of I/O pins, an estimated area (based on performing behavioral, RTL and logic synthesis in isolation), and an estimated execution time (obtained by simulating that initial implementation, and considering communication delay as well). The area estimate can be changed if more leaves are mapped onto the same physical entity, due to potential sharing. The cost model is attached to a graph, in which nodes represent leaves and edges represent control (activation/deactivation) and data (communication) dependencies. Classical clustering and partitioning algorithms are then applied, followed by a refinement phase. During refinement, each partition is synthesized, to get better area and timing estimates, and "peripheral" graph nodes are moved among partitions greedily to reduce the overall cost. The cost of a given partition is a simple weighted sum of area, pin, chip count, and performance constraint satisfaction measures.

Steinhausen *et al.* [106], [91], [115] describe a complete co-synthesis environment in which a CDFG representation is derived from an array of specification formats, such as Verilog, VHDL and C. The CDFG is partitioned by hand, based on the results of profiling, and then mapped onto an architecture that can include general-purpose micro-processors, ASIPs (application-specific instruction processor, software-programmable components designed ad hoc for an application), and ASICs (application-specific integrated circuits). An interesting aspect of this approach is that the architecture itself is not fixed, but synthesis is driven by a user-defined structural description. ASIC synthesis is done with a commercial tool, while software synthesis, both for general-purpose and specialized processors, is done with an existing retargetable compiler developed by Hoogerbrugge et al. [116].

Ben Ismail et al. [107] and Voss et al. [117] start from a system specification described in SDL ([118]). The specification is then translated into the Solar internal representation, based on a hierarchical interconnection of communicating processes. Processes can be merged and split, and the hierarchy can be changed by splitting, moving and clustering of subunits. The sequencing of these operations is currently done by the user.

Finally, Chou et al. [96] and Walkup and Borriello [119] describe a specialized, scheduling-based algorithm for interface partitioning. The algorithm is based on a graph model derived from a formalized timing diagram. Nodes represent low-level events in the interface specification. Edges represent constraints, and can either be derived from causality links in the specification, or be added during the partitioning process (for example to represent events that occur on the same wire, and hence should be moved together). The cost function is time for software and area for hardware. The algorithm is based on a min-cut procedure applied to the graph, in order to reduce congestion. Congestion in this case is defined as software being required to produce events more rapidly than the target processor can do, which implies the need for some hardware assistance.

C. Hardware and Software Synthesis

After partitioning (and sometimes before partitioning, in order to provide cost estimates) the hardware and software components of the embedded system must be implemented. The inputs to the problem are a specification, a set of resources and possibly a mapping onto an architecture. The objective is to realize the specification with the minimum cost.

Generally speaking, the constraints and optimization criteria for this step are the same as those used during partitioning. Area and code size must be traded off against performance, which often dominates due to the real-time characteristics of many embedded systems. Cost considerations generally suggest the use of software running on off-the-shelf processors, whenever possible. This choice, among other things, allows one to separate the software from the hardware synthesis process, relying on some form of pre-designed or customized interfacing mechanism.

One exception to this rule are authors who propose the simultaneous design of a computer architecture and of the program that must run on it (e.g., Menez et al. [120], Marwedel [121], and Wilberg et al. [115]). Since the designers of general-purpose CPUs face different problems than the designers of embedded systems, we will only consider those authors who synthesize an Application-Specific Instruction Processor (ASIP, [122]) and the micro-code that runs on it. The designer of a general-purpose CPU must worry about backward compatibility, compiler support, and optimal performance for a wide variety of applications, whereas the embedded system designer must worry about addition of new functionality in the future, user interaction, and satisfaction of a specific set of timing constraints.

Note that by using an ASIP rather than a standard Application Specific Integrated Circuit (ASIC), which generally has very limited programming capabilities, the embedded system designer can couple some of the advantages of hardware and software. For example, performance and power consumption can be improved with respect to a software implementation on a general-purpose micro-controller or DSP, while flexibility can be improved with respect to a hardware implementation. Another method to achieve the same goal is to use reprogrammable hardware, such as Field Programmable Gate Arrays. FPGAs can be reprogrammed either off-line (just like embedded software is upgraded by changing a ROM), or even on-line (to speed up the algorithm that is currently being executed).

The hardware synthesis task for ASICs used in embedded systems (whether they are implemented on FPGAs or not) is generally performed according to the classical high-level and logic synthesis methods. These techniques have been worked on extensively; for example, recent books by De Micheli [123], Devadas, Gosh and Keutzer [124], and Camposano and Wolf [125] describe them in detail. Marwedel and Goossens [126] present a good overview of code generation strategies for DSPs and ASIPs.

The software synthesis task for embedded systems, on the other hand, is a relatively new problem. Traditionally, software synthesis has been regarded with suspicion, mainly due to excessive claims made during its infancy. In fact, the problem is much more constrained for embedded systems compared to general-purpose computing. For example, embedded software often cannot use virtual memory, due to physical constraints (e.g., the absence of a swapping device), to real-time constraints, and to the need to partition the specification between software and hardware. This severely limits the applicability of dynamic task creation and memory allocation. For some highly critical applications even the use of a stack may be forbidden, and everything must be dealt with by polling and static variables. Algorithms also tend to be simpler, with a clear division into cooperating tasks, each solving one specific problem (e.g., digital filtering of a given input source, protocol handling over a channel, and so on). In particular, the problem of translating cooperating finite-state machines into software has been solved in a number of ways.

Software synthesis methods proposed in the literature can be classified, as shown in Table IV, according to the following general lines:
- the specification formalism,
- interfacing mechanisms (at the specification and the implementation levels),
- when the scheduling is done, and
- the scheduling method.

Almost all software synthesis methods perform some sort of scheduling—sequencing the execution of a set of originally concurrent tasks. Concurrent tasks are an excellent specification mechanism, but cannot be implemented as such on a standard CPU. The scheduling problem (reviewed e.g. by Halang and Stoyenko [127]) amounts to finding a linear execution order for the elementary operations composing the tasks, so that all the timing constraints are satisfied. Depending on how and when this linearization is performed, scheduling algorithms can be classified as:

- Static, where all scheduling decisions are made at design- or compile-time.
- Quasi-static, where some scheduling decisions are made at run-time, some at compile-time.
- Dynamic, where all decision are made at run-time.

Dynamic schedulers take many forms, but in particular they are distinguished as preemptive or non-preemptive, depending on whether a task can be interrupted at arbitrary points. For embedded systems, there are compelling motivations for using static or quasi-static scheduling, or at least for minimizing preemptive scheduling in order to minimize scheduling overhead and to improve reliability and predictability. There are, of course, cases in which preemption cannot be avoided, because it is the only feasible solution to the problem instance ([127]), but such cases should be carefully analyzed to limit preemption to a minimum.

Many static scheduling methods have been developed. Most somehow construct a precedence graph and then apply or adapt classical methods. We refer the reader to Bhattacharyya *et al.* [32] and Sih and Lee [128], [129] as a starting point for scheduling of dataflow graphs.

Many approaches to software synthesis for embedded systems divide the computation into cooperating tasks that are scheduled at run time. This scheduling can be done

1. either by using classical scheduling algorithms,
2. or by developing new techniques based on a better knowledge of the domain. Embedded systems with fairly restricted specification paradigms are an easier target for specialized scheduling techniques than fully general algorithms written in an arbitrary high-level language.

The former approach uses, for example, Rate Monotonic Analysis (RMA [113]) to perform schedulability analysis. In the pure RMA model, tasks are invoked periodically, can be preempted, have deadlines equal to their invocation period, and system overhead (context switching, interrupt response time, and so on) is negligible. The basic result by Liu and Layland states that under these hypotheses, if a given set of tasks can be successfully scheduled by a static priority algorithm, then it can be successfully scheduled by sorting tasks by invocation period, with the highest priority given to the task with the shortest period.

The basic RMA model must be augmented to be practical. Several results from the real-time scheduling literature can be used to develop a scheduling environment supporting process synchronization, interrupt service routines, context switching time, deadlines different from the task invocation period, mode changes (which may cause a change in the number and/or deadlines of tasks), and parallel processors. Parallel processor support generally consists of analyzing the schedulability of a given assignment of tasks to processors, providing the designer with feedback about potential bottlenecks and sources of deadlocks.

Chou *et al.* [96] advocate developing new techniques based on a better knowledge of the domain. The problem they consider is to find a valid schedule of processes specified in Verilog under given timing constraints. This approach, like that of Gupta et al. described below, and unlike classical task-based scheduling methods, can take into account both fine-grained and coarse-grained timing constraints. The specification style chosen by the authors uses Verilog constructs that provide structured concurrency with watchdog-style preemption. In this style, multiple computation branches are started in parallel, and some of them (the watchdogs) can "kill" others upon occurrence of a given condition. A set of "safe recovery points" is defined for each branch, and preemption is allowed only at those points. Timing constraints are specified by using modes, which represent different "states" for the computation as in SpecCharts, e.g., initialization, normal operation and error recovery. Constraints on the minimum and maximum time separation between events (even of the same type, to describe occurrence rates) can be defined either within a mode or among events in different modes. Scheduling is performed within each mode by finding a cyclic order of operations which preserves I/O rates and timing constraints. Each mode is transformed into an acyclic partial order by unrolling, and possibly splitting (if it contains parallel loops with harmonically unrelated repetition counts). Then the partial order is linearized by using a longest-path algorithm to check feasibility and assign start times to the operations.

The same group describes in [132] a technique for device driver synthesis, targeted towards microcontrollers with specialized I/O ports. It takes as input a specification of the system to be implemented, a description of the function and structure of each I/O port (a list of bits and directions), and a list of communication instructions. It can also exploit specialized functions such as parallel/serial and serial/ parallel conversion capabilities. The algorithm assigns communications in the specification to physical entities in the micro-controller. It first tries to use special functions, then assigns I/O ports, and finally resorts to the more expensive memory-mapped I/O for overflow communications. It takes into account resource conflicts (e.g. among different bits of the same port), and allocates hardware components to support memory-mapped I/O. The output of the algorithm is a netlist of hardware components, initialization routines and I/O driver routines that can be called by the software generation procedure whenever a communication between software and hardware must take place.

Gupta *et al.* [56], [109] started their work on software synthesis and scheduling by analyzing various implementation techniques for embedded software. Their specification model is a set of threads, extracted from a Control and DataFlow Graph (CDFG) derived from a C-like HDL called Hardware-C. Threads are concurrent loop-free routines, which invoke each other as a basic synchronization mechanism. Statements within a thread are scheduled statically, at compile-time, while threads are scheduled dynamically, at run-time. By using a concurrent language rather than C, the translation problem becomes easier, and the authors can concentrate on the scheduling problem, to simulate the concurrency of threads. The authors compare the inherent advantages and disadvantages of two main techniques to implement threads: coroutines and a single case statement (in which each branch implements a thread). The coroutine-based approach is more flexible (coroutines can be nested, e.g. to respond to urgent interrupts), but more expensive (due to the need to switch context) than the case-based approach.

The same group developed in [133] a scheduling method for reactive real-time systems. The cost model takes into account the processor type, the memory model, and the instruction exe-

TABLE IV
A COMPARISON OF SOFTWARE SCHEDULING METHODS.

Author	Model	Interface	Constraint Granularity	Scheduling Algorithm
Cochran [130]	task list	none	task	RMA (runtime)
Chou [96]	task list	synthesized	task operation	heuristic (static)
Gupta [109]	CDFG	?	operation	heuristic with look-head (static+runtime)
Chiodo [131]	task list	synthesized	task	RMA (runtime)
Menez [120]	CDFG	?	operation	exhaustive

cution time. The latter is derived bottom-up from the CDFG by assigning a processor and memory-dependent cost to each leaf operation in the CDFG. Some operations have an unbounded execution time, because they are either data-dependent loops or synchronization (I/O) operations. Timing constraints are basically data rate constraints on externally visible Input/Output operations. Bounded-time operations within a process are linearized by a heuristic method (the problem is known to be NP-complete). The linearization procedure selects the next operation to be executed among those whose predecessors have all been scheduled, according to: whether or not their immediate selection for scheduling can cause some timing constraint to be missed, and a measure of "urgency" that performs some limited timing constraint lookahead. Unbounded-time operations, on the other hand, are implemented by a call to the runtime scheduler, which may cause a context switch in favor of another more urgent thread.

Chiodo et al. [134] also propose a software synthesis method from extended asynchronous Finite State Machines (called Co-design Finite State Machines, CFSMs). The method takes advantage of optimization techniques from the hardware synthesis domain. It uses a model based on multiple asynchronously communicating CFSMs, rather than a single FSM, enabling it to handle systems with widely varying data rates and response time requirements. Tasks are organized with different priority levels, and scheduled according to classical run-time algorithms like RMA. The software synthesis technique is based on a very simple CDFG, representing the state transition and output functions of the CFSM. The nodes of the CDFG can only be of two types: TEST nodes, which evaluate an expression and branch according to its result, and ASSIGN nodes, which evaluate an expression and assign its result to a variable. The authors develop a mapping from a representations of the state transition and output functions using Binary Decision Diagrams ([81]) to the CDFG form, and can thus use a body of well-developed optimization techniques to minimize memory occupation and/or execution time. The simple CDFG form permits also an easy and relatively accurate prediction of software cost and performance, based on cost assignment to each CDFG node ([135]). The cost (code and data memory occupation) and performance (clock cycles) of each node type can be evaluated with a good degree of accuracy, based on a handful of system-specific parameters (e.g., the cost of a variable assignment, of an addition, of a branch). These parameters can be derived by compiling and running a few carefully designed benchmarks on the target processor, or on a cycle-accurate emulator or simulator.

Liem et al. [64] tackle a very different problem, that of retargetable compilation for a generic processor architecture. They focus their optimization techniques towards highly asymmetric processors, such as commercial Digital Signal Processors (in which, for example, one register may only be used for multiplication, another one only for memory addressing, and so on). Their register assignment scheme is based on the notion of classes of registers, describing which type of operation can use which register. This information is used during CDFG covering with processor instructions [136] to minimize the number of moves required to save registers into temporary locations.

Marwedel [121] also uses a similar CDFG covering approach. The source specification can be written in VHDL or in the Pascal-like language Mimola. The purpose is micro-code generation for Very Long Instruction Word (VLIW) processors, and in this case the instruction set has not been defined yet. Rather, a minimum encoding of the control word is generated for each control step. Control steps are allocated using an As Soon As Possible policy (ASAP, meaning that each micro-operation is scheduled to occur as soon as its operands have been computed, compatibly with resource utilization conflicts). The control word contains all the bits necessary to steer the execution units in the specified architecture to perform all the micro-operations in each step. Register allocation is done in order to minimize the number of temporary locations in memory due to register spills.

Tiwari et al. [137] describe a software analysis (rather than synthesis) method aimed at estimating the power consumption of a program on a given processor. Their power consumption model is based on the analysis of single instructions, addressing modes, and instruction pairs (a simple way of modeling the effect of the processor state). The model is evaluated by running benchmark programs for each of these characteristics, and measuring the current flow to and from the power and ground pins.

V. CONCLUSIONS

In this paper we outlined some important aspects of the design process for embedded systems, including specification models and languages, simulation, formal verification, partitioning and hardware and software synthesis.

The design process is iterative—a design is transformed from an informal description into a detailed specification usable for manufacturing. The specification problem is concerned with the representation of the design at each of these steps; the validation problem is to check that the representation is consistent both within a step and between steps; and the synthesis problem is to transform the design between steps.

We argued that formal models are necessary at each step of

a design, and that there is a distinction between the language in which the design is specified and its underlying model of computation. Many models of computation have been defined, due not just to the immaturity of the field but also to fundamental differences: the best model is a function of the design. The heterogeneous nature of most embedded systems makes multiple models of computation a necessity. Many models of computation are built by combining three largely orthogonal aspects: sequential behavior, concurrency, and communication.

We presented an outline of the tagged-signal model [8], a framework developed by two of the authors to contrast different models of computation. The fundamental entity in the model is an event (a value/tag pair). Tags usually denote temporal behavior, and different models of time appear as structure imposed on the set of all possible tags. Processes appear as relations between signals (sets of events). The character of such a relation follows from the type of process it describes.

Simulation and formal verification are two key validation techniques. Most embedded systems contain both hardware and software components, and it is a challenge to efficiently simulate both components simultaneously. Using separate simulators for each is often more efficient, but synchronization becomes a challenge.

Formal verification can be roughly divided into theorem proving methods, finite automata methods, and infinite automata methods. Theorem provers generally assist designers in constructing a proof, rather than being fully automatic, but are able to deal with very powerful languages. Finite-automata schemes represent (either explicitly or implicitly) all states of the system and check properties on this representation. Infinite-automata schemes usually build finite partitions of the state space, often by severely restricting the input language.

In this paper, synthesis refers to a step in the design refinement process where the design representation is made more detailed. This can be manual and/or automated, and is often divided into mapping to architecture, partitioning, and component synthesis. Automated architecture mapping, where the overall system structure is defined, often restricts the result to make the problem manageable. Partitioning, where sections of the design are bound to different parts of the system architecture, is particularly challenging for embedded systems because of the elaborate cost functions due to their heterogeneity. Assigning an execution order to concurrent modules, and finding a sequence of instructions implementing a functional module are the primary challenges in software synthesis for embedded systems.

VI. ACKNOWLEDGEMENTS

Edwards and Lee participated in this study as part of the Ptolemy project, which is supported by the Advanced Research Projects Agency and the U.S. Air Force (under the RASSP program, contract F33615-93-C-1317), the State of California MICRO program, and the following companies: Cadence, Dolby, Hitachi, LG Electronics, Mitsubishi, Motorola, NEC, Philips, and Rockwell. Lavagno and Sangiovanni-Vincentelli were partially supported by grants from Cadence, Magneti Marelli, Daimler-Benz, Hitachi, Consiglio Nazionale delle Ricerche, the MICRO program, and SRC. We also thank Harry Hsieh for his help with a first draft of this work.

REFERENCES

[1] G. Berry, *Information Processing*, vol. 89, chapter Real Time programming: Special purpose or general purpose languages, pp. 11–17, North Holland-Elsevier Science Publishers, 1989.

[2] R. Milner, M. Tofte, and R. Harper, *The definition of Standard ML*, MIT Press, 1990.

[3] W. Wadge and E.A. Ashcroft, *Lucid, the dataflow programming language*, Academic Press, 1985.

[4] A. Davie, *An introduction to functional programming systems using Haskell*, Cambridge University Press, 1992.

[5] N. Halbwachs, *Synchronous Programming of Reactive Systems*, Kluwer Academic Publishers, 1993.

[6] K. McMillan, *Symbolic model checking*, Kluwer Academic, 1993.

[7] J. E. Stoy, *Denotational Semantics: The Scott-Strachey Approach to Programming Language Theory*, The MIT Press, Cambridge, MA, 1977.

[8] E. A. Lee and A. Sangiovanni-Vincentelli, "The tagged signal model - a preliminary version of a denotational framework for comparing models of computation," Tech. Rep., Electronics Research Laboratory, University of California, Berkeley, CA 94720, May 1996.

[9] J. E. Hopcroft and J. D. Ullman, *Introduction to Automata Theory, Languages, and Computation*, Addison-Wesley, 1979.

[10] J. T. Buck, *Scheduling Dynamic Dataflow Graphs with Bounded Memory Using the Token Flow Model*, Ph.D. thesis, University of California, Berkeley, 1993, Dept. of EECS, Tech. Report UCB/ERL 93/69.

[11] T. M. Parks, *Bounded Scheduling of Process Networks*, Ph.D. thesis, University of California, Berkeley, Dec. 1995, Dept. of EECS, Tech. Report UCB/ERL 95/105.

[12] J.C. Shepherdson and H. E. Sturgis, "Computability of recursive functions," *Journal of the ACM*, vol. 10, no. 2, pp. 217–255, 1963.

[13] G. Kahn, "The semantics of a simple language for parallel programming," in *Proc. of the IFIP Congress 74*. 1974, North-Holland Publishing Co.

[14] J. T. Buck, S. Ha, E. A. Lee, and D. G. Messerschmitt, "Ptolemy: A framework for simulating and prototyping heterogeneous systems," *Int. Journal of Computer Simulation*, vol. 4, no. 155, pp. 155–182, Apr. 1994. Special issue on simulation software development. http://ptolemy.eecs.berkeley.edu/papers/JEurSim.ps.Z.

[15] D. Harel, H. Lachover, A. Naamad, A. Pnueli, M. Politi, R. Sherman, A. Shtull-Trauring, and M. Trakhtenbrot, "Statemate: A working environment for the development of complex reactive systems," *IEEE Trans. on Software Engineering*, vol. 16, no. 4, Apr. 1990.

[16] D. Drusinski and D. Harel, "On the power of bounded concurrency. I. Finite automata," *Journal of the Association for Computing Machinery*, vol. 41, no. 3, pp. 517–539, May 1994.

[17] M. von der Beeck, "A comparison of statecharts variants," in *Proc. of Formal Techniques in Real Time and Fault Tolerant Systems*. 1994, vol. 863 of *LNCS*, pp. 128–148, Springer-Verlag.

[18] W. Takach and A. Wolf, "An automaton model for scheduling constraints in synchronous machines," *IEEE Tr. on Computers*, vol. 44, no. 1, pp. 1–12, Jan. 1995.

[19] M. Chiodo, P. Giusto, H. Hsieh, A. Jurecska, L. Lavagno, and A. Sangiovanni-Vincentelli, "A formal methodology for hardware/software codesign of embedded systems," *IEEE Micro*, Aug. 1994.

[20] W.-T. Chang, A. Kalavade, and E. A. Lee, "Effective heterogeneous design and cosimulation," in *NATO Advanced Study Institute Workshop on Hardware/Software Codesign*, Lake Como, Italy, June 1995, http://ptolemy.eecs.berkeley.edu/papers/effective.

[21] Jr C. N. Coelho and G. De Micheli, "Analysis and synthesis of concurrent digital circuits using control-flow expressions," *IEEE Trans. on CAD*, vol. 15, no. 8, pp. 854–876, Aug. 1996.

[22] A. Benveniste and G. Berry, "The synchronous approach to reactive and real-time systems," *Proc. of the IEEE*, vol. 79, no. 9, pp. 1270–1282, 1991.

[23] F. Boussinot and R. De Simone, "The ESTEREL language," *Proc. of the IEEE*, vol. 79, no. 9, 1991.

[24] N. Halbwachs, P. Caspi, P. Raymond, and D. Pilaud, "The synchronous data flow programming language LUSTRE," *Proc. of the IEEE*, vol. 79, no. 9, pp. 1305–1319, 1991.

[25] A. Benveniste and P. Le Guernic, "Hybrid dynamical systems theory and the SIGNAL language," *IEEE Transactions on Automatic Control*, vol. 35, no. 5, pp. 525–546, May 1990.

[26] F. Maraninchi, "The Argos language: Graphical representation of automata and description of reactive systems," in *Proc. of the IEEE Workshop on Visual Languages*, Kobe, Japan, Oct. 1991.

[27] D. Harel, "Statecharts: A visual formalism for complex systems," *Sci. Comput. Program.*, vol. 8, pp. 231–274, 1987.

[28] G. Berry, "A hardware implementation of pure Esterel," in *Proc. of the Int. Workshop on Formal Methods in VLSI Design*, Jan. 1991.

[29] F. Rocheteau and N. Halbwachs, "Implementing reactive programs on circuits: A hardware implementation of LUSTRE," in *Real-Time, Theory in Practice, REX Workshop Proceedings*, Mook, Netherlands, June 1992, vol. 600 of *LNCS*, pp. 195–208, Springer-Verlag.

[30] T. R. Shiple, G. Berry, and H. Touati, "Constructive analysis of cyclic circuits," in *Proc. of the European Design and Test Conference*, Mar. 1996.

[31] E. A. Lee and T. M. Parks, "Dataflow process networks," *Proc. of the IEEE*, May 1995, http://ptolemy.eecs.berkeley.edu/papers/processNets.

[32] S. S. Bhattacharyya, P. K. Murthy, and E. A. Lee, *Software Synthesis from Dataflow Graphs*, Kluwer Academic Press, Norwood, Mass, 1996.

[33] W.-T. Chang, S.-H. Ha, and E. A. Lee, "Heterogeneous simulation - mixing discrete-event models with dataflow," *J. on VLSI Signal Processing*, 1996, to appear.

[34] R. M. Karp and R. E. Miller, "Properties of a model for parallel computations: Determinacy, termination, queueing," *SIAM Journal*, vol. 14, pp. 1390–1411, Nov. 1966.

[35] E. A. Lee and D. G. Messerschmitt, "Synchronous data flow," *IEEE Proceedings*, Sept. 1987.

[36] R. Lauwereins, P. Wauters, M. Adé, and J. A. Peperstraete, "Geometric parallelism and cyclostatic dataflow in GRAPE-II," in *Proc. 5th Int. Workshop on Rapid System Prototyping*, Grenoble, France, June 1994.

[37] G. Bilsen, M. Engels, R. Lauwereins, and J. A. Peperstraete, "Static scheduling of multi-rate and cyclo-static DSP applications," in *Proc. 1994 Workshop on VLSI Signal Processing*. 1994, IEEE Press.

[38] D. J. Kaplan et al., "Processing graph method specification version 1.0," The Naval Research Laboratory, Washington D.C., Dec. 1987.

[39] R. Jagannathan, "Parallel execution of GLU programs," in *2nd Int. Workshop on Dataflow Computing*, Hamilton Island, Queensland, Australia, May 1992.

[40] W. B. Ackerman, "Data flow languages," *Computer*, vol. 15, no. 2, 1982.

[41] N. Carriero and D. Gelernter, "Linda in context," *Comm. of the ACM*, vol. 32, no. 4, pp. 444–458, Apr. 1989.

[42] F. Commoner and A. W. Holt, "Marked directed graphs," *Journal of Computer and System Sciences*, vol. 5, pp. 511–523, 1971.

[43] P. A. Suhler, J. Biswas, K. M. Korner, and J. C. Browne, "Tdfl: A task-level dataflow language," *J. on Parallel and Distributed Systems*, vol. 9, no. 2, June 1990.

[44] Arvind and K. P. Gostelow, "The U-Interpreter," *Computer*, vol. 15, no. 2, 1982.

[45] J. Rasure and C. S. Williams, "An integrated visual language and software development environment," *Journal of Visual Languages and Computing*, vol. 2, pp. 217–246, 1991.

[46] C. A. R. Hoare, "Communicating sequential processes," *Comm. of the ACM*, vol. 21, no. 8, 1978.

[47] R. Milner, *Communication and Concurrency*, Prentice-Hall, Englewood Cliffs, NJ, 1989.

[48] J. L. Peterson, *Petri Net Theory and the Modeling of Systems*, Prentice-Hall Inc., Englewood Cliffs, NJ, 1981.

[49] W. Reisig, *Petri Nets: An Introduction*, Springer-Verlag, 1985.

[50] A. Valmari, "A stubborn attack on state explosion," *Formal Methods in System Design*, vol. 1, no. 4, pp. 297–322, 1992.

[51] P. Godefroid, "Using partial orders to improve automatic verification methods," in *Proc. of the Computer Aided Verification Workshop*, E.M Clarke and R.P. Kurshan, Eds., 1990, DIMACS Series in Discrete Mathematica and Theoretical Computer Science, 1991, pages 321-340.

[52] E. Dijkstra, "Cooperating sequential processes," in *Programming Languages*, E. F. Genuys, Ed. Academic Press, New York, 1968.

[53] R. P. Kurshan, *Automata-Theoretic Verification of Coordinating Processes*, Princeton University Press, 1994.

[54] J. Burch, E. Clarke, K. McMillan, and D. Dill, "Sequential circuit verification using symbolic model checking," in *Proc. of the Design Automation Conf.*, 1990, pp. 46–51.

[55] R. Alur and T.A. Henzinger, "Logics and models of real time: A survey," in *Real-Time: Theory in Practice. REX Workshop Proc.*, J.W. de Bakker, C. Huizing, W.P. de Roever, and G. Rozenberg, Eds., 1992.

[56] R. K. Gupta, C. N. Coelho Jr., and G. De Micheli, "Synthesis and simulation of digital systems containing interacting hardware and software components," in *Proc. of the Design Automation Conf.*, June 1992.

[57] J. Rowson, "Hardware/software co-simulation," in *Proc. of the Design Automation Conf.*, 1994, pp. 439–440.

[58] J. Wilson, "Hardware/software selected cycle solution," in *Proc. of the Int. Workshop on Hardware-Software Codesign*, 1994.

[59] D.E. Thomas, J.K. Adams, and H. Schmitt, "A model and methodology for hardware-software codesign," *IEEE Design and Test of Computers*, vol. 10, no. 3, pp. 6–15, Sept. 1993.

[60] K. ten Hagen and H. Meyr, "Timed and untimed hardware/software cosimulation: application and efficient implementation," in *Proc. of the Int. Workshop on Hardware-Software Codesign*, Oct. 1993.

[61] A. Kalavade and E. A. Lee, "Hardware/software co-design using Ptolemy – a case study," in *Proc. of the Int. Workshop on Hardware-Software Codesign*, Sept. 1992.

[62] S. Sutarwala and P. Paulin, "Flexible modeling environment for embedded systems design," in *Proc. of the Int. Workshop on Hardware-Software Codesign*, 1994.

[63] S. Lee and J.M. Rabaey, "A hardware-software co-simulation environment," in *Proc. of the Int. Workshop on Hardware-Software Codesign*, Oct. 1993.

[64] C. Liem, T. May, and P. Paulin, "Register assignment through resource classification for ASIP microcode generation," in *Proc. of the Int. Conf. on Computer-Aided Design*, Nov. 1994.

[65] D.L. Dill, *Trace Theory for Automatic Hierarchical Verification of Speed-Independent Circuits*, The MIT Press, Cambridge, Mass., 1988, An ACM Distinguished Dissertation 1988.

[66] M.J.C. Gordon and T.F. Melham, Eds., *Introduction to HOL: a theorem proving environment for higher order logic*, Cambridge University Press, 1992.

[67] R.S. Boyer, M. Kaufmann, and J.S. Moore, "The Boyer-Moore theorem prover and its interactive enhancement," *Computers & Mathematics with Applications*, pp. 27–62, Jan. 1995.

[68] S. Owre, J.M. Rushby, and N. Shankar, "PVS: a prototype verification system," in *11th Int. Conf. on Automated Deduction*. June 1992, Springer-Verlag.

[69] O. Coudert, C. Berthet, and J. C. Madre, "Verification of Sequential Machines Using Boolean Functional Vectors," in *IMEC-IFIP Int'l Workshop on Applied Formal Methods for Correct VLSI Design*, November 1989, pp. 111–128.

[70] E. M. Clarke, E. A. Emerson, and A. P. Sistla, "Automatic verification of finite-state concurrent systems using temporal logic specifications," *ACM TOPLAS*, vol. 8, no. 2, 1986.

[71] J. P. Queille and J. Sifakis, "Specification and verification of concurrent systems in Cesar," in *Int. Symposium on Programming*. April 1982, LNCS 137, Springer Verlag.

[72] A. Pnueli, "The temporal logics of programs," in *Proc. of the 18th Annual Symposium on Foundations of Computer Science*. May 1977, IEEE Press.

[73] Z. Manna and A. Pnueli, *The temporal logic of reactive and concurrent systems*, Springer-Verlag, 1992.

[74] R. Alur and D. Dill, "Automata for Modeling Real-Time Systems," in *Automata, Languages and Programming: 17th Annual Colloquium*, 1990, vol. 443 of *Lecture Notes in Computer Science*, pp. 322–335, Warwick University, July 16-20.

[75] P. Cousot and R. Cousot, "Abstract interpretation: a unified lattice model for static analysis of programs by construction or approximation of fixpoints," in *4th ACM Symp. on Principles of Programming Languages*, Los Angeles, January 1977.

[76] J. McManis and P. Varaiya, "Suspension automata: a decidable class of hybrid automata," in *Proc. of the Sixth Workshop on Computer-Aided Verification*, 1994, pp. 105–117.

[77] J. R. Burch, *Automatic Symbolic Verification of Real-Time Concurrent Systems*, Ph.D. thesis, Carnegie Mellon University, Aug. 1992.

[78] E. Clarke, O. Grumberg, and D. Long, "Model checking and abstraction," *ACM Trans. on Programming Languages and Systems*, vol. 16, no. 5, pp. 1512–1542, Sept. 1994.

[79] A. Mazurkiewicz, "Traces, histories, graphs: Instances of a process monoid," in *Proc. Conf. on Mathematical Foundations of Computer Science*, M. P. Chytil and V. Koubek, Eds. 1984, vol. 176 of *LNCS*, Springer-Verlag.

[80] M. L. de Souza and R. de Simone, "Using partial orders for verifying behavioral equivalences," in *Proc. of CONCUR '95*, 1995.

[81] R. Bryant, "Graph-based algorithms for boolean function manipulation," *IEEE Trans. on Computers*, vol. C-35, no. 8, pp. 677–691, August 1986.

[82] J.R. Burch and D.L. Dill, "Automatic verification of pipelined microprocessor control," in *Proc. of the Sixth Workshop on Computer-Aided Verification*, 1994, pp. 68–80.

[83] R.E. Bryant and Y-A Chen, "Verification of arithmetic circuits with Binary Moment Diagrams," in *Proc. of the Design Automation Conf.*, 1995, pp. 535–541.

[84] F. Balarin and A. Sangiovanni-Vincentelli, "A verification strategy for timing-constrained systems," in *Proc. of the Fourth Workshop on Computer-Aided Verification*, 1992, pp. 148–163.

[85] R. Alur, A. Itai, R. Kurshan, and M. Yannakakis, "Timing verification by successive approximation," in *Proc. of the Computer Aided Verification Workshop*, 1993, pp. 137–150.

[86] J. Buck, S. Ha, E.A. Lee, and D.G. Masserschmitt, "Ptolemy: a framework for simulating and prototyping heterogeneous systems," *Interntional Journal of Computer Simulation*, vol. special issue on Simulation Software Development, January 1990.

[87] D. Harel, H. Lachover, A. Naamad, A. Pnueli, et al., "STATEMATE: a working environment for the development of complex reactive systems," *IEEE Trans. on Software Engineering*, vol. 16, no. 4, Apr. 1990.

[88] P. J. Ramadge and W. M. Wonham, "The control of discrete event systems," *Proc. of the IEEE*, vol. 77, no. 1, January 1989.

[89] G. Hoffmann and H. Wong-Toi, "Symbolic synthesis of supervisory controllers," in *American Control Conference, Chicago*, June 1992.

[90] M. Di Benedetto, A. Saldanha, and A. Sangiovanni-Vincentelli, "Strong model matching for finite state machines," in *Proc. of the Third European Control Conf.*, Sept. 1995.

[91] M. Theissinger, P. Stravers, and H. Veit, "CASTLE: an interactive environment for hardware-software co-design," in *Proc. of the Int. Workshop on Hardware-Software Codesign*, 1994.

[92] S. Kumar, J. H. Aylor, B. W. Johnson, and W. A. Wulf, "A framework for hardware/software codesign," in *Proc. of the Int. Workshop on Hardware-Software Codesign*, Sept. 1992.

[93] S. Kumar, J. H. Aylor, B. Johnson, and W. Wulf, "Exploring hardware/software abstractions and alternatives for codesign," in *Proc. of the Int. Workshop on Hardware-Software Codesign*, Oct. 1993.

[94] S. Prakash and A. Parker, "Synthesis of application-specific multiprocessor architectures," in *Proc. of the Design Automation Conf.*, June 1991.

[95] F. Vahid and D. G. Gajski, "Specification partitioning for system design," in *Proc. of the Design Automation Conf.*, June 1992.

[96] P. Chou, E.A. Walkup, and G. Borriello, "Scheduling for reactive real-time systems," *IEEE Micro*, vol. 14, no. 4, pp. 37–47, Aug. 1994.

[97] J. Henkel, R. Ernst, U. Holtmann, and T. Benner, "Adaptation of partitioning and high-level synthesis in hardware/software co-synthesis," in *Proc. of the Int. Conf. on Computer-Aided Design*, Nov. 1994.

[98] K. Olokutun, R. Helaihel, J. Levitt, and R. Ramirez, "A software-hardware cosynthesis approach to digital system simulation," *IEEE Micro*, vol. 14, no. 4, pp. 48–58, Aug. 1994.

[99] X. Hu, J.G. D'Ambrosio, B. T. Murray, and D-L Tang, "Codesign of architectures for powertrain modules," *IEEE Micro*, vol. 14, no. 4, pp. 48–58, Aug. 1994.

[100] E. Barros, W. Rosenstiel, and X. Xiong, "Hardware/software partitioning with UNITY," in *Proc. of the Int. Workshop on Hardware-Software Codesign*, Oct. 1993.

[101] E. Barros and A. Sampaio, "Towards provably correct hardware/software partitioning using OCCAM," in *Proc. of the Int. Workshop on Hardware-Software Codesign*, Oct. 1994.

[102] A. Kalavade and E.A. Lee, "A global criticality/local phase driven algorithm for the constrained hardware/software partitioning problem," in *Proc. of the Int. Workshop on Hardware-Software Codesign*, 1994.

[103] J.K. Adams, H. Schmitt, and D.E. Thomas, "A model and methodology for hardware-software codesign," in *Proc. of the Int. Workshop on Hardware-Software Codesign*, Oct. 1993.

[104] P. Eles, Z. Peng, and A. Doboli, "VHDL system-level specification and partitioning in a hardware/software cosynthesis environment," in *Proc. of the Int. Workshop on Hardware-Software Codesign*, Sept. 1994.

[105] W. Luk and T. Wu, "Towards a declarative framework for hardware-software codesign," in *Proc. of the Int. Workshop on Hardware-Software Codesign*, 1994.

[106] U. Steinhausen, R. Camposano, H Gunther, P. Ploger, M. Theissinger, et al., "System-synthesis using hardware/software codesign," in *Proc. of the Int. Workshop on Hardware-Software Codesign*, Oct. 1993.

[107] T.B. Ismail, M. Abid, and A.A. Jerraya, "COSMOS: a codesign approach for communicating systems," in *Proc. of the Int. Workshop on Hardware-Software Codesign*, 1994.

[108] S. Antoniazzi, A. Balboni, W. Fornaciari, and D. Sciuto, "A methodology for control-dominated systems codesign," in *Proc. of the Int. Workshop on Hardware-Software Codesign*, 1994.

[109] R. K. Gupta, C. N. Coelho Jr., and G. De Micheli, "Program implementation schemes for hardware-software systems," *IEEE Computer*, pp. 48–55, Jan. 1994.

[110] R. Ernst and J. Henkel, "Hardware-software codesign of embedded controllers based on hardware extraction," in *Proc. of the Int. Workshop on Hardware-Software Codesign*, Sept. 1992.

[111] J. Henkel, T. Benner, and R. Ernst, "Hardware generation and partitioning effects in the COSYMA system," in *Proc. of the Int. Workshop on Hardware-Software Codesign*, Oct. 1993.

[112] J.G. D'Ambrosio and X.B. Hu, "Configuration-level hardware/software partitioning for real-time embedded systems," in *Proc. of the Int. Workshop on Hardware-Software Codesign*, 1994.

[113] C. Liu and J.W Layland, "Scheduling algorithms for multiprogramming in a hard real-time environment," *Journal of the ACM*, vol. 20, no. 1, pp. 44–61, Jan. 1973.

[114] D. D. Gajski, S. Narayan, L. Ramachandran, and F. Vahid, "System design methodologies: aiming at the 100 h design cycle," *IEEE Trans. on VLSI*, vol. 4, no. 1, Mar. 1996.

[115] J. Wilberg, R. Camposano, and W. Rosenstiel, "Design flow for hardware/software cosynthesis of a video compression system," in *Proc. of the Int. Workshop on Hardware-Software Codesign*, 1994.

[116] J. Hoogerbrugge and H. Corporaal, "Transport-triggering vs. operation-triggering," in *5th Int. Conf. on Compiler Construction*, Apr. 1994.

[117] M. Voss, T. Ben Ismail, A.A. Jerraya, and K-H. Kapp, "Towards a theory for hardware-software codesign," in *Proc. of the Int. Workshop on Hardware-Software Codesign*, 1994.

[118] S. Saracco, J. R. W. Smith, and R. Reed, *Telecommunications Systems Engineering Using SDL*, North-Holland - Elsevier, 1989.

[119] E. Walkup and G. Borriello, "Automatic synthesis of device drivers for hardware-software codesign," in *Proc. of the Int. Workshop on Hardware-Software Codesign*, Oct. 1993.

[120] G. Menez, M. Auguin, F Boèri, and C. Carrière, "A partitioning algorithm for system-level synthesis," in *Proc. of the Int. Conf. on Computer-Aided Design*, Nov. 1992.

[121] P. Marwedel, "Tree-based mapping of algorithms to predefined structures," in *Proc. of the Int. Conf. on Computer-Aided Design*, Nov. 1993.

[122] P. Paulin, "DSP design tool requirements for embedded systems: a telecommunications industrial perspective," *Journal of VLSI Signal Processing*, vol. 9, no. 1-2, pp. 22–47, Jan. 1995.

[123] G. De Micheli, *Synthesis and optimization of digital circuits*, McGraw-Hill, 1994.

[124] S. Devadas, A. Ghosh, and K. Keutzer, *Logic synthesis*, McGraw-Hill, 1994.

[125] R. Camposano and W. Wolf, Eds., *High-level VLSI synthesis*, Kluwer Academic Publishers, 1991.

[126] P. Marwedel and G. Goossens, Eds., *Code generation for embedded processors*, Kluwer Academic Publishers, 1995.

[127] W.A. Halang and A.D. Stoyenko, *Constructing predictable real time systems*, Kluwer Academic Publishers, 1991.

[128] G. C. Sih and E. A. Lee, "Declustering: A new multiprocessor scheduling technique," *IEEE Trans. on Parallel and Distributed Systems*, vol. 4, no. 6, pp. 625–637, June 1993.

[129] G. C. Sih and E. A. Lee, "A compile-time scheduling heuristic for interconnection-constrained heterogeneous processor architectures," *IEEE Trans. on Parallel and Distributed Systems*, vol. 4, no. 2, Feb. 1993.

[130] M. Cochran, "Using the rate monotonic analysis to analyze the schedulability of ADARTS real-time software designs," in *Proc. of the Int. Workshop on Hardware-Software Codesign*, Sept. 1992.

[131] M. Chiodo, P. Giusto, H. Hsieh, A. Jurecska, L. Lavagno, and A. Sangiovanni-Vincentelli, "Hardware/software codesign of embedded systems," *IEEE Micro*, vol. 14, no. 4, pp. 26–36, Aug. 1994.

[132] P. Chou and G. Borriello, "Software scheduling in the co-synthesis of reactive real-time systems," in *Proc. of the Design Automation Conf.*, June 1994.

[133] R.K. Gupta and G. De Micheli, "Constrained software generation for hardware-software systems," in *Proc. of the Int. Workshop on Hardware-Software Codesign*, 1994.

[134] M. Chiodo, P. Giusto, H. Hsieh, A. Jurecska, L. Lavagno, and A. Sangiovanni-Vincentelli, "Synthesis of software programs from CFSM specifications," in *Proc. of the Design Automation Conf.*, June 1995.

[135] K. Suzuki and A. Sangiovanni-Vincentelli, "Efficient software performance estimation methods for hardware/software codesign," in *Proc. of the Design Automation Conf.*, 1996.

[136] C. Liem, T. May, and P. Paulin, "Instruction set matching and selection for DSP and ASIP code generation," in *European Design and Test Conf.*, Feb. 1994.

[137] V. Tiwari, S. Malik, and A. Wolfe, "Power analysis of embedded software: a first step towards software power minimization," *IEEE Trans. on VLSI Systems*, vol. 2, no. 4, pp. 437–445, Dec. 1994.

SpecSyn: An Environment Supporting the Specify-Explore-Refine Paradigm for Hardware/Software System Design

Daniel D. Gajski, *Fellow, IEEE,* Frank Vahid, *Member, IEEE,* Sanjiv Narayan, and Jie Gong

Abstract— System-level design issues are gaining increasing attention, as behavioral synthesis tools and methodologies mature. We present the SpecSyn system-level design environment, which supports the new specify-explore-refine (SER) design paradigm. This three-step approach to design includes precise specification of system functionality, rapid exploration of numerous system-level design options, and refinement of the specification into one reflecting the chosen option. A system-level design option consists of an allocation of system components, such as standard and custom processors, memories, and buses, and a partitioning of functionality among those components. After refinement, the functionality assigned to each component can then be synthesized to hardware or compiled to software. We describe the issues and approaches for each part of the SpecSyn environment. The new paradigm and environment are expected to lead to a more than ten times reduction in design time, and our experiments support this expectation.

Index Terms— Embedded systems, estimation, exploration, hardware/software codesign, hierarchical modeling methodology, partitioning, refinement, specification, system design.

I. INTRODUCTION

THE focus of design effort on higher levels of abstraction, driven by increasing system complexity and shorter design times, has led to the need for a system-level design methodology and supporting tools. To better understand the system design problem, we can isolate three distinct tasks. First, we must specify the system's functionality and constraints. Second, we must explore various system-level design alternatives, each consisting of an interconnection of system components and an assignment of functionality to them. System components include standard processors, custom application specific integrated circuit (ASIC) processors, memories, and buses. Third, we must refine the original specification into a new system-level description, which designers will use to create an implementation for each component.

In current practice, these three steps are carried out in an informal and *ad hoc* manner. Specifications are usually written informally in English or some other natural language. Exploration is done manually using mental or hand-calculated estimations of quality metrics such as performance, size, and power. The refined description is then created informally using block diagrams and English. Drawbacks of such informal techniques include the lack of early simulation, the lack of rapid feedback of quality metrics that result from design decisions, the lack of automated tools to explore more design alternatives while requiring less design time, and the lack of good documentation of each component's functionality as well as of the design decisions to aid in concurrent design, component integration and redesign.

The response in the research community to the above drawbacks has been to introduce simulatable specifications earlier into the design process, and to use automated tools to assist in the exploration of design alternatives. The specify-explore-refine paradigm, which can also be thought of as a hierarchical modeling methodology, may further improve the situation. In such an approach, we first precisely specify the system's functionality, explore numerous system-level implementations with the aid of tools, and then automatically generate a refined description representing any implementation decisions.

More specifically, the following tasks, illustrated in Fig. 1, are necessary to create a system-level design.

- *Specification Capture:* To specify the desired system functionality, we decompose the functionality into pieces by creating a conceptual model of the system. We generate a description of this model in a language. We validate this description by simulation or verification techniques. The result of specification capture is a *functional specification*, which lacks any implementation detail.
- *Exploration:* We explore numerous design alternatives to find one that best satisfies our constraints. To do this, we transform the initial specification into one more suitable for implementation. We allocate a set of system components and specify their physical and performance constraints. We partition the functional specification among allocated components. For guidance in these exploration

---

Manuscript received March 17, 1995; revised July 3, 1996. This work was supported by the National Science Foundation under Grant MIP-8922851 and the Semiconductor Research Corporation under Grant 92-DJ-146.

D. D. Gajski is with the Department of Information and Computer Science, University of California, Irvine, CA 92664 USA.

F. Vahid is with the Department of Computer Science, University of California, Riverside, CA 92502 USA.

S. Narayan is with Ambit Design Systems, Santa Clara CA 95053 USA.

J. Gong was with the Semiconductor Systems Design Technology Group, Motorola, Inc., Tempe, AZ 85281 USA. She is now with Qualcomm, Inc., San Diego, CA 92121 USA.

Publisher Item Identifier S 1063-8210(98)01308-0.

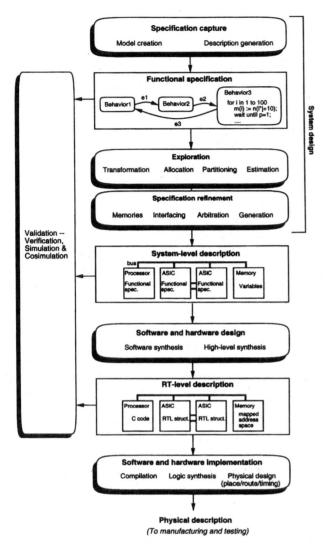

Fig. 1. The specify-explore-refine (SER) approach to system design.

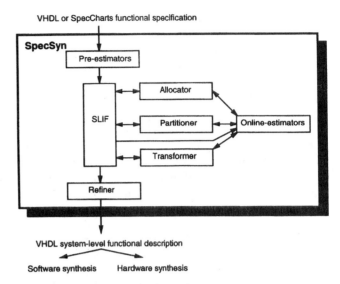

Fig. 2. The SpecSyn system-design environment.

subproblems, we estimate each alternative design's quality.

- *Specification Refinement:* We refine the initial specification into a new description reflecting the decisions that we have made during exploration. To do this, we move variables into memories, insert interface protocols between components, and add arbiters to linearize concurrent accesses to a single resource. Then, we generate a system description detailing the system's processors, memories, and buses and the functionality assigned to each. We use cosimulation to verify that this refined description is equivalent to the initial specification. The result of specification refinement is a *system-level description*, which possesses some implementation details of the system-level architecture we have developed, but otherwise is still largely functional.

Afterwards, we perform *software and hardware design*, where we create a design for each component, using software and hardware design techniques. A standard processor component requires software synthesis, which determines software execution order to satisfy resource and performance constraints. We can obtain a custom processor's design through high-level (behavioral) synthesis [1], [2], which converts the behavioral description into a data path structure of register-transfer (RT) components from a library, such as arithmetic and logic units, registers, counters, register files and memories, along with a finite-state machine (FSM) controller that sequences the flow of data through the data path. The result of software and hardware design is an *RT-level description*, which may contain C code for each software component, and an FSM plus an RT-level netlist for each custom component. The RT-level description is then passed to *software and hardware implementation* for final implementation. Software components require compilation, while custom components require FSM and logic synthesis [3] followed by physical design, in which fine-grained digital components like gates or transistors are placed, routed and timed on an integrated circuit (IC).

We have developed the SpecSyn environment to support the specify, explore, and refine steps—the SER paradigm. The various parts of SpecSyn, illustrated in Fig. 2, correspond to the various system-design subtasks described above; each part will be discussed in detail in upcoming sections. Discussion of how SpecSyn differs from many related efforts is found in Section VI; however, we point out two key differences here. First, SpecSyn outputs a system-level description, which differs from the input only by the addition of system-level architectural features. This output can thus be treated as though it were hand-written. Specifically, it can be easily read and understood, used as documentation, input to simulators, input to behavioral synthesis, input to real-time schedulers (and ideally compilers), or designed manually. SpecSyn thus fits in well with current practice. Second, SpecSyn was developed as a general tool intended to support a wide variety of implementation component technologies, architectures, and heuristics, and new versions of such items can be added.

In this paper, we present an overview of the SpecSyn environment, discussing relevant issues, previous work, and solutions for each part. We then present industry experiments using SpecSyn and the specify-explore-refine paradigm.

II. SPECIFICATION CAPTURE

A. Models and Languages

Specifying a system's functionality is a difficult task, because the functionality is often complex and poorly understood. To ease the specification task, one decomposes the functionality into pieces according to some model, and captures that model in some language. This distinction between a model and a language is important, since the choice of a model affects the ease of the specification task much more than does the choice of a language. Common models include communicating sequential processes (CSP) [4], dataflow graphs, hierarchical FSM's, Petri-nets, and object-oriented models. Common languages include C, C++, VHDL, Verilog, Statecharts [5], and Java. Each language can capture many models, but certain languages excel for particular models. For example, Statecharts excels at capturing FSM's, even though VHDL and Verilog can also capture FSM's, albeit with more effort.

We observed that no existing model or language catered to the capture of embedded systems. Embedded systems are those systems whose functionality is determined mostly by interactions with the environment. Examples include most controller and telecommunication systems. We found that many such systems possess several characteristics, including *state-transitions, exceptions, forking*, and *program-like computations*, which are not all supported by any one existing model. State-transitions, exceptions and forking are supported by the hierarchical FSM model, while forking and program-like computations are supported by the CSP model. To overcome this lack of support, we developed the program-state machine (PSM) model, which is essentially a combination of hierarchical FSM's (Statecharts) and CSP. The model consists of a hierarchy of program-states. Each program-state can be decomposed into concurrent program-substates or sequential program-substates sequenced by arcs, as in Statecharts. However, unlike Statecharts, a third option is to decompose a program-state into sequential program statements. Because a program-state is not just a state but also a computation, two types of arcs are required: transition-on-completion (TOC), which is traversed when the computation has completed, and transition-immediately (TI), which is traversed when the arc event occurs, regardless of the computation stage. We also developed the SpecCharts language, which is an extension to VHDL, to capture the PSM model [6]. SpecCharts can be translated automatically to VHDL, which will be more complex than the original SpecCharts, but is simulatable and (ideally) synthesizable in a VHDL environment. Of course, the PSM model can also be captured directly in VHDL (with some additional effort); we are currently investigating techniques to capture the PSM model in Java and C++.

The choice of a language depends on more than just supported system characteristics, so SpecSyn accepts the industry standard of VHDL as input, as well as SpecCharts.

Though languages such as VHDL and Verilog lack support for certain embedded system characteristics, most notably for state-transitions, one can always use some more complex combination of other constructs, which of course is more time-consuming and error-prone, but not impossible. For example, we can always capture state transitions using sequential program constructs. Such capture using less appropriate constructs is analogous to capturing a record using multiple scalar variables, capturing recursion using a stack, or capturing a parser using C's sequential constructs; all such captures are possible (and in fact support tools usually translate to such constructs during processing), but are tedious for humans to perform directly.

There are many other system characteristics that are not directly supported by languages such as SpecCharts, VHDL, Verilog, and C, including synchronous dataflow [7], queuing, complex timing constraints, and mixed analog/digital parts. No one language directly supports all characteristics, but hybrid models and languages that extend the number of supported characteristics, such as PSM and SpecCharts, seem to be a step in the right direction. For more information on PSM and SpecCharts, we refer the reader to [6] and [8].

In addition to specifying functionality, the designer must also specify design constraints. SpecSyn permits minimum and maximum constraints to be specified on behavior execution times and channel bit rates. Ideally, one would also be able to specify overall design constraints, such as power, board size, dollar cost, and design cost (if these items could be quantified). More specific design constraints, such as a component's size and I/O limitations, will be derived from each component's library entry later.

B. Internal Representation

The captured specification must be converted into an internal representation on which subsequent tools can operate. Representations commonly used for behavioral synthesis, including the control/dataflow graph (CDFG) and Value Trace [1], expose control and data dependencies between arithmetic-level operations, which may be too fine-grained for system design tasks. Most good partitioning heuristics would require long run times on the resulting large numbers of objects, and estimators could not obtain meaningful preestimates (see Section III-C) for each object. Refinement into a readable system-level description also becomes a nearly impossible task. Thus, we chose to create a representation based on the coarser-granularity of procedural-level computations.

A second drawback of using behavioral synthesis representations stems from their focus on dependencies. Such dependencies are necessary for scheduling during behavioral synthesis, but are not essential to performing system design tasks. Representing dependencies between procedural-level objects requires us to replicate each object at each place that a procedure is called, since dependencies will differ for each call. This replication makes the system design task much more complex. Instead, we developed a representation that focuses on representing the accesses, rather than dependencies, among objects.

```
entity FuzzyControllerE is
    port ( in1, in2 : in integer; out1: out integer );
end;
...
FuzzyMain: process
        variable in1val, in2val : integer;
        type mr_array is array (1 to 384) of integer;
        variable mr1, mr2: mr_array; -- membership rules
        type tmr_array is array (1 to 128) of integer;
        variable tmr1, tmr2: tmr_array; -- truncated memb. rules
        function Min ...
        ...
begin
        in1val := in1;  in2val := in2;
        EvaluateRule(1);
        EvaluateRule(2);
        Convolve;
        out1 <= ComputeCentroid;
        wait until ...
end process;

procedure EvaluateRule(num : in integer) is
    variable trunc : integer;  -- truncated value
begin
    if (num = 1) then
        trunc := Min(mr1(in1val), mr1(128+in1val));
    elsif (num = 2) then
        trunc := Min(mr2(in2val), mr2(128+in2val));
    end if;

    for i in 1 to 128 loop
        if (num = 1) then
            tmr1(i) := Min(trunc, mr1(256+i));
        elsif (num = 2) then
            tmr2(i) := Min(trunc, mr2(256+i));
        end if;
    end loop;
end;
```

Fig. 3. Partial VHDL specification of a fuzzy-logic controller example.

For example, consider the partial VHDL specification of a fuzzy-logic controller in Fig. 3. Inputs $in1$ and $in2$ must be converted to output $out1$ using fuzzy logic. The main process *FuzzyMain* first samples input values by writing them into variables $in1val$ and $in2val$. It then calls procedure *EvalRule* twice, once for each input, and that procedure fills an array ($tmr1$ or $tmr2$) based on the input and on another predefined array ($mr1$ or $mr2$). After convolving the tmr arrays, a centroid value is computed and output. The process repeats after a time interval.

We represent this specification as the directed graph in Fig. 4. Each graph node represents a *behavior* or a *variable* from the specification, where a behavior is a process or procedure, though for finer granularity we can consider statement blocks like loops by creating new procedures using a technique called exlining [9]. Each graph directed-edge represents a communication *channel* from the specification, where a channel represents a procedure call, a variable/port read or write, or a message pass specified using send/receive constructs. For example, process *FuzzyMain*, procedure *EvalRule* and variable $in1val$ are each represented by a node. The write of $in1val$ in *FuzzyMain* translates to a single edge, while the two calls of *EvalRule* by *FuzzyMain* translate to another single edge. Nodes representing processes are tagged to distinguish them from procedure nodes (hence the *FuzzyMain* node is shown in bold).

We refer to the representation as the *Specification-level intermediate format (SLIF)* since its granularity is that of behaviors and variables explicit in the specification. We refer to the part of SLIF shown so far as an *access graph (AG)* since the relations between the behaviors/variables are defined by the accesses among those objects. The AG is similar to a procedure call-graph commonly used for software profiling, where an edge represents an access rather than a flow of data; the AG is more general since it also includes variables. Note that the AG uses only one node for *EvalRule* and one for *Min*, even though each behavior is called more than once with different dependencies for each call; thus, a large increase in the number of nodes is prevented using the AG. Sometimes

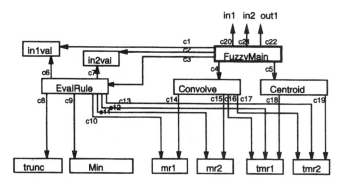

Fig. 4. Basic SLIF-AG for the example.

we do want multiple nodes, however, which can be handled using a procedure cloning transformation [10].

SLIF is annotated with numerous values, as shown in Figs. 5 and 6. We annotate each behavior and variable object with a list of size weights, one weight for each type of component to which the object may be assigned. For example, a variable object is annotated with the number of memory words required for storage in each library memory. A behavior is annotated with numbers of square microns, gates, and combinational-logic blocks for each custom chip, ASIC, and FPGA, respectively, on which the behavior could be implemented. [More complex annotations can be used to consider hardware sharing; see Section III-C3).] In addition, a behavior is annotated with the number of bytes for each possible standard processor.

We annotate each behavior and variable object with internal computation time (ict) weights for each possible component, corresponding to a variable's access time, or to a behavior's execution time excluding communication time. Times can be obtained with the aid of profiling and static estimation techniques [11]. We also annotate each edge with access frequency weights, which can also be obtained through profiling. Furthermore, we associate a bits weight with each edge, representing the number of bits sent during each transfer. For

Object	lct_8051	lct_XC4020	lct_V100	size_8051	size_XC4020	size_V100
FuzzyMain	5	8		80	500	
in1val	0	0	0	2	80	2
in2val	0	0	0	2	80	2
EvalRule	778	522		500	1600	
Convolve	800	600		900	2000	
Centroid	2,500	2000		700	4500	
trunc	0	0	0	2	80	2
Min	8	3		30	850	
mr1	0	0	0	768	30720	768
mr2	0	0	0	768	30720	768
tmr1	0	0	0	256	10240	256
tmr2	0	0	0	256	10240	256

Fig. 5. SLIF behavior/variable annotations for the example.

Object	accfreq	bits	src	dst
c1	1	6	FuzzyMain	in1val
c2	1	6	FuzzyMain	in2val
c3	2	8	FuzzyMain	EvalRule
c4	1	0	FuzzyMain	Convolve
c5	1	0	FuzzyMain	Centroid
c6	1	16	EvalRule	in1val
c7	1	16	EvalRule	in2val
c8	129	16	EvalRule	trunc
c9	129	32	EvalRule	Min
c10	65	32	EvalRule	mr1
c11	65	32	EvalRule	mr2
c12	32	16	EvalRule	tmr1
c13	32	16	EvalRule	tmr2

Fig. 6. SLIF channel annotations for the example.

each annotation, we might associate average, minimum and maximum values.

Annotations are computed during preestimation, and are combined into quality metric estimates during online estimation; Section III-C discusses these two estimation steps further.

III. EXPLORATION

Given a functional specification, we must proceed to create a system-level design of interconnected components, each component implementing a portion of that specification. A design's acceptability is evaluated by how well it satisfies constraints on design metrics, such as performance, size, power and cost. Since substantial time and effort are needed to evaluate a potential design, designers usually examine only a few potential designs, often those that they can evaluate quickly because of previous experience.

By using a machine-readable specification, we can automatically explore large numbers of potential designs rapidly. Exploration of potential designs can be decomposed into four interdependent subproblems: allocation, partitioning, transformation and estimation. We need not solve these problems in the given order; in fact, we will usually need to iterate many times before we are satisfied with our system-level design.

A. Allocation

Allocation is the task of adding components to the design. Many possible components exist. A standard processor is programmable and comes with widely used compilers and debuggers, but is usually slow or large. A special-purpose processor, such as a DMA controller or Fourier transformer, performs a specific function. A custom processor is synthesized to quickly execute a set of functions, but is harder to design and modify. An application-specific instruction-set processor (ASIP) is a programmable processor optimized for a particular class of applications, such as telecommunications. A memory stores variables. A bus implements communication between processors/memories.

The SpecSyn allocator permits allocation of any number of standard processors, custom processors, memories, and buses. Of course, allowing any allocation is only useful if the exploration tool understands the allocation; specifically, if the tool knows how to partition functionality among the components, knows how to estimate for such a partition, and can generate a refined description with behavior for each component. Incorporating such knowledge, especially that required for estimation, is very difficult, which is the reason that current tools only support a subset of possible allocations, such as a particular interconnection of a standard processor, memory, bus and custom processor [12], [13]. While SpecSyn permits a variety of allocations, its estimation models and heuristics must continually be improved to better apply to each.

Each component is characterized in a library by its constraints, and by a technology file. For example, a custom processor might be characterized by the maximum I/O pins and gates, and by a technology file describing an RT-component library. A standard processor is characterized by a maximum program memory size, a bus size, a maximum bus bitrate, and a technology file describing how to map a generic instruction set to the processor's instruction set [11]. A memory is characterized by the number of ports, number of words, word width, and access time. A bus is characterized by the number of wires, protocol, and maximum bit rates.

Ideally, we would also be able to allocate special-purpose processor components (e.g., DMA controllers), as well as hierarchical components, such as an ASIC which itself contains a standard processor core, memory, and several custom processor blocks.

Fig. 7 demonstrates an example allocation. *StandardProc1* is an Intel 8051 with 4 kb of on-chip memory, and *CustomProc1* is a Xilinx XC4010 FPGA with 160 I/O pins and 10 000 gates. Two 1 kB memories are also allocated.

B. Partitioning

Given a functional specification and an allocation of system components, we need to partition the specification and assign each part to one of the allocated components. In fact, we can distinguish three types of *functional objects* that must be partitioned. One type is a *variable*, which stores data values. Variables in the specification must be assigned to memory components. The second is a *behavior*, which transforms data values. A behavior may consist of programming statements, such as assignment, if and loop statements, and it generates a new set of values for a subset of variables. Behaviors must be assigned to custom or standard processors. The third is the

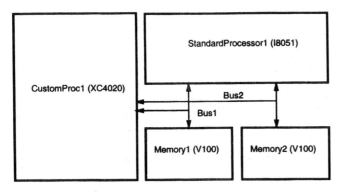

Fig. 7. An example allocation of components.

channel, which transfers data from one behavior to another. Channels must be assigned to buses. Specification partitioning strives to satisfy constraints, specified by the user as well as associated with allocated components.

1) Hardware and Hardware/Software Partitioning: A variety of techniques have evolved to assist the designer perform functional partitioning. We can consider two categories of techniques: hardware partitioning and hardware/software partitioning. The hardware partitioning techniques aim to partition functionality among hardware modules, such as among ASIC's or among blocks on an ASIC. Most such techniques partition at the granularity of arithmetic operations, differing in the partitioning heuristics employed. Clustering heuristics are used in [14] and [15], integer-linear programming in [16] and [17], manual partitioning in [18], and iterative-improvement heuristics in [19] and [20]. Other techniques for hardware partitioning operate at a higher level of granularity, such as in [21] where processes and subroutines are partitioned among ASIC's using clustering, iterative-improvement, and manual techniques. Experiments have shown tremendous advantages of functional partitioning over the current practice of structural partitioning [22].

Hardware/software partitioning techniques form the second functional partitioning category. These techniques focus on partitioning functionality among a hardware/software architecture. The techniques in [12], [13], [23], and [24]–[27] partition at the statement, statement sequence and subroutine/task levels, respectively.

In SpecSyn, both the hardware and hardware/software partitioning techniques are supported, since one can allocate any combination of hardware and software components and assign pieces of the specification to those components.

2) Heuristics: Instead of using one particular partitioning heuristic, SpecSyn uses a partitioning engine called GPP (general purpose partitioner). GPP is a library of functions with uniform interfaces, implementing the basic control strategies of numerous common heuristics, including clustering, group migration (an extension of Kernighan/Lin), simulated annealing, clique partitioning, genetic evolution, as well as custom heuristics. These control strategies are distinct from data structures and cost functions. A particular partitioning problem can be solved by calling a heuristic with the appropriate data structure and cost function—for example, circuit partitioning can be solved by passing a hypergraph data structure and a min-cut cost function. Each SpecSyn partitioning problem, including variables to memories, channels to buses, and behaviors to processors, is performed by passing the appropriate data structure and cost function and then applying the existing heuristics.

SpecSyn's approach to partitioning thus addresses the fact that heuristics, data structures, and cost functions are continually evolving. A new partitioning problem can initially be solved using a general heuristic. Then, once the problem definition has matured, one can develop and easily integrate a new custom heuristic. A user, after some experimentation, can choose the heuristic(s) with the appropriate result quality and runtime.

3) Manual Partitioning and Hints: We have also focused on supporting manual partitioning because of the importance placed on designer interaction. Such support not only involves providing the ability to manually relocate objects, but also allowing user control of the relative weights of various metrics in the cost function (see below), and automatically providing hints of what changes might yield improvements to the current partition. SpecSyn currently supports two types of hints. Closeness hints provide a list of object pairs, sorted by the closeness of the objects in each pair. Closeness is based on a weighted function of various closeness metrics. There are currently seven behavior closeness metrics supported [28].

- *Connectivity* is based on the number of wires shared between the sets of behaviors. Grouping behaviors that share wires should result in fewer pins.
- *Communication* is based on the number of bits of data transferred between the sets of behaviors, independent of the number of wires used to transfer the data. Grouping heavily communicating behaviors should result in better performance, due to decreased communication time.
- *Hardware sharing* is based on the estimated percentage of hardware that can be shared between the two sets of behaviors. Grouping behaviors that can share hardware should result in a smaller overall hardware size.
- *Common accessors* is based on the number of behaviors that access both sets of behaviors. Grouping such behaviors should result in fewer overall wires.
- *Sequential execution* is based on the ability to execute behaviors sequentially without loss in performance.
- *Constrained communication* is based on the amount of communication between the sets of behaviors that contributes to each performance constraint. Grouping such behaviors should help ensure that performance constraints are met.
- *Balanced size* is based on the size of the sets of behaviors. Grouping smaller behaviors should eventually lead to groups of balanced size.

  There are also three closeness metrics supported for variables and for channels.
- *Common accessors* is based on the number of behaviors that access both sets of variables/channels. Grouping such variables/channels should result in fewer overall wires.
- *Sequential access* is based on the occurrence of sequential, rather than concurrent, access of the variables/channels by behaviors. Grouping sequentially

accessed variables/channels into the same memory does not decrease performance, whereas grouping concurrently accessed ones might decrease performance due to access conflicts.

- *Width similarity* is based on the similarity of the variables'/channels' bit widths. Grouping variables/channels with similar bitwidths should result in fewer wasted memory/bus bits.

The other type of hint is called lookahead. Here, we generate all possible n modifications of the current partition, where an n modification is a sequence of n moves of any objects from one group to another (n is user-defined). We again provide a list of such modifications, sorted by the partition improvement gained by each as measured by a cost function.

4) Cost Functions: Partitioning heuristics are guided by cost functions. A variety of cost functions can be supported. The following supported cost function focuses on satisfying constraints:

$$\begin{aligned}
Costfct = &\ k_1 \cdot F(component1.size, \\
&\qquad component1.size\_constr) \\
&+ k_2 \cdot F(component2.size, \\
&\qquad component2.size\_constr) \\
&+ k_3 \cdot F(component1.IO, \\
&\qquad component1.IO\_constr) \\
&+ k_4 \cdot F(behavior1.exectime, \\
&\qquad behavior1.exectime\_constr) \cdots \quad (1)
\end{aligned}$$

where the k's are user-provided constants indicating the relative importance of each metric, and F is a function indicating the desirability of a metric's value. A common form of F returns the degree of constraint violation, normalized such that zero indicates no violation, and one indicates very large violation. This form of F causes the cost function to return zero when a partition meets all constraints, making the goal of partitioning to obtain a cost of zero.

The above cost function is very general, permitting us to satisfy constraints as well as to optimize certain metrics, without requiring specific knowledge in a heuristic of the constraints or optimization metrics. For example, if we wish to optimize execution time while satisfying size and I/O constraints, we can simply weigh size and I/O very heavily, so that violations of those constraints will not be tolerated. If we wish to focus first on just execution time, and then later on power, we can give the power constraint an initial weight of zero.

As an example of the results of partitioning, Fig. 8 shows a partition of several of the previous example's nodes among two memories, an ASIC, a processor and a bus. Note that four communication channels have been partitioned onto *bus1*.

C. Estimation

Estimation of values for design quality metrics is required to determine if a particular system-level design (a partition of functions among allocated components) satisfies constraints, and to compare alternative designs. In this section, we describe

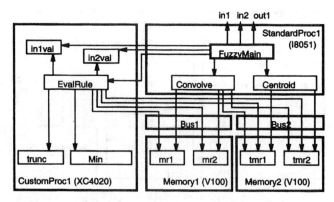

Fig. 8. Partitioning AG nodes among system components.

our two-level approach for fast and accurate estimation, and we provide details of our estimation models.

1) Preestimation and Online-Estimation: In general, more accurate estimates require more time, but time is very limited during exploration. (When comparing alternative options, fidelity is often more important than accuracy; see [8] and [29]). High accuracy can be achieved through synthesis, compilation, and simulation, i.e., by generating a refined description, creating an RT-level design using synthesis and compilation, measuring gates or bytes for size metrics, and performing simulations for performance metrics. However, the minutes or hours required by such an approach makes it unsuitable during exploration, when hundreds to tens of thousands of designs must be examined.

To decrease estimation time, an implementation *model* can be used, which is an implementation abstraction from which metric values can be derived, but which does not contain complete implementation details. SpecSyn uses a two-level technique to obtain metric values, as illustrated in Fig. 9.

1) **Preestimation:** Each functional object (behavior, variable and channel) is annotated with information (see Section II-B), such as the number of bytes for a behavior when compiled to a particular processor, the average frequency of channel access, or the number of channel bits. Preestimation occurs only once at the beginning of exploration, is independent of any particular partition and allocation, and may take seconds to minutes.

2) **Online-estimation:** Preestimated annotations are combined in complex expressions to obtain metric values for a particular partition and allocation. Online-estimation occurs hundreds or thousands of times during manual or automated exploration, so it must be completed in just milliseconds.

In most other approaches, exploration consists of only one level of estimation (or two levels where one is trivial), with another level coming only after RT-level design.

We now discuss SpecSyn estimation models for three metric types: performance, hardware size, and software size.

2) Performance: In SpecSyn's performance model, a behavior's execution time is calculated as the sum of the behavior's *internal computation time (ict)* and *communication time*. The *ict* is the execution time on a particular component, assuming all accessed behaviors and variables take zero time.

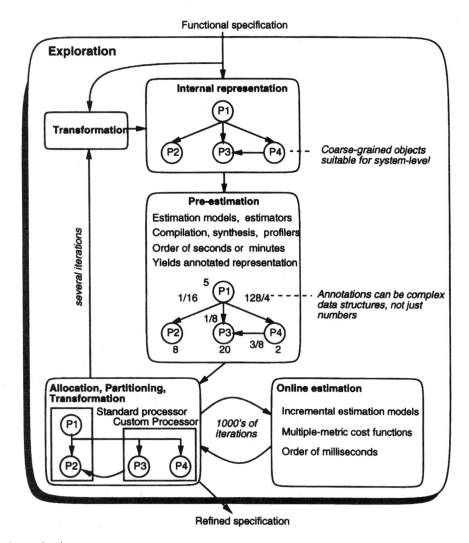

Fig. 9. Subtasks during exploration.

The communication time includes time to transfer data to/from accessed behaviors and variables, as well as the time for such accessed behaviors to execute (e.g., the time for a called procedure to execute and return). This model leads to some inaccuracy, since some computation and communication could occur in parallel, but the model seems to provide reasonable accuracy while enabling rapid estimations.

More precisely, execution time is computed as follows:

$$b.exectime = b.ict_p + b.commtime$$
$$b.commtime = \sum_{c_k \in b.outchannels} c_k.accfreq$$
$$\times (c_k.ttime_{bus} + (c_k.dst).exectime)$$
$$c_k.ttime_{bus} = [bus.time \times (c_k.bits \div bus.width)]$$
$$bus.time = bus.timesame$$
$$\text{if}(c_k.dst).p = p,$$
$$= bus.timediff \text{ otherwise.} \quad (2)$$

In other words, a behavior's execution time equals its ict on the current component ($b.ict_p$), plus its communication time ($b.commtime$). The communication time equals the transfer time over a channel for each accessed object ($c_k.ttime_{bus}$), plus the execution time of each accessed object (($c_k.dst).exectime$), times the number of such accesses ($c_k.accfreq$). The transfer time over a channel is determined from the bus data transfer time ($bus.time$) and the width of that bus ($bus.width$); if the data bits exceeds the bus width, then multiple transfers are used (as computed by the division). The bus_time is usually less when the communication is within one component.

Fig. 10 shows the execution-time equation for *FuzzyMain* of Fig. 4. For simplicity, the example uses fixed numbers for *Convolve* and *Centroid* communication times, whereas actually further equations should be used.

a) Preestimation: A behavior's internal computation time can be computed during preestimation through profiling and scheduling. Profiling determines the execution count of each basic block where a basic block is a sequence of statements not containing a branch. A schedule for each basic block is then estimated for each possible processor component, using compilation for standard processors and synthesis for custom processors. [Compilation techniques are discussed further in Section III-C4.] The summation over all blocks

```
FuzzyMain.et     = FuzzyMain.ict
                 + c1.accfreq * (c1.tt + in1val.et)
                 + c2.accfreq * (c2.tt + in2val.et)
                 + c3.accfreq * (c3.tt + EvalRule.et)
                 + c4.accfreq * (c4.tt + Convolve.et)
                 + c5.accfreq * (c5.tt + Centroid.et)
inv1val.et       = in1val ict + 0
inv2val.et       = in2val ict + 0
EvalRule.et      = EvalRule.ict
                 + c8.accfreq  * (c8.tt + trunc.et)
                   c9.accfreq  * (c9.tt + Min.et)
                   c10.accfreq * (c10.tt + mr1.et)
                   c11.accfreq * (c11.tt + mr2.et)
                   c12.accfreq * (c12.tt + tmr1.et)
                   c13.accfreq * (c13.tt + tmr2.et)
Convolve.et      = Convolve.ict +333
Centroid         = Centroid.ict +454
trunc            = trunc ict + 0
Min              = Min ict + 0
mr1              = mr1 ict + 0
mr2              = mr2 ict + 0
tmr1             = tmr1 ict + 0
tmr2             = tmr2 ict + 0
```

Fig. 10. Execution-time equations for the example.

Object	comp	bind	ict	et
FuzzyMain	StdProc1	8051	5	8,494
in1val	CustProc1	XC4020	0	0
in2val	CustProc1	XC4020	0	0
EvalRule	CustProc1	XC4020	522	2,197
Convolve	StdProc1	8051	800	1,133
Centroid	StdProc1	8051	2500	2,954
trunc	CustProc1	XC4020	0	0
Min	CustProc1	XC4020	3	3
mr1	Mem1	V100	0	0
mr2	Mem1	V100	0	0
tmr1	Mem2	V100	0	0
tmr2	Mem2	V100	0	0

Fig. 11. Evaluating execution times for the example.

of each block's execution count times steps yields the total steps for the behavior. Multiplying by the step time, i.e., the clock period, yields an *ict* value. Note that processors using pipelining, caching or interrupts would require further refinements of the *ict* model. Each behavior is annotated with an *ict* value for each possible component.

Channel access frequencies are also determined through profiling. Any variable accesses or procedure call parameters can be encoded into bits as during synthesis. Bus times and widths are already associated with each bus.

Figs. 5 and 6 showed the annotations obtained during preestimation for the fuzzy-logic controller example.

b) Online estimation: Given a partition of every functional object to a component, the actual *ict*, bus values, and bus times become known. Thus, a behavior's execution time equation can be evaluated. When a partitioning heuristic moves an object, the object's *ict* value will change, and bus times may also change since objects previously on the same component will now be on different components, and possibly vice-versa. We only need to change those values and reevaluate the equation. In addition, any other equations that include the object's execution time must also be updated. If care is taken to maintain links from an object to all terms that change when the object is moved, then the updates can be done very quickly.

Fig. 11 shows the results of evaluating the execution time equations for the fuzzy controller example. Using the allocation and partition of Fig. 8, each object is assigned to a component (*comp*), each of which was bound to a library item (*bind*); based on this assignment, the current *ict* values are shown. Using these *ict*'s, and the communication times based on the transfer times (not shown), the execution time (*et*) equations of Fig. 10 are evaluated. Thus, *FuzzyMain* executes in 8494 time units for the given allocation and partition.

3) Hardware Size: When several behaviors are assigned to a custom processor, we must estimate the size (e.g., number of gates) required by that processor. The most accurate estimate is achieved by performing synthesis, but as discussed above, such an approach is too slow during exploration. Instead, some tools use a *weight-based* approach, in which preestimation consists of annotating each behavior and variable with a weight, and then a simple online-estimation sums the weights [12], [13]. Such an approach is fast, but may be inaccurate since it does not consider hardware sharing. Other research efforts [14], [15], [18], [30] use a *design-based* approach, in which an online-estimation roughly synthesizes a design for a given partition, omitting time-consuming synthesis tasks such as logic optimization. While more accurate, such estimators may require tens of seconds, which may be too slow for exploration of thousands of options.

SpecSyn uses an incremental update technique to achieve both the accuracy of design-based estimators and the speed of weight-based estimators. The technique takes advantage of the fact that many iterative-improvement partitioning heuristics, while exploring thousands of partitions, move only a few objects between one iteration and the next. Thus, using extensive information gathered during preestimation, we incrementally modify a custom processor's design in just milliseconds (constant-time).

SpecSyn uses a hardware design model similar to those in [8], [14], and [15], consisting of a control-unit/data path (CU/DP) as shown in Fig. 12. The CU/DP area can be computed as the sum of the following terms: *Functional-unit (FU) size*; *Storage-unit size* including registers, register files and memories; *Multiplexer size*; *State-register size*; *Control-logic size*; and *Wiring-size*. As shown in Fig. 13, each term is a function of basic parameters, including the number of possible states, the number of control lines, the number of states each control line is active, the number of bits and words for each storage unit, the number of bits and type of each functional unit, the number of sources of each storage-unit input, functional-unit input, and data path output, the number of data path connections, and the number of data path components. For example functions, see [31].

a) Preestimation: The parameters are computed for each functional object during preestimation, by performing rough synthesis on each object. Each object is then annotated with the computed parameters. Such computation can take seconds or

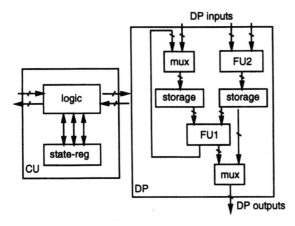

Fig. 12. CU/DP area model.

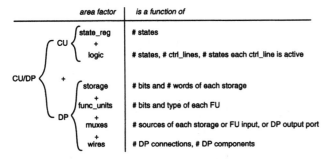

Fig. 13. Equation and terms for computing CU/DP area.

minutes. Given an initial partition of functional objects among custom processors, we can obtain a rough design of each processor by intelligently combining its objects' parameter annotations. For example, we can determine the number of possible custom processor states S by summing the objects' possible states (in our model, a custom processor implements sequential objects from one process; multiple processes would require multiple processors) and then creating a state register of size $\log(S)$ bits. As another example, we can determine the number of FU's by taking the union of the objects' FU's (since sequential behaviors can share FU's). Note that the terms, such as state register size and number of FU's, are not obtained by simple addition; in fact, terms may actually be nonlinear with respect to the parameters. See [31] for details on computing all the terms from the objects' parameters.

b) Online estimation: When a partitioning heuristic removes an object from a processor, we update that processor's terms. Some terms can be updated simply by examining the object's annotations. For example, the number of possible processor states is reduced by the object's number, and the state register size recomputed using the log function. On the other hand, other terms require further examination. For example, an object might require a particular FU, but removing that object only removes that FU if no other object uses the FU; thus, we keep track of which objects use each FU. Likewise, removing an object might not eliminate a multiplexor, but might reduce its size since certain sources are no longer needed; thus, we keep track of which objects require each source. Updating a processor's design for removal of an object, as well as the complementary action of adding an object, can be done in constant time [31].

Note that we can merge the information from the functional objects because of their coarse granularity; otherwise, the ignored interobject effects would result in poor accuracy.

4) Software Size: A straightforward model of a processor's software size is that of the summation of the processor's functional objects' sizes. While neglecting interprocedural optimization, such optimization is likely not large, so this model yields fairly accurate estimates.

a) Preestimation: Ideally, we could determine a functional object's size by simply compiling the object for each possible target standard processor, as shown in Fig. 14(a). Unless the target processor is the same as the host machine processor on which SpecSyn is running, such compilation will require a cross-compiler, i.e., a compiler that runs on one processor but generates code for another. However, a cross-compiler may not be available on the host machine. For example, suppose the host machine is a Sparc and the target processor an Intel 8051. We probably do not have an 8051 compiler that runs on the Sparc; instead, we probably have one that runs on an x86 processor.

SpecSyn supports a method for estimating software size even when a cross-compiler is not available. The method uses a generic processor model and a single compiler, as shown in Fig. 14(b). A functional object's size is first compiled into generic three-address instructions. Using available processor-specific technology files listing the number of bytes that each generic instruction would require in each processor, the estimator computes the software size. A target processor's technology file can be developed based on the size information of the processor's instruction set; note that developing such a file is substantially simpler than developing a back-end compiler. Details on deriving technology files for specific processors are given in [11].

Note that the same generic processor approach would be applied for software performance estimation. Specifically, the technology file of the target processor would include not only the bytes but also the number of steps for each generic instruction.

Some experiments comparing the generic model with the processor-specific model yielded inaccuracy of roughly 7% [11].

b) Online estimation: Online software size estimation consists simply of increasing or decreasing the processor size by the size of the added or removed functional object.

D. Transformations

A functional specification serves the purpose of precisely defining a system's intended behavior. Such a specification usually will be read by humans as well as input to synthesis tools. Unfortunately, a specification written for readability may not directly lead to the best synthesized design. As a result, designers often try to juggle synthesis considerations with readability considerations while writing the initial functional specification. Such juggling usually leads to lower readability, less portability, and more functional errors; hence, many of

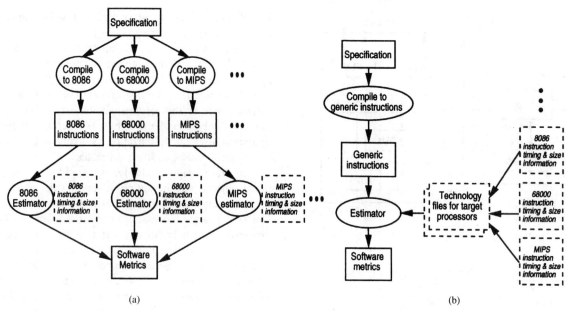

Fig. 14. Software size estimation: (a) processor-specific model and (b) generic model.

the advantages of a top-down approach are greatly diminished, ultimately leading to longer design times.

To solve this problem, SpecSyn provides a suite of automated transformations. As shown in Fig. 9, transformations can be applied on the SLIF or on the specification. SLIF transformations occur in an "inner loop" along with allocation, partitioning and online estimation, being applied thousands of times. Specification transformations occur in an "outer loop," which is followed by rebuilding of the SLIF and reannotation.

One specification transformation is *procedure exlining* [9]. Exlining is the inverse of procedure inlining; namely, replacing sequences of statements by procedure calls. Since procedures determine SLIF granularity, exlining is a means for achieving finer-granularity. There are two types of exlining. *Redundancy exlining* seeks to find and replace redundant statement sequences. *Distinct-computation exlining* seeks to break a large procedure into several smaller procedures, even though each may only be called once. Redundancy exlining is a very hard problem; presently, we encode each statement into a character string indicating the statement type, symbolic target and sources, concatenate each such string into one large one, and then use the *agrep* approximate pattern matching tool to find potential redundancies. Not all matches found by such an approach are necessarily redundancies, so user interaction is required. Distinct-computation exlining is in fact very similar to the problem addressed in [15]. Statements can be clustered together based on a number of closeness metrics. Simulated annealing can be used to further improve the statement clusterings.

A second specification transformation is *procedure inlining*, which achieves coarser granularity and distributes computations among calling behaviors, eliminating potential computation bottlenecks. Other possible transformations include *process merging* [32], where two processes are sequentialized into one to reduce hardware size, and *process splitting* [33], where one process is split into two concurrent ones. We plan to investigate such process transformations. A variety of other optimizing transformations with origins in software compilation could also be applied [34], [35].

Turning to SLIF transformations, *preclustering* [28] merges nodes that should probably never be separated, thus achieving coarser granularity. *Procedure cloning* [10] duplicates procedure nodes so that each calling behavior has its own copy, without necessarily inlining that copy; such cloning is analogous to logic duplication during logic-level partitioning. *Port calling* [36] inserts a node for sending or receiving data to external input/output ports; such nodes enable better distribution of I/O among components, similar in idea to parallel I/O chips.

IV. REFINEMENT

Refinement is the generation of a new specification for each system component after exploration has yielded a suitable allocation and partition. The refined specification should be both readable and simulatable, enabling further verification and synthesis. We now describe specification refinement tasks required after system design.

A. Interfacing

An important task is interface generation. Abstract communication channels were assigned to physical buses. *Interface refinement* determines the buswidth and the protocol for the bus that will implement the channels. A bus (such as a PC ISA bus) may already have these items fixed, in which case they are simply looked up. Alternatively, a bus may be flexible, in which case the best width and protocol must still be determined; algorithms and techniques have been reported in [37], [38]. After determining the protocol to meet design constraints, structure can be created for the protocol using techniques in [39]–[41].

```
entity FuzzyControllerE is
  port ( in1, in2 : in integer;  out1: out integer );
end;
...
component ASIC1E is
  port ( in1, in2 : in integer; startEvalRule : in bit;
         doneEvalRule : out bit;  num_chan : int_chan;
         mr_chan, tmr_chan : addr_int_chan; ...);
end;
component Memory1E is
  port (mr_chan : addr_int_chan);
end;
component Memory2E is ...
component Processor1E is ...

< port maps > ...
...
entity ASIC1E is
  port ( in1, in2 : in integer; startEvalRule : in bit;
         doneEvalRule : out bit;  num_chan : int_chan;
         mr_chan, tmr_chan : addr_int_chan; ...);
end;
...
process
  variable in1val, in2val : integer;
  function Min ...
  variable num : integer;
  ...
begin
  wait until startEvalRule='1';
  num := ReadNum(num_chan);
  EvaluateRule(num);
  doneEvalRule:='1';
  ....

procedure EvaluateRule(num : in integer) is
  variable trunc : integer; -- truncated value
  variable mr_val1, mr_val2 : integer;
  variable tmr_val : integer;
begin
  if (num = 1) then
    mr_val1 := ReadMemory1(in1val + MR1OFFSET);
    mr_val2 := ReadMemory1(128 + in1val + MR1OFFSET);
    trunc := Min(mr1_val1, mr1_val2));
  elsif (num = 2) then
    mr_val1 := ReadMemory1(in1val + MR2OFFSET);
    mr_val2 := ReadMemory1(128 + in1val + MR2OFFSET);
    trunc := Min(mr_val1, mr_val2);
  end if;

  for i in 1 to 128 loop
    if (num = 1) then
      mr_val1 := ReadMemory1(256+i + MR1OFFSET);
      tmr_val := Min(trunc, mr_val1);
      WriteMemory2(i + TMR1OFFSET, tmr_val);
    elsif (num = 2) then
      mr_val1 := ReadMemory1(256+i + MR2OFFSET);
      tmr_val := Min(trunc, mr_val1);
      WriteMemory2(i+TMR2OFFSET, tmr_val);
    end if;
  end loop;
end;
```

Fig. 15. Refined fuzzy-logic controller VHDL partial specification.

B. Memories

Another task is memory refinement associated with the implementation of variables assigned to memories. The variable accesses must be replaced by references to the corresponding memory locations.

C. Arbitration

A third task, arbiter generation, inserts an arbiter behavior where there is a resource contention, i.e., where two behaviors could access the same memory or bus simultaneously.

Note that, while during partitioning we abstracted communication implementation to the problem of mapping channels to buses, during refinement we must now deal with more complex communication issues involving protocols and arbitration. Such complex communication results in new behaviors (protocols and arbiters), which may later be synthesized, or possibly mapped to existing communication components like serial communication controllers or direct-memory-access controllers.

D. Generation

The final task of refinement is the actual generation of a refined description. The new description should be readable, modifiable, simulatable, and synthesizable. We use the following technique to generate a refined description. First, we create a VHDL entity for each system component. Second, for each behavior that represented a process in the original specification, we create a VHDL process inside the component to which the behavior has been assigned. Third, we describe activation for separated behaviors, i.e., those behaviors that have been assigned to a component different from their calling behaviors. The simplest approach to achieving such activation would be to create a single process for each such behavior, where the process would wait until it was activated via a control signal, would execute the behavior, and then would indicate completion via another control signal. However, such an approach results in an excessive number of processes (one for each separated behavior) and control signals. A better approach is to combine all separated behaviors that we know to be sequential (i.e., all those behaviors that belong to the same process), and that have been assigned to the same component, into a single process. This process would wait until it was activated, would execute one of its behaviors based on a newly introduced mode signal, and would indicate its completion. Fourth, we insert communication protocols and arbiters, as described above. We use VHDL send/receive procedures to hide the protocol details, and use additional VHDL processes to describe the arbiters.

E. Validation

To verify the system-design decisions, we can simulate the refined specification. When certain components use different models of computation than other components or contain different levels of details, different simulation approaches must be combined to obtain a simulation of the complete system. Such combination is called cosimulation. A variety of approaches to cosimulation are described in the literature, such as in [42]–[45]. The refined specification can serve as input to most of these approaches.

In Fig. 15, we show a refined specification for the system design shown in Fig. 8. Due to space limitations, the figure shows only a part of the refined specification. The interface of the fuzzy controller remains unchanged. However, its contents now consist of many more details than in the original specification of Fig. 3. For example, the top-level view of the controller now consists of instantiations of an ASIC, two memories, and a processor component, along with the interconnections among those components. The ASIC component, in turn, is defined as an entity with several ports. The first two ports, $in1$ and $in2$, simply connect with the external inputs with the same names. The next two ports, *startEvalRule* and *doneEvalRule*, would be used by the *FuzzyMain* process on the processor to activate the *EvalRule* procedure on the ASIC. The last three ports shown, num_chan, mr_chan and tmr_chan, are composite data types that describe the signals necessary for fetching the num parameter from *FuzzyMain*, for fetching $mr1$ and $mr2$ data from *Memory1*, and for storing $tmr1$ and $tmr2$ data to *Memory2*. The ASIC's behavior consists of a single process, which waits for an activation signal, fetches the num parameter, and calls *EvalRule* with that parameter.

EvalRule is a procedure found in this process, identical to the procedure in Fig. 3, except that the mr and tmr arrays can no longer be accessed as global variables. Instead, they must be accessed using new subroutines that read data from *Memory1* and write data to *Memory2*. Those subroutines describe the detailed communication protocol for such memory accesses, and would usually be found in a communication-protocol VHDL package. Note that since the $mr1$ and $mr2$ arrays have been merged into the same memory *Memory1*, offsets ($MR1OFFSET$ and $MR2OFFSET$) must be added to any array addresses; likewise for $tmr1$ and $tmr2$, which both reside in *Memory2*.

There are two important points to note in this example. First, note the large amount of detail that must be added to the specification as a result of creating a system-level design. Presently, designers must manually incorporate this detail, resulting in longer specification times. Moreover, if the system-level design serves as the first captured specification, then we can expect many more functional errors, since the specification writer must consider many detailed issues that detract from a focus on the system's functionality. Second, it is crucial that the designer be given access to these newly introduced details. Many of those details involve important design decisions that the designer must be aware of and must be able to change; for these reasons, generation of a refined specification can be seen as extremely important. After refinement, the functional specification of each component is just that—a specification, not an implementation. This means that for a software component (as well as a hardware component), there may be more than one process in the component's functional specification. These processes will need to be merged into a single control thread, but such merging is part of the implementation task for the component. Thus, the refined specification is a unique and important intermediate representation of functionality, necessary to verify the system-level allocation and partitioning decisions we have made, without yet requiring detailed implementation decisions for each component. Further details on refinement can be found in [8] and [46].

V. EXPERIMENTS

We have conducted a series of experiments to explore design alternatives for several industrial examples. Here we present results for one particular example: a fuzzy-logic controller [47].

Four library components were available: a standard processor (Intel 8051) and three custom processors with 50, 100, and 150 k gates. Each component had an associated dollar cost. For the experiment, we automatically generated all possible allocation combinations of these components below a certain dollar cost. For each allocation, we partitioned automatically using simulated annealing and a cost function that sought to meet all size and pin constraints while minimizing execution time.

Fig. 16 shows results for the fuzzy-logic controller for 35 different allocations. Allocation 1 consisted of just the 8051 standard processor, and had an execution time of over 150 000 ms, so its point is not shown on the graph. Allocation 2 consisted of just one 50 k gate custom processor, but the processor's size constraint was violated so that point is not shown either. Allocation 3 consisted of one 8051 standard processor and one 50-k gate custom processor, resulting in an execution time of 18 115 ms. Allocation 4 consisted of just one 100-k gate processor, but again this resulted in a size violation, so the point is not shown. Allocation 5 consisted of one 8051 and one 100-k gate custom processor, yielding an execution time of 7721 ms. Subsequent higher cost allocations yield no better execution time. For example, allocation 31 consisted of one 8051, one 50-k custom processor, one 100-k custom processor, and two 150-k custom processors, and yielded an execution time of 9785 ms. Conceptually, we should have been able to achieve 7721 ms by just using the 100-k custom processor, but the simulated annealing formulation simply did not find a solution using just that custom processor along with the 8051; instead, functions were assigned to multiple custom processors, requiring interprocessor communication and hence the longer execution time.

SpecSyn thus aids the designer to get a feel for the design space, enabling him to focus on promising points. The above data was generated automatically in 1 h running on a Sparc 2. There are numerous other types of tradeoffs that can also be generated.

SpecSyn was used by an industry engineer to design the fuzzy-logic controller. The partitioning results obtained matched favorably with those obtained by another engineer who did a manual partition. The system-level design obtained by SpecSyn consisted of 5 FPGA's. Each was implemented using high-level synthesis, and NeoCAD tools were used to complete the design. Details of this experiment can be found in [47]. We summarize them briefly in Fig. 17. The SpecCharts language was used for the initial specification. Note the reduction in the number of lines when using SpecCharts as opposed to VHDL for the specification (see [8] for other experiments which demonstrate the reduction in specification time, specification errors, comprehension time, and lines of code). Also note the large increase in the number of lines for the refined specification; since this is automatically generated, the designer is relieved from the tedious effort of having to write the refined specification himself. Finally, note the very large size of the VHDL after its structural implementation; such a large amount of

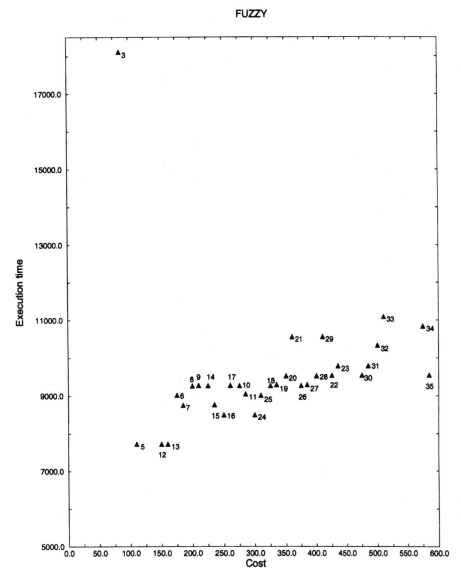

Fig. 16. Exploration for the fuzzy-logic controller.

information is very difficult to work with, so starting with a functional specification enables a tremendous increase in designer comprehension. The entire implementation was obtained in roughly 100 man-hours with the aid of SpecSyn and high-level synthesis, which is nearly a ten times reduction in design time from the six months required to obtain the design manually.

VI. RELATED WORK, CURRENT STATUS, AND FUTURE WORK

Several other system-level design environments have also evolved. TOSCA [48], [49] focuses on control-dominated systems. A hierarchical FSM input is converted to a process algebra internal format based on a CSP-like model, which is partitioned among an architecture consisting of a standard processor, memory, system bus, and some number of custom processors that can share local buses. Partitioning is performed manually or using a hierarchical clustering heuristic,

SpecChart spec	350
VHDL spec	598
Refined VHDL spec	1495
Structural VHDL spec	17500

Fig. 17. Fuzzy-logic controller industry design summary.

incorporating formal transformations such as parallelization. Several metrics guide the partitioning. Processes partitioned to software are output in a virtual instruction set (VIS), which is later translated for a particular processor, thus achieving some processor independence. Synthesis is applied to the output and the results used to guide further iterations. The VIS is similar to SpecSyn's generic instruction set, except that SpecSyn only uses the set for estimation purposes; SpecSyn outputs software at the algorithmic level, in accordance with the SER methodology.

COSYMA [12] focuses on microcontroller-based systems. An extended C input is converted to a basic-block and statement-level graph, which is partitioned among an architecture consisting of a standard processor, custom processor, memory and bus. Fast indirect metrics guide the simulated annealing partitioning, the resulting implementation is then analyzed using more complex metrics, and the results are used to guide further iterations. Vulcan II [13] uses a similar architecture and applies a greedy partitioning heuristic with fast indirect metrics. Recent focus has been on analyzing input constraints for use during partitioning and synthesis.

A large number of other approaches exist. Summaries can be found in [29] and [50].

SpecSyn possesses many unique features. First, SpecSyn outputs a system-level description in order to support the SER methodology. Second, SpecSyn is intended to support a variety of system architectures, heuristics, estimation models, and cost functions; no one version of any of these items is advocated for all possible systems. For example, a suite of heuristics is provided, with easy ability to add new ones. Third, SpecSyn uses a two-level estimation method in which considerable effort is spent on both preestimation and online-estimation.

SpecSyn currently consists of over 150 000 lines of C code, and has been under development since 1989. Its main interface consists of a spreadsheet-like display showing each component and functional object along with annotations, constraints and metric values for each. Menu options permit designers to perform any of a number of design tasks, whose results are then reflected by updating values in the display; violated constraints are flagged for the user. SpecSyn has been released to several universities and to over 20 companies, and experiments with industry examples are ongoing.

Some limitations lend themselves to future work. First, SpecSyn does not currently support scheduling of the coarse-grained behaviors on the processors to which they are assigned, since in manual design, the system-level allocation and partition decisions are usually made before such scheduling decisions. However, in an automated approach, such scheduling might prove useful. Second, SpecSyn does not currently incorporate the postsynthesis metric values back into subsequent explore/refine iterations. Such incorporation could prove very useful. Third, a method should be introduced to allow designers to provide manual metric estimations. Such a method could be as simple as accepting numbers for use during preestimation, or as complex as using designer-defined expressions for combining annotations during online-estimation. Fourth, a method for design from partial specifications should be implemented. The method for allowing manual metric estimations would likely form a large part of this method. Fifth, estimation models must be continually improved to account for additional architectural features, such as pipelining, caching, and real-time operating systems, and to model fixed-processors like DMA controllers, Fourier transform blocks, Ethernet controllers, MPEG decoders, etc. Some work on pipelining has been reported in [51] and [52]. Sixth, exploration might be improved by considering ranges of designs during partitioning, rather than a single point in the range as is currently done. Seventh, transformations, such as parallelization, need to be developed and integrated with partitioning, as they play a key role in enabling good final implementations. Eighth, as package borders continually change and more components find their way onto a chip, a general method of partitioning and estimating for hierarchical components needs to be developed. Finally, a variety of input languages, such as C, Statecharts, and synchronous-dataflow-based languages, need to be supported.

VII. CONCLUSIONS

We have introduced a specify-explore-refine paradigm for system design. Our specification technique focuses on understandable specifications, which in turn encourages the use of front-end languages such as SpecCharts. Our approach to exploration uses preestimation and online-estimation to achieve both fast and accurate estimates, supports a variety of partitioning heuristics, and is intended to be continually extended, enabling a designer to examine numerous alternative designs quickly. Our refinement techniques automatically insert details into the specification that would otherwise have been manually written by the designer, thus relieving the designer of tedious effort. We expect that this paradigm and tool will eventually result in a 100-h design cycle, and our experiments demonstrate the feasibility of such a dramatic reduction in design time from current practice.

REFERENCES

[1] D. D. Gajski, N. D. Dutt, C. H. Wu, and Y. L. Lin, *High-Level Synthesis: Introduction to Chip and System Design.* Boston, MA: Kluwer-Academic, 1991.
[2] J. Vanhoof, K. VanRompaey, I. Bolsens, and H. DeMan, *High-level Synthesis for Real-Time Digital Signal Processing.* Boston, MA: Kluwer-Academic, 1993.
[3] G. DeMicheli, A. Sangiovanni-Vincentelli, and P. Antognetti, *Design Systems for VLSI Circuits: Logic Synthesis and Silicon Compilation.* Amsterdam, The Netherlands: Martinus Nijhoff, 1987.
[4] C. A. R. Hoare, "Communicating sequential processes," *Commun. ACM*, vol. 21, no. 8, pp. 666–677, 1978.
[5] D. Harel, H. Lachover, A. Naamad, A. Pnueli, M. Politi, R. Sherman, and A. Shtul-Trauring, "STATEMATE: A working environment for the development of complex reactive systems," in *Proc. Int. Conf. Software Eng.*, 1988, pp. 396–406.
[6] F. Vahid, S. Narayan, and D. Gajski, "SpecCharts: A VHDL front-end for embedded systems," *IEEE Trans. Comput.*, pp. 694–706, 1995
[7] E. Lee and D. Messerschmitt, "Synchronous data flow," *Proc. IEEE*, vol. 75, pp. 1235–1245, Sept. 1987.
[8] D. D. Gajski, F. Vahid, S. Narayan, and J. Gong, *Specification and Design of Embedded Systems.* Englewood Cliffs, NJ: Prentice-Hall, 1994.
[9] F. Vahid, "Procedure exlining: A transformation for improved system and behavioral synthesis," in *Proc. Int. Symp. Syst. Synthesis*, 1995, pp. 84–89.
[10] ——, "Procedure cloning: A transformation for improved system-level functional partitioning," in *Proc. European Design Test Conf. (EDTC)*, 1997, pp. 487–492.
[11] J. Gong, D. Gajski, and S. Narayan, "Software estimation using a generic processor model," in *Proc. European Design Test Conf. (EDTC)*, 1995, pp. 498–502.
[12] R. Ernst, J. Henkel, and T. Benner, "Hardware-software cosynthesis for microcontrollers," *IEEE Design Test Comput.*, pp. 64–75, Dec. 1994.

[13] R. Gupta and G. DeMicheli, "Hardware-software cosynthesis for digital systems," *IEEE Design Test Comput.*, pp. 29–41, Oct. 1993.
[14] M. C. McFarland and T. J. Kowalski, "Incorporating bottom-up design into hardware synthesis," *IEEE Trans. Comput.*, pp. 938–950, Sept. 1990.
[15] E. D. Lagnese and D. E. Thomas, "Architectural partitioning for system level synthesis of integrated circuits," *IEEE Trans. Comput.*, vol. 10, pp. 847–860, July 1991.
[16] C. H. Gebotys, "An optimization approach to the synthesis of multichip architectures," *IEEE Trans. VLSI Syst.*, vol. 2, pp. 11–20, Mar. 1994.
[17] Y. Y. Chen, Y. C. Hsu, and C. T. King, "MULTIPAR: Behavioral partition for synthesizing multiprocessor architectures," *IEEE Trans. VLSI Syst.*, vol. 2, pp. 21–32, Mar. 1994.
[18] K. Kucukcakar and A. Parker, "CHOP: A constraint-driven system-level partitioner," in *Proc. Design Automation Conf.*, 1991, pp. 514–519.
[19] R. Gupta and G. DeMicheli, "Partitioning of functional models of synchronous digital systems," in *Proc. Int. Conf. Computer-Aided Design*, 1990, pp. 216–219.
[20] P. Eles, Z. Peng, K. Kuchcinski, and A. Doboli, "Hardware-software partitioning with iterative improvement heuristics," in *Proc. Int. Symp. Syst. Synthesis*, 1996, pp. 71–76.
[21] F. Vahid and D. Gajski, "Specification partitioning for system design," in *Proc. Design Automation Conf.*, 1992, pp. 219–224.
[22] F. Vahid, T. D. M. Le, and Y. C. Hsu, "A comparison of functional and structural partitioning," in *Proc. Int. Symp. Syst. Synthesis*, 1996, pp. 121–126.
[23] X. Xiong, E. Barros, and W. Rosentiel, "A method for partitioning UNITY language in hardware and software," in *Proc. European Design Automation Conf. (EuroDAC)*, 1994.
[24] F. Vahid, J. Gong, and D. D. Gajski, "A binary-constraint search algorithm for minimizing hardware during hardware-software partitioning," in *Proc. European Design Automation Conf. (EuroDAC)*, 1994, pp. 214–219.
[25] P. Eles, Z. Peng, and A. Doboli, "VHDL system-level specification and partitioning in a hardware/software co-synthesis environment," in *Proc. Int. Workshop on Hardware-Software Co-Design*, 1992, pp. 49–55.
[26] A. Kalavade and E. A. Lee, "A global criticality/local phase driven algorithm for the constrained hardware/software partitioning problem," in *Proc. Int. Workshop on Hardware-Software Co-Design*, 1994, pp. 42–48.
[27] J. G. D'Ambrosio and X. Hu, "Configuration-level hardware/software partitioning for real-time embedded systems," in *Proc. Int. Workshop Hardware-Software Co-Design*, 1994, pp. 34–41.
[28] F. Vahid and D. D. Gajski, "Clustering for improved system-level functional partitioning," in *Proc. Int. Symp. Syst. Synthesis*, 1995, pp. 28–33.
[29] D. D. Gajski and F. Vahid, "Specification and design of embedded hardware-software systems," *IEEE Design Test Comput.*, vol. 12, pp. 53–67, 1995.
[30] J. V. Rajan and D. E. Thomas, "Synthesis by delayed binding of decisions," in *Proc. Design Automation Conf.*, 1985.
[31] F. Vahid and D. D. Gajski, "Incremental hardware estimation during hardware/software functional partitioning," *IEEE Trans. VLSI Syst.*, vol. 3, pp. 459–464, Sept. 1995.
[32] J. W. Hagerman and D. E. Thomas, "Process transformation for system level synthesis," Tech. Rep. CMUCAD-93-08, 1993.
[33] R. A. Walker and D. E. Thomas, "Behavioral transformation for algorithmic level IC design," *IEEE Trans. Comput.*, pp. 1115–1128, Oct. 1989.
[34] A. Nicolau and R. Potasman, "Incremental tree height reduction for high level synthesis," in *Proc. Design Automation Conf.*, 1991, pp. 770–774.
[35] M. Girkar and C. D. Polychronopoulos, "Automatic extraction of functional parallelism from ordinary programs," *IEEE Trans. Parallel Distrib. Syst.*, pp. 166–178, 1992.
[36] F. Vahid, "Port calling: A transformation for reducing I/O during multipackage functional partitioning," in *Int. Symp. Syst. Synthesis*, 1997.
[37] S. Narayan and D. D. Gajski, "Synthesis of system-level bus interfaces," in *Proc. European Conf. Design Automation (EDAC)*, 1994.
[38] ———, "Protocol generation for communication channels," in *Proc. Design Automation Conf.*, 1994, pp. 547–551.
[39] G. Borriello and R. H. Katz, "Synthesis and optimization of interface transducer logic," in *Proc. Int. Conf. Computer-Aided Design*, 1987.
[40] J. Akella and K. McMillan, "Synthesizing converters between finite state protocols," in *Proc. Int. Conf. Computer Design*, 1991.
[41] J. S. Sun and R. W. Brodersen, "Design of system interface modules," in *Proc. Int. Conf. Computer-Aided Design*, 1992, pp. 478–481.
[42] D. Becker, R. K. Singh, and S. G. Tell, "An engineering environment for hardware/software co-simulation," in *Proc. Design Automation Conf.*, 1992, pp. 129–134.

[43] R. Gupta, C. N. Coelho, and G. DeMicheli, "Synthesis and simulation of digital systems containing interacting hardware and software components," in *Proc. Design Automation Conf.*, 1992, pp. 225–230.
[44] A. Kalavade and E. A. Lee, "A hardware/software codesign methodology for DSP applications," *IEEE Design Test Comput.*, 1993.
[45] S. Sutarwala and P. Paulin, "Flexible modeling environment for embedded systems design," in *Proc. Int. Workshop Hardware-Software Co-Design*, 1994, pp. 124–130.
[46] J. Gong, D. Gajski, and S. Bakshi, "Model refinement for hardware-software codesign," in *Proc. European Design Test Conf. (EDTC)*, 1996.
[47] L. Ramachandran, D. D. Gajski, S. Narayan, F. Vahid, and P. Fung, "Toward achieving a 100-hour design cycle: A test case," in *Proc. European Design Automation Conf. (EuroDAC)*, 1994, pp. 144–149.
[48] A. Balboni, W. Fornaciari, and D. Sciuto, "Partitioning and exploration strategies in the TOSCA co-design flow," in *Proc. Int. Workshop Hardware-Software Co-Design*, 1993, pp. 62–69.
[49] S. Antoniazzi, A. Balboni, W. Fornaciari, and D. Sciuto, "A methodology for control-dominated systems codesign," in *Proc. Int. Workshop Hardware-Software Co-Design*, 1994, pp. 2–9.
[50] W. H. Wolf, "Hardware-software co-design of embedded systems," *Proc. IEEE*, vol. 82, pp. 967–989, July 1994.
[51] S. Bakshi and D. D. Gajski, "A component selection algorithm for high-performance pipelines," in *Proc. European Design Automation Conf. (EuroDAC)*, 1994, pp. 400–405.
[52] S. Bakshi and D. D. Gajski, "A memory selection algorithm for high-performance pipelines," in *Proc. European Design Automation Conf. (EuroDAC)*, 1994, pp. 124–129.

Daniel D. Gajski (M'77–SM'83–F'94) received the Dipl.Ing. and M.S. degrees in electrical engineering from the University of Zagreb, Croatia, and the Ph.D. degree in computer and information sciences from the University of Pennsylvania, Philadelphia.

After ten years of industrial experience in digital circuits, switching systems, supercomputer design, and VLSI structures, he spent ten years in academia with the Department of Computer Science at the University of Illinois, Urbana-Champaign. Presently, he is a Professor in the Department of Information and Computer Sciences at the University of California, Irvine. His interests are in multiprocessor architectures and science of design. He is editor of the book *High-Level Synthesis: An Introduction to Chip and System Design* (New York: Kluwer-Academic, 1992) and *Specification and Design of Embedded Systems* (Englewood Cliffs, NJ: Prentice-Hall, 1994), and the author of *Principles of Digital Design* (Englewood Cliffs, NJ: Prentice-Hall, 1985).

Frank Vahid (S'89–M'93) received the B.S. degree in electrical and computer engineering from the University of Illinois, Urbana-Champaign, in 1988. He received the M.S. and Ph.D. degrees in computer science from the University of California, Irvine, in 1990 and 1994, respectively, where he was an SRC fellow.

He has worked as an Engineer at Hewlett-Packard and AMCC. He is currently an Assistant Professor in the Department of Computer Science at the University of California, Riverside. His research interests include hardware/software codesign of embedded systems, intellectual property development and use, and functional partitioning. He is coauthor of the book *Specification and Design of Embedded Systems*.

Dr. Vahid served as Program Chair for the International Symposium on System Synthesis in 1996 and as General Chair in 1997.

Sanjiv Narayan received the B.S. degree in computer science from the Indian Institute of Technology, New Delhi, in 1988. He received the M.S. and Ph.D. degrees in computer science as a Chancellor's Fellow at the University of California, Irvine, in 1990 and 1994, respectively.

He is currently with Ambit Design Systems, Santa Clara, CA, where he is associated with the research and development of behavioral synthesis tools. His current research interests include behavioral synthesis, system specification and modeling, and interface synthesis. He is also a coauthor of *Specification and Design of Embedded Systems* (Englewood Cliffs, NJ: Prentice-Hall, 1994).

Jie Gong received the M.S. and Ph.D. degrees in computer science from the University of California, Irvine. She received the B.S. degree in computer engineering from the Tsinghua University, Beijing, People's Republic of China.

She was working at the Unified Design System Laboratory of Motorola, Inc., and currenlty she is with Qualcomm, Inc. Her research interests include behavioral synthesis and system-level design. She is a coauthor of the book, *Specification and Design of Embedded Systems* (Englewood Cliffs, NJ: Prentice-Hall, 1994).

Dr. Gong is a member of the ACM.

VHDL generation from SDL specifications

Jean-Marc Daveau, Gilberto Fernandes Marchioro, Carlos Alberto Valderrama and Ahmed Amine Jerraya

TIMA laboratory
TIMA/INPG 46 Avenue Felix Viallet, 38031 Grenoble cedex, France
Email {daveau, marchior, valderr, jerraya}@verdon.imag.fr
FAX : (+33) 4 76 47 38 14

Abstract

The aim of this paper is to present an approach that allows the generation of VHDL from system level specifications in SDL. Our approach overcome the main known problem encountered by previous work which is the communication between different processes. We allow SDL communication to be translated into VHDL for synthesis. This is made possible by the use of an intermediate form that support a powerful communication model which enable the representation in a synthesis oriented manner of most communication schemes. This intermediate form allows the refinement of the system in order to obtain the desired solution. The main refinement step, called communication synthesis, is aimed at fixing the protocol and the interface used by the different processes to communicate. The refined specification is translated into VHDL for synthesis using existing CAD tools. We illustrate the feasibility of our approach through two SDL to VHDL translation examples.

Keywords

Hardware/Software codesign, SDL, System level specification, VHDL, generation, Communication synthesis

1 INTRODUCTION

As the system complexity grows there is the need for new methods to handle large system design. One way to manage that complexity is to rise the level of abstraction of the specifications by using system level description languages. On the other side, as the level of abstraction rise the gap between the concepts used for the specifications at the system level (communication channels, interacting processes, data types) and those used for hardware synthesis becomes wider. Although these languages are well suited for the specification and validation of complex real time distributed systems, the concepts manipulated are not easy to map onto hardware description languages. It is thus necessary to defines methods for system level synthesis enabling efficient synthesis from system level specifications.

1.1 Objective

System level specification language offers concepts and methods adapted to the description of complex systems. They provide formal methods for verifying and validating the system behaviour. As a system level specification serves as a basis for deriving an implementation, it should abstract from implementation details in order to postpone implementation decisions and not to exclude any valid realisation. Therefore many intermediate refinement steps are needed to achieve a realisation. Each of this steps will fixes implementation details closing the gap between the specification and the realisation. Several concepts supported by system level specification languages (finite state machine, communication through high level schemes, exceptions) are not easily represented in hardware description languages and need a cumbersome implementation. Therefore, having an automatic translation is then an efficient and errors free way of deriving an implementation from system level specifications.

When translating high level languages for implementation the main problem is to convert high level communication model. Direct implementation of system communication models inevitably leads to infeasible solution as system communication models are abstract and general. To achieve efficient solutions different communication schemes and protocols may be needed in embedded systems as well as different interconnection topologies.

In this paper we introduce a new approach for generating VHDL code from SDL system level specifications that overcome the problem of mapping system level concepts into hardware. The main objective for our method are :

1. to have an automatic VHDL code generation from system level specifications. Concepts that have no efficient hardware semantics will not be handled. The code produced should be acceptable by existing simulation and synthesis tools.
2. to have an efficient implementation of system level communication schemes.
3. to be able to choose between different communication schemes through a library.
4. to be able to model the system behaviour independently of the communication in a modular way. System specification should be independent of the communication specification in order to allow changes in the communication scheme without any changes in the system specification.

In addition our methodology should be compatible with others system design tools such as hardware/software partitioning and software code generation from SDL.

1.2 Previous Work

Several previous work on system level synthesis are reported in the literature [Gajski 95], [Narayan 91] but only a few of them address the field of system synthesis from SDL specification [Bonatti 95], [Glunz 93], [Pulkkinen 92]. Although SDL [TU-T 93] is widely used in the software and telecommunication community [Bochmann 93], it did not gain acceptance among the hardware designers. Many approaches try to use or extend existing hardware description languages such as VHDL [Eles 94], OO-VHDL [Swamy 95] by adding some object oriented and high level communication features.

Several approaches have extended single threaded languages to support hardware and communication concepts. Most of them have used the C language such as HardwareC [Mooney 96] or C^x [Ernst 93]. Another approach is to create a new system level specification language as SpecChart [Narayan 93], [Vahid 95].

Other approaches use synchronous specification languages [Halbwachs 93] such as Esterel [Boussinot 91] [Chiodo 96], Signal [Le Guernic 91], Alpha [Le Moenner 96] or StateCharts [Buchenrieder 96].

Only few approaches have tried to use existing distributed system specification language such as SDL [Bonatti 95], [Glunz 93], [Pulkkinen 92], Lotos [Carreras 96], [Delgado Kloos 95] or Estelle [Wytrebwicz 95]. This is mainly due to the gap existing between the concepts manipulated by such languages and those used in hardware description languages. These languages offers concepts like concurrency and abstract communication. We believe that this gap can be closed by the use of progressive refinements [Ben Ismail 95], [Krueger 92]. However most of the work has concentrated on straightforward translation. Specification refinements are needed as the abstraction level of system level specifications is often too high to be executed directly and efficiently. The goal in this phase is to produce an executable system that satisfies the high level specification and that also exhibits acceptable performances. This transformational phase can be thought as an interactive, human guided compilation. Human interaction is necessary because such automatic algorithms are beyond compiler technology [Krueger 92], [Gajski 94], [Gong 96] uses SpecChart as an intermediate form for progressive refinements although this language does not allows to model easily complex communication schemes such as message passing.

[Bonatti 95], [Glunz 93] and [Pulkkinen 92] generate VHDL from SDL specification. In [Pulkkinen 92], strong restrictions to the communication model are made. The translation to VHDL does not provide a queue into which incoming signals of a process are stored (see section 2). Instead, it translates each SDL signal into a VHDL signal changing the communication model from message passing to signals (see section 3). Each signal can have at most one parameter. Although this approach allows an easy synthesis, only one implementation of the SDL communication model is possible. It provides a correct implementation of the SDL execution model only when each state of the finite state machine has one transition. In [Bonatti 95], the mapping algorithm also simplifies the communication model to obtain synthesisable hardware. Three protocols are available from the library :

1. one single position queue shared by all signals.
2. one single position queue for each signal. In this case a process may have several queues
3. one N positions queue for all signals.

Any of the three protocols can be used and new protocols can be added to the library. As in [Pulkkinen 92] it assigns one VHDL signal for each SDL signal. When using the second protocol, the algorithm requires the designer interaction to assign priorities to signals. This model does not respect the SDL communication model as signals are consumed in the order of their priorities and not in the order of their arrival. Glunz [Glunz 93] presents a more powerful approach for SDL to VHDL translation. The communication model can be changed through the use of a protocol library but it support only a subset of SDL. It does not support transition in procedures, labels and doesn't seem to support states with different transitions fired by signals having a different number of parameters.

To our knowledge none of the previous approaches overcome the main encountered translation problems related to communication. The major contribution of this paper is to present an approach where the synthesis is made through an intermediate form which allows transformations and refinements on the system. This allows to support a wide subset of SDL and to overcome the problem of communication.

In the following sections we present our approach to system level synthesis from SDL specifications. The next section gives an overview of the main SDL concepts used for system specification. In section 3 we emphasize the main differences between SDL and VHDL concept that may cause translation problems. Section 4 presents our intermediate representation and the different design steps. Section 5 introduces the communication model used for intermediate refinement and the concept of communication units. In this section we also detail the steps needed to overcome the problem of communication in system level synthesis from high level communication specification. Section 6 describe synthesis from SDL and give the supported subset. Finally we present some results before concluding.

2 SYSTEM SPECIFICATIONS WITH SDL

SDL (specification and description language) is intended for the modelling and simulation of real time, distributed and telecommunication systems and is standardised by the ITU [ITU-T 93]. A system described in SDL is regarded as a set of concurrent processes that communicate with each others using signals. SDL support different concepts for describing systems such as structure, behaviour and communication. SDL is intended for describing large designs at the system level. There are two SDL formats, a textual and a graphical one.

2.1 Structure

The static structure of a system is described by a hierarchy of blocks. A block can contain other blocks, resulting in a tree structure or a set of processes to describe the behaviour of a terminal block. Processes are connected with each other and to the boundary of the block by signalroutes. Blocks are connected together by channels. Channels and signalroutes are a way of conveying signals that are used by the processes to communicate. Signals exchanged by the processes follow a communication path made up of signalroutes and channels from the sending to the receiving process (Figure 2). SDL also support dynamic feature that are software oriented like dynamic process creation and dynamic addressing.

2.2 Behaviour

The behaviour of a system is described by a set of autonomous and concurrent processes. A process is described by a finite state machine that communicate asynchronously with other processes by signals. Each process has an input queue where signals are buffered on arrival. Signals are extracted from the input queue by the process in the order in which they arrived. In other words, signals are buffered in a first-in-first-out order.

Each process is composed of a set of states and transitions. The arrival of an expected signal in the input queue validate a transition and the process can then execute a set of actions such as manipulating variables, procedures call and emission of signals. The received signal determines the transition to be executed. When a signal has initiated a transition it is removed from the input queue. In SDL, variables are owned by a specific process and cannot be modified by others processes. The synchronisation between processes is achieved using the exchange of signals only. SDL includes communication through revealed and exported shared variables. However they are single-writer-multiple-readers. Shared variables are not recommended in the SDL92 standard. Each process has an unique address (Pid) which identify it. A signal always carries the address of the sending and the receiving processes in addition to possible values. The destination address may be used if the destination process cannot be determined statically and the address of the sending process may be used to reply to a signal. Figure 1 represents an SDL process specification. State *start* represents the default state. *Input* represents the guard of a transition. This transition will be triggered when the specified signal is extracted from the input queue. *Task* represent an action to perform when the transition is executed and *output* emit a signal with its possible parameters.

```
PROCESS SpeedControl;
DCL Vin integer;
DCL Vout, Vout_1 integer;
DCL CtrlConst integer;
START ;
        TASK Vout:=0, Vout_1:=0, Vin:=0;
        OUTPUT NewSpeed1(0);
        NEXTSTATE WaitK;
STATE WaitK;
        INPUT ControlConst1(CtrlConst);
        NEXTSTATE WaitSpeed;
ENDSTATE;
STATE WaitSpeed;
INPUT MDReady1;
        TASK Vout_1:=Vout;
        TASK Vout:=Vout_1 + CtrlConst*(Vin - (Vout_1/UPSCALE) );
        OUTPUT NewSpeed1(Vout/UPSCALE);
        NEXTSTATE WaitSpeed;
INPUT SpeedCmd(Vin);
        NEXTSTATE WaitSpeed;
INPUT ControlConst1(CtrlConst);
        NEXTSTATE WaitSpeed;
        ENDSTATE;
ENDPROCESS SpeedControl;
```

Figure 1 SDL process specification

2.3 Communication

Signals are transferred between processes using signalroutes and channels. If the processes are contained in different blocks, signals must traverse channels. The main difference between channels and signalroutes are :

- channels may perform a routing operation on signals, it routes a signal to different channels (signalroutes) connected to it at the frontier of a block depending on the receiving process.
- a communication through signalroutes is timeless while a communication through channel is delayed nondeterministically. No assumption can be made on the delay and no ordering can be presumed for signals using different delaying paths.

Figure 2 represents the structure and communication specification of an SDL system.

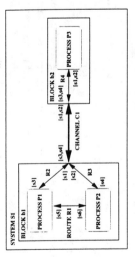

Figure 2 SDL signalroutes and channels

Channels and signalroutes may be both uni and bidirectional. If many signals are transferred on the same channel or signalroute their ordering is preserved. When going through a channel or signal route, signals are not allowed to overtake each other. However there is no specific ordering of signals arriving in the input queue of a process that have followed different channels and signalroutes.

3 DISTANCE BETWEEN SDL AND VHDL CONCEPTS

In this section we emphasize the main differences between SDL an VHDL concepts that may generate translation problems. These include :

(a) Execution Model

Every language is based on a computation model that specify the control or data flow and the synchronisation [Halbwachs 93]. SDL and VHDL are both control flow oriented.

In SDL, each process evolve independently according to the signals received. The execution of parallel processes can be non deterministic. For example when a process receive at the same time two signals coming from two different processes their ordering in the input queue cannot be predicted.

In VHDL, the execution of parallel processes is scheduled by the simulator. Every Δ-cycle, all processes are evaluated. Signals assignement are instantaneous and deterministic as conflicts are resolved through resolution functions. With VHDL93 nondeterminism can be introduced using shared variables.

When going from an SDL specification to a VHDL implementation signals have to be scheduled in the input queues, one has then to ensure that the ordering of the signals is valid.

(b) Communication Abstraction

Interprocess communication relies basically on two models : message passing and shared memory [Andrews 83]. SDL uses the former while VHDL uses the latter. In message passing, processes communicate through messages send with a specific protocol. With shared memory processes communicate through data stored in a common memory. In VHDL communication can also be carried using signals.

Modelling SDL communication in VHDL requires an expansion of the communication protocol and input queue that are implicit in SDL.

(c) Behavioural Description

The behavioural model specify how to describe the behaviour of the system.

In SDL, the basic construct is the finite state machine. SDL also provides dynamic features such as process creation or dynamic addressing.

In VHDL the number of component instances is fixed and behaviour is specified through processes in an algorithmic form. Moreover VHDL does not provide facilities for control flow specification such as *exception*, *reset*. Representing these concepts in VHDL requires cumbersome descriptions [Narayan 93].

(d) Time

In SDL, a time reference is offered by a global time server. This server manage the set of timers by providing *set* and *reset* primitives. Timers can be used to synchronise processes on an external event. The global time is available to every process through the variable *now*.

In VHDL, the time is also available through the global simulation time. Processes can use this global time for the synchronisation and the scheduling of signals assignment (*for* and *after* clause). The global simulation time is available through the variable *now* although it is not supported for synthesis. The translation of SDL timers implies choices concerning their realisation. In SDL the different timers are independent and are not synchronised by a common clock.

(e) Data Type

SDL offers the possibility to define abstract data types and generic operators for the specification of data types. Operators can be defined in an algorithmic form in SDL or C or through a state machine in SDL. VHDL only provides simple data types but SDL abstract data type can be translated in VHDL without introducing changes in the original program.

As shown in table 1, SDL support most of the system specification concepts as defined in [Vahid 95]. The main restrictions come from the behavioural hierarchy that is not supported and from a single available communication model. VHDL does not support directly some of these concepts (finite state machines, communication through high level schemes, exception handling)

language	hierarchy	concurrency	behaviour	synchronisation	communication	exception handling	timing
SDL	structural	single level of process	finite state machines	global signals	message passing, FIFO protocol	yes STATE *	timers
VHDL	structural	statement level parallelism, process	algorithm, data flow equation	WAIT statement, Common events	shared memory, signals	no	AFTER clause

Table 1 VHDL and SDL supported concepts

but they can be implemented using cumbersome description. A more complete comparison of several specification languages can be found in [Narayan 93].

4 AN SDL BASED HARDWARE/SOFTWARE CODESIGN ENVIRONMENT

In this section we present COSMOS, a methodology and an environment for the specification and the synthesis of mixed systems containing hardware and software. COSMOS starts with an SDL specification and produce a C/VHDL distributed architecture. In this paper we will concentrate on the VHDL generation only.

Our approach is based on an intermediate form on which interactive and incremental refinements are performed. The use of an intermediate representation permits the unification of different specifications described in hardware, software or system description languages. The codesign process starts with a functional specification which is translated into the intermediate form. The next steps are partitioning, communication synthesis and architecture generation.

The partitioning decompose the initial specification into abstract processors (partition) that may be transposed on the target architecture composed of hardware parts (ASIC, FPGA), software parts (processor + code) and communication modules (FIFO, memories, buses, IPC, interrupts). Each abstract processor may execute in hardware or in software.

Communication synthesis generally follows the system partitioning. Communication synthesis aims at fixing the protocol and interfaces used by the communicating subsystems. It is detailed in section 5. System are specified using the communication model offered by the specification language. This communication model may not suit the requirement of the final design and can be changed during communication synthesis.

The architecture generation step produces an executable description in C and VHDL for each abstract processor resulting of the partitioning step. The communication modules are extracted from a library.

5 COMMUNICATION SYNTHESIS

In this section we describe our communication modelling scheme for system level synthesis. This model aims at representing and implementing the communication scheme used in specification languages. Our model should be general enough to accommodate different communication schemes such as message passing or shared memory and allow an efficient implementation of a system level communication specifications.

5.1 Communication Model

In this paper we will use the communication modelling strategy described in [Ben Ismail 95]. At the system level, a system is represented by a set of

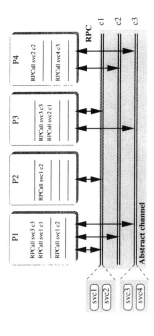

Figure 3 Specification of communication with abstract channels

processes communicating through abstract channels (figure 3). An abstract channel is an entity able to execute a communication scheme invoked through a procedure call mechanism. It offers high level communication primitives that are used by the processes to communicate. Access to the channel is controlled by this fixed set of communication primitives and relies on remote procedures call [Andrews 91] of these primitives. A process that is willing to communicate through a channel makes a remote procedure call to a communication primitive of that channel. Once the remote procedure call is done the com-

130   CHAPTER 2: Modeling

munication is executed independently of the calling process by the channel unit. The communication primitives are transparent to the calling processes. This allows processes to communicate by means of high level communication schemes while making no assumption on the implementation of the communication.

There is no predefined set of communication primitives, they are defined as standard procedures and are attached to the abstract channel. Each application may have a different set of communication primitives (*send_int*, *send_short*, *send_atm*, *etc*). The communication primitives are the only visible part of an abstract channel.

The use of remote procedures call allows to separate communication specification from the rest of the system. These communication schemes can be described separately. In our approach the detailed I/O structure and protocols are hidden in a library of communication components. Figure 3 shows a conceptual communication over an abstract communication network. The processes communicate through three abstract channels *c1*, *c2* and *c3*. *c1* and *c2* offers services *svc1*, *svc2* and *c3* offers services *svc3*, *svc4* (services *svc1* and *svc2* offered by abstract channel *c2* are not represented).

(a) Protocol Selection and Communication Unit Allocation

Allocation of communication units starts with a set of processes communicating through abstract channels (figure 3) and a library of communication units (figure 4). These communication units are an abstraction of some physical used for data exchange. This step is called protocol selection or communication unit allocation. The second step, called interface synthesis, adapts the interface of the different processes to the selected communication network.

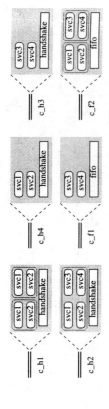

Figure 4 Library of communication units

components. This step chooses the appropriate set of communication units from the library in order to provide the services required by the communicating processes. The communication between the processes may be executed by one of the schemes described in the library. The choice of a given communication unit will not only depend on the communication to be executed but also on the performances required and the implementation technology of the communicating processes. This step fixes the protocol used by each communication primitive by choosing a communication unit with a specific protocol for each abstract channel. It also determines the interconnection topology of the processes by fixing the number of communication units and the abstract channels executed on it.

5.2 Communication Unit Modelling

We define a communication unit as an abstraction of a physical component. Communication units are selected from the library and instantiated during the communication synthesis step.

From a conceptual point of view, the communication unit is an object that can execute one or several communication primitives with a specific protocol. A communication unit is composed of a set of primitives, a controller and an interface. The complexity of the controller may range from a simple handshake to a complex layered protocol. This modular scheme hides the details of the realisation in a library where a communication unit may have different implementations depending on the target architecture (hardware/software).

Communication abstraction in this manner enables a modular specification, allowing communication to be treated independently from the rest of the design.

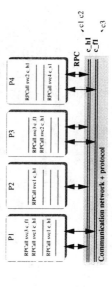

Figure 5 System after allocation of communication units

An example of communication unit allocation for the system of figure 3 is given in figure 5. Starting with the library of communication units of figure 4, the communication unit *c_h1* has been allocated for handling the communica-

5.3 Communication Synthesis

Communication synthesis aims to transform a system composed of processes that communicate via high level primitives through abstract channels into a set of interconnected processors that communicate via signals and share communication control. Starting from such a specification two steps are needed. The first is aimed to fix the communication network structure and protocols

tion offered by the two abstract channels c1 and c2. Communication unit c_h1 is able to execute two independent communication requiring services svc1 and svc2. Communication unit c_f1 has been allocated for abstract channel c3.

(b) Interface Synthesis

Interface synthesis selects an implementation for each of the communication units from the implementation library (figure 6) and generates the required interfaces and interconnections for all the processes using the communication units (figure 7). The library may contain several implementations of the same

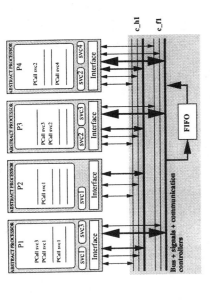

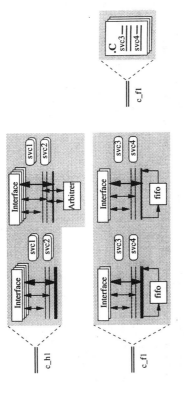

Figure 6 Implementation library

communication unit. Each communication unit is realised by a specific implementation selected from the library with regard to data transfer rates, memory buffering capacity, and the data bus width. The interface of the different processes are adapted according to the implementation selected and interconnected. The result of interface synthesis is a set of interconnected processors communicating through signals, buses and possible additional dedicated components selected from the implementation library such as bus arbiter, fifo, etc. With this approach it is possible to map communication specification into any protocol, from a simple handshake to a complex protocol.

Starting from the system of figure 5, the result of interface synthesis task is detailed in figure 7. The communication unit c_h1 has two possible implementations, one with an external bus arbiter for scheduling the two communication, the other with the arbiter distributed in the interfaces. Any of the two implementation may be selected.

6 HARDWARE SYNTHESIS FROM SDL SPECIFICATIONS

This section details the refinement steps and the models used by COSMOS in order to transform an SDL model into VHDL. This process support a large

subset of SDL. Only the concepts that are difficult to implement in hardware are excluded from the supported subset.

Figure 7 System after interface synthesis

6.1 Restriction for Hardware Synthesis

SDL support a general and abstract communication model that is not well suited for hardware synthesis. This is mainly due to the fact that signals can be routed through channels. In other words the destination of a signal can be determined dynamically by the address of the receiver. In SDL, the dynamic routing scheme is mainly intended for use with the dynamic process creation feature. This feature is very software oriented and is difficult to map in hardware. Nevertheless we can restrict the SDL communication model for hardware synthesis without loosing too much of its generality and abstraction. The restriction imposed on SDL will concern its dynamical aspects such as process creation and message routing.

6.2 Supported Subset

A wide subset of SDL is supported including :

- *system*, *block*, *process*, multiple instances.
- *state*, *state **, *state *()*, *save*, *save **, continuous signals, enabling condition.
- *input*, *output*, signals with parameters, *task*, *label*, *join*, *nextstate*, *stop*, *decision*, procedure call, imported and exported variables.

132 CHAPTER 2: Modeling

the abstract channel to read and write the signal and its parameters in the channel.

Feature not supported includes : dynamic creation of processes, *Pid* (supported for multiple instances processes), channel substructure, non determinism (*input any, input none, decision any*).

6.3 Correspondence Model Between SDL and VHDL

In this section we present the translation patterns for the main SDL concepts.

(a) Structure

As stated in paragraph 6.1 dynamic aspects of SDL are not considered for hardware synthesis. To avoid any routing problem and obtain an efficient communication, we will restrict ourselves to the case where the destination process of a signal can be statically determined. Communication structure can then be flattened at compile time. A signal emitted by a process through a set of channels must have a single receiver among the processes connected to these channels. In such a case, channels only forward signals from one boundary of a block to another. No routing decision may be taken as there is only one path for a signal through a set of channels. Therefore channels and signalroutes won't be represented in the final system. A process that is emitting a signal will write it directly in the input queue of the destination process without going through several channels. Flattening the communication eliminates the communication overhead that occurs when traversing several channels.

(b) Behaviour

Each SDL process will be translated into the corresponding finite state machine. During the partitioning step state machines may be splitted and merged to achieved the desired solution. This step may generate additional communication steps like shared variables. All the communication protocols and implementation details will be fixed by the communication synthesis step regardless from where it has been generated (initial specification or partitioning).

(c) Communication

In SDL, each process has a single implicit queue used to store incoming messages. Therefore we will associate one abstract channel to each process (figure 8). This abstract channel will stand for the input queue and will offer the required communication primitives. During the communication synthesis steps a communication unit able to execute the required communication scheme will be selected from the library. This approach allows the designer to choose from the library a communication unit that provide an efficient implementation of the required communication. Despite the fact that SDL offers only one communication model, several different protocols may be allocated from the library for different abstract channels (see paragraph 5.3.a).

Each signal will be translated as two communication primitives offered by

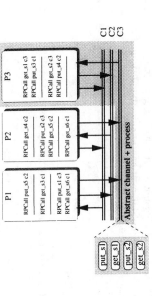

Figure 8 Modelling SDL communication with abstract channels

Figure 8 represents the refined SDL model corresponding to the system of figure 2 for synthesis. Each SDL process is mapped to a process containing the behavioural part of the specification and an abstract channel that offers communication primitives to send and receive signals. Each process will read from its own channel and write into other processes channel. An SDL specification is therefore represented by a set of processes and abstract channels. As stated before channels and signalroutes are not represented.

7 RESULTS

We present here some results concerning VHDL generation from system level specifications.

Figure 9 give the generated code for the process of figure 1. Figure 10 gives an implementation of the communication primitives implementing the SDL communication. The input queue of the process is not detailed in the example below. It is a standard fifo. Communication primitives (figure 10) read and write to the fifo ports.

```
entity speedcontrol is
   Generic ( IPCKEY: INTEGER := 1 );
   Port (
      CLK: IN BIT;
      RST: IN BIT;
      motorsender_wr_req: OUT BIT;
      motorsender_wr_rdy: IN BIT;
      motorsender_wr_blk: OUT BIT;
      motorsender_rd_req: OUT BIT;
      motorsender_rd_rdy: IN BIT;
      motorsender_data_io: INOUT INTEGER;
      speedcontrol_wr_req: OUT BIT;
      speedcontrol_wr_rdy: IN BIT;
      speedcontrol_wr_blk: OUT BIT;
      speedcontrol_rd_req: OUT BIT;
      speedcontrol_rd_rdy: IN BIT;
      speedcontrol_data_io: INOUT INTEGER
   );
end speedcontrol;

architecture behaviour of speedcontrol is
begin
```

```
process
  variable sdl_signal: INTEGER;
  variable vin: INTEGER;
  variable vout: INTEGER;
  variable vout_1: INTEGER;
  variable ctrlconst: INTEGER;
  variable PCALL: INTEGER:= 1;
  procedure motorsender_put_int(
    sdl_signal: IN INTEGER; param_1: IN INTEGER );
  procedure speedcontrol_get_int(
    param_1: INOUT INTEGER );
  type StateType is (initial, waitk, waitspeed);
  variable NextState: StateType:= initial;
begin
  wait until (rising_edge(CLK)) OR (RST='1');
  if (RST='1') then
    NextState:= initial;
    wait until (rising_edge(CLK));
  end if;
  StateTable_speedcontrol: loop
    case NextState is
      when(initial) =>
        vout:= 0;
        vout_1:= 0;
        vin:= 0;
        motorsender_put_int(
          sdl_signal=> 2,
          param_1=> 0 );
        NextState:= wait;
        exit StateTable_speedcontrol;
      when(wait) =>
        speedcontrol_get_int(
          sdl_signal=> sdl_signal );
        if (sdl_signal = 14) then
          speedcontrol_get_int(
          param_1=> ctrlconst );
        motorsender_wr_req<= '0';
        if NOT(motorsender_wr_rdy = '0') then
```

```
          NextState:= waitspeed;
          exit StateTable_speedcontrol;
        end if;
      when(waitspeed) =>
        speedcontrol_get_int(
          sdl_signal=> sdl_signal );
        if (sdl_signal = 3) then
          vout_1:= vout;
          vout:= (vout_1 + (ctrlconst *
            (vin - (vout_1 / upscale))));
          motorsender_put_int(
            sdl_signal=> 2,
            param_1=> (vout / upscale));
          NextState:= waitspeed;
          exit StateTable_speedcontrol;
        else
          if (sdl_signal = 15) then
            speedcontrol_get_int(
              param_1=> vin);
            NextState:= waitspeed;
            exit StateTable_speedcontrol;
          end if;
        end if;
      end case;
      exit StateTable_speedcontrol;
    end loop StateTable_speedcontrol;
  end process;
end behaviour;
```

Figure 9 generated VHDL code

```
procedure motorsender_put_int(
  sdl_signal: in INTEGER; param_1: in INTEGER ) is
  type StateType is (SPIDLE, request, signalio, paramio);
  variable NextState: StateType:= request;
begin
  PCALL:= 1;
  while (PCALL = 1) loop
    StateTable_put_integer: loop
      case NextState is
        when(request) =>
          motorsender_wr_req<= '1';
          motorsender_wr_blk<= '1';
          if NOT(motorsender_wr_rdy = '1') then
            wait until (motorsender_wr_rdy = '1');
          end if;
          motorsender_data_io<= sdl_signal;
          NextState:= signalio;
          exit StateTable_put_integer;
        when(signalio) =>
          motorsender_wr_req<= '0';
          if NOT(motorsender_wr_rdy = '0') then
```

```
            wait until
              (motorsender_wr_rdy = '0');
          end if;
          motorsender_data_io<= 0;
          motorsender_wr_req<= '1';
          if NOT(motorsender_wr_rdy
            = '1') then
            wait until
              (motorsender_wr_rdy = '1');
          end if;
          motorsender_data_io<= param_1;
          motorsender_wr_blk<= '0';
          NextState:= paramio;
          exit StateTable_put_integer;
        when(paramio) =>
          motorsender_wr_req<= '0';
          if NOT(motorsender_wr_rdy
            = '0') then
            wait until
              (motorsender_wr_rdy = '0') then
          end if;
```

```
          motorsender_data_io<= 0;
          NextState:= SPIDLE;
        when OTHERS =>
          PCALL:= 0;
          NextState:= request;
      end case;
      exit StateTable_put_integer;
    end loop;
  end loop;
end motorsender_put_int;
```

```
          end loop StateTable_put_integer;
          if (PCALL=1) then
            wait until (rising_edge(CLK));
          end if;
        end loop;
      end motorsender_put_int;
      exit StateTable_put_integer;
```

Figure 10 Implementation of communication primitives in VHDL

We can see from table 2 the line increase when going from SDL specification to VHDL implementation. Communication which represents only 10-20 % of the SDL specification represent more than 50 % of the implementation in VHDL. This is mainly due to the the high level of abstraction of the communication provided by SDL. The VHDL size is more than seven times the size of the corresponding SDL model.

design	complexity	SDL lines		VHDL lines		lines increase
		behaviour	communication	behaviour	communication	
pid controller	4 processes 34 states 33 transitions	331	73 (22 %)	2403	1194 (50 %)	726 %
fuzzy logic controller	9 processes 16 states 29 transitions	560	88 (15 %)	4765	2856 (60%)	850 %

Table 2 SDL to VHDL translation results

In SDL, communication requires one instruction to send a signal. The protocol, signal conveying and input queue are implicit. When going at the implementation level communication becomes explicit requiring a specific protocol, communication controller and buses.

8 CONCLUSION

In this paper we have described an approach whereby the Specification and Description Language (SDL) can be used for system level synthesis to produce an implementation in VHDL. We have emphasised on the necessity of interactive and progressive refinement steps to close the gap between the concepts used in system description languages and those of hardware description language. Our approach support a large subset of SDL, i.e all concepts that may be used for hardware specification. The generated VHDL code is acceptable by existing simulation and high level synthesis tools. Efficient implementation of system communication is achieved through a library of communication models.

ACKNOWLEDGEMENTS

This work was supported by France-Telecom/CNET under grant 94 1B 113, ESPRIT programme under project COMITY 23015, SGS-Thomson and Aerospatiale. The SDL to Solar translator was developed using the Verilog GEODE SDL environmement.

REFERENCES

G.R. Andrews and F.B. Schneider, *Concepts and Notation for Concurrent Programming*, Computing Survey, Vol 15, No 1, March 1983.

G.R. Andrews, *Concurrent Programming, Principles and Practice*, Benjamin/Cummings (eds) Redwood City, Calif, 1991.

T. Ben Ismail and A.A. Jerraya, *Synthesis Steps and Design Models for CoDesign*, IEEE Computer, special issue on rapid-prototyping of microelectronic systems, Vol. 28, No. 2, February 1995.

G.V. Bochmann, *Specification Languages for Communication Protocols*, Proceedings of the Conference on Hardware Description Languages, April 1993.

I.S. Bonatti and R.J.O. Figuerido, *An Algorithm for the translation of SDL into Synthesizable VHDL*, Current Issue in Electronic Modelling, Vol 3, August 1995.

F. Boussinot and R. De Simone, *The ESTEREL Language*, Proceedings of the IEEE, Vol. 79, No. 9, September 1991.

K. Buchenrieder, A. Pyttel and C. Veith, *Mapping StateCharts Models onto an FPGA Based ASIP Architecture*, Proceedings of the European Design Automation Conference with Euro-VHDL, September 1996.

C. Carreras, J.C. López et all, *A Codesign Methodology Based on Formal Specifications and High Level Estimation*, Proceedings of the CODES/CASHE workshop, March 1996.

M. Chiodo, D. Engels et all, *A case Study in Computer Aided Codesign of Embedded Controllers*, Design Automation for Embedded Systems, Vol. 1, No. 1-2, January 1996.

C. Delgado Kloos, A. Marin López et all, *From Lotos to VHDL*, Current Issue in Electronic modelling, Vol. 3, September 1995.

P. Elcs, Z. Peng and A. Doboli, *VHDL System Level Specification and Partitioning in a Hardware/Software Co-Synthesis environment*, Proceedings of International Workshop on Hardware/Software Codesign, April 1994.

R. Ernst, J. Henkel and T. Benner, *Hardware/Software Co-Synthesis for Microcontrollers*, IEEE Design & Test of Computers, Vol. 10 No. 4, pp. 64-75, December 1993.

D. Gajski, F. Vahid and S. Narayan, *A Design Methodology for Systems Specification Refinement*, Proceedings of the European Design Automation Conference (EDAC), February 1994.

D. Gajski and F. Vahid, *Specification and Design of Embedded Hardware/Software Systems*, IEEE Design & Test of Computers, Spring 1995.

W. Glunz, T. Kruse, T. Rossel and D. Monjau, *Integrating SDL and VHDL for System Level Specification*, Proceedings of the Conference on Hardware Description Languages, April 1993.

J. Gong and D. Gajski, *Model Refinement For Hardware Software Codesign*, Proceedings of the European Design & Test Conference, March 1996.

P. Le Guernic, T. Gautier et all, *Programming Real-Time Applications with SIGNAL*, Proceedings of the IEEE, Vol. 79, No. 9, September 1991.

N. Halbwachs, *Synchronous programming of reactive systems*, Kluwer Academic Publishers, ISBN 0-7923-9311-2, 1993.

C. Krueger, *Software reuse*, ACM computer survey, Vol. 24, No. 2, June 1992.

V.J. Mooney, C.N. Coelho, T. Sakamoto and G. De Micheli, *Synthesis From Mixed Specifications*, Proceedings of the European Design Automation Conference with Euro-VHDL, September 1996.

P. Le Moenner, L. Perraudeau et all, *Generating Regular Arithmetic Circuit with ALPHAHARD*, Proceedings of International Conference on Massively Parallel Computing Systems, May 1996.

S. Narayan and D. Gajski, *Features Supporting System-Level Specification in HDLs*, Proceedings of the European Design Automation Conference with Euro-VHDL, September 1993.

S. Narayan, F. Vahid and D. Gajski, *Translating System Specifications to VHDL*, Proceedings of the European Design Automation Conference (EDAC), February 1991.

O. Pulkkinen and K. Kronlöf, *Integration of SDL and VHDL for High Level Digital Design*, Proceedings of the European Design Automation Conference with Euro-VHDL, September 1992.

S. Swamy, A. Molin, and B. Covnot, *OO-VHDL Object Oriented Extension to VHDL*, IEEE Computer, Vol. 28, No. 10, October 1995.

F. Vahid, S. Narayan and D. Gajski, *SpecCharts: A VHDL Front End for Embedded Systems*, IEEE Transactions on Computer-Aided Design of Integrated Circuits and Systems, Vol. 14, No. 6, June 1995.

J. Wytrebwicz and S. Budkowski, *Communication Protocols Implemented in Hardware : VHDL Generation from Estelle*, Current Issue in Electronic Modelling, Vol 3, September 1995.

ITU-T, *Z.100 Functional Specification and Description Language*, Recommendation Z.100 - Z.104, March 1993.

STATEMATE: A Working Environment for the Development of Complex Reactive Systems

DAVID HAREL, MEMBER, IEEE, HAGI LACHOVER, AMNON NAAMAD, AMIR PNUELI, MICHAL POLITI, RIVI SHERMAN, AHARON SHTULL-TRAURING, AND MARK TRAKHTENBROT

Abstract—This paper provides an overview of the STATEMATE® system, constructed over the past several years by the authors and their colleagues at Ad Cad Ltd., the R&D subsidiary of i-Logix, Inc. STATEMATE is a set of tools, with a heavy graphical orientation, intended for the specification, analysis, design, and documentation of large and complex reactive systems, such as real-time embedded systems, control and communication systems, and interactive software or hardware. It enables a user to prepare, analyze, and debug diagrammatic, yet precise, descriptions of the system under development from three interrelated points of view, capturing *structure*, *functionality*, and *behavior*. These views are represented by three graphical languages, the most intricate of which is the language of *statecharts* [4], used to depict reactive behavior over time. In addition to the use of statecharts, the main novelty of STATEMATE is in the fact that it "understands" the entire descriptions perfectly, to the point of being able to analyze them for crucial dynamic properties, to carry out rigorous executions and simulations of the described system, and to create running code automatically. These features are invaluable when it comes to the quality and reliability of the final outcome.

Index Terms—Code-generation, executable specifications, functional decomposition, propotyping, reactive systems, statecharts, STATEMATE.

I. INTRODUCTION

REACTIVE systems (see [18], [6]) are characterized as owing much of their complexity to the intricate nature of reactions to discrete occurrences. The computational parts of such systems are assumed to be dealt with using other means, and it is their reactive, control-driven parts that are considered here to be the most problematic. Examples of reactive systems include most kinds of real-time computer embedded systems, control plants, communication systems, interactive software of varying nature, and even VLSI circuits. Common to all of these is the notion of *reactive behavior*, whereby the system is not adequately described by specifying the output that results from a set of inputs, but, rather, requires specifying the relationship of inputs and outputs over time. Typically, such descriptions involve complex sequences of events, actions, conditions and information flow, often with explicit timing constraints, that combine to form the system's overall behavior.

It is fair to say that the problem of finding good methods to aid in the development of such systems has not been satisfactorily solved. Standard structured analysis and structured design methods do not adequately deal with the dynamics of reactive systems, since they were proposed to deal primarily with nonreactive, data-driven applications, in which a good functional decomposition and data-flow description are sufficient. Some of these methods have recently been extended to deal with real-time systems (see, e.g., [8], [9], [16], [17], [20]–[22]), and our approach, developed independently,[1] can be viewed as being consistent with many of the ideas in these. See the comparisons in the recent [22]. As to commercially available tools for real-time system design, most are, by and large, but sophisticated graphics editors, with which one can model certain aspects of reactive systems, but with which a user can do little with the resulting descriptions beyond testing them for syntactic consistency and completeness and producing various kinds of output reports. These systems are often helpful in organizing a designer's thoughts and in communicating those thoughts to others, but they are generally considered severely inadequate when it comes to the more difficult task of preparing reliable specifications and designs that satisfy the requirements, that behave over time as expected, and from which a satisfactory final system can be constructed with relative ease.

If we were to draw an analogy with the discipline of conventional programming, there is an acute need for the reactive system's analog of a programming environment that comes complete with a powerful programming language, a useful program editor and syntax checker, but, most importantly, also with a working compiler and/or interpreter, and with extensive debugging facilities. Programs are not only to be written and checked for syntax errors; they must also be run, tested, debugged, and thoroughly analyzed before they are set free to do their thing in the real world.

As it turns out, the problems arising in the design of a typical reactive system are far more difficult than those

---

Manuscript received May 12, 1988; revised November 13, 1989. Recommended by L. A. Belady. This work was supported in part by the Bird Foundation and the Israel Ministry of Industry and Commerce.

D. Harel and A. Pnueli are with i-Logix Inc., Burlington, MA 01803, Ad Cad Ltd., Rehovot, Israel, and the Department of Applied Mathematics and Computer Science, The Weizmann Institute of Science, Rehovot 76100, Israel.

H. Lachover, A. Naamad, M. Politi, R. Sherman, A. Shtull-Trauring, and M. Trakhtenbrot are with i-Logix Inc., Burlington, MA 01803, and Ad Cad Ltd., Rehovot, Israel.

IEEE Log Number 8933740.

*STATEMATE is a registered trademark of i-Logix, Inc.

[1]Most of the ideas described in this paper were conceived between 1983 and 1985.

arising in the preparation of a typical computational or data-processing program. Most reactive systems are highly concurrent and distributed; they fall quite naturally into multiple levels of detail, and usually display unpredictable, often catastrophic, behavior under unanticipated circumstances. More often than not, the development phases of such systems are laden with misunderstandings between customers, subcontractors, and users, as well as among the various members of the design team itself, and their life-cycle is replete with trouble-shooting, modifications, and enhancements.

The languages in which reactive systems are specified ought to be clear and intuitive, and thus amenable to generation, inspection and modification by humans, as well as precise and rigorous, and thus amenable to validation, simulation, and analysis by computers. Such languages ought to make it possible to move easily, and with sufficient semantic underpinnings, from the initial stages of requirements and specification to prototyping and design, and to form the basis for modifications and maintenance at later stages. One of the underlying principles adopted in this paper is that clarity and intuition can be greatly enhanced by the adoption of visual languages for the bulk of the description effort, behavioral aspects included. This, together with the need for precision and rigor, leads naturally to the notion of *visual formalisms* [5], i.e., languages that are highly visual in nature, depending on a small number of carefully chosen diagrammatic paradigms, yet which, at the same time, admit a formal semantics that provides each feature, graphical and nongraphical alike, with a precise and unambiguous meaning. For reactive systems, this means that it should be possible to prepare intuitive and comprehensive specifications that can be analyzed, simulated, and debugged at any stage with the aid of a computerized support system.

This paper describes the ideas behind STATEMATE, a computerized environment for the development of reactive systems, which adheres to these principles. The reader is also referred to additional material about the system, particularly [12]-[14].

II. STATEMATE at a Glance

The underlying premise of STATEMATE is the need to specify and analyze the system under development (SUD in the sequel) from three separate, but related, points of view: *structural*, *functional*, and *behavioral*. The latter two are closely linked, as we shall see later, and constitute together the *conceptual model* of the SUD. See Fig. 1.

In the structural view, one provides a hierarchical decomposition of the SUD into its physical components, called *modules* here, and identifies the *information* that flows between them; that is, the "chunks" of data and control signals that flow through whatever physical links exist between the modules. The word "physical" should be taken as rather general, with a module being anything from an actual piece of hardware in some systems to the

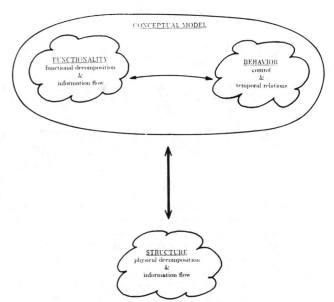

Fig. 1. Structure of a STATEMATE model.

subroutines, packages and tasks in the software parts of others.

The conceptual model of the SUD consists of a hierarchy of *activities*, complete with the details of the *data items* and *control signals* that flow between them, and, significantly, *control activities* that specify behavior. Let us be a little more explicit here. The activity hierarchy and flow information (without the control activities) constitute our functional view, and are essentially what is often called the *functional decomposition* of the SUD. However, in the functional view we do not specify dynamics; we do not say when and why the activities are activated, whether or not they terminate on their own, and whether they can be carried out in parallel. The same is true of the data-flow; in the functional view we specify only that data *can* flow, and not whether and when it will. For example, if we have identified that two of the subactivities of an automatic teller machine are **identify-customer** and **report-balance**, and that the data item **account-number** can flow from the former to the latter, then no more and no less than that is implied; we still have not specified when that item will flow, how often will it flow, and in response to what, and, indeed, whether the flow will be initiated by the former activity or requested by the latter. In other words, the functional view provides the decomposition into activities and the possible flow of information, but it says virtually nothing about how those activities and their associated inputs and outputs are controlled during the continued behavior of the SUD.

It is the behavioral view, our third, that is used to specify the control activities. These can be present on any level of the activity hierarchy, controlling that particular level. It is these controllers that are responsible for specifying when, how and why things happen as the SUD reacts over time. Among other things, a controlling statechart can start and stop activities, can generate new events, and can change the values of variables. It can also sense whether activities are active or data has flowed, and it can respond to events and test the values of conditions and variables. These connections between activities and control will be seen in Section III to be rather elaborate and multifaceted, so that the conceptual model should be regarded as a closely knit aggregate. The relationship between this conceptual model and the physical view, on the other hand, is far simpler, and consists essentially of specifying which modules implement which activities.

For these three views, the structural, functional, and behavioral, STATEMATE provides graphical, diagrammatic languages, *module-charts*, *activity-charts*, and *statecharts*, respectively. All three languages are based on a common set of simple graphical conventions (see [5]) and come complete with graphics editors that check for syntactic validity as the specifications are developed, and, more importantly, with formal semantics that are embedded within. The languages are described in some detail in Section III, and in more detail in [12] (statecharts are described in [4]).

Fig. 2 illustrates the overall structure of STATEMATE. The database is central, and obtains much of its input from the three graphics editors, and also from an editor for a *forms language*, in which additional information is specified, as we shall see later.

The most interesting parts of STATEMATE, however, are the analysis capabilities, described in Sections IV and V and in [13]. As mentioned, the entire approach is governed by the desire to enable the user to run, debug and analyze the specifications and designs that result from the graphical languages. To this end, the database has been constructed to make it possible to rigorously execute the specification and to retrieve information of a variety of kinds from the description of the SUD provided by the user. Some of the special tools provided for these purposes are 1) a means for querying the database and retrieving information from it; 2) an execution ability with a simulation control language, allowing the user to emulate the SUD's environment and execute the specifications, interactively or in batch or programmed mode, with or without graphic animated response, and using breakpoints if desired; 3) a set of dynamic tests, e.g., for reachability and the detection of deadlock and nondeterminism, which are based on exhaustive executions; 4) an automatic translation of the specification into a high-level programming language, such as Ada or C, yielding code that can be linked to a real or simulated target environment.

STATEMATE has been under development and extension since early 1984, and has been commercially available since late 1987. The currently available versions run on Sun, Apollo and Vax color[2] workstations (or networks of such). Many of the ideas and methods embodied in STATEMATE have been field-tested successfully in a number of large real-world development projects, among which is the mission-specific avionics system for the Lavi

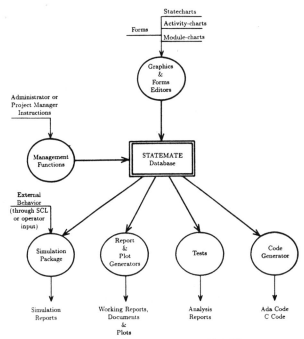

Fig. 2. Overall structure of STATEMATE.

fighter aircraft designed by the Israel Aircraft Industries, which was specified in part using statecharts (see [4]). The reader is also referred to [19], a case study of using STATEMATE, to [11], in which an application to process modeling is described, and to the recent comparative evaluation [22].

III. THE MODELING LANGUAGES OF STATEMATE

In this section we present the highlights of the three graphical languages and the forms language that the user of STATEMATE employs to specify the SUD. No formal syntax or semantics are given here, neither are all of the features presented. The reader is referred to [12] for a more comprehensive description, and to [4], [14] for a detailed treatment of the language of statecharts. The languages are described with the help of a simple example of an early warning system (EWS in the sequel), which has the ability to take measurements from an external sensor, compare them to some prespecified upper and lower limits, and warn the user when the measured value exceeds these limits.

The structural view of the SUD is described using the language of *module-charts*, which describe the SUD *modules* (i.e., its physical components), the environment modules (i.e., those parts that for the purpose of specification are deemed to be external to the SUD), and the clusters of data and/or control signals that may flow among them. Modules are depicted as rectilinear shapes and storage modules as rectangles with dashed sides. Encapsulation is used to capture the submodule relationship. Environment modules appear as dashed-line rectangles external to that of the SUD itself. Information flow is represented by labeled arrows or hyperarrows.[3] Various kinds

---

[2] While color appears to significantly enhance the appeal of STATEMATE, monochrome versions are also available.

[3] A hyperarrow has more than two endpoints.

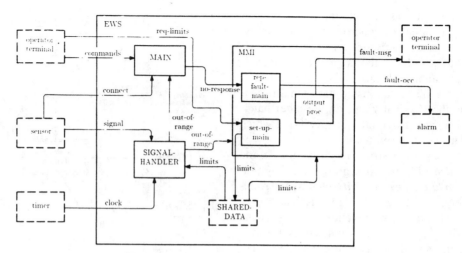

Fig. 3. Module-chart of the early warning system.

of connectors can appear in these charts, both to abbreviate lengthy arrows and to denote compound chunks of data.

Fig. 3 is (part of) the module-chart of our early warning system. It specifies in a self-explanatory fashion that the modules, or subsystems, of the EWS are a **main** component, a **man–machine-interface** (MMI), and a **signal-handler**, and that the **operator-terminal, sensor, timer,** and **alarm** are considered to be external to the system. The MMI is further decomposed into submodules, as shown. There is also a storage module, by the name of **shared-data,** and the information flowing between the modules is specified as well.

Turning to conceptual modeling, the functional decomposition of the SUD is captured by the language of *activity-charts*. Graphically, these are very similar to module-charts, but here the rectilinear shapes stand for the *activities*, or the functions, carried out by the system. Solid arrows represent the flow of data items and dashed arrows capture the flow of control items.[4] See Fig. 4. A typical activity will accept input items and produce output items during its active time-spans, its inner workings being specified by its own lower level decomposition. Activities that are atomic, or *basic* (i.e., they reside on the lowest level) may be described as simple input/output transformations using other means, such as code in a high-level programming language.

Activity-charts may contain two additional kinds of objects: *data-stores* and *control activities*. Data-stores can be thought of as representing databases, data structures, buffers, and variables of various kinds, or even physical containers or reservoirs, and typically correspond to the storage modules in the module-chart. They represent the ability to store the data items that flow into them and to produce those items as outputs upon request.

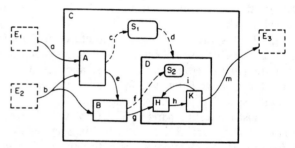

Fig. 4. An activity-chart.

The control activities constitute the behavioral view of the system and they appear in the activity-chart as empty boxes only. A control activity may appear inside an activity on any level, as shown in Fig. 4. The contents of the control activities are described in the third of the graphical languages, *statecharts*, which we discuss below. In general, a control activity has the ability to control its sibling activities by essentially sensing their status` and issuing commands to them. Thus, for example, in Fig. 4 the control activity S_1 can, among other things, perform *actions* that cause subactivities A, B, and D to start and stop, and can sense whether those subactivities have started or stopped by appropriate *events* and *conditions*. Various consequences of such occurrences are integrated into the semantics of the activity-charts language, such as the fact that all subactivities stop (respectively, suspend) upon the stopping (respectively, suspension) of the parent activity.

We now turn to the behavioral view. Statecharts, which were introduced in [4] (see also [5]), are an extension of conventional finite-state machines (FSM's) and their visual counterpart, state-transition diagrams. Conventional state diagrams are inappropriate for the behavioral description of complex control, since they suffer from being flat and unstructured, are inherently sequential in nature, and give rise to an exponential blow-up in the number of states (i.e., small extensions of a system cause unacceptable growth in the number of states to be considered). These problems are overcome in statecharts by supporting

---

[4]In displaying module-charts and activity-charts on the screen, we employ different conventions regarding color and arrow type, so that a user can distinguish between them quite easily. Thus, for example, the arrows in module-charts are drawn using rectilinear segments parallel to the axes, whereas in activity-charts they are drawn using smooth spline functions.

the repeated decomposition of states into substates in an AND/OR fashion, combined with an instantaneous broadcast communication mechanism. A rather important facet of these extensions is the ability to have transitions leave and enter states on any level.

Consider Fig. 5, in which (a) and (b) are equivalent. In Fig. 5(b) states S and T have been clustered into a new state U so that to be in U is to be either in S or in T. The f-arrow leaving U denotes a high-level interrupt, and has the effect of prescribing an exit from U, i.e., from whichever of S or T the system happens to be in, to the new state V. The h-arrow entering U would appear to be underspecified, as it must cause entry to S or T; in fact, its meaning relies on the internal default arrow attached to T, which causes entrance to T.

Turning to AND decomposition, consider Fig. 6, in which, again, Fig. 6(a) and (b) are equivalent. Here, to be in state U the system must be in *both* S and T. An unspecified entrance to U relies on both default arrows to enter the pair $\{V, W\}$, from which an occurrence of e, for example, would lead to the new pair $\{X, Y\}$, and k would lead to $\{V, Z\}$. The meaning of the other transitions appearing therein, including entrances and exits, can be deduced by comparing Fig. 6(a) and (b). It is worth mentioning that this AND decomposition, into what we call *orthogonal* state components, can be carried out on any level of states and is therefore more convenient than allowing only single-level sets of communicating FSM's. Orthogonality is the feature statecharts employ to solve the state blow-up problem, by making it possible to describe independent and concurrent state components; see [4], [5]. Also, orthogonal state decomposition eliminates the need for multiple control activities within a single activity, as is done, e.g., in [9], [21].

The general syntax of an expression labeling a transition in a statechart is

$$\alpha[C]/\beta$$

where α is the event that triggers the transition, C is a condition that guards the transition from being taken unless it is true when α occurs, and β is an action that is carried out if, and precisely when, the transition is taken. All of these are optional. Events and conditions can be considered as inputs, and actions as outputs, except that here this correspondence is more subtle than in ordinary FSM's, due to the intricate nature of the statecharts themselves and their relationship with the activities. For example, if β appears as an action along some transition, but it also appears as a triggering event of a transition in some orthogonal component, then executing the action in the first transition will immediately cause the second transition to be taken simultaneously. Moreover, in the expression α/β, rather than being simply a *primitive* action that might cause other transitions, β can be the special action **start**(A) that causes the activity A to start. Similarly, rather than being simply an external, primitive event, α might be the special event **stopped**(B) that occurs (and hence causes the transition to take place) when

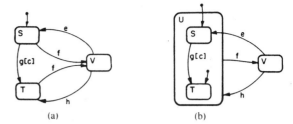

Fig. 5. OR-decomposition in a statechart.

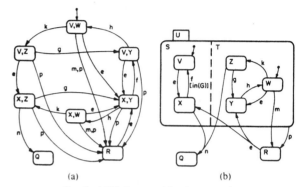

Fig. 6. AND-decomposition in a statechart.

B stops or is stopped. Table I shows a selection of the special events, conditions, and actions that can appear as part of the labels along a transition. It should be noted that the syntax is also closed under boolean combinations, so that, for example, the following is a legal label:

entered(S) $[$**in**(T) **and not active**$(C)]/$

suspend$(C); X := Y + 7$

Notice that we have incorporated another extension of the FSM approach—the use of conventional variables. The changing of a value is now allowed as an event, standard comparisons are allowed as conditions, and assignment statements are allowed as actions.

Besides allowing actions to appear along transitions, they can also appear associated with the entrance to or exit from a state (any state, of course, on any level).[5] This association is currently specified nongraphically, in the forms language discussed below. Thus, if we associate the action **resume**(A) with the entrance to state S, activity A will be resumed whenever S is entered.

Some of the special constructs appearing in Table I thus serve to link the control activities with the other objects appearing in an activity-chart, and, as such, are part of the way behavior is associated with functionality and dataflow. There are other facets to this association, one of which is the ability to specify an activity A as taking place **throughout** state (S), which is the same as saying that A is started upon entering state S and is stopped upon leaving it. This connection is also stated via forms.

The power to control and sense the status of activities is limited by a scoping rule to the control activity appear-

---

[5]In this way, statecharts can be seen to generalize both Mealy and Moore automata; see [10].

140 CHAPTER 2: Modeling

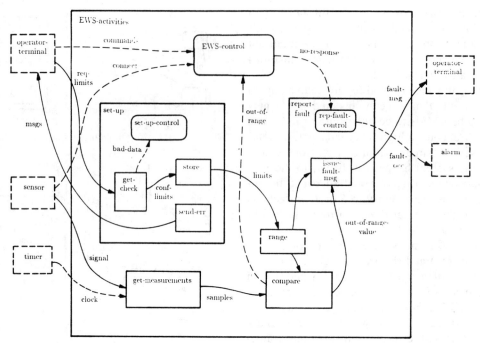

Fig. 7. Activity-chart of the early warning system.

TABLE I
SOME SPECIAL EVENTS, CONDITIONS, AND ACTIONS

REFERRING TO	EVENTS	CONDITIONS	ACTIONS
state S	entered(S) exited(S)	in(S)	
activity A	started(A) stopped(A)	active(A) hanging(A)	start(A) stop(A) suspend(A) resume(A)
data items D, F condition C	read(D) written(D) true(C) false(C)	D=F D<F D>F	D:=exp make_true(C) make_false(C)
event E action A n-time units	timeout(E,n)		schedule(A,n)

ing on the same level as the activities and flow in question. Thus, in Fig. 4, for example, some of the events and actions that can appear in the statechart S_1 are:[6] **st**(A), **rs!**(B) and **wr!**(d), but ones referring to, say, H and K, such as **st!**(H), cannot, and would appear only in S_2. This scoping mechanism for hiding information is intended to help in making specifications modular and amenable to the kind of division of work that is required in large projects. The scoping rule can easily be overridden by explicitly-flowing events and actions, but we shall not get into the details here.

Fig. 7 shows the activity-chart of the early warning system. The user, via the operator terminal, can send **com-**

---

[6]Here, and also in Fig. 8, we use abbreviations for the elements appearing in Table I, such as **st** instead of **started**, **rs!** instead of **resume**, and **tm** instead of **timeout**. STATEMATE recognizes these abbreviations too.

mands to the control activity; this is an *information flow*, which, via a form, is specified to consist of **set-up, execute,** and **reset** instructions. The operator can also send the upper and lower required limits to the **get-check** subactivity of **set-up.** These limits can be stored in the data-store **range,** and can subsequently be used by the **compare** and **report-fault** activities. (The item **req-limits** is a compound data item, and stands for the pair containing the required upper and lower limits.) A special activity, **get-measurements,** can receive the **signal** from the sensor and a **clock** reading from the timer, and translates these into a time-stamped digital value sample, which can be sent to the comparing activity. If out of range, a signal and value can be sent to the controller and the **report-fault** activity, respectively. The latter is responsible for sending out an alarm and formatting and sending the user an appropriate message. The second level of Fig. 7 is self explanatory.

It is important to emphasize that Fig. 7 is not required to provide dynamic, behavioral information about the EWS; that is the role of the controlling statecharts. Fig. 8, for example, shows one possible statechart for the high-level control activity of Fig. 7, i.e., EWS-**control,** and the reader should be able to comprehend it quite easily.

The connections between activity-charts and statecharts are rather intricate, resulting in a tightly knit conceptual model. In contrast, the connections between this model and the structural view are more straightforward. What we have to do is to assign implementational responsibility for each part of the former to appropriate parts of the latter. This is done by associating modules with activities, and storage modules with data stores. In our example, some of these associations are that the MAIN module implements the EWS-**control** activity, SIGNAL-HANDLER

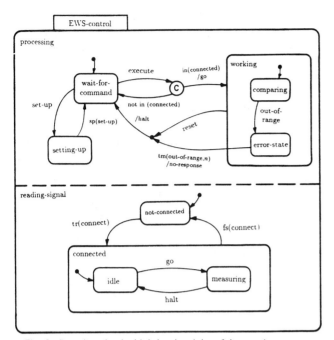

Fig. 8. Statechart for the high-level activity of the warning system.

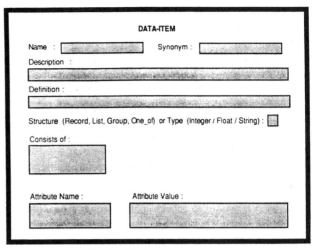

Fig. 9. The form for a data item.

implements **get-measurements** and **compare,** and MMI implements **set-up** and **report-fault.** Within the MMI association, the **send-err** subactivity is implemented by the **output-proc** submodule and the other three by **set-up-main.** The associations themselves are input in the forms of the activities.

We now turn to the *forms language* itself. A special form is maintained for each of the elements in the description, in which additional information can be input. This includes details that are nongraphical in nature, such as lengthy definitions of compound events and conditions, or the type and structure of data items. Fig. 9 shows an example of the form for a data item, in which most fields are self-explanatory. The "Consists of" field therein makes it possible to structure data items into components, and the "Attribute" fields make it possible to associate attributes with the items (e.g., units and precision for certain kinds of data-items, or the names of the personnel responsible for the specification for certain high-level elements). The attributes are recognizable by the retrieval tools of STATEMATE and are therefore able to play a role in the evaluation and documentation of the model, as we shall see later.

The color graphical editors for all three charts languages continuously check the input for syntactic soundness, and the database is updated as graphical elements are introduced. The editors are mouse- and menu-based, and support a wide range of possibilities, including move, copy, stretch, hide, reveal, and zoom options, all applicable to single or multiple elements in the charts, that can be selected in a number of ways. The form for a selected element can be viewed and updated not only from the special forms editor, but from the appropriate graphical editor as well.

Extensive consistency and completeness tests, as well as more subtle *static logic* tests can be carried out during a session. Examples include checking whether information flow in the module-chart is consistent with that in the activity-chart, listing modules that have no outputs, or activities that are never started, and identifying cyclic definitions of nongraphical elements (e.g., events and conditions).

IV. QUERIES, REPORTS, AND DOCUMENTS

In this section, we describe some of the tools that are available for retrieving and formatting information from the model.

STATEMATE provides a querying tool, the *object list generator*, with which the user can retrieve information from the database. It works by generating lists of elements that satisfy certain criteria. At all times it keeps a *pending list* that gets modified as the user refines the criteria or asks for a list of elements of another type. For example, starting with an empty pending list, one can ask for all states in the controlling statechart of activity A, and the resulting list promptly becomes the new pending list. This list might then be refined by asking for those states therein that have an attribute named **"responsibility-of"** whose value is **"Jim Brown."** Then one might ask for all activities that are started within any of those states, and so on. This query language, on the face of it, might appear to be bounded in its expressive power by that of the conjunctive queries of [2]. However, since it actually supports certain kinds of transitive closures (such as the ancestor and descendent relationships between states or activities), it is not directly comparable with the conjunctive queries, and can be shown to be a subset of the more general fixpoint queries (see [1]).

The charts that constitute the SUD's description can be plotted. The user can control the portion of the chart to be plotted, as well as its size and depth. In addition, the user can ask for several kinds of fixed-format **reports** that are compiled directly from the description of the SUD in the database, and which can be displayed on the workstation screen or output to an alphanumeric terminal or printer. Each of these can be projected, so to speak, on any part of the description that is retrievable by the query language. In other words, the user may first use queries to capture, say, a set of activities of particular interest, and then request the report; it will be applied only to the activities in the list. Among the reports currently implemented are *data dictionaries* of various kinds, textual *protocols* of states or activities that contain all the information relevant to them, *interface diagrams*, *tree versions* of various hierarchies, and so-called N^2-diagrams of [15]. Using certain parameters, the user can control various aspects of the reports produced, such as the depth of the trees in the tree reports, and the keys by which the dictionaries are to be sorted.

In addition to fixed-format reports, STATEMATE has a *document generation language* with which users can tailor their own documents. Programs can be written in this language to produce documents with particular structure, contents and appearance. One uses the language to design a document template, containing formatting commands for one's desired word processor,[7] interleaved with instructions to incorporate information from the model. These instructions activate queries in the query language to retrieve information, or routines to extract graphical charts, and then format these according to the template. A document generation program can therefore be prepared once, in advance, and can then be run whenever the document is needed. The templates for some particular documents have been prepackaged, and are available ready-made to the user. They include the main parts of the US DoD Standards 2167 and 2167A. Programmed documents too can be generated at any stage of the development, and for the complete model or portions thereof.

V. EXECUTIONS AND DYNAMIC ANALYSIS

We now turn to the analysis capabilities of STATE-MATE, which constitute one of its main novelties. In [13] we have tried to set out the underlying philosophy in some detail, emphasizing the analysis capabilities.

The heart of these is the ability to carry out a *step* of the SUD's dynamic behavior, with all the consequences taken into account. A step, briefly, is one unit of dynamic behavior, at the beginning and end of which the SUD is in some legal *status*. A status captures the system's currently active states and activities, the current values of variables and conditions, etc. During a step, the environment activities can generate external events, change the truth values of conditions, and update variables and other data items. Given the potentially intricate form that a STATEMATE description of the SUD might take on, such changes can have a profound effect on the status, triggering transitions in statecharts, activating and deactivating activities, modifying other data items, and so on. Clearly, each of these changes, in turn, may cause many others.

The portion of STATEMATE that is responsible for calculating the effect of a step contains involved algorithmic procedures, which reflect the formal semantics that have been defined mathematically for the modeling languages. The particular semantics of statecharts that has been adopted is described in [14], and is somewhat different from that described in [7], although on most standard examples the two are equivalent.

The most basic way of "running" the SUD is in a step-by-step interactive fashion. At each step the user generates external events, changes conditions and carries out other actions (such as changing the values of variables) at will, thus emulating the environment of the system. All of these are assumed to have occurred within a single step, the most recent one. When the user then gives the "go" command, STATEMATE responds by transforming the SUD into the new resulting status. Typically, there will be one or more statecharts on the screen while this is happening, and often also an activity-chart. The currently active states and activities will be highlighted with special coloring.[8]

This ability to run through dynamic scenarios has obvious value as a debugging mechanism in the specification stage. If we find that the system's response is not as expected we go back to the model, change it (by modifying a statechart, for example), and run the same scenario again.

At times, however, we want to be able to see the model executing noninteractively, and under circumstances that we do not care to spell out in detail ourselves. We would like to see it perform under random conditions, and in both typical and less typical situations. This more powerful notion of executing the model is achieved by the idea of *programmed executions*. To that end, a specially tailored *simulation control language* (SCL) has been designed and incorporated into STATEMATE, enabling the user to retain general control over how the executions proceed, yet exploit the tool to take over many of the details.

Programs in SCL look a little like conventional programs in a high-level language: they employ variables and support several control structures that can be combined and nested. They are used to control the simulation by reading events and changes from previously prepared files, and/or generating them using, say, random sampling from a variety of probability distributions. Several kinds of *breakpoints* can be incorporated into the program, causing the execution to stop and take certain actions when particular situations come up. These actions can range from incrementing counters (e.g., to accumulate statistics about performance), through switching to interactive mode (from which the user can return to the programmed execution by a simple command), and all the way to executing a lengthy calculation constituting the inners of a basic activity that was left unspecified when modeling the SUD.

---

[7]Several standard word processors are supported.

[8]Actually, the system will highlight only those states and activities that are on the lowest level visible.

Executions can thus be stopped and restarted, and intervening changes can be made; the effects of events generated with prescribed probabilities can be checked, and the computational parts of the SUD and its environment can be emulated. Moreover, during such simulated executions a *trace database* is maintained, which records changes made in the status of the SUD. The trace database can later be reviewed, filed away, printed or discarded, and, of course, is important for inspecting the execution and its effects off-line. A variety of *simulation reports* can be produced, in which parts of the information are gathered as the execution proceeds, via instructions in the SCL program, and other parts are taken from the trace database after the execution ends. Moreover, we may view the progress of a programmed execution graphically just as in the interactive case; the same color codes are used to continuously update the displayed charts. The result is a visually pleasing discrete animation of the behavior of the SUD.[9]

The part of the SUD that is simulated (in either interactive or programmed mode) can be restricted in scope. For example, one can simulate an activity and its inners, and the rest of the STATEMATE specification is considered to be nonexistent for the duration of that simulation. Moreover, there is no need to wait until the entire SUD is specified before initiating executions and simulations; a user can start simulating, or running, a description from the moment the portion that is available is syntactically intact (and this can be checked by the static tests). In the simulation the user will typically provide those events and other items of information that are external to the specified portion, even though later they might become internal to the complete specification.

In general, then, a carefully prepared SCL program can be used to test the specification of the SUD under a wide range of test data, to emulate both the environment and the as-of-yet unspecified parts of the SUD, to check the specification for time-critical performance and efficiency, and, in general, to debug it and identify subtle run-time errors. Needless to say, the kinds of errors and misconceptions that can be discovered in this way are quite different from the syntactic completeness and consistency checks that form the highlights of most of the other available tools for system design, and which STATEMATE carries out routinely.

It is important to keep in mind that the role of the SCL programs is to oversee the execution of the model; they are not intended to replace it. Thus, SCL is not a modeling language but a meta-language that serves as a vehicle for some of our analysis capabilities. It should not be compared with simulation languages in the sense that term is often used, where the programs themselves constitute the model.

Now, since STATEMATE can fully execute steps of dynamic behavior, and since SCL programs can be writ-ten to control the execution of many scenarios, it becomes tempting to provide the ability to execute *all* scenarios—as long as the number of possibilities is manageable—in order to test for crucial dynamic properties. STATEMATE has been programmed to provide a number of these dynamic tests, all of which proceed essentially by carrying out exhaustive, brute-force, sets of executions. They include *reachability*, *nondeterminism*, *deadlock*, and *usage of transitions*. For the first of these, given an initial configuration and a target condition, the test seeks sequences of external events and other occurrences that lead from the initial status to one that satisfies the condition, producing these sequences if they exist and stating that there are none otherwise. It is important to stress that this is run-time, dynamic, reachability, not merely a test for whether two boxes in some diagram are connected by arrows. The same applies to the other dynamic tests too.

One must realize, however, that even if we limit the values of variables to finite sets, the number of scenarios that have to be tested in an exhaustive execution quickly becomes unmanageable. This means that unless the portion of the model that we are testing is sufficiently small and has only a few external connections, we will not always be able to complete our exhaustive test. Indeed, these dynamic tests should be used only on very critical, well isolated parts of our model. When larger parts require exhaustive testing, we may limit the scope of the test by instructing it, for example, to ignore some of the external events, or to avoid simulating the details of certain activities. We have used the reachability test successfully on a number of occasions. In one real-world situation, when analyzing part of the specification of the trigger mechanism in a certain deployed missile system, our reachability test discovered a new sequence of events (that was unknown to the design team!) leading to the firing of a missile.

The reachability test can be used in a more sophisticated way, by attaching *watchdog* statecharts to the model being tested. Thus, we can test whether it is possible to reach situations of temporal, dynamic nature, by adding a watchdog statechart that enters a special state S when the situation in case arises. A reachability test is then run on the original statechart with the new one added as an orthogonal component, and the condition being sought for is specified to be **in**(S).

An additional feature that is planned for a future version is the ability to verify a STATEMATE specification against a formula in temporal logic.

VI. CODE-GENERATION AND RAPID PROTOTYPING

Once a model of the SUD has been constructed, and has been executed and analyzed to the satisfaction of the designer, STATEMATE can be instructed to translate it automatically into code in a high-level programming language. This is analogous to the compilation of a program in a high-level language, whereas the executability of the model is analogous to its interpretation. Currently, trans-

---

[9]There are other visual tools that support animated executions. See, for example, [3].

lations into Ada and C are supported. Technically, any activity-chart (together with its controlling statecharts) can be translated. which, again, means that one need not wait until the entire model is ready but can produce code from portions thereof. If code was supplied by the bottom-level basic activities, it can be appropriately linked to the generated code, resulting in a complete running version of the system.

We term the result *prototype code*, since it is generated automatically, and reflects only those design decisions made in the process of preparing the conceptual model. It may thus not be as efficient as final real-time code, though it runs much faster than the executions of the model itself, just as compiled code runs faster than interpreted code. Future plans call for enhancing the code generator with the ability to incorporate decisions made interactively by the human designer, as well as with various further optimization features. We might add that an interesting way to further exploit STATEMATE for analyzing the model is to construct special statecharts, which are not part of the model itself, and whose role is to test the model. Of course, for these test suites (and also for the watchdog statecharts described earlier) the output from the code-generation is actually final code.

One of the main uses of the prototype code is in observing the SUD performing in circumstances that are close to its final environment. The code can be ported and executed in the actual target environment, or—as is more realistic in most cases—in a simulated version of the target environment. Often we have linked the prototype code with "soft" panels, graphical mock-ups of control panels, dials, gauges, etc., that represent the actual user interface of the final system. These panels appear on the screen and are manipulated with the mouse and keyboard. Unlike conventional prototypes of such systems, however, here the soft panels are not driven by hastily-written code prepared especially for the prototype, but by code generated automatically from the STATEMATE model, which typically will have been thoroughly tested and analyzed before being subjected to code-generation. The idea is to use this feature for goals that go beyond the development team. We envision mock-ups of the SUD driven by our prototype code being used as part of the communication between customer and contractor or contractor and subcontractor. It is not unreasonable to require such a running version of the system to be one of the deliverables in certain development stages, such as the preliminary design review.

Associated with the code-generation facility is a debugging mechanism, with which the user can trace the executing parts of the code back up to the STATEMATE model. Breakpoints can be inserted to stop the run of the code when chosen events occur, at which point one may examine the model's configuration (states, activities, etc.) and modify elements (conditions, data-items, etc.), prior to resuming the run. Of course, if substantial problems arise in the running of the code, changes can be made in the STATEMATE model itself, which is then recompiled down into Ada or C, and rerun. As in simulations, trace files can be requested, in which the changes in desired elements can be recorded. Continuing the analogy between conventional compilation and our generation of code from a STATEMATE model, this debugging facility might be termed *source-level* debugging.

Finally, the code-generation facility can be used for bringing the model gradually closer to a final software implementation. This is done by *incremental substitution*, whereby increasingly larger parts of the system are replaced by code, the process being interleaved with the making of design decisions. This procedure, which we hope to discuss more fully in a subsequent paper, is different from conventional integration in that the medium is changed (from conceptual model to code) as the integration is being carried out. As a consequence, there is a need for testing and validation in intermediate steps, much of which can be carried out in STATEMATE.

In the future, we plan to enrich the code-generator with the ability to yield VHDL code. This will enable hardware designers to use STATEMATE not only for the specification and early design stages, but also for the later stages. Silicon compilation would then be carried out from code that is generated automatically from a STATEMATE specification.

VII. CONCLUSIONS

In conclusion, we might say that the STATEMATE system combines two principles, or theses, that we feel should guide future attempts to design support tools for system development. The first is the long-advocated need for *executable specifications*, and the second is the advantage of using *visual formalisms*.

As far as the first of these goes, the development of complex systems must not be allowed to progress from untested requirements or specifications. Rather, ways should be found to model the SUD on any desired level of detail in a manner that is fully executable and analyzable, and which allows for deep and comprehensive testing and debugging, of both static and dynamic nature, prior to, and in the process of, building the system itself. We might add that the dynamic analysis capabilities of STATEMATE go far beyond what is normally taken as the meaning of the term executable specification, i.e., the simple ability to animate a diagram in a step-by-step fashion.

As to the second principle, we believe that visual formalisms will turn out to be a crucial ingredient in the continuous search for more natural and powerful ways to exploit computers. It is our feeling that the progress made in graphical hardware, combined with the capabilities of the human visual system, will result in a significant change in the way we carry out many of our complex engineering activities. The surviving approaches will be, we believe, of diagrammatic nature, yet will be formal and rigorous, in both syntax and semantics.

ACKNOWLEDGMENT

We would like to thank J. Lavi and his group at the Israel Aircraft Industries for their suggestions, their time, and their constructive criticism during the lengthy period in which the STATEMATE system was being developed. In a way, this project would not have gotten started had Dr. Lavi not lured the first-listed author into consulting for IAI in early 1983. This action led to the invention of statecharts in mid-1983, and to the decision to form Ad-Cad Ltd. and to start work on STATEMATE in early 1984.

We are grateful to all the technical staff members of Ad-Cad Ltd., past and present, who were indispensible in turning the ideas described here into a real working system. They include R. Arnan, E. Bahat, S. Barzilai, A. Bernstein, M. Cohen, R. Cohen, D. Falkon, A. Farjou, N. Fogel, L. Gambom, E. Gery, O. Hay, R. Heiman, M. Hirsch, R. Kazmirski, D. Levin, H. Libreich, R. Livne, A. Maimon, L. Maron, Y. Partosh, S. Pnueli, Y. Pnueli, A. Polyack, J. Prozan-Schmidt, Y. Rubinfain, A. Sarig, R. Shaprio, A. Sharabi, I. Shimshoni, M. Trachtman, Y. Yochai, and B. Yudowitz. In addition, I. Lachover deserves special thanks for being the most pleasant manager imaginable, contributing his experience and expertise to all phases of the work.

We would like to thank the Bird Foundation, and the office of the chief scientist of Israel's Ministry of Industry and Commerce for financial help. One of the referees provided many helpful comments on the penultimate version of this paper.

References

[1] A. K. Chandra and D. Harel, "Structure and Complexity of Relational Queries," *J. Comput. Syst. Sci.*, vol. 25, pp. 99-128, 1982.
[2] A. K. Chandra and P. Merlin, "Optimal implementation of conjunctive queries in relational databases," in *Proc. 9th ACM Symp. Theory of Computing*, Boulder, CO, 1977, pp. 77-90.
[3] M. Graf, "Building a visual designer's environment," in *Principles of Visual Programming Systems*, S.-K. Chang, Ed. Englewood Cliffs, NJ: Prentice-Hall, 1990, pp. 291-325.
[4] D. Harel, "Statecharts: A visual formalism for complex systems," *Sci. Comput. Program.*, vol. 8, pp. 231-274, 1987 (appeared in preliminary form as Rep. CS84-05, Weizmann Inst. Sci., Rehovot, Israel, Feb. 1984).
[5] —, "On visual formalisms," *Commun. ACM*, vol. 31, no. 5, pp. 514-530, 1980.
[6] D. Harel and A. Pnueli, "On the development of reactive systems," in *Logics and Models of Concurrent Systems*, K. R. Apt, Ed. New York: Springer-Verlag, 1985, pp. 477-498.
[7] D. Harel, A. Pnueli, J. P. Schmidt, and R. Sherman, "On the formal semantics of statecharts," in *Proc. 2nd IEEE Symp. Logic in Computer Science*. New York: IEEE Press, 1987, pp. 54-64.
[8] D. J. Hatley, "A structured analysis method for real-time systems," in *Proc. DECUS Symp.*, Dec. 1985.
[9] D. J. Hatley and I. Pirbhai, *Strategies for Real-Time System Specification*. New York: Dorset, 1987.
[10] J. E. Hopcroft and J. D. Ullman, *Introduction to Automata Theory, Languages, and Computation*. Reading, MA: Addison-Wesley, 1979.
[11] W. S. Humphrey and M. I. Kellner, "Software process modeling: Principles of entity process models," in *Proc. 11th Int. Conf. Software Eng.*, Pittsburgh, PA. New York: IEEE Press, 1989, pp. 331-342.
[12] "The languages of STATEMATE," i-Logix Inc., Burlington, MA, Tech. Rep., 1987.
[13] "The STATEMATE approach to complex systems," i-Logix Inc., Burlington, MA, Tech. Rep., 1989.
[14] "The semantics of statecharts," i-Logix Inc., Burlington, MA, Tech. Rep., 1989.
[15] R. J. Lano, *A Technique for Software and Systems Design (TRW Series on Software Engineering)*. Amsterdam, The Netherlands: North-Holland, 1979.
[16] J. Z. Lavi and E. Kessler, "An embedded computer systems analysis method," Manuscript, Israel Aircraft Industries, Nov. 1986.
[17] J. Z. Lavi and M. Winokur, "ECSAM—A method for the analysis of complex embedded systems and their software," in *Proc. Structured Techniques Assoc. Conf. STA5*, Univ. Chicago, Chicago, IL, May 1989, pp. 50-63.
[18] A. Pnueli, "Applications of temporal logic to the specification and verification of reactive systems: A survey of current trends," in *Current Trends in Concurrency (Lecture Notes in Computer Science, vol. 224)*, de Bakker et al., Eds. Berlin: Springer-Verlag, 1986, pp. 510-584.
[19] S. L. Smith and S. L. Gerhart, "STATEMATE and cruise control: A case study," in *Proc. COMPAC '88, 12th Int. IEEE Comput. Software and Applicat. Conf.* New York: IEEE Press, 1988, pp. 49-56.
[20] P. Ward, "The transformation schema: An extension of the data flow diagram to represent control and timing," *IEEE Trans. Software Eng.*, vol. SE-12, pp. 198-210, 1986.
[21] P. Ward and S. Mellor, *Structured Development for Real-Time Systems*. New York: Yourdon, 1985.
[22] D. P. Wood and W. G. Wood, "Comparative evaluations of four specification methods for real-time systems," Software Eng. Inst., Carnegie-Mellon Univ., Pittsburgh, PA, Tech. Rep. CMU/SEI-89-TR-36, Dec. 1989.

David Harel (M'84) received the B.Sc. degree in mathematics from Bar-Ilan University in 1974, the M.Sc. degree in computer science from Tel-Aviv University in 1976, and the Ph.D. degree in computer science from the Massachusetts Institute of Technology in 1978.

He is currently a Professor at the Weizmann Institute of Science in Israel, and Chairman of its Department of Applied Mathematics and Computer Science. He is also a co-founder and Chief Scientist of i-Logix, Inc., Burlington, MA. He has been on the research staff of IBM's Research Center at Yorktown Heights, NY, and a Visiting Professor at Carnegie-Mellon University's Department of Computer Science. His research interests include logics of programs, computability theory, systems engineering, and visual languages, topics in which he has published widely. He is on the editorial boards of *Information and Computation* and the ACM-Press/Addison-Wesley book series. His most recent book, *The Science of Computing: Exploring the Nature and Power of Algorithms*, was published by Addison-Wesley in 1989.

Dr. Harel is a member of the Association for Computing Machinery and the IEEE Computer Society.

Hagi Lachover received the B.Sc. degree in applied mathematics from Tel-Aviv University in 1967.

In previous positions, he developed operating systems at the Weizmann Institute of Science and was Vice President for product development at Mini Systems, Ltd., a company that developed the software for Scitex, Inc., Herzelia, Israel. He is a co-founder and Vice President for Operations at Ad Cad, Ltd., the R&D subsidiary of i-Logix, Inc., Burlington, MA.

Amnon Naamad received the B.Sc. degree in mathematics and the M.Sc. degree in computer science from Tel-Aviv University in 1976 and 1979, respectively, and the Ph.D. degree in computer science from Northwestern University in 1981.

He is currently a Project Leader at Ad Cad, Ltd., the R&D subsidiary of i-Logix, Inc., Burlington, MA. He was responsible for the development of the simulation and dynamic analysis tools of the STATEMATE system, and is currently developing a translator from STATEMATE descriptions into hardware specification languages such as VHDL.

Amir Pnueli received the Ph.D. degree in applied mathematics from the Weizmann Institute of Science, Rehovot, Israel, in 1967.

He is currently a Professor of Computer Science at the Weizmann Institute of Science. He is also a co-founder and Chief Scientist of i-Logix, Inc., Burlington, MA. He has been a Chief Scientist at Mini Systems, Ltd., and a Visiting Professor at the Departments of Computer Science of Stanford University, Harvard University, and Brandeis University. His research interests include specification and verification of reactive systems, with a special emphasis on temporal logic, which he introduced into computer science in 1977. He has published widely on these topics. He is on the editorial boards of *Science of Computer Programming* and Springer-Verlag's Lecture Notes in Computer Science series.

Dr. Pnueli is a member of the Association for Computing Machinery and the IEEE Computer Society.

Aharon Shtull-Trauring received the B.A. degree in urban studies from Columbia University in 1975, and the M.Sc. degree in public management from Carnegie-Mellon University in 1979.

For many years he worked in software development, particularly of database systems. From 1984 to 1988 he was one of the project leaders at Ad Cad, Ltd., the R&D subsidiary of i-Logix, Inc., Burlington, MA, where he was responsible for the database and systems aspects of the STATEMATE system. He is now involved in the international marketing of STATEMATE.

Michal Politi received the B.Sc. degree in mathematics and physics from the Hebrew University in 1969, and the M.Sc. degree in computer science from the Weizmann Institute of Science.

She has had many years of experience in developing complex real-time systems in various places. Since 1986 she has been Product Manager for the STATEMATE system at Ad Cad, Ltd., the R&D subsidiary of i-Logix, Inc., Burlington, MA. Her interests are in methods and languages for the specification and design of real-time systems.

Rivi Sherman received the B.Sc. degree in mathematics from Tel-Aviv University in 1974, and the M.Sc. degree and Ph.D. degrees in computer science from the Weizmann Institute of Science in 1978 and 1984, respectively.

She is currently on the technical staff of Orbot, Inc., Yavne, Israel, and has spent three years as a researcher at the University of Southern California/Information Sciences Institute in Los Angeles. She was the first project leader at Ad Cad, Ltd., the R&D subsidiary of i-Logix, Inc., Burlington, MA, from 1984 to 1986, and was responsible for the development of the first version of the STATEMATE system.

Mark Trakhtenbrot received the M.Sc. degree in computer science from the University of Novosibirsk in 1971, and the Ph.D. degree from the Kiev Institute of Cybernetics in 1978.

He has been a Project Manager at Mayda, Ltd., Rehovot, Israel, developing and implementing an Ada-based PDL. He is currently a project leader at Ad-Cad, Ltd., the R&D subsidiary of i-Logix, Inc., Burlington, MA, where he was responsible for the development of the prototyping and code-generation capabilities of STATEMATE. His interests are in methodologies and tools for software and systems engineering.

The Synchronous Approach to Reactive and Real-Time Systems

ALBERT BENVENISTE, FELLOW, IEEE, AND GÉRARD BERRY

Invited Paper

This special issue is devoted to the synchronous approach to reactive and real-time programming. This introductory paper presents and discusses the application fields and the principles of synchronous programming. The major concern of the synchronous approach is to base synchronous programming languages on mathematical models. This makes it possible to handle compilation, logical correctness proofs, and verifications of real-time programs in a formal way, leading to a clean and precise methodology for design and programming.

I. Introduction: Real-Time and Reactive Systems

It is commonly accepted to call *real-time* a program or system that receives external interrupts or reads sensors connected to the physical world and outputs commands to it. Real-time programming is an essential industrial activity whose importance keeps increasing. Factories, plants, transportation systems, cars, and a wide variety of everyday objects are or will be computer controlled.

However, there is still little agreement about what the precise definition of a real-time system should be. Here, we propose to call *reactive* a system that maintains a permanent interaction with its environment[1] and to reserve the word *real-time* for reactive systems that are in addition subject to externally defined *timing constraints*. The broad class of reactive applications, therefore, contains all real-time applications as well as non-real-time applications such as classical communication protocols, man–machine interfaces, etc.

Safety is a crucial concern for reactive and real-time programs. In this area, a simple bug can have extreme consequences. *Logical correctness* is the respect of the input/output specification; it is essential in all cases. *Temporal correctness* is a further requirement of real-time applications: a logically correct real-time program can fail to adequately control its environment if its outputs are not produced on time. Notice that the expressions "timing constraints" and "on time" should not be taken too literally, since constraints are not necessarily expressed in terms of physical time; for example, "stop in less than 30 meter" is a timing constraint expressed by a distance.

Historically, reactive and real-time applications evolved mostly from the use of analog machines and relay circuits to the use of microprocessors and computers. They did not benefit from the recent progress in programming technology as much as did other fields. Although strongly technically related, the various application fields are treated by different groups of people having their own methods and vocabulary, and little relation has been established between them. The programming tools are still often low-level and specific. For instance, one uses calls to specific operating systems to monitor the communications between modules written in standard languages, such as Assembly or C, and one writes nonportable programs designed to drive very specific hardware units.

The present situation must change rapidly. Modern applications will require strong interactions between application fields that used to be separated, and specific vocabularies or tools must be unified whenever possible to keep large systems tractable. Low-level programming techniques will not remain acceptable for large safety-critical programs, since they make behavior understanding and analysis almost impracticable. As in all other fields of computing, hardware independence will be forced by the fact that software has a much longer lifetime than hardware. Finally, it will be necessary and sometimes even required to formally verify the correctness of programs at least with respect to their crucial safety properties. All these new requirements call for rigorous concepts and programming tools and for the use of automatic verification systems.

The goal of this special issue is to present the *synchronous* approach to reactive and real-time systems, as well as the associated software tools and verification techniques. The synchronous approach is based on a relatively small variety of concepts and methods based on deep, elegant, but simple mathematical principles. Roughly, the main idea is to first consider ideal systems that produce their

---

Manuscript received September 15, 1990; revised March 9, 1991.
A. Benveniste is with IRISA-INRIA, Campus de Beaulieu, France.
G. Berry is with Ecole des Mines, Centre de Mathématiques Appliquées Sophia-Antipolis, France.
IEEE Log Number 9102298.

[1] The notion of a reactive system was first introduced in [14], [23].

outputs synchronously with their inputs. Such synchronous systems compose very well and turn out to be easier to describe and analyze that asynchronous ones. Furthermore, sophisticated algorithms can take advantage of the synchrony hypothesis to produce highly efficient code. Of course, the object codes are not really synchronous, but they are often of predictable behavior unlike fully asynchronous code (predictability is a key to correctly deal with speed issues of actual implementation; we shall not study this point here, referring to the specific papers). Automatic algorithms can adapt the resulting code to distributed architectures.

The synchronous programming concept was first introduced for software in [14]–[17], but one must say that it bears many similarities with classical hardware concepts: in a clocked digital circuit, communication between subcomponents behaves as fully synchronous provided the clock is not too fast. Clock speed is predictable and all CAD tools can actually report to which clock speed a precise circuit can work.

Before presenting synchronous programming, we shall review the area of real-time systems and the presently prevalent programming tools

II. Reactive and Real-Time Systems: Examples and Main Issues

It is not our purpose to be exhaustive, but we feel it is necessary to analyze some examples of how diverse reactive and real-time systems can be. We shall first present the main application areas. We shall then present two case studies in more detail. Finally, we shall mention the main issues in reactive and real-time system development.

A. Application Areas

We list the applications areas in increasing order of complexity:

1. **Pure task sequencers** are typically encountered in command boards, man–machine interfaces, or more generally computer integrated manufacturing (CIM). They deal with *sequence of tasks* such as

   PUT_OBJECT_ON_BELT; BELT_IN_MOTION;
   DETECT_OBJECT; GRASP_OBJECT.

   Several elementary sequences may occur *in parallel* and cooperate for instance via shared events (PUT_OBJECT_ON_BELT can refer to events shared by a robot and by a belt). Task sequencers can be objects of high combinatorial complexity, so that the main issue here is to provide a formal method to convert a *specification*, i.e., a description that is easily understandable, into an efficient *implementation*, for instance the transition table of an automaton.
2. **Communication protocols** are encountered in various kinds of networks, and in particular in real-time local-area networks. Similar comments may be drawn as for tasks sequencers, in particular as far as combinatorial complexity is concerned.
3. **Low level signal processing** of which sensor data processing and signal processing in digital communication systems are typical instances. Digital filtering is here the basic item. At first sight, it can be considered as the direct adaptation of analog filtering to digital computing techniques. But the rapidly growing use of *adaptive* filtering makes digital signal processing evolve toward a computationally intensive real-time activity. The main issue is to achieve high throughput, so that it is desirable to handle both *algorithm* and *architecture* within the same framework.
4. **Industrial process control** involves regulators that are supervised via internally or externally generated interruptions and sequential tasks. The main challenge is to provide a tool that is flexible enough to support an easy specification, and powerful enough to guarantee that the actual implementation meets the specification.
5. **Complex signal processing systems** such as radar and sonar involve preprocessing of signals, followed by drastic data-compression via detection-and-labeling, and then by logically complex data-processing modules (data fusion, decision handling, etc.). This results in computationally intensive real-time systems where many events are generated and further combined to fire new computations. The same remarks hold as for process control. The issue of speed becomes much more important.
6. **Complex Control-and-Monitoring systems** govern aircraft and transportation systems as well as hazardous industrial plants. They can involve thousands of sensors, hundreds of actuators, and dozens of interconnected computer systems. Data can be processed in numerous operating modes, for example for maintenance or safety purposes. Heuristics of high combinatorial complexity typically may compose up to 90% of the application software code. Highly distributed target architectures must be considered. The safety constraints are obviously critical.
7. C^3-**systems** (Command-Control-Communicate) or even C^3I-systems ('I' for "Intelligent") are encountered in military systems, in air traffic control systems, and also in large ground transportation systems. A further difficulty here is the highly distributed nature of the architecture supporting the real-time system: subsystems are moving, so that communication links cannot be considered as time-invariant.

B. A First Case Study: Automobile Control

Transportation systems involve numerous reactive systems, some of which bear severe real-time constraints. Let us take an automobile as an example.

There are or will be specific controllers for fuel injection, brakes, suspension, direction, etc. Each of those involves reactive programs that do numerical computations and have numerous functioning states, in particular because of hardware failure handling.

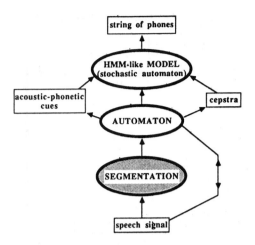

Fig. 1. A speech-to-phoneme recognition system.

In the future, all these controllers will not stay independent of each other. They will have to be linked together for global coordination, for instance, to make cars lean inwards in curves. Coordination can be performed in two ways: either by distributing information from each controller to the other ones, thus making each of them much more complex, or by building a centralized controller that is itself a complex reactive system. In both approaches, there will be no easy solution and the safety problems will greatly increase. Linking the controllers together will be done by local area networks, involving themselves with fast protocols which are nontrivial reactive programs.

At the user end, panels and man–machine interfaces will be computerized. Again, this will involve numerous reactive programs. Furthermore, one of the essential functions in car automation will be failure detection and reporting. This difficult area is often underestimated: the messages to the user or repairer should be simple and should not involve dozen of individual failures. This will require a clever mixture of reactive programming, signal processing, and heuristics.

Similar situations of course appear in almost all transportation systems. For automobiles, there is a rather strong additional constraint: the price of hardware should be as small as possible, which means that programs are also subject to severe size constraints.

C. A Second Case Study: Speech Recognition Systems

Speech recognition systems are do not bear hard real-time constraints: the time response between the input (spoken language) and the output (text on screen or input to some other system) may be only loosely constrained. Nevertheless, the continuous speech signal must be processed on-line to avoid unbounded buffering. Hence, continuous speech recognition is a good prototype of application where high-speed numerical preprocessing as well as complex symbolic postprocessing is required. Similar examples are found in data communication, pattern recognition, military systems, process monitoring, and troubleshooting systems. We describe here briefly the speech-to-phoneme recognition system developed at IRISA [7]. Its overall organization is shown in the Fig. 1. The originality of this system lies in its use of a *segmentation* of the continuous speech signal prior to any recognition. The *automaton* supervises the segmentation; it fires small modules to compute *cepstra*, a representation of the spectral characteristics of the signal, associated with detected segments as well as some *acoustic/phonetic cues*. All these modules are numerically oriented. Finally, high level processing is performed following a technique close to *Hidden-Markov Model* (HMM) methods [22]: maximum likelihood decoding based on a stochastic automaton. This is again a numerically as well as logically oriented module.

To illustrate further how signal processing algorithms may give rise to reactive systems, let us give additional details on the segmentation module. The outcome of this processing is shown in the Fig. 2. The segmentation procedure is mainly numerically oriented and is performed on-line. Detection of change occurs with a bounded delay, so that the speech signal must be reprocessed from the estimated change time. Furthermore, some local backward processing of the speech signal is also needed. Hence, while this is still a real-time processing of speech signal, its timing is far from being trivial. Therefore, writing a real-time oriented programming of this processing in C or FORTRAN is a tedious and error-prone task.

To summarize, this example is a good prototype of a complex real-time signal processing application. It may be compared to radar systems for example.

D. Reactive and Real-time Systems—Major Issues

Most reactive and real-time systems naturally decompose into communicating concurrent components. The programming architecture must follow this decomposition. Hence, all aspects related to concurrency are important: communication, synchronization, and organization of the computational flow. We shall refer to these aspects as qualitative ones. The timing constraints imposed on real-time systems also impose to consider quantitative aspects mostly related to the speed of computations. Here are the major issues related to these aspects:

1. **Use modular and formal techniques to specify, implement, and verify programs.** The specification-implementation cycle is a major issue in the software life cycle. Modular programming is necessary to reflect the conceptual architecture into the programs themselves. Relying on a discipline of programming based on manual translations from specification to implementation is known not to guarantee enough safety. One should therefore provide modular tools that formally and inherently guarantee the equivalence preserving throughout the specification → implementation process and give access to formal verification techniques. Notice that these tools must perform nontrivial transformations, since there is usually no perfect match between the functional architecture and the target computer architecture.

2. **Encompass within a single framework all reactive aspects,** i.e., communication, synchronization, logic,

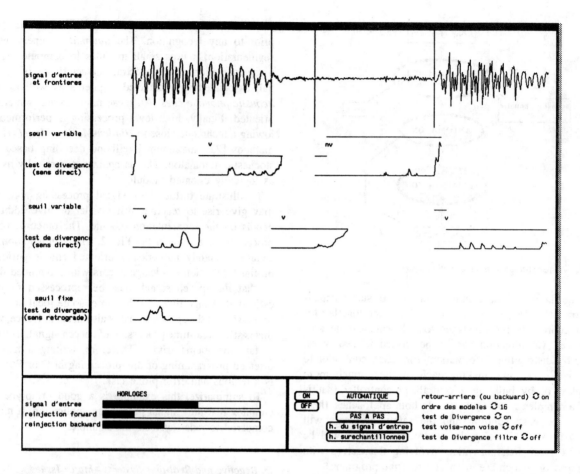

Fig. 2. The segmentation module. The detected segments are superimposed on the signal (top line). Subsequent lines show the behavior of several auxiliary quantities (the divergence tests) that are computed on-line to perform the segmentation. As a by-product of the processing, the auxiliary labels "v" and "nv" indicate voiced and unvoiced segments, respectively.

and computational flow. Having to deal with several frameworks can break the coherence of the global chain. This constraint may be somewhat relaxed if the interface between frameworks is very cleanly defined and permits useful reasoning.
3. **Deal with distributed target architectures.** The need for distributed architecture can come either from performance requirements or from geographical constraints within the application.
4. **Preserve determinism whenever possible**. A system is said to be deterministic if a given sequence of inputs always produces the same sequence of outputs. Any sensible functional description of the kind of real-time system we discussed (information processing, control, C^3, etc.) should be obviously deterministic in this sense: there is no reason the engineer should *want* its procedure to behave in some unpredictable manner. Furthermore, even when the implementation of a complex system is globally nondeterministic, most parts of it are individually deterministic. Since deterministic programs are much simple to analyze and debug that nondeterministic ones, tools should not force nondeterminism unless specifically required

to. There are obviously subtle trade-offs between determinism and concurrency when implementation issues are considered.
5. **Consider issues of speed**. In all cases, the executable codes should be efficient and avoid overheads due to unnecessary run-time communications. Execution times should be predictable whenever possible. For real-time systems, if object code efficiency is not enough to guarantee the respect of timing constraints, timing issues should be incorporated in the model.

III. REAL-TIME PROGRAMMING: THE STATE OF THE ART

We review the techniques classically used for real-time according to the previously mentioned issues (see [9] for a more complete presentation):

1. *Connecting classical programs by making them communicate using OS primitives.* This is the most common way of doing things. There is presently a lot of experience of using this technique, but its drawbacks are rather numerous and severe. There is no *single* object to study, but a set of more or less loosely connected programs. Understanding, debugging, and maintaining applications is hard. For the same rea-

son, there is little room for clean automatic program behavior analysis, and therefore no way of formally guaranteeing safety properties. Last, operating systems are generally somewhat nondeterministic, unless they are reduced to trivial sequencers, which in turn makes programming harder.

2. *Using finite-states machine*, also called *finite automata*. These objects have numerous advantages: they are deterministic, efficient, they can be automatically analyzed by numerous available verification systems. However, they have a severe drawback: they do not directly support hierarchical design and concurrency. A small change to a specification can provoke a complete transformation of an automaton. When they are put into cooperation, separately small and pretty automata can yield a big ugly one. As soon as they are large, automata become impossible to understand for human beings.

3. Using *Petri Nets* or Petri-Net based formalisms such as the GRAFCET [24], [11]. Such formalisms are commonly used for comparatively small applications. They naturally support concurrency, but they lack modular structure and often lack determinism. They do not scale up well to big applications.

4. Using classical *Concurrent Programming Languages* such as ADA [6] or OCCAM [13]. These languages take concurrency as a primary concern and support modularity. They permit their user to see a single program for a concurrent application. However, they are essentially asynchronous and nondeterministic: although a communication is seen as a synchronization between two processes, the time taken between the *possibility* of a communication and its actual *achievement* can be arbitrary and is unpredictable. When several communications can take place, their actual order is also unpredictable. For all these reasons, such languages are hardly adequate for real-time programming. Finally, automatic program verification is often not feasible since asynchrony makes the programs state spaces explode. See [9] for more details.

IV. THE SYNCHRONOUS APPROACH TO REACTIVE AND REAL-TIME SYSTEMS SPECIFICATION, DESIGN, AND IMPLEMENTATION

We now turn to the synchronous approach and show that it reconciles all aspects discussed in the previous sections: it makes deterministic hierarchical concurrent specification and programming possible, it leads to efficient and controllable object code, and it makes it possible to use automatic verification tools by avoiding or at least reducing the state space explosion problem.

The basic idea is very simple: we consider *ideal* reactive systems that produce their outputs *synchronously* with their inputs, their reaction taking no observable time. This is akin to the instantaneous interaction hypothesis of Newtonian mechanics or standard electricity, a hypothesis which is well-known to make life simple and to be valid in most practical cases. The main simplification lies in the fact that sets of ideal systems compose very well into other ideal systems. In the synchronous model, a system can be decomposed into concurrent subcomponents at will without affecting its observable behavior even with respect to timing issues.

To illustrate the synchrony hypothesis, we shall start from two extreme examples. First, we discuss the case of sequential tasks. Then, we discuss the case of regulators in process control or adaptive filtering in signal processing. Based on the first example we introduce the synchronous model as an idealization of reactive systems where internal actions and communications are instantaneous. Based on the second example, we introduce the synchronous model as dealing with systems of interconnected dynamical equations (the block-diagrams of signal processing or control sciences), or, equivalently, as a description of the traces. Then we show how both points of view may be interchanged or mixed together, leading to an idealized picture of *general* real-time systems.

Note that it is not our purpose to be formal in this introductory paper. We simply present an intuitive picture of the synchronous style of modeling we want to promote. Information on related formal models and their properties can be found in the subsequent papers and references therein.

A. A First Example: Clicking on a Mouse

We consider a mouse handler that has two inputs:
1. CLICK: a push-button;
2. TICK: a clock signal.

A first CLICK fires the GO module that watches for the elapsed time to decide whether a SINGLE, or a DOUBLE CLICK has been received (on the diagram of Fig. 3 the maximum elapsed time is 4). The end of the enabling period where the CLICKs are watched for is indicated by the signal RELAX.

Obvious modularity considerations lead to consider this small system as the composition of two communicating subsystems, namely:

1. a module GO that is fired by the first click and delivers RELAX at the end of the enabling period;
2. a module SIMPLE_MOUSE that outputs signals SINGLE, or DOUBLE according to the above specification when it receives RELAX.

Both modules and their resulting communication we call MOUSE are shown in the modular state transition diagram of Fig. 3. This figure should be read as follows. Each of the two modules contains a state transition diagram; transitions are labeled with words that list the events which must occur simultaneously with the considered transition. When two different words are assigned to a transition, then any one of them may cause the transition to occur. The two modules share RELAX as a common event, which means that each time one module executes a transition involving RELAX, then the other one must execute simultaneously

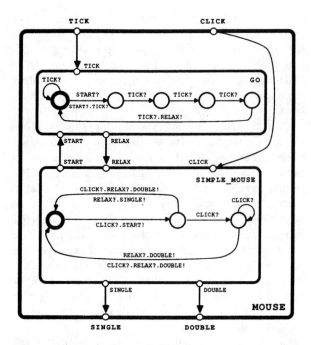

Fig. 3. The modules GO, SIMPLE_MOUSE, and their communication MOUSE.

some transition involving the same event. This presentation roughly follows the STATECHARTS style [3].

Such a specification of this toy system can be intuitively accepted by the reader. This diagram, however, should be interpreted according to the following rules.

1. Changes of state in each of the modules should be considered as *synchronous* (or simultaneous) with the reception of the mentioned input signals.
2. The emission of output signals in each of the modules should be considered as *synchronous* (or simultaneous) with the associated change of state.
3. The communications follow the principle of "instantaneous broadcast" of the signals emitted by the modules, which means that their reception is *synchronous* (or simultaneous) with their emission.
4. The output behavior of MOUSE is entirely fixed whenever the *global interleaving* of the two input signals TICK, CLICK is given by the environment.

To summarize the three first points, *internal actions and communications are instantaneous*. As a by-product, outputs are synchronous with inputs as requested above. The fourth point follows and implies that determinism is preserved by synchronous concurrent composition.

An example of a global interleaving is given in the following chronogram, where signals written on the same column are simultaneous and events are ordered from left to right:

TICK	TICK	TICK	TICK		TICK	TICK
	CLICK			CLICK		

This chronogram must be understood as a *discrete event* one. Only the global ordering makes sense, the interval between successive events does not need to be constant with respect to some externally given notion of absolute time. Actually, no physical notion of time is referred to in the mouse specification, although in practice the TICK input will often be generated by actual quartz clocks.

The synchronous model does *not* specify how an input chronogram is generated by the environment. This relies on the actual implementation of the mouse as an electronic device, using simple sensors and A/D converters. Then providing a global input interleaving can depend on some comparison of the actual instants of arrival of physical signals actually bound to continuous time.

The mouse example reveals a fundamental feature of our approach to real-time programming: thanks to the above idealization of synchrony, the reactive part of our system is made *implementation independent*, and only a relatively very small part—building the global interleaving—is implementation dependent and bound to physical time. Most programming difficulties actually arise in the reactive part in actual reactive problems. Later on, we shall see that powerful formal reasoning can be performed on the implementation-independent part, while some formal reasoning can be still also performed on the implementation-dependent depending on the cases.[2]

We must recognize that we left aside the issue of *computation speed* in this discussion, since we assumed an infinitely fast machine was at hand. But it turns out that this is too dogmatic an interpretation of the synchronous model and that we can be more flexible. As an illustration, consider again the chronogram above augmented with the outputs corresponding to each input:

TICK	TICK	TICK	TICK		TICK	TICK
	CLICK			CLICK		
	START					RELAX
						DOUBLE

Now, assume the mouse system has been actually implemented in some environment subject to physical continuous "real" time, and that the real time unit is plotted on the horizontal axis. A realistic picture is to consider that the separating vertical lines are *elastic* ones, i.e., that they may be redrawn as oblique curves, provided that causality be preserved (outputs must follow inputs). This is exactly what is done when considering clock cycles in digital circuits. In some cases, we can even make slots overlap to perform pipelining. Taking into account physical time consumption at the implementation level amounts to reason about such a flexibility.

[2] For instance, we may prove here that any global interleaving is a possible input to this system.

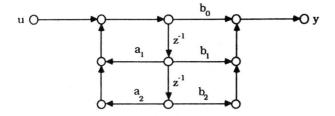

Fig. 4. A second order filter.

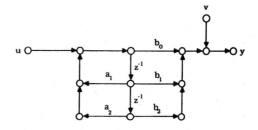

Fig. 5. A two-port filter.

Altogether, we hope to have convinced the reader that there are two distinct issues: implementation-independent logical synchronization and qualitative timing on the one hand and implementation-dependent physical time consumption on the other hand. We further discuss this point in the Section V. It should be remembered that our synchronous model deals only with qualitative timing and synchronization and not physical time consumption. Our claim is that one should stay within the ideal synchronous model as much as possible and consider actual timing dependencies only when needed and where needed.

B. A Second Example: Digital Filtering

The signal flow graph of a "second order digital filter" in the classical direct form [21] is shown in Fig. 4. At the nodes of this graph, incoming signals are added and their result is broadcast along the outgoing branches. The labels z^{-1} and a_i, b_j on the arcs denote a shift register and a multiplication by the mentioned constant gain, respectively. Accordingly, the signal flow graph of Fig. 4 is a coding of the following formula:

$$w_n = u_n + a_1 w_{n-1} + a_2 w_{n-2}$$
$$y_n = b_0 w_n + b_1 w_{n-1} + b_2 w_{n-2}$$

where n denotes the time index. A little algebra yields equivalently:

$$y_n = a_1 y_{n-1} + a_2 y_{n-2} + b_0 u_n + b_1 u_{n-1} + b_2 u_{n-2}.$$

We can read this mathematical expression as describing a machine which performs the specified filtering *according to the principles 1, 2, and 3 of synchronicity* we have introduced while discussing the mouse. This is certainly a well-accepted idealization of a digital filter.

A slightly more subtle example is the signal flow graph of Fig. 5, which represents a two-port filter derived from the preceding one. It corresponds to the formula

$$y_n = a_1 y_{n-1} + a_2 y_{n-2} + b_0 u_n + b_1 u_{n-1} + b_2 u_{n-2} + v_n \quad (1)$$

where v is a second input signal. Two input ports are needed at the interface, as in the MOUSE example, and principle 4 applies here. But, what is new here is that *not every global*

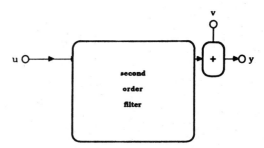

Fig. 6. A two port filter: modular specification.

interleaving is allowed for the two input signals u, v: to each sample of u must correspond a unique sample of v.

Now, interconnecting digital filters is usually specified by linking graphs, or equivalently by writing systems of equations. For instance, the filter of Fig. 5 may be redrawn in a modular way as shown in Fig. 6. But this corresponds to replacing (dynamical or recurrent) (1) by a *system* of equations in the usual mathematical sense:

$$z_n = a_1 y_{n-1} + a_2 y_{n-2} + b_0 u_n + b_1 u_{n-1} + b_2 u_{n-2}$$
$$y_n = z_n + v_n$$

where common names denote the same signal.

C. Toward the Synchronous Modeling Approach

The mouse example was naturally described using state transition diagrams. The digital filter example was naturally described in the mathematical framework of systems of recurrent equations. Formal models corresponding to these different frameworks can be shown equivalent. We find it illustrative to perform the following exercise on these two examples: crisscross the models, i.e., describe the digital filter via a state transition diagram and the mouse via a system of recurrent equations.

A state transition diagram for the digital filter. To simplify our presentation, we shall replace the filter (1) by the simpler one

$$y_n = a_1 y_{n-1} + a_2 y_{n-2} + u_n \quad (2)$$

Introduce the vector signal

$$X_n = \begin{bmatrix} y_n \\ y_{n-1} \end{bmatrix}$$

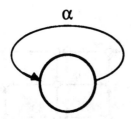

Fig. 7. State transition diagram of the filter.

and rewrite (2) in the "state space" form

$$X_n = \begin{bmatrix} a_1 & a_2 \\ 1 & 0 \end{bmatrix} X_{n-1} + \begin{bmatrix} u_n \\ 0 \end{bmatrix}$$
$$y_n = [1 \ 0] X_n. \qquad (3)$$

One time step of the system (3) would be written as follows in a standard sequential programming language:

$$X := \begin{bmatrix} a_1 & a_2 \\ 1 & 0 \end{bmatrix} X + \begin{bmatrix} u \\ 0 \end{bmatrix}; \qquad (4)$$

$$y := [1 \ 0] X \qquad (5)$$

This program is of the form (4);(5), i.e., it is composed of two instructions separated by the PASCAL-like sequencer ";". Denote by α the action performed by this program. Then the state transition diagram corresponding to the system (3) is shown in Fig. 7.

In this diagram, the state just counts the occurrences of the input signal. The task is in fact entirely summarized by the α label of the action (4);(5) which corresponds to a single iteration of the recurrent equation.

A system of recurrent equations for the mouse. To simplify our discussion, we shall only consider the SIMPLE_MOUSE. We shall term an *event* the occurrence of at least one of the input signals CLICK and RELAX. Events will be indexed using the integers $N = \{1, 2, 3, \ldots\}$. Then, we denote the subsequences of events where CLICK and RELAX are respectively received by $C = \{C_1, C_2, \ldots, C_m, \ldots\}$ and $R = \{R_1, R_2, \ldots, R_k, \ldots\}$. This simple mouse can be specified by the following system of equations, where the running index n denotes the current event:

$$N = C \cup R \qquad (6)$$

$$X_n = \text{if } n \in R, \text{ then } 0 \text{ else } \min\{2, X_{n-1} + 1\} \qquad (7)$$

$$M_{R_k} = \text{if } R_k \in C, \text{ then } \min\{2, X_{R_k-1} + 1\}$$
$$\text{else } X_{R_k-1} \qquad (8)$$

$$\text{if } R_k \in C, \text{ then } X_{R_k-1} \neq 0 \qquad (9)$$

- Equation (6) specifies that events consist of the occurrence of at least one of the inputs CLICK, RELAX.
- X denotes the internal state of the counter. Equation (7) expresses that X is reset to 0 whenever RELAX is received and incremented whenever CLICK is received but not RELAX. Note that the specification (6) is used for (7) to be correct: since, according to (6), the index n of events is incremented only if at least one input signal has been delivered, the "else" in equation (7) means $n \notin R$ and thus $n \in C$.
- The integer M_{R_k}, whose possible values are 1, 2 is the output. Equation (8) specifies that the output M has the same index as R; the value carried by M is either the previous value of the state (when RELAX is received alone), or the previous value of the state incremented by one (when both CLICK, RELAX are received).
- Finally, equation (9) asserts that RELAX cannot occur when the counter is in its initial state 0.

Hence we should call this a *Multiple Clocked Recurrent System (MCRS)*, since different time indices are used here. Obviously, handling more than 3 different indexes in such a pedestrian way becomes intractable. The model (6,7,8,9) also reveals clearly that the two subsequences $C_1, C_2, \ldots$ and $R_1, R_2, \ldots$ are used. But knowing these consists precisely in knowing the global interleaving of the two input signals: this is precisely point 4 of the principles of synchronicity. Again, no physical notion of time is used here. Finally the model (6,7,8,9) consists of describing *relations* between various signals rather than constructing a machine whose behavior represents that of the desired mouse. In particular, (9) specifies a *constraint* on the input signal RELAX.

D. Summary of the Synchronous Model

The discussion above illustrates that two different in style but equivalent forms of *synchronous modeling* may be used. Both specify an ideal real-time machine with the following features:

1. *Output is synchronous with input, internal actions are instantaneous, communications are performed via instantaneous broadcasting,*
2. *The global interleaving of the external communications may be partially chosen by the environment and is essential in analyzing the behavior of the system.*

The two styles are:

State based formalisms. In the mouse example, we used state transition diagrams where arrows were labeled by communication actions. The Statecharts generalize this kind of presentation. The CSML and ESTEREL formalisms have a fairly similar but more implicit notion of state based on control positions in an imperative program. All these formalisms will be presented in this special issue. The corresponding formal models are discussed in the papers above or in the references therein.

Multiple Clocked Recurrent Systems (MCRS's). They are a way to describe the legal traces of a system and are generalizations of the usual models of dynamical systems used in digital signal processing or control. This generalization is needed to handle different timings and their relations, which naturally arise in complex real-time applications. The languages LUSTRE and SIGNAL, [4], [5] presented in this special issue section mainly rely on this style of modeling; proper references to corresponding formal models can be found in these articles.

State-based formalisms are easy and natural to use in problems where control flow is prevalent, for example for systems that often jump between many distinct functioning modes (man–machine interfaces, protocols, control panels, etc.). Writing concurrent components is easy at a syntactic level, but defining the behavior of a concurrent composition is not easy: broadcasting signals has the effect that concurrent components constrain each other in a nontrivial way at each reaction. The overall behavior is given by a fixpoint of a set of constraints, generally computed using formal semantics given in Plotkin's *Structural Operational Semantics* inference-rules based style. Roughly speaking, SOS are the convenient framework to handle state-based formalisms in a modular style, just as if they were systems of equations.

MRCS are clearly well-adapted to problems where data flow is prevalent, signal processing being an obvious example. The composition of MRCS is very easy to define since they are standard mathematical equation systems. Conversely, MRCS are weak where state-based approaches are strong, that is when the complexity is in functioning mode changes. Then the user must handle explicit control variables to record the current mode, not an easy task.

It is shown in [8], [12] that both styles allow to describe the reactive aspects of all real-time system. In practice, each style tends to be weak where the other one is strong. Since we do not know yet how to combine both styles in a common formalism nor whether this makes sense, we need to use both in real applications, depending on the style of individual parts. There is some present work not reported in this special issue to make both styles as compatible as possible, for example at the object code level.

E. Solving Communication Equations

Be it in the state-based approach or in the MCRS approach, communication equations may have:

1. **no solution:** the constraints contradict each other, or cycles of causality may exist that cannot be solved using finite algorithms. Such contradictions or deadlocks may involve the whole system, or only a subsystem of it.
2. **infinitely many solutions:** the timing of the various signals is not completely determined by the given inputs, we get nondeterminism.
3. **a single solution** which is also an input-output map: our program is deterministic, and is thus a suitable candidate for proper execution.

All languages presented in this special issue have specific algorithms to check these properties. In particular *determinism can be checked and guaranteed,* an important feature as we have discussed before.

F. Program Verification

In most reactive or real-time applications, it is important to be able to formally verify program properties: liveness of safety properties, respect of total or partial specifications. There are various available software tools to perform such verifications for the formalisms described in this special issue. Some use model checkers to compare the infinite sequence of events of a given program with a list of specified properties that are stated using a different formalism, see for instance [1], [3] where temporal logic is used for this purpose, and also [2]. Some other tools provide the user with abstractions of the program, i.e., with reduced programs that behave as the original one but involve only a (small) subset of signals, see [2], [4] for such an approach. Finally, in MCRS formalisms such as SIGNAL [5] and LUSTRE [4], constraints or properties can be specified just as further dynamical equations that must be implied by the given system. Then there is no deep distinction between program and safety properties and the standard program compilers can act as verifiers.

V. SYNCHRONOUS MODELS VERSUS ASYNCHRONOUS SYSTEMS

Actual machines for which the ideal synchronous model is realistic do exist. For instance, strongly synchronized hardware or VLSI architectures are such that internal actions and communications occur within a clock cycle, that is within a "tick" in our sense. The only difference is that outputs are given to the environment at the end of the cycle and not synchronously with the inputs. Since the cycle time is very short, say 100 ns, this is the best approximation we can get. The language CSML [1] or the hardware implementation of ESTEREL and LUSTRE [10] implement this point of view.

However, most of the machines used to support the applications we listed in the Section I should be certainly considered as *asynchronous* in any reasonable sense. Furthermore, real-time systems are often implemented on distributed architecture, that is on sets of processors connected by asynchronous means. Synchronous models as introduced before can hardly be considered as realistic for such target architectures.

In this section, we discuss implementation issues when asynchronism must be considered. We first consider the case of the digital filter and exhibit different *realistic* implementations for which we can prove equivalence with the original specification. Then, we consider a simple example of token-based architecture as an instance of asynchronous machine and show how reasoning on its synchronization may be performed via considering an associated synchronous model.

A. Implementing the Digital Filter

An infinitely fast machine implementing (3) is certainly a correct implementation of the digital filter of Fig. 7, but it is obviously an unrealistic one. We shall discuss two relevant alternatives.

A purely sequential implementation can be derived from the signal flow graph of Fig. 5 in the following classical way. First consider the associated *dependency graph* obtained by cutting the branches labeled with a delay z^{-1} as shown in Fig. 8.

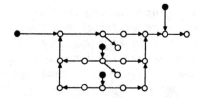

T input:	T_1		...
F input:		F_2	...
boolean:	true	false	...
output:	T_1	F_2	...

Fig. 8. The dependency graph corresponding to Fig. 5.

We get an acyclic directed graph. Peeling this graph by removing first the input nodes and then subsequent ones yields a sequential execution scheme of each single time step of the system. This is depicted in Fig. 9.

A **data–flow (asynchronous) execution** can be simply derived by interpreting each node and branch in the graph of Fig. 5 according to the data–flow mechanism shown in Fig. 10.

What is important here is that *we know before execution that this token mechanism will be nonblocking and with bounded files.* This property is well-known; it is already used to guarantee well-behaved executions for simple data–flow machines, see [19]. Note that similar arguments can be used to justify asynchronous executions à la Petri net of this filter.

This ability to validate asynchronous executions of our synchronous ideal machines generalizes to the fully general reactive systems we can model with our approach. It is beyond the scope of this paper to formally justify this claim in a general fashion. We just present a simple example and show how to associate a synchronous model with a "generalized" data-flow machine [20] to validate it.

B. Validating Asynchronous Machines with Synchronous Models

Figure 11 depicts the data-flow actors introduced in [20].[3] Let us concentrate on the **SELECT** operator, and consider the run depicted in Fig. 12. We construct a global "time indexing" of the tokens which is be consistent in the following sense: *the tokens that are consumed or produced in a given firing must have the same time index.* By inspecting the run of Fig. 12, one easily checks that the time indexing shown in Fig. 13 is consistent in the above sense.

Let us collect the tokens with the same label into successive slots. We get a global interleaving of the four signals involved in this actor shown as follows:

What we have derived here is a synchronous model associated with the data–flow actor. Generally speaking, given a data–flow graph built with the above primitive actors, we can automatically build a synchronous model as an interconnection of synchronous subsystems associated with each actor. Then any of the formal verification methods presented in this special issue can be applied to the obtained synchronous model. It turns out that correctness of this synchronous model[4] guarantees a satisfactory execution of the original data–flow graph for any input data sequence.

C. The Synchronous Approach to Asynchronous Implementations

1. When feasible, strictly synchronous executions of synchronous systems are certainly valid (cf. VLSI and hardware).
2. Verification and proofs of correct synchronization and logic are available in the synchronous approach to real-time programming,
3. A sequential execution scheme can be derived at compile time for any synchronous system.

---

[3]They were in fact inspired by the primitive operators of the SIGNAL synchronous language we present in this special issue.

[4]cf. The remark at the very end of the Section 4.

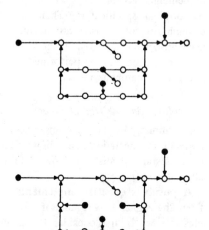
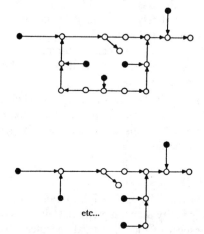

Fig. 9. Peeling the graph of Fig. 8.

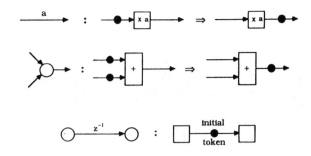

Fig. 10. Data–flow mechanisms for the graph of Fig. 5.

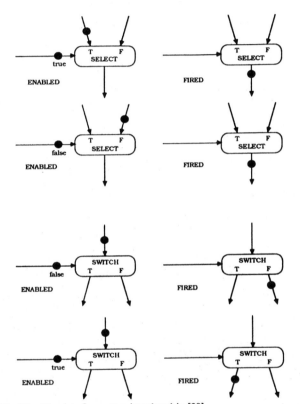

Fig. 11. The data-flow actors introduced in [20].

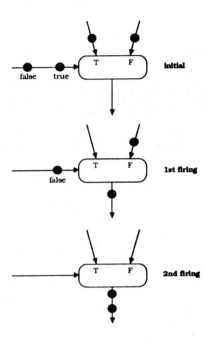

Fig. 12. A run of SELECT.

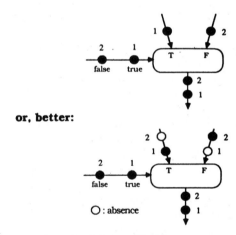

Fig. 13. A consistent time indexing of the tokens.

4. The idealized strict synchronicity hypothesis can be relaxed to yield fully *asynchronous* executions of synchronous systems that are guaranteed correct.
5. The formal verification tools based on the synchronous approach provide a way to validate asynchronous executions.

Since both purely sequential (e.g., Von Neumann) and purely asynchronous execution schemes cam be associated with synchronous systems, it is easy to believe that *mixed sequential/asynchronous* execution schemes cam be derived as well. To conclude, using the synchronous and asynchronous frameworks in the above suggested way yields a much cleaner treatment of the specification → implementation process. Again, we should point out that issues of physical time consumption are not considered here as such; however, we think that our approach facilitates their proper handling. This special issue reports various experiments along this line.

VI. Possible Impact of the Synchronous Approach on the Activity of Real-Time Programming

The techniques we presented here are clearly novel. This has some consequences we discuss now.

The synchronous formalisms are based on very advanced and powerful concepts and have clean mathematical semantics. This is clearly a big progress compared to previous tools. However, two questions are still largely open: that of user interfaces and that of programming methodology.

Consider first user-interfaces. Some formalisms are purely graphical (Statecharts), some are purely textual (CSML,

ESTEREL), and others can use both graphical and textual presentations indifferently (SIGNAL, LUSTRE). Speaking first of graphical interfaces, STATECHARTS are state-oriented while the block-diagram interface of SIGNAL is data-flow oriented. None of these two choices covers the whole area of reactive and real-time systems: state-oriented diagrams are poor for signal processing and block-diagrams are poor for state machines. When using textual formalisms, one often needs to draw pictures to explain program architectures, but there is yet no clear way to make these drawings formal rather than simply explanatory. Therefore, while the principles of the synchronous approach have a wide applicability, this is hardly the case for the particular user interfaces available so far. The development of rich and well-targeted user interfaces for synchronous languages must be a technical priority.

Let us now turn to methodology. At least in the area of real-time systems most potential users have a process-oriented background[5] rather than a computer science oriented one. Furthermore, most of them are used to a particular way of thinking, say for example to state-based reasoning rather than to equation manipulation. Since the synchronous approach yields new design and programming styles, one should develop methodologies that make these styles easy to master. Such methodologies do not really exist yet and their development will take some time. They should of course be based on elaborate software development environments and on fancy user-interfaces.

Tools that are considered as user-friendly in a particular application domain do exist: we can cite for example the GRAFCET. However, their associated formalisms definitely lack precise semantics. While this can be accepted in simple situations, it becomes unacceptable when safety is critical. There might actually be a reasonable way to make a smooth transition from existing tools to really rigorous ones: to build programming environments externally based on existing formalisms but internally based on the synchronous approach and on rigorous semantics.

Finally, it is important to note that synchronous languages are not completely bound to nondeterminism. Some of the synchronous languages perfectly well accept nondeterministic programs as modules, although they refuse to produce deterministic code out of them. Nondeterministic modules can be useful to model the environment or the controlled physical process. This might be the basis for a design methodology of real-time software based on a joint handling of the application and of a model of the physical process. Such an approach is standard in control systems design; it is interesting to note that it might become valid for real-time programming as well.

VII. CONCLUSION

We have first discussed the major issues in the area of reactive and real-time programming, insisting particularly on safety constraints. We have then informally presented the new synchronous programming approach. Based on simple examples, we have discussed two orthogonal synchronous styles and their semantics: a state-based style and a data-flow based style. Each style applies to a particular class of problems; complex applications will certainly require the cooperation of both. We have briefly discussed how to verify program properties and how to make asynchronous implementations look like synchronous ones.

The other papers in this Special Issue will present the existing specific synchronous formalisms and the associated software tools for program simulation, compiling, and verification. They will support our general claim that synchronous programming opens a new path toward powerful, rigorous, and usable methodologies for reactive and real-time programming.

ACKNOWLEDGMENT

The authors are indebted to several reviewers who pointed out misleading and obscure claims in the first version. They would like to thank especially E. Clarke for his careful reading and criticism of the manuscript.

REFERENCES

[1] CSML, see this issue.
[2] ESTEREL, see this issue.
[3] STATECHARTS, see this issue.
[4] LUSTRE, see this issue.
[5] SIGNAL, see this issue.
[6] ADA, *The Programming Language* ADA *Reference Manual.* New York: Springer Verlag, LNCS 155, 1983.
[7] R. André-Obrecht, "A new statistical approach for the automatic segmentation of continuous speech signals," *IEEE Trans. Acoust., Speech, Signal Processing,* vol. 36, pp. 29–40, 1988.
[8] A. Benveniste, P. Le Guernic, Y. Sorel, and M. Sorine, "A denotational theory of synchronous communicating systems," *Inform. Comput.,* to be published.
[9] G. Berry, "Real time programming: Special purpose languages or general purpose languages," presented at the 11th IFIP World Congress, San Francisco, CA, 1989.
[10] ——, "A hardware implementation of pure Esterel," in *Proc. Workshop on Formal Methods in VLSI Design,* Miami, FL, 1991.
[11] M. Blanchard, *Comprendre, maitriser et appliquer le* GRAFCET. Cepadues Editions, 1979.
[12] P. Caspi, "Clocks in data–flow languages," *Theoretical Comp. Sci.,* 1990.
[13] Inmos Ltd., *The* OCCAM *Programming Manual.* Englewood Cliffs, NJ: Prentice-Hall, 1984.
[14] D. Harel and A. Pnueli, "On the development of reactive systems" in *Logics and Models of Concurrent Systems,* NATO ASI Series, vol. 13, K. R. Apt, Ed. New York: Springer-Verlag, pp. 477–498, 1985.
[15] G. Berry, S. Moisan, and J-P. Rigault, "Esterel: Toward a synchronous and semantically sound high level language for real time applications," in *Proc. IEEE Real Time Systems Symp.,* 1983.
[16] J.-L. Bergerand, P. Caspi, N. Halbwachs, D. Pilaud, and E. Pilaud, "Outline of a real-time data-flow language," in *1985 Real-Time Symp.,* San Diego, CA, 1985.
[17] P. Le Guernic, A. Benveniste, P. Bournai, and T. Gautier, "SIGNAL: A data-flow oriented language for signal processing," *IEEE Trans. Acoust., Speech, Signal Processing,* vol. ASSP-34, pp. 362–374, 1986.
[18] D. Harel, H. Lachover, A. Naamad, A. Pnueli, M. Politi, R. Sherman, A. Shtul-Trauring, and M. Trakhtenbrot, "STATE-MATE: A working environment for the development of complex 14 systems," *IEEE Trans. Software Eng.* vol. 16, pp. 403–414, 1990.

---

[5]They are typically chemical, mechanical, aircraft, control engineers, etc.

[19] E. A. Lee and D. G. Messerschmitt, "Static scheduling of synchronous data flow programs for digital signal processing," *IEEE Trans. Computers,* vol. C-36, Jan. 1987.
[20] E. A. Lee, "Consistency in data–flow graphs", Research Report UCB/ERL M89/125, Electronics Research Lab., College of Eng., U. C. Berkeley, 1989; also, *IEEE Trans. Parallel Distributed Syst.,* vol. 2, pp. 223–235, Apr. 1991.
[21] A. V. Oppenheim and R. W. Schafer, *Discrete-Time Signal Processing.* Englewood Cliffs, NJ: Prentice Hall, 1989.
[22] J. Picone, "Continuous speech recognition using hidden Markov models," *IEEE ASSP Mag.,* vol. 7, pp. 26–41, 1990.
[23] A. Pnueli, "Applications of temporal logic to the specification and verification of reactive systems: A survey of current trends", in *Current Trends in Concurrency,* de Bakker *et al.*, Eds., Lecture Notes in Comput. Sci., vol. 224, Berlin, Germany: Springer-Verlag, pp. 510–584, 1986.
[24] W. Reisig, *Petri Nets.* New York: Springer, 1985.

Albert Benveniste (Fellow, IEEE), for a photograph and biography please see page 1269 of this issue.

Gérard Berry, for a photograph and biography please see page 1269 of this issue.

CHAPTER THREE

Analysis and Estimation

Performance Estimation of Embedded Software with Instruction Cache Modeling 167
    Y.-T. S. Li, S. Malik, and A. Wolfe

Scheduling Algorithms for Multiprogramming in a Hard-Real-Time Environment 179
    C. L. Liu and J. W. Layland

Performance Estimation for Real-Time Distributed Embedded Systems .195
    T.-Y. Yen and W. Wolf

Rate Analysis for Embedded Systems 207
    A. Mathur, A. Dasdan, and R. K. Gupta

Power Analysis of Embedded Software: A First Step Towards Software Power Minimization 222
    V. Tiwari, S. Malik, and A. Wolfe

A Survey of Design Techniques for System-Level Dynamic Power Management 231
    L. Benini, A. Bogliolo, and G. De Micheli

Power Estimation of Embedded Systems: A Hardware/Software Codesign Approach 249
    W. Fornaciari, P. Gubian, D. Sciuto, and C. Silvano

A Framework for Estimating and Minimizing Energy Dissipation of
Embedded HW/SW Systems 259
    Y. Li and J. Henkel

Hardware/Software Co-Synthesis with Memory Hierarchies 265
    Y. Li and W. Wolf

System Level Memory Optimization for Hardware-Software Co-design .278
    K. Danckaert, F. Catthoor, and H. De Man

A Path-Based Technique for Estimating Hardware Runtime in HW/SW-Cosynthesis 283
    J. Henkel and R. Ernst

INTRODUCTION

Any decision in the co-design process relies on assumptions concerning the decision consequences, be it the resulting timing, cost, or power consumption. Therefore, good assumptions are required to be able to control the design process.

Assumptions are founded on analysis or estimation. We distinguish analysis techniques that formally derive system properties and estimation techniques that are "educated guesses" possibly based on analysis steps. Analysis is not only used to control design decisions but also for design verification, such as for formal analysis of timing or power consumption. Other than simulation, formal analysis covers all possible behaviors of a system that lead to more reliable verification results.

When maximum timing and power consumption of a system are given as constraints, as they are in many embedded systems, analysis precision is crucial to avoid costly, overly conservative designs that might not be competitive.

The papers in this chapter belong to three topics. The first part consists of papers that present analysis and estimation techniques for single processes running on a single hardware component, such as a processor, with a simple memory architecture. The second set of papers assumes that analysis and estimation techniques for single processes running on single components are available as a basis for analysis and estimation of parallel processes and multiprocessors and contains some classical papers in the field of real-time operating systems. The third set of papers treats a topic that is particularly interesting to memory-intensive high-performance designs: the analysis and estimation of memory architectures.

SINGLE-PROCESSOR SYSTEMS WITH SIMPLE MEMORY ARCHITECTURES

Process execution depends on the process description and on input data, on the one hand, and on the target architecture, on the other. Process description and input data are technology independent and are evaluated in a process-path analysis, whereas target architecture effects are technology dependent and require architecture modeling and analysis.

A *process path* is a sequence of process statements that is executed for given input data. If there are loops, statements can be executed several times on a path. Data-dependent control statements in the process decide which of the possible paths is taken. The determination of the set of possible process paths and, therfore, the frequency of execution of each single statement is in the most general case a known noncomputable problem. Fortunately, practical embedded system processes are bounded in their running time and, hence, path length.

Many approaches have been proposed to determine upper bounds on the set of possible process paths, ranging from loop bounding to explicit path enumeration via regular expressions. Most of them require a fair amount of user interaction, which makes the approaches hard to use. An important step forward was the introduction of the implicit path enumeration technique presented by Li *et al.* [Li99a]. First, the program is divided into basic blocks, that is, short sequences of statements in a program that include only one entry point at the first statement and one exit point at the end [Aho86]. The running time for these basic blocks is determined by architecture analysis, which is described later. Here, path constraints are implicitly given by equations and inequalities that describe the relative frequency of basic block execution. Basic block running times and equations and inequalities form an ILP problem that is solved to obtain the maximum execution time. Part of the statements are derived from the process structure, others can be provided by the user. The solution is always a correct upper bound, which can be tightened by additional constraints. Later, the precision of this approach was increased by extending architecture analysis from basic blocks to general program segments with a single path [Yen98].

A major problem of process-path analysis is the memory architecture. The behavior of an instruction cache does not fall under the ILP approach since dependencies between statements depend on their memory addresses and not on the control flow. Therefore, Li *et al.* [Li99a] provide a cache-conflict graph (CCG), which represents conflicts between cache lines of a direct mapped cache based on the process control flow. From this CCG, additional equations and inequalities can be derived such that the ILP approach is applicable again. The computation times for the running time analysis of larger processes have demonstrated that this approach is practical. In another publication [Li99b], the authors have also proposed an approach to analyze set associative cache behavior, but this turns out to be more computation intensive.

Process-path analysis can easily be extended to cost functions other than timing by simply changing the data provided by the architecture model from timing to, for example, power consumption. Besides techniques for worst case analysis, there are statistical methods that assume branching probabilities to obtain statistical timing. The reader is referred to the paper by Gong *et al.* [Gon94].

Architecture modeling and analysis is the second component of process analysis and estimation. General purpose computer architectures expose a high degree of internal parallelism that is for the most part data dependent. One should be aware that analyzing the behavior of a single process on such an architecture is, in principle, comparable to the analysis of a parallel architecture. Therefore, precise modeling of such architectures is confined to simple examples, if an appropriate processor model is available at all. Fortunately, embedded system processors typically have a much simpler structure in which most of the parallelism is controlled by a program or a finite-state machine.

Because architecture modeling is used together with path analysis, it can be limited to segments with a single path, such as basic blocks. There are two basic techniques to determine the execution cost (*i.e.*, power or running time) of such a process segment. In simple microcoded architectures such as the 8-bit 8051, it is sufficient to use a table in which the execution cost of each instruction is contained and then simply add up the cost of the individual instructions along a path. The authors of [Li99a] have successfully used this technique for running time analysis of an Intel i960 processor.

Power analysis is more complicated even for smaller architectures, because in CMOS technology, most of the power consumption is caused by transistor and wire switching activities that depend on the sequence of operations rather than on a single instruction. This effect has been investigated for several architectures with strikingly different results. The paper [Tiw94], by Tiwari, Malik, and Wolfe, investigated the Intel 486DX2 as an example of a general-purpose architecture. The authors developed a straightforward technique to isolate the effects of individual instructions and short instruction sequences on power consumption. They found that the internal state of the processor has little to no influence on the power consumption of such an architecture due to complex internal control sequences. Similar architectures with complex internal control sequences are used for many embedded control applications, from user interfaces to automotive electronics to washing machines. Pipeline stall and cache misses must be treated separately.

For processor architectures with simpler control sequences and wide data paths, such as digital signal processors, the influence of the instruction sequence is significantly higher and can even dominate the overall power consumption, as shown in a second investigation by Tiwari et al. [Lee97]. Such effects can be captured by simulating the instruction sequence with a cycle-accurate processor model (see Chapter 6, "Co-simulation and Emulation") [Yen98].

For those parts of the target architecture that have not yet been implemented, only estimation is possible. Here, estimation includes assumptions on the design process. The paper by Fornaciari et al. [For98] proposes an approach to power estimation of hardware/software systems consisting of a processor and several custom hardware components described in a behavioral VHDL description. The custom hardware components are divided into the data path, the memory, and the controller. For each of these parts, a different power estimation technique is selected. The data path power estimation assumes that the operator schedule, that is, the sequence of operations, has already been fixed. Given the hardware process, a variable lifetime analysis is executed followed by a register allocation, known from compiler design or high-level synthesis. This mimics part of the design process providing an estimate of the necessary size of the register file and of the number of register file accesses. To account for the input data dependent part of power consumption, an estimated average signal switching activity of the register variables is added that is derived from simulation or provided by the user. Register file sizes, number of register accesses and switching activity are combined to estimate the register file power consumption. The same combination of estimated results of the design process and statistics for data switching activities is used to derive power estimations for the function units and multiplexers in the data path as well as for the memory.

The situation is slightly more complicated for the controller since the switching activities are determined by the input data as well as by the control sequence and state assignment that are defined in the design process. In this case, the authors resort to a Markov model to capture controller state transition probabilities that are then used to estimate the switching activity.

It should be noted that this power estimation approach is based on a predefined architecture template with a data path, a register file, multiplexers for communication, and an FSM controller. Other target architectures might lead to very different results.

Similar to the power estimation approach just described, estimation methods for hardware running time and cost (in VLSI: area) can be developed as well. In a paper by Henkel and Ernst [Hen95], a path-based scheduling algorithm is used to anticipate the potential effects of globally optimizing synthesis tools. It is used in co-synthesis [Hen98]. In this estimation approach, scheduling is included. Path-based scheduling is computation intensive, and there is the risk that estimation becomes time consuming as synthesis. Therefore, simplifications are applied, which are shown to have a minor impact on result precision. As in the previous paper, the estimation techniques mimic part of the design process. The same holds for the paper [Vah95] that is discussed in Chapter 5, "Implementation Generation." In this paper, the hardware cost is estimated. It models the allocation process of hardware synthesis, applying an incremental design approach to save computation time.

The paper by Li and Henkel [Li98] presents an example of how to use power estimation to heuristically control high-level transformations, such as loop unrolling and procedure inlining. This combination of power estimation and transformation control is then used in design space exploration where the size and type of caches is modified, each time automatically applying high-level transformations where suitable.

MULTIPROCESSOR ANALYSIS

So far, we have considered single processes and single components only. The primary step to system analysis is the *estimation or analysis of parallel process execution*. Whereas a single process runs uninterrupted, the execution of parallel processes can be delayed. The first reason for delay is process dependency, either because a process, p_i, waits for the output of another process, p_j, which is a data dependency, or because a process, p_j, blocks a shared resource (shared memory, I/O channel, etc.) that p_i needs to continue execution. The second reason is that processes running on one component (processor or custom hardware component) interrupt each other. While data dependencies are predefined by the system of processes, the other two dependencies are a result of the design process.

We distinguish the *computation time* of a process, which is the execution time of a process when it is run without interruption as discussed before, and the *response time*, which is the time between the request for process execution to the instant when a process has finished execution, including all delays by interrupts and dependencies. A *deadline* is the instant in which a process must have finished.

Process scheduling decides in which order processes are executed. *Preemptive scheduling* interrupts running processes to execute other processes, whereas *nonpreemptive scheduling* algorithms do not support interruptions. The scheduling algorithm can determine a fixed order of process execution (*static scheduling*) or assign priorities to processes. *Process priorities* can be fixed (*static priority*) or assigned at run time (*dynamic priority*). Scheduling can be done off-line or at run time, the latter requiring a run-time scheduler process.

The timing of parallel processes *running on one component* is a classical problem in real-time computing. Many applications require *periodic process execution* (signal processing, control engineering with periodic sampling), or they can be mapped to periodic process execution (signal polling). In 1973, Liu and Layland [Liu73] presented a milestone solution that could guarantee response times of a system of periodically executed independent parallel processes with statically assigned priorities. It requires that the process deadlines are equal to the individual process periods and that processes have a known maximum computation time. They proved that the solution they found, rate-monotonic scheduling (RMS), is optimal for statically assigned process priorities on uniprocessors. Given this optimal solution, rules are derived to determine whether the system of processes is schedulable, given the process computation times. So, RMS also provides an analysis technique. In the same paper, the authors investigate a dynamic priority scheduling algorithm that they call *deadline driven* scheduling algorithm, more commonly known as *earliest deadline first* scheduling. Again, they prove that this dynamic priority assignment is optimal and give rules to guarantee schedulability of periodic independent processes.

There are many papers on timing analysis of parallel processes running on a single or on parallel components. Most approaches in hardware/software co-design use static or static priority scheduling. Whereas static scheduling leads to sequential execution that can be analyzed with graph algorithms, process order in static priority scheduling depends on the execution time of the processes, which, as we have seen, is data dependent. This requires specific analysis approaches described in the paper by Yen and Wolf [Yen98], which represents the current state in the field. A more general overview of the field is found in the paper edited by Krishna and Lee [Kri94].

First, Yen and Wolf [Yen98] extend the problem. In many applications, processes are grouped in sets of data-dependent processes without cycles, called *tasks*. They are represented by acyclic directed task graphs. The processes of a task are executed with the same period. They may have individual *deadlines* that are not necessarily at the end of a period. Based on an earlier result by Leung and Whitehead [Leu82], it is known that all processes will reach all deadlines if they reach their first deadline, given all non–data-dependent processes of a task (*i.e.*, the first processes in the task graph) are ready to be executed at time 0. This is no conservative assumption, since in any system of independent tasks, there can always be a future instant when this situation occurs. Using the data dependencies, the paper proposes an approach to derive earliest and latest starting and finishing times of processes in the first and second periods. The solution is based on a fix-point solution of the original problem of Liu and Layland, developed by Lehoczky, that is again solved for the first period. Iteratively, data dependencies and start and finish times are evaluated to tighten the timing bounds. The approach works on single and parallel components and mimics the parallel process executions covering all possible cases. This gives a good impression of the complicated situations that occur in systems involving parallel processes with different periods and data dependencies.

Rate analysis is another problem that must be solved to ensure the feasibility of a design. Mathur *et al.* [Mat98] developed the RATAN algorithm to check rate constraints. A constraint on the rate at which data is processed may be imposed by the environment (input data rates, for example) or by the designer (system resource limitations). Their algorithm computes bounds on the rate at which a process can execute. Those results are then checked against the rate constraints to determine whether the design is feasible.

Power analysis for multiple processes and components has a large impact on system design. It does not only influence design decisions but, just like run-time process scheduling, is also used to control the system at run time. It is the basis of the new field of dynamic power management. An embedded system with dynamic power control has different activity states with major differences in power consumption and computing performance. The transition time between these states is significantly higher than the context switching time between processes that requires precise estimation of the expected performance requirements. This problem necessitates new control approaches that are extensively discussed in the tutorial paper by Benini *et al.* [Ben00].

MEMORY SYSTEM ANALYSIS

Memories are a major factor of cost, performance, and power consumption in many integrated systems. We included two papers that demonstrate the effect of memory architectures and show how to use estimation of memory utilization in an automated or manual design process. The paper by Danckert, Catthoor, and De Man [Dan97] explains how to manually transform loops and split large data arrays in the description of a single process to reduce buffer memory requirements as well as background memory transfers. They use a video compression algorithm as an example. Memory and transfer costs are estimated by adding up the variable sizes or references to memory variables, respectively. The authors conclude that these transformations must occur before hardware/software partitioning to be fully effective. They developed a tool environment, ADOPT, to support such transformations.

The othre paper, by Li and Wolf [Li99c], assumes an environment of multiple periodic processes running on multiple components with processes grouped in tasks, as explained above. The paper is primarily concerned with cache optimization. It assumes a direct-mapped data cache per component and an additional direct-mapped instruction cache for all processor components. As in the previous paper, all program transformations have been executed, and all program and data addresses of the program are known at design time. The first step is to identify the cache lines that a program might use during execution. Continuous cache lines are grouped in regions to reduce the analysis problem size. If cache regions of two tasks overlap, then compulsory misses will occur when switching from one task to another. These compulsory misses add to the context switching time between processes. The authors present a co-synthesis algorithm that derives a static task schedule and performs heuristic local optimizations on the processor type and cache size.

ADDITIONAL READINGS IN ANALYSIS AND ESTIMATION

[Dic00] R. P. Dick, G. Lakshminarayana, A. Rangunathan, and N. K. Jha, "Power analysis of embedded operating systems," in *Proceedings, 37th Design Automation Conference*, ACM Press, New York, 2000, 312–15. *Analyzes the power consumption of RTOSs and the influence of the RTOS on overall system power requirements.*

[Wuy99] S. Wuytack, F. Catthoor, G. de Jong, and H. J. De Man, "Minimizing the required memory bandwidth in VLSI system realizations," *IEEE Transactions on VLSI Systems* 7, no. 4 (Dec. 1999): 433–41. *Analyzes relationships between memory accesses using a conflict hypergraph to optimize storage bandwidth.*

[Lah99] K. Lahiri, A. Ragunathan, and S. Dey, "Performance analysis of bus-based system-on-chip communication architectures," in *Proceedings, ICCAD 99*, IEEE, 1999, New York, 566–72. *Presents a trace-driven methodology for analyzing the behavior of bus-based systems.*

[Had99] G. Hadjiyiannis, P. Russo, and S. Devadas, "A methodology for accurate performance evaluation in architecture exploration," in *Proceedings, 36th Design Automation Conference*, ACM Press, New York, 1999, 927–932. *Describes a system that can automatically generate a cycle-accurate instruction-level simulator and a hardware model from a description of the target machine.*

[DeV99] G. De Veciana, M. Jacome, and J.-H. Guo, "Assessing probabilistic timing constraints on system performance," *Design Automation for Embedded Systems* 5, no. 1 (Feb. 1999): 61–81. *Presents a method for analyzing systems of components with probabilistic execution times; develops a method for probabilistic relaxation of those constraints.*

[Chu99] E. Chung, G. De Micheli, L. Benini, and A. Boglilo, "Dynamic power management for non-stationary service requests," in *Proceedings, DATE 99*, IEEE Computer Society Press, Los Alamitos, 1999, 77–81. *Uses sliding windows to characterize non stationary service requests.*

[Mae98] J. A. Maestro, D. Mozos, and H. Mecha, "A macroscopic time and cost estimation model allowing task parallelism and hardware sharing for the codesign partitioning process," in *Proceedings, DATE 98*, IEEE Computer Society Press, Los Alamitos, 1998, 218–25. *Presents a high-level model for temporal behavior that can be used to estimate the results of later stages of co-synthesis.*

[Ger98] J. Gerlach and W. Rosenstiel, "A scalable methodology for cost estimation in a transformational high-level design space exploration environment," in *Proceedings, DATE 98*, IEEE Computer Society Press, Los Alamitos, 1998, 226–32. *Uses transformations to reduce the computation time required to estimate the costs of a modification to a candidate design; uses a system-level simulator to investigate the relationships between energy consumption, hardware architecture, and software.*

[Tom98] H. Tomiyama, T. Ishihara, A. Inoue, and H. Yasuura, "Instruction scheduling for power reduction in processor-based system design," in *Proceedings, DATE 98*, IEEE Computer Society Press, Los Alamitos, 1998, 855–60. *Schedules instructions to minimize bus transitions during a cache miss.*

[Gup97] R. K. Gupta and G. De Micheli, "Specification and analysis of timing constraints for embedded systems," *IEEE Transactions on CAD of Itegrated and Systems* 16, no. 3 (Mar.) 1997: 240–56. *Presents techniques for analyzing systems of operation delay and execution rate constraints.*

[Bal97] F. Balarin and A. Sangiovanni-Vincentelli, "Schedule validation for embedded reactive real-time systems," in *Proceedings, 34th Design Automation Conference*, ACM Press, New York, 1997, 52–57. *Presents an efficient algorithm for checking a reactive system schedule against external constraints.*

[Ye97] W. Ye and R. Ernst, "Embedded program timing analysis based on path clustering and architecture classification," *Proceedings, ICCAD 97*, IEEE, New York, 1997, 598–604. *Describes a running time analysis approach which combines cycle-true processor simulation with formal path analysis.*

[Li99b] Y. T. S. Li and S. Malik, "Performance analysis of real-time embedded software," *Kluwer Academic Publishers*, 1999. *A detailed description of the implicit path enumeration approach to program running time analysis including direct mapped and set associative Caches.*

[Gon94] J. Gong, D. D. Gajski, S. Narayan, "Software execution from executable specification," *The Journal of Computer and Software Engineering* 2, no. 3 (1994): 239–58. *A probabilistic approach to software running time analysis.*

[Aho86] A. V. Aho, R. Sethi, and J. D. Ullman, *Compilers: Principles, Techniques, and Tools*, Addison-Wesley, Reading, 1986. *A widely used textbook on compiler construction.*

[Kri94] C. M. Krishna, Y. H. Lee, ed., "Special issue on real-time systems," *Proceedings of the IEEE* 82, no. 1 (Jan. 1994). *A collection of overview papers, on the development and status of real-time systems.*

[Leu82] J. Y.-T. Leung and J. Whitehead, "On the complexity of fixed priority scheduling of periodic, real-time tasks," *Performance Evaluation* 2, no. 4 (1982): 237–250. *A rigorous paper providing various proofs on the complexity of real-time scheduling.*

[Hen98] J. Henkel and R. Ernst, "High-level estimation techniques for usage in hardware/software co-design," *Proceedings, Asia and South Pacific Design Automation Conference*, 1998, 353–60. *A paper on using estimation tools in co-synthesis with a number of experiments.*

[Kri94] C. M. Krishna, Y. H. Lee, ed., "Special issue on real-time time systems," *Proceedings of the IEEE* 82, no. 1 (Jan. 1994). *A collection of overview papers on the development and status of real-time systems.*

Performance Estimation of Embedded Software with Instruction Cache Modeling

YAU-TSUN STEVEN LI, SHARAD MALIK, and ANDREW WOLFE
Princeton University

Embedded systems generally interact in some way with the outside world. This may involve measuring sensors and controlling actuators, communicating with other systems, or interacting with users. These functions impose real-time constraints on system design. Verification of these specifications requires computing an upper bound on the worst-case execution time (WCET) of a hardware/software system. Furthermore, it is critical to derive a tight upper bound on WCET in order to make efficient use of system resources.

The problem of bounding WCET is particularly difficult on modern processors. These processors use cache-based memory systems that vary memory access time based on the dynamic memory access pattern of the program. This must be accurately modeled in order to tightly bound WCET. Several analysis methods have been proposed to bound WCET on processors with instruction caches. Existing approaches either search all possible program paths, an intractable problem, or they use highly pessimistic assumptions to limit the search space. In this paper we present a more effective method for modeling instruction cache activity and computing a tight bound on WCET. The method uses an integer linear programming formulation and does *not* require explicit enumeration of program paths. The method is implemented in the program cinderella and we present some experimental results of this implementation.

Categories and Subject Descriptors: C.4 [**Computer Systems Organization**]: Performance of Systems—*Modeling techniques*

General Terms: Performance

---

1. INTRODUCTION

The execution time of a program can often vary significantly from one run to the next on the same system. Even given a known program and a known system, the actual execution time depends on the input data values and the initial state of the system. In many cases it is essential to know the worst-case execution time (WCET) for a hardware/software system. In hard real-time systems, the programmer must guarantee that the WCET satisfies the timing deadlines. Many real-time operating systems rely on this for process scheduling. In embedded system designs, the WCET of the software is often required for deciding how hardware/software partitioning is done.

The *actual* WCET of a program cannot be determined unless we simulate all possible combinations of input data values and initial system states. This is clearly impractical due to the large number of simulations required. As a result, we can only obtain an estimate on the actual WCET by performing a static analysis of the program. For it to be useful, the *estimated* WCET must be tight and conservative such that it bounds the actual WCET without introducing undue pessimism.

WCET analysis can be divided into two components: *program path analysis*, which determines the sequence of instructions to be executed in the worst-case scenario, and *microarchitecture modeling*, which models the underlying hardware systems and computes the WCET of a known sequence of instructions. Both components are important in determining tight estimated WCETs.

The program path analysis has been discussed extensively in our previous work [Li and Malik 1995]. It deals with computing the estimated WCET of a program efficiently and making use of the user-provided program path annotations to eliminate infeasible program paths. We observed that while the user annotations do tighten the estimated WCET significantly, a large amount of pessimism still exists in the estimated WCET because of the simple microarchitecture modeling.

Microarchitecture modeling is particularly difficult for modern microprocessors. These processors usually include pipelined instruction execution and cache-based memory systems. These features speed up the typical performance of the system, but complicate timing analysis. The exact execution time of an instruction depends on many factors and varies more than in the previous generation of microprocessors. The cache memory system is particularly difficult to model and is becoming the dominant factor in the pessimism. Incorporating accurate cache modeling into the worst-case timing analysis is essential in order to effectively use modern processors in real-time systems. Our goal is to devise an instruction cache modeling method that accurately represents cache activity and provides enough information for the timing analysis tool to tightly bound the WCET.

We propose a method to model instruction cache memory. Unlike other cache analysis methods, it does not require explicit program path enumeration, yet it provides a tighter bound on the worst-case cache miss penalties than other practical estimation methods that we know of. In this paper, we limit our method to model a direct-mapped instruction cache. However, it can be extended to handle set associative instruction cache memory.

This paper is organized as follows: We first discuss some related work in this area in Section 2. Then, in Section 3, we summarize our previous work in program path analysis. In Section 4 and 5, we describe how this work is extended to model direct-mapped instruction cache. Implementation issues

---

Authors' address: Department of Electrical Engineering, Princeton University, Princeton, NJ 08544; email: yauli@ee.princeton.edu; sharad@ee.princeton.edu; awolfe@ee.princeton.edu.
Permission to make digital/hard copy of part or all of this work for personal or classroom use is granted without fee provided that the copies are not made or distributed for profit or commercial advantage, the copyright notice, the title of the publication, and its date appear, and notice is given that copying is by permission of the ACM, Inc. To copy otherwise, to republish, to post on servers, or to redistribute to lists, requires prior specific permission and/or a fee.
© 1999 ACM 1084-4309/99/0700-0257 $5.00

CHAPTER 3: Analysis and Estimation

are discussed in Section 6. This is followed by the experimental results shown in Section 7. Finally, we present the conclusions in Section 8.

2. RELATED WORK

The problem of finding a program's worst-case execution time is in general undecidable and is equivalent to a halting problem. This is true even with a constant-access-time instruction memory. Kligerman and Stoyenko [1986], as well as Puschner and Koza [1989], listed the conditions for this problem to be decidable. These conditions are bounded loops, absence of recursive function calls, and absence of dynamic function calls. These researchers, together with Mok et al. [1989] and Park and Shaw [1992], have proposed a number of methods to determine the estimated WCET. These methods assume a simple hardware model such that the execution time of every instruction in the program is a constant equal to the instruction's worst-case execution time. No cache analysis is performed.

The presence of cache memory complicates the WCET analysis significantly. The reason is that to determine the worst-case execution path, the execution times of individual instructions are needed. Yet without knowing the worst-case execution path, the cache hits and misses of instructions, and hence the execution times of the instructions, cannot be determined. As a result, program path analysis and cache memory analysis are interrelated.

Several WCET analyses with direct-mapped instruction cache modeling methods have recently been proposed. Liu and Lee [1994] noted that a *sufficient* condition for determining the *exact* worst-case cache behavior is to search through all feasible program paths exhaustively. This becomes an intractable problem whenever there is a conditional statement inside a while loop, which unfortunately happens frequently. Lim et al. [1994], who extended Shaw's timing schema methodology [Shaw 1989] to incorporate cache analysis, also encountered a similar problem. To deal with this intractable problem, the above researchers trade-off cache prediction accuracy for computational complexity by proposing different pessimistic heuristics. Even so, the size of the program for analysis is still limited. Arnold et al. [1994] proposed a less aggressive cache analysis method. They used flow analysis to identify the *potential* cache conflicts and classified each instruction as first miss, always hit, always miss, or first hit categories. This results in fast but less accurate cache analysis. Rawat [1993] handled data cache performance analysis by using graph-coloring techniques. However, this approach had limited success even for small programs. A severe drawback of all the methods above is that they do not accept any user annotations describing infeasible program paths, which are essential in tightening the estimated WCET.

Explicit path enumeration is *not* a necessity in obtaining a tight estimated WCET. An important observation here is that the WCET can be computed by methods other than path enumeration. We propose a method that determines the worst-case *execution counts* of the instructions and, from these counts, computes the estimated WCET. The main advantage of this method is that it reduces the solution search space significantly. Further, as we show in Section 4, only minimal necessary sequencing information is kept in performing the cache analysis. No path enumeration is needed. The method supports user annotations that is at least as powerful as Park's Information Description Language (IDL) [Park 1992] and, at the same time, computes the cache memory activity that is far more accurate than Lim's work. To the best of our knowledge, our research is the first to address both issues together.

3. ILP FORMULATION

Our previous work [Li and Malik 1995] focused on path analysis given a simple microarchitecture model, which assumes that every instruction takes a constant time to execute. Instead of searching all program paths, the path analysis analytically determines the dynamic execution count of each instruction under the worst-case scenario. There are similarities between our analysis technique and the one used by Avrunin et al. [1994] in determining time bounds for concurrent systems.

Since we assume that each instruction takes a constant time to execute, the total execution time can be computed by summing up the product of instruction counts by their corresponding single execution times. Furthermore, since the instructions within a basic block are always executed together, their execution counts must be the same. Hence, they can be considered as a single unit. If we let variable x_i be the execution count of a basic block B_i, and constant c_i be the execution time of the basic block, then the total execution time of the program is given as

$$\text{Total execution time} = \sum_{i=1}^{N} c_i x_i \qquad (1)$$

where N is the number of basic blocks in the program. Clearly, x_is must be integer values. The possible values of x_i are constrained by the program structure and the possible values of the program variables. If we can represent these constraints as linear inequalities, then the problem of finding the worst-case execution time of a program is transformed into an integer linear programming (ILP) problem which can be solved by many existing ILP solvers.

The linear constraints are divided into two parts: (1) *program structural constraints*, which are derived automatically from the program's control flow graph (CFG), and (2) *mprogram functionality constraints*, which are provided by the user to specify loop bounds and other path information. The construction of these constraints is best illustrated by an example shown in Figure 1, in which a conditional statement is nested inside a while loop. Figure 1(ii) shows the CFG. Each node in the CFG represents a basic block B_i. A basic block execution count, x_i, is associated with each node. Each

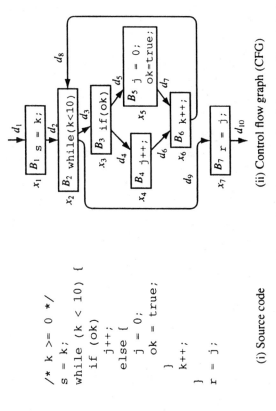

```
/* k >= 0 */
s = k;
while (k < 10) {
    if (ok)
        j++;
    else {
        j = 0;
        ok = true;
    }
    k++;
}
r = j;
```

(i) Source code

(ii) Control flow graph (CFG)

Fig. 1. An example code fragment showing how the structural and functionality constraints are constructed.

edge in the CFG is labeled with a variable d_i which serves both as a label for that edge and as a count of the number of times that the program control passes through that edge. Analysis of the CFG is equivalent to a standard network-flow problem. Structural constraints can be derived from the CFG from the fact that, for each node B_i, its execution count is equal to the number of times that the control enters the node (inflow) and is also equal to the number of times that the control exits the node (outflow). The structural constraints extracted from this example are

$$d_1 = 1 \tag{2}$$

$$x_1 = d_1 = d_2 \tag{3}$$

$$x_2 = d_2 + d_8 = d_3 + d_9 \tag{4}$$

$$x_3 = d_3 = d_4 + d_5 \tag{5}$$

$$x_4 = d_4 = d_6 \tag{6}$$

$$x_5 = d_5 = d_7 \tag{7}$$

$$x_6 = d_6 + d_7 = d_8 \tag{8}$$

$$x_7 = d_9 = d_{10}. \tag{9}$$

Here, the first constraint (2) specifies that the code fragment is to be executed once. The structural constraints do not provide any loop bound information. This information is provided by the user by using functionality constraints. In this example, we note that since variable k is positive before the program control enters the loop, the loop body will be executed between 0 and 10 times each time the loop is entered. The constraints to specify this information are

$$0x_1 \le x_3 \le 10x_1. \tag{10}$$

The functionality constraints can also be used to specify other path information. For example, we observe that the else statement (B_5) can be executed at most once inside the loop. This information can be specified as

$$x_5 \le 1x_1. \tag{11}$$

All of these constraints—(2) through (11)—are passed to the ILP solver with the goal of maximizing the cost function (1). The ILP solver returns a bound on the worst-case execution time and the execution counts of the basic blocks.

4. DIRECT-MAPPED INSTRUCTION CACHE ANALYSIS

To incorporate cache memory analysis into our ILP model, shown in the previous section, we need to modify the cost function (1) and add a list of linear constraints, denoted *cache constraints*, representing cache memory behavior. These are described in the following sections.

4.1 Modified Cost Function

With cache memory, each instruction fetch will result in either a cache hit or a cache miss, which may in turn result in two very different instruction execution times. The simple microarchitecture model that each instruction takes a constant time to execute no longer models this situation accurately. We need to subdivide the original instruction counts into counts of cache hits and misses. If we can determine these counts, and the hit and miss execution times of each instruction, then a tighter bound on the execution time of the program can be established.

As in the previous section, we can group adjacent instructions together. We define a new type of atomic structure for analysis; the *line-block* or simply *l-block*. An *l-block* is defined as a contiguous sequence of code within the same basic block that is mapped to the same cache set in the instruction cache. In other words, the *l-blocks* are formed by the intersection of basic blocks with the cache set line size. All instructions within a *l-block* are always executed together in sequence. Further, since the cache controller always loads a line of code into the cache, these instructions are either

CHAPTER 3: Analysis and Estimation

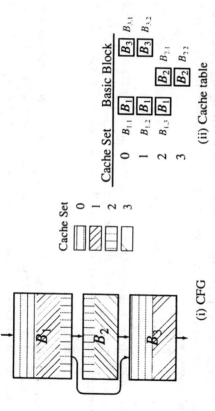

Fig. 2. An example showing how the *l-blocks* are constructed. Each rectangle in the cache table represents a *l-block*.

in the cache completely or not in the cache at all. These are denoted as a cache hit or a cache miss, respectively, of the *l-block*.

Figure 2(i) shows a CFG with 3 basic blocks. Suppose that the instruction cache has 4 cache sets. Since the starting address of each basic block can be determined from the program's executable code, we can find all cache sets that each basic block is mapped to, and add an entry on these cache lines in the cache table (Figure 2(ii)). The boundary of each *l-block* is shown by the solid line rectangle. Suppose a basic block B_i is partitioned into n_i *l-blocks*. We denote these *l-blocks* $B_{i,1}, B_{i,2}, \ldots, B_{i,n_i}$.

For any two *l-blocks* that are mapped to the same cache set, they will *conflict* with each other if they have different address tags. The execution of one *l-block* will displace the cache content of the other. For instance, *l-block* $B_{1,1}$ conflicts with *l-block* $B_{3,1}$ in Figure 2. There are also cases where two *l-blocks* do not conflict with each other. This situation happens when the basic block boundary is not aligned with the cache line boundary. For instance, *l-blocks* $B_{1,3}$ and $B_{2,1}$ in Figure 2, each occupies a partial cache line and they do not conflict with each other. They are called *nonconflicting l-blocks*.

Since *l-block* B_{ij} is inside the basic block B_i, its execution count is equal to x_i. The cache hit and the cache miss counts of *l-block* B_{ij} are denoted x_{ij}^{hit} and x_{ij}^{miss}, respectively, and

$$x_i = x_{ij}^{hit} + x_{ij}^{miss}, \quad j = 1, 2, \ldots, n_i. \quad (12)$$

The new total execution time (cost function) is given by

$$\text{Total execution time} = \sum_{i=1}^{N} \sum_{j=1}^{n_i} (c_{ij}^{hit} x_{ij}^{hit} + c_{ij}^{miss} x_{ij}^{miss}) \quad (13)$$

where c_{ij}^{hit} and c_{ij}^{miss} are, respectively, the hit cost and the miss cost of the *l-block* B_{ij}.

Equation (12) links the new cost function (13) with the program structural constraints and the program functionality constraints, which remain unchanged. In addition, the cache behavior can now be specified in terms of the new variables x_{ij}^{hit}'s and x_{ij}^{miss}'s.

4.2 Cache Constraints

These constraints are used to constrain the hit/miss counts of the *l-blocks*. Consider a simple case. For each cache line, if there is only one *l-block* $B_{k,l}$ mapped to it, then once $B_{k,l}$ is loaded into the cache it will permanently stay there. In other words, only the first execution of this *l-block* may cause a cache miss and all subsequent executions will result in cache hits. Thus,

$$x_{k,l}^{miss} \leq 1. \quad (14)$$

A slightly more complicated case occurs when two or more *nonconflicting l-blocks* are mapped to the same cache line, such as $B_{1,3}$ and $B_{2,1}$ in Figure 2. Since the cache controller always fetches a line of code into the cache, the execution of any of the *l-blocks* will result in the cache controller loading all of them into the cache line. Therefore, the sum of their cache miss counts is at most one. In this example, the constraint is

$$x_{1,3}^{miss} + x_{2,1}^{miss} \leq 1. \quad (15)$$

When a cache line contains two or more *conflicting l-blocks*, the hit/miss counts of these *l-blocks* will be effected by their execution sequence. An important observation is that the execution of any other *l-blocks* mapped to other cache sets will have no effect on these counts. This leads us to examine the control flow of *l-blocks* mapped to a particular cache set by using a *cache conflict graph*.

4.3 Cache Conflict Graph

A cache conflict graph (CCG) is constructed for every cache set containing two or more conflicting *l-blocks*. It contains a start node '*s*', an end node '*e*', and a node '$B_{k,l}$' for every *l-block* $B_{k,l}$ mapped to the cache set. The start node represents the start of the program and the end node represents the end of the program. For every node '$B_{k,l}$', a directed edge is drawn from node $B_{k,l}$ to node $B_{m,n}$ if there exists a path in the CFG from basic block B_k to basic block B_m *without* passing through the basic blocks of any other *l-blocks* of the same cache set. If there is a path from the start of the CFG to basic block B_k without going through the basic blocks of any other

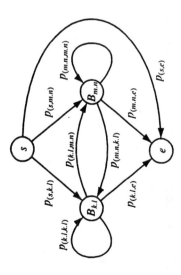

Fig. 3. A general cache conflict graph containing two conflicting *l-blocks*.

l-blocks of the same cache set, then a directed edge is drawn from the start node to node $B_{k,l}$. The edges between nodes and the end node are constructed analogously. Suppose that a cache line contains only two conflicting *l-blocks* $B_{k,l}$ and $B_{m,n}$, a possible CCG is shown in Figure 3. The program control begins at the start node. After executing some other *l-blocks* from other cache lines, it will eventually reach node $B_{k,l}$, node $B_{m,n}$, or the end node. Similarly, after executing $B_{k,l}$, the program control may pass through some *l-blocks* from other cache lines and then reach node $B_{k,l}$ again, or it may reach node $B_{m,n}$ or the end node.

For each edge from node $B_{i,j}$ to node $B_{u,v}$, we assign a variable $p_{(i,j,u,v)}$ to count the number of times that the program control passes through that edge. At each node $B_{i,j}$, the sum of control flow going into the node must be equal to the sum of control flow leaving the node, and it must also be equal to the execution count of *l-block* $B_{i,j}$. Therefore, two constraints are constructed at each node $B_{i,j}$:

$$x_i = \sum_{u,v} p_{(u,v,i,j)} = \sum_{u,v} p_{(i,j,u,v)}, \quad (16)$$

where '$u.v$' may also include the start node 's' and the end node 'e'. This set of constraints is linked to the program structural and functionality constraints via the x-variables.

The program is executed once, so at start node:

$$\sum_{u,v} p_{(s,u,v)} = 1. \quad (17)$$

The variable $p_{(i,j,i,j)}$ represents the number of times that the control flows into *l-block* $B_{i,j}$ after executing *l-block* $B_{i,j}$ without entering any other *l-blocks* of the same cache line in between. For a direct mapped cache, each cache set has one cache line. Therefore, the contents of *l-block* $B_{i,j}$ are still in the cache every time the control follows the edge $(B_{i,j}, B_{i,j})$ to reach node $B_{i,j}$, and it will result in a cache hit. Thus, there will be at least $p_{(i,j,i,j)}$ cache hits for *l-block* $B_{i,j}$. In addition, if both edges $(B_{i,j}, e)$ and $(s, B_{i,j})$ exist, then the contents of $B_{i,j}$ may already be in the cache at the beginning of program execution, as its content may be left by the previous program execution. Thus, variable $p_{(s,i,j)}$ *may* also be counted as a cache hit. Hence,

$$p_{(i,j,i,j)} \leq x_{i,j}^{hit} \leq p_{(s,i,j)} + p_{(i,j,i,j)}. \quad (18)$$

Otherwise, if any of edges $(s, B_{i,j})$ and $(B_{i,j}, e)$ does not exist, then

$$x_{i,j}^{hit} = p_{(i,j,i,j)}. \quad (19)$$

Equations (14) through (19) are the possible cache constraints for bounding the cache hit/miss counts. These constraints, together with (12), the structural constraints, and the functionality constraints, are passed to the ILP solver with the goal of maximizing the cost function (13). Because of the cache information, a tighter estimated WCET is returned. Further, some path-sequencing information can be expressed in terms of p-variables as extra functionality constraints. The CCGs are network flow graphs, and thus the cache constraints are typically solved rapidly by the ILP solver. In the worst case, there is one CCG for each cache set.

The above constraints can also be used to solve the best-case execution time. The objective is to minimize cost function (13), subject to the same structural constraints, functionality constraints, and cache constraints. In this case the ILP solver will try to increase the value of $x_{i,j}^{hit}$ as much as possible. If $p_{(i,j,i,j)}$ (self-edge variable) exists, then the ILP solver may set $p_{(i,j,i,j)} = x_{i,j}^{hit} = x_i$. However, this is not possible in any execution trace. Before this path can occur, the program control must first flow into node $B_{i,j}$ from some other node. To handle this problem, an additional constraint is required for all nodes $B_{i,j}$ with a self-edge:

$$x_i \leq Z \sum_{u,v, u,v \neq i,j} p_{(u,v,i,j)}, \quad (20)$$

where Z is a large positive integer constant. The addition of this kind of constraints may generate some nonintegral optimal variable values when the whole constraint set is passed to an LP solver. If the ILP solver uses branch and bound techniques for solving the ILP problem, the computational time may be lengthened significantly.

4.4 A Simple Example

Section 3 shows how the structural constraints and functionality constraints are constructed for the example shown in Figure 1. For simplicity, assume that each basic block will only be partitioned into one *l-block*. Consider the cases where the `if` statement ($B_{4,1}$) and `else` statement ($B_{5,1}$) conflict with each other and the loop preheader ($B_{1,1}$) conflicts with the loop body statement ($B_{6,1}$).

$$x_6 = p_{(1,1,6.1)} + p_{(6.1,6.1)} = p_{(6.1,e)} + p_{(6.1,6.1)} \quad (32)$$

$$p_{(s,1.1)} = 1 \quad (33)$$

$$x_{1.1}^{hit} \leq p_{(s,1.1)} \quad (34)$$

$$x_{6.1}^{hit} = p_{(6.1,6.1)}. \quad (35)$$

Since all other *l-blocks* are nonconflicting *l-blocks*, their cache constraints are

$$x_2 = x_2^{hit} + x_2^{miss} \quad (36)$$

$$x_3 = x_3^{hit} + x_3^{miss} \quad (37)$$

$$x_7 = x_7^{hit} + x_7^{miss} \quad (38)$$

$$x_2^{miss} \leq 1 \quad (39)$$

$$x_3^{miss} \leq 1 \quad (40)$$

$$x_7^{miss} \leq 1. \quad (41)$$

4.4.1 Bounds on *p-Variables*. In this section, we discuss bounds on the *p*-variables. Without the correct bounds, the ILP solver may return an infeasible *l-block* count and an overly pessimistic estimated WCET. This is demonstrated by the example in Figure 5. In this example, the CFG contains two nested loops. Suppose that there are two conflicting *l-blocks*, $B_{4.1}$ and $B_{7.1}$. A CCG will be constructed (Figure 5(ii)) and the following cache constraints generated:

$$x_4 = p_{(s,4.1)} + p_{(4,1,4.1)} + p_{(7.1,4.1)} = p_{(4.1,e)} + p_{(4,1,4.1)} + p_{(4.1,7.1)} \quad (42)$$

$$x_7 = p_{(s,7.1)} + p_{(7.1,7.1)} + p_{(4.1,7.1)} = p_{(7.1,e)} + p_{(7.1,7.1)} + p_{(7.1,4.1)} \quad (43)$$

$$p_{(s,4.1)} + p_{(s,7.1)} + p_{(s,e)} = 1 \quad (44)$$

$$p_{(4.1,4.1)} \leq x_{4.1}^{hit} \leq p_{(s,4.1)} + p_{(4.1,4.1)} \quad (45)$$

$$p_{(7.1,7.1)} \leq x_{7.1}^{hit} \leq p_{(s,7.1)} + p_{(7.1,7.1)}. \quad (46)$$

Suppose that the user specifies that both loops will be executed 10 times each time they are entered and that basic block B_4 will be executed 9 times each time the outer loop is entered. The functionality constraints for this information are

$$x_3 = 10x_1, \quad x_7 = 10x_5, \quad x_4 = 9x_1. \quad (47\text{-}49)$$

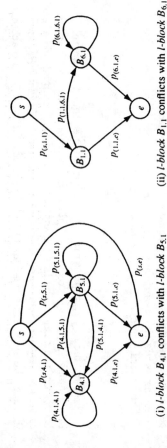

(i) *l-block* $B_{4.1}$ conflicts with *l-block* $B_{5.1}$

(ii) *l-block* $B_{1.1}$ conflicts with *l-block* $B_{6.1}$

Fig. 4. The two CCGs of the example shown in Figure 1.

Figure 4 shows the CCGs for these two cases. For *l-blocks*, $B_{4.1}$ and $B_{5.1}$ (Figure 4(i)), the constraints for the worst-case execution estimation are

$$x_4 = x_{4.1}^{hit} + x_{4.1}^{miss} \quad (21)$$

$$x_5 = x_{5.1}^{hit} + x_{5.1}^{miss} \quad (22)$$

$$x_4 = p_{(s,4.1)} + p_{(4.1,4.1)} + p_{(5.1,4.1)} = p_{(4.1,e)} + p_{(4.1,4.1)} + p_{(4.1,5.1)} \quad (23)$$

$$x_5 = p_{(s,5.1)} + p_{(5.1,5.1)} + p_{(4.1,5.1)} = p_{(5.1,e)} + p_{(5.1,5.1)} + p_{(5.1,4.1)} \quad (24)$$

$$p_{(s,4.1)} + p_{(s,5.1)} + p_{(s,e)} = 1 \quad (25)$$

$$p_{(4.1,4.1)} \leq x_{4.1}^{hit} \leq p_{(s,4.1)} + p_{(4.1,4.1)} \quad (26)$$

$$p_{(5.1,5.1)} \leq x_{5.1}^{hit} \leq p_{(s,5.1)} + p_{(5.1,5.1)}. \quad (27)$$

Some further path information can be provided here by the user. We note that if the if statement is executed, it implies that variable ok is true, and therefore the else statement will never be executed again. So there will never be a control flow from basic block B_4 to basic block B_5. This information can be expressed as

$$p_{(4.1,5.1)} = 0. \quad (28)$$

The cache constraints for the second case are

$$x_1 = x_{1.1}^{hit} + x_{1.1}^{miss} \quad (29)$$

$$x_6 = x_{6.1}^{hit} + x_{6.1}^{miss} \quad (30)$$

$$x_1 = p_{(s,1.1)} = p_{(1.1,6.1)} + p_{(1.1,e)} \quad (31)$$

of loop iterations. This is the upper bound on $p_{(i,j,u,v)}$. Since l-blocks B_{ij} and $B_{u,v}$ are inside the loop, x_i and x_u can at most be equal to the total number of loop iterations. Therefore, (16) is bound $p_{(i,j,u,v)}$ correctly.

Suppose that there are two nested loops such that l-block B_{ij} is in the outer loop while $B_{u,v}$ is in the inner loop. If edge $(B_{iJ}, B_{u,v})$ exists, all paths represented by this edge go from basic block B_i to basic block B_u in the CFG. They must pass through the loop preheader,[1] say basic block B_h, of the inner loop. Since the execution count of basic block B_h, x_h, may be smaller than x_i and x_u, a constraint

$$p_{(i,j,u,v)} \leq x_h \qquad (51)$$

is needed to properly bound $p_{(i,j,u,v)}$.

In general, a constraint is constructed at each loop preheader. All paths going from outside the loop to inside the loop must pass through the loop preheader. Therefore, the sum of these flows can at most be equal to the execution count of the loop preheader. In our example, a constraint at loop preheader B_5 is needed:

$$p_{(s,7.1)} + p_{(4.1,7.1)} \leq x_5. \qquad (52)$$

With this constraint, the ILP solver will generate a correct solution.

5. INTERPROCEDURAL CALLS

So far, our cache analysis discussion has been limited to a single function. In this section we show how cache analysis is performed when there are function calls in the program.

A function may be called many times from different locations of the program. The variable x_i represents the *total* execution count of the basic block B_i when the whole program is executed once. Similarly, x_{ij}^{hit} and x_{ij}^{miss} represents the total hit and miss counts, respectively, of the l-block B_{iJ}. Equation (12) is still valid and (13) still represents the total execution time of the program.

In performing cache analysis, we need to consider the cache conflicts among l-blocks from different functions and the bounds of the p-variables. For these reasons, every function call is treated as if it were inlined. During the construction of CFG, when a function call occurs, an f-edge that contains an instance of the callee function's CFG is used. The edge has a variable f_k that represents the number of times that a particular instance of the callee function is executed. Each variable and name in the callee

---

[1] A loop preheader is the basic block just before entering the loop. For instance, in the example shown in Figure 5, basic block B_1 is the loop preheader of the outer loop and basic block B_5 is the loop preheader of the inner loop.

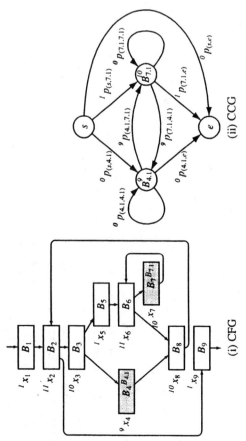

Fig. 5. Example showing two conflicting l-blocks ($B_{4.1}$ and $B_{7.1}$) from two different loops. Italicized numbers on the left of the variables are the pessimistic worst-case solution returned from ILP solver.

If we feed the above constraints and the structural constraints into the ILP solver, it will return a worst-case solution in which the counts are shown on the upper left corner of the variables in the figure.

From the CCG, we observe that these p-values imply that l-blocks $B_{4.1}$ and $B_{7.1}$ will be executed alternately, with l-block $B_{7.1}$ executed first. This execution sequence generates the maximum number of cache misses, and hence the WCET. However, if we look at the CFG, we know that this sequence is impossible because the inner loop is entered only once. Once the program control enters the inner loop, l-block $B_{7.1}$ must be executed 10 times before the program control exits the inner loop. Hence, there must be at least 9 cache hits for l-block $B_{7.1}$. The ILP solver overestimates the number of cache misses based on the given constraints. Upon closer investigation, we find that the correct solution also satisfies the above set of constraints. This implies that some constraints for tightening the solution space are missing.

The reason for producing such pessimistic worst-case solution is that the p-variables are not properly bounded. The flow equations (16) generated from the CCG implicitly bound the p-variables as follows: For any variable $p_{(i,j,u,v)}$, its bounds are

$$0 \leq p_{(i,j,u,v)} \leq \min(x_i, x_u). \qquad (50)$$

Consider the case where two conflicting l-blocks B_{ij} and $B_{u,v}$ are in the same loop and at the same loop nesting level. In this case, the maximum control flow allowed between these two l-blocks is equal to the total number

another instance of the same l-block $B_{i,j}$, as it represents cache hits of the l-block $B_{i,j}$, as it represents the execution of l-block $B_{i,j}$ at f_l after the same l-block has just been executed at f_k. The cache constraints derived from the example's CCG are

$$x_1 = x_{1.1}^{hit} + x_{1.1}^{miss} \quad (61)$$

$$x_2 = x_{2.1}^{hit} + x_{2.1}^{miss} \quad (62)$$

$$x_3 = x_{3.1}^{hit} + x_{3.1}^{miss} \quad (63)$$

$$x_{2.1}^{miss} \leq 1 \quad (64)$$

$$x_1 = p_{(s,1.1)} = p_{(1.1,3.1,f_1)} \quad (65)$$

$$x_3.f_1 = p_{(1.1,3.1,f_1)} = p_{(3.1,f_1,\,3.1,f_2)} \quad (66)$$

$$x_3.f_2 = p_{(3.1,f_1,\,3.1,f_2)} = p_{(3.1,f_2,\,e)} \quad (67)$$

$$x_{1.1}^{hit} = 0 \quad (68)$$

$$x_{3.1}^{hit} = p_{(3.1,f_1,\,3.1,f_2)} \quad (69)$$

$$p_{(s,1.1)} = 1. \quad (70)$$

6. IMPLEMENTATION AND HARDWARE MODELING

The above cache analysis method has been integrated into our original tool cinderella, which estimates the WCET of programs running on an Intel i960KB development board [Intel Corporation 1990] containing a 20MHz Intel i960KB processor, 128KB of main memory, and several I/O peripherals. The i960KB processor is a 32-bit RISC processor used in many embedded systems (e.g., in laser printers). The processor contains an on-chip 512-byte direct-mapped instruction cache organized as 32×16-byte lines. It also features a floating point unit, a 4-stage instruction pipeline, and 4 register windows for faster execution of function call/return instructions [Intel Corporation 1991; Myers and Budde 1988].

The hit cost c_{ij}^{hit} of a l-block B_{ij} is determined by adding up the effective execution times of the instructions in the l-block. Since the effective execution times of some instructions, especially the floating point instructions, are data-dependent, a conservative approach is taken by assuming the worst-case effective execution time. This may induce some pessimism in the final estimated WCET. Additional time is also added to the last l-block of each basic block to ensure that all buffered load/store instructions [Intel Corporation 1991] are completed when the program control reaches the end of the basic block. Note that the instruction boundary may not be aligned with the cache line boundary, i.e., an

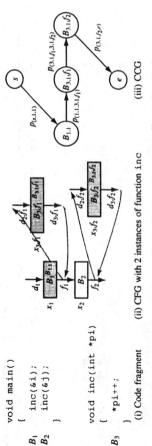

Fig. 6. An example code fragment showing how function calls are handled.

function has a suffix '.f_k' to distinguish it from other instances of the same callee function.

Consider the example in Figure 6. Here, function inc is called twice in the main function. The CFG is shown in Figure 6(ii), where two instances of function inc's CFG are created. The structural constraints are

$$d_1 = 1 \quad (53)$$

$$x_1 = d_1 = f_1 \quad (54)$$

$$x_2 = f_1 = f_2 \quad (55)$$

$$d_2.f_1 = f_1 \quad (56)$$

$$x_3.f_1 = d_2.f_1 = d_3.f_1 \quad (57)$$

$$d_2.f_2 = f_2 \quad (58)$$

$$x_3.f_2 = d_2.f_2 = d_3.f_2 \quad (59)$$

$$x_3 = x_3.f_1 + x_3.f_2. \quad (60)$$

The last equation above links the total execution counts of basic block B_3 with its counts from two instances of the function. Based on these variables, the user can provide path information among different functions. The CCG is constructed as before, by treating each instance of the l-block $B_{i,j}.f_k$ as independent from other instances of the same l-block. In the example shown in Figure 6, if l-block $B_{1.1}$ conflicts with l-block $B_{3.1}$, then, since l-block $B_{3.1}$ has 2 instances ($B_{3.1}.f_1$ and $B_{3.1}.f_2$), there will be 5 nodes in the CCG (Figure 6(iii)).

The cache constraints and the bounds on p variables are modified slightly. In addition to the self edges, the edge going from one instance of a l-block (say $B_{i,j}.f_k$) to

Table I. Benchmark Examples: Descriptions, Source File Line and i960KB Binary Code Sizes

Program	Description	Lines	Bytes
check data	Check if any of the elements in an array is negative, from Park [1992]	23	88
circle	Circle drawing routine, from Gupta [1993]	100	1,588
des	Data Encryption Standard	192	1,852
dhry	Dhrystone benchmark	761	1,360
djpeg	Decompression of 128 × 96 color JPEG image	857	5,408
fdct	JPEG forward discrete cosine transform	300	996
fft	1024-point Fast Fourier Transform	57	500
line	Line drawing routine, from Gupta [1993]	165	1,556
matcnt	Summation of 2 100 × 100 matrices, from Arnold [Arnold, Mueller, Whalley, and Harmon 1994]	85	460
matcnt2	Matcnt with inlined functions	73	400
piksrt	Insertion sort of 10 elements	19	104
sort	Bubble sort of 500 elements, from Arnold [Arnold, Mueller, Whalley, and Harmon 1994]	41	152
sort2	Sort with inlined functions	30	148
stats	Calculate the sum, mean and variance of two 1,000-element arrays, from Arnold [Arnold, Mueller, Whalley, and Harmon 1994]	100	656
stats2	Stats with inlined functions	90	596
whetstone	Whetstone benchmark	196	2,760

instruction may span two cache sets, and consequently may span two *l-blocks*. When this happens, the effective execution time of this instruction is counted in the hit cost of the second *l-block*. Since these two *l-blocks* must come from the same basic block, they have the same total execution count. Therefore, the total execution time spent on this instruction is correctly accounted for. The miss cost c_{ij}^{miss} of the *l-block* is equal to the hit cost c_{ij}^{hit}, plus the time needed to load the line of code into the cache memory.

Cinderella[2] now contains about 20,000 lines of C++ code. The tool reads the subject program's executable code and constructs the CFGs and the CCGs. It then outputs the annotation files in which the xs and fs are labeled along with the program's source code. The user is then asked to provide loop bounds. A WCET bound can be computed at this point. The user can provide additional path information, if available, to tighten this bound. We use a public domain ILP solver lp_solve[3] to solve the constraints generated by cinderella. The solver uses the branch and bound procedure to solve the ILP problem.

An optimization implemented in cinderella actually reduces the number of variables and CCGs. If two or more adjacent cache lines hold instructions from the same set of basic blocks, e.g., cache lines 0 and 1 in Figure 2(ii), then the corresponding *l-blocks* can be combined together and only one CCG is drawn for those cache lines.

7. EXPERIMENTAL RESULTS

In this section, we evaluate the accuracy and performance of our cache analysis method. Since there are no standard benchmark programs, we selected a set of benchmark programs from a variety of sources. They included programs from academic sources, DSP routines, standard software benchmarks, and a JPEG decompression program, which is the largest and most complicated one used in this kind of analysis. Table I shows for each program, its name, description, source code line size, and i960KB binary code size in bytes.

7.1 Measurement Methods

Ideally, we would like to compare each program's estimated WCET with its actual WCET. But since it is impractical to simulate every possible input data set and every initial system state, a program's actual WCET may not be determined. In fact, if we can determine a program's actual WCET, then we do not need its estimated WCET anymore!

To resolve this problem, we tried to identify each program's *worst-case input data set* and compared its execution time, denoted *measured WCET*, with the estimated WCET. We assumed that the worst-case initial system state was the one with empty cache contents, since this generates the maximum number of cache misses. For most programs, the worst-case input data set could be determined. For instance, the worst-case input data set for the sorting programs is an array of descending elements. For these programs, the measured WCET should be very close to the actual WCET. But for more complicated programs, this became a nontrivial task. These programs have instructions whose execution times are data-dependent, such as the floating point instructions presented in programs fft and fdct; and/or complicated input data-dependent execution paths, such as programs des and djpeg. For these four programs, the worst-case data input sets are unknown. We generated a series of random input data sets, measured their corresponding execution times, and picked the longest one as the measured WCET of the program. In this case, the difference between the measured WCET and the actual WCET may be larger. To determine the *measured WCET* accurately, we executed each program on the Intel QT960 evaluation board and used a logic analyzer to measure its execution time. The difference between a program's estimated WCET and its measured WCET was equal to the difference between the estimated WCET and the actual WCET, due to pessimism in path analysis, cache modeling, and execution unit modeling, plus the difference between the actual WCET and the measured WCET.

---

[2] Details of this tool can be obtained via http://www.ee.princeton.edu/nyauli/cinderella-3.0/.
[3] lp_solve is written by Michel Berkelaar and can be retrieved from ftp://ftp.es.ele.tue.nl/pub/lp_solve.

input image was so random that no compression was achieved in the Huffman encoding process. Therefore, the Huffman decoding function in djpeg needs to loop more in reading and decoding the Huffman symbols. But for all random images we generated for determining the measured WCET, some sort of compression was still achieved. The larger differences between the loop bounds in the estimation and the actual loop iterations in measurements accounted for this pessimism. In this program, the measured WCET might not be as close to its actual WCET as other programs are. This illustrates that the actual WCET is in some cases very hard to be attained through simulation, whereas static analysis always guarantees bounding the actual WCET.

A few simple programs were also used by Arnold et al. [1994] and Lim et al. [1994]. It is natural to compare our estimated WCETs to theirs. However, the above researchers used different hardware platforms for modeling. Arnold et al. used a Sparc simulator and Lim et al. used a MIPS R3000 evaluation board. Since the binary codes were different and the model of each processor was different, there is no direct way to compare the results. One main drawback of the above researchers' methods is that they cannot accept path information other than loop bounds. Therefore, for programs like sort and fft, which have nested loops in which the loop iteration of the inner loop depends on the loop index of the outer loop, they reported estimated WCETs that are roughly two times the measured WCETs. Our analysis method is superior in that it accepts path information even in the presence of instruction cache analysis. This results in much tighter estimation, and our method can analyze more complicated programs.

Since a large amount of pessimism shown in Table II is due to the pessimism in modeling the execution unit, we would like to factor it out. For programs whose code size is greater than 512-bytes, we executed each program with its worst-case input data set to generate the instruction address trace. This was passed to a cache simulator DineroIII to determine the number of cache misses. We then used cinderella to estimate the program's worst-case cache misses by using a hardware model in which a cache miss incurs one unit of time and a cache hit and other execution times incur zero execution times. Table III shows the results. For many programs, the simulator and cinderella reported the same number of cache misses. The pessimism in other programs is mainly due to inaccuracy in path analysis. In particular, program djpeg has exceptionally large pessimism because the Huffman decoding function contains conflicted code. Since the execution count of this function is conservatively overestimated, a large number of cache misses resulted.

7.3 Performance Issues

The structural and cache constraints are derived from the CFG and CCGs that are very similar to network flow graphs. We therefore expect that the ILP solver can solve the problem efficiently. Table IV shows, for each

Table II. Estimated WCETs of Benchmark Programs. Estimated WCETs and Measured WCETs In Units of Clock Cycles

Program	Measured WCET	Estimated WCET	Ratio
check data	4.30×10^2	4.91×10^2	1.14
circle	1.45×10^4	1.54×10^4	1.06
des	2.44×10^5	3.70×10^5	1.52
dhry	5.76×10^5	7.57×10^5	1.31
djpeg	3.56×10^7	7.04×10^7	1.98
fdct	9.05×10^3	9.11×10^3	1.01
fft	2.20×10^6	2.63×10^6	1.20
line	4.84×10^3	6.09×10^3	1.26
matcnt	2.20×10^6	5.46×10^6	2.48
matcnt2	1.86×10^6	2.11×10^6	1.13
piksrt	1.71×10^3	1.74×10^3	1.02
sort	9.99×10^6	27.8×10^6	2.78
sort2	6.75×10^6	7.09×10^6	1.05
stats	1.16×10^6	2.21×10^6	1.91
stats2	1.06×10^6	1.24×10^6	1.17
whetstone	6.94×10^6	10.5×10^6	1.51

7.2 Results

Table II shows the results of our experiments. The second and third columns show, respectively, the measured WCET and estimated WCET with cache analysis. The fourth column shows the ratio of the estimated WCET to the measured WCET. All ratios are larger than one, meaning that all estimated WCETs bound their corresponding measured WCETs. Smaller ratios mean tighter estimates.

For small programs like check data and piksrt, the estimated WCETs are very close to their corresponding measured WCETs. Programs sort, matcnt, and stats have larger than expected pessimism. This is because we did not model the register windows featured in the i960KB processor. We conservatively assumed that the register window overflowed (underflowed) on each function call (return). This pessimism incurred about 50 clock cycles on each function call and function return. Since the above programs had lots of small function calls, a large amount of pessimism resulted. In order to factor out this pessimism, we inlined the frequently called functions in these programs. The modified programs are sort2, matcnt2, and stats2. Their estimated WCETs are much tighter than the original ones. We are currently working on this problem to reduce the pessimism.

The pessimism for programs with floating point instructions, such as fft and whetstone, is also higher. The reason is that the execution time of an i960KB floating point instruction is data-dependent. For our worst-case estimation, we conservatively assumed that each floating point instruction took its worst-case execution time to complete, which is typically 30%–40% more than its average execution time [Intel Corporation 1991].

Finally, the reason for large pessimism in program djpeg is due to the loose measured WCET. For the worst-case estimation, we assumed that the

Table III. Estimated Worst-Case Number of Cache Misses of Benchmark Programs. The instruction cache is 512-byte direct-mapped, its line size is 16 bytes

Program	DineroIII simulation	Est. worst case cache misses	Ratio
circle	443	458	1.03
des	3,872	4,188	1.08
dhry	8,304	8,304	1.00
djpeg	230,861	316,394	1.37
fdct	63	63	1.00
line	99	101	1.02
stats	47	47	1.00
stats2	44	44	1.00
whetstone	18,678	18,678	1.00

Table IV. Performance Issues in Cache Analysis

Program	No. of Variables				No. of Constraints			ILP branches	ILP Time (sec.)
	d's	f's	p's	x's	Struct.	Cache	Funct.		
check_data	12	0	0	40	25	21	5+5	1+1	0+0
circle	8	1	81	100	24	186	1	1	0
des	174	11	728	560	342	1,059	16+16	13+13	171+197
dhry	102	21	503	504	289	777	24×4+26×4	1×8	0×3+2+0 +1×2+4
djpeg	296	20	1,816	416	613	2,568	64	1	87
fdct	8	0	18	34	16	49	2	1	0
fft	27	0	0	80	46	46	11	1	3
line	31	2	264	231	73	450	2	1	0
matcnt	20	4	0	106	59	61	4	1	0
matcnt2	20	2	0	92	49	54	4	1	0
piksrt	12	0	0	42	22	26	4	1	0
sort	15	1	0	58	35	31	6	1	0
sort2	15	0	0	50	30	27	6	1	0
stats	28	13	75	180	99	203	4	1	0
stats2	28	7	41	144	75	158	4	1	0
whetstone	52	3	301	388	108	739	14	1	2

program, the number of variables and constraints, the number of branches in solving the ILP problem, and the CPU time required to solve the problem. Since each program may have more than one set of functionality constraints [Li and Malik 1995], a + symbol is used to separate the number of functionality constraints in each set. For a program having n sets of functionality constraints, the ILP is called n times. The + symbol is used again to separate the number of ILP branches and the CPU time for each ILP call.

We found that even with thousands of variables and constraints, the branch and bound ILP solver could still find an integer solution within the first few calls to the linear programming solver. The time taken to solve the problem ranged from less than a second to a few minutes on a SGI Indigo2 workstation. With a commercial ILP solver, CPLEX, the CPU time reduced significantly to a few seconds.

In order to evaluate how the cache size affects solving time, we doubled the number of cache lines (and hence the cache size) from 32 lines to 64 lines and determined the CPU time needed to solve the ILP problems. Table V shows the results. From the table, we determined that the number of variables and constraints changed little when the number of cache lines is doubled. The time to solve the ILP problem is of the same order as before. The primary reason is that although increasing the number of cache lines increases the number of CCGs, each CCG has fewer nodes and edges. As a result, there are fewer cache constraints in each CCG. These two factors roughly cancel each other out.

Table V. Complexity of the ILP Problem: Number of Cache Lines Doubled to 64

Program	No. of variables				No. of constraints			ILP branches	ILP Time (sec.)
	d's	f's	p's	x's	Struct.	Cache	Funct.		
des	174	11	809	524	342	1,013	16+16	7+10	90+145
whetstone	52	3	232	306	108	559	14	1	1

8. CONCLUSIONS AND FUTURE WORK

In this paper we presented a method to determine a tight bound on the worst-case execution time of a given program. The method includes a direct-mapped instruction cache analysis and uses an integer linear programming formulation to solve the problem. This approach avoids enumeration of program paths. Furthermore, it allows the user to provide additional program path information so that a tighter bound may be obtained. The method is implemented in cinderella, and the experimental results show that the estimated WCETs tightly bound the corresponding measured WCETs. Since the linear constraints are mostly derived from the network flow graphs, the ILP problems are typically solved efficiently.

We extended this method to analyze a set-associative instruction cache. cinderella has been ported to model the Motorola M68000 architecture. We are now working on data cache modeling, as well as refining our microarchitecture modeling to model register windows and other advanced microarchitecture features.

ACKNOWLEDGMENTS

This research work was supported by a grant from ONR (grant N00014-95-0274). We gratefully acknowledge numerous useful suggestions from Wayne Wolf, Margaret Martonosi, and Janak Patel. We also thank Rajesh Gupta and David Whalley for providing some of the benchmark programs.

REFERENCES

ARNOLD, R., MUELLER, F., WHALLEY, D., AND HARMON, M. 1994. Bounding worst-case instruction cache performance. In *Proceedings of the 15th IEEE Symposium on Real-Time Systems* (Dec.). IEEE Computer Society Press, Los Alamitos, CA, 172–181.

AVRUNIN, G. S., CORBETT, J. C., DILLON, L. K., AND WILEDEN, J. C. 1994. Automated derivation of time bounds in uniprocessor concurrent systems. *IEEE Trans. Softw. Eng. 20*, 9 (Sept. 1994), 708–719.

GUPTA, R. K. 1994. Co-synthesis of hardware and software for digital embedded systems. Ph.D. Dissertation. Stanford University, Stanford, CA.

INTEL CORPORATION, 1990. QT960 User Manual. Intel Corp., Santa Clara, CA.

INTEL CORPORATION, 1991. i960KA/KB Microprocessor Programmers's Reference Manual. Intel Corp., Santa Clara, CA.

KLIGERMAN, E AND STOYENKO, A D 1986. Real-time Euclid: a language for reliable real-time systems. *IEEE Trans. Softw. Eng. SE-12*, 9 (Sept. 1986), 941–949.

LI, Y.-T. S. AND MALIK, S. 1995. Performance analysis of embedded software using implicit path enumeration. In *Proceedings of the 32nd ACM/IEEE Conference on Design Automation* (DAC '95, San Francisco, CA, June 12–16, 1995), B. T. Preas, Ed. ACM Press, New York, NY, 456–461.

LIM, S., BAE, Y. H., JANG, G. T., RHEE, B., MIN, S. L., PARK, C. Y., SHIN, H., PARK, K., AND KIM, C. S. 1994. An accurate worst case timing analysis technique for RISC processors. In *Proceedings of the 15th IEEE Symposium on Real-Time Systems* (Dec.). IEEE Computer Society Press, Los Alamitos, CA, 97–108.

LIU, J. AND LEE, H. 1994. Deterministic upperbounds of the worst-case execution times of cached programs. In *Proceedings of the 15th IEEE Symposium on Real-Time Systems* (Dec.). IEEE Computer Society Press, Los Alamitos, CA, 182–191.

MOK, A. K., AMERASINGHE, P., CHEN, M., AND TANTSIRIVAT, K. 1989. Evaluating tight execution time bounds of programs by annotations. In *Proceedings of the Sixth IEEE Workshop on Real-Time Operating Systems and Software* (May). IEEE Computer Society Press, Los Alamitos, CA, 74–80.

MYERS, G. J. AND BUDDE, D. L. 1988. *The 80960 Microprocessor Architecture*. John Wiley & Sons, Inc., New York, NY.

PARK, C. Y. 1992. Predicting deterministic execution times of real-time programs. Ph.D. Dissertation. University of Washington, Seattle, WA.

PUSCHNER, P. AND KOZA, CH. 1989. Calculating the maximum, execution time of real-time programs. *Real-Time Syst. 1*, 2 (Sep. 1989), 159–176.

RAWAT, J. 1993. Static analysis of cache performance for real-time programming. Master's Thesis. Iowa State Univ., Ames, IA.

SHAW, A. C. 1989. Reasoning about time in higher-level language software. *IEEE Trans. Softw. Eng. 15*, 7 (July 1989), 875–889.

Received: October 1995; revised: September 1996; accepted: December 1997

Scheduling Algorithms for Multiprogramming in a Hard-Real-Time Environment

C. L. LIU

Project MAC, Massachusetts Institute of Technology

AND

JAMES W. LAYLAND

Jet Propulsion Laboratory, California Institute of Technology

ABSTRACT. The problem of multiprogram scheduling on a single processor is studied from the viewpoint of the characteristics peculiar to the program functions that need guaranteed service. It is shown that an optimum fixed priority scheduler possesses an upper bound to processor utilization which may be as low as 70 percent for large task sets. It is also shown that full processor utilization can be achieved by dynamically assigning priorities on the basis of their current deadlines. A combination of these two scheduling techniques is also discussed.

KEY WORDS AND PHRASES: real-time multiprogramming, scheduling, multiprogram scheduling, dynamic scheduling, priority assignment, processor utilization, deadline driven scheduling

CR CATEGORIES: 3.80, 3.82, 3.83, 4.32

1. Introduction

The use of computers for control and monitoring of industrial processes has expanded greatly in recent years, and will probably expand even more dramatically in the near future. Often, the computer used in such an application is shared between a certain number of time-critical control and monitor functions and a non-time-critical batch processing job stream. In other installations, however, no non-time-critical jobs exist, and efficient use of the computer can only be achieved by a careful scheduling of the time-critical control and monitor functions themselves. This latter group might be termed "pure process control" and provides the background for the combinatoric scheduling analyses presented in this paper. Two

Copyright © 1973, Association for Computing Machinery, Inc. General permission to republish, but not for profit, all or part of this material is granted, provided that reference is made to this publication, to its date of issue, and to the fact that reprinting privileges were granted by permission of the Association for Computing Machinery.

This paper presents the results of one phase of research carried out at the Jet Propulsion Laboratory, California Institute of Technology, under Contract No. NAS-7-100, sponsored by the National Aeronautics and Space Administration.

Authors' present addresses: C. L. Liu, Department of Computer Science, University of Illinois at Urbana-Champaign, Urbana, IL 61801; James W. Layland, Jet Propulsion Laboratory, California Institute of Technology, 4800 Oak Grove Drive, Pasadena, CA 91103.

scheduling algorithms for this type of programming are studied; both are priority driven and preemptive; meaning that the processing of any task is interrupted by a request for any higher priority task. The first algorithm studied uses a fixed priority assignment and can achieve processor utilization on the order of 70 percent or more. The second scheduling algorithm can achieve full processor utilization by means of a dynamic assignment of priorities. A combination of these two algorithms is also discussed.

2. Background

A process control computer performs one or more control and monitoring functions. The pointing of an antenna to track a spacecraft in its orbit is one example of such functions. Each function to be performed has associated with it a set of one or more *tasks*. Some of these tasks are executed in response to events in the equipment controlled or monitored by the computer. The remainder are executed in response to events in other tasks. None of the tasks may be executed before the event which requests it occurs. Each of the tasks must be completed before some fixed time has elapsed following the request for it. Service within this span of time must be guaranteed, categorizing the environment as "hard-real-time" [1] in contrast to "soft-real-time" where a statistical distribution of response times is acceptable.

Much of the available literature on multiprogramming deals with the statistical analysis of commercial time-sharing systems ([2] contains an extensive bibliography). Another subset deals with the more interesting aspects of scheduling a batch-processing facility or a mixed batch-time-sharing facility, usually in a multiple processor configuration [3–8]. A few papers directly attack the problems of "hard-real-time" programming. Manacher [1] derives an algorithm for the generation of task schedules in a hard-real-time environment, but his results are restricted to the somewhat unrealistic situation of only one request time for all tasks, even though multiple deadlines are considered. Lampson [9] discusses the software scheduling problem in general terms and presents a set of ALGOL multiprogramming procedures which could be software-implemented or designed into a special purpose scheduler. For the allocation of resources and for the assignment of priorities and time slots, he proposes a program which computes estimated response time distributions based on the timing information supplied for programs needing guaranteed service. He does not, however, describe the algorithms which such a program must use.

The text by Martin [10] depicts the range of systems which are considered to be "real-time" and discusses in an orderly fashion the problems which are encountered in programming them. Martin's description of the tight engineering management control that must be maintained over real-time software development is emphatically echoed in a paper by Jirauch [11] on automatic checkout system software. These discussions serve to emphasize the need for a more systematic approach to software design than is currently in use.

3. The Environment

To obtain any analytical results about program behavior in a hard-real-time environment, certain assumptions must be made about that environment. Not all of these assumptions are absolutely necessary, and the effects of relaxing them will be discussed in a later section.

(A1) The requests for all tasks for which hard deadlines exist are periodic, with constant interval between requests.

(A2) Deadlines consist of run-ability constraints only—i.e. each task must be completed before the next request for it occurs.

(A3) The tasks are independent in that requests for a certain task do not depend on the initiation or the completion of requests for other tasks.

(A4) Run-time for each task is constant for that task and does not vary with time. Run-time here refers to the time which is taken by a processor to execute the task without interruption.

(A5) Any nonperiodic tasks in the system are special; they are initialization or failure-recovery routines; they displace periodic tasks while they themselves are being run, and do not themselves have hard, critical deadlines.

Assumption (A1) contrasts with the opinion of Martin [2], but appears to be valid for pure process control. Assumption (A2) eliminates queuing problems for the individual tasks. For assumption (A2) to hold, a small but possibly significant amount of buffering hardware must exist for each peripheral function. Any control loops closed within the computer must be designed to allow at least an extra unit sample delay. Note that assumption (A3) does not exclude the situation in which the occurrence of a task τ_j can only follow a certain (fixed) number, say N, of occurrences of a task τ_i. Such a situation can be modeled by choosing the periods of tasks τ_i and τ_j so that the period of τ_j is N times the period of τ_i and the Nth request for τ_i will coincide with the 1st request for τ_j, and so on. The run-time in assumption (A4) can be interpreted as the maximum processing time for a task. In this way the bookkeeping time necessary to request a successor and the costs of preemptions can be taken into account. Because of the existence of large main memories out of which programs are executed and the overlapping of transfers between main and auxiliary storage and program execution in modern computer systems, assumption (A4) should be a good approximation even if it is not exact. These assumptions allow the complete characterization of a task by two numbers: its request period and its run-time. Unless stated otherwise, throughout this paper we shall use $\tau_1, \tau_2, \cdots, \tau_m$ to denote m periodic tasks, with their request periods being $T_1, T_2, \cdots, T_m$ and their run-times being $C_1, C_2, \cdots, C_m$, respectively. The *request rate* of a task is defined to be the reciprocal of its request period.

A scheduling algorithm is a set of rules that determine the task to be executed at a particular moment. The scheduling algorithms to be studied in this paper are preemptive and *priority driven* ones. This means that whenever there is a request for a task that is of higher priority than the one currently being executed, the running task is immediately interrupted and the newly requested task is started. Thus the specification of such algorithms amounts to the specification of the method of assigning priorities to tasks. A scheduling algorithm is said to be *static* if priorities are assigned to tasks once and for all. A static scheduling algorithm is also called a *fixed* priority scheduling algorithm. A scheduling algorithm is said to be *dynamic* if priorities of tasks might change from request to request. A scheduling algorithm is said to be a *mixed scheduling algorithm* if the priorities of some of the tasks are fixed yet the priorities of the remaining tasks vary from request to request.

4. A Fixed Priority Scheduling Algorithm

In this section we derive a rule for priority assignment that yields an optimum static scheduling algorithm. An important concept in determining this rule is that of the *critical instant* for a task. The *deadline* of a request for a task is defined to be the time of the next request for the same task. For a set of tasks scheduled according to some scheduling algorithm, we say that an *overflow* occurs at time t if t is the deadline of an unfulfilled request. For a given set of tasks, a scheduling algorithm is *feasible* if the tasks are scheduled so that no overflow ever occurs. We define the *response time* of a request for a certain task to be the time span between the request and the end of the response to that request. A *critical instant* for a task is defined to be an instant at which a request for that task will have the largest response time. A *critical time zone* for a task is the time interval between a critical instant and the end of the response to the corresponding request of the task. We have the following theorem.

THEOREM 1. *A critical instant for any task occurs whenever the task is requested simultaneously with requests for all higher priority tasks.*

PROOF. Let $\tau_1, \tau_2, \cdots, \tau_m$ denote a set of priority-ordered tasks with τ_m being the task with the lowest priority. Consider a particular request for τ_m that occurs at t_1. Suppose that between t_1 and $t_1 + T_m$, the time at which the subsequent request of τ_m occurs, requests for task τ_i, $i < m$, occur at t_2, $t_2 + T_i$, $t_2 + 2T_i$, $\cdots$, $t_2 + kT_i$ as illustrated in Figure 1. Clearly, the preemption of τ_m by τ_i will cause a certain amount of delay in the completion of the request for τ_m that occurred at t_1, unless the request for τ_m is completed before t_2. Moreover, from Figure 1 we see immediately that advancing the request time t_2 will not speed up the completion of τ_m. The completion time of τ_m is either unchanged or delayed by such advancement. Consequently, the delay in the completion of τ_m is largest when t_2 coincides with t_1.

Repeating the argument for all τ_i, $i = 2, \cdots, m - 1$, we prove the theorem.

One of the values of this result is that a simple direct calculation can determine whether or not a given priority assignment will yield a feasible scheduling algorithm. Specifically, if the requests for all tasks at their critical instants are fulfilled before their respective deadlines, then the scheduling algorithm is feasible. As an example, consider a set of two tasks τ_1 and τ_2 with $T_1 = 2$, $T_2 = 5$, and $C_1 = 1$, $C_2 = 1$. If we let τ_1 be the higher priority task, then from Figure 2(a) we see that such a priority assignment is feasible. Moreover, the value of C_2 can be increased at most to 2 but not further as illustrated in Figure 2(b). On the other hand, if we let τ_2 be the higher priority task, then neither of the values of C_1 and C_2 can be increased beyond 1 as illustrated in Figure 2(c).

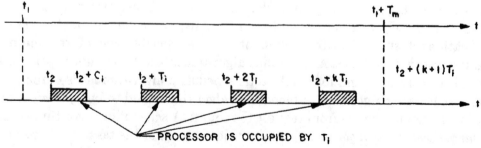

FIG. 1. Execution of τ_i between requests for τ_m

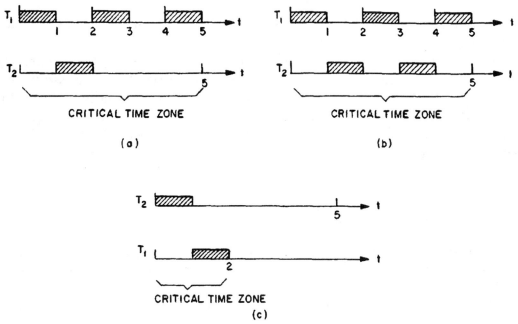

Fig. 2. Schedules for two tasks

The result in Theorem 1 also suggests a priority assignment that is optimum in the sense that will be stated in Theorem 2. Let us motivate the general result by considering the case of scheduling two tasks τ_1 and τ_2. Let T_1 and T_2 be the request periods of the tasks, with $T_1 < T_2$. If we let τ_1 be the higher priority task, then, according to Theorem 1, the following inequality must be satisfied:[1,2]

$$\lfloor T_2/T_1 \rfloor C_1 + C_2 \leq T_2. \qquad (1)$$

If we let τ_2 be the higher priority task, then, the following inequality must be satisfied:

$$C_1 + C_2 \leq T_1. \qquad (2)$$

Since

$$\lfloor T_2/T_1 \rfloor C_1 + \lfloor T_2/T_1 \rfloor C_2 \leq \lfloor T_2/T_1 \rfloor T_1 \leq T_2,$$

(2) implies (1). In other words, whenever the $T_1 < T_2$ and C_1, C_2 are such that the task schedule is feasible with τ_2 at higher priority than τ_1, it is also feasible with τ_1 at higher priority than τ_2, but the opposite is not true. Thus we should assign higher priority to τ_1 and lower priority to τ_2. Hence, more generally, it seems that a "reasonable" rule of priority assignment is to assign priorities to tasks according to their request rates, independent of their run-times. Specifically, tasks with higher request rates will have higher priorities. Such an assignment of priorities will be known as the *rate-monotonic priority assignment*. As it turns out, such a priority assignment is optimum in the sense that no other fixed priority assignment rule can schedule a task set which cannot be scheduled by the rate-monotonic priority assignment.

[1] It should be pointed out that (1) is necessary but not sufficient to guarantee the feasibility of the priority assignment.
[2] $\lfloor x \rfloor$ denotes the largest integer smaller than or equal to x. $\lceil x \rceil$ denotes the smallest integer larger than or equal to x.

THEOREM 2. *If a feasible priority assignment exists for some task set, the rate-monotonic priority assignment is feasible for that task set.*

PROOF. Let $\tau_1, \tau_2, \cdots, \tau_m$ be a set of m tasks with a certain feasible priority assignment. Let τ_i and τ_j be two tasks of adjacent priorities in such an assignment with τ_i being the higher priority one. Suppose that $T_i > T_j$. Let us interchange the priorities of τ_i and τ_j. It is not difficult to see that the resultant priority assignment is still feasible. Since the rate-monotonic priority assignment can be obtained from any priority ordering by a sequence of pairwise priority reorderings as above, we prove the theorem.

5. Achievable Processor Utilization

At this point, the tools are available to determine a least upper bound to processor utilization in fixed priority systems. We define the *(processor) utilization factor* to be the fraction of processor time spent in the execution of the task set. In other words, the utilization factor is equal to one minus the fraction of idle processor time. Since C_i/T_i is the fraction of processor time spent in executing task τ_i, for m tasks, the utilization factor is:

$$U = \sum_{i=1}^{m} (C_i/T_i).$$

Although the processor utilization factor can be improved by increasing the values of the C_i's or by decreasing the values of the T_i's it is upper bounded by the requirement that all tasks satisfy their deadlines at their critical instants. It is clearly uninteresting to ask how small the processor utilization factor can be. However, it is meaningful to ask how large the processor utilization factor can be. Let us be precise about what we mean. Corresponding to a priority assignment, a set of tasks is said to *fully utilize* the processor if the priority assignment is feasible for the set and if an increase in the run-time of any of the tasks in the set will make the priority assignment infeasible. For a given fixed priority scheduling algorithm, the *least upper bound* of the utilization factor is the minimum of the utilization factors over all sets of tasks that fully utilize the processor. For all task sets whose processor utilization factor is below this bound, there exists a fixed priority assignment which is feasible. On the other hand, utilization above this bound can only be achieved if the T_i of the tasks are suitably related.

Since the rate-monotonic priority assignment is optimum, the utilization factor achieved by the rate-monontonic priority assignment for a given task set is greater than or equal to the utilization factor for any other priority assignment for that task set. Thus, the least upper bound to be determined is the infimum of the utilization factors corresponding to the rate-monotonic priority assignment over all possible request periods and run-times for the tasks. The bound is first determined for two tasks, then extended for an arbitrary number of tasks.

THEOREM 3. *For a set of two tasks with fixed priority assignment, the least upper bound to the processor utilization factor is $U = 2(2^{\frac{1}{2}} - 1)$.*

PROOF. Let τ_1 and τ_2 be two tasks with their periods being T_1 and T_2 and their run-times being C_1 and C_2, respectively. Assume that $T_2 > T_1$. According to the rate-monotonic priority assignment, τ_1 has higher priority than τ_2. In a critical time zone of τ_2, there are $\lceil T_2/T_1 \rceil$ requests for τ_1. Let us now adjust C_2 to fully utilize the available processor time within the critical time zone. Two cases occur:

Case 1.   The run-time C_1 is short enough that all requests for τ_1 within the critical time zone of T_2 are completed before the second τ_2 request. That is,

$$C_1 \leq T_2 - T_1 \lfloor T_2/T_1 \rfloor.$$

Thus, the largest possible value of C_2 is

$$C_2 = T_2 - C_1 \lceil T_2/T_1 \rceil.$$

The corresponding processor utilization factor is

$$U = 1 + C_1[(1/T_1) - (1/T_2) \lceil T_2/T_1 \rceil].$$

In this case, the processor utilization factor U is monotonically decreasing in C_1.

Case 2.   The execution of the $\lceil T_2/T_1 \rceil$th request for t_1 overlaps the second request for τ_2. In this case

$$C_1 \geq T_2 - T_1 \lfloor T_2/T_1 \rfloor.$$

It follows that the largest possible value of C_2 is

$$C_2 = -C_1 \lfloor T_2/T_1 \rfloor + T_1 \lfloor T_2/T_1 \rfloor$$

and the corresponding utilization factor is

$$U = (T_1/T_2) \lfloor T_2/T_1 \rfloor + C_1[(1/T_1) - (1/T_2) \lfloor T_2/T_1 \rfloor].$$

In this case, U is monotonically increasing in C_1.

The minimum of U clearly occurs at the boundary between these two cases. That is, for

$$C_1 = T_2 - T_1 \lfloor T_2/T_1 \rfloor$$

we have

$$U = 1 - (T_1/T_2)[\lceil T_2/T_1 \rceil - (T_2/T_1)][(T_2/T_1) - \lfloor T_2/T_1 \rfloor]. \quad (3)$$

For notational convenience,[3] let $I = \lfloor T_2/T_1 \rfloor$ and $f = \{T_2/T_1\}$. Equation (3) can be written as

$$U = 1 - f(1-f)/(I+f).$$

Since U is monotonic increasing with I, minimum U occurs at the smallest possible value of I, namely, $I = 1$. Minimizing U over f, we determine that at $f = 2^{\frac{1}{2}} - 1$, U attains its minimum value which is

$$U = 2(2^{\frac{1}{2}} - 1) \simeq 0.83.$$

This is the relation we desired to prove.

It should be noted that the utilization factor becomes 1 if $f = 0$, i.e. if the request period for the lower priority task is a multiple of the other task's request period.

We now derive the corresponding bound for an arbitrary number of tasks. At this moment, let us restrict our discussion to the case in which the ratio between any two request periods is less than 2.

[3] $\{T_1/T_2\}$ denotes $(T_2/T_1) - \lfloor T_2/T_1 \rfloor$, i.e. the fractional part of T_2/T_1.

Theorem 4. *For a set of m tasks with fixed priority order, and the restriction that the ratio between any two request periods is less than 2, the least upper bound to the processor utilization factor is $U = m(2^{1/m} - 1)$.*

Proof. Let $\tau_1, \tau_2, \cdots, \tau_m$ denote the m tasks. Let $C_1, C_2, \cdots, C_m$ be the run-times of the tasks that fully utilize the processor and minimize the processor utilization factor. Assume that $T_m > T_{m-1} > \cdots > T_2 > T_1$. Let U denote the processor utilization factor. We wish to show that

$$C_1 = T_2 - T_1.$$

Suppose that

$$C_1 = T_2 - T_1 + \Delta, \quad \Delta > 0.$$

Let

$$\begin{aligned} C_1' &= T_2 - T_1 \\ C_2' &= C_2 + \Delta \\ C_3' &= C_3 \\ &\vdots \\ C_{m-1}' &= C_{m-1} \\ C_m' &= C_m. \end{aligned}$$

Clearly, $C_1', C_2', \cdots, C_{m-1}', C_m'$ also fully utilize the processor. Let U' denote the corresponding utilization factor. We have

$$U - U' = (\Delta/T_1) - (\Delta/T_2) > 0.$$

Alternatively, suppose that

$$C_1 = T_2 - T_1 - \Delta, \quad \Delta > 0.$$

Let

$$\begin{aligned} C_1'' &= T_2 - T_1 \\ C_2'' &= C_2 - 2\Delta \\ C_3'' &= C_3 \\ &\vdots \\ C_{m-1}'' &= C_{m-1} \\ C_m'' &= C_m. \end{aligned}$$

Again, $C_1'', C_2'', \cdots, C_{m-1}'', C_m''$ fully utilize the processor. Let U'' denote the corresponding utilization factor. We have

$$U - U'' = -(\Delta/T_1) + (2\Delta/T_2) > 0.$$

Therefore, if indeed U is the minimum utilization factor, then

$$C_1 = T_2 - T_1.$$

In a similar way, we can show that

$$\begin{aligned} C_2 &= T_3 - T_2 \\ C_3 &= T_4 - T_3 \\ &\vdots \\ C_{m-1} &= T_m - T_{m-1}. \end{aligned}$$

Consequently,
$$C_m = T_m - 2(C_1 + C_2 + \cdots + C_{m-1}).$$

To simplify the notation, let
$$g_i = (T_m - T_i)/T_i, \quad i = 1, 2, \cdots, m.$$

Thus
$$C_i = T_{i+1} - T_i = g_i T_i - g_{i+1} T_{i+1}, \quad i = 1, 2, \cdots, m-1$$

and
$$C_m = T_m - 2g_1 T_1$$

and finally,
$$\begin{aligned}
U = \sum_{i=1}^{m} (C_i/T_i) &= \sum_{i=1}^{m-1} [g_i - g_{i+1}(T_{i+1}/T_i)] + 1 - 2g_1(T_1/T_m) \\
&= \sum_{i=1}^{m-1} [g_i - g_{i+1}(g_i + 1)/(g_{i+1} + 1)] + 1 - 2[g_1/(g_1 + 1)] \\
&= 1 + g_1[(g_1 - 1)/(g_1 + 1)] + \sum_{i=2}^{m-1} g_i[(g_i - g_{i-1})/(g_i + 1)].
\end{aligned} \quad (4)$$

Just as in the two-task case, the utilization bound becomes 1 if $g_i = 0$, for all i.

To find the least upper bound to the utilization factor, eq. (4) must be minimized over the g_j's. This can be done by setting the first derivative of U with respect to each of the g_j's equal to zero, and solving the resultant difference equations:

$$\partial U/\partial g_j = (g_j^2 + 2g_j - g_{j-1})/(g_j + 1)^2 - (g_{j+1})/(g_{j+1} + 1) = 0,$$
$$j = 1, 2, \cdots, m-1. \quad (5)$$

The definition $g_0 = 1$ has been adopted for convenience.

The general solution to eqs. (5) can be shown to be
$$g_j = 2^{(m-j)/m} - 1, \quad j = 0, 1, \cdots, m-1. \quad (6)$$

It follows that
$$U = m(2^{1/m} - 1),$$

which is the relation we desired to prove.

For $m = 2$, eq. (6) is the same bound as was found directly for the set of two tasks with no restrictions on the request periods. For $m = 3$, eq. (6) becomes
$$U = 3(2^{1/3}) - 1) \simeq 0.78$$

and for large m, $U \simeq \ln 2$.

The restriction that the largest ratio between request period less than 2 in Theorem 4 can actually be removed, which we state as:

THEOREM 5. *For a set of m tasks with fixed priority order, the least upper bound to processor utilization is $U = m(2^{1/m} - 1)$.*

PROOF. Let $\tau_1, \tau_2, \cdots, \tau_i, \cdots, \tau_m$ be a set of m tasks that fully utilize the processor. Let U denote the corresponding utilization factor. Suppose that for some i, $\lfloor T_m/T_i \rfloor > 1$. To be specific, let $T_m = qT_i + r$, $q > 1$ and $r \geq 0$. Let us replace the task τ_i by a task τ_i' such that $T_i' = qT_i$ and $C_i' = C_i$, and increase C_m by the amount needed to again fully utilize the processor. This increase is at most $C_i(q-1)$, the time within the critical time zone of τ_m occupied by τ_i but not by τ_i'. Let U' denote the utilization factor of such a set of tasks. We have

$$U' < U + [(q-1)C_i/T_m] + (C_i/T_i') - (C_i/T_i)$$

or

$$U' \leq U + C_i(q-1)[1/(qT_i + r) - (1/qT_i)].$$

Since $q - 1 > 0$ and $[1/(qT_i + r)] - (1/qT_i) \leq 0$, $U' \leq U$. Therefore we conclude that in determining the least upper bound of the processor utilization factor, we need only consider task sets in which the ratio between any two request periods is less than 2. The theorem thus follows directly from Theorem 4.

6. *Relaxing the Utilization Bound*

The preceding section showed that the least upper bound imposed upon processor utilization by the requirement for real-time guaranteed service can approach $\ln(2)$ for large task sets. It is desirable to find ways to improve this situation, since the practical costs of switching between tasks must still be counted. One of the simplest ways of making the utilization bound equal to 1 is to make $\{T_m/T_i\} = 0$ for $i = 1, 2, \cdots, m - 1$. Since this cannot always be done, an alternative solution is to buffer task τ_m and perhaps several of the lower priority tasks and relax their hard deadlines. Supposing that the entire task set has a finite period and that the buffered tasks are executed in some reasonable fashion—e.g. in a first come first served fashion—then the maximum delay times and amount of buffering required can be computed under the assumptions of this paper.

A better solution is to assign task priorities in some dynamic fashion. The remaining sections of this paper are devoted to one particular method of dynamic priority assignment. This method is optimum in the sense that if a set of tasks can be scheduled by some priority assignment, it can also be scheduled by this method. In other words, the least upper bound on the processor utilization factor is uniformly 100 percent.

7. *The Deadline Driven Scheduling Algorithm*

We turn now to study a dynamic scheduling algorithm which we call the *deadline driven scheduling algorithm*. Using this algorithm, priorities are assigned to tasks according to the deadlines of their current requests. A task will be assigned the highest priority if the deadline of its current request is the nearest, and will be assigned the lowest priority if the deadline of its current request is the furthest. At any instant, the task with the highest priority and yet unfulfilled request will be executed. Such a method of assigning priorities to the tasks is a dynamic one, in contrast to a static assignment in which priorities of tasks do not change with time. We want now to establish a necessary and sufficient condition for the feasibility of the deadline driven scheduling algorithm.

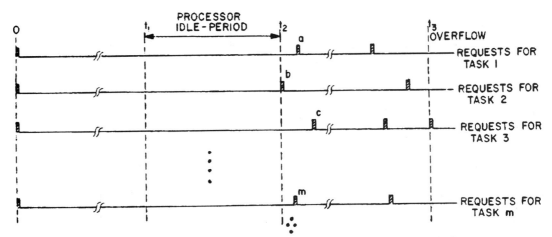

FIG. 3. Processing overflow following a processor idle period

THEOREM 6. *When the deadline driven scheduling algorithm is used to schedule a set of tasks on a processor, there is no processor idle time prior to an overflow.*

PROOF. Suppose that there is processor idle time prior to an overflow. To be specific, starting at time 0, let t_3 denote the time at which an overflow occurs, and let t_1, t_2 denote the beginning and the end, respectively, of the processor idle period closest to t_3 (i.e. there is no processor idle time between t_2 and t_3.) The situation is illustrated in Figure 3, where the times of the first request for each of the m tasks after the processor idle period $[t_1, t_2]$ are denoted $a, b, \cdots, m$.

Suppose that from t_2 on we move all requests of task 1 up so that a will coincide with t_2. Since there was no processor idle time between t_2 and t_3, there will be no processor idle time after a is moved up. Moreover, an overflow will occur either at or before t_3. Repeating the same argument for all other tasks, we conclude that if all tasks are initiated at t_2, there will be an overflow with no processor idle period prior to it. However, this is a contradiction to the assumption that starting at time 0 there is a processor idle period to an overflow. This proves Theorem 6.

Theorem 6 will now be used to establish the following theorem:

THEOREM 7. *For a given set of m tasks, the deadline driven scheduling algorithm is feasible if and only if*

$$(C_1/T_1) + (C_2/T_2) + \cdots + (C_m/T_m) \leq 1.$$

PROOF. To show the necessity, the total demand of computation time by all tasks between $t = 0$ and $t = T_1 T_2 \cdots T_m$, may be calculated to be

$$(T_2 T_3 \cdots T_m) C_1 + (T_1 T_3 \cdots T_m) C_2 + \cdots + (T_1 T_2 \cdots T_{m-1}) C_m.$$

If the total demand exceeds the available processor time, i.e.

$$(T_2 T_3 \cdots T_m) C_1 + (T_1 T_3 \cdots T_m) C_2 + \cdots + (T_1 T_2 \cdots T_{m-1}) C_m > T_1 T_2 \cdots T_m \tag{7}$$

or

$$(C_1/T_1) + (C_2/T_2) + \cdots + (C_m/T_m) > 1,$$

there is clearly no feasible scheduling algorithm.

To show the sufficiency, assume that the condition

$$(C_1/T_1) + (C_2/T_2) + \cdots + (C_m/T_m) \leq 1$$

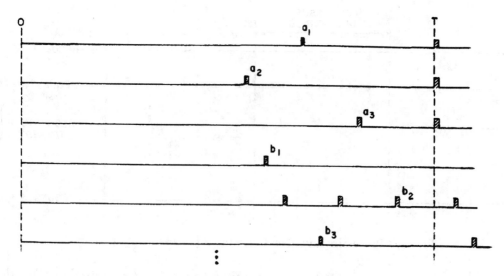

FIG. 4. Processing overflow at time T

is satisfied and yet the scheduling algorithm is not feasible. That is, there is an overflow between $t = 0$ and $t = T_1 T_2 \cdots T_m$. Moreover, according to Theorem 6 there is a $t = T$ ($0 \leq T \leq T_1 T_2 \cdots T_m$) at which there is an overflow with no processor idle time between $t = 0$ and $t = T$. To be specific, let $a_1, a_2, \cdots,$ $b_1, b_2, \cdots,$ denote the request times of the m tasks immediately prior to T, where $a_1, a_2, \cdots$ are the request times of tasks with deadlines at T, and $b_1, b_2, \cdots$ are the request times of tasks with deadlines beyond T. This is illustrated in Figure 4.

Two cases must be examined.

Case 1. None of the computations requested at $b_1, b_2, \cdots$ was carried out before T. In this case, the total demand of computation time between 0 and T is

$$\lfloor T/T_1 \rfloor C_1 + \lfloor T/T_2 \rfloor C_2 + \cdots + \lfloor T/T_m \rfloor C_m .$$

Since there is no processor idle period,

$$\lfloor T/T_1 \rfloor C_1 + \lfloor T/T_2 \rfloor C_2 + \cdots \lfloor T/T_m \rfloor C_m > T.$$

Also, since $x \geq \lfloor x \rfloor$ for all x,

$$(T/T_1)C_1 + (T/T_2)C_2 + \cdots + (T/T_m)C_m > T$$

and

$$(C_1/T_1) + (C_2/T_2) + \cdots + (C_m/T_m) > 1,$$

which is a contradiction to (7).

Case 2. Some of the computations requested at $b_1, b_2, \cdots$ were carried out before T. Since an overflow occurs at T, there must exist a point T' such that none of the requests at $b_1, b_2, \cdots$ was carried out within the interval $T' \leq t \leq T$. In other words, within $T' \leq t \leq T$, only those requests with deadlines at or before T will be executed, as illustrated in Figure 5. Moreover, the fact that one or more of the tasks having requests at the b_i's is executed until $t = T'$ means that all those requests initiated before T' with deadlines at or before T have been fulfilled before T'. Therefore, the total demand of processor time within $T' \leq t \leq T$ is less than or equal to

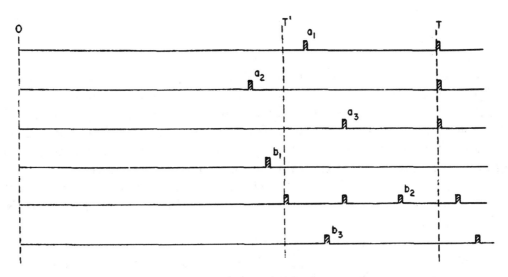

REQUESTS WITH DEADLINES AT a_1 AND a_3 WERE FULFILLED BEFORE T'

FIG. 5. Processing overflow at time T without execution of $\{b_i\}$ following T'

$$\lfloor (T - T')/T_1 \rfloor C_1 + \lfloor (T - T')/T_2 \rfloor C_2 + \cdots + \lfloor (T - T')/T_m \rfloor C_m.$$

That an overflow occurs at T means that

$$\lfloor (T - T')/T_1 \rfloor C_1 + \lfloor (T - T')T_2 \rfloor C_2 + \cdots + \lfloor (T - T')/T_m \rfloor C_m > T - T',$$

which implies again

$$(C_1/T_1) + (C_2/T_2) + \cdots + (C_m/T_m) > 1,$$

and which is a contradiction to (7). This proves the theorem.

As was pointed out above, the deadline driven scheduling algorithm is optimum in the sense that if a set of tasks can be scheduled by any algorithm, it can be scheduled by the deadline driven scheduling algorithm.

8. A Mixed Scheduling Algorithm

In this section we investigate a class of scheduling algorithms which are combinations of the rate-monotonic scheduling algorithm and the deadline driven scheduling algorithm. We call an algorithm in this class a mixed scheduling algorithm. The study of the mixed scheduling algorithms is motivated by the observation that the interrupt hardware of present day computers acts as a fixed priority scheduler and does not appear to be compatible with a hardware dynamic scheduler. On the other hand, the cost of implementing a software scheduler for the slower paced tasks is not significantly increased if these tasks are deadline driven instead of having a fixed priority assignment. To be specific, let tasks $1, 2, \cdots, k$, the k tasks of shortest periods, be scheduled according to the fixed priority rate-monotonic scheduling algorithm, and let the remaining tasks, tasks $k + 1$, $k + 2, \cdots, m$, be scheduled according to the deadline driven scheduling algorithm when the processor is not occupied by tasks $1, 2, \cdots, k$.

Let $a(t)$ be a nondecreasing function of t. We say that $a(t)$ is sublinear if for all

t and all T

$$a(T) \leq a(t+T) - a(t).$$

The availability function of a processor for a set of tasks is defined as the accumulated processor time from 0 to t available to this set of tasks. Suppose that k tasks have been scheduled on a processor by a fixed priority scheduling algorithm. Let $a_k(t)$ denote the availability function of the processor for tasks $k+1, k+2, \cdots, m$. Clearly, $a_k(t)$ is a nondecreasing function of t. Moreover, $a_k(t)$ can be shown to be sublinear by means of the critical time zone argument. We have:

THEOREM 8. *If a set of tasks are scheduled by the deadline driven scheduling algorithm on a processor whose availability function is sublinear, then there is no processor idle period to an overflow.*

PROOF. Similar to that of Theorem 6.

THEOREM 9. *A necessary and sufficient condition for the feasibility of the deadline driven scheduling algorithm with respect to a processor with availability function $a_k(t)$ is*

$$\lfloor t/T_{k+1} \rfloor C_{k+1} + \lfloor t/T_{k+2} \rfloor C_{k+2} + \cdots + \lfloor t/T_m \rfloor C_m \leq a_k(t)$$

for all t's which are multiples of T_{k+1}, or $T_{k+2}, \cdots$, or T_m.

PROOF. The proof is quite similar to that of Theorem 7. To show the necessity, observe that at any moment the total demand of processor time cannot exceed the total available processor time. Thus we must have

$$\lfloor t/T_{k+1} \rfloor C_{k+1} + \lfloor t/T_{k+2} \rfloor C_{k+2} + \cdots + \lfloor t/T_m \rfloor C_m \leq a_k(t)$$

for any t.

To show the sufficiency, assume that the condition stated in the theorem is satisfied and yet there is an overflow at T. Examine the two cases considered in the proof of Theorem 7. For Case 1,

$$\lfloor T/T_{m+1} \rfloor C_{k+1} + \lfloor T/T_{k+2} \rfloor C_{k+2} + \cdots + \lfloor T/T_m \rfloor C_m > a_k(T),$$

which is a contradiction to the assumption. Note that T is multiple of T_{k+1}, or $T_{k+2}, \cdots$, or T_m. For Case 2,

$$\lfloor (T-T')/T_{k+1} \rfloor C_{k+1} + \lfloor (T-T')/T_{k+2} \rfloor C_{k+2} + \cdots + \lfloor (T-T')/T_m \rfloor C_m > a_k(T-T').$$

Let ϵ be the smallest nonnegative number such that $T - T' - \epsilon$ is a multiple of T_{k+1}, or $T_{k+2}, \cdots$, or T_m. Clearly,

$$\lfloor (T - T' - \epsilon)/T_{k+j} \rfloor = \lfloor (T - T')/T_{k+j} \rfloor \quad \text{for each } j = 1, 2, \cdots, m - k$$

and thus

$$\lfloor (T - T' - \epsilon)/T_{k+1} \rfloor C_{k+1} + \lfloor (T - T' - \epsilon)/T_{k+2} \rfloor C_{k+2} + \cdots + \lfloor (T - T' - \epsilon)/T_m \rfloor C_m > a_k(T - T') \geq a_k(T - T' - \epsilon),$$

which is a contradiction to the assumption. This proves the theorem.

Although the result in Theorem 9 is a useful general result, its application involves the solution of a large set of inequalities. In any specific case, it may be advantageous to derive sufficient conditions on schedule feasibility rather than work directly from Theorem 9. As an example, consider the special case in which three tasks are scheduled by the mixed scheduling algorithm such that the task with the shortest period is assigned a fixed and highest priority, and the other two tasks are scheduled by the deadline driven scheduling algorithm. It may be readily verified that if

$$1 - (C_1/T_1) - \min\left[(T_1 - C_1)/T_2, (C_1/T_1)\right] \geq (C_2/T_2) + (C_3/T_3),$$

then the mixed scheduling algorithm is feasible. It may be also verified that if

$$C_2 \leq a_1(T_2), \quad \lfloor T_3/T_2 \rfloor C_2 + C_3 \leq a_1(\lfloor T_3/T_2 \rfloor T_2), \text{ and}$$
$$(\lfloor T_3/T_2 \rfloor + 1) C_2 + C_3 \leq a_1(T_3),$$

then the mixed scheduling algorithm is feasible.

The proof of these statements consists of some relatively straightforward but extensive inequality manipulation, and may be found in Liu [13]. Unfortunately, both of these sufficient conditions correspond to considerably lower processor utilization than does the necessary and sufficient condition of Theorem 9.

9. Comparison and Comment

The constraints in Theorem 9 strongly suggest that 100 percent utilization is not achievable universally by the mixed scheduling algorithm. The following simple example will illustrate this. Let $T_1 = 3$, $T_2 = 4$, $T_3 = 5$, and $C_1 = C_2 = 1$. Since $a_1(20) = 13$, it can be easily seen that the maximum allowable C_3 is 2. The corresponding utilization factor is

$$U = \tfrac{1}{3} + \tfrac{1}{4} + \tfrac{2}{5} = 98.3\%.$$

If these three tasks are scheduled by the deadline driven scheduling algorithm, C_2 can increase to $2.0833\cdots$ and achieve a 100 percent utilization. If they are all scheduled by the fixed priority rate-monotonic scheduling algorithm, C_3 is restricted to 1 or less, and the utilization factor is restricted to at most

$$U = \tfrac{1}{3} + \tfrac{1}{4} + \tfrac{1}{5} = 78.3\%,$$

which is only slightly greater than the worst case three task utilization bound.

Although a closed form expression for the least upper bound to processor utilization has not been found for the mixed scheduling algorithm, this example strongly suggests that the bound is considerably less restrictive for the mixed scheduling algorithm than for the fixed priority rate-monotonic scheduling algorithm. The mixed scheduling algorithm may thus be appropriate for many applications.

10. Conclusion

In the initial parts of this paper, five assumptions were made to define the environment which supported the remaining analytical work. Perhaps the most important and least defensible of these are (A1), that all tasks have periodic requests, and (A4), that run-times are constant. If these do not hold, the critical time zone for each task should be defined as the time zone between its request and deadline during which the maximum possible amount of computation is performed by the tasks having higher priority. Unless detailed knowledge of the run-time and request periods are available, run-ability constraints on task run-times would have to be computed on the basis of assumed periodicity and constant run-time, using a period equal to the shortest request interval and a run-time equal to the longest run-time. None of our analytic work would remain valid under this circumstance, and a severe bound on processor utilization could well be imposed by the task aperiodicity. The fixed priority ordering now is monotonic with the shortest span between request and deadline for each task instead of with the undefined request period. The same will be true if some of the deadlines are tighter than assumed in (A2), although the impact on utilization will be slight if only the highest priority tasks are involved. It would appear that the value of the implications of (A1) and (A4) are great enough to make them a design goal for any real-time tasks which must receive guaranteed service.

In conclusion, this paper has discussed some of the problems associated with multiprogramming in a hard-real-time environment typified by process control and monitoring, using some assumptions which seem to characterize that application. A scheduling algorithm which assigns priorities to tasks in a monotonic relation to their request rates was shown to be optimum among the class of all fixed priority scheduling algorithms. The least upper bound to processor utilization factor for this algorithm is on the order of 70 percent for large task sets. The dynamic deadline driven scheduling algorithm was then shown to be globally optimum and capable of achieving full processor utilization. A combination of the two scheduling algorithms was then discussed; this appears to provide most of the benefits of the deadline driven scheduling algorithm, and yet may be readily implemented in existing computers.

REFERENCES

1. MANACHER, G. K. Production and stabilization of real-time task schedules. *J. ACM 14,* 3 (July 1967), 439–465.
2. MCKINNEY, J M. A survey of analytical time-sharing models. *Computing Surveys 1,* 2 (June 1969), 105–116.
3. CODD, E. F. Multiprogram scheduling. *Comm ACM 3,* 6, 7 (June, July 1960), 347–350; 413–418.
4. HELLER, J. Sequencing aspects of multiprogramming. *J. ACM 8,* 3 (July 1961), 426–439.
5. GRAHAM, R. L. Bounds for certain multiprocessing anomalies. *Bell System Tech. J. 45,* 9 (Nov. 1966), 1563–1581.
6. OSCHNER, B. P. Controlling a multiprocessor system. *Bell Labs Record 44,* 2 (Feb. 1966), 59–62.
7. MUNTZ, R. R., AND COFFMAN, E. G., JR. Preemptive scheduling of real-time tasks on multiprocessor systems. *J. ACM 17,* 2 (Apr 1970), 324–338.
8. BERNSTEIN, A. J., AND SHARP, J. C. A policy-driven scheduler for a time-sharing system. *Comm. ACM 14,* 2 (Feb. 1971), 74–78.
9. LAMPSON, B. W. A scheduling philosophy for multiprocessing systems. *Comm. ACM 11,* 5 (May, 1968), 347–360.
10. MARTIN, J. *Programming Real-Time Computer Systems*, Prentice-Hall, Englewood Cliffs, N.J., 1965.
11. JIRAUCH, D. H. Software design techniques for automatic checkout. *IEEE Trans. AES-3,* 6 (Nov. 1967), 934–940
12. MARTIN, J. Op. cit., p. 35 ff
13. LIU, C. L. Scheduling algorithms for hard-real-time multiprogramming of a single processor. JPL Space Programs Summary 37-60, Vol. II, Jet Propulsion Lab., Calif. Inst. of Tech., Pasadena, Calif., Nov. 1969.

Performance Estimation for Real-Time Distributed Embedded Systems

Ti-Yen Yen, *Member, IEEE*, and Wayne Wolf, *Fellow, IEEE*

Abstract—Many embedded computing systems are distributed systems: communicating processes executing on several CPUs/ASICs. This paper describes a performance analysis algorithm for a set of tasks executing on a heterogeneous distributed system. Tight bounds are essential to the synthesis and verification of application-specific distributed systems, such as embedded computing systems. Our bounding algorithms are valid for a general problem model: The system can contain several tasks with hard real-time deadlines and different periods; each task is partitioned into a set of processes related by data dependencies. The periods of tasks and the computation times of processes are not necessarily constant and can be specified by a lower bound and an upper bound. Such a model requires a more sophisticated algorithm, but leads to more accurate results than previous work. Our algorithm both provides tighter bounds and is faster than previous methods.

Index Terms—Embedded systems, distributed systems, real-time systems, performance analysis, periodic tasks

---

1 INTRODUCTION

THIS paper describes new methods for the performance analysis of an embedded application executing on multiple processors. The performance analysis algorithm is useful in the design of any distributed system in which the task structure is known in advance. Accurate performance analysis is especially important for the **hardware/software co-synthesis** of distributed embedded systems [1] in which hardware and software are designed together to meet performance and cost goals [2]. Performance analysis is a critical step in the inner loop of co-synthesis algorithms, where it is used to judge the quality of a scheduling and allocation of processes in the embedded system. Since performance analysis is performed many times during the course of co-synthesis, it must be efficient. Performance analysis must also be accurate to ensure high-quality results from co-synthesis.

An embedded computing system is an *application-specific* computing system. The hardware platform consists of one or more *processing elements* (PEs)—programmable CPUs and application-specific integrated circuits (ASICs). The software executing on the programmable CPUs is, in general, split into multiple concurrent processes. An embedded system is designed to execute a relatively stable body of code, unlike general-purpose systems which may execute code which was not available to the system designers for characterization. Many embedded systems have *hard real-time performance constraints*. Shin and Ramanathan [3] provide a good survey of real-time computing. A real-time application is usually composed of a set of periodic **tasks**. Each task has a **deadline** by which it must complete the execution. The application-specific nature of the design problem means that, unlike in time-sharing operating systems, the job characteristics are known when the system is designed. This favors static design and analysis over dynamic analysis for predictability and reducing overhead.

Given the computation time of the uninterrupted execution of processes, the allocation of processes, and the priority assignment for process scheduling, the goal of our analysis algorithm is to statically estimate the worst-case delay of a task to see whether the deadline is satisfied. A sophisticated performance analysis algorithm is important for hardware/software co-design because many embedded systems are distributed heterogeneous computing engines: Modern automobiles include up to 60 microcontrollers of various sizes; many cellular phones contain multiple CPUs which execute both signal processing and control-oriented code; many 35mm cameras include several microprocessors. Rosebrugh and Kwang [4] described a pen-based system built from four processors of different types.

While the scheduling and allocation of a nonperiodic task consisting of predefined processes is NP-complete [5] (multiprocessor scheduling), the performance analysis problem is polynomially solvable given an allocation and schedule of processes. On the other hand, for periodic tasks running on a distributed system, we can show that even the analysis problem is NP-hard based on the results proved by Leung and Whitehead [6]. This paper presents a new performance analysis algorithm for multirate tasks on multiprocessors which is both faster and more accurate than previous methods. Given the complexity of the problem, we adopt *conservative* delay estimation algorithms which give *strict upper bounds* on delay, but which also give *tight* bounds on delay. In some cases, we can prove that our schedule bounds are tighter than those provided by other algorithms, since our algorithm uses a more general model of the set of tasks. Many algorithms for hard real-time distributed systems enumerate all the occurrence of processes in a cycle with a length equal to the least common multiple

---

- *T.-Y. Yen is with Quickturn Design Systems, 55 W. Trimble Rd., San Jose, CA 95131-1013. E-mail: tyen@quickturn.com.*
- *W. Wolf is with the Department of Electrical Engineering, Princeton University, Princeton, NJ 08544. E-mail: wolf@princeton.edu.*

Manuscript received 8 June 1995.
For information on obtaining reprints of this article, please send e-mail to: tpds@computer.org, and reference IEEECS Log Number 101201.

of all the task periods. This approach is not practical for co-synthesis, as we will mention in Section 2. Our algorithm does not rely on unrolling the schedule to the least common multiple of the periods. Our algorithm is also considerably faster on practical problems than previous methods, in part because it extends previous constraint-generation methods and uses multiple constraint-solution algorithms to solve the system of constraints which describes the multirate scheduling problem.

Our algorithm has several advantages: It handles both upper and lower bounds on process execution time [7], it considers data dependencies between processes, and it handles preemption and task pipelining. In general, the initiation times for processes may vary from iteration to iteration; these variations ripple throughout the schedule and complicate the analysis. The traditional way to handle this problem is to unroll the schedule to the least-common multiple of the periods of the tasks, but that method both takes a large amount of CPU time and creates obstacles for scheduling heuristics. Our algorithm can compute a tight bound on the schedule without unrolling. Previous publications [8], [9] provide earlier descriptions of this algorithm.

The next section surveys previous work on performance analysis for hard real-time systems. Section 3 gives our formulation of the problem. Section 4 describes our algorithm in detail. Section 5 describes the results of experiments with that algorithm.

2 Previous Work

The performance analysis of a single program has been studied by Park [10], Ye et al. [11], and Li and Malik [7], among others. These papers describe the calculation of bounds on the running time of uninterrupted execution of a sequence of code. In most embedded systems, several processes can run concurrently on the same CPU and interfere with one another according to a certain scheduling criterion. In this case, the *response time*—the time between the request and the finish of a process—consists of the whole execution time of the process itself and portions of the execution time of some other processes. The previous work at the program level provides a foundation for the performance analysis at the process level; in this paper, we assume the *computation time*—the uninterrupted execution time of each process—has been given in advance. We need to bear in mind the computation time for a process is usually not a constant and should be modeled by a bounded interval due to factors such as conditional behavior in the control flow, cache access, and the inaccuracy of the analysis techniques [7].

Rate-monotonic scheduling [12] (RMS) is a foundational scheduling method for real-time systems. It gives a fixed-priority assignment for periodic processes on a single processor. RMS assumes that the processes are *independent* with no data dependencies between them. Each process P_i is characterized by a computation time c_i and a period p_i. The deadline of a process is always at the end of its period. The processes on the PE may have different periods. Liu and Layland showed that the CPU was optimally utilized when processes are given priorities according to their rates. The deadlines of n processes can be met if the processor utilization

$$U \equiv \sum_{j=1}^{i} c_j / p_j \leq n(2^{1/n} - 1). \quad (1)$$

RMS has been generalized in several ways as surveyed by Sha et al. [13].

There is a large amount of literature on real-time distributed systems. Some of this work uses models which are not suitable for embedded systems. For instance, Liu and Shyamasundar [14] and Amon et al. [15] assumed that there can be only one process on each processor; Chu et al. [16] applied probabilistic approach which is not appropriate to handle hard deadlines. Many scheduling or allocation algorithms for distributed systems focus only on a single non-periodic task and cannot handle the RMS model. Chu and Lan [17] reviewed some of these works and categorize them as graph-theoretic, integer 0-1 programming, and heuristic approaches. However, in most real-time embedded systems, different tasks running in different rates mix together. For instance, Chiodo et al. [18] gave a seatbelt example to demonstrate multiple-rate tasks in embedded systems.

A useful result by Lehoczky et al. [19] bounds the response times for a set of independent processes; we will take advantage of this result in Section 4 to compute bound the response times of processes with data dependencies. Suppose $P_1, P_2, \ldots$ are a set of priority-ordered processes allocated on the same CPU, with P_1 being the process with the highest priority. There is no data dependency between one another so the initial phase of the processes can be arbitrary. For a process P_i, its minimum period is p_i, and its longest computation time on the CPU is c_i. Let the worst-case response time from a request of P_i to its finish be w_i. Lehoczky et al. showed that w_i is the smallest nonnegative root of the equation

$$x = g(x) = c_i + \sum_{j=1}^{i-1} c_j \cdot \lceil x/p_j \rceil. \quad (2)$$

The function $g(x)$ represents the computation time required for higher priority processes and for P_i itself: If the response time is x, there are at most $\lceil x/p_j \rceil$ requests from P_j. The total computation time for these requests is $c_j \cdot \lceil x/p_j \rceil$, so $g(x)$ includes these terms for all j as well as the computation time c_i for P_i itself. The iteration technique used to solve this equation has been mentioned by Sha et al. [13]. It can be stated as a *fixed-point iteration* technique:

1) $x = \lceil c_i / \left(1 - \sum_{j=1}^{i-1} c_j / p_j \right) \rceil$;
2) **while** $(x < g(x))$ $x = g(x)$;

It is assumed that $\left(1 - \sum_{j=1}^{i-1} c_j / p_j \right) > 0$; otherwise, the schedule must be infeasible and such an allocation should be given up by the synthesis algorithm because the processor utilization $U \equiv \sum_{j=1}^{i} c_j / p_j > 1$. We can prove that the value of x must converge to w_i in finite steps.

EXAMPLE 1. Suppose that $p_1 = 5$, $c_1 = 1$, $p_2 = 37$, $c_2 = 3$, $p_3 = 51$, $c_3 = 16$, $p_4 = 134$, $c_4 = 42$. Fixed-point iteration tells us that we only need four steps to know that $w_4 = 128$; the x-values during iterations are 104, 120, 126 and 128.

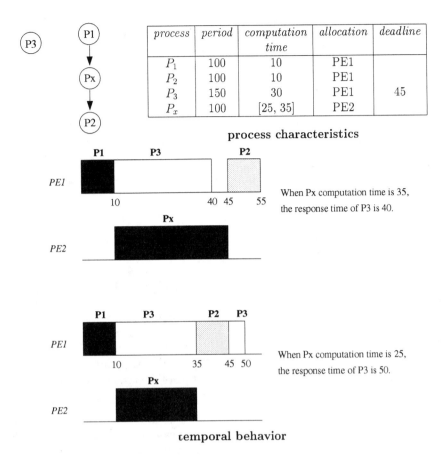

Fig. 1. Using worst-case execution times in unrolled schedules may lead to erroneous results.

The restricting case occurs when the deadline is equal to the period. By rate monotonic analysis in (1) the processor utilization for this case is

$$U = \frac{1}{5} + \frac{3}{37} + \frac{16}{51} + \frac{42}{134} = 0.908 > 4\left(2^{1/4-1}\right) = 0.76$$

and the schedule may be misjudged to be infeasible. But fixed-point iteration determines that the deadlines are satisfied.

Pure RMS is not, however, often used to schedule distributed systems with data dependencies. Surveys of scheduling algorithms for periodic tasks in real-time distributed systems can be found in several valuable survey papers [3], [20]. Many algorithms [21], [22], [23] solve the problem by *unrolling* the schedule—forming a single large task whose length is the least common multiple (LCM) of all the periods. The LCM period allows the scheduler to evaluate interactions between different-rate processes. We decided that it was important to design an algorithm that did not require the periods to be unrolled for several reasons. First, since the analysis algorithm is run in the inner loop of a synthesis algorithm, efficiency is important and we believe that unrolling is inherently less efficient. Second, schedule unrolling cannot easily handle cases in which the period and computation time are bounded but not constant. If we use the upper bound of the computation time in the simulation over the length of the LCM, a deadline thought to be satisfied may actually be violated, as shown in the example of Fig. 1. In this example, the three processes P_1, P_2, and P_3 share the same CPU and P_3 has lowest priority. The deadline of P_3 is satisfied when P_x runs for 35 time units, but not if P_x runs for 25 time units. This phenomenon was also mentioned by Gerber et al. [24]. Using a static table [20] to fix all the process request time in the length of LCM can handle nonconstant computation times, but cannot handle nonconstant periods (as in variable-speed engines and motors) and can lead to large tables which are expensive to implement in memory-limited embedded systems.

Leinbaugh and Yamani [25] derived analytic bounds for response times of a set of tasks. However, their approach uses some pessimistic assumption so the bounds are not tight enough. D'Ambrosio and Hu [26] used simulation to judge the feasibility of a schedule during co-synthesis. Extensive simulation is often time consuming and not guaranteed to prove feasibility.

Prakash and Parker [27] formulated distributed system co-synthesis as an integer linear program (ILP). Their ILP formulation cannot handle periodic processes and preemptive scheduling. A great deal of recent work has studied hardware-software partitioning, which targets a one-CPU-one-ASIC topology. The Vulcan system of Gupta and De Micheli [28] and the COSYMA system of Ernst et al. [29] move operations between software and hardware. They schedule and allocate operations inside a process to satisfy timing constraints between operations but handle only single-rate problems and single-threaded implementations.

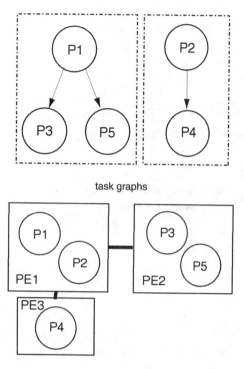

Fig. 2. A task graph and its implementation.

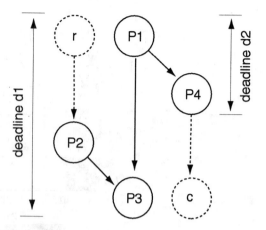

Fig. 3. How to transform release times and multiple deadlines into single-deadline form.

Our work may be applied to one-CPU-one-ASIC model but also holds for more general system topologies.

3 Problem Formulation

Our problem formulation is similar to those used in distributed system scheduling and allocation problems. A **process** P_i is a single thread of execution, characterized by bounds on its **computation time**—the bounds may be written as $[c_i^{lower}, c_i^{upper}]$, where c_i^{lower} is the lower bound and c_i^{upper} is the upper bound. These bounds are a function of the processor type to which P_i is allocated. A **task** is a partially ordered set of processes. The **task graph** is a directed acyclic graph which represents the structure of a task (or a set of tasks). A directed edge from P_i to P_j represents that the output of P_i is the input of P_j. A process is not initiated until all its inputs have arrived; it issues its outputs when it terminates. (Delay processes may be added to the model to accommodate data which arrives or leaves the main computation processes at different times.) A problem specification may contain several concurrently running tasks. (An embedded system may perform several tasks which are nearly decoupled, such as running several relatively independent peripherals; in such cases, it may be useful to describe the system as unconnected subsets of processes.)

Processes are illustrated on the top of Fig. 2 as nodes labeled with their names. The processes and data dependency edges form tasks. Each task has two implicit nodes—the start node and the end node. There is a dependency from the start node to each process, and a dependency from each process to the end node. The start node and the end node are not drawn in the examples and will be used only to explain the algorithm. Each task is given two characteristics: a **period** (also known as a **rate constraint**) which is the time between two consecutive initiations; and a **deadline**, the maximum time allowed from initiation to termination of the task. If a task τ is not issued in a constant rate, the period is modeled by an interval $[p_\tau^{lower}, p_\tau^{upper}]$. A task's deadline is satisfied if it is greater than or equal to the worst-case delay through the task. Release times and multiple deadlines can be modeled by inserting dummy processes—processes with delay but not allocated on any physical PE—in the task graph, as described in Fig. 3. We therefore assume each task has a single deadline.

Synthesis produces an embedded system architecture. As illustrated in the bottom of Fig. 2, the *hardware engine* architecture is a labeled graph whose nodes represent **processing elements (PEs)** and whose edges represent communication links. A PE may represent a CPU executing software or an ASIC which can execute a particular function. The edges and nodes of the graph are labeled with the type of link or PE, as appropriate. The **allocation** is given by a mapping of processes onto PEs. The **schedule** of processes is an assignment of priorities to processes. Some processes may be implementable by either a CPU or an ASIC; we assume that the processes have been partitioned so that they do not cross CPU-ASIC or CPU-CPU boundaries.

We assume static allocation of processes—a process does not move to a different PE during the course of execution. Since processes may share a CPU, we must model the interaction of co-allocated processes. Each process is given an integral, fixed priority; the CPU always executes the highest-priority ready process, which continues execution until it completes or is preempted by a higher-priority process. We neglect operating system overhead in this analysis; with fixed priority scheduling, OS overhead is frequently negligible, but its effects can be straightforwardly incorporated into the computation time of a process.

We can show that the analysis problem under this model is NP-hard, even though the schedule and allocation of processes have been given.

THEOREM. *Given the task graphs and an embedded system architecture (the hardware engine, schedule, and allocation of processes), the problem to decide whether the deadline of each task is satisfied is NP-hard.*

PROOF. Leung and Whitehead [6] proved that deciding whether a priority assignment schedule is valid for an asynchronous system on a single processor is NP-hard. In their formulation, an asynchronous system contains a set of processes. Each process P_i has a period p_i, an initial request time s_i, a deadline d_i measured relative to the initial request time, and a computation time c_i.

We prove that our analysis problem is NP-hard by showing that Leung and Whitehead's problem is polynomial-time reducible [30] to our analysis problem. For each process P_i in the asynchronous system, create a task graph τ_i as follows: Task τ_i contains P_i, another process Q_i, and an directed edge from Q_i to P_i. The computation time of Q_i is s_i and the computation time of P_i is c_i; the period of τ_i is p_i and the deadline of τ_i is $d_i + s_i$. Schedule and allocate the processes such that each Q_i on a different PE such that only Q_i is executed on that PE, all the processes P_is in the original asynchronous system on the same PE, the priority assignment for the original asynchronous system are used to schedule the processes P_is. The deadline of task τ_i is satisfied if and only if the deadlines of process P_i in the original asynchronous system is satisfied. Because the analysis problem of an asynchronous system is NP-hard, the performance analysis of task graphs on an embedded system architecture is also NP-hard. □

The theorem is different from the NP-completeness of the multiprocessor scheduling problem [5] because:

- scheduling and allocation is known a priori;
- processes are periodic;
- preemptive scheduling is allowed.

4 OUR ALGORITHM

This section describes our core algorithm, which uses a *fixed-point iteration* based on *phase adjustment* and *separation analysis* to compute tight bounds on the worst-case delay through a task graph executing on multiple PEs, including complications caused by data dependencies in the task graph.

4.1 Algorithm Overview

Our algorithm iteratively applies two techniques—phase adjustment and separation analysis—to tighten the bounds on process delay. A simple example illustrates the need for both types of analysis.

EXAMPLE 2. Consider the task graph of Fig. 4 in which the three processes share the same CPU and P_1 have highest priority. If we ignore data dependencies between P_2 and P_3, as is done in (2), their worst-case response times are 35 for P_2 and 45 for P_3. But the worst-case total delay along the path from P_2 to P_3 is actually 45 instead of 80 (the sum of 35 and 45) because of two conditions. First, P_1 can only preempt either P_2 or P_3, but not both in a single execution of the task. Second, P_2 cannot preempt P_3.

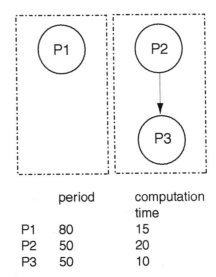

	period	computation time
P1	80	15
P2	50	20
P3	50	10

Fig. 4. An example of worst-case task delay estimation.

This example shows that the delays among processes in disjoint tasks are not independent, unlike many critical-path problems in CAD. Since processes in separate tasks may be co-allocated to the same processor, the execution times of processes in separate tasks can affect each other. As a result, we cannot use simple longest-path algorithms [30] to solve for the worst-case delays of the processes. We must take into account combinations of process activation's to generate tight bounds on worst-case delays.

Fig. 5 outlines our complete algorithm. G_i is a subgraph of the task graph which contains process P_i and its successors. Each connected subgraph of the complete task graph is referred to as a G_i which contains a process P_i and all of its successors in the task graph. The result of the algorithm is a set of upper and lower bounds on process separation times *maxsep*[·, ·] which provide the bounds on process execution times. The algorithm repeatedly applies two steps to tighten the bounds, starting with bounds of ∞:

- `EarliestTimes()` and `LatestTimes()` use a modified longest-path algorithm to take into account data dependencies, handling the first phenomenon observed in Example 2.
- `MaxSeparations()` uses a modified max-constraint algorithm to take into account preemption, handling the second phenomenon of Example 2.

The algorithm terminates when the bounds do not change over the course of an iteration. It is easy to show that the algorithm terminates, since the bounds always tighten at each iteration and termination occurs when the tightening of every bound is zero. We may also set a limit on the number of iterations if faster delay estimation is desirable.

The algorithm computes *phase adjustments* which model the constraints imposed by data dependencies in the task graph. It computes two types of phases:

- The *request phase* ϕ_{ij}^r between processes P_i and P_j captures the smallest interval between the request time of the current P_i and the first request time of P_j following it.

```
1   maxsep[·, ·] = ∞; /* initialize separations */
2   step = 0; /* count tightening iterations */
3   do {
4     for (each P_i) { /* longest path */
5       EarliestTimes(G_i);
6       LatestTimes(G_i);
7     }
8     for (each P_i) /* max constraints */
9       MaxSeparations(P_i);
10    step++;
11  } while (maxsep[·, ·] is changed and step < limit);
```

Fig. 5. Our delay estimation algorithm.

```
1   LatestTimes(a task graph G)
2   /* Compute latest[P_i.request] and latest[P_i.finish] for all P_i in a task graph G. */
3   {
4     for (each process P_i) { /* initialize */
5       latest[P_i.request] = 0;
6       for (each process P_j) φ^r_{ij} = 0;
7     }
8     for (each process P_i in topologically sorted order) {
9       w_i = worst-case response time of P_i with phase adjustment of φ^r_{ij}
10        for each process P_j with higher priority than P_i;
11      latest[P_i.finish] = latest[P_i.request] + w_i;
12      Calculate the phases φ^f_{ij} relative to latest[P_i.finish] for each j;
13      for (each immediate successor P_k of P_i) {
14        δ = latest[P_k.request] - latest[P_i.finish];
15        if (latest[P_k.request] < latest[P_i.finish])
16          latest[P_k.request] = latest[P_i.finish];
17        Update phases φ^r_{kj} for each process P_j according to φ^f_{ij} and δ;
18      }
19    }
20  }
```

Fig. 6. The LatestTimes algorithm.

- Similarly, the *finishing phase* ϕ^f_{ij} between processes P_i and P_j captures the smallest interval between the finish time of the current P_i and the first request time of P_j following it.

These phases capture the minimum distance between a preempted process and a preempting process. As we saw in Example 2, the phases of a pair of processes may be influenced by both data dependencies and preemptions caused by co-allocation of processes to a PE. In a pure rate-monotonic model, phase relationships between processes do not exist since there are no constraints on the relative timing of pairs of processes. However, given the existence of data dependencies which limit the timing relationships between processes, determining the relative phase of a pair of processes allows the algorithm to tighten the schedule bounds.

The next two sections describe each step of the algorithm in more detail. We will then summarize the relationships between these steps. Finally, we will show how our algorithm can be used to analyze pipelined task sets.

4.2 Latest/Earliest Times Calculation

LatestTimes, one of the two algorithms used to analyze data dependencies, is listed in Fig. 6. This procedure computes the *latest request time* and *latest finish time* of each process P_i in a task. (Given the LatestTimes procedure, it is easy to transform that program into the EarliestTimes procedure to compute earliest request and finish times.) If the times are relative to the start of the task, the latest finish time of the end node of the task is the worst-case delay of the whole task.

LatestTimes is a modified longest-path algorithm—it traces through the processes in topological order, as is typically done in a longest-path algorithm, but it uses the current bounds, which include preemption information, to compute new bounds on execution time.

The first step in the algorithm is to initialize the request phase relationships and latest request times for each process. The algorithm considers the processes in topological order as defined by the task graph. Line 9 in Fig. 6 calculates the worst-case response time of a process P_i using the fixed-point iteration for w_i given by (2). However, the terms $\lceil x/p_j \rceil$ in $g(x)$ shown in (2) are modified into

$$\left\lceil (x - \phi_{ij}^r)/p_j \right\rceil,$$

where ϕ_{ij}^r is the phase of P_j relative to the request time of P_i. In other words, x is adjusted by the request phase ϕ_{ij}^r.

After w_i is computed, line 12 calculates the phases relative to $latest[P_i.finish]$, the ϕ_{ij}^fs. If P_j preempts P_i,

$$\phi_{ij}^f = \left(\phi_{ij}^r - w_i\right) \bmod p_j.$$

We subtract w_i from ϕ_{ij}^r because $latest[P_i.finish] = latest[P_i.request] + w_i$. Otherwise,

$$\phi_{ij}^f = \max\left(\phi_{ij}^r - w_i, 0\right).$$

Updating the request phases (the ϕ_{kj}^rs) is more complex—the algorithm must look ahead one iteration to determine the request time for a process on its next iteration. Line 17 uses the finishing phases and δ calculated at line 14 to update the request phases; it does so by examining each immediate successor P_k of P_i. If P_i is the first visited immediate predecessor of P_k, $\phi_{kj}^r = \phi_{ij}^f$ for each j because $latest[P_k.request] = latest[P_i.finish]$. If $\delta > 0$, there is slack between $latest[P_i.finish]$ and $latest[P_k.request]$; that slack is used to increase the finishing phase ϕ_{ij}^f. If $\delta < 0$, increase ϕ_{kj}^r similarly. Finally, $\phi_{kj}^r = \min\left(\phi_{kj}^r, \phi_{ij}^f\right)$. We choose the smaller phase, which may give longer delay to P_k for the worst case. The final ϕ_{kj}^r values are used to adjust the phases in fixed-point iteration to get more accurate value for w_k when P_k is visited.

We can modify **LatestTimes** as follows to obtain the earliest request time $earliest[P_i.request]$ and the earliest finish time $earliest[P_i.finish]$:

- Replace $latest[\cdot]$ with $earliest[\cdot]$. Replace the ceiling operators $\lceil \cdot \rceil$ with the floor operators $\lfloor \cdot \rfloor$ in (2) for fixed-point iteration. Let $c_i = c_i^{lower}$ and $p_i = p_i^{upper}$ for the best-case delay estimation.
- At line 12, set ϕ_{ij}^f to 0 if P_j are not allocated to the same CPU as P_i. Otherwise, calculate ϕ_{ij}^f in a way similar to that in Section 4 but keep it in the range $(-p_j, 0]$. At line 17, make ϕ_{kj}^r equal to ϕ_{ij}^f only when

  $earliest[P_k.request] = earliest[P_i.finish]$.

  Otherwise, leave ϕ_{kj}^r unchanged.

Suppose the modified algorithm is **EarliestTimes**.

Processes P_js or P_ks visited by **LatestTimes** belong to the same task graph. However, the worst-case delay of the task graph may be affected by processes P_js from the other tasks, if those processes share a CPU. For instance, the delay of the task graph composed of P_2 and P_3 can be lengthened by P_1 in another task.

The following example explains how **LatestTimes** algorithm solves the problem in Fig. 4 and Example 2.

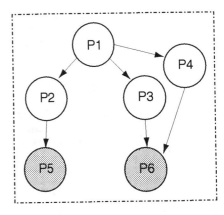

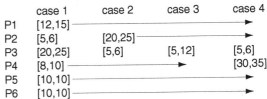

Fig. 7. Several different schedules for a task showing different combinations of execution time overlaps.

EXAMPLE 3. The situation is illustrated in Fig. 4. Initially, $\phi_{21}^r = 0$. When the algorithm **LatestTimes** visits P_2, by solving the equation

$$x = g(x) = 20 + 15 \cdot \lceil x/80 \rceil,$$

it determines that $latest[P_2.finish] = latest[P_3.request] = w_2 = 35$ and

$$\phi_{31}^r = \phi_{21}^f = \left(\phi_{21}^r - w_2\right) \bmod p_1 = -35 \bmod 80 = 45.$$

If we know P_2 will not preempt P_3, then the phase adjustment is described by

$$x = g(x) = 10 + 15 \cdot \lceil (x - 45)/80 \rceil.$$

In this case, we get $w_3 = 10$ and $latest[P_3.finish] = 35 + 10 = 45$, which is the worst-cast task delay we expect.

4.3 Separation Analysis

The **MaxSeparations** procedure determines what combinations of process activation's cannot occur, since one process cannot preempt another if they cannot be activated simultaneously. The role of max constraints in describing limitations on preemptions was illustrated in Example 2. While it is easy to know that a process will not preempt its predecessors or successors, such as with P_2 and P_3 in Fig. 4, it is not obvious how to decide whether two processes in disjoint paths of a task graph can overlap. This problem is illustrated in the following example.

EXAMPLE 4. Fig. 7 gives four different combinations of process computation times, with the lower and upper bounds listed as $[l, u]$. P_5 and P_6 are on the same CPU, where P_5 has higher priority. Even if the processes are not allowed to be allocated to different PEs, we can see substantial changes in their computation times as the schedule changes. In Cases 1 and 2, P_5 will not preempt P_6 because they are *separated*—that is, they

```
 1  MaxSeparations(a process P_i)
 2  /* Compute maxsep[P_i.request, P_j.finish] for all P_j in the same task graph */
 3  {
 4    for (each process P_j in topologically sorted order) {
 5      Enqueue(Q, P_j); /* initialize queue */
 6      tmp = ∞; /* initialize time */
 7      while (Q is not empty) {
 8        P_k = Dequeue(Q); /* get node to evaluate */
 9        for (each immediate predecessor P_l of P_k) {
10          if (P_l is a predecessor of P_i)
11            tmp = max(tmp, upper[P_k.request, P_j.finish]
12                    −lower[P_l.finish, P_i.request]);
13          if (P_j is a predecessor of P_i)
14            tmp = min(tmp, −lower[P_j.finish, P_i.request]);
15          if (maxsep[P_i.request, P_l.finish] == −lower[P_l.finish, P_i.request])
16            continue;
17          if (P_l ∉ Q) Enqueue(Q, P_l); /* keep traversing */
18        }
19        if (tmp == −lower[P_j.finish, P_i.request]) break;
20      }
21      maxsep[P_i.request, P_j.finish] = tmp;
22    }
23  }
```

Fig. 8. The MaxSeparations algorithm.

cannot execute simultaneously. But in Cases 3 and 4, P_5 can preempt P_6. This possible overlap must be taken into account during worst-case task delay estimation.

The separation analysis illustrated in Example 4 depends on, but is not the same as, the phase analysis performed by **LatestTimes**. Phase analysis looks at the data dependencies between processes, but does not fully take into account the effects of preemption. The purpose of **MaxSeparations** is to use the results of phase analysis, along with allocation information, to determine the separations between pairs of processes.

The relationship between the start of a process and its predecessors in the task graph can be modeled by *max* constraints [31], [32], [15]. *Max* constraints are introduced by the co-allocation of processes on a processing element. The initiation time of a process is computed by a *max* function of the finish times of its immediate predecessors in the task graph. For example, the completion of a lower priority process depends on both the execution time of that process and the possible execution of higher priority processes. *Max* constraints, unlike data dependencies, are nonlinear and the combinatorics of solving systems of *max* constraints is more challenging than that of a system of linear constraints. *Max* constraints cannot be efficiently processed using the critical-path algorithms exemplified by **LatestTimes**. McMillan and Dill's $O(ne)$ algorithm [32] can deal with *max* constraints and calculate pairwise separations. However, in their algorithm, the delay along a path is the sum of the bounds of individual constraints, which is not true in our case, as mentioned in Example 2.

The algorithm **MaxSeparations**, listed in Fig. 8, finds the maximum separations from P_i to all other processes in the same task graph. It is a modified version of McMillan and Dill's maximum separation algorithm. Like McMillan and Dill's algorithm, **MaxSeparations** traverses the task graph from sink to source to evaluate the maximum separation constraints. The efficiency of a sink-to-source traversal when evaluating max constraints becomes clearer when one considers the alternative of source-to-sink traversal, which would require node values to be repeatedly pushed forward in time to satisfy max constraints.

MaxSeparations uses the information computed by **LatestTimes** and **EarliestTimes** to calculate two time instants for a process P—$P.request$ is the request time of P relative to the beginning of the task graph and $P.finish$ is the time P finishes its execution. Given two time instants x and y, $upper[x, y]$ is an upper bound on the delay from x to y and $lower[x, y]$ is a lower bound on the delay from x to y. Let G_i be a subgraph composed of P_i and all its successors. The modifications to McMillan and Dill's algorithms are required because we are not computing a single value for a node, but rather the upper and lower bounds on request and finish times.

We compute bounds on delays based on request and finish times as follows. After calling **LatestTimes**(G_i) we can assign

$$upper[P_i.request, P_j.request] = latest[P_j.request]$$

$$upper[P_i.request, P_j.finish] = latest[P_j.finish]$$

for all successors P_j of P_i. Similarly, we can call **EarliestTimes**(G_i) and let

$$lower[P_i.request, P_j.request] = earliest[P_j.request]$$

$$lower[P_i.request, P_j.finish] = earliest[P_j.finish]$$

The bound from a finish time can be derived from the bounds from the request time. For instance,

$$lower\big[P_i.finish, P_j.request\big] = \max_k lower\big[P_k.request, P_jrequest\big],$$

where P_k is an immediate successor of P_i. These bounds are used in `MaxSeparations` to derive the maximum separations.

Given a source node i in McMillan and Dill's algorithm, the maximum separation $maxsep[i, j]$ can be calculated only after $maxsep[i, k]$ is known for all predecessors k of j through recursive calls. In Fig. 8, line 4 searches the task graph in topological order for the same reason. In McMillan and Dill's algorithm, for each immediate predecessor k of j,

$$maxsep[i,j] = \min\Big(\max_k\big(maxsep[i,k] + upper[k,j]\big), -lower[j,i]\Big).$$

Similarly, we apply the $\max_k$ and min operators at lines 11 and 14, respectively. But when a path delay is not the sum of bounds, it is not accurate enough to consider only the immediate predecessors and we use the formula $maxsep[i, k] + upper[k, j]$ to calculate upper bounds. Instead, we try to consider all the predecessors of P_j by a backward breadth-first-search in lines 7-20. The breadth-first-search is trimmed at line 15 and terminated at line 19 when the lower bounds determine the maximum separation value; it is not necessary to trace further back to know the upper bounds along a path. The maximum separation between two request times can be calculated by:

$$maxsep\big[P_i.request, P_j.request\big] = \max_k maxsep\big[P_i.request, P_k.finish\big],$$

where P_k is an immediate predecessor of P_j.

4.4 Iterative Improvement

Separation analysis (performed by `MaxSeparations`) and phase analysis (performed by `LatestTimes` and `EarliestTimes`) compute distinct but related pieces of information about the system schedule. The complete analysis algorithm uses the result from one to improve the results obtained by the other. We use maximum separations to improve delay estimation in `LatestTimes`, but we need to call `LatestTimes` to derive maximum separations. Therefore, we get successively tighter delay bounds and maximum separations iteratively. Initially, to be pessimistic but feasible, we set the maximum separations to ∞.

Maximum separations are used to improve delay estimation in `LatestTimes` as follows:

- If $maxsep[P_i.request, P_j.finish] \leq 0$ or $maxsep[P_j.request, P_i.finish] \leq 0$, the execution of P_i and P_j will not overlap. The corresponding terms are eliminated from the function $g(x)$ in (2) when the worst-case response time w_i is computed at line 9 in Fig. 6.
- In `LatestTimes`,

$$\phi_{ij}^r = \max\big(\phi_{ij}^r, -maxsep\big[P_j.request, P_i.request\big]\big)$$

for phase adjustment. Similarly, in `EarliestTimes`,

$$\phi_{ij}^r = \min\big(\phi_{ij}^r, -maxsep\big[P_j.request, P_i.request\big] - p_j\big)$$

for phase adjustment.

The use of improved phase estimates to tighten separations computed by `MaxSeparations` is more straightforward—lines 11 through 20 in Fig. 8 directly use the latest values of the finish and request times to update the separations.

4.5 Period Shifting and Task Pipelining

This section shows how our algorithm automatically handles pipelined task execution—pipelining causes more complex, nonconstant relationships between process executions which our algorithm automatically handles *without* unrolling to the least-common multiple of the periods. Our earlier examples assumed for simplicity that the period of a process is the same as that of the task to which the process belongs. While this is true for a process with no predecessors in a task graph, this assumption is not accurate in general. The delay for the predecessors may vary from period to period, making the request period of a process different from the period of the task.

EXAMPLE 5. Consider the task graphs and a system implementation shown in Fig. 9. In this figure, an upward arrow represents the request of a process, while a downward dotted arrow stands for a data dependency. P_1 and P_2 share one CPU, with P_1 having higher priority; P_3 and P_4 share the other CPU, with P_3 having higher priority. If we consider the period of P_3 to be 70, which is the same as that of τ_2, the worst case delay of τ_3 should be 50. However, the worst case delay of τ_3 can be 80. Note a process cannot start before its request arrives or before its predecessors in the task graph finish.

Suppose there is no task pipelining, so that every process finishes before its next request. In (2), the maximum number of requests for the processes P_j is $\lceil x/p_j \rceil$, where p_j is the period of the task containing P_j. Before any preemption from P_j occurs, the term for the number of requests should be modified into

$$\lceil (x + latest[P_j.request] - earliest[P_j.request])/p_j \rceil$$

We call such modification *period shifting*. Similarly, when we calculate the earliest times, the minimum number of requests should be

$$\lfloor (x - latest[P_j.request] + earliest[P_j.request])/p_j \rfloor$$

In the iterative tightening procedures of Fig. 5, we use as an initial worst-case estimate $latest[P_j.request] - earliest[P_j.request] = p_j - c_j$ because, otherwise, P_j may not finish before its next request. Later on, as the values for $latest[P_j.request]$ and $earliest[P_j.request]$ are tightened, period shifting is modeled more and more accurately.

The other phenomenon handled by our algorithm is *task pipelining*. Although the computation time of a process should be smaller than the period of the task containing the process, we allow the deadline or the delay of a task to be longer than its period. As a result, some processes may not finish before the beginning of some processes in the next execution of the same task. To make the techniques discussed so far valid in spite of task pipelining, we require two conditions to be satisfied:

- If two processes P_i and P_j belong to the same task with a minimum period p and are allocated on the same CPU, it

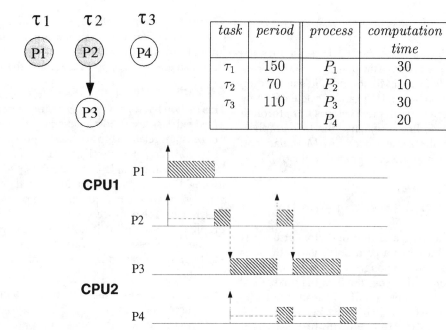

Fig. 9. An example of period shifting.

TABLE 1
THE BOUNDED COMPUTATION TIME ON i960 FOR SEVERAL ROUTINES (AFTER LI AND MALIK)

function	description	[lower bound, upper bound]
checkdata	Park's example	[32, 1039]
piksrt	Insertion Sort	[146, 4333]
des	Data Encryption Standard (DES)	[42302, 604169]
line	line drawing	[336, 8485]
circle	circle drawing	[502, 16652]
jpegfdct	JPEG forward discrete cosine transform	[4583, 16291]
jpegidct	JPEG inverse discrete cosine transform	[1541, 20665]
recon	MPEG2 decoder reconstruction	[1824, 9319]
fullsearch	MPEG2 encoder frame search routine	[43082, 244305]
matgen	matrix generating routine	[5507, 13933]

TABLE 2
THE BOUNDED COMPUTATION TIME ON DSP3210 FOR SEVERAL ROUTINES (AFTER LI AND ONG)

Function	Description	[lower bound, upper bound]
arccos	arc cosine	[166, 706]
sqrt	square root	[460, 460]
gran	random number generator	[1128, 1128]
matmul	matrix multiplication	[810, 810]
fft	fast Fourier transform	[103688, 103688]

is not allowed that $latest[P_i.finish] > latest[P_j.request] + p$. If this requirement is not satisfied, P_i will delay the request time of P_j, which may in turn delay the request time of the next iteration of P_i further and there is chance that the delay will continue to grow.

- We will avoid $latest[P_i.finish] > earliest[P_j.request] + p$. When this does happen, we implement a dummy process with a delay $latest[P_i.finish] - p$ between the start of the task and the initiation of P_j. If this requirement is not satisfied, when $P_i = P_j$, the peak frequency of P_i may get too high due to period-shifting effect, endangering the deadlines of other tasks.

As a matter of fact, such requirements are conservative. However, in most practical pipelining designs, different stages are allocated to different resources (PEs). The execution time of each stage is smaller than the period and it is unlikely that a process will overlap the next execution of the same stage, so these requirements are reasonable in practice.

5 EXPERIMENTAL RESULTS

Li and Malik estimated the computation time for some real programs on an Intel i960 [7] and Li and Ong performed a similar task for a Lucent DSP3210 [33]. We repeat their data in Table 1 and Table 2. Their data reveals that, in many real

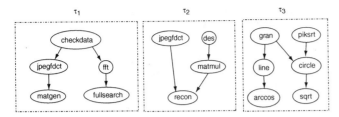

Fig. 10. Three task graphs and their periods.

TABLE 3
THE ALLOCATION AND SCHEDULE OF THE PROCESSES IN FIG. 10

PE	processes (priority-ordered)
i960-1	piksrt, line, circle, jpegidct
i960-2	jpegdct, matgen, fullsearch, checkdata
i960-3	des, recon
DSP3210	sqrt, arccos, matmul, gran, fft

TABLE 4
THE DELAY ESTIMATION FOR THE THREE TASKS IN THE EXAMPLE CREATED FROM LI AND MALIK'S DATA

method	τ_1	τ_2	τ_3	CPU time
our algorithm	356724	615464	29930	0.12s
simulation	355914	615004	29930	641.76s

problems, computation time is not constant and is sufficiently large to make the LCM method inefficient. We constructed three task graphs containing these processes as shown in Fig. 10. The processes are allocated in four CPUs: one DSP3210s and three i960s. The allocation and priority assignment of the processes is shown in Table 3. We compared our algorithm to extensive simulations using an interval of length equal to the LCM of the periods, the lower bound value for each period, and the upper bound value for each computation time. The results are given in Table 4 with the CPU time for our analysis algorithm on a Sun SS20 workstation. The results show that simulation requires much more CPU time than our analysis, even though we did not perform exhaustive simulation, which would require possible values between the lower bound and upper bound should be used. Such an exhaustive simulation is too expensive to be implemented.

Some examples in other literature are not directly comparable: The example by Ramamritham [34] did not use static allocation; the example by Peng and Shin [21] used synchronization to make three tasks equivalent to a single nonperiodic task. Both examples have small periods and the LCM of the periods happen to be equal to the largest period. We compare our algorithm with Leinbaugh and Yamini's algorithm [25] using their two examples. In each of their examples, all the tasks have the same period, but the initial phases can be random. The results are given in Table 5. Our algorithm gave better bounds because it does not rely on their pessimistic assumptions. For example, they assume a process with high priority can preempt a task during the whole interval of the task's execution, even though the task only spends a portion of time on the same CPU the high-priority process is allocated to.

Table 6 shows the analysis results for three designs in D'Ambrosio and Hu's example [26]. In this table, "yes" means

TABLE 5
THE ESTIMATED TASK DELAYS FOR LEINBAUGH AND YAMINI'S EXAMPLES

Example	Method	Task 1	Task 2	Task 3	Task 4	CPU time
#1	L & Y	1116	1110	1114		NA
	ours	1093	1084	1072		0.03s
#2	L & Y	959	845	863	912	NA
	ours	655	586	820	637	0.03s

TABLE 6
DEADLINE SATISFACTION RESULTS FOR D'AMBROSIO AND HU'S EXAMPLE

PEs	cost	D&H's simulation	Our algorithm	CPU time	Our simulation
P1, PIO	3.00	no	no	0.04s	no
MC2	3.25	yes	no	0.04s	no
MC1	3.50	yes	yes	0.04s	yes

that the deadlines of all nine processes were satisfied, while "no" means that at least one was not. In their example, the largest period is the LCM of all the periods. There are no data dependencies between processes, but each process has both a release time and a deadline. We also ran a simulation in a length equal to the largest period and compare the results.

6 CONCLUSIONS

Distributed computers are often the most cost-effective means of meeting the performance requirements of an embedded computing application. We have proposed an algorithm for tight yet easy-to-compute timing bounds on the tasks. This work does not address all the modeling issues in distributed embedded systems. In other work, we have studied the problem of communication link contention [35], however, more work remains in integrating communication link scheduling with processing element scheduling. We have also not considered the effects of preemption overhead. We have used this analysis algorithm to develop a hardware/software co-synthesis algorithm [1] which simultaneously designs a hardware topology and allocates and schedules processes on CPUs to meet hard real-time deadlines. Once again, there is more work to be done in this area. We believe that algorithms such as this are an important tool for the practicing embedded system designer.

ACKNOWLEDGMENTS

This work was supported in part by the U.S. National Science Foundation under Grant MIP-9424410.

REFERENCES

[1] T.-Y. Yen and W. Wolf, "Sensitivity-Driven Co-Synthesis of Distributed Embedded Systems," *Proc. Eighth Int'l Symp. System Synthesis*, pp. 4–9, 1995.
[2] W. Wolf, "Hardware-Software Co-Design of Embedded Systems," *Proc. IEEE*, vol. 82, no. 7, July 1994.
[3] K.G. Shin and P. Ramanathan, "Real-Time Computing: A New Discipline of Computer Science and Engineering," *Proc. IEEE*, vol. 82, no. 1, Jan. 1994.
[4] C. Rosebrugh and E.-K. Kwang, "Multiple Microcontrollers in an Embedded System," *Dr. Dobbs J.*, Jan. 1992.
[5] C.H. Papadimitriou and K. Steiglitz. *Combinatorial Optimization: Algorithms and Complexity*. Prentice Hall, 1982.

[6] J.Y.-T. Leung and J. Whitehead, "On the Complexity of Fixed-Priority Scheduling of Periodic, Real-Time Tasks," *Performance Evaluation*, vol. 2, 1982.

[7] S. Li and S. Malik, "Performance Analysis of Embedded Software Using Implicit Path Enumeration," *Proc. Design Automation Conf.*, 1995.

[8] T.-Y. Yen and W. Wolf, "Performance Estimation for Real-Time Distributed Embedded Systems," *Proc. IEEE Int'l Conf. Computer Design*, 1995.

[9] T.-Y. Yen and W. Wolf. *Hardware-Software Co-Synthesis of Distributed Embedded Systems*. Norwell, Mass.: Kluwer Academic, 1996.

[10] C.Y. Park, "Predicting Deterministic Execution Times of Real-Time Programs," PhD thesis, Univ. of Washington, Seattle, Aug. 1992.

[11] W. Ye, R. Ernst, T. Benner, and J. Henkel, "Fast Timing Analysis for Hardware-Software Co-Synthesis," *Proc. IEEE Int'l Conf. Computer Design*, 1993.

[12] C.L. Liu and J.W. Layland, "Scheduling Algorithms for Multiprogramming in a Hard-Real-Time Environment," *J. ACM*, vol. 20, no. 1, Jan. 1973.

[13] L. Sha, R. Rajkumar, and S.S. Sathaye, "Generalized Rate-Monotonic Scheduling Theory: A Framework for Developing Real-Time Systems," *Proc. IEEE*, vol. 82, no. 1, Jan. 1994.

[14] L.Y. Liu and R.K. Shyamasundar, "Static Analysis of Real-Time Distributed Systems," *IEEE Trans. Software Eng.*, vol. 16, no. 4, Apr. 1990.

[15] T. Amon, H. Hulgaard, S.M. Burns, and G. Borriello, "An Algorithm for Exact Bounds on the Time Separation of Events in Concurrent Systems," *Proc. IEEE Int'l Conf. Computer Design*, 1993.

[16] W.W. Chu, C.-M. Sit, and K.K. Leung, "Task Response Time for Real-Time Distributed Systems with Resource Contentions," *IEEE Trans. Software Eng.*, vol. 17, no. 10, Oct. 1991.

[17] W.W. Chu and L.M.-T. Lan, "Task Allocation and Precedence Relations for Distributed Real-Time Systems," *IEEE Trans. Computers*, vol. 36, no. 6, June 1987.

[18] Chiodo, Guisto, Hsieh, Jurecska, Lavagno, and Sangiovanni-Vincentelli, "Configuration-Level Hardware/Software Partitioning for Real-Time Embedded Systems," *Proc. Int'l Workshop Hardware-Software Co-Design*, 1993.

[19] J. Lehoczky, L. Sha, and Y. Ding, "The Rate Monotonic Scheduling Algorithm: Exact Characterization and Average Case Behavior," *Proc. IEEE Real-Time Systems Symp.*, 1989.

[20] K. Ramamritham and J.A. Stankovic, "Scheduling Algorithms and Operating Systems Support for Real-Time Systems," *Proc. IEEE*, vol. 82, no. 1, Jan. 1994.

[21] D.-T. Peng and K.G. Shin, "Static Allocation of Periodic Tasks with Precedence Constraints," *Proc. Int'l Conf. Distributed Computing Systems*, 1989.

[22] K. Ramamritham, "Allocation and Scheduling of Precedence-Related Periodic Tasks," *IEEE Trans. Parallel and Distributed Systems*, vol. 6, no. 4, Apr. 1995.

[23] C.J. Hou and K.G. Shin, "Allocation of Periodic Task Modules with Precedence and Deadline Constraints in Distributed Real-Time Systems," *Proc. Real-Time Systems Symp.*, 1982.

[24] R. Gerber, W. Pugh, and M. Saksena, "Parametric Dispatching of Hard Real-Time Tasks," *IEEE Trans. Computers*, vol. 44, no. 3, pp. 471-479, Mar. 1995.

[25] D.W. Leinbaugh and M.-R. Yamini, "Guaranteed Response Times in a Distributed Hard-Real-Time Environment," *Proc. Real-Time Systems Symp.*, 1982.

[26] J.G. D'Ambrosio and X. Hu, "Configuration-Level Hardware/Software Partitioning for Real-Time Embedded Systems," *Proc. Int'l Workshop Hardware-Software Co-Design*, 1994.

[27] S. Prakash and A.C. Parker, "SOS: Synthesis of Application-Specific Heterogeneous Multiprocessor Systems," *J. Parallel and Distributed Computing*, vol. 16, 1992.

[28] R.K. Gupta and G. De Micheli, "Hardware-Software Cosynthesis for Digital Systems," *IEEE Design and Test of Computers*, vol. 10, no. 3, pp. 29-41, Sept. 1993.

[29] R. Ernst, J. Henkel, and T. Benner, "Hardware-Software Co-Synthesis for Microcontrollers," *IEEE Design and Test of Computers*, vol. 10, no. 4, pp. 61-75, Dec. 1993.

[30] T.H. Cormen, C.E. Leiserson, and R.L. Rivest, *Introduction to Algorithms*. McGraw-Hill, 1990.

[31] P. Vanbekbergen, G. Goossens, and H. De Man, "Specification and Analysis of Timing Constraints in Signal Transition Graphs," *Proc. European Conf. Design Automation*, 1992.

[32] K. McMillan and D. Dill, "Algorithms for Interface Timing Verification," *Proc. IEEE Int'l Conf. Computer Design*, 1992.

[33] S. Li and P.-W. Ong, "Cinderella for DSP3210," unpublished report, 1994.

[34] K. Ramamritham, "Allocation and Scheduling of Complex Periodic Tasks," *Proc. Int'l Conf. Distributed Computing Systems*, 1990.

[35] T.-Y. Yen and W. Wolf, "Communication Synthesis for Distributed Embedded Systems," *Proc. Int'l Conf. Ccomputer-Aided Design-95*, pp. 288-294, 1995.

Ti-Yen Yen received his BS degree in electrical engineering from National Taiwan University in 1989 and his PhD degree in electrical engineering from Princeton University in 1996. He served as an electronic engineering officer in the Navy of Taiwan from 1989 to 1991. He joined Quickturn Design Systems, San Jose, California, in 1995 and is now the HDL-ICE project manager. His research interests include synthesis, design verification, hardware/software co-design, emulation, and reconfigurable computing.

Wayne Wolf received the BS, MS, and PhD degrees in electrical engineering from Stanford University in 1980, 1981, and 1984, respectively. He was with AT&T Bell Laboratories from 1984 through 1989. He joined the Department of Electrical Engineering at Princeton University in 1989, where he is now a professor. His research interests include hardware/software co-design and embedded computing, multimedia computing systems, and video libraries. He is a fellow of the IEEE and a member of the ACM and SPIE.

Rate Analysis for Embedded Systems

ANMOL MATHUR
Silicon Graphics, Inc.
ALI DASDAN
University of Illinois—Urbana-Champaign
and
RAJESH K. GUPTA
University of California—Irvine

Embedded systems consist of interacting components that are required to deliver a specific functionality under constraints on execution rates and relative time separation of the components. In this article, we model an embedded system using concurrent processes interacting through synchronization. We assume that there are rate constraints on the execution rates of processes imposed by the designer or the environment of the system, where the execution rate of a process is the number of its executions per unit time. We address the problem of computing bounds on the execution rates of processes constituting an embedded system, and propose an interactive rate analysis framework. As part of the rate analysis framework we present an efficient algorithm for checking the consistency of the rate constraints. Bounds on the execution rate of each process are computed using an efficient algorithm based on the relationship between the execution rate of a process and the maximum mean delay cycles in the process graph. Finally, if the computed rates violate some of the rate constraints, some of the processes in the system are redesigned using information from the rate analysis step. This rate analysis framework is implemented in a tool called RATAN. We illustrate by an example how RATAN can be used in an embedded system design.

Categories and Subject Descriptors: C.4 [**Computer Systems Organization**]: Performance of Systems—*modeling techniques; performance attributes*

General Terms: Algorithms, Design, Performance, Theory

Additional Key Words and Phrases: Average execution rate, concurrent system modeling, embedded systems, interactive rate violation debugging, rate analysis, rate constraints

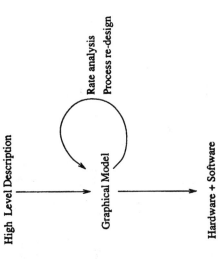

Fig. 1. Interaction between rate analysis and synthesis in the design of an embedded system.

1. INTRODUCTION

The design of embedded systems has become an increasingly difficult problem due to increased design complexity and shortened time-to-market. Since such systems consist of interacting hardware and software components, the designers have to validate these components not only individually but also the interfaces between them. The design of such a system entails mapping a high-level description of the system in a hardware description language into hardware and software so that all the constraints such as timing, resource, and power are satisfied. This mapping typically consists of three main stages. The system is captured in a high-level description, and an architecture of the system with software and hardware parts is selected during the first stage. The second stage includes the independent design of hardware, software, and the interface between them. The third stage is the integration and test stage. During this stage, a hardware prototype is built and the software is tested to make sure that the hardware–software interface functions correctly. However, interfacing software with hardware is likely to cause many timing constraint violations, and unfortunately, any such errors found in this stage are very costly to correct due to the amount of commitment already in the design. Consequently, it is becoming extremely important to take timing constraints into consideration at higher levels in the design flow. This article is an attempt in this direction.

An embedded system consists of concurrent components interacting under timing constraints. It is customary to generate an intermediate graphical model of the system during the design of such systems as illustrated in Figure 1. We use a *process graph* as our model of an embedded system in which each component corresponds to a process. Processes are active concurrently, and synchronization between the pro-

---

The first author's work was partially supported by NSF under grant MIP 92-22408 and by Silicon Graphics. We also acknowledge support from NSF Career Award 95-01615 and a grant from NSF Engineering Research Center ECD 89-43166.
Authors' current addresses: A. Mathur, Cadence Design Systems, Ambit Group, 2500 Augustine Dr., Santa Clara, CA 95054 (mathura@cadence.com); A. Dasdan, Department of Computer Science, University of Illinois at Urbana-Champaign, Urbana, IL 61801; R. K. Gupta, Department of Information and Computer Science, University of California, Irvine, CA 92697.
Permission to make digital/hard copy of part or all of this work for personal or classroom use is granted without fee provided that the copies are not made or distributed for profit or commercial advantage, the copyright notice, the title of the publication, and its date appear, and notice is given that copying is by permission of the ACM, Inc. To copy otherwise, to republish, to post on servers, or to redistribute to lists, requires prior specific permission and/or a fee.

This article not only proposes a rate analysis framework but also presents its underlying system model, theoretical basis, and implementation via RATAN. The main contributions can be summarized as follows.

—A two-level system model in which the top level models the processes in the system using a process graph and the bottom level models each process using a sequencing graph. We introduce the concept of an *enable signal* to capture the synchronization between processes. This abstraction allows us to model systems with pipelined processes. The two-level model is useful in developing efficient algorithms for rate analysis.

—The notion of *average execution rate* of a process, defined as the inverse of the asymptotic mean of the sequence of time intervals between successive invocations of the process. We present a purely graph-theoretic proof showing that the average execution rate is well defined for all processes in a finite process graph, irrespective of the initial start times of the processes. This proof also gives more accurate bounds on the periodicity of interexecution times for a process than previously reported in the literature. We present efficient algorithms for computing bounds on the average execution rates of processes in a process graph.

—The rate analysis framework for using the bounds on process execution rates to interactively modify the design of an embedded system to satisfy all the rate constraints. Our rate analysis framework is implemented in a tool, RATAN. We demonstrate the utility of RATAN using an example.

The rest of the article is organized as follows. Section 2 describes our two-level system model, focusing mainly on the process graph and the modeling of synchronization. Section 3 gives an overview of the rate analysis framework, defines the average execution rate, and the main problems addressed in the article. Each of the remaining sections examines one of these problems. Section 4 shows that the average execution rate is well defined and presents efficient algorithms for computing bounds on the average execution rates of processes in a process graph. The proof of this result is fairly long and given in the Appendix. Section 5 defines the notion of consistency of rate constraints and presents an efficient algorithm for consistency checking. Section 6 discusses how rate analysis can be used to debug rate constraint violations and redesign the embedded system to satisfy the rate constraints.

2. THE SYSTEM MODEL

We model an embedded system as a set of concurrent interacting processes. Our model is a hierarchical two-level model. The top level is the *process graph* that captures the interaction between the processes. Each process is modeled using a *sequencing graph* [De Micheli 1994] that represents the data and control flow dependencies between the operations within a process. These sequencing graphs form the bottom level in our two-level representation.

cesses occurs according to a statically defined dependency relation between them. Timing constraints are usually in two forms: constraints on the execution rates of processes and constraints on the time separation between a pair of processes. In this article, we are concerned with those on the execution rates, called *rate constraints*. Rate constraints are imposed by the designer to guarantee the conformance of the system to its environment. Our ultimate objective is to make sure that all the rate constraints are satisfied, which holds if each process executes at a rate as constrained. We propose an interactive *rate analysis framework* to realize this objective. This framework includes four main steps: checking the consistency of the rate constraints using an efficient algorithm; finding bounds on the execution rate of each process using an efficient algorithm based on the relationship between the execution rate of a process and the maximum mean delay cycles in the process graph; checking to see if the rate constraints are satisfied; and redesigning some parts of the system, attempted if the set of the rate constraints is found to be inconsistent during the first step or if there are some rate constraints that are not satisfied (*i.e.*, violated) during the third step. After any redesigns, these steps are repeated. This rate analysis framework is implemented in a tool called RATAN. We illustrate by an example how RATAN can be used in an embedded system design.

The problem of determining execution rates has been studied in several different contexts. Gupta and De Micheli [1997] have examined the problem of rate analysis in embedded systems, but they consider very limited interaction/synchronization between the component processes. Furthermore, their algorithms require the processes to be implemented only in a nonpipelined manner. Rate analysis has also been studied for asynchronous, concurrent systems modeled using timed Petri nets [Burns and Martin 1991; Magott 1984; Ramamoorthy and Ho 1980]. However, such analysis is based on restrictive assumptions, such as the vector of start times for the processes is a specially chosen vector. This assumption is not valid if an embedded system software is implemented as a set of coroutines where each coroutine consists of an initial process that is executed only once and a repeating body. Hulgaard et al. [1995] have addressed the problem of finding tight bounds on the time interval between events in a process graph using implicit unfolding of the process graph. These bounds can be converted to bounds on the execution rates of processes by inversion. However, the process graphs that can be analyzed using their techniques need to be strongly connected or satisfy other restrictive conditions. Furthermore, the proposed algorithms can be computationally expensive in the worst case.

Bacelli et al. [1992] have used algebraic techniques for the analysis of event graphs arising from discrete event dynamic systems (DEDS). They have shown that several results from traditional theory of linear systems can be extended to the analysis of DEDS. The key to this is the fact that the timing semantics of DEDS can be expressed as linear equations using a new algebra that replaces multiplication by addition and addition by the *max* operation.

—*Ability to model several different synchronization mechanisms.* The basic primitive for synchronization in our model is an enable signal from one process to another. A process starts executing once it has received an enable signal from all its predecessors in the process graph. This allows us to model systems with several different kinds of synchronization and communication paradigms in a unified manner. Some examples are:

(1) *Operation-based enable signal.* Such an enable signal is issued by a process when it executes a particular operation in its sequencing graph. A vertex in the sequencing graph whose execution results in the generation of an enable signal is called an *enabling vertex*. The delay between the start of the execution of a process and the generation of an operation-based enable signal can vary for different executions of the process because it may be value dependent.

(2) *Time-based enable signal.* Such an enable signal is generated after a fixed time following the start of the execution of a process. It is not associated with the execution of a particular operation in the process. Such enable signals are useful in modeling a pipelined process for which a new execution starts after a fixed delay.

—*Modeling pipelined processes.* A new instance of a pipelined process can start executing before its previous execution has finished. Our process graph model can handle such pipelined processes using a self-loop with delay less than the execution time of the process. Thus, the process graph model allows us to model multiple parallel and pipelined execution instances of a process. If the delay associated with a self-loop is larger than the execution time of the process then a new execution of the process cannot begin until the previous execution has terminated. Consequently, the process cannot be pipelined.

2.2 Limitations

In order to develop efficient algorithms for rate analysis, we need to impose some restrictions on the way enable signals can be issued by processes. These are not inherent to our process graph model, but are limitations introduced due to the algorithmic techniques we use for rate analysis. Basically, these limitations arise due to the requirement that one execution of a process should generate exactly one enable signal for each of its successors in the process graph. This results in the following restrictions on the generation of enable signals.

—*Enable signals should not be generated from inside loops in the sequencing graph.* Since loop bodies can be executed multiple times for one execution of a process, if there are enable vertices in a loop body then multiple enable signals would be generated for the same successor process in one execution. Rate analysis for such systems is an interesting problem that would require new techniques.

—*Enable signals should not be generated from conditionally executed parts of the sequencing graph for a process.* The presence of enable vertices in

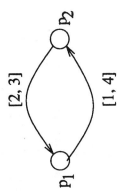

Fig. 2. A process graph with two processes.

In the process graph $G_P(V_P, E_P)$, each vertex p_i in V_P represents a process. An edge (p_i, p_j) indicates that the process p_i enables the execution of process p_j by sending an enable signal to process p_j. Each edge (p_i, p_j) in the process graph is associated with a delay interval $\Delta_{ij} = (d_{ij}, D_{ij})$ that bounds the time after the initiation of an execution of process p_i when p_j receives the enable signal from p_i. Let δ_{ij} be the actual delay after the start of an execution of p_i when p_j receives the enable signal from p_i; then $d_{ij} \leq \delta_{ij} \leq D_{ij}$. Figure 2 shows a simple process graph with two process.

Each process represents an independent thread of control. We assume that all the processes are concurrently active. The execution semantics of our model is as follows. Let $x_i(k)$ denote the time at which process p_i starts its $(k+1)$st execution. In particular, $x_i(0)$ is the initial start time of p_i. Then, the following rules govern the subsequent executions of the processes.

—*Independence.* Initially, each process p_i starts its first execution at $x_i(0)$ independently of the other processes.

—*AND causality.* A new instance of process p_j starts executing after all its predecessors in the process graph have issued enable signals for p_j. Consequently,

$$x_i(k) = \max_{p_j \in Pred(p_i)} \{x_j(k-1) + \delta_{ij}\},$$

or, since $\delta_{ij} \in [d_{ij}, D_{ij}]$,

$$\max_{p_j \in Pred(p_i)} \{x_j(k-1) + d_{ij}\} \leq x_i(k) \leq \max_{p_j \in Pred(p_i)} \{x_j(k-1) + D_{ij}\},$$

where $k > 0$ and $Pred(p_i)$ is the set of predecessors of p_i in the process graph.

2.1 Highlights

Our process graph model and the associated enable signal-based communications/synchronization is general enough to represent most embedded system specifications. Here are some of the main highlights of our model.

rizing the performance of a process in such a system (see Bacelli et al. [1992] and Ramamoorthy and Ho [1980]). We use the same definition and define the *average interexecution time* T_i and the *average execution rate* r_i of a process p_i as

$$T_i = \lim_{n \to \infty} \frac{\sum_{k=0}^{n-1} x_i(k+1) - x_i(k)}{n} = \lim_{n \to \infty} \frac{x_i(n)}{n} \quad \text{and} \quad r_i = T_i^{-1}, \quad (2)$$

if the preceding limit exists. We show in Section 3.1 that for a finite process graph with finite edge delays, the preceding limit exists and can be efficiently computed. Thus, in this article we focus on asymptotic rates of execution. Note that the time between successive invocations of a process (interexecution time) is not constant, hence the instantaneous execution rate of a process keeps changing. The following example illustrates our definition of average rate of execution.

Example 3.1. Consider the process graph shown in Figure 2. Assuming that the processes start executing at time 0, and the edge delays equal their lower bounds ($\delta_{12} = 1, \delta_{21} = 2$), the sequence of initiation times of the processes are:

Process p_1: 0, 2, 3, 5, 6, 8 $\cdots$
Process p_2: 0, 1, 3, 4, 6, 7 $\cdots$.

Thus, the sequence of interexecution times for both the processes are:

Process p_1: 2, 1, 2, 1 $\cdots$
Process p_2: 1, 2, 1, 2 $\cdots$,

and the average interexecution time is 3/2. Thus, using the definition of average rate of execution given previously, the execution rates of both processes in this example are 2/3. Notice that the limit in our definition of the average rate of execution exists in this case because both sequences of interexecution times are periodic (with period 2).

3.2 Rate Constraints

We assume that the designer specifies upper and lower bounds on the average execution rates of all the processes in the system. Thus, each process p_i in the process graph is associated with a *constraint interval* $I_i = [L_i, U_i]$. Constraint intervals for processes in a process graph can be arbitrary (since they are specified independently for each process by the designer). If there is no lower bound constraint on the rate of a process then $L_i = 0$, and if there is no upper bound constraint then $U_i = \infty$. For the specified rate constraints to be satisfied, the computed execution rate for each process must lie within its constraint interval; that is

$$L_i \leq r_i \leq U_i.$$

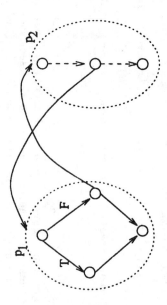

Fig. 3. Two processes (with the corresponding sequencing graphs shown in the dotted regions); process p_1 issues a conditional enable signal for process p_2.

conditional branches would imply that when the conditional branch is not executed no enable signal would be generated for some successor process. At first glance, this appears to be a severe restriction on the expressive power of our process graph model. However, any deadlock-free, strongly connected process graph that uses our synchronization semantics must have this property. The possibility of deadlock in the presence of conditional enable signals is illustrated in the following example. It is possible to have conditional enable signals without causing deadlock if they span two different strongly connected components in the process graph.

Example 2.1. Consider the processes shown in Figure 3. Process p_1 issues an enable signal for process p_2 from an enabling vertex in the FALSE branch of a conditional branch and process p_2 issues an unconditional enable signal for process p_1. If the computation ever takes the TRUE branch in process p_1, no enable signal is issued for p_2. Thus, p_2 is not invoked and consequently p_1 is not invoked, leading to a deadlock. The same scenario can occur in any strongly connected process graph that has enable vertices in conditional branches.

3. RATE ANALYSIS FRAMEWORK

In this section we define average execution rate, give a precise formulation of the problems that are addressed in the article, and then give a brief overview of our rate analysis framework.

3.1 Average Execution Rate

The rate of execution of a process is defined as the number of executions of the process per unit time. Let

$$x_i(k) = \text{time at which process } p_i \text{ starts executing for the } (k+1)\text{th time.} \quad (1)$$

We are concerned with systems that exhibit infinite behavior. Such systems behave in a cyclic fashion in steady state after the initial transients. The following limit has been used by researchers as a standard way of summa-

Usually the environment in which an embedded system works imposes rate constraints on various components (processes) of the system. So the rates at which certain events happen in the environment place execution rate constraints on the components of the embedded system that are supposed to process those events.

3.3 Problem Formulation

Given a description of an embedded system (process graph and the sequencing graphs of the processes), along with the associated rate constraints, the following problems need to be addressed in the rate analysis framework.

Delay Analysis. Compute bounds on the execution times of operations in the sequencing graphs, and use these estimates to find bounds on the delays of the edges in the process graph. Delay analysis requires computations of bounds on the time after the initiation of a process when it issues an enable signal for another process, and the estimation of the communication delay between the process generating the enable signal and the one receiving it. This problem has been addressed by Gupta [1996] and Mathur et al. [1996], and is not the focus of this article.

Consistency Checking of Rate Constraints. This problem arises because the designer usually specifies the rate constraints independently for each process. A set of rate constraints is said to be inconsistent if they cannot be simultaneously satisfied for a given process graph topology, irrespective of the delay intervals on the process graph edges. Thus, if a set of rate constraints is inconsistent, the computed rate intervals can never satisfy all the rate constraints. Since consistency of a set of rate constraints is independent of the actual delay intervals in the process graph, we can state the consistency checking problem as follows: Given a process graph and the rate constraint intervals associated with each process in the process graph, are the constraint intervals consistent?

Section 5 describes our consistency checking algorithm.

Rate Analysis. The rate analysis problem is stated as follows. Given a description of an embedded system as a process graph and the associated sequencing graphs, find upper and lower bounds on the average execution rate of each process in the process graph.

So, rate analysis finds an interval $[r_l(p_i), r_u(p_i)]$ for each process p_i such that the average rate of execution of the process is guaranteed to lie in this interval. The rate constraints on p_i are said to be satisfied if the rate interval computed by rate analysis is contained in $[L_i, U_i]$. If the computed rate interval is not contained in $[L_i, U_i]$, then one or both of the rate constraints of p_i are violated. In Section 4 we present our algorithms for rate analysis.

Rate Constraint Debugging and Process Redesign. If rate analysis finds that some of the rate constraints are violated, the designer needs to redesign certain processes and/or change the process graph topology by

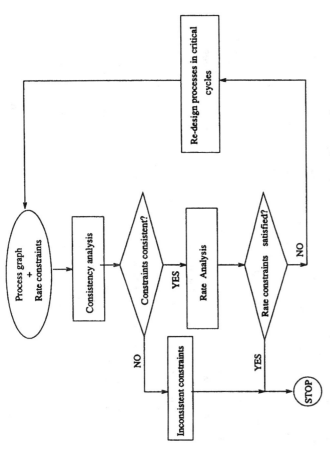

Fig. 4. An overview of our rate analysis framework.

altering the manner in which the processes communicate. The rate analysis tool needs to give adequate information about the cause of the rate constraint violation to help in this step. We discuss some possible approaches in Section 6.

Figure 4 shows our framework for rate analysis. The design specification is first translated from a high-level description to a process graph along with the associated sequencing graphs. First, the rate constraints are checked for consistency. If the rate constraints are consistent, rate analysis is performed on the process graph. If all the computed rate intervals are contained in the intervals defined by the rate constraints, then the system satisfies all the rate constraints and no redesign is required. If a rate constraint is violated, the tool gives the user the reasons for the violation and this information can be used to redesign the relevant processes. Although consistency analysis of the rate constraints precedes rate analysis in the flow, we discuss rate analysis before consistency analysis in this article. This is motivated by the fact that many of the results required for describing our consistency-checking algorithm are more natural to discuss in the context of rate analysis.

4. RATE ANALYSIS

In this section we show that our notion of average execution rate is well defined and present algorithms for rate analysis of process graphs. For the sake of clarity, some of our results are stated for strongly connected process graphs. However, we do generalize our results to arbitrary process graphs and there is no limitation on the topology of the process graphs that our rate analysis algorithms can handle.

4.1 Existence of Average Execution Rate

In order to prove that our asymptotic definition of average execution rate is well defined, we first examine the case when the process graph is strongly connected (i.e., there is a path from each process p_i to all other processes in the graph) and there is a unique delay δ_{ij} associated with each edge in the process graph. The extension to the case when the process graph has several strongly connected components and the process graph edges have delay intervals associated with them becomes clear when we discuss the algorithms for rate analysis for such process graphs in Section 4.2.

We define the delay of a cycle C in the process graph as

$$d(C) = \sum_{(i,j) \in C} \delta_{ij} \qquad (3)$$

The number of edges in a cycle C is denoted by $|C|$. The *mean delay* of a cycle C is given by

$$\frac{d(C)}{|C|}. \qquad (4)$$

The maximum mean cycle delay is denoted by λ. A cycle is said to be *critical* if it has the maximum mean delay among all the cycles in the graph.

The following theorem establishes that our definition of execution rate in Equation (2) is well defined, and can be related to the maximum mean cycle in the process graph. Weaker forms of this theorem can be found in Bacelli et al. [1992], Burns and Martin [1991], Ramamoorthy and Ho [1980], and Reiter [1968].

THEOREM 1. *Consider a strongly connected process graph and let $x_i(k)$, $k \geq 0$ be the sequence of time instances at which process p_i executes. Then there exists some $N \geq 0$ such that the following are true.*

(1) *The sequence $x_i(k) - x_i(k-1)$, $k \geq N$ is periodic with period equal to $\mathcal{L}$, where $\mathcal{L}$ is equal to the least common multiple of the lengths of all the critical cycles in the process graph.*

(2) *For any $q \geq N$,*

$$\frac{\sum_{j=q}^{q+\mathcal{L}-1} x_i(j+1) - x_i(j)}{\mathcal{L}} = \lambda,$$

where λ is the maximum mean cycle delay in the process graph.

(3) *The average interexecution time is well defined and*

$$T_i = \lim_{n \to \infty} \frac{\sum_{k=0}^{n-1} x_i(k+1) - x_i(k)}{n} = \lambda.$$

The proof of this theorem is based on the characterization of critical paths in the process graph and is given in the Appendix. The main idea used in the proof is that $x_i(k)$ (the time when the $(k+1)$th execution of process p_i starts) is determined by the delay of the longest path in the process graph with exactly k edges that ends at process p_i, and that this path can be characterized using the maximum mean delay cycles in the process graph.

Notice that T_i is not average in the probabilistic sense. As this theorem shows, the interexecution time of a process in a process graph may not stay constant but a sequence of its successive interexecution times repeats itself with a certain period and T_i is the mean of the interexecution times within such a sequence.

4.2 Algorithms for Rate Analysis

Theorem 1 shows that for a process graph with one strongly connected component (SCC), if all the edge delays are exact then the execution rate of all the processes is equal to the inverse of the maximum mean cycle delay in the process graph. In this section, we first show how to compute upper and lower bounds on execution rates of processes in the presence of uncertainty in the edge delays. Then, we give an efficient algorithm for computing execution rates for the case when the process graph is strongly connected (or, equivalently, has one SCC) and, finally, we extend our algorithms to the case when the process graph has multiple SCCs. This case handles any process graph.

Handling Delay Intervals. We assume that we have a process graph G_P with a delay interval associated with each edge. The following theorem allows us to compute the rate interval $[r_l(p_i), r_u(p_i)]$ for each process p_i in the process graph from the delay intervals of the edges.

THEOREM 2. (*Monotonicity Theorem*). *Increase (decrease) in the delay of an edge cannot increase (decrease) the average execution rate of any process.*

PROOF. From Theorem 1, we know that the average execution rate of a process in a strongly connected process graph is equal to the inverse of the maximum mean cycle delay in the process graph. Increasing (decreasing) the delay of an edge in the process graph increases (decreases) the mean delay of any cycle in the process graph. It follows that increasing (decreasing) the delay of an edge in the process graph cannot increase (decrease) the average execution rate of any process. □

From the monotonicity theorem it follows that we can compute $r_u(x)$ by setting all the edge delays to their lower bounds and $r_l(x)$ by setting all the edge delays to their upper bounds. Hence, if the process graph is strongly connected then all the nodes have the same rate interval $[\lambda_u^{-1}, \lambda_l^{-1}]$, where λ_l and λ_u are the maximum mean cycle delays of the process graph computed by setting the edge delays of all the edges to their lower bounds and upper bounds, respectively. Hence, the rate interval for a strongly connected process graph is computed by two invocations of the algorithm for computing the maximum mean delay cycle in a graph.

Notice that the lower and upper rate bounds are the tightest bounds on the average execution rate but they do not bound the best and worst case execution rates. If the latter are desired, our rate analysis framework would still apply; however, the average interexecution time, which is used to compute the average execution rate, should be replaced with the best and worst case interexecution times. Loose bounds on them are simply the minimum and maximum arc delays in the process graph. The tightest bounds on them are given by the time separation algorithm of Hulgaard et al. [1995].

Rate Analysis: Single SCC. Using the result in Theorem 1, we need to compute the maximum mean cycle delay to compute the average execution rate of processes in a SCC. The following theorem due to Karp [1978] allows the design of an efficient algorithm for finding the maximum mean cycle delay. Its proof can be found in Bacelli et al. [1992, p. 47].

THEOREM 3. *Consider a strongly connected graph $G(V, E)$ with n nodes. Let s be an arbitrary chosen vertex. For every $v \in V$, and every nonnegative integer k, define $D_k(v)$ as the maximum delay of a path of length k from s to v; if no such path exists, then $D_k(v) = -\infty$. Then the maximum cycle mean λ of G is given by*

$$\lambda = \min_{v \in V} \max_{0 \leq k < n} \frac{D_n(v) - D_k(v)}{n - k}.$$

Thus, for a strongly connected process graph the average execution rates of all the processes are equal to the inverse of the maximum mean cycle delay, and they can be computed using Karp's characterization of the maximum mean cycle delay in $O(|V| \cdot |E|)$ time.

Rate Analysis: Multiple SCCs. We now consider a process graph that has several strongly connected components. We define the *component graph* of the process graph to be the graph in which there is a vertex for each SCC and an edge from u to v if and only if there is an edge from a vertex in the SCC represented by u to a vertex in the SCC represented by v in the process graph. Note that the component graph is a directed acyclic graph. The following is the key observation on which the algorithm for computing rate intervals for a process graph with multiple SCCs hinges.

RATE_ANALYSIS(G)
  Find the maximal SCCs in G
  for each SCC, C
    $r_l(C) = \textbf{RATE}(C : t(x) = t_u(x) \, \forall x \in C)$
    $r_u(C) = \textbf{RATE}(C : t(x) = t_l(x) \, \forall x \in C)$
  Construct the component graph : $G_c(V_c, E_c)$
    $r_l(C_j) = \min\{r_l(C_j), \min_{(C_i, C_j) \in E_c}\{r_l(C_i)\}\}$
    $r_u(C_j) = \min\{r_u(C_j), \min_{(C_i, C_j) \in E_c}\{r_u(C_i)\}\}$
end RATE_ANALYSIS

Fig. 5. Algorithm for rate analysis for a process graph with multiple SCCs; **RATE** is the algorithm for computing λ^{-1} using Karp's characterization of λ.

THEOREM 4. *Let P and C be two maximal strongly connected components in a process graph with some edges from vertices in P to vertices in C (so P is a "producer" and C is a "consumer"). Let $[r_l(P), r_u(P)]$ and $[r'_l(C), r'_u(C)]$ be the rate intervals for P and C, respectively, computed assuming that there are no edges between P and C. Then the actual rate interval for C is $[r_l(C), r_u(C)]$, where*

$$r_l(C) = \min\{r_l(P), r'_l(C)\},$$

$$r_u(C) = \min\{r_u(P), r'_u(C)\}.$$

PROOF. Any cycle in P has a path to any process $p_i \in C$ through edges connecting P to C. Consequently, the k critical paths for p_i (for sufficiently large values of k) are determined by the larger of the maximum mean delay cycle in P and C (refer to the proof of Theorem 1). Hence, the average execution rate of any process in C is the minimum of the rate computed assuming that there are no dependencies from P to C (this is the inverse of the maximum mean cycle delay in C) and the average execution rate of any process in P (this is the inverse of the maximum mean cycle delay in P). These observations along with the monotonicity theorem prove this theorem. □

Using the preceding theorem we develop the algorithm in Figure 5 for rate analysis of a process graph with multiple SCCs. The following example illustrates the steps involved in the rate analysis for process graphs.

Example 4.1. Consider the process graph shown in Figure 6. The delay intervals for the edges are shown. Notice that we do not associate a delay interval with the edge connecting the two strongly connected components of the graph. This is because such inter-SCC edges are not part of any cycles in the process graph, and consequently their delay does not affect any execution rates. We now consider the steps involved in the rate analysis of the process graph in Figure 6.

214 CHAPTER 3: Analysis and Estimation

Thus,

$$r_u = (7)^{-1} = 0.142.$$

Hence, the rate interval for SCC_1 is $[0.068, 0.142]$.
For SCC_2:

$$r_l = \left[\max\left\{\frac{20+8+4}{3}, \frac{10+5+6+8+4}{5}\right\}\right]^{-1} = 0.094$$

and

$$r_u = \left[\max\left\{\frac{7+5+1}{3}, \frac{4+3+3+5+1}{5}\right\}\right]^{-1} = 0.231.$$

So, the rate interval for SCC_2 is $[0.094, 0.231]$. Notice that the rate intervals of the two SCCs overlap. The rate analysis was carried out assuming that the two SCCs are completely disjoint. The rates in SCC_1 are not affected by the edge from SCC_1 to SCC_2; however, the rate interval for SCC_2 needs to take into consideration the rate interval of the "producer" SCC. In fact, the actual rate interval for SCC_2 is

$$[\min\{0.094, 0.068\}, \min\{0.231, 0.142\}] = [0.068, 0.142].$$

Thus, the rate interval of SCC_2 is the same as that of SCC_1. Notice that for clarity of exposition, we have computed the maximum mean cycle delay using explicit enumeration of the cycles in this example. In our implementation, instead of explicit cycle enumeration, we use Karp's characterization of maximum mean cycle delay to compute the rates.

5. CONSISTENCY CHECKING

A set of rate constraints is said to be *inconsistent* if they cannot be simultaneously satisfied for a given process graph topology, irrespective of the delay intervals on the process graph edges. Thus, if a set of rate constraints is inconsistent, the computed rate intervals can never satisfy all the rate constraints. Note that a consistent set of constraints may not be satisfied because some of the computed rate intervals may not be contained in the corresponding constraint intervals. Theorem 4 gives sufficient conditions for a set of rate constraints with the consistency analysis, we need a few definitions. Consider n rate constraint intervals in the form of $I_i = [L_i, U_i]$ for $1 \leq i \leq n$.

—Their minimum is $\min_i\{I_i\} = [\min_i\{L_i\}, \min_i\{U_i\}]$.
—Their intersection is $\cap_i\{I_i\} = [\max_i\{L_i\}, \min_i\{U_i\}]$.
—Given intervals I_i and I_j, $I_i < I_j$, if $U_i < L_j$.

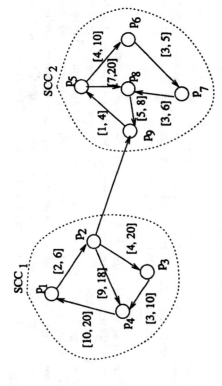

Fig. 6. Process graph used in Example 4.1.

For SCC_1:
For computing r_l, set all edge delays to their upper bounds.

λ_l = maximum mean delay cycle in SCC_1

$$= \max\left\{\frac{20+18+6}{3}, \frac{6+20+10+20}{4}\right\}$$

$$= \max\left\{\frac{44}{3}, 14\right\}$$

$$= 14.67.$$

The critical cycle is $(p_1 \rightarrow p_2 \rightarrow p_4 \rightarrow p_1)$ and

$$r_l = (14.67)^{-1} = 0.068.$$

For computing r_u, we use the lower bounds on the edge delays.

λ_u = maximum mean delay cycle in SCC_1

$$= \max\left\{\frac{10+9+2}{3}, \frac{2+4+3+10}{4}\right\}$$

$$= \max\{7, 4.75\}$$

$$= 7.$$

Now consider a strongly connected component in the process graph C_j. Then the following hold.

— The intersection of the rate intervals of the processes in C_j is

$$I_j^\cap = \cap_{p_i \in C_j} I_i.$$

— The minimum of all the intersections that belong to C_j and all of its predecessors is

$$I_j^{\min} = \min(I_j^\cap, \min_{C_i \in pred(C_j)} \{I_i^{\min}\}), \quad (5)$$

and for a component with no predecessors, $I_j^{\min} = I_j^\cap$. More intuitively, $I_j^{\min}$ is obtained by propagating the $I_j^\cap$ intervals in the component graph in topological order (this is similar to the propagation of rate intervals during rate analysis).

THEOREM 5. *A set of rate constraints S that define the constraint intervals I_i for each process p_i in a process graph G_P is inconsistent if any of the following conditions is satisfied.*

(1) *There exists a strongly connected component C_j of the process graph such that*

$$I_j^\cap = \Phi,$$

(2) *There exists a component C_j for which*

$$I_j^{\min} < I_j^\cap.$$

PROOF. (1) From Theorems 1, 2, and 4, we know that the computed rate interval of all processes in a strongly connected component, C_j, of G_P is identical. Let $[r_l(C_j), r_u(C_j)]$ be the computed rate interval. If $I_j^\cap = \Phi$, then there must be some process $p_i \in C_j$ for which $[r_l(C_j), r_u(C_j)]$ is not contained in I_i (otherwise the intersection of the I_is contains $[r_l(C_j), r_u(C_j)]$ and is not empty). Hence, the rate constraints for p_i are violated. Since the preceding argument does not depend on any particular choice of the delay ranges of edges in G_P, it follows that if $I_j^\cap = \Phi$ for any C_j, then S is inconsistent.

(2) From Theorem 4, we know that the average execution rate of a SCC is constrained by the average execution rate of its predecessors in the component graph. In particular, the rate interval for a process is the minimum of its own rate interval (assuming no dependencies across SCCs), and the rate intervals of its predecessors. If we assume that rate constraints are satisfied for all SCCs that are predecessors of C_j, then the largest possible rate interval for C_j is equal to $I_j^{\min}$. Furthermore, if rate constraints are satisfied for all the processes in C_j, then the largest

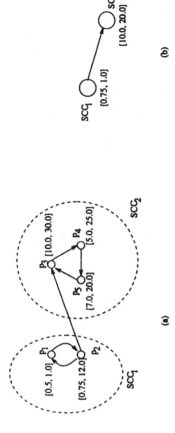

Fig. 7. (a) Process graph used in Example 5.1; (b) corresponding component graph.

possible rate interval for C_j is $I_j^\cap$. Consequently, if

$$I_j^{\min} < I_j^\cap,$$

then any assignment of delay intervals that satisfies the rate constraints at all the predecessors of C_j will violate the rate constraints at some process in C_j. Hence, the constraint set S is inconsistent. □

The preceding theorem gives us a characterization of a set of inconsistent rate constraints. Computing $I_j^\cap$ for all the SCCs in the process graph takes time linear in the size of the process graph. Hence, the first condition in this theorem can be checked in linear time. Also, the component graph can be constructed in linear time, and $I_j^{\min}$ can be computed by a topological traversal of the component graph. So, the second condition can also be checked in linear time. Thus, Theorem 5 yields a linear time algorithm for checking whether the specified rate constraints are consistent.

Example 5.1. Consider the process graph along with the constraint intervals for all the processes shown in Figure 7.

$$I_1^\cap = [0.5, 1.0] \cap [0.75, 12.0]$$
$$= [0.75, 1.0]$$
$$I_2^\cap = [10.0, 30.0] \cap [5.0, 25.0] \cap [7.0, 20.0]$$
$$= [10.0, 20.0].$$

Also,

$$I_1^{\min} = I_1^\cap = [0.75, 1.0],$$

and

$$I_2^{\min} = \min([0.75, 1.0], [10.0, 20.0]) = [0.75, 1.0].$$

216 CHAPTER 3: Analysis and Estimation

Since $[0.75, 1.0] < [10.0, 20.0]$, the given rate constraints are inconsistent due to Condition 2 in Theorem 5. More intuitively, the rate constraints on process p_1 force the constraint interval for SCC_1 to be at most 1. Furthermore, since the constraint intervals for all the processes in SCC_2 are strictly larger than 5, the constraint interval for SCC_2 has a lower bound of 5. Hence, Condition 2 in Theorem 5 is satisfied and the rate constraints are inconsistent. □

6. RATE CONSTRAINT DEBUGGING AND PROCESS REDESIGN

Our algorithms for rate analysis and for checking consistency of rate constraints can be used as part of a system for interactive debugging of embedded system designs. Figure 4 shows one such framework. The design specification is first translated from a high-level description to a process graph along with the associated sequencing graphs. First, the rate constraints are checked for consistency. If the rate constraints are consistent, rate analysis is performed on the process graph. If all the computed rate intervals are contained in the intervals defined by the rate constraints, then the system satisfies all the rate constraints and no redesign is required.

If a rate constraint is violated, the system gives the user the reasons for the violation along with the critical cycles responsible for the violation. This information can be used to redesign the processes that are involved in the critical cycles. If an upper bound rate constraint is violated for process p_i, then it means that p_i executes faster than required by the constraint. This situation is easier to remedy because additional delay can be introduced on some of the process graph edges to slow down the execution rate of p_i. In this case, the "best" places where additional delay can be introduced to avoid the constraint violation can be identified by the rate analysis program. If a lower bound rate constraint is violated, the program outputs all the critical cycles in the process graph that affect the rate at the process where the constraint violation occurs. Potential candidates for pipelining are identified by the self-loops in the critical cycles responsible for rate constraint violation. Pipelining will reduce the delay of the self-loop and possibly avoid the constraint violation. In general, the tool outputs the bottlenecks in the current design (in the form of critical cycles) and the designer then needs to redesign the processes involved to reduce the delay intervals on the edges involved in the critical cycles. In some cases it may even be necessary to alter the communication and synchronization between the component processes to change the topology of the process graph.

All our algorithms for checking the consistency of rate constraints and for rate analysis have been implemented in C++ as a tool called RATAN. The following example illustrates the utility of this interactive rate analysis framework in redesigning a system to meet specified rate constraints.

Example 6.1. Consider the process graph in Figure 8 containing 18 processes and 32 edges. The interval of real numbers on an edge is the delay interval associated with that edge. This process graph has 6 strongly connected components labeled C0, C2, ... C5, and grouped with a dashed circle. The darker lines between components are also edges in the process graph. Since the delay intervals on these edges are not used in rate analysis, they are not shown in the figure. There can be more than one edge between two components, but only one is enough to show the precedence relation between a pair of components. We now trace the steps involved in interactive rate analysis (as shown in Figure 4) on the process graph in Figure 8.

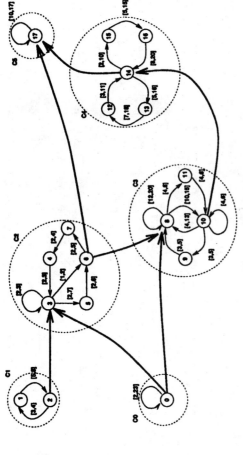

Fig. 8. Process graph used in Example 6.1.

(1) *Step 1: [Check if the given rate constraints are consistent].* For simplicity, Figure 8 does not show the rate constraints for each process. Suppose that the given rate constraints are consistent, and the constraint interval for C4 is $[0.05, 0.10]$ (this is the intersection of the constraint intervals of all the processes in C4).

(2) *Step 2: [Rate analysis].* Tables I and II give the computed rate bounds for each component before and after rate propagation. These tables also show the critical cycle(s) that determine a particular rate bound. Notice that the critical cycle that determines the lower bound can be different from the one that determines the upper bound (e.g., C2 in Table II). Also, after rate propagation, the cycles that determine the rate bound for a component may be contained in a predecessor of the component in the component graph.

(3) *Step 3: [Check if the computed rate constraints are satisfied].* The lower bound rate constraint for C4 is not satisfied since the computed rate interval is $[0.043, 0.083]$, and the constraint interval is $[0.05, 0.10]$. This means that we need to speed up some processes on the critical

Table I. Step 2: Before Rate Propagation

SCC	r_l	r_u	Critical cycle
C0	0.043	0.500	$0 \to 0$
C1	0.167	0.250	$1 \to 2 \to 1$
C2	0.200	0.500	$3 \to 5 \to 6 \to 7 \to 4 \to 3$
C3	0.050	0.083	$8 \to 8$
C4	0.067	0.200	$12 \to 14 \to 13 \to 12$
C5	0.059	0.100	$17 \to 17$

Table II. Step 2: After Rate Propagation

SCC	r_l	r_u	Critical cycle
C0	0.043	0.500	$0 \to 0$
C1	0.167	0.250	$1 \to 2 \to 1$
C2	0.043	0.250	$1 \to 2 \to 1$
C3	0.043	0.083	$8 \to 8$
C4	0.043	0.083	$8 \to 8$
C5	0.043	0.083	$8 \to 8$

Table III. Steps 4,5: Before Rate Propagation

SCC	r_l	r_u	Critical cycle
C0	0.050	0.500	$0 \to 0$
C1	0.167	0.250	$1 \to 2 \to 1$
C2	0.200	0.500	$3 \to 5 \to 6 \to 7 \to 4 \to 3$
C3	0.050	0.083	$8 \to 8$
C4	0.067	0.200	$12 \to 14 \to 13 \to 12$
C5	0.059	0.100	$17 \to 17$

Table IV. Steps 4,5: After Rate Propagation

SCC	r_l	r_u	Critical cycle
C0	0.050	0.500	$0 \to 0$
C1	0.167	0.250	$1 \to 2 \to 1$
C2	0.050	0.250	$1 \to 2 \to 1$
C3	0.05	0.083	$8 \to 8$
C4	0.05	0.083	$8 \to 8$
C5	0.05	0.083	$8 \to 8$

cycle that constrains the lower bound to be less than 0.05. Assume that all other rate constraints are satisfied.

(4) *Steps 2,3: [Pipeline a process in a critical cycle responsible for violating a rate constraint and re-do rate analysis].* The critical cycle that determines the rate lower bound of 0.043 for C4 is $0 \to 0$. This suggests that by speeding up process 0, we can avoid violation of the rate constraint. Indeed, if the process 0 is pipelined and the delay on the 0 $\to$ 0 self-loop is reduced to [2, 20], the rate interval for C4 becomes [0.05, 0.083] and the violated rate constraint is now satisfied. Tables III and IV show the rate intervals for the modified process graph (after pipelining process 0) before and after rate propagation, respectively.

(5) *Step 6: [Check if the computed rate constraints are satisfied].* We now check if all the rate constraints are satisfied. In this case, all the rate constraints are satisfied because the only effect of pipelining process 0 is to increase the rate lower bounds for components C0, C2, C3, C4, and C5. If there were still some violated rate constraints, we would have incrementally pipelined processes on critical paths to reduce delays on critical self-loops. If even pipelining fails to prevent constraint violation, more drastic redesign of the processes on the critical paths is needed. In fact, even the communication/synchronization patterns of the processes may need to be changed in order to alter the topology of the process graph.

This example illustrates that using our interactive rate analysis, we can explore bottlenecks in the current design and interactively modify the design to obtain one that satisfies all the rate constraints. Some of the modifications suggested by the interactive system are nontrivial to discover otherwise. For instance, to remove the constraint violation at C4 consisting of processes 12 through 16, process 0 needs to be pipelined.

7. CONCLUSIONS

In this article we have examined the problem of estimating execution rates of concurrent processes modeled as sequencing graphs that interact through process level synchronization. We show that the average execution rate can be efficiently computed using a relation between average execution rate and the critical cycles in the process graph. A linear time algorithm was developed for checking the consistency of a set of rate constraints. We have developed a tool, RATAN, for using our rate analysis algorithms for debugging violations of rate constraints.

Our future plans are to seek effective integration of RATAN in the design of embedded systems. Another interesting area of research is to study the rate analysis problem under more general timing semantics, such as allowing some processes to start executing as soon as they receive one enable signal, that is, OR causality. We also plan to study the rate analysis problem when enable vertices are allowed inside loops and conditional branches in sequencing graphs.

APPENDIX: PROOF OF THEOREM 1

In order to prove Theorem 1, we need a few preliminary results.

We define the *k-critical paths* for process p_i to be the paths whose delay determines $x_i(k)$. A *k-critical path* for p_i is a maximum delay path with exactly k edges ending at p_i. For any *k*-critical path $\pi: p_j = v_0, v_1, \ldots, v_k = p_i$, the *delay of the path* is

$$d(\pi) = x_j(0) + \sum_{l=0}^{k-1} \delta_{v_l v_{l+1}} = x_i(k).$$

For any cycle $C: p_j = v_0, v_1, v_2, \ldots, v_{k-1}, v_k = p_j$,

$$d'(C) = \sum_{l=0}^{k-1} \delta'_{v_l v_{l+1}}$$

$$= \sum_{l=0}^{k-1} (\delta_{v_l v_{l+1}} + x_{v_l}(0) - x_{l+1}(0))$$

$$= d(C) + \sum_{l=0}^{k-1} (x_{v_l}(0) - x_{v_{l+1}}(0))$$

$$= d(C) + (x_{v_0}(0) - x_{v_k}(0))$$

$$= d(C).$$

Since the delay of all the cycles remains unchanged, it is clear that the critical cycles and maximum mean cycle delay also remain unchanged. □

Henceforth, we assume that the transformation on edge delays in Lemma A.1 has been performed and the vector of initial start times is zero. The following three lemmas establish important characteristics of "sufficiently long" *k*-critical paths that enable us to prove the theorem establishing the relation between the average rate of execution and the maximum mean cycle delay of the process graph. In the following lemmas we assume that the process graph has m critical cycles: $C_1, C_2, \ldots, C_m$ each with mean delay λ.

LEMMA A.2. *A k-critical path, π, for process p_i that includes a vertex of a critical cycle C_j has less than $lcm(|C_j|, |C|)/|C|$ occurrences of any noncritical cycle C. Furthermore, there exists a k-critical path for p_i that has fewer than $lcm(|C_j|, |C'|)/|C'|$ occurrences of any cycle C' other than C_j.*

PROOF. Let S_j be the delay of the critical cycle C_j (this is the sum of the edge delays of the edges in C_j) and let S be the delay of the noncritical cycle C. Since C is not critical, its mean delay is less than that of C_j. Hence,

$$\frac{S_j}{|C_j|} > \frac{S}{|C|},$$

or

$$\frac{lcm(|C_j|, |C|) \cdot S_j}{|C_j|} > \frac{lcm(|C_j|, |C|) \cdot S}{|C|}. \tag{6}$$

Consider any path ending at p_i passing through a vertex of C_j that has more than $lcm(|C_j|, |C|)/|C|$ occurrences of C. Due to the relation in the

---

LEMMA A.1. *The k-critical paths for all processes remain unchanged when we change the delay on all the edges using the transformation $\delta'_{ij} = \delta_{ij} + x_i(0) - x_j(0)$ and the initial vector to $x'(0) = [00\ldots 0]$. Furthermore, this transformation also leaves the critical cycles and the maximum mean cycle delay in the process graph unchanged.*

PROOF. The length of a path $\pi: p_j = v_0, v_1, v_2, \ldots, v_k = p_i$ using the new edge costs is

$$d'(\pi) = \sum_{l=0}^{k-1} \delta'_{v_l v_{l+1}}$$

$$= \sum_{l=0}^{k-1} (\delta_{v_l v_{l+1}} + x_{v_l}(0) - x_{v_{l+1}}(0))$$

$$= \sum_{l=0}^{k-1} \delta_{v_l v_{l+1}} + x_j(0) - x_i(0)$$

$$= d(\pi) - x_i(0).$$

Since the length of all the paths ending at p_i gets decreased by $x_i(0)$, the set of *k*-critical paths remains unchanged.

inequality (6) we can replace $lcm(|C_j|, |C|)/|C|$ occurrences of C with $lcm(|C_j|, |C|)/|C|$ occurrences of C_j, with an accompanying increase in the total delay of the path. Notice that this replacement does not alter the total number of edges in the path. Consequently, a k-critical path for process p_i that contains a vertex of critical cycle C_j will have fewer than $lcm(|C_j|, |C|)/|C|$ occurrences of a noncritical cycle C.

Since we have already bounded the number of occurrences of noncritical cycles in π, we only need to show the existence of a k-critical path where the occurrences of critical cycles other than C_j are bounded. Let C' be another critical cycle in π with delay S'. Then,

$$\frac{S_j}{|C_j|} = \frac{S'}{|C'|},$$

or

$$\frac{lcm(|C_j|, |C'|) \cdot S_j}{|C_j|} = S_j = \frac{lcm(|C_j|, |C'|) \cdot S'}{|C'|}.$$

Hence, the path π' obtained by repeatedly replacing $lcm(|C_j|, |C'|)/|C'|$ occurrences of C' by $lcm(|C_j|, |C'|)/|C_j|$ occurrences of C_j, for all critical cycles C' in π has the same length and delay as π. Consequently, π' is a k-critical path for process p_i that has the property required in the lemma. □

A k-critical path that contains a bounded number of occurrences of all cycles except a critical cycle C_j is defined to be in *canonical form with respect to* C_j. Note that a k-critical path can be transformed to canonical form with respect to any of the critical cycles that it touches. The part of a k-critical path that is canonical with respect to C_j, which is not included in the complete occurrences of C_j, is referred to as the *stem* of the canonical k-critical path (see Figure 9). Note that the stem of a k-critical path that is canonical with respect to C_j has bounded length because it can have at most $|C_j| - 1$ occurrences of any cycle.

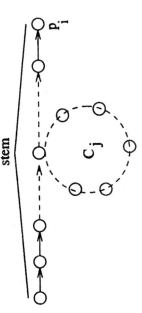

Fig. 9. Canonical path with critical cycle C_j.

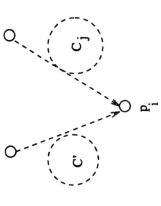

Fig. 10. Canonical paths with respect to a noncritical cycle C' and a critical cycle C_j ending at p_i.

LEMMA A.3. *There exists a constant N such that for $k \geq N$, there is a k-critical path for process p_i that is canonical with respect to some critical cycle C_j.*

PROOF. We first show that for sufficiently large k, the k-critical path for p_i will touch a critical cycle. Suppose there is no k-critical path for p_i that touches a critical cycle. Let π' be a k-critical path that uses only noncritical cycles. Let C' be the cycle with maximum mean delay used in π' and let $\lambda' < \lambda$ be its mean delay.

Using the result in Lemma A.2 applied to the path π, we claim that π must be canonical with respect to C'. Hence,

$$d(\pi') = w' + n' \cdot \lambda' \cdot |C'|,$$

where w' is the delay of the stem of π' and n' is the number of occurrences of C' in π'. Furthermore, if the length of the stem is l', then $k = l' + n' \cdot |C'|$.

Consider any critical cycle, C_j. Since the process graph is strongly connected there is a path from C_j to p_i. Consider the path π of length k consisting of n occurrences of C_j along with a stem of delay W and length l ending at p_i (see Figure 10). Then

$$d(\pi) = w + n \cdot \lambda \cdot |C_j|,$$

and $k = l + n \cdot |C_j|$. Now, $d(\pi) > d(\pi')$, if

$$n > \frac{w - w' + (l - l') \cdot \lambda'}{|C_j| \cdot (\lambda - \lambda')}.$$

Consequently, there exists a constant N such that for $k \geq N$, we get a contradiction to the claim that all the k-critical paths for p_i avoid all the critical cycles. Hence, for sufficiently large k, there is a k-critical path for p_i that touches a critical cycle C_j. Now, using Lemma A.2, we can claim

CHAPTER 3: Analysis and Estimation

that we can transform this k-critical path to one that is canonical with respect to C_j. □

Let $C_1, C_2, \ldots, C_m$ be the critical cycles in G_P and let $\mathcal{L} = lcm(|C_1|, |C_2|, \ldots, |C_m|)$.

LEMMA A.4. *For all $k \geq N$, there are k- and $(k+\mathcal{L})$-critical paths that are canonical with respect to the same critical cycle C_j and the stems of the canonical k- and $(k+\mathcal{L})$-critical paths are identical. Thus,*

$$x_i(k+\mathcal{L}) = x_i(k) + \mathcal{L} \cdot \lambda, \quad \forall k \geq N.$$

PROOF. From Lemma A.3 we know that for $k \geq N$, there exists a k-critical path for any process p_i in the process graph that is canonical with respect to some critical cycle C_j. Notice that the length of the stem of a canonical k-critical path is bounded (using the result of Lemma A.2). So, there are only a finite number of different stems. This observation plays a crucial role in this proof.

Consider a critical cycle C_r. Let $\pi_{k,r}$ be the longest path with k edges ending at p_i that is canonical with respect to C_r and let $\pi^s_{k,r}$ denote the stem of this canonical path. The canonical k-critical path for p_i is the longest of all these paths. Let $C_{\phi(j)}$ be the critical cycle with respect to which the k-critical path is canonical, where $k \equiv j \pmod{\mathcal{L}}$ and ϕ provides a mapping from j to a critical cycle (the justification for this mapping follows from this lemma). Consider $\pi_{k+L,r}$, the longest path with $k + \mathcal{L}$ edges that is canonical with respect to C_r. Since k is large, and the lengths of the stems $\pi^s_{k,r}$ and $\pi^s_{k+L,r}$ are bounded, any stem that is reachable from p_i in $k+\mathcal{L}$ steps is also reachable in k steps. Thus, if the stem $\pi^s_{k+L,r}$ has more delay than $\pi^s_{k,r}$, then we could replace the stem of $\pi_{k,r}$ by the stem of $\pi_{k+L,r}$ to obtain a new path with k edges and larger delay than $\pi_{k,r}$. This contradicts the definition of $\pi_{k,r}$. It follows that $\pi_{k,r}$ and $\pi_{k+L,r}$ have the same stem. Consequently,

$$d(\pi_{k+L,r}) = d(\pi_{k,r}) + \mathcal{L} \cdot \lambda.$$

Thus, if $C_{\phi(j)}$ is the critical cycle with respect to which the k-critical path is canonical, then the $(k+\mathcal{L})$-critical path will also be canonical with respect to $C_{\phi(j)}$ and as observed earlier both these paths have the same stem. Since the delays of these canonical critical paths determine $x_i(k)$ and $x_i(k+L)$, it follows that

$$x_i(k+\mathcal{L}) = x_i(k) + \mathcal{L} \cdot \lambda.$$

□

With the preceding results in hand, we are now ready to prove the theorem that shows that the average execution rate of processes is well defined irrespective of the initial vector of start times.

THEOREM A.1. *Consider a strongly connected process graph and let $x_i(k)$, $k \geq 0$ be the sequence of time instances at which process p_i executes. Then there exists some N such that the following are true.*

(1) *The sequence $x_i(k) - x_i(k-1)$, $k \geq N$ is periodic with period equal to L, where L is equal to the least common multiple of the lengths of all the critical cycles in the process graph.*

(2) *For any $q \geq N$,*

$$\frac{\sum_{j=q}^{q+\mathcal{L}-1} x_i(j+1) - x_i(j)}{\mathcal{L}} = \lambda,$$

where λ is the maximum mean cycle delay in the process graph.

(3) *The average interexecution time is well defined and*

$$T_i = \lim_{n \to \infty} \frac{\sum_{k=0}^{n-1} x_i(k+1) - x_i(k)}{n} = \lambda.$$

PROOF.

(1) From Lemma A.4 we know that for $k \geq N$, $x_i(k + \mathcal{L}) = x_i(k) + \mathcal{L} \cdot \lambda$ and $x_i(k+1+\mathcal{L}) = x_i(k+1) + \mathcal{L} \cdot \lambda$. Consequently,

$$x_i(k+1) - x_i(k) = x_i(k+1+\mathcal{L}) - x_i(k+\mathcal{L}).$$

Hence, the sequence of interexecution times for any process p_i is periodic with period equal to $\mathcal{L}$.

(2) When consecutive terms in the sequence of interexecution times are added, the sum telescopes; consequently,

$$\frac{\sum_{j=q}^{q+\mathcal{L}-1} x_i(j+1) - x_i(j)}{\mathcal{L}} = \frac{x_i(q+\mathcal{L}) - x_i(q)}{\mathcal{L}}$$

$$= \frac{\mathcal{L} \cdot \lambda}{\mathcal{L}}$$

$$= \lambda.$$

(3) Let W be the sum of the first N terms of the sequence of interexecution times. After the first N terms the sequence is periodic with period $\mathcal{L}$. Therefore,

$$\lim_{n \to \infty} \frac{\sum_{k=0}^{n-1} x_i(k+1) - x_i(k)}{n} = \lim_{t \to \infty} \frac{W + t \cdot \lambda \cdot \mathcal{L}}{N + t \cdot \mathcal{L}}$$

$$= \lim_{t \to \infty} \frac{W/t + \lambda \cdot \mathcal{L}}{N/t + \mathcal{L}}$$

$$= \lambda.$$

□

REFERENCES

BACELLI, F., COHEN, G., OLSDER, G. J., AND QUADRAT, J.-P. 1992. *Synchronization and Linearity*. Wiley, New York.

BURNS, S. M. AND MARTIN, A. J. 1991. Performance analysis and optimization of asynchronous circuits. In *Advanced Research in VLSI, Proceedings of the 1991 University of California/Santa Cruz Conference*, 71–86.

DE MICHELI, G. 1994. *Synthesis and Optimization of Digital Circuits*. McGraw-Hill, New York.

GUPTA, R. K. 1993. Co-synthesis of hardware and software for digital embedded systems. Ph.D. Thesis, Stanford University.

GUPTA, R. K. 1996. A framework for interactive analysis of timing constraints in embedded systems. In *Proceedings of the International Workshop on Hardware/Software Codesign* (Pittsburgh, PA, March), 44–51.

GUPTA, R. K. AND DE MICHELI, G. 1997. Specification and analysis of timing constraints for embedded systems. *IEEE Trans. CAD/ICAS 16*, 3, 240–256.

HULGAARD, H., BURNS, S. M., AMON, T., AND BORRIELLO, G. 1995. An algorithm for exact bounds on the time separation of events in concurrent systems. *IEEE Trans. Comput. 44*, 1306–1317.

KARP, R. M. 1978. A characterization of the minimum cycle mean in a digraph. *Discrete Math. 23*, 309–311.

MAGOTT, J. 1984. Performance evaluation of concurrent systems using Petri nets. *Inf. Process. Lett. 18*, 7–13.

MATHUR, A., DASDAN, A., AND GUPTA, R. K. 1996. Rate analysis for embedded systems. Tech. Rep. UIUCDCS-R-96-1952, University of Illinois.

OLSDER, G. J. 1989. Performance analysis of data-driven networks. In *Systolic Array Processors*, J. McCanny, J. McWhirter, and E. Swartzlander Jr, Eds. Prentice-Hall, Englewood Cliffs, NJ, 33–41.

RAMAMOORTHY, C. V. AND HO, G. S. 1980. Performance evaluation of asynchronous concurrent systems using Petri nets. *IEEE Trans. Softw. Eng. SE-6*, 5, 440–449.

REITER, R. 1968. Scheduling parallel computations. *J. ACM 15*, 4, 590–599.

Received February 1996; revised April 1997; accepted September 1997

Power Analysis of Embedded Software: A First Step Towards Software Power Minimization

Vivek Tiwari, Sharad Malik, and Andrew Wolfe

Abstract—Embedded computer systems are characterized by the presence of a dedicated processor and the software that runs on it. Power constraints are increasingly becoming the critical component of the design specification of these systems. At present, however, power analysis tools can only be applied at the lower levels of the design—the circuit or gate level. It is either impractical or impossible to use the lower level tools to estimate the power cost of the software component of the system. This paper describes the first systematic attempt to model this power cost. A power analysis technique is developed that has been applied to two commercial microprocessors—Intel 486DX2 and Fujitsu SPARClite 934. This technique can be employed to evaluate the power cost of embedded software. This can help in verifying if a design meets its specified power constraints. Further, it can also be used to search the design space in software power optimization. Examples with power reduction of up to 40%, obtained by rewriting code using the information provided by the instruction level power model, illustrate the potential of this idea.

I. Introduction

EMBEDDED COMPUTER systems are characterized by the presence of a dedicated processor which executes application specific software. Recent years have seen a large growth of such systems. This growth is driven by several factors. The first is an increase in the number of applications as illustrated by the numerous examples of "smart electronics" around us. A notable example is automobile electronics where embedded processors control each aspect of the efficiency, comfort and safety of the new generation of cars. The second factor leading to their growth is the increasing migration from application specific logic to application specific code running on existing processors. This in turn is driven by two distinct forces. The first is the increasing cost of setting up and maintaining a fabrication line. At over a billion dollars for a new line, the only components that make this affordable are high volume parts such as processors, memories and possibly FPGA's. Application specific logic is getting increasingly expensive to manufacture and is the solution only when speed constraints rule out programmable alternatives. The second force comes from the application houses, which are facing increased pressures to reduce the time to market as well as

Manuscript received June 15, 1994; revised August 23, 1994. The work of V. Tiwari was supported by an IBM Graduate Fellowship. The work of S. Malik was supported by an IBM Faculty Development Award.
The authors are with the Department of Electrical Engineering, Princeton University, Princeton, NJ 08540 USA.
IEEE Log Number 9406371.

to have predictable schedules. Both of these can be better met with software programmable solutions made possible by embedded systems. Thus, we are seeing a movement from the logic gate being the basic unit of computation on silicon, to an instruction running on an embedded processor.

A large number of embedded computing applications are power critical, i.e., power constraints form an important part of the design specification. This has led to a significant research effort in power estimation and low power design. However, there is very little available in the form of design tools to help embedded system designers evaluate their designs in terms of the power metric. At present, power measurement tools are available for only the lower levels of the design-at the circuit level and to a limited extent at the logic level. At the least these are very slow and impractical to use to evaluate the power consumption of embedded software, and often cannot even be applied due to lack of availability of circuit and gate level information of the embedded processors. The embedded processors currently used in designs take two possible shapes. The first is "off the shelf" microprocessors or digital signal processors (DSP's). The second is in the form of embedded cores which can be incorporated in a larger silicon chip along with program/data memory and other dedicated logic. In the first case, the processor information available to the designer is whatever the manufacturer cares to make available through data books. In the second case, the designer has logic/timing simulation models to help verify the designs. In neither case is there lower level information available for power analysis.

This paper describes a power analysis technique for embedded software. The goal of this research is to present a methodology for developing and validating an instruction level power model for any given processor. Such a model can then be provided by the processor vendors for both off the shelf processors as well as embedded cores. This can then be used to evaluate embedded software, much as a gate level power model has been used to evaluate logic designs. The technique has so far been applied to two commercial microprocessors—the Intel 486DX2 and the Fujitsu SPARClite 934. This paper uses the former as a basis for illustrating the technique. The application of this technique for the latter is described in [9]. The ability to evaluate software in terms of the power metric helps in verifying if a design meets its specified power constraints. In addition, it can also be used to search the design space in software power optimization. Examples with power reduction of up to 40% on the 486DX2, obtained by rewriting code using the information provided by the instruction level power model, illustrate the potential of this idea.

II. EXPERIMENTAL METHOD

The power consumption in microprocessors has been a subject of intense study lately. Attempts to model the power consumption in processors often adopt a "bottom-up" approach. Using detailed physical layouts and sophisticated power analysis tools, isolated power models are built for each of the internal modules of the processor. The total power consumption of the processor is then estimated using these individual models. No systematic attempt, however, has been made to relate the power consumption of the processor to the software that executes on it. Thus, while it is generally recognized that the power consumption of a processor varies from program to program, there is a complete lack of models and tools to analyze this variation. This is also the reason why the potential for power reduction through modification of software is so far unknown and unexploited. The goal of our work is to overcome these deficiencies by developing a methodology that would provide a means for analyzing the power consumption of a processor as it executes a given program. We want to provide a method that makes it possible to talk about the "power/energy cost of a given program on a given processor." This would make it possible to very accurately evaluate the power cost of the programmable part of an embedded system.

We propose the following hypothesis that forms the basis for meeting the above goal: *By measuring the current drawn by the processor as it repeatedly executes certain instructions or certain short instruction sequences, it is possible to obtain most of the information that is needed to evaluate the power cost of a program for that processor.*

The intuition that guides this hypothesis is as follows: Modern microprocessors are extremely complex systems consisting of several interacting functional blocks. However, this internal complexity is hidden behind a simple interface—the instruction set. Thus to model the energy consumption of this complex system, it seems intuitive to consider individual instructions. Further, each instruction involves specific processing across various units of the processor. This can result in circuit activity that is characteristic of each instruction and can vary with instructions. If a given instruction is executed repeatedly, then the power consumed by the processor can be thought of as the power cost of that instruction. In a given program, certain inter-instruction effects also occur, such as the effect of circuit state, pipeline stalls and cache misses. Repeatedly executing certain instruction sequences during which these effects occur may provide a way to isolate the power cost of these effects. Thus the sum of the power costs of the each instruction that is executed in a program enhanced by the power cost of the inter-instruction effects can be an estimate for the power cost of the program.

The above hypothesis, however, is of no use until it is validated. We have empirically validated the hypothesis for two commercial microprocessors using actual physical measurements of the current drawn by them. The validation of the hypothesis, and based on it, the derivation of the parameters of an instruction level power model for the Intel 486DX2, is the subject of the next few sections.

Given that the above hypothesis has been validated for two processors using physical measurements, there is an alternative way for deriving the parameters of the instruction level power model. Instead of physically measuring the current drawn by the CPU, it can be estimated using accurate, simulation based power analysis tools. The execution of the given instruction/instruction sequence is simulated on lower level (circuit or layout) models of the CPU, and the power analysis tool provides an estimate of the current drawn. The advantage of this method is that since detailed internal information of the CPU is available, it may be possible to relate the power cost of the instructions to the micro-architecture of the CPU. This could provide cues to the CPU designer for optimizing the designs for low power.

However, in the case of embedded system design, detailed layout information of the CPU is often not available to the designer of the system. Even if it is available, the simulation based tools and techniques are expensive and difficult to apply. A methodology based on laboratory measurements, like the one described below, is inexpensive and practical, and often may be the only option available. Given a setup to measure the current being drawn by the microprocessor, the only other information required can be obtained from the widely available manuals and handbooks specific to that microprocessor. The specifics of the measurement methodology are described next.

A. Power and Energy

The average power consumed by a microprocessor while running a certain program is given by: $P = I \times V_{CC}$, where P is the average power, I is the average current and V_{CC} is the supply voltage. Since power is the rate at which energy is consumed, the energy consumed by a program is given by: $E = P \times T$, where T is the execution time of the program. This in turn is given by: $T = N \times \tau$, where N is the number of clock cycles taken by the program and τ is the clock period.

In common usage the terms power consumption and energy consumption are often interchanged, as has been done in the above discussion. However it is important to distinguish between the two in the context of programs running on mobile applications. Mobile systems run on the limited energy available in a battery. Therefore the energy consumed by the system or by the software running on it determines the length of the battery life. Energy consumption is thus the focus of attention. We will attempt to maintain a distinction between the two terms in the rest of the paper. However, in certain cases the term power may be used to refer to energy, in adherence to common usage.

B. Current Measurement

For this study, the processor used was a 40 MHz Intel 486DX2-S Series CPU. The CPU was part of a mobile personal computer evaluation board with 4 MB of DRAM memory. The reason for the choice of this processor was that its board setup allowed the measurement of the CPU and

DRAM subsystem current in isolation from the rest of the system. *We would like to emphasize that while the numbers we report here are specific to this processor and board, the methodology used by us in developing the model is widely applicable.* The current was measured through a standard off the shelf, dual-slope integrating digital ammeter. Execution time of programs was measured through detection of specific bus states using a logic analyzer.

If a program completes execution in a short time, a current reading cannot be obtained visually. To overcome this, the programs being considered were put in infinite loops and current readings were taken. The current consumption in the CPU will vary in time depending on what instructions are being executed. But since the chosen ammeter averages current over a window of time (100 ms), if the execution time of the program is much less than the width of this window, a stable reading will be obtained.

The main limitation of this approach is that it will not work for programs with larger execution times since the ammeter may not show a stable reading. However, in this study, the main use of this approach was in determining the current drawn while a particular instruction (instruction sequence) was being executed. A program written with several instances of the targeted instruction (instruction sequence) executing in a loop, has a periodic current waveform which yields a steady reading on the ammeter. This inexpensive approach works very well for this. However, the main concepts described in this paper are independent of the actual method used to measure average current. If sophisticated data acquisition based measurement instruments are available, the measurement method can be based on them.

For our setup, V_{CC} was 3.3 V and τ was 25 ns, corresponding to the 40 MHz internal frequency of the CPU. Thus, if the average current for an instruction sequence is I A, and the number of cycles it takes to execute is N, the energy cost of the sequence is given by: $E = I \times V_{CC} \times N \times \tau$, which equals: $(8.25 \times 10^{-8} \times I \times N)$ J. Throughout the rest of the paper, in order to specify the energy cost of an instruction (instruction sequence), the average current will be specified. The number of cycles will either be explicitly specified, or will be clear from the context.

III. INSTRUCTION LEVEL MODELING

Based on the hypothesis described in Section II, an instruction level energy model has been developed and validated for the 486DX2. Under this model each instruction in the instruction set is assigned a fixed energy cost called the *base energy cost*. The variation in base costs of a given instruction due to different operand and address values is then quantified. The base energy cost of a program is based on the sum of the base energy costs of each executed instruction. However, during the execution of a program, certain inter-instruction effects occur whose energy contribution is not accounted for if only base costs are considered. The first type of inter-instruction effect is the effect of circuit state. The second type is related to resource constraints that can lead to stalls and cache misses. The energy cost of these effects is also modeled and used to obtain the total energy cost of a program.

Fig. 1. Internal pipelining in the 486DX2

The instruction-level energy model described here is based on actual measurements and evolved as a result of extensive experimentation. The various components of this model are described in the subsections below.

A. Base Energy Cost

The base cost for an instruction is determined by constructing a loop with several instances of the same instruction. The average current being drawn is then measured. This current multiplied by the number of cycles taken by each instance of the instruction is proportional to the total energy as described in Section II.

While this method seems intuitive if the CPU executes only one instruction at a given time, most modern CPU's, including the 486DX2, process more than one instruction at a given time due to pipelining. However, the following discussion shows that the concept of a base energy cost per instruction and its derivation remains unchanged.

The 486DX2 CPU has a five-stage pipeline as shown in Fig. 1 [6]. Let Ej_{I_k} be the average energy consumed by pipeline stage j, when instruction I_k executes in that stage. Pipeline stages are separated from each other by latches. Thus, if we ignore the effect of circuit state and resource constraints for now, the energy consumption of different stages is independent of each other. Let us assume that in a given cycle, instruction I_1 is being processed by stage 1, I_2 by stage 2, and so on. The total energy consumed by the CPU in that cycle would be: $E_{\text{cycle}} = E1_{I_1} + E2_{I_2} + E3_{I_3} + E4_{I_4} + E5_{I_5}$. On the other hand, the total energy consumed by a given instruction I_1, as it moves through the various stages is: $E_{\text{ins}} = \sum_j Ej_{I_1}$. This quantity actually refers to the base cost in the sense described above. Our method of forming a loop of instances of instruction I_1, results in $E_{\text{cycle}} = E_{\text{ins}}$, since in that case, $I_1 = I_2 = I_3 = I_4 = I_5$. The average current in this case is $\sum_j Ej_{I_1}/(V_{CC} \times \tau)$, which is the same as the ammeter reading obtained.

Some instructions take multiple cycles in a given pipeline stage. All stages are then stalled. The reasoning applied above, however, remains unchanged. The base energy cost of the instruction is just the observed average current value multiplied by the number of cycles taken by the instruction in that stage. For instance, consider a loop of instruction I_1, where I_1 takes m cycles in the 4th stage. Therefore, $E4_{I_1}$ is spread over m cycles. Energy consumption in any of the stalled stages can be considered as a part of $E4_{I_1}$. Then the current value observed on the ammeter will be $\sum_j Ej_{I_1}/(V_{CC} \times \tau \times m)$. This quantity multiplied by m yields $\sum_j Ej_{I_1}/(V_{CC} \times \tau)$, the base energy cost of the instruction. m represents the "number of cycles" parameter specified in instruction timing tables in microprocessor manuals.

TABLE I
SUBSET OF THE BASE COST TABLE FOR THE 486DX2[1]

Number	Instruction	Current (mA)	Cycles
1	NOP	275.7	1
2	MOV DX,BX	302.4	1
3	MOV DX,[BX]	428.3	1
4	MOV DX,[BX][DI]	409.0	2
5	MOV [BX],DX	521.7	1
6	MOV [BX][DI],DX	451.7	2
7	ADD DX,BX	313.6	1
8	ADD DX,[BX]	400.1	2
9	ADD [BX],DX	415.7	3
10	SAL BX,1	300.8	3
11	SAL BX,CL	306.5	3
12	LEA DX,[BX]	364.4	1
13	LEA DX,[BX][DI]	345.2	2
14	JMP label	373.0	3
15	JZ label	375.7	3
16	JZ label	355.9	1
17	CMP BX,DX	298.2	1
18	CMP [BX],DX	388.0	2

TABLE II
BASE COSTS OF MOV BX, DATA

data	0	0F	0FF	0FFF	0FFFF
No. of 1's	0	4	8	12	16
Current(mA)	309.5	305.2	300.1	294.2	288.5

Table I is a sample table of CPU base costs for some 486DX2 instructions. The numbers in Column 3 are the observed average current values. The overall base energy cost of an instruction is the product of the numbers in Columns 3 and 4 and the constants V_{CC} and τ. A rigorous confidence interval was not determined for the current measurement apparatus. However, it was observed that repeated runs of an experiment at different times resulted in only a very small variation in the observed average current values. The variation was in the range of ±1 mA.

Care should be taken in designing the experiments used to determine the base costs. The loops that are used to determine the base costs of instructions have to satisfy certain size constraints. As more of the target instructions are put in the loop, the impact of the branch statement at the bottom of the loop is minimized. The observed current value thus converges with increasing loop size. Thus, the loop size should be large enough in order to obtain the converged value. Very large loops, on the other hand, may cause cache misses, which are undesirable during determination of base costs. A loop size of 120, which satisfies both the above constraints, was chosen. Only the target instructions should execute on the CPU during experiments, and thus system effects like multiple time-sharing applications and interrupts cannot be allowed during the experiments.

Variations in Base Cost: As Table I shows, instructions with differing functionality and different addressing modes can have very different energy costs. This is to be expected since different functional blocks are being affected in different ways by these instructions. Within the same family of instructions, there is variability in base costs depending on the value of operands used. For example, consider the MOV

[1] All instructions are executed in "Real Mode". All registers contain 0, except in entry 11, where CL contains 1. Entry 15 is a "taken" jump while entry 16 is "fall through". Entries 5, 6, and 9 show *normalized* costs [11].

register,immediate family. Use of different *registers* results in insignificant variation since the register file is probably a symmetric structure. Variation in the *immediate* value, however, leads to measurable variation. For example, for MOV BX, *immediate*, the costs seem to be almost a linear function of the number of 1's in the binary representation of the immediate data—the more the 1's, the lesser the cost. Table II illustrates this through some sample values. Similarly, for the ADD instruction, the base costs are a function of the two numbers being added. The range of variation in all cases, however, is small. It is observed to be about 14 mA, which corresponds to less than a 5% variation.

For instructions involving memory operands, there is a variation in the base cost depending upon the address of the operand. The variation is of two kinds. The first is due to operands that are misaligned [6]. Mis-aligned accesses lead to cycle penalties and thus energy penalties that are added to the base cost. Within aligned accesses there is variation in the base cost depending upon the value of the address. For example, for MOV DX, [BX], the base cost can be greater than the cost shown in Table I by about 3.5%. This variation is a function of the number of, and position of, 1's in the binary representation of the address.

Given the operand value and address, exact base costs can be obtained through direct measurements. However, these exact values will be of little use since typically a data or address value can be known only at run-time. Thus, from the point of view of program energy cost estimation, the only alternative is to use average base cost values. This is reasonable given that the variation in base costs is small and thus the discrepancy between the average and actual values will be limited.

B. Inter-Instruction Effects

When sequences of instructions are considered, certain inter-instruction effects come into play, which are not reflected in the cost computed solely from base costs. These effects are discussed below.

Effect of Circuit State: The switching activity in a circuit is a function of the present inputs and the previous state of the circuit. Thus, it can be expected that the actual energy cost of executing an instruction in a program may be different from the instruction's base cost. This is because the previous instruction in the given program and in the program used for base cost determination may be different. For example, consider a loop of the following pair of instructions:

XOR BX,1
ADD AX, DX

The base costs of the XOR and ADD instructions are 319.2 mA and 313.6 mA. The expected base cost of the pair, using the individual base costs would be their average, i.e., 316.4

TABLE III
AN EXAMPLE INSTRUCTION SEQUENCE

Number	Instruction	Current(mA)	Cycles
1	MOV CX,1	309.6	1
2	ADD AX,BX	313.6	1
3	ADD DX,8[BX]	400.2	2
4	SAL AX,1	308.3	3
5	SAL BX,CL	306.5	3

mA, while the actual cost is 323.2 mA. It is greater by 6.8 mA. The reason is that the base costs are determined while executing the same instruction again and again. Thus each instruction executes in what we expect is a context of least change. At least, that is what the observations consistently seem to indicate. When a pair of two different instructions is considered, the context is one of greater change. The cost of a pair of instructions is always greater than the base cost of the pair and the difference is termed as the *circuit state overhead*.

As another example, consider the sequence of instructions shown in Table III. The current cost and the number of cycles of each instruction is listed alongside. The measured cost for this sequence is 332.8 mA (avg. current over 10 cycles). Using base costs we get:

$$(309.6 + 313.6 + 400.2 \times 2 + 308.3 \times 3 + 306.5 \times 3)/10$$
$$= 326.8 \qquad (1)$$

The circuit state overhead is thus 6.0 mA.

It is possible to get a closer estimate if we consider the circuit state overhead between each pair of consecutive instructions. This is done as follows. Consider a loop of the targeted pair, e.g., instructions 2 and 3. The estimated cost for the pair is $(2 \times 400.2 + 313.6 \times 1)/3 = 371.3$ mA, while the measured cost is 374.8 mA. Thus, the circuit state overhead is 3.5 mA. Now the overhead occurs twice in every 3 cycles, once between instructions 2 & 3, and once between 3 & 2. Since these two different cases cannot be resolved, let us assume that they are the same. Thus, the overhead each time it occurs would be $3.5 \times \frac{3}{2} = 5.25$ mA. Similarly, the overhead between the pairs 1 and 2, 3 and 4, 4 and 5, and 5 and 1 is found to be 17.9, 12.25, 3.3, and 17.2 mA, respectively. When these overheads are added to the numerator in (1), we get an estimated cost of 332.38 mA, which is within 0.12% of the measured value.

This example illustrates that by determining costs of pairs of instructions, it is possible to improve upon the results of the estimation obtained with base costs alone. However, extensive experiments with pairs of instructions revealed that the circuit state overhead has a limited range—between 5.0 mA and 30.0 mA and most frequently occurred in the vicinity of 15.0 mA. This motivates an efficient yet fairly accurate way to account for the circuit state overhead. Calculate the average current for the program using the base costs. Then, add 15.0 mA to it, to account for circuit state overhead.

A specific manifestation of the effect of circuit state is the effect of switching that occurs on address and data lines. Our experiments revealed that the overall impact of this effect was small. For back-to-back data reads from the cache, greater switching of the address values led to at most a 3% increase in the energy cost. For back-to-back data writes (which go to both the cache and the memory bus since the cache is write-through), the impact of greater switching of the address values was less than 5%.

The limited variation in the circuit state overhead is contrary to popular belief. In fact, a recent work [8], talks about scheduling instructions to reduce this overhead. But as our experiments reveal, the methods described in this work will not have much impact for the 486DX2. The probable explanation for the limited variation in circuit state overhead is that a major part of the circuit activity in a complex processor like the 486DX2, is common to all instructions, e.g., instruction prefetch, pipeline control, clocks etc. While the circuit state may cause significant variation within certain modules, its impact on the overall energy cost is swamped by the much greater common cost. However, we would not like to rule out the impact of circuit state overhead for all processors. It may well be the case that it is a significant part of the energy consumption in processors like RISC's (Reduced Instruction Set Computers) DSP's, and processors with complex power management features. An investigation of this issue is the subject of our future study.

Effect of Resource Constraints: Resource constraints in the CPU can lead to stalls e.g. pipeline stalls and write buffer stalls [6], [7]. These can be considered as another kind of inter-instruction effect. They cause an increase in the number of cycles needed to execute a sequence of instructions. For example, a sequence of 120 MOV DX, [BX] instructions takes about 164 cycles to execute, instead of 120 due to prefetch buffer stalls. While determining the base cost of instructions, it is important to avoid stalls, since they represent a condition that ought not to be reflected in the base cost. Thus, for MOV DX, [BX] a sequence consisting of 3 MOV instructions followed by a NOP is used since there are no stalls during its execution [7]. Knowing the cost of the NOP and the measured value for the sequence, the base cost of the MOV is determined.

The energy cost of each kind of stall is experimentally determined through experiments that isolate the particular kind of stall. For example, an average cost of 250 mA for stall cycles was determined for the prefetch buffer stall.

It has been observed that the cost of stalls can show some variation depending upon the instructions involved in the stall. Through extensive experimentation it may be possible to subdivide each stall type into specific cases and to assign a cost to each case. However, in general, the use of a single average cost value for each stall type suffices.

To account for the energy cost of the above stalls during program cost estimation, the number of stall cycles has to be multiplied by the experimentally determined stall energy cost. This product is then added to the base cost of the program. The number of stall cycles is estimated through a traversal of the program code.

Effect of Cache Misses: Another inter-instruction effect is the effect of cache misses. The instruction timings listed in manuals give the cycle count assuming a cache hit. For a cache miss, a certain cycle penalty has to be added to the instruction execution time. Along the same lines, the base costs for instructions with memory operands are determined in the context of cache hits. A cache miss will lead to extra cycles being consumed, which leads to an energy penalty. For experimentation purposes, a cache miss scenario is created by accessing memory addresses in an appropriate order. An average penalty of 216 mA for cache miss cycles has been experimentally obtained. This has to be multiplied by the average number of miss penalty cycles to get the average energy penalty for one miss. The average penalty multiplied by the cache miss rate is added to the base cost estimate to account for the cache misses during execution of a program.

IV. Estimation Framework

In this section we describe a framework for energy estimation of programs using the instruction level power model outlined in the previous section. We start by illustrating this estimation process for the program shown in Table IV. The program has three basic blocks as shown in the figure[2]. The average current and the number of cycles for each instruction are provided in two separate columns. For each basic block, the two columns are multiplied and the products are summed up over all instructions in the basic block. This yields a value that is proportional to the base energy cost of one instance of the basic block. The values are 1713.4, 4709.8, and 2017.9, for B1, B2, and B3, respectively. B1 is executed once, B2 4 times and B3 once. The `jmp main` statement has been inserted to put the program in an infinite loop. Cost of the `jl L2` statement is not included in the cost of B2 since its cost is different depending on whether the jump is taken or not. It is taken 3 times and not taken once. Multiplying the base cost of each basic block by the number of times it is executed and adding the cost of the unconditional jump `jl L2`, we get a number proportional to the total energy cost of the program. Dividing it by the estimated number of cycles (72) gives us an average current of 369.1 mA. Adding the circuit state overhead offset value of 15.0 mA we get 384.0 mA. The actual measured average current is 385.0 mA. This program does not have any stalls and thus no further additions to the estimated cost are required. If in the real execution of this program, some cold-start cache misses are expected, their energy overhead will have to be added.

To validate the estimation model described in the previous section, experiments were conducted with several programs. A close correspondence between the estimated and measured cost was obtained. It was observed that the main reasons for the discrepancy in the estimated and actual cost are as follows: First, for instructions that require operands, the operand values and addresses are often not known until runtime. Thus, average base costs may have to be used instead of exact costs. Second, the circuit state overhead for pairs of consecutive instructions in the program may differ from the default value used. Third,

---

[2] A basic block is defined as a contiguous section of code with exactly one entry and exit point.

TABLE IV
ILLUSTRATION OF THE ESTIMATION PROCESS

Program	Current(mA)	Cycles
; Block B1		
main:		
mov bp,sp	285.0	1
sub sp,4	309.0	1
mov dx,0	309.8	1
mov word ptr -4[bp],0	404.8	2
;Block B2		
L2:		
mov si,word ptr -4[bp]	433.4	1
add si,si	309.0	1
add si,si	309.0	1
mov bx,dx	285.0	1
mov cx,word ptr _a[si]	433.4	1
add bx,cx	309.0	1
mov si,word ptr _b[si]	433.4	1
add bx,si	309.0	1
mov dx,bx	285.0	1
mov di,word ptr -4[bp]	433.4	1
inc di, 1	297.0	1
mov word ptr -4[bp],di	560.1	1
cmp di,4	313.1	1
jl L2	405.7(356.9)	3(1)
;Block B3		
L1:		
mov word ptr _sum,dx	521.7	1
mov sp,bp	285.0	1
jmp main	403.8	3

the penalty due to stalls and cache misses is difficult to predict statically. As discussed in Section III, the first two effects are limited in their impact on the overall cost. The inability to predict the penalty due to stalls and cache misses, on the other hand, can potentially have a greater impact on the accuracy of the estimate. However, for programs with no stalls and cache misses, the maximum difference between the estimated and the measured cost was less than 3% of the measured cost.

A. Overall Flow

The overall flow of the estimation procedure is shown in Fig. 2. Given an assembly or machine level program, it is first split up into basic blocks. The base cost of each instance of the basic block is determined by adding up the base costs of the instructions in the block. These costs are provided in a base cost table. The energy overhead due to pipeline, write buffer and other stalls is estimated for each basic block and added to the basic block cost. Next, the number of times each basic block is executed has to be determined. This depends on the path that the program follows and is dynamic, run-time information that is obtained from a program profiler. Given this information, each basic block is multiplied by the number of times it will be executed. The circuit state overhead is added to the overall sum at this stage, or alternatively, it could have been determined for each basic block using a table of energy costs for pairs of instructions. An estimated cache penalty is added to get the final estimate. The cache penalty overhead

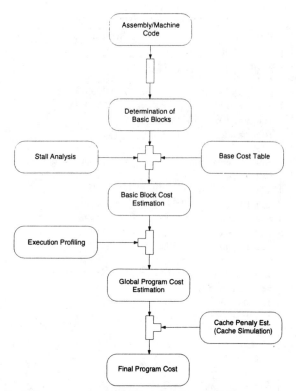

Fig. 2. Software energy consumption estimation methodology.

computation needs an estimate of the miss ratio, which is obtained through a cache simulator.

V. MEMORY SYSTEM MODELING

The energy consumption in the memory system is also a function of the software being executed. The salient observations regarding the DRAM system current on our experimental setup are briefly described here. Details are provided in [11].

The DRAM system draws constant current when no memory access is taking place. This current value was determined to be 77.0 mA or 5.3 mA, depending on whether page mode was active or not.[3] Greater current is drawn during a memory access. The exact value of this current depends on the address of the present and previous memory access. For example, for writes, when both the previous and the present access map to the same page, i.e., for a page hit, the cost is 122.8 mA (for 3 cycles including 1 wait state). For a page miss, the cost is 247.8 mA (for 6 cycles including 4 wait states). For page hits, a smaller variation was observed depending on the number of bits that change from the previous address to the present.

Let X be the sum of the energy costs of each individual memory access. Let n and m be the number of memory idle cycles during which the page mode is active and inactive, respectively. The total memory system energy cost is given by, $(X + (77.0 \times n + 5.3 \times m) \times 8.25 \times 10^{-8})J$. As discussed above, the quantity X depends on the location and sequence of memory accesses made by the program. Along with n and m, this is dynamic, run-time information, which can only

[3] "Page mode active" refers to the condition when the row address has been latched and the Row Address Strobe (RAS) signal is active.

be loosely estimated by static analysis. Thus, modeling of memory system energy consumption is difficult if only static analysis is used. However, as the above discussion shows, analysis of this consumption is feasible. This is significant, given that for systems with tight energy budgets, it is important to understand all sources of energy consumption.

VI. SOFTWARE POWER OPTIMIZATION

In recent years there has been a spurt of research activity targeted at reducing the energy consumption in systems. This research, however, has by and large not recognized the potential energy savings achievable through optimization of software. This was mainly due to the lack of practical techniques for analyzing the energy consumption of programs. This deficiency has been alleviated by the measurement and estimation methodology described in the previous sections. The growing trend towards tight energy budgets necessitates identification and exploration of every possible source of energy reduction, forcing us to examine the design of energy efficient software.

The energy formula described in Section II-A shows that the energy cost of a program is proportional to the product of the average current and the running time of the program. Thus, the value of this product has to be reduced in order to reduce the energy cost. This section examines some alternatives for this, in the context of the 486DX2, using the results of the instruction level analysis that was described earlier.

A. Instruction Reordering

A recent work [8] presents a technique for scheduling instructions on an experimental RISC processor in such a way that the switching on the control path is minimized. In terms of the energy formula, this technique is trying to reduce the average current for the program through instruction reordering.

Our experiments based on actual energy measurements on the 486DX2, however, reveal that this technique does not translate into very significant overall energy reduction. This technique is trying to reduce what we termed as the circuit state overhead. As we saw earlier, this quantity is bounded by a small range and does not show a great amount of variation. In fact, it was observed that different reorderings of several sequences of instructions showed a variation of only up to 2% in their current cost. It can be concluded that this technique is not very effective for the 486DX2. However, its effectiveness on other architectures and processors should be investigated further.

B. Generation of Energy Efficient Code

While reordering of a given set of instructions in a piece of code may have only a limited impact on the energy cost, the actual choice of instructions in the generated code can significantly affect the cost. As a specific example, an inspection of the energy costs of 486DX2 instructions reveals that instructions with memory operands have very high average current compared to instructions with register operands. Instructions using only register operands cost in the vicinity of 300 mA. Memory reads that hit the cache cost upwards of 430

TABLE V
RESULTS OF ENERGY OPTIMIZATION OF SORT AND CIRCLE

Program	hlcc.asm	hht1.asm	hht2.asm	hht3.asm
Avg. Current (mA)	525.7	534.2	507.6	486.6
Execution Time (μsec)	11.02	9.37	8.73	7.07
Energy ($10^{-6} J$)	19.12	16.52	14.62	11.35
Program	clcc.asm	cht1.asm	cht2.asm	cht3.asm
Avg. Current (mA)	530.2	527.9	516.3	514.8
Execution Time (μsec)	7.18	5.88	5.08	4.93
Energy ($10^{-6} J$)	12.56	10.24	8.65	8.37

mA. Memory writes cost upwards of 530 mA and also incur a memory system current cost since the cache is write-through. Thus, reduction in the number of memory operands can lead to a reduction in average current.

The reduction in energy cost, i.e., in the product of average current and running time would be greater still, since use of memory operands incurs more cycles. For example, ADD DX, [BX] takes two cycles, even in the case of a cache hit, while ADD DX, BX takes just one cycle. Potential pipeline stalls, misaligned accesses, and cache misses, further add to the running time. Reduction in number of memory operands can be achieved by adopting suitable code generation policies, e.g. saving the least amount of context during function calls. However, the most effective way of reducing memory operands is through better utilization of registers. This entails techniques akin to optimal global register allocation of temporaries and frequently used variables [1] [2].

The impact of the above ideas on the energy cost of programs is illustrated here using examples. The first program considered is a *heapsort* program in C, called "sort" [3]. hlcc.asm is the assembly code for this program generated by lcc, an ANSI C compiler [4]. The sum of the observed average CPU and memory currents is given in the table above. The program execution times and overall energy costs are also reported. lcc is a general purpose compiler and while it produces good code, it leaves room for further improvement of running time. Hand tuning of the code for shorter running time (hht1) leads to a 15% reduction in running time. The average current goes up a little since of all the instructions that were eliminated, a greater proportion had lower average currents. However, due to the reduction in running time, the overall energy cost goes down by 13.5%. So far only temporary variables had been allocated to registers. In hht2, 3 local variables are allocated to registers and the appropriate memory operands are replaced by register operands. Even though redundant instructions are not removed, there is a 5% reduction in current and a 7% reduction in running time. In hht3, 2 more local variables are allocated to registers and all redundant instructions are removed. Compared to hlcc, hht3 has 40.6% lower energy consumption. Results for another program derived from the circle program [5] are also shown in Table V. Significant energy reduction, about 33%, are observed for this program too.

The specific optimizations used in the above examples were prompted by the results of the instruction level analysis of the 486DX2. They are discussed in greater detail in [10]. In general, the ideas used for energy efficient code for one processor may not hold for another. An instruction level analysis, using the methodology described earlier, should therefore be performed for each processor under consideration. That methodology provides a way for assigning energy costs to instructions. The idea behind energy driven code generation is to select instructions using these costs, such that the overall energy cost of a program is minimized. An investigation of this issue for different architectural styles will be pursued further as part of research in the area of software power optimization.

VII. ANALYSIS OF SPARClite 934

The previous sections describe the application of the power analysis methodology for the 486DX2, a CISC processor. To verify the general applicability of this methodology, it was decided to apply the methodology to a processor with a different architectural style. The Fujitsu SPARClite 934, a RISC processor targeted for embedded applications was chosen for this purpose. A power analysis of this processor has been performed using the measurement and experimentation techniques described in the previous sections. The basic model of a base energy cost per instruction, enhanced by the inter-instruction effects remains valid for this processor, though the actual costs differ in value. The details of this analysis are described in [9].

VIII. SUMMARY AND FUTURE WORK

This paper presents a methodology for analyzing the energy consumption of embedded software. It is based on an instruction level model that quantifies the energy cost of individual instructions and of the various inter-instruction effects. The motivation for the analysis methodology is threefold. It provides insights into the energy consumption in processors. It can be used to help verify if an embedded design meets its energy constraints and it can also be used to guide the design of embedded software such that it meets these constraints. Initial attempts at code re-writing demonstrate significant power reductions—justifying the motivation for such a power analysis technique.

The methodology has so far been applied to two commercial processors, a CISC and a RISC. Future work will extend this to other architecture styles to characterize and contrast their energy consumption models. DSPs, superscalar processors, and processors with internal power management will be considered. Finally, we hope to use this analysis in automatic techniques for the reduction of power consumption in embedded software.

ACKNOWLEDGMENT

We would like to thank D. Singh, S. Rajgopal, and T. Rossi of Intel for providing us with the 486DX2 evaluation board; M. Tien-Chien Lee, M. Fujita, and D. Maheshwari of Fujitsu for helping make the SPARClite analysis possible; C. Fraser of AT&T Bell Labs and D. Hanson of Princeton University for the 486 code generator.

References

[1] A. V. Aho, R. Sethi, and J. D. Ullman, *Compilers, Principles, Techniques and Tools*. Reading, MA: Addison Wesley, 1988.

[2] M. Benitez and J. Davidson, "A retargetable integrated code improver," *Tech. Rep. CS-93-64*, Univ. of Virginia, Dept of Computer Sci., Nov. 1993.

[3] Press *et al.*, *Numerical Recipes in C*. Cambridge, MA: Cambridge Univ., 1988.

[4] C. W. Fraser and D. R. Hanson, "A retargetable compiler for ANSI C," *SIGPLAN Notices*, pp. 29–43, Oct., 1991.

[5] R. Gupta, "Co-synthesis of hardware and software for digital embedded systems," Ph.D. dissertation, Dept. of Electrical Eng., Stanford University, CA, 1993.

[6] Intel Corp., *i486 Microprocessor, Hardware Reference Manual*, 1990.

[7] Intel Corp., *Intel486 Microprocessor Family, Programmer's Reference Manual*, 1992.

[8] C. L. Su, C. Y. Tsui, and A. M. Despain, "Low power architecture design and compilation techniques for high-performance processors," in *IEEE COMPCON*, Feb. 1994.

[9] V. Tiwari, T. C. Lee, M. Fujita, and D. Maheshwari, "Power analysis of the SPARClite MB86934," *Tech. Rep. FLA-CAD-94-01*, Fujitsu Labs of America, Aug. 1994.

[10] V. Tiwari, S. Malik, and A. Wolfe, "Compilation techniques for low energy: An overview," in *Proc. 1994 Symp. Low Power Electron.*, Oct. 1994.

[11] V. Tiwari, S. Malik, A. Wolfe, "Power analysis of the Intel 486DX2," *Tech. Rep. CE-M94-5*, Princeton Univ., Dept. of Elect. Eng., June, 1994.

Vivek Tiwari received the B. Tech degree in computer science and engineering from the Indian Institute of Technology, New Delhi, India in 1991. Currently he is working towards the Ph.D. degree in the Department of Electrical Engineering, Princeton University, Princeton, NJ.

His research interests are in the areas of computer aided design of VLSI and embedded systems and in microprocessor architecture. The focus of his current research is on tools and techniques for power estimation and low power design. He has held summer positions at NEC Research Labs, Intel Corporation, and Fujitsu Labs of America, in 1992, 1993, and 1994, respectively, where he worked on the above topics.

Mr. Tiwari received the IBM Graduate Fellowship award in 1993 and 1994.

Sharad Malik received the B. Tech. degree in electrical engineering from the Indian Institute of Technology, New Delhi, India in 1985 and the M.S. and Ph.D. degrees in computer science from the University of California, Berkeley in 1987 and 1990 respectively.

Currently he is an Assistant Professor with the Department of Electrical Engineering, Princeton University. His current research interests are in the synthesis and verification of digital systems.

Dr. Malik has received the President of India's Gold Medal for academic excellence (1985), the IBM Faculty Development Award (1991), an NSF Research Initiation Award (1992), a Best Paper Award at the IEEE International Conference on Computer Design (1992), the Princeton University Engineering Council Excellence in Teaching Award (1993, 1994), the Walter C. Johnson Prize for Teaching Excellence (1993), Princeton University Rheinstein Faculty Award (1994), and the NSF Young Investigator Award (1994).

Andrew Wolfe received the B.S.E.E. from the Johns Hopkins University in 1985 and the M.S. and Ph.D. degrees from Carnegie Mellon University in 1987 and 1992, respectively. His doctoral dissertation introduced a new model for instruction-level parallel processor architecture called XIMD.

He was a Semiconductor Research Corporation Fellow from 1986 to 1991. He has also worked as a processor designer at ESL/TRW in Sunnyvale, CA and as a product design consultant for numerous companies. Since 1991, he has been an Assistant Professor at Princeton University. His current research interests include embedded systems architectures and design tools, instruction-level parallelism, and video-signal processors.

Dr. Wolfe has served as General Chair of Micro-26 and as Program Chair of Micro-24 as well as serving on the technical committees of several ICCD and Micro conferences. He has presented tutorials on instruction-level parallelism at ASPLOS V and ISCA 20 as well as a tutorial on embedded systems at ICCD '93.

A Survey of Design Techniques for System-Level Dynamic Power Management

Luca Benini, *Member, IEEE*, Alessandro Bogliolo, *Member, IEEE*, and Giovanni De Micheli, *Fellow, IEEE*

Abstract—Dynamic power management (DPM) is a design methodology for dynamically reconfiguring systems to provide the requested services and performance levels with a minimum number of active components or a minimum load on such components. DPM encompasses a set of techniques that achieves energy-efficient computation by selectively turning off (or reducing the performance of) system components when they are idle (or partially unexploited).

In this paper, we survey several approaches to system-level dynamic power management. We first describe how systems employ power-manageable components and how the use of dynamic reconfiguration can impact the overall power consumption. We then analyze DPM implementation issues in electronic systems, and we survey recent initiatives in standardizing the hardware/software interface to enable software-controlled power management of hardware components.

Index Terms—Energy conservation, energy management, optimization methods.

I. INTRODUCTION

MOST ELECTRONIC circuits and system designs are confronted with the problem of delivering high performance with a limited consumption of electric power. High performance is required by the increasingly complex applications (e.g., multimedia) that are running even on portable devices. Low-power consumption is required to achieve acceptable autonomy in battery-powered systems, as well as to reduce the environmental impact (e.g., heat dissipation, cooling-induced noise) and operation cost of stationary systems. In other words, achieving highly energy-efficient computation is a major challenge in electronic design.

Electronic systems can be viewed as collections of components, which may be heterogeneous in nature. Some components may have mechanical parts, e.g., hard-disk drives (HDD's), or optical parts, e.g., displays. For example, a cellular telephone has a digital very large scale integration (VLSI) component, an analog radio-frequency (RF) component, and a display. Such components may be active at different times, and correspondingly consume different fractions of the telephone power budget. Similarly, main components of portable computers are VLSI chips, HDD, and display. It is often the case that the HDD and the display are the most power-hungry components [1], and thus their effective use is key to achieving long operating times between battery recharges.

To be competitive, an electronic design must be able to deliver peak performance when requested. Nevertheless, peak performance is required only during some time intervals. Similarly, system components are not always required to be in the active state. The ability to enable and disable components, as well as of tuning their performance to the *workload* (e.g., user's requests), is key in achieving energy-efficient designs.

Dynamic power management (DPM) is a design methodology that dynamically reconfigures an electronic system to provide the requested services and performance levels with a minimum number of active components or a minimum load on such components [1], [2]. DPM encompasses a set of techniques that achieve energy-efficient computation by selectively turning off (or reducing the performance of) system components when they are *idle* (or partially unexploited). DPM is used in various forms in most portable (and some stationary) electronic designs; yet its application is sometimes primitive because its full potentials are still unexplored and because the complexity of interfacing heterogeneous components has limited designers to simple solutions.

The fundamental premise for the applicability of DPM is that systems (and their components) experience nonuniform workloads during operation time. Such an assumption is valid for most systems, both when considered in isolation and when internetworked. A second assumption of DPM is that it is possible to predict, with a certain degree of confidence, the fluctuations of workload. Workload observation and prediction should not consume significant energy.

Dynamic power managers can have different embodiments, according to the level (e.g., component, system, network) where DPM is applied and to the physical realization style (e.g., timer, hard-wired controller, software routine). Typically, a *power manager* (PM) implements a control procedure based on some observations and/or assumptions on the workload. The control procedure is often called *policy*. An example of a simple policy, ubiquitously used for laptops and palmtops, is the *timeout* policy, which shuts down a component after a fixed inactivity time, under the assumption that it is highly likely that a component remains idle if it has been idle for the timeout time. We shall show in this paper how this simple-minded policy may turn out to be inefficient and how it can be improved.

This paper has the objective to cover and relate different approaches to system-level DPM. We begin by describing how systems employ power-manageable components and how the

---

Manuscript received February 14, 1999; revised September 23, 1999. This work was supported in part by NSF under Contract CCR-9901190 and by the MARCO/DARPA Gigascale Silicon Research Center.
L. Benini is with the Dip. di Elettronica, Informatica e Sistemistica, Università di Bologna, Bologna 40136, Italy.
A. Bogliolo is with the Department of Engineering, Università di Ferrara, Ferrara 44100, Italy.
G. De Micheli is with the Computer Systems Laboratory, Stanford University, Stanford, CA 94305 USA.
Publisher Item Identifier S 1063-8210(00)04347-X.

use of their dynamic reconfiguration can impact the overall power consumption. Next, we review and compare different approaches to DPM. We use a mathematical framework to highlight the benefits and pitfalls of different power management policies. We classify power management approaches into two major classes, where policies are based on *predictive schemes* and *stochastic optimum control* respectively. Within each class, we survey the approaches being applied to system design and/or described in the literature. Last, we present the means of implementing DPM in electronic systems, and we describe in particular the recent initiatives in standardizing hardware/software interface to enable software-controlled power management of hardware components.

II. MODELING POWER-MANAGED SYSTEMS

We model a power-managed system as a set of interacting *power manageable components* (PMC's) controlled by a *power manager* (PM). We model PMC's as *black boxes*. We are not concerned on how PMC's are designed (this topic will be deferred to Section IV), but we focus instead on how they interact with the environment. The purpose of this analysis is to understand what type and how much information should be exchanged between a power manager and system components in order to implement effective policies. We take a bottom-up view. We consider PMC's in isolation first. Then we describe DPM for systems with several interacting components. Finally, we analyze the problem of managing power for a *network* of communicating systems.

A. Power Manageable Components

Our working definition of *component* is general and abstract. A component is an atomic block in a complete system. Notice that the granularity of this definition is arbitrary, hence components can be as simple as a functional unit within a chip, or as complex as a board. The characterizing property of our definition is *atomicity*. At the system level, a component is seen as an indivisible functional block: no detailed knowledge of its internal structure is assumed. The fundamental characteristic of a PMC is the availability of multiple *modes of operation* that span the power-performance tradeoff. Nonmanageable components are designed for a given performance target and power budget. In contrast, with PMC's it is possible to dynamically switch between high-performance high-power modes of operation and low-power low-performance ones.

It is possible to think that a PMC may have a continuous range of operation modes, or that the number of modes can be very large. Intuitively, the availability of many operation modes gives fine control on how to operate a PMC in such a way that power waste is minimized and performance is perfectly calibrated on the task. In practice, the number of modes of operation tends to be quite small because the increased design complexity and hardware overhead for supporting power management must be tightly controlled. Several implementation techniques for PMC's are surveyed in Section IV. Here, we just stress the fact that the increased flexibility offered by PMC's may have a cost that should be taken into account.

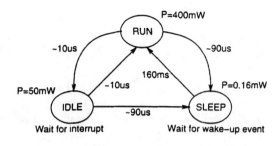

Fig. 1. Power state machine for the StrongARM SA-1100 processor.

Another important characteristic of real-life PMC's is that transitions between modes of operation have a cost. In many cases, the cost is in terms of delay, or performance loss. If a transition is not instantaneous, and the component is not operational during a transition, performance is lost whenever a transition is initiated. Transition cost depends on PMC implementation: in some cases (see Section IV) the cost may be negligible, but, generally, it is not. There might also be a transition power cost: this is often the case when transitions are not instantaneous. It is important not to neglect transition costs when designing a PMC's. Excessive costs may make one or more low-power operation states almost useless because it is very hard to amortize the cost of transitioning in and out of them.

In most practical instances, we can model a PMC by a finite-state representation called *power state machine* (PSM). States are the various modes of operation that span the tradeoff between performance and power. State transitions have a power and delay cost. In general, low-power states have lower performance and larger transition latency than states with higher power. This simple abstract model holds for many single-chip components like processors [14] and memories [7] as well as for devices such as disk drives [18], wireless network interfaces [19], displays [18], which are more heterogeneous and complex than a single chip.

Example 2.1: The StrongARM SA-1100 processor [3] is an example of PMC. It has three modes of operation: Run, IDLE, and SLEEP. Run mode is the normal operating mode of the SA-1100: every on-chip resource is functional. The chip enters run mode after successful power-up and reset. IDLE mode allows a software application to stop the CPU when not in use, while continuing to monitor interrupt requests on or off chip. In idle mode, the CPU can be brought back to run mode quickly when an interrupt occurs. SLEEP mode offers the greatest power savings and consequently the lowest level of available functionality. In the transition from Run or IDLE, the SA-1100 performs an orderly shutdown of on-chip activity. In a transition from SLEEP to any other state, the chip steps through a rather complex wake-up sequence before it can resume normal activity.

The PSM model of the StrongARM SA-1100 is shown in Fig. 1. States are marked with power dissipation and performance values, edges are marked with transition times. The power consumed during transitions is approximatively equal to that in Run mode. Notice that both Idle and SLEEP have null performance, but the time for exiting SLEEP is much longer than that for exiting Idle (10 μs versus 160 ms). On the other hand, the power consumed by the chip in SLEEP mode (0.16 mW) is much smaller than that in Idle (50 mW). □

Power-manageable components can be managed *internally* or *externally*, according to the physical location of the implementation of the corresponding policy. Internally managed components (also called *self-managed* components) use conservative policies because of the lack of observability of the overall system operation and of the need of tolerating little or no performance degradation, since no assumptions can be made on how demanding the component's environment will be. Nevertheless, there are several examples of components that are either partially of completely self-managed.

Example 2.2: IBM's Travelstar [4] hard disk drives have three low-power inactive states called Performance Idle, Active Idle, and Low Power Idle. When the disk is idle, the drives employ a proprietary internal management technology called "Enhanced Adaptive Battery Life Extender" for selecting the appropriate idle mode to minimize power usage. Idle-mode selection is based on the current disk drive access patterns, and IBM claims that automatic adaptation helps in improving access times. The disk does not need an external power manager and no configuration or set up is needed. Travelstar drives have also two additional very low-power states, namely, Stand-by and Sleep. The times required for entering and exiting these two states are much longer than those needed for transitioning to and from the first three. Decisions on transitions to Stand-by or Sleep are left to external control. □

B. Power-Managed Systems

From our viewpoint, a system is a set of interacting components, some of which (at least one) are externally controllable PMC's. Notice that this generic definition does not pose any limitation on the size and complexity of a system. The activity of components is coordinated by a system controller. In complex systems, control is often implemented in software. For instance, in computer systems, global coordination is performed by the *operating system* (OS).

The system controller has precise and up-to-date control on the status of system components, hence, the power manager is naturally implemented as a module of the system controller. A power-manageable system should provide a clean abstraction of its components to the power manager. Standardization of the interface between PM and system is an important feature for decreasing design time.

The choice and realization of a DPM scheme requires modeling both the components' power/performance behavior and their workload. The former model is captured well by the power state machine model. On the other hand, models for the workload may vary in complexity, and range from the simple assumption used in timeout schemes to complex statistical models. As we shall see in Section III, workload information is required for all advanced power management approaches. Hence, we postulate the existence of a system-monitoring module which is capable of collecting run-time workload data and extracting the relevant information required to drive the PM. The abstract structure of a generic system-level PM is shown in Fig. 2. The

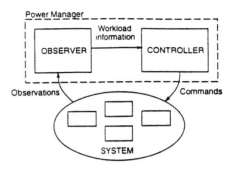

Fig. 2. Abstract structure of a system-level power manager.

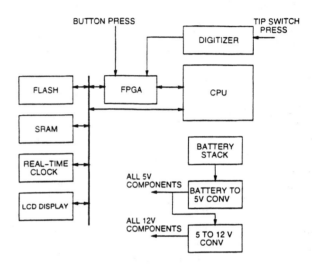

Fig. 3. PaperClip hardware diagram.

observer block collects workload information for all PMC's in the system, while the *controller* takes care of issuing commands for forcing state transitions.

Not all components in a power-managed system have to be PMC's. The power consumption of all noncontrollable components makes up a baseline power consumption that cannot be reduced by power management. Self-managed components appear as noncontrollable to the PM. Even though the functionality of the PM is clearly defined, its implementation is not constrained in any way. In some systems, the PM is a hardware block, while in others it is a software routine. Hybrid hardware–software implementations are also possible. PM implementation issues are analyzed in Section IV.

Example 2.3: The PaperClip, a hand-held electronic clipboard developed by HP Laboratories, is an example of a power-managed system [5]. The high-level hardware organization of PaperClip is shown in Fig. 3. All major components are power-manageable: the CPU, memory, LCD, and digitizer can be put in a low-power sleep state. Some components, like the real-time clock and the FPGA-based control logic, are always active. PaperClip's inputs come either from the control buttons situated on the clipboard or from the digitizer's pen. PaperClip can operate as a digitizer and as data-transfer unit. During digitize, PaperClip stores digitized handwriting on FLASH memory, while the user writes on a sheet of paper on the clipboard. During data transfer, the digitized handwriting is transferred to a host PC via either a serial or an IR interface.

Power management for PaperClip is based on a hybrid hardware–software implementation. The core PM functionality is implemented as firmware running on the CPU. PaperClip's workload can be widely varying over time. If the user is not writing on the clipboard, the system is idle. However, PaperClip should not be turned off as soon as writing stops because resuming normal operation after a sleep period requires a few milliseconds. If the PM puts the system to sleep too greedily, a significant amount of data can be lost when writing resumes, and the quality of handwriting digitization may be compromised. Power state transitions for non-CPU components are forced by the PM module running on the CPU by writing to memory-mapped I/O locations. PM commands are then decoded by control circuitry implemented with an FPGA and distributed to the components. CPU shutdown is software based. Wake-up is interrupt driven: interrupts are generated by pressing control buttons or by pressing the pen on the clipboard. Notice that sleep power cannot be reduced to zero because some of the system components are not power manageable. □

C. Power-Managed Networks

In many cases, systems are not isolated, but they actively communicate among themselves. We call *network* a set of communicating systems. While network design has been traditionally focused on communication quality and throughput, the increased emphasis on low-power portable systems with communication capabilities has spurred several research initiatives targeting power-efficient networking [22].

Energy-conscious communication protocols based on power management have been extensively studied [23]–[25]. The main purpose of these protocols is to regulate the access of several communication devices to a shared medium trying to obtain maximum power efficiency for a given throughput requirement. Even when interference is not an issue, point-to-point communication can be made more power efficient by increasing the predictability of communication patterns [26]: if it is possible to accurately predict the arrival time of messages (packets), idle times can be exploited to force communication devices into a low-power inactive state.

The main challenge in network power management is that it is generally not realistic to assume that power control is centralized. Hence, we must rely on distributed algorithms that take autonomous decisions for each system in the network based either on local information, or on incomplete global network status data. Even though network power management is an interesting and relevant topic, we focus on system-level centralized power management.

III. Dynamic Power Management Techniques

In this section, we analyze techniques for controlling the power state of a system and its components. We consider components as black boxes, whose behavior is abstracted by the PSM model. We defer to Section IV the description of the interfacing layers for component control as well as the implementation technical details. We focus on how to design effective power management policies. For the sake of

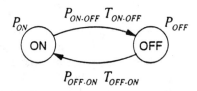

Fig. 4. PSM of a two-state power-manageable component.

simplicity, we shall focus on the problem of controlling a single component (or, equivalently, the system as a whole).

First, we want to clarify why the search for a DPM policy is not a simple problem to solve. For this reason, we give an example of a trivial problem first. Consider a system where transitions between power states are instantaneous: negligible power and performance costs are paid for performing state transitions. In such a system, DPM is a trivial task, and the optimum policy is greedy: as soon as the system is idle, it can be transitioned to the deepest sleep state available. On the arrival of a request, the system is instantaneously activated.

Unfortunately, most PMC's have nonnegligible performance and power costs for power state transitions. For instance, if entering a low-power state requires power-supply shutdown, returning from this state to the active state requires a (possibly long) time for: 1) turning on and stabilizing the power supply and the clock; 2) reinitializing the system; and 3) restoring the context. When power state transitions have a cost, as it is typically the case, we are faced with a difficult optimization problem. In rough but intuitive words, we need to decide when (if at all) it is worthwhile (performance and power-wise) to transition to a low-power state and which state should be chosen (if multiple low-power states are available).

Example 3.1: Consider the StrongARM SA-1100 processor described in Example 2.1. Transition times between Run and Idle states are so fast that the Idle state can be optimally exploited according to a greedy policy possibly implemented by an embedded PM.

On the other hand, the wake-up time from the Sleep state is much larger and has to be carefully compared with the environment's time constants before deciding to shut the processor down. In the limiting case of a workload with no idle periods longer than the time required to enter and exit the Sleep state, a greedy policy shutting down the processor as soon as an idle period is detected would reduce performance without saving any power (the power consumption associated with state transitions is of the same order of that of the Run state). An external PM controlling transitions of the SA-1100 processor to the Sleep state has to observe the workload and take decisions according to a policy whose optimality depends on workload statistics and on predefined performance constraints. Notice that the policy becomes trivial if there are no performance constraints: the PM could keep the processor always in the Sleep state.

An SA-1100 processor with embedded control for the Idle state and external control for the Sleep state is a partially self-managed PMC whose PSM model (shown in Fig. 4) has only two states: On and Off. The On state is a macrostate representing both the Run and Idle states of the processor, with a greedy policy autonomously controlling transitions between them. The power consumption associated with the On state is the sum of the power consumptions of the Run and Idle states, weighted by the workload activity and idleness probabilities. The Off state corresponds to the actual Sleep state. Transitions between On and Off represent transitions between the Run and Sleep states. □

Example 3.1 leads to two observations. First, policy optimization is a *power optimization* problem under *performance constraints*, or vice versa. Second, the achievable power savings depend on the workload (which must be bursty at some degree), and system characteristics (i.e., the PSM of the system). The general applicability of DPM is discussed in the next section as a property of a system-workload pair. Existing techniques for DPM and policy optimization are surveyed and discussed in Sections III-B and C, focusing on *predictive techniques* and *stochastic control*, respectively.

A. Applicability of DPM

Putting a PMC into an inactive state causes a period of inactivity whose duration T_n is the sum of the actual time spent in the target state and the time spent to enter and exit it. We define the *break-even time* for an inactive state S (denoted by $T_{BE,S}$) as the minimum inactivity time required to compensate the cost of entering state S. The break-even time $T_{BE,S}$ is inferred directly from the power state machine of a PMC. If $T_n < T_{BE,S}$, either there is not enough time to enter and exit the inactive state, or the power saved when in the inactive state does not amortize the additional power consumption typically required to turn-on the component. Intuitively, DPM aims at exploiting idleness to transition a component to an inactive low-power state. If no performance loss is tolerated, the length of the idle periods of the workload is an upper bound for the inactivity time of the resource. On the other hand, if some performance loss is tolerated, inactivity times may be longer than idle periods.

In this section, we analyze the *exploitability* of the inactive states of a PMC, that is the possibility of saving power by transitioning the component to the inactive states. Exploitability depends on the power states, on the workload, on the performance constraints, on the DPM policy and on the PM implementation. Techniques for policy optimization and implementation will be discussed later, together with the impact of performance constraints. Here, we focus only on *inherent exploitability*, which represents the possibility of exploiting an inactive state under the assumption that: 1) no performance penalty is tolerated and 2) an *ideal PM* is available that has complete (*a priori*) knowledge of the entire workload trace. Inherent exploitability is a property of a system-workload pair.

For example, consider the two-state PSM of a component, as shown in Fig. 4. For the sake of clarity, when there is only one inactive state, we will use the shorthand notation T_{BE} instead of $T_{BE,S}$. The optimum policy for an ideal PM controlling the transitions between states On and Off consists of shutting down the component at the beginning of all idle periods longer than $T_{BE} = T_{BE,\text{Off}}$ and waking it up right in time to serve upcoming requests with no delay. The resulting power consumption (denoted by P_{ideal}) is a lower bound for the power consumption that can be achieved by a PM exploiting inactive state Off. The potential power saving (P_{saved}), defined as the gap between P_{ideal} and the power consumption of the system when in the active state (P_{On}), represents the inherent exploitability of the Off state for the given workload. The larger P_{saved} the larger the potential advantage of exploiting state Off for DPM. If $P_{\text{saved}} = 0$, no power savings can be achieved by entering the inactive state without impairing performance. Needless to say, the inactive state can always be exploited in practice if arbitrary performance degradation is tolerated.

We are interested in studying the dependence of P_{saved} on power-state parameters and workload statistics. The parameters of a power state S are represented by its break-even time $T_{BE,S}$, while workload statistics are represented by the probability distribution of the idle periods $F(T_{\text{idle}})$. Intuitively, the larger $T_{BE,S}$ (with respect to the average idle time), the smaller P_{saved}. In the limiting situation where all idle periods are shorter than $T_{BE,S}$, no power savings would be achieved by means of DPM: an ideal PM implementing the optimum policy would never shut the resource down, thus providing $P_{\text{ideal}} = P_{\text{On}}$ and $P_{\text{saved}} = 0$.

In general, T_{BE} is the sum of two terms: the total transition time (i.e., the time required to enter and exit the inactive state, T_{TR}) and the minimum time that has to be spent in the low-power state to compensate the additional transition power (P_{TR}). For our example PMC (Fig. 4), T_{TR} and P_{TR} can be computed as

$$T_{TR} = T_{\text{On,Off}} + T_{\text{Off,On}} \quad (1)$$

$$P_{TR} = \frac{T_{\text{On,Off}} P_{\text{On,Off}} + T_{\text{Off,On}} P_{\text{Off,On}}}{T_{TR}} \quad (2)$$

while T_{BE} can be expressed as

$$T_{BE} = T_{TR} + T_{TR}\frac{P_{TR} - P_{\text{On}}}{P_{\text{On}} - P_{\text{Off}}} \text{ if } P_{TR} > P_{\text{On}}$$
$$T_{BE} = T_{TR} \text{ if } P_{TR} \leq P_{\text{On}}. \quad (3)$$

In practice, T_{BE} grows linearly with transition time and cost (T_{TR} and P_{TR}) and depends hyperbolically on the power saved ($P_{\text{On}} - P_{\text{Off}}$) when in the inactive state When $P_{TR} \leq P_{\text{On}}$, T_{BE} reduces to T_{TR} (this is, for instance, the case of the ARM SA-1100 processor), while it is greater than T_{TR} when $P_{TR} > P_{\text{On}}$ (as for components with mechanical inertia, such as hard disk drives). In this case, we need to add to T_{TR} the term $T_{TR}(P_{TR} - P_{\text{On}})/(P_{\text{On}} - P_{\text{Off}})$, which represents the additional time that we need to spend in the Off state to compensate the excess power consumed during state transition.

For systems with multiple inactive states, a different break-even time $T_{BE,S}$ and, consequently, a different value of $P_{\text{saved},S}$, has to be defined for each state S. Deeper sleep states have lower power consumption at the cost of longer and more expensive transitions. When designing power-manageable components, a tradeoff between P_S, P_{TR} and T_{TR} has to be found for each sleep state S to obtain small values of $T_{BE,S}$ and high exploitability. Sleep states with smaller break-even times are more likely to be successfully exploited by DPM.

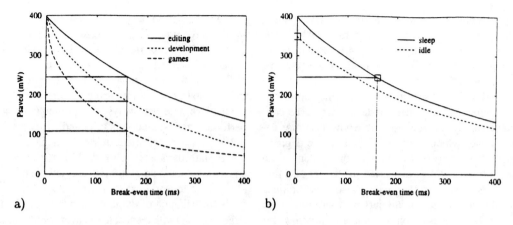

Fig. 5. (a) Plot of $P_{\text{saved}}(T_{BE})$ for the Sleep state of the StrongARM SA-1100 processor. The three curves refer to three different workload statistics, computed from real-world CPU traces provided by the *IPM monitoring package* [5]. (b) Comparison of $P_{\text{saved}}(T_{BE})$ for the two inactive states of the SA-1100 processor. The two curves refer to the same workload.

The energy saved by entering state S during an idle period $T_{\text{idle}} > T_{BE,S}$ is

$$E_S(T_{\text{idle}}) = (T_{\text{idle}} - T_{TR})(P_{\text{On}} - P_S) + T_{TR}(P_{\text{On}} - P_{TR}). \quad (4)$$

Its average value is given by

$$E_S^{\text{avg}} = \int_{T_{BE}}^{\infty} E_S(T_{\text{idle}}) f(T_{\text{idle}}) \, dT_{\text{idle}} \quad (5)$$

where $f(T_{\text{idle}})$ is the probability density of the idle periods. The exploitability of S (in symbols, $P_{\text{saved},S}$) is the ratio between E_S^{avg} and the average length of the idle periods ($T_{\text{idle}}^{\text{avg}}$). By replacing the expression of $E_S(T_{\text{idle}})$ from (4) into (5) and dividing by $T_{\text{idle}}^{\text{avg}}$, we obtain a formula for $P_{\text{saved},S}$

$$P_{\text{saved},S} = \frac{1}{T_{\text{idle}}^{\text{avg}}} \int_{T_{BE}}^{\infty} [(T_{\text{idle}} - T_{TR})(P_{\text{On}} - P_S) + T_{TR}(P_{\text{On}} - P_{TR})] f(T_{\text{idle}}) \, dT_{\text{idle}} \quad (6)$$

which can be integrated and rewritten as the product of three terms: the power saving of state S, the expected idle time in excess of $T_{BE,S}$ (normalized at the average idle period), and the probability of going to state S (assuming that we perform the transition only when it is convenient)

$$P_{\text{saved},S} = (P_{\text{On}} - P_S) \frac{\left(T_{\text{idle}>T_{BE,S}}^{\text{avg}} - T_{BE,S}\right)}{T_{\text{idle}}^{\text{avg}}} \cdot (1 - F(T_{BE})) \quad (7)$$

where F is the probability distribution of T_{idle} and $T_{\text{idle}>T_{BE,S}}^{\text{avg}}$ is the average length of idle periods longer than $T_{BE,S}$. The power saved P_{saved} is always a decreasing function of $T_{BE,S}$: it takes maximum value for $T_{BE,S} = 0$ and asymptotically tends to zero for increasing values of $T_{BE,S}$. The way it goes to zero depends on the first-order statistics of the workload, namely, on the distribution of T_{idle}.

Example 3.2: We want to evaluate the exploitability of the inactive states of the StrongARM SA-1100 processor. We start by computing their break-even times according to (4). Since the power consumption associated with all state transitions is equal to P_{Run}, $T_{BE} = T_{TR}$

$$T_{BE,\text{Idle}} = 0.01 \text{ ms} + 0.01 \text{ ms}$$
$$T_{BE,\text{Sleep}} = 160 \text{ ms} + 0.09 \text{ ms}.$$

As intuitively observed at the beginning of this section, the Idle state has a break-even time much smaller than the Sleep state.

As reference workloads to evaluate exploitability, we take real-world CPU usage traces provided by the IPM monitoring system [5] described in Section IV. From each trace, we compute the probability distribution function $F(T_{\text{idle}})$ and we evaluate (7) for different values of T_{BE}. The behavior of $P_{\text{saved, Sleep}}$ as a function of the break-even time is shown in Fig. 5(a) for three different CPU workloads, corresponding to three different user sessions: editing, software development, and graphical interactive games. The dependence on the workload is evident: graphical interactive games require more CPU usage than text editors, thus reducing the opportunity of putting the CPU to the Sleep state. Notice that, if the break-even time for the Sleep state were null, $P_{\text{saved, Sleep}}$ would have been of about 400 mW independently of the workload. Corresponding to the actual value of $T_{BE,\text{Sleep}}$, instead, $P_{\text{saved, Sleep}}$ is much smaller and strongly dependent on the workload.

Fig. 5(b) compares the P_{saved} curves of both inactive states for the same workload (namely, the editing trace). $P_{\text{saved, Idle}}$ is always below $P_{\text{saved, Sleep}}$. Since the Sleep state has lower power consumption than the Idle state, if the two states had the same break-even time the deepest one would have been more exploitable. However, taking into account the actual break-even times we find that the inherent exploitability of the Idle state is greater than that of the Sleep state (the points to be compared are shown by square boxes on the graph). □

As mentioned at the beginning of the section and formally expressed by (7), the exploitability of an inactive state depends both on the characteristics of the inactive state and on the workload. If typical workload information is not available when designing a PMC, the exploitability of its low-power states cannot be computed. To represent the properties of an inactive state S independently of the workload, we use the time-power product

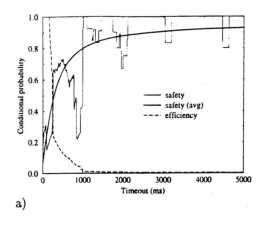
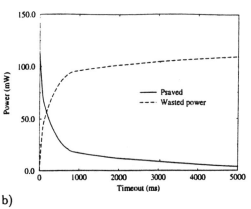

Fig. 6. Quality of a timeout-based predictor evaluated as a function of timer duration. (a) Safety and efficiency of the timeout used to predict idle periods longer than $T_{BE} = 160$ ms. (b) Saved and wasted power consumption. Data refer to the PSM of Example 3.1 and to a CPU usage trace provided by the IPM monitoring package [5].

$C_S = T_{BE,S} \cdot P_S$. Inactive states with lower C_S are likely to lead to larger power savings. Incidentally, we remark that C_S has the same dimension of the well-known power-delay product used as a cost metric for comparing different electronic devices and circuits.

B. Predictive Techniques

In most real-world systems, there is little knowledge of future input events and DPM decisions have to be taken based on uncertain predictions. The rationale in all predictive techniques is that of exploiting the correlation between the past history of the workload and its near future in order to make reliable predictions about future events. We denote by p the future event that we want to predict. We denote by o the past event whose occurrence is used to make predictions on p. For the purpose of DPM we are interested in predicting idle periods long enough to go to sleep, in symbols: $p = \{T_{\text{idle}} > T_{BE}\}$.

Good predictors should minimize the number of mispredictions. We call *overprediction* (*underprediction*) a predicted idle period longer (shorter) than the actual one. Overpredictions give rise to a performance penalty, while underpredictions imply power waste but no performance penalty. To represent the quality of a predictor we define two figures: *safety*, that is the complement of the risk of making overpredictions, and *efficiency*, that is the complement of the risk of making underpredictions. Safety and efficiency can be expressed in terms of conditional probabilities $\text{Prob}(p|o)$ and $\text{Prob}(o|p)$. A totally safe predictor never makes overpredictions ($\text{Prob}(p|o) = 1$), and a totally efficient predictor never makes underpredictions ($\text{Prob}(o|p) = 1$). A predictor with maximum safety and efficiency is an *ideal predictor*, whose availability would enable the actual implementation of the ideal PM discussed in the previous section. Predictors of practical interest are neither safe nor efficient, thus causing suboptimum control. Their quality (and the quality of the resulting control) depends on the choice of the observed event o and on the second-order workload statistics.

1) Static Techniques:

Fixed Timeout: The most common predictive PM policy is the *fixed timeout*, which uses the elapsed idle time as observed event ($o = \{T_{\text{idle}} > T_{TO}\}$) to be used to predict the total duration of the current idle period ($p = \{T_{\text{idle}} > T_{TO} + T_{BE}\}$). The policy can be summarized as follows: when an idle period begins, a timer is started with duration T_{TO}. If after T_{TO} the system is still idle, then the PM forces the transition to the Off state. The system remains off until it receives a request from the environment that signals the end of the idle period. The fundamental assumption in the fixed timeout policy is that the probability of T_{idle} being longer than $T_{BE} + T_{TO}$, given that $T_{\text{idle}} > T_{TO}$, is close to one: $\text{Prob}(T_{\text{idle}} > T_{TO} + T_{BE} | T_{\text{idle}} > T_{TO}) \approx 1$. The critical design decision is obviously the choice of the timeout value T_{TO}.

Timeouts have two main advantages: they are general (their applicability slightly depends on the workload) and their safety can be improved simply by increasing the timeout values. Unfortunately, they tradeoff efficiency for safety: large timeouts cause a large number of underpredictions, which represent a missed opportunity of saving power, and a sizeable amount of power is wasted waiting for the timeout to expire.

Example 3.3: Consider one of the CPU usage traces described in Example 3.2 (namely, the game trace) as a typical workload for the StrongARM SA-1100 processor. We want to evaluate the quality of a timeout-based shutdown policy for the processor. Since the break-even time for the Sleep state is of 160 ms, we evaluate the safety and efficiency of a timeout used to predict idle periods longer than 160 ms. The two figures are plotted on Fig. 6(a) as a function of the timer duration. As the timeout increases, predictions become safer but less efficient (efficiency is almost null for timeouts greater than 1 s). It is also worth noting that safety has a highly nonsmooth instance-dependent behavior that makes it difficult to choose optimal timeout values [the irregular curve in Fig. 6(a) refers to a 1-h trace, while the smooth one refers to the average of several traces collected during equivalent user sessions].

Fig. 6(b) shows the power savings obtained by applying the timeout policy to the SA-1100 and the wasted power evaluated with respect to the ideal power savings. The effect of T_{TO} on the actual power savings is similar to the effect of T_{BE} on the ideal ones. Both parameters reduce the portion of idle time that can be effectively exploited to save power. □

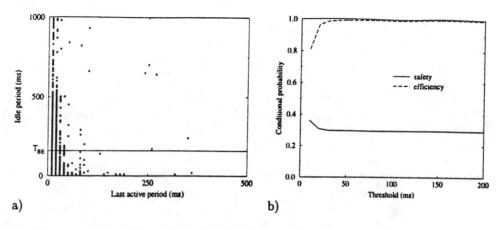

Fig. 7. (a) Scatter plot of T_{idle} versus T_{active} for the workload of the CPU of a personal computer running Linux. (b) Safety and efficiency of a predictive shutdown scheme plotted as a function of the threshold value T_{Thr}.

Karlin et al. [31] proposed to use $T_{TO} = T_{BE}$ and showed that this choice leads to an energy consumption which is at worse twice the energy consumed by an ideal policy. The rationale of this strong result is related to the fact that the worst case happens for traces with repeated idle periods of length $T_{\text{idle}} = 2T_{BE}$ separated by pointwise activity. In this case, Karlin's algorithm provides no power saving, while an ideal algorithm saves power during half of each idle interval. Indeed, the ideal algorithm performs a shutdown for each idle period, but half of the period is spent in state transition.

Timeout schemes have two more limitations: they waste a sizeable amount of power (during user's idleness) waiting for the timeout to expire and they always pay a performance penalty upon wakeup. The first issue is addressed by *predictive shutdown policies* [30], [32] that take PM decisions as soon as a new idle period starts, based on the observation of past idle and busy periods. The second issue is addressed by predictive wakeup, described later.

Predictive Shutdown: Two predictive shutdown schemes have been proposed by Srivastava et al. [32]. In the first scheme, a nonlinear regression equation is obtained from the past history

$$T_{\text{pred}} = \phi\left(T_{\text{active}}^n, T_{\text{idle}}^{n-1}, \cdots, T_{\text{active}}^{n-k}, T_{\text{idle}}^{n-k-1}\right) \quad (8)$$

and used to make predictions. We use superscripts to indicate the sequence of past idle and active periods; n indicates the current idle period (whose length has to be predicted) and the most recent active period. If $T_{\text{pred}} > T_{BE}$, the system is immediately shut down as soon as it becomes idle. According to our notation, the observed event is

$$o = \left\{\phi\left(T_{\text{active}}^n, T_{\text{idle}}^{n-1}, \cdots, T_{\text{active}}^{n-k}, T_{\text{idle}}^{n-k-1}\right) > T_{BE}\right\}. \quad (9)$$

The format of the nonlinear regression is decided heuristically, while the fitting coefficients can be computed with standard techniques. The main limitations of this approach are: 1) there is no automatic way to decide the type of regression equation and 2) offline data collection and analysis are required to construct and fit the regression model.

The second approach proposed by Srivastava et al. [32] is based on a *threshold*. The duration of the busy period immediately preceding the current idle period is observed. If $o = \{T_{\text{active}}^{n-1} < T_{Thr}\}$, the idle period is assumed to be larger than T_{BE} and the system is shut down. The rationale of this policy is that for the class of systems considered by Srivastava et al. (interactive graphic terminals), short active periods are often followed by long idle periods. Clearly, the choice of T_{Thr} is critical. Careful analysis of the scatter plot of T_{idle} versus T_{active} is required to set it to a correct value, hence, this method is inherently offline (i.e., based on extensive data collection and analysis). Furthermore, the method is not applicable if the scatter plot is not L-shaped.

Example 3.4: Fig. 7(a) shows the scatter plot of T_{idle} versus T_{active} for the development trace of Example 3.2. From the plot, we observe that: 1) the time is discretized (both T_{idle} and T_{active} are multiple of 10 ms, that is the duration of the time slots assigned by the Linux scheduler to the active process); 2) the large majority of the idle periods are shorter than 1000 ms (this is due to the presence of a system daemon that required the CPU at every second independently of the state of user's application); and 3) the scatter plot is L-shaped (thus enabling the use of threshold-based predictors). The horizontal line shows the break-even time of the sleep state of the StrongARM SA-1100 processor. Safety and efficiency of a threshold-based predictor used to shut down the SA-1100 are plotted in Fig. 7(b) as a function of T_{Thr}. Interestingly, efficiency becomes almost one even for small threshold values (in fact, most of the exploitable idle periods are preceded by short active periods), but there is no way of improving safety. In our example, threshold-based predictions are unsafe due to the presence of a dense region in the bottom-left corner of the scatter plot. A threshold on T_{active} does not help us in distinguishing between idle periods longer or shorter than T_{BE}. □

The applicability and the quality of history-based predictors depend on the correlation between past and future events, that is, not under designer's control. As a matter of fact, short-term correlation has been observed in many real-world workloads, but the nature and strength of such correlation is strongly instance dependent. For a given workload, history-based predictors are usually more efficient and less safe than timeouts.

Predictive Wakeup: The DPM strategy proposed by Hwang et al. [33] addresses the second limitation of timeout policies, namely the performance penalty that is always paid on wakeup.

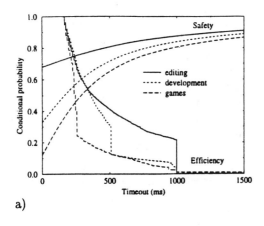 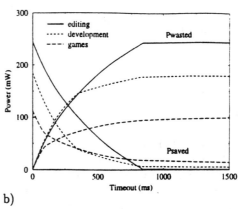

Fig. 8. Effect of the workload on the quality of a timeout-based power manager. (a) Safety and efficiency. (b) Saved and wasted power.

To reduce this cost, the power manager performs *predictive wakeup* when the predicted idle time expires, even if no new requests have arrived. This choice may increase power dissipation if T_{idle} has been underpredicted, but decreases the delay for servicing the first incoming request after an idle period.

2) Adaptive Techniques: Since the optimality of DPM strategies depends on the workload statistics, static predictive techniques are all ineffective (i.e., suboptimal) when the workload is either unknown *a priori*, or nonstationary. Hence, some form of adaptation is required. While for timeouts the only parameter to be adjusted is the timer duration, for history-based predictors even the type of observed events could in principle be adapted to the workload.

Example 3.5: Fig. 8 shows the same graphs of Fig. 6 plotted for three different workloads. All the parameters used in Example 3.3 to represent the quality of a timeout-based estimator are shown to be strongly dependent on the workload. Suppose, for instance, that a target power saving (e.g., of 50 mW) has to be guaranteed regardless of the performance degradation. For a given workload (namely, the editing trace) the timeout value to be used to meet the constraint can be obtained from the corresponding curve of Fig. 8(b): about 550 ms. However, as the workload changes (becoming for instance similar to the development trace), the fixed timeout does not guarantee the required power savings any longer (for the development trace, the power savings provided by a timeout of 550 ms are of about 25 mW). □

Several adaptive predictive techniques have been proposed to deal with nonstationary workloads. In the work by Krishnan *et al.* [27], a set of timeout values is maintained and each timeout is associated with an index indicating how successful it would have been. The policy chooses, at each idle time, the timeout that would have performed best among the set of available ones. Another policy, presented by Helmbold *et al.* [28], also keeps a list of candidate timeouts and assigns a weight to each timeout based on how well it would have performed relatively to an optimum offline strategy for past requests. The actual timeout is obtained as a weighted average of all candidates with their weights. Another approach, introduced by Douglis *et al.* [29], is to keep only one timeout value and to increase it when it is causing too many shutdowns. The timeout is decreased when more shutdowns can be tolerated. Several predictive policies are surveyed and classified in Douglis' paper.

Another aggressive shutdown policy has been proposed by Hwang *et al.* [33]. This policy is capable of online adaptation, since the predicted idle time T_{pred}^n is obtained as a weighted sum of the last idle period T_{idle}^{n-1} and the last prediction T_{pred}^{n-1}

$$T_{\text{pred}}^n = aT_{\text{idle}}^{n-1} + (1-a)T_{\text{pred}}^{n-1}. \qquad (10)$$

This recursive formula dynamically changes the actual observed event: $o = \{aT_{\text{idle}}^{n-1} + (1-a)T_{\text{pred}}^{n-1} > T_{BE}\}$.

Underprediction impact is mitigated by employing a timeout scheme to reevaluate T_{pred} periodically if the system is idle and it has not been shut down. Overprediction impact is reduced by imposing a saturation condition on predictions: $T_{\text{pred}}^n < C_{\max}T_{\text{pred}}^{n-1}$.

Workload prediction accuracy can be increased by specializing predictors to particular classes of workload. Specialization restricts the scope of applicability, but it also reduces the difficulties of predicting completely general workloads. A recently proposed adaptive technique [34] is specifically tailored toward hard-disk power management and it is based on the observation that disk accesses are clustered in *sessions*. Sessions are periods of relatively high disk activity separated by long periods of inactivity. Under the assumption that disk accesses are clustered in sessions, adaptation is used only to predict *session length*. Prediction of a single parameter is easily accomplished and the reported accuracy is high.

C. Stochastic Control

Policy optimization is an optimization problem under uncertainty. Predictive approaches address workload uncertainty, but they assume deterministic response and transition times for the system. However, the system model for policy optimization is very abstract, and abstraction introduces uncertainty. Hence, it may be safer, and more general, to assume a stochastic model for the system as well. Moreover, predictive algorithms are based on a two-state system model, while real-life systems have multiple power states. Policy optimization involves not only the choice of *when* to perform state transitions, but also the choice of *which* transition should be performed. Furthermore, predictive algorithms are heuristic, and their optimality can only be gauged

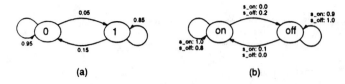

Fig. 9. Markov model of a power-managed system and its environment.

through comparative simulation. Parameter tuning for these algorithms can be very hard if many parameters are involved. Finally, predictive algorithms are geared toward power minimization, and cannot finely control performance penalty.

The stochastic control approach addresses the generality and optimality issues outlined above. Rather than trying to eliminate uncertainty by prediction, it formulates policy optimization as an optimization problem under uncertainty. More specifically [39], power management optimization has been studied within the framework of *controlled Markov processes* [42], [43]. In this flavor of stochastic optimization, it is assumed that the system and the workload can be modeled as Markov chains. Under this assumption, it is possible to: 1) model the uncertainty in system power consumption and response (transition) times; 2) model complex systems with many power states, buffers, queues, etc.; 3) compute power management policies that are globally optimum; and 4) explore tradeoffs between power and performance in a controlled fashion. The Markov model postulated by the stochastic control approach [39] consists of the following.

- A *service requester* (SR), a Markov chain with state set R, which models the arrival of service requests for the system (i.e., the workload).
- A *service provider* (SP), a controlled Markov chain with S states that models the system. Its states represent the modes of operation of the system (i.e., its power states), its transitions are probabilistic, and probabilities are controlled by commands issued by the power manager.
- A *power manager* (PM), which implements a function $f: S \times R \rightarrow A$ from the state set of SR and SP to the set of possible commands A. Such function is an abstract representation of a decision process: the PM observes the state of the system and the workload, takes a decision, and issues a command to control the future state of the system.
- *Cost metrics*, which associate power and performance values with each system state-command pair in $S \times R \times A$.

In the work by Paleologo *et al.* [39], the general Markov model is specialized by assuming finite state set, finite command set, and discrete (or slotted) time. Continuous-time Markov models have been studied as well [37], [38], [40].

Example 3.6: A simple Markov model for a power-managed system [39] is shown in Fig. 9. The SR is a two-state Markov chain with two states: zero (no request is issued to the service provider) and one (a request is issued to the provider). The transition probabilities between states are represented as edge weights in Fig. 9(a). The chain models a "bursty" workload. There is a high probability (0.85) of receiving a request during period $n + 1$ if a request was received during period n, and the mean duration of a stream of requests is equal to $1/0.15 = 6.67$ periods.

The SP model has two states as well, namely $S = \{\text{on}, \text{off}\}$. State transitions are controlled by two commands that can be issued by the power manager. The commands are, respectively, s_on and s_off, with the intuitive meaning of "switch on" and "switch off." When a command is issued, the SP will move to a new state in the next period with a probability dependent only on the command, and on the departure and arrival states. The Markov chain model of the SP is shown in Fig. 9(b). Edge weights represent transition probabilities. Notice that their values depend on the command issued by the power manager. A power management policy can be represented as a table that associates a command with each pair of states of SP, SR. For instance, a simple deterministic policy is: $f: \{(0, \text{on}) \rightarrow \text{s\_off}, (1, \text{on}) \rightarrow \text{s\_on}, (0, \text{off}) \rightarrow \text{s\_off}, (1, \text{off}) \rightarrow \text{s\_on}\}$. □

1) Static Techniques: To perform policy optimization, the Markov chains of SR and SP are composed to obtain a global controlled Markov chain. Then, the problem of finding a minimum-power policy that meets given performance constraints can be cast as a linear program (LP). The solution of the LP produces a *stationary randomized* policy. Such a policy is a nondeterministic function which, given a present system state, associates a probability with each command. The command to be issued is selected by a random trial based on the state-dependent probabilities. It can be shown [43] that the policy computed by LP is *globally optimum*. Furthermore, LP can be solved in polynomial time in the number of variables. Hence, policy optimization for Markov processes is exact and computationally efficient.

Stochastic control based on Markov models has several advantages over predictive techniques. First, it captures the global view of the system, thus allowing the designer to search for a global optimum that possibly exploits multiple inactive states of multiple interacting resources. Second, it enables the exact solution (in polynomial time) of the performance-constrained power optimization problem. Third, it exploits the strength and optimality of randomized policies.

However, several important points need to be understood. First, the performance and power obtained by a policy are *expected* values, and there is no guarantee that results will be optimum for a specific workload instance (i.e., a single realization of the corresponding stochastic process). Second, policy optimization requires a Markov model for SP and SR. If we can safely assume that the SP model can be precharacterized, we cannot assume that we always know the SR model beforehand. Third, policy implementation in practice may not be straightforward. We have always implicitly assumed that the power consumption of the PM is negligible, but this assumption needs to be validated on a case-by-case basis. Finally, the Markov model for the SR or SP can be just an approximation of a much more complex stochastic process. If the model is not accurate, then the "optimal" policies are just approximate solutions.

Example 3.7: We apply stochastic control to our example system, namely, the two-state PSM of the SA-1100 processor. The only decision to be taken by the PM is when to shut down the component. We stress that this is not a typical application of stochastic control (whose main strength is the capability of managing multiple states and finding a global optimum in a

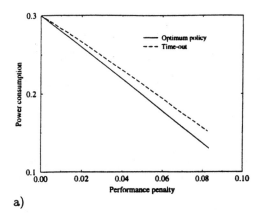 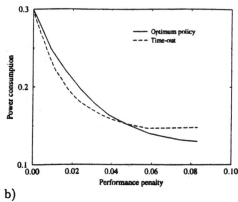

Fig. 10. Power-performance tradeoff curves for the SA-1100 with (a) a realization of a stationary Markovian workload and (b) a highly non-Markovian/nonstationary workload. Solid and dashed lines refer to stochastic control and timeout-based shutdown policies, respectively.

large design space) since there is only one sleep state and the PM cannot control the wake-up. This simple example, however, allows us to make a fair comparison between stochastic control and predictive techniques based on timeouts. The optimal Markov policy is computed by formulating a Markov chain model for the workload, composing it with the controlled Markov model extracted from the PSM of the SA-1100 and solving the LP problem associated with the controlled Markov model of processor and workload under performance constraints [39].

Comparative results for a static Markovian workload are shown in Fig. 10(a): the solid line is the performance versus power Pareto curve of optimum stochastic control (obtained by varying the performance constraint), while the dashed line is the tradeoff curve of a timeout policy (obtained by varying the timer duration). We remark that optimum stochastic control performs better than a timeout heuristic even if the degrees of freedom available for optimization are exactly the same. The difference in power is proportional to the timeout time, which represents a wasted opportunity of saving power.

The same comparison is repeated in Fig. 10 for a highly nonstationary non-Markovian workload. For several timer values, timeout-based shutdown outperforms stochastic control. In fact, policy optimization is not guaranteed to provide optimum results if the modeling assumptions are not verified. □

The class of application of stochastic control is that of computer systems subject to performance constraints. We remark, however, that policy optimization can be used as a tool for design exploration even when stochastic control is not the target DPM technique. In fact, once Markov models have been constructed for the system and the workload, the Pareto curve of optimum tradeoff points can be drawn on the power-performance plane by repeatedly solving policy optimization while varying performance constraints. The Pareto curve provides valuable information to evaluate and improve the quality of any power management strategy.

2) Adaptive Techniques: One limitation of the stochastic optimization technique described in the previous section is that it assumes complete *a priori* knowledge of the system (i.e., the SP) and its workload (SR). Even though it is generally possible to construct a model for the SP once for all, system workload is generally much harder to characterize in advance. Furthermore, workloads are often nonstationary. An adaptive extension of the static stochastic optimization approach has been presented by Chung *et al.* [41]. Adaptation is based on three simple concepts: *policy precharacterization, parameter learning*, and *policy interpolation*. A simple two-parameter Markov model for the workload is assumed, but the value of the two parameters is initially unknown.

Policy precharacterization constructs a two-dimensional (2-D) table addressed by values of the two parameters. The table element uniquely identified by a pair of parameters contains the optimal policy for the system under the workload uniquely identified by the pair. The table is filled by computing optimum policies under different workloads. During system operation, *parameter learning* is performed online. Short-term averaging techniques are employed to obtain run-time estimates of workload parameters based on past history. The parameter values estimated by learning are then used for addressing the lookup table and obtain the power management policy. Clearly, in many cases the estimated parameter values do not correspond exactly to values sampled in the table. If this is the case, *policy interpolation* is employed to obtain a policy as a combination of the policies in table locations corresponding to parameter values close to the estimated ones.

Experimental results reported by Chung *et al.* [41] indicate that adaptive techniques are advantageous even in the stochastic optimization framework. Simulations of power-managed systems under highly nonstationary workloads show that the adaptive technique performs nearly as well as the ideal policy computed offline, assuming perfect knowledge of workload parameters over time.

IV. IMPLEMENTATION OF DYNAMIC POWER MANAGEMENT

In this section, we address how different DPM schemes have been implemented in circuits and systems. At the same time, we describe the infrastructure that will enable the implementation of complex power management policies in electronic systems. The section is organized as follows. We describe first the physical mechanisms for power management of digital and other types of components. We review how DPM is implemented in hardware circuits that include power-manageable components. We address next system-level design, and we describe how power management is implemented in hardware/software systems, with particular reference to operating system-based power management. We conclude by presenting some experimental results on software-managed personal computers.

A. Power Management in System Components

Our working definition of system component has been provided in Section II. The complexity of a component may vary and it is irrelevant for this discussion. In Section II-A, components are considered as black boxes. Here, we are concerned with their internal structure, and we outline several techniques that can be exploited to design power-manageable components (PMC's).

1) Clock Gating: We consider first digital components that are clocked. This class of components is wide, and it includes most processors, controllers and memories. Power consumption in clocked digital components (in CMOS technology) is roughly proportional to the clock frequency and to the square of the supply voltage. Power can be saved by reducing the clock frequency (and in the limit by stopping the clock), or by reducing the supply voltage (and in the limit by powering off a component). Note that the two limiting cases (clock freezing and powering off) are applicable only to idle components. For components that are in an active state but whose response is not performance critical, power consumption can be traded off for performance by reducing the clock frequency or the supply voltage. The latter solution is usually preferred because of the quadratic dependence of power consumption on supply voltage, and it is often combined with frequency downscaling.

When considering possibly idle digital components, clock gating (or freezing) is the most common technique for power management. Namely, the clock of an idle component can be stopped during the period of idleness. Power savings are achieved in the registers (whose clock is halted) and in the combinational logic gates where signals do not propagate due to the freezing of data in registers.

Example 4.1: Clock gating has been implemented in several processors [14]–[17]. The Alpha 21 264 microprocessor uses a hierarchical clocking scheme with gated clocks [17]. In particular, the 21 264 Floating Point Unit has a controller that can freeze the clock to its components, such as the adder, multiplier, divider, etc., according to the instructions to be executed, so that the idle components do not waste power.

The PowerPC 603 processor [14] has both local and global clock control. We highlight here a feature of global clock control. When the processor is in a Sleep state, the clock to all units may be disabled. On the other hand, the PLL is not necessarily disabled in the Sleep state, so that the system controller can choose from different levels of power savings, depending on the wake-up response time requirements. For example, if a quick wake-up is required, the processor can wake up from Sleep in ten system clock cycles, if the PLL is active. On the other hand, for maximum power savings, the PLL can be shut off in the Sleep state. In this case, the wake-up time can be as long as 100 μs, to allow the PLL to relock to the external clock. □

Clock gating has a small performance overhead: the clock can be restarted by simply deasserting the clock-freezing signal. Hence, clock gating is ideally suited for implementing self-managed components. In this case, the clock is *always* stopped as soon as some custom-designed idleness detection logic signals that the component (or some of its subunits) is idle. Several CAD tools have been developed to support design with local clock (or signal) gating [8]–[12], [47]. These tools aim at generating automatically the circuit that detects idleness and that issues the signal to freeze the clock. The tools implement various methods of realizing clock gating, which differ according to the type of unit to be controlled (e.g., sequential controller, data path, pipelined circuit) and to the type of idleness being monitored (e.g., state/output pair of a sequential circuit, external observability of some signals).

Clock gating is widely used because it is conceptually simple, it has a small overhead in terms of additional circuits and often zero performance overhead because the component can transition from an idle to an active state in one (or few) cycles. The main design challenges in the implementation of clock gating are: 1) to construct an idleness-detecting circuit which is small (and thus consuming little power) and accurate (i.e., able to stop the clock whenever the component is idle) and 2) to design gated-clock distribution circuitry that introduces minimum routing overhead and keeps clock skew under tight control [13]. In some cases, as seen in the previous example, power dissipation can be further reduced by stopping not only clock distribution, but also clock generation (i.e., by stopping the master clock PLL or the internal oscillator). This choice implies nonnegligible shutdown and restart delays and it is generally not automated. Sleep states where global clock generation is stopped can only be entered by issuing external commands. For processors, shutdown can be initiated by either a dedicated instruction or by asserting a dedicated signal.

2) Supply Shutdown: It is important to stress that clock-gating does not eliminate power dissipation. First, if clock gating is local, or if the clock generator is active, there is still dynamic power dissipation on the active clock circuitry. Second, leakage currents dissipate power even when all clocks are halted. As a result, the objective of achieving minimum power dissipation, as required by some battery-powered hand-held devices, may not be achieved by clock gating.

Power consumption of idle components can be avoided by powering off the unit. This radical solution requires controllable switches on the component supply line. An advantage of this approach is the wide applicability to all kind of electronic components, i.e., digital and analog units, sensors, and transducers. A major disadvantage is the wake-up time recovery time, which is typically higher than in the case of clock gating because the component's operation must be reinitialized.

When thinking of a microelectronic circuit (e.g., processor, controller), such a component is typically structured as a hierarchical compositions of subcomponents. Thus, power shutdown is applied to a selected number of subcomponents. In the case of complex circuits, usually a portion of the circuit is not powered down, so that it can run a set of minimal monitoring and control functions, and wake up the powered-down components when needed.

Example 4.2: The StrongARM SA-1100 [3] chip has two power supplies: a VDDI 1.5-V internal power supply and a VDDX 3.3-V interface voltage supply. VDDI powers the CPU core and the majority of the functional units on the chip (DMA controller, MMU, LCD controller, etc.). VDDX powers the input–output drivers, an internal 32-KHz crystal oscillator, the system control unit, and a few critical circuits.

The Sleep state the SA-1100 is an example of power supply shutdown. Power in Sleep is reduced to 0.16 mW (as opposed to 400 mW in Run state) by switching off the VDDI supply. The shutdown sequence for entering the Sleep state goes through three phases: 1) flush to memory all state information that should be preserved throughout the sleep period; 2) reset all internal processor state and program wakeup events; and 3) shutdown the internal clock generator. Each phase takes approximatively 30 μs. During Sleep, the SA-1100 only watches for preprogrammed wake-up events. Processor wake-up goes through three phases: 1) ramp-up VDDX and processor clock startup; 2) wait time for stabilizing processor clock; and 3) CPU boot sequence. The first two phases take, respectively, 10 and 150 ms. The third phase has negligible duration compared to the first two. The Sleep state can be entered either by rising a dedicated pin (called BATT_FAULT) or by a software procedure that writes to the power manager control register PMCR of the CPU. □

Power down is applicable to electrooptical and electromechanical system components, such as displays and HDD's. For systems with mechanical moving parts, like HDD's, the time constants involved in accelerating and decelerating moving parts are usually much larger than those involved in powering up and down electronic components. Furthermore, acceleration and deceleration tend to decrease the expected lifetime of the component [34]. Lifetime reduction can be seen as another cost associated with state transitions.

Example 4.3: We consider again the IBM Travelstar 14GS disk drive [4], mentioned in Example 2.2. In this component, we can highlight as main subunits: the spindle motor, the head positioning subsystem, and the host interface. The IBM Travelstar HDD has nine power states: a spin-up state to initialize the drive from power down, three operational states (seek, write and read), and five inactive states (Performance Idle, Active Idle, Low power idle, Standby, and Sleep). Different physical mechanisms are used to reduce power in the inactive states. In the Performance Idle state, all electronic components are powered while in the Active Idle state, some circuitry is in power saving mode, and in the Low power idle the head is unloaded. Whereas the spindle motor is rotating in the three idle states, the motor is spun down in the Standby and Sleep states. In the Standby state the host interface is active, while in the Sleep it is turned off.

The power consumption in the active states (in average 2.6 W) decreases in the inactive states to the values of 2, 1.3, 0.85, 0.25, and 0.1 W, respectively. Restarting the HDD requires a peak power of 5 W, due to the acceleration of the disks. Finally, note that the lower the power consumption is, the longer the corresponding wake up time is. Thus, DPM strategies need to take advantage of the low-power states while minimizing the impact on performance. □

3) Multiple and Variable Power Supplies: DPM is also applicable to components that are not idle, but whose performance (e.g., I/O delays) requirements varies with time. The implementation technology can then be based on the *slowdown* of non-critical components. The slowdown is achieved by lowering the voltage supply, such that the component becomes performance critical.

Early implementations of multivoltage chips used a static power-directed partitioning into subunits, each powered by a different supply voltage. Most often two voltage levels were used, and level shifters were employed at the border of subunits running on different supplies [44]. The extension of this approach to the realm of DPM is to enable dynamic adjustment of power supply voltage during system operation. One of the main challenges in implementing this extension is to guarantee that clock frequency tracks the speed changes caused by dynamic voltage supply adjustments.

In the pioneering work by Nielsen *et al.* [45], self-timed circuits were employed in conjunction with variable supply voltage. Self-timed circuits synchronize using local handshake signals, hence, they do not need adjustable clocks. Unfortunately, self-timed circuits are not mainstream technology. Alternative approaches employ standard synchronous logic [46], [48], [49] coupled with adjustable clocks that adapt their frequency to the speed of the critical path under different supply voltages. Another issue in systems with dynamically variable supply voltage is that they require high-efficiency dc–dc converters that can be programmed over a wide range of output voltages. Several adjustable dc–dc converters have been described in the literature [50]–[53]. The variable supply voltage approach can be complemented by dynamic threshold-voltage adjustment, achieved by controlling the body back bias [48], [49].

Dynamically varying supply voltages may be quantized [46] and thus be restricted to a finite number of values, or may take values in a continuous range. In the former case it is possible to identify a finite number of power states for the system; in the latter the concept of finite state is not applicable. State transition take a finite time because dc–dc converters cannot support arbitrarily fast changes in supply voltage.

B. System-Level Power Management Implementation

We consider DPM at the system level, and the corresponding implementation issues. Note that DPM schemes at the system level can coexist with local power management of components.

When considering electronic systems implemented in hardware, the power manager is a specialized control unit that acts in parallel and in coordination with the system control unit. In other words, the power manager may be a hardwired or microprogrammed controller, and possibly merged with the system controller. Policies based on timeouts are easily implemented by timers. Stochastic policies can be implemented by lookup tables (when stationary) or by sequential circuits. Randomized policies require the use of pseudorandom number generators, that can be implemented by *linear feedback shift registers* (LFSR's).

Typical electronic systems are software programmable, and a majority have an operating system ranging from a simple run-time scheduler or real-time operating system (RTOS) (for embedded applications) to a full-fledged operating system (as in the case of personal computers or workstations).

There are several reasons for migrating the power manager to software. Software power managers are easy to write and to reconfigure. In most cases, the designer cannot, or does not want to, interfere with and modify the underlying hardware platform. DPM implementations are still a novel art, and experimentation with software is easier than with hardware.

In general, the operating system is the software layer where the DPM policy can be implemented best. *OS-based power management* (OSPM) has the advantage that the power/performance dynamic control is performed by the software layer (the OS) that manages the computational, storage and I/O tasks of the system. Implementing OSPM is a *hardware/software codesign* problem because the hardware resources need to be interfaced with the OS-based software power manager, and because both the hardware resources and the software application programs need to be designed so that they cooperate with OSPM.

Recent initiatives to handle system-level power management include Microsoft's *OnNow* initiative [20] and the *advanced configuration and power interface* (ACPI) standard proposed by Intel, Microsoft, and Toshiba [21]. The former supports the implementation of OSPM and targets the design of personal computers with improved usability through innovative OS design. The latter simplifies the codesign of OSPM by providing an interface standard to control system resources. On the other hand, the aforementioned standards do not provide procedures for optimal control of power-managed system.

1) Industrial Design Standards: Industrial standards have been proposed to facilitate the development of operating system-based power management. Intel, Microsoft and Toshiba proposed the open standard called *advanced configuration and power interface* (ACPI) [21]. ACPI provides an OS-independent power management and configuration standard. It provides for an orderly transition from *legacy* hardware to ACPI-compliant hardware. Although this initiative targets *personal computers* (PC's), it contains useful guidelines for a more general class of systems. The main goals of ACPI are to: 1) enable all PC's to implement motherboard dynamic configuration and power management; 2) enhance power management features and the robustness of power-managed systems; and 3) accelerate implementation of power-managed computers, reduce costs and time to market.

The ACPI specification defines most interfaces between OS software and hardware. The software and hardware components relevant to ACPI are shown in Fig. 11. Applications interact with the OS kernel through *application programming interfaces* (API's). A module of the OS implements the power management policies. The power management module interacts with the hardware through kernel services (system calls). The kernel interacts with the hardware using device drivers. The front-end of the ACPI interface is the *ACPI driver*. The driver is OS-specific, it maps kernel requests to ACPI commands, and ACPI responses/messages to kernel signals/interrupts. Notice that the kernel may also interact with non-ACPI-compliant hardware through other device drivers.

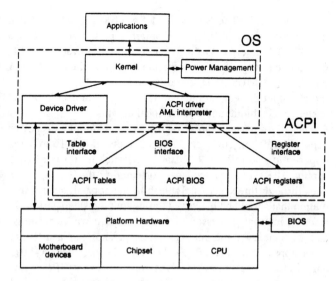

Fig. 11. ACPI interface and PC platform.

At the bottom of Fig. 11 the hardware platform is shown. Although it is represented as a monolithic block, it is useful to distinguish three types of hardware components. First, hardware resources (or *devices*) are the system components that provide some kind of specialized functionality (e.g., video controllers, modems, bus controllers). Second, the *CPU* can be seen as a specialized resource that need to be active for the OS (and the ACPI interface layer) to run. Finally, the *chipset* (also called core logic) is the motherboard logic that controls the most basic hardware functionalities (such as real-time clocks, interrupt signals, processor busses) and interfaces the CPU with all other devices. Although the CPU runs the OS, no system activity could be performed without the chipset. From the power management standpoint, the chipset, or a critical part of it, should always be active because the system relies on it to exit from sleep states.

It is important to notice that ACPI specifies neither how to implement hardware devices nor how to realize power management in the operating system. No constraints are imposed on implementation styles for hardware and on power management policies. Implementation of ACPI-compliant hardware can leverage any technology or architectural optimization as long as the power-managed device is controllable by the standard interface specified by ACPI.

In ACPI, the system has five *global power states*. Namely, the following.

- `Mechanical off` state $G3$, with no power consumption.
- `Soft off` state $G2$ (also called $S5$). A full OS reboot is needed to restore the working state.
- `Sleeping` state $G1$. The system appears to be off and power consumption is reduced. The system returns to the working state in an amount of time which grows with the inverse of the power consumption.
- `Working` state $G0$, where the system is On and fully usable.
- `Legacy` state, which is entered when the system does not comply with ACPI.

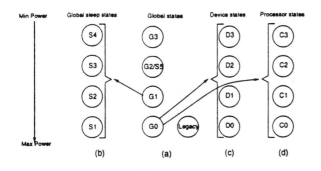

Fig. 12. State definitions for ACPI.

The global states are shown in Fig. 12(a). They are ordered from top to bottom by increasing power dissipation.

The ACPI specification refines the classification of global system states by defining four sleeping states within state $G1$, as shown in Fig. 12(b).

- $S1$ is a sleeping state with low wake-up latency. No system context is lost in the CPU or the chipset.
- $S2$ is a low wake-up latency sleeping state. This state is similar to the $S1$ sleeping state with the exception that the CPU and system cache context is lost.
- $S3$ is another low wake-up latency sleeping state where all system context is lost except system memory.
- $S4$ is the sleeping state with the lowest power and longest wake-up latency. To reduce power to a minimum, all devices are powered off.

Additionally, the ACPI specification defines states for system components. There are two types of system components, *devices* and *processor*, for which power states are specified. Devices are abstract representations of the hardware resources in the system. Four states are defined for devices, as shown in Fig. 12(c). In contrast with global power states, device power states are not visible to the user. For instance, some devices can be in an inactive state, but the system appears to be in a working state. Furthermore, state transitions for different devices can be controlled by different power management schemes. The processor is the central processing unit that controls the entire PC platform. The processor has its own power states, as shown in Fig. 12(d). Notice the intrinsic asymmetry of the ACPI model. The central role of the CPU is recognized, and the processor is not treated as a simple resource.

2) ACPI-Based DPM Implementations: A set of experiments were carried out by Lu et al. [35], [36] to measure the effectiveness of different DPM policies. Lu used two ACPI-compliant computers, running a beta version of Windows NT V5, which is also ACPI compliant. The first computer is a VarStation 2861A desktop, using a Pentium II processor and an IBM DTTA 350–640 HDD. The second is a Sony VAIO PCG F-150 laptop, with a Pentium II and a Fujitsu MHF 2043AT HDD. The experiments aimed at controlling the HDD unit using different policies.

For this purpose, Lu implemented *filter drivers* (Fig. 13) to control the power states of the HDD's, to record disk accesses and to analyze the performance impact of the power management overhead of each algorithm. The power lines of the disks

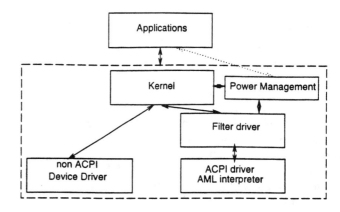

Fig. 13. DPM using filter drivers.

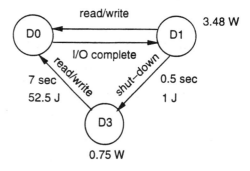

Fig. 14. PSM for IBM DTTA HDD.

TABLE I
DISK PARAMETERS: SUBSCRIPTS sd AND wu DENOTE SHUT DOWN AND WAKE UP, RESPECTIVELY

Model	P_{Off}	P_{On}	T_{sd}	E_{sd}	T_{wu}	E_{wu}
	Watt	Watt	sec	J	sec	J
IBM	0.75	3.48	0.51	1.08	6.97	52.5
Fujitsu	0.13	0.95	0.67	0.36	1.61	4.39

were monitored by digital multimeters, connected to a PC via a RS-232 port to record the measurements.

The IBM HDD can be in one of three states: `PowerDeviceD0` when it is reading or writing, `PowerDeviceD1` when the plates are spinning and `PowerDeviceD3` when the plates stop spinning. I/O requests only wait for seek and rotation delays when the disk is at `PowerDeviceD1` (see Fig. 14). If a request arrives when the hard disk is at `PowerDeviceD3`, it has to wait for the wake-up procedure in addition to the seek and rotation delays. The disk consumes 3.48 and 0.75 W in states D1 and D3, respectively. It takes approximately 7 s and 52.5 J to wake up from D3 to D0. It takes (in average) 0.5 s to enter D3 from D1. The behavior of the Fujitsu HDD is similar, but with different parameters (see Table I). The break-even times of the IBM and Fujitsu HDD's are 17.6 and 5.43 s, respectively.

Experimental results are reported in [36], where a comparative analysis of different algorithms is presented. For comparison purposes, both computers execute the same trace of input data (an 11-h-long execution trace). Results show that all algorithms spend less than 1% of computation on power management itself, thus validating a fundamental premise of this body of work. For the laptop (desktop) computer, power reductions have been measured up to 55% (43%) (as compared to the always on case) and up to 34% (23%) (as compared to the default 3-min timeout policy of Windows OS). Larger power savings are achieved on the laptop computer because of the shorter break-even time of its disk.

3) Observer Implementation: As seen in Section III, power management requires information on the usage of each hardware resource, such as: 1) distribution of interarrival times of request to the resources and 2) distribution of service times for the requests. The *observer* module (Fig. 2) of the PM takes care of data collection. In ACPI-compliant PC's, the observer may rely on ACPI messages to obtain the data needed to drive the policies. However, not all computers are ACPI-compliant. In this section, we shall analyze the implementation of a power manager observer module that does not exploit ACPI, nor it is based on a proprietary Microsoft operating system. The basic requirements for the implementation of the observer are as follows.

- *Low perturbation of normal system activity*: Monitoring should be transparent to the end user and should modify the usage patterns of hardware resources as little as possible.
- *Flexibility*: It should be easy to monitor multiple types of resources. Moreover, the number and types of observed resources should be dynamically controllable. This feature is particularly useful for laptop computers where new devices can be installed during system operation (i.e., plug-and-play capability).
- *Accuracy*: Well-known system utilities give access to cumulative counts of accesses to system resources. This functionality is not sufficient to obtain accurate statistics of interarrival times and service times. One important feature of the observer is the capability of time-stamping the events with high resolution.

The software-based observer architecture analyzed in this section is called IPM [6], and it has been implemented as an extension of the Linux operating system [54]. The observer monitors the accesses to system resources and stores them in form of time-stamped events. The core data structure is located in kernel memory space, that is forced to reside in physical-address space. Hence, storing events in kernel space prevents the usage of memory paging, thus avoiding the severe performance penalty possibly caused by TLB misses.

On the other hand, storing the event list in kernel space imposes a tight limitation on its maximum size. The list cannot grow larger than 64 KB, which corresponds to $L_{\max} = 4096$ events. The event list is implemented as a circular buffer and it is allocated once for all (for performance reasons). The circular structure protects against memory violations. If the number of unprocessed events stored in the list grows larger than the number of slots, older events are overwritten. Event loss causes a decrease in accuracy in monitoring but does not damage normal system operation.

The size limitation of the event list in kernel memory is not a concern if events are processed and discarded as soon as they are registered (online monitoring). However, event loss should be avoided if the observer is collecting long event traces for offline processing. The observer supports offline

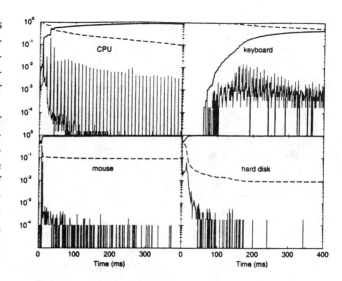

Fig. 15. Statistical analysis of the interarrival time. For each device, three curves are plotted in lin-log scale: the probability density (solid line), the probability distribution (bold line), and its complement to one (dashed line). Data refer to software development.

monitoring through a simple dumping mechanism that can be summarized as follows. Whenever the number of unprocessed events reaches a value $L_{\text{low}} < L_{\max}$, a wake-up signal is sent to a dedicated process. The process is normally inactive, waiting for the wake-up signal, thus it does not alter normal system activity. Whenever the wake-up signal is asserted, the process becomes active and can be scheduled. Clearly, the execution of this process does alter normal system activity. However, the perturbation is limited by the fact that the list is processed only when it is almost full.

Devices that are controlled by the OS through device drivers are monitored by inserting standard function calls that update the event list in the device driver routines that are run whenever the component is accessed. Monitoring does not change the flow of execution of the device driver, and it has minimal impact on the execution time. At boot time, the observer is initialized by specifying which resources should be monitored.

The CPU and all hardware components required for its operation (chipset, RAM, bus controllers, etc.) are not controlled through device drivers. Fortunately, it is possible to monitor the CPU and its ancillary components by observing that the OS kernel itself is nothing else than executable code running on the CPU. Whenever the kernel is running, the CPU is active. When there is nothing to do, the kernel schedules a dummy process, called *idle task*. Hence, to detect CPU idleness, it is sufficient to monitor the scheduling of *idle task*.

Monitor installation requires kernel recompilation, and supports monitoring of CPU, keyboard, serial and parallel ports, PS2 mouse, IDE hard disk, and CD-ROM. During the system boot, a data structure is created for each IPM-compliant resource, containing its name, type, configuration flags, unique identifier, and resource-specific information (such as the type of events to be monitored). Monitoring can be selectively enabled for each resource by setting the corresponding flags.

Several experiments [5] (run on a HP Omnibook 5500 CT with 133-MHz Pentium processor and 48 MB of RAM) showed that system operation is slowed down by less than 0.38% in average, even when all available system components are monitored, thus showing convincing evidence of the nonintrusiveness of the monitor. Examples of the data collected by the monitoring system are reported in Fig. 15, where the probability densities and distributions of request interarrival times are plotted for CPU, keyboard, mouse, and hard disk. Data was collected during a code development user session. Several different usage patterns were also tested (such as editing, game playing, etc.).

V. CONCLUSION

DPM is a powerful methodology for reducing power consumption in electronic systems. In a power-managed system, the state of operation of various components is dynamically adapted to the required performance level, in an effort to minimize the power wasted by idle or underutilized components. For most system components, state transitions have nonnegligible power and performance costs. Thus, the problem of designing power management policies that minimize power under performance constraints is a challenging one.

We surveyed several classes of power-managed systems and power management policies. Furthermore, we analyzed the tradeoffs involved in designing and implementing power-managed systems. Several practical examples of power-managed systems were analyzed and discussed in detail. Even though DPM has been successfully employed in many real-life systems, much work is required for achieving a deep understanding on how to design systems that can be optimally power managed.

ACKNOWLEDGMENT

The authors would like to thank E.-Y. Chung, Y.-H. Lu, G. Paleologo, and T. Šimunić at Stanford University and S. Cavallucci and A. Gordini at Bologna University for their help and useful suggestions.

REFERENCES

[1] J. Lorch and A. Smith, "Software strategies for portable computer energy management," *IEEE Personal Commun.*, vol. 5, pp. 60–73, June 1998.
[2] L. Benini and G. De Micheli, *Dynamic Power Management: Design Techniques and CAD Tools*. Norwell, MA: Kluwer, 1998.
[3] *SA-1100 Microprocessor Technical Reference Manual*, Intel, 1998.
[4] *2.5-Inch Travelstar Hard Disk Drive*, IBM, 1998.
[5] L. Benini, R. Hodgson, and P. Siegel, "System-Level power estimation and optimization," in *Int. Symp. Low Power Architecture and Design*, Aug. 1998, pp. 173–178.
[6] L. Benini, A. Bogliolo, S. Cavallucci, and B. Riccó, "Monitoring system activity for OS-directed dynamic power management," in *Int. Symp. Low Power Architecture and Design*, Aug. 1998, pp. 185–190.
[7] "Advanced micro devices," in *AM29SLxxx Low-Voltage Flash Memories*, 1998.
[8] M. Alidina, J. Monteiro, S. Devadas, A. Ghosh, and M. Papaefthymiou, "Precomputation-based sequential logic optimization for low power," *IEEE Trans. VLSI Syst.*, vol. 2, pp. 426–436, Dec. 1994.
[9] S. Malik, V. Tiwari, and P. Ashar, "Guarded evaluation: Pushing power management to logic synthesis/design," in *Int. Symp. Low Power Design*, Apr. 1995, pp. 221–226.
[10] L. Benini and G. De Micheli, "Transformation and synthesis of FSM's for low power gated clock implementation," *IEEE Trans. Computer-Aided Design*, vol. 15, pp. 630–643, June 1996.
[11] F. Theeuwen and E. Seelen, "Power reduction through clock gating by symbolic manipulation," in *Symp. Logic and Architecture Design*, Dec. 1996, pp. 184–191.
[12] M. Ohnishi *et al.*, "A method of redundant clocking detection and power reduction at RT-level design," in *Int. Symp. Low Power Electronics and Design*, Aug. 1997, pp. 131–136.
[13] J. Oh and M. Pedram, "Gated clock routing minimizing the switched capacitance," in *Design Automation and Test in Europe Conf.*, Feb. 1998, pp. 692–697.
[14] S. Gary *et al.*, "PowerPC 603, a microprocessor for portable computers," *IEEE Design & Test of Computers*, vol. 11, pp. 14–23, 1994.
[15] G. Debnath, K. Debnath, and R. Fernando, "The pentium processor-90/100, microarchitecture and low-power circuit design," in *Int. Conf. VLSI Design*, Jan. 1995, pp. 185–190.
[16] S. Furber, *ARM System Architecture*. Reading, MA: Addison-Wesley, 1997.
[17] M. Gowan, L. Biro, and D. Jackson, "Power considerations in the design of the alpha 21 264 microprocessor," in *Design Automation Conf.*, June 1998, pp. 726–731.
[18] E. Harris *et al.*, "Technology directions for portable computers," *Proc. IEEE*, vol. 83, pp. 636–657, Apr. 1996.
[19] M. Stemm and R. Katz, "Measuring and reducing energy consumption of network interfaces in hand-held devices," *IEICE Trans. Commun.*, vol. E80-B, pp. 1125–1131, Aug. 1997.
[20] Microsoft. (1997) On now: The evolution of the PC platform. [Online] http://www.microsoft.com/hwdev/pcfuture/OnNOW.HTM.
[21] Intel, Microsoft, and Toshiba. (1996) Advanced configuration and power interface specification. [Online] http://www.intel.com/ial/powermgm/specs.html.
[22] N. Bambos, "Toward power-sensitive network architectures in wireless communications: Concepts, issues and design aspects," *IEEE Personal Commun.*, vol. 5, pp. 50–59, June 1998.
[23] J. Rulnick and N. Bambos, "Mobile power management for wireless communication networks," *Wireless Networks*, vol. 3, no. 1, pp. 3–14, Jan. 1997.
[24] K. Sivalingham *et al.*, "Low-power access protocols based on scheduling for wireless and mobile ATM networks," in *Int. Conf. Universal Personal Communications*, Oct. 1997, pp. 429–433.
[25] M. Zorzi and R. Rao, "Energy-constrained error control for wireless channels," *IEEE Personal Commun.*, vol. 4, pp. 27–33, Dec. 1997.
[26] B. Mangione-Smith, "Low-power communication protocols: Paging and beyond," in *IEEE Symp. Low-Power Electronics*, Apr. 1995, pp. 8–11.
[27] P. Krishnan, P. Long, and J. Vitter, "Adaptive disk spindown via optimal rent-to-buy in probabilistic environments," in *Int. Conf. Machine Learning*, July 1995, pp. 322–330.
[28] D. Helmbold, D. Long, and E. Sherrod, "Dynamic disk spin-down technique for mobile computing," in *IEEE Conf. Mobile Computing*, Nov. 1996, pp. 130–142.
[29] F. Douglis, P. Krishnan, and B. Bershad, "Adaptive disk spin-down policies for mobile computers," in *2nd USENIX Symp. Mobile and Location-Independent Computing*, Apr. 1995, pp. 121–137.
[30] R. Golding, P. Bosh, and J. Wilkes, "Idleness is not sloth," HP Laboratories Tech. Rep. HPL-96-140, 1996.
[31] A. Karlin, M. Manasse, L. McGeoch, and S. Owicki, "Competitive randomized algorithms for nonuniform problems," *Algorithmica*, vol. 11, no. 6, pp. 542–571, June 1994.
[32] M. Srivastava, A. Chandrakasan, and R. Brodersen, "Predictive system shutdown and other architectural techniques for energy efficient programmable computation," *IEEE Trans. VLSI Syst.*, vol. 4, pp. 42–55, Mar. 1996.
[33] C.-H. Hwang and A. Wu, "A predictive system shutdown method for energy saving of event-driven computation," in *Int. Conf. Computer-Aided Design*, Nov. 1997, pp. 28–32.
[34] Y. Lu and G. De Micheli, "Adaptive hard disk power management on personal computers," in *Great Lakes Symp. VLSI*, Feb. 1999, pp. 50–53.
[35] Y. Lu, T. Šimunić, and G. De Micheli, "Software controlled power management," in *Hardware–Software Codesign Symp.*, May 1999, pp. 151–161.
[36] Y. Lu, E. Y. Chung, T. Šimunić, L. Benini, and G. De Micheli, "Quantitative comparison of power management algorithms," in *DATE, Proc. Design Automation and Test in Europe*, Mar. 2000.
[37] T. Šimunić, L. Benini, and G. De Micheli, "Event-driven power management of portable systems," in *ISSS, Proc. Int. Symp. System Synthesis*, Nov. 1999, pp. 18–23.
[38] T. Šimunić, L. Benini, P. Glynn, and G. De Micheli, "Dynamic power management of portable systems using semi-Markov decison processes," in *DATE, Proc. Design Automation and Test in Europe*, Mar. 2000.
[39] L. Benini, G. Paleologo, A. Bogliolo, and G. De Micheli, "Policy optimization for dynamic power management," *IEEE Trans. Computer-Aided Design*, vol. 18, pp. 813–33, June 1999.

[40] Q. Qiu and M. Pedram, "Dynamic power management based on continuous-time Markov decision processes," in *Design Automation Conf.*, June 1999, pp. 555–561.

[41] E. Chung, L. Benini, A. Bogliolo, and G. De Micheli, "Dynamic power management for nonstationary service requests," in *Design and Test in Europe Conf.*, Mar. 1999, pp. 77–81.

[42] S. Ross, *Introduction to Probability Models*, 6th ed. New York: Academic, 1997.

[43] M. Puterman, *Finite Markov Decision Processes*. New York: Wiley, 1994.

[44] K. Usami *et al.*, "Automated low-power technique exploiting multiple supply voltages applied to a media processor," *IEEE J. Solid-State Circuits*, vol. 33, pp. 463–472, Mar. 1998.

[45] L. Nielsen, C. Niessen, J. Sparso, and K. van Berkel, "Low-power operation using self-timed circuits and adaptive scaling of supply voltage," *IEEE Trans. VLSI Syst.*, vol. 2, pp. 425–435, Dec. 1994.

[46] A. Chandrakasan, V. Gutnik, and T. Xanthopoulos, "Data driven signal processing: An approach for energy efficient computing," in *Int. Symp. Low Power Electronics and Design*, Aug. 1996, pp. 347–352.

[47] H. Kapadia, G. De Micheli, and L. Benini, "Reducing switching activity on datapath buses with control-signal gating," in *Custom Integrated Circuit Conf.*, May 1998, pp. 589–592.

[48] K. Suzuki *et al.*, "A 300 MIPS/W RISC core processor with variable supply-voltage scheme in variable threshold-voltage CMOS," in *Custom Integrated Circuits Conf.*, May 1997, pp. 587–590.

[49] K. Usami *et al.*, "Design methodology of ultra low-power MPEG4 codec core exploiting voltage scaling techniques," in *Design Automation Conf.*, June 1998, pp. 483–488.

[50] A. Stratakos, S. Sanders, and R. Brodersen, "A low-voltage CMOS dc–dc converter for a portable battery-operated system," in *Power Electronics Specialists Conf.*, June 1994, pp. 619–626.

[51] G. Wei and M. Horowitz, "A low power switching power supply for self-clocked systems," in *Int. Symp. Low Power Electronics and Design*, Aug. 1996, pp. 313–317.

[52] W. Namgoong, M. Yu, and T. Meng, "A high-efficiency variable-voltage CMOS dynamic dc–dc switching regulator," in *Int. Solid-State Circuits Conf.*, Feb. 1997, pp. 380–381.

[53] V. Gutnik and A. Chandrakasan, "Embedded power supply for low-power DSP," *IEEE Trans. VLSI Syst.*, vol. 5, pp. 425–435, Dec. 1997.

[54] L. Torvalds, "The Linux operating system," *Commun. ACM*, vol. 42, no. 4, pp. 38–39, Apr. 1999.

Luca Benini (M'93) received the Dr.Eng. degree in electrical engineering from the University of Bologna, Bologna, Italy, in 1991 and the M.S. and Ph.D. degrees in electrical engineering from Stanford University, Stanford, CA, in 1994 and 1997, respectively.

Since 1998, he has been an Assistant Professor in the Department of Electronics and Computer Science, University of Bologna. He also holds visiting professor positions at Stanford University and Hewlett-Packard Laboratories, Palo Alto, CA. His research interests are in all aspects of computer-aided design of digital circuits, with special emphasis on low-power applications and in the design of portable systems.

Dr. Benini has been a member of technical program committees for several technical conferences, including the Design and Test in Europe Conference and the International Symposium on Low Power Design.

Alessandro Bogliolo (M'95) received the Laura degree in electrical engineering and the Ph.D. degree in electrical engineering and computer science from the University of Bologna, Bologna, Italy, in 1992 and 1998, respectively.

From 1992 to 1999, he was with the Department of Electronics, Computer Science and Systems (DEIS), University of Bologna. In 1995 and 1996, he was a Visiting Scholar at the Computer Systems Laboratory (CSL), Stanford University, Stanford, CA. Since then he has cooperated with the research group of Prof. De Micheli at Stanford. In 1999, he joined the Department of Engineering (DIF), University of Ferrara, Ferrara, Italy, as an Assistant Professor. His research interests are in the area of computer-aided design of digital integrated circuits and systems, with particular emphasis on high-level power modeling, power optimization, and intellectual property protection.

Giovanni De Micheli (F'94) is a Professor of Electrical Engineering and Computer Science at Stanford University, Stanford, CA. His research interests include several aspects of the computer-aided design of integrated circuits and systems, with particular emphasis on automated synthesis, optimization, and validation. He is the author of *Synthesis and Optimization of Digital Circuits* (New York: McGraw-Hill, 1994) and a coauthor of *Dynamic Power Management: Circuit Techniques and CAD Tools* (Norwell, MA: Kluwer, 1998) and three other books. He is the Editor-in-Chief of the IEEE TRANSACTIONS ON COMPUTER-AIDED DESIGN.

Dr. De Micheli received the 1987 IEEE TRANSACTIONS ON COMPUTER-AIDED DESIGN/ICAS Best Paper Award, a Presidential Young Investigator Award in 1988, and two Best Paper Awards at the Design Automation Conference in 1983 and in 1993. He is Vice President (for publications) of the IEEE CAS Society. He is the General Chair of the 37th Design Automation Conference. He was Program and General Chair of the International Conference on Computer Design (ICCD) in 1988 and 1989, respectively. He was also Codirector of the NATO Advanced Study Institutes on Hardware/Software Co-design, Tremezzo, Italy, in 1995 and the Logic Synthesis and Silicon Compilation, L'Aquila, Italy, in 1986.

Power Estimation of Embedded Systems: A Hardware/Software Codesign Approach

William Fornaciari, *Member, IEEE,* Paolo Gubian, *Member, IEEE,* Donatella Sciuto, *Member, IEEE,* and Cristina Silvano

Abstract— The need for low-power embedded systems has become very significant within the microelectronics scenario in the most recent years. A power-driven methodology is mandatory during embedded systems design to meet system-level requirements while fulfilling time-to-market. The aim of this paper is to introduce accurate and efficient power metrics included in a hardware/software (HW/SW) codesign environment to guide the system-level partitioning. Power evaluation metrics have been defined to widely explore the architectural design space at high abstraction level. This is one of the first approaches that considers globally HW and SW contributions to power in a system-level design flow for control dominated embedded systems.

Index Terms— Embedded systems, hardware/software codesign, low-power design, power estimation.

I. INTRODUCTION

EMBEDDED systems are those computing and control systems designed for dedicated applications [1] where *ad hoc* software routines are provided to respond to specific requirements. The diffusion on the semiconductor market of standard processors characterized by high performance and reasonable prices contributed to increase the importance of embedded systems. The typical embedded system architecture is constituted by one or more dedicated hardware units such as application specific integrated circuits (ASIC's) to implement the hardware part and a set of software routines running on a dedicated processor or application specific instruction processor (ASIP) for the software part. Exploiting the advantages offered by submicron complementary metal–oxide–semiconductor (CMOS) technologies, the entire embedded system can be implemented on a single ASIC, including the processor core, the on-chip memory, the input/output (I/O) interface and the custom hardware part.

Innovative codesign techniques emerged as a new computer-aided design (CAD) discipline in the recent past, to cope with the complexity of a comprehensive exploration of the design alternatives in the hardware/software design space. Codesign aims at meeting the system-level requirements by using a concurrent design and validation methodology, thus exploiting the synergism of the hardware and the software parts.

Several design tasks are covered during the codesign process, mainly system-level modeling, capture of the functional cospecification, analysis and validation of the cospecification, system-level partitioning, exploration and evaluation of several architectures with respect to given design metrics, cosynthesis and cosimulation. The availability of a codesign methodology, covering all these design phases, is mandatory during embedded systems design to meet the system-level requirements.

The overall system costs and performance are greatly impacted by the effects of the partitioning task, that targets the assignment of operations to the hardware (HW) or software (SW) parts. To guide the partitioning process, design metrics should be defined to compare alternative partitionings and to evaluate their conformance with respect to the system requirements, typically defined in terms of performances, area, power, costs, etc. Moreover, the design of embedded systems is often over-constrained. Thus, a solution satisfying all those constraints is difficult to be identified in a reasonable design time. As a result, only a partial exploration of the architectural design space can be usually carried out, to get to an acceptable solution, far from the optimal one.

The importance of the power constraints during the design of embedded systems has continuously increased in the past years, due to technological trends toward high-level integration and increasing operating frequencies, combined with the growing demand of portable systems. Despite of the increasing importance of power consumption in most of the embedded applications, only a few codesign approaches take into account such a goal at the higher levels of abstraction.

While several power estimation techniques have been proposed in literature at the gate, circuit and layout levels [2], a few papers have been published addressing the power estimation problem at high-level until recently [3], [4], despite the increasing interest in the system and behavioral levels. According to [3], high-level power estimation techniques can be classified depending on their abstraction level.

The average power is strongly related to the switching activity of the circuit nodes, hence power estimation can be considered a pattern-dependent process. In particular, the input pattern-dependency of the power estimation approaches can be classified as strong or weak pattern-dependency [4]. Main advantages of the strongly pattern-dependent process, based on extensive simulations, derive from their accuracy and wide applicability. However, to obtain a complete and accurate power estimation, the designer should provide a

---

Manuscript received March 15, 1997; revised July 1, 1997.
W. Fornaciari and D. Sciuto are with Politecnico di Milano, Dipartimento di Elettronica e Informazione, Milano 20133 Italy.
P. Gubian and C. Silvano are with the Università di Brescia, Dipartimento di Elettronica per l'Automazione, Brescia 25123 Italy.
Publisher Item Identifier S 1063-8210(98)02948-5.

comprehensive amount of input patterns to be simulated, thus making this approach very time consuming and computationally very costly. To avoid the need of a large amount of input patterns, the weakly pattern-dependent approaches require input probabilities, reflecting the typical input behavior, but the estimated results will depend on the user-supplied input probabilities.

High-level power estimation is a key issue in the early determination of the power budget for embedded systems. However, high-level power estimation methods [5] have not yet achieved the maturity necessary to enable their use within current industrial CAD environments. Our work is an attempt to fill such a gap, by providing a set of metrics based on a high-level power model, to cover the different parts composing the basic architecture of embedded systems. The goal is to widely explore the architectural design space during the system-level partitioning and to early retarget architectural design choices. Accuracy and efficiency should be the driving forces to meet the power requirements, avoiding redesign processes. In general, the relative accuracy in high-level power estimation is much more important than the absolute accuracy, the main objective being the comparison of different design alternatives [3].

The aim of this paper is to define a power evaluation codesign methodology. The method is part of a more general HW/SW codesign approach for control dominated embedded systems. The related CAD environment, called TOSCA (TOols for System Codesign Automation) [6], among other design quality estimation techniques, provides accurate and efficient power metrics to guide the system-level partitioning. Metrics suitable for power evaluation of both the hardware and software parts are defined.

The availability of a high-level power analysis is of paramount importance to obtain early estimation results, while maintaining an acceptable accuracy and a competitive global design time. Based on these results, tradeoff considerations can be carried out in a reasonable time, by avoiding to follow the entire design flow to get power comparison results. Our approach can be considered as one of the first attempts to cover power estimation issues from a HW/SW comprehensive perspective, mainly focusing on the hardware part and considering a general architecture adopted by most industrial synthesis systems.

The paper is organized as follows. Foundations and notations constituting the background of our analysis are shown in Section II. Power metrics to guide the system-level partitioning are derived in Section III, while the proposed power models for the HW and SW parts are addressed in Section IV and V, respectively. Simulation results are also provided in Section VI, to demonstrate the advantages offered by the proposed methodology during the development of control dominated embedded systems. Finally, concluding remarks are drawn in Section VII.

II. BACKGROUND OF THE ANALYSIS

Let us introduce the general formalism to express power dissipation, the TOSCA codesign framework and the target system architecture.

A. Power Dissipation in CMOS Circuits

Power dissipation in CMOS devices is composed of both a static and a dynamic component. Anyway, the dominant part [7] is the dynamic part, expressed by the switching activity power $P = V_{DD}^2 f_{\text{CLK}} C_{\text{EFF}}$ where V_{DD} is the supply voltage, f_{CLK} is the system clock frequency and C_{EFF} is the effective switched capacitance (that is the product of the total physical capacitance C_{Li} of each node in the circuit and the switching activity factor α_i of each node summed over all the N nodes in the circuit).

The switching activity of each signal is fully characterized by a *static* and a *dynamic* component. The static component can be expressed in terms of the *static signal probability* (p_n^1) of each node n, that is the probability of the node to be at one (therefore, $p_n^1 \leq 1$ and $p_n^0 = 1 - p_n^1$). A signal is called *equiprobable* when $p_n^1 = p_n^0 = 0.5$. The *transition probability* (p_n^{01}) is the probability of a zero to one transition at node n. In the spatial and temporal independence assumption [4], p_n^{01} is given by the probability that the current state is zero times the probability that the next state is one $p_n^{01} = p_n^0 p_n^1 = (1-p_n^1)p_n^1$. Under the same assumption, the *switching activity* of a node n (α_n) is $\alpha_n = p_n^{01} + p_n^{10} = 2p_n^1(1 - p_n^1)$, while the *toggle rate* (TR_n) is $TR_n = \alpha_n f_{\text{CLK}}$.

B. The TOSCA Codesign Flow

The design flow of the TOSCA codesign environment, where the present work is going to be integrated, is shown in Fig. 1. Main goal is to reduce the impact of the system integration and design constraints verification bottlenecks on the global design time, thus allowing a cost-effective evaluation of alternative designs.

The design capture is performed via a mixed textual/graphical editor based on a OCCAMII customization [6] improving the user friendliness and gathering in the same design database timing constraints, design requirements, design goals and possibly an initial HW versus SW allocation of the modules composing the system. If the latter information is left unspecified by the user, an initial allocation is decided based on the results of an heuristic, by statically inspecting the properties of the system description. The main part of the codesign flow is represented by the design space exploration, i.e., a "what if" analysis of alternative architectural solutions to discover an acceptable final system modularization and HW versus SW allocation fulfilling the initial requirements and goals. This is obtained by evaluating system properties through a set of metrics, by applying system-level transformations, producing new modularization of the system specification semantically equivalent to the original one. When an acceptable partitioning is found, synthesis of the HW and SW parts can be performed. The SW synthesis passes through an intermediate uncommitted format, called virtual instruction set (VIS) [8], allowing the designer to consider the timing performance when different CPU cores are employed and to make possible a flexible simulation of the cooperating HW and SW based on the same VHDL simulator engine. HW-bound modules and interfaces are automatically converted into suitable VHDL templates. Finally, simulation

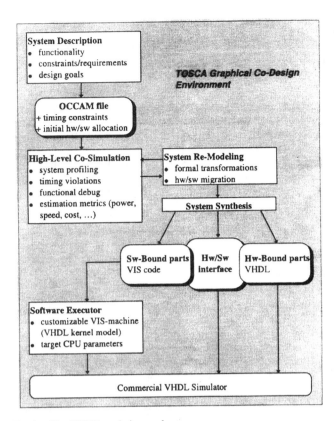

Fig. 1. The TOSCA codesign roadmap.

of the HW/SW system is performed, considering the side-effects due to the HW/SW bused communication and the different performance of HW and SW technologies.

The task of system-level partitioning should provide alternative solutions in terms of the cost/performance ratio. To afford the partitioning process with respect to the design constraints, it is necessary to define a *cost function*, based on some metrics. Thus, a preliminary and iterated phase is a metric-based analysis of the system-level description. Design metrics, considering the contribution of both the HW and SW parts, can be conceived to evaluate the quality of a partitioning solution in terms of fulfillment of several design optimization criteria [6], such as performance, cost, resource exploitation, communication and power consumption. The current version of TOSCA evaluates a set of static and dynamic metrics, based on the analysis of the object oriented representation of the specification, high-level simulation and profiling. Metrics to evaluate area and performances are described in [6], while metrics for power analysis are the subject of such paper.

C. The Target System Architecture

The system-level architecture of the embedded system is implemented within a single ASIC, including both the HW and SW parts. The target architecture is presented in Fig. 2.

The single ASIC architecture is defined at the RT-level and it is composed of the following parts.

1) *Data Path*—including storage units, functional units, and multiplexers. A two-level multiplexer structure is considered for the interconnection among registers and functional units and the typical operations imply a register-to-register transfer;
2) *Main Memory*—to be accessed through input/output registers;
3) *Control Unit*—implemented as a set of finite state machines (FSM's);
4) *Embedded Core Processor*—such as a general-purpose standard processor, a microcontroller, a DSP, etc., with its memory (even if part of the memory can be external) implementing the SW part;
5) *Clock Distribution Logic*—including the buffers of the clock distribution network;
6) *Crossbar Network*—to interface the architectural units by using a communication protocol at the system-level;
7) *Primary I/O's*—to interface with the external environment.

III. HIGH-LEVEL POWER ESTIMATION METRICS

Our goal is to define power metrics to be applied at the system-level to measure and to compare the power consumption of several design alternatives. In general, it is quite difficult to define a single metric suitable for accurate and efficient power assessment for all the embedded systems applications. Thus, first we classify the embedded systems depending on their constraints and computational modes, then we propose a set of metrics for each class of systems.

We can divide the embedded systems in *timing-constrained* systems, if the speed is the most important design constraint, and *area-constrained* systems, if the area is the most important constraint. Several computational modes characterize the *timing-constrained* systems, depending on the *system throughput* T defined as the number of operations performed in a given time [7]. For microprocessor-based embedded systems, we can define three main modes of computation: *fixed* throughput mode, *maximum* throughput mode, and *burst* throughput mode, the latter characterized by a fraction of time performing useful computations, during which the maximum throughput is required, while during the rest of the time the system is in idle state, such as among user requests. Since the power budget strictly depends of the computational mode for which the embedded system is dedicated, a specific power metric can be defined for each one of the above defined operating modes [7].

For fixed throughput systems, a suitable metric is represented by the power/throughput ratio or equivalently the energy per operation. Since the throughput is fixed, if a partitioning solution leads to a reduction of such metric with respect to an initial partitioning, the corresponding power dissipation is reduced.

For maximum throughput systems, the most appropriate metric should account for both the low power and high performance needs. A suitable metric is thus the energy to throughput ratio (ETR) defined as in [7] $\text{ETR} = E_{\text{MAX}}/T_{\text{MAX}}$ where E_{MAX} is the energy per operation or equivalently the power per throughput and T_{MAX} is the maximum throughput. Hence, the ETR metric can also be expressed as $\text{ETR} = \text{Power}/T^2$.

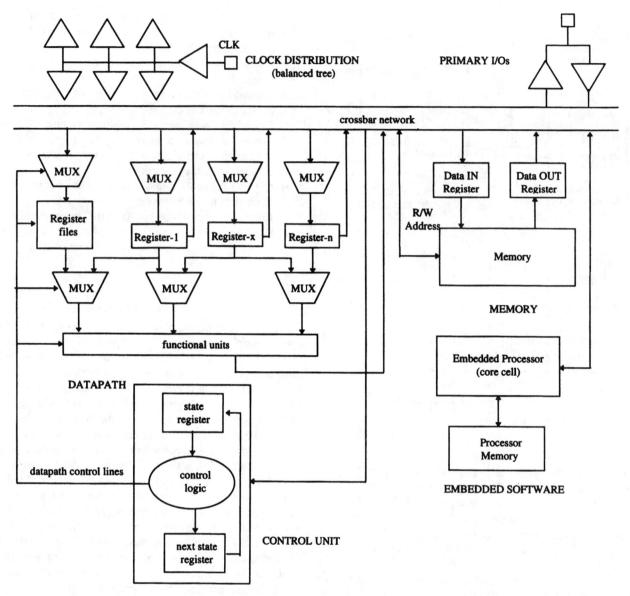

Fig. 2. The target system architecture at the RT-level.

The ETR metric expresses the concept of optimization of both the throughput and the power dissipation. A partitioning corresponding to a lower value of ETR represents a solution with lower energy per operation for equal throughput as well as a solution with greater throughput for the same amount of energy per operation.

For systems operating in the burst throughput mode, the power metric should provide power reduction, during both the idle and computing time, and throughput optimization when computing. For those systems applying power shut down techniques during idle cycles, an efficient metric is just ETR, since the power dissipation has been completely eliminated when idling. For those systems not supporting power saving modes, a most effective metric is [7]

$$M_{\text{BURST}} = (E_{\text{MAX}} + E_{\text{IDLE}})/T_{\text{MAX}} \qquad (1)$$

where $E_{\text{MAX}}/E_{\text{IDLE}}$ is the total energy dissipated when computing/idling per total operations and T_{MAX} is the maximum throughput.

For those area-constrained systems for which the target area is fixed, a valid metric M_A is represented by the power by area product (or equivalently the power/area ratio). Since the area is fixed, a reduction in the value of M_A corresponds to a minimization in the power consumption.

In general, for those area-constrained systems aiming at both power and area reduction, a good metric is given by the product of the energy per operation by area EAP $= E_{\text{MAX}} * A$ where E_{MAX} is the energy per operation or equivalently the power per throughput and A is the area. Hence, the EAP metric can also be expressed as EAP $= (\text{Power} * A)/T$. The EAP metric expresses the concept of optimization of both the area and the power dissipation. A partitioning with a lower value of EAP represents a solution with lower energy per operation for the same area as well as a solution with lower area for the same energy per operation.

The models used to estimate the *power* terms (for both the SW and HW parts) contained in the above equations are detailed in the next sections. The power assessment of the SW side is based on the system-level specification described at the VIS level, while the analysis of the HW side is related to the VHDL description of the ASIC model at the behavioral/RT level. The methodology proposed in [6] can be used to evaluate the area and throughput terms in the above metrics.

IV. POWER ESTIMATION FOR THE HW PART

The power model for the HW-bound part is based on the VHDL description of the ASIC at the behavioral/RT levels and the probabilistic estimation of the internal switching activity. The proposed approach is based on the following general assumptions:

1) the supply and ground voltage levels in the ASIC are fixed, although it is worth noting the impact of supply voltage reduction on power;
2) the design style is based on synchronous sequential circuits;
3) the data transfer occurs at the register-to-register level;
4) a zero delay model (ZDM) has been adopted, thus ignoring the contribution of glitches and hazards to power.

The inputs for the estimation are as follows:

1) *the ASIC specification*—consisting of a hierarchical VHDL description of the target system architecture;
2) *the allocation library*—composed of the available components implementing the macro-modules (such as adders, multipliers, etc.) and the basic modules (such as registers, multiplexers, logic gates, I/O pads, etc.).
3) *the technological parameters*—such as frequency, power supply, derating factors, etc.;
4) *the switching activity*—of the ASIC primary I/O's.

The power model is an analytical model, where the average power of the VHDL descriptions is related to the physical capacitance and the switching activity of the nets. The estimation approach is hierarchical: at the highest hierarchical level, *ad hoc* analytical power models for each part of the target system architecture are proposed; these models are in turn based on a macro-module library, at the lowest hierarchical levels. Furthermore, to avoid a large amount of input patterns to be simulated, our approach is weakly pattern-dependent. User-supplied input probabilities are required, reflecting the typical input behavior and derived from the system-level specification.

In the proposed single ASIC architecture, the total average power dissipated P_{AVE} is given by

$$P_{\text{AVE}} = P_{\text{IO}} + P_{\text{CORE}} \quad (2)$$

where P_{IO} and P_{CORE} are the average power dissipated by the I/O nets and the core internal nets, respectively. The power model of the core logic is based on the models of the different components of the target system architecture, therefore the P_{CORE} term can be in turn expressed as

$$P_{\text{CORE}} = P_{DP} + P_{\text{MEM}} + P_{\text{CNTR}} + P_{\text{PROC}} \quad (3)$$

where the single terms represent the average power dissipated by the data-path, the memory, the control logic and the embedded core processor. The power models related to the single terms in the above equations will be detailed in the following subsections, except for the P_{PROC} term, that is considered to be part of the power dissipated by the SW-bound part, detailed in Section V.

A. P_{IO} Estimation

Although a presynthesis analysis is performed, we assume the knowledge of the ASIC interface in terms of primary I/O pads characteristics and related switching activity from the system-level specifications. The set S of input, output and bidirectional nets of the ASIC can be partitioned into N sets, such as $S = \{s_1, s_2, \cdots, s_k, \cdots, s_N\}$ where the kth set s_k is composed of the same type t_k of I/O pads. Considering for example a set of output pads, the average power of the set s_k can be estimated as

$$P_{s_k} = \sum_{i=1}^{n_k} P_i(C_i) TR_i \quad (4)$$

where n_k is the number of output pads in the set s_k; TR_i is the toggle rate of the ith output pad, derived from the system-level specifications and $P_i(C_i)$ is the average power consumption per MHz of the ith output pad in s_k as a function of the output load C_i at a given reference frequency f_0.

B. P_{DP} Estimation

The average power dissipated by the data-path can be expressed as

$$P_{DP} = P_{\text{REG}} + P_{\text{MUX}} + P_{\text{FU}} \quad (5)$$

where the single terms represent the average power dissipated by the registers, the multiplexers and the functional units.

Concerning the P_{REG} term, the live variable analysis has been applied to the behavioral-level VHDL code to estimate the number of required registers and the maximum switching activity of each register. The preliminary step is the estimation of the number of required registers and, consequently, the values of the toggle rate TR_i for each of them. According to the abstraction level, such data are directly available from the RT-level description or the live variable analysis can be applied to the behavioral-level specifications.

The algorithm [9] examines the life of a variable over a set of VHDL code statements to derive information concerning the registers switching activity and it can be summarized as follows.

1) Compute the lifetimes of all the variables in the given VHDL code, composed of S statements. A variable v_j is said to live over a set of sequential code statements $\{i, i+1, i+2, \cdots, i+n\}$ when the variable is written in statement i and it is last accessed in statement $(i+n)$. When a variable is written in a statement $(i+k)$ in the

set, but last used in the same statement $(i + k)$ of the next iteration, it is assumed to live over the entire set.

2) Represent the lifetime of each variable as a vertical line from statement i through statement $(i+n)$ in the column j reserved for the corresponding variable v_j.
3) Determine the maximum number N of overlapping lifetimes, computing the maximum number of vertical lines intersecting with any horizontal cut-line.
4) Estimate the minimum number N of set of registers necessary to implement the code by using register sharing, that has to be applied whenever a group of variables, with the same bit-width b_i, can be mapped to the same register. The total number of registers is given by the sum of all b_i.
5) Select a possible mapping of variables into registers by using registers sharing.
6) Compute the number w_i of write to the variables mapped to the same set of registers.
7) Estimate α_i of each set of registers dividing w_i by S: $\alpha_i = w_i/S$; hence, $TR_i = \alpha_i f_{\text{CLK}}$.

The value of P_{REG}, considers that the power of latches and flip/flops is consumed not only during output transitions, but also during all clock edges by the internal clock buffers, even though the data stored in the register does not change. Thus, our analytical model of registers takes into account both the *switching* and *nonswitching* power. Let the set of registers S be composed of N sets, such as $S = \{s_1, s_2, \cdots, s_k, \cdots, s_N\}$, where the kth set s_k is composed of the same type t_k of registers, the average register power can be estimated as

$$P_{\text{REG}} = \sum_{k=1}^{N} (Ps_k + P_{Nsk}) \quad (6)$$

where Ps_k is the average power of each set s_k and P_{NSk} is the corresponding average nonswitching power, that is the average power dissipated by the internal clock buffers when there are no output transitions. The estimated value of Ps_k accounts for TRs_k, while the estimated values of the P_{NSk} should consider a toggle rate of $(f_{\text{CLK}} - TRs_k)$. The estimated values of Ps_k and P_{Nsk}, for the kth set s_k (constituted by an estimated number of registers n_k) are respectively given by

$$P_{s_k} = \sum_{i=1}^{n_k} P_i(C_i)TR_i \quad P_{Ns_k} = P_{0k} \sum_{i=1}^{n_k} (f_{\text{CLK}} - TR_i) \quad (7)$$

where $P_i(C_i)$ is the average power consumption per MHz of the ith register in s_k, and P_{0k} is the nonswitching power consumption per MHz of a single register of type t_k, that is load-independent.

Let us consider the estimation of the power related to multiplexers. First, to estimate the size and number of multiplexers from the VHDL code, it is necessary to determine the number of paths in the data-path. Then, the approach is based on the definition of the power model of a two-input noninverting multiplexer, based on both static signal probability of the selection net and the switching activities of the input nets. Given the pass-gate model of the two-input noninverting multiplexer, a simplified model for the maximum switching activity of the output Z of a two-input noninverting multiplexer is

$$\alpha_Z = \alpha_A(1 - p_s^1) + \alpha_B p_s^1 \quad (8)$$

where α_A and α_B are the switching activity of inputs A and B, respectively, while p_s^1 is the static signal probability of the selection net S. Globally, the average power dissipated by the multiplexers can be estimated as the sum of the average power of the single multiplexer contributions.

For the estimation of the average power of the functional units, we use complexity-based analytical models [3], where the complexity of each functional unit is described, in a library of macromodules, in terms of equivalent gates. Then, the estimated power dissipated by the functional units can be expressed as the sum of the contributions of the average power consumption P_i of the ith macromodule given by

$$P_i = n_i P_{\text{TECH}} TR_i \quad (9)$$

where P_{TECH} is a technological parameter expressed in $(\mu\text{W/(gate MHz)}]$; n_i is the estimated number of logic gates in the ith macrofunction; TR_i is the toggle rate of the output net of the ith macromodule.

C. P_{MEM} Estimation

Considering a fully CMOS single port static RAM, at a high-level of abstraction, we assume to have in the target library the information related to the power consumption of a single memory cell P_{cell} and of a single memory output buffer.

The average power dissipation during a read access to a single row of the array, composed of n rows and m columns, is proportional to the inverse of the read access time t_a and to the sum of the average power dissipated by the following blocks: the row decoder, the m memory cells composing the ith row and the output buffers. In particular, the power dissipated by the row decoder can be estimated with a complexity-based model, where the number of equivalent gates is proportional to the product $(nXlg_2n)$ and the load capacitance is the word line capacitance.

D. P_{CNTR} Estimation

This section describes the contribution to the power consumption due to the control part of the target system architecture, described as a set of finite-state machines (FSM's) represented by state transition graphs (STG's). The proposed FSM power model is a probabilistic model, where we approximate the average switching activities of the FSM nodes by using the switching probabilities (or transition probabilities) derived by modeling the FSM as a Markov chain. Given a typical implementation of a FSM, composed of a combinational circuit and a set of state registers, we consider the different contributions to the global average power

$$P_{\text{CNTR}} = P_{\text{IN}} + P_{\text{STATE\_REG}} + P_{\text{COMB}} + P_{\text{OUT}} \quad (10)$$

where P_{IN} is the average power dissipated by the primary inputs $P_{\text{STATE\_REG}}$ is the average power dissipated by the state registers, P_{COMB} is the average power dissipated by the combinational logic and finally P_{OUT} is the average power dissipated by the primary outputs.

The input static signal probabilities and the input switching activity factors are obtained from the system-level specifications, being derived by either simulating the FSM at a high abstraction level or by direct knowledge of the typical input behavior. Furthermore, we assume a ZDM for the logic gates and synchronous primary inputs. Under these assumptions, we can ignore the effects of glitches and hazards on the state bit lines, therefore the switching activity of the present and next state bit lines are equal.

Let the FSM, composed of n_s states, described by using a STG composed of n_s vertices, corresponding to the states in the set $S = \{s_1, s_2, \cdots, s_{nS}\}$, and the related directed edges. The edges are labeled with the set of input configurations that cause a transition from the source state to the destination state. Considering a transition from state s_i to state s_j, we can compute the factor p_{ij}, called *conditional state transition probability*, that represents the conditional probability of the transition from state s_i to state s_j, given that the FSM was in state s_i: $p_{ij} = \text{Prob}(\text{Next} = s_j|\text{Present} = s_i)$. The computation of the p_{ij}'s can be carried out as in [10], assuming totally independent primary inputs $P_I = \{x_1, x_2, \cdots, x_k, \cdots, x_{nI}\}$ and being p_{xk} the static signal probability of input x_k. The *steady-state probability* P_i of a state s_i is defined as the probability to be in the state s_i in an arbitrarily long random sequence [11]. Computing the P_i's implies solving the system composed of the Chapman–Kolmogorov equations and the equation representing the normality condition:

$$P^T = P^T p \qquad \sum_{i=1}^{N_s} P_i = 1 \qquad (11)$$

where $P^T = (P_1, \cdots, P_k, \cdots, P_{ns})$ is the row vector of the steady-state probabilities and p is the matrix of the conditional state transition probabilities p_{ij}. Note that the above system has $(n_s + 1)$ equations and n_s unknowns, thus one of the Chapman-Kolmogorov equations can be dropped [10]. Given the state probabilities P_i's and the conditional state transition probabilities p_{ij}'s, the *total state transition probabilities* P_{ij} between the two states s_i and s_j can be expressed as $P_{ij} = p_{ij} P_i$.

Given a state encoding, the next steps are represented by the estimation of the switching activity of the state bit lines and the primary outputs. The switching activity of the state bit lines depends on both the state encoding and the total state transition probabilities between each pair of states in the STG. Let us generalize the concept of state transition probability to transitions occurring between two distinct subsets of disjoint states, S_i and S_j, contained in the set of states $S = \{s_1, s_2, \cdots, s_{ns}\}$, as defined in [11]

$$TP(Si \leftrightarrow Sj) = \sum_{si \in Si} \sum_{sj \in Sj} (Pij + Pji) \qquad (12)$$

Being b^i the ith bit ($1 \leq i \leq n_{\text{var}}$) of the state code (called state bit) and n_{var} the number of state bits ($\lceil lg_2 n_s \rceil \leq n_{\text{var}} \leq n_s$), we consider the two sets of substates in which the ith state bit assumes the value one and zero, respectively. The switching activity α_b^i of the state bit line b_i is given by [11]

$$\alpha_b^i = TP\Big(\text{States}\big(b^i = 1\big) \leftrightarrow \text{States}\big(b^i = 0\big)\Big).$$

In a Moore-type FSM, the total state transition probabilities P_{ij} between the two states s_i and s_j are equal to the total transition probabilities between the corresponding outputs o_i and o_j where the output row vector o_i ($i = 1, 2, \cdots, n_s$.) is composed of the n_O primary outputs $(y_i^1, \cdots, y_i^l, \cdots, y_i^{nO})$. Let us define the transition probability of the transitions occurring between two distinct subsets of disjoint outputs O_i and O_j contained in the set of the outputs $O = \{o_1, o_2, \cdots, o_{ns}\}$, as

$$TP(O_i \leftrightarrow O_j) = \sum_{o_i \in O_i} \sum_{o_j \in O_j} (P_{ij} + P_{ji}) \qquad (13)$$

Being y^m the mth output bit ($1 \leq m_O$) and n_O the number of primary outputs, we consider the two sets of outputs in which the mth output bit assumes the value one and zero, respectively. The switching activity α_{ym} of primary outputs y_m is given by $\alpha_y^m = TP(\text{Outputs}(y^m = 1) \leftrightarrow \text{Outputs}(y^m - 0))$.

At this point of the analysis, we can detail the different power terms contained in the expression of P_{CNTR}.

The average power dissipated by the kth primary input belonging to the set $P_I = \{x_1, x_2, \cdots, x_k, \cdots x_{nI}\}$ depends on the switching activity factors α_{xk} and the input load capacitance C_{xk}, the latter being proportional to the number of literals, n_{litxk}, that the kth primary input is driving in the combinational part, and the estimated capacitance C_{lit} due to each literal [11]. Therefore, the average power PIN can be estimated as

$$P_{\text{IN}} = \sum_{x_k \in PI} P_{xk}(C_{xk}) TR_{xk} \qquad (14)$$

where $C_{xk} = n_{litxk} C_{lit}$; $TR_{xk} = \alpha_{xk} f_{\text{CLK}}$ and $P_{xk}(C_{xk})$ is the average power consumption per MHz of the cell driving the kth input.

The average power dissipated by the state registers $P_{\text{STATE\_REG}}$ can be derived by using the switching activity α_{bi} of the ith state bit line b_i where $1 \leq i \leq n_{\text{var}}$ and the corresponding toggle rate is $TR_{bi} = \alpha_{bi} f_{\text{CLK}}$. The term $P_{\text{STATE\_REG}}$ accounts for the switching and nonswitching power of the state registers

$$P_{\text{STATE\_REG}} = \sum_{i=1}^{n_{\text{var}}} (P_i + P_{NSi}) \qquad (15)$$

where n_{var} is the number of state registers and P_i and P_{NSi} are the average switching and nonswitching power dissipated by each state register. The terms P_i should account for a toggle rate given by TR_{bi}, while the terms P_{NSi} should consider a toggle rate of $(f_{\text{CLK}} - TR_{bi})$.

The average power dissipated by the combinational logic P_{COMB} has been estimated by considering a two-level logic implementation, before the minimization step. The ith state bit line b_i (where $1 \leq i \leq n_{\text{var}}$) can be expressed by using the canonical form as the sum of N_{bi} minterms ($N_{bi} \leq 2^{nlit}$ where n_{lit} is the number of literals and 2^{nlit} is the maximum number of minterms). Similarly, the mth output bit y^m ($1 \leq m \leq n_O$) can be expressed in the canonical form as the sum of N_{ym} minterms ($N_{ym} \leq 2^{nlit}$).

Let us assume to use a single AND gate to represent the generic minterm, hence the maximum number of AND gates in the AND-plane is 2^{nlit}, while in general $n_{\text{AND}} \leq 2^{nlit}$. Given the probabilistic model of the switching activity of the generic n_{lit}-input AND gate, we can derive an upper bound for the estimated power of the AND-plane

$$P_{\text{COMB}} = \sum_{i=1}^{n_{\text{AND}}} P_i(C_i) TR_i \qquad (16)$$

where $P_i (C_i)$ is the average power consumption per MHz of the ith n_{lit}-input AND gate; C_i is the capacitance driven by the ith n_{lit}-input AND gate and $TR_i = \alpha_i f_{\text{CLK}}$ is the toggle rate of the ith n_{lit}-input AND gate (derived by using the switching activity model of the n_{lit}-input AND gate).

P_{OUT} is the average power dissipated by the OR-plane, that is composed of n_{var} N_{bi}-input OR gates corresponding to the state bit lines, driving the input capacitance of the state registers, and n_O N_{ym}-input OR gates corresponding to the primary outputs, driving the output load capacitances.

Therefore, the upper bound for the power of the OR-plane is composed of two terms. The first term is thus proportional to the switching activity factors α_{bi} of the state bit line b_i, while the second term is proportional to the switching activity factors α_{yi} of the primary outputs:

$$P_{\text{OUT}} = \sum_{i=1}^{n_{\text{var}}} P_i(C_{\text{IN\_REG}}) TR_{bi} + \sum_{i=1}^{n_O} P_i(C_{yi}) TR_{yi} \qquad (17)$$

where $P_i (C_{\text{IN\_REG}})$ is the average power consumption per MHz of the ith N_{bi}-input OR gate driving the ith state bit line, $C_{\text{IN\_REG}}$ is the input capacitance of each state register; $TR_{bi} = \alpha_{bi} f_{\text{CLK}}$ is the toggle rate of the ith state bit line b_i, $P_i(C_{yi})$ is the average power consumption per MHz of the ith N_{yi}-input OR gate driving the ith primary output, C_{yi} is the output load capacitance of the ith primary output and finally $TR_{yi} = \alpha_{yi} f_{\text{CLK}}$ is the toggle rate of the ith primary output.

V. POWER ESTIMATION FOR THE SW PART

The software power assessment in TOSCA is performed by following a bottom-up approach. Each software-bound part of the OCCAM2 specification is considered in terms of basic blocks and it is compiled in the VIS. Hence, the power analysis has been performed at the VIS-level, by considering the average power consumption of each VIS instruction during the execution of a given program. The choice to work at the VIS-level is motivated by the goal to make our analysis processor-independent.

In general, the average power dissipated by a processor while running a program is $P_{SW} = I_{\text{AVE}} * V_{DD}$, where I_{AVE} is the average current and V_{DD} is the supply voltage. The associated energy is given by $E_{SW} = P_{SW} * t_{SW}$, where t_{SW} is the execution time of the software program, that can be expressed as: $t_{SW} = N_{\text{CLK}} * \tau_{\text{CLK}}$, being N_{CLK} the number of clock cycles to execute the program and τ_{CLK} the clock period. To compute the average current drawn during the execution of each instruction, it is necessary to perform some measurements on the energy cost of each instruction, such those proposed in [12], [13], or to have detailed power information provided by the processor supplier, in terms of the energy dissipated by each type of instruction in the instruction-set. This latter power information can be derived by the processor supplier by simulating the execution of instruction sequences on a lower level (circuit or layout) or gate level model of the processor, to obtain an estimate of the current drawn. Based on this information, a power table can be derived for each processor, reporting the energy consumption for each instruction in the instruction-set and for all the possible addressing modes associated with each instruction type.

Additional contributions to the global energy derive from to interinstruction effects, not considered computing the base cost of each instruction. The possible interinstruction effects are mainly related to the previous state of the processor, the limited number of resources leading to pipeline and write buffer stalls and the rate of cache misses [12], [13]. The condition of the processor in the previous clock cycle may cause an energy overhead due to the different switching activities on data and address busses and the different processors internal behavior. In general, the previous state of the circuit is different during program execution, since there is a switching from an instruction to another, with respect to the execution of the program used for the measurements of the base energy, where the same instruction was executed many times. The circuit state overhead has been measured in [12] by considering all the possible instruction pairs and it results approximately less than 5% of the base energy per instruction. This overhead has been considered in [12], as an average constant value to be added to the base cost, without a significant loss of precision. The effects of resource constraints and cache misses on the power budget have been measured in [12]. However, these effects can be usually neglected in embedded software based on both simple microcontrollers (e.g., M68000, Intel 8051, Z80, $\cdots$,) where such advanced features can be absent, and advanced processors, achieving cache hit-rate over the 98% and providing a fully exploitation of the pipeline stages.

Once the power analysis is completed for all the basic VIS-level instructions, the analysis is extended to upper-level software modules, by weighting the power consumption of each basic block according to the execution frequencies.

VI. SIMULATION RESULTS

Since we are focusing on control dominated embedded systems, we report some results derived from the application of the proposed power model to a set of 35 FSM's derived from the MCNC-91 benchmark suite. The measures have been derived by using the HCMOS6 technology, featuring 0.35 μm and 3.3 V, supplied by SGS-Thomson Microelectronics at the target operating frequency of 100 MHz. First we applied the area-oriented state assignment program NOVA to the selected benchmarks, then the encoded FSM's have been synthesized by the Synopsys Design Compiler tool targeting the HCMOS6 technology. The estimation results obtained by the proposed

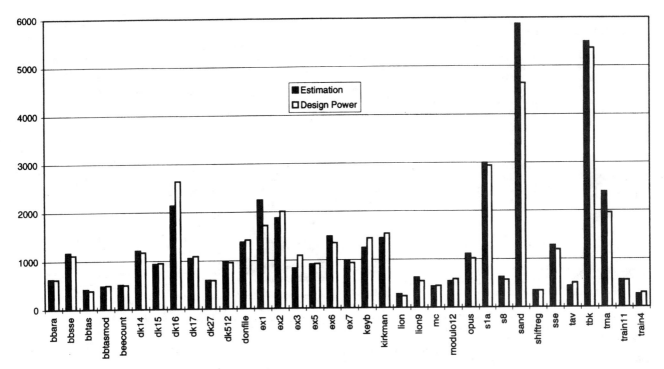

Fig. 3. Total power: estimated versus Design Power results.

methodology at presynthesis level have been compared with the results derived by using the Synopsys Design Power tool, based on the synthesized gate-level netlist. Note that both methods are based on a ZDM.

Fig. 3 summarizes the results. Considering the sequential power, the proposed model shows an average percentage error of 9.52% (ranging from 0.01 to 25.8%) with respect to the design power estimates. Concerning the combinational and total power, the average percentage errors is equal to 9.21 and 8.17%, respectively. Globally, the relative accuracy of our results compared with the design power results is considered satisfactory at this level of abstraction.

VII. CONCLUSIONS

The proposed analysis affords the problem of power estimation for control oriented embedded systems, implemented into a single ASIC. The main goal has been to offer a power-oriented codesign methodology, with particular emphasis on power metrics, to compare different design solutions described at high abstraction levels. Power models for both the HW and SW parts have been presented. The paper covers in more detail the HW part, since it is usually the more complicated part to be estimated with an acceptable precision, due to its heterogeneous nature. As it has been shown, the proposed approach is quite general, since it considers both the implementation domains as well as all the subparts, which typically constitute the HW side of an embedded system. The value-added has been to introduce a third dimension, power, to the speed versus area space, where the architectural design exploration is usually carried out. Finally, experimental results on benchmark circuits have shown a sufficient relative accuracy with respect to gate-level power estimates.

The approach is limited by the fact that at present the proposed power model is tailored to the target system architecture shown in Fig. 2 and that only the average power consumption is considered. However, the inclusion of the peak power could be performed by considering maximum switching activity values at input/output nodes. Moreover, work is in progress aiming at defining a power model suitable for the HW/SW communication part.

REFERENCES

[1] G. De Micheli and M. G. Sami, Eds., *Hardware/Software Co-Design*. New York: Kluwer Academic, NATO ASI Series, 1996.
[2] D. Singh, J. Rabaey, M. Pedram, F. Catthoor, S. Rajgopal, N. Sehgal, and T. Mozdzen, "Power conscious CAD tools and methodologies: A perspective," *Proc. IEEE*, vol. 83, pp. 570–594, Apr. 1995.
[3] P. Landman, "High-level power estimation," in *Proc. ISLPED-96: Int. Symp. Low Power Electron. Design*, Monterey, CA, 1996, pp. 29–35.
[4] F. N. Najm, "A survey of power estimation techniques in VLSI circuits," *IEEE Trans. VLSI Syst.*, vol. 2, pp. 446–455, Dec. 1994.
[5] P. E. Landman and J. M. Rabaey, "Activity-sensitive architectural power analysis," *IEEE Trans. Computer-Aided Design*, vol. 15, pp. 571–587, June 1996.
[6] A. Balboni, W. Fornaciari, and D. Sciuto, "Partitioning of HW-SW embedded systems: A metrics-based approach," in *Integrated Computer-Aided Engineering*. IOS Press, 1998, vol. 5, no. 1, pp. 39–55.
[7] T. D. Burd and R. W. Brodersen, "Energy efficient CMOS microprocessor design," in *Proc. 28th Hawaii Int. Conf. System Sci.*, HI, 1995.
[8] A. Balboni, W. Fornaciari, and D. Sciuto, "Co-synthesis and co-simulation of control dominated embedded systems," in *International Journal Design Automation for Embedded Systems*, vol. 1, no. 3, July 1996.
[9] W. Fornaciari, P. Gubian, D. Sciuto, and C. Silvano, "A conceptual analysis framework for low power design of embedded systems," in *Proc. ISIS-96: IEEE 8th Int. Conf. Innovative Syst. Silicon*, Austin, TX, 1996, pp. 170–179.
[10] E. Macii, "Sequential synthesis and optimization for low power," in *Low Power Design in Deep Submicron Electronics*. New York: Kluwer Academic, NATO ASI Series, 1997.

[11] C. Y. Tsui, M. Pedram, C. A. Chen, and A. M. Despain, "Low power state assignment targeting two- and multi-level logic implementations," in *Proc. IEEE/ACM Int. Conf. Computer-Aided Design*, 1994, pp. 82–87.

[12] V. Tiwari, S. Malik, and A. Wolfe, "Power analysis of embedded software: A first step toward software power minimization," *IEEE Trans. VLSI Syst.*, vol. 2, pp. 437–445, Dec. 1994.

[13] V. Tiwari, S. Malik, A. Wolfe, M. T.-C. Lee, "Instruction level power analysis and optimization of software," in *Journal of VLSI Signal Processing*. New York: Kluwer Academic, 1996, pp. 1–18.

Donatella Sciuto (S'84–M'87) received the Laurea in electronic engineering in 1984 and the Ph.D. degree in electrical and computer engineering from University of Colorado, Boulder, in 1988.

She has been an Assistant Professor at the Dipartimento di Elettronica per l'Automazione, University of Brescia, Italy, until 1992. She is currently an Associate Professor at the Dipartimento di Elettronica e Informazione of the Politecnico di Milano, Italy, and she is Secretary of the Special Interest Group in VHDL. Her research interests include VLSI synthesis and testing, VHDL system specification and design, and hardware/software codesign.

William Fornaciari (S'92–M'95) received the Laurea (cum laude) in electronic engineering and the Ph.D. degree in automation engineering and computer sciences from the Politecnico di Milano, Milano, Italy.

In 1993, he joined the CEFRIEL Research Center in Milano, where he currently supervises the Electronic Design Automation (EDA) area. Since 1995, he has been an Assistant Professor at the Politecnico di Milano, Department of Electronic Engineering and Information Sciences. His research interests covered algorithms for electrical circuit simulation, VLSI design with particular emphasis on the problems related to the digital implementation of artificial neural networks. Currently, his main research is in the field of the design automation for embedded systems, hardware/software codesign and low-power system-level analysis/design.

Dr. Fornaciari is member of the IEEE Computer Society. He has organized a special session on hardware/software codesign for the ICRAM'95 and CESA'96 conferences. During the IEEE-ICONIP'95 and IEEE-IJCNN'92 conferences, he received the Best Paper Award. In 1996, he received the Certification of Appreciation from the IEEE Circuits and Systems Society.

Cristina Silvano received the Dr.Ing. degree in electronic engineering from the Politecnico di Milano, Italy, in 1987. She is currently working towards the Ph.D. degree at the Università di Brescia, Italy, where her dissertation is on advanced design and estimation techniques for low-power circuits.

From 1987 to 1995, she held the position of Senior Design Engineer in the ASIC Development and Validation Group, PowerPC Platform Department, Bull Research and Development Laboratories, Pregnana M., Italy. In 1996, she joined the Department of Electronics of the Università di Brescia, Italy. Her current research interests are in the area of computer-aided design of integrated circuits and systems, with particular emphasis on low power and codesign techniques for embedded systems.

Ms. Silvano is a member of the IEEE Computer Society.

Paolo Gubian (M'88) received the Dr.Ing. degree (summa cum laude) from Politecnico di Milano, Italy, in 1980.

After an initial period as a Research Associate at the Department of Electronics of the Politecnico di Milano, he started consulting for SGS-Thomson Microelectronics (then SGS-Microelectronics) in the areas of electronic circuit simulation and CAD system architectures. During this period, he worked at the design and implementation of ST-SPICE, the company proprietary circuit simulator. He also worked in European initiatives to define a standard framework for integrated circuit CAD systems. From 1984 to 1986, he was a Visiting Professor at the University of Bari, Italy, teaching a course on circuit simulation. In 1987, he joined the Department of Electronics at the University of Brescia, Italy as an Assistant Professor in the Depatment of Electrical Engineering, where he is now an Associate Professor. His research interests are in statistical design and optimization, modeling of frameworks for IC CAD environments and low-power design of IC's.

A Framework for Estimating and Minimizing Energy Dissipation of Embedded HW/SW Systems

Yanbing Li
Department of Electrical Engineering
Princeton University, Princeton, NJ 08544.
yanbing@ee.princeton.edu

Jörg Henkel
C&C Research Laboratories, NEC USA
4 Independence Way, Princeton, NJ 08540
henkel@ccrl.nj.nec.com

Abstract Embedded system design is one of the most challenging tasks in VLSI CAD because of the vast amount of system parameters to fix and the great variety of constraints to meet. In this paper we focus on the constraint of low energy dissipation, an indispensable peculiarity of embedded mobile computing systems. We present the first comprehensive framework that *simultaneously* evaluates the tradeoffs of energy dissipations of software and hardware such as caches and main memory. Unlike previous work in low power research which focused only on software or hardware, our framework optimizes system parameters to minimize energy dissipation of the overall system. The trade-off between system performance and energy dissipation is also explored. Experimental results show that our *Avalanche* framework can drastically reduce system energy dissipation.

1 Introduction

The design of embedded systems is a challenging task for today's VLSI CAD environments. As opposed to a general purpose computing system, an embedded system performs just *one* particular application that is known a priori. Therefore, the system can be designed with respect to the particular application to have lower cost, higher performance, or be more energy-efficient. Energy efficiency is a hot topic in embedded system design. As mobile computing systems (e.g. cellular phones, laptop computers, video cams, etc.) become more popular, how to length the battery life of these systems becomes a critical issue.

From the design process point of view, many of the embedded systems can be integrated on just one chip (*systems on a chip*) using core based design techniques. Previous work in core-based system design has mainly focused on performance and cost constraints. Some recent work has been presented in co-synthesis for low power [1, 2]. However, the *trade-off* in energy dissipation among software [1], memory and hardware has not yet been explored. This is a challenging and indispensable task for the design of low power embedded systems. Consider for example, that the use of a bigger cache can reduce the number of cache misses and speed up the software execution, which may cause less energy dissipation on the processor. On the other hand, a larger cache size also causes bigger switching capacitance for cache accesses and therefore increases the cache energy dissipation per access.

In this paper we present our framework *Avalanche*, the first framework that explores the design space of hardware/software systems in terms of overall system energy dissipation. Since embedded system design usually has multiple constraints such as performance and power, our framework

---
[1] We use the term *software energy dissipation* for the energy that is dissipated within a processor core.

Permission to make digital/hard copy of all or part of this work for personal or classroom use is granted without fee provided that copies are not made or distributed for profit or commercial advantage, the copyright notice, the title of the publication and its date appear, and notice is given that copying is by permission of ACM, Inc. To copy otherwise, to republish, to post on servers or to redistribute to lists, requires prior specific permission and/or a fee.
DAC 98, San Francisco, California
©1998 ACM 0-89791-964-5/98/06..$5.00

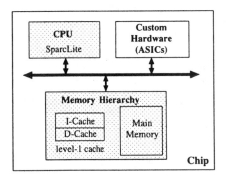

Figure 1: Target architecture of an embedded system

evaluates performance as well and optimizes for the best energy-performance trade-off.

This paper is structured as follows: Sec.2 reviews some of the related work in energy estimation and optimization for embedded systems. Sec.3 describes our model for embedded system energy dissipation. In Sec.4 we present our approach for energy dissipation optimization under timing constraints, and energy and performance trade-off optimization. Experimental results are presented in Sec.5.

2 Related Research

Energy estimation and optimization has been studied for both software and hardware. Tiwari and Malik [3] investigated the energy dissipation during the execution of programs running on different processor cores. Ong and Ynn [4] showed that the energy dissipation may drastically vary depending on the algorithms running on a dedicated hardware. A power and performance simulation tool for a RISC design has been developed by Sato et al. [5]. Their tool can be used to conduct architecture-level optimizations.

Further work deals with energy dissipation from a hardware point of view. Gonzales and Horowitz [6] explored the energy dissipation of different processor architectures (pipelined, un-pipelined, super-scalar). Kamble and Ghose [7] analyzed cache energy consumption. Itoh et al. studied SRAM and DRAM energy dissipation and low power RAM design techniques [14]. Panda et al [8] presented a strategy for exploring on-chip memory architecture in embedded systems with respect to performance only. Optimizing energy dissipation by means of high-level transformations has been addressed by Potkonjak et al. [9].

While estimating or optimizing power, these previous work only focuses on one component of the system at a time. A comprehensive approach that takes into consideration the mutual impacts of software *and* hardware in terms of energy dissipation — as it is actually the case in an embedded hardware/software system — has not been addressed so far.

3 System Model and Design Flow

In this section we present our *energy estimation model* of an embedded *system-on-a-chip*. It is based on an architecture template shown in Fig.1, which comprises a processor core, an instruction cache, a data cache, a main memory, and a custom hardware part (ASICs). We assume that hardware/software partitioning has already been performed and the custom hardware is fixed, therefore it adds a *constant* amount of energy to our model. During the design space exploration, we change the software and the cache/memory part, by performing high-level transformations on software and changing the cache and/or main memory parameters. When either of these components changes, the energy dissipation of other components is influenced and so is the overall system energy.

3.1 Analytical Cache Memory Model

We deploy a cache energy model based on transistor-level analysis. The model consists of an input decoder, a tag array and a data array. Attached to the tag array are column multiplexers whereas data output drivers are attached to the data array. A SRAM cell in data and tag array comprises six CMOS transistors. The switching capacitances in the equations derived below, are obtained by the tool *cacti* [10].

Only the energy portions in the bit lines for read and write ($E_{bit,rd}$ and $E_{bit,wr}$), in the word lines ($E_{word,rd/wr}$), in the decoder (E_{dec}) and in the output drivers (E_{od}) contribute essentially to the total energy. The according effective capacitances are:

$$C_{bit,rd} = N_{bitl} \cdot N_{rows} \cdot (C_{SRAM,pr} + C_{SRAM,rd}) + N_{cols} \cdot C_{pr\_logic} \quad (1)$$

where $C_{SRAM,pr}$, $C_{SRAM,rd}$ and C_{pr_logic} are the capacitances of the SRAM cell affected by precharging and discharging and the capacitance of the precharge logic itself, respectively. N_{rows} is the number of rows (number of sets) in the cache. The number of bit lines is given by N_{bitl}:

$$N_{bitl} = (T \cdot m + St + 8 \cdot L \cdot m) \cdot 2$$
$$N_{cols} = m \cdot (8 \cdot L + T + St)$$

where m means a m-way set associative cache, L is the line size in bytes, T is the number of tag bits and St is the number of status bits in a block frame. $C_{bit,wr}$ is defined in a similar manner as $C_{bit,rd}$.

The effective wordline capacitance is given by:

$$C_{word} = N_{cols} \cdot C_{word,gate} \quad (2)$$

where $C_{word,gate}$ is the sum of the two gate capacitances of the transmission gates in the 6-transistor SRAM cell. For simplification, we do not include the equations for C_{dec} and C_{od} here. Apparently, the switched capacitance is directly related to the cache parameters (Eq. 2).

Finally, the total energy dissipated within the cache (i-cache or d-cache) during the execution of a software program is related to the number of total cache accesses N_{acc}, as well as the number of hits and misses for cache reads and writes:

$$E_c = 0.5 \cdot V_{DD}^2 (N_{acc} \cdot C_{bit,rd} + N_{acc} \cdot C_{word} + a \cdot C_{bit,wr} + b \cdot C_{dec} + c \cdot C_{od}) \quad (3)$$

where a, b and c are complex expressions that depend on read/write accesses and, in parts on statistical assumptions. $a \cdot C_{bit,write}$, $b \cdot C_{dec}$ and $c \cdot C_{od}$ [2] are the effective capacitances to switch when writing one bit, during decoding of an access and during output, respectively.

The implemented cache model has a very high accuracy (compared to the real hardware) since every switching transistor within the cache has been taken into consideration

---
[2] The capacitances of the output drivers are derived for an on-chip cache implementation i.e. we assume that all resources like processor, cache and main memory are implemented on just one chip.

(even if this is not transparent through our equations because of the simplification). All the capacitances are obtained by running *cacti* [10] and are derived for a $0.8\mu m$ CMOS technology. The calculation of the capacitances within *cacti* has been proofed against a *Spice* simulation.

3.2 Main Memory Energy Model

For energy analysis of the main memory, we use the model for DRAM described by Itoh, *et al.* [14]. The energy source for DRAM mainly includes: the RAM array, the column decoder, the row decoder and peripherals.

$$I_a = m \cdot i_{act} + m(n-1) \cdot i_{hld} + m \cdot i_{dec} + n \cdot i_{dec} + I_{peri} \quad (4)$$

Eq.4 shows the current drawn during each memory access. Note that during each access, m cells are selected. $m \cdot i_{act}$ is the active current of the m selected cells. $m(n-1) \cdot i_{hld}$ is the data retention current of the $m \cdot (n-1)$ cells that are not selected. $m \cdot i_{dec}$ and $n \cdot i_{dec}$ are the currents drawn on column and row decoder, respectively. I_{peri} represents the current on peripheral circuits. The equations show that energy dissipation of each memory access is directly related to the size of the memory. For the total energy dissipation, i_{active} is the dominating component. At high clock frequencies, i_{hld} is negligible [14].

3.3 Software Energy and Performance Model

For software energy estimation we deploy a behavioral simulator ([16]) that we enhanced by values of the current drawn during the execution of an instruction. Those current values are obtained from [12]. The total SW program energy is:

$$E_{prg} = T_{w\_c} \cdot V_{DD} \cdot \sum_{i=0}^{N-1}(I_{instr,i} \cdot N_{cyc,i}) + $$
$$T_{cyc} \cdot V_{DD} \cdot (\underbrace{N_{miss,rd} \cdot N_{cyc,rd\_pen} \cdot I_{instr,nop}}_{\text{data write miss penalty}} + $$
$$\underbrace{N_{miss,wr} \cdot N_{cyc,wr\_pen} \cdot I_{instr,nop}}_{\text{data write miss penalty}} + $$
$$\underbrace{N_{miss,fetch} \cdot N_{cyc,fet\_pen} \cdot I_{instr,nop}}_{\text{instruction fetch miss penalty}}) \quad (5)$$

where V_{DD} is the voltage supply, I_{instr} is the current that is drawn during the execution of instruction i at the processor pins, $N_{cyc,i}$ is the number of cycles the instruction needs for execution and N is the total number of instructions of the program. T_{w_c} is the execution time of the application assumed that there is a cache as specified.

The three additional portions within the brackets refer to the energy dissipated in the penalty cycles when occurs a data cache write miss, a data read miss and an instruction fetch miss, respectively. We assume that the energy dissipated within processor is negligible after the program has been executed (through gated clock).

Let T_{w/o_c} be the execution time of a program running on the processor core (simulated by a behavior compiler) without cache, the corrected execution time (i.e. including cache behavior) is estimated by:

$$T_{w\_c} = T_{w/o\_c} + T_{cyc} \cdot (N_{miss,rd} \cdot N_{cyc,rd\_pen} + N_{miss,wr} \cdot N_{cyc,wr\_pen} + N_{miss,fet} \cdot N_{cyc,fet\_pen}) \quad (6)$$

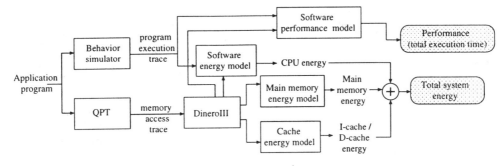

Figure 2: Design flow of the estimation part of our *Avalanche* framework

3.4 Design Flow of Our Framework

Using the above energy models and timing models, the estimation design flow (the energy optimization part is not shown) of our framework is shown in Fig.2. The input is an application program. It is fed into a behavioral model of the target processor that simulates the program and delivers a program trace to the *software energy model* and the *software performance model*. At the mean time, the input program is also fed into the memory trace profiler *QPT* [13] which generates the memory access trace to be used by *Dinero*[13]. *Dinero* provides the number of demand fetches and demand misses (for data and instructions). These numbers are then used: by the *software performance model* to get the total execution time with cache miss penalty considered (Eq.6); by the *software energy model* to adjust the software energy with the stalls caused by cache misses (Eq.5); and by the *cache* and *main memory energy models* (Eq.3 and Eq.4) to calculate the energy dissipation by the memory components based on the actual number of instruction/data cache accesses and main memory accesses.

4 System-level Energy Optimization

To optimize the system energy, we explore the design space in the dimensions of software and cache/memory. As mentioned in Sec.3, our framework assumes that the hardware (ASIC) is fixed. It changes the software by performing various high-level transformations. It changes the cache/main memory by modifying their parameters such as size, associativity, etc. When one component (software, cache or memory) changes, it not only affects the energy consumption of itself, but also that of other components in the system; it not only affects the power, but also the performance. The interesting aspect is that the change of overall system energy and performance can not be easily predicted unless comprehensive system analysis is performed. We now discuss some scenarios of software and cache/memory changes and their possible impacts on energy and performance:

- **Software transformation:** suppose a transformation can be performed on the software to lower the *software energy*. However, this transformation may change the cache/main memory access pattern and result in ambiguous changes of the caches or main memory energy and the performance. In some cases, software transformations may increase the code size so that a larger main memory is required to accommodate the new program; therefore, the energy of each memory access increases.

- **Cache:** when a larger instruction and/or data cache is used, in general, there are less cache misses and the *system performance* is improved. The *software energy* decreases because less cache misses imply less main memory access penalties. The energy of the main memory is decreasing because of less accesses. However, the energy dissipated by the caches increases due to its increased size, and the system energy change is ambiguous.

```
test1(...)                        test2()
{ ... ...                         { ... ... }
  test2();      /*call 3*/
  ... ... }
main()
{ int i, j;
  for (i=0; i<100; i++) {         /* loop 1 */
    test1(...);                   /* A */
    for(j=0; i<100; j++)          /* loop 2 */
      test1(...);                 /* B */
  }
  ... ... }
```

Figure 3: Program example for software transformations.

- **Main memory:** When a bigger main memory is used, the energy dissipation of the main memory increases because of its larger size (Eq. 4), but the energy of other parts is usually not affected.

4.1 Software Transformation and Energy

Many source-level transformations have been proposed for the purpose of improving performance. However, they may have some side-effects other than performance improvement, such as a bigger main memory requirement due to increased code size. This will lead to larger energy dissipation due to larger capacitances to switch for each access. Here we have a brief look at some of the commonly used transformation techniques and analyze their impacts on energy and performance.

Procedure calls are costly in most architectures. *Procedure in-lining* can help improve performance and save software energy by eliminating the overhead associated with calls and returns. For example, suppose we have a SPARC architecture that features up to 8 register windows. For each new procedure call a new window is required and released after the return from the procedure. However, if the depth of procedure calls (i.e. a consecutive number of calls without returns) exceeds the available number of register windows, an interrupt is released for the operating system to process the spilling of register contents to the main memory. This is time consuming. A side effect of in-lining is the increased code size, especially when the procedure is called from different points within the program.

Loop unrolling is another transformation technique. It can help to increase the instruction level parallelism and eliminate control overhead. Similar to procedure in-lining, it also results in code size increase. Another possible impact is that an unrolled loop may no longer fit in the instruction cache so that it possibly will be slowed down. Other techniques include *software pipelining, recursion elimination, loop optimization*, etc. [15], whose impacts on both the software and cache/memory accesses may make it hard to judge the change of the overall system energy dissipation.

4.2 Software Transformation Selection Algorithm

When a designer is concerned about both performance and power, a sophisticated approach is mandatory to choose which transformations to perform, and in what order. In order to find the combination and sequences of transformations that yield the most energy savings under memory size constraints, we designed a *transformation-selection* algorithm. Given a

262 CHAPTER 3: Analysis and Estimation

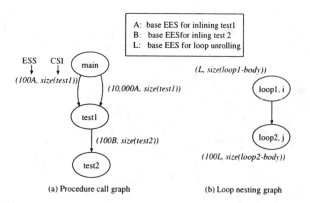

Figure 4: Procedure calling graph and loop graph of the program example.

set of available transformations techniques, the algorithm needs to:

1. identify *which* transformations can be applied and *where*, and evaluate these choices of transformations.

2. choose the combination and the order of the transformations that obtain the best energy improvement without violating a memory size limit.

Currently, we have implemented procedure in-lining and loop unrolling using SUIF [11]. However, our *transformation-selection* algorithm is applicable to general types of transformations as long as their particular characteristics are defined (see later). The algorithm is independent of the transformations themselves.

In the first step of the algorithm, to evaluate the impacts of the transformations, we developed some heuristic measures to characterize the estimated-energy-saving (EES) and code size increase (CSI) incurred by these transformations. EES is the estimated energy improvement while performing a certain transformation. Fig.3 shows a code segment that contains two loops and three procedure calls. The EES for inlining the procedure *test1* at location A is 100 times the base EES of inlining *test1*. At location B, EES is 10,000 times the base EES. Similar considerations apply to loop unrolling.

To identify the calling relationships, a *procedure calling graph* is constructed (Fig.4) for each program. In the calling graph, a node represents a procedure and a directed edge represents a procedure call. Multiple edges between nodes may exist, reflecting that a procedure can be called from different locations. The edges have been assigned the attributes *EES* and *CSI*. Since our algorithm does not support recursion, the procedure calling graph is *acyclic*. After inlining has been applied, the edge corresponding to the call is removed. For loop unrolling, a similar graph is created, in which a node represents a loop, an edge indicates one loop is nested in another. However, unlike the procedure calling graph, the nodes are labeled instead of the edges because the nodes are where the transformations are applied to.

Note that the possible transformations are not independent of each other. For the example in Fig.3: if *loop 1* is unrolled, 100 new instances of *test1* calls will be generated and new calling edges in the procedure calling graph need to be added. It is important for the algorithm to not only choose the best combination of the transformations, but also the right order.

In the second step, the algorithm, 1) prioritizes all possible transformations according to a heuristic measure — the EES/CSI ratio; 2) a probability is assigned to each transformation according to its priority value; 3) in each transformation step, randomly select a transformation based on the probabilities, perform the transformation, and update the procedure and loop graphs; 4) repeat 3) until the memory limit is reached. This algorithm is called repeatedly by the system-level energy optimization algorithm (Sec.4.3).

```
Inputs: source_software, design_goal;
Variable: solution_pool, current_sw, new_sw,
          current_design, new_design, tmp_design;
1.  Static analysis of program:
2.     identify all possible transformations;
3.     construct procedure graphs / loop graphs;
4.     generate possible cache / memory sizes;
5.  Energy optimization:
6.     for each memory size m_size {
7.        current_sw = source_sw;
8.        current_design = best design with
                    current_sw from solution_pool;
9.        do{
10.          new_sw = transformation_select
                          (current_sw, m_size);
11.          new_design = (new_sw,0,0,m_size);
12.          A=set of i_cache/d_cache sizes for new_sw;
13.          for each (dcache, icache) in A {
14.             tmp_design = (new_sw,d_cache,
                              i_cache,m_size);
15.             new_design = choose one by design_goal
                              (tmp_design, new_design);
16.          }
17.          if new_design better than current_design{
18.             save new_design in solution_pool;
19.             current_sw = new_sw;
                 current_design= new_design; }
20.          else  continue;
21.       } while( !stop_condition)
22.    }
23. output: designs from solution_pool
               that satisfies design_goal.
```

Figure 5: System-level energy optimization algorithm.

4.3 System-Level Energy Optimization Algorithm

We now formally define the problem of our system-level energy optimization algorithm. We assume that:
1. Hardware/software partitioning has already been done and application specific hardware is synthesized and therefore fixed.
2. A processor has been chosen.
3. We are given an initial version of the software.
4. The user specifies one *optimization goal*. The algorithm is designed for minimizing energy. However, as power is usually not the sole concern in the design process, we allow three different optimization goals:

- *Goal I*: minimized power.
- *Goal II*: minimized power under performance constraints.
- *Goal III*: multiple objective optimization

Goal III is to find a set of solutions within performance *and* energy constraints. This will provide important trade-off information to the designer. The designer can review different design options and choose the most suitable one. For example, there are two designs A and B, with design A being 20% faster than design B, but Design B consuming just 1% less energy. They both meet the performance constraints. *Goal I and II* will discard A, although it might be a better choice for the designer.

The algorithm returns the optimized new system configuration of the target system architecture (Fig.1): the transformed program, the data cache and instruction cache sizes and other parameters, and the main memory size. The energy dissipation of each component and the performance is also delivered. For *Goal-III*, a set of designs is returned, with percentage data indicating energy and performance difference between two designs adjacent in terms of energy dissipation.

Fig.5 shows the pseudo-code for the optimization algorithm. It consists of two main steps:

1. **Static analysis of the application program** (lines 1-4), includes

    - generating the procedure calling graph and loop graph, as described in Sec.4.2, and
    - generating the set of feasible cache and memory sizes and configurations based on the current version of the program.

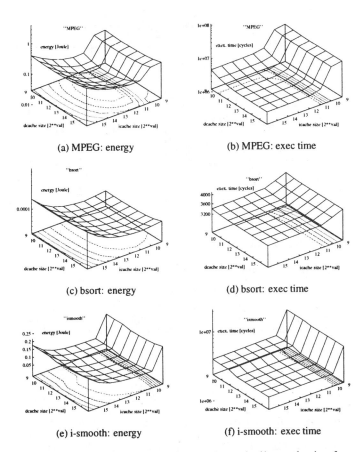

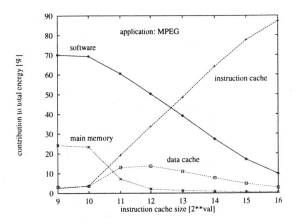

(a) MPEG: energy
(b) MPEG: exec time
(c) bsort: energy
(d) bsort: exec time
(e) i-smooth: energy
(f) i-smooth: exec time

Figure 6: Energy and execution time vs. instruction/data cache size, for applications *MPEG*, *bsort* and *ismooth*.

Figure 7: Contribution of software, d-cache, i-cache and main memory to total energy dissipation, at fixed data cache size (4k).

2. **Optimization step** (lines 6-23): choose the design, i.e. set of transformations and the cache and memory parameters, to meet the constraints and optimization goal.

In the algorithm, we limit the maximum memory size to four times of the original memory size (of the original, not transformed software program) because as shown by our experiments, the energy overhead of a very large memory usually out-weighs the energy saving provided by software transformations. We generate a set of designs for each possible memory size (lines 6-22), and select design(s) that meet the design goal (*I, II or III*) in line 23. A design is represented as a quadruple of software, instruction cache, data cache and main memory.

To construct designs for a certain memory size, we perform software transformations using the algorithm described in Sec. 4.2 (line 10), and then decide the subset of feasible instruction/data caches for the transformed software (lines 11-12). The best instruction/data caches are chosen based on the designer's goal (line 13-16). The transformed software, the best suited cache sizes and parameters and the new memory size makes up a new design.

If the new design has a better quality than the previous one, then it is saved in a solution pool (line 17-19) and will be used in the next iteration. Otherwise, the transformation is discarded (line 20) and a new transformation is performed on the previous version of the software. The process is repeated until a stop criteria is met (line 21): there is no improvement in a given number of consecutive iterations, or the total number of iterations reaches a preset limit.

An important issue in the algorithm is evaluating the quality of two designs. The evaluation depends on the design goal: for *minimizing energy* (*Goal I*), energy is the sole standard; for minimized energy under a performance constraints (*Goal II*), the performance constraint is to be met first then energy is considered; for *Goal III*, for designs falling within energy and performance constraints, we use the *Pareto optimality* measure to discard solutions that are both higher in energy and slower in performance. Note the energy and performance data are obtained using the models described in Sec.3.

5 Experiments and Results

As will be shown in this section, our framework can be deployed to support a system designer through a design space exploration or for automated optimization according to the designers goals (energy, performance). We used data-dominated applications (including an MPEG encoder consisting of about 200kB of C source code), in which caches and memory play a key role in energy and performance.

5.1 Design space explorations

Since the variety of system parameters to choose is very large, we fixed all parameters except for the sizes of data cache and instruction cache. Each application in Fig.6 has been dedicated two figures showing the total energy dissipation of the whole system (left) and the number of clock cycles to perform that application on our target architecture (right). The varied parameters in each figure are the data cache size (left axis) and the instruction cache size right axis). A number of 12 for example means a cache size of 4K (= 2^{12}) byte. Figures a) and b) show the results of the MPEG encoder. Here, both large and small cache sizes lead to a high system energy dissipation. In case of large caches, the caches' energy dominates the system energy; while in case of smaller cache sizes, the software energy is dominating — from Eq.5, large number of cache misses (due to small caches) result in poor performance and large energy consumed in the miss penalty cycles. The right figure shows in fact that the program execution time raises drastically for small instruction cache sizes ($<$ 1024 byte). Remarkably, the least energy consuming configuration (data cache size and instruction cache size 4k each) is also one of those with the highest performance (i.e. small number of clock cycles). This is a behavior that would possibly not be expected (and is not the case for the other applications). In addition, Fig.7 reveals the contribution (in percent) of each component to whole system energy dissipation (i.e. software program, caches, main memory). In that figure, the data cache size has been fixed whereas the instruction cache size varies.

The experiments conducted with the *bsort* (c) and d)) application (bubble sort) show mainly that there is almost no dependency on data cache size in terms of system energy dissipation and system performance. More dependencies can be observed by changing the instruction cache size. Obviously, a large instruction cache size leads to a large system energy

appl.	objective	orig. architecture		optim arch. Goal I
		w/o cache	fixed cache	
bsort	energy [J]	0.33	0.30	23.21E-3
	energy improv. [%]	n/a	-9.09	-93.21
	time [# cyc × 10^6]	19.4	17.6	1.4
	exec. improv. [%]	n/a	-9.52	-92.98
eg2	energy [J]	0.31	0.28	19.41E-3
	energy improv. [%]	n/a	-9.68	-93.73
	time [# cyc × 10^6]	17.9	16.5	1,186.8
	exec. improv. [%]	n/a	-8.34	-93.39
ismooth	energy [J]	1.03	0.96	67.411E-3
	energy improv. [%]	n/a	-6.80	-93.45
	time [# cyc × 10^6]	60.1	56.2	3.9
	exec. improv. [%]	n/a	-6.60	-93.46
itimp	energy [J]	2.97	2.78	186.01E-3
	energy improv. [%]	n/a	-6.40	-93.73
	time [# cyc × 10^6]	173.8	162.5	8.8
	exec. improv. [%]	n/a	-6.50	-94.91

Table 1: Optimization of architecture through *GOAL I* compared to original architecture (no cache) and an achitecture with non–optimized cache size

appl.	objective	w/o cache	optimized architecture		
			GOAL II	GOAL III	
bsort	energy [J]	0.33E-3	22.4E-3	0.27	0.24	0.21
	e-improv. [%]	n/a	-93.2	-17.6	-26.8	-36.1
	time [# cyc × 10^6]	19.4	1.4	15.9	14.1	12.3
	t-improv. [%]	n/a	-93.0	-18.4	-27.5	-36.8
eg2	energy [J]	0.31	19.4E-3	0.25	0.23	-
	e-improv. [%]	n/a	-93.7	-18.2	-24.8	-
	time [# cyc × 10^6]	18.0	1.2	14.8	13.6	-
	t-improv. [%]	n/a	-93.4	-17.6	-24.3	-
ismooth	energy [J]	1.03	67.4E-3	0.10	0.72	0.48
	e-improv. [%]	n/a	-93.4	-90.1	-29.8	-53.5
	time [# cyc × 10^6]	60.1	3.9	3.6	42.1	28.0
	t-improv. [%]	n/a	-93.5	-94.0	-30.0	-53.5
itimp	energy [J]	2.97	0.19	2.4	2.2	-
	e-improv. [%]	n/a	-93.7	-19.9	-25.3	-
	time [# cyc × 10^6]	173.8	8.8	139.1	129.5	-
	t-improv. [%]	n/a	-94.9	-20.0	-25.5	-

Table 2: Optimization of architecture through *GOAL II* and *GOAL III* compared to original architecture that has no cache

dissipation also. But as opposed to the *MPEG* encoder, a small instruction cache size does not lead to a larger system energy dissipation as a consequence of a larger program execution time. Rather than that, the performance decreases (more cycles due to the mid-right figure on page 6).

An additional different behavior is shown by the application *ismooth*, (e) f)) an image smoothing application. As could be observed, the behavior of a system in terms of energy and performance is hard to predict and therefore needs powerful tools for analyzing and optimizing.

5.2 Optimizing system-level energy dissipation

In Sec.4.3 we have presented our algorithms for three different design goals. For all following experiments we have chosen the clock cycle time to 30ns. The behavior simulation tool for evaluating software performance is a SPARC simulator [16]. The same conventions were used for the experiments in Sec.5.1. All other system parameters are subject to change through the optimization process.

Table.1 shows the results for *Goal I* compared to two original architectures called *w/o cache* (no cache) and the architecture called *fixed cache* (a small standard cache; same size for i-cache and d-cache). For all applications, system energy dissipation (Joule) and execution time (number of clock cycles) is given. Additionally, the relative improvement $(value - value_{ref})/value_{ref} * 100$ for both objectives is given. Apparently, a negative percentage number means an improvement.

As shown in Table.1, *Goal I* yields remarkable improvements in energy and performance. The "fixed cache" architecture is somewhere between "w/o cache" and the optimized architecture. As investigations have shown, in parts, the drastic improvements in performance are due to the architecture: we assume a cache miss penalty of 20 clock cycles, which is a quite typical value. The contribution of software transformation techniques solely (as described in section 4.1) to energy and performance improvements varies in most of the shown cases between 5% and 10%.

Table.2 shows the results yielded with our algorithms for improving energy dissipation under performance constraints (*Goal II* and a multiple objective optimization *Goal III*). In the latter case, the designer is provided with a set of different solutions where he can choose from since design constraints are not completely defined every time. The algorithm for *Goal II* is searching the design space around a given performance constraints i.e. it searches for design configurations with minimum energy dissipation while not exceeding the budget of clock cycles to execute. Here also, large improvements could be yielded as shown in Table.2.

The computation time for determining *one* design point (fixed system parameters) is in the range of 3-5 minutes. A whole optimization run is between 2 and 10 hours on an Ultra Sparc.

6 Conclusions

We have presented our *Avalanche* framework for estimating and optimizing the energy dissipation of embedded systems. It is the first approach that trades off the energy dissipation of software against the energy dissipation of system resources like caches and main memory. Through various experiments we have shown that it is not straightforward to judge the change of the total system energy when various system parameters are varied and software transformation are performed. Our *Avalanche* framework provides a powerful tool for low power design at system level. Experimental results have shown significant improvements (up to $\approx$ 95% energy cut) in energy dissipation.

References

[1] D. Kirovski, M. Potkonjak, *System-Level Synthesis of Low-Power Hard Real-Time Systems*, Proc. DAC'97, pp.697-702, 1997.
[2] B.P. Dave, G. Lakshminarayana, N.K. Jha, *COSYN: Hardware-Software Co-Synthesis of Embedded Systems*' Proc. DAC'97, pp.703-708, 1997.
[3] V. Tiwari, S. Malik, A. Wolfe, *Instruction Level Power Analysis and Optimization of Software*, Kluwer Academic Publishers, Journal of VLSI Signal Processing, pp. 1-18, 1996.
[4] P.-W. Ong, R.-H. Ynn, *Power-Conscious Software Design - a framework for modeling software on hardware*, IEEE Proc. of Symp. on Low Power Electronics, pp. 36-37, 1994.
[5] T. Sato, M. Nagamatsu, H. Tago, *Power and Performance Simulator: ESP and its Application for 100 MIPS/W Class RISC Design*, IEEE Proc. of Symp. on Low Power Electronics, pp. 46-47, 1994.
[6] R. Gonzales, M. Horowitz, *Energy Dissipation in General Purpose Processors*, IEEE Proc. of Symp on Low Power Electronics, pp. 12-13, 1995.
[7] M.B. Kamble, K. Ghose, *Analytical Energy Dissipation Models For Low Power Caches*, IEEE Proc. of Symposium on Low Power Electronics and Design, pp. 143-148, 1997.
[8] P.R. Panda, N. D. Dutt, A. Nicolau, *Architectural Exploration and Optimization of Local Memory in Embedded Systems*, Proc. of IEEE International Symposium on System Synthesis, pp. 90-97, 1997.
[9] I. Hong, D. Kirovski, M. Potkonjak, *Potential-Driven Statistical Ordering of Transformations*, Proc. DAC'97, pp.347-352, 1997.
[10] S.J.E Wilton, N.P. Jouppi, *An Enhanced Access and Cycle Time Model for On-Chip Caches*, DEC, WRL Research Rep. 93/5, 1994.
[11] Stanford Compiler Group, *The SUIF Library: A set of core routines for manipulating SUIF data structures*, Stanford University, 1994.
[12] V. Tiwari, *Logic and system design for low power consumption*, PhD thesis, Princeton University, Nov. 1996.
[13] M. D. Hill, J. R. Laurus, A. R. Lebeck et al., *WARTS: Wisconsin Architectural Research Tool Set*, Computer Science Department University of Wisconsin.
[14] K. Itoh, K. Sasaki and Y. Nakagome, *Trends in Low-Power RAM Circuit Technologies*, Pro. of the IEEE, VOL. 83, No. 4, 1995.
[15] H. Mehta, R. Owens, M.J. Irwin, R. Chen and D. Ghosh, *Techniques for Low Power Software*, IEEE Proc. of Symposium on Low Power Electronics and Design, pp. 72-75, 1997.
[16] W. Ye, R. Ernst, Th. Benner, J. Henkel, *Fast Timing Analysis for Hardware-Software Co-Synthesis*, Proc. ICCD, pp.452-457, 1993.

Hardware/Software Co-Synthesis with Memory Hierarchies

Yanbing Li, *Member, IEEE*, and Wayne H. Wolf, *Fellow, IEEE*

Abstract—This paper introduces the first hardware/software co-synthesis algorithm of distributed real-time systems that optimizes the memory hierarchy along with the rest of the architecture. Memory hierarchies (caches) are essential for modern embedded cores to obtain high performance. They also represents a significant portion of the cost, size and power consumption of many embedded systems. Our algorithm synthesizes a set of real-time tasks with data dependencies onto a heterogeneous multiprocessor architecture that meets the performance constraints with minimized cost. Unlike previous work in co-synthesis, our algorithm not only synthesizes the hardware and software portions of the applications, but also the memory hierarchies. It chooses cache sizes and allocates tasks to caches as part of co-synthesis. The algorithm is built upon a task-level performance model for memory hierarchies. Experimental results, including examples from the literature and results on real-life examples such as an MPEG-2 encoder, show that our algorithm is efficient, and compared with existing algorithms, it can reduce the overall cost of the synthesized system.

Index Terms—Hardware/software co-synthesis, memory hierarchy, real-time, scheduling.

I. INTRODUCTION

This paper describes a new system-level algorithm for **hardware/software co-synthesis** of multirate **real-time systems** on **heterogeneous multiprocessors**. Unlike most of the previous work in hardware/software co-synthesis, the algorithm not only synthesizes the hardware and software parts of the applications, but also the memory hierarchy: it takes into account the impact of the memory hierarchy on system performance and cost in the co-synthesis process. The algorithm targets periodic real-time applications running at multiple rates. The target architecture is a heterogeneous multiprocessor architecture that consists of multiple processing elements (PE's) of various types (i.e., general-purpose processors, domain-specific CPU's such as digital signal processors (DSP's), and custom hardware), memory components at different levels of memory hierarchy, and communication links. The algorithm synthesizes the hardware, software and memory hierarchy based on a multiprocessor target architecture (Fig. 1) to meet the performance constraints with minimal cost.

Manuscript received October 1, 1998; revised February 24, 1999. This work was supported by grants from the National Science Foundation. A preliminary version of this work appeared in the *Proceedings of International Conference on Computer-Aided Design*, November 1998. This paper was recommended by Associate Editor R. Gupta.
Y. Li is with Synopsys Inc., Mountain View, CA 94043 USA (e-mail: yanbing@synopsys.com).
W. H. Wolf is with the Department of Electrical Engineering, Princeton University, Princeton, NJ 08544 USA.
Publisher Item Identifier S 0278-0070(99)07722-2.

With embedded CPU cores becoming increasingly common in very large scale integration (VLSI) systems, and with increasing use of multiple embedded cores on a single chip (*systems-on-a-chip*), system designers need to implement major subsystems using real-time system design techniques such as multiple, prioritized tasks sharing CPU's. Multirate systems are usually most efficiently implemented as a set of concurrent tasks, which may run on a single CPU or on a multiprocessor consisting of multiple CPU's and application—specific integrated circuits (ASIC's). The design of these systems (*core-based systems*) is complex and requires sophisticated analysis and optimization. Hardware/software co-synthesis can be used to explore the design space and synthesize the application into hardware and software cores that meet design constraints (performance, cost, power, etc.).

Memory hierarchies, in particular caches, are essential for modern RISC-embedded cores to obtain sustained high performance. Some architectures (such as Power PC) are defined to always have caches. Even relatively small microsystems often utilize caches to improve system performance. As the functionality of embedded systems increases, caches and memories represent a significant portion of the cost, size, weight, and power consumption of many embedded systems. Ineffective use of the memory hierarchy requires extra transfers of data and program and can significantly increase both execution time and power consumption.

Memory hierarchy must be taken into consideration in system-level design to minimize the overall system cost. For example, to improve the performance of a system, the designer may use a faster and usually more expensive CPU, or add a piece of custom hardware, or use a bigger cache. It is important for the designer to evaluate the tradeoffs among these different design options in order to find the optimized design. Although many processor chips already include caches, they still provide several choices of cache sizes for the same CPU type. In *core-based design* for *systems-on-a-chip*, the designer has the option of adjusting the cache sizes of the CPU cores. However, most previous research in co-synthesis has ignored the cache's impact and only concentrated on the synthesis of PE's for software (processors) and hardware (ASIC's). So far, there is no systematic approach for the design of memory hierarchies in co-synthesis. In our previous work [11], we designed a task-level cache performance model and concentrated on analysis and scheduling with memory hierarchy but not co-synthesis. Some previous work [14] has introduced techniques for analyzing the caching behavior of a single program. Besides not addressing co-synthesis, these

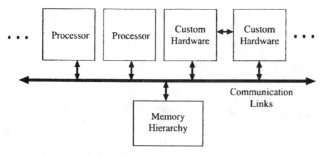

Fig. 1. The target architecture.

methods are insufficient for systems implemented as multiple tasks, running at multiple rates.

To handle memory hierarchies in a multitasking environment, we need a high-level model that can efficiently model the application performance in presence of memory hierarchy. Performance analysis with multiple levels of memory hierarchy is difficult, and it is even worse for *preemptive real-time systems* with *multiple tasks*, in which *preemptions* keep changing the state of cache and make it harder to give a tight bound of the task execution time. We have designed a task-level model that efficiently bounds the cache performance of tasks running in a *multitasking* environment. The model is incorporated into the process or hardware/software co-synthesis.

This paper is organized as follows. Section II reviews related work. We then present our *task-level* cache performance model. Section IV describes our co-synthesis algorithm that uses the cache-performance model and optimizes the use of memory hierarchy and synthesizes the cache memory together with hardware and software. Section V discusses the experimental results of our co-synthesis algorithm.

II. Previous Work

Related work includes studies from hardware/software partitioning, hardware/software co-synthesis, performance analysis with caches, and real-time computing.

Hardware/software partitioning [4], [6], [22], [24] has been a major topic in the area of hardware/software co-design. Most of the partitioning algorithms implement the system based on a template of a CPU (software) and an ASIC (hardware). Recent work in co-synthesis has used a more generalized model consisting of heterogeneous multiprocessors with arbitrary communication links. The SOS algorithm developed by Prakash and Parker [18] uses an integer linear programming (ILP) approach. Yen and Wolf's work [23], [25] uses a faster iterative improvement approach. The co-synthesis algorithms developed by Dave *et al.* [2], [3] can handle multiple objectives such as cost, performance, power and fault tolerance. However, all of these algorithms ignore memory hierarchy.

Due to the vast design space in system level synthesis, fast and accurate evaluation of design quality (execution time, area, etc.) is important. Ernst *et al.* [4] use preprocessing steps to estimate design metrics such as communication time overhead and these steps need not be repeated during inner-loop simulated annealing. Gajski *et al.* [5] utilize a two-level technique to estimate design quality metrics: preestimation which occurs once at the beginning of design space exploring, and online estimation which uses complex expressions of the preestimation results to rapidly obtain metric values for a particular partition and allocation.

Recent research, such as the path-based analysis algorithm of Li *et al.* [14], has developed cache models for analyzing the performance of a *single program*. While such models provide accurate estimates of the performance of a single program, they do not take into account the effects of preemptions between multiple tasks, and they are much too expensive to be used in system-level synthesis and design exploration. When one task preempts another, it may (or may not) change the state of the cache at a point in a way that compromises the performance of the originally-executing model. For preemptive real-time systems, such interactions are critical to evaluate during system-level architecture design.

Lee *et al.* [9] proposed a technique to analyze cache-related preemption delays of tasks that cause unpredictable variation in task execution time for preemptive scheduling. Kirk and Strosnider [8] developed a strategic memory allocation for real-time (SMART) cache design that partitions the cache to provide predictable cache performance. Danckaert *et al.* [1] studied memory optimization aiming to reduce the dominant cost of memory in hardware/software co-design of multimedia and DSP applications. Their algorithm concentrated on reducing data storage and did not consider multilevel memory hierarchy. Li and Henkel [10] designed a framework that synthesizes caches and memory used in single-CPU embedded systems to optimize the overall system energy dissipation. Panda *et al.* [16] proposed techniques for application-specific on-chip data memory sizing and partitioning. Rawat [20] studied cache analysis and data placement for real-time programming. All these approaches [1], [8], [9], [14] relies on program-level analysis, and are too expensive to be used in design space exploration of multiple tasks.

Research in the area of *real-time scheduling* provides an important foundation to our co-synthesis algorithm which targets multirate real-time tasks. In a uniprocessor environment, real-time systems commonly use one of two scheduling policies to schedule periodic tasks: *earliest-deadline-first (EDF)* and *rate-monotonic scheduling (RMS)* [15]. For distributed real-time systems, Peng and Shin [17] used a branch-and-bound approach for allocation of task graphs onto heterogeneous architecture; Ramamritham [19] used an task-graph unrolling approach and developed a heuristic allocation and scheduling algorithm that considered data dependencies, communication, and fault-tolerance requirements; Li and Wolf [12] developed an efficient hierarchical algorithm to schedule and allocate multirate tasks with precedence constraints.

III. Task-Level Memory Hierarchy Performance Model

Accurate estimation of memory hierarchy (cache) behaviors requires *program-level* or *trace-level* analysis. However, program-level or trace-level analysis is much too expensive to be used in the design exploration of *multiple tasks* on

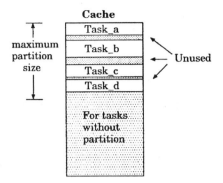

Fig. 2. Cache partitioning: Mapping of tasks onto mutually exclusive partitions of the cache.

a *multiprocessor architecture*. An embedded application can easily have tens of thousands of lines of instructions in its program and a trace size of millions or even billions. A *high-level model* of memory hierarchy performance is critical for integrating memory hierarchy into co-synthesis of multiple tasks.

In order for a cache performance model to be efficiently used by a co-synthesis algorithm which handles multiple tasks and needs to evaluate different cache sizes and configurations, the model should be able to:
1) efficiently model the *multitasking* environment, where tasks may execute in an arbitrary sequence, and the environment may be further complicated by preemption between tasks;
2) efficiently model cache behavior (hits/misses) when *cache size* or *configuration* changes.

In our earlier work, we proposed the first *task-level model* of memory hierarchy performance for system-level synthesis, and allocation/scheduling algorithms with memory hierarchies [11]. The model treats each task as an entity, partitions the caches, and reserves some partitions exclusively for certain tasks to guarantee predictable performance of these tasks. An example of cache partitions is shown in Fig. 2. We designed an algorithm to select the set of tasks with partitions chosen to maximize the performance gain (reduction of overall system workload), given caches of certain sizes. While this model provides a fast means to bound the cache performance of tasks running in a *multitasking* environment, the cache partitioning/reservation approach may result in inefficient utilization of the caches. Furthermore, the model is not flexible in terms of the memory allocation of tasks: for tasks with cache partitions on the same cache, the compiler has to make sure that they do not map to overlapped cache locations.

We have developed a new task-level cache performance model that handles *arbitrary mapping* of tasks to caches. Fig. 3 shows how four tasks map to a cache of 1-kbyte. For simplicity, we make the following assumptions about the tasks and the caches:

Assumption 1: Only one-level cache is modeled and tasks are well-contained in the level-1 cache (each task's program size and data size are no bigger than the instruction and data cache size, respectively). This may not be a reasonable assumption in a general-purpose system, but it is plausible

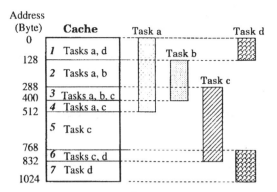

Addresses of tasks in the main memory (Byte)
Task a: 2048-2560
Task b: 3200-3472
Task c: 4384-4928
Task d: 6912-7296

Fig. 3. Mapping of tasks onto a 1-kbyte direct-mapped cache.

for many embedded systems. The kernels of time-critical operations are frequently small enough to fit into a modest-sized cache. Even when a task is too large to be contained in a level-1 cache, it can be specified at a finer granularity to satisfy this assumption.

Assumption 2: The caches are direct-mapped. We make this assumption to simplify the analysis, because in a direct-mapped cache, each data block is loaded into a deterministic location in the cache.

Assumption 3: The cache sizes are powers of two. This is usually true for most direct-mapped caches.

Assumption 4: A task's program is allocated a continuous region of the main memory and is, therefore, mapped into a continuous region of the cache. A task's data can be scattered in several regions of the main memory.

Due to the first assumption, when a task executes on a processor, if not preempted by other tasks, the only cache misses are *compulsory misses* [30]. A compulsory miss refers to the cache miss that happens when the first access to a block is not in the cache, so the block must be brought into the cache. As opposed to *capacity misses* (which occur when the cache cannot contain all the blocks needed during execution of a program and some blocks are discarded and later retrieved) and *conflict misses* (which occur when too many blocks map to one cache set, they are also called interference misses), a nice feature about compulsory misses is that their number does not change with cache size [30].

We now analyze the cache performance in two situations that the model must handle in order for it to be useful in co-synthesis: multiple tasks on a fixed-size cache, and changing the cache size.

A. Multiple Tasks on a Fixed-Size Cache

First, we look at multiple tasks running on a processor with a fixed cache size. Note that only compulsory misses can happen because of Assumption 1. The performance of a task depends not only on itself and the processor, but also on the history of task execution on the processor:

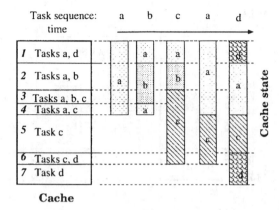

Fig. 4. Cache state transition during the execution of task sequence a, b, c, a, d.

- if the task is executed on the processor for the first time, it is initially loaded into the cache (i.e., cold start), with all the necessary compulsory misses;
- if the task has been executed before and has not been overwritten by other tasks, then there are no cache misses;
- if it has been partly overwritten by other tasks, then there are compulsory misses associated with the cache regions that were overwritten.

It is important to monitor the change of the cache status to tightly bound the cache performance of tasks.

As shown in Fig. 3, when tasks are mapped to a cache, there can be overlaps between tasks. These overlaps determine all the possibilities of task overwriting. We divide the cache into several regions according to distinct task boundaries. Suppose there are n tasks mapped to the cache. Since each task has lower and upper address bounds, the number of tasks boundaries are bounded by $O(2n)$, which means that the cache is divided into at most $O(2n + 1)$ regions. In the example of Fig. 3, the cache is divided into seven regions by four tasks, with each task spanning several regions of the cache.

Definition 1: **Cache state.** Suppose a cache is divided into a number of regions by the overlapping tasks mapped to it. We define the *state* of a cache region as the task currently loaded in that region, and the *cache state* as a tuple of the states of all the regions.

Example 1: Fig. 3 shows an example of four tasks mapped to a cache. The cache is divided into seven regions due to task overlapping. Task a spans regions 1–4, b 2–3, c 3–6, and d spans regions 1, 6, and 7. Suppose we start executing a sequence of tasks: a, b, c, a, d. Fig. 4 shows the cache state transition during the execution of the tasks. After executing a for the first time, the cache state is $\{a, a, a, a, 0, 0, 0\}$, where zero indicates a cache region has not been loaded. The final cache state is $\{d, a, a, a, c, d, d\}$.

During a multitasking execution, we can look up the current cache state to determine a task's number of misses and, therefore, its execution time. Let *WCET_base* be the *worst case execution time* of a task assuming no cache misses, *#misses* be the number of misses. Note that *WCET_base* is constant for the task on a particular type of PE, no matter what the cache size is. The actual *WCET* considering cache misses is shown in (1).

It is equal to *WCET_base* plus the total cache miss penalty. Because of Assumption 1, compulsory misses are the only type of cache misses. Therefore, the number of cache misses for a task is the sum of the number of its compulsory misses associated with all the cache regions in which it is not loaded. It is shown in (2), where *#misses_comp(i)* is the number of the task's (say task x) compulsory misses associated with region i

$$WCET_x = WCET\_base_x + \#misses_x \cdot miss\_penalty \quad (1)$$

$$\#misses_x = \sum_{state(i) \neq task\_x} \#misses\_comp_x(i). \quad (2)$$

Example 2: In the task sequence of Fig. 4, the number of cache misses for the second execution of task a (after a, b, c) is

$$\#misses\_comp_{a,2} + \#misses\_comp_{a,3} + \#misses\_comp_{a,4}$$

where $\#misses\_comp_i$ is the number of task a's compulsory misses associated with region i. ∎

Although this model only analyzes the compulsory misses inside each task, it implicitly models conflict and capacity misses by the contentions (overlap) among tasks. In Example 2, from an application point of view (tasks a–d are parts of an application), the compulsory misses for task a ($\#misses\_comp_{a,2} + \#misses\_comp_{a,3} + \#misses\_comp_{a,4}$) are in fact conflict and capacity misses caused by tasks b and c overwriting a.

In summary, for a fixed cache, the cache performance model works in these following steps:

1) it first maps tasks to the cache and divides the cache into regions according to the task overlaps;
2) for each task and each of its related regions, it obtains the number of compulsory misses of that task associated with that region; these numbers are constants (because they are compulsory misses) and do not need to be recomputed;
3) in the case of multiple task execution, it monitors the cache state to compute the number of cache misses and *WCET*'s for the tasks in their execution context, using (1) and (2).

B. Changing Cache Size

We now analyze how cache performance changes when cache size changes. Note that because of Assumption 3, the cache size is changed only by doubling it or cutting it in half. When changing the cache size, the overlap between tasks may change. We try to infer the cache performance of a bigger cache based on an analysis of a smaller cache (half of its size).

In Fig. 5, we double the cache size of Fig. 3 and tasks a–d will map differently onto the new cache and generate different divisions of the cache. However, an important observation is that doubling the cache size does not incur more divisions on the cache: the number of regions that a task spans can only stay the same, or decrease. This is because tasks that used to overlap may not overlap in the new bigger cache. As the number of compulsory misses of a task on a particular region does not change with cache size [30], we do not need to recompute the compulsory miss numbers for the tasks.

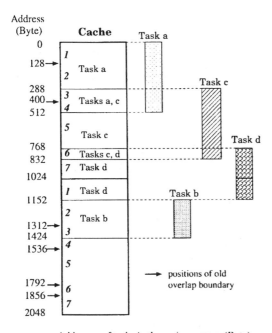

Fig. 5. Mapping of tasks onto a 2-kbyte direct-mapped cache.

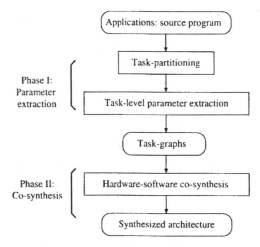

Fig. 6. Hardware/software co-synthesis system flow.

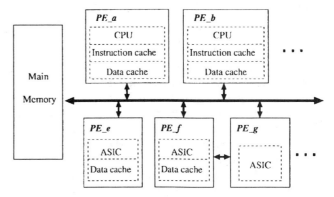

Fig. 7. An example multiprocessor architecture.

Example 3: Suppose we double the cache size in Fig. 3. The new cache and task mapping are shown in Fig. 5. Task *a* spans four regions 1–4 in the smaller cache; when the cache size is doubled, as task *b* no longs overlaps *a*, task *a* now spans two regions (1, 2) and (3, 4). The compulsory misses of *a* for these two new regions can be easily computed by adding up the compulsory misses of their corresponding subregions 1–4. ∎

Based on the above observation, to analyze all possible cache sizes, we can start from the smallest cache that satisfies Assumption 1, the analysis of any other cache size can be inductively done from the cache half of its size. For example, suppose the smallest cache size that satisfies Assumption 1 is 1-kbyte. The analysis of a cache with size 2 kbytes can be done based on the analysis results of the 1-kbyte cache. The analysis of a 4-kbyte cache can be based on that of the 2-kbyte cache, and so on.

The above discussion is based on the assumption that each task is mapped to one continuous region of the cache. While this is true for instructions, it is usually not valid for task data which may occupy several disjoint regions (Assumption 3). In this case, we can treat each data region the same way we treat an instruction region, the only difference is that multiple data regions for one task will result in more divisions on the data cache, but a similar analysis still applies.

IV. HARDWARE/SOFTWARE CO-SYNTHESIS WITH MEMORY OPTIMIZATION

Based on the task-level model for cache performance, we build a framework for hardware/software co-synthesis with caches. Fig. 6 shows the flow graph of our framework. It has two main phases: the first phase, *parameter extraction*, prepare for co-synthesis—it extracts task-level parameters from the original application specifications (source programs); these parameters are then used by the second phase—*co-synthesis* phase (design space exploration) to synthesize the multiprocessor architecture.

A. Problem Specification

The **problem specification** of our co-synthesis algorithm includes the following components: an architecture template, a set of real-time applications, and a *technology library*.

We use a heterogeneous *shared memory multiprocessor* as the template architecture (see Fig. 7). The architecture has a number of PE's (programmable processors or ASIC's) of various types. Each programmable processor has its private instruction cache and data cache. An ASIC may have a private data cache. Lower-level caches and memory are shared. PE's and memory components are linked by a shared bus. Private connections between ASIC's are allowed.

The real-time applications are periodic, running at multiple rates. Initially, each application is represented by a source program-level specification. We partition an application into an *acyclic task graph*, as shown in Fig. 8. In a task graph, nodes represent tasks that may have moderate to large granularity; the directed edges represent data dependencies between tasks.

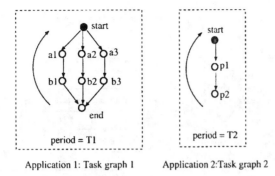

Fig. 8. A task graph example.

TABLE I
AN EXAMPLE TECHNOLOGY LIBRARY (a) PROGRAMMABLE PROCESSORS, (b) ASIC'S, (c) CACHES/MEMORIES, AND (d) COMMUNICATION LINKS

	Cost
Processor type 1	c1
Processor type 2	c2
...	...

(a)

	Cost
ASIC type 1	c3
ASIC type 2	c4
...	...

(b)

	Unit Cost	access time
Memory type 1	c5	t5
Memory type 2	c6	t6
...	...	...

(c)

	Cost	Speed (data amount/sec)
Link type 1	c7	s7
Link type 2	c8	s8
...	...	...

(d)

The data dependencies can be either read-after-write (RAW), write-after-read (WAR) or write-after-write (WAW). In any case, an edge, say $a \rightarrow b$, implies that task b cannot start execution until a is finished. Data dependency edges ensure the correct order of execution.

While generating task graphs, in order to expose as much parallelism in the application as possible while maintaining a moderate granularity of the generated task graphs, it is important to not only partition the functionality, but also to partition the data. Different tasks may share the same program or data in the memory. One example is that while partitioning an MPEG video encoding application, we partition the program into different functionality such as motion estimation, discrete cosine transform (DCT), and inverse discrete cosine transform (IDCT) etc.; the data are partitioned into blocks of 8×8; and each task node represents an operation on a block of data, such as an 8×8 DCT.

Tasks in one application run at the same rate. We assume that the deadlines of the tasks are the same as their periods.

Example 4: Fig. 8 shows an input of two applications represented by task graphs 1 and 2. In task graph 1, nodes $a1, a2$, and $a3$ could be of the same functionality (same program) running with different data. Nodes $a1$ and $b1$ could be of different functionality, but sharing data. ∎

Each task can have several implementation options differing in area cost and execution time. The *technology library* provides the tasks with a number of choices of the types of processors, ASIC's, and caches to be used in the target architecture, each associated with a certain cost. An example technology library is shown in Table I. Caches and memories are also parameterized with access times. Communication links have different speeds.

The **goal** of the co-synthesis algorithm is to:
1) choose the number and types of components in the target architecture from the technology library, e.g., the PE's and caches, such that the applications can be scheduled to meet their performance constraints (deadlines) and the total cost of the result system is minimized;
2) return the allocation and scheduling of the applications on the resultant architecture.

B. Task-Level Parameter Extraction

After the source applications have been partitioned into task graphs, for each task, from its program-level description (such as a C program), we extract *task-level parameters* that are essential for evaluating the task's execution and caching behaviors. As shown in Fig. 6, the core of our co-synthesis algorithm uses the task-level parameters as its inputs. These task-level parameters include **software parameters** and **hardware parameters**. Software parameters highlight a task's execution behavior on a programmable CPU core. They include the following.

- $WCET\_base$: worst case execution time when there are no cache misses. It is constant for a task on a CPU.
- The task's program and data address ranges in the memory: $program\_region$, and $data\_region1$, $data\_region2, \ldots$ Note that we have assumed a task's program occupies a continuous region, but may have multiple data regions. Tasks with the same (or overlapped) program regions share the same (or part of) functionality.
- Cache-related parameters: these are the tasks' compulsory misses associated with cache regions. They are computed based on the task-level cache performance model presented in Section III. We compute the smallest cache size that satisfies Assumption 1, separately for data and instruction caches. Assuming all tasks are allocated to this one cache, we divide the cache into regions according to task overlaps in the cache and compute the tasks' compulsory misses on each of their relevant regions (as described in Section III). During the co-synthesis process, only a subset (say T) of all tasks are allocated to a given PE (say P) in the architecture. This results in fewer regions in P's cache. The compulsory misses for each task in T associated with each cache region can be obtained by removing boundaries related to tasks that are not allocated to P.

TABLE II
AN EXAMPLE TECHNOLOGY DESCRIPTION

	Task1	Task2	...
PE type 1 (Processor)	$WCET\_base_{11}$ $program\_region_{11}$ $data\_regions_{11}$ $\#instr\_miss\_comp_{11}$ $\#data_miss\_comp_{11}$	$WCET\_base_{12}$ $program\_region_{12}$ $data\_regions_{12}$ $\#instr\_miss\_comp_{11}$ $\#data\_miss\_comp_{12}$	... ...
PE type 2 (ASIC)	∞ − − − −	$WCET_{22}$ − $data\_regions_{22}$ − $\#data\_miss\_comp_{22}$	... ...
...	...	...	...

Hardware parameters model tasks' behaviors on ASIC's. While a core-based design methodology usually tries to map tasks to available CPU or ASIC cores in the technology library, sometimes it is impossible to have a library of ASIC's that can implement all the functionality in the applications. Therefore, it may be necessary to synthesize ASIC's for some tasks. A task may have many different hardware implementations of various size and performance. We use high-level synthesis to obtain three possible implementations of a task: fastest, average, slowest. The fastest implementation is based on the assumption that it can use as much resources as it needs to achieve the highest speed, this usually results in a costly solution. The slowest implementation is the one with the least number of necessary resources of every type (adders, registers, etc.). The fastest and slowest implementation may not be finally chosen by the co-synthesis algorithm, but they provide bounds on the performance and cost of all the possible hardware implementations. For each task on each ASIC, the parameters mainly include *WCET_base* and data cache parameters if the ASIC has a data cache. They are defined similarly to those of the software parameters.

Parameter extraction is performed for *all tasks on all PE types*. All these parameters are stored in a table called *technology description*, where each entry of the table stores the task-level parameters of one task on one PE. Table II shows an example technology description. Since a PE (such as an ASIC) may not be suitable to run all tasks, we use a *WCET* of infinity to indicate this situation.

In our framework, a task's execution time and its memory mapping on a CPU can be obtained by either simulation or analysis. The CPU's behavior simulation tools are used to obtain the task execution times. The number of cache compulsory misses are easily obtained with a cache simulator. These parameters can also be obtained by performance analysis tools such as *Cinderella* [14]. Hardware parameters can be estimated with the help of high-level synthesis tools.

C. Cache Coherency

In a shared-memory multiprocessor architecture, caching of shared data introduces the *cache coherency* problem. The data dependencies (RAW, WAW, and WAR) in the task graph enforces that two tasks with data dependencies do not execute at the same time. This ensures the correct order of execution. However, a task may still write a data in its local cache that has several copies in the caches of other processors.

In our algorithm, we use the *write invalidate protocol*. A write on one processor will invalidate all other copies of the same data on other processors to ensure this processor has exclusive access to the data. After a task finishes its execution, if the data are "dirty" (have been written), they are written back to the main memory such that the updated data can be used by other tasks. Note that there is no need to write to the main memory during the execution of a task (say a), because any other tasks that are data-dependent on a do not start running until a is finished. When a task accesses its data through its local cache, an invalid flag associated with a block of data indicates the data needs to be reloaded from the main memory.

D. Hardware/Software Co-Synthesis Algorithm

Hardware/software co-synthesis of distributed real-time systems is an NP-complete problem. In our problem formulation, synthesizing cache memory adds another dimension to the problem and makes it even more complicated. Based on the task-level cache model described in Section III, we have designed an *iterative improvement* algorithm that uses the task-level parameters described in Section IV-B as inputs and outputs a design based on the architecture template (see Fig. 7) that meets the performance constraints with *minimal cost*. The major aspects of the co-synthesis algorithm include *analysis* and *synthesis*.

Analysis refers to the evaluation of the quality of a system design, including evaluating both its *cost* and its *performance*. **Synthesis** refers to the exploration of the design space. Synthesis is integrated with the cost/performance analysis and allocation/scheduling algorithm to find the optimized design.

1) Cost Analysis: The total cost of the system is evaluated as the sum of the component costs

$$cost(system) = \sum_{i \in CPU's} (cost(CPU_i) + cost(I\_cache_i) \\ + cost(D\_cache_i)) \\ + \sum_{j \in ASIC's} (cost(ASIC_j) \\ + cost(D\_cache_j)) \\ + \sum_{k \in links} cost(commu\_link_k). \quad (3)$$

It includes the costs of all CPU's, ASIC's, instruction and data caches, and communication links. Since the algorithm does not co-synthesize the lower-level memory (main memory), its cost is considered constant and not included in the total cost.

2) Performance Analysis: **Performance evaluation** is far more complicated. We use two different methods at different points of the design process. One method is to *allocate and schedule* all the tasks and see if the deadlines can be met. This method is accurate but also time-consuming. Section IV-C5 will describe the allocation and scheduling algorithm.

The other method is to compute the workload [(4)] on each PE to quickly check the current design's feasibility. The workload on a PE is the sum of the workloads of all the tasks allocated to this PE

$$Workload(PE) = \sum_{i \in Tasks\_on\_PE} WCET(task_i, PE)/Period(task_i). \quad (4)$$

If any PE in the current design has a workload of higher than 100%, then the design is not feasible. Workload analysis is used in the intermediate steps of the design space search to quickly weed out infeasible designs. However, due to data dependencies and bus contentions, a PE can rarely achieve a 100% utilization. A design is validated only when a schedule can be constructed without violating the task deadlines.

3) Task Allocation and Scheduling: Task allocation and scheduling are important aspects of the co-synthesis algorithm. The scheduling routine is used not only to generate the allocation and schedules in the final design, but also to evaluate the performance of intermediate solutions, and to help generate new solutions. Both its result quality and speed are critical to the success of the co-synthesis algorithm. A schedule of good quality that utilizes the PE's well is essential for lowering the system cost. A fast scheduler is important to shorten the performance evaluation time of a design and, therefore, allows the design space to be more thoroughly searched, which eventually helps in finding a lower cost design.

Scheduling of multiple real-time tasks onto heterogeneous multiprocessors is a difficult problem in itself. The addition of caches further complicates it because instead of having a constant execution time, each task now has widely varying execution times depending on the cache states.

We built our scheduling algorithm based on the *hierarchical scheduling* algorithm (HS-algorithm) that we have developed [12]. The HS-algorithm is a preemptive static scheduling algorithm that uses the hierarchical structure of the system's task graphs to hierarchically allocate and schedule tasks on the multiprocessors and memory transfers on the bus, to meet the real-time constraints.

The HS-algorithm targets similar task model to that used by our co-synthesis framework. It allows a more general architecture model in which PE's may have an arbitrary communication topology, while our co-synthesis architecture template (Fig. 7) is restricted to a bus connection and private connections only between ASIC's. However, the HS-algorithm did not originally consider memory hierarchies. We added caches to the PE's and slightly modified the HS-algorithm by adding our memory hierarchy performance model presented in Section III.

In the HS-algorithm, a task's execution time on a given PE was assumed to be fixed. This is no longer valid when caches are added—the execution time of a task $task_i$ on a PE PE_j not only depends on the speed of the PE, but also the speed of the cache and the current cache size and cache state. Therefore, instead of using a fixed $WCET(task_i, PE_j)$, we dynamically compute it according to the current cache state using (1) (see Section III). This change is reflected in the calculation of *dynamic urgency*, a measure used by the HS-algorithm to determine the next task to schedule and where to schedule it. In the following equation, $WCET(task_i, PE_j)$ should be computed according to the current cache state. *Dynamic urgency* encourages a task to reuse the cache state to reduce cache misses

$$\begin{aligned}DU(task_i, PE_j) = &SU(task_i) \\ &- \max\bigl(ready\_time(task_i), \\ &\qquad\qquad available\_time(PE_j)\bigr) \\ &+ \bigl(median\_WCET\_base(task_i) \\ &\qquad - WCET(task_i, PE_j)\bigr). \quad (5)\end{aligned}$$

Other parts of the equation, as well as other parts of the scheduling algorithm remain the same.

4) Outline of the Co-Synthesis Algorithm: Our co-synthesis algorithm uses an iterative improvement strategy to search the design space. The outline of our algorithm consists of the following steps:
1) find an initial solution;
2) iteratively reduce PE and cache cost;
3) allocate and schedule tasks and data transfers for the final design.

In step 1, the *initial solution* is constructed by assigning each task in the task graphs the fastest PE that is available for the task. This is done by looking up the corresponding entry for a task in the technology description. The PE entry with the least *WCET_base* is chosen. If the PE chosen is a processor, instruction and data caches of the task's program or data size are added to the PE; if it is an ASIC, a data cache of the size of the task's data size is added if necessary. The performance of the initial solution is evaluated, assuming the communication delay between PE's is zero. If the performance constraints are satisfied, we proceed to the next step. If it cannot meet the real-time deadlines, then for the given task graphs, there exists no feasible design given the current technology library, and the algorithm returns without a solution.

The PE and cache cost reduction step is the core step of the whole algorithm. Section IV-D5 describes the details of this step.

5) PE and Cache Cost Reduction: PE and cache cost reduction is the most critical step in the co-synthesis algorithm. We used an *iterative improvement* strategy to search for the optimized design by cutting PE and cache cost interactively.

A single iteration of cost reduction is shown in Fig. 9. The idea is to try to eliminate lightly loaded PE's by moving the tasks on those PE's to other PE's. The PE's in the current design are ordered by their workload (line 3). We start from the most lightly loaded PE. For each PE, we identify the tasks on it that can be executed on other PE's (line 6); these tasks are then moved to the other PE's that provide the best performance for the tasks (line 7); the cache sizes of the other PE's increase to accommodate the tasks that are newly moved there (line 8). The PE is removed if it becomes empty (lines 10–11). When there are tasks on a PE that cannot be moved to other PE's, the algorithm tries to implement the remaining tasks with a cheaper PE (lines 12–13). If such a PE cannot be found, the current PE in the design is kept, but an attempt is made to cut its instruction and data cache sizes (lines 14–16).

```
1.  PE_&_cache_cost_reduction(design) {
2.      foreach PE_i in design, calculate workload;
3.      sort PEs by increasing workload;
4.      foreach PE_i in sorted list {
5.          foreach task_j allocated to PE_i {
6.              other_PEs = other PEs in design with enough
                            workload left to execute task_j;
7.              move task_j to fastest PE_x in other_PEs;
8.              increase PE_x's I-cache/D-cache size by
                            task_j's program/data size;
9.          }
10.         if PE_i is empty
11.             remove PE_i and its caches;
12.         else if there is a cheaper PE_x available to
                        implement all tasks left on PE_i
13.             replace PE_i with PE_x;
14.         else
15.             keep PE_i;
16.             if feasible cut PE_i's cache size by half;
17.     }
18.     return the new design;
19. }
```

Fig. 9. One iteration of PE/cache cost reduction.

```
iterative_pe_cache_cost_reduction(initial_design) {
    last_cost = cost(initial_design);
    last_design = initial_design;
    do {
        this_design =PE_&_cache_cost_reduction(last_design);
        last_design =allocate_and_schedule(this_design);
    } while(!stop_condition);
    /*stop condition: no cost improvement in 3
      consecutive iterations*/
}
```

Fig. 10. The iterative PE/cache cost reduction procedure.

In a single-iteration procedure, when we move tasks from one PE to another, the performance constraint may be violated. We use the quick workload bound method [(4)] to check the utilization of PE's. In summary, a single iteration of cost reduction is achieved by:

- elimination of PE's that become empty after moving all their allocated tasks to other PE's;
- replacing PE's with cheaper ones;
- reducing cache cost.

The iterative algorithm is shown in Fig. 10. Starting from the initial design, the algorithm performs PE/cache cost reduction step-by-step, until there is no improvement in three consecutive iterations. For each new design returned by a single iteration of PE and cache cost reduction, we call the allocation and scheduling procedure to:

- check the validity of the design;
- if it is valid, we generate a new allocation and schedule that is customized to the current system. This is important because the single iteration of cost reduction moves tasks between PE's, eliminates and replaces some PE's. The resultant design may not have a balanced allocation of tasks on the PE's included in the design. We reallocate and reschedule the task graphs to achieve a better utilization of the PE's in the current architecture. The newly reallocated design is used as the starting point of the next cost reduction iteration.

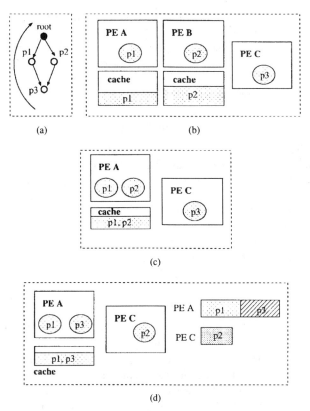

Fig. 11. An illustrative example of the co-synthesis procedures. (a) A task graph, (b) initial solution, (c) arter PE/cache cost reduction, and (d) final solution after reallocation and rescheduling.

Example 5: Fig. 11 gives an illustrative example of the synthesis process. Starting from the task graph in Fig. 11(a), an initial solution of three PE's and two caches are generated [Fig. 11(b)]. The algorithm then iteratively reduces the PE and cache cost to obtain a new solution with one less PE and smaller cache [Fig. 11(c)]. Fig. 11(d) shows the result of the final design after the tasks are reallocated and rescheduled.

E. Complexity of the Co-Synthesis Algorithm

To determine the time complexity of our framework, we recognize that the dominant part is the parameter extraction phase, where program-level estimation or simulation is needed to estimate the *WCET_base* of tasks, and the program/data memory locations for tasks on different types of PE's. For one task, the complexity of parameter extraction is either related to the size of its program-level representation if estimation tools are used, or related to the size of its execution trace if simulation tools are used. In our framework, program-level or trace-level analysis is only needed once to extract task-level parameters; the design space search is performed on a task-level abstraction which is much more manageable.

We analyze the worst case complexity of our co-synthesis algorithm. Suppose there are m task graphs, each with at most k tasks. So the total number of tasks, n, is bounded by mk. Let P be the number of different PE types. Let p be the number of PE's in a design. Because the maximum number of PE's in any design will not exceed the number of tasks, $p = O(n)$. Each full allocation/scheduling step has the complexity of $O(n^2 p) =$

$O(n^3)$. The complexity for a single iteration of PE/cache cost reduction is $O(pnP) = O(n^2P)$. The total number of iterations is bounded by $O(pP) = O(nP)$ because for each PE, it is either eliminated or can be replaced by a cheaper PE at most P times. Therefore, the worst case complexity of the co-synthesis algorithm is $O(nP \times (n^2P + n^3)) = O(n^4P + n^3P^2)$.

V. Experimental Results

To test the effectiveness of the co-synthesis algorithm, we have run a number of experiments and obtained promising results. We compared the result quality of our algorithm with co-synthesis algorithms that do not exploit the benefits of cache. Results show that co-synthesis with memory hierarchy results in significantly lower-cost implementations.

We conducted three sets of experiments: synthetic task graphs from the literature, generated task graphs, and real-life examples including a real MPEG-2 encoder.

A. Validation of the Cache Performance Model

To validate the cache performance model, we designed the following experimental procedure.

1) An application written in a source-level representation (C) is partitioned into tasks represented in a task graph.
2) A SPARC behavior simulator *Sparcsim* [29] developed at Technical University of Braunschweig is then used to extract the worst case execution times of the tasks. A memory trace profiler *QPT* [28] generates the memory access trace to be used by the cache simulator *Dinero* [28], which extracts cache-related parameters of the tasks.
3) A schedule is generated for the tasks to run on a SPARC processor, using the hierarchical scheduling algorithm with the cache performance model included. The schedule shows the sequence of task execution and the estimated execution times of the tasks with cache.
4) To validate the estimated task execution times, the programs of the tasks are combined into a single program based on the schedule. For example, if the task schedule is A, B, C, A, C, the new program has the following format:

```
A(...) {... ...}
B(...) {... ...}
C(...) {... ...}
main()
{
  A(...);
  B(...);
  C(...);
  A(...);
  C(...);
}
```

5) The program is simulated with *Sparcsim*, *QPT*, and *Dinero* to obtain the execution times and cache behavior (hits/misses) for each of its calls to the task functions. The simulation results are compared to our estimation results.

We applied the above procedure on several examples. The results are shown in Table III. One example is an image processing application consisting of procedures for image filtering, computing histogram, edge detection, etc. Another example is an integer array processing program that performs array sorting, splitting, etc. The schedule length column in Table III shows the scheduling results, in terms of the numbers of task instances scheduled, and the total WCET's for these instances. The simulated execution times and the simulation trace length are given. The last two column of the table compares the estimation and the simulation results. The average estimation error in percentage for all task instances and the standard deviation of these errors are shown.

B. Results for Examples from the Literature

To compare with existing co-synthesis algorithms, we used examples from the literature [2], [7], [8], as shown in Table IV. We used the same technology library (PE library) as those used in the corresponding references. Table IV(a) shows the results (CPU time and the synthesized system cost) of these examples using several existing algorithms: Prakash and Parker's algorithm [18], Yen and Wolf's algorithm [7], and COSYN by Dave *et al.* [2]. We ran the same examples on our algorithm, but with three different setups [see Table IV(b)]

- **Without cache:** while running our algorithm, we set the cache part in the technology library to be null, so that the synthesized architecture does not have caches. The results show that even without the benefits of caches, our algorithm can achieve comparable results.
- **With fixed-size caches** associated with each processor: Similar to a typical design practice, we manually picked fixed cache sizes to be used in the target architecture. The results show improvements in term of system cost, compared to the no-cache results.
- **Co-synthesis with cache optimization:** This allows the full potential of our algorithm to synthesize software, hardware as well as caches simultaneously. The results show further cost reduction over the fixed-size cache approach.

For easier comparison of our results and those of previous work, we have plotted the results in Table IV in Fig. 12. The examples $ex1$–$ex5$ are the five examples in Table IV. The costs of the synthesized architectures are normalized in order to put the results of all the five examples in the same plot.

For the second and third setups, we needed more input parameters required by our algorithm, such as the memory regions of the program and data for the tasks. These parameters were generated because the examples from the literature only provide the task-graph representations and task execution times.

C. Results for an MPEG-2 Encoder

We applied our algorithm to a real MPEG-2 video encoding algorithm. We use the MPEG-2 encoding software in C from *MPEG Software Simulation Group*. The compiled code has a size of 200 kbytes. We use the image frame size of 720 × 560.

TABLE III
EXPERIMENTAL RESULTS FOR VALUDATION OF THE CACHE PERFORMANCE MODEL

Example	#tasks	Schedule length WCET (cycles) / #task_instances	Simulated execution time (cycles)	Trace length	Avg. error	Std deviation
image processing	7	1,814,375/32	1,679,822	1,078,139	7.6%	2.3%
array	3	3,843,337/11	3,656,839	3,071,293	4.7%	1.2%

TABLE IV
EXPERIMENTAL RESULTS FOR EXAMPLES FROM THE LITERATURE EXPERIMENTAL RESULTS FOR (a) THREE EXISTING CO-SYNTHESIS ALGORITHMS AND (b) OUR SYNTHESIS ALGORITHM IN THREE SETUPS: WITHOUT CACHE, WITH FIXED CACHE, AND WITH CACHE

Examples,#tasks	Prakash/Parker		Yen/Hou/Wolf		COSYN	
	#PEs / Cost($)	CPU time on Solbourne 5/e/900 (sec)	#PEs / Cost($)	CPU time on Sparc 20 (sec)	#PEs / Cost($)	CPU time on Sparc 20 (sec)
Prakash&Parker, 4	1/5	37	N/A	N/A	1/5	0.20
Prakash&Parker, 9	1/5	3691.20	1/5	59.15	1/5	0.40
Prakash&Parker, 9	2/10	7.2hrs	3/10	56.79	2/10	0.54
Yen&Wolf Ex, 6	N/A	N/A	3/1765	10.63	3/1765	0.74
Hou&Wolf Ex1, 20	N/A	N/A	2/170	14.96	2/170	5.10

(a)

Examples	Our algorithm					
	Without cache		With fixed cache		With cache	
	#PEs / Cost($)	CPU time (sec)	#PEs / Cost($)	CPU time (sec)	#PEs / Cost($)	CPU time (sec)
Prakash/Parker (0)	1/5	0.30	1/4.2	0.36	1/2.6	0.45
Prakash/Parker (1)	1/5	0.71	1/4	0.73	1/2.4	0.89
Prakash/Parker (2)	2/10	0.75	2/7.4	0.75	1/4.8	1.10
Yen/Wolf Ex	3/1765	1.16	3/1640	2.02	2/1220	2.38
Hou&Wolf Ex1	2/170	6.59	2/190	6.60	2/145	7.12

(b)

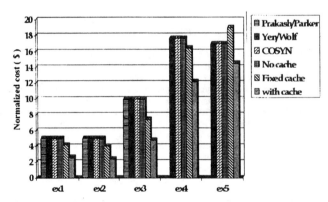

Fig. 12. Plot of experimental results for examples from the literature.

We first extract the task graph. The functionality of MPEG is partitioned into motion estimation, motion compensation, DCT, quantization, various-length encoder (VL-encoder), inverse quantization and IDCT etc. The data of each frame is partitioned into blocks of 16 × 16. The generated task graph is composed of 1350 blocks with 12 tasks per block. The graph is huge but the blocks share the same structure, of which our algorithm can take advantage.

The technology library consists of SPARC processors, ASIC's for DCT, IDCT, VL-encoder and motion estimation, and SRAM to be used as first-level caches. For each task on the SPARC processors, *WCET_base*, program and data memory regions are obtained using the SPARC behavior simulator *Sparcsim* [29]. *QPT* is used to generate the memory access trace of each task and a cache simulator similar to *DineroIII*[1] is used to obtain the compulsory miss numbers. We assume a cache and memory access time ratio of 1 : 20. The retail prices of SPARC processors and SRAM's are used as their costs. *WCET*'s and the cost for ASIC's are estimated with high-level synthesis.

Synthesis results of the MPEG encoder is shown in Table V. Even in this example, with the huge number of tasks in the task graph, our algorithm was able to find a solution of good quality in a short period of time. The short CPU times of our algorithm on such a big design is made possible by our efficient task-level cache performance model, and the hierarchical scheduling methodology which takes advantage of the task graph structures.

An interesting fact of the MPEG experiment is the CPU time spent in different phases of our framework: in the parameter extraction phase, for all the tasks, generating their execution traces (about 100M instructions in total), computing *WCET_base* and program/data memory mapping took about about 4 h in total; using the task execution traces, it took a little less than 1 h to compute compulsory misses for all tasks. In contrast, the second phase—the co-synthesis algorithm itself only took minutes (see Table V). This shows that the task-level abstraction and the task-level cache model greatly speed up the design space exploration, which would have been impossible

[1] M. D. Hill, DineroIII cache simulator, 1989.

TABLE V
CO-SYNTHESIS RESULTS FOR THE MPEG-2 VIDEO ENCODER

Example/Results	Our algorithm					
	Without cache		Fixed caches		Co-synthesis w/ caches	
	#PEs Cost($)	CPU time (sec)	#PEs Cost($)	CPU time (sec)	#PEs Cost($)	CPU time (sec)
MPEG video encoder	6/840	121	5/680	157	4/520	203

TABLE VI
CO-SYNTHESIS RESULTS FOR SEVERAL REAL-LIFE APPLICATIONS

name	inputs		co-synthesis results		
	#tasks	#dependencies	# PEs	cost	CPU time (sec)
3D − image	7	8	1	30	0.12
FFT	16	20	4	200	25.2
dfloat	12	15	2	65	4.89
wavelet	18	32	2	120	5.23

with program-level analysis tools that spend hours to evaluate just one single design for the MPEG encoder.

D. Results for Other Examples

Other than the examples from the literature and the MPEG encoder example, we experimented with more real-life examples with small-to-moderate sizes (smaller than MPEG). The real-life examples include: a small three-dimensional (3-D) image processing application, *3D-image*; fast Fourier transformation; *dfloat*, an application with intensive floating point operations; and *wavelet*, a wavelet transformation. These examples are simulated on SPARC processors using *Sparcsim* as well as the cache simulator, to obtain the execution time estimation and cache-related parameters on SPARC. Table VI summarizes the co-synthesis results of these applications.

VI. CONCLUSIONS

In this paper, we described a task-level model for bounding cache performance of tasks in a multitasking environment. This model is used by our algorithm for hardware/software co-synthesis with cache memory optimization. Although it is used only in our co-synthesis algorithm which targets multirate real-time applications, the cache performance model itself is not limited to real-time applications. It is applicable to all applications that execute in a multitasking environment.

The algorithm is the first co-synthesis algorithm that considers the impact of memory hierarchy on both the system performance and the system cost. Our algorithm synthesizes complex multirate real-time applications onto a heterogeneous multiprocessor architecture to meet real-time deadlines at minimal cost. The co-synthesis algorithm works at the task level, does not require a detailed program analysis, and, therefore, is very computationally efficient. Our co-synthesis algorithm achieves improved results (in terms of lower cost of the synthesized system) compared to existing algorithms.

Future work may include developing co-synthesis algorithms with a more generalized memory hierarchy model. We plan to model set associative caches, and extend the one-level cache model to multiple level caches. Currently our algorithm assumes fixed memory allocation for tasks. A more optimal algorithm needs to find a optimal placement of tasks in memory to reduce the overlapping of tasks in caches [26]. We plan to extend the algorithm to optimize task placement and cache sizes at the same time. As the experimental results showed that the co-synthesis phase is very fast compared to the parameter extraction phase. We plan to use a more sophisticated approach such as genetic algorithms to further improve the quality of co-synthesis results. Our memory-hierarchy model optimizes context switching at task-level, which not only helps reduce computation time, but also power consumption. We plan to develop a quantitative model for power consumption at system level and use power as another objective of co-synthesis.

REFERENCES

[1] K. Danckaert, F. Catthoor, and H. De Man, "System level memory optimization for hardware-software co-design," in *Proc. Co-Design*, 1997, pp. 55–59.
[2] B. Dave, G. Lakshminarayana, and N. Jha, "COSYN: Hardware-software co-synthesis of embedded systems," in *Proc. 34th Design Automation Conf.*, 1997, pp. 703–708.
[3] B. Dave and N. K. Jha, "COFTA: Hardware-software co-synthesis of heterogeneous distributed embedded system architectures for low overhead fault tolerance," in *Proc. IEEE Fault-Tolerant Computing Symp.*, 1997, pp. 339–348.
[4] R. Ernst, J. Henkel, and T. Benner, "Hardware-software cosynthesis for microcontrollers," *IEEE Design Test Comput.*, vol. 10, pp. 64–75, Dec. 1993.
[5] D. Gajski, F. Vahid, S. Narayan, and J. Gong, "System-level exploration with SpecSyn," in *Proc. 35th Design Automation Conf.*, 1998, pp. 812–817.
[6] R. Gupta and G. De Micheli, "Hardware-software cosynthesis for digital systems," *IEEE Design Test Comput.*, vol. 10, pp. 29–41, Sept. 1993.
[7] J. Hou and W. Wolf, "Process partitioning for distributed embedded systems," in *Proc. Int. Workshop Hardware/Software Co-Design*, 1996, pp. 70–76.
[8] D. Kirk and J. Strosnider, "SMART (strategic memory allocation for real-time) cache design using the MIPS R3000," in *Proc. 11th Real-time Systems Symp.*, 1990, pp. 322–330.
[9] C.-G. Lee, J. Hahn, Y.-M. Seo, S. L. Min, R. Ha, S. Hong, C. Y. Park, M. Lee, and C. S. Kim, "Analysis of cache-related preemption delay in fixed-priority preemptive scheduling," in *Proc. 17th Real-Time Systems Symp.*, 1996, pp. 264–274.
[10] Y. Li and J. Henkel, "A framework for estimating and minimizing energy dissipation of embedded HW/SW systems," in *Proc. 35th Design Automation Conf.*, 1998, pp. 188–193.
[11] Y. Li and W. Wolf, "A task-level hierarchical memory model for system synthesis of multiprocessors," in *Proc. 34th Design Automation Conf.*, 1997, pp. 153–156.

[12] ——, "Hierarchical scheduling and allocation of multirate systems on heterogeneous multiprocessors," in *Proc. European Design and Test Conf.*, 1997, pp. 134–139.

[13] ——, "Hardware/software co-synthesis with Memory Hierarchies," in *Proc. Int. Conf. Computer-Aided Design*, 1998, pp. 430–436.

[14] Y.-T. Li, S. Malik, and A. Wolfe, "Performance estimation of embedded software with instruction cache modeling," in *Proc. Int. Conf. Computer-Aided Design*, 1995, pp. 380–387.

[15] C. L. Liu and J. W. Layland, "Scheduling algorithms for multiprogramming in a hard real time environment," *J. ACM*, vol. 20, no. 1, pp. 46–61, 1973.

[16] P. Panda, N. Dutt, and A. Nicolau, "Architectural exploration and optimization of local memory in embedded systems," in *Proc. Int. Symp. System Synthesis*, 1997, pp. 90–97.

[17] D.-T. Peng and K. G. Shin, "Static allocation of periodic tasks with precedence constraints in distributed real-time systems," in *Proc. Int. Conf. Distributed Computing Systems*, 1989, pp. 190–198.

[18] S. Prakash and A. Parker, "SOS: Synthesis of application-specific heterogeneous multiprocessor systems," *J. Parallel Distributed Computing*, vol. 16, pp. 338–351, 1992.

[19] K. Ramamritham, "Allocation and scheduling of complex periodic tasks," in *Proc. Int. Conf. Distributed Computing Systems*, 1990, pp. 108–115.

[20] J. Rawat, "Static analysis of cache performance for real-time programming," master's thesis, Iowa State Univ. Sci. Technol., Ames, IA, Nov. 1993, TR93-19.

[21] J. A. Stankovic, M. Spuri, M. Di Natale, and G. C. Buttazzo, "Implication of classical scheduling results for real-time systems," *IEEE Comput.*, vol. 28, pp. 16–25, June 1995.

[22] F. Vahid, J. Gong, and D. Gajski, "A binary-constraint search algorithm for minimizing hardware during hardware/software partitioning," in *Proc. European Design Automation Conf.*, 1994, pp. 214–219.

[23] W. Wolf, "An architectural co-synthesis algorithm for distributed, embedded computing systems," *IEEE Trans. Very Large Scale Integration (VLSI) Syst.*, vol. 5, pp. 218–229, June 1997.

[24] ——, "Hardware/software co-design of embedded systems," *Proc. IEEE*, vol. 82, pp. 967–989, July 1994.

[25] T.-Y. Yen and W. Wolf, "Communication synthesis for distributed systems," in *Proc. Int. Conf. Computer-Aided Design*, 1995, pp. 288–294.

[26] H. Tomiyama and H. Yasuura, "Size-constrained code placement for cache miss rate reduction," in *Proc. Int. Symp. System Synthesis*, 1996, pp. 96–101.

[27] Motion Pictures Experts Group, "Information technology-Coding of moving pictures and associated audio for digital media at up to about 1.5 Mbit/s," Tech Rep. ISO-IEC/JTC1/SC29/WG11, 1992.

[28] J. R. Larus, "WARTS: Wisconsin Architectural Research Tool Set," Computer Science Dept., Univ. Wisconsin, Madison, 1997.

[29] W. Ye *et al.*, "Fast timing analysis for hardware-software co-synthesis," in *Proc. Int. Conf. Computer Design*, 1993, pp. 452–457.

[30] J. Hennessy and D. Patterson, "Computer architecture, a quantitative approach," 2nd ed. San Mateo, CA: Morgan Kaufmann, 1995.

Yanbing Li (M'95) received the Ph.D. degree from Princeton University, Princeton, NJ, in 1998, the M.S. degree from Cornell University, Ithaca, NY, in 1995, and the B.S. degree form Tsinghua University, Beijing, China, in 1992, all in electrical engineering.

Since August 1998, she has been with the Advanced Technology Group of Synopsys Inc., Mountain View, CA. Her research interests include hardware/software co-design, performance modeling, cache and memory issues in system-level synthesis, design for low power, and reconfigurable computing.

Wayne H. Wolf (S'78–A'80–M'83–SM'91–F'98) received the B.S., M.S., and Ph.D. degrees in electrical engineering from Stanford University, Stanford, CA, in 1980, 1981, and 1984, respectively.

He is Professor of Electrical Engineering, Princeton University, Princeton, NJ. Before joining Princeton, he was with AT&T Bell Laboratories, Murray Hill, NJ. His research interests include hardware/software co-design and embedded computing, very large scale integration (VLSI) CAD, and multimedia computing systems.

Dr. Wolf has been elected to Phi Beta Kappa and Tau Beta Pi. He is a member of the ACM and SPIE.

System level memory optimization for hardware-software co-design

Koen Danckaert   Francky Catthoor‡   Hugo De Man‡

IMEC, Kapeldreef 75, B-3001 Leuven, Belgium
‡Professor at the Katholieke Universiteit Leuven

Abstract

Application studies in the areas of image and video processing systems indicate that between 50 and 80% of the area cost in (application-specific) architectures for real-time multi-dimensional signal processing (RMSP) is due to data storage and transfer of array signals. This is true for both single- and multi-processor realizations, both customized and (embedded) programmable targets. This paper has two main contributions. First, to reduce this dominant cost, we propose to address the *system-level storage organization* for the *multi-dimensional (M-D) signals* as a first step in the overall methodology to map these applications, before the HW/SW-partitioning decision. Secondly, we will demonstrate the usefulness of this novel approach based on a realistic test-vehicle, namely a quad-tree based image coding application.

1 Introduction and related work

In multi-media applications and others that make use of large multi-dimensional array-type data structures, a considerable amount of memory is required which is dominant in the system cost. This is especially true for embedded systems [12].

A system designer crafting an image or video processing system faces a large design space at the specification level. Up to now, only few hardware synthesis systems (see refs in [12]) try to reduce the storage requirements for array-type data structures, always focussed on single-processor realizations and with (severe) model limitations. Also in our own previous work on ATOMIUM [12], we have focussed mainly single-processor storage, dealing with loop transformations, memory allocation and in-place storage reduction for complex M-D array signal processing. Only recently, we have started studying the effect in a parallel processor context [4], but then focussed on the parallelisation issue and not on the hardware-software (HW/SW) co-design aspects.

Many papers have been published on the HW/SW co-design issues, including modeling and simulation [10], generic integration and interfaces [3, 5, 7], custom HW/SW synthesis [8], and especially partitioning. The latter category includes manual approaches: coarse-grain [2] or fine-grain [1], and automatic approaches: starting from hardware allocation first [9] or from software allocation [6]. All of these approaches ignore however the heavy impact of the data storage cost if they would be applied on data-dominated applications as in image processing.

As a result, the number of transfers to large memories or the amount of cache misses in the software part is not minimized at all. Consequently, there is a large potential loss in power consumption and a significant overhead in cycles (due to cache misses or off-chip access). This is especially undesirable in an embedded application.

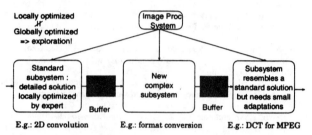

Figure 1: Data transfer and storage exploration for heterogeneous data dominated multi-process systems: possibilities for design support and optimization

Conventional HW/SW co-design approaches tackle the partitioning and load balancing issues as the only key point so they perform these first in the overall methodology. For the typical image processing system in figure 1, this means that all the submodules are first assigned to the best matched processors, and afterwards they are treated fully separately where they will be compiled in an optimized way onto the corresponding HW or SW processor. This strategy leads to a good load balancing solution but unfortunately, it will typically give rise to a significant buffer overhead for the mismatch between the data produced and consumed in the different submodules. To remedy this situation, the system-level memory management (SLMM) oriented methodology presented in this paper, first applies storage and transfer oriented optimizations *between* the different systems. Initially, all the submodules containing M-D processing are combined into one global specification model, and then optimized as a whole in terms of SLMM. It has to be stressed that it is indeed not required that the actual processor organization or even the processor partitioning is known initially in order to apply this SLMM methodology. We also apply more aggressive loop and data flow transformations than previously done. These transformations are able to significantly reduce the storage requirements for statically allocated memory in a multi-processing context.

Our SLMM techniques are complementary to the existing partitioning and load balancing techniques (as discussed earlier). In that way, they typically have little effect on the finally obtained partitioning or load balancing properties, whereas a large storage size and/or data transfer gain can be obtained. They are also fully complementary to the traditional high-level synthesis step known as "register allocation/assignment" [11]. The latter should be applied after partitioning still because they are too much related to the detailed scheduling stage.

It should be emphasized too that decisions made at the SLMM level do translate into constraints on the M-D signal access, which directly influence the search space of the subsequent partitioning and processor mapping tasks. This is for instance true due to the restrictions on loop ordering and index expressions. Still, *only* the relative ordering of blocks of statements is decided and not yet the fully sequential execution or the "scheduling". Typically, these restrictions do not negatively affect the final outcome itself (see section 3)!

The overall approach will be illustrated with a real application in section 3. The application is described first in section 2.

2 The QSDPCM algorithm

2.1 Algorithm description

QSDPCM (Quadtree Structured Difference Pulse Code Modulation) is a compression technique for video [13]. It involves a motion estimation step, and a quadtree encoding of the motion compensated frame-to-frame difference signal. The algorithm optimizes both the displacement vector and the quadtree mean decomposition jointly such that the total frame-to-frame update information can be coded with a minimum number of bits. In this paper, we will assume that the images are in CIF format (528 x 288 for the luminance/chrominance signals together), and that the frame rate is 25 Hz.

A global view of the algorithm is given in figure 2. In a first step, the actual image is 4×4 mean subsampled, and matched with a 4×4 subsampled version of the reconstructed previous image. The initial guess of the displacement is computed using a 4×4 block matching (BM) algorithm with a search interval of +/- 4 pixels (full search) in the subsampled images. The resulting displacement vector is used as an inital displacement in the second stage, where an 8×8 BM algorithm with a search interval of +/- 2 pixels is applied on 2×2 mean subsampled versions. The displacement vector obtained in this way provides the initial guess for the QSDPCM algorithm.

The optimum displacement vector and the best quadtree decomposition are finally determined in a joint optimization procedure. For each displacement in a +/- 1 interval around the initial guess, the 16×16 difference signal is computed and 2×2 mean subsampled. The resulting 8×8 difference signals are quadtree encoded (with the local block means being Huffman coded). The displacement which requires the minimum number of bits for the quadtree decomposition is selected.

In a bottom-up quadtree decomposition of a two-dimensional signal, four adjacent subblocks are tested if they can accurately be represented by their mean value.

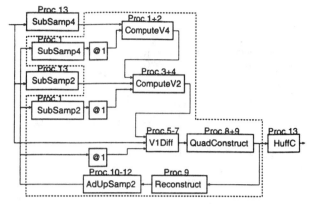

Figure 2: The QSDPCM video encoding algorithm and one processor partitioning option

If so, they are merged to a $4\times$ larger subblock. The procedure can then be repeated recursively until the largest possible block size (8×8) is reached.

2.2 Algorithm code and cycles

From figure 2, it is clear that many submodules of the algorithm operate in a cycle with an iteration period bound (IPB) of 1 (i.e. one frame). Indeed, to compute the motion vectors in the 4×4 subsampled images, the previous frame must already have been reconstructed (and 4×4 subsampled too). The following submodules are not in this critical cycle: the computation of the 4×4 and 2×2 subsampled versions of the initial image, and the Huffman coding of the displacement vectors and quadtrees.

Figure 3 illustrates the algorithm structure as Silage code. In the main function, we see that the incoming and the reconstructed image are first 4×4 and 2×2 subsampled. Then, the estimated motion vectors are computed, first in the 4×4 and then in the 2×2 subsampled image. Based on these, the final motion vectors are computed with pixel accuracy. First, the nine possible 2×2 subsampled difference images are computed, and then they are quadtree encoded to determine which one requires the fewest bits. Finally everything is Huffman coded. The image is then reconstructed, and 2×2 adaptive upsampled. It is this upsampled image which will be the reference image for the next frame to be encoded. Also a 2×2 and 4×4 subsampled version of this reference are needed. Only when these reference images are available, we can start computing the motion vectors of the next frame. The following table gives the number of arithmetic operations in each function, for one block (first line) and for a whole image (second line).

Sub4	Sub2	V4	V2	V1	Quad	Rec	AdUp2
272	320	2673	3225	5184	2646	384	4608
161K	190K	1587K	1915K	3079K	1571K	228K	2737K

3 SLMM approach illustration

3.1 Design based on initial description

When a design is made based on this initial description and when flexibility is desired in the final implementation,

```
func main(image: P[N][N]) : P =
begin
  sub2[][]=SubSamp2(image[][]); sub4[][]=SubSamp4(image[][]);
  (v4x[][],v4y[][])=ComputeV4(sub4[][],rec4[][]@1);
  (v2x[][], v2y[][])=ComputeV2(sub2[][],rec2[][]@1,v4x[][],v4y[][]);
  (diffs[][][][])=V1Diff(image[][],rec[][]@1,v2x[][],v2y[][]);
  (quadmeans[][][], quadcode[][][], v1x[][], v1y[][]) =
       QuadConstruct(diffs[][][][]);
  huffcode[] = HuffCoding(quadmeans[][][], quadcode[][][],
                          v1x[][], v1y[][]);
  recsub[][] = Reconstruct(quadmeans[][][], quadcode[][][],
                           rec2[][]@1, v1x[][], v1y[][]);
  rec[][] = AdUpSamp2(rec2[][]);
  rec2[][] = SubSamp2(rec[][]); rec4[][] = SubSamp4(rec[][]);
end;

func SubSamp2(image: P[N][N]) sub: P[][] =
begin
  (i: 0 .. N div 2 -1) ::
  (j: 0 .. N div 2 -1) ::
    sub[i][j] = (image[i][j] + image[i+1][j] + ...)/4;
end;

func ComputeV2(act2, prev2: P[N div 2][N div 2];
       v4x,v4y: A[N div Nb][B div Nb]) v2x, v2y: A[][] =
begin
  (xb : 0 .. N div Nb -1) :: /* for each block */
  (yb : 0 .. N div Nb -1) ::
     (vx[xb][yb], vy[xb][yb]) = V2_block(act2[][],
             prev2[][], xb, yb, v4x[xb], v4y[yb]);
end;

func V2_block(act2, prev2: P[N div 2][N div 2]; xb, yb: A;
       v4x, v4y: A) v2x, v2y : A =
begin
  (vx : -2 .. 2) :: /* Scan through search region */
  (vy : -2 .. 2) :: /* Keep 8x8 current block + 8x12 region */
    begin            /* of prev frame in foreground      */
      (i : 0 .. 7) :: /* Accumulate differences over */
      (j : 0 .. 7) :: /* 8x8 block                    */
        SumAbsDiff[vx][vy][i*8+j+1] =
          SumAbsDiff[vx][vy][i*8+j] + abs(act2[xb*8+i][yb*8+j]
            -prev2[xb*8+v4x+2*vx+i][yb*8+v4y+2*vy+j]);
    /* Select vx,vy with minimum SumAbsDiff */
    end;
end;
```

Figure 3: Original Silage code

typically some submodules will be implemented in hardware and some in software. In this case, the submodules in the cycle can be assigned to hardware due to the high computation complexity and the high throughput requirement in this critical cycle. An exception can be made for SubSamp2, SubSamp4 and Reconstruct because these do not contain many operations.

When we take into account that programmable digital signal processors (SW) run at about 50 to 100 MHz, that the frame rate is 25 fr/s and that the arithmetic operation efficiency of these DSP processors is usually about 25-50% (the rest is lost in overhead for condition and address handling and the like), we arrive at a maximal load of 1 million operations per frame per SW processor. Given the operations in table 2.2, we need about 12 SW processors for the operations in the critical cycle. On the other hand, the functions which are not in the cycle can be combined into a single SW software processor.

Several approaches are feasible now for the critical cycle. We will illustrate that the data storage cost has a major effect on the cost related to HW/SW partitioning. Indeed, in the initial description of this algorithm, each submodule operates on a whole frame of the incoming video stream. This means that between two submodules, buffers are needed to store the results for a whole frame. For example, between SubSamp4 and ComputeV4, the two 4 × 4 subsampled images (actual and reconstructed previous frame) must be stored in a buffer. This has to be a background buffer as it is too big to be stored in foreground. If we have assigned SubSamp4 to software and ComputeV4 to hardware, then this buffer cannot be optimized away anymore. In the global initial QSDPCM description this leads to an overhead of buffers for 742K words, and an overhead of 2245K transfers operating on these frame size buffers. This number already assumes that a memory hierarchy is present, and that it is used in an optimal way. Without memory hierarchy (caching), there would be even 9599K background memory transfers.

If we do not need the flexibility, one or more dedicated hardware processor(s) can be designed to perform the functions which are in the cycle. How many will depend on the used hardware synthesis methodology. The IPB of 1 precludes simple pipelining. However, by performing a pipeline interleaving combined with loop folding operation such that each of the processors works on 1/12 of the frame successively, it is still possible to break this cycle which allows more freedom in processor partitioning.

When the flexibility is needed in all the functions, we again have several options. We can use data level parallelism by partitioning the frame into 12 equal parts and distributing the processing of these pixels over 12 processors. The advantage of this approach is that it is simple to program but the memory overhead is high, namely still 742K (540K with in-place mapping) words in total i.e. 61K (45K) per processor. The amount of transfers is 2245K. Moreover, each processor has to run the full code for all the functions. Alternatively, we can use task level parallelism by the more complex pipeline interleaving manipulation and by assigning the different functions (or parts of them) in chunks of 1 million operations over the different SW processors. This leads to the processor partitioning indicated in figure 2 by the processor numbers. The advantages are that the code size per processor is relatively low and especially that we need only 325K words with our memory management approach. The reason for this is that most buffers need only be present between two stages (although double-buffered). E.g. the buffer which contains the array diffs, is $342/12 = 28K$, and is only present (twice) between V1Diffs and QuadConstruct. In the data parallel case, each processor needs this 28K (although not double-buffered), which equals 342K total. The disadvantage is that the design time will be much higher due to the complex processor partitioning and memory management.

In summary, if we do not take into account the optimized storage related costs during the evaluation of the processor partitioning decisions, the data parallel option could have been selected. If later on the individual processor designers are faced with the given partitioning they would not be able to return to the much less costly task parallel case.

However, this is not the end of the story. This way of partitioning a system based on the initial description

```
func main(image: P[N][M]) : P =
begin
  (xb : 0 .. N div Nb -1) ::   /* for each block */
  (yb : 0 .. M div Mb -1) ::
  begin
    sub2[xb][yb][][] = SubSamp2_block(image[][],xb,yb);
    sub4[xb][yb][][] = SubSamp4_block(image[][],xb,yb);
    (v4x[xb][yb], vec4y[xb][yb]) = V4_block(sub4[xb][yb][][],
        rec4[xb][][]);
    (v2x[xb][yb], vec2y[xb][yb]) = V2_block(sub2[xb][yb][][],
        rec2[xb][yb][][],v4x[xb][yb], v4y[xb][yb]);
    ....
end;
```

Figure 4: Globally transformed code

and only afterwards evaluating the data storage cost will lead to suboptimal designs. Typically it still gives rise to large buffers between the different submodules, even if it is already optimized towards memory as described above. Unfortunately, if the HW/SW partitioning is performed first in the design trajectory, these remaining buffers afterwards cannot be optimized away anymore.

For the QSDPCM application, we can do much better still by *applying aggressive storage oriented transformations before the HW/SW partitioning*.

3.2 Global optimizations

To apply our system-level memory optimizations, all functions (submodules) are first taken together in one big function. In this way, global transformations can be done which have a very big impact on the memory cost (and thus on the power and area cost).

We can apply a loop merging operation to this description, so that we have two outer loops that iterate over the block indices (see figure 4). Indeed, there are no dependences between two blocks of the same frame at all, so it is easy to see that this is a valid transformation[1].

Now we have an algorithm that operates block per block. All computations are done on the first block before we begin processing the second one. In this way, buffer memory for only one block (instead of one frame) will be required between the submodules. This reduces both the area and power requirements of the application because these small buffers can be stored in foreground memories.

The pipeline interleaving transformation is still possible. This will now allow pipelining at the level of blocks. While ComputeV4 is being executed on block x, ComputeV2 is executed on block $x-1$, and so on.

3.3 Optimizations between modules

Between V1Diff and QuadConstruct, nine difference blocks have to be kept in memory. It is obviously much better to merge the loops which iterate over the nine possible displacements in these functions. Then after computing one difference block, it is immediately quadtree encoded. Note however, that these quadtrees (which occupy less memory) have to be written to background anyway (only one of them will have to be read back). A possible

---

[1] Note that also a loop tiling transformation of the loops in SubSamp2 and SubSamp4 has been applied to make the global loop merging possible. Hence, the subsampled images are now 4-dimensional signals.

choice would be not to write them to background, but only remember how many bits they took, and to recompute the best one afterwards. Then however, the 16×16 and 18×18 blocks from which the difference image was computed, would have to be read back, so here this is not good.

In ComputeV4, it is possible to interchange the loop which iterates over all possible displacements and the loop which scans over the 4×4 block itself. If the displacement loop is the outer one, the 4×4 block of the actual image and a 12×4 region of the previous image must be kept in foreground (if we work row-wise or column-wise) to avoid duplicate transfers from background memory to the datapath. If the block-scanning loop is the outer one, we can compute for each individual pixel the contribution to the mean absolute difference, and this for all $9 \times 9 = 81$ positions (see figure 5). This will obviously not be the best solution in this case, as it requires 81 values to be kept in foreground instead of 16.

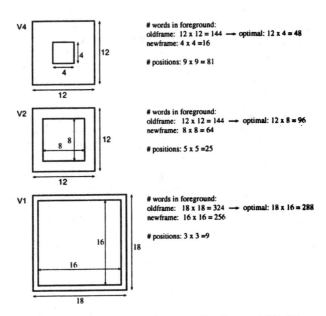

Figure 5: Memory requirements for ComputeV4,2,1

In ComputeV2 however, this loop interchange transformation is beneficial w.r.t. memory. If the displacement loop is the outer one here (figure 3), an 8×8 block of the actual image and a 12×8 region of the previous image must be kept in foreground. If the block-scanning loop is the outer one (figure 6), we need only storage for $5 \times 5 = 25$ positions of the displacement vector. Moreover, only a 12×5 region of the previous image must be in foreground (because each new pixel must be compared with all old pixels in a 5×5 square).

Another advantage of this modification is that, by merging the block-scanning loop (which is now the outer loop) with the block-scanning loop of SubSamp2, the 2×2 subsampled values do not have to be stored in background memory between SubSamp2 and ComputeV2. Note that this would also not be possible if we had assigned these functions to different chips in the initial partitioning. On

```
func V2_block(act2:P[8][8];prev2: P[N][M];v4x,v4y:A) v2x,v2y: A=
begin
  (i: 0 .. 7) :: /* For each pixel in current block, compute */
  (j: 0 .. 7) :: /* contrib to 5x5 possible SumAbsDiff values */
  begin
    (vx : -2 .. 2) :: /* Scan through search region */
    (vy : -2 .. 2) :: /* Keep 5x5 SumAbsDiff values + 5x12 */
    begin           /* region of prev frame in foreground */
      SumAbsDiff[vx][vy][i*8+j+1] = SumAbsDiff[vx][vy][i*8+j]
        +abs(act2[i][j]-prev2[xb*8+v4x+2+vx+i][yb*8+v4y+2+vy+j]);
    end;
  end;
  /* Select vx,vy with minimum SumAbsDiff */
end;
```

Figure 6: Transformed code for V2_block

the other hand, it influences the way we will partition the new transformed algorithm: SubSamp2 and ComputeV2 must now be kept together.

In V1diff and Quadconstruct, this analysis is a bit more difficult to make, as for every possible displacement, not the mean absolute difference is computed (which would require only $3 \times 3 = 9$ values), but the quadtree decomposition. So if we want to reduce the required memory (18×18 pixels of the previous and 16×16 of the actual image), we have to merge the loops which compute the difference signal and the quadtree decomposition.

If we work line per line, when 2 lines of the difference signal have been computed, the first level of the bottom-up construction of the quadtree can already be applied, and the results written to background memory. Only four values are needed for the further construction of the quadtree (and must be kept in foreground). So we need to keep 2 rows of 8 values, 2 rows of four values, and 2 rows of 2 values in foreground, and this for all nine possible quadtree decompositions. Instead of a 16×16 block, we then only have to keep two rows (2×16) of the actual image block in foreground (note that one line is not enough because the quadtree is constructed on the 2×2 subsampled difference signal). Likewise, we need only four rows (4×18) of the previous image block.

3.4 Memory optimized design

The only background memories we still need are the actual and previous frame buffer (2 x 152K, which can be reduced to 166K in total by appropriate in-place mapping between these two frames). The number of transfers to background has been reduced from 2245K to 1238K.

If we choose for a data parallel solution in this case, each of the 12 processors will be working on another block. So each processor has much code to execute. The frame memory has to be organised such that it allows simultaneous accesses from all processors. One solution is to use a 12-port memory. A much better solution is to use 12 memories, and store 1/12 of the number of blocks in each memory, in an interleaved way.

In our optimizations, we have imposed the constraint that following pairs of functions must be on the same chip (so without pipelining between them): Sub4 & V4, Sub2 & V2, V1 & Quad. This means that a purely algorithmic parallel solution is not possible here. A mixed data/algorithmic parallel solution is possible

though, where e.g. two processors execute Sub2 & V2, each on another block. Between the pipelined functions, double buffers are still needed, but our optimizations have made those very small.

4 Conclusion

In this paper, we have demonstrated that the HW/SW partitioning approach which is typically followed in conventional HW/SW co-design papers does not lead to good results for data-dominated applications as image and video processing. Instead of performing the processor partitioning prior to the hardware synthesis or software compiling steps per processor, first a system-level memory management approach should be applied to the global algorithm, leading to significant reshuffling and modification of the initial processes or submodules. Only then the partitioning step should be applied. The feasibility and effect of this new approach has been substantiated on a realistic image processing application, leading to a reduction of the storage size from 742K 12-bit words to 166K words and a decrease of the number of memory accesses from 2245K to 1238K.

References

[1] E.Barros, W.Rosenstiel, "A method for hardware/software partitioning", *Proc. CompEuro Conf.*, Den Haag, The Netherlands, May 1992.

[2] K.Buchenrieder, A.Sedlmeier, C.Veith, "HW/SW codesign with PRAMs using Codes", *Proc. IFIP Conf. Hardware Description Languages*, Elsevier, Amsterdam, pp.55-68, 1993.

[3] P.Chou, R.Ortega, G.Borriello, "The Chinook hardware/software co-synthesis system", *Proc. 8th ACM/IEEE Intnl. Symp. on System-Level Synthesis*, Cannes, France, Sep. 1995.

[4] K.Danckaert, F.Catthoor, H.De Man, "System-level memory management for weakly parallel image processing", *Proc. EuroPar Conference*, Lyon, France, August 1996. "Lecture notes in computer science" series, Springer Verlag, pp.217-225, 1996.

[5] H.De Man, I.Bolsens, B.Lin, K.Van Rompaey, S.Vercauteren, D.Verkest, "Co-design of DSP systems", NATO Advanced Study Institute on "Hardware/Software Co-design", Tremezzo, Italy, June 1995.

[6] R.Ernst, J.Henkel, T.Benner, "Hardware-software cosynthesis for microcontrollers", *IEEE Design and Test of Computers*, Vol.10, No.4, pp.64-75, Dec. 1993.

[7] D.Gajski, F.Vahid, S.Narayan, J.Gong, "Specification and design of embedded systems", Prentice Hall, 1994.

[8] G.Goossens, F.Catthoor, H.De Man, "Integration of signal processing systems on IC architectures with mixed hardware/software", *IFIP Intnl. Workshop on Hardware/Software Co-design*, Grassau, Germany, May 1992.

[9] R.Gupta, G.De Micheli, "Hardware-software cosynthesis for digital systems", *IEEE Design and Test of Computers*, Vol.10, No.3, pp.29-41, Sep.1993.

[10] A.Kalavade, E.Lee, "A hardware-software codesign methodology for DSP applications", *IEEE Design and Test of Computers*, Vol.10, No.3, pp.16-28, Sep.1993.

[11] M.C.McFarland, A.C.Parker, R.Camposano, "The high-level synthesis of digital systems", special issue on computer-aided design in Proc. of the IEEE, Vol.78, No.2, pp.301-318, Feb. 1990.

[12] L.Nachtergaele, F.Catthoor, F.Balasa, F.Franssen, E.De Greef, H.Samsom, H.De Man, "Optimisation of memory organisation and hierarchy for decreased size and power in video and image processing systems", *Proc. Intnl. Workshop on Memory Technology, Design and Testing*, San Jose CA, pp.82-87, Aug. 1995.

[13] P. Strobach, "QSDPCM - A New Technique in Scene Adaptive Coding," *Proc. 4th Eur. Signal Processing Conf.*, EUSIPCO-88, Grenoble, France, Elsevier Publ., Amsterdam, pp.1141-1144, Sep. 1988.

A Path–Based Technique for Estimating Hardware Runtime in HW/SW-Cosynthesis

Jörg Henkel, Rolf Ernst

Institut für Datenverarbeitungsanlagen
Technische Universität Braunschweig
Hans-Sommer-Str. 66, D–38106 Braunschweig, Germany
Henkel@ida.ing.tu–bs.de

Abstract
One of the key issues in hardware/software-cosynthesis is precise estimation. The usual local estimation techniques are inadequate for globally optimising compilers and synthesis tools. We present a path based estimation technique which allows a computation time/quality tradeoff. The results show acceptable computation times while revealing much more potential parallelism than local list scheduling.

1 Introduction
System level design becomes more important since the time to market (e.g. about 18 months for complex HW/SW systems [Keu94]) decreases at a continuously increasing complexity of mixed hardware/software systems. As a consequence, uniform specification of HW/SW systems, HW/SW partitioning, HW synthesis, SW synthesis, cosimulation etc. become important research areas.

In the ambitious area of cosynthesis, hardware software partitioning plays a key role. There are some constraint–driven approaches which focus on this problem: The VULCAN system [GuMi92] is a hardware–oriented approach to HW/SW-cosynthesis. In [VaGaGo94] a software–oriented approach (starting with an all–software–solution) decides about the HW/SW tradeoff using a binary search algorithm. The approach described in [KaLe94] uses an algorithm called GCLP that takes into consideration a global time critical measure and a set of local criteria in order to determine the HW/SW tradeoff. COSYMA [ErHeBe93] also belongs to the class of software–oriented approaches and uses the simulated annealing algorithm for automating the HW/SW partitioning process. Other approaches [BaRoXi94], [JaElOb+94] also focus on HW/SW partitioning but still need some user interaction.

All these approaches have in common that they need sophisticated techniques for estimating parameters (time, area,...) that will decide on the hardware/software partitioning.

We present a precise hardware runtime estimation technique that can even evaluate global optimization potential and that has acceptable computation time.

The next section introduces to the estimation problem in the context of the COSYMA system. In section 3 the use of the path–based technique for estimating hardware runtime is presented. The results are discussed in section 4 while section 5 gives a conclusion.

2 Estimation in COSYMA
A very simplified design flow of COSYMA is shown in figure 1. Input is a real-time system description in a superset of C that is translated to an internal representation, the extended syntax graph (ESG).

HW/SW–partitioning in COSYMA is solved with simulated annealing [OG89]. The iterative annealing process is called *Inner partitioning Loop* (IPL). Simulated annealing generates several thousands of designs that must be evaluated by the cost function. The cost function is based on estimation of hardware and software runtimes, HW/SW–communication time and on trace data. The path–based estimation technique presented in this paper provides the hardware runtime estimation. After partitioning, hardware and software synthesis are executed and the actual values for hardware runtime, chip area, ... are fed back. For more details on COSYMA see [ErHeBe93]. If the constraints (CS) have not been met, the whole procedure is repeated. Reason for a deviation from the given constraints is that estimation cannot predict all local and global optimization effects in the computation intensive hardware and software synthesis processes.

As shown in figure 2, COSYMA takes those effects into account by correcting the set of estimation values E_j when the real values C_j have been determined. The result is a set of rules from which a set of new estimation values E_{j+1} is derived. Then, again a hardware/software partition P_j is generated and so on. We call this process the *Outer Partitioning Loop OPL*. Iteration through the OPL should be done until all constraints are met.

As shown in [HeHeEr94] a convergence – i.e. meeting all constraints – can be achieved after a few iterations. *Prerequisite are sophisticated estimation algorithms*: the closer the result of an estimation to the real value the faster the convergence and the final re-

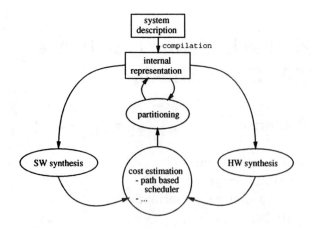

Figure 1: Simplified design flow of COSYMA.

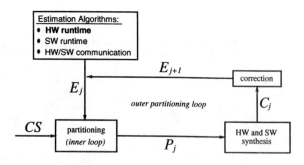

Figure 2: The role of estimation in the Outer Partitioning Loop.

sult (see [HeHeEr94]). This estimation is only executed *once* in the beginning of inner loop computation to derive all estimation values including high order values as E_{ij} [HeHeEr94].

The requirements for developing an adequate algorithm that estimates the hardware runtime, are (implied by the arguments above):

- *high precision*
- *low computational effort*
- *completely automatic*

The first requirement excludes all estimation approaches that are limited to the scope of basic blocks because they are not able to identify the global optimization potential in hardware synthesis. Path–based scheduling could be used for estimation instead as it reveals global optimization potential of basic block sequences.

The scheduling algorithm described in [Cam91] furthermore promises a high flexibility since the handling of resource constraints is integrated into the global concept. Nevertheless the major disadvantage is that some of the steps in path–based scheduling are *NP-complete* thereby preventing its use for larger programs. In [ObRaJe93] an approach is presented that uses an algorithm in order to avoid a path explosion. There paths end if a *wait* statement is encountered or a node is found that has already been inserted in a path. This approach is not able to decide between different alternatives to limit a path since the conditions are fixed (i. e. always end a path if the conditions are true).

We present a path–based estimation technique that reduces the number of paths drastically with a minimum loss of quality[1] (schedule) since our algorithm can decide where to end a path (given a set of possibilities from which only that subset is taken that leads to a small loss of quality) A further advantage is that the user can decide on the *quality/computation time trade-off*.

3 A Path–Based Estimation Technique

Path–based scheduling consists of the following passes:

I. Transforming a CDFG into a directed acyclic graph.
II. **Collecting ALL paths.**
III. Scheduling all paths *As–Fast–As–Possible* (AFAP see [Cam91]).
IV. Overlapping all paths.

Computation time intensive steps are III and IV as a consequence of step II.
The AFAP schedule in step III makes use of a clique partitioning algorithm [TsSi86] that has been proved to be *NP-complete*. The computation time depends on the number of operations per path N_O.
Assuming the worst case i.e. each path has at least one basic block with each other path in common the computation effort for step IV results to $O(N_P{}^2)$ with N_P the total number of paths found.

So the goal is to minimize the total numbers of paths as well as the number N_O of operations (or basic blocks) per path. Therefore the whole graph representation of an application is split and each part is scheduled by itself. This section deals with determining the so called *cut points* in a sophisticated way.

Let $G = \{V, E\}$ be a directed acyclic graph DAG where each node $v_i \in V$ represents a basic block that contains at least one single operation and where a directed edge $e_i \in E$ specifies the direction of the control flow. Fork nodes correspond to an *if-else* statement in the origin program code. Feedback edges denoting *loop* statements are already removed. Each node v_i has two attributes: *it* (i. e. iterations) is the number of times this node has been visited at simulation time. The nesting level nl of a node increases by one if the predecessor is a fork node and it decreases accordingly if the predecessor is a join node.

Example 1:
Calculating all paths in the graph representation given by figure 3 leads to a number of $N_P = 10$ paths. Each path P contains a number of $N_O = \sum_{v_i \in V} N_{O_i}$ operations.

---

[1] The original path–based scheduling by [Cam91] does not consider a re–ordering of operations in a path during scheduling. We have overcome this problem by executing a pre–scheduling phase. We do not focus on this problem here due to lack of space.

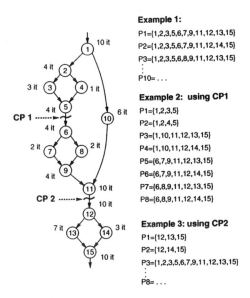

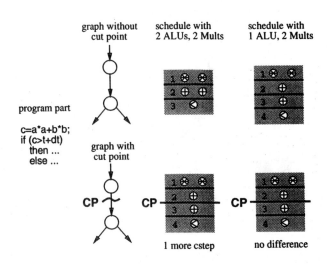

Figure 3: Calculating the number of paths with different cut points set.

Figure 4: Comparison of schedules without (top) and with (bottom) cut points for different constraints.

Example 2:
Now assume the graph has been split into two parts split by a *cut point CP1*. Determining all paths for each subgraph[2] leads to a total number of $N_P = 8$ possible paths.

Example 3:
Instead of *CP1* cut point *CP2* is set and all possible paths are calculated again. Hereby there is $N_P = 8$ also.

Compared to example 1, example 2 and 3 are expected to gain a near optimum scheduling result because a *cstep* (control step) ends at each cut point and a new cstep starts behind the cut point.

The loss in quality measured in terms of an additional number of csteps depends on the *data dependencies* of operations before and behind a cut point. Assuming that the operations have already been optimally ordered, there is no way to influence this effect.

Another aspect are the hardware constraints (number of available hardware resources). The larger the number of resources the larger is the additional number of control steps since a potential high parallelism is prevented (see example in figure 4). Calculating the number of additional csteps as a result of cut points would require a data flow analysis *through* the according cut point. The computation time saved by reducing the number of paths would have to be re-invested and nothing is gained.

A better measure for the loss of quality is the increase of execution time (measured in clock cycles) implied by the schedule. Let it_j be the number of times an operation scheduled in control step c_j (C is the set of all control steps) is executed. Then

$$t_{ex\_cut} = \sum_{g \subset G} \sum_{c_j \in C} it_j \qquad (1)$$

gives the total execution time of an program whose graph representation G has been cut into subgraphs g. In spite of the fact that example 2 and 3 lead to the same (reduced) number of paths, example 2 is expected to imply a smaller execution time (only 4 iterations at cut point *CP1* against 10 iterations at *CP2*). That leads to the formulation of rule 1.

Rule 1:
Locate the cut points at positions in the graph representation where a minimum number of additional clock cycles Δt_{ex} compared to a non-cut graph is expected.

$$\Delta t_{ex} = min(t_{ex\_cut} - t_{ex\_org}) \qquad (2)$$

There are t_{ex_cut} and t_{ex_org} the execution times with and without cut points set. Preferred candidates are those with the lowest iterations (executions).

When rule 1 is executed it is assumed that a selection of cut points has already taken place. In order to simplify the optimization procedure the total number of possible cut points should be minimized by limitation to those cut points that will really reduce the complexity:

Rule 2:
A possible cut point CP_i is located behind a node $v_i \in V$ if v_i is a join point *and* if there exists a path P where v_i is the starting node *and* where

$$\bigvee_{v_j \neq v_i, v_j \in P} (v_j\ is\ join\ point) \wedge \bigwedge_{v_n \in P} nl(v_n) \geq nl(v_i).$$

Here $nl(v)$ is the nesting level of node v. The **nesting level increases by one after a fork node and decreases**

---

[2] A *subgraph* is part of the origin graph G with a cut point before the first node and after the last node set but without any cut point inside.

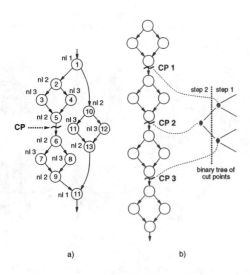

Figure 5: a) Searching for possible cut points. b) Hierarchical reducing of cut points.

when a join node is reached (see figure 5 a) attribute "nl". The path P ends if a node v_k is encountered with $nl(v_k) \leq nl(v_j)$.

Figure 5 a) shows the result of rule 2 for a small example. Only node 5 fulfills all conditions and therefore a cut point is set accordingly. It is obvious that cut points behind nodes 9 and 13 would not reduce the number of paths.

For the case rule 2, rule 1 and an AFAP schedule have been applied and the user wants to improve the result[3] a reduction of cut points is necessary.

Rule 3:
Search for subgraphs $g \subset G$ that could possibly contain (according to rule 1) more than one cut point at the same nesting level. Find that cut point that would split such a subgraph best, i.e. the resulting 2 pieces are of same length (a measure is the number of operations). Handle each piece in the same way etc. A binary tree is built up where each node represents a cut point and each edge represents a piece of the subgraph of the original program graph G. Then step by step, beginning at the leafs of the binary tree, the cut points are removed. The user determines how many cut points are removed since reduction of cut points implies an increase of computation time (*quality/computation time tradeoff*).

Figure 5 b) shows this procedure for a small subgraph with only 3 cut points. Step 1 would remove cut points 1 and 3 and step 2 would remove cut point 2.
The hierarchical reduction of cut points takes into account that a minimum quality loss at a maximum reduction of complexity (number of paths) shall be guaranteed.

Figure 6 shows how rules 1 to 3 are applied within the path–based estimation technique. The set of cut

---

[3]The user does not interact with the individual scheduling process but defines the maximum number of cut points as a control parameter.

```
( 1 )  path_based_estim_tech()
( - )  {
( 2 )      CP := {};
( - )
( 3 )      collect_profiling_data(CDFG);
( 4 )      DAG := convert_to_DAG(CDFG);
( 5 )      #paths := compute_num_of_paths(DAG);
( - )
( 6 )      if (#paths < max_paths ) {
( 7 )          CP := compute_cutpoints(DAG);
( 8 )          DAG := split_DAG(DAG, CP);
( - )      }
( - )
( 9 )      for each dag_i ∈ DAG {
( 10 )         P := calculate_all_paths(dag_i);
( 11 )         CS := {};
( 12 )         for each p ∈ P {
( 13 )             CS := CS ∪ do_AFAP_schedule(p);
( - )         }
( 14 )         superpose_all_schedules(P, CS);
( - )     }
( - )  }

( 15 ) compute_cutpoints(DAG)
( - )  {
( 16 )     CP_list.initialize();
( - )
( 17 )     for each v_i ∈ V { /* apply rule 2 */
( 18 )         if ( fulfills_rule2(v_i) ) {
( 19 )             CP_list.insert(v_i);
( - )         }
( - )     }
( - )
( 20 )     sort_by_profiling(CP_list); /* apply rule 1 */
( - )
( 21 )     #cut_pts := input();
( 22 )     if (len(CP_list) < #cut_pts) {
( 23 )         if ( ambiguous_cut(CP_list, #cut_pts) )
( 24 )             CP_list := apply_rule3(CP_list, #cut_pts);
( - )     }
( - )
( 25 )     return(CP_list);
( - )  }
```

Figure 6: Path–based estimation technique applying rule 1 to 3.

points is initialized with the empty set, profiling data are collected and written to the CDFG-representation, the CDFG is transformed into a directed acyclic graph DAG and the number of a all paths *#paths* is computed (lines 2–5). If the number of paths would exceed the computation time (table 2 says that a number of ≈ 1000 leads to acceptable computation time of a few minutes only) cut points are calculated (l. 7, l. 15ff, see below). Then the DAG is split at the according locations (l. 8) and for all dag's in $\mathcal{DAG}$ a path based scheduling is executed. First all paths are calculated and for each path a AFAP-schedule is performed (l. 9–13). Then the set of all constraints $\mathcal{CS}$ is taken in order to superimpose all constraints of all paths (l. 14).

Cut points are computed in the function *compute_cutpoints*. It starts with scanning all nodes v_i of the DAG (l. 17). If a node fulfills the conditions formulated by rule 1, the node is inserted to the list of potential cut points *CP_list* (l. 18,19). Now the cut points are sorted in such a way that those that are located at less often executed parts of the graph have the highest priority since they lead to the smallest deviation from the optimum schedule (l. 20).
Now the user can determine the quality/computation-

benchm	loC	List-Schedule [cycles]
fuzzy	100	80,353
distance	695	256,680
contour	127	360,524
median	302	26,680,323
table	664	17,623,269

Table 1: Benchmarks scheduled with a simple List-Schedule using 4 ALUs, 4 Multipliers.

-time-tradeoff by choosing the number of cut points to apply (l. 21). If the number of potential cut points found exceeds this number (l. 22) a selection is necessary: for the case there are more than one cut points in the list which would lead to the same loss of quality — assuming only rule 1 and 2 have been applied — rule 3 will decide (l. 23,24) which of them to delete from the list in order to hit exactly the user-defined #*cut_pts*.

4 Experimental Results

For the experiments 5 benchmarks have been selected: *fuzzy* is a fuzzy controller, *distance*, *contour* and *table* are parts of a complex chromakey-algorithm (digital image processing) and *median* is a median noise reducer. The variety in lines of C-code ("loC" in table 1) allows to find the *optimum solution* for the smaller benchmarks (since the computation time is small enough even if all paths are scheduled and superposed) and by means of the larger benchmarks the functionality of heuristics described in chapter 3 can be shown. As a reference, all benchmarks have first been scheduled using a simple List-Schedule[4]. Table 1 shows the result in terms of clock cycles. This is possible since a profiling has already taken place. Remember that one of the ideas is to reduce the total execution time (equation 1). Reducing the number of control steps will possibly not lead to the best result. First result is that the number of clock cycles for a specified benchmark using the path-based estimation technique (column "schedule" in table 2) in all cases is smaller than the according minimum for a List-Scheduling — independent from the number of cut points set.
This is mainly due to the principle of a path-based schedule. In terms of HW/SW-cosynthesis in COSYMA it means that the hardware/software trade-off can be computed more precisely.
The remaining question is, how close the described estimation method approaches the optimum (path-based) schedule. If the number of cut points ("cpt" in table 2) is chosen to 1 the estimation technique is identical to the path-based schedule[5]. So, the line in bold face letters for benchmark "*contour*" represents the optimum solution. The number of total paths detected (2,430) is still acceptable since the computation time

---

[4]Hardware constraints have been selected to 4 ALUs and 4 multipliers in order to achieve a fast schedule.
[5]By definition, a single cut point means that the according program graph is *not* split since in every case one cut point is set behind the last node in the graph. This comes from the algorithm of the implementation.

benchm	#pth	#cpt	schedule [cycles]	ctime [sec]
fuzzy	21	11	72,321	2
	22	8	69,567	3
	27	6	67,049	7
	41	3	64,445	12
	43	**2**	**57,562**	**12**
distance	123	41	184,255	697
	403	10	178,864	957
	448	9	178,876	1,558
	2,463	**8**	**178,876**	**3,728**
contour	25	9	261,441	4
	102	3	231,583	82
	813	2	231,654	1,257
	2,430	**1**	**231,653**	**3,426**
median	44	21	21,980,162	5
	55	16	20,321,282	6
	72	11	19,077,122	16
	74	10	18,662,402	16
	80	9	18,247,682	19
	93	8	17,832,962	20
	437	7	17,832,962	317
	819	6	17,418,242	823
	1,585	5	16,588,801	1,732
	3,119	**4**	**16,174,082**	**3,640**
table	140	45	10,108,341	363
	146	43	10,100,459	399
	183	36	10,076,203	748
	238	27	10,076,236	749
	309	**25**	**10,076,257**	**946**

Table 2: Benchmarks scheduled with path-based estimation technique using 4 ALUs, 4 multipliers.

using a SPARC20 is about 1 an hour (3,426 seconds). For most of the other benchmarks an optimum solution (*cpts* = 1) could *not* be computed (too many paths). The goal is to find a solution that results in a good schedule for a given amount of paths.
Each cut point should reduce the complexity, it should lead to a smaller computation time. Figure 7 reflects the result implied by rules 1 to 3 described above. For each of the benchmarks an increase of cut points (horizontal axis) leads to a reduction of computation time (vertical axis). A drastic reduction is gained when the first cut points are set. A saturation is reached when more cut points do not lead to a profitable reduction of computation time. Such points (marked by arcs) are assumed to lead to a good compromise between precision and computation time. Therefore figure 8 shows the quality of a schedule (deviation of a specified schedule from the according best schedule of this benchmark) as a function of the number of paths (a measure for the complexity). Assuming that e.g. a deviation of 15% for estimation during partitioning phase in HW/SW Cosynthesis is acceptable, 4 of the 5 *saturation points* are within this limit. The figure shows furthermore the non-linear dependency of precision and number of paths: the small improvement when passing the *saturation point* does not justify the large increase in computation time (number of paths).
Even quite large benchmarks could be scheduled with

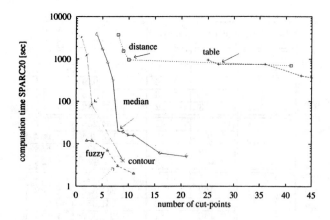
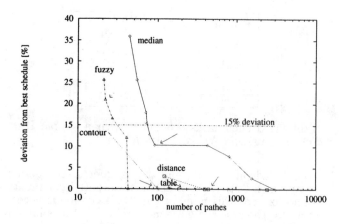

Figure 7: Computation time (using a SPARC20) versa number of cut points.

Figure 8: Tradeoff between quality (deviation from according best schedule) and complexity (number of paths).

the path–based estimation technique and lead to better results than a simple list schedule. So, real benchmarks like *distance* and *table* can make use of a path–based approach whereas the computation time of a pure path–based schedule would (in most cases and especially in HW/SW Cosynthesis) not be acceptable (> 1 day since the number of paths ≫ 10000).

5 Conclusion

The advantage of a good schedule as well as the flexibility makes path–based scheduling interesting for HW/SW–cosynthesis. The disadvantage of large computation times for real benchmarks could be overcome by the described path–based estimation technique. We demonstrated that with a few heuristic rules a sophisticated placement of cut points can reduce the complexity with only a small loss of quality. As a result the path–based estimation technique provides a reasonable tradeoff between quality and computation time.

References

[BaRoXi94] E. Barros, W. Rosenstiel, X. Xiong, *A Method for Partitioning UNITY Language in Hardware and Software*, Proc. of Euro–DAC'94, pp. 220–225, 1994.

[Cam91] R. Camposano, *Path–Based Scheduling for Synthesis*, IEEE Transactions on Computer–Aided Design, Vol. 10, No.1, pp. 85–93, Jan. 1991.

[ErHeBe93] R. Ernst, J. Henkel and Th. Benner, *Hardware/Software Co-Synthesis for Microcontrollers*, IEEE Design & Test Magazine, Vol. 10, No. 4, Dec. 1993.

[GuMi92] R.K. Gupta and G.D. Micheli, *System-level Synthesis using Re-programmable Components*, Proc. of EDAC'92, IEEE Comp. Soc. Press, pp. 2–7, 1992.

[HeErHo+94] J. Henkel, R. Ernst, U. Holtmann, Th. Benner, *Adaptation of Partitioning and High-Level Synthesis in Hardware/Software Co-Synthesis*, Proc. of ICCAD'94, pp. 96–100, 1994.

[HeHeEr94] D. Herrmann, J. Henkel, R. Ernst, *An approach to the adaptation of estimated cost parameters in the COSYMA system*, Proc. of 3rd IEEE International Workshop on Hardware/Software Codesign, pp. 100–107, 1994.

[JaElOb+94] A. Jantsch, P. Ellervee, J. Öberg et. al., *Hardware/Software Partitioning and Minimizing Memory Interface Traffic*, Proc. of Euro–DAC'94, pp. 220–225, 1994.

[KaLe94] A. Kalavade, E. Lee, *A Global Criticality/Local Phase Driven Algorithm for the Constraint Hardware/Software Partitioning Problem*, Proc. of 3rd IEEE Int. Workshop on Hardware/Software Codesign, pp. 42–48, 1994.

[Keu94] K. Keutzer, *Hardware-Software Co-Design and ESDA*, Proc. of 31st Design Automation Conference, pp. 435–436, 1994.

[ObRaJe93] K. O'Brien, M. Rahmouni, A. Jerraya, *DLS: A Scheduling Algorithm For High-Level Synthesis in VHDL*, Proc. of EDAC'93, pp. 393–397, 1993.

[OG89] R. Otten, P. van Ginneken, *The Annealing Algorithm*, Kluwer, 1989.

[PeKu93] Z. Peng, K. Kuchcinski, *An Algorithm for Partitioning of Application Specific System*, Proc. of The European Conference on Design Automation 1993, pp. 316–321, 1993.

[TsSi86] C.J. Tseng, D.P. Siewiorek, Automated Synthesis of Data Paths in Digital Systems, IEEE Trans. on CAD, Vol. 5, No. 3, pp. 379–395, 1986.

[VaGaGo94] F. Vahid, D.D. Gajski, J. Gong, *A Binary-Constraint Search Algorithm for Minimizing Hardware during Hardware/Software Partitioning*, Proc. of Euro–DAC'94, pp. 214–219, 1994.

CHAPTER FOUR

System-Level Partitioning, Synthesis, and Interfacing

The Extended Partitioning Problem: Hardware/Software Mapping, Scheduling, and
Implementation-bin Selection 293
    A. Kalavade and E. A. Lee

Hardware-Software Codesign of Embedded Systems 313
    M. Chiodo, P. Giusto, A. Jurecska, H. C. Hsieh, A. Sangiovanni-Vincentelli,
    and L. Lavagno

SOS: Synthesis of Application-Specific Heterogeneous Multiprocessor Systems 324
    S. Prakash and A. C. Parker

An Architectural Co-Synthesis Algorithm for Distributed, Embedded Computing Systems 338
    W. Wolf

Control Generation for Embedded Systems on Composition of Modal Processes 350
    P. Chou, K. Hines, K. Partridge, and G. Borriello

Interface Co-Synthesis Techniques for Embedded Systems 358
    P. Chou, R. B. Ortega, and G. Borriello

Protocol Selection and Interface Generation for HW-SW Codesign 366
    J.-M. Daveau, G. Fernandes Marchioro, T. Ben-Ismail, and A. Amine Jerraya

Clairvoyant: A Synthesis System for Production-Based Specification 375
    A. Seawright and F. Brewer

Real-Time Multi-Tasking in Software Synthesis for Information Processing Systems 389
    F. Thoen, M. Cornero, G. Goossens, and H. De Man

Co-Synthesis and Co-Simulation of Control-Dominated Embedded Systems 395
    A. Balboni, W. Fornaciari, and D. Sciuto

CoWare—A Design Environment for Heterogeneous Hardware/Software Systems 412
    D. Verkest, K. Van Rompaey, I. Bolsens, and H. De Man

INTRODUCTION

The design of hardware/software systems involves modeling, validation, and implementation. This section focuses on system implementation, which is often strongly biased by the modeling style. System implementation involves several (automated) choices, that include hardware/software partitioning and hardware and software synthesis.

A hardware/software *partitioning* problem can be stated as finding those parts of the model best implemented in hardware and those best implemented in software. Partitioning can be decided by the designer, with a successive refinement and annotation of the initial model, or determined by a CAD tool. This problem is relevant when the initial model is homogeneous, that is, a single functional modeling style is used for the system. Research in this area started in the early 1990s. The partition of a system into hardware and software is of critical importance because it has a first order impact on the cost/performance characteristics of the final design. Therefore any partitioning decision, performed either by a designer or by a CAD tool, must take into account the properties of the resulting hardware and software blocks.

The formulation of the hardware/software partitioning problem differs according to the co-design problem being confronted. In the case of embedded systems, a hardware/software partition represents a physical partition of system functionality into application-specific hardware and software executing on one (or more) processor(s). Various formulations of this partitioning problem can be compared on the basis of the architectural assumptions, partitioning goals, and solution strategy.

TECHNIQUES

The paper by Kalavade and Lee [Kal97] takes a global view of the partitioning problem. They assume that a homogeneous procedural model is compiled into task graphs and determines the implementation choice (hardware or software) for each task graph node while scheduling these nodes at the same time so that real-time constraints are met. Kalavade and Lee stress the intimate relation between partitioning and scheduling. This intimacy is caused by wide variation in timing properties of the hardware and software implementations of a task, which affects the overall latency significantly.

Chiodo *et al.* [Chi94] describe the Polis system. Designs are described as networks of co-design finite-state machines (CFSMs). A CFSM design's components are assigned to implementation in either hardware or software. Hardware units are fully synchronous; each software component is implemented as a standalone C program. This paper also provides a good overview of the Polis system as a whole; the book by Balarin *et al.* [Bal97] provides a more recent and thorough description of the system.

Synthesis of hardware units involves several subtasks. First and foremost is operation scheduling, which may or may not be combined with system-level partitioning, as mentioned earlier. Different scheduling approaches are used, often borrowed from the operating systems and real-time systems communities. Prakash and Parker [Pra92] describe a formal method of design, based on a mixed-integer linear programming model. The method provides a static schedule, as well as an assignment of tasks to processors. Although the paper targets heterogeneous multiprocessor systems, it may also be applicable to other types of designs.

Wolf [Wol97] addresses hardware/software co-synthesis in distributed systems. He describes a method to simultaneously synthesize the hardware and software architectures of a distributed system to satisfy performance requirements and minimize cost. The hardware consists of a network of processors with an arbitrary communication topology; the software consists of an allocation of processes to processors and a schedule for the processes. His approach provides a high-quality solution and is faster than ILP methods.

When considering embedded systems, their operation often can be envisioned as mode-specific. Thus hardware control synthesis requires the identification of the modal processes and the control of the transitions among them, as well as scheduling within each modal process. Chou *et al.* [Cho98] provide a framework for describing modal processes and the corresponding hardware synthesis algorithms. Among these, they provide a way of synthesizing a mode manager, which regulates the operation of the system in different modes and during modal transition.

System-level synthesis must also encompass the design of the interfaces among hardware and software modules. Automatic synthesis of interfaces allows designers to use plug-and-play methodologies and re-use existing components. The Chinook system, developed at the University of Washington, provides the user with tools for synthesis of interfaces. Chou *et al.* [Cho95] describe how interfaces can be synthesized in hardware and in software. Daveau *et al.* [Dav97a] describe instead how the inter-module communication problem can be stated as an allocation problem. They show how models expressed in terms of communicating processes through abstract channels can be executed by interconnected processors that communicate via signals and share communication control. Overall, they propose both a communication protocol selection scheme and an interface generation method.

Synthesis from protocol specification is addressed by Seawright and Brewer [Sea94]. The Clairvoyant system, a precursor of Synopsys's Protocol Compiler, allows designers to specify complex communication protocols using a production-based specification system that captures the essence of a protocol without specifying states and transitions. The Clairvoyant system automatically constructs from the production-based specification the controlling machine that implements a protocol.

Daveau [Dav97] describes a methodology and an environment for the specification and synthesis of mixed systems using the COSMOS system. COSMOS starts with an SDL specification and produces a C/VHDL distributed architecture. Specific co-design steps are partitioning, communication synthesis, and architecture generation. Partitioning generates processes that can execute in hardware or software. Communication synthesis aims at generating the protocols and the interfaces used by the subsystems. Eventually, VHDL descriptions are synthesized for all hardware components.

Software design and synthesis is extremely important in system-level design, since systems are predominantly implemented in software. Software synthesis focuses on the support of embedded systems without the use of operating systems. Compared to traditional, OS-based, design approaches, software synthesis achieves better utilization of time and resources because the system specification information is fully exploited in the automatic generation of an application-specific software solution. Thoen *et al.* [Tho95] propose an approach to software synthesis for real-time information processing systems, where multiple concurrent processes are executed on a single processor.

Overall system-level design requires both tools and methodologies. Balboni *et al.* [Bal96] describe both tools and methods for co-design with particular emphasis on concurrent simulation and synthesis of hardware and software components. The co-design methodology aims at unifying the tools for validation and synthesis, thus enabling concurrent design. This methodology is oriented toward the application domain of control-dominated embedded systems on a chip. Verkest *et al.* [Ver96] describe the design methodology with *CoWare*, a design environment for application-specific architectures targeting telecommunication applications. The design of systems based on such architectures is very challenging. Their contribution is to outline both tools and methodologies for these applications.

ADDITIONAL READINGS IN SYSTEM-LEVEL PARTITIONING, SYNTHESIS, AND INTERFACING

[Bal97] F. Balarin, M. Chiodo, P. Giusto, H. Hsieh, A. Jurecska, L. Lavagno, C. Passerone, A. Sangiovanni-Vincentelli, E. Sentovich, K. Suzuki, and B. Tabbara, *Hardware-Software Co-Design of Embedded Systems: The Polis Approach*, Kluwer Academic Press, Dordecht, 1997. *Describes the Polis system and methodology in detail.*

[Cha00] J.-M. Chang and M. Pedram, "Codex-dp, co-design of communicating systems using dynamic programming," *IEEE Transactions on CAD of Integrated Circuits and Systems* 19, no.7 (July 2000): 732–44. *Uses dynamic programming to create a coarse-grain hardware/software allocation for a system using a task graph as the system specification.*

[Omn00] T. J.-F. Omnes, T. Franzetti, and F. Catthoor, "Interactive co-design of high throughput embedded multimedia," in *Proceedings, 37th Design Automation Conference*, ACM Press, New York, 2000, 328–31. *Describes the use of a form of force-directed scheduling to improve the results of co-synthesis.*

[DiN00] M. Di Natale, A. L. Sangiovanni-Vincentelli, and F. Balarin, "Task scheduling with RT constraints," in *Proceedings, 37th Design Automation Conference*, ACM Press, New York, 2000, 483–88. *Presents scheduling methods for communicating finite-state machines with real-time deadlines.*

[Cor00] J. Cortadella, A. Kondratyev, L. Lavagno, M. Massot, S. Moral, C. Passerone, Y. Watanabe, and A. L. Sangiovanni-Vincentelli, "Task generation and compile-time scheduling for mixed data-control embedded software," in *Proceedings, 37th Design Automation Conference*, ACM Press, New York, 2000, 489–94. *Uses a Petri net model to schedule processes.*

[Shi00] Y. Shin, D. Kim, and Kiyoung Choi, "Schedulability-driven performance analysis of multiple mode embedded real-time systems," in *Proceedings, 37th Design Automation*

Conference, ACM Press, New York, 2000, 489–94. *Analyzes system behavior of systems that allow multiple operational modes.*

[Bak99] S. Bakshi and D. D. Gajski, "Partitioning and pipelining for performance-constrained hardware/software sytsems," *IEEE Transactions on VLSI Systems* 7, no. 4 (Dec. 1999): 419–32. *Presents algorithms for the synthesis of pipelined heterogeneous multiprocessors.*

[Dav99] B. P. Dave, G. Lakshminarayana, and N. K. Jha, "COSYN: Hardware-software co-synthesis of heterogeneous distributed embedded systems," *IEEE Transactions on VLSI Systems* 7, no. 1 (March 1999): 92–104. *Presents a co-synthesis system that can synthesize large task sets.*

[Rho99] David L. Rhodes and Wayne Wolf, "Co-synthesis of heterogeneous multiprocessor systems using arbitrated communication," in *Proceedings, ICCAD 99*, IEEE, New York, 1999, 339–42. *Models the effect of arbitrated communication between processes and factors these effects into co-synthesis.*

[Qu99] Gang Qu and Miodrag Potkonjak, "Power minimization using system-level partitioning of applications with quality of service requirements," in *Proceedings, ICCAD 99*, IEEE, New York, 1999, 343–46. *Partitions a system description among processors to meet quality of service requirements and minimize power consumption.*

[Leu99] R. Leupers and P. Marwedel, "Function inlining under code size constraints for embedded processors," in *Proceedings, ICCAD 99*, IEEE, New York, 1999, 253–56. *Presents a branch-and-bound algorithm for selecting functions to inline.*

[Shi99] Y. Shin and K. Choi, "Power conscious fixed priority scheduling for hard real-time systems," in *Proceedings, 36th Design Automation Conference*, ACM Press, New York, 1999, 134–39. *Exploits slack times to reduce power consumption.*

[Dav98] B. P. Dave and N. K. Jha, "COHRA: Hardware-software cosynthesis of hierarchical heterogeneous distributed embedded systems," *IEEE Transactions on CAD of Integrated Circuits and Systems* 17, no. 10 (Oct. 1998): 900–19. *Uses synthesis methods that take advantage of hierarchical specifications to handle very large system specifications.*

[Dic98] R. P. Dick and N. K. Jha, "MOGAC: A multiobjective genetic algorithm for the co-synthesis of hardware-software embedded systems," *IEEE Transactions on CAD* 17, no. 10 (Oct. 1998): 920–35. *Presents a genetic algorithm optimization approach to co-synthesis.*

[Kal98] A. Kalavade and P. A. Subrahmanyam, "Hardware/software partitioning for multifunction systems," *IEEE Transactions on CAD of Integrated Circuits and Systems* 17, no. 9 (Sept. 1998): 819–37. *Presents synthesis techniques for platforms that can run any of several different applications.*

[Gro98] J. Grode. P. V. Knudsen, and J. Madsen, "Hardware resource allocation for hardware/software partitioning in the LYCOS system," in *Proceedings DATE 98*, IEEE Computer Society Press, Los Alamitos, 1998, 22–27. *Describes allocation methods used in the LYCOS co-synthesis system.*

[Sri98] J. V. Srinivasan, S. Radhakrishnan, and R. Vemuri, "Hardware software partitioning with integrated hardware design space exploration," in *Proceedings DATE 98*, IEEE Computer Society Press, Los Alamitos, 1998, 28–34. *Presents a genetic algorithm for hardware/software partitioning.*

[Ele98] P. Eles, K. Kuchinski, Z. Peng, A. Doboli, and P. Pop, "Scheduling of conditional process graphs for the synthesis of embedded systems," in *Proceedings DATE 98*, IEEE Computer Society Press, Los Alamitos, 1998, 132–38. *Describes an algorithm for scheduling a graph that allows conditional execution of data flow graph components.*

[Kar98] I. Karkowski and H. Corporaal, "Design space exploration algorithm for heterogeneous multiprocessor embedded system design," in *Proceedings, 35th Design Automation Conference*, ACM Press, New York, 1998, 82–85. *Describes methods for extracting parallelism from an algorithm for use in evaluating potential processor architectures.*

[Tir97] Y. G. Tirat-Gefen, D. C. Silva and A. C. Parker, "Incorporating imprecise computation into system-level design of application-specific heterogeneous multiprocessors," in *Proceedings, 34th Design Automation Conference*, ACM Press, New York, 1997, 58–63. *Uses a mixed-integer linear programming formulation to design systems that trade imprecision in results for implementation cost.*

The Extended Partitioning Problem:
Hardware/Software Mapping, Scheduling, and Implementation-bin Selection

ASAWAREE KALAVADE kalavade@eecs.berkeley.edu
Dept. of EECS, University of California at Berkeley, Berkeley, CA

EDWARD A. LEE eal@eecs.berkeley.edu
Dept. of EECS, University of California at Berkeley, Berkeley, CA

Abstract. In system-level design, applications are represented as task graphs where tasks (called nodes) have moderate to large granularity and each node has several implementation options differing in area and execution time. We define the extended partitioning problem as the joint determination of the mapping (hardware or software), the implementation option (called implementation bin), as well as the schedule, for each node, so that the overall area allocated to nodes in hardware is minimum and a deadline constraint is met. This problem is considerably harder (and richer) than the traditional binary partitioning problem that determines just the best mapping and schedule. Both binary and extended partitioning problems are constrained optimization problems and are NP-hard.

We first present an efficient ($O(N^2)$) heuristic, called GCLP, to solve the binary partitioning problem. The heuristic reduces the greediness associated with traditional list-scheduling algorithms by formulating a global measure, called global criticality (GC). The GC measure also permits an adaptive selection of the optimization objective at each step of the algorithm; since the optimization problem is constrained by a deadline, either area or time is optimized at a given step based on the value of GC. The selected objective is used to determine the mapping of nodes that are "normal", i.e. nodes that do not exhibit affinity for a particular mapping. To account for nodes that are not "normal", we define "extremities" and "repellers". Extremities consume disproportionate amounts of resources in hardware and software. Repellers are inherently unsuitable to either hardware or software based on certain structural properties. The mapping of extremities and repellers is determined jointly by GC and their local preference.

We then present an efficient ($O(N^3 + N^2 B)$, for N nodes and B bins per node) heuristic for extended partitioning, called MIBS, that alternately uses GCLP and an implementation-bin selection procedure. The implementation-bin selection procedure chooses, for a node with already determined mapping, an implementation bin that maximizes the area-reduction gradient of as-yet unmapped nodes. Solutions generated by both heuristics are shown to be reasonably close to optimal. Extended partitioning generates considerably smaller overall hardware as compared to binary partitioning.

1.0 Introduction

System-level design usually involves designing an application specified at a large granularity. A typical design objective is to minimize cost (in terms of area or power) while the performance constraints are usually throughput or latency requirements. The basic component of the system-level specification is called a *task* or a *node*.

The key issues in system-level design are *partitioning, synthesis, simulation,* and *design methodology management*. The *partitioning* process determines an appropriate hardware or software mapping and an implementation for each node, given several hardware and software implementation options for every node in the task-level specification. A partitioned application has to be *synthesized* and *simulated* within a unified framework that involves the hardware and software components as well as the generated interfaces. The system-level design space is quite large and the system-level design problem cannot, in general, be posed as a single well-defined optimization problem. Typically, the designer needs to explore the possible options, tools, and architectures. A *design methodology management* framework helps to manage the design space exploration process. We have developed a software environment, called the *Design Assistant*, that addresses these issues [1]. The Design Assistant consists of: (1) specific tools for partitioning, synthesis, and simulation that are configured for a particular hardware-software codesign flow, and (2) an underlying design methodology management infrastructure for design space exploration. In this paper we will focus on the partitioning problem.

A very important aspect of system-level design is the multiplicity of design options available for every node in the task-level specification. Each node can be implemented in several ways in both hardware and software mappings. The *partitioning* problem is to select an appropriate combination of mapping and implementation for each node. For instance, a given task can be implemented in hardware using design options at several levels.

1. *Algorithm level*: Several algorithms can be used to describe the same task. For instance, a finite impulse response filter can be implemented either as an inner product or using the FFT in a shift-and-add algorithm. Figure 1-a shows the direct and transform forms for a biquad.

2. *Transformation level*: For a particular algorithm, several transformations [2] can be applied on the original description. Figure 1-b shows two such transformations.

3. *Resource level*: A task, for a specified algorithm and transformation set, can be implemented using varying numbers of resource units. Figure 1-c shows two resource-level implementation options for the direct form biquad.

A particular task can thus be implemented in several ways. To illustrate this further, Figure 2 shows the Pareto-optimal points in the area-time trade-off curves for the hardware implementation of typical nodes. The sample period is shown on the X axis, and the corresponding hardware area required to implement the node is shown on the Y axis. The left-most point on the X axis for each curve corresponds to the fastest possible implementation of the node. The right-most point on the X axis for each curve corresponds to the smallest possible area. Thus, the curve represents the design space for the task in a hardware mapping.[1] Similarly, different software synthesis strategies can be used to implement a given node in software. For instance, inline code is faster than code using subroutine calls, but has a larger code size. Thus, there is a trade-off between code size and execution time.

In summary, each node in the task-level description can be implemented in several ways in either hardware or software. It is not sufficient to just determine whether a node is to be mapped to hardware or software—the appropriate implementation needs to be determined as well. A system-level specification consists of a number of tasks and the goal is to optimize the *overall* design. Clearly, it is not enough to optimize each task independently. For example, if each task in the task-level specification were fed to a high-level hardware synthesis tool that is optimized for speed (i.e., generates the fastest implementation), then

294 CHAPTER 4: System-Level Partitioning, Synthesis, and Interfacing

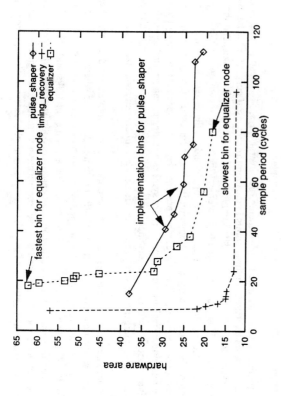

Figure 2. Typical hardware implementation curves.

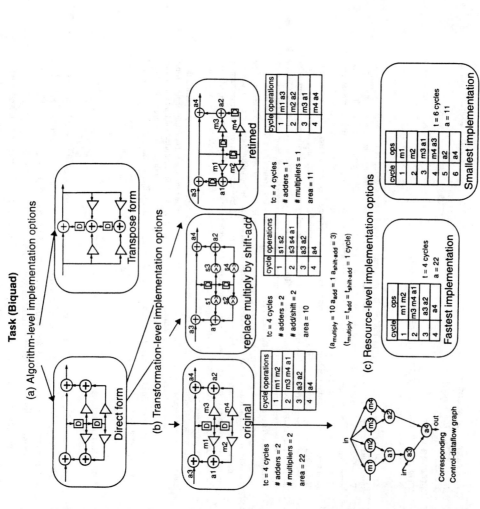

Figure 1. Hardware design options for a "node".

the overall area of the system might be too large. Thus, a mapping and implementation that optimizes the overall design should be selected for each node.

In addition to mapping and implementation selection, a third aspect of partitioning is to *schedule* the application, i.e., determine when each nodes executes. Scheduling after fixing a mapping and implementation leaves little flexibility in meeting the timing constraints; hence scheduling should be done simultaneously with mapping and implementation selection.

Thus, the goal of partitioning is to determine three parameters for each task: mapping (hardware or software), implementation (*type* of implementation to use with respect to the algorithm, transformation, and area-time value), and schedule (*when* it executes, relative to other tasks).

Partitioning is a non-trivial problem. Consider a task-level specification, typically in the order of 50 to 100 tasks. Each task can be mapped to either hardware or software. Furthermore, within a given mapping, a task can be implemented in one of several options, as shown in Figure 2. Consider, for example, a design with 100 nodes and suppose that for each node there are 5 design options in hardware and software each. Thus there are $(2*5)^{100}$ design options in the worst case! Although a designer may have a preferred implementation for some (say p) nodes, there is still a larger number of design alternatives with respect to the remaining nodes ($(2*5)^{100-p}$). Determining the *best* design option for *all* the nodes is, in fact, a constrained optimization problem. The design parameters can often be used to formulate this problem as an integer optimization problem. Exact solutions to such formulations (typically using integer linear programming (ILP)) are intractable for even moderately small problems. In this paper, we propose and evaluate heuristic solutions. The heuristics will be shown to be comparable to the ILP solution in quality, with a much reduced solution time.

We study the partitioning problem in two stages, binary partitioning and extended partitioning. *Binary partitioning* is the problem of determining, for each node, a hardware or a software mapping and a schedule. *Extended partitioning* is the problem of selecting an appropriate implementation, over and above binary partitioning. Currently published approaches on hardware/software partitioning focus only on the binary partitioning problem; one of the contributions of this work is the formulation of the extended partitioning problem. Before we formally define these two problems, we digress briefly to outline the key assumptions in our work.

Assumptions

System-level design is a very broad problem. We restrict our attention to the design of embedded systems with real-time signal processing components. Examples of such systems include modems for both tethered and wireless communication, cordless phones, disk drive controllers, printers, digital audio systems, data compression systems, etc. The partitioning techniques discussed in this paper are based on the following assumptions:

1. The precedences between the tasks are specified as a direct acyclic graph (DAG $G = (N, A)$).[2] Assuming a non-pipelined implementation, the throughput constraint on the graph translates to a deadline D ($D = 1/throughput$), i.e., the execution time of the DAG should not exceed D clock cycles.

2. The target architecture consists of a single programmable processor (which executes the software component) and a custom datapath (the hardware component). The software and hardware components have capacity constraints—the software (program and data) size should not exceed AS (memory capacity) and the hardware size should not exceed AH. The communication costs of the hardware-software interface are represented by three parameters: ah_{comm}, as_{comm}, and t_{comm}. Here, ah_{comm} (as_{comm}) is the hardware (software) area required to communicate one sample of data across the hardware-software interface and t_{comm} is the number of cycles required to transfer the data. The parameter ah_{comm} represents the area of the interface glue logic and as_{comm} represents the size of the code that sends or receives the data. In our implementation we assume a self-timed blocking memory-mapped interface. We neglect the communication costs of software-to-software and hardware-to-hardware interfaces.

3. The area and time estimates for the hardware and software implementation bins of every node are assumed to be known; the specific techniques used to estimate these values are described in Section 4.0 and Section 8.0. Associated with every node i, is a hardware implementation curve CH_i, and a software implementation curve CS_i. The implementation curve plots all the possible design alternatives (referred to as *implementation bins*) for the node. $CH_i = \{(ah_i^j, th_i^j), j \in NH_i\}$, where ah_i^j and th_i^j represent the area and execution time when node i is implemented in hardware bin j, and NH_i is the set of all the hardware implementation bins. $CS_i = \{(as_i^j, ts_i^j), j \in NS_i\}$, where as_i^j and ts_i^j represent the program size and execution time when node i is implemented in software bin j, and NS_i is the set of all the software implementation bins. Within a mapping, the fastest implementation bin is called L bin, and the slowest implementation bin is called H bin. In the case of binary partitioning, where a single implementation bin is assumed, th_i, ah_i, ts_i, and as_i represent the best-case execution time and the corresponding area in hardware and software respectively.

4. We assume that there is no reuse between nodes mapped to hardware.

Problem Definition

The binary partitioning problem ($P1$): Given a DAG, area and time constraints for software and hardware mappings of all nodes, and communication costs, subject to resource capacity constraints and a deadline D, determine for each node i, the hardware or software mapping (M_i) and the start time for the execution of the node (schedule t_i), such that the total area occupied by the nodes mapped to hardware is minimum. $P1$ is NP-hard and can be formulated exactly as an ILP [1].

The extended partitioning problem ($P2$): Given a DAG, hardware and software implementation curves for all the nodes, communication costs, resource capacity constraints, and a required deadline D, find a hardware or software mapping (M_i), the implementation bin (B_i^*), and the schedule (t_i) for each node i, such that the total area occupied by the nodes mapped to hardware is minimum. It is obvious that $P2$ is a much harder problem than $P1$. It has $(2B)^{|N|}$ alternatives, given B implementation bins per mapping. $P2$ can be formulated exactly as an integer linear program, similar to $P1$. An ILP formulation for $P2$ is given in [1].

The motivation for solving the extended partitioning problem is that the flexibility of selecting an appropriate implementation bin for a node, instead of assuming a fixed implementation, is likely to reduce the overall hardware area. In this paper, we investigate, with examples, the pay-off in using extended partitioning over just mapping (binary partitioning).

The rest of the paper is organized as follows. In Section 2.0, we discuss some of the related work in the area of hardware/software partitioning. In Section 3.0, we present the GCLP algorithm to solve the binary partitioning problem. Its performance is analyzed in Section 4.0. In Section 5.0, we present the MIBS heuristic to solve the extended partitioning problem. The MIBS algorithm essentially solves two problems for each node in the precedence graph: hardware/software mapping and scheduling, followed by implementation-bin selection for this mapping. The first problem, that of mapping and scheduling, is solved by the GCLP algorithm. For a given mapping, an appropriate implementation bin is selected using a bin selection procedure. The bin selection procedure is described in Section 6.0. The details of the MIBS algorithm are described in Section 7.0, and its performance is analyzed in Section 8.0.

2.0 Related Work

Binary Partitioning

The binary partitioning problem has been studied quite extensively in the past couple of years. We discuss a sampling of the work in this area. Gupta *et al.* [6] discuss a scheme where all data-independent nodes are initially mapped to hardware. Nodes are at an instruction level of granularity. Nodes are progressively moved from hardware to software if the resultant solution is feasible and the cost of the new partition is smaller than the earlier cost. The scheme proposed by Henkel *et al.* [7] also assumes an instruction level of granularity. All the nodes are mapped to software at the start and then moved to hardware (using simulated annealing) until timing constraints are met. Baros *et al.* [8] present a two-stage clustering approach to the mapping problem. Clusters are characterized by attribute values and are assigned hardware and software mappings based on their attribute values. D'Ambrosio *et al.* [9] describe an approach for partitioning applications where each node has a deadline constraint. The input specification is transformed into a set of constraints that is solved by an optimizing tool called GOPS, which uses a branch and bound approach, to determine the mapping. Thomas *et al.* [10] propose a manual partitioning approach for task-level specifications. They discuss the properties of tasks that render them suitable to either hardware or software mapping. In their approach, the designer has to qualitatively evaluate these properties and make a mapping decision.

Next, we briefly discuss some work in related areas such as software partitioning, hardware partitioning, and high-level synthesis to evaluate the possibility of extending it to the binary partitioning problem. The heterogeneous multiprocessor scheduling problem is to partition an application into multiple heterogeneous processors. Approaches used in the literature [11, 12] to solve this problem ignore the area dimension while selecting the mapping; they cannot be directly applied to the hardware/software mapping and scheduling problem. Considerable attention has been directed towards the hardware partitioning problem in the high-level hardware synthesis community. The goal in most cases is to meet the chip capacity constraints; timing constraints are not considered. Most of the proposed schemes (for example [13, 14]) use a clustering-based approach first presented by Camposano *et al.* [15]. The approaches used to solve the throughput-constrained scheduling problem in high-level hardware synthesis, (such as force directed scheduling by Paulin *et al.* [16]), do not directly extend to the hardware/software mapping and scheduling problem.

Extended Partitioning

The authors are not aware of any published work that *formulates or solves* the extended hardware/software partitioning problem in system-level design. The problem of selecting an appropriate bin from the area-time trade-off curve is reminiscent of the technology mapping problem in physical CAD [17], and the module selection (also called resource-type selection) problem in high-level synthesis [18], both of which are known to be NP-hard problems.

The technology mapping problem is to bind nodes in a Boolean network, representing a combinational logic circuit, to *gates* in the library such that the area of the circuit is minimized while meeting timing constraints. Gates with different area and delay values are available at the library. Several approaches ([19], among others) have been presented to solve this problem. The module selection problem is the search for the best resource type for each *operation*. For instance, a multiply operation can be realized by different implementations, e.g., fully parallel, serially parallel, or fully serial. These resource types differ in area and execution times. A number of heuristics ([20], among others) have been proposed to solve this problem.

3.0 The Binary Partitioning Problem: GCLP Algorithm

In this section, we present the Global Criticality/Local Phase (GCLP) algorithm to solve the binary partitioning problem ($P1$).

3.1. Algorithm Foundation

The underlying scheduling framework in the GCLP algorithm is based on *list scheduling* [21]. The general approach in list scheduling is to serially traverse a node list (usually from the source node to the sink node in the DAG[3]) and for each node to select a mapping that minimizes an objective function. In the context of $P1$, two possible objective functions could be used: (1) minimize the *finish time* of the node (i.e., sum of the start time and the execution time), or (2) minimize the *area* of the node (i.e., the hardware area or software size). Neither of these objectives by itself is geared toward solving $P1$, since $P1$ aims to minimize area and meet timing constraints at the same time. For example, an objective function that minimizes finish time drives the solution towards feasibility from the viewpoint of deadline constraints. This solution is likely to be suboptimal (increased area). On the other hand, if a node is always mapped such that area is minimized, the final solution is quite likely infeasible. Thus a fixed objective function is incapable of solving $P1$, a constrained optimization problem. There is also a limitation with list scheduling; mapping based on serial traversal tends to be greedy, and therefore globally suboptimal.

The GCLP algorithm tries to overcome these drawbacks. It *adaptively* selects an appropriate *mapping objective* at each step to determine the mapping and the schedule. (A step corresponds to the mapping of a particular node in the DAG.) As shown in Figure 3, the mapping objective for a particular node is selected in accordance with:

1. *Global Criticality* (GC): GC is a global look-ahead measure that estimates the time criticality at each step of the algorithm, by looking at *all* the as-yet unmapped nodes at each step. (Details on computing GC will be given in Section 3.2). GC is compared to a threshold to determine if time is critical. If time is critical, an objective function that minimizes finish time is selected, otherwise one that minimizes area is selected. GC may change at every step of the algorithm. The adaptive selection of the mapping objective overcomes the problem associated with a hardwired objective function. The "global" time criticality measure also helps overcome the "horizon-effect" that is typically a limitation of serial traversal. Since GC selects the optimization objective based on the expected mappings of unmapped (or future) nodes, it is called a look-ahead measure.

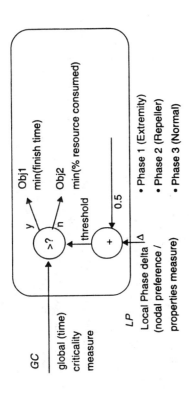

Figure 3. Selection of the mapping objective at each step of GCLP.

2. *Local Phase (LP)*: LP is a classification of nodes based on their heterogeneity and intrinsic properties. Each node is classified as an extremity (local phase 1), repeller (local phase 2), or normal (local phase 3) node. A measure called *local phase delta* quantifies the local mapping preferences of the node under consideration and accordingly modifies the threshold used in GC comparison. (Details on the local phase delta will be given in Section 3.3.)

The flow of the GCLP algorithm is shown in Figure 4. N represents the set of nodes in the graph. $N_U(N_M)$ is the set of unmapped (mapped) nodes at the current step. N_U is initialized to N. The algorithm maps one node per step. At the beginning of each step, the global time criticality measure GC is computed. GC is a global measure of time criticality at each step of the algorithm, based on the currently mapped and unmapped nodes and the deadline requirements. The details of this computation will be given in Section 3.2. Unmapped nodes whose predecessors have already been mapped and scheduled are called *ready* nodes. A node is selected for mapping from the set of ready nodes using an urgency criterion, i.e., a ready node that lies on the critical path is selected for mapping. Details of this selection are given in Section 3.4. The local phase of the selected node is identified and the corresponding local phase delta is computed. The details of this computation will be given in Section 3.3. GC and the local phase delta are then used to select the mapping objective. Using this objective, the selected node is assigned a mapping (M_i). The mapping is also used to determine the start time for the node (t_i). The process is repeated $|N|$ times until no nodes are left unmapped. Next, we describe the computation of GC.

3.2. *Global Criticality (GC)*

GC is a global look-ahead measure that estimates time criticality at each step of the algorithm. Figure 5 illustrates the computation of GC with the help of an example. At a given

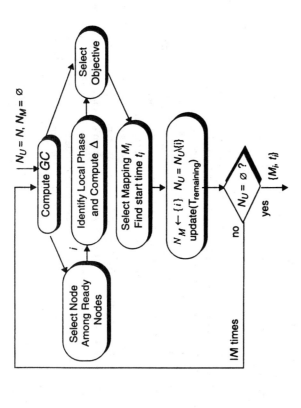

Figure 4. The GCLP Algorithm.

step, the hardware/software mapping and schedule for the already mapped nodes is known (Figure 5-a). Using this schedule and the required deadline D, the remaining time T_{rem} is first determined. Next, all the unmapped nodes (nodes 4 and 5 in this example) are mapped to software and the corresponding finish time T^S is computed, as shown in Figure 5-b. Suppose that T^S exceeds the allowed deadline D. Some of the unmapped nodes have to be moved from software to hardware to meet the deadline[5]. Define this to be the set $N_{S \to H}$. Suppose that in the example, $N_{S \to H} = \{5\}$. The new finish time (T^H) is then recomputed as shown in Figure 5-c and suppose that it meets the timing constraint. GC at this step of the algorithm is defined as the fraction of unmapped nodes that have to be moved from software to hardware, so as to meet feasibility. A high value of GC indicates that many as-yet unmapped nodes need to be mapped to hardware so as to get a feasible solution, or in other words time, as a resource, is more critical. GC is thus a measure of global time criticality at each step. The following procedure summarizes the computation of GC.

Procedure: **Compute_GC**
Input: Mapped (N_M) and Unmapped (N_U) nodes, D, ts_i, th_i, $size_i$, $\forall i \in N$
Output: GC

298 CHAPTER 4: System-Level Partitioning, Synthesis, and Interfacing

(ts_i/th_i) ordering gives the best results. S1.2 determines whether moving this set $N_{S \rightarrow H}$ to hardware meets feasibility by computing the actual finish time T^H. The finish time can be computed by an $O(|A|+|N|)$ algorithm. If the result is infeasible, additional nodes are moved by repeating steps S1.1 to S1.3. GC is computed in S2 as a ratio of the sum of the sizes of the nodes in $N_{S \rightarrow H}$ to the sum of the sizes of the nodes in N_U. The size of a node is taken to be the number of elementary operations (add, multiply, etc.) in the node.

As indicated earlier, GC is a measure of global time criticality; a high GC indicates a high global time criticality. GC has yet another interpretation; it is the likelihood that any unmapped node is mapped to hardware. This likelihood may change at each step of the algorithm.

3.3. Local Phase (LP)

GC is an averaged measure over all the unmapped nodes at each step. This desensitizes GC to the local properties of the node being mapped. To emphasize their local characteristics, we classify nodes as *extremities* (local phase 1 nodes), *repellers* (local phase 2 nodes), or *normal nodes* (local phase 3 nodes).

3.3.1. Motivation for Local Phase Classification

Since nodes are at a *task* level of granularity, they are likely to exhibit area and time heterogeneity in hardware and software mappings. Nodes that consume a disproportionately large amount of resource on one mapping as compared to the other mapping are called *extremities* or local phase 1 nodes. For instance, a hardware extremity requires a large area when mapped to hardware, but could be implemented inexpensively in software. The mapping preference of such nodes, quantified by an *extremity measure*, modifies the threshold used in GC comparison.

Once a feasible solution is obtained, it is usually possible to further swap nodes between hardware and software so as to reduce the allocated hardware area. GCLP uses the concept of *repellers* or local phase 2 nodes to swap similar nodes between hardware and software. To do this, we identify certain intrinsic nodal properties (called repeller properties) that reflect the inherent suitability of a node to either a hardware or a software mapping. For instance, bit operations are handled better in hardware, while memory operations are better suited to software. As a result, a node with many bit manipulations, relative to other nodes, is a software repeller, while a node with a lot of memory operations, relative to other nodes, is a hardware repeller. Moving a node with many bit manipulation operations out of software is thought of as generating a *repelling force* from the software mapping. Hence the proportion of bit manipulation operations in a node is a software repeller property. Similarly, the proportion of memory operations in a node is a hardware repeller property. A repeller property is quantified by a *repeller value*. The combined effect of all the repeller properties in a node is expressed as the *repeller measure* of the node. All nodes are ranked according to their repeller measures. Given two nodes N1 and N2 with similar software characteristics, if N1 has a higher software repeller measure than N2, and given the choice

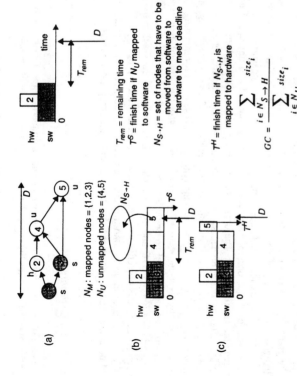

Figure 5. Computation of Global Criticality.

S1. Find the set $N_{S \rightarrow H}$ of unmapped nodes to be moved from software to hardware to meet deadline D

  S1.1. Select a set of nodes in N_U, using a priority function Pf, to move from software to hardware

  S1.2. Compute the actual finish time (T^H) based on these $N_{S \rightarrow H}$ nodes being mapped to hardware

  S1.3. If $T^H > D$ go to S1.1

S2. $GC = \dfrac{\sum_{i \in N_{S \rightarrow H}} size_i}{\sum_{i \in N_U} size_i}, \ 0 \leq GC \leq 1$

In S1.1, the set of nodes to be moved to hardware is selected on the basis of a priority function Pf. One obvious Pf is to rank the nodes in the order of decreasing execution times ts_i. A second possibility is to use (ts_i/th_i) as the function to rank the nodes. This has the effect of first moving nodes with the greatest relative gain in time when moved to hardware. A third possibility is to rank the nodes in increasing order of ah_i; nodes with smaller hardware area are moved out of software first. Our experiments indicate that the

of mapping one of them to hardware, N1 is preferred. The details of the computation of the repeller measure are deferred to Section 3.3.3. One way of partitioning nodes to hardware and software is to map them based on their area and time values only. The mapped nodes can then be swapped between each other, based on their repeller values, so as to improve the overall solution. However, this step adds overhead to the partitioning process. In our approach, we incorporate the effect of swapping after mapping into the mapping process itself. This is done by tweaking the mapping decision of each node relative to its repeller value. The result is a single-step partitioning algorithm.

Normal nodes (local phase 3) do not modify the default threshold value; their mapping is determined by GC consideration only. In the following sections, we outline procedures to classify nodes into local phases and quantify their local phase measures.

3.3.2. Local Phase 1 or Extremity Nodes

The bottleneck resource in hardware is area, while the bottleneck resource in software is time. Extremities are nodes that consume a disproportionately large amount of the bottleneck resource on a particular mapping (relative to the other mapping). A *hardware extremity* node is defined as a node that consumes a large area in hardware, but a relatively small amount of time in software. A *software extremity* node is defined as a node that takes up a large amount of time in software, but a relatively small amount of area when mapped to hardware. The rationale in moving a hardware (software) extremity node to software (hardware) is obvious.

The disparity in the resources consumed by an extremity node i is quantified by an *extremity measure* E_i. The extremity measure is used to modify the threshold to which GC is compared when selecting the mapping objective (as shown in Figure 3); i.e., E_i is the local phase delta for an extremity node.

Extremity Measure

We now describe a procedure to identify extremity nodes in a graph and compute the extremity measure E_i for all such nodes.

Procedure: **Compute Extremity Measure**
Input: $ts_i, ah_i, \forall i \in N, \alpha, \beta$ percentiles
Output: $E_i, \forall i \in N, -0.5 \leq E_i \leq 0.5$

S1. Compute the histograms of all the nodes with respect to their software execution times (ts_i) and hardware areas (ah_i)

S2. Determine $ts(\alpha)$ and $ah(\beta)$ corresponding to α and β percentiles of ts and ah histograms respectively

S3. Classify nodes into software and hardware extremity sets EX_s and EX_h respectively:
   If $(ts_i \geq ts(\alpha))$ and $ah_i < ah(\beta)$), $i \in EX_s$ (software extremity)
   If $(ah_i \geq ah(\beta))$ and $ts_i < ts(\alpha)$), $i \in EX_h$ (hardware extremity)

S4. Determine the extremity value x_i for node i:
   If $i \in EX_s$, $x_i = \dfrac{ts_i/ts_{max}}{ah_i/ah_{max}}$, else $x_i = \dfrac{ah_i/ah_{max}}{ts_i/ts_{max}}$
   where $ts_{max} = max_i\{ts_i\}$ and $ah_{max} = max_i\{ah_i\}$

S5. Order the nodes in EX_s (EH_h) by x. Denote the maximum and minimum extremity values as xs_{max} (xh_{max}) and xs_{min} (xh_{min}) respectively.

S6. Compute the extremity measure E_i for node i:
   If $i \in EX_s$, $E_i = -0.5 \times \dfrac{x_i - xs_{min}}{xs_{max} - xs_{min}}, -0.5 \leq E_i \leq 0$
   else if $i \in EX_h$, $E_i = 0.5 \times \dfrac{x_i - xh_{min}}{xh_{max} - xh_{min}}, 0 \leq E_i \leq 0.5$

In S1, we compute a distribution of the nodes with respect to their software execution times ts, and hardware areas ah_i. Parameters α and β represent percentile cut-offs for these distributions. For instance, in S3, a node i is classified as a software extremity node if it lies above α percentile in the ts histogram ($ts_i > ts(\alpha)$) and below β percentile in the ah histogram ($ah_i < ah(\beta)$). Similarly, a node i is classified as a hardware extremity if it lies above β percentile in the ah histogram ($ah_i > ah(\beta)$) and below α percentile in the ts histogram ($ts_i < ts(\alpha)$). Figure 6 shows typical histograms and the identification of extremities. For the examples that we have considered, values of α and β in the range (0.5, 0.75) are used. A value outside this range tends to reduce the number of nodes that fit this behavior and consequently the extremities do not play a significant role in biasing the local preferences of nodes. The extremity value of a node is computed in S4. The extremity measure E_i of a node i is computed in S6, $-0.5 \leq E_i \leq 0.5$.

Threshold Modification Using the Extremity Measure

Let GC_k denote the value of GC at step k when an extremity node i is to be mapped. If E_i is ignored, the threshold assumes its set value of 0.5. Since GC_k is averaged over all unmapped nodes, mapping of node i in this case is based just on GC_k. This leads to:

1. *Poor mapping:* Suppose node i is a hardware extremity. If $GC_k \geq 0.5$, Obj1 is selected in Figure 3 (minimize time), and i could get mapped to hardware based on time-criticality. However, i is a hardware extremity and mapping it to hardware is an obviously poor choice for P1.

CHAPTER 4: System-Level Partitioning, Synthesis, and Interfacing

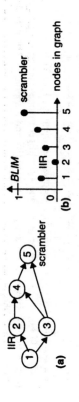

Figure 6. Hardware (EX_h) and software (EX_s) extremity sets.

2. *Infeasible mapping*: Suppose node i is a software extremity. If $GC_k < 0.5$, Obj2 is selected in Figure 3 (minimize area) and i could get mapped to software. Node i is a software extremity, however, and mapping it to software could exceed the deadline.

To overcome these problems, the extremity measure E_i is used to modify the default threshold in the direction of the preferred mapping. The new threshold is $0.5 + E_i$. GC_k is compared to this modified threshold. For software extremities, $-0.5 \leq E_i \leq 0$, so that $0 \leq \text{Threshold} \leq 0.5$, and for hardware extremities, $0 \leq E_i \leq 0.5$, so that $0.5 \leq \text{Threshold} \leq 1$.

3.3.3. Local Phase 2 or Repeller Nodes

The use of repellers to reduce the overall hardware area was discussed in Section 3.3.1. In this section, we quantify a repeller node with a repeller measure and describe its use in GCLP.

Several repeller properties can be identified for each node. Bit-level instruction mix and precision level are examples of software repeller properties; while memory-intensive instruction mix and table-lookup instruction mix are possible hardware repeller properties. Each property is quantified by a property value. The cumulative effect of all the properties of a node is expressed by a repeller measure.

Let us consider the **bit-level instruction mix**, a software repeller property, in some detail. This property is quantified through its property value called $BLIM$. $BLIM_i$ is defined as the ratio of bit-level instructions to the total instructions in a node i ($0 \leq BLIM_i \leq 1$). For instance, consider the DAG shown in Figure 7-a. Suppose that node 2 in the graph is an IIR filter and node 5 is a scrambler. Figure 7-b shows the hypothetical $BLIM$ values plotted

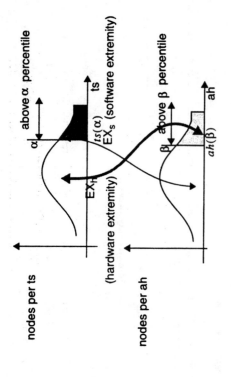

Figure 7. An example repeller property.

for all the nodes in the DAG in Figure 7-a. Node 5, the scrambler, has a high $BLIM$ value. Node 2, the IIR filter, does not have any bit manipulations, and hence its $BLIM$ value is 0. The higher the $BLIM$ value, the worse is the suitability of a node to software mapping.

Consider two nodes N_1 and N_2, with software (hardware) areas as_1 (ah_1) and as_2 (ah_2) respectively. Suppose $BLIM_1 > BLIM_2$. Now, if $as_1 \approx as_2$, then $ah_1 < ah_2$ (because bit-level operations can be typically done in a smaller area in hardware). Thus N_1 is a software repeller relative to N_2, based on the bit-level instruction mix property. Given the choice of mapping one of N_1 or N_2 to hardware, N_1 is preferred for hardware mapping on the basis of the $BLIM$ property.

Other repeller properties mentioned at the beginning of Section 3.3.3 are similarly quantified through their property values. The cumulative effect of all the repeller properties in a node is considered when mapping a node. The *repeller measure* R_i of a node captures this aggregate effect. It is expressed as a convex combination of all the repeller property values of the node. The repeller measure is used to modify the threshold against which GC is compared when selecting the mapping objective (as shown in Figure 3); i.e., R_i is the local phase delta for repeller nodes.

Repeller Measure

The procedure outlined below describes the computation of the repeller measure (R_i) for each node i. Let RH be the set of hardware repeller properties, and RS be the set of software repeller properties. Let $P = RH \cup RS$ be the complete set of repeller properties.

Procedure:	**Compute Repeller Measure**
Input:	$v_{i,p}$ = value of repeller property p for node i, $i \in N$, $p \in P$
Output:	Repeller measure R_i, $\forall i \in N$, $-0.5 \leq R_i \leq 0.5$

S1. Computer for each property p:

$$\sigma^2(v_{i,p}) = \text{variance of } v_{i,p} \text{ over all } i$$
$$min(v_{i,p}) = \text{minimum of } v_{i,p} \text{ over all } i$$
$$max(v_{i,p}) = \text{maximum of } v_{i,p} \text{ over all } i$$

Let $RX = RH$ if $p \in RH$ or $RX = RS$ if $p \in RS$

$$a_p = \frac{\sigma^2(v_{i,p})}{\sum_{p \in RX} \sigma^2(v_{i,p})} = \text{weight of repeller property } p, \sum_{p \in RX} a_p = 1,$$

$$0 \leq nv_{i,p} \leq 1.$$

S2. Compute the normalized property value $nv_{i,p}$ for each property p, of node i

$$nv_{i,p} = \frac{v_{i,p} - min(v_{i,p})}{max(v_{i,p}) - min(v_{i,p})}, \quad 0 \leq nv_{i,p} \leq 1.$$

S3. Compute the repeller measure R_i for each node i

$$R_i = \frac{1}{2} \cdot \left(\sum_{p \in RH} a_p \cdot nv_{i,p} - \sum_{p \in RS} a_p \cdot nv_{i,p} \right), \quad -0.5 \leq R_i \leq 0.5.$$

The value $v_{i,p}$ of each repeller property p for node i is obtained by analyzing the node. For instance, consider the bit-level instruction mix property. The bit-level operations (such as OR, AND, EXOR) are first identified in the node. The *BLIM* value of a node i is simply the ratio of the number of bit-level operations to the total number of operations in that node. Repeller property values for other repeller properties mentioned at the beginning of Section 3.3.3 have also been similarly quantified.

In S1 of the above procedure, the variance, minimum, and maximum of each repeller property value are computed. The property values are normalized in S2. In S3, the repeller measure for each node is computed as a convex combination of the normalized repeller property values. The weight a_p of a property p is proportional to the variance of its value. This deemphasizes properties with small varainces in their values. When the repeller measure is used to swap repeller nodes with comparable property values, there is hardly any area reduction; they are not worth swapping. The variance weight ensures this.

Threshold Modification Using the Repeller Measure

As described in Section 3.3.1, one way to partition nodes between hardware and software is to first use area and time values only to make the mapping decision. The overall solution can then be improved by swapping nodes between hardware and software. Since the repeller measure quantifies the inherent unsuitability for a particular mapping, it can be used for swapping. However, this method adds an additional step in the partitioning process. Instead, in our approach, we incorporate the effect of swapping after mapping into the mapping process itself. This is done by tweaking the mapping decision of each node relative to its repeller value. In particular, the repeller measure R_i is used to modify the threshold so that the new threshold is $0.5 + R_i$. For software repellers, $-0.5 \leq R_i \leq 0$, so that $0 \leq$ Threshold ≤ 0.5, and for hardware repellers, $0 \leq R_i \leq 0.5$ so that $0.5 \leq$ Threshold ≤ 1. The modified threshold is used to select the optimization objective and hence the mapping.

3.3.4. Local Phase 3 or Normal Nodes

A node that is neither an extremity nor a repeller is defined to be a **local phase 3** node or a **normal** node. The threshold is set to its default value (0.5) when a normal node is mapped. Thus the mapping objective is governed by GC alone.

In summary, nodes are classified into three disjoint sets: extremity nodes, repeller nodes, and normal nodes. The local preference of each node is quantified by its measure, represented by a *local phase delta* (Δ). In particular, $\Delta = E_i$ for extremity nodes, $\Delta = R_i$ for repeller nodes, and $\Delta = 0$ for normal nodes. This local phase delta is used to compute the modified threshold; threshold $= 0.5 + \Delta$.

3.4. GCLP Algorithm

Algorithm: **GCLP**
Input: $ah_i, as_i, th_i, ts_i, E_i$ (extremity measure), and R_i (repeller measure)
$\forall i \in N$
Communication costs: $ah_{comm}, as_{comm},$ and t_{comm}
constraints: $AH, AS,$ and D.
Mapping $M_i (M_i \in \{\text{hardware, software}\})$, start time $t_i, \forall i \in N$
Output: $N_U = \{\text{unmapped nodes}\} = N$, $N_M = \{\text{mapped nodes}\} = \phi$.
Initialize:
Procedure: while $\{|N_U| > 0\}\{$

S1. Compute GC

S2. Determine N_R, the set of *ready* nodes

S3. Compute the effective execution time $t_{exec}(i)$ for each node i

If $i \in N_U$ $t_{exec}(i) = GC \cdot th_i + (1 - GC) \cdot ts_i$
else if $i \in N_M$ $t_{exec}(i) = th_i \cdot I(M_i == \text{hw}) + ts_i \cdot I(M_i == \text{sw})$[6]

S4. Compute the longest path $longestPath(i), \forall i \in N_R$ using $t_{exec}(i)$

S5. Select node i, $i \in N_R$, for mapping: $\max(longestPath(i))$

S6. Determine mapping M_i for i:

S6.1. if ($E_i \neq 0$) $\Delta = \gamma \cdot E_i$ (local phase 1)
                     where γ is extremity measure weight, $0 \leq \gamma \leq 1$
     else if ($R_i \neq 0$) $\Delta = \nu \cdot R_i$ (local phase 2)
                     where ν is repeller measure weight, $0 \leq \nu \leq 1$
     else $\Delta = 0$; (local phase 3)

Obj1 selects a mapping that minimizes the finish time of the node. A node can begin execution only after all of its predecessors have finished execution and the data has been transferred to it from its predecessors. Also, a node cannot begin execution on the software resource until the last node mapped to software has finished execution.

Obj2 uses a "percentage resource consumption" measure. This measure is the fraction of the resource area of a node (nodal area plus communication area) to the total resource area. The area ah_{comm}^{tot} (as_{comm}^{tot}) takes into account the total cost of communication (glue logic in hardware and code in software) between node i in hardware (software) and all its predecessors. For the hardware resource, the resource area required by the node is divided by the available hardware area ($AH_{remaining}$). Obj2 thus favors software allocation as the algorithm proceeds.

GCLP has a quadratic complexity in the number of nodes [1]. The performance of the algorithm is analyzed in the next section.

4.0 Performance of the GCLP Algorithm

We first describe the two classes of examples used to analyze the performance of the algorithm: practical examples, and random graphs. Next, we present two sets of experiments. The first experiment (Section 4.1) is a comparison of the solution obtained with GCLP to the optimal solution generated by an ILP formulation. The second experiment (Section 4.2) demonstrates the effectiveness of classifying nodes into extremities and repellers. Section 4.3 discusses the algorithm behavior with the help of an example trace.

Practical Examples

We consider practical signal processing applications with periodic timing constraints. Two examples are used: 32KHz 2-PSK modem, and 8 KHz bidirectional telephone channel simulator (TCS). These applications are specified in Ptolemy [22]. Figure 8 shows the receiver section of the modem example. A DAG is generated from the SDF graph representation. Nodes in the DAG are at a task level of granularity. Typical nodes in the modem include carrier recovery, timing recovery, equalizer, descrambler, etc. in the receiver section, and pulse shaper, scrambler etc. in the transmitter section. The nodes in the TCS include linear distortion filter, Gaussian noise generator, harmonic generator, etc. In the modem and TCS examples considered, the DAGs consist of 27 and 15 nodes respectively[8].

The area and time estimates (in hardware and software mappings) for each node in these DAGs are obtained by using the Ptolemy and Hyper environments. We assume a target architecture consisting of: (1) Motorola DSP 56000 custom hardware for the software component, (2) standard-cell based custom hardware generated by Hyper, and (3) self-timed memory mapped I/O for hardware-software communication. The code generation feature of Ptolemy is used to synthesize 56000 assembly code and Silage code for each node in the DAG. Estimates of the software area (as_i) and software execution time (ts_i) for each node i are obtained by using simple scripts that analyze the generated DSP 56000 assembly code. The Silage code for each node i is input to Hyper, which generates estimates of the hardware

---

S6.2. Threshold = $0.5 + \Delta$, $0 \leq$ Threshold ≤ 1

S6.3. If ($GC \geq$ Threshold) m: minimize($Obj1$);
 else m: minimize($Obj2$);

S6.4. $M_i = m$; Set(t_i); $N_U = N_U \setminus \{i\}$; $N_M \leftarrow \{i\}$;[7]
 Update($T_{remaining}$, $AH_{remaining}$, $AS_{remaining}$);
}

The algorithm maps one node per step. In S1, GC is computed using the procedure described in Section 3.2. In S2, we determine the set of ready nodes, i.e., the set of unmapped nodes whose predecessors have been mapped. One of these ready nodes is selected for mapping in S5. In particular, we select the node on the maximum longest path, the critical path of the graph. The critical path generally involves unmapped nodes; computing it can present problems since the execution times of such nodes is not known at the current step. To overcome this difficulty, we define the effective execution time ($t_{exec}(i)$) of an unmapped node i as the mean execution time of the node, assuming it is mapped to hardware with probability GC and to software with probability $(1 - GC)$. Here we use the notion of GC as a node-invariant hardware mapping likelihood (see Section 3.2). In S6, the mapping and schedule are determined for the selected node. If the node is an extremity (or a repeller) its extremity (or repeller) measure is used to modify the threshold. The contribution of the extremity and repeller measures can be varied by weighting factors γ and ν. In Section 8.3, we discuss the tuning of these weights. The mapping objective is scheduled in S6.3 by comparing GC against the threshold. If time is critical, an objective that minimizes the finish time is selected, otherwise one that minimizes resource consumption is selected. The objective functions are:

Obj1: $t_{fin}(i, m)$, where $m \in \{$software, hardware$\}$

$$t_{fin}(i, m) = max(max_{P(i)}(t_{fin}(p) + t_c(p, i)), tf_{last}(m)) + t(i, m)$$

where

$P(i)$ = set of predecessors of node i, $p \in P(i)$
$t_{fin}(p)$ = finish time of predecessor p
$t_c(p, i)$ = communication time between predecessor p and node i
$tf_{last}(m)$ = finish time of the last node assigned to mapping m
 = 0 if m corresponds to hardware
$t(i, m)$ = execution time of node i on mapping m

Obj2: $\dfrac{(as_i + as_{comm}^{tot})}{AS} \cdot I(m = sw) + \dfrac{(ah_i + ah_{comm}^{tot})}{AH_{remaining}} \cdot I(m = hw)$

Table 1. Results from ILP and GCLP algorithm.

example	size	algorithm	total hardware area (normalized with respect to hardware area required in ILP solution)	DSP utilization $(1 - idle\_time/D)*100$	solution time
modem	27	ILP	1.0	93.8%	19190 s
		GCLP	1.1935	84.89%	0.535 s
TCS	15	ILP	1.0	73.5%	6656 s
		GCLP	1.0	73.5%	0.387 s

4.1. Experiment 1: GCLP vs. ILP

The examples are first partitioned using the GCLP algorithm. The ILP formulation for these examples is then solved using the ILP solver CPLEX. Table 1 lists the GCLP and ILP solutions for the modem and TCS examples. The total hardware area (normalized with respect to the optimal solution), DSP utilization, and solution time for all the cases are compared. The solution time represents the CPU time required to generate the solution on a SPARCstation 10. The total hardware area obtained with the GCLP algorithm is quite close to the ILP solution. In the modem example, the GCLP mapping has all but one node identical with the ILP mapping. The GCLP mapping for the TCS is identical to the ILP mapping.

Figure 9 compares the total hardware area obtained with the GCLP algorithm to the optimal solution obtained with ILP formulation for a number of random examples. For all tested examples the generated GCLP solution is within **30%** of the optimal solution. Examples larger than 20 nodes could not be solved by ILP in reasonable time[10]. GCLP has been used to solve examples with up to 500 nodes with relative ease.

4.2. Experiment 2: GCLP With and Without Local Phase Nodes

To examine the effect of local phase nodes on the GCLP performance, the GCLP algorithm is applied under three cases:

Case 1. The local phase classification is not used—all nodes are normal nodes with $\Delta = 0$. The objective function is selected by comparing GC with the default threshold = 0.5.

Case 2. Nodes are classified as either repellers ($\Delta = R_i$) or normal nodes ($\Delta = 0$).

Case 3. Complete local phase classification, using extremities, repellers, and normal nodes. For extremity nodes $\Delta = E_i$, for repeller nodes $\Delta = R_i$, and for normal nodes $\Delta = 0$.

In the modem example, it was found that:

1. Repellers reduce the hardware area (the solution obtained in case 2 is 13% smaller than the solution obtained in case 1).

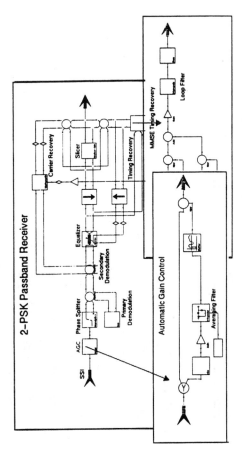

Figure 8. Receiver section of a modem, described in Ptolemy. Hierarchical descriptions of the AGC and timing recovery blocks are shown.

execution time (th_i) and hardware area (ah_i) for the node. The hardware execution time is computed as the best-case execution time (corresponding to the critical path of the control-dataflow graph associated with the node[9]). The hardware area is computed by setting the sample period to the critical path. Generating these area and time estimates is quite time-consuming since it involves a partial synthesis of the hardware and software components. For example, for the 27-node modem example, about 30 minutes of wall-clock time were needed to generate the area and time estimates. In the Design Assistant [1] we have developed mechanisms that automatically invoke the appropriate synthesis tools to generate the estimates.

Random Examples

A random graph generator is used to generate a graph with a random topology for a given number of nodes (graph size). The hardware-software area and time estimates of the nodes in the random graph are generated by taking into account the trend observed in real examples. Details of the techniques used to generate the random graphs are given in [1, Appendix A7]. For each size, we generate 10 random graphs differing in topology and area and time metrics. The heuristic is applied for each random graph and the average value of the result is reported for that size.

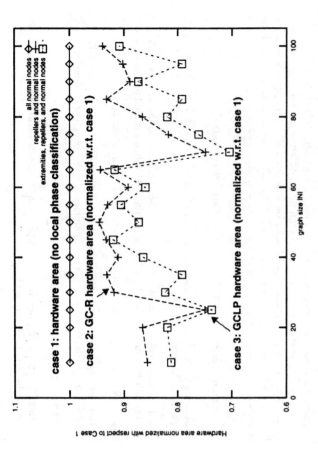

Figure 10. Effect of local phase classification on GCLP performance: case 1: mapping based on *GC* only, case 2: threshold modified for repellers, case 3: complete local phase classification.

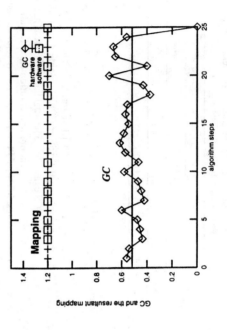

Figure 11. Algorithm trace: *GC* and the Mapping. All normal nodes, threshold = 0.5.

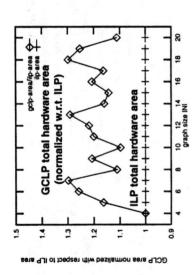

Figure 9. GCLP vs. ILP: Random examples.

2. Extremities are seen to match their expected mappings (ex: *Pulse Shaper*, a hardware extremity, is mapped to software. *Carrier Recovery*, a software extremity, is mapped to hardware).

3. Repeller nodes are also mapped to their intuitively expected mappings (ex: *Scrambler*, a high *BLIM* software repeller, is mapped to hardware).

Figure 10 plots the results of these three cases when applied to random examples. The total hardware areas are normalized with respect to the total hardware area obtained in case 1. It is seen that the use of repellers (case 2) significantly reduces the hardware area as compared to a purely *GC*-based selection in case 1. This verifies our premise that using the repeller measure reduces the total hardware area. Using both extremity and repeller nodes further improves the quality of the solution. On an average, the complete classification of local phase nodes reduces the total hardware area by **16.82%**, when compared with case 1.

4.3. Algorithm Trace

The behavior of GCLP with complete local phase classification of nodes is quite complex. To understand the relation between node classification, threshold, *GC*, and the actual mapping at each step of the algorithm, we illustrate these key parameters in algorithm traces for specific examples.

Figure 11 illustrates the *GC* variation and the mapping at each step, ignoring the local phase classification. When *GC* > 0.5, time is critical. Almost always, nodes get mapped to hardware. Eventually, this reduces the time criticality and *GC* reduces. When it drops below 0.5, area minimization is selected as the objective. In most cases, this objective selects software mapping. Subsequently, time becomes critical, *GC* increases, and further nodes get mapped to hardware. Thus *GC* (and the mapping) adapts continually.

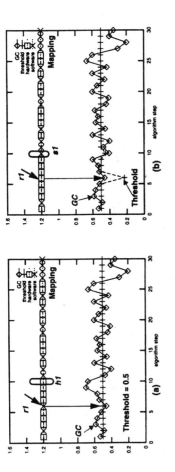

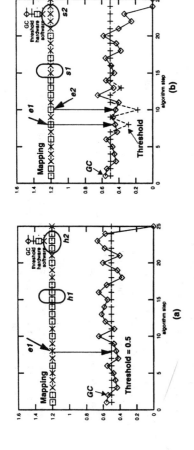

Figure 12. GC and mapping: (a) without extremity measures (b) with extremity measures.

Figure 13. GC and mapping: (a) without repeller measures (b) with repeller measures.

Figure 12 illustrates the effect of adding extremity nodes to the above example. Nodes mapped in steps 8 and 10 are software extremities. In Figure 12-a, the extremity measure is not considered, in Figure 12-b, it is. We assume that nodes are mapped in the same order in both these cases. Mapping marked by a cross means software mapping and by a square means hardware mapping. In Figure 12-a, the threshold assumes its default value (0.5). The software extremity node mapped in step 8 (market $e1$) gets mapped to software, hence, time criticality increases. When compared to the corresponding mapping in Figure 12-b, nodes mapped subsequently in steps 15 and 16 (marked $h1$) get mapped to hardware. A similar effect is observed while mapping nodes in steps 22, 23, and 24 (marked $h2$ in Figure 12-a). The generated solution has a total hardware area of 1253, and 14 nodes are mapped to hardware. Also, the sample mean of the GC over all steps is 0.50448. In Figure 12-b, extremity measures are used to change the default threshold. The extremity measure for nodes mapped in steps 8 and 10 lowers the threshold at the points marked $e1$ and $e2$ in Figure 12-b. This induces a hardware mapping. Mapping these software extremities to hardware reduces time criticality. Subsequently, nodes mapped in steps 15 and 16 (marked $s1$) get mapped to software. The total hardware area is 756, and 10 nodes are mapped to hardware. Thus by taking into account the local preference of nodes 8 and 10, the quality of the solution is improved by 40%. Also, the sample mean of the GC over all the steps is 0.4288.

Figure 13 illustrates the effect of repellers on GC and mapping at each step of the algorithm applied to a particular example. In this example, nodes mapped in steps 6 and 10 are software repellers; the node mapped in step 6 has a larger repeller measure than the node mapped in step 10. In Figure 13-a repellers are not considered, in Figure 13-b, they are. We assume that nodes are mapped in the same order in both the cases. In Figure 13-a, the repeller measures are not considered when mapping—the threshold assumes its default value of 0.5. In this case, node mapped in step 6 is mapped to software and the node mapped in step 10 is mapped to hardware. Clearly, this mapping can be improved. In Figure 13-b, repeller measures are taken into consideration; they modify the default threshold and hence the mapping. The repeller measure for the node mapped in step 6 lowers the threshold at the point marked $r1$ in Figure 13-b. This forces the node to get mapped to hardware. The threshold for the node in step 10 is not lowered as much and it gets mapped to software. The mapping of nodes in steps 6 and 10 is thus exactly opposite to that in Figure 13-a. Thus nodes in steps 6 and 10 were in effect *swapped* in Figure 13-b—the node with a larger repeller measure displaced the one with a smaller measure and this reduced the overall area (1803 in Figure 13-a vs. 1677 in Figure 13-b, 17 nodes are mapped to hardware in both cases).

5.0 Algorithm for Extended Partitioning: Design Objectives

The GCLP algorithm described so far solves the binary partitioning problem $P1$. The extended partitioning problem $P2$ is to jointly optimize the mapping as well as implementation bin for each node. Consider the implementation-bin curve of a node as shown in Figure 2. Denote L to be the fastest (left-most) implementation bin, and H to be the slowest (right-most) implementation bin. As the implementation-bin curve is traversed from bins L to H, the hardware area required to implement the node decreases. From the viewpoint of minimizing hardware area, each node mapped to hardware can be set at its H bin (lowest area). This might, however, be infeasible since the H bins correspond to the slowest implementations. The extended partitioning problem is to select an "appropriate" implementation bin and mapping for each node such that the total hardware is minimized, subject to deadline and resource constraints. This problem is obviously far more complex than the binary partitioning problem. Our goal is to design an efficient algorithm to solve the extended partitioning problem. There are two guiding objectives used in the design of this algorithm.

1. *Design Objective 1: Complexity that scales reasonably:* The binary partitioning problem has $2^{|N|}$ mapping possibilities for $|N|$ nodes in the graph. Given B implementation bins within a mapping, the extended partitioning problem has $(2B)^{|N|}$ possibilities in the worst-case. The algorithm complexity should not scale with the dimensionality (number of design alternatives per node) of the partitioning process, i.e., if a binary par-

titioning algorithm has complexity $O(|N|^2)$, the extended partitioning algorithm should not have complexity $O(|N|^{2B})$, since B is typically in the range 5 to 10. Obviously the binary partitioning algorithm cannot be extended directly to solve the extended partitioning problem, since the implementation possibilities explode.

2. *Design Objective 2: Reuse of GCLP:* Since we already have an efficient algorithm for binary partitioning, the algorithm for extended partitioning should reuse it. This suggests that extended partitioning can be decomposed into two blocks: mapping and implementation selection. GCLP can be used for mapping.

It is not enough, however, to decompose the extended partitioning problem into two isolated steps, namely that of mapping followed by implementation-bin selection. The serial traversal of nodes in a graph means that the implementation bin of a particular node affects the mapping of as-yet unmapped nodes. Since there is a correlation between mapping and implementation selection, they cannot be optimized in isolation. This dependence has to be captured in the algorithm.

Our approach to solving the extended partitioning problem is summarized in Figure 14. The heuristic is called MIBS. In the final solution, each node in the graph is characterized by three attributes: mapping, implementation bin, and schedule. As the algorithm progresses, depending on the extent of information that has been generated, each node in the DAG passes through a sequence of three states: (1) free, (2) tagged, and (3) fixed. Before the algorithm begins, all three attributes are unknown. Such nodes are called *free* nodes. Assuming median area and time values, GCLP is first applied to get a mapping and schedule for all the free nodes in the graph. A particular free node is then selected (called a *tagged* node). Assuming its mapping to be that determined by GCLP, an appropriate implementation bin is then chosen for the tagged node. In the following section, we describe a bin selection procedure that determines the implementation bin for the tagged node. Once the mapping and implementation bin are known, the tagged node becomes a *fixed* node. GCLP is then applied on the remaining nodes and this process is repeated until all nodes in the DAG become fixed; the MIBS algorithm has $|N|$ steps[11] for $|N|$ nodes in the DAG.

The MIBS approach subscribes closely to the design objectives outlined. GCLP is used for mapping (according to Design Objective 2). Since GCLP and bin selection are applied alternately within each step of the MIBS algorithm, there is continuous feedback between the mapping and implementation-bin selection stages. The MIBS algorithm will be shown to be reasonably efficient ($O|N|^3 + B \cdot |N|^2$), where B is the number of implementation bins per mapping. Thus it scales polynomially with the dimensionality of the problem (Design Objective 1). In the next section, we describe the bin selection procedure to solve the implementation-bin selection problem.

6.0 Implementation-Bin Selection

6.1. Overview

In the following, we restrict ourselves to the problem of selecting the implementation bin for hardware-mapped nodes only. The concepts introduced here can be extended to software implementation-bin selection as well.

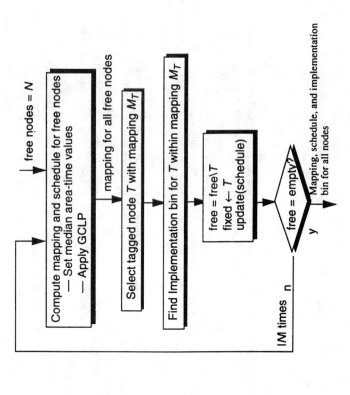

Figure 14. MIBS approach to solving extended partitioning.

Recall from Figure 14 that, in each step of the MIBS algorithm, GCLP is first applied to determine the revised mapping of free nodes. Let the free nodes mapped to hardware at the current step be called $free^h$ nodes. A tagged node is selected from the set of free nodes. Assuming its mapping to be that determined by GCLP, the bin selection procedure is applied to select an implementation bin for the tagged node.

Figure 15 shows the flow of the bin selection procedure. The key idea is to use a lookahead measure to correlate the implementation bin of the tagged node with the hardware area required for the $free^h$ nodes. It selects the most *responsive* bin in this respect as the implementation bin for the tagged node.

Computing the lookahead measure can be very complex since the final implementation bins of the $free^h$ nodes are not known at this step. To simplify matters, we assume that $free^h$ nodes can be in either L or H bins[12]. All $free^h$ nodes are assumed to be in their H bins initially. The lookahead measure (called *bin fraction* BT_T^j) computes, for each bin j of the tagged node T, the fraction of $free^h$ nodes that need to be moved from H bins to L bins in order to meet timing constraints. A high value of BF_T^j indicates that if the tagged node T

were to be implemented in bin j, a large fraction of $free^h$ nodes would likely get mapped to their fast implementations (L bins), hence increasing the overall area. The *bin fraction curve* (BFC_T) is the collection of the all bin fraction values of the tagged node T.

Bin sensitivity is the gradient of BFC_T. It reflects the responsiveness of the bin fraction to the bin motion of node T. Suppose that the maximum slope of the bin fraction curve is between bins $k-1$ and k (Figure 15). Moving the tagged node from bin $k-1$ to k shifts the largest fraction of $free^h$ nodes to their L bins. Equivalently, the k to $k-1$ motion for the tagged node results in the latest reduction of the area of $free^h$ nodes. Hence the $(k-1)$th bin is selected as the implementation bin for the tagged node (B_T^*). The computation of the BFC and bin sensitivity is described next.

6.2. Bin Fraction Curve (BFC)

Assuming node T is implemented in bin j, BF_T^j is computed as the fraction of $free^h$ nodes that have to be moved from their H bins to their L bins in order to meet feasibility. The bin fraction curve BFC_T is the plot of the bin fraction BF_T^j for each bin j of the tagged node T. The procedure to compute the BFC is described next. The underlying concept is similar to that used in GC calculation (Section 3.2). For simplicity, we apply the bin selection procedure only for a tagged node mapped to hardware by GCLP. A single implementation bin is assumed when the tagged node is mapped to software.

Procedure:	**Compute_BFC**
Input:	N_{fixed} = {fixed nodes}, N_{free}^h = {$free^h$ nodes}, T = tagged node, mapping M_T (assumed hardware), hardware implementation curve CH_T
Output:	$BFC_T = \{(BF_T^j, j), \forall j \in NH_T\}$
Initialize:	$N_{H \to L} = \phi$, $t_{exec}(p)$ known for all fixed nodes p, $p \in N_{fixed}$.

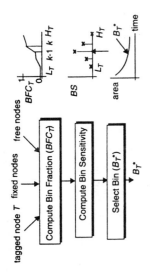

Figure 15. The bin selection procedure.

for $(j = 1; j \leq |NH_T|, j++)\{$

S1. Set $t_{exec}(T) = th_T^j$

S2. For all $k \in N_{free}^h$, set $t_{exec}(k) = th_k^H$ (all $free^h$ nodes at H bins)

S3. Compute T_{finish}, given the mapping and t_{exec} for all nodes

S4. Find the set $N_{H \to L}$ of $free^h$ nodes that need to be moved to their L bins in order to meet deadline

S4.1. $N_{H \to L} \leftarrow next(N_{free}^h)$

S4.2. $t_{exec}(f) = th_f^L$, $\forall f \in N_{H \to L}$ (set to L bins)

S4.3. Update(T_{finish})

S4.4. If $T_{finish} > D$ go to S4.1

S5. $BF_T^j \frac{\sum_{i \in N_{H \to L}} size_i}{\sum_{i \in N_{free}^h} size_i}$, $0 \leq BF_T^j \leq 1$.

$\}$

The sequence S1 to S5 outlines the procedure used to compute the bin fraction BF_T^j for particular bin j, N_{fixed} is the set of fixed nodes and N_{free}^h is the set of free nodes that has been mapped to hardware by GCLP at the current step of the MIBS algorithm. In S1, the execution time of the tagged node is set to the execution time for the jth bin. In S2, the execution times for all the $free^h$ nodes are set corresponding to their respective H bins. The finish time for the DAG (T_{finish}) is computed in S3. In S4, we compute $N_{H \to L}$, the set of $free^h$ nodes that need to be moved to their L bins in order to meet the timing constraints. Various ranking functions can be used to order the $free^h$ nodes. One obvious choice is to rank the nodes in the order of decreasing H bin execution times th_i^H. A second possibility is to use (th_i^H/th_i^L) as the function to rank the nodes. This has the effect of moving nodes with the greatest relative gain in time when moved from H to L bin. BF_T^j is computed in S5 as a ratio of the sum of the sizes of the nodes in $N_{H \to L}$ to the sum of the sizes of the nodes in N_{free}^h. Recall that the *size* of a node is the number of elementary operations (add, multiply, etc.) in the node.

In summary, a high value of BF_T^j, the bin fraction for node T in implementation bin j, indicates that selecting the jth implementation bin is likely to result in a large fraction of $free^h$ nodes being subsequently assigned to their L bins.

6.3. Implementation-Bin Selection

Figure 16-a plots a typical bin fraction curve for a tagged node T. Let $L_T (H_T)$ denote the $L(H)$ bin for node T. How is the desired bin B_T^* to be selected for this node? An intuitive

308 CHAPTER 4: System-Level Partitioning, Synthesis, and Interfacing

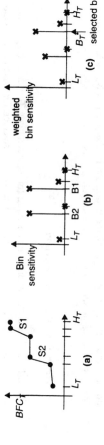

Figure 16. Bin fraction and bin sensitivity for implementation-bin selection.

choice is to set $B_T^* = H_T$, since this corresponds to the smallest hardware area for node T. At H_T, however, BF_T^H is high, i.e., a large fraction of the $free^h$ nodes are in L bins so that the total hardware area might be unnecessarily large. As the tagged node shifts from bin H_T downwards, the resulting decrease in BF implies that the fraction of $free^h$ nodes at their L bin decreases, and consequently the allocated hardware area of $free^h$ nodes reduces. The slope of BFC_T represents how fast the $free^h$ node area reduces with the (leftward) bin motion of node T. This slope is called bin sensitivity BS; it reflects the correlation between bin motion of the tagged node and the overall area reduction of the $free^h$ nodes. That is, $BS_T^j = BF_T^{(j+1)} - BF_T^j$, $L \le j \le H - 1$, where $BS_T^H = 0$.

Let the maximum bin sensitivity be BS_{max} (Figure 16-b). The implementation bin (B_T^*) for the tagged node T is selected to be the bin with bin sensitivity equal to BS_{max}, if $BS_{max} > 0$. If BFC_T is constant, then $BS_{max} = 0$, and the tagged node is mapped to its H bin, since moving it from its slowest to fastest implementations does not affect the $free^h$ nodes.

Consider the plot of bin sensitivity in Figure 17-a, where regions marked S1 and S2 have identical slopes, i.e., same bin sensitivity. In this case, bin B1 which is closer to the H_T bin is preferred over bin B2 since it corresponds to a smaller area of node T. To incorporate this effect in general, the bin sensitivity values are weighted by the area of node T. In particular, the weighted bin sensitivity is plotted by multiplying the bin sensitivity at each bin j by ah_T^H/ah_T^j (Figure 17-c). B_T^* is then selected to be the bin with the maximum weighted bin sensitivity. In case of a tie for the maximum weighted bin sensitivity, the bin closer to H_T bin is selected.

In summary, the strategy for implementation-bin selection is to plot the weighted bin sensitivity and set B_T^* to be the bin with the maximum bin sensitivity that is closest to the H_T bin. The bin selection procedure has complexity $O(B \cdot (|N| + |A|))$, as shown in [1]. The procedure is outlined below:

Procedure **bin_selection**
Input $N_{fixed} = \{\text{fixed nodes}\}$, $N_{free}^h = \{free^h \text{ nodes}\}$

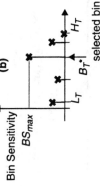

Figure 17. Weighted bin sensitivity.

T = tagged node, with mapping M_T (assumed hardware), hardware implementation curve CH_T

Output B_T^*

S1. Compute BFC_T (Section 6.2)
S2. Compute bin sensitivity
S3. Compute weighted bin sensitivity
S4. Determine bin B_T^* corresponding to the bin with the maximum weighted bin sensitivity

In the next section, we present the MIBS algorithm to solve the extended partitioning problem P2.

7.0 The Extended Partitioning Problem: MIBS Algorithm

Algorithm: **MIBS**
Input: $\forall i \in N$: CH_i, CS_i, E_i (extremity measure), and R_i (repeller measure). Software-hardware interface communication costs: ah_{comm}, as_{comm}, and t_{comm}.
Constraints: AH, AS, and D.
Output $\forall i \in N$: mapping M_i ($M_i \in \{\text{hardware, software}\}$), implementation bin B_i^*, and start time t_i.
Initialization $N_{fixed} = \{\text{fixed nodes}\} = \phi$, $N_{free} = \{\text{free nodes}\} = \{N\}$.
Procedure Compute median area and time values for all nodes in software and hardware.
while ($|N_{free}| > 0$) {

S1. Determine M_i and t_i for all $i \in N_{free}$

    S1.1. For all $i \in N_{free}$, set area and time values to their median values

    S1.2. Use GCLP to compute M_i and t_i for $i \in N_{free}$. (Section 3.0)

S2. Determine the set of ready nodes N_R

S3. Select tagged node T ($T \in N_R$) using urgency measures

S4. Determine the implementation bin B_T^* for node T assuming mapping M_T

    S4.1. Use the bin selection procedure to determine bin B_T^* (Section 6.0)

S5. $N_{free} = N_{free} \setminus \{T\}$; $N_{fixed} \leftarrow \{T\}$, Update t_T based on the selected implementation bin B_T^*.

}

N represents the set of nodes in the graph. N_{free} is the set of free nodes; it is initialized to N. N_{fixed} is the set of fixed nodes and is empty at start. The median values of the area and time on hardware and software mappings are computed in the initialization phase. For each step, the MIBS algorithm computes the mapping, the implementation bin, and the schedule of one node. In S1 of each step, the mapping and schedule for all the free nodes is first computed. This is done by applying GCLP over the set of free nodes assuming median area and time values. The set of ready nodes is determined in S2. This represents the set of nodes whose predecessors are fixed nodes. One of these ready nodes is selected as a tagged node in S3. In particular, we select a ready node on the critical path. In S4, the bin selection procedure is applied to determine the implementation bin for this tagged node. Finally, in S5, the schedule of the tagged node is updated depending on the implementation bin selected. The tagged node then becomes fixed. The sequence S1–S5 is repeated $|N|$ times until all the nodes in the graph become fixed.

Note that in the MIBS algorithm, the mapping of all the nodes is not finalized in one iteration; future mappings of the remaining free nodes are allowed to change depending on the implementation bin selected for a tagged node. At any step, the known mappings and implementation bins of the fixed nodes affect the mappings of the free nodes. The complexity of the MIBS algorithm is $O(|N|^3 + B \cdot |N|^2)$, where B is the number of implementation bins per mapping ([1, Appendix A6]).

8.0 Performance of the MIBS Algorithm

The performance of the MIBS algorithm is examined in this section. As in Section 4.0, we will use both practical examples (the modem and TCS) as well as random graphs to evaluate the performance.

Table 2. Comparison of ILP and MIBS solutions for the modem example.

Scenario	hardware area	solution time
ILP	316	3.5 hours
MIBS	362	3 minutes
Comparison	1.1456 times bigger	70 times faster

To generate the hardware implementation bins, the Silage description for each node is passed through Hyper. The best-case execution time (corresponding to the critical path) is first estimated and the corresponding area is computed. This corresponds to the L bin. Next, the execution time is incremented and the corresponding area is computed. This process is repeated until the required hardware corresponds to just one resource of each type. This corresponds to the smallest hardware area (H bin). Points in between correspond to the other implementation bins. In our experiments we assume only one software implementation bin, but techniques described in [23] can be used to estimate the software bins. Implementation options corresponding to various algorithmic choices are assumed to be specified by the designer. In the estimation tool in the Design Assistant [1], Hyper is automatically invoked with different design constraints (by stepping through the range of execution times and applying different transformations) to generate the hardware implementation curves.

In Section 8.1, the solutions observed with the MIBS algorithm are compared to the optimal solutions obtained with the ILP formulation. In Section 8.2, we demonstrate the effectiveness of the MIBS algorithm in reducing the hardware area relative to the GCLP algorithm.

8.1. Experiment 1: MIBS vs. ILP

ILP formulations of the modem and TCS examples become impossible to solve in a reasonable time. A simplified version of the modem example with 15 nodes and 5 hardware implementation bins per node is considered here. The ILP formulation for this example requires 718 constraints and 396 variables. Table 2 summarizes the solutions obtained with ILP and with MIBS algorithm. The closeness of the solutions is encouraging, especially since ILP becomes formidable for even slightly larger problems.

Figure 18 plots the MIBS and ILP hardware areas for a number of random examples. For the examples tested, the MIBS solution is within **18%** of the optimal solution obtained by ILP. Larger examples could not be solved by ILP in reasonable time. In these examples, ILP failed to give even a single feasible integer solution.

310 CHAPTER 4: System-Level Partitioning, Synthesis, and Interfacing

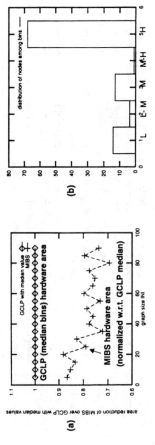

Figure 18. Comparison of MIBS and ILP solutions.

Table 3. Area improvement using MIBS vs. GCLP (modem example).

case	Scenario	hardware area	area reduction normalized with respect to case 1	solution time
1	GCLP, L implementation bin	736	1.0	0.0525s
2	GCLP, median implementation bin	530	0.7201	0.0525s
3	MIBS	362	0.4918	0.7974s

8.2. *Experiment 2: Binary Partitioning vs. Extended Partitioning*

Our next objective is to evaluate the effectiveness of the extended partitioning approach in reducing the total hardware area compared with binary partitioning. Three cases are considered. In the first case, mapping is done based on GCLP, assuming that the execution times and areas for the nodes mapped to hardware are set to the values corresponding to their L bins. In the second case, this mapping is recomputed, now with the area and execution time values corresponding to the median implementation bins. In the third case, extended partitioning is done based on the MIBS algorithm. Table 3 shows the results for the three cases applied to the modem example. The MIBS solution is observed to be much superior to both the GCLP solutions (50% less hardware compared to case 1, and 32% less than case 2). This strengthens our premise that implementation flexibility can be used at the partitioning level to reduce the overall hardware area.

In Figure 19-a, we compare, for random graphs, the hardware area obtained with MIBS to that obtained with GCLP (median area and time values). On average, the area generated by MIBS is **26.4%** smaller than that generated by GCLP.

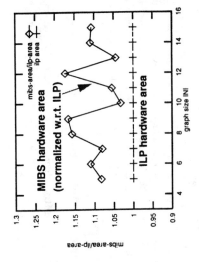

Figure 19. (a) MIBS vs. GCLP (extended partitioning vs. binary partitioning); (b) Node distribution among implementation bins.

Figure 19-b shows the distribution of the nodes among the implementation bins selected by the MIBS algorithm. This distribution is averaged over a number of random examples for a fixed graph size of 25 nodes. The bins are classified into 5 categories: L bin, L to median bin, median bin, median to H bin, and the H bin. It is seen that the nodes in hardware are distributed among all the implementation bins. This flexibility reduces time criticality at every mapping decision and improves DSP utilization, i.e., the number of nodes mapped to software increases. This combined effect (reduced number of hardware nodes and their distribution over several bins) reduces the total hardware area.

8.3. *Parameter Tuning*

Several user-settable parameters come into play in the MIBS algorithm. These include: (1) the cut-off percentiles (α, β) used for classifying extremities in GCLP, (2) the extremity measure weight (γ) and the repeller measure weight (ν) in GCLP, (3) the ranking function for GC calculation ($ts, ts/th$, or ah), and (4) the ranking function for BF calculation (th^H, th^H/th^L, or ah^L).

Parameters α, β, γ, and ν are tuned by a simple search between 0 and 1. We have incorporated this automated search mechanism in our algorithm implementation. Since the MIBS algorithm is extremely fast, such an exploration is computationally viable. Typically, α and β in the range (0.5, 0.75) are used since a value outside this range tends to reduce the number of nodes that fit this behavior and consequently the extremities do not play a significant role in biasing the local preferences of nodes. Typically, γ and ν are set to 1. To further improve the solution, their values are varied in steps of 0.1 in the range [0,1] and the values that give the best solution are selected. The ts/th and th^H/th^L ranking functions have been found to perform best for GC and BF calculations respectively.

9.0 Summary

At the system-level, designs are typically represented modularly, with moderate to large granularity. Each node can be implemented using a variety of algorithms and/or synthesis mechanisms in hardware or software. These implementations typically differ in area and execution time. We define *extended partitioning* as the joint problem of mapping nodes in a precedence graph to hardware or software, scheduling, and selecting a particular implementation (called implementation bin) for each node. The end-objective is to minimize the total hardware area subject to throughput and resource constraints.

In this paper, we first presented the GCLP algorithm to solve the *binary partitioning* (mapping and scheduling) problem. It uses a global time criticality measure to adaptively select a mapping objective at each step—if time is critical, it selects a mapping that minimizes the finish time of the node, otherwise it minimizes the resource consumption. This time criticality measure overcomes the inherent drawback with list scheduling. In addition to global consideration, local optimality is sought by taking into account the preferences of nodes that consume disproportionate amounts of resources in hardware and software mappings. This effect is quantified by classifying nodes as extremities. The hardware area is further reduced by using a concept of repellers. Repellers take into account the relative preferences of nodes, based on intrinsic algorithmic properties that dictate a preferred hardware or software mapping. The GCLP algorithm is computationally efficient ($O(|N|^2)$). For the examples tested, the GCLP solution was found to be no more than 30% larger than the optimal solution. The effectiveness of local phase nodes (extremities and repellers) in reducing the overall hardware area was experimentally verified. On an average, the use of local phase nodes reduces the hardware area by 17%, relative to solutions obtained without using local phase classification of nodes.

The MIBS algorithm uses the GCLP heuristic to solve the extended partitioning problem. The strategy is to classify nodes in the graph as free, tagged, and fixed. Initially all nodes in the graph are free—their mappings and implementation bins are unknown. GCLP is applied over the set of free nodes. A tagged node is then selected from this set; its mapping is assumed to be that determined by GCLP. A bin selection procedure is used to compute an appropriate implementation bin for the tagged node. The procedure uses a look-ahead measure, called bin fraction, which estimates for each bin of the node, the fraction of unmapped nodes that need to move to their fastest implementations so that timing constraints are met. The bin fraction is used to compute a bin sensitivity measure that correlates the implementation bin with the overall hardware area reduction. The procedure selects the bin with maximum bin sensitivity. The procedure simplifies this computation by assuming that the remaining free nodes are either in their slowest or fastest implementations. The tagged node becomes a fixed node once its implementation bin is determined. GCLP is then applied over the remaining free nodes and the sequence is repeated until all nodes in the graph become fixed. In the examples tested, the MIBS solution is found to be within 18% of the optimal solution. Experimental results also indicate that implementation bins can be used effectively to reduce the overall area by as much as 27% over solutions generated using binary partitioning. The complexity of the MIBS algorithm is $O(|N|^3 + B \cdot |N|^2)$, where B is the number of implementation bins per mapping.

Acknowledgements

The authors would like to thank Pratyush Moghé for many stimulating discussions and detailed feedback on the manuscript. The authors also gratefully acknowledge Prof. Jan Rabaey; the problem of selecting from among implementation bins was motivated by multiple discussions with him.

This research was part of the Ptolemy project, which is supported by the Advanced Research Projects Agency and the U.S. Air Force (under the RASSP program F33615-93-C-1317), the Semiconductor Research Corporation (SRC) (project 95-DC-324-016), the National Science Foundation (MIP-9201605), the State of California MICRO program, and the following companies: Bell Northern Research, Cadence, Dolby, Hitachi, Luckygoldstar, Mentor Graphics, Mitsubishi, Motorola, NEC, Philips, and Rockwell.

Notes

1. We generated each of these curves by running a task-level Silage [3] description of the node through Hyper [4].
2. Such a DAG can be generated from a synchronous dataflow (SDF) graph, which allows loops and multirate operations, thus making it possible to represent a reasonably large class of applications [5].
3. Note that we are not restricted to a single source (sink) node. If there are multiple source (sink) nodes in the DAG, they can all be assumed to originate from (terminate into) a dumy source (sink) node.
4. A *step* corresponds to the mapping of a particular node in the DAG.
5. Assuming there is at least one feasible solution to $P1$ satisfying the deadline constraint.
6. $I(expr)$ is an indicator function that evaluates to 1 when $expr$ is true, 0 else.
7. Using set-theoretic notation, $N_U = N_U \setminus \{i\}$ means element i is deleted from set N_U, and $N_M \leftarrow \{i\}$ means element i is added to set N_M.
8. Much larger examples have been easily solved with the GCLP algorithm (as will be shown in Section 4.2). Here, we consider these relatively small examples that can be solved by ILP as well. The intent is to compare the GCLP solution to the optimal ILP solution to evaluate the quality of the heuristic.
9. This control-dataflow graph is generated by Hyper during the hardware synthesis process.
10. Using techniques such as polyhedral theory, the ILP solution time can be improved slightly, but the size of problems that can be solved using ILP is still limited.
11. Each *step* of the MIBS algorithm constitutes the determination of the mapping, implementation bin, and schedule of a node.
12. A *free[h]* node loses this restriction when it becomes tagged later on.

References

1. A. Kalavade. System-level codesign of mixed hardware-software systems, Ph.D. Dissertation, University of California, Berkeley, CA, 1995 (http://ptolemy.eecs.berkeley.edu/~kalavade).

2. M. Potkonjak and J. Rabaey. Optimizing resource utilization using transformations. *IEEE Transactions of Computer-Aided Design of Integrated Circuits and Systems* 13(3): 277–292, March 1994.
3. P. Hilfinger. A high-level language and silicon compiler for digital signal processing. In *Proc. of IEEE 1985 Custom Integrated Circuits Conference*, Portland, OR, pp. 213–216, May 20–23, 1985.
4. J. M. Rabaey et al. Fast prototyping of datapath-intensive architectures. *IEEE Design & Test*, 40–51, June 1991.
5. E. A. Lee and D. G. Messerschmitt. Sunchronous data flow. *Proc. of the IEEE* 75(9): 1235–1245, Sept. 1987.
6. R. Gupta and G. De Micheli. System-level synthesis using re-programmable components. In *Proceedings of the European Conference on Design Automation*, Brussels, Belgium, pp. 2–7, Feb. 1992.
7. R. Ernst and J. Henkel. Hardware/software codesign of embedded controllers based on hardware extraction. In *Handouts of the 1st Intl. Workshop on Hardware/Software Codesign*, Estes Park, Colorado, Sept. 1992.
8. E. Baros and W. Rosential. A method for hardware/software partitioning. In *Proc. of COMPUERO'92, IEEE Intl. Conference on Computer and Software Engineering*, The Hague, The Netherlands, pp. 580–585, May 4–8, 1992.
9. J. G. D'Ambrosio and X. Hu. Configuration-level hardware/software partitioning for real-time embedded systems. In *Proc. of Third Intl. Workshop on Hardware/Software Codesign*, Grenoble, France, pp. 34–41, Sept. 1994.
10. D. E. Thomas et al. A model and methodology for hardware/software codesign. *IEEE Design & Test*, Sept. 1993.
11. G. Sih and E. A. Lee. A compile-time scheduling heuristic for interconnection-constrained heterogeneous processor architectures. *IEEE Transactions on Parallel and Distributed Systems* 4(2): 175–187, Feb. 1993.
12. T. Hamada et al. Macripipelining based heterogeneous multiprocessor scheduling. In *Proc. of IEEE Intl. Conference on Acoustics, Speech and Signal Processing (ICASSP)*, Vol. 5, San Francisco, CA, pp. 597–600, March 23–26, 1992.
13. E. D. Lagnese and D. E. Thomas. Architectural partitioning for system-level synthesis of ICs. *IEEE Transactions on Computer Aided Design* 10(7): 847–860, July 1991.
14. M. C. McFarland and T. J. Kowalski. Incorporating bottom-up design into hardware synthesis. *IEEE Transactions on Computer Aided Design* 9(9): 938–950, Sept. 1990.
15. R. Camposano and R. K. Brayton. Partitioning before logic synthesis. In *Proc. of the Intl. Conference on Computer Aided Design (ICCAD)*, pp. 324–326, 1987.
16. P. G. Paulin and J. P. Knight. Force-directed scheduling for the behavioral synthesis of ASICS. *IEEE Trans. on CAD* 8(6): 661–679, June 1989.
17. R. K. Brayton et al. Multilevel logic synthesis. *Proceedings of the IEEE* 78(2): 264–300, Feb. 1990.
18. G. De Micheli. *Synthesis and Optimization of Digital Circuits*. McGraw-Hill, New York, 1994.
19. K. Chaudhary and M. Pedram. A near optimal algorithm for technology mapping minimizing area under delay constraints. In *Proc. of 29th Design Automation Conference*, Anaheim, CA, pp. 492–498, June 1992.
20. M. Ishikawa and G. De Micheli. A module selection algorithm for high-level synthesis. In *Proc. of 1991 IEEE International Symposium on Circuits and Systems*, Vol. 3, Singapore, pp. 1777–1780, June 11–14, 1991.
21. T. C. Hu. Parallel sequencing and assembly line problems. *Operations Research* 9(6): 841–848, Nov. 1961.
22. J. Buck et al. Ptolemy: a framework for simulating and prototyping heterogeneous systems. *International Journal of Computer Simulation* 4, 155–182, Apr. 1994. Special issue on "Simulation Software Development."
23. S. Ritz et al. High-level software synthesis for the design of communication systems. *IEEE Journal on Selected Areas in Communications* 11(3): 348–358, April 1993.

Hardware-Software Codesign of Embedded Systems

Designers generally implement embedded controllers for reactive real-time applications as mixed software-hardware systems. In our formal methodology for specifying, modeling, automatically synthesizing, and verifying such systems, design takes place within a unified framework that prejudices neither hardware nor software implementation. After interactive partitioning, this approach automatically synthesizes the entire design, including hardware-software interfaces. Maintaining a finite-state machine model throughout, it preserves the formal properties of the design. It also allows verification of both specification and implementation, as well as the use of specification refinement through formal verification.

Massimiliano Chiodo

Paolo Giusto

Attila Jurecska

Magneti Marelli

Harry C. Hsieh

Alberto Sangiovanni-Vincentelli

University of California, Berkeley

Luciano Lavagno

Politecnico di Torino

Current approaches to the hardware-software codesign problem fall short, we believe, on one of two counts. The formal model they define is not abstract enough for use as an implementation-independent representation during the system design process. Otherwise, the model is not sufficiently detailed for efficient synthesis as a mix of hardware and software components.

Our formalism, an extension of classical finite-state machines called Codesign Finite State Machine (CFSM), is equally expressive for hardware or software implementations of control-dominated systems. It is also formally defined, hence we can directly use it to verify properties that all implementations will share.[1]

For our purposes, we take hardware-software codesign to mean the design of a special-purpose system composed of a few application-specific integrated circuits that cooperate with software procedures on general-purpose processors. A single, well-defined purpose at a definite point in time and a generally long lifetime also characterize such embedded systems. Development of these systems cannot proceed by trial and error after deployment, so designers must optimize them as completely as possible during early design phases.

Though restricted, this definition is still too broad to allow a useful formalization of generally applicable automated design methodologies.

Embedded controllers serve in everything from portable compact-disc players to the navigation control units of battle aircraft. Consequently, we limit our present focus to relatively small, real-time control systems composed of software on one (or few) microcontrollers and some semi-custom hardware components.

Ignored here as well are large systems requiring the coordination of many boards and hundreds of thousands of lines of code. Nor do we directly address computation-dominated tasks, such as robotics and vision, that require, for example, digital signal processors or powerful general-purposes computers. Typical applications of our proposed methodology include automotive electronics (as the accompanying box describes) and household appliance control (from elevators to microwave ovens).

Some current approaches to the codesign problem concern methods to implement software programs in hardware. For example, designers have translated various flavors of Hoare's Communicating Sequential Processes (CSP) into synchronous or asynchronous circuits. Languages for real-time software specification, such as Esterel,[2] StateCharts,[3] or some modification of C[4] have served directly or indirectly as hardware description languages. Conversely, investigators have proposed methods to implement hardware specifications in software.[5] Some research has focused on particular aspects of

Automotive electronics

One application field deriving the greatest gains from the coming of age of codesign techniques is automotive electronics. Here, high production volumes go hand in hand with a demand for high quality and reliability, low costs and maintenance needs, and short time-to-market. The end product—usually a box with some connectors—must meet stringent physical constraints, such as weight and size.

The demand for embedded controllers in this application has steadily increased for the past few years, both in terms of the range of applications and the sophistication of the functions performed. In virtually all vehicles manufactured since the mid 1980s, an electronic device—the engine control unit (ECU)—controls fuel injection and ignition. Most medium- to high-range cars come equipped with microcontroller-based dashboards. Also electronically controlled and monitored are automatic transmissions, air-conditioning systems and, recently, shock absorbers. The boom of safety devices, such as air bags and anti-lock braking systems (ABS), has boosted the demand for in-vehicle electronics.

The increase in the number and complexity of electronic devices in vehicles is affecting the way designers conceive the entire automobile. For example, a high-range car equipped with a rich set of options can have over 100 wires tied to a dashboard (including 30 to 35 wires entering each front door), for a total length of about 3 miles and a weight of about 100 pounds (Mercedes S-series and Renault Safrane). Effectively replacing such a bundle of hard-wired devices is a local area network implemented, usually, with a serial bus (see Figure A). This bus replaces the numerous wires, allocating the functions to CPUs that no longer need be topologically close to the controlled part, such as a window or mirror. Compensating for the added cost of the electronics are savings in material (wires and connectors), manufacturing time, and reliability of the links.

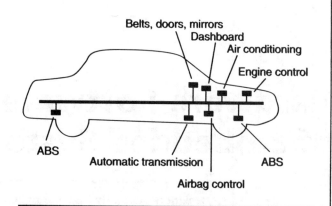

Figure A. An on-board local area network.

The complexity of these functions and the precision dictated, for example, by the exhaust emission control laws, require the use of specialized fast microcontrollers. Such controllers, like the Motorola MC68332, feature 32-bit architectures (versus the 8 or 16 bits of older microcontrollers) along with specialized microprogrammable processors (time processing units) to handle hard real-time tasks more easily.

---

hardware-software cooperation, such as design of interfaces between hardware and software components[6] or formal specification of hardware-software system properties.[7]

Our basic model, by contrast, is a network of interacting CFSMs that communicate through a very low-level primitive: events. A CFSM, or the environment in which the system operates, emits events that one or more CFSMs or the environment can later detect. This scheme assumes a broadcast communication model, rather than point-to-point channels as in CSP.

Note that events are quite similar to the valued-token model used to model computation-intensive applications;[8] events can also serve to interface the two domains. CFSMs also bear some resemblance to behavioral finite-state machines,[9] because both are based on finite-state causal reaction. Our model, however, offers a more flexible communication mechanism, by using events with an arbitrary propagation time, rather than instantaneous broadcast.

Events directly implement a communication protocol that does not require an acknowledgment. The receiver waits for the sender to emit the event, but the sender can proceed immediately after emission. An implicit one-place buffer between the sender and each receiver saves the event until it is detected or overwritten. This approach lends itself to an efficient hardware implementation with synchronous circuits, as well as a software implementation, either polling- or interrupt-based. If required, our approach can easily model an explicit full handshake mechanism in terms of event exchange.

The notion of communication our proposed model uses implies that the sender does not remove the event immediately after emitting it, but only when emitting another one. Each CFSM can detect an event at most once any time after the event's emission, until another event of the same type overwrites it. Thus, the event can be correctly received even with the rather unpredictable reaction times associated with a software implementation. Correct reception is ensured as long as either the sender data rate is lower than the receiv-

Applying our methodology

As an example of the application of our methodology, let's look at a simplified subsystem of a car dashboard. The functions considered here are the odometer and the speedometer. The system is structured as follows: a proximity sensor placed near the wheel shaft sends a pulse to the dashboard when an indentation goes by it. The dashboard then

- measures the instantaneous speed by counting wheel pulses in a given time interval;
- filters the speed value to improve resolution and reduce sensitivity to noise;
- drives a pulse width-modulated signal proportional to the value of the filtered speed; accumulates speed pulses and every K pulses refreshes the odometer display.

Figure B depicts a data-flow diagram of the system. Dashed arrows represent pure events. Solid lines represent data flows. Rectangles represent memories. Ellipses represent transformations. We can also see the diagram as an interconnection of CFSMs, where data flows are represented by valued events, and the memories are implicitly implemented by the input and output buffers of the CFSMs. We omit the details of the CFSM behavior for reasons of space.

The synthesis system we are describing produced various choices of implementation for each CFSM. Table A describes the cost of a hardware implementation of each CFSM (separately optimized) in terms of square microns in a 3-μm technology. The delay of this implementation is almost negligible, and is supposed to be the same as the clock cycle of the microcontroller (a reasonable choice in an embedded system). The other tables describe the cost in terms of memory occupation (bytes) and execution time (average clock cycles over a set of random inputs) of a software implementation of the CFSMs, excluding the scheduler and I/O drivers, on a Motorola 68HC11 microcontroller. Table B refers to a straightforward implementation of each CFSM as a logic expression for each output and state variable.

Table A. Cost of hardware implementation.

CFSM	Area (μm^2)
AcqSpeed	163,792
OdoAcq	31,088
OdoDisplay	59,392
PWMDriver	31,088
StackFilter	128,064

Table B. Cost of direct software implementation of hardware function.

CFSM	Size (bytes)	Time (cycles)
AcqSpeed	117	130
OdoAcq	59	82
OdoDisplay	120	181
PWMDriver	177	250
StackFilter	104	152

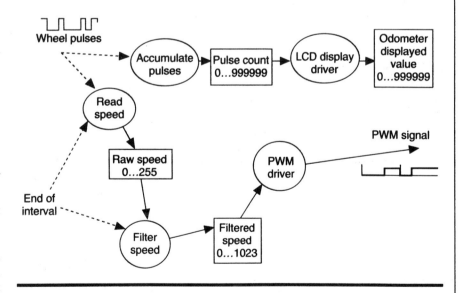

Figure B. Dashboard flowchart.

er processing ability, or the designer explicitly introduces some possibly complex form of synchronization between the two, using events as basic building blocks.

In our methodology, we use a discrete model of time, in which each computing element takes a nonzero unbounded (at least before an implementation is chosen) time to perform its task. This model is quite realistic for synchronous systems and lends itself to efficient formal verification techniques.[1]

The synthesis methodology uses two auxiliary models, derived from CFSM specifications, to describe a hardware and a software component. The first model is a standard logic netlist used by logic synthesis systems. The second model, which is new, is an abstraction of the basic instructions of a very simple computer model, called an s-graph (for software graph).

Since the s-graph is much simpler than a full-blown programming or assembly language, it lets us perform optimizations that real compilers and instruction schedulers could not easily do. They must solve a much more difficult and general optimization problem. Our approach then can map the s-graph into a high-level or assembly language implementation for a specific microcontroller, compile it, and load it.

Completing the methodology is a validation paradigm allowing us to verify that a synthesized design satisfies its specification. We use formal verification to debug both the specification with respect to high-level properties—safety constraints—and the implementation with respect to lower-level properties—timing constraints. It can also help the designer fix errors and try alternate solutions, by providing error traces that describe the reason for failing to satisfy a desired property. Designers can use simulation to complement verification, thus quickly ruling out special cases that are considered potentially troublesome by formal verification, but that are actually impossible in the specified operating conditions. (For an example of this approach in action, see the accompanying Applying our methodology box.)

Codesign finite-state machines

A CFSM, like a standard FSM, transforms a set of inputs into a set of outputs with only a finite amount of internal state. The difference between the two models is that the standard definition of concurrent FSMs implies that all the FSMs change state exactly at the same time. On the other hand, a software implementation of a set of FSMs generally interleaves them in time. Hence replacing the synchrony hypothesis (which is often quite satisfactory for synchronous hardware) in our model is a finite, nonzero, a priori unbounded reaction time.

In this article, we describe the set of assumptions that we chose to add to this basic intuition to obtain a powerful general model for control-dominated reactive systems. For a more extensive treatment, see Chiodo et al.[10]

Suppose we want to specify a simple safety function of an automobile: a seat belt alarm. A typical specification a designer receives would be: "Five seconds after the key is turned on, if the belt has not been fastened, an alarm will beep for ten seconds or until the key is turned off." We can represent the

Applying our methodology (continued)

Tables C and D refer to two different s-graph-based implementations of the same behavior. The former uses multivalued tests (implemented as switch statements, hence the large size of one case that required a 256-way jump). The latter uses binary tests on individual bits of each variable. No method has a clear advantage over the other in all cases, so both strategies should be part of the design toolbox.

To evaluate the trade-off between hardware and software implementations of this subsystem, we can estimate the RAM/ROM occupation of the implementation in Table D at around 100,000-μm (in a 0.5-μm technology). Hence it is about eight times smaller (neglecting the microcontroller area, since the microcontroller is supposed to be required by other functions anyway), but also approximately 100 times slower than the hardware implementation.

Table C. Cost of multiway s-graph implementation.

CFSM	Size (bytes)	Time (cycles)
AcqSpeed	62	32
OdoAcq	33	27
OdoDisplay	55	82
PWMDriver	581	77

Table D. Cost of bit test s-graph implementation.

CFSM	Size (bytes)	Time (cycles)
AcqSpeed	55	45
OdoAcq	36	34
OdoDisplay	97	107
PWMDriver	94	83
StackFilter	63	40

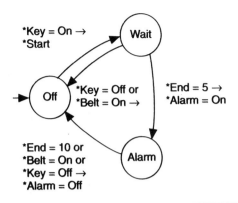

Figure 1. Codesign finite-state machine specification of a simple system.

specification in a reactive finite state form as shown in Figure 1. Input events, such as the fact that the key has been turned on or that a 5-second timer has expired, trigger reactions, such as the starting of the timer or the beeping of the alarm.

The basic observable entities defining the behavior of the system that we want to model are events. Sequences of time-stamped events are timed traces; defining the behavior of the system are the set of timed traces that can be observed when it interacts with the environment. Modeling the system itself and possibly its environment will be a set of CFSMs that produce those traces.

Identifying an event are a name (such as, *Key), a value from a finite set (such as On, Off), and a time of occurrence. We also refer to the event-name, set-of-values pair as an event type. Some events, such as the user hitting the reset button, may not have an interesting value.

Each element of a network of CFSMs describes a component of the system to be modeled. (For the sake of clarity, we give the definition here in terms of a flat view, even though both the methodology and its implementation support hierarchical decomposition.) A CFSM consists of sets of input and output event types (the latter with an optional initial value), and a transition relation (a set of cause-reaction pairs, in which each cause is a set of event names and values and each reaction is also a set of events and values). Triggered by the input events, each transition emits, after an unbounded nonzero time, the output events. (Response bounds must be assumed when we want to verify time-dependent constraints of the system, as we will discuss later.) The state of the CFSM consists of the set of those event types that are at the same time input and output for it. The nonzero reaction time provides the storage capability required to implement the concept of state.

For example, in Figure 1, the fact that the state event has value Off and that input event *Key occurs with value On causes the state event value to become Wait and the value-

less event *Start to be emitted. We model causality by a relation rather than a function, because the specification may be nondeterministic. We can use this to abstract implementation details in the early phases of a design or during validation, or to model the unpredictable behavior of the environment.

Defining the behavior of the system is the evolution of the CFSM network in time, governed by a set of rules that define valid timed traces of a network of CFSMs. Such rules ensure that the transitions of each CFSM are atomic; all output events of a given transition must be emitted (not necessarily at the same time) before the next transition can occur. Note that a CFSM may ignore events, if it is not ready to accept them when they occur. Our methodology requires only that reactions to successive events with the same name be ordered, thus ensuring that one-place buffers can serve to implement events.

The behavior defined by a CFSM network does not assume fairness per se, because this would impose too tight a constraint on the software implementation. (Loosely speaking, fairness means that each CFSM that is enabled to react will do so within a finite amount of time.) However, a suitable software scheduler may impose fairness in practice.

For showing implementation correctness and performing design validation, we can also interpret the behavior of a CFSM network as a (less compact) network of nondeterministic FSMs. Each CFSM corresponds to a main FSM, which represents the desired reactive behavior, surrounded by a set of FSMs (one for each input and output event type) implementing one-place buffers modeling input (detection) and output (reaction) delays.

Synthesis of a CFSM network

Figure 2 represents our complete framework for hardware-software codesign. Before describing the system validation approach, we need to briefly discuss the design flow through the synthesis portion of the framework.

Specification language translation. Due to its relatively low-level view of the world, the CFSM model is not meant to be used directly by designers. They will conceivably write their specifications in a higher level language—Esterel, StateCharts, or a subset of VHDL[11]—that directly translates into CFSMs.

These languages or language subsets all share a common zero-delay hypothesis, also called the perfect synchrony hypothesis. We assume that the system reacts infinitely fast to environmental stimuli. This allows us to eliminate all internal communication between interacting system components, and produces very fast software implementations, at the expense of relatively large code size.[2]

Our CFSM model comes into play after this collapsing of functions into a single reactive block has produced the desired level of granularity. We take into account the nonzero response time typical of a software implementation of the reaction, and study how an interconnection of such reactive blocks, each represented by a CFSM, behaves. In this

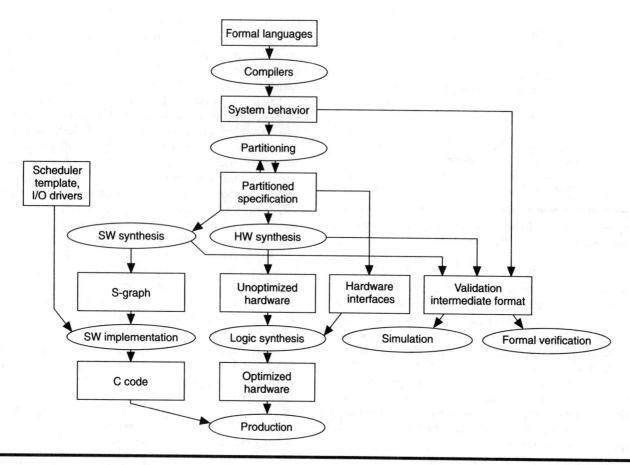

Figure 2. Codesign framework.

sense our proposed methodology is orthogonal to compilation issues for synchronous languages.

Design partitioning. The second step of the design process is design partitioning, that is, choosing the software or hardware implementation for each component of the system specification. The CFSM specification is totally implementation-independent in our approach, a key point that allows designers to experiment with a number of implementation options.

This article does not address directly the issue of automated partitioning; rather it describes a framework where algorithms to solve it can be transparently embedded.

Hardware synthesis. The third step of the proposed design process is to implement each CFSM in the chosen style. The synthesis algorithms we propose are based on restrictions common to the design of most industrial embedded control systems:

- Each hardware partition is implemented as a fully synchronous circuit.
- Each software partition is implemented as a C standalone program (with an operating system skeleton that includes the scheduler and I/O drivers) embedded in a microcontroller.
- All partitions have the same clock.

In the case of hardware synthesis, we map a CFSM into an abstract hardware description format. We implement[12] each transition function with a combinational circuit, latching the circuit outputs to ensure the nonzero reaction delay.

At a given point in time, the significant information elements regarding an event name are its presence or absence, and its optional value. A straightforward hardware mapping of this model uses a wire that has value 1 in all the clock cycles when an event with that name is present and 0 when it is absent. (That is, if the signal stays at 1 for n cycles, there are n successive events with the same name.) The value, if present, is encoded on a bundle of auxiliary wires. Unlike other communication paradigms used originally for software specifications—channels or rendezvous—this communication scheme imposes almost no overhead due to event detection in hardware.

Software synthesis. We map a CFSM subnetwork into a software structure that includes a number of procedures and a simple operating system.

CFSM implementation. A two-step process implements the reactive behavior:

- Implementing and optimizing the desired behavior in a high-level, technology-independent representation of the decision process (called s-graph).
- Translating the s-graph into portable C code and using any available compiler to implement and optimize it in a specific, microcontroller-dependent instruction set.

The methodology-specific, processor-independent first step allows a much broader exploration of the design space than a general-purpose compiler can generally achieve. We can take advantage of the fact that CFSMs compute a finite state reaction to a set of events, which is much simpler to optimize than a generic high-level program. The second step, conversely, allows us to capitalize on predeveloped, microcontroller-specific optimizations such as register allocation or instruction selection and scheduling.

Another major advantage of our proposed approach is a much tighter control of software cost than generally possible with a general-purpose compiler. For this discussion, the cost of a software program is a weighted mixture of code size and execution speed, as real-time reactive systems usually have precise memory occupation as well as timing constraints. With these requirements, the s-graph needs to be detailed enough to make prediction of code size and execution times easy and accurate. On the other hand, it must be high-level enough for easy translation into various dialects of programming languages for the target microcontrollers (whose interpretation even of a standardized language such as C may vary widely).

Hence the s-graph is a reduced form of the control-flow graphs used in compiler technology (see, for example, Aho, Sethi, and Ullman[13]). As such, it is amenable to the standard set of optimizations done by compilers, plus some specific ones.

An s-graph is a directed acyclic graph (DAG), containing Begin, End, Call, Test, and Assign vertices. It is associated with a set of finite-valued variables, corresponding to the input and output events of the CFSM it implements.

An s-graph has one source vertex Begin, and one sink vertex End. Each Test vertex v has two children, *true(v)* and *false(v)*. (We use the limit of two children for the sake of explanation only. The implementation caters to multiway branching.) Each Begin or Assign vertex v has one child *next(v)*. Each Call vertex v has two children, *sub(v)* and *next(v)*. Any nonroot vertex can have one or more parents. A label associates each Test vertex with a Boolean-valued function that determines which child is traversed. It also associates each Assign vertex with a CFSM output variable and with a function defined on the s-graph variables.

The semantics of the s-graph is simply defined by a traversal from Begin to End. The s-graph execution process visits the next vertex at every step, except for the Call and Test vertices. Every time it reaches an Assign vertex, it evaluates the Assign vertex's associated function and assigns its value to the labeling variable. Every time it reaches a Test vertex, it evaluates the function and visits the true or false child. Every time it reaches a Call vertex, it visits the sub vertex of the Call vertex, traverses until the End vertex, then visits the next vertex of the last visited parent Call (no recursion is allowed).

Figure 3 shows an example of a simple s-graph, computing the transition function of Figure 1 (variable S denotes the CFSM state).

We deal with speed and size requirements at the s-graph level. The components of the cost function we consider are:

- the total number of vertices, which is related to the program code (ROM) size,
- the maximum distance between Begin and End vertices, which is related to the execution time, and
- the number of variables, which is proportional to the data size (RAM, including CPU registers).

Speed optimization makes the s-graph as flat as possible without exceeding a bound on the number of vertices.

Driving the software synthesis procedure is a cost estimation done on the s-graph. We use appropriately chosen benchmarks to obtain a cost (code/data size and time) estimation for the various software constructs corresponding to s-graph vertices in various combinations.

We can perform local optimization by collapsing groups of s-graph vertices with one entry point and two exit points into a single Test vertex, whose label we can obtain by function composition. We can estimate the potential gain of this collapsing as the reduction in code size and execution time due to the use of Boolean operations (used to compute the function) rather than tests and jumps.

Finally, we can perform more global optimizations across multiple CFSMs, because composing CFSMs together can reduce the execution time and RAM occupation, thus eliminating the variables used for communication.[2]

Real-time operating system. The customized operating system for each microcontroller consists of a scheduler and drivers for the I/O channels. Hence it is extremely small and imposes little overhead, compared with standard operating systems for real-time applications.

To correctly implement the CFSM behavior, the operating system must satisfy the following constraints:

- Each transition of a task must be performed atomically; that is, the values of the input event buffers for that task must not change once it has been started.

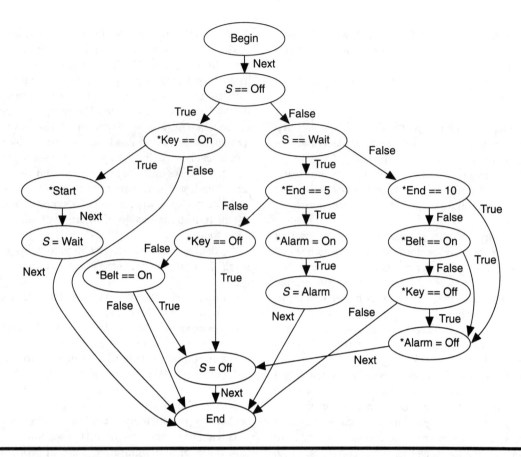

Figure 3. An s-graph implementing the seat belt system.

- The operating system must reset consumed events before invoking a task again.
- The operating system must transfer all output events from a task by setting the signal or variable denoting the event presence only after it has updated the corresponding value.

This scheme lends itself both to polling and interrupt implementations of event detection, as it can suspend and resume an active task at any time. We are still investigating means of specifying real-time constraints, and scheduling algorithms used to satisfy them.

Handling the communication mechanism between a task and the external world—other tasks or external devices—are two layers of software services:

- a general event-driver layer that implements the CFSM event emission/detection primitives, and
- a microcontroller-specific peripheral-driver layer that interfaces the software tasks with the physical I/O channels such as parallel I/O ports, serial ports, and analog-to-digital and digital-to-analog converters.

The latter, which is generally implemented via memory-mapped peripherals, also constitutes the software side of the interfacing mechanism we describe later.

Modeling data flow. Although general in terms of expressiveness, CFSMs are not specifically designed for computation-intensive tasks, but only for control-dominated ones. The idea is that a CFSM specifies the reactive part of the behavior, whereas standard functions can specify the details of the algorithms associated with the actions invoked. This model corresponds to the classic data/control dichotomy both compilers and high-level synthesis use. Libraries thus are made available that provide standard components—adders, counters—already mapped in hardware and software. Designers can incorporate netlists in the hardware implementation and optimize them with it. Similarly, software macros can occur as Test and Assign vertex labels in the s-graph; we must provide cost estimates for them to the s-graph optimizer.

Interfacing implementation domains. Event emission and detection are implemented differently in each domain, so we need an interfacing mechanism.

Conceptually, we can think of an interface mechanism as

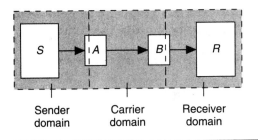

Figure 4. Interface between heterogeneous domains.

a three-layer block (see Figure 4 and Chou, Ortega, and Borriello[6]). A carrier here can be, for example, a printed circuit board track or a bus. Each block acts as a translator between representations in different domains. For example, Figure 5a describes the A and B blocks of a hardware-to-hardware interface (a simple wire). Figure 5b describes the B block of a software-to-hardware interface. Figure 5c describes the A block of a hardware-to-software interface. The software counterparts are embedded in the real-time operating system (for example, as an interrupt handler or an output port driver).

System validation

Partially driving the CFSM model was our desire to use formal verification techniques, which essentially involve proving mathematically that a certain formally specified property is true of a design.

Among the several methods proposed for formal verification, which is best suited for the task at hand, was an approach based on modeling the system as a network of FSMs. We can formally define the time behavior of a CFSM in terms of an equivalent FSM network. Any implementation of the CFSM network exhibits a behavior (allowed sequences of events) contained in the behavior of its specification.

Verification, for example, involves checking whether an undesirable behavior, expressed as a timed sequence of events σ, is consistent with the specification. If σ cannot occur in the specification, neither can it occur in a correctly derived implementation; the latter defines a subset of behaviors of the former. Examples of properties of our seat-belt system are "The alarm will not be on forever" (untimed) and "The alarm will not be on for more than 6 seconds" (timed). After modeling both the system and the properties, we can perform implementation-independent verification with existing formal verification tools, such as Kurshan[1] describes.

Between the abstracted behavior of a specification (an FSM network in our case) and the actual behavior of a given implementation there are a number of intermediate models that we can use as input to a formal verification algorithm. We can obtain one such intermediate model by composing the specification (as proposed in Alur, Courcourbetis, and

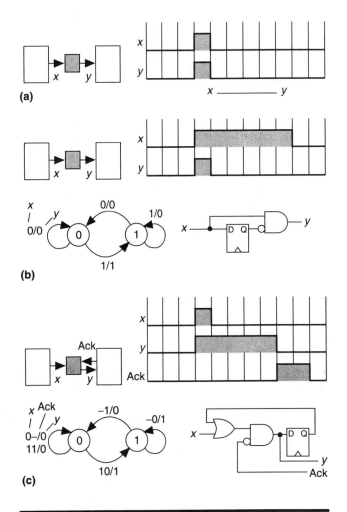

Figure 5. Interface types: the A and B blocks of a hardware-to-hardware interface (a); B block of a software-to-hardware interface (b); and A block of a hardware-to-software interface (c).

Dill[14]) with an implementation-specific component called a timing descriptor. The timing descriptor captures information about the allowed delays in a given implementation. Obtained trivially as 1-clock delays are portions of the timing descriptor related to hardware. For software, computing the maximum/minimum/average runtime, or giving a probability distribution, is desirable.

Specification refinement is a novel way of using formal verification. Initially, the designer specifies a set of properties that the system should satisfy, along with the description of the system in the form of a network of CFSMs with unbounded delays. Then, the designer checks the model with respect to some properties; the results define the information required to build the timing descriptor.

One major obstacle in formal verification is that deciphering an error trace and determining the exact cause of the failure is generally difficult. Active research is underway to efficiently return a set of minimal error traces that can help the designer pinpoint the cause of the failure.

Another obstacle is the complexity of models (also known as the state explosion problem). The size of a model can easily grow, especially when precise timing information must be considered. As an example, we modeled the seat-belt system described earlier as an implementation-independent network of two CFSMs, plus a CFSM that models the unpredictable behavior of the user. There, hardware, software, and human speeds differ by several orders of magnitude. Even with an unrealistically coarse base clock of 0.1 seconds, we have a total of 60,000,000 states. The longest run requires about 6.5 hours of CPU time on a DEC5000/125 with 64 Mbytes of memory. Dense-time algorithms[14] may be one way to cope with complexity, but more research needs to be done to make these algorithms applicable to problems of real-life magnitude.

Our methodology for designing hardware-software systems exhibits the following characteristics:

- It is well-suited to small control-dominated embedded systems.
- It is based on events as a basic communication primitive. Events are low-level enough to be efficiently implemented both in hardware and software, without imposing unnecessary overheads, and yet general enough to allow the construction of more powerful communication schemes.
- Since both hardware and software can be transparently derived from the same CFSM specification, we need not commit ourselves to a particular mix of software-hardware implementation a priori.
- We use an FSM-based model throughout the design process, thus preserving formal properties. The FSM model derived from a CFSM is compatible with the input format of many formal verification algorithms.
- Verification can proceed both at the specification and implementation levels. In addition, the results of formal verification can serve as a guide in specification refinement.

Already in place are many of the tools necessary for a complete synthesis system. In particular, an early version of the ESTEREL translator and of the synthesis environment described in Figure 2, including hardware and software synthesis, are functional.

In the future, we plan to explore the possibility of adopting formal verification methods that do not require an expensive translation of a CFSM into equivalent FSMs. We would like to exploit different time scales pertaining to different implementation and environment domains.

We also want to investigate the possibility of automated constraint-driven partitioning algorithms for mixed hardware-software systems.

References

1. R.P. Kurshan, "Analysis of Discrete Event Coordination," *Lecture Notes in Computer Science*, J.W. de Bakker, W.P. de Roever, and G. Rozenberg, eds., Springer-Verlag, Berlin, Heidelberg, Germany, 1990, pp. 414-453.
2. A. Benveniste and G. Berry, "The Synchronous Approach to Reactive and Real-Time Systems," *Proc. IEEE*, Vol. 79, No. 9, IEEE, Piscataway, N.J., 1991, pp. 1270-1282.
3. D. Druzinski and D. Har'el, "Using Statecharts for Hardware Description and Synthesis," *IEEE Trans. Computer-Aided Design*, Vol. 8, No. 7, 1989, pp. 798-807.
4. N. Woo, A. Dunlop, and W. Wolf, "Codesign from Cospecification," *Computer*, Vol. 27, No. 1, Jan. 1994, pp. 42-47.
5. R.K. Gupta, C.N. Coelho, Jr., and G. DeMicheli, "Program Implementation Schemes for Hardware-Software Systems," *Computer*, Vol. 27, No. 1, Jan. 1994, pp. 48-55.
6. P. Chou, R. Ortega, and G. Borriello, "Synthesis of Hardware/Software Interface in Microcontroller-Based Systems," *Proc. Int'l Conf. Computer-Aided Design*, IEEE Computer Society Press, Los Alamitos, Calif., 1992, pp. 488-495.
7. M.C. McFarland, T.J. Kowalski, and M.J. Peman, "Language and Formal Semantics of the Specification System CPA," *Proc. Int'l Workshop Hardware-Software Codesign*, CS Press, 1991, pp. 342-345.
8. N. Halbwachs et al., "The Synchronous Data Flow Programming Language LUSTRE," *Proc. IEEE*, Vol. 79, No. 9, IEEE, Sept. 1991, pp. 1305-1320.
9. W. Wolf et al., "The Princeton University Behavioral Synthesis System," *Proc. 29th ACM/IEEE Design Automation Conf.*, Assn. Computing Machinery, June 1992, pp. 182-187.
10. M. Chiodo et al., "A Formal Specification Model for Hardware/Software Codesign," Tech. Report UCB/ERL M93/48, University of California at Berkeley, Berkeley, Calif., June 1993.
11. W. Baker, "Application of the Synchronous/Reactive Model to the VHDL Language," Tech. Report, UCB/ERL-93-10, U.C. Berkeley, 1993.
12. E.M. Sentovich et al., "Sequential Circuit Design Using Synthesis and Optimization," *Proc. Int'l Conf. Computer Design*, CS Press, Oct. 1992, pp. 328-333.
13. A.V. Aho, R. Sethi, and J.D. Ullman, *Compilers, Principles, Techniques, and Tools*, Addison-Wesley, Reading, Mass., 1988.
14. R. Alur, C. Courcoubetis, and D. Dill, "Model-Checking in Dense Real Time," *Information and Computation*, Vol. 104, No. 1, May 1993, pp. 2-34.

Massimiliano Chiodo currently serves as a software area leader at Magneti Marelli Electronics Division, Pavia, Italy. Recently, he was a visiting industrial fellow for Magneti Marelli at the University of California, Berkeley, where he worked on formal verification and hardware-software codesign.

Chiodo received his doctorate in physics from the Universitá degli Studi di Milano, Italy. He is a member of the IEEE.

Paolo Giusto has been working for Magneti Marelli, Turin, as software engineer. He is currently a Visiting Industrial Fellow for Magneti Marelli at the University of California, Berkeley, where is working with the hardware-software codesign group

Giusto received the Doctor of Information Sciences from Universitá di Torino, Italy, and received his MSc degree in hardware engineering from CEFRIEL in Milan, where he developed a tool for synthesis of PLAs. He is a member of the IEEE.

Attila Jurecska works for Magneti Marelli, Turin, Italy, as a software engineer, where he is currently participating in the Formal Languages project. He is also working on the development of a codesign environment, together with the hardware-software codesign group of the University of California, Berkeley.

Jurecska received his first MSc degree in electrical engineering from the Technical University of Budapest. He received his second M.Sc. degree in hardware engineering from CEFRIEL in Milan.

Harry C. Hsieh is currently a PhD student in the Electrical Engineering and Computer Science Department at the University of California, Berkeley. He has been a member of the technical staff at Hewlett-Packard's Mainline Systems Laboratory, and has worked at IBM's Federal System Division and T. J. Watson Research Center. His primary research interests include system-level design methodologies, logic synthesis, and hardware-software codesign.

Hsieh received a BS degree from University of Wisconsin, Madison, and an MS degree from Stanford University. He is a member of the IEEE.

Alberto Sangiovanni-Vincentelli is a professor of electrical engineering and computer sciences at the University of California, Berkeley, where he recently received the Distinguished Teaching Award. He has been a visiting professor at the Universities of Torino, Bologna, Pavia, Pisa, and Rome, and has served as advisor, founder, or director with a number of companies. He has published over 250 papers and three books in the area of CAD for VLSI.

Sangiovanni-Vincentelli holds a D.Eng. degree from the Politecnico di Milano, Italy. He is on the International Advisory Board of the Institute for Micro-Electronics of Singapore, is a Fellow of the IEEE, and belongs to the Berkeley Roundtable for International Economy (BRIE). He has also been the technical program chair and the general chair of the International Conference on CAD. He is a member of the IEEE and the IEEE Computer Society.

Luciano Lavagno is an assistant professor at the Politecnico di Torino, Italy, where his current research interests include synthesis of asynchronous and low-power circuits, concurrent design of mixed hardware and software systems, and formal verification of digital systems.

Lavagno received the D.Eng. from the Politecnico di Torino and his PhD in electrical engineering from the University of California, Berkeley. In 1991, he received the Best Paper award at the 28th Design Automation Conference. He is a member of the IEEE and the IEEE Computer Society.

Direct questions concerning this article to Luciano Lavagno, Dip. di Elettronica, Politecnico di Torino, C. Duca degli Abruzzi 24, 10129, Torino, Italy; lavagno@polito.it.

Reader Interest Survey
Indicate your interest in this article by circling the appropriate number on the Reader Service Card.

Low 159   Medium 160   High 161

SOS: Synthesis of Application-Specific Heterogeneous Multiprocessor Systems*

SHIV PRAKASH

Mentor Graphics

ALICE C. PARKER

University of Southern California

This paper describes a formal synthesis approach to design of optimal application-specific heterogeneous multiprocessor systems. The method generates a static task execution schedule along with the structure of the multiprocessor system and a mapping of subtasks to processors. The approach itself is quite general, but its application is demonstrated with a specific style of design. The approach involves creation of a Mixed Integer–Linear Programming (MILP) model and solution of the model. A primary component of the model is the set of relations that must be satisfied to ensure proper ordering of various events in the task execution as well as to ensure completeness and correctness of the system. Several experiments and tradeoff studies have been performed using the approach. These results indicate that the approach can be a useful tool in designing application-specific multiprocessor systems. © 1992 Academic Press, Inc.

1. INTRODUCTION

With VLSI systems becoming more and more commonplace, and with myriads of new applications for VLSI systems, there is a growing need for design of hardware systems for specific applications (i.e., hardware systems that will perform given tasks efficiently). This paper addresses a technique for design of *heterogeneous multiprocessor systems* for given applications. Example application tasks where heterogeneous multiprocessor systems are desirable can be found in many domains, including digital signal processing, robotics, and control of power systems.

We consider a heterogeneous multiprocessor system to be a system which makes use of several different types of processors, processing components, and/or connectivity paradigms to optimize performance and/or cost-effectiveness of the system. For example, different processor/processing component types could include vector processors, SIMD processors, MIMD processors, special purpose processors, and data-flow processors. Similarly, different connectivity paradigms could include bus, point-to-point, ring, or a mixture of these. The Purdue mixed-mode PASM system [38] is an example of a heterogeneous system.

1.1. Motivation for Synthesis

Some questions that come up during the design of application-specific multiprocessor systems are the following (the list is not exhaustive):

• how to consider all the relevant factors, costs, constraints, and objectives during the design,
• how to decide the number and types of processors to be included in the system,
• how to decide the interconnection between the selected processors,
• how to use the designed system effectively to perform the given application task, and
• how to map and schedule the subtasks onto the processors.

Obviously, the answers to these questions are difficult to obtain. It is important to devise systematic methods for designing such systems. As a matter of fact, answers to several design questions depend on the characteristics of the specific application task under consideration. Hence, it seems appropriate to consider such task characteristics while designing the system; i.e., the system should be specifically tuned to the application at hand. With this in mind, we describe an "automatic synthesis approach" for design of application-specific multiprocessor systems. In such an approach, one starts with a given application and designs a complete system considering the application characteristics and all other relevant factors.

1.2. Overview of the SOS Approach

Some of the questions mentioned in Section 1.1 relate to the design of the system while others relate to how to effectively use the system. It is our view that in order to optimize overall performance and/or cost-effectiveness

---

* This work was supported in part by the Department of the Air Force, the Department of the Army, and the Department of the Navy, Contract N00039-87-C-0194, and in part by the Defense Advanced Research Projects Agency, monitored by the Federal Bureau of Investigation, under Contract JFBI90092. The views and conclusions considered in this document are those of the authors and should not be interpreted as necessarily representing the official policies, either expressed or implied, of the Defense Advanced Research Projects Agency or the U.S. Government.

of the system, it is imperative to consider issues related to both types of questions while designing the system. The SOS (Synthesis Of Systems) approach reflects this view. One of the prime concerns relating to the effective usage of the system is the issue of scheduling/mapping the application task onto the system. Indeed, the SOS approach is scheduling-driven and it deals with scheduling/mapping as a primary issue. The synthesis technique described here produces a custom multiprocessor system, maps the subtasks onto the system, and provides a static schedule for the task execution.

SOS assumes the application domain is specified in terms of a task data flow graph (Fig. 1). The task data flow graph specifies a set of subtasks (nodes in the graph) that need to be performed and the data precedence between them (arcs in the graph). Given the task data flow graph, the goal is to synthesize a multiprocessor system which meets various cost and performance constraints. The multiprocessor system is specified in terms of a set of processors and the interconnections between them. An example system is shown in Fig. 2. Synthesizing a system involves making decisions about the number and types of processors, the overall interconnection between the processors, and the scheduling of subtasks on the processors.

The SOS approach involves creation of a formal model of the multiprocessor synthesis problem using mathematical programming and the solution of this model. This approach is a natural outgrowth of the work described by Chu *et al.* [6], Mehrotra and Talukdar [30], and Hafer and Parker [19]. Hafer's notation has been adopted wherever it is meaningful to do so. *Our research focuses on the automatic design of the multiprocessor system itself, not merely the mapping of tasks onto a given system.* The SOS approach can be used to explore different intercon-

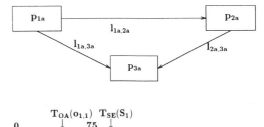

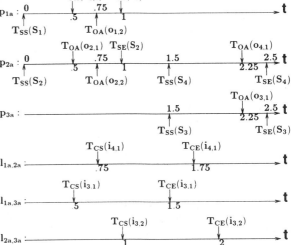

FIG. 2. Synthesized multiprocessor system I and schedule for Example 1.

nection styles; e.g., bus, point-to-point, ring, or a mixture of these. SOS assumes there is no global clock and communications between subtasks are asynchronous at the task level. A distinguishing feature of the research is the fact that SOS designs a truly heterogeneous system, which allows a more precise tailoring of the synthesized system to a specific application. SOS is capable of handling two types of heterogeneity:

- *Heterogeneity of Type I.* This refers to heterogeneity in terms of the functionality of the processors. Two processors could be different in terms of the types of subtasks they are capable of performing. This notion allows inclusion of special-purpose processors in the system.

- *Heterogeneity of Type II.* This refers to heterogeneity in terms of the cost-speed characteristics of the processors. Two processors could be capable of performing a given subtask, but the speeds of execution are different.

A complete mathematical programming formulation of the problem requires specification of an objective function that has to be optimized and a set of constraints that have to be satisfied. The objective function can be any function which can be linearized; e.g., the total system cost, or the overall system performance. The set of constraints consists of the correctness constraints that must be satisfied for the overall task to be performed correctly

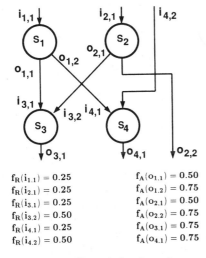

FIG. 1. Example 1 task graph.

as well as the arbitrary timing and cost constraints imposed by the designer. The correctness constraints consist primarily of the relations that ensure proper ordering of the subtasks and the data transfers, taking into account the timing involved and the relations that express the conditions for complete and correct system configuration. In order to express the various constraints and the objective function, SOS defines certain variables related to the system. The necessary variables fall into two basic categories: the *timing variables* (real variables which represent timings of various critical events in the operation of the system) and the *binary variables* (0–1 variables which represent the implementation decisions regarding the system configuration). Several constraints composing the mathematical programming model turn out to be nonlinear relations. These relations are linearized and the model is converted into an MILP (Mixed Integer–Linear Programming) formulation. *Bozo*[1] [18] solves the MILP model by invoking a commercial linear programming package, XLP, developed by XMP Software, Inc.

SOS is being developed as part of the USC (Unified System Construction) Project [33]. The strength of SOS lies in the fact that it is quite general and flexible. The approach allows us to modify, extend, and enhance the model to include more design possibilities and variations easily. The exact form of constraints used can be tailored to meet the characteristics of the design problem at hand. Also, the approach offers a great degree of flexibility in handling arbitrary constraints as they can be expressed using the timing and binary variables defined in the model.

The organization of the rest of the paper is as follows. Section 2 briefly surveys some of the related research. Section 3 describes the SOS approach in detail by applying it to a specific style of design; Section 3.1 presents the computation model used to represent the application task to be executed on the system, Section 3.2 describes the architecture style chosen for the system to be designed, Section 3.3 describes the complete SOS mathematical programming model for the style under consideration, and Section 3.4 describes how to linearize the specific SOS model and solve it as an MILP problem. Section 4 describes some examples and experimental results in detail; Section 4.1 presents some synthesis experiments with an example of four subtasks, Section 4.2 describes some tradeoff studies using the same example, and Section 4.3 describes some synthesis experiments with another example (nine subtasks). Section 5 comments on the usefulness and significance of the SOS approach. Section 6 outlines possible applications of the SOS approach and how the specific SOS model can be extended to deal with more complex design problems. Finally, Section 7 summarizes the paper and concludes that SOS can be a useful tool.

2. PREVIOUS RELATED RESEARCH

SOS is a scheduling-driven synthesis approach for application-specific multiprocessor systems. Synthesis methodologies for such systems are not well researched yet. The related past research of others covers a broad range of topics, which we briefly review here.

The multiprocessor scheduling problem has been researched quite extensively [21, 11, 8, 1, 14, 25]. However, most of the solutions concentrate on homogeneous systems and assume an existing multiprocessor architecture. Earlier solutions did not consider communication overhead. Many solutions are based on the *List Scheduling* (LS) heuristic. Fernandez and Bussell [11] propose a lower and an upper bound on the number of processors required to execute a task precedence graph in a time not exceeding the length of the critical path. They also determine a lower bound on the execution time for a given number of processors. Kasahara and Narita [25] describe heuristic algorithms, combining critical path ideas with branch-and-bound, for scheduling to minimize the execution time. However, neither of the efforts includes communication overhead. Some scheduling heuristics considering communication overhead are also reported; e.g., *ELS heuristic* [23], *ETF heuristic* [23], and *MH heuristic* [10]. Al-Mouhamed [3] proposes an approximate lower bound on the completion time, and approximate lower bounds on the number of processors and the number of communication links required to process a task precedence graph within this completion time. An approximate lower bound on the completion time is also estimated for a given number of processors.

There have been a number of research efforts directed towards the problem of task allocation for a given system. Several variants of the problem have been considered and several different approaches have been investigated. Inspired by Stone's work on the two-processor problem [39], graph-theoretic techniques have been researched for serially partitioned tasks (i.e., even though there are *m* subtasks, only one is active at one time); e.g., [36, 4]. In [5], Bokhari extends the prior research for serially partitioned tasks [4] to parallel tasks by explicitly taking concurrency into account. Shen and Tsai [37] model the task assignment problem as a graph matching problem. In [24], Indurkhya *et al.* use an analytical approach for modeling and optimization of multiprocessing execution time for random-graph models of programs. They derive an optimal task-assignment policy by optimizing the execution time and confirm intuitive results for the 2-processor and *n*-processor cases. Nicol [32] and

---

[1] A branch-and-bound program to solve MILP problems; developed by L. J. Hafer of Simon Fraser University.

Haddad [15] describe similar research. Heuristic approaches have also been applied to the task allocation problem [9, 7, 20]. Houstis [20] describes heuristic algorithms for task allocation to homogeneous bus connected systems, along with an iterative algorithm to determine the optimal number of processors.

Mathematical programming has also been applied to the problem of task allocation for a given system. Chu *et al.* [6] described an integer 0–1 programming approach to the problem. They considered the problem of optimal allocation of a set of m subtasks to a set of p (fixed) processors already interconnected in some fashion. Ma *et al.* [28] also report an integer programming model for task allocation. However, the models described in [6, 28] do not consider the effects of precedence relations in the data flow among the subtasks. We are using a similar approach for synthesis and we take into account the precedence relations. Nonlinear programming has also been used for task allocation under an assumption that the given task can be split into arbitrary size subtasks [2, 16]. A limitation of such research is that it is not directly applicable to practical situations where partitioning can usually be done only at specific points.

One research effort by Talukdar and Mehrotra [30] is oriented towards synthesis of multiprocessors. In this work, a simplified and similar version of our problem is described, and the goal is to find a minimum execution time system which meets the system cost constraint. The problem is modeled using mathematical programming, though the solution procedure is heuristic and iterative. The core of the solution procedure consists of an interactive program that estimates the minimum execution time of the task for a given system. In this work, no explicit consideration is given to the delays/costs associated with the communication links. Our research models the communication links explicitly.

Mathematical programming has also been applied to the data path synthesis problem. Hafer and Parker [19] used a mixed integer–linear programming approach to automatically synthesize register-transfer level datapaths, given a data flow/control flow graph description of the hardware. Hwang *et al.* [22] have described an integer–linear programming model for the scheduling problem in data path synthesis under resource constraints and time constraints.

There have been research efforts directed towards synthesis of array-processor architectures [26, 12, 31, 27]. Such architectures are usually characterized by synchronized operation, and all the processors perform nearly identical and relatively simple computations. Synchronous operation makes array processors best suited for computations displaying reasonably regular structure and flow of data. However, more often a task contains a mix of quite different subtasks with differing processing requirements and consequently heterogeneous systems are more suitable. Our research is geared toward the synthesis of such heterogeneous systems.

Superconcurrency [13] is a research effort directed towards heterogeneous processing. It is a form of distributed heterogeneous processing developed to support a variety of Navy High Performance Computing requirements. It is a general technique for matching and managing a heterogeneous suite of superspeed processors.

3. A SPECIFIC SOS MODEL

As mentioned in Section 1.2, the SOS approach can be applied to varying design situations and design styles. The approach involves creation of a mathematical programming model and solution of the model. Depending on the specific design problem at hand, a specific model can be created. The challenge is to come up with the specific mathematical programming model applicable to the design problem at hand. The answer lies in the general characteristics of the application tasks as well as the systems being considered. Let us refer to the relevant characteristics of the application tasks as the *task model*, and those of systems as the *system model*. The task model describes the computational model underlying the application task. The system model describes the style of architecture used to implement the task. The task model and the system model together determine the mathematical programming model to be created. The application task itself determines the specific constraints to be used to solve a particular problem. In this paper, we describe application of the approach to a specific task model and system model.

3.1. A Representative Task Model

The task consists of a set of subtasks. Each subtask requires certain input data and produces certain output data. Inputs to a subtask may come from other subtasks and outputs from a subtask may go to other subtasks. The set of subtasks and the input–output relationships among them can be expressed by a task data flow graph (directed acyclic graph) as shown in Fig. 1. The subtask nodes are labeled S_1, S_2, etc. (S_a in general). The input end of a data arc is labeled $i_{a,b}$ if it provides the bth input to subtask S_a, and the output end is labeled $o_{a,c}$ if it transmits the cth output from the subtask S_a. Although we represent the task by a data flow graph, we consider a subtle distinction between our model and the traditional data flow model. With the traditional meaning, a subtask would require all the inputs before starting its execution and none of the outputs would be available until after its execution was over. However, in our model subtasks do not require all the inputs before starting their execution and they may produce some outputs even before their completion. To express this possibility, each input $i_{a,b}$ has a parameter

$f_R(i_{a,b})$ associated with it which is the fraction of the subtask S_a that can proceed without requiring the input $i_{a,b}$. Similarly, each output $o_{a,c}$ has a parameter $f_A(o_{a,c})$ associated with it which specifies that the output $o_{a,c}$ becomes available when $f_A(o_{a,c})$ fraction of the subtask S_a is completed. For each subtask S_a, a set P_a represents the set of processors capable of executing it. A data arc from node S_{a1} to node S_{a2} implies that some data are transferred from the subtask S_{a1} to the subtask S_{a2}. The volume of data transferred varies from arc to arc, and a parameter $V_{a1,a2}$ specifying the volume is associated with each arc.

3.2. A Representative System Model

The multiprocessor system is specified in terms of the processors selected and the interconnection architecture between them. For the specific style under consideration, we assume point-to-point interconnection; i.e., if a processor p_{d1} needs to send data to another processor p_{d2}, then there must be a direct communication link from p_{d1} to p_{d2}. Each processor is assumed to have local memory, and all the interprocessor communication takes place by message passing over communication links. The subtasks get executed on the processors and the necessary data transfers take place over the communication links.

A processor could be executing at most one subtask at any given time. Also, one and only one processor performs a given subtask. So, once execution of a subtask begins on a processor, the subtask occupies the processor for an uninterrupted duration of time before it completes. The length of the duration is equal to the execution time of the subtask, which depends on the processor type on which it is performed. A parameter, denoted as $D_{PS}(P_t, S_a)$, specifies the execution time for the subtask S_a if processor type P_t is selected to perform it. If two subtasks are to be executed by the same processor, one must be scheduled to begin after the other is completed.

The data transfer corresponding to an arc from subtask S_{a1} to subtask S_{a2} may be a *remote transfer* (if S_{a1} and S_{a2} are mapped to different processors); or it may be a *local transfer* within the same processor (if S_{a1} and S_{a2} are mapped to the same processor). Delay associated with a data transfer depends on whether it is a remote transfer or a local transfer.[2] The local transfer delay is represented by the parameter D_{CL} which specifies the time taken in transferring a unit volume of data locally. The remote transfer delay is represented by the parameter D_{CR} which specifies the time taken in transferring a unit volume of data remotely. In practice, the time spent in performing a remote data transfer depends on the amount of traffic in the interconnection network; if two data transfers are supposed to take place over the same communication link at the same time, then the second can only start after the first is completed (the second set of data will remain held in the local memory of the processor producing it). Essentially, the time spent in remote transfer consists of the *waiting time* and the *actual transfer time*. The parameter D_{CR} only captures the actual transfer time component. The waiting time component is captured in the mathematical programming model as a delay in scheduling the communication by enforcing exclusion in the usage of the communication links. Similar to subtask execution, once a data transfer operation begins, the communication link is released only after the operation is completed; i.e., the link is busy for an uninterrupted duration of $D_{CR}V_{a1,a2}$ time units if $V_{a1,a2}$ is the volume of data associated with the operation.

Our system model assumes overlap between computation and I/O operations. Data transfer operations are taken care of by I/O modules. A subtask can produce output data at intermediate points of its execution. Transfer of such output data can start as soon as they are available (obviously, only if required communication links are available) without delaying the completion of the subtask. It is not necessary to wait for the completion of the subtask before starting the transfer of the output data, since it is assumed that the processor executing this subtask does not get involved in the data transfer operation. We assume for this specific model that each processor in the system will have the necessary I/O modules. Similarly, the processor receiving the data does not get involved in the data transfer operation, and could be performing computations while the data is being received by its I/O module (and so the inputs of the subtask could arrive after the processor has already started executing the subtask).

A set P represents the set of all the processors (with varying functionality, cost and performance) available for selection as part of the synthesized system, where $P = \cup_a P_a$. Associated with each processor $p_d \in P$ is a parameter C_d which specifies the cost of the processor. C_L specifies the cost of creating a communication link between two processors.

3.3. The Mathematical Programming Model

3.3.1. The Constraints

output data value $o_{a,c}$ computed by subtask S_a has become available.

Timing Variables. There are three classes of timing variables.

- Data availability timing variables:
  —Input data availability, $T_{IA}(i_{a,b})$. Time when the data required by input $i_{a,b}$ of subtask S_a are available for use.
  —Output data availability, $T_{OA}(o_{a,c})$. Time when the

---
[2] Local transfer delay could be negligible compared to the remote transfer delay.

output data value $o_{a,c}$ computed by subtask S_a has become available.

- Subtask execution timing variables:
  —Subtask execution start, $T_{SS}(S_a)$. Time when the execution of subtask S_a actually begins.
  —Subtask execution end, $T_{SE}(S_a)$. Time when the execution of subtask S_a is completed.
- Data transfer timing variables:
  —Data transfer start, $T_{CS}(i_{a,b})$. Time when the transfer of the data required by input $i_{a,b}$ of subtask S_a actually begins.
  —Data transfer end, $T_{CE}(i_{a,b})$. Time when the transfer of the data required by input $i_{a,b}$ of subtask S_a ends.

Binary Variables. There are two types of binary variables.

- Subtask-to-processor-mapping variable, $\sigma_{d,a}$: The variables of this type specify the mapping between the subtasks and the processors. $\sigma_{d,a} = 1$ indicates processor p_d will implement subtask S_a.
- Data-transfer-type variable, $\gamma_{a1,a2}$: The variables of this type specify the data transfer type for the various data arcs. $\gamma_{a1,a2} = 1(0)$ indicates that data transfer from subtask S_{a1} to subtask S_{a2} is a remote (local) transfer.

The necessary constraints have been classified into ten categories as follows.

- Processor-selection constraint: For each subtask S_a, a set of processors P_a is available to implement it. In order for the implementation to be correct, one and only one processor should be selected to implement the subtask. Thus, for each subtask S_a, the following must be satisfied:

$$\sum_{d | p_d \in P_a} \sigma_{d,a} = 1 \quad (3.3.1)$$

- Data-transfer-type constraint: $\gamma_{a1,a2}$ is a variable which indicates whether the data transfer from the subtask S_{a1} to the subtask S_{a2} is a local transfer or a remote transfer. Now, if the subtasks S_{a1} and S_{a2} are mapped to the same processor (say p_d, where $p_d \in P_{a1}$ and $p_d \in P_{a2}$), then we know that it is a local transfer, and thus $\gamma_{a1,a2} = 0$. However, if they are mapped to different processors, then the data transfer is remote, and thus $\gamma_{a1,a2} = 1$. Thus, the defining equation for $\gamma_{a1,a2}$ is

$$\gamma_{a1,a2} = 1 - \sum_{d | p_d \in P_{a1} \cap P_{a2}} \sigma_{d,a1} \sigma_{d,a2}. \quad (3.3.2)$$

We have such an equation for each pair of subtasks communicating with each other.

- Input-availability constraint: $T_{IA}(i_{a,b})$ is the time the data required at input $i_{a,b}$ will be available, which will be the time $T_{CE}(i_{a,b})$ when the data transfer has ended. So, for each input $i_{a,b}$, we have

$$T_{IA}(i_{a,b}) = T_{CE}(i_{a,b}). \quad (3.3.3)$$

- Output-availability constraint: Once execution of the subtask S_a begins, a certain time elapses before an output data value $o_{a,c}$ produced by the subtask becomes available. The time elapsed would be the time taken in executing $f_A(o_{a,c})$ fraction of the subtask; and so the time $T_{OA}(o_{a,c})$ must satisfy the following relation (we will have such a relation for each output):

$$T_{OA}(o_{a,c}) = T_{SS}(S_a) + f_A(o_{a,c})(T_{SE}(S_a) - T_{SS}(S_a)). \quad (3.3.4)$$

- Subtask-execution-start constraint: $T_{SS}(S_a)$ is the time the subtask S_a begins execution. There must be a certain relationship between the time a given subtask begins its execution and the times at which its various inputs become available. Since $f_R(i_{a,b})$ fraction of the subtask S_a can proceed without requiring the input $i_{a,b}$, the following relation must be satisfied for all the inputs $i_{a,b}$ to the subtask:

$$T_{IA}(i_{a,b}) \leq T_{SS}(S_a) + f_R(i_{a,b})(T_{SE}(S_a) - T_{SS}(S_a)). \quad (3.3.5)$$

- Subtask-execution-end constraint: Once execution of a subtask begins, a time equal to the execution time of the subtask must elapse before the subtask is completed. Execution time of the subtask depends on the processor type being used for it. A priori we do not know which processor type a given subtask S_a is going to be mapped to. Any processor from the set P_a could be selected to execute the subtask S_a. The uncertainty can be expressed by the following relation (where $\text{Typ}(p_d)$ represents the type of the processor p_d). The summation acts as a selection since only one $\sigma_{d,a} = 1$ for each a (for each subtask S_a, we need such a relation):

$$T_{SE}(S_a) = T_{SS}(S_a) + \sum_{d | p_d \in P_a} \sigma_{d,a} D_{PS}(\text{Typ}(p_d), S_a). \quad (3.3.6)$$

- Data-transfer-start constraint: The time at which transfer of data begins must be after the output data are produced. Except for external inputs, for each input datum $i_{a2,b2}$ (to the subtask S_{a2}) being supplied by another subtask's output, if the output supplying the datum is $o_{a1,c1}$, the following relation must be satisfied by $T_{CS}(i_{a2,b2})$, the start of the data transfer:

$$T_{CS}(i_{a2,b2}) \geq T_{OA}(o_{a1,c1}). \quad (3.3.7)$$

- Data-transfer-end constraint: The time at which transfer of data ends, T_{CE}, depends on whether the transfer is remote or local. A priori we do not know which case will occur. However, the two possibilities can be combined into one single relation using the variable $\gamma_{a1,a2}$. Thus, for each input datum $i_{a2,b2}$ being supplied by another subtask S_{a1}, we have

$$T_{CE}(i_{a2,b2}) = T_{CS}(i_{a2,b2}) + \gamma_{a1,a2}D_{CR}V_{a1,a2} \\ + (1 - \gamma_{a1,a2})D_{CL}V_{a1,a2}. \quad (3.3.8)$$

The next two categories of constraints ensure that the hardware resources (processors, communication links) are shared correctly. These constraints ensure that the same hardware resource is not scheduled to perform more than one function during any given time interval. In order to express these constraints concisely, we define a special function called an overlap function L (as defined in [19]). The function is defined on two closed intervals of time, $[t1, t2]$ and $[t3, t4]$ (where $t1 < t2$ and $t3 < t4$), as

$$L([t1, t2], [t3, t4]) = \begin{cases} 1, & \text{if the intervals overlap} \\ 0, & \text{otherwise.} \end{cases}$$

- Processor-usage-exclusion constraint: If two subtasks S_{a1} and S_{a2} are being executed by the same processor p_d, then the two subtasks must not be scheduled to be executed at the same time. The situation that two subtasks S_{a1} and S_{a2} are being implemented by the same processor p_d implies $\sigma_{d,a1} = \sigma_{d,a2} = 1$. For each processor p_d and each pair of subtasks S_{a1} and S_{a2} such that the sets of processors P_{a1} and P_{a2} available to implement the subtasks contain the processor p_d, the following relation ensures that the overlap in the usage of the processor by the two subtasks is prevented:

$$\sigma_{d,a1}\sigma_{d,a2}L([T_{SS}(S_{a1}), T_{SE}(S_{a1})], [T_{SS}(S_{a2}), T_{SE}(S_{a2})]) = 0. \quad (3.3.9)$$

- Communication-link-usage-exclusion constraint: If the data required by two inputs $i_{a1,b1}$ and $i_{a2,b2}$ are being transmitted over the same communication link, then the two data transfers must not be scheduled at the same time. Let us say the input datum $i_{a1,b1}$ is supplied by the subtask S_{a3} and the input datum $i_{a2,b2}$ is supplied by the subtask S_{a4}. The two inputs $i_{a1,b1}$ and $i_{a2,b2}$ will be transmitted over the same communication link if the two subtasks S_{a1} and S_{a2} are mapped to the same processor, say p_{d2}, and also the subtasks S_{a3} and S_{a4} are mapped to the same processor, say p_{d1} (in that case, both the inputs will be transmitted over the communication link from processor p_{d1} to processor p_{d2}). So, for each processor pair (p_{d1}, p_{d2}) and each pair of inputs $i_{a1,b1}$ and $i_{a2,b2}$, if the input $i_{a1,b1}$ is being supplied from S_{a3} to S_{a1} and the input $i_{a2,b2}$ from S_{a4} to S_{a2} then the following relation ensures that the overlap in the usage of the communication link from processor p_{d1} to processor p_{d2} by the two data transfers is prevented:

$$\sigma_{d2,a1}\sigma_{d2,a2}\sigma_{d1,a3}\sigma_{d1,a4}L([T_{CS}(i_{a1,b1}), T_{CE}(i_{a1,b1})], \\ [T_{CS}(i_{a2,b2}), T_{CE}(i_{a2,b2})]) = 0. \quad (3.3.10)$$

The above constraint also captures the waiting times associated with the remote data transfers.

3.3.2. Objective Functions

Two of the most important goals that the designer may wish to optimize are the overall system performance and the total system cost.

Overall System Performance. The performance is frequently measured by how fast the system can perform the given task, the time at which the task is completed (or all the subtasks are completed). If T_F is a real variable representing the time at which the task is completed, then the objective is to *minimize* T_F. To ensure that T_F represents the time at which all the subtasks are completed, we need to introduce the following constraint in the model (for each subtask S_a):

$$T_F \geq T_{SE}(S_a). \quad (3.3.11)$$

Total System Cost. The total cost of the system can be expressed as the sum of the costs of the processors selected and the costs of the links created. In order to do so, we need to define two types of binary variables as follows.

- Processor-selection variable, β_d: The variables of this type specify which processors have been selected in the synthesized architecture. $\beta_d = 1$ indicates that the processor p_d is included in the system.
- Communication-link-creation variable, $\chi_{d1,d2}$: The variables of this type specify what communication links are present in the synthesized architecture. $\chi_{d1,d2} = 1$ indicates there exists a communication link from the processor p_{d1} to the processor p_{d2} in the designed system.

Using the variables defined above, the objective is to

$$\text{MINIMIZE} \sum_{d | p_d \in P} \beta_d C_d + \sum_{d1,d2 | p_{d1} \in P \wedge p_{d2} \in P} \chi_{d1,d2} C_L,$$

where C_d is the cost of a processor p_d and C_L is the cost of building a link between two processors, as defined in Section 3.2. The variables of type β_d are related to the variables of type $\sigma_{d,a}$. A processor p_d will be included in the system if and only if at least one of the subtasks S_a ($p_d \in P_a$) is mapped to it, which implies that the variable β_d is the logical OR of all the $\sigma_{d,a}$ variables. This can be expressed by introducing the following constraint into the model (for all a such that $p_d \in P_a$):

$$\beta_d \geq \sigma_{d,a}. \qquad (3.3.12)$$

The variables of type $\chi_{d1,d2}$ are also related to the variables of type $\sigma_{d,a}$. A communication link is created from processor p_{d1} to processor p_{d2} if and only if at least one of the subtasks S_{a1} ($p_{d1} \in P_{a1}$) mapped to the processor p_{d1} needs to send data to at least one of the subtasks S_{a2} ($p_{d2} \in P_{a2}$) mapped to the processor p_{d2}. So the variable $\chi_{d1,d2}$ is the logical OR of all the product terms of the form ($\sigma_{d1,a1}\sigma_{d2,a2}$), where the subtask S_{a1} supplies some data to the subtask S_{a2}. This condition leads to the introduction of following constraint in the model (for all $a1$, $a2$ such that $p_{d1} \in P_{a1}$ and $p_{d2} \in P_{a2}$ and subtask S_{a1} sends data to subtask S_{a2}):

$$\chi_{d1,d2} \geq \sigma_{d1,a1}\sigma_{d2,a2}. \qquad (3.3.13)$$

The essence of the model has been presented. It is easy to see that *arbitrary constraints imposed by the designer (within the semantics of the model) can be expressed using the timing and binary variables defined in the model.*

3.4. Synthesis Using the Model

3.4.1. Linearization of the Model

Several constraints comprising the mathematical programming model presented in Section 3.3 are nonlinear relations. In order to solve the model as an MILP, these relations must be linearized and the model converted into an MILP formulation.

Equation (3.3.2) is nonlinear. It can be linearized by defining a binary variable of the form $\delta_{d,a1,a2}$ for each product of the form ($\sigma_{d,a1}\sigma_{d,a2}$). Using the new variables defined, Eq. (3.3.2) can be replaced by the following set of linear relations:

$$\gamma_{a1,a2} = 1 - \sum_{d \mid p_d \in P_{a1} \cap P_{a2}} \delta_{d,a1,a2} \qquad (3.4.14)$$

$$\delta_{d,a1,a2} \leq \sigma_{d,a1} \qquad (3.4.15)$$

$$\delta_{d,a1,a2} \leq \sigma_{d,a2}. \qquad (3.4.16)$$

Now, let us consider linearization of Eq. (3.3.9). The constraint says that if two subtasks S_{a1} and S_{a2} are executed on the same processor p_d, then there must be no overlap in their execution time intervals. This implies that either the start time of S_{a1} is sometime after the completion time of S_{a2} or the start time of S_{a2} is sometime after the completion time of S_{a1}. Let us define a binary variable $\alpha_{a1,a2}$ whose value decides which of the two pos-

sibilities occurs. $\alpha_{a1,a2} = 1$ implies S_{a1} is executed first. Using this variable, Eq. (3.3.9) can be rewritten as the following pair of nonlinear relations:

$$T_{SS}(S_{a2}) \geq \alpha_{a1,a2}\sigma_{d,a1}\sigma_{d,a2}T_{SE}(S_{a1})$$

$$T_{SS}(S_{a1}) \geq (1 - \alpha_{a1,a2})\sigma_{d,a1}\sigma_{d,a2}T_{SE}(S_{a2}).$$

To linearize the above pair, let us define a constant T_M whose value is larger than the possible values of all the timing variables in the model. Now, the following two linear relations express the desired constraint:

$$T_{SS}(S_{a2}) \geq T_{SE}(S_{a1}) - (3 - \alpha_{a1,a2} - \sigma_{d,a1} - \sigma_{d,a2})T_M \qquad (3.4.17)$$

$$T_{SS}(S_{a1}) \geq T_{SE}(S_{a2}) - (2 + \alpha_{a1,a2} - \sigma_{d,a1} - \sigma_{d,a2})T_M. \qquad (3.4.18)$$

Similarly, to linearize Eq. (3.3.10), we need to define a binary variable $\phi_{a1,b1,a2,b2}$. $\phi_{a1,b1,a2,b2} = 1$ indicates that the data transfer for $i_{a1,b1}$ takes place before the data transfer for $i_{a2,b2}$ if the same communication link is used for both the transfers. Using this variable, Eq. (3.3.10) can be rewritten as the following pair of linear relations:

$$T_{CS}(i_{a2,b2}) \geq T_{CE}(i_{a1,b1}) - (5 - \phi_{a1,b1,a2,b2} - \sigma_{d2,a1} - \sigma_{d2,a2} - \sigma_{d1,a3} - \sigma_{d1,a4})T_M \qquad (3.4.19)$$

$$T_{CS}(i_{a1,b1}) \geq T_{CE}(i_{a2,b2}) - (4 + \phi_{a1,b1,a2,b2} - \sigma_{d2,a1} - \sigma_{d2,a2} - \sigma_{d1,a3} - \sigma_{d1,a4})T_M. \qquad (3.4.20)$$

Finally, nonlinear Eq. (3.3.13) can be simply rewritten in the following linear form:

$$\chi_{d1,d2} \geq \sigma_{d1,a1} + \sigma_{d2,a2} - 1. \qquad (3.4.21)$$

3.4.2. Solution of the Model

The linearized MILP model is solved using the *Bozo* program [18]. As a result of solving the model, we get the following information as outputs:

- A multiprocessor system; i.e., the chosen set of processors and the interconnection architecture,
- A schedule for the subtasks, and
- Detailed timing information for computation and transfer of data.

4. EXPERIMENTS AND RESULTS

The specific model described in Section 3 was used to experiment with two example task graphs. The first example consists of four subtask nodes, while the second consists of nine. Some of the data related to these examples are taken from [30].

TABLE I
Processor Characteristics: Example 1

Proc.	Cost	\multicolumn{4}{c}{Execution time}
		S_1	S_2	S_3	S_4
p_1	4	1	1	—	3
p_2	5	3	1	2	1
p_3	2	—	3	1	—

4.1. Example 1. Four-Subtask Task Graph

This example data flow graph is shown in Fig. 1. Associated f_R and f_A parameters are also given in the figure, constraining input/output timing for the subtasks. We assume we have available three types of processors: p_1, p_2, and p_3. The costs of these processors and the execution times of various subtasks on the processors are given in Table I. An entry of "—" in the table implies that the particular processor is functionally not capable of performing the particular subtask. As is obvious from the table, different processors have different cost–speed–functionality characteristics. In this example the volume of data that needs to be communicated is one unit at each arc in the graph. Local transfer delay is given to be negligible; i.e., $D_{CL} = 0$. We are also given the communication link characteristics. The cost of a link, C_L, is one unit; and the remote transfer delay for a unit volume of data over a link, D_{CR}, is also one unit.

The MILP model for the example consists of 21 timing and 72 binary variables and 174 constraints. Bozo was used to generate four noninferior[3] systems. These different systems were generated by changing the constraint value for the total cost of the system and optimizing the overall performance of the system. Bozo's runtime to generate each of these designs is on the order of a few seconds. These runtimes are on a Solbourne Series5e/900 (similar to Sun SPARCsystem 4/490) with 128 MB of memory. Cost, performance, and runtime for the four designs are given in Table II. Note that the performance of the target system is measured by the time at which the overall task is completed. A brief discussion of these designs follows.

Design 1 consists of three processors: p_{1a}, a processor of type p_1; p_{2a}, a processor of type p_2; and p_{3a}, a processor of type p_3. Processor p_{1a} performs subtask S_1, processor p_{2a} performs subtasks S_2 and S_4 in that order, and processor p_{3a} performs subtask S_3. There are three communication links: $l_{1a,2a}$, $l_{1a,3a}$, and $l_{2a,3a}$. Data $i_{4,1}$ get transmitted

[3] A system (characterized by its cost and performance) is considered noninferior if cost (performance) cannot be improved without degrading performance (cost).

on link $l_{1a,2a}$, data $i_{3,1}$ get transmitted on link $l_{1a,3a}$, and data $i_{3,2}$ get transmitted on link $l_{2a,3a}$. As an illustration, this system is shown in Fig. 2. A detailed schedule for the various events is also shown in the figure. *Design 2* is similar to design 1, and also consists of three processors: p_{1a}, p_{2a}, and p_{3a}. However, it has only two links: $l_{1a,2a}$ and $l_{1a,3a}$. The presence of fewer links forces a change in the mapping between the resources and the events. Processor p_{1a} performs subtasks S_1 and S_2 in that order, processor p_{2a} performs subtask S_4, and processor p_{3a} performs subtask S_3. Data $i_{4,1}$ get transmitted on link $l_{1a,2a}$; data $i_{3,1}$ and data $i_{3,2}$ get transmitted on link $l_{1a,3a}$ in that order. *Design 3* consists of two processors: p_{1a}, a processor of type p_1, and p_{3a}, a processor of type p_3. Processor p_{1a} performs subtasks S_1 and S_4 in that order, and processor p_{3a} performs subtasks S_2 and S_3 in that order. There is a communication link: $l_{1a,3a}$. Data $i_{3,1}$ get transmitted on link $l_{1a,3a}$. *Design 4* consists of just one processor: p_{2a}, a processor of type p_2. The processor performs the subtasks S_2, S_1, S_3, and S_4 in that order.

4.2. Tradeoff Studies Using the Four-Subtask Graph

Some tradeoff studies were performed using the example in Section 4.1. We studied the role of intersubtask communication in synthesis of the systems. The study was performed by varying the ratio between communication times and execution times.

4.2.1. Experiment 1. Increase the Communication Time

In this experiment, we increased the volume of data to be transferred for each arc in the four-subtask task graph. All the other parameters remained as given in Section 4.1.

When the volume of data is doubled for each of the arcs (i.e., the volume is two units instead of one), three-processor designs become inferior. Only two designs remain noninferior: the two-processor design and the uniprocessor design.

The two-processor design also becomes inferior when the volume of data is made six times the original volume (i.e., the volume is six units for each arc). Only the uniprocessor design remains noninferior.

TABLE II
Example 1 Systems

Design	Runtime (s)	Cost	Performance (time units)
1	11	14	2.5
2	24	13	3
3	28	7	4
4	37	5	7

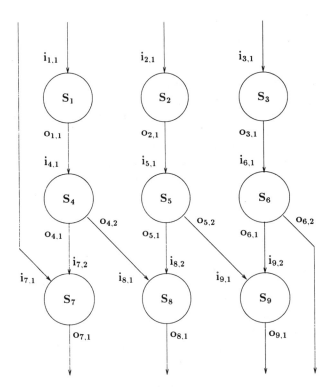

FIG. 3. Example 2 task graph.

4.2.2. Experiment 2. Increase the Execution Time

In this experiment, we increased the size of each of the subtasks (and thus the execution times in Table I). All the other parameters remained as given in Section 4.1.

When the size of each of the subtasks is doubled (and hence the execution time is doubled for each of the processor types), the number of noninferior designs becomes 5 (instead of 4). The new noninferior design consists of three processors: p_{1a}, p_{1b}, two processors of type p_1, and p_{3a}, a processor of type p_3. Processor p_{1a} performs subtasks S_1 and S_2 in that order, processor p_{1b} performs subtask S_4, and processor p_{3a} performs subtask S_3. There are two communication links: $l_{1a,1b}$ and $l_{1a,3a}$. Data $i_{4,1}$ get transmitted on link $l_{1a,1b}$, and data $i_{3,2}$ and data $i_{3,1}$ get transmitted on link $l_{1a,3a}$ in that order.

When the size of each of the subtasks is further increased and made three times the original size, the number of noninferior designs becomes 7 (as opposed to 5 for the double-size case above). The two new additions are a four-processor design and a new two-processor design. The four-processor design consists of p_{1a}, p_{1b}, two processors of type p_1, p_{2a}, a processor of type p_2, and p_{3a}, a processor of type p_3. Processor p_{1a} performs subtask S_1, processor p_{1b} performs subtask S_2, processor p_{2a} performs subtask S_4, and processor p_{3a} performs subtask S_3. There are three communication links: $l_{1a,2a}$, $l_{1a,3a}$, and $l_{1b,3a}$. Data $i_{4,1}$ get transmitted on link $l_{1a,2a}$, data $i_{3,1}$ gets transmitted on link $l_{1a,3a}$, and data $i_{3,2}$ gets transmitted on link $l_{1b,3a}$. The new two-processor design consists of p_{1a}, a processor of type p_1, and p_{2a}, a processor of type p_2. Processor p_{1a} performs subtasks S_1 and S_2 in that order, and processor p_{2a} performs subtasks S_3 and S_4 in that order. There is a communication link: $l_{1a,2a}$. Data $i_{3,1}$, data $i_{3,2}$, and data $i_{4,1}$ get transmitted on link $l_{1a,2a}$ in that order.

The results of experiments 1 and 2 essentially indicate what is known intuitively, that as the ratios between the intersubtask communication (in time units) and the sizes of subtasks (in time units) increase, designs with fewer processors are synthesized as they can achieve the desired performance with lower costs. However, as the sizes of subtasks increase (and thus intersubtask communication becomes relatively less important), multiprocessing becomes useful and designs with more processors are synthesized as they can provide better performance.

4.3. Example 2: Nine-Subtask Task Graph

The data flow graph is shown in Fig. 3. For this example, we assumed that a subtask requires all the inputs before it can start and that none of the outputs from a subtask become available until its execution is over. Again, there are three types of processors, with the costs and the execution times given in Table III. The volume of data is one unit for each arc. We are given $D_{CL} = 0$, $D_{CR} = 1$. For this graph, we synthesized systems for two different styles of interconnection.

4.3.1. Point-to-Point Interconnection Experiments

Here, as before, if two processors need to communicate, then there must be a direct link between them, and the cost of building a link $C_L = 1$. The MILP model consists of 47 timing and 225 binary variables, and 1081 constraints. We generated five noninferior systems by changing the constraint value for the total system cost, and optimizing the system performance. Bozo's runtime for each of these designs is on the order of a few hours, except for design 5. Cost, performance, and runtime for the five designs are given in Table IV. A brief discussion of the designs follows.

TABLE III
Processor Characteristics: Example 2

Proc.	Cost	Execution time								
		S_1	S_2	S_3	S_4	S_5	S_6	S_7	S_8	S_9
p_1	4	2	2	1	1	1	1	3	—	1
p_2	5	3	1	1	3	1	2	1	2	1
p_3	2	1	1	2	—	3	1	4	1	3

TABLE IV
Example 2 Systems (Point-to-Point)

Design	Runtime (min)	Cost	Performance (time units)
1	62.2	15	5
2	445.17	12	6
3	538.67	8	7
4	75.18	7	8
5	6416.87	5	15

Design 1 consists of three processors: p_{1a}, a processor of type p_1, p_{2a}, a processor of type p_2, and p_{3a}, a processor of type p_3. Processor p_{1a} performs subtasks S_3, S_6, and S_4 in that order, processor p_{2a} performs subtasks S_2, S_5, S_9, and S_7 in that order, and processor p_{3a} performs subtasks S_1 and S_8 in that order. There are four communication links: $l_{1a,2a}$, $l_{1a,3a}$, $l_{2a,3a}$, and $l_{3a,1a}$. Data $i_{9,2}$ and data $i_{7,2}$ get transmitted on link $l_{1a,2a}$ in that order, data $i_{8,1}$ get transmitted on link $l_{1a,3a}$, data $i_{9,1}$ get transmitted on link $l_{2a,3a}$, and data $i_{4,1}$ gets transmitted on link $l_{3a,1a}$. *Design 2* also consists of three processors: p_{1a}, p_{1b}, two processors of type p_1, and p_{3a}, a processor of type p_3. Processor p_{1a} performs subtasks S_1, S_4, and S_7 in that order, processor p_{1b} performs subtasks S_3, S_6, and S_9 in that order, and processor p_{3a} performs subtasks S_2, S_5, and S_8 in that order. There are two communication links: $l_{1a,3a}$, and $l_{3a,1b}$. Data $i_{8,1}$ get transmitted on link $l_{1a,3a}$, and data $i_{9,1}$ get transmitted on link $l_{3a,1b}$. *Design 3* consists of two processors: p_{1a}, a processor of type p_1, and p_{3a}, a processor of type p_3. Processor p_{1a} performs subtasks S_3, S_6, S_4, S_7, and S_9 in that order, and processor p_{3a} performs subtasks S_1, S_2, S_5, and S_8 in that order. There are two communication links: $l_{1a,3a}$, and $l_{3a,1a}$. Data $i_{8,1}$ gets transmitted on link $l_{1a,3a}$, and data $i_{4,1}$ and data $i_{9,1}$ get transmitted on link $l_{3a,1a}$ in that order. *Design 4* is similar to design 3, and also consists of two processors: p_{1a} and p_{3a}. However, it has only one link: $l_{1a,3a}$. Presence of only one link forces a change in the mapping between the resources and the events. Processor p_{1a} performs subtasks S_3, S_6, S_1, S_4, and S_7 in that order, and processor p_{3a} performs subtasks S_2, S_5, S_9 and S_8 in that order. Data $i_{9,2}$ and data $i_{8,1}$ get transmitted on link $l_{1a,3a}$ in that order. *Design 5* consists of just 1 processor: p_{2a}, a processor of type p_2. The processor performs the subtasks S_2, S_1, S_4, S_5, S_8, S_3, S_7, S_6, and S_9 in that order.

4.3.2. Bus-Style Interconnection Experiments

In this interconnection style, the system consists of a set of processors and a bus connecting all the processors to each other. The cost of the system is dominated by the costs of the processors selected. The SOS approach is capable of modeling such a system. the MILP bus-architecture model for the nine-subtask graph example consists of 47 timing and 153 binary variables, and 416 constraints. Three noninferior systems were generated by changing the constraint value for the total system cost, and optimizing the system performance. Runtime for each of these designs is on the order of a few hours. Table V gives the statistics for the three designs. A brief discussion of the designs follows.

Design 1 consists of three processors: p_{1a}, p_{1b}, two processors of type p_1, and p_{3a}, a processor of type p_3. Processor p_{1a} performs subtasks S_1, S_4, and S_7 in that order, processor p_{1b} performs subtasks S_3, S_6, and S_9 in that order, and processor p_{3a} performs subtasks S_2, S_5, and S_8 in that order. Data $i_{8,1}$ and data $i_{9,1}$ get transmitted on the common bus in that order. *Design 2* consists of two processors: p_{1a}, a processor of type p_1, and p_{3a}, a processor of type p_3. Processor p_{1a} performs subtasks S_3, S_6, S_4, S_7, and S_9 in that order, and processor p_{3a} performs subtasks S_1, S_2, S_5, and S_8 in that order. Data $i_{4,1}$, data $i_{8,1}$ and data $i_{9,1}$ get transmitted on the common bus in that order. *Design 3* consists of just one processor: p_{2a}, a processor of type p_2. The processor performs the subtasks S_2, S_1, S_4, S_3, S_5, S_8, S_6, S_9, and S_7 in that order.

5. SOME COMMENTS ON THE USEFULNESS OF THE APPROACH

By looking at the examples discussed in Section 4, it is clear that if we increased the number of subtasks and/or the number of processor types, the size of the MILP model could grow fairly quickly, and solving such a large MILP model could become impractical or impossible. However, we find applications which require heterogeneous systems and for which the number of subtasks and processor-types involved are relatively small. As an example, in [30], the problem of optimum power flow in power systems has been modeled as a task graph consisting of eight subtasks, and the system to solve the problem has been designed using four types of processors. The SOS approach can definitely be used to perform synthesis for such applications.

As we go to larger applications, the amount of computer time to solve the MILP model would grow. However, we believe that the approach may still be usable

TABLE V
Example 2 Systems (Bus-Style)

Design	Runtime (min)	Cost	Performance (time units)
1	107.3	10	6
2	89.53	6	7
3	61.52	5	15

since it ensures an optimal design in return. A human designer may actually require more design time than the computer time required by SOS, if it is necessary to ensure the optimality of the design. The human designer may still not be sure about the optimality and the correctness of the design. One thing which is definitely clear is that as the application size grows, it would be very cumbersome to generate the MILP model manually. For this reason, an automatic tool is under development which will generate the MILP model from the application specification. This tool will be very useful in dealing with large applications. Once the tool is ready, we will perform extensive experimentation with the approach and solve much larger examples to investigate if the approach is still practical and how far we can take it.

As we continue to increase the application size, it is obvious that a point will be reached at which the computer time to solve the MILP model is prohibitive. In other words, for very large applications, the MILP approach cannot be used directly. However, the research described here is still of great significance, as it provides a complete in-depth model for the synthesis problem. From the understanding provided by the model created, several directions of research are possible. One possibility is to devise better solution strategies for the MILP model to reduce the runtime. This could involve development of some theory, heuristics, and/or design knowledge to be incorporated into the branch-and-bound search process used for MILP solution. In the area of operations research, such strategies for improving the MILP solution time have been very successfully used. A similar approach was developed by Prakash [34] for an MILP model for the data path synthesis problem [19], and the runtime could be reduced to half its original value on the average. Another possible direction is to develop some theory using the understanding gained from the MILP model and use it in building algorithmic/heuristic procedures for the synthesis problem. Both directions of research are being pursued by us, and some theory has been developed. We strongly believe in this evolution, as the field of *high-level synthesis* [29] witnessed a similar evolution. First, when Hafer and Parker [19] applied MILP to the data path synthesis problem, only very small problems could be solved using the approach and there was a great deal of skepticism about the usefulness of their research. But over the last several years, modified versions of Hafer's approach have been successfully applied to data path synthesis; e.g., [22]. The runtime performance of Hafer's original model has also been improved [17], and much larger problems can be solved now. Also, Hafer's model provided a basic understanding of the data path synthesis problem, which led to development of several algorithmic/heuristic procedures for the problem.

6. APPLICATION OF THE APPROACH TO OTHER DESIGN SCENARIOS

In Section 3, we described application of the SOS approach to a specific task model and system model. In Section 4, we reported the supporting experimental results for the specific model. It must be emphasized that the approach can be applied to several other design scenarios. As reported in Section 4.3.2, the approach has already been applied to a system model for bus-style interconnection, and the corresponding MILP model can be found in [35]. The approach can be applied to other interconnection styles. The MILP model for ring interconnection is being developed. Future work would involve development of the MILP models for different interconnection styles and their combinations.

As the reader might note, in the specific model of Section 3, each processor is assumed to have local memory, but the cost of memory is not included in the system cost explicitly. The MILP model has been extended to perform local memory design. The extended model takes care of this cost explicitly. Solution of the model includes how much local memory is required at each processor in the synthesized system. Shared-memory systems can also be modeled using the SOS approach. The MILP model for shared-memory systems is being developed. Future work involves dealing with more complex memory issues/structures.

The specific model of Section 3 assumes overlap between computation and I/O operations. An MILP model can also be developed for the situation when such an overlap is not possible. Again, the specific model does not explicitly consider the costs associated with the I/O modules. Future work involves extension of the model to handle costs associated with I/O modules and memory buffers required at the I/O modules.

7. CONCLUSIONS

In this paper, we have presented a scheduling-driven approach for synthesizing optimal multiprocessor systems for given applications. The approach is applicable to several design situations, and we have discussed how to apply it to a specific task model and system model. The crux of the approach lies in a mathematical programming model reflecting the design problem.

Several experiments have been conducted using the approach, and the results are reported. Most of the experiments were performed for the specific model discussed in the paper. The experiments indicate that the approach can indeed be used for synthesizing different systems for a given application, depending on the cost–performance requirements imposed by the designer. The approach has also been applied to a system model for bus-style interconnection, and some experiments with this model are reported.

Some tradeoff studies were also performed to study the role of intersubtask communication. The reported results verify the intuitive expectation that heavy intersubtask communication leads to designs with fewer processors and multiprocessing is more useful only when intersubtask communication is reasonable.

The synthesis approach described here may not be directly applicable to very large applications. However, the model created and the research performed provide a basic understanding of the synthesis problem, which would be useful in developing more practical approaches for the larger applications.

The remaining challenges include developing techniques for partitioning an application task into subtasks and techniques for determining the performance of each available processor when it executes each subtask.

REFERENCES

1. Adam, T. L., Chandy, K. M., and Dickson, J. R. A comparison of list schedules for parallel processing systems. *Comm. ACM* **17,** 12 (Dec. 1974), 685–690.
2. Agrawal, R., and Jagadish, H. V. Partitioning techniques for large-grained parallelism. *IEEE Trans. Comput.* **37,** 12 (Dec. 1988), 1627–1634.
3. Al-Mouhamed, M. A. Lower bound on the number of processors and time for scheduling precedence graphs with communication costs. *IEEE Trans. Software Engng.* **16,** 12 (Dec. 1990), 1390–1401.
4. Bokhari, S. H. A shortest tree algorithm for optimal assignments across space and time in a distributed processor system. *IEEE Trans. Software Engrg.* **SE-7,** 6 (Nov. 1981), 583–589.
5. Bokhari, S. H. Partitioning problems in parallel, pipelined, and distributed computing. *IEEE Trans. Comput.* **37,** 1 (Jan. 1988), 48–57.
6. Chu, W. W., Hollaway, L. J., Lan, M.-T., and Efe, K. Task allocation in distributed data processing. *Computer* **13,** 11 (Nov. 1980), 57–69.
7. Chu, W. W., and Lan, L. M.-T. Task allocation and precedence relations for distributed real-time systems. *IEEE Trans. Comput.* **C-36,** 6 (June 1987), 667–679.
8. Coffman, E. G., Jr., and Denning, P. J. *Operating Systems Theory.* Prentice–Hall, Englewood Cliffs, NJ, 1973.
9. Efe, K. Heuristic models of task assignment scheduling in distributed systems. *Computer* **15,** 6 (June 1982), 50–56.
10. El-Rewini, H. and Lewis, T. G. Scheduling parallel program tasks onto arbitrary target machines. *J. Parallel Distrib. Comput.* **9,** 2 (1990), 138–153.
11. Fernandez, E. B., and Bussell, B. Bounds on the number of processors and time for multiprocessor optimal schedules. *IEEE Trans. Comput.* **C-22,** 8 (Aug. 1973), 745–751.
12. Fortes, J. A. B., and Moldovan, D. I. Parallelism detection and transformation techniques useful for VLSI algorithms. *J. Parallel Distrib. Comput.* **2,** 3 (Aug. 1985), 277–301.
13. Freund, R. F. Superconcurrent processing, a dynamic approach to heterogeneous parallelism. *Proceedings of the Parallel/Distributed Computing Networks Seminar.* San Diego Section, IEEE, Feb. 1990.
14. Garey, M. R., Graham, R. L., and Johnson, D. S. Performance guarantees for scheduling algorithms. *Oper. Res.* **26,** 1 (Jan.–Feb. 1978), 3–21.
15. Haddad, E. K. Analysis, modeling and optimization of multiprocessing execution time. Tech. Rep. TR 89-11, Department of Computer Science, Virginia Polytechnic Institute and State University, Falls Church, VA, 1989.
16. Haddad, E. K. Partitioned load allocation for minimum parallel processing time. *Proceedings 1989 International Conference on Parallel Processing.* IEEE Computer Society, Aug. 1989.
17. Hafer, L. J. Constraint improvements for MILP-based hardware synthesis. *Proceedings 28th Design Automation Conference.* ACM/IEEE, June 1991, pp. 14–19.
18. Hafer, L. J., and Hutchings, E. Bringing up Bozo. Tech. Rep. CMPT TR 90-2, School of Computing Science, Simon Fraser University, Burnaby, British Columbia, Canada V5A 1S6, Mar. 1990.
19. Hafer, L. J., and Parker, A. C. A formal method for the specification, analysis, and design of register-transfer level digital logic. *IEEE Trans. Comput. Aided Design* **CAD-2,** 1 (Jan. 1983), 4–17.
20. Houstis, C. E. Module allocation of real-time applications to distributed systems. *IEEE Trans. Software Engrg.* **16,** 7 (July 1990), 699–709.
21. Hu, T. C. Parallel sequencing and assembly line problems. *Oper. Res.* **9** (Nov. 1961), 841–848.
22. Hwang, C.-T., Lee, J.-H., and Hsu, Y.-C. A formal approach to the scheduling problem in high level synthesis. *IEEE Trans. Comput. Aided Design* **10,** 4 (Apr. 1991), 464–475.
23. Hwang, J.-J., Chow, Y.-C., Anger, F. D., and Lee, C.-Y. Scheduling precedence graphs in systems with interprocessor communication times. *SIAM J. Comput.* **18,** 2 (Apr. 1989), 244–257.
24. Indurkhya, B., Stone, H. S., and Xi-Cheng, L. Optimal partitioning of randomly generated distributed programs. *IEEE Trans. Software Engrg.* **SE-12,** 3 (Mar. 1986), 483–495.
25. Kasahara, H., and Narita, S. Practical multiprocessor scheduling algorithms for efficient parallel processing. *IEEE Trans. Comput.* **C-33,** 11 (Nov. 1984), 1023–1029.
26. Kung, S.-Y. On supercomputing with systolic/wavefront array processors. *Proc. IEEE* **72,** 7 (July 1984), 867–884.
27. Li, G.-J., and Wah, B. W. The design of optimal systolic arrays. *IEEE Trans. Comput.* **C-34,** 1 (Jan. 1985), 66–77.
28. Ma, P.-Y. R., Lee, E. Y. S., and Tsuchiya, M. A task allocation model for distributed computing systems. *IEEE Trans. Comput.* **C-31,** 1 (Jan. 1982), 41–47.
29. McFarland, M. C., Parker, A. C., and Camposano, R. The high-level synthesis of digital systems. *Proc. IEEE* **78,** 2 (Feb. 1990), 301–318.
30. Mehrotra, R., and Talukdar, S. N. Task scheduling on multiprocessors. Tech. Rep. DRC-18-55-82, Department of Electrical Engineering, Carnegie–Mellon University, Pittsburgh, PA, Dec. 1982.
31. Miranker, W. L., and Winkler, A. Spacetime representations of computational structures. *Computing* **32,** 2 (1984), 93–114.
32. Nicol, D. M. Optimal partitioning of random programs across two processors. *IEEE Trans. Software Engng.* **15,** 2 (Feb. 1989).
33. Parker, A. C., Küçükçakar, K., Prakash, S., and Weng, J.-P. Unified System Construction (USC). In Camposano, R., and Wolf, W. (Eds.). *High-Level VLSI Synthesis.* Kluwer Academic, Boston, 1991, Chap. 14, pp. 331–354.
34. Prakash, S. Guiding design decisions in RT-level logic synthesis. Master's thesis, School of Computing Science, Simon Fraser University, Burnaby, British Columbia, Canada, Apr. 1987.
35. Prakash, S., and Parker, A. C. A mathematical programming model

for synthesis of multiprocessor systems: Linearization, an example model, and some tradeoff studies. CEng Tech. Rep. 91-17, Department of EE–Systems, University of Southern California, Los Angeles, CA, July 1991.

36. Rao, G. S., Stone, H. S., and Hu, T. C. Assignment of tasks in a distributed processor system with limited memory. *IEEE Trans. Comput.* **C-28,** 4 (Apr. 979), 291–299.

37. Shen, C.-C., and Tsai, W.-H. A graph matching approach to optimal task assignment in distributed computing systems using a minimax criterion. *IEEE Trans. Comput.* **C-34,** 3 (Mar. 1985), 197–203.

38. Siegel, H. J., Schwederski, T., Kuehn, J. T., and Davis IV, N. J. An overview of the PASM parallel processing system. In Gajski, D. D., Milutinovic, V. M., Siegel, H. J., and Furht, B. P. (Eds.). *Computer Architecture.* IEEE Computer Society, Washington, D.C., 1987, pp. 387–407.

39. Stone, H. S. Multiprocessor scheduling with the aid of network flow algorithms. *IEEE Trans. Software Engng.* **SE-3,** 1 (Jan. 1977), 85–93.

SHIV PRAKASH received his bachelor's degree (B. Tech.) in electrical engineering from the Indian Institute of Technology, Kanpur,

Received December 1, 1991; revised May 21, 1991; accepted June 9, 1992

India in 1982, and his master's degree in computing science from Simon Fraser University in Canada in 1987. He was recently a Ph.D. candidate in the department of electrical engineering at the University of Southern California, Los Angeles. His areas of interest include high-level synthesis, system-level synthesis, and multiprocessor systems. He is a member of the IEEE Computer Society as well as the IEEE Circuits and Systems Society. He is currently with Mentor Graphics.

ALICE C. PARKER received the B.S.E.E. and Ph.D. degrees from North Carolina State University and an M.S.E.E. from Stanford University. Dr. Parker is a professor of electrical engineering at the University of Southern California. She was previously on the faculty at Carnegie–Mellon University. She is on the board of advisers of *CAD/CAM Abstracts,* and is an associate editor for *IEEE Transactions on Computer Aided Design of Circuits and Systems*. Dr. Parker has been involved in high-level synthesis research since 1975. Her current research interests are in system-level synthesis and partitioning, CAD frameworks, and design representation. She was elected a Fellow of the IEEE for her contributions to design automation in the areas of high-level synthesis, hardware description languages, and design representation.

An Architectural Co-Synthesis Algorithm for Distributed, Embedded Computing Systems

Wayne H. Wolf, *Senior Member, IEEE*

Abstract—Many embedded computers are distributed systems, composed of several heterogeneous processors and communication links of varying speeds and topologies. This paper describes a new, heuristic algorithm which simultaneously synthesizes the hardware and software architectures of a distributed system to meet a performance goal and minimize cost. The hardware architecture of the synthesized system consists of a network of processors of multiple types and arbitrary communication topology; the software architecture consists of an allocation of processes to processors and a schedule for the processes. Most previous work in co-synthesis targets an architectural template, whereas this algorithm can synthesize a distributed system of arbitrary topology. The algorithm works from a technology database which describes the available processors, communication links, I/O devices, and implementations of processes on processors. Previous work had proposed solving this problem by integer linear programming (ILP); our algorithm is much faster than ILP and produces high-quality results.

Index Terms— Co-synthesis, embedded computing systems, hardware/software co-design.

I. INTRODUCTION

THIS paper describes a new algorithm for the *architectural co-synthesis* of embedded hardware and software architectures. The algorithm synthesizes a distributed multiprocessor architecture and allocates software processes to the CPU's in the multiprocessor such that the combined hardware-software architecture is of minimal cost to meet hard deadlines. The synthesized multiprocessor may have an arbitrary topology, as determined by the design requirements; the synthesis algorithm selects appropriate CPU's and communication channels from a technology-specific library.

Previous work in VLSI CAD, distributed systems, and real-time systems have addressed various aspects of this problem and will provide a valuable foundation to this work. However, most previous work has concentrated on solving for only one or two variables at a time: allocating processes for a given partitioning, scheduling processes for a given hardware configuration, etc. In contrast, our goal is to study multiple-parameter system design: changing the partitioning, scheduling, and allocation of software processes while simultaneously optimizing the underlying hardware which is executing the software.

Manuscript received December 21, 1994; revised October 6, 1995. This work was supported in part by the National Science Foundation under Grant MIP-9121901. Equipment support for this work was provided by the National Science Foundation under Grant CDA-9216171.

The author is with the Department of Electrical Engineering, Princeton University, Princeton, NJ 08544 USA.

Publisher Item Identifier S 1063-8210(97)01954-9.

The algorithm described in this paper constructs a cost-minimal distributed processing system which meets all specified performance constraints and simultaneously allocates and schedules the software processes onto the processing elements (PE's) in the distributed system. Once the architecture has been designed, other synthesis algorithms or manual design can be used to complete the lower levels of abstraction of the design. A co-synthesis algorithm is useful, beyond its obvious use for architecture design, as a product planning tool. Embedded computing systems are frequently designed as families, with successive generations developed using the previous generation as a starting point. Designers can use a co-synthesis tool to determine the cost and performance of implementations of an incompletely specified proposed product. For example, the co-synthesis tool can help determine whether projected memory costs will allow a particular feature to be added to the next-generation system. Co-synthesis allows the design space to be much more thoroughly explored than is possible than by manual methods.

The next section describes the characteristics of embedded computing systems and the role architectural co-synthesis plays in the design process. Section III describes previous research on problems related to architectural co-synthesis. Section IV describes our formulation of the architectural co-synthesis problem in detail. Section V describes the co-synthesis algorithm and Section VI describes the results of experiments with the algorithms.

II. EMBEDDED COMPUTING SYSTEM DESIGN

The ability to co-synthesize a distributed multiprocessor with a custom interconnect architecture is important to the embedded system designer because many embedded systems are distributed systems. Examples include: a pen-based computer which used four microprocessors, each of a different type [25]; a high-performance signal processing machines, such as radar processors, which are implemented using multiple 32-bit processors along with some custom components; a robot arm controller designed by Srivastava *et al.* [31] which was implemented by microprocessors connected to a work station bus; 35 mm cameras which use two or more microprocessors; and automobiles such as the Mercedes S-class, which uses over 60 microprocessors; most navigation and communications systems for boats and aircraft communicate via RS-232 serial connections. Distributed embedded computers exhibit a wide range of architectures: loosely coupled systems which communicate via RS-232; microprocessor networks which use higher-speed serial communication systems such as the I^2C bus

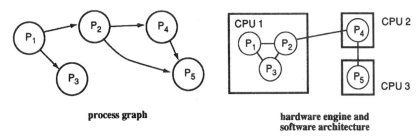

Fig. 1. The input and output of architectural co-synthesis.

[29] or the Echelon Neuron architecture; or microprocessors which communicate via a shared parallel bus [25]. Slater [32] describes the hardware design of multimicroprocessor systems.

An application may be implemented as a distributed system for any of several reasons. In many cases, using several 8-bit microcontrollers is often cheaper than using one 32-bit embedded microprocessor. Even if a more expensive microprocessor is required for some computation-intensive tasks, smaller microcontrollers may be used as device handlers to off-load the main CPU. If the design includes several I/O devices, enough on-board I/O devices or timers may be required that more than one embedded controller is necessaryusing several microcontrollers which include on-board I/O logic may be the lowest-cost design. Finally, there are cases in which even the largest single CPU cannot handle the computation load and processes must be put on separate CPU's and/or ASIC's to meet all the hard deadlines.

An embedded computing system consists of a *hardware engine* which executes *application software* [35]. If we limit our design requirements to cost and performance for the sake of argument, the architectural design problem for the hardware engine is to determine how much hardware is needed to make sure that the system meets its deadlines and its soft performance goals, while minimizing the engine's cost. The computing elements of the hardware engine are PE's, which may be general-purpose CPU's, digital signal processors (DSP's), floating-point units, ASIC's, etc.. In the simplest case of a single-CPU engine, the PE must be fast enough to run all the processes fast enough to meet all their deadlines under the worst-case input combinations. Even in a single-CPU design, the designer is faced with several choices within a CPU family (different bus widths, different clock speeds, different amounts of execution parallelism) as well as choices across families (different architectures and manufacturers). When designing a distributed hardware engine, the designer faces the PE selection choice at each node as well as the choice of communication channels between the PE's.

However, the hardware engine cannot be designed without simultaneously considering the application software architecture. The allocation of processes to PE's and the scheduling of those processes and their communications determines the cost of both the PE's and communications network. Therefore, the software architecture must be optimized simultaneously with the hardware architecture to ensure that arbitrary choices in the software design have not foreclosed attractive hardware design options. Our co-synthesis algorithm allocates processes to PE's while simultaneously allocating PE's and communication channels in the hardware engine and it schedules the processes to determine the execution demands of the processes on the CPU's and communication system.

The input and output of architectural co-synthesis are shown in Fig. 1. An embedded system's specification includes both functional and nonfunctional elements [10]: a model for the functional specification is a *process graph*; the nonfunctional specification of interest in this work is a *rate constraint*, or the maximum time from initiation to termination of the process graph execution. (The inverse of the process graph's rate is its *period*.) The product of architectural co-synthesis is a pair of architectures: the hardware engine architecture consists of the component PE's and their interconnections; the software architecture consists of an allocation of processes to the PE's, priorities for process execution, and assignment of interprocess communication to physical communication links. Detailed design of the hardware and software components is guided by the structure of these architectures. The goal of architectural co-synthesis is to estimate and predict the results of detailed design decisions well enough to guide the construction of an effective, efficient architecture. Co-design is necessary at several different levels of the design hierarchy. For example, Chou *et al.* [5] developed an algorithm which synthesizes a complete device interface using a combination of instructions executing on the host CPU and external interface logic. Architectural co-synthesis works at the top level of the design hierarchy; it does not produce a complete implementation of the hardware and software components of the system, but it does a combined hardware-software architecture for the complete system.

The design of a hardware–software (HW/SW) architecture for an embedded system requires consideration of a great deal of information. Each software process executes at different speeds on different PE's. PE types also vary in their available communication topology and bandwidth and their on-chip devices. Architectural design requires considering the utilization of PE's, interprocess communication, component cost, and other factors. While simple systems can be designed on the back of an envelope, sophisticated systems which execute more complex functions and which have stricter performance and cost constraints require tools which can efficiently search through architectural choices to find an efficient design.

A useful architectural co-synthesis algorithm must be able to handle incomplete functional specifications. There are many reasons why a designer may not be able to completely specify the function to be executed on the hardware engine: while some software may be lifted from previous designs, new

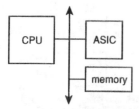

Fig. 2. Target architecture of hardware–software partitioning algorithms.

software will by definition not be fully implemented when system architecture design begins; the engine may be designed as a platform for several product generations, and only budgets for the maximum computational cost of possible features are available when the engine is under design; the designer may need to flesh out several architectures to determine possible price-performance points for the product. The process graph serves as a useful abstraction for incompletely specified systems as follows: a well-understood or previously implemented operation can be represented by a process with measured execution times or a poorly understood function can be modeled as a process with estimated execution times.

III. Previous Work

Related previous work includes studies of architectural partitioning, hardware-software partitioning, hardware–software co-synthesis, and distributed system scheduling and allocation.

Architectural partitioning algorithms model the design as a marked graph and partition the graph into several smaller subgraphs to optimize performance and interconnect cost. Partitioning algorithms rely primarily on the structure of the graph during optimization. APARTY [19] is an architectural partitioner targeted mainly to hardware designs thanks to its emphasis on a large number of relatively small operators; it uses a hierarchical clustering algorithm. PARTIF [18] is an interactive partitioning tool based on the SOLAR design representation of communicating processes.

Hardware–software partitioning algorithms implement a system from an architectural template: a CPU and a custom ASIC communicating over a bus, as illustrated in Fig. 2. These algorithms either move operations from hardware to software to minimize cost, as does the algorithm of Gupta and De Micheli [17], or moves operations from software to hardware to satisfy performance goals, as does the algorithm of Ernst et al. [11] Vahid et al. [34] use a multi-phase partitioning algorithm to improve the results of hardware–software partitioning.

SIERA [31] is a template-based synthesizer of board-level controllers; the system description is successively refined by having one generator build a system from components created by smaller generators. At each stage of abstraction, two templates—one for hardware and another for software—describe the basic structure of the unit to be synthesized. Generators are used to create detailed designs of the components, which may themselves invoke generators at the next-lower level of abstraction. Properties of the specification are used as parameters to the generators. SIERA does not feed back results of hardware or software synthesis to modify the architecture generated by the template. SIERA has been used to design a robot arm controller, among other projects.

Some recent work in co-synthesis has developed techniques for synthesizing engines with arbitrary topologies. In the SOS algorithm [23], Prakash and Parker formulated the hardware engine design problem as a software process set implemented on a hardware architecture and solved the resulting problem using mixed integer linear programming (MILP) techniques. D'Ambrosio and Hu [8] simulated a set of processes to determine the feasibility of a given hardware-software architecture on a single-CPU system. Barros et al. [2] use a clustering algorithm to synthesize an engine and allocate processes to the engine.

Research on the scheduling and allocation of processes in distributed systems is relevant to our research. Distributed systems scheduling algorithms assume that the processes have already been partitioned and that the hardware architecture of the distributed system is given. Leinbaugh and Yamani [20] developed algorithms to bound the amount of time required to execute a set of processes on a distributed system. Ramamritham et al. [24] developed a heuristic scheduling algorithm for real-time multiprocessors. Sih and Lee developed a multiprocessor scheduling algorithm called declustering [30] which reclusters processes on CPU's to trade off concurrency for interprocess communication time.

Distributed systems allocation algorithms assume that the processes have been allocated and the topology of the distributed computing engine is given. Stone [33] developed the first algorithm for allocation of processes to processors on distributed systems. Dasarathy and Feridun [9] developed extensions for real-time constraints. Chu et al. [7] developed heuristics for taking interprocess communication times into account during the allocation process. Chu and Tan [6] developed heuristics to include precedence relations between processes during optimization; they used process size as an approximation for important precedence relationships. Shen and Tsai [27] used a graph matching heuristic to allocate processes; their algorithm minimized interprocessor communication and balanced system load. Gopinath and Gupta [15] applied a combination of static and dynamic techniques to improve processor utilization. They statically analyze process code and assign two predictability/unpredictability and monotonicity/nonmonotonicity values to each process, which they use to move less-predictable code earlier in the schedule. They then use software monitors to keep track of actual execution time of processes and adjust the schedule on-line.

Our co-synthesis algorithm has several advantages over previous work. Unlike distributed system optimization algorithms, we do not assume that the topology of the hardware engine is given. Unlike template-driven schemes or hardware–software partitioning algorithms, our algorithm can synthesize an engine with an arbitrary topology. It also selects the proper PE type at each node. We will see that the difficulty of predicting performance of a process before the PE it will run on has been selected is the greatest single problem in the design of our co-synthesis algorithm. Unlike architectural partitioning algorithms, it evaluates system performance based on nongraph-theoretic properties of the design; we schedule and

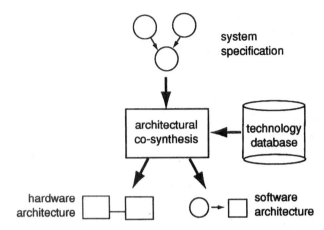

Fig. 3. The synthesis process.

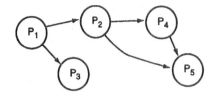

Fig. 4. An example process graph.

allocate processes to evaluate the hardware engine architecture. D'Ambrosio and Hu consider only architectures with a single CPU. Barros *et al.* take advantage of properties of the Unity language to simplify analysis of the system specification.

The work of Prakash and Parker is closest to our own, since they co-synthesize a distributed engine of arbitrary topology. However, our algorithm is heuristic and can therefore produce a solution very quickly. We believe that a heuristic algorithm is an important step in the development of architectural co-synthesis algorithms because the development of heuristics both offers the promise of much shorter execution times and helps identify the key relationships between subproblems and further refine the solution method. The experimental results of Section VI demonstrate that our heuristic algorithm gives results comparable to those generated by ILP on small problems and can handle larger problems due to its low execution times. Our algorithm also allocates devices along with processes. When PE's include on-chip devices, it is important to allocate those with processes: a process and its device must be on the same chip, and the number of on-chip devices required may expand the number of PE's of a given type available, allowing different allocations of processes to PE's.

IV. PROBLEM FORMULATION

As illustrated in Fig. 3, the co-synthesis process takes as input the system specification along with a set of technology parameters; it produces both the hardware architecture, consisting of PE's and communication channels connecting them, and the software architecture, which gives the allocation of processes to PE's, the scheduling of processes, and the scheduling and allocation of communication on channels. The formulation of our problem can be divided into three components: the problem specification; the definition of the hardware and software architectures; and the technology-dependent descriptions of the hardware and software components.

A. Problem Specification

The problem specification (which Prakash and Parker called the task model) includes both the functional and nonfunctional requirements, as shown in Fig. 4. A *process* is the atomic unit of specification. A process may begin execution when all its inputs arrive and emits its outputs when execution terminates. The execution time for a process depends on the type of PE to which it is allocated, as described in Section IV-C. A *process graph* defines the system's functional requirements: is a directed acyclic graph whose nodes represent processes and whose edges (*data dependencies*) represent data communication between processes and devices. The system of processes described by the process graph is repeatedly executed. Each edge is labeled with the *size* of the datum transmitted in units of bits; data is transmitted at each termination of the process. In the example, $s_{1:3}$ specifies the number of bits transmitted from process P_1 to P_3 in a single communication. An input device is represented by a node with no inward edges and an output device by a node with no outgoing edges. Prakash and Parker model processes which can start executing before all of their inputs have been received using additional variables to model the execution times at various stages of processing; we prefer to represent such processes as a network of processes, with some processes receiving initial inputs and passing partial computations onto later processes. Similarly, we can model system inputs which arrive after execution has begun by adding pseudo-processes which delay time-zero-arrival inputs by the appropriate amount.

The minimum *rate* at which the process graph must be executed is a nonfunctional requirement of the system. The rate is measured from the process graph inputs to the computation of the last output of the process graph. The inverse of the rate is the maximum *period* of one process graph execution. The rate is a *hard* constraint—it must be satisfied for the implementation to be feasible. We refer to schedule of processes which ensures that all processes complete with the period as a *feasible schedule*.

B. Architecture Model

The architecture of the implementation consists of the software architecture and hardware engine architecture. The hardware engine architecture is built from three kinds of primitives: *PE's*, I/O *devices*, and communication *channels*. The hardware architecture is specified as a labeled hypergraph: nodes represent PE's or devices, with labels giving the type of component represented; communication channels are specified by hyperedges (since a communication channel may connect more than two devices, an edge may connect more than two nodes).

The software architecture implemented by co-synthesis consists of *processes* and *interprocess communication (IPC) channels* (also known as *communication channels*). Each software process in the implementation corresponds to a process in the specification. Interprocess communication links are implemented over communication channels (capped with software interfaces) for processes executing on different PE's; IPC links are implemented by shared memory communication mediated by the operating system when the communicating processes execute on the same PE. The software architecture may be described in terms of the problem specification: the process allocation is given by a mapping from the nodes in the process graph to processors in the hardware engine architecture; the communication allocation is given by a mapping from edges in the process graph to communication channels in the hardware architecture.

C. Technology Description

A technology database describes the characteristics of the hardware and software component types. A communication channel connects to a PE or a device through a port. A channel type's technology model includes three parameters: the cost (in dollars, ECU's, etc.) of the hardware required to implement a port, the channel's throughput, and the maximum number of ports which can be connected to the channel. A device type's technology model includes the type of channel to which the device is connected and the cost of the device. The technology model for a PE type describes its manufacturing cost, its internal devices, and its communication ports. Manufacturing cost is a monetary value which can include the cost of printed circuit board real estate required by the PE and other indirect costs, so long as the indirect cost per PE is fixed. Any on-chip devices and communication ports have their costs included in the total PE cost, so that using an on-chip device or port is cheaper than adding an external equivalent.

The technology database must also specify the implementation characteristics of the processes. Execution times for individual processes are specified by the designer. The technology model gives the maximum execution time of a process for each PE type on which it can run. The execution time can be found by measurement of code running on a processor or through analysis techniques such as those of Park and Shaw [21]. The execution time of a function implemented on an ASIC can be estimated using high-level synthesis techniques like those of Henkel and Ernst [12]; if an ASIC preemptively executes several processes, the techniques of Potkonjak and Wolf [22] can be used to determine worst case performance and to synthesize the shared data path. A process's worst case execution time may also be estimated by the designer if the process has not yet been implemented. If a process does not have a bounded execution time, then it cannot be used to meet a hard rate constraint. It is possible, however, to use an average execution time to represent the process and treat the rate as a soft constraint.

V. ENGINE/SOFTWARE ARCHITECTURE CO-SYNTHESIS

A. Summary of the Algorithm

Our architectural co-synthesis algorithm's primary objective is to meet the rate constraint and the secondary objective is to minimize total implementation cost

$$\sum_{i \in \text{CPU's}} \text{cost}(\text{CPU}_i) + \sum_{j \in \text{devices}} \text{cost}(\text{device}_j) + \sum_{k \in \text{channels}} \text{cost}(\text{channel}_k). \qquad (1)$$

Co-design includes four major procedures [35]: partitioning of the functional description into a set of processes; scheduling the processes; allocating the processes to PEs; and mapping PE's into particular component types. Our synthesis algorithm assumes that the description has been partitioned into processes and it implements a process on a single PE. The most important steps to architectural co-synthesis are allocation and mapping; scheduling information serves to compute the most accurate PE utilization to guide allocation.

Synthesis is easiest when scheduling, allocation, partitioning, and mapping can be cleanly separated. However, these steps are much more closely tied in co-synthesis than in high-level synthesis because process execution times vary in small increments, depending on the mapping to a particular type of PE. The circular reasoning required due to the relationship between mapping and the other two tasks can be easily seen: we want to schedule processes and allocate them to PE's so as to maximize PE utilization and minimize communication costs; but the execution time of a process, which determines utilization, is not known until the process is not only mapped to a particular node in the multiprocessor network but also mapped to a particular type of PE; and we cannot allocate and schedule processes until we know their execution times. The greatest challenge in the development of an efficient co-synthesis algorithm is to break this circular process in allows the algorithm to find a good hardware–software architecture.

We have chosen to break the circularity by first performing an initial allocation and mapping which has enough resources to ensure that all the specification's deadlines are met, then refining the design to reduce system cost. The co-synthesis algorithm is designed to satisfy design criteria in this order: first, satisfy all deadlines; second, minimize PE cost; third, minimize communication port cost; and fourth, minimize device cost. The algorithm assumes that I/O operations have been assigned to different physical ports; the algorithm allocates devices to minimize system cost, but it does not try to combine several logical I/O operations onto one physical device. The techniques of Amon and Borriello [1] can be used to schedule I/O among and determine the number of physical I/O devices required.

Synthesis proceeds through five major steps.

1) Generate an initial solution: allocate processes to PE's such that all tasks are placed on PE's fast enough to ensure that all deadlines are met; schedule the processes to determine process exclusivity and communication rates.
2) Reallocate processes to PE's to minimize PE cost.
3) Reallocate processes again to minimize inter-PE communication.
4) Allocate communication channels.

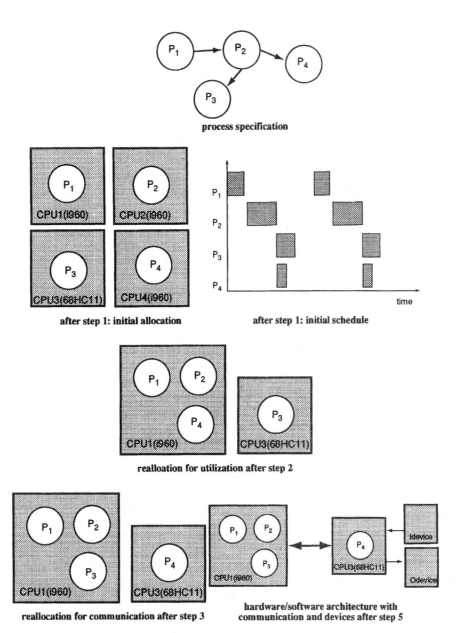

Fig. 5. The major steps in our co-synthesis algorithm.

5) Allocate devices, either internally to PE's or externally to communication channels.

While we have described these steps as scheduling or allocation for descriptive purposes, we schedule to test feasibility during several of the allocation phases. The sequence of synthesis steps is designed to refine the design from a feasible one to a minimal-cost architecture.

We found that several elements were important in achieving high-quality results. This synthesis heuristic first tries to minimize PE cost, then communication channel cost, and finally device cost; this sequence of optimizations reflects the relative importance of these components of cost in the examples that we have studied. Our experiments have shown that Step 2 is the most important for achieving minimum cost, so that step performs an iterative refinement; other steps in the algorithm are greedy, as described below. Our algorithm moves several processes at a time when re-allocating. In our experiments with various heuristics, we found that moving several processes at a time in order to eliminate or cost-reduce a PE is also very important to quickly finding a good architecture. Finally, since Step 2 carries most of the burden of reducing the PE cost of the system, it is important to use an optimization strategy which goes beyond simple greedy allocation. As described in detail below, we alternate between trying to eliminate excess PE's and balancing the load across the existing PE's in order to perform a more complete search of the design space.

The operation of the algorithm is illustrated in Fig. 5. The process specification includes four processes, an input operation, and an output operation; the input and output operations each require their own devices. The initial allocation of processes to PE's is conservative, requiring three powerful, expensive processors (i960s) and one slower, cheaper processor

```
Edge_set ordering_constraints(spec,allocation,last_schedule) {
    Edge_set order_edges;
    foreach_PE c in spec
        foreach_process pi in spec
            foreach_process pj in spec
                if (timeof(pi,last_schedule) < timeof(pj,last_schedule))
                    order_edges.add(Edge(end(pi),start(pj.),0));
                else
                    order_edges.add(Edge(end(pj),start(pi),0));
    return order_edges;
}

double schedule(spec,allocation,last_schedule) {
    graph = merge(spec.process_graph ,
                  ordering_constraints(spec,allocation,last_schedule));
    return longest_path(graph);
}
```

Fig. 6. The scheduling procedure.

(a 68HC11). The scheduling performed in Step 1 reveals that processes P_1, P_2, and P_4 are mutually exclusive in time and thus can share a priority in a single PE; that change is made in Step 2. Step 3 tries to minimize communication cost by swapping P_3 and P_4, since P_2 communicates a larger volume of data with P_3. The final steps in the algorithm allocate the communication link between the two PE's and the I/O devices which implement the input and output operations.

We refer to the process graph and rate requirement as the *specification*, the current hardware architecture as the *engine*, and the current software architecture as the process *allocation*. A useful measure in guiding heuristic choices is the *utilization* of a PE, which we define here as the ratio of execution time required by currently allocated processes to the specified period; note that this ratio will never be greater than one in a feasible solution.

This algorithm concentrates on microprocessor-based architectures. The algorithm can be extended to synthesize into ASIC's as well as CPU's by using a more sophisticated timing model for the PE's. In a CPU, only one process can run at a time, but an ASIC can support two processes which execute concurrently. The performance estimation procedures of this algorithm could be extended to handle multiple processes executing simultaneously on a PE. Other hardware-software partitioning algorithms, like those of Ernst *et al.* [11], make similar simplifying assumptions, such that the CPU and ASIC do not execute concurrently.

B. Steps in Co-Synthesis

We will describe the steps in more detail using pseudocode. The first two steps assume that sufficient communication capacity will be available to support the chosen allocation of processes to PE's.

Step 1 first performs an initial allocation of processes to PE's-the algorithm assigns only one process to a PE and chooses the fastest type of PE available to execute that process. It then schedules processes on the initially allocated hardware engine; if scheduling does not find a feasible schedule for this system (assuming zero communication time) then the problem does not have a feasible solution in the given technology.

The scheduling procedure used throughout the co-synthesis algorithm is shown in Fig. 6. During Step 1, since the initial allocation has just been selected, the scheduler is called to find an initial feasible schedule. Our goal is to find a feasible schedule quickly, not necessarily an optimal schedule, and multiprocessor scheduling is NP-complete [14]. However, since we separately determine the allocation of processes to PE's and our process graphs are acyclic, we can use a simple scheduling approximation as the core of our algorithm. We use Dijkstra's algorithm [13] to find the longest path through the process graph. However, the longest-path algorithm operating only on the precedence constraints in the process graph will not give a feasible schedule, since processes allocated to the same PE must be scheduled to have nonoverlapping execution times. The allocation of processes to PE's is given. We approximate the solution to the multiprocessor scheduling problem by inserting extra constraints to force an order of process execution. We use the last computed schedule to choose the order in which the processes on a PE should be executed. As shown in the figure, an ordering constraint is generated to keep the processes executing in the same order and ensuring that the later process's start time is no sooner than the earlier process's completion time. (During Step 1 of the algorithm, although we do not have a previous schedule, we also do not need to generate any ordering constraints since each PE is allocated only one process.)

During Step 2, we reallocate processes to minimize PE cost, still assuming that communication is unrestricted. At a single step in the iterative procedure, we try to remove all processes from a lightly loaded PE so that it can be removed from the current engine. The improvement step procedure is outlined in Fig. 7. We consider the PE's from least to most utilized. Given a PE c, we first identify processes which it may be feasible to move to another, existing PE in the engine. We must check the feasibility of the schedule to determine whether the processes can in fact be moved, so we use utilization as an approximation. We may move different processes to various different PE's in the engine. Some processes may not be movable, so we try creating one additional PE to hold all the leftover processes; that PE is chosen as the cheapest

```
void PE_cost_reduction_step(spec,engine,allocation) {
    sorted_PEs = sort_PEs_by_utilization(engine,least_first); /* sort with least-utilized first */
    foreach_PE c in sorted_PEs {
        reallocatable = processes in allocation(c) which can be executed on
                        other existing PEs;
        /* reducible is the set of all processes allocated to PE c which cannot be moved
           to another process */
        reducible = allocation(c) - reallocatable;
        xtype = cheapest PE type which can implement all processes in reducible;
        /* new allocation moves some processes of c to other, existing PEs and moves
           the remaining processes to a new, cheaper PE */
        new_allocation = old allocation with reallocatable and reducible modifications;
        if (size(reallocatable | reducible) == size(allocation(c)) /* can move all processes */
            && schedule(spec,new_allocation) <= period) {
            if (size(reducible) > 0)
                engine.add_PE(new_PE(xtype)); /* add the new, cheaper PE */
            remove_PE(engine,c); /* get rid of the old PE */
            reallocate(new_allocation); /* actually reallocate the processes */
        }
    }
}
```

Fig. 7. The PE cost reduction step procedure.

```
void iteratively_reduce_PE_cost(spec,engine,allocation) {
    lastcost = large_value;
    first = YES;
    do {
        if (!first) lastcost = cost(engine);
        first = NO;
        PE_cost_reduction_step(spec,engine);
        pairwise_merge(spec,engine);
        balance_load(spec,engine);
    } while (cost(engine) < lastcost);
}
```

Fig. 8. The iterative PE cost reduction procedure.

type which implements all the processes. Using a single, cheap PE to hold leftover processes is a good heuristic for minimizing hardware engine cost, since it allows noncritical processes to migrate to cheaper PE's without creating too many additional PE's. If some processes in c cannot be moved to some combination of existing PE's and the newly created PE, we move on to the next PE for reallocation. We then check the feasibility of this allocation by rescheduling the processes (using, of course, the execution times for the new allocation). If the new allocation is feasible, we move the processes, delete the now-empty c, and add the new PE if one was necessary.

The iterative PE cost reduction procedure is summarized in Fig. 8. This procedure first applies the basic PE cost reduction step, then tries to merge process sets by replacing two PE's with a single PE of smaller total cost, and finally reallocates processes in the existing engine to balance load, and continues so long as the engine cost is reduced. The pairwise merger and load balancing procedures are shown in Fig. 9. Pairwise merging complements the other optimizations by identifying a single PE which can cover a larger set of processes. Load-balancing iteratively tries to move processes from the most heavily utilized PE's to less-utilized PE's; however, the procedure does not remove more than half the PE's load as a heuristic to avoid eliminating this PE. Our experiments show that the load balancing step helps move processes to less-expensive PE's.

Step 3 reallocates processes to reduce communication requirements, since allocation decisions in Step 2 were made without consideration of the required communication rates. This procedure, which is outlined in Fig. 10, does not explicitly take channel capacities into account, but only tries to reduce total communication between PE's. The rate at which interprocess communication occurs is fundamentally determined by the process graph, but the rate at which communication between PE's occurs depends on the allocation of processes to PE's. Before allocating channels, Step 3 reallocates processes to minimize inter-PE communication rates. The algorithm considers processes one at a time, starting with the process p which conducts the most interprocess communication. The nearest-neighbor processes to p in the process are identified. Given a neighboring process q, the algorithm either move directly q onto p's current PE or to swap q with some other process which currently resides on p's PE.

Step 4 actually allocates the communication channels between the PE's. The type of channel used for each link is determined by the types of ports supported by each PE and device and port cost. The procedure, illustrated in Fig. 11, identifies communications which span PE's and allocates channels as necessary. Any data dependency which connects processes allocated to different PE's requires a communications channel. Each data dependency edge is labeled with the size of datum transmitted at each execution, as was described in Section IV-A. From that information the required data rate can be computed. We assume that the communication is scheduled at the termination time of the process at the source of the data dependency. If the communication can be permitted on an existing channel, taking into account both the rate and the schedule, it is allocated to the channel, otherwise another channel is created. The number and types of channels which can be created for the PE are specified

```
void pairwise_merge(spec,engine) {
    for (i=0; i < size(PEs(engine)); i++) {
        for (j=i+1; j < size(PEs(engine); j++) {
            mergedprocs = merge(processes(ith_PE(i,engine)),
                                processes(ith_PE(j,engine)));
            repl_types = PE types which implement all processes in mergedprocs;
            if (size(repl_types) == 0) continue;
            cheapest = PE(cheapesttype(repl_types));
            if (cost(cheapest) > cost(ith_PE(i,engine)) + cost(ith_PE(j,engine))) continue;
            new_allocation = old_allocation with i and j processes moved to cheapest;
            if (schedule(spec,new_allocation,last_schedule(engine)) <= period)
                reallocate(new_allocation); /* actually reallocate the processes */
        }
    }
}

void balance_load(spec,engine) {
    sorted_PEs = sort_PEs_by_utilization(engine,most_first); /* sort with most-utilized first */
    foreach_PE c in sorted_PEs
        do {
            p = process in c not yet considered;
            x = less-utilized PE in engine which can implement p;
            new_allocation = old allocation with p moved to x;
            if (schedule(spec,new_allocation,last_schedule(engine)) <= period)
                reallocate(new_allocation); /* actually reallocate the processes */
        } while ((less than half of processes in c moved) ||
                 (more processes can be moved));
}
```

Fig. 9. The load balancing and merging procedures.

```
void reallocate_for_communication(spec,engine,allocation) {
    /* sort from most to least output communication rate */
    sorted_processes = sort_processes_by_communication(spec);
    foreach_process p in sorted_processes {
        this_cpu = assignment(allocation,p); /* convenient alias for CPU to which p is assigned */
        /* nearby is the set of processes adjacent to p in the data flow graph */
        nearby = processes adjacent to p in process_graph + {p};
        new_allocation = allocation;
        foreach_process q in nearby {
            if (q can be implemented on this_cpu)
                new_allocation = q moved to this_cpu;
            else if (q can be swapped with a process r currently allocated to this_cpu)
                new_allocation = q swapped with r;
        }
        if (schedule(spec,new_allocation,last_schedule(engine)) <= period)
            reallocate(new_allocation); /* actually reallocate the processes */
    }
}
```

Fig. 10. The communication minimization procedure.

as devices in the technology description. Step 5 may fail to produce a feasible design if communication channels cannot be allocated to handle the required inter-PE communication. We have not encountered this difficulty in practice, but if it were encountered, it would be possible to reallocate processes and possibly allocate new PE's to make the communication network feasible.

At this point, process allocation is complete, and the last step of the algorithm is straightforward. Step 5 allocates devices around the engine to ensure that each process has a communication channel to the devices it reads and writes. To minimize cost, on-chip devices are used when possible.

We have analyzed the complexity of this algorithm. Let n be the number of processes, d the number of data dependencies in the process graph, p the number of PE's, P be the maximum number of PE types which can implement any one process, c be the number of channels, and x be the number of devices specified. Since we use the scheduling procedure of Fig. 6 as a building block in several steps, we will analyze it first. Adding execution ordering constraints requires $O(n^2)$ time, and Dijkstra's algorithm also requires $O(n^2)$ time. The allocation phase of Step 1 is linear in the number of processes; the scheduling procedure used in Step 1 requires $O(n^2)$ time. The PE cost reduction procedure of Fig. 7, which is used as

```
void allocate_channels(spec,engine,allocation) {
    D = set of dependencies d in spec.process_graph where d.source and d.sink
        are allocated to different PEs;
    foreach_dependency d in D {
        ca = PE to which d.source is allocated; cz = PE to which d.sink is allocated;
        if ((existing channel connects ca and cz) &&
            (existing channel has capacity))
            allocate d to existing channel;
        else {
            allocate new channel of compatible type;
            allocate d to new channel;
        }
    }
}
```

Fig. 11. The communication channel allocation procedure.

TABLE I
A COMPARISON OF OUR ALGORITHM WITH PRAKASH AND PARKER

example	# processes	period	implementation cost		CPU time (sec)	
			Wolf	P&P	Wolf	P&P
pp1	4	2.5	14	14	0.05	11
		3	14	13	0.05	24
		4	7	7	0.05	28
		7	5	5	0.05	37
pp2	9	5	15	15	0.7	3732
		6	12	12	1.1	26710
		7	8	8	1.6	32320
		8	8	7	1.0	4511
		15	5	5	1.1	385012

the inner loop of Step 2, is dominated by the scheduling check performed on each PE, and has complexity $O(pn^2)$. The load balancing procedure of Fig. 9 has the same complexity and the pairwise merger procedure has complexity $O(p^2n^2)$. The full, iterative PE cost reduction procedure will be executed at most pP times, since we must either eliminate a PE or replace it with a lower-cost PE at each step, so the complete procedure requires $O(p^3n^2P)$ time. Step 3, which reallocates to minimize communication cost, has complexity $O(pd)$ since an iteration may have to examine all the PE's to determine the system connectivity. Step 5 is linear in the number of communication devices.

VI. RESULTS

We have implemented our architectural co-synthesis algorithm, which required about 6000 lines of C++, using the NIH Class Library. Execution times for processes in all our examples were either measured from separately implemented C code or were estimated. All of our experiments were run on SGI Indigo work stations.

We used examples from related co-synthesis research and from software engineering texts to evaluate our algorithm: $pp1$ and $pp2$ are Prakash and Parker's examples 1 and 2 [23], the two examples they used to test their ILP formulation; $cfuge$ is the centrifuge example of Calvez [3]; dye is the dyeing machine example of Selic et al. [26]; $juice$ is the juice plant example of Shlaer and Mellor [28]. For all these examples, we used the process graph structure given by the authors. For the examples of Prakash et al. and D'Ambrosio et al., we were also able to use those authors' technology parameters: process execution times for various PE's and component costs. For the other examples, we estimated process execution times based on the description of the functions to be executed and based our cost values on the catalog, costs of known components.

Table I compares our results to those of Prakash and Parker's algorithm, with $pp1$ synthesized for four different specified periods and $pp2$ synthesized for five different periods corresponding to the point-to-point interconnection experiments of Prakash and Parker. The data for Prakash and Parker's experiments is taken from their paper. In two cases, $pp1$ with period = 3 and $pp2$ with period = 8, our algorithm found a slightly higher cost implementation. In all other cases it found the same implementation as Prakash and Parker's algorithm, resulting in the same implementation cost. The iterative search of Step 2, which alternates between cost reduction and load balancing, is essential to obtaining high-quality results. Our algorithm required substantially less execution time than theirs. Even though the execution times are reported for different processors, the large difference in execution time required for heuristic versus ILP solutions to co-synthesis suggest that heuristic algorithms become attractive even for relatively small examples.

TABLE II
ADDITIONAL RESULTS FROM OUR ALGORITHM

example	# processes	implementation cost	PEs	channels	CPU time (sec)
cfuge	3	17	HC11: servo_speed, control_speed, speed-clock	none	0.1
dye	15	59	i486: dyeing_parameters, solution_level, device_position, run_parameters, operator_command, timeout, start_timer, run_status, parameter_request, command_dye, command_drain, command_heater HC11: dyevalve, drainvalve, heaterctrl	i486-HC11 (serial link)	7.2
juice	4	41	68000: ctank, tramp, abatch HC11: heater	68000-HC11 (serial link)	0.1

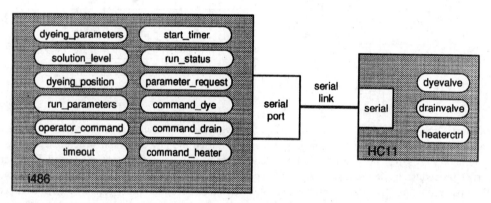

Fig. 12. The synthesized hardware and software architectures of the *dye* example.

Table II summarizes the results of our experiments with the other examples. The table summarizes the hardware and software architectures of the synthesized implementations by listing the PE's, channels, and process allocation. Fig. 12 shows the architecture generated for the *dye* example as an illustration of the results of our algorithm. Synthesis placed the three driver routines for the external devices in the smaller HC11 and the remaining processes in an i486. Our technology file specified that the driver processes could be implemented only on an HC11, while the other processes could be implemented either on an i386 or i486. Our algorithm determined through scheduling that all the processes could not be implemented on an i386 and chose to use one i486 rather than two i386s to reduce cost. It also determined that all the driver processes could be feasibly executed on a single HC11. The i486 required an external serial port, while the HC11's internal serial port could be used to implement that side of the connection to the communications channel. This example has the largest number of processes because object-oriented specifications tend to include many small processes. Most of the CPU time required for synthesis went into iterative optimization for PE cost (Step 3 in the algorithm). In the *juice* example, we specified that the *ctank* and *abatch* processes could be implemented only on the 68 000 but that the other processes could be implemented on either type of CPU. The algorithm chose to cluster as many processes as possible on the 68 000 to minimize interprocess communication delays.

VII. CONCLUSIONS

Architectural co-synthesis is an important tool for the embedded system designer. Architectural decisions made early strongly influence the ease and even the feasibility of the detailed hardware and software implementations. The choice of a hardware-software architecture requires balancing many factors: what operations can be implemented on each available PE type; PE cost; allocation of processes to PE and utilization; interprocess communication requirements; communications capacity; and device cost, among others. An architectural co-synthesis algorithm is essential for quickly assessing the design space, particularly when system architects and customers must evaluate candidate architectures to help refine the system's specification.

Our co-synthesis algorithm does not assume an architectural template. As a result, it can synthesize the range of designs to which embedded system architects have been accustomed to being able to implement. The heuristic nature of the algorithm makes it significantly more efficient than mathematical programming, making it feasible for system architects to use the algorithm to evaluate a number of system specifications and component choices. The algorithm handles more sophisticated component models, taking into account not only CPU times but also the savings afforded by integrated devices and ports. Our heuristics show that the complex relationship between allocation, scheduling, and mapping in co-synthesis can be managed by allocating first for deadline feasibility, then refining the design to reduce its cost. Our experiments show that the heuristics applied by our algorithm find the optimal solution in many cases and close-to-optimal solutions in many others.

Much work remains to be done in architectural co-synthesis as well as the co-analysis and coverification tasks which support architectural design. However, we believe that this co-synthesis algorithm is an important step in developing an understanding the tradeoffs involved in the design of complex, multiple-processor embedded computing systems.

REFERENCES

[1] T. Amon and G. Borriello, "Sizing synchronization queues: A case study in higher level synthesis," in *Proc. 28th Design Automat. Conf.*, Los Alamitos, CA, IEEE Computer Society Press, 1991, pp. 690–693.
[2] E. Barros, W. Rosenstiel, and X. Xiong, "A method for partitioning UNITY language in hardware and software," in *Proc. EuroDAC '94*, Los Alamitos, CA, IEEE Computer Society Press, 1994, pp. 220–225.
[3] J. P. Calvez, *Embedded Real-Time Systems: A Specification and Design Methodology*. New York: Wiley, 1993.
[4] M. Chiodo, P. Giusto, A. Jurecska, H. Hsieh, A. Sangiovanni-Vincentelli, and L. Lavagno, "Hardware-software codesign of embedded systems," *IEEE Micro*, vol. 14, no. 4, pp. 26–36, Aug. 1994.
[5] P. Chou, R. Ortega, and G. Borriello, "Synthesis of the hardware/software interface in microcontroller-based systems," in *Proc. ICCAD-92*, Los Alamitos, CA, IEEE Computer Society Press, 1992, pp. 488–495.
[6] W. W. Chu and L. M.-T. Tan, "Task allocation and precedence relations for distributed real-time systems," *IEEE Trans. Comput.*, vol. C-36, pp. 667–679, June 1987.
[7] W. W. Chu, L. J. Holloway, M.-T. Lan, and Kemal Efe, "Task allocation in distributed data processing," *IEEE Comput.*, pp. 57–69, Nov. 1980.
[8] J. G. D'Ambrosio, Xiaobo Hu, and Almon Tang, "Configuration-level hardware/software partitioning for real-time embedded systems," in *Proc. Int. Workshop Hardware/Software Codesign*, Los Alamitos, CA, IEEE Computer Society Press, 1994, pp. 34–41.
[9] B. Dasarathy and M. Feridun, "Task allocation problems in the synthesis of distributed real-time systems," in *Proc. IEEE 1984 Real-Time Syst. Symp.*, 1984, pp. 135–144.
[10] A. M. Davis, *Software Requirements: Analysis and Specification*. Englewood Cliffs, NJ: Prentice Hall, 1990.
[11] R. Ernst, J. Henkel, and T. Benner, "Hardware-software co-synthesis for microcontrollers," *IEEE Design & Test Comput.*, vol. 10, Dec. 1993.
[12] J. Henkel and R. Ernst, "A path-based technique for estimating hardware runtime in HW/SW-cosynthesis," in *Proc. 8th Int. Symp. Syst. Synth.*, Los Alamitos, CA, IEEE Computer Society Press, 1995, pp. 116–121.
[13] S. Even, *Graph Algorithms*. Los Alamitos, CA: Computer Science Press, 1979.
[14] M. R. Garey and David S. Johnson, *Computers and Intractability: A Guide to the Theory of NP-Completeness*. San Francisco, CA: W. H. Freeman, 1979.
[15] P. Gopinath and R. Gupta, "Applying compiler techniques to scheduling in real-time systems," in *Proc. 1990 IEEE Real-Time Syst. Symp.*, pp. 247–256.
[16] A. P. Gupta, W. P. Birmingham, and D. P. Siewiorek, "Automating the design of computer systems," *IEEE Trans. Computer-Aided Design*, vol. 12, pp. 473–487, Apr. 1993.
[17] R. K. Gupta and G. De Micheli, "Hardware-software cosynthesis for digital systems," *IEEE Design & Test Comput.*, vol. 10, pp. 29–41, Sept. 1993.
[18] T. B. Ismail, K. O'Brien, and A. Jerraya, "Interactive system-level partitioning with PARTIF," in *Proc. EDAC '94*, Los Alamitos, CA, IEEE Computer Society Press, 1994.
[19] E. D. Lagnese and D. E. Thomas, "Architectural partitioning of system level synthesis of integrated circuits," *IEEE Trans. Computer-Aided Design*, vol. 10, pp. 847–860, July 1991.
[20] D. W. Leinbaugh and M.-R. Yamani, "Guaranteed response times in a distributed hard-real-time environment," in *Proc. 1982 Real-Time Syst. Symp.*, Los Alamitos, CA, IEEE Computer Society Press, 1982, pp. 157–169.
[21] C. Y. Park and A. C. Shaw, "Experiments with a program timing tool based on source-level timing scheme," *IEEE Comput.*, vol. 24, pp. 48–57, May 1991.
[22] M. Potkonjak and W. Wolf, "Cost optimization in ASIC implementation of periodic hard-real time hardware systems using behavioral synthesis techniques," in *Proc. ICCAD-95*, Los Alamitos, CA, IEEE Computer Society Press, 1995.
[23] S. Prakash and A. C. Parker, "SOS: Synthesis of application-specific heterogeneous multiprocessor systems," *J. Parallel Distrib. Comput.*, vol. 16, pp. 338–351, 1992.
[24] K. Ramamritham, J. A. Stankovic, and P.-F. Shiah, "Efficient scheduling algorithms for real-time multiprocessor systems," *IEEE Trans. Parallel Distrib. Syst.*, vol. 1, pp. 184–194, Apr. 1990.
[25] C. Rosebrugh and E.-K. Kwang, "Multiple microcontrollers in an embedded system," *Dr. Dobbs J.*, pp. 48–57, Jan. 1992.
[26] B. Selic, G. Gullekson, and P. T. Ward, *Real-Time Object-Oriented Modeling*. New York: Wiley, 1994.
[27] C.-C. Shen and W.-H. Tsai, "A graph matching approach to optimal task assignment in distributed computing systems using a minimax criterion," *IEEE Trans. Comput.*, vol. C-34, pp. 197–203, Mar. 1985.
[28] S. Shlaer and S. J. Mellor, *Object Lifecycles: Modeling the World in States*. New York: Yourdon, 1992, ch. 5.
[29] Signetics, "The I2C-bus and how to use it (including specification)," Jan. 1992.
[30] G. C. Sih and E. A. Lee, "Declustering: A new multiprocessor scheduling technique," *IEEE Trans. Parallel Distrib. Syst.*, vol. 4, pp. 625–637, June 1993.
[31] M. B. Srivastava, T. I. Blumenau, and R. W. Brodersen, "Design and implementation of a robot control system using a unified hardware-software rapid-prototyping framework," in *Proc. ICCD '92*, Los Alamitos, CA, IEEE Computer Society Press, 1992.
[32] M. Slater, *Microprocessor-Based Design*. Englewood Cliffs, NJ: Prentice Hall, 1989.
[33] H. S. Stone, "Multiprocessor scheduling with the aid of network flow algorithms," *IEEE Trans. Software Eng.*, vol. SE-3, pp. 85–93, Jan. 1977.
[34] F. Vahid, J. Gong, and D. D. Gajski, "A binary-constraint search algorithm for minimizing hardware during hardware/software partitioning," in *Proc. EuroDAC '94*, Los Alamitos, CA, IEEE Computer Society Press, 1994, pp. 214–219.
[35] W. Wolf, "Hardware-software co-design of embedded systems," *Proc. IEEE*, July 1994.
[36] W. Wolf, A. Wolfe, S. Chinatti, R. Koshy, G. Slater, and S. Sun, "TigerSwitch: A case study in embedded system design," in *Proc. Int. Workshop Hardware/Software Codesign*, Los Alamitos, CA, IEEE Computer Society Press, 1994.

Wayne H. Wolf (S'78–M'83–SM'91) for a photograph and biography, see this issue, p. 210.

Control Generation for Embedded Systems Based on Composition of Modal Processes *

Pai Chou, Ken Hines, Kurt Partridge, and Gaetano Borriello

Department of Computer Science and Engineering, Box 352350
University of Washington, Seattle, WA 98195-2350 USA
{chou,hineskj,kepart,gaetano}@cs.washington.edu

Abstract

In traditional distributed embedded system designs, control information is often replicated across several processes and kept coherent by application-specific mechanisms. Consequently, processes cannot be reused in a new system without tailoring the code to deal with the new system's control information. The *modal process* framework [5] provides a high-level way to specify the coherence of replicated control information independently of the behavior of the processes. Thus multiple processes can be composed without internal tailoring and without suffering from errors common in lower-level specification styles. This paper first describes a kernel-language representation for the high-level composition operators; it also presents a synthesis algorithm for the *mode manager*, the runtime code that maintains control information coherence within and between distributed processors.

1 Introduction

To handle the ever-increasing complexity of distributed embedded systems, modern design methodologies must support system *composition*. For this reason, most distributed embedded systems are modeled as communicating *processes*. Process composition has been particularly successful in data-dominated applications, because a set of dataflow processes can be composed as long as they agree on the protocol and data format of their communication.

However, existing process models, based on the idea of *functional decomposition*, do not compose control very well. Control information shared among multiple processes must be encoded as data and communicated using messages.

---

*This work was supported by PYI MIP-8858782, DARPA DAAH04-94-G-0272, and a Mentor fellowship.

Permission to make digital or hard copies of all or part of this work for personal or classroom use is granted without fee provided that copies are not made or distributed for profit or commercial advantage and that copies bear this notice and the full citation on the first page. To copy otherwise, to republish, to post on servers or to redistribute to lists, requires prior specific permission and/or a fee.
ICCAD98, San Jose, CA, USA
© 1998 ACM 1-58113-008-2/98/0011..$5.00

Transmissions, receipts, and tests of control information must then be sprinkled throughout the data-processing code. This approach is error-prone. For example, an update may be accidentally omitted, and deadlock or other synchronization problems may occur. Furthermore, although processes with control information are composable, they are not very modular. Any change involving shared control information requires changing multiple processes [3]. Control-dominated languages such as Esterel [1] and StateCharts [6] attempt to address these problems by also supporting the *temporal decomposition* style of specification. Unfortunately, this results in monolithic, centralized control with no modularity.

Thus, code is rarely reused as is. Since a process must make fixed assumptions about what control interface it wishes to have, it must anticipate the control interactions of any other process with which it is composed. If its interface does not match what is expected by other processes, it cannot be composed with them. Instead, it or some of the other processes must be modified, or an application-specific translation process must be inserted between them. Modification is sometimes impossible for intellectual property reasons, and translation processes tend to be inefficient. Moreover, both techniques require an intimate understanding of what, when, and how control is shared, thus potentially introducing new coherence maintenance errors every time supposedly "reusable" processes are composed.

We introduce the *modal process* framework [5] with an emphasis on enabling *control composition*. Each modal process consists of a set of run-to-completion *handlers* and *modes*. A mode is an enable bit for a set of handlers and is also a basis for spanning the control state space of the system. Rather than keeping modes coherent by communicating their values at the application level, the designer composes the control aspect of the system by applying instances of *abstract control types* (ACTs) to modes of different modal processes. A set of runtime *mode managers* ensures that control is kept coherent on all processes in the system, communicating between themselves as needed. Because the ACTs handle system-level control through mode managers, the modal processes are free to focus on specific modular, reusable behaviors. Modal processes also enhance *retargetability* by synthesizing the runtime system for a specific distributed target architecture, potentially with different processes-to-processor allocations, without requiring the designer to write low-level synchronization primitives.

This paper describes the semantics of modal processes and the synthesis of mode managers. For synthesis, the coherence requirements are expanded into basic constraint primitives and checked for consistency. Depending on the constraint topology, various optimizations are possible for greater run-time efficiency in terms of both space and time.

2 Programming model

This section describes the two fundamental aspects of our programming model: modal processes and abstract control types. We illuminate this discussion with aspects of a mobile robot example, with control composed from processes for controlling its wheels, its sonar, and its bumper sensor.

2.1 modal processes

A modal process contains a set of code segments called *handlers*, which can be triggered by *events*. Examples of events are notifications of elapsed times and message arrivals. Similar to ROOM [7], the handlers execute with run-to-completion semantics, such that once a handler begins execution, no other handler in that process may execute until it completes. In addition, a modal process also has a number of *modes* that govern the behavior of the process. The state of a mode is called its *status*, which can be either *active* or *inactive*. When a mode is active, it can enable the invocation of a set of handlers to respond to events. A vector that represents the active/inactive status of all modes is known as a *configuration*. Associated with each configuration is a *scheduling policy* that manages the processing of events.

When a handler finishes execution, it may return a request for a configuration change. Changes to the configuration on one modal process may affect the configuration of another modal process. Hence configuration changes are negotiated using a mechanism called a *vote*. In a single-processor architecture, the vote may be processed immediately, but in a distributed architecture, multiple votes may be requested simultaneously, and they must be resolved before being allowed to proceed.

A vote contains a set of pairs, each of which names a mode in the handler's modal process, and the desired new value for the mode. Formally, each component of a vote $v \in V$ is defined to be a member of $M \times \{$'+', '−'$\}$, where + means to *activate* the mode (change its status to active), and − means to *deactivate* the mode (change its status to inactive), and M is the set of modes. Any modes in the modal process unmentioned by the vote are treated as "don't cares." However, these modes as well as modes of other modal processes may still be indirectly affected by this vote through composed control.

ACT	input cond.	output cond.
unify($m[1:N]$)	$\pm m[i]$	$\pm m[\forall j]$
mutex($m[1:N]$)	$m[i] \wedge +m[j]$	$-m[i]$
mutexLock($m[1:N]$)	$m[i] \wedge +m[j]$	deny $+m[j]$
parent($p, m[1:N]$)	$\neg p \wedge +m[i]$	$+p$
	$-p$	$-m[1:N]$
(with default)	$+p$	$+m[1]$
guardian($p, m[1:N]$)	$\neg p \wedge +m[i]$	deny $+m[i]$
	$-p$	$-m[1:N]$
(with default)	$+p$	$+m[1]$
preempt($p, m[1:N]$)	$p \wedge +m[i]$	deny $+m[i]$
sequencing($m[1:N]$)	$-m[i]$	$+m[(i\%N)+1]$
seqLoop($s, m[1:N]$)	$+s$	$+m[1]$
	$s \wedge -m[i]$	$+m[(i\%N)+1]$

Table 1: Examples of ACTs

2.2 abstract control types

Control composition is accomplished by means of instantiating abstract control types (ACTs), each of which defines a pattern for constraining how control should flow between a set of modes. This view is similar to the Livingstone [8] approach to reactive self-configuring systems used in the NASA Deep-Space One Probe (DS1) project. However, instead of solving the general satisfiability problem with a fast heuristic for the purpose of reconfiguring the system in response to failed valves, modal processes solve a more restricted problem for the purpose of propagating mode changes imperatively. ACTs can also be prioritized, allowing behavioral composition similar to the subsumption architecture [2]. While handlers are allowed to change only those modes that are local to their process, ACTs allow the local effects to be propagated to other processes globally, as well as customizing the behavior of individual processes.

Some commonly used ACTs are shown in Table 1. The most common way control is composed is to use the `unify` ACT, which correlates modes in different processes and keeps their status the same. In addition, ACTs can relate a set of modes as a flat FSM with the `mutex` ACT, or as superstates/substates with the `parent` ACT; the `sequencing` ACT can be used to express structured control flow. Moreover, `mutexLock` and `guardian` ACTs refine the semantics of `mutex` and `parent` with their ability to *deny* activation requests when locked or when the designated superstate is inactive. The key point is that the framework enables control composition using ACTs as high-level operators that are user definable in terms of simpler ACTs.

example: mobile robot

Consider the example of a bumper process in a mobile robot. The robot normally moves forward until the bumper is hit. Whenever the bumper is hit, the robot should go in reverse until two seconds after the bumper has been released, then it turns 45 degrees before going forward again. Fig. 1(a) shows a StateChart that captures this behavior. The states are F (forward), B (bumped), W (waiting for 2 second since release), and T (turn).

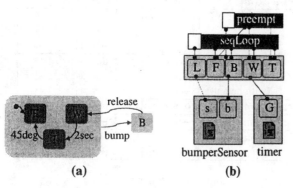

composed mode	hidden mode	component process	mode binding
F		(none)	(none)
B		bumperSensor	b
	L		s
W		timerProcess	G
T		(none)	(none)
ACTs for control composition			
preempt(B, [F, W, T])			
seqLoop(L, [F, B, W, T])			

Table 2: Control composition of the bumper process from two reusable components.

Figure 1: (a) The bumper process described in StateCharts; (b) composition of the bumper process from two reusable components.

The same behavior can be obtained by composition from two reusable components: a bumper sensor and a timer process (Fig. 2) and Table 2. Note that the preempt ACT is assigned a higher priority than the seqLoop.

mode	handler
	bumper sensor
s	on (bumping) vote(+b);
	on (releasing) vote(−b);
b	(no handler)
	timer process
G	on (modeEntry) $t := 2$ sec; enableTimer();
	on (tick) if $(--t \leq 0)$ vote(−G);
	on (modeExit) disableTimer();

Figure 2: Reusable modal processes to be composed for the bumper process.

Fig. 3 shows how the composition works. On powerup (Fig. 3(a)), the system initializes to the desired configuration. In this case, mode s should be activated to sense the bumper (bubble (0)). Because L is bound to s and serves as the scope mode in seqLoop, +L implies +F, the first body mode of seqLoop (bubble (1)), resulting in the configuration shown in Fig. 3(b). When the bumper is hit, mode b is activated by the bumper-sensing handler (bubble (2)). Since b is bound to B and serves as the preempting condition for preempt, it forces the deactivation of [F, W, T] (bubble 3). When the bumper is released, the bumper-sensing handler deactivates b (bubble 4), which also deactivates B, and seqLoop activates the next mode in sequence, namely W (bubble 5). Since W is unified with the timer's G, it effectively starts the count-down timer. When the timer finishes counting down, it deactivates G (bubble 6) and therefore votes for −W, causing seqLoop to activate T for turning (bubble 7). When

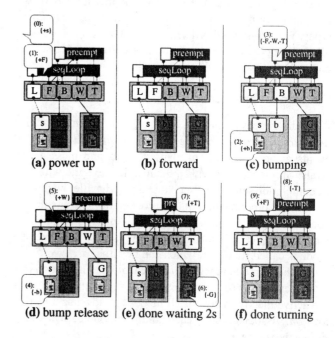

(a) power up (b) forward (c) bumping
(d) bump release (e) done waiting 2s (f) done turning

Figure 3: Illustration of operation of the composed bumper process.

turning is completed, the turning handler (not shown) deactivates T mode (bubble 8), causing seqLoop to activate F mode (bubble 9). The resulting configuration in Fig. 3(f) is identical to Fig. 3(b).

3 A kernel language

In this section we discuss one perspective on the evaluation semantics for *stateless* ACTs, or ACTs whose behavior is purely functional. The current tool uses a simple *kernel language* for representing ACTs, consisting of only a single simple constraint (Γ) which operates on a sensitivity list, an activity, and an environment. The environment contains consistent configurations for modes in the system. Each primitive constraint is associated with a priority, which may or may not coincide with the evaluation order.

This representation is useful for a couple of reasons: first, it simplifies the evaluation semantics, and pushes the complexity to the compiler instead of the runtime environment, and second, it simplifies many of the consistency checks that we may want to run on a system before committing to a runtime system.

$\Gamma : senselist \to action \to Z \to 2^M \to M \to env \to env$

In the following:

- P represents a modelist of all source modes.
- S represents a senselist representing (parameterized) sensitivity.
- a represents the target mode of the constraint
- A represents the action to be performed on the target mode.
- E represents the environment in which this constraint is evaluated.
- and as indicated above, the final return value is an environment.

$[[(P,S)\Gamma(a,A)]](E) = if(E \cap S(a) = S, E \uplus (a,A), E)$

$A \uplus B = A \cup B - \{\text{values that contradict B}\}$

Figure 4: Semantics of the primitive constraint.

As shown in Fig 4, the primitive constraint Γ is a function that takes the following curried parameters: a sensitivity list ($\subset senselist = \{(m,p) \| m \in \text{Modes}, p \in \{'+','-','T','F'\}\}$), an action to be performed on a mode ($\in action = \{'+','-'\}$), a priority ($\in Z$), an input list ($\in 2^M$), an output ($\in M$) and an environment ($\in env$) and returns an environment.

So–if all of the conditions of the sensitivity list are met by the environment when the constraint is evaluated, then the constraint performs the appropriate action on the environment–but only if this action has not already been preempted by a constraint with a higher priority. Notice that this implies that the conditions in a sensitivity list for a single constraint are related through conjunction. We can achieve a disjunctive relationship by using multiple constraints.

It is important to note that the evaluation order and the priority of constraints are specified separately. A significant effect of this is that constraints can cause changes in the environment that may not appear directly in the new configuration. For example, a particular mode may be associated with activation at some point during the evaluation, and this apparent activation may be propagated through the system – but later this same mode may be deactivated by a constraint with higher priority. This allows modes to be used as temporary place-holders in determining a new configuration.

The curried parameters in the functional definition of the primitive constraint allow us to specialize this for certain general applications. For example, one interesting set of primitive constraints are called the *force* constraints. These

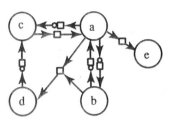

Figure 5: A bipartite digraph representation of modes with primitive constraints.

are constraints with single input and output modes, and are sensitive only to changes. This type of constraint is commonly given a two letter designation indicating the input sensitivity and output action (e.g. AA for activation ('+') sensitivity and an activation action, DA for deactivation ('−') sensitivity and an activation action etc.) Force constraints are actually sufficient for representing many ACTs, so they will appear often in the following discussion.

3.1 graph formulation

A system of modes and primitive constraints can be represented as a bipartite graph $G(M, C, E)$, where M is a set of vertices representing modes, C is a set of vertices representing primitive constraints, and E represents the edges. An example of a graphic representation is shown in figure 5, in which modes are represented by round vertices and constraints are represented by square vertices. Some shorthand is employed in this example: edges entering constraints with small circles indicate '−' sensitivity, edges exiting constraints with small circles indicate a '−' action, and edges without the small circles indicate '+' sensitivity or actions. Note: this graph does not show any information pertaining to evaluation order or to priority. This information was left off for clarity. Also note that most constraints shown in this graph are simple force constraints, with the only exception being the conjunctive constraint between a, b and d (as explained earlier, the evaluation semantics consider the conjunction of all edges entering a constraint vertex, and the disjunction of all edges entering a mode vertex)

3.2 ACT expansion

Building a constraint graph from a set of modes and stateless ACTs is performed by treating each ACT as a constraint macro, and expanding it into its relevant constraints. Both priority and evaluation order are derived from the original ACT description.

As an example, consider the composition of the bumper and wheels processes in Fig. 6. The bumper process is internally constrained as a composition of a seqLoop(F, R, W, T) at priority 1 and preempt(R, F, W, T) at priority 2. It is possible to apply ACTs across the processes, such as the or that designates R and W of the bumper process as the chil-

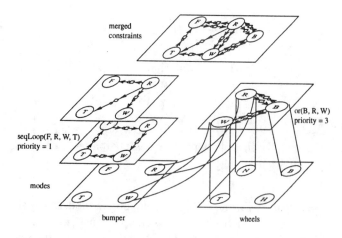

Figure 6: example of ACT expansion on the bumper and wheels processes

dren of mode B of the wheels process. These constraints are merged as shown at the top of Fig 6.

checking consistency

In many applications, the reduction of ACTs to simple constraints makes it possible to perform a variety of consistency checks. An example of one such check is the finding of constraint conflicts, which may result in race conditions. Constraint conflicts occur when the change of one mode propagates through the constraint graph over two separate paths which result in conflicting votes for a single mode. Although this may be desired behavior in some circumstances, such as when the conflict is used to maintain some temporary state, if both paths have the same priority and execution order is arbitrary, this situation may cause an indeterminate system.

To perform a conservative constraint conflict check, it is only necessary to take a transitive closure of the constraints, and compare constraints with a match between left hand side and right hand side arguments.

optimization

There are several optimizations available for a constraint graph, and although many of these depend on the target architecture of the system and will be addressed in later sections, there are some optimizations that may be performed directly when transforming ACTs to constraint graphs. For example, an optimization that may be performed with unification ACTs is to collapse the unified modes into a single *supermode*.

4 Centralized mode manager

Following the transformation of ACTs and constraints into their runtime form, the mode manager code that implements the constraints must be produced. The implementation depends significantly on whether the target architecture is a uniprocessor or a distributed architecture. The discussion of distributed architecture implementations is postponed to the next section.

The centralized mode manager has a notion of a discrete *step*, which defines a sequential boundary for a set of votes to be accumulated and resolved as a single externally visible change of configuration. We support two possible step semantics: event-triggered and time-triggered. Both share the same engine that computes the next configuration.

4.1 computing a new configuration

Algorithm 4.1 Centralized mode manager configuration selection.

foreach vote $V = \{(m_i, s_i, p_i) \in M \times \{+,-\} \times Z\}$
  foreach $((m_i, s_i, p_i) \in V)$
    $m_i.\text{set}(s_i, p_i)$
foreach constraint $C = (\{(m_j, s_j) \in M \times \{+,-,'T','F'\}\},$
  $(m_i, s_i, p_i))$
  ifall $m_j.\text{polarity} == s_j$ **and** $p_i > m_i.\text{priority}$
    $m_i.\text{set}(s_i, p_i)$

Algorithm 4.1 shows how the next configuration is computed. At the end of a step, the mode manager is given an ordered set of requests, or votes, to change either part or all of the configuration. Each vote is a set of tuples $V = \{(m_i, s_i, p_i) \in M \times \{A, D\} \times Z\}$, where m_i is the specific mode to change, and s_i indicates whether it should be activated or deactivated. Each mode with a pending vote is set to the vote's value, and flagged with the priority of the vote. If there are multiple votes for a single mode, then the mode is set to the value of the highest priority vote. (Since potential votes must be totally ordered, there is always a uniquely chosen vote.)

In the next step, the mode manager evaluates each primitive constraint according to the evaluation order specified by the designer (or the source ACTs) depending on whether or not the constraint has higher priority than the vote already placed on the target mode. Higher priority constraints are always evaluated, even if their result would not conflict with the state of the target since these may change the priority of the state.

Example

To illustrate the operation of the mode manager algorithm, we consider an example based on the bumper process of the robot (Fig. 7). Note that the mode manager maintains the configurations without using any knowledge about what processes the modes belong to. Therefore, the mechanism for managing modes within a process is exactly the same as that for a set of processes.

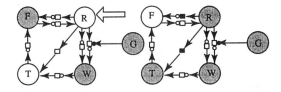

Figure 7: Example for computing the next configuration.

Assume the current configuration is { F, W, G }, and a handler votes for activation of R. The algorithm first marks R active, then iterates over all constraints in the system that are sensitive to this change. These constraints are AD(R, F), AA(R, T), and the conjunctive constraint sensitive to +R and $'F'G$. DA(R, W) is not applicable because the vote is for activation, not deactivation. The result: F is deactivated and T is activated, however, since G is active, the conjunctive constraint is not satisfied and therefore W does not change. The resulting configuration is therefore { R, T, W, G }.

4.2 voting steps

The execution of a modal process system with centralized control can be viewed as a sequence of discrete steps. All events generated during a step are consumed during a later, though not necessarily the next, step. Furthermore, no handler execution crosses a step boundary. Several handlers may be invoked in a given step. If they requests mode changes, the requests are queued until the end of the step when they are processed collectively for the next step. We provide the mechanism for defining a variety of steps, ranging from event-driven steps to dataflow and time-triggered steps.

The simplest step is defined by an event occurrence. That is, the designer may assume no simultaneous events and that a mode change request is serviced right after dispatching an event to a set of handlers. Discrete event models are more general in that events are not only completely ordered but can also be simultaneous, such that vote processing is performed after all (logically) simultaneous events have triggered their handlers.

Another way of defining steps is to mark certain event types as step-delimiting events. For synchronous dataflow (SDF) models, a reasonable step would be to process votes after an entire iteration of the dataflow graph has been invoked. This allows the dataflow graph to be invoked according to a static schedule without using the more expensive event dispatch mechanism. Although dataflow models are untimed, dispatching according to a static schedule can be extended for real-time systems by replacing dataflow events with timer events. In general, statically scheduled, time-triggered systems offer the best determinism and can make the strongest guarantee in meeting hard real-time constraints.

5 Distributed mode manager

When mapping a design to a distributed architecture, control may be implemented in a centralized or a distributed style. If the designer desires a centralized control process, the centralized mode manager described in the previous section can be used, with slight extension to communicate votes explicitly in a message. However, such an organization is not very efficient and defeats the very advantages offered by distributed architectures, because the centralized mode manager must handle and generate communication to all processes even if most are not affected by a localized mode change.

To exploit the architectural distribution, we support *distributed mode managers*, which maintain consistent mode configurations between processes residing on different processors—without centralized control. With distributed mode managers, each processor in the system is given its own mode manager and each of these coordinate activation and deactivations between themselves. In this case, however, there is no single notion of step. In fact, the rate of step progression may be different for each specific mode manager. To avoid over-specification, the modal process model does not impose specific *synchrony* semantics on the interactions between mode managers; instead, several synchrony options can be supported, as described in [4]. This section focuses on one on synchrony option called *mode synchronous* semantics, where a mode change blocks progress of only those processes whose modes are affected until their mode managers agree to it.

The synthesis steps for a distributed mode manager can be divided into graph partitioning, control communication synthesis, and local mode-manager synthesis. Local mode-managers are centralized mode managers whose inputs are their respective partitioned graphs. This section reviews the graph partitioning algorithm that has been described previously and addresses the extensions to the mode managers needed for distributed control coordination.

5.1 mode manager partitioning

In distributed implementations of a modal process system, it isn't necessary for all parts of the system to maintain the complete constraint graph. In fact, each subsystem needs only a projection of the constraint graph containing the portions relevant to the processes in that subsystem. Specifically, these are the modes that occur within these processes (the local modes), and the modes that appear as the source end of a primitive constraint that terminates at a local mode (see Figure 8 *b)* and *c)*). For more information, see [5].

5.2 control communication

Upon completion of the partitioning step, the mode manager residing on each subsystem is aware of which *voted* activations and deactivations of modes need to be transmitted to the rest of the system. Using mode synchronous semantics, the requesting subsystem is not able to perform the changes until each of the relevant subsystems acknowledges this request. Assuming reliable communication between all mode managers, there is a three phase handshake (request, acknowledge, commit) such that the requester transmits the desired activations and deactivations as a special vote to all relevant mode managers and it waits for the remote subsystems to acknowledge the requests.

The receiving subsystem mode managers include this vote in calculating the next configuration (based on this subsystem's own version of steps). In considering this sort of vote local mode managers must determine whether there were any internally generated conflicting votes—and if there were and they had higher priority than the remote vote, it must send a request of its own to the original requester before acknowledging the original request.

If it finds no such conflict, it simply acknowledges the request and places itself into a provisional state until it receives the corresponding *commit* message. From the perspective of the requester, the actual transition to a new configuration is blocked until all requests have been acknowledged. When the requester receives acknowledgments from all subsystems over all parts of the vote, it performs the action locally (provided there were no conflicts received before getting all acknowledgments) and sends *commit* messages to all relevant subsystems. If it received a conflict in the mean time, and it decided that the conflict had higher priority, then it sends *abort* messages to each of the participants.

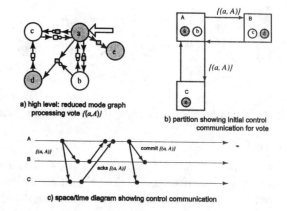

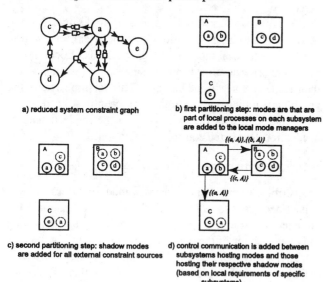

Figure 8: Shown are the steps involved in partitioning the constraint graph for individual mode managers (based on a preexisting process partition), and in synthesizing control communication.

To insure consistent choices in the event of several concurrent requests, there should be system wide total ordering of priorities that allow all subsystems to independently but

Figure 9: a) shows a system constraint graph, b) shows the mapping of nodes from this to processes in a distributed implementation and c) shows the control communication required to insure mode synchrony.

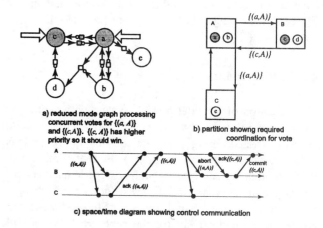

Figure 10: This shows the control communication between the processes in Figure 9 in the presence of an inter-process vote conflict.

consistently choose from among conflicting requests.

Identification of the required control communication is straightforward given the partitioning step. Any constraint such that the source mode is on one subsystem, and the terminal mode is on another implies a communication.

All subsystem mode managers are essentially centralized mode managers, and can be synthesized as demonstrated in the previous section, with some minor modifications.

5.3 Examples

In Figure 8 we show a system constraint graph, and the steps required to build consistent distributed mode managers for this. First the mode graph is partitioned across the subsystems and then the control communication is synthesized.

Next we subject this system to various conditions that might occur in choosing a new consistent configuration (shown in Figures 9 and 10). In Figure 9 the system hosts a single request for mode activation, and this is easily resolved. In Figure 10 case, there are two concurrent requests for activation, where one request has a higher priority than the the other. In this case, each of the requesting managers must evaluate the relative priority of the requests, and independently (but consistently) choose the winner. The subsystem that requested the losing activation (subsystem A in this case) is then responsible for sending abort messages to all subsystems that received the original request.

6 Results

In this section we present some results from a slightly different implementation of the wall-following robot from the one described in this paper. We look at two implementations - one with a centralized mode manager and one with a distributed mode manager. For the distributed mode manager we look at the communication bandwidth consumed by control communication, and for both we look at the percentage of computation required for maintaining mode consistent modes.

The complete example required forty-five primitive constraints and on average, sixty-three percent of these were ignored during the evaluation step because their priority was less than that of their target mode. For a centralized implementation, on average thirty percent of each scheduling cycle was spent in the mode manager, with occasional peaks of up to fifty percent. It is important to note that this time is not entirely overhead, since the mode manager replaces some activity that would normally be included in the scheduled code.

For a distributed implementation with mode synchronous communication, the average cycle time required by the mode managers rose to approximately fifty percent, with occasional spikes of up to ninety percent.

7 Conclusions

This paper describes a control generation technique for embedded systems specified as a composition of modal processes. Modal processes improve upon traditional programming models in their ability to support control composition using high-level, user-definable operators called abstract control types. The advantages include better re-use of intellectual property and also greatly enhanced retargetability of behavioral specification to heterogeneous distributed architectures. To support this design methodology, implementation techniques are developed for the automatic synthesis of the composed control, called the mode manager, for both single processor and distributed architectures, including all low-level synchronization details. While many implementations of the modal processes abstraction are possible, this paper presented an approach based on a small set of well-defined primitives, or a kernel-language, that can be composed to build up the high-level, user-definable abstractions.

Future work must progress in several directions. The approach here is applicable to *stateless* ACTs, which cover a large class of practical ACTs and enable the generation of highly efficient runtime control, but a more powerful kernel language is needed to represent those ACTs with internal states, such as a mutex that queues requests for serial activation. The mode manager implements composed control by *interpretation* of mode constraints. While this is adequate for most distributed systems where communication cost dominates the overhead, better code generation may be needed to enable low-cost embedded systems to take full advantage of this methodology. An improved user interface will greatly enhance the usability of this methodology. Graphic primitives corresponding to common ACTs can be used to provide an environment where components can be composed and the hierarchy and priority of ACTs can be more intuitively described. Finally, this approach presents new opportunities for formal verification, which may be able to take advantage of the high-level knowledge explicitly specified within the ACTs instead of rederiving it from embedded code. With careful design of the kernel language, it may be possible to extend the idea of composition from control to formal verification.

References

[1] G. Berry and G. Gonthier. The ESTEREL synchronous programming language: design, semantics, implementation. *Science of Computer Programming*, 19(2):87–152, November 1992.

[2] R. A. Brooks and J. H. Connell. Asynchronous distributed control system for a mobile robot. In *Proceedings of the SPIE - The International Society for Optical Engineering*, volume 727, pages 77–84, 1987.

[3] P. Chou. *Control Composition and Synthesis of Distributed Real-Time Embedded Systems*. PhD thesis, University of Washington, 1998.

[4] P. Chou and G. Borriello. An analysis-based approach to composition of distributed embedded systems. In *Proc. International Workshop on Hardware/Software Codesign (CODES/CACHE)*, 1998.

[5] P. Chou and G. Borriello. Modal processes: Towards enhanced retargetability through control composition of distributed embedded systems. In *Proc. Design Automation Conference*, pages 88–93, June 1998.

[6] D. Harel. StateCharts: a visual formalism for complex systems. *Science of Programming*, 8(3):231–274, June 1987.

[7] B. Selic, G. Gullekson, and P. T. Ward. *Real-Time Object-Oriented Modeling*. Wiley, 1994.

[8] B. C. Williams and P. P. Nayak. A model-based approach to reactive self-configuring systems. In *Proceedings of AAAI-96*, 1996.

Interface Co-Synthesis Techniques for Embedded Systems [*]

Pai Chou, Ross B. Ortega, Gaetano Borriello
Department of Computer Science & Engineering, Box 352350
University of Washington, Seattle, WA 98195-2350
{chou,ortega,gaetano}@cs.washington.edu

Abstract

A key aspect of the synthesis of embedded systems is the automatic integration of system components. This entails the derivation of both the hardware and software interfaces that will bind these elements together and permit them to communicate correctly and efficiently. Without the automatic synthesis of these interfaces, designers are not able to fully simulate and evaluate their systems. Frequently, they are discouraged from exploring the design space of different hardware/software partitions because practical concerns mandate minimizing changes late in the design cycle, thus leading to more costly implementations than necessary. This paper presents a set of techniques that form the basis of a comprehensive solution to the synthesis of hardware/software interfaces. Software drivers and glue logic are generated to connect processors to peripheral devices, hardware co-processors, or communication interfaces while meeting bandwidth and performance requirements. We use as examples a set of devices that communicate over an infrared local communications network (highlighting a video wrist-watch display) to explain our techniques and the need for design space exploration tools for embedded systems.

1 Introduction

Designers of task-specific systems must deal with a wide collection of interfaces. Applications range from medical instrumentation to communication and networking devices to controllers in automobiles. There are many optimization opportunities because these systems have narrower and more specialized operational requirements, and users place fewer restrictions on the components that constitute the system. Optimizing the designs leads to an emphasis on design space exploration and system integration. Designers need to rapidly evaluate implementation options, that is, they must consider different partitionings and mixes of components. The most common activity in this type of exploration is integration of the components, *i.e.*, generating the interfaces between them.

As an example, consider the class of devices that can be used with an infrared local-area network [10]. The types of possible devices range from transceivers connected to a workstation or a laptop all the way to simple identification tags for tracking people and objects. Each device must implement the same communication protocol but within very different cost constraints. For instance, identification tags must be small and inexpensive while a PC-Card (PCMCIA) transceiver for a laptop can use more expensive components that support more robust and efficient communication.

To help identify the possible optimizations, consider the video wrist-watch system shown in Fig. 1. It has a grayscale video camera whose images are scaled to the size of the wrist-watch display (128x128 8-bit pixels), compressed using pixel and frame differencing techniques, and then transmitted over the omni-directional infrared link. The images are received at the wrist-watch, decompressed, and rendered on a small LCD screen. These pieces have a wide range of implementation choices. For example, either the decompression algorithm or the display controller could be implemented in custom hardware, or on the microprocessor that will also be handling the reception of IR packets. On the camera end, the camera controller, scaler, and compressor could also be in hardware, software, or a combination depending on the capabilities of the components used.

To decide on the lowest cost mix of components and feasibility, designers must iteratively map the device's functionality to a particular hardware/software partition and target architecture (*i.e.*, the processors and devices to be used). Every time the designer explores a different system architecture, the interfaces must be redesigned. For instance, changing from a 16-bit processor to a 32-bit processor requires new glue logic and new device drivers. Alternatively, a slower processor may require additional interface logic to meet the timing constraints of a fast peripheral device. Interfacing components requires managing many details in both hardware and software; however, no CAD tools are currently available to help designers with these interfacing issues. This is unfortunate as managing all of these details is so time consuming that designers typically cannot afford to evaluate many different implementations. The tendency is to make incremental changes that keep interfaces and device drivers fixed. This leads to *overdesign*, that is, the building in of extra capacity to handle unforeseen design changes, thereby increasing the cost.

Automating the interface generation and system integration tasks is a critical part of the development of embedded system synthesis tools. Designers are quite capable of considering different global partitionings of their designs but need help in evaluating them. Interfacing and integrating system components are not only highly cumbersome and error-prone processes but also must be performed repeatedly. A tool that can manage these details and demonstrate the efficacy of the partition on a particular target architecture is critical to enabling a more complete exploration of

---
[*] This work was supported by ARPA DAAH04-94-G-0272

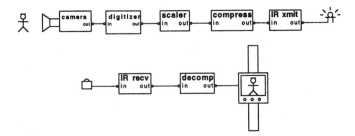

Fig. 1: The infrared video-wristwatch system. The camera unit transmits compressed video packets to a wrist-watch display.

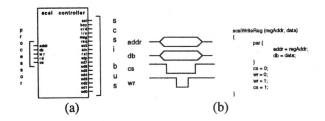

Fig. 2: SCSI controller along with access waveform and corresponding SEQ.

the design space.

This paper presents various techniques for the synthesis of the interface between hardware and software components in embedded systems. Section 2 describes the representation and main algorithm for synthesizing the interface using the processor's I/O resources (I/O ports and memory bus). Sections 3 and 4 describe the allocation of I/O ports and address/data ports for performing direct I/O. These techniques will introduce all of the necessary glue logic and generate device driver software. Section 5 describes the synthesis of the I/O sequencers (FSMs) for cases where direct I/O cannot meet the performance requirements of the device. The sequencer itself is in turn interfaced as any other device.

2 Hardware/Software Interface Synthesis

The main goal in hardware/software interface synthesis is to generate a communication link using minimal glue logic while respecting timing constraints. Automating the hardware/software interface allows designers to focus on higher-level decisions. To accomplish this requires developing the appropriate abstractions for device interfaces so that device drivers can be generated automatically. The description of the interface requirements must include detailed timing and bandwidth information for the tool to determine how the interface should be generated. The I/O capabilities of processors must also be specified in a general form. These include directly manipulable I/O pins, interrupt mechanisms, and system bus interfaces. Given the two sides of the interface (device and processor), the tool should then be able to determine the best way to interconnect them and generate the corresponding interface software and hardware.

The processor may use either *direct I/O* or *indirect I/O*. Direct I/O manipulates the interface directly without glue logic, resulting in minimum hardware cost. Indirect I/O means the processor communicates with the devices via auxiliary hardware. This may be necessary for three main reasons. First, if the processor does not have sufficient I/O resources, then it requires multiplexing logic. Second, the processor is restricted to instruction cycle timing and may require an I/O sequencer to guarantee intricate low-level device signaling constraints such as latching requirements and fast reaction times. Third, auxiliary hardware can be used as co-processors for special purposes such as bit manipulation instructions, algorithmic computations, or even coarse-grained processes to reduce the load on the processor.

After glue logic and partitioning decisions have been finalized, the device-drivers must be updated to reflect the binding of I/O resources and the introduction of the interface hardware. In this section, we describe the representation and the algorithm for interface synthesis.

2.1 Representation

The designer writes a high-level specification describing the behavior and lists the processors and peripheral devices used to implement the system. The input to the algorithm consists of descriptions for the processors, peripheral devices, and computations (in the form of control flow graphs). The first two are stored in the processor and device libraries, while the latter is derived from the behavioral description.

2.1.1 Processor Description

Each processor's I/O resources and access routines are described in the processor library. One resource is I/O ports which are listed with their directionality (input, output, or bidirectional), the physical pins that constitute the logical port, and the different ways they can be addressed. For example, the Intel 87c51 microcontroller has four 8-bit bidirectional I/O ports P0, P1, P2 and P3, each of which is also bit-addressable. Other processors, such as the Intel i960, do not have built-in I/O ports, but may use external ones created with port expander chips. Templates for connecting these expander chips to the processor are also defined in the processor library.

Another resource that can be used for I/O is the memory bus, which consists of an address port and a data port. Additionally, the library includes the I/O instructions and auxiliary hardware needed to produce the waveforms for a memory transaction. The library also captures other I/O resources such as a serial line controller (UART or I^2C bus interface), or an A/D converter which may be built into the processor.

2.1.2 Device Description

The device library contains for each device a description of its ports, interface properties, and low-level access routines. A device port is said to be *guarded* if it is able to isolate itself from a shared bus. A guarded port is not active unless its associated control signals, called *guards*, enable it. That is, the device does not sample or drive the guarded ports until the guard becomes true. The guards, by definition, are always active. As an example, the SCSI Controller shown in Fig. 2a has five ports that must be connected to a processor: DB (8-bit data port), ADDR (4-bit address port),

CS (1-bit chip select), WR (1-bit write mode), and RD (1-bit read mode). Port CS guards DB, ADDR, WR, and RD.

To communicate with a peripheral device, the processor must generate a sequence of signals that read and write the device's ports. These signal sequencings, called *SEQs*, are atomic routines that comprise a low-level procedural interface to the device. The SEQs can be viewed as a textual representation of the waveforms the processor will generate. SEQs are derived from the timing diagrams for the device's interfaces and are customized to the capabilities of the processor in question [3]. SEQs are basic-block primitives. All control constructs such as loops and conditionals are expressed in *higher-level device drivers*. Another difference between SEQs and drivers is that only SEQs may directly access device ports whereas drivers must access them via calls to SEQs. Timing constraints can be specified on signaling events within a SEQ as well as between two SEQs invoked by a driver.

Consider the example of a SEQ that writes a parameter to an internal register in the SCSI Controller (see Fig. 2b). First, the register's address and the data to be written are placed on the ADDR and DB ports, respectively. Second, the chip is selected (enabled) by setting CS. Next, WR is pulsed to clock the data into the chip. Finally, the chip is deselected.

2.1.3 Control Flow Graphs

At the high level, the behavioral description of the system is parsed and transformed into control flow graphs (CFGs) which call the device-drivers to perform I/O. By default, the CFGs are implemented in software. The designer may tag portions of the CFGs to be implemented in hardware. These will be synthesized by a behavioral synthesis tool after an interfacing mechanism to software is added (*i.e.*, an I/O sequencer for passing input and output parameters).

2.1.4 Output

The interface synthesizer outputs all the information necessary for the construction of the system. This includes a complete hardware netlist and software for the processors. In addition, the hardware output consists of interface glue logic modules described in structural Verilog to be synthesized by a behavioral compiler. The software output consists of access routines for all of the peripheral devices and I/O sequencers. The access routines contain either I/O port instructions or load/store instructions mapped to I/O addresses. Using the output from the interface synthesizer along with the compiled control algorithms specified in the behavioral description, a designer can construct and power-up a fully functional system.

2.2 Main Algorithm

The main algorithm (Fig. 3) is called with four parameters: CFG_{SW}, CFG_{HW}, *DeviceList*, and *ProcessorList*. CFG_{SW} is the set of control flow graphs to be implemented in software. CFG_{HW} are the control flow graphs implemented in hardware and requiring I/O sequencers. *DeviceList* is the list of peripheral devices to be connected to the processors in *ProcessorList*. Each device is connected to one and only one processor and each processor may control multiple devices.

The first step of the algorithm synthesizes hardware sequencers for CFG_{HW} and their access routines from

```
SynthesizeInterface( CFG_SW, CFG_HW, DeviceList, ProcessorList)
{ foreach Processor ∈ ProcessorList
    // generate I/O hardware and new software access routines
    SequencerList := SynthesizeSequencer(CFG_SW, CFG_HW);
    DeviceList := DeviceList ∪ SequencerList;
    // First, use processor's I/O ports
    ConnectedPorts := AllocIOPorts(Processor, DeviceList);
    // Connect remaining ports with MMIO
    if (MMIO(Processor, DeviceList − ConnectedPorts, IOPrefix) == fail)
        return fail;
    GenerateSoftware();
    return success;
}
```

Fig. 3: Main algorithm for interface synthesis

CFG_{SW}. The next step allocates I/O resources for the devices controlled by direct I/O, including the newly synthesized sequencers. The algorithm first attempts to use I/O ports if the processor has them. If there are any unconnected device ports remaining, then the algorithm connects them using memory-mapped I/O. Finally, the algorithm generates the device drivers by binding device ports in the SEQs to the I/O resources of the processors. In the next section, we summarize the port allocation algorithm (described in detail in [1]) and present a preprocessing step called port-width partitioning. Memory-mapped I/O and sequencer synthesis are described in sections 4 and 5.

3 Interface Synthesis using I/O Ports

The I/O port allocation algorithm assigns processor I/O ports for communication with peripheral devices. Interface synthesis using I/O ports has been described in [1] with an $O(n^2)$ greedy sharing heuristic, where n is the number of device ports. The algorithm assumes that oversized device ports, if any, have been partitioned manually. In this section, we review this algorithm, introduce a new automated port partitioning technique, and illustrate their application with an example.

3.1 I/O Port Allocation

The algorithm considers the n device ports in order of decreasing size. This order maximizes sharing opportunities among device ports. The greedy sharing heuristic is based on the observation that guarded ports from different devices cannot be simultaneously active and therefore may share the same I/O port without multiplexing logic or a performance penalty. Unguarded device ports, including all guard ports, are always active, and so the algorithm allocates dedicated I/O ports for them.

If there are not enough I/O ports, the algorithm adds multiplexing logic to enable some unguarded device ports to share I/O resources with other device ports. Two techniques for this are *forced sharing* and *encoding transformation*. Forced sharing adds a latch or a tristate, depending on the directionality of the device port, to free up a dedicated I/O port, at the expense of a newly introduced guard signal. For single-bit device ports, such a scheme is actually a loss. Instead, encoding transformation adds a decoder or a multiplexor to encode the address for a group of single-bit ports.

After the device ports have been allocated I/O resources, the SEQs are customized to reflect the choice of processor ports and any interface logic that has been introduced. The algorithm outputs assembly code constituting the I/O primitives for the higher-level device drivers.

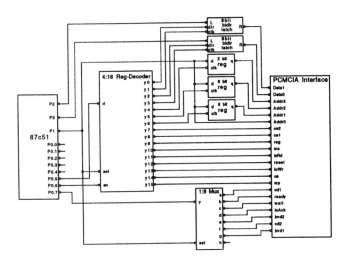

Fig. 4: Automatic I/O Port Allocation and Port-Splitting for connecting an 8-bit Microcontroller to a PC-Card Interface

3.2 Port-Width Partitioning

The main port allocation algorithm assumes that none of the device ports are larger than the largest processor I/O port. If one is, then the preprocessing step described in this subsection divides it into several smaller ones, by introducing an interface component if needed. Many microcontroller families include processor versions with very different I/O port capabilities, hence, automating this task is necessary to facilitate experimentation with different processors.

A device port is called *splittable* if it can be read or written in pieces without data consistency problems. For example, a touchtone generator is a combinational device with an input port that requires valid tone codes. Writing only to a slice of the input port may cause an invalid tone to be emitted. A register placed in front of the tone generator can act as a staging area for data delivered in slices. An output port is splittable if its value remains stable while the guard is true. Unguarded output ports are not splittable because the data values may change between sampling the different slices. Bidirectional device ports can be split using a register in each direction with complementary output enables. The device library contains an attribute that indicates whether a device port is splittable.

3.3 Example: I/O Port Allocation after Device Port Splitting

As an example where splitting ports is necessary consider connecting an 8-bit microcontroller directly to a PC-Card bus, which is treated as a peripheral device (see Fig. 4). The PC-Card device has a 26-bit address port and a 16-bit bidirectional data port along with card enables CE1, CE2, and other control ports.

Either CE1 or CE2 guards the remaining PC-Card ports. Therefore, the preprocessor partitions the address port into three 8-bit ports (ADDR0, ADDR1, ADDR2) and one 2-bit port (ADDR3). The data port is partitioned into two 8-bit ports (DATA0, DATA1). Note that, because of the guards, this is a logical partitioning and the ports require no extra hardware to make them splittable.

The I/O port allocation algorithm first attempts to dedicate processor I/O ports to each of the 8-bit ports. Upon de-

```
MMIO(Processor c, DeviceList L, ioPrefix I)
{
    n := 0;
    foreach (d ∈ L) {
        n := n + 1;
        foreach (p ∈ portList(d))
            if (guarded(p)) continue;
            if p can output or p used in reading seqs of d
                or allocateDataBits(d, p) fails then
                allocateAddressBits(d, p);
        availDevSelect[d] := addrWidth(c) − #usedAddrBits(d)
    m = min_{i∈L} (#availDevSelect[i]);
    if (m ≥ n) return one-hot-encode
    if (m ≥ ⌈lg(n)⌉) return binary-encode
    return Huffman-encode
}
```

Fig. 5: Memory-Mapped I/O Algorithm

pleting I/O ports, the algorithm introduces interface hardware to force some of the 8-bit ports to share the same processor I/O port. A multiplexor is used for reading single-bit output ports. A registered decoder is used to assert one control line at a time.

4 Memory-Mapped I/O

Memory-mapped I/O (MMIO) is attempted when I/O port allocation has failed due to the lack of I/O ports. Memory-mapped devices are accessed through the address/data bus of the processor. This is more expensive than using I/O ports because it requires address matching logic. Yet, MMIO is less flexible than I/O ports because all accessing must be expressed in terms of load/store instructions, whereas I/O instructions allow for arbitrary sequencing. However, MMIO can be applied effectively to interfacing with a large class of devices when I/O ports are not available. This section presents a technique for memory-mapped I/O that introduces minimal address matching logic by efficiently assigning the address bits to the devices.

4.1 Representation

Input to the MMIO algorithm consists of a hardware template for the processor, a range of addresses reserved for I/O, and a list of devices to be connected. The output contains the address matching logic, connections made to the processor, and the updated SEQs for the devices.

Each processor in the library has a template for translating memory control signals into a waveform required by the MMIO algorithm. It assumes that memory transactions have an address cycle followed by a data cycle. The address must be valid throughout both the address and data cycles. A pulse during the data cycle causes data to be either read or written.

Each device is assigned a range of addresses. If the current memory transaction falls within its address range, then it responds according to its inputs, which are connected to the address bus and the data bus.

4.2 Memory-mapped I/O Algorithm

The MMIO algorithm has several steps (Fig. 5). First, it ensures that every device port except the guards can share the memory bus by applying *forced sharing* [1] if necessary. Second, all guarded device ports are assigned bits in the processor's data port or the remaining bits in the address port. Third, it allocates address bits to uniquely identify each device, and generates the address matching logic.

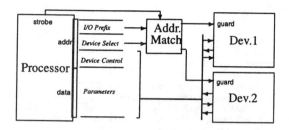

Fig. 6: Partitioning of the address space.

```
Huffman-encode(DeviceList D)
{  const m = min_{j ∈ D}(#availDevSelect[j]);
   L := ∅;
   foreach i ∈ D
      weight[i] := -#availDevSelect[i] + m + 1;
      insert i into L
   while (|L| ≥ 2)
      {i,j} := extractMin(L)
      k := makeTree(i,j)
      weight[k] := weight[i]+weight[j];
      insert k into L
   foreach i ∈ D
      devSelect[i] := pathLabel(head(L), i)
}
```

Fig. 7: Huffman Encoding

The guard for each device is connected to the *data strobe* qualified by the output of its address matching bit. The memory-mapped architecture is shown in Fig. 6. Finally, the algorithm generates software from SEQs in terms of load/store instructions.

The MMIO algorithm partitions the address word into three fields: *I/O prefix*, *device-select*, and *device-control*. The *I/O prefix* field distinguishes I/O addresses from data memory addresses. Its width is fixed, possibly zero. The *device-select* field identifies devices within the I/O address space. The *device-control* field, together with the data port, can be used to control the non-guard device pins.

The algorithm must decide whether to assign each non-guard device port to either the *device-control* field or the data port. If the device port can output, then it must be assigned data bits. If the device port is input only, and if it is used in any SEQ that also reads any port from the device, then it must be assigned to the *device-control* field. This is because it must be written to with a load instruction, which reads from but cannot write to data pins. All other device ports may be allocated either way. The algorithm will attempt allocating data bits first in order to maximize the available *device-select* field, whose size is bounded by the remaining address bits after all other fields have been assigned.

The *device-select* field is computed using one of three schemes, from the least expensive to the most expensive in terms of address matching logic: *one-hot*, *binary*, and *Huffman encoding*. If these schemes fail then the SEQs requiring the largest device-control field is divided into multiple transfers, thereby freeing address bits needed for the device-select field.

In one-hot encoding, each device is selected by one address bit qualified by the *I/O prefix*. The advantage of this technique is that it requires very simple address comparator logic (an AND gate). A binary encoding technique of the *device-select* field encodes n devices with $\lceil \log n \rceil$ bits. This technique frees $(n - \lceil \log n \rceil)$ bits from one-hot encoding by using a single $\lceil \log n \rceil$ input decoder to implement n address comparators.

If the two approaches above fail, then the algorithm attempts Huffman encoding [4] of the *device-select* field. Huffman encoding uniquely identifies each device with a variable number of address bits. It exploits situations where the devices require different numbers of bits in the *device-control* field. A device requiring more *device-control* bits is addressed by a shorter *device-select* pattern, and vice versa.

The widths of the available *device-control* fields are used as the cost parameters to Huffman encoding (Fig.7). If a device has more available *device-select* bits, then it is assigned a smaller weight, which yields a longer Huffman encoding.

If all three techniques fail to package the SEQs into single load/store instructions, then a transformation step divides the unpackageable SEQs into multiple memory instructions. This involves introducing registers and tristates to hold values for a subset of the ports in the SEQ. The remaining ports are accessed in subsequent load/store instructions. After all ports have been allocated, the MMIO algorithm generates the driver software by replacing the body of each SEQ with the appropriate memory operation(s).

4.3 Example: Wrist-watch Display by Memory Mapped I/O

We demonstrate the application of the MMIO algorithm with a video display on a wristwatch via an infrared link. The display is pieced together in quadrants using four square LCDs, each with 64x64 pixels. The peripherals include four LCDs and the IR receiving logic as well as an external 16K data memory connected to a Motorola 68hc11 microcontroller. To illustrate the MMIO algorithm, only the data and address ports of the microcontroller are considered.

The *I/O prefix* is given as zero in address bit 15 so the width of this field is one. The algorithm detects that the LCD's DB port is bidirectional and assigns it to the data port (Fig. 8). The RS and RW ports are input-only, used in reading SEQs, and are not *guards*. Therefore, they are assigned address bits 1 and 0 in the *device-control* field. The E port is a guard and is therefore connected to the output of the address comparator logic. Similarly for the receive logic, the **control** port is assigned address bits 5 through 0 and the DB port is assigned the data port. The remaining address bits are available for the *device-select* field. The one-hot test returns success because there are five memory-mapped components and nine free bits. Fig. 9 shows how the software is updated.

4.4 Electronic Rolodex by Memory-Mapped I/O

This example demonstrates how the algorithm uses Huffman encoding. It uses the 87c51 microcontroller without the I/O ports, an LCD, a tone generator, a 16K external RAM, a UART, and four individual switches. The UART is mapped to the built-in function. The other devices are memory-mapped.

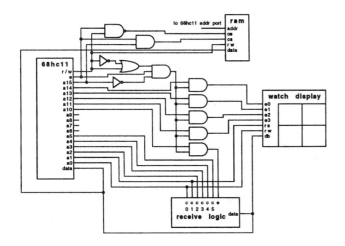

Fig. 8: Implementation of a wrist-watch display by one-hot encoded memory-mapped I/O.

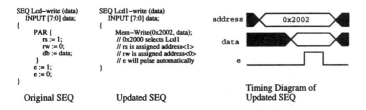

Fig. 9: Updated SEQ after memory-mapping.

First, the switches and the tone generator are not sharable, so the forced-sharing transformation is applied to make them sharable. Both one-hot and binary encodings fail because there are seven external devices (including the RAM) but only two address bits are available for the I/O prefix and the device-select fields. Therefore the Huffman encoding technique is attempted.

To perform Huffman encoding, the devices are sorted by the width of their device-control field. Note that the switches and the tone generator require no bits in the device-control field. A Huffman tree is created based on the widths of the device-control fields (see Fig. 10). This tree represents the I/O prefix and device-select fields. These address bits are connected to the address comparator logic.

5 I/O Sequencer Generation

The chosen processor may not be able to satisfy all timing constraints by direct-I/O. At the low level (SEQs), the constraints include minimum and maximum separation be-

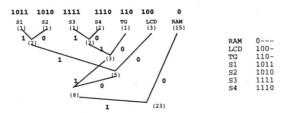

Fig. 10: Huffman tree created for electronic rolodex along with the high order address bits required to select a device.

tween signaling events. At the higher level, there may be response time and rate requirements. To meet these constraints, the designer or automated tools may move some functionality from software to hardware by tagging particular CFGs. For example, the infrared transmission protocol has intricate fine-grained timing constraints on the order of microseconds. Although it is possible to implement the protocol in software, a slow processor would not be able to service other devices at the same time. By creating a sequencer that implements the transmit protocol, the processor needs only to initiate a send command to the sequencer and can proceed to other tasks. This section describes the synthesis of this kind of hardware, which we refer to as I/O sequencers.

An I/O sequencer communicates with a peripheral on behalf of the processor. In the simplest case, a sequencer is a slave FSM that waits for the processor to pass in-parameters, invokes one of the SEQs, and returns out-parameters, if any. This requires that the processor initiate every I/O primitive. In the more sophisticated case, the sequencer autonomously interacts with the peripheral devices and the environment. The sequencer must in parallel communicate with the device and the processor. An example would be a sequencer that receives an infrared packet. This sequencer autonomously decodes the packet header, receives the specified number of bytes, calculates a checksum, and requests retransmission if necessary. After reading in the packet, the sequencer notifies the processor that a packet has arrived. After the I/O sequencer is synthesized, it is treated as a peripheral device to be connected to the processor using I/O port allocation or MMIO.

The input to the I/O sequencer generator consists of the control flow graphs to be implemented in software (CFG_{SW}) and hardware (CFG_{HW}). The output is a synthesizable description of the hardware sequencer, the connection between the sequencer and the devices it controls, and the software routines called by CFG_{SW} to access the sequencer. In addition to meeting performance requirements, the algorithm attempts to minimize the amount of hardware and the number of pins on the sequencer. We divide the problem into processor/sequencer protocol synthesis and finite state machine generation.

5.1 Algorithm for Sequencer Synthesis

The algorithm generates an I/O sequencer for each peripheral device that is accessed by a CFG tagged as hardware. An assumption of the algorithm is that if a device is accessed via a SEQ that must be implemented in hardware, then all of that device's SEQs must also be implemented in hardware. The first step is to extract all entry points from the software into the hardware to be synthesized. For each peripheral device, the extracted entry points and the reachable CFG_{HW} form an *entry cluster*.

The algorithm transforms each cluster into an I/O sequencer with customized access routines. First, it converts the hardware CFGs into FSMs using behavioral synthesis and then connects the FSMs to the corresponding peripheral device ports. The algorithm next synthesizes the communication protocol between the processor and the I/O sequencer. The protocol involves selecting the appropriate entry point, passing the parameters, and synchronization between the processor and sequencer. Finally, the algorithm connects the protocol engine and the FSM, and updates the software entry points to reflect the synthesized

```
SynthesizeSequencer(CFG_SW, CFG_HW)
{
    form entry clusters
    for each cluster
        generate FSM for CFG_HW
        generate interface to device
        encode commands with required parameters
        generate param-latching FSM
        add transitions from param FSM to CFG_HW FSM
        update CFG_SW
}
```

Fig. 11: Algorithm for sequencer synthesis

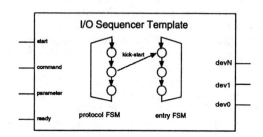

Fig. 12: I/O Sequencer template

protocol.

5.2 Protocol Synthesis

Protocol synthesis generates new SEQs for the processor to use to control the I/O sequencer as a peripheral device. These SEQs represent the new entry points into CFG_{HW}. Note that the I/O sequencer must implement all communication between the processor and the peripheral device. Furthermore, it must also provide the processor with a means of obtaining status information for the sequencer.

The template for a sequencer is shown in Fig. 12. Each entry point is encoded on the **command** port. In-parameters are passed in by selecting the appropriate entry point and pulsing the **start** signal. When invoking a call in the sequencer, the parameters can be transmitted individually or in groups. A protocol FSM reads in the parameters. The last parameter passed in kick-starts the selected entry's FSM. While the FSM is executing, the **ready** bit is set false to prevent reentrant calls to the sequencer. Upon completion, the **ready** bit is set true. The processor can now read the out-parameters in a similar manner.

The main problem in protocol synthesis is encoding the entry points and determining how to pass and retrieve parameters from the sequencer. Encoding of entry points may be done using techniques similar to encoding the *device-select* field in memory-mapped I/O (section 4.2). Unlike memory-mapped I/O, the parameters can be packaged many different ways from sending each parameter bit serially to passing all parameters simultaneously. The choice of a parameter passing protocol is influenced by timing constraints.

The algorithm's objective is to minimize the number of I/O sequencer pins required while still meeting timing constraints. The algorithm first determines W, the size of the

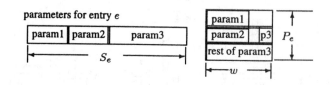

Fig. 13: Determining the number of pins required for parameter passing

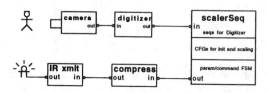

Fig. 14: Example of Sequencer Synthesis: Video Camera Scaler/Compressor with IR Transmitter

parameter port. There are two things to consider, P_e the number of time steps for passing parameters and S_e the size of data to be transferred for each entry e (see Fig. 13). The width of the **parameter** port must allow all parameters to be transferred within the allotted number of time steps. Formally, the inequality $W * P_e \geq S_e$ must hold for all entries e. Therefore, the algorithm chooses W such that:

$$W = \max_{e \in \text{cluster}} \left\lceil \frac{S_e}{P_e} \right\rceil \quad (1)$$

5.3 Example: Video Camera with Scaling

We illustrate the application of I/O sequencers with a video camera which transmits images to a host via an infrared link. It digitizes a 256x256 8-bit grayscale image, scales it down to 128x128 pixels, applies video compression using frame differencing, and then transmits the image with the IR protocol. This system has many possible implementations. We consider a partitioning where an I/O sequencer is introduced to perform scaling for the processor, in addition to handling interfacing with the digitizer. This partitioning allows the compression algorithm and the IR transmission protocol to be implemented entirely in software.

On input to the sequencer synthesizer, the control flow graph for the scaler process has been tagged as hardware. This CFG accesses the digitizer, therefore all of the digitizer's SEQs must be implemented as hardware as well. The first step of the algorithm forms the entry clusters by extracting the entry points from software. The four entries are initialization, enable-scaling, disable-scaling, and read-pixel.

For each cluster, the algorithm first generates the FSM for the CFG_{HW} by calling behavioral synthesis on the scaler process and the SEQs it invokes. The algorithm connects this FSM to the peripheral device (the digitizer in this case). Next, the algorithm encodes the commands with the required parameters. Even though the digitizer's

SEQs are also implemented in hardware, they are not directly invoked by software but rather through the sequencer and thus need not be encoded as separate commands. The only way for software to invoke the digitizer's functions is through the four entry points into the scaler's I/O sequencer which are encoded using two bits in the command field. The initialization, enable-scaling, and disable-scaling commands require no parameters, while the read-pixel command transmits an 8-bit pixel to the processor.

The state machine for handling parameter transmission and interfacing with the CFG_{HW} is generated next. It has three main states. The first state waits for the processor to send a command. The next state sends the start signal to the corresponding entry in CFG_{HW}. After the completion of the invoked entry, the third state waits for the processor to read the pixel before making a transition back to the first state. Finally, the algorithm generates the software to initialize the sequencer and to read a pixel using this synthesized protocol. The block diagram is shown in Fig. 14.

6 Conclusion

This paper presents a comprehensive set of techniques for the synthesis of hardware-software interfaces for embedded systems. Embedded system designers are challenged with meeting performance constraints while minimizing cost. Tools are needed to help designers explore the design space of possible solutions while being freed from the cumbersome tasks required for finalizing an implementation. This is crucial as it enables proper evaluation of design decisions early in the process.

Synthesis of the interfaces between system components is one of these cumbersome tasks. An interface synthesis tool incorporating the techniques presented in this paper produces the glue logic and device drivers needed to connect processors to their peripheral devices. Hardware is introduced only when necessary for handling intricate timing constraints and for multiplexing I/O resources. Once hardware decisions are finalized, device drivers are automatically customized to reflect the I/O resource bindings and auxiliary hardware introduced. We presented I/O port allocation and memory-mapped I/O for allocating I/O resources found on general purpose microprocessors. Furthermore, we presented techniques for interfacing to elements of the system's functionality that are implemented in hardware. This requires the synthesis of a parameter passing protocol that achieves the communication in the time allotted. These ideas have been validated with practical examples used throughout the paper, including several embedded systems that interact over an IR network.

The techniques and algorithms presented in this paper are part of the Chinook co-synthesis tool for embedded systems under development at the University of Washington [2]. Future work includes development of interfacing techniques that permit sharing of communication resources between processors and interprocessor communication and synchronization mechanisms that will permit exploration of software/software partitions.

References

[1] P. Chou, R. Ortega, and G. Borriello. Synthesis of the hardware/software interface in microcontroller-based systems. In *Proc. ICCAD*, pp.488–495, Nov. 1992.

[2] P. Chou, R. B. Ortega, and G. Borriello. The Chinook Hardware/Software Co-Synthesis System. In *Proc. ISSS*, Sept. 1995.

[3] P. Chou, E. A. Walkup, and G. Borriello. Scheduling for Reactive Real-Time Systems. In *IEEE Micro*, 14(4):37–47, August 1994.

[4] T. Cormen, C. Leiserson, and R. Rivest. *Introduction to Algorithms*. The MIT Press, 1990.

[5] R. Ernst, J. Henkel, and T. Benner. Hardware-software cosynthesis for microcontrollers. *IEEE Design & Test of Computers*, 10(4):64–75, Dec. 1993.

[6] R. Gupta and G. De Micheli. Hardware-software cosynthesis for digital systems. *Computers and Electrical Engineering*, 10(3):29–41, Sept. 1993.

[7] S. Narayan and D. D. Gajski. Interfacing system components by generation of interface processes. In *Proc. 32nd DAC*, June 1995.

[8] M. Srivastava, B. C. Richards, and R. W. Brodersen. System level hardware module generation. *IEEE Transactions on VLSI Systems*, 3(1), March 1995.

[9] J. S. Sun and R. W. Brodersen. Design of system interface modules. In *Proc. ICCAD*, pp.478–481, Nov. 1992.

[10] M. Weiser. Some computer science issues in ubiquitous computing. *CACM*, 36(7):74–84, July 1993.

Protocol Selection and Interface Generation for HW–SW Codesign

Jean-Marc Daveau, Gilberto Fernandes Marchioro, Tarek Ben-Ismail, *Member, IEEE*, and Ahmed Amine Jerraya, *Member, IEEE*

Abstract— The aim of this paper is to present a communication synthesis approach stated as an allocation problem. In the proposed approach, communication synthesis allows to transform a system composed of processes that communicate via high-level primitives through abstract channels into a set of processes executed by interconnected processors that communicate via signals and share communication control. The proposed communication synthesis approach deals with both protocol selection and interface generation and is based on binding/allocation of communication units. This approach allows a wide design space exploration through automatic selection of communication protocols. We present a new algorithm that performs binding/allocation of communication units. This algorithm makes use of a cost function to evaluate different allocation alternatives. We illustrate through an example the usefulness of the algorithm for allocating automatically different protocols within the same application system.

Index Terms— Communication synthesis, hardware/software codesign, interface generation, protocol selection/allocation.

I. INTRODUCTION

RECENTLY, the synthesis community has moved toward the highest level of abstraction commonly known as the system level [4], [9], [15], [16], [20], [32]. This move was motivated by the increasing complexity of systems and by the need for a unified approach to allow the development of systems containing both hardware and software. As the level of abstraction rise, some problems heretofore nonexisting appear [12], [38]. At the system level, some of the main concepts are behavior and communication [25]. These two concepts have brought new problems known as partitioning and communication synthesis. The goal of partitioning is to distribute a system functionality over a set of subsystems where each subsystem is to be executed either in software or in hardware processors [33]. The problem of communication synthesis [2], which appears after system-level partitioning, is to fix the protocols and interfaces needed by the different subsystems for the communication.

A. Objective

When designing distributed embedded systems, communication synthesis becomes essential as different subsystems inevitably need to communicate. Different communication schemes and protocols may be needed in embedded systems, as well as different interconnection topologies. Communication topologies and protocol greatly influence the overall system performances and may lead to infeasible design if the designer underestimate communication load. Decision based on the average load only tend to forget peak load or communication delay due to bus sharing, which may degrade the system performances. Therefore a large design space exploration have to be explored to find a feasible solution. In this paper we describe a paradigm that allows a wide range of communication schemes to be modeled in a synthesis oriented approach. The main objective for our communication synthesis method are as follows.

- To be able to choose between differents communication schemes.
- To be able to model the system behavior independantly of the communication. System specification should be independant of the communication specification in order to allow changes in the communication scheme without any changes in the system specification.
- To be able to reuse existing communication models through a library.
- To have an automatic communication synthesis method based on a cost function and some constraints.

This paper introduces a new approach for communication synthesis. This task is formulated as an allocation problem aimed at selecting, from a library, a set of communication units that implement the data exchange between the subsystems.

B. Previous Work

Most of the work in communication synthesis for codesign has focussed on interface synthesis assuming a fixed network structure [9], [15]. Only few works in codesign handle network synthesis [7], [13] [37]. In [13] Gong's network synthesis is guided by the mapping of variables (shared or private) to memory (local or global). In [37], Yen create a new processing element and a bus when it is not possible to assign a process to an already existing processing element or a communication on a bus without violating real time constraints. In [5] and [30], Chou and Srivastava use a set of predefined interconnection models during communication synthesis. Several works on protocol selection are reported in the software synthesis for distributed systems [29]. Much previous work has focused on interface synthesis [6], [8], [21], [22], [26]–[28], and [35]. In [6], Ecker presents a method

---

Manuscript received July 31, 1996. This work was supported by France-Telecom/CNET under Grant 94 1B 113 and SGS-Thomson.

The authors are with TIMA/INPG Laboratory, Institut National Polytechnique de Grenoble, Grenoble F-38031, France.

Publisher Item Identifier S 1063-8210(97)00736-1.

for transforming and optimising protocols. In [26], Narayan addresses the problem of bus interface generation between two different hardware modules of a partitioned specification. The focus is to optimize the bus utilization by interleaving different point to point communications on it. As described in [21], [27], Lin and Nayaran consider the problem of interface synthesis with automatic protocol conversion with one or both sides having a fixed interface. Madsen interface synthesis approach [22] consider the problem of interface adaptation between a fixed interface and a communication medium chosen during partitioning. A state based model that describes both functional and timing properties of an interface is detailed by Ravn in [28]. Another model using extended signal transition graph allowing the specification of complex synchronous/asynchronous interface is proposed by Vanbekbergen in [35]. Approaches where communication is done through shared memory are detailed in [17], [14], and [5]. In [17], the problem of interface between a memory and a coprocessor or I/O processor is addressed. In [14], Gupta also address the problem of communication between a processor (software) and a coprocessor (hardware). In that approach the communication may be done through memory or through a direct bus between the processor and an ASIC. Different communication models (blocking, non blocking) are available. These approaches mainly address the hardware/software interface. In [30], Srivastava starts after partitioning with a process graph, an architecture template and map the communication on the physically available communication resources. Only one communication model is supported, the single reader single writer first in-first out (FIFO). When the available communication resources does not directly support the FIFO protocol it is emulated. This work mainly address the field of real time distributed heterogeneous systems.

To our knowledge none of the existing work tackle communication synthesis as an allocation problem. The main contribution of this paper is to present communication synthesis as an allocation problem.

Compared to classical communication synthesis approach the main advantages of our approach are as follows:
1) wide design space exploration through automatic selection of communication protocols;
2) formulation as an allocation problem which allows numerous algorithm to solve it;
3) complete communication synthesis approach as follows:
   a) network synthesis and protocol selection;
   b) interface synthesis.
4) component reuse through library.

The limitations of our approach are as follows.
1) The need for a library of communication that must be provided by the user. It is not possible to use a protocol that is not described in the library.
2) The need for a realistic cost function for the algorithm and the need for communication estimator [37] [34] to lead network synthesis and protocol selection.

In the following sections, we present our proposed communication synthesis method. The next section introduces the

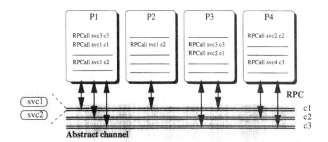

Fig. 1. Processes communicating through abstract channels.

communication model. Section II introduces the concept of communication unit. The communication synthesis problem is detailed in Section III. Section IV describes an algorithm for communication unit allocation. Finally, we will present the application of the communication synthesis method on an example before concluding the paper.

II. COMMUNICATION MODEL

In this paper, we will use the communication modeling strategy described in [19].

At the system level, a system is represented by a set of processes communicating through abstract channels (Fig. 1). An abstract channel is an entity able to execute a communication scheme invoked through a procedure call mechanism. These abstract channels offer high-level communication primitives (services) that are used by the processes to communicate. Access to a channel is controlled by a fixed set of primitives and relies on remote procedures call [1], [3] of these communication primitives. A process that is willing to communicate through a channel makes a remote procedure call to a communication primitive (*send, receive*) of that channel. Once the remote procedure call is done the communication is executed independently of the calling process by the channel unit. The communication primitives are transparent to the calling processes and are the only visible part of a channel unit. This allows processes to communicate by means of high level communication schemes. There is no predefined set of communication primitives, they are defined as standard procedures and are attached to the abstract network. Each application may have different set of communication primitives (*send_int, send_short, send_atm, etc.*). This model allows to hide the implementation details of the communication and separate communication from the rest of the design behavior. In our approach, the detailed I/O structure and protocols are hidden in a library of communication components. Fig. 1 shows a conceptual communication over an abstract communication network. The processes communicate through three abstract channels $c1$, $c2$ and $c3$. $C1$ and $c2$ offers services *svc1*, *svc2* and $c3$ offers services *svc3*, *svc4*.

III. COMMUNICATION UNIT MODELING

We define a communication unit as an abstraction of a physical component. Communication units are selected from the library and instantiated during the communication synthesis step.

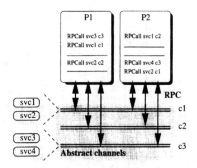

Fig. 2. Specification of communication with abstract channels.

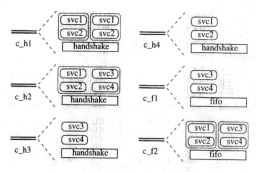

Fig. 4. Library of communication units.

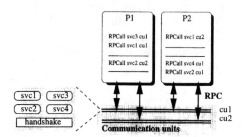

Fig. 3. Merge of abstract channels on a communication unit.

From a conceptual point of view, the communication unit is an object that can execute one or several communication primitives with a specific protocol. These services can share some common resources (bus arbiter, buffering memory, buses) provided by the communication unit. The communication unit can include a controller which determines the protocol of the communication. The complexity of the controller may range from a simple handshake to a complex layered protocol. The services interact with the controller which modifies the communication unit state and synchronizes the communication. All accesses to the interface of the communication unit are made through these services. Such services also fix the protocol of exchanging parameters between the processes and the communication unit. The use of services allows to hide the details of the protocol in a library where a service may have different implementations depending on the target architecture (hardware/software).

Communication units differs from abstract channels in the way that they implement a communication with a specific protocol and realization (hardware/software). An abstract channel just specify the required services for a communication (Fig. 2).

Therefore, several abstract channels may be implemented by a single communication unit if it is able to provide all the required services. This operation is called a *merge* of abstract channels. Fig. 3 represent a merge of two abstract channels *c1* and *c3* on a communication unit *cu1*. Communication unit *cu2* implement the communication offered by abstract channel *c2*.

This models enable the user to describe a wide range of communication schemes and most system level communication such as message passing or shared memory. Communication abstraction in this manner enables a modular specification, allowing communication to be treated independently from the rest of the design.

IV. COMMUNICATION SYNTHESIS

Communication synthesis aims to transform a system with processes that communicate via high level primitives into a set of interconnected processors that communicate via signals and share communication control. At this level the system is represented as a process graph [38]. The nodes represent the processes and the edges the communication. Communication through abstract channels is based on the remote procedure call of communication primitives (Fig. 1). Starting from such a specification two steps are needed. The first is aimed to fix the communication network structure and protocols used for data exchange. This step is called protocol selection or communication unit allocation. The second step adapt the interface of the different processes to the selected communication network.

A. Protocol Selection and Communication Unit Allocation

Allocation of communication units starts with a set of processes communicating through abstract channels (Fig. 1) and a library of communication units (Fig. 4).

These communication units are an abstraction of some physical components. This step chooses the appropriate set of communication units from the library in order to provide the services required by the communicating processes. The communication between the processes may be executed by one of the schemes described in the library. This step fixes the protocol used by each communication primitive by choosing a communication unit with a specific protocol for each abstract channel.

Several abstract channels may be executed by a single communication unit if it is able to handle several independent communications. Merging several abstract channels on a single communication unit allows to share a single communication medium among several abstract communications. The different abstract channels will be time multiplexed over the communication unit. This step also determines the interconnection topology of the processes by fixing the number of communication units and the abstract channels executed on it.

Allocation of communication units to abstract channels is related to the classical speed/area trade off. The choice of a given communication unit will not only depend on the communication to be executed but also on the performances required and the implementation technology of the communicating processes. These features may be packed into a cost function to be reduced by the allocation algorithm. This is

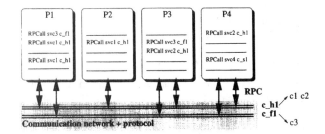

Fig. 5. System after allocation of communication units.

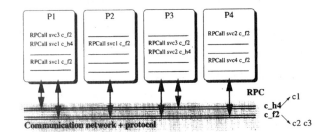

Fig. 6. Communication unit allocation alternative.

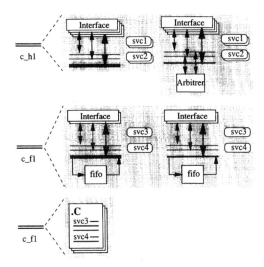

Fig. 7. Implementation library.

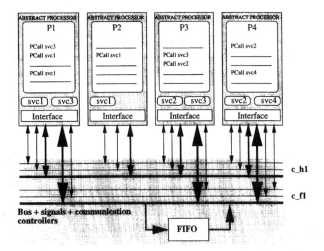

Fig. 8. System after interface synthesis.

similar to the binding/allocation of functional units in classic high-level synthesis tools [11] [18]. Most of the allocation algorithms used in high-level synthesis may be used to solve this problem [24].

An example of communication unit allocation for the system of Fig. 1 is given in Fig. 5. Starting from the library of communication units of Fig. 4, the communication unit c_h1 has been allocated for handling the communication offered by the two abstract channels $c1$ and $c2$. Communication unit c_h1 is able to execute two independent communication requiring services $svc1$ and $svc2$. Communication unit c_f1 has been allocated for abstract channel $c3$. Another solution could have been to merge $c2$ and $c3$ and allocate c_f2 for handling that communication. C_h4 could have been allocated for $c1$. This solution is represented on Fig. 6.

B. Interface Synthesis

Interface synthesis selects an implementation for each of the communication units from the implementation library (Fig. 7) and generates the required interfaces for all the processes using the communication units (Fig. 8). The library may contain several implementations of the same communication unit. Each communication unit is realized by a specific implementation selected from the library with regard to data transfer rates, memory buffering capacity, and the number of control and data lines. The interface of the different processes are adapted according to the implementation selected and interconnected. An approach for determining the width of a bus that will implement a group of channels is presented in [10] and [26] or for interfacing incompatible protocol in [27]. The result of interface synthesis is a set of interconnected processors communicating through signals, buses, and possible additional dedicated components selected from the implementations library such as bus arbiter, FIFO. With this approach it is possible to map communication specification into any protocol, from a simple handshake to a complex protocol.

Starting from the system of Fig. 5, the result of interface synthesis task is detailed in Fig. 8. The communication unit c_h1 has two possible implementations, one with an external bus arbiter for scheduling the two communications, one with the arbiter distributed in the interfaces. Any of the two implementation may be selected.

C. Statement of Communication Synthesis as an Allocation Problem

The communication synthesis is formulated as an allocation problem aimed at fixing the number and type of communication units needed to implement the abstract network. Given 1) a set of processes communicating via a set of primitives (Fig. 1) and 2) a library of functional communication units with their services and specific protocols (Fig. 4), the objective is to allocate a set of communication units that perform the task of the abstract network (Figs. 5 and 6). Each communication unit hides a special kind of communication implementation. This scheme allows more than one form of communication protocol to exist within the same framework. The interface

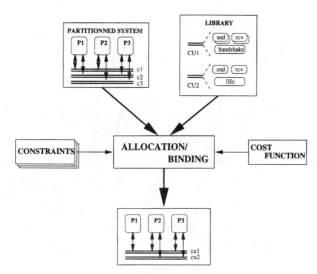

Fig. 9. Channel allocation/binding.

synthesis allows to fix the implementation (actual signals and possible communication components) of the communication scheme (Fig. 8). Currently there is no system in our knowledge that performs the selection of the physical communication structure automatically.

V. COMMUNICATION UNIT ALLOCATION/BINDING ALGORITHM

A. Introduction

The proposed allocation/binding algorithm starts with a library of functional communication units and a process graph. The nodes of this graph are the processes and the edges are the abstract channels. The main task of the algorithm is to allocate from the library a set of instances of communication units to perform the task of the abstract network (Fig. 9). Allocation is based on a cost function that is to be reduced and some constraints that have to be met.

For each abstract channel M_i, we will use the same set of constraints defined in [26] as follows.

- The protocol requested for the communication over that abstract channel noted $Protocol(M_i)$;
- The services provided to the processes noted $Services(M_i)$.
- The average transfer rate $AveRate(M_i)$. It is defined as the rate at which data is sent over the bus.
- The peak transfer rate $PeakRate(M_i)$. It is defined as the rate at which a single transfer occurs over the bus.

Both $AveRate(M_i)$ and $PeakRate(M_i)$ are specified in bits/clock. Those constraints can be set by the user or given by an estimation tool. With each communication unit C_j from the library are given a set of properties as follows.

- Its cost noted $Cost(C_j)$ which represents the intrinsic cost of the component due to its complexity, silicon area, buffering capacity, etc.
- The protocol implemented by that communication unit noted $Protocol(C_j)$.

- The maximum bus rate $MaxBusRate(C_j)$ at which the data can be transferred across the communication unit.
- The services offered noted $Services(C_j)$.
- The maximum number of independent communications it can support noted $MaxCom(C_j)$.

Given an abstract channel, a communication unit can be a candidate for allocation if it satisfies the three following conditions:

- it provides the required services : $Services(M_i) \subseteq Services(C_j)$;
- it provides the right protocol : $Protocol(M_i) = Protocol(C_j)$;
- it provides the minimum required bus bandwidth: $MaxBusRate(C_j) > AveRate(M_i)$.

During allocation of communication units we attempt to assign several abstract channels on the same instance of a communication unit to reduce cost. If some abstract channels need to transfer data at a certain average rate, after being merged onto the same communication unit they should be able to transfer data at the same rate [26]. If the MaxBusRate is greater than the sum of the AveRate of all the abstract channels merged on that communication unit we have a feasible implementation. All processes using that communication unit will be able to transfer data without being slowed by an insufficient bus bandwidth. Therefore, we must have

$$MaxBusRate(C_j) \geq \sum_{\text{All } M_i \text{ merged on } C_j} AveRate(M_i).$$

To ensure that a single data transfer does not take unnecessarily long time, the peak rate should be satisfied. This can be expressed as

$$MaxBusRate(C_j) \geq PeakRate(M_i), \forall M_i \text{ merged on } C_j.$$

If this constraint is not satisfied then the cost of that solution will increase. Since a finite number of abstract channels can be merged on a single instance of a communication unit we must have

$$\text{number of abstract channels } M_i \text{ merged on a}$$
$$\text{communication unit } C_j \leq MaxCom(C_j).$$

B. Algorithm

The proposed algorithm first builds the tree of all possible implementations. This decision tree enumerates for each abstract channel all the communication units from the library that are candidate for allocation (Section IV-A). The nodes of the tree are the abstract channels and the edges represent communication units. Each node will have as many candidates as communication units that may implement that abstract channel. The leaves of the tree correspond to empty nodes. Each path in the tree from the root to a leaf node is a possible solution.

The second step of the algorithm is to perform a depth first exploration of the tree in order to select the best solution. In order to handle the case where several abstract channels are assigned on the same instance of a communication unit from the library, we use a procedure called *merge*. This procedure is used during the tree exploration in order to assign several abstract channels on the same instance of a communication unit. If a *merge* attempt fails, a new instance of a communication unit will be created. The algorithm is detailed in the rest of this section. The main program builds the tree. The procedure *traversal* explores the tree and procedure *merge* allows the assignment of several abstract channels on the same communication unit during the tree exploration.

The cost function to be reduced by the allocation algorithm takes into account a selected communication unit C_j from the library and several abstract channels M_i merged on it. This cost function is given as follows:

$$costfunction = K_1 * cost(C_j) + K_2 * \sum_{\text{All } M_i \text{ merged on } C_j} [PeakRate(M_i) - MaxBusRate(C_j)]^2.$$

The second term of the cost function is taken into account only if the constraint on *PeakRate* is violated, i.e., only if $PeakRate(M_i) > MaxBusRate(C_j)$. K_1 and K_2 are user set parameters used to weight each term of the cost function. These allow trade-offs between component cost and performance. Let M_i be an abstract channel offering a set of services, called $Services(M_i)$, that have to be allocated on the same communication unit. Let C_j be an element of the library of communication units. C_j is a communication unit that offers a set of services, called $Services(C_j)$. Let $\mathcal{A}$ be a solution for the allocation/binding of the abstract channel network and *total_cost* its cost. Let $\mathcal{I}$ be a list of instances of communication units that have already been allocated along a path in the tree : $\mathcal{I} = \{I_1, I_2, ..I_f\}$. With each I_k comes a set of variables as follows.

1) The current bus load of that communication unit noted $BusRate(I_k)$. It is the sum of the *AveRate* of all abstract channels allocated on that instance.
2) The number of communications handled by that communication unit called $CurrentCom(I_k)$. It correspond to the number of abstract channels merged on that communication unit.

With each node of the tree is associated an abstract channel noted *AbstractChannel(node)* and to each outgoing decision edge a communication unit noted *CommunicationUnit(edge)*. Each edge is terminated by a node noted *Nextnode(edge)*.

ALGORITHM

Algorithm Allocation/Binding {
  build the decision tree
  $\mathcal{A} = \{\emptyset\}$
  $total\_cost = +\infty$
  $current\_cost = 0$
  TRAVERSAL (root, $\mathcal{I}$, *current_cost*)
}
Procedure MERGE (InstanceList $\mathcal{I}$, Instance CU : IN, Instance V, Integer *merge_cost* : OUT) {
  $merge\_cost = \infty$
  $V = \emptyset$
  For each instance $I_k == CU$, $I_k \in \mathcal{I}$ **Do** {
    If $protocol(CU) = protocol(I_k)$ **and**
    $BusRate(I_k) + AveRate(M_i) \leq MaxBusRate(I_k)$ **and**
    $CurrentCom(I_k) + 1 \leq MaxCom(I_k)$ **Then** {
      If $PeakRate(M_i) > MaxBusRate(I_k)$ **Then** {
        $current\_merge\_cost =$
        $K_2 * [PeakRate(M_i) - MaxBusRate(I_k)]^2$
      }
      Else
        $current\_merge\_cost = \infty$
      If $current\_merge\_cost < merge\_cost$ **Then** {
        $merge\_most = current\_merge\_cost$
        $V = I_k$
      }
    }
  }
  Return V **and** *merge_cost*
}

Procedure TRAVERSAL (Node n : IN, InstanceList $\mathcal{I}$, Integer *current_cost* : OUT) {
  If n is a leaf **Then**
    If $current\_cost < total\_cost$ **Then** {
      /* new better solution found */
      $\mathcal{A} = \mathcal{I}$
      $total\_cost = current\_cost$
    }
  }
  Else {
    $V = \emptyset$
    $M_i = AbstractChannel(n)$
    For every edge e of n **Do** {
      CU = CommunicationUnit(e)
      MERGE ($\mathcal{I}$, CU, V, *merge_cost*)
      If ($V \neq \emptyset$)**Then** {   /* merge successful */
        bind M_i to V
        $BusRate(V) += AveRate(M_i)$
        $CurrentCom(V)++$
        $current\_cost += merge\_cost$
        TRAVERSAL (Nextnode(e), $\mathcal{I}$, *current_cost*)
      }
      Else {   /* allocate a new instance */
        If $AveRate(M_i) \leq MaxBusRate(CU)$ **Then** {
          /* feasible solution */
          If $PeakRate(M_i) > MaxBusRate(CU)$ **Then** {
            /* *PeakRate* constraint violated */
            $alloc\_cost = K_1 * Cost(CU) +$
            $K_2 * [PeakRate(M_i) -$
            $MaxBusRate(CU)]^2$
          Else   /* no constraint violated */
            $alloc\_cost = K_1 * Cost(CU)$
          bind M_i to CU
          $\mathcal{I} += \{CU\}$
          $BusRate(CU) = AveRate(M_i)$
          $CurrentCom(CU)++$
          $current\_cost += alloc\_cost$
          TRAVERSAL (Nextnode(e), $\mathcal{I}$, *current_cost*)
        }

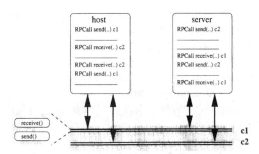

Fig. 10. Send and receive system

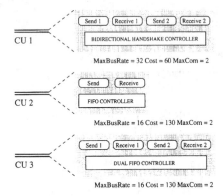

Fig. 11. Functional communication units library

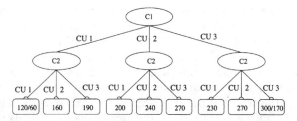

Fig. 12. Decision tree for the allocation/binding of system send-and-receive

```
      Else      /* not a feasible solution */
                current_cost = +∞
        }
      }
    }
  }
```

VI. RESULTS

In this section we show the results of applying our allocation algorithm onto a simple example. We consider a send and receive system. It is composed of two processes, a server, a host and two abstract channels ensuring a bi-directional communication. Let us assume that the communication synthesis starts with the system of Fig. 10. We give the following set of constraints on the abstracts channels:

- $AveRate(c1) = 12$ bits/clock, and $PeakRate(c1) = 18$ bits/clock.
- $AveRate(c2) = 4$ bits/clock, and $PeakRate(c2) = 8$ bits/clock.
- $Protocol(c1) = Protocol(c2) = $ any.

We set $K_1 = 1$ and $K_2 = 10$, therefore we favor the performance by setting its weight to 10 times the weight of the component cost. The communication library used for allocation is detailed on Fig. 11. It contains three communication units:

- a bidirectional handshake protocol.
- a single FIFO.
- a dual FIFO.

Fig. 12 shows the decision tree corresponding to the system described in Fig. 10 with the communication units library of Fig. 11. Each node of the tree correspond to an abstract channel. The edges corresponds to the different possible allocations for the abstract channel. The leaf nodes give the cost of the solution. When a communication unit can handle several abstract channels the leaf node contains two numbers corresponding to the path before/after *merge*. The first corresponds to the cost obtained by associating one communication unit for each abstract channel. The second is the cost obtained by sharing the communication unit. In Fig. 12, cu1 is a bidirectional handshake that can handle the communication of the two abstract channels c1 and c2. The leaf node includes two costs: 120 is the cost of two instances of cu1 assuming that the two abstract channels do not share the same communication unit and 60 is the cost of the corresponding solution with one shared instance of communication unit cu1.

Five of the possible allocation/binding alternatives are listed below and described in Fig. 13:

- (a) both c1 and c2 with a handshake, and total_cost = 60;
- (b) both c1 and c2 with a FIFO, and total_cost = 240;
- (c) c1 with a handshake and c2 with a FIFO, and total_cost = 160;
- (d) c1 with a FIFO and c2 with a handshake, and total_cost = 200;
- (e) both c1 and c2 with a dual FIFO, and total_cost = 170.

These alternatives, presented on Fig. 13, make use of the functional communication units library presented in Fig. 11. From Fig. 13, we see that the allocation/binding of communication units determines the topology of the interconnection network. The total_cost is obtained by applying the cost function detailed above. The algorithm is going to choose the solution with the lowest cost, therefore solution in Fig. 13(a) will be retained. The two abstract channels will be physically implemented as a single bidirectional bus that multiplexes both accesses from abstract channel c1 and abstract channel c2. The interface synthesis is going to map a predefined generic interface onto the processes to obtain abstract processors using the implementation library (Fig. 14). Thus, it will generate one bus with its control signals (Fig. 15). This step generates all the interfaces. This corresponds to an expansion (inlining) of procedure calls into the processes according to the communication units selected. The size of the bus will be fixed by the interface synthesis algorithm depending on the data transfer rate.

Table I gives a summary of the allocation/binding alternatives with their cost. The number of buses and external

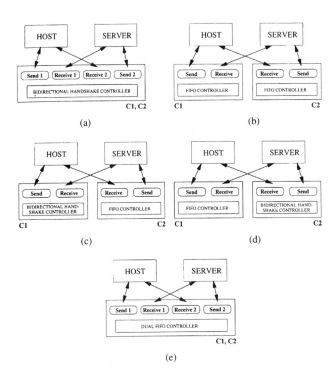

Fig. 13. Channel allocation/binding alternatives

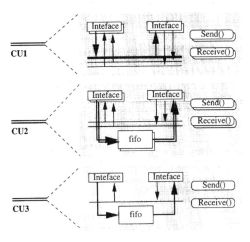

Fig. 14. Implementation library.

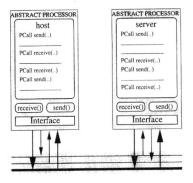

Fig. 15. System send and receive after interface synthesis

controllers neddeed are also reported. It includes the data and control lines. We assume the following interface for the library

TABLE I
ALLOCATION/BINDING COST

protocol		cost	buses	controller
channel c1	channel c2			
handshake		60	1	none
handshake	single FIFO	160	3	1
handshake	dual FIFO	190	3	1
single FIFO	handshake	200	3	1
single FIFO	single FIFO	240	4	2
single FIFO	dual FIFO	270	4	2
dual FIFO	handshake	230	3	1
dual FIFO	single FIFO	270	4	2
dual FIFO		170	4	1

communication unit (Fig. 14):

- bidirectional handshake: one in and one out data port and two control ports;
- single FIFO: one in and one out ports and one control port;
- dual FIFO: two in and two out ports and two control ports.

VII. CONCLUSION

We have presented in this paper a means whereby communication synthesis is stated as an allocation problem. This approach allows a wide design space exploration through automatic selection of communication protocols. This problem can be solved by using most of the allocation algorithms used in high level synthesis. We have presented one possible algorithm for communication units allocation/binding. This algorithm is based on a decision tree. The interface synthesis task may be performed automatically. The key issue in this scheme is the use of an abstract and general communication model. The separation between communication and computation allows the reuse of existing communication models. A library of communication units offers a wide range of communication mechanisms allowing the designer to select the appropriate communication protocol for his application. Since no restrictions are imposed to the communication models this process can be applied to a large class of codesign applications.

REFERENCES

[1] G. R. Andrews, *Concurrent Programming, Principles and Practice*, Benjamin and Cummings, Eds. Redwood City, CA: 1991, pp. 484-494.
[2] T. B. Ismail, and A. A. Jerraya, "Synthesis steps and design models for codesign," IEEE Computer, Special Issue on Rapid-Prototyping of Microelectronic Systems, vol. 28, no. 2, pp. 44-52, Feb. 1995.
[3] A. D. Birrell, and B. J. Nelson, "Implementing remote procedure call," *ACM Trans. Comput. Syst.*, vol. 2, no. 1, pp. 39-59, Feb. 1984.
[4] K. Buchenrieder, "A prototyping environment for control oriented hardware/software systems using state-charts, activity-charts and FPGA," in *Proc. European Design Automat. Conf. Euro-VHDL*, Sept. 1994, pp. 60-65.
[5] P. H. Chou, R. B. Ortega, and G. Borriello, "The Chinook hardware/software co-synthesis system," in *Proc. 8th Int. Symp. Syst. Synth.*, Sept. 1995, pp. 22-27.
[6] W. Ecker, M. Glesner, and A. Vombach, "Protocol merging : A VHDL based method for clock cycle minimizing and protocol preserving scheduling of IO operations," in *Proc. European Design Automat. Conf. Euro-VHDL*, Sept. 1994, pp. 624-629.
[7] W. Ecker and M. Huber, "VHDL based communication and synchronization synthesis," in *Proc. European Design Automat. Conf. Euro-VHDL*, Sept. 1995, pp. 458-462.

[8] W. Ecker, "Semi dynamic scheduling of synchronization mechanisms," *Proc. European Design Automat. Conf. Euro-VHDL*, Sept. 1995, pp. 374-379.

[9] R. Ernst, J. Henkel, and T. Benner, "Hardware/software co-synthesis for microcontrollers," *IEEE Design & Test Comput.*, vol. 10, pp. 64-75, Dec. 1993.

[10] D. Filo, D. Ku, C. N. Coelho, and G. de Micheli, "Interface Optimization for Concurrent Systems Under Timing Constraints," *IEEE Trans. VLSI*, vol. 1, pp 268-281, Sept. 1993.

[11] C. H. Gebotys, "Optimal scheduling and allocation of embedded VLSI chips," in *Proc. IEEE Design Automat. Conf.*, June 1992, pp. 116-120.

[12] D. Gajski and F. Vahid, "Specification and design of embedded hardware/software systems," *IEEE Design & Test Comput.*, pp. 53-67, Spring 1995.

[13] J. Gong and D. Gajski, "Model refinement for hardware software codesign," in *Proc. European Design & Test Conf.*, Mar. 1996, pp 270-274.

[14] R. K. Gupta, C. N. Coelho, and G. de Michelli, "Synthesis and simulation of digital systems containing interacting hardware and software components," in *Proc. IEEE Design Automation Conf.*, June 1992, pp. 225-230.

[15] _____, "Program implementation schemes for hardware software systems," *IEEE Design & Test Comput.*, vol. 27, pp. 48-55, Jan. 1994.

[16] R. K. Gupta and G. de Michelli, "Hardware/software cosynthesis for digital systems," *IEEE Design & Test Comput.*, vol. 10, pp. 29-41, Dec. 1993.

[17] J. Henkel, R. Ernst, U. Holtman, and T. Benner, "Adaptation of partitioning and high level synthesis in hardware/software co-synthesis," in *Proc. IEEE Int. Conf. Computer-Aided Design*, Nov. 1994, pp. 96-100.

[18] C. Y. Huang, Y. S. Chen, Y. L. Lin, and Y. C. Hsu, "Data path allocation based on bipartite weighted matching," in *Proc. IEEE Design Automat. Conf.*, June 1990, pp. 499-504.

[19] A. A. Jerraya and K. O'Brien, "SOLAR: An intermediate format for system-level modeling and synthesis," in *Computer Aided Software/Hardware Engineering*, J. Rozenblit, K. Buchenrieder, Eds. Piscataway, NJ: IEEE Press, 1994, pp. 147-175.

[20] A. Kalavade and E. A. Lee, "Hardware/software codesign methodology for DSP applications," *IEEE Design & Test Comput.*, vol. 10, pp. 16-28, Dec. 1993.

[21] B. Lin, and S. Vercauteren, "Synthesis of concurrent system interface modules with automatic protocol conversion generation," in *Proc. IEEE Int. Conf. Computer-Aided Design*, Nov. 1994, pp. 395-399.

[22] J. Madsen and B. Hald, "An approach to interface synthesis," in *Proc. 8th Int. Symp. Syst. Synth.*, Sept. 1995, pp. 16-21.

[23] A. J. Martin, "Synthesis of asynchronous VLSI circuits," *Formal Methods for VLSI Design*, J. Staunstrup, Ed. Amsterdam, The Netherlands: North Holland, 1990.

[24] P. Michel, U. Lauther, and P. Duzy, *The Synthesis Approach to Digital System Design*. New York: Kluwer-Academic, 1992.

[25] S. Narayan and D. Gajski, "Features supporting system-level specification in HDLs," in *Proc. European Design Automat. Conf. Euro-VHDL*, Sept. 1993, pp. 540-545.

[26] S. Narayan and D. Gajski, "Synthesis of system-level bus interfaces," in *Proc. European Design Automat. Conf. Euro-VHDL*, Feb. 1994, pp. 395-399.

[27] _____, "Interfacing incompatible protocols using interface process generation," in *Proc. IEEE Design Automat. Conf.*, June 1995, pp. 468-473.

[28] A. P. Ravn and J. Staunstrup, "Interface models," in *Proc. IEEE Codes/Cashe Workshop*, Sept. 1994, pp. 157-164.

[29] K. Salah and R. Probert, "A service-based method for the synthesis of communication protocols," *Int. J. Mini Microcomput.*, vol. 12, no. 3, pp. 97-103, 1990.

[30] M. B. Srivastava and R. W. Brodersen, "SIERA: A unified framework for rapid prototyping of system level hardware and software," *IEEE Trans. Computer-Aided Design Integr. Circuits Syst.*, vol. 14, June 1995.

[31] A. Takach and W. Wolf, "Scheduling constraint generation for communicating processes," *IEEE Trans. VLSI Syst.*, vol. 3, June 1995.

[32] D. E. Thomas, J. K. Adams, and H. Schmit, "A model and methodology for hardware/software codesign," *IEEE Design & Test Comput.*, vol. 10, pp. 6-15, Dec. 1993.

[33] F. Vahid, and D. Gajski, "Specification partitioning for system design," in *Proc. IEEE Design Automat. Conf.*, June 1992, pp. 219-224.

[34] F. Vahid, and D. Gajski, "Closeness metrics for system level functional partitioning," in *Proc. European Design Automat. Conf. Euro-VHDL*, Sept. 1995, pp. 328-333.

[35] P. Vanbekbergen, C. Ykman-Couvreur, B. Lin, and H. de Man, "A generalized signal transition graph model for specification of complex interfaces," in *Proc. European Design & Test Conf.*, Feb. 1994, pp. 378-384.

[36] S. Vercauteren, B. Lin, and H. de Man, "Constructing application specific heterogeneous embedded architecture from custom HW/SW application," in *Proc. IEEE Design Automat. Conf.*, June 1996, pp. 521-526.

[37] T. Yen, and W. Wolf, "Communication synthesis for distributed embedded systems," in *Proc. Int. Conf. Computer-Aided Design*, Nov. 1995, pp. 288-294.

[38] W. Wolf, "Hardware/software co-design of embedded systems," *Proc. IEEE*, vol 82, pp 967-989, July 1994.

[39] X. Xiong, P. Gutberlet, and W. Rosenstiel, "Automatic generation of interprocess communication in the PARAGON system," in *Proc. IEEE Int. Workshop on Rapid Syst. Prototyping*, June 1996, pp. 24-29.

Jean-Marc Daveau is working toward the Ph.D. degree in microeletronics at the University of Grenoble (INPG) since 1994. He received the opto & microelectronics engineer degree from the National Superior Engineering School in Caen (ISMRA), France, 1992 and the Master's degree in computer architecture from the National Superior Engineering School of Telecommunication in Paris (ENST), 1993.

He is now working on system level specifications and communication synthesis for hardware/software codesign. His research interest include computer architecture, VLSI design, and CAD tools.

Gilberto Fernandes Marchioro is working towards the Ph.D. degree in microeletronics at the University of Grenoble (INPG) since 1994. He received the Master's degree in microlelectronics from the Federal University of Rio Grande do Sul, Brazil, South America in 1991 (UFRGS-Brasil).

He worked as a researcher in the field of frameworks and CAD tools integration. He is now working on semi-automatic models for hardware software codesign. His research interest include hardware/software partitionning and system level estimations.

Tarek Ben-Ismail (M'96) He received the Master and Ph.D. degrees in computer science from the University of Grenoble (INPG), France.

He is a Researcher at Hewlett-Packard Laboratories, Bristol, England. His research interests include system-level specification, synthesis and codesign of mixed hardware/software systems. He is the author of several papers on system level synthesis.

Ahmed Amine Jerraya (A'94) for a photograph and biography, see this issue, p. 58.

Clairvoyant: A Synthesis System for Production-Based Specification

Andrew Seawright, *Member, IEEE* and Forrest Brewer, *Member, IEEE*

Abstract— This paper describes a new high-level synthesis system based on the hierarchical Production Based Specification (PBS). Advantages of this form of specification are that the designer does not describe the control flow in terms of explicit states or control variables and that the designer does not describe a particular form of implementation. The production-based specification also separates the specification of the control aspects and data-flow aspects of the design. The control is implicitly described via the production hierarchy, while the data-flow is described as action computations. This approach is a hardware analog of popular software engineering techniques. The Clairvoyant system automatically constructs a controlling machine from the PBS and this process is not impacted by the possibly exponentially larger deterministic state space of the designs. The encodings generated by the constructions compare favorably to encodings derived using graph-based state encoding techniques in terms of logic complexity and logic depth. These construction techniques utilize recent advances in BDD techniques.

Index Terms— Binary decision diagrams, control dominated synthesis, hardware description languages, high-level synthesis, reactive systems, state encoding.

I. Introduction

IN CONVENTIONAL high-level and register-transfer-level hardware description languages, the control structure of a design is typically specified using conditional language constructs such as *if-then-else* and *case* statements. Conditional branching in the control flow is determined by the evaluation of program state variables which are explicitly specified. For many problems, however, the specification of the machine behavior in this format is cumbersome. The designer may wish to work at a higher level of abstraction in which the detailed interaction of the sub-components is resolved automatically. This is especially true for problems in which the time sequence behavior is complex or the control state space is large or difficult to describe explicitly. These design problems include the specification of protocol controllers, communication devices, and computer interface subsystems. The high-level synthesis system described in this paper addresses these types of specification problems. This synthesis system is based on the Production-Based Specification (PBS) [29] [30] [31].

Manuscript received December 14, 1992; revised May 14, 1993 and October 15, 1993. This work was supported by Synopsys, Inc. and the California MICRO Program #92-019.
A. Seawright was with the University of California, Santa Barbara, CA. He is now with Synopsys, Inc., 700 E. Middlefield Rd., Mountain View, CA 94043 USA.
F. Brewer is with the University of California, Santa Barbara, CA 93016 USA.
IEEE Log Number 9400592.

In a production-based specification, the control structure of the design is specified as a hierarchical set of productions. Each production is viewed as a submachine or, more precisely, a nondeterministic automation. Productions are defined through hierarchical compositions of other productions. The hierarchical composition defines the control structure of a design *implicitly*. Data-flow computations called "actions" are hooked into this implicitly described control-flow by associating them with productions. A data-flow action is "executed" when its associated submachine is "recognized". The recognition of a production may span many levels of abstraction. For example, the recognition of a production may correspond to the occurrence of a single signal transition, or to the termination of an entire protocol transaction.

Clairvoyant is a new high-level synthesis system intended for two areas of design. These areas are the specification and synthesis of designs:

1) that are naturally specified with the use of a grammar-based decomposition of the design's behavior. These machines include those that perform computations in response to complex communication protocols.
2) that are naturally described as hierarchical compositions of interacting submachines. These machines include complex data-path controllers.

This manner of specification is intended to be a hardware analogy of a popular software engineering techniques and tools such as those used to create parsers, compiler control structures, and lexical analyzers, applied to high-level synthesis. Consider the design of an ASIC interface to Ethernet. The sequential structure of the Ethernet protocol can be described using a set of productions in the Backus-Naur Form (BNF) commonly used for specifying language grammars [1], [14]. These productions define the syntax for correct Ethernet transactions as well as those transactions performed on the machine interface side of the interface. Every possible combination of machine behavior on all interfaces is implicitly described this way as the set of recognizable sequences of the productions. It is then natural to attach data-path operations (actions) describing the desired semantics to this production framework since we assume that each action will be triggered on valid recognition of the underlying annotated production. For example, in the Ethernet interface, the action of storing a received data byte is triggered by the recognition of the production describing required sequence for a valid serial byte. This direct association between actions and the recognition of valid high level behavior allows for specifications where the required actions for a given behavior are described locally, but other possibly simultaneous actions necessary for other behaviors are described elsewhere. This property and the reusable hierarchy of productions provide the means for very concise and simpler behavioral specifications of these complex machines. Of particular utility is the ability to specify the desired behavioral response of a machine to a set of sequential stimuli without specifying a particular state machine implementation.

The Clairvoyant system is targeted toward the design of sequential machine controllers with associated data-paths for use in ASIC designs where the constructed control structures aim for high performance and/or low power characteristics. These ASIC designs are typically multilevel logic circuits implemented using gate array or FPGA technology. Mapping the output into such implementations can be performed by any number of commercial synthesis packages, for example [7], because the output of Clairvoyant is a directly synthesizable subset of the VHDL [15] hardware description (HDL) language. Thus, Clairvoyant works as an HDL generator. The user describes the behavior of a design entity in the form of a PBS description. This description is compiled and a hardware architecture is synthesized. In this process, both the control structure and the data-path register transfers required to implement the actions are created. The output is an HDL description of the architecture at the register-transfer level (sequential VHDL processes) with the required control machine described as a sequential logic network (structural VHDL). The Clairvoyant system aims to handle large designs with large state spaces. The control machine is output in a structural format to avoid the possibility that a deterministic state table output would require exponential space. This possibility arises from the nondeterministic nature of the input specification [14], [20].

The designs specified using PBS are entities that are typically components of larger systems. The PBS specified design entity is assumed to interact with other design entities described at different levels of abstraction and using different specification techniques. In this way, the HDL generation can be applied to large constructions in exactly those places where it is most useful; i.e., submachines responding to complex sequential protocols or submachines connected to several other concurrently communicating sequential machines. An added advantage of the VHDL output is the ability of the designer to simulate and verify the synthesized design in the same way that conventional VHDL designs are constructed.

The next section of this paper describes the model and form of the PBS. Related work is discussed in Section III. In Section IV, the symbolic construction algorithms of the Clairvoyant system are described. In Section V experimental results are presented. Conclusions and future work are presented in Section VI.

II. THE PRODUCTION-BASED SPECIFICATION

The PBS describes the behavior of a single design entity with a well defined boundary and interface. It is assumed that the design entity contains synchronous logic and that at least one of the input signals is a global clock signal. The PBS specification assumes a monorate sampling paradigm that allows multiple clocks for multiphase synchronous clocking. Each PBS entity can be specified over a unique synchronous domain. The global clock(s) are assumed to be shared with other design entities in the complete system. It is assumed that other the entities in the system interact with the synthesized entity only through its interface. The implementation of the entity is not important so long as it meets the desired sequential constraints of the interface and design constraints of area, cycle time, and power consumption. Thus all implementations of the design entity which satisfy the PBS specification are behaviorally equivalent, and differ only when characterized by implementation costs or other design metrics.

A *production* is a named composition of symbols, operators, and action clauses. There are two types of productions, those specifying sequential behaviors and those specifying combinational Boolean functions. The symbols in a *sequential production* are either references to other sequential productions or they are *tokens*. A token is a reference to a *Boolean Production* or a *Boolean composition* in a sequential production. The symbols in a Boolean production are either references to other Boolean production or they are atomic symbols. These atomic symbols either represent the input interface signals (primary inputs) or they are other language defined symbols.

Composition operators are used to compose the productions. They are used to build more abstract or complex productions from simpler productions. The composition operators are similarly grouped into sequential and Boolean types for use in the two kinds of productions. Thus Boolean composition operators are used to define complex Boolean functions from simpler Boolean functions and sequential composition operators define abstract sequential behaviors from more primitive sequential behaviors. Table I describes the available composition operators.

A token is "recognized" or "accepted", if its Boolean function is satisfied in the context (clock cycle) in which the token appears in the productions. A production is accepted during the clock cycle in which the time sequence behavior dictated by its *composition* is satisfied. Thus, token recognition provides the mechanism for a machine's sequencing behavior. The productions are annotated with action clauses or *actions* for short. An action is a specified data-flow computation that is executed when its antecedent symbol, composition, or production is recognized. In general, any number of productions may be active or simultaneously in the state of acceptance. A production may also accept several times in its execution.

Recursive productions in the PBS specification are illegal since the intent is the specification of state machine controllers and data-paths of finite size. Although some recursive production sets can be constructed as FSM's, these cases are not currently allowed to simplify the implementation. This does not restrict the language capability since tail recursive behavior can be concisely described using the Kleene closure operator. A production, however, may be referenced by any number of *other* productions.

Fig. 1, illustrates an example design entity. The top portion [Fig. 1(a)] depicts the design entity and its signal interface. The PBS specification for this design's behavior is shown in Fig. 1(b). In the description, there are seven productions:

TABLE I
COMPOSITION OPERATORS

operator	name	type	composition example	meaning
,	concatenation	sequential	a,b	Recognized if a is recognized followed by the recognition of b, in time sequence.
^	multiple concatenation	sequential	a^n	n concatenations of the sub-machine a. n is an integer constant.
||	sequential or	sequential	a||b	Recognized if a or b or both are recognized.
&&	sequential and	sequential	a&&b	Recognized if a and b are simultaneously recognized in the same clock cycle.
!	sequential not	sequential	!a	Recognized if a is not currently in the state of recognition.
!!	exception-handler	sequential	a!!b	Sub-machine a is initiated. If a is about to enter a state from which it can *never* be recognized, then handler machine b is initiated.
!R	exception-reset	sequential	a!R	Restart sub-machine a if initiated and a is about to enter a state from which it can *never* accept.
*	Kleene Closure	sequential	a*	Recognizes all sequences consisting of zero or more concatenations of a.
+	one-or-more	sequential	a+	Recognizes sequences of one or more a's. Equivalent to a*,a.
|	Boolean or	Boolean	a|b	Represents the Boolean function a∨b.
&	Boolean and	Boolean	a&b	Boolean function a∧b.
~	Boolean complement	Boolean	~a	Boolean function ¬a.
:	qualification	special	a:b	Modify the behavior of the sub-machine b such that for b to be recognized, the Boolean function represented by a must be true throughout the execution of b.

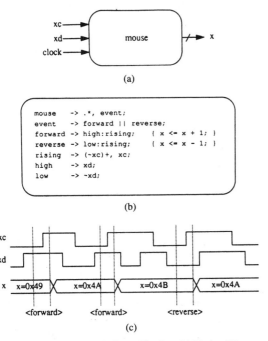

Fig. 1. (a) Design entity. (b) PBS specification. (c) Timing Diagram.

mouse, event, forward, reverse, rising, high, and low. Of these, the first five are sequential productions, and the last two are Boolean productions. The Boolean composition (~xc) is a token as it appears in the rising production. The symbols xc and xd refer to the input interface signals. By default, the first production in the PBS (mouse) is the *top-level production*. The top-level production encompasses the behavior of the whole design entity.

This description specifies the behavior of a 1-D positioning machine such as that used in a computer mouse pointing device. It continuously updates the signal x with a current 1-D position based on the quadrature encoding of the signals xc and xd received from external motion sensors. Updating the position occurs if one of the productions forward or reverse are recognized. The rising production recognizes a rising edge occurring on the signal xc. It is recognized if xc is in a high state following a sequence of one or more cycles in which the signal xc has remained low since the initiation of rising. The productions forward and reverse are defined as qualified versions of the rising submachine. HDL action clauses are attached to these two productions. For example, if forward is recognized the signal x is incremented. The sequential composition ".*, event" represents the behavioral idiom "any input sequence followed by event" since "." denotes the Boolean function that is always true. Thus, a new recognition of event is attempted on each clock cycle so that both the forward and reverse submachines are concurrently enabled to recognize motion of the mouse. Fig. 1(c) shows an example time sequence behavior of the mouse design.

Production-Based Specifications are convenient to the designer since it is often possible to implicitly specify very complex sequential constraints in a concise format. Additionally, this specification is local in the sense that additional desired behaviors can be specified by adding additional concurrent productions. For example, the *rate* of mouse motion can be measured by adding a production which counts idle clock cycles and adding two more actions to the forward and reverse productions. In general, such changes to FSM state descriptions require global modification of the entire design. Another valuable property is the ability to reuse previously defined productions representing key activities without regard to the possible concurrency of their execution. For example, a `read` production defined for a bus protocol can be used in the definition of all desired bus activities even if those activities might occur concurrently. A similar description as a deterministic FSM would potentially require the cartesian multiplication of all of the possibly concurrent `read` sub-machines to describe the possible states.

The PBS language was designed to allow flexible specification of finite state machine controllers. Although it contains a superset of the regular expression operators, the language remains in the class of finite automata. This is because all finite PBS specifications imply finite controllers. The controller does not require unbounded storage as is the case, for example, of a LALR parser which requires a stack [1], [14]. The extended operator set allows for more convenient expression of behaviors that would require exponentially larger specification in the form of traditional regular expressions, however each specification remains finite with respect to the controller.

A. Execution Model

The behavior of the PBS design is defined by execution of the implied control-flow where the actions are executed at their respective points in the protocol and the execution of each action concludes on the accepting clock cycle. This model describes the external behavior of the design not how the design is implemented. The PBS language model assumes sufficient resources to execute all potential simultaneous actions over all possible input excitation sequences. There may be considerable freedom to schedule the actions without violating the sequential interface constraints and thus optimize the resources or other design constraints. The PBS language doesn't preclude action execution overlapped with recognition of productions so long as these transformations result in equivalent behavior. Techniques to exploit this freedom is the topic of current research and will be described in a separate publication.

Because of the nature of production recognition, it is possible that several actions may be triggered simultaneously (during the same clock cycle). Since such actions may have data dependencies, the conceptual ordering of their execution within the accepting cycle is important. Consider the actions: $\{x := 0;\}$ and $\{x := x + 1;\}$. In one ordering, the resulting value of x is 0, while in the other order x is 1. *Action precedence* is defined for two actions if one of their respective productions is in the execution *scope* of the other respective production. The *scope* of a production includes all of the more primitive productions from which it is defined. The precedence ordering specifies that actions of more primitive productions conceptually occur before those of less primitive productions. Thus, the set of actions has a partial order imposed by the production hierarchy. Actions whose productions have unrelated scopes do not have a defined precedence ordering.

This concept is best illustrated with an example. Consider the following PBS fragment of two productions:

$$\text{block} \rightarrow \text{word}^\wedge 8; \{x := 0;\}$$
$$\text{word} \rightarrow \text{bit}^\wedge 32; \{x := x + 1;\}$$

In this example, every time a `word` is recognized, the variable x is incremented. When a `block` is recognized, however, both of the actions are executed, since the recognition of the `block` occurs synchronously with the recognition of the last `word`. The action precedence rules imply that in the acceptance of the `block` production, the net result is that x is 0, since the reset action is conceptually last. The designer can exploit action precedence by crafting actions that supplant the results of other. When no action precedence is defined, dependencies between actions can be ambiguous. The synthesis system, however, can warn the user of a possible action conflict. This behavior is not forbidden so as to not limit the expressability of the language.

Synthesis of the controller in the Clairvoyant system does not rely on predicting the external world's response to the execution of an action. Thus, actions that "side-effect" via feedback from the external world and through the primary inputs, by design or otherwise, don't present synthesis problems. For example, an action may assert a signal on an output that is fed back to a primary input, thus changing how tokens are interpreted in subsequent cycles. These effects are considered in the construction because, effectively, every possible input sequence is assumed possible.

B. Operators

The sequential operators are a superset of the classical regular expression operators [1], [14], [20]. These operators include generalizations such as the *sequential not* "!" operator, and the *sequential and* "&&" operator useful for specifying synchronization.

The exception operators are designed for specifying exception handling, re-synchronization, and recovery mechanisms. These operators are used to specify behaviors based on the conditions in which a sub-machine enters a state in which it can *never* accept. They are used to construct productions which recognize when a dependent production cannot accept and then take appropriate action. Exception operators may be nested hierarchically, as they operate on a general sub-machine which could contain other exception operators. An exception operator is defined over the production scope of all more primitive productions used to construct its dependent part. For example, consider the following nested productions:

$$a \rightarrow b! \ !c;$$
$$b \rightarrow d! \ !e;$$
$$d \rightarrow \ldots$$

If the production d receives an input for which it has no more possible accepting sequences it is said to have failed. The b production can then be accepted only if the e production (the exception handler) is accepted. If e succeeds, b is accepted and so a is accepted as well. If e fails, then b fails and since b is in the scope of a, the exception handler c is activated. This type of behavior greatly simplifies the problem of specifying exceptional behavior since the alternative would be to specify every possible failure sequence for a production. This could require an exponentially larger regular expression.

The Boolean operators *and* "&", *or* "|", and *not* "~", are used in Boolean compositions for the specification of Boolean functions which are used as tokens in sequential productions and used as the left-hand operand in the qualification operator. A sequential production or composition may be *qualified* with a Boolean production or composition using the *qualification* operator. For a qualified production to accept, the Boolean part must remain true during any accepting sequence of the sequential part. In other words, the behavior of the qualified submachine is the same as the unqualified submachine in which all of its tokens have been *and*ed with the qualifying Boolean function. The qualification operator is useful because it can modify or refine the behavior of a production in different contexts. For example, a "generic" submachine can be referenced from several other productions in different contexts and its behavior refined through qualification in each instance.

III. Related Work

Jackson [16] championed a methodology for specification and design of software programs and software interfacing between programs using constructive methods. Similar ideas are manifest in the successful compiler construction tools such as YACC [17] and LEX [21]. In these tools, the specification of the language to be complied is described as a set of productions representing the language grammar. The semantic actions performed by the compiler are specified as code annotations to the grammar. The tools compile this specification into the control structure of a compiler program to parse the specified language. This provides an enormous simplification in the complexity of constructing compilers since the designer need not consider the all the concurrent combinations of productions which are possible when the compiler is executed. PBS mimics this specification approach, however, fundamentally different operators and construction techniques are applied since the constraints differ between hardware and software. PBS achieves the economy of specification characteristic of these tools.

Ullman *et al.* [10], [18], [35] studied the use and compilation of regular expressions in the design of hardware controllers. In this work, the design is specified as a single regular expression which is then implemented as a nondeterministic PLA. The nondeterminism was expressed as feedback terms in the PLA, each of which indicating the validity of a given nondeterministic state. The system chose encodings based on an algorithm to minimize the number of feedback terms in the PLA. The PLA was minimized to produce the smallest number of cubes in the final design. Trickey [34] proposed a dynamic programming algorithm for optimizing the layout of these PLA pattern recognizers.

Although there are similarities between Ullman's approach and PBS, particularly in the use of regular expression operators, there are several differences in the specification form, construction techniques, and goal. In PBS, the notion of explicit productions which are re-used in central and allows more concise specification. The modeling of actions in PBS is that of arbitrary high level data-flow behaviors instead of output signal transitions and PBS targets multilevel logic models for the control.

STATEMATE [13] is a system for the design and documentation of reactive systems for use in interactive software and embedded systems. Designs are specified in the form of a hierarchical statechart [12]. In this specification, a state is active if *any* of its child states are active, for example, or alternatively if *all* of its child states are active. Transitions between states occur on events and are allowed between states at different levels of abstraction. The statecharts are converted directly into software code. SpecCharts [27] addresses the behavioral specification of whole systems by combining hierarchical state charts and VHDL in a graphical specification methodology. The SADE system [23] uses graphical entry and underlying petri net models for design specifications that are converted into HDL code. The PUBSS system [38] specifies designs in the form of several interacting, but not hierarchical, cooperative VHDL processes that are modeled as behavioral finite state machines. Its synthesis focuses on scheduling the communication and computation in the design under the ensemble constraints induced from the individual process constraints. In all of these techniques, the designer *either* describes the behavior in terms of *explicit states* or the designer explicitly partitions the problem into interacting procedural processes that contain *explicitly defined state variables.* PBS, instead, describes the decomposition of the control behavior as a hierarchical listing of the possibly concurrent desired behaviors. This difference is similar to differences between C [19] and PROLOG [8] programs.

ESTEREL is a reactive programming language from which hardware specification has been recently studied [3], [11]. ESTEREL includes language constructs for parallelism and includes a powerful trap mechanism. There are several differences between PBS specification and ESTEREL. The primary difference is that the ESTEREL language is an *imperative* style language [11] and PBS is an *applicative* language for control specification. In an applicative language, the basic statements are definitions as opposed to assignments or sequences of tasks. Another difference is that a PBS specification has an explicit partitioning of the behavioral specification between the productions and the actions. Productions represent the implicit control behaviors the designer wants to specify at a very high level without describing the detailed state transitions or the linking of the control and data-paths. The ensemble of actions implicitly describe the data-path requirements. Thus, control of the data-path is implicit in PBS which simplifies the specification and allows more freedom in the final design implementation. ESTEREL's trapping mechanism is different from PBS's exception mechanism, however, both allow for the description of exceptional behaviors and both mechanisms use the notion of lexical scope.

```
p1 -> p2 || p3; { action₂ }
p2 ->(z1 & z2), p4
p3 -> p4 && p5; { action₁ }
p4 -> z2+;
p5 -> z3 | ~z4;
```

Fig. 2. Example productions.

In our previous work [29], we proposed the use of PBS for use in high-level synthesis. In this earlier system, the execution model of the implied nondeterministic machine includes action clauses of VHDL code. These concepts have been expanded in the synthesis system described in this paper. Clairvoyant incorporates improvements to the expressive power of the production specification language as well as more powerful synthesis techniques. The addition of new production composition operators, combinational Boolean productions, and the incorporation of recent BDD and symbolic representation techniques allows an efficient re-formulation of the synthesis task.

IV. Clairvoyant Implementation

A. Design Representation

The synthesis process begins with the parsing of the PBS. A *production representation* is created which captures the hierarchical structure of the description and it is derived from the production parse trees [1]. This representation is the starting point for further synthesis tasks and is retained throughout the synthesis process as an important representation of the high-level design structure. To describe the production representation and subsequent construction we will use a small example shown in Fig. 2.

The symbols, z1, z2, z3, and z4 represent external interface signals. The productions p1, p2, p3, p4 are sequential productions while production p5 is a Boolean production. Tokens are atomic sequential productions and represent the sampling of the interface signals for the desired Boolean function on a synchronous clock. For example, the composition "(z1 & z2)" is a token which is recognized if both z1 and z2 are true during the sample period. Production p3 is recognized (and action₁ is triggered) if productions p4 and p5 are simultaneously recognized. i.e., z2 became true at least one clock before the current clock and z3 is true while z4 is false. Production p2 first requires z1 and z2 to be simultaneously valid and then p4 is recognized, while p1 is recognized if either p2 or p3 are recognized. Note that if p3 is recognized, both *action₁* and *action₂* will be triggered simultaneously, with *action₂* conceptually occurring after *action₁* due to action precedence (this precedence ordering can be easily seen for this example in Fig. 3).

A collapsed production structure called the *production DAG* is subsequently constructed from the parse tree. Each node in the DAG represents a sequential composition operator. It is constructed from the production representation by propagating all Boolean operators toward the leaves of the DAG and then

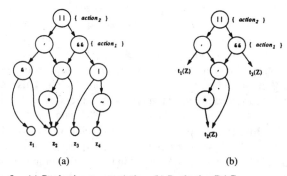

Fig. 3. (a) Production representation. (b) Production-DAG.

representing the resulting complex Boolean composition dags as combinational Boolean functions. For example, $t_1(Z) = z_1 z_2$, and $t_2(Z) = z_2$. This construction is always possible because it is illegal for sequential productions or compositions to be used in Boolean compositions. Reference to a Boolean function from a sequential composition node implies token recognition if the function is valid during that clock cycle. Practically speaking, these functions are represented by an ROBDD [5], [6] using the external signals as the basis variables. The example production representation and the collapsed production DAG are illustrated in Fig. 3(a) and (b), respectively. Here, the sequential composition operator nodes are represented by unshaded nodes, while the Boolean composition nodes are shaded. It is important to note that each sub-DAG from a sequential node to its leaves represents a sub-machine of the design. Thus, the production DAG represents a hierarchical finite-state machine partitioning of the entire design. This property is exploited by the deterministic machine construction process detailed in the following sections.

B. Intermediate Machine Representation

The production DAG represents the input behavioral specification of the desired state machine. Construction of a physical implementation from this description passes through an intermediate stage in which state encodings have been made and the control can be described as a set of combinational functions taking the current state and inputs into the next state and outputs. This description is output as register-transfer level VHDL for later logic synthesis and optimization by conventional tools. The internal design representation of this level is called the *intermediate machine representation*. The construction of this representation by conventional algorithms is hampered by the possibly exponential growth of the state transition table due to the parallelism of the input specification. For this reason, an implicit construction technique was devised allowing more flexible and larger problem instances than can be handled conventionally.

The intermediate machine representation consists of two parts, a state transition function and an output function for the machine. In what follows, B represents the set $\{0, 1\}$. The transition function Δ is a function mapping: $B^n \times B^k \to B^n$. This mapping is written:

$$\Delta : \{(x_1, x_2, x_3, \ldots, x_n)\} \times \{z_1, z_2, z_3, \ldots, z_k\}$$
$$\to \{(y_1, y_2, y_3, \cdots, y_n)\},$$

```
Input : production-DAG node pointer n, Boolean Function f(X)
Output : Boolean Function h(X)

Build (n, f(X)) {
    if (node n is a terminal function, t_j(Z)) {
        g(X, Z) = and(f(X), t_j(Z));
        x_t = RecallControlPoint(g(X, Z));
        if (x_t is not null) {
            x_i = x_t;
        } else {
            x_i = new control point;
            SaveControlPoint(x_i, g(X, Z));
        }
        y_i = f_i(X, Z) = g(X, Z)
        h(X) = x_i;
    } else if (node n is a "concatenation" node) {
        g(X) = Build(node->left, f(X));
        h(X) = Build(node->right, g(X));
    } else if (node n is a "sequential and" node) {
        g(X) = Build(n->left, f(X));
        h(X) = Build(n->right, f(X));
        h(X) = and(g(X),h(X));
    } else if (node n is a "sequential or" node) {
        g(X) = Build(n->left, f(X));
        h(X) = Build(n->right, f(X));
        h(X) = or(g(X),h(X));
    } else if (node n is a "sequential not" node) {
        g(X) = Build(n->right, f(X));
        h(X) = not(g(X));
    } else if ...

        ... the other cases ...

    }
    if (action a_k attached to n) {
        set c_k(X) = or(c_k(X),h(X));
    }
    return h(X);
}
```

Fig. 4. Build algorithm.

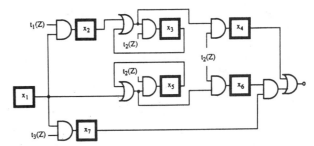

Fig. 5. Example circuit.

where X, Y, and Z are Boolean vectors. X represents the present state of the machine, Z represents the input interface signals, and Y the next state of the machine. The transition function Δ represents a deterministic state transition function. The representation, however, is unconventional in that each state bit is associated with token recognition of a leaf of the production DAG. In this encoding of state, a true bit implies that control has been transferred to this bit and that the corresponding token (Boolean function of the signals) was recognized. Since the machine is non-deterministic, it is possible for several such bits (called *control points*) to be simultaneously true. Looking ahead, Δ can be viewed as a circuit—in the example in Fig. 3, recognition of the function $t_1(Z)$ is associated with state bit x_2 in the circuit in Fig. 5. This representation has two views. As a whole, Δ represents the transition function of a deterministic FSM, while each function $y_i = f_i(X, Z)$ in Δ represents the excitation of an individual nondeterministic control point.

The Moore output function $\Lambda : B^n \to B^m$ is defined as a mapping:

$$\Lambda : \{(x_1, x_2, x_3, \ldots, x_n)\} \to \{(a_1, a_2, a_3, \ldots, a_m)\}.$$

where X is the present state and $a_i \in A$ represent each of the individual actions. Each action is triggered by the condition $a_i = c_i(X)$ corresponding to its location in the production DAG. Because many actions may be triggered simultaneously, action precedence enforces the execution sequence. The ordering of the a_i's in the vector A satisfy the partial order action precedence relations implied by the production DAG.

Alternatively, a Mealy form output representation Λ' is derived from Λ. In this case Λ' maps $B^n \times B^k \to B^m$, with the individual action conditions a function of X and Z, e.g., $c_i(X, Z)$. The action execution in the Moore form of the output function lags by a cycle vs. the Mealy form of the output function. The choice between the two forms of output function is selected prior to construction by the designer.

C. Construction of the Intermediate Machine

The construction is a recursive procedure on the production DAG building the intermediate machine. This procedure applies a particular construction rule at each composition node of the DAG, based on the node's type. These rules are templates for the application of a sequence BDD operations. Each time a leaf of the production DAG is reached, a new control point is added to the intermediate machine state vector. Since the production DAG may have several paths to a leaf from production re-use the number of control points may be larger than the number of leaves in the DAG. This can be seen in the example in which the $t_2(Z)$ leaf denotes 4 distinct control points x_3, x_4, x_5 and x_6 in Fig. 5. These control points represent sequentially distinct recognitions of the $t_2(Z)$ Boolean function of the input signals. Unlike Thompson's construction [1], [14], [20], here there is no need for ε-transitions to link the machine components. This is a consequence of the symbolic (ROBDD) representation of the control points excitation function which allows direct manipulation by the construction rules for both the conventional and generalized regular expression operators.

The construction is performed by the recursive procedure Build() illustrated in Fig. 4. At each level of the recursion, the routine is passed a pointer to a node of the production DAG and a Boolean function (BDD node pointer) representing an excitation function $f(X)$ passed from other recursion levels. The routine returns a Boolean function $h(X)$ which is true on recognition of the current sub-DAG. At leaf nodes, new control points are allocated and their excitation functions are determined. When a leaf node is traversed, if a prior allocated control point exists with identical excitation, this prior control point is used instead of allocating a new control point. This is implemented using a memory function and is illustrated by the SaveControlPoint() and RecallControlPoint() calls in the pseudocode. At intermediate nodes, left and right submachines are composed via operations on the passed returned functions.

The construction process is initiated by allocating an initial control point x_1 and calling Build (n = top-level-node, $f(X) = x_1$).

The time complexity of this algorithm depends on the representation used for Boolean functions. Although ROBDD representations can exhibit exponential growth in general, in this algorithm, the variable support of the excitation functions returned from the left and right submachines is disjoint in all cases other than in the exception operator constructions. The BDD growth is additive under the variable ordering implied by the sequential allocation of control point variables for these cases. As well, each constructed excitation function typically has very small variable support. Thus, for a DAG representing a regular expression, the time complexity of this construction is typically linear in the size of the regular expression.

The construction for the closure operator case is somewhat subtle. A temporary variable x_{tmp} is allocated and used in lieu of $f(X)$ for construction of the operand submachine. This is done because the complete excitation function for the submachine depends on the function $g(X)$ returned from Build(), which is unknown until the operand sub-machine is constructed. After Build() returns with $g(X)$, the function $h(X) = f(X) + g(X)$ is calculated. At this point, this function is substituted for x_{tmp} in every function in which x_{tmp} appears in the structure of the sub-machine. These substitutions are nicely performed by composing BDD functions e.g. $f(x = g()) = \text{ite}(g(), f_x, f_{\bar{x}})$ [5], [6]. Note, a unique x_{tmp} variable must be used for each simultaneously open closure in the construction process.

Special sequential operators called *exception operators* are implemented. In an exception construction, a handler machine $\mathcal{M}_h$ is initiated when its associated submachine $\mathcal{M}$, once initiated, will enter a state in the next cycle from which it can *never* accept. Note this is a different notion than the *sequential not* operation in which both the cases of "active but not presently accepting" and "will never accept" are recognized. The function $e(X, Z)$ represents the excitation that triggers $\mathcal{M}_h$. Consider the following equation for $e_x(X, Z)$, which is used to calculate $e(X, Z)$:

$$e_x(X, Z) = \overline{g(X)} \cdot \prod_{f_i \in \mathcal{M}} \overline{f_i(x, z)} \quad (1)$$

This equation describes the conditions in which $\mathcal{M}$ is not in a state of recognition, $\overline{g(X)}$, and will contain no active control points in the next cycle since each excitation function is false. To calculate $e(X)$ we also need knowledge that $\mathcal{M}$ is active. This information can be computed as summation of the present control points in $\mathcal{M}$ and $\mathcal{M}$'s excitation. Thus $e(X, Z)$ can be calculated as:

$$e(X, Z) = \left(\sum_{x_i \in \mathcal{M}} x_i + f(X) \right) \cdot e_x(X, Z) \quad (2)$$

An alternative calculation for $e(X, Z)$ can be derived using an extra control point to denote that control was passed to $\mathcal{M}$. This reduces the necessary logic necessary but introduces control points that do not purely represent token recognition. To derive $e(X, Z)$ in this case, let x_h represent this control point. Then,

$$e(X, Z) = (x_h + f(X)) \cdot e_x(X, Z) \quad (3)$$

The excitation of x_h is $f_h(X, Z)$ and can be computed as follows:

$$f_h(X, Z) = (x_h + f(X)) \cdot \overline{e_x(X, Z)} \cdot \overline{h(X)} \quad (4)$$

These exception operator constructions are valid for a general sub-machine, including sub-machines containing exception operators, and thus implement the notion of exception scope described in Section II.

The circuit illustrated in Fig. 5 represents the constructed intermediate machine for the example in Fig. 3. Note that x_2 becomes valid after the machine is initialized only if $t_1(Z)$ is seen on the inputs in the next cycle. The control points x_3 and x_5 correspond to repetitive recognitions of $t_2(Z)$ required by the closure operator.

D. Action Conditions

In the Build() algorithm, the action execution conditions $c_k(X)$'s are constructed using the current $h(X)$ at production operator nodes with the respective associated actions. The Moore output function Λ is constructed in this process. The Mealy output function can be created from the Moore output function. This is done by substituting $f_i(X, Z)$ for all x_i's in $c_k(X)$ forming a new $c_k(X, Z)$ by composing BDD functions. The Moore and Mealy machines are not equivalent; actions are triggered a cycle earlier in the Mealy format machine than in the Moore machine. In the Clairvoyant system, the designer chooses between the two forms of the action conditions before writing the PBS specification.

The action execution conditions for the Moore and Mealy implementations of the example design are as follows:
- Moore: action condition $c_1(X) = x_7 x_6$.
                action condition $c_2(X) = x_7 x_6 + x_4$.
- Mealy: action condition $c_1(X, Z) = t_2 t_3 x_1 (x_5 + x_1)$.
                action condition $c_2(X, Z) = t_2 t_3 x_1 (x_5 + x_1)$
                                     $+ t_2(x_3 + x_2)$.

E. Action Ordering and Resources

Actions are register transfer operations destined for execution on data-paths associated with the synthesized controller. Action precedence from the production DAG is used to constrain the conceptual ordering of these executions. However, the output HDL must be carefully structured to allow subsequent synthesis procedures to take full advantage of exclusive control paths in the design to minimize resource usage [36]. In conventional high-level synthesis, the exclusive nature of the different control paths are usually apparent from the input description HDL code. In Clairvoyant, however, the control structure can be analyzed to find which actions can execute simultaneously and thus cannot share resources. The output HDL is structured to indicate the exclusive use of the register transfers and to meet the constraints of the partial ordering relations from action precedence. Note, if actions are further broken into operations, detailed scheduling could be performed using data-flow precedence as well, however, discussions of detailed scheduling in this context is the topic of future research.

To determine if two actions can share resources, we need to determine if states exist in the machine in which both actions are simultaneously triggered. Since the action execution conditions are functions of the control points (state) and, in the Mealy case, the input interface signals, we can use the symbolic Boolean representation to determine if such states exist. Two actions a_i and a_j are mutually exclusive if the following equation holds:

$$c_i(X, Z)c_j(X, Z)R(X) = 0 \qquad (5)$$

In this equation, $R(X)$ is a *characteristic function* [9], [22], [33] representing the set of possible deterministic states reachable from the initial state of the intermediate machine. This function, mapping $B^n \rightarrow B$, is true if and only if the input vector $X \in B^n$ is a reachable state.

Assessing action conflicts between all pairs of actions is not sufficient, however, to determine the complete action conflict information. For example, consider three action conditions all executable on a common type of operator resource. If each pair of actions is used simultaneously in some state, but all three never occur together, only 2 data-path resources are needed even though no pair of actions are exclusive. This sharing cannot be predicted from a pair-wise analysis but is correctly handled in the Clairvoyant model which represents all action conflict information in a characteristic function $A(Q)$. Q is a vector of variables $(q_1, q_2, \ldots, q_m)$ corresponding to the set of actions $(a_1, a_2, \ldots, a_m)$. $A(Q)$ is true if there is a state in which the set of actions corresponding to true variables q_i occur simultaneously and thus can't be shared. $A(Q)$ is computed as follows:

$$A(Q) = \exists(Z)\exists(X)\left(\prod_{i=1}^{m}(c_i(X,Z) \equiv q_i) \cdot R(X)\right) \qquad (6)$$

The existential quantification (smoothing) [9], [22], [33] operation above is defined as:

$$\exists(X)f = \exists(x_1)\exists(x_2)\cdots\exists(x_n)f \qquad \exists(x)f = f_x + f_{\bar{x}} \qquad (7)$$

The characteristic function $A(Q)$ represents the image [9], [33] of the reachable state set $R(X)$ projected onto the space B^m through the action condition functions.

To see how $A(Q)$ can be used to construct the output control structure, consider $A(Q)$ as a BDD. We can impose an order on the variables Q that minimizes the BDD size and that is compatible with the partial order required by the precedence relations. It is very likely that the actions naturally occur in independent sets which have no state overlap with other such sets. If the variables are ordered into such sets, the canonical nature of the ROBDD representation forces all the paths from the previous set into a unique node at the start variable of the next set. Then, since the BDD can be interpreted as a network of *if-then-else* constructs, we can construct a feasible control structure for the output using if statements and procedures which is no more complex than the BDD representation of $A(Q)$, and correctly represents all possible resource sharing of the actions. This can be done in time proportional to the size of $A(Q)$, even though the number of complete paths through the entire control structure may grow exponentially fast. Alternatively, $A(Q)$ can be used to generate a table of overlaps for pair-wise exclusion or other approximate analysis. Conflict analysis utilizing $A(Q)$ is used to generate the output VHDL coded to maximize the effectiveness of subsequent high level synthesis allocation and resource sharing algorithms in processing the generated VHDL code.

F. Reachable State Analysis

Clairvoyant is equipped to perform a reachable state analysis on the constructed intermediate machine to compute the set of possible deterministic states reachable from the initial reset state of the intermediate machine: $x_1\bar{x}_2\bar{x}_3\bar{x}_4\cdots\bar{x}_n$. *Reachable state analysis is not required for the synthesis of the intermediate machine*, but it is useful in several ways. In particular, knowledge of the reachable states is needed for the exact construction of $A(Q)$ shown previously. Reachable state information can also be used to simplify portions of the intermediate machine, for example, simplifying (1). The essential use is to describe all deterministic states of the machine. All state bit combinations not in this set are not states and therefore specify don't care conditions for any of the functions depending on the control points.

The computation method is based on the recent implicit fixed-point iteration techniques [9], [22], [33] with custom heuristics based on properties of the intermediate machine. Even using these techniques, calculation of the set of reachable states is usually far more time consuming than the construction of the intermediate machine.

Recall that the set of reachable states is used in calculating the action relation. An approximate action conflict characteristic function can be calculated assuming all states are reachable in the event the reachable state computation is not invoked. For the Mealy model machines, this approximation is useful because particular actions are often strongly correlated to the current inputs. For example, in the mouse example described earlier, the increment and decrement actions are selected by the level of a signal input, so they are clearly exclusive.

G. Intermediate Machine Locality Property

A useful property of the intermediate machine representation is that any node of the production DAG can be directly related to specific portions of the intermediate machine representation, and each control point and excitation function can be related back to specific productions and compositions. Specifically, each production and each composition node is associated with a set of closed intervals $[a, b]$ of control points created on each call to build() for the node. A new interval of control points is created each time the production is re-used since control points are allocated sequentially. This property is important for debugging, high-level optimization, and design information tracking. It can be used to provide links between the specification and structure similar to the CORAL II approach [4]. For example, the example productions in Fig. 2 can be related to the circuit in Fig. 5 as shown in Table II.

TABLE II
PBS ⟷ INTERMEDIATE MACHINE LINKAGE

sequential production	control points	interval(s)
p1	{x2, x3, x4, x5, x6, x7}	[2,7]
p2	{x2, x3, x4}	[2,4]
p3	{x5, x7}	[5,7]
p4	{x3, x4, x5, x6}	[3,4] [5,6]

TABLE III
DESIGN CHARARCTERISTICS

design	number of productions	number of actions	number of inputs	number of outputs
mouse(a)	4	2	4	8
xymouse(a)	7	4	6	16
mouse(b)	8	2	4	8
xymouse(b)	15	4	6	16
count0	6	3	3	4
qr42	4	3	4	2
i8251ar	16	4	8	10
midi	30	12	3	16
mismatch	7	1	4	1

H. Implementation Details

Clairvoyant synthesis system was developed in C++ and is comprised of approximately 7600 total lines. Of this, 3160 lines represents reusable classes including a 1485 line BDD manipulation package. The output of the Clairvoyant PBS compiler is VHDL code describing the synthesized machine architecture. This VHDL is composed of structural elements that describe the logic structure of the controller, and processes that implement the register transfers and data-path logic required by the actions. The structure of the VHDL action processes satisfy the partial ordering required by action precedence.

The tool uses BDD's for the symbolic Boolean manipulations. During the synthesis, BDD variables are allocated dynamically as the machine construction proceeds. This construction process also naturally develops a reasonable heuristic variable ordering based on circuit topology arguments [25]. BDD variables are grouped into classes based on use and are interleaved. The following three-way ordering is used: $z_1 < x_1 < y_1 < z_2 < x_2 < y_2 < z_3 < x_3 < y_3 \cdots$. The y_i's represent an additional set of state variables used by the reachable state analysis, and in computing the action conflict relation $A(Q)$.

In the Clairvoyant system, after the intermediate machine is constructed, redundant registers may exist. These arise for several reasons. Boundary registers with lack of fan-out may exist if action conditions are converted from Moore to Mealy form. Registers with identical excitation may exist that were not filtered by the memory function described in Section IV-C. This is due to the existence of temporary variables allocated in the construction process preventing identification. Finally, if the reachable state analysis is invoked, additional redundant registers may be identified using techniques similar to those described in [28]. Post-processing steps manipulate the intermediate machine to ensure that all registers (control points) identified as reductant will be eliminated by later logic synthesis. For example, after logic synthesis, the registers x_4, and x_6 will be removed (equivalent fan-in to x_3, x_5). If Mealy action conditions are used, register x_7 (output unused) will be removed as well, in the circuit in Fig. 5.

V. EXPERIMENTAL RESULTS

A. Examples

Several example designs were specified using Production-Based Specifications. These designs and their characteristics are tabulated in Table III. The number of inputs includes the clock signal and the reset signal. Each design was verified by simulation of VHDL output from Clairvoyant. The several mouse designs are different versions of the 1-D quadrature decoder machine described in the introduction of this paper. The "mouse(a)" design is identical to this earlier example. The "mouse(b)" design recognizes a complete quadrature sequence as an event and so is a more restrictive version, although, both versions correctly interpret quadrature data. The "xymouse" designs are 2-D versions of the respective 1-D mouse decoder examples. The xymouse designs are specified as a single set of productions using the expressive power of the Boolean representation in the language. Using the early version of the PBS language [29], the xymouse designs would require a symbolic alphabet consisting of the cartesian product of the 1-D mouse alphabets, and would be far more difficult to express. Using arbitrary Boolean functions as tokens allows representation of enormous symbolic alphabets, and makes specification of realistic designs possible.

The "count0" example is a design that counts sequential zero's in a valid input frame format. This example is based on the procedural VHDL design in [7]. The "qr42" design is a handshake conversion protocol. This design is a standard asynchronous example specified as a synchronous machine. This design connects two interfaces together, one side operating with two-phase (nonreturn-to-zero) signaling and the other with four-phase (return-to-zero) signaling. This machine uses the "&&" operator for synchronization. The "i8251ar" example is the asynchronous receiver protocol in the i8251 high-level synthesis benchmark [2]. This example uses the Boolean qualification operators in the specification of the different modes of operation. This design also uses an exception operator to reset the machine if invalid stimulus is encountered. The "midi" design is a large design example. It is an interface controller which interprets the MIDI [26] music protocol for a digital synthesizer chip controller. The specification of this design also includes an exception operator to restart the machine in case of invalid input sequences. The "mismatch" example is the pathological regular expression described in [18] which detects mismatches between first and the last symbols in the input sequence. This example is expected to produce very large numbers of deterministic states.

B. Results

Results for compiling the example designs to the intermediate machine form are illustrated in Table IV. In this table, the number of control points in the intermediate machine

TABLE IV
INTERMEDIATE MACHINE SYNTHESIS

design	control points	build time	ite calls
mouse(a)	8	0.08	306
xymouse(a)	15	0.12	1,047
mouse(b)	14	0.08	688
xymouse(b)	26	0.17	2,136
count0	7	0.10	1,004
qr42	21	0.19	3,421
i8251ar	14	0.34	10,004
midi	182	4.09	112,545
mismatch	69	0.28	7,465

TABLE V
OPTIONAL REACHABLE STATE ANALYSIS

design	reachable states	diameter	computaion time	ite calls
mouse(a)	8	2	0.23	8,761
xymouse(a)	50	2	1.52	64,396
mouse(b)	14	4	0.71	28,863
xymouse(b)	170	4	10.72	408,505
count0	5	3	0.17	5,663
qr42	62	12	3.49	126,158
i8251ar	17	12	3.17	114,765
midi	166	40	1,791	37,331,185
mismatch	8062	16	5,191	172,797,476

representation after construction are listed. Also listed in Table IV are the construction times in CPU seconds (Solbourne Series 5e/906 machine) and construction complexity measured in terms of the numbers of calls to the primitive BDD function ite() for the entire construction.

Table V shows the results of the reachable state analysis. The number of reachable states represent the total number of unique deterministic states in the intermediate machine representation of the controller. The diameter measures the shortest path from the initial state of the controller to the furthest reachable state. This number is directly related to the number of fixed point iterations required to compute the reachable states. The ite call numbers reflect the total number of calls to ite() during the reachable state analysis. Times are CPU seconds (Solbourne Series 5e/906 machine).

Action conflict data is given in Table VI. In this table, "conflict states" refers to the number of points in the Boolean space B^m covered by $A(Q)$ in each of the designs. This represents the number of combinations of possible simultaneous action execution. For example, in the mouse designs three states are possible for its two actions. Neither action can execute, or each action can execute individually, however, both can never execute simultaneously. The table also indicates the number of BDD nodes in the function $A(Q)$ and the time (CPU seconds for Solbourne 5e/906) and number ite calls recorded to construct $A(Q)$.

The intermediate machine is used in Clairvoyant for representation, analysis, and optimization of the design. It is also utilized in derivation of a circuit realization of the design's controller. This is advantageous because the construction naturally creates machine implementations with very small excitation functions. In practice, the excitation function for a given control point tends to depend on a very small number of other control points. Results showing the size of the average and maximum literal support for the control points is tabulated in Table VII. This table reflects the variable support of the control point excitation functions (the $f_i(X, Z)$'s in Δ) and the action conditions (the $c_i(X, Z)$'s in Λ) after redundant registers are removed. Average and maximum numbers are reported in the table. The relatively large maximum support for the i8251ar and midi examples is a consequence of the exception operators in these designs.

Comparisons of the encodings present in the Clairvoyant implementations of the example designs to conventional state assignment techniques are presented in Tables VIII(a) and VIII(b). These comparisons were performed as follows. BLIF files describing the controller portion of the designs were generated from the intermediate machine representation by the Clairvoyant system. These BLIF files were read into the SIS sequential and logic synthesis system [32] for analysis. Comparisons were made between the SIS circuit network optimizations of the Clairvoyant implementations and the implementations generated by extracting the State Transition Graphs (STG's) and performing state assignment. Three state assignment algorithms were used in the comparisons: NOVA [37], JEDI [22], and one hot. These algorithms were invoked from within SIS. Table VIII(a) shows the comparision of the Clairvoyant encodings to state assignments of the extracted STG. Table VIII(b) shows the same comparisons, however, the extracted STG's were state minimized before state assignment. In these comparisons, standard SIS minimization scripts were invoked for the network optimization.

In the tables, "L" refers to the number of literals in the factored form of the optimized technology independent network. A measure for performance comparison of the encodings was obtained by mapping the optimized network to two input logic gates and recording the maximum levels of logic required. These numbers are listed in the columns labeled "D". The number of required registers for each of the encodings is also listed in the table in columns labeled "R". The STG for the mismatch example could not be extracted due to the large number of deterministic states. State minimization for the midi STG failed due to the example's size. Note, in the extraction of the STG's from the networks, not all of the network reachable states are significant due to the presence of redundant registers which don't fan out. This is why the number of STG states differs from the number reachable states in the intermediate form. The SIS command "xdc" reports the number reachable states of the network which are identical to those listed in Table V.

Results for further VHDL and logic synthesis of the output RTL implementations generated by the Clairvoyant system for each of the example designs is shown in Table IX. Gate level circuit implementations of the designs were synthesized using the Synopsys® VHDL and logic synthesis tools. In these results, no additional sequential optimizations such as state assignment, re-timing, or re-encoding were invoked. The logic synthesis was directed to optimize for speed (critical path delay) and the synthesized circuits were optimized for

TABLE VI
ACTION CONFLICT DATA

example design	number of actions	conflict states	A(Q) BDD nodes	computation time	ite calls
mouse(a)	2	3	2	0.04	1,075
xymouse(a)	4	9	4	0.35	7,531
mouse(b)	2	3	2	0.06	1,701
xymouse(b)	4	9	4	0.9	18,869
count0	3	3	4	0.03	825
qr42	3	3	2	0.39	9,203
i8251ar	4	6	5	0.38	8,885
midi	12	11	26	49.0	676,379
mismatch	1	2	0	2.21	53,087

TABLE VII
VARIABLE SUPPORT OF INTERMEDIATE MACHINE FUNCTIONS

design	Variable Support			
	Δ		Λ	
	avg.	max.	avg.	max.
mouse(a)	2	4	4	4
xymouse(a)	2	4	4	4
mouse(b)	3	4	4	4
xymouse(b)	3	4	4	4
count0	3	5	4	5
qr42	3	6	11	18
i8251ar	5	20	7	12
midi	3	167	11	27
mismatch	2	4	10	10

TABLE VIII
STATE MACHINE ENCODING COMPARISON #1 (a). COMPARISON #2 (b).

example design	Clairvoyant			Extract STG, State Assign									
	L	D	R	STG states	nova			jedi			one hot		
					L	D	R	L	D	R	L	D	R
mouse(a)	18	5	4	5	21	7	3	19	8	3	26	4	5
xymouse(a)	36	5	8	25	100	29	5	99	21	5	168	14	25
mouse(b)	36	5	10	11	42	19	4	35	9	4	61	10	11
xymouse(b)	72	5	20	121	1948	33	7	1844	67	7	943	18	121
count0	16	5	4	5	12	8	3	16	6	3	16	6	5
qr42	77	6	21	62	359	68	6	317	54	6	382	19	62
i8251ar	84	16	14	17	74	16	5	112	25	5	95	12	17
midi	604	22	166	166	743	81	8	1098	89	8	705	23	166
mismatch	114	6	62	unable									

(a)

example design	Clairvoyant			Extract STG, State Minimize, State Assign									
	L	D	R	STG states	nova			jedi			one hot		
					L	D	R	L	D	R	L	D	R
mouse(a)	18	5	4	3	10	4	2	10	4	2	10	3	2
xymouse(a)	36	5	8	9	46	12	4	35	8	4	59	4	9
mouse(b)	36	5	10	7	29	10	3	26	16	3	41	8	7
xymouse(b)	72	5	20	49	528	65	6	515	50	6	636	22	49
count0	16	5	4	4	12	5	2	11	5	2	13	6	3
qr42	77	6	21	16	54	20	4	84	28	4	121	12	16
i8251ar	84	16	14	14	71	24	4	75	14	4	95	11	14
midi	604	22	166	unable									
mismatch	114	6	62										

(b)

and mapped to LSI 10k gate array library cells [24]. The data for the path delay (in nS), relative area, total number of LSI 10k cells, and total number of flip flops is given. These numbers include both the control as well as the data-path portions of the designs. The relative area numbers are the area estimates based on LSI 10k library cells returned by the synthesis tool.

Some conclusions can be drawn from these results. In comparing the mouse machines with the xymouse machines, the number of productions and control points roughly doubles while the state space of the machine is squared. It is clear that the machine construction complexity is not proportional to the growth of the machine's state space as would be expected from conventional algorithms. The execution speed of the two designs (which includes the data-path delay as well as the control delay) is nearly the same (the Clairvoyant design for the xy-version consists essentially of two of the single machines in parallel thus the delay differences are artifacts of the further synthesis). The midi design was much more complicated in its behavior and included an exception handling routine so that any valid data imbedded in arbitrary invalid data would be correctly interpreted. Considering this, the design's cycle time was an impressive 13.96 nS. Also, note that this design required only 30 productions for the entire specification, which fit comfortably on 2 pages of text. Finally, the pathological mismatch design had 8062 deterministic states, but was constructed in 0.28 CPU seconds, showing the relative independence of the construction time from the size of the deterministic state space. Table VI shows that our optimal technique for generation of operation exclusion information is both feasible and is simple to map into the output VHDL, as shown by the very small ROBDD representations needed to represent the functions $A(Q)$. Use

TABLE IX
VHDL AND LOGIC SYNTHESIS RESULTS

design	delay	area	#cells	total #FF
mouse(a)	6.43	277	61	12
xymouse(a)	7.15	514	123	24
mouse(b)	5.98	324	83	18
xymouse(b)	6.56	601	159	36
count0	4.74	116	41	7
qr42	4.65	235	77	21
i8251ar	6.82	365	138	22
midi	13.96	1,927	532	194
mismatch	3.65	656	175	62

of this information is critical in allowing subsequent logic optimization to minimize the required resources.

It is of interest to note the relatively high performance of the designs derived directly from the intermediate form. These designs typically have more registers than conventional designs but generally have very simple excitation logic between the control points. This is due to the direct use of the specification in constructing the logic and selecting the deterministic codes. In effect, the control points provide a set of signals from which the excitation functions can be derived with very small literal support. These considerations are demonstrated by the differences in logic complexity (as reflected by factored literal counts) and in controller logic delay (as reflected by the mapped logic depth) shown for Clairvoyant designs and designs created by symbolic state extraction, state assignment, minimization and identical synthesis. In particular, in the small state machines with little parallelism: mouse(a), mouse(b), i8251ar, and count0, the Clairvoyant designs are comparable to the state assigned designs. However, for larger and more parallel cases such as xy-mouse and qr42, the quality of the distributed encoding becomes much more impressive. Note that even when the minimal machine encodings have comparable literal counts, the logic depth (and hence the controller delay) of these machines is greater. In the typical case, the logic depth of Clairvoyant was smaller than any of the other encodings, state minimized or not. Finally, it is important to note that the mismatch design complexity is relatively simple even though it could not be synthesized at all using state-graph based techniques.

The register costs for the Clairvoyant designs must be measured relative to the implementation technology. The encodings are ideal for FPGA implementation where registers are virtually free since they typically occur in every FPGA cell. In these designs, the small average literal support and logic depth should allow efficient, high performance designs. In other technologies where high performance is required, these encodings may be desirable, regardless of the register costs.

VI. CONCLUSION AND FUTURE WORK

We have presented a new high-level synthesis system directed toward the synthesis of complex designs that are specified concisely using hierarchical grammar-like decompositon of their behavior. These specifications are of practical use in synthesis problems that are control dominated or require complex concurrent protocols. The use of productions enables the specification to span many levels of complexity, and to describe what actions should be taken in each case. Nondeterminism in the language frees the designer from the onerous task of determining the precise behavior required of each deterministic state. Instead, the designer needs only to specify the kinds of behaviors expected and what actions should take place. The direct use of Boolean functions in both the token recognition and production qualification processes greatly expand the expressability of engineering design specifications in this format. The resulting specifications are very concise and allow the designer to specify the design at high levels of abstraction in which the detailed interaction of the submachines is automatically derived. The system synthesizes a hardware architecture with VHDL register-tranfer output allowing system assembly with VHDL modules from many sources and use of commercially available tools.

The Clairvoyant system implementation makes extensive use of symbolic construction techniques to perform this synthesis. These techniques include a new direct machine construction algorithm which is not directly impacted by the size of the deterministic state space and hence is applicable to very large designs. The constructed intermediate machine form is a convenient representation base for further analysis and optimization using both classical and more recent symbolic techniques. With little additional optimization, this form yields sequential machines with favorable performance characteristics. Techniques for evaluating resources conflicts for designs in this representation have also been described.

In future work, further optimization of the intermediate machine to reduce the number of registers without reducing the high level of performance achieved in the design will be studied and applied to the Clairvoyant synthesis tool. Additional studies and possible future work includes operation scheduling and optimization in conjuction with the controller and protocol constraints as well as optimizations to simplify the productions.

ACKNOWLEDGMENT

The authors wish to acknowledge E. Girczyc and M. Marek-Sadowska for helpful suggestions and discussion. The authors also thank the reviewers for their constructive feedback.

REFERENCES

[1] A. V. Aho, R. Sethi, and J. D. Ullman, *Compilers Principles, Techniques and Tools.* Reading, MA: Addison-Wesley 1988.
[2] Benchmarks of the Fourth International Workshop on High-Level Synthesis,1989.
[3] G. Berry, "A Hardware implementation of pure ESTEREL," *Sādhanā*, vol. 17, Part 1, pp. 95–130, Mar. 1992.
[4] R. L. Blackburn, D. E. Thomas, and P. M. Koenig, "CORAL II: Linking behavior and structure in an IC design system," *Proc. 25th DAC,* pp. 529–535, June 1988.
[5] K. S. Brace, R. L. Rudell, and R. E. Bryant, "Efficient implementation of a BDD Package," *Proc. 27th DAC,* pp. 40–45, June 1990.
[6] R. E. Bryant, "Graph based algorithms for Boolean function manipulation," *IEEE Trans. Comput.,* pp. 677–691, Aug. 1986.

[7] S. Carlson, Introduction to HDL-Based Design Using VHDL. Mountain View, CA: Synopsys, 1990.
[8] W. F. Clocksin and C. S. Mellish, Programming in PROLOG. Berlin: Springer-Verlag, 1984, second ed.
[9] O. Coudert and J. C. Madre, "A unified framework for the formal verification of sequential circuits," *Proc. ICCAD-90*, pp. 126–129, Nov. 1990.
[10] R. W. Floyd and J. D. Ullman, "The compilation of regular expressions into integrated circuits," *J. of the ACM*, pp. 603–622, vol. 29, no. 3, July 1982.
[11] N. Halbwachs, Syncronous Programming of Reactive Systems. Dordrecht: Kluwer, 1993.
[12] D. Harel, "Statecharts: A visual approach to complex systems," *Sci. of Comput. Program.*, vol. 8, pp. 231–274, 1987.
[13] D. Harel et al., "STATEMATE: A working environment for the development of complex reactive systems," *Proc. Int. Conf. Software Engin.*, pp. 396–406, 1988.
[14] J. E. Hopcroft and J. D. Ullman, Introduction to Automata Theory, Languages, and Computation. Reading, MA: Addison-Wesley, 1986.
[15] IEEE Standard VHDL Language Reference Manual. IEEE Std. 1076–1987.
[16] M. A. Jackson, "Constructive methods of program design," in *Lecture Notes in Computer Science*. Springer-Verlag, 1976, vol. 44, pp. 236–262.
[17] S. C. Johnson, "Yacc: Yet another compiler compiler," *Computing Science Tech. Rep. 32*, AT&T Bell Lab., Murray Hill, NJ, 1975.
[18] A. R. Karlin, H. W. Trickey, and J. D. Ullman, "Experience with a regular expression compiler," *Proc. ICCD*, pp. 656–665, 1983.
[19] B. W. Kernighan and D. M. Ritchie, The C Programming Language. Englewood Cliffs, NJ: Prentice-Hall, 1988, second ed.
[20] Z. Kohavi, Switching and Finite Automata. New York: McGraw-Hill, 1978.
[21] M. E. Lesk, "Lex—A lexical analyzer generator," *Computing Science Tech. Rep. 39*, AT&T Bell Lab., Murray Hill, NJ, 1975.
[22] B. Lin, "Synthesis of VLSI designs with symbolic techniques," *Ph.D. Thesis*, Univ. California, Berkeley, UCB/ERL M91/105, Nov. 1991.
[23] J. Lathi, M. Sipola, and J. Kivelä, "SADE: A graphical Ttool for VHDL-based systems analysis," *Proc. ICCAD-91*, pp. 262–265, Nov. 1991.
[24] LSI Logic Corporation, "1.5-Micron Compacted Array Technology, Databook, July 1987.
[25] S. Malik, A. R. Wang, R. K. Brayton, and A. Sangiovanni-Vincetelli, "Logic verification using binary decision diagrams in a logic synthesis environment," *Proc. ICCAD-88*, pp. 6–9, Nov. 1988.
[26] MIDI Specification Version 1.0, International MIDI Assoc., 1983.
[27] S. Narayan, F. Vahid, and D. D. Gajski, "System specification with the SpecCharts language," *Proc. ICCAD-91*, pp. 266–269, Nov. 1991.
[28] H. Savoj, H. Touati, and R. K. Brayton. "Extracting local don't cares for network optimization," *Proc. ICCAD-91*, pp. 514–517, Nov. 1991.
[29] A. Seawright and F. Brewer, "Synthesis from production-based specification," *Proc. 29th DAC*, pp. 194–199, June 1992.
[30] ——, "PBS 2.x Users Guide," *ECE Tech. Rep. #92-21*, UCSB, Oct. 1992.
[31] ——, "High-level symbolic construction techniques for high performance sequential synthesis," *Proc. 30th DAC*, pp. 424–428, June 1993.
[32] E. M. Sentovich, K. J. Singh, L. Lavagno, C. Moon, R. Murgai, A. Saldanha, H. Savoj, P. R. Stephan, R. K. Brayton, and A. Sangiovanni-Vincentelli, "SIS: A system for sequential circuit synthesis," *Electron. Res. Lab. Memo. No. UCB/ERL M92/41*, May 1992.
[33] H. J. Touati, H. Savoj, B. Lin, R. K. Brayton and A. Sangiovanni-Vincentelli, "Implicit State Enumeration of Finite State Machines using BDD's," *proc. ICCAD-90*, pp. 130–133, November 1990.
[34] H. W. Tricky, "Good layouts for pattern recognizers," *IEEE Trans. Comput.*, vol. 31, pp. 514–520, June 1982.
[35] J. D. Ullman, Computational Aspects of VLSI. Rockville: Computer Science Press, 1984.
[36] K. Wakabayashi and H. Tanaka, "Global scheduling independent of control dependencies based on condition vectors," *Proc. 29th DAC*, pp. 112–115, June 1992.
[37] T. Villa, T. and A. Sangiovanni-Vincentelli, "NOVA: State assignment of finite state machines for optimal two-level logic implementation," *IEEE Trans. Computer-Aided Des.*, vol. 9, pp. 905–924, Sept. 1990.
[38] W. Wolf et al., "The Princeton University behavioral synthesis system," *Proc. 29th DAC*, pp. 182–187, June 1992.

Andrew Seawright (M'93) was born in Manhattan, NY. He received the B.S. degree in electrical engineering from Rutgers University, NJ, in 1989 and the M.S. and Ph.D. degrees in electrical and computer engineering from the University of California, Santa Barbara, in 1992 and 1994, respectively.

Presently, he is with Synopsys, Inc., Mountain View, CA. His current research interests include system level computer-aided design, high-level synthesis, design specification and entry, and the use of BDD techniques for analysis and synthesis of digital systems.

Dr. Seawright is a member of the Association for Computing Machinery, Tau Beta Pi, and Eta Kappa Nu.

Forrest Brewer (M'87) received the Bachelor of Science degree with honors in physics from the California Institute of Technology, Pasadena, in 1980 and the M.S. and Ph.D. degrees in computer science in 1985 and 1988, respectively, from the University of Illinois, Urbana-Champaign.

Since 1988, he has served as an Assistant Professor with the University of California, Santa Barbara. From 1981 to 1983, he was a Senior Engineer at Northrop Corp. and consulted there until 1985. He co-authored Chippe, which was the first demonstrated closed loop high level synthesis system. Recently, his research work has been in the application of logic synthesis techniques to high level synthesis, specification, and scheduling of control dominated designs.

Dr. Brewer is a member of the ACM and APS.

Real-Time Multi-Tasking in Software Synthesis for Information Processing Systems*

Filip Thoen, Marco Cornero†, Gert Goossens and Hugo De Man

IMEC, Leuven, B-3001, Belgium
† SGS-Thomson Microelectronics, Crolles, 38921, France

Abstract

Software synthesis is a new approach which focuses on the support of embedded systems without the use of operating-systems. Compared to traditional design practices, a better utilization of the available time and hardware resources can be achieved, because the static information provided by the system specification is fully exploited and an application specific solution is automatically generated.

On-going research on a software synthesis approach for real-time information processing systems is presented which starts from a concurrent process system specification and tries to automate the mapping of this description to a single processor. An internal representation model which is well suited for the support of concurrency and timing constraints is proposed, together with flexible execution models for multi-tasking with real-time constraints. The method is illustrated on a personal terminal receiver demodulator for mobile satellite communication.

1 Introduction

The target application domain of our approach is advanced real-time information processing systems, such as consumer electronics and personal communication systems. The distinctive characteristic of these systems is the coexistence of two different types of functionalities, namely *digital signal processing* and *control functions*, which require different timing constraint support. Specifically, signal processing functions operate on sampled data streams, and are subject to the *real-time* constraint derived from the required sample frequency or throughput. Control procedures vary in nature from having to be executed as soon as possible (like e.g. a man-machine interface), but an eventual execution delay does not usually compromise the integrity of the entire system (*soft deadline*), to having very stringent constraints, like e.g. a critical feedback control loop (*hard deadline*).

Traditionally, real-time kernels, i.e. specialized operating systems, are used for software support in the design of embedded systems [5]. These small kernels, often stripped-down versions of traditional time-sharing operating-system, are in the first place designed to be *fast* (e.g. fast context switch). Above all, real-time kernels provide the run-time support for *real-time multi-tasking* to perform software scheduling, and primitives for inter-process communication and synchronization, and for accessing the hardware resources. Since processes are considered as black boxes,

---

* This work was supported by the European Commission, under contract Esprit-9138 (Chips)

---

most kernels apply a *coarse grain* model for process scheduling. Most kernels tend to use a fixed priority preemptive scheduling mechanism, where process priorities have to be used to mimic the timing constraints. Alternatively, traditional process scheduling approaches use timing constraints, specified as process period, release time and deadline [11]. From the designer viewpoint however, these constraints are more naturally specified with respect to the occurrence of observable events. Moreover, the scheduler has no knowledge about the time stamps when the events are generated by the processes, and consequently can not exploit this. Assignment of the process priorities, as in the case of the fixed priority scheduling scheme, is a *manual* task to be performed without any tool support. Typically, an iterative, error-prone design cycle, with a lot of code and priority tuning, is required. Not only is this inflexible and time consuming, but it also restricts the proof of correctness to the selected stimuli. Additionally, the behavior of the scheduler under peak load conditions is hard to predict, resulting often in under-utilized systems to stay on the safe side. It is safer to guarantee timeliness pre-runtime, as new family of kernels tend to attain [5]. Moreover, kernels trade optimality for generality, causing them to be associated with run-time and memory overhead.

Software synthesis [1][2][7] is an alternative approach to real-time kernels: starting from a system specification, typically composed of concurrent communicating processes, the aim of software synthesis is the automatic generation of the *source code* which realizes 1) the specified functionalities while satisfying the timing constraints and 2) the typical run-time support required for real-time systems, such as multi-tasking, and the primitives for process communication and synchronization. A better utilization of the available time and hardware resources can be achieved with software synthesis, because the static information provided by the system specification is fully exploited; as a consequence the automatically generated run-time support is customized for and dedicated to each particular application, and does not need to be general, as in the case of real-time kernels. Moreover, an accurate static analysis provides an early feedback to the designer on the feasibility of the input specifications. In this way the iterative design cycle typical for real-time kernels is avoided, and satisfaction of the timing constraints can be guaranteed automatically. Besides, the transformations and optimizations envisioned in the software synthesis approach, try to automate this code tuning. Finally, since the output of software synthesis is source code, portability can be easily achieved by means of a retargetable compiler [6].

The software synthesis approach in the VULCAN framework [7] allows to specify latency and rate timing constraints. *Program threads* are extracted from the system specification, in order to isolate operations with an unknown timing delay. A simple non-preemptive, control-FIFO based run-time scheduler alternates their execution, but provides only a restricted support for satisfying these constraints, since threads are executed as they are put at run-time in the FIFO and are not reordered. Moverover, interrupts are not supported, due to the choice of the non-preemptive scheduler.

The approach taken in the CHINOOK [2] system suffers from a similar restriction: although preemption is allowed based on the watchdog paradigm, resuming at the preemption point is difficult, and hence interrupts are not supported. The system, targetted towards reactive control systems, only supports timing constraints on state transitions and on latency between operations. No rate constraints are supported, as is typical for DSP applications.

The rest of this paper is structured as follows. Section 2 introduces the system representation and the concepts used. In section 3, two different execution models and the steps of a possible software synthesis script are discussed. A real-life illustration of the approach is the subject of section 4. Finally, section 5 draws some conclusions.

2 System Representation - Model

We assume that the target application can be modeled in a concurrent process description, which captures operation behavior, data dependencies between operations, concurrency and communication [8][9]. The precise semantics of such a specification are beyond the scope of this paper. From this specification, a *constraint graph* can be derived that contains sufficient information for the software synthesis problem, as will be introduced below.

We define a **program thread** as *a linearized set of operations which may or may not start with a non-deterministic (ND) time delay operation* [7]. Examples of ND-operations are synchronization with internal and external events, wait for communication and unbounded loops. The purpose of extracting program threads from the concurrent process input specification is to isolate all the uncertainties related to the execution delay of a given program at the beginning of the program threads. Program threads, which can be executed using a single thread of control (as present in most contemporary processors), have the property that their execution latency can be computed statically. Besides being defined by the ND-operations, program threads can also capture concurrency and multi-rate transitions. A new representation model, based on **constraint graphs** [10], is then built up from the extracted threads. This model allows a static analysis, both of the imposed timing constraints and of the thread scheduling. The *vertexes* represent program threads and the *edges* capture the data dependency, control precedence and the timing constraints between threads. Specifically, let $\delta(v_i)$ the execution delay of the thread represented by vertex v_i; a forward edge $e_{i,j}$ with weight $w_{i,j} = \delta(v_i)$, represents a minimum timing constraint between v_i and v_j,

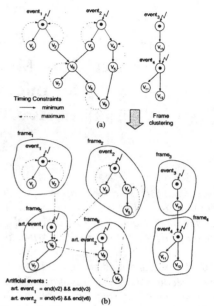

Figure 1: Example of a Constraint Graph

i.e. the requirement that the start time of v_j must occur *at least* $w_{i,j}$ units of time later than v_i. Similarly, a *maximum* timing constraint between two threads v_i and v_j is indicated as a backward edge with negative weight $w_{i,j}$, representing the requirement that the end time of v_i must occur no later than $\mid w_{i,j} \mid$ units of time later than the end time of v_j. Finally, *ND*-operations are represented by separate **event nodes**. An example is given in figure 1 (a).

Our model differs from [10] in the abstraction level of a CG node: in our approach a CG node isolates a group of operations which corresponds to static program parts, while in [10] individual operations are the CG entities. Moreover, in [10] a CG is restricted to being a single connected graph, not able to capture process concurrency. This restriction is lifted in our approach and internal events are introduced to synchronize between concurrent graphs capturing process concurrency. Also, we support multi-rate by placing relative execution rate numbers on control edges.

By definition, all the uncertainties related to the timing behavior of a system specification are captured by event nodes. Since the arrival time of an event is unknown at compile time, event nodes limit the extent of analysis and synthesis which can be performed statically.

In a second step, threads are clustered into so-called **thread frames** (figure 1 (b)). The purpose of identifying thread frames is to partition the initial constraint graphs into disjoint clusters of threads triggered by a single event, so that static analysis and synthesis (e.g. scheduling) can be performed for each cluster *relatively* to the associated event. Remark that sequence edge(s) can exist between frames according to the original system specification.

The *event set* $E(v_i)$ of a node v_i is defined as the set of event nodes which are predecessors of v_i. Artificial events are introduced for threads with an event set which contains at least two elements between which there does not exist a path in the graph. These events are in fact internal events, which must be observed and taken care of by the execution model in a similar way as the external events which are triggered directly by the environment.

The execution model will take care of the activation at run-time of the different thread frames according to the original specification while taking into account the sequence of occurred events and the imposed timing constraints. In this way the unknown delay in executing a program thread appears as a delay in scheduling the program thread, and is not considered as part of the thread latency.

3 Execution Models and Implementation

In this section the execution models and the implementation, i.e. the mapping of the representation model to the single thread of control of the target processor, are described. Although the CG model is target independent, in this paper we focuss on a single processor target.

3.1 Execution Models

Blocking Model - Cyclic Executive Combined with Interrupt Routines A simple, but cost effective solution for the run-time thread frame activation consists of using a simple *event loop* in background combined with tying different thread frames to processor interrupts. The assignment of frames to the event loop and the (internal) scheduling of the frames is done at compile-time. The event loop in the background polls in a round-robin fashion the occurrence of the events triggering the different thread frames and accordingly starts executing the appropriate frames sequentially. Processor interrupts present a cheap way, supported by hardware, to asynchronously start up thread frames which suspend the currently executing frame. The processor interrupt masking and priority levels can be used to selectively allow interruption of time critical thread frame sections and to favor high priority frames.

Only frames which are triggered by an event corresponding to interrupts (either the external hardware or the internal peripheral interrupts) can be started up asynchronously, while the other frames are to be placed in the background event loop. Moreover, a background frame started up by the event loop will block the processor till the end of its execution preventing other frames in the event loop to be started up. Hence, the name "blocking execution model". The execution length of the frames limits the response time of events in the event loop, and therefore limits the scope of this model.

Non-blocking Model using a Run-time Scheduler Figure 2 (a) outlines the execution model which takes a two-level scheduling approach. *Static* scheduling (i.e. at compile-time) is performed after thread clustering to determine a relative ordering of threads *within* each thread frame, and by assumption this ordering is not changed anymore in the dynamic scheduling phase. At *run-time*, a small *pre-emptive* and *time-driven* scheduler takes care of the composition and interleaving of the different thread frames according to the system evolution and the timing constraints. Additionally, it tries to avoid active waiting by scheduling other frames when the next frame is not ready to be executed, in this way maximizing processor utilization.

This run-time behavior is illustrated in the lower part of fig-

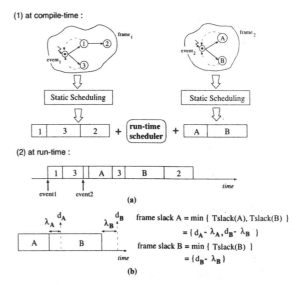

Figure 2: The run-time execution model (a) and the *frame slack* scheduling metric (b)

ure 2 (a): starting from an idle state, suppose that $event_1$ occurs; this event activates the run-time scheduler, and since no other frames are currently active, the threads of the first frame are executed with the order determined previously with static scheduling (order 1-3-2). Occurrence of $event_2$, while executing $thread_3$ of the first frame, causes the following actions: 1) $thread_3$ is interrupted; 2) the run-time scheduler is invoked for determining the subsequent execution order, in the example: A, rest of $thread_3$, B, 2; and 3) execution proceeds with the newly determined thread ordering. As indicated the *relative ordering* between the threads of the same frame is not changed allowing an efficient implementation of the run-time scheduler, which must be necessarily very fast.

The scheduling metric used by the run-time scheduler is the *frame slack* time. This information is derived statically based on the imposed timing constraints and on the relative thread ordering within each frame. The frame slack indicates the amount of time the end of an individual thread in a thread frame can be postponed, relatively to its static schedule, before violating a timing constraint. As illustrated in figure 2 (b), the frame slack is defined as the minimum of all *thread slacks*, i.e. the remaining time between the end of the thread and its timing constraint, of all the succeeding threads in the static schedule. The frame slack derived at compile time, is used and updated at run-time. For a more formally description of this model, we refer to [3].

3.2 Script

Figure 3 gives an overview of the proposed approach. From the concurrent process specification, the different program threads are extracted and the non-deterministic timing delay is isolated in event nodes. During this step, a code generator can provide a static estimate of the thread execution times. These execution times are placed together with the timing constraints in a constraint graph, the abstraction model used in the sequel of the approach. The assignment of external processor interrupts to event nodes in the constraint

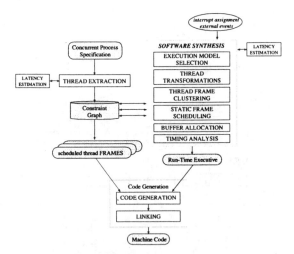

Figure 3: Possible software synthesis script

graph, which is determined by the context of the system, is to be provided by the user.

After selection of one of the two execution models explained above, five tasks, which are phase coupled, have to be performed. *Thread frame clustering* tries to cluster the constraint graph into disjoint groups of threads which are triggered by the same event set. These thread frames are to be activated *at run-time* by the selected execution model. Since events introduce an overhead during frame scheduling, we also want to minimize the number of clusters, without violating timing constraints. *Static frame scheduling* will determine *at compile-time* the relative order of the threads *inside* each of the identified thread frames. Occasionally, the timing constraints can not be met by the identified frames. In this case, *a transformation step* on the threads or the frames can resolve the problem or can provide a more optimal solution. An example of these transformations will be given in the illustration in section 4. *Buffer allocation* will insert the required buffers in between communicating frames, by deriving the buffer sizes from the execution rates of the frames. *Timing analysis* is used in different phases : once upon entry of the tool, to check for consistency of the user specified timing constraints, and subsequently during the execution of the tool, to verify whether a result of a synthesis task still satisfies all constraints.

The outcome of software synthesis are scheduled thread frames and possibly (depending on the execution model chosen) a small run-time executive, which activates the appropriate frames at run-time; both have to be compiled with the code generator and linked together afterwards.

4 Illustration of the Approach

System Description - Concurrent Communicating Process Specification   Figure 4 outlines the process specification of a mobile terminal receiver *demodulator* to be used in the MSBN satellite communication network [4]. This network allows a bi-directional data and voice communication in a star network consisting of a fixed earth station and multiple mobile stations. Two different data channels, called *pilot* and *traffic* channel, are sent over on the same transmission carrier using the CDMA technique, i.e. correlating the channels with orthogonal pseudo-noise codes enabling them to use the same frequency spectrum without interference. The former channel carries network system information (e.g. average channel bit error rate), the latter carries the actual user data. Acquisition and tracking of the transmission carrier is performed on the pilot channel in cooperation with an intelligent antenna.

Triggered by an external interrupt, the `read_decorr` process reads periodically (at a rate of 3.4 kHz) the memory mapped decorrelator FPGA. This process sends data to the `track_pilot&demod` and the `traffic_demod` processes, which perform the tracking of the transmission carrier and the demodulation (i.e. gain, carrier phase and bit phase correction). After a 1:3 rate conversion the demodulated traffic data is formatted by the `traffic_manage-_data` process and via the `send_vocoder` process transmitted to a second, memory mapped processor. In contrast, the demodulated pilot data will be further processed on the same processor.

The `track_pilot&demod` process not only delivers its demodulated data to the `pilot_manage_data` process, it steers the frequency of the NCO *(numerical controlled oscillator)* in the preceeding analog demodulation part through use of the on-chip *serial peripheral*. Moreover, together with `traffic_demod` process it sends information concerning carrier synchronization to the `display_LEDs` process and `write_antenna` process. The channel decoding of demodulated pilot data is carried out by the `pilot_DSP-_functions` process, which operates on a 1024 element *frame* basis, so a multi-rate transition is present between the `pilot_manage_data` and this latter process. The output data of the pilot channel decoding is sent to a PC computer using the on-chip DMA engine. The `setup_DMA` process is triggered when output data is available from the `pilot-_DSP_functions` process and sets up and starts the DMA process.

Asynchronously with this chain of periodic processes, the `read_sys_cmd` and `read_antenna` process control the internal parameters of the demodulation processes. They respectively perform the man-machine interface connected to the system using a memory mapped flag, allowing the user to alter the system operating parameters, and the interface with the antenna controller which is connected via an external interrupt. The former is a *sporadic* process, since a user will adapt the parameters only once in a while, and is allowed to have a large response time. The latter is a *time-critical* process: when the antenna controller looses the beam, it will signal this immediately to the demodulator, which must take special re-tracking actions.

Constraint Graph Representation   Figure 5 outlines the constraint graph (after thread frame clustering) for the demodulator capturing the threads, their dependency and their timing constraints. For reasons of clarity, the thread execution times are not indicated.

Three event nodes are introduced to capture the timing uncertainty of the periodic interrupt from the decorrelator (ev_{decorr}), the interrupt from the antenna controller (ev_{ant}) and the setting of the polling flag of the man-machine in-

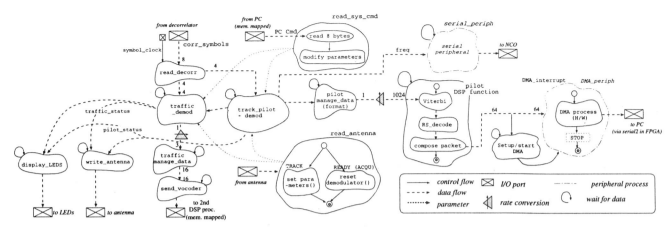

Figure 4: Concurrent Process Specification of the MSBN demodulator

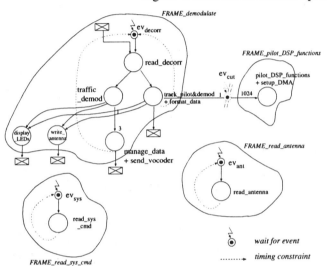

Figure 5: The constraint graph of the MSBN demodulator (after frame clustering)

terface (ev_{sys}). The extra event ev_{cut} was not present in the original CG, but was introduced during frame clustering (see below). Remark that the event nodes make abstraction from whether they are implemented as an interrupt or as a polling loop. Program threads capture also concurrency and the rate conversion. Some processes in the original user specification have been combined into one program thread (e.g. manage_data+send_vocoder).

Timing constraints are added as backward edges, e.g. the edge from the manage_data+send_vocoder to the (periodic) event node expresses that the end of that thread must be executed before the start of the occurrence of the next event, and thus the next period.

Thread Frame Clustering and Transformations In first instance, the cyclic executive based execution model was tried, which proved satisfactory for this application. *Thread frame clustering* and *transformation* were already added in the CG of figure 5. Four different thread frames are identified, three according to the original events and one by an artificial event introduced by the *frame cutting transformation*. Although the event set of the pilot_DSP_functions-+setup_DMA thread is the same as e.g. track_pilot-&demod+format_data thread, it had to be placed in a separate frame because of timing constraints: the execution time of the frame triggered by the decorrelator event in its 1024th execution (according to the relative rate of 1:1024 of the last thread) would become longer than the period of the periodic event and thus conflicts with the timing constraints. Cutting the pilot_DSP_functions-+setup_DMA frame off and introducing an artificial event ev_{cut} which checks for the 1024th execution of preceeding frame, will allow the execution model to overlap the 1024 executions of the FRAME_demodulate with the FRAME-_pilot_DSP_functions.

Another transformation, called *rate matching* is applied on the manage_data_send_vocoder thread: by inserting a rate counter which checks for the relative event occurrence, and based on this causes a conditional execution, the rate of this thread is matched to its frame rate.

Implementation The final implementation after static *frame scheduling* and *introduction of the communication buffers* and with inclusion of the *execution model* is shown in figure 6. Both the FRAME_read_sys_cmd and FRAME_pilot_DSP_functions frame are placed in the background event loop of cyclic executive based execution model, and thus in a round-robin schedule. For the man-machine frame, this is possible because of its non-stringent timing constraint. Its response time to a user setting new system commands will be limited by the execution time of FRAME_pilot_DSP_functions. The two other frames are triggered and activated by the environment using the corresponding hardware interrupt. Remark that in the frame FRAME_demodulate the interrupts are unmasked again (the target processor by default did not allow interrupt nesting) to allow interrupt by FRAME_read_antenna, in order to reduce the response time to the antenna loosing the carrier. At the bottom of figure 6 the behavior of both the CPU and the processor peripherals are outlined on a time-axis. It can be seen clearly that while the FRAME_pilot_DSP-_functions frame is processing the previous data frame in background, the FRAME_demodulate frame (activated by a hardware interrupt) is processing consecutively the 1024 data samples of the next frame. This can be considered as a kind of *process time-folding*. It can also be seen that in-

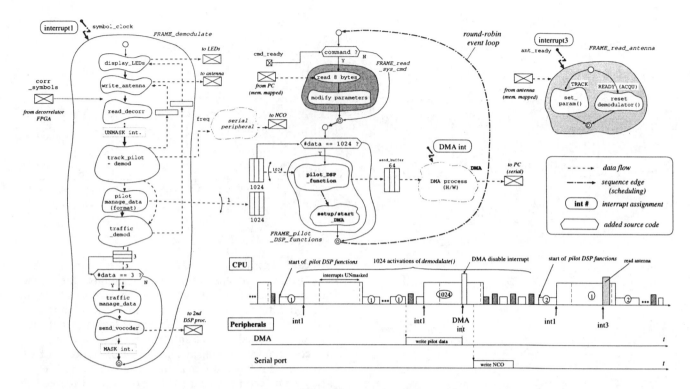

Figure 6: The Final Implementation of the MSBN demodulator

terrupt nesting of both the `FRAME_read_antenna` frame and the DMA interrupt routine (which disables the DMA engine after transfer completion), can occur in the `FRAME_demodulate` frame.

Results The overhead implied by the use of the blocking execution model is *minimal*: it only requires an infinite loop and two conditional tests for the background event loop, and a (register) context save/restore (supported by the processor hardware) for each interrupt routine.

This overhead has to be compared the situation when a realtime kernel is used to implement the run-time behavior of figure 4. The original specification consists of twelve concurrent user processes, and when this hierarchy is straight-forwardly implemented, using the kernel's semaphore primitives to signal between two tasks when data is available, this will result in a considerable (run-time) overhead compared with the solution proposed above. Additionally, it requires extra program memory to hold the kernel's program code. However, with careful manual tuning of the orginal specification and by collapsing a number of user processes, the kernel solution could approach ours. This tuning is however a manual task in contrast the automated tuning and transformation process in our approach, which works across the division of the specification into processes by the user.

5 Conclusions

The approach in this paper tackles the software support problem at the source level in contrast to contemporary coarse-grain, black-box approaches.

The proposed approach tries to exploit the knowledge of the application at hand, applies transformations and optimizations to the specification and generates an application specific solution, with the automatic support for timeliness. The method, based on a representation model composed of program threads and constraint graphs, features a selectable execution model which combines a detailed static analysis of the input specifications, resulting in a static partitioning of the input specifications and a static schedule for each partition, and a run-time activation for the dynamic composition of the specification partitions.

References

[1] M. Chiodo, et al., "Hardware-Software Co-design of Embedded Systems," IEEE Micro, Vol. 14, No. 4, Aug., 1994.

[2] P. Chou, G. Borriello, "Software Scheduling in the Co-Synthesis of Reactive Real-Time Systems," Proc. DAC-94, Jun., 1994.

[3] M. Cornero, et al., "Software Synthesis for Real-Time Information Processing Systems," Code Generation for Embedded Processors, Kluwer, 1995.

[4] European Space Agency (ESA), "Mobile Satellite Business Network (MSBN) - System Requirement Specification," Issue 3.1, ESA-Estec, Nov. 17, 1992.

[5] K. Ghosh, et al.,"A Survey of Real-Time Operating Systems," report GIT-CC-93/18, College of Computing, Georgia Institute of Technology, Atlanta, Georgia, Feb. 15, 1994.

[6] D. Lanneer, et al., "CHESS: Retargetable Code Generation for Embedded DSP Processors," Code Generation for Embedded Processors, Kluwer, 1995.

[7] R. K. Gupta, "Co-Synthesis of Hardware and Software for Digital Embedded Systems," PhD. Dissertation, Stanford University, Dec., 1993.

[8] N. Gehani, W. D. Roome, "The Concurrent C Programming Language," Prentice Hall, 1989.

[9] IEEE Inc., "IEEE Standard VHDL Language Reference Manual," IEEE Standard 1076-1987, Mar., 1982.

[10] D. Ku, G. De Micheli, "Relative Scheduling Under Timing Constraints," Proc. DAC-90, Orlando, FL, Jun., 1990.

[11] J. Xu, D. L. Parnas, "Scheduling Processes with Release Times, Deadlines, Precedence and Exclusion Relations," IEEE Trans. on Softw. Eng., Vol. 16, No. 3, Mar., 1990.

Co-synthesis and Co-simulation of Control-Dominated Embedded Systems

ALESSANDRO BALBONI   fornacia@mailer.cefriel.it, fornacia@elet.polimi.it
ITALTEL-SIT, Central Research Labs, CLTE, 20019 Castelletto di Settimo m.se (MI), Italy

WILLIAM FORNACIARI
Politecnico di Milano, Dip. Elettronica e Informazione, P.zza L. Da Vinci 32, Milano, Italy; CEFRIEL, via Emanueli 15, 20126 Milano (MI), Italy

DONATELLA SCIUTO   sciuto@elet.polimi.it
Politecnico di Milano, Dip. Elettronica e Informazione, P.zza L. Da Vinci 32, Milano, Italy

Abstract. This paper presents a methodology for hardware/software co-design with particular emphasis on the problems related to the concurrent simulation and synthesis of hardware and software parts of the overall system. The proposed approach aims at overcoming the problem of having two separate simulation environments by defining a VHDL-based modeling strategy for software execution, thus enabling the simulation of hardware and software modules within the same VHDL-based CAD framework. The proposed methodology is oriented towards the application field of control-dominated embedded systems implemented onto a single chip.

Keywords: Control dominated systems, hw-sw co-design, application-specific software synthesis, real-time process scheduling, hw-sw cosimulation.

1. Introduction

Many application areas, spanning from telecom systems, automotive equipment to consumer electronics, aim at tradeoff implementation costs and performance requirements, through the use of heterogeneous hardware/software architectures. In particular, for many application fields requiring an ASIC approach to the design, the interest of the CAD developers in methodologies and support tools balancing the performance of customized hardware with the low cost and flexibility of software components has been steadily increasing in the past few years. Therefore, new design automation methodologies should complete current ASIC design flows in order to integrate dedicated logic obtained from behavioral (or Register-Transfer Level) synthesis with programmable parts.

A wide class of computing systems requiring such a detailed design of both hardware and software subparts, fall in the category of *embedded systems*. In the following we will refer to the class of embedded systems which are dedicated to a specific application. For this term we adopt the most restrictive view [28] of a system based on a programmable instruction-set processor which executes a fixed software program, connected to hardware dedicated modules which interact with the external environment and with the processor. They are usually characterized by a *reactive* behavior to the environment stimuli, also conditioned by *real-time* constraints, sometimes requiring a high-performance non-conventional design of the software. Although a certain flexibility/modifiability of the system is always a desirable property, the significant level of customization required by the application, the absence of notable interactions with users and the physical nature of the final product (e.g. a digital switching system, a remote automotive fuel injection controller, small-size portable equipment....) lead to an almost impossible on-line after production tuning of the system. These reasons, in addition to the time-to-market pressure on delivering as soon as possible the final product, force the designers to freeze the system-level design once the refinement of the initial specification becomes synthesizable. As a consequence, the space for trade-off analysis of different architectural solutions is dramatically shrunk.

The result is that a traditional design flow is usually far from a quantitative approach, it is basically driven by a minimum design effort strategy, generating problems during the final modules integration, due to the lack of a concurrent design strategy. The presence of programmable components acts both as a leverage for reducing costs and as a bare support for patching the missing system functionality, since the impact of software modifications is less expensive in comparison with hardware redesign. However, improving the design process is not only a matter of modifying the designer's view of system-level analysis, the activity of combining mixed hw/sw systems is fairly complex since there is a number of preliminary problems and positions to be carefully considered to successfully obtain an effective overall system synthesis. In fact, to take full advantage from concurrent design of mixed hw/sw architectures, new design automation strategies should be designed to allow a smooth integration with available industrial design environments and standards (e.g. VHDL). One of the challenges/requirements is to achieve *cooperation* instead of *competition* with the EDA (Electronic Design Automation) tools composing the ESDA (Electronic System Design Automation) arena.

A basic path for the concurrent design process (*co-design*) starts from capturing the functionality of the whole system (*co-specification*), possibly avoiding any implementation bias. Such a model constitutes the basis for the *system-level exploration*, i.e. the activity of experimenting/evaluating different architectural solutions that will produce two sets of subsystems to be implemented one as hardware and the other as software modules (*partitioning* and *binding*). The final stage consists of the actual synthesis of both the hardware-bound and programmable parts (*co-synthesis*). Some important aspects to be considered along the co-design process are the early prediction of the final results, the possibility of performing a global analysis formally or by simulation (*co-simulation*), the managing and evaluation of different design alternatives, and the reusability support.

Although hardware/software co-design goals and techniques will not probably converge to a single common interpretation, due to the wide spectrum of application fields and design requirements, the potential value-added provided by the automation of co-design tasks has been shown by a number of recent research works. The proposed approaches can be roughly partitioned in strategies starting from a fully software system implementation moving pieces of software toward the hardware domain and, viceversa, strategies aiming at obtaining the minimum cost by replacing pieces of hardware with software code. Two pioneer researches, representing this duality of goals, are COSYMA [6] and VULCAN-II [15], [16].

The first assumes as input of the co-design flow a textual specification written in the C^x language, a C extension supporting task-level concurrence and timing constraints. Such a specification is translated into an internal representation (Extended Syntax Graph) on

for DSP-oriented applications only [7] [24]. A survey of alternative strategies for more general applications is presented in [1] and [26] while [28] provides an extensive survey of the existing open research issues and projects on embedded system co-design. A specific approach is proposed in [15] through the Poseidon system, an event-driven scheduler able to manage mixed hw/sw models. Hardware models are simulated at gate-level (i.e. after synthesis and optimization) by the Mercury logic simulator, while the generated software in C language is first compiled into assembly code and managed by a target-specific assembly code executor. In fact, Poseidon acts as a higher-level integrator of multiple heterogeneous simulators.

A different approach showing the different points of view on co-design related issues, can be found in [27]. This research work tends to unify embedded system co-design and distributed systems design within a common conceptual framework.

However, despite the number of proposals appeared in literature, usually they are still too advanced for being considered in current industrial environments. In particular, these approaches do not consider in a unified way the activities of co-simulation and co-synthesis under the point of view of obtaining system representations compatible with current industrial standards. Main purpose of our research is to define a pragmatic approach that could be accepted as prototype in the R&D department of an Italian telecom company. Therefore main requirement is the possibility of integration within an industrial design flow and to allow human intervention on all decisions pertaining system exploration, with the possibility of backtracking along the design process and of reusing already designed submodules.

The paper introduces a novel methodology to manage the co-design process for a specific application field, i.e. control-dominated ASICs, such as those embedded into telecom digital switching subsystems. Usually this class of systems is composed of interacting hardware and software components where a mix of algorithm and event-driven control/communication functions (e.g. protocol stacks) are affected by real-time constraints and have to be captured/processed in an integrated manner.

The development of such a methodology is currently in progress within a research project called TOSCA (TOols for System Co-design Automation), in which one of the main activities is the definition of a support environment by integrating commercial EDA software with new experimental tools [2], [3], [4]. One of the main characteristics of the TOSCA framework over other literature proposals is the high level of integration with the existing commercial EDA tools through the direct interfacing to an existing design entry environment (e.g. speedChart), a VHDL representation of the hardware-bound parts, the direct synthesis of the software modules and the possibility of achieving co-simulation of the entire mixed hw/sw system within the same VHDL-based environment. Moreover, the CAD environment allows the user to cover the whole design process, ranging from the system-level specification capture down to the synthesis, by considering low level effects of the software timing properties (at the assembly level), by providing the code for software processes as well as the necessary operating system support and, finally, by generating the interfaces among hw and sw modules. In addition, the internal representation paradigm, based on process algebra [19], [21], provides the possibility of extending the analysis to include formal verification capabilities.

The two main phases of the TOSCA co-design environment discussed in this paper are which preliminary simulation and profiling can be carried out. The environment provides an automatic partitioning stage based on a simulated annealing algorithm. Candidate solutions are compared by applying a cost function to the marked graph. After hw/sw partitioning, hardware-bound parts of the ESG are translated into HardwareC language and implemented via the Olympus high-level synthesis system [11], while C source code is generated from software-bound parts.

The front-end and back-end stages of VULCAN are conceptually similar to the ones provided by COSYMA: a textual specification (written in HardwareC) is translated into an internal graph-based representation (System Graph); after hw/sw partitioning, parts targeted to hardware are synthesized by Olympus while C code is produced for software by exploiting a coroutine-based multiprocessing scheme. The main difference can be found in the strategy adopted by the partitioner, based on iterative process moving of operations between the partitions with the goal of reducing communication overhead while satisfying timing, bus/processor utilization and feasibility constraints.

In the SpecSyn system-design environment [13], specifications are captured via the Spec-Charts visual language and translated into an internal representation called PSM. Partitioning is performed through algorithms based on clustering or simulated annealing and results are evaluated by estimation tools providing metrics for software and hardware speed, silicon area and code size. An approach to interface synthesis is discussed in [14]. A discussion on the importance of having a suitable intermediate format to represent system-level specifications can be found in [25]. The PARTIF tool ([20]) allows the user to explore alternative system-level partitions by manipulating a hierarchical concurrent finite-state model (SO-LAR). A primitive set of transformation (moving states, merging states) and decomposition (splitting/cutting macro-states) rules has been defined.

An alternative solution to hw/sw binding is shown in the CASTLE project [23]. Systems are modeled in standard languages such as VHDL, Verilog and C. The internal representation (Software View) is hierarchical and composed of control-flow graphs and basic blocks. The CASTLE approach is based on the concept of a library of complex components (processors, memories, special-purpose off-the-shelf chips as well as ASICs) and a library-driven mapping strategy.

In [10] a co-design environment is presented, called Chinook, tailored to implement reactive real-time controllers with particular emphasis on the problems of modules interfacing and synchronization. The system goal is to cover the problems of partitioning, device synthesis, low level scheduling, code generation and performance estimation. The top-level system specification is captured via a Verilog description while the output consists of all the elements necessary to build the embedded system: the netlist of coprocessor and glue logic together with the assembly code retargeted to the specific microprocessor.

Finally, a co-design environment not emphasizing the automation of the hw/sw partitioning stage based on an extension of the well know FSM paradigm, has been proposed in [8], [9]. The system specifications are modeled by asynchronous non-deterministic finite-state machines (CFSM) which, in perspective, will be obtained from a VHDL or ESTEREL front-end. The internal representation of CFSM (SHIFT) is suitable for preliminary analysis by formal verification techniques.

The research area concerning hardware/software co-simulation has been widely explored

requirements of the designer. The co-design process supported by the TOSCA CAD environment is composed of the following, partially interleaved, coarse-grain phases:

1. *System description*, including functional requirements, performance goals and feasibility constraints.
2. *Analysis of the system specification* through a set of metrics for early prediction of the implementation results.
3. *System-level partitioning and binding*, to identify a decomposition in modules of the initial specification together with their implementation technology. Manipulations of the system specification, preserving its functionality, are performed. They are driven by the set of metrics which estimate the final results and by the design constraints.
4. *System-synthesis*, producing the assembly code for the software part and VHDL for the hardware-bound modules.
5. *Co-simulation* of the final system and user-level *back-annotation* of the results.

The acquisition of the specifications requires the possibility of integrating elements obtained from different sources, since often most designs are realized starting from previous product releases or make use of existing, or third party, modules. Therefore, the value added of a co-design methodology is tightly conditioned by the achievement of a realistic integration with current trends of specification standards. The characteristics of most project specifications, which are not unconstrained, can be summarized as follows:

- Some parts can be *a priori* hardware or software bound; this can derive from direct intervention of experienced designers or forced by top-level specifications/requirements.
- Some parts can be not only hardware or software bound but already synthesized, e.g. because of reusability of proprietary (or widely accepted) software algorithms and hardware subsystems (e.g. belonging to the company library of VHDL models).
- Design centers with up to date CAD environments can produce models captured via a mixed graphical/textual formalism, based on concurrent and hierarchical FSMs (e.g. the statecharts family [17] [18]), or at least through a HDL (basically VHDL and Verilog).
- Some parts can be designed without any particular bias, currently in our system this is realized by using a process algebra computational model; however different solutions can be envisaged without loss of generality.
- Non purely functional requirements, such as area, total cost, power are given by considering the system as a whole, regardless of its modules composition and unbalanced granularity. This sometimes catches the co-design process in local optimums, because design optimization is usually performed onto a limited subset of the modules composing the system.

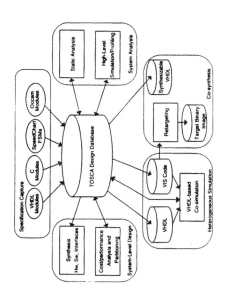

Figure 1. The architecture of the TOSCA co-design environment.

the hardware and software co-synthesis and the co-simulation of the system obtained. Therefore the paper is organized as follows: section two gives an overview of the TOSCA design flow and defines the objectives of the supported co-design activities. Then section three introduces the target system architecture and details the synthesis of software and hardware modules, it also discusses the problems related with direct synthesis of interfaces and software retargeting. An example of software synthesis is reported in Appendix 1. Section four introduces the co-simulation engine while showing the strategies adopted to simulate both hardware and software modules by using the same VHDL-based environment.
The final section outlines the main results of our approach and points out the future research guidelines.

2. The TOSCA Design Flow

System design companies need methodologies and tools suitable to be integrated within existing design flows, usable by designers with a low training effort and able to move down from abstract specification toward the actual implementation, while maintaining the capability of performing an efficient global co-simulation at any considered level. The *state of the art* of research in this field, tends to focus on specific aspects of the problem or to be affected by an high level of customization, making difficult a significant cooperation with existing design environments.

The methodology we are proposing aims at providing a complete stand-alone design framework, whose main structure is shown in fig. 1, allowing a realistic integration with commercial EDA tools as back-end or front-end to the global framework.

The analysis of the basic design flow followed by system designers has allowed us to identify the proposed automated methodology which takes into account the needs and

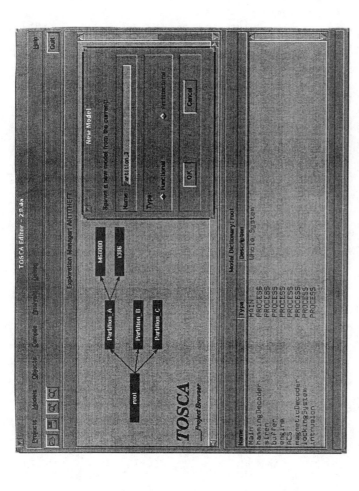

Figure 2. The Project Editor framework.

To adjust to such an industrial practice, the methodology developed in TOSCA allows the concurrent existence of multiple formalisms able to cover hardware oriented models, intrinsically software parts as well as specification parts without any particular implementation bias. To manage such a variety of formalisms, a uniform internal representation has been created based on a process algebra computational model with an OCCAMII more pragmatic syntax [21], [5]. Modules which are already synthesized and cannot be modified in the following phases of system exploration are only encapsulated, while other modules described through different formalisms can be mapped (up to now only speedCHART and OCCAMII, but any formalism can be easily translated into the formal internal representation adopted). The overall system representation is stored within an object oriented database (TOSCA DB) tailored to support high-level architectural exploration, shared by all the tools composing the TOSCA environment.

System designs can also be specified by means of a graphical front- end for OCCAMII specifications developed in TCL (Tools Command Language). Three different editors have been developed to manage the design complexity.

1. A Project editor/Exploration Manager, that is the user interface aiming at providing a complete management of the co-design flow (e.g. saving/restoring of different versions of the project, documentation of the analysis results, ...); fig. 2 depicts the graphical front-end gathering all the tools composing the TOSCA environment.
2. A Process editor, allowing the specification of graphical state-based processes, including an editor for the textual parts; fig. 3 shows the capturing of a system description through the built-in process editor.
3. A Hierarchy editor, whose main purpose is to manage the specification of a complex system in terms of connections between hierarchical modules, possibly belonging to heterogeneous domain (e.g. existing VHDL library models, graphical FSMs descriptions, ...).

A simulation tool based on Petri Nets, written in C, has been developed for early functional validation and profiling.

The entire co-design process evolution is controlled by an Exploration Manager (EM) tool whose goal is to maintain a complete history of the multiple alternative design paths explored by the user. All the data are stored within a common design database whose user-friendly interface enables direct intervention in each of the steps composing system-level design, simulation and synthesis. The EM allows the user to manage:

- The internal representation of the system specification;
- The evaluation of different design alternatives at system level;
- A step by step visualization of statistics and results concerning the transformations performed onto the system representation;
- The documentation of the design flow spanning from the system specification to the synthesis data.

After the preliminary phase of design capture, the main activity managed by the EM is the manipulation of the initial system modularization to produce a new set of system partitions and their association (if still *floating*) either with software or dedicated hardware units. Our approach, apart from possible bindings forced by users, does not start from an *a priori* default solution (e.g. initially fully software bound).

The system exploration and partitioning process can be viewed as an incremental activity of modification of the initial specification through the application of transformations. The TOSCA project has considered this process through:

- The definition and implementation of formal transformation rules working onto the internal model stored within the design database [12], [4];
- The definition of a partitioning algorithm and its implementation within the Exploration Manager framework to obtain a tool allowing both direct intervention of the user and automatic selection of the strategies by following the built-in evaluation criteria [4];

The activity of identifying some closeness properties among parts of the system specification, can be performed as a static analysis based on metrics for early prediction of cost/performance. It aims at producing an initial nearly-optimum allocation and binding to be iteratively improved by the user until design goals are satisfied. The final exploration stage, including at least one actual synthesis cycle, is the most time consuming and it is strongly sensitive to the quality of the pre-allocation performed during the former phases; it returns information that will be back-annotated as a replacement of predicted data.
The metrics consider the system analysis from a threefold point of view:

- *Statically*, by analyzing composition and structure of the description contained within the database.
- *Dynamically*, but still independent of the implementation, through an high-level execution and profiling of the specification in order to extract information such as communication bottlenecks and statistics on operators applications to better tune the decision on the initial partitioning and binding.
- *After-synthesis*, requiring at least a complete synthesis cycle. This returns information that will be back-annotated as a replacement of predicted data and will also contribute to the final design evaluation.

A proper set of metrics for early prediction of cost/performance, as well as to evaluate the system synthesis results, has been developed and constitutes the basis for the partitioning process. The following types of parameters have been considered in the definition of the cost/performance metrics.

- *Communication*: costs related to the number of lines and bandwidth for hardware-hardware and software-hardware communication.
- *Interfacing*: according to the adopted communication/synchronization technique among different modules (e.g. between hardware and software, one interface unit per coprocessor vs. a common bus manager/arbiter queuing messages), costs can be affected by number and granularity of modules. Alternative bus protocol templates can be evaluated.
- *Area*: this is the most important aspect because of the single chip implementation. Overall optimization takes into account possible user-defined binding along the evaluation and comparison among different alternatives.
- *Resources exploitation*: on the software side, since the microprocessor is anyhow present, it is important to increase as much as possible the CPU utilization while fulfilling the temporal requirements of the programmed modules and the effectiveness of memory. Another relevant issue is related to the power consumption that is improved by a modularization able to identify the minimum set of coprocessors with the lowest amount of idle time.
- *Reuse*: expressed by the number and complexity of different subsections used to build the modules and by the quota of the system covered by library components or existing modules.

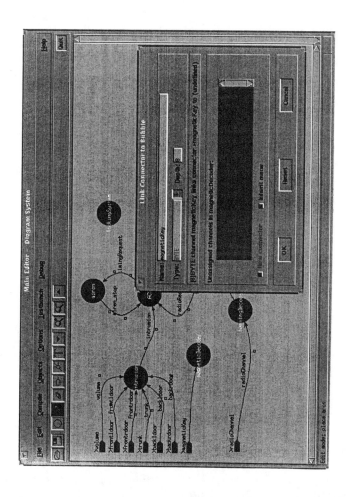

Figure 3. The Process Editor.

- The definition and implementation of a set of metrics to drive the partitioning process [4], [5], [12].

The user can organize these actions either along customizable schedules called *recipes* or can proceed under his own direct control. The output of this activity is a set of monolithic architectural units with a binding establishing either a hardware or a software implementation. Each architectural unit is then passed as input to the following co-synthesis stages.

The criteria guiding the selection of the transformations to be applied to the system description (in order to fulfill the target design requirements) are supported by a quantitative evaluation. Such an evaluation is performed by means of a set of metrics which drive both the definition of a coarse-grain initial solution and an iterative fine tuning until all the design constraints are met.

The basic transformation applied is processes collapsing. This will occur whenever the measure of a closeness criteria, during the selection of the closest processes, will remain under a certain *a priori* defined threshold. This solution is particularly flexible since it is possible to consider a set of criteria, with different priorities that will be changed dynamically, according to the current processes granularity or user choice.

More specific information on the definition and use of metrics can be found in [4], [5], since it does not represent the main focus of this paper.

The co-synthesis step is constituted by two different tools: a tool for VHDL description generation for hardware-bound architectural units including interface generation, and a software synthesis tool for software-bound architectural units, including the Operating System support.

The class of embedded systems we are considering, characterized by real-time reactive requirements, and the typical application size enabling the use of a single ASIC including a CPU, has led to discard a C-language based solution for the software parts since we believe that software needs to be considered at a lower level, to carefully control time delay, code size and low level interfacing alternative schemes. Easy retargeting and portability are frequently advocated as some of the main advantages of high-level languages with respect to assembly, our solution is to consider the software description at the level of a virtual assembly instruction set (VIS) whose structure can be mapped onto different CPU cores with fully predictable translation rules and, consequently, reliable performance estimation. As shown in the following, this solution provides the possibility of achieving a fully VHDL based co-simulation of each proposed hardware/software architecture, in order to get feedback on the effectiveness of the implementation. In fact a suitable VHDL model for VIS instruction-level execution, has been developed [3], so that the entire system can be co-simulated through a unified VHDL-based environment. The model is parametrizable in order to make possible the analysis of low-level timing/cost/performance, for different classes of microprocessors.

Up to now studies devoted to include a C-based real-time preemptive microkernel have been postponed. According to the needs of the application field, requiring simplicity and predictability, a static schedule approach with a coroutine scheme has been adopted as the target software structure.

Hardware synthesis is performed by generating behavioral VHDL for synthesis from the internal OCCAMII representation of the selected modules. It is also possible to generate RTL level VHDL for logic synthesis for finite state machine descriptions. Interfaces are generated with respect to the adopted model of communication. At this time a fixed protocol is implemented, coherent with the target architecture adopted as discussed in section 3.

3. System Synthesis

In our approach, the system is intended to be implemented onto a single chip including an off-the-shelf microprocessor core with its memory (even if part of the memory can be external) and the dedicated logic implementing a set of coprocessors, i.e. the set of synthesized hardware-bound modules identified during system exploration (see fig. 4).

In this discussion the term coprocessor includes also arithmetic/logic operations and possible private storage capability, while high-level synthesis tools typically separate controllers from data-paths. The master processor is programmable and the software can be either on-chip resident or read from an external memory; dedicated units operate as peripheral coprocessors. Hardware and software bound elements are interfaced by means of a master-slave shared bus communication strategy. All hardware to hardware communications are

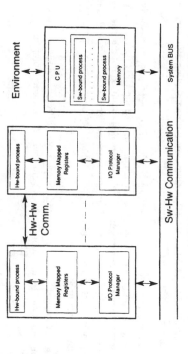

Figure 4. The hardware-software target architecture.

managed through dedicated lines. The RAM memory required for program/data storage shares the main data bus with the coprocessors, but can be accessed only by the master CPU. Communications among CPU and coprocessors are based on a memory mapped I/O scheme with one bus interface manager per coprocessor based on a common I/O buffered protocol manager.

Before committing to a specific implementation, the initial system specification can be manipulated to fulfill the target design requirements. This partitioning process, can be viewed as an incremental activity of modification of the initial specification through the application of transformations [12], [5], briefly summarized in section 2.

Once a pair of hardware and software bound sets of modules have been defined, the following step is to produce their implementations. The synthesis stage will produce a mapping of the system onto the target architecture reported in Fig. 4, i.e.:

- assembly-level code for each sw-bound process, according to the target microprocessor instruction set;
- operating system support for process to process communication (both between sw to sw and sw to hw), as well as for CPU scheduling;
- VHDL code for each architectural unit (coprocessor) corresponding to hw-bound processes; this includes also the implementation of the hardware side of the interfacing subsystem, allowing the mapping of the abstract process to process communication onto an actual system architecture.

3.1. Software Synthesis

The software system has to be designed according to the reference architecture that is itself strongly influenced in terms of programming paradigm and hardware by the application field and the cost/performance goals. The basic requirements of an embedded system are the performing of activities according to a set of precise timing constraints (*timeliness*) and the *flexibility*, that in our case means that system configuration and software behavior have to be easy to update. These requirements are crucial to enhance maintenance, possibility of customization and re-use of the system and design methodology. Low-cost embedded systems characterized by small/medium size applications require the development of a light-weight software in terms of typical operating system services provided, but with an high degree of reliability and predictability. The run-time support provided in TOSCA has been kept minimal and includes only those features that are actually needed to support exception handling, configuration control, communication management and process activation, chosen during the customization phase. The operating system micro-kernel actually acts as a high-level process manager whose evolution is controlled by a deterministic algorithm, with synchronization among processes or with the environment (i.e. the coprocessors or external devices connected to the system).

Since the current target architecture considers just one microprocessor, concurrence is emulated through interleaving of processes, each corresponding to a software-bound part of the system modularization, whose ordering is statically defined, i.e. a pre-runtime schedule has been adopted. This solution has been chosen because high processor utilization is foreseen to reduce implementation costs, so that there is not much spare CPU available. As a consequence, a solution able to guarantee *a priori* that all the stringent timing constraints will be met, seems to be the only viable. We found many advantages of this solution compared to the presence of an on-line schedule policy, such as the significant reduction in the share of run-time resources necessary to implement context switching and the scheduling itself, but the most important is that it is easier to satisfy our primary goal of meeting the real-time deadline.

Software-bound processes, that are viewed as a set of sequential cooperating threads with shared memory similar to a coroutine scheme, are constituted by operations that must be executed in a prescribed order. The number of processes is known in advance, and it will never change run-time. This implies that the operating system does not require a dynamic scheduling since the scheduling policy can be computed off-line and *code-wired*. Therefore, the solution proposed requires only a small operating system providing the mechanisms for process activation and the communication support.

In general, two classes of processes can be present: *periodic*, whose computation is executed repeatedly in a fixed amount of time and *asynchronous*, that usually consist of computations responding to an event (internal or external). A typical example of periodic process is the sampling of external data with the consequent updating of state internal variables and outputs as it happens in a transmission frame manager of a telecom digital switching system. For a number of real-time applications, periodic processes where the sequencing and timing constraints are known in advance, seem to constitute the bulk of computation. The number of asynchronous processes is usually limited, requiring short computation times. Moreover, information due to external or internal events can be recorded and buffered until they can be handled by periodic processes tailored to serve them. Different and more general techniques for mapping asynchronous processes onto an equivalent set

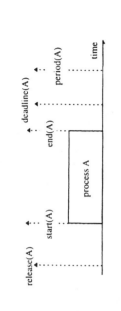

Figure 5. Timing characterization of a process.

of periodic processes can be found in [22], therefore we considered only the problem of scheduling periodic processes.

The algorithm we implemented, given the set of processes constituting the sw-bound part of the system, determines a schedule (whenever it exists) such that each process is activated after its release time and carries out its computation before its deadline. Fig. 5 reports the timing characterization of a periodic process. Even though the exact timing characteristics of system components and events sometimes cannot be predicted, we overcome such a problem by using a worst case estimation of these parameters so that the scheduling algorithm can guarantee a predictable behavior.

The methodology we adopted to obtain the pre-run time schedule is based upon a systematic improvement of an initial schedule until a feasible (near optimal) schedule is found. The analysis of the VIS code corresponding to each software-bound part allows the VIS scheduler to consider each software process characterized by a *release* time, the *duration* and a *deadline*, which can be broken into a set of code segments. An analysis of the internal composition of the process provides the start time of each code segment relative to the beginning of the process it belongs. Exclusion relations may be present among segments when some of them must avoid interruption by others to prevent possible errors caused by simultaneous access to shared resources, e.g. data structures, I/O devices, coprocessors. Precedence relations, that occur when a segment requires some information produced by other process segments, are also considered.

The scheduler produces an ordered set of code segments fulfilling deadlines and constraints (if they exist) where the lateness of all segments is minimized. The context switching overhead has been considered by including an additional delay to the purely computational time. To characterize the scheduler the software running onto the microprocessor, other information is produced by the scheduler by inspecting the final schedule produced: the level of process fragmentation and the relative overhead, the slack time, the CPU utilization and, in case of non feasible schedule, the critical segments responsible of the algorithm failure.

The starting point of the algorithm is a valid initial schedule satisfying release times, exclusion and precedence constraints obtained through an heuristic belonging to the class *earliest-deadline-first*. Through a branch and bound technique a search-tree is built where each node is a schedule. Nodes are obtained from their parents by introducing new additional properties (preemption and exclusion): by computing the lower bound of the lateness of any schedule deriving from that node the best solution among all candidates is selected. A skeleton of the algorithm is depicted in fig. 6.

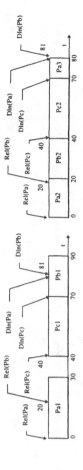

```
repeat {
    select child-node with min-lateness among unexpanded nodes;
    compute SG1, SG2;
    for each segment ∈ SG1 and SG2 create new schedule;
    compute lateness lower-bound of each schedule;
} until (lateness - LowerBound) ≤ ε
```

Figure 6. The scheduling strategy. ε is the maximum acceptable error.

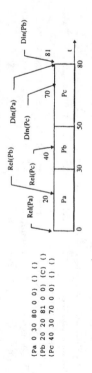

```
{Pa  0 30 80 0 0} () ()
{Pb 20 20 81 0 0} {C} ()
{Pc 40 30 70 0} () ()
```

Figure 7. An example of scheduling problem associated with its textual and graphical representation. Rel(P) and Dln(P) indicates *release* and *deadline* of the process P.

A *valid solution$_i$* (VS_i) computed through an earliest-deadline-first policy and its latest segment (LS_i) are associated with the generic node i of the search tree. In order to produce new solutions improving the current one, two groups of segments $SG1_i$, $SG2_i$ are determined such that:

a) $SG1_i$: VS_i can be improved if the latest segment is *scheduled before* a segment of $SG1_i$;

b) $SG2_i$: VS_i can be improved if the latest segment *preempts* a segment of $SG2_i$.

According to the properties a) and b), for each segment belonging to the two groups SG1 and SG2, a new schedule (successor node) is created. The result of this step consists of two sets of new schedules (nodes), that are dominated by the node$_i$, associated with the lower bound on the lateness for each schedule obtained during this stage. Among the unexpanded nodes, the one with the lowest bound is considered the best candidate to achieve an optimal solution (i.e. lateness equal to a goal value LowerBound) for a new branching. The search proceeds until either a feasible solution is determined or no unexpanded node exists with a lower bound less than the least lateness of all the valid solutions computed up to now (that will constitute an optimal solution). In such a way, all the possible improvements of the initial schedule are considered, so that the optimal solution is determined, if one exists. Moreover, in the case of algorithm failure, the responsible segment (the one with the least lateness) and consequently the owner process is determined and can be used as starting point for actions aiming at making the implementation of the software-bound parts feasible. As an example let us consider the simple case of the following input file (left) for the scheduler and the corresponding graphical representation (right) of fig. 7.

The problem is composed of three processes (Pa, Pb, Pc) where, the items of the corresponding list represent the name, the release time, the computation time, the deadline

Figure 8. The schedules originated by the SG1 and SG2 expanding sets.

	Schedule of fig 8 (left)	Schedule of fig 8 (right)
ListSortedSegments	Pa1, Pc1, Pb1	Pa2, Pb2, Pc2, Pa3
Sections	Pa1, Pc1, Pb1	Pa2, Pb2, Pc2, Pa3
LatenessSchedule	9	0
LatestSegment	Pb1	Pa3, Pc2
CPUinactivity	10	0
MaxSlackTime	10	0
EndSchedule	90	80
StartSchedule	0	0
TotalTimeSchedule	90	80
LowerBound	9	0

Figure 9. Data computed at each step of the schedule, TotalTimeSchedule is the overall execution time of the schedule and the Sections field contains the sets of contiguous segments.

and two values to mimic the delay necessary to restore and save the process context (for simplicity set to zero), respectively. The other lists report possible constraints (exclusion and preemption), in the proposed example Pb excludes Pc. The expanding sets are $SG1 = \{Pb\}$ and $SG2 = \{Pa\}$, therefore the two sets of new schedules are composed only by one element each. The actual schedules are obtained from the characteristic properties of SG1, i.e. {Pc precedes Pb} (fig. 8-left) and similarly for SG2, i.e. {Pc Preempts Pa, Pb Preempts Pa} (fig. 8-right).

For each schedule the report file includes a section containing the information summarized in fig. 9. In the leftmost schedule the latest segment is Pb1 and the Lateness evaluates End(Pb1) − Deadline(Pb1) = 9 that is a local optimum. The latest segments of the second open node of the search tree, i.e. the rightmost schedule, are Pa3 and Pc2, the Lateness evaluates End(Pa3) − Deadline(Pa) = End(Pc2) − Deadline(Pc) = 0. No further expansion of the tree is possible, therefore the rightmost schedule represents a global optimum since Lateness is equal to least LowerBound of all the open nodes considered up to now. The output of the scheduler is thus the process segmentation and ordering on the right of fig. 8.

The software part of the system is implemented by means of a generic Virtual Instruction Set (VIS) which allows a better control of time delays, code size and a low level characterization of I/O interfaces. The VIS is an intermediate language between OCCAMII and the target CPU assembly aiming at capturing the minimum set of features shared by microcontrollers for embedded applications. This solution allows us to achieve the following goals:

- integrated simulation of the mixed hardware-software system;
- extension of the analysis to cover also multiple processor families;
- good predictability of the final running software behavior;
- integrated synthesis flow able to cover the entire system development in terms of hardware, interfaces, software and operating system support.

The VIS is defined in terms of a customizable and orthogonal register-oriented machine with a common address space for both code and data. This means that each register can act as accumulator and all the operations (e.g. addressing, arithmetic-logic, data transfer) can be performed no matter which register is used as operand. The instruction set has been designed in order to be easily retargeted onto different CPUs: a mix of CISC and RISC typical instructions are included. A generic VIS instruction can either be one-to-one mapped on a native target assembly instruction or correspond to a group of assembly instructions. In such a way, if the selected CPU does not match the VIS instruction, the retargeting of the code is performed via an alternative definition of the instruction using only the RISC-side of the VIS, thus reducing the effort to reconfigure the software whenever alternative CPUs are evaluated.

The VIS supports unsigned/signed integer data types (BIT, BYTE, INT16 or *word* and 32-bits integer called *longword*) as well as all typical arithmetic/logic operations. The address space spans over 32 bits so that each VIS argument is always contained within a longword. The memory format for the data is aligned in terms of 32-bits words, as a consequence four memory locations are necessary to store a byte. Boolean variables can be packed to save memory space.

The instruction format is similar to the one of the MC68000 with a suffix indicating the operand type, e.g. MOVE.B R1, R2 copies a byte from R1 to R2. Three types of instruction formats have been defined:

- `op destination, source`
- `op arg1, arg2`
- `op`

where both destination and source can be registers or memory references (*source* can also be an immediate operand) and arg1, arg2 model operations where the argument order is not relevant.

The generation of the VIS code as well as the final implementation of the software running on the target microprocessor follows the phases depicted in fig. 10. Three main steps compose the top part of such an activity: initialization, code generation, estimation of time delays and binary code size.

At the beginning the system is initialized by reading from a technology file the information characterizing the selected CPU, e.g. the clock period, the instruction set, the registers

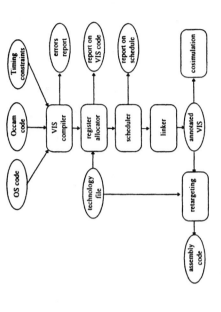

Figure 10. The software generation process.

number, type and size of the registers, the number of clock per instruction, etc. The code generation involves register usage optimization and automated packing of bit variables. The estimation of timing performance and memory requirements for back-annotation towards the system design exploration phase can be obtained for several possible microprocessor cores. In fact, its actual behavior is represented by the following three groups of information (for each foreseen CPU):

- retargeting rules (RR): specifying the rules for mapping VIS code onto the target microprocessor instruction set;
- time/size table (TST): reporting for each VIS instruction the number of clock cycles and bytes of the corresponding target CPU mapping (which, in general, is not composed of a single instruction).
- technology (TF): containing information on the adopted CPU as the BUS width, the power consumption, the pin-out of the microprocessor, the particular characteristics of the adopted model of microprocessor with respect to the rest of the CPU family, such as, for instance the memory size.

The first step is the compilation of the OCCAMII specification in VIS. Although the entire system specification will not probably be implemented in software, the estimation of the VIS performance and cost is initially carried out for all the OCCAMII modules composing the description. The obtained result is employed during the system partitioning to compare/drive alternative modularizations and hardware vs software bindings. The obtained code is not executable since the following decisions have yet to be taken: register mapping, process scheduling, system bootstrap, memory allocation including symbolic vs actual address determination.

CHAPTER 4: System-Level Partitioning, Synthesis, and Interfacing

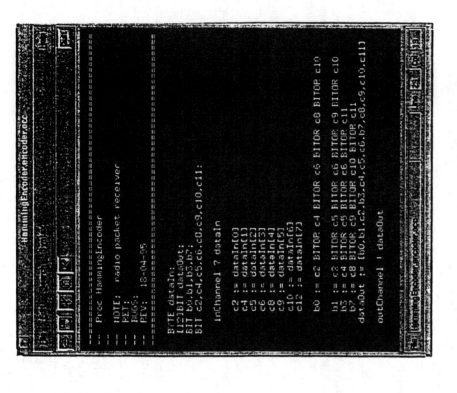

Figure 11. Screen-dump of the description of a Hamming decoder described by using the TOSCA OCCAMII process editor.

A pre-allocation of the register to extract execution times and memory requirements is performed according to the information included within the technology file. The VIS code is then annotated with the information needed by the scheduler to produce a correct ordering of the processes execution, by adding some bracket- encapsulated tags. A simple example of VIS compilation for a sub-part (Hamming encoder) belonging to a car antitheft system that we use as a small benchmarking, is shown in appendix 1. The example is composed of a process receiving data from the channel dataIn where two parallel sections allow the system to compute the Hamming encoding of the input to be transmitted on the dataOut channel (see fig. 11).

The VIS code maintains a structure similar to the original OCCAMII model: the body of each process is identified through the <process> and </process> tags while concurrent processes (corresponding to the PAR construct of OCCAM) fall within the scope of a <group> identifier.

As reported above, the scheduler may require to break the processes to meet time deadlines; as a consequence, it is necessary to consider the impact of additional context-switching overheads. The scheduler performs such an analysis by considering the <USE Regs-List> and <LEAVE Regs-List> tags which represent, incrementally, the registers necessary to be saved at any point in time. Critical sections, corresponding to non-breakable actions such as an interrupt handling, are enclosed within <atomic> </atomic> to prevent a possible preemption.

Data transfer from software to hardware and viceversa is modeled via memory-mapped coprocessor registers, associated with each port. In this example, the 12-bits channel has been mapped onto a 16 bits word corresponding to a pair of contiguous memory locations. Timing characterization is also performed with a fine granularity to improve the freedom of the scheduler to choose the point where to break processes. The left-most tags of each VIS instruction contains the computation of <minimum typical maximum> delays to execute the operation according to the target CPU. Up to now, according to the most common types of embedded system microprocessors, effects concerning pipelined instruction execution or parallel fetch have not been considered. For an analysis on how these issues can be managed for DSP applications, see [24].

During software synthesis, processes as well as the operating system microkernel are directly assembled into VIS code. As reported above, the software system is composed of processes and of a kernel basically operating as a context switcher: although no sophisticated mechanisms for memory protection are necessary, particular attention has been devoted to the software section responsible for communication by adopting *ad-hoc* solutions to suit each specific circumstance. Our software synthesis system has to implement two different communication schemes: software to software, hardware to software (and viceversa). Processes communication takes place through buffered channels that will be implemented according to the type of data protocol and the hw/sw binding of the source and target processes.

Protocol implementation of complex data types is defined in terms of composition of basic types, such as BOOL, BYTE, INT16 (16-bit integer). The needs for communication involving the system bus have been reduced during the system partitioning phase since, under the scheduling algorithm viewpoint, the bus is a shared resource that will originate

a *critical section* within the software-bound process requiring its use, thus increasing the difficulty to determine a feasible schedule.

Even though the basic OCCAMII model is composed of direct, point-to-point, asynchronous channels, our implementation has been extended to provide also a broadcasting node by expanding its definition into a software process able to copy the datum on all the target channels. The channel is mapped onto a pair (memory variable, data ready flag) shared by all processes. Since communication rates can vary across different processes, no matter if they belong to the same hardware or software partition, appropriate FIFO buffering capability has been introduced. Hardware/software interface is performed via memory mapped registers.

A parametrizable retargeting tool, able to map VIS code on different target CPU has been implemented and tested for a Motorola 68000 microprocessor family, the extension towards the PowerPC architecture is part of the current effort.

3.2. Hardware and Interface Synthesis

Concerning the *hardware mapping* strategy adopted in TOSCA, it should be pointed out that control-oriented specifications cannot easily be managed by classical high-level synthesis approaches involving operators scheduling. In fact, circuit speed estimation is very difficult when dealing with descriptions dominated by conditional functions, where arithmetic operations are typically restricted to a few sums and comparisons (if anyone of them is present at all). During the next stage involving VHDL translation into a generic netlist, technology mapping and logic implementation, any direct relation between functional specification and synthesized implementation is lost. Estimating area is also a very hard task. As a consequence, scheduling operators according to estimated propagation delays cannot be considered a realistic approach. In the previous version of the TOSCA module devoted to hardware mapping, each hardware-bound architectural unit is implemented by generating a finite state machine VHDL description, together with its bus interface [3]. If the starting point is a synchronous model (as those obtained from speedCHART), no additional scheduling step is needed. The VHDL code generator translates the internal representation of each FSM into a VHDL template (block-encapsulated processes) compliant to the guidelines for synthesis enforced by commercial tools such as Mentor Graphics Autologic and Synopsys VHDL Compiler. The data flow graphs modeling conditions and actions are translated into VHDL statements included in the related template. The algorithm adopted is able to produce a very readable description by building expressions whenever possible, instead of basic assignments for each DFG node. Parameters such as the logic types to be used can be customized by the user. In particular cases, such as for instance counters, predefined library components may be preferred to RTL synthesis in order to guarantee an efficient implementation.

However, recently several commercial VHDL behavioral synthesis tools are emerging (Synopsys, Synthesia). This opportunity is particularly valuable to cope with system-level architectural exploration needing fast speed/cost prediction techniques, avoiding as much as possible to move down to the gate-level netlist. The current version of TOSCA is oriented towards a direct compilation of process algebra description into behavioral VHDL, that is becoming the target abstraction level for synthesis. In summary, three different hardware synthesis paths can be applied:

1. transparent passing of the initial VHDL description to the synthesis tool;
2. RTL synthesizable VHDL description of the modules such as FSM;
3. behavioral VHDL descriptions of the hardware-bound modules.

A suitable VHDL generator has been developed, starting from the OCCAMII description stored within the database and building a tree modeling the statements nesting. It produces a set of modules corresponding to the hardware bound architectural units (coprocessors) with their communication interfaces. The VHDL code generator performs a depth-first scan of the tree representing the OCCAMII structure and produces two output files: the first contains the entities declarations with the corresponding behavioral description while the second is a package containing all the procedures necessary to realize the communication among processes.

Since channels are not supported by VHDL, *ad hoc* fully hardware interface structures covering both buffered and unbuffered communication have been introduced.

In case of hardware-to-hardware communication, the realization of each channel requires the instance of three signals to implement the negotiation process `s_req` (send-request), `s_data` (send-data) and `r_ack` (receive-ack)- that will be used to expand each OCCAMII declaration of channel—`CHAN OF TYPE ChannelName`—into the following VHDL code:

```
signal ChannelName_s_req:boolean:=false;
signal ChannelName_s_data:=0;
signal ChannelName_r_ack:boolean:=false;
```

These variables are used to generate an handshake mechanism with the semantic defined by the following VHDL code:

```
if not s_req then
    wait until s_req;
else
    wait for 0 ns;
end if;
```

The OCCAMII statements for message passing *ChannelName!variable* and *ChannelName?variable* are translated into the following two procedures, respectively:

`send_unbuffered(ChannelName_s_req, ChannelName_r_ack, ChannelName_s_data, variable)`
`recv_unbuffered(ChannelName_s_req, ChannelName_r_ack, ChannelName_s_data, variable)`

The unbuffered communication needs an additional pair of signals, `full_f` (fifo full) and `empty_f` (fifo empty), modeling the availability of free positions within the FIFO buffer, as input to the sender and the receiver processes, respectively. The VHDL procedure for buffered communication thus becomes:

`send_f(ChName_s_req, ChName_r_ack, ChName_s_data, ChName_full_f, variable)`
`recv_f(ChName_s_req, ChName_r_ack, ChName_s_data, ChName_empty_f, variable)`

In addition to the above procedure, a VHDL process *fifo_ChName* will be instanced to actually implement the message storage and management unit. This element can be customized according to the desired buffer size (N) and channel type (e.g. INT).

- VHDL methodologies and tools are already available in most design centers;
- in any case, VHDL models have to be generated as input to commercial register-transfer level synthesis tools for the dedicated coprocessors and interfaces;
- VHDL language features allow the concise modeling of programmable cores as well as the simulation-oriented representation of the related software;
- existing hardware modules can be easily included in new projects developed by using the proposed hw/sw co-design methodology.

Co-simulation is more critical for the programmable subsystem with respect to the dedicated hardware parts because it requires VHDL models for the selected CPU core cells whose acquisition can be difficult and/or expensive. Moreover, a conventional CPU core model (as provided, for instance, by third-part developers) is able to run target binary code only. As a consequence, a specific binary code generator has to be developed for each target CPU (or an assembly code generator if an assembler tool is supplied in addition to the VHDL model).

The proposed approach focuses on minimizing the retargeting effort as well as reducing the number of intermediate steps required to obtain an architectural model ready for co-simulation. The underlying concept exploits the characteristics of the virtual instruction set. In fact, VIS code obtained from software mapping is already optimized for the selected target CPU core and can be executed with no *a priori* partitioning of the code/data memory space due to the virtual addressing scheme adopted.

For simulation purposes only, each target CPU core model will be implemented through

- a basic *kernel* executing VIS code that is target-CPU independent;
- a customizable target-dependent *I/O module*, tailored to manage the bus-based interface to/from the dedicated coprocessors;
- the time/size table (TST) of the selected target CPU.

In such a way, coprocessors are interfaced to the CPU core through the target bus protocol, while code/data memory representation and access are not explicitly handled at bus level but encapsulated within the virtual kernel.

For instance, the internal structure of the M68000 core model is shown in fig. 12. The vkernel module represents the virtual part, performing the fetch/decode/exec loop. The io.manager process translates I/O requests from the virtual kernel into the target-specific bus protocol (read and write bus cycles). An abstract representation of the memory space is embedded in the virtual kernel.

A VHDL view of the entire hw/sw system for simulation underlying the architecture depicted on fig. 12 is reported in fig. 13; the Motorola 68000 has been adopted as target CPU core.

Each coprocessor unit is composed of a bus protocol manager, a set of memory-mapped registers and the finite-state machine as obtained from the previous restructuring, allocation, binding and hardware mapping stages. The protocol manager is synchronized with the CPU

Each entity description of the modules connected via hardware channels contains the declaration of a set of ports corresponding to the signals used to implement the communication protocol.

The hardware side of the hw-to-sw communication has been implemented by studying an additional BUS interface unit to be added to the coprocessor (see fig. 4). Such a module contains a pair (input and output) of FIFO buffers used to store the messages that processor and coprocessor need to exchange. The entire communication is mastered by the processor which triggers the reading of data from the output queue or the sending of messages to the input queue according to the data flow direction of the original OCCAMII channel. When a message is sent out on the BUS, the coprocessor protocol manager performs a decoding of the BUS address to discover if it has to be processed. A maximum of 255 coprocessors are allowed with at most eight bi-directional channels per each. For each queue, a pair of status registers (in, out) storing the information on FIFO content (e.g. empty) are foreseen, their information can be accessed by the processor communication primitives. In summary, for the target architecture we are considering, the ADDRESS BUS bits have been associated with the following information:

A0...A2   coprocessors or other peripheral selection;
A3   data BUS contains a datum or the status register;
A4   selection of the status register to put on the data bus;
A5...A7   FIFO selection among the possible eight per coprocessor;
A8...A15 coprocessor selection among the possible 255.

The customization of such a scheme onto the MC68000 is straightforward, the only additional control signals to be taken into account are R/W, BUSREQ and MEMREQ. When a software-bound process needs to send a datum to the *n-th* coprocessor, the software communication procedures will put on A8...A15 the binary encoding of the coprocessor number, on A5...A7 the FIFO identifier corresponding to the channel considered, A0...A2 = 1 to select the coprocessors address space, A3 = 0, R/W = 0 and MEMREQ = BUSREQ = 1. The datum on the data bus will be acquired by the addressed coprocessor and placed within the proper input FIFO queue which is assumed to be sufficiently large to contain all the incoming messages (this is a matter of correct design, not impacting the suitability of the proposed scheme). The hw-to-sw communication takes place in a similar way.

4. Simulation of Interacting Hardware and Software Subparts

Although a preliminary validation of the initial system-level specification is performed during the initial design phases, an additional simulation step at the hw/sw architectural level still represents a significant value-added to obtain feedback on the effectiveness of the selected design-space exploration recipes. Furthermore, already existing components may be excluded from the specification-level (or managed as *black boxes*) and considered during the co-simulation and logic synthesis stages only.

The co-simulation task involves four main entities: the dedicated coprocessors, the programmable core, the software running on the core and the interface logic. An homogeneous simulation environment based on VHDL has been adopted due to the following reasons:

```
entity system is
    port(
        clk:     in std_ulogic;
        reset:   in std_ulogic;
        ........
    );
end;

architecture system_arc of system is
    signal   a:       std_ulogic_vector(22 downto 0);
    signal   as:      std_ulogic;
    signal   rw:      std_ulogic;
    signal   uds:     std_ulogic;
    signal   lds:     std_ulogic;
    signal   dtack:   std_ulogic;
    signal   d:       std_ulogic_vector(31 downto 0);
    signal   ipl:     std_ulogic_vector(2 downto 0);
    ...
begin
    cpu: m68k generic map(4096,256,8192)
            port map(clk,reset,a,as,rw,uds,lds,dtack,d,ipl);
    c1: coprocessor1 port map(clk,reset,a,as,uds,lds,dtack,d,....);
    ...
    cN: coprocessorN port map(clk,reset,a,as,uds,lds,dtack,d,....);
end;
```

Figure 13. VHDL top-level representation of a mixed hw/sw system.

VIS instructions are modeled by the `vis_instruction` record data type containing the opcode (as defined by the enumerative type `opcodes`) and the source/destination operands. Legal types for source operands are register (`reg`), memory (`mem`), bit vector/integer immediate (`bv_imm`, `int_imm`) or memory-mapped I/O (`io`), while destination types are restricted to register, memory or I/O. Since according to the VIS definition each data transfer has to involve at least one register, direct transfers from memory to memory (or I/O) are not supported.

The code segment (`code` signal) is implemented as an array of `vis_instruction` records. The current instruction can be referenced through the instruction pointer `ip`. An auxiliary pointer `aux_ip` is used for indirect jumps.

Program variables are implemented via a `vis_variable` record data type whose fields specify content and size (byte, word, long word). The data segment is represented by an array of records. The virtual kernel also includes a general purpose register bank (`dbr`), whose cardinality is parametrized through the DBANK_SIZE generic.

Instruction fetch/decode tasks are reported in fig. 16. The fetch operation is implemented by referencing the location in the code array pointed by `ip`. A case construct selects the proper action according to the VIS opcode.

To give a flavor of how the typical VIS instruction can be simulated, the corresponding VHDL source code is shown in fig. 17. Such a model has to deal with three main issues:

- the different addressing modes as specified by operand types;

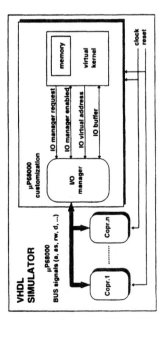

Figure 12. Virtual and target-specific parts in the CPU model and their connection with the rest of the system architecture.

clock and it is sensitive to a subset of the configurations on the address bus, each of them selecting a particular entry in the register bank.

An overview of the VHDL code implementing the entire CPU entity is presented in fig. 14. The source code follows the modularization depicted in fig. 12. The `io_manager` process communicates with the `vkernel` instance through the following signals:

`io_manager_enabled`: used by the vkernel to enable the `io_manager` during the I/O stages;
`io_manager_request`: specifies the kind of vkernel request (read or write);
`io_buffer`: used for data transfer;
`io_virtual_address`: used by the vkernel to communicate the VIS code addresses that must be translated into physical addresses on the system bus.

The `io_manager` process is composed of two sections modeling the read and the write I/O requests, respectively. Note that bus protocols and transfer speed are strictly dependent on the target CPU. For instance, a complete unidirectional transfer carried out by the M68000 is completed in four clock cycles. As a consequence, the bus managers belonging to the coprocessors have to be synthesized according to such behavioral constraints. The statement:

`a <= io_base + io_virtual_address;`

implements the generation of target physical I/O addresses from virtual offsets.

The software mapping stage produces an ASCII file containing a virtual assembly code description. Such a file is loaded during the initialization phase of a simulation session into the internal data structures. Code and data segments are managed in different ways (fig. 15).

408 CHAPTER 4: System-Level Partitioning, Synthesis, and Interfacing

```vhdl
entity m68k is
  generic(
    code_size: integer := 1024;
    data_size: integer := 512;
    io_base: std_ulogic_vector(22 downto 0)
  );
  port(
    clk:    in std_ulogic;
    reset:  in std_ulogic;
    a:      out std_ulogic_vector(22 downto 0);
    as:     out std_ulogic;
    rw:     out std_ulogic;
    uds:    out std_ulogic;
    lds:    out std_ulogic;
    dtack:  in std_ulogic;
    d:      inout std_ulogic_vector(31 downto 0);
    ipl:    in std_ulogic_vector(2 downto 0)
  );
end;

package core_pack is
  type io_man_req is (read,write);
  type sizes is (byte,word,long);
end;

use work.core_pack.all;
use work.m68k_pack.all;

architecture m68k_arc of m68k is
  signal io_manager_enabled: boolean:= false;
  signal io_manager_request: io_man_req;
  signal io_buffer: std_ulogic_vector(31 downto 0);
  signal io_virtual_address: integer;
begin
  io_manager: process
  begin
    if io_manager_enabled then
      if io_manager_request = read then
        a<="zzzzzzzzzzzzzzzzzzzzzzz";
        rw<= '1';
        wait until clk='1' and clk'last_value =
          '0' and clk'event;
        a <=io_base + io_virtual_address;
        wait until clk='0' and clk'last_value =
          '1' and clk'event;
        as <= '0';
        uds <= '0';
        lds <= '0';
        wait until clk='1' and clk'last_value =
          '0' and clk'event;
        wait until clk='0' and clk'last_value =
          '1' and clk'event;
```

```vhdl
        and clk'event and dtack = '0';
        wait until clk='1' and clk'last_value =
          '0' and clk'event;
        wait until clk='0' and clk'last_value =
          '1' and clk'event;
          io_buffer <= d;
        wait until clk='1' and clk'last_value =
          '0' and clk'event;
          as <= '1';
          uds <= '1';
          lds <= '1';
          a<="zzzzzzzzzzzzzzzzzzzzzzz";
        else -- write
          rw<= '1';
        wait until clk='1' and clk'last_value =
          '0' and clk'event;
          a <=io_base +
            std_ulogic_vector(io_virtual_address);
        wait until clk='0' and clk'last_value =
          '1' and clk'event;
          uds <= '0';
          lds <= '0';
        wait until clk='1' and clk'last_value =
          '0' and clk'event;
          d <= io_buffer;
        wait until clk='0' and clk'last_value =
          '1' and clk'event;
          as <= '0';
          uds <= '1';
          lds <= '1';
          a<="zzzzzzzzzzzzzzzzzzzzzzz";
          rw <= '1';
        wait until clk='1' and clk'last_value =
          '0' and clk'event;
          and clk'event and dtack = '0';
        wait until clk='0' and clk'last_value =
          '1' and clk'event;
          d<="zzzzzzzzzzzzzzzzzzzzzzzzzzzzzzzz";
        wait until clk='1' and clk'last_value =
          '0' and clk'event;
          io_manager_enabled <= false;
        end if;
      end if;
    end process;
    vk: vkernel generic
      map(8,code_size,data_size,4)
      port
      map(clk,reset,io_buffer,io_manager_enabled,
        io_manager_request,io_virtual_address);
end;
```

Figure 14. VHDL code for the CPU entity.

```vhdl
entity vkernel is
  generic(
    DBANK_SIZE: integer := 10;
    code_size: integer := 1024;
    data_size: integer := 1024;
    BUS_READ_DELAY :integer
  );
  port(
    clk:               in std_ulogic;
    reset:             in std_ulogic;
    io_buffer:         inout std_ulogic_vector(31 downto 0);
    io_manager_enabled: inout boolean;
    io_manager_request: out io_man_req;
    io_virtual_address: out integer
  );
end;

use work.core_pack.all;

architecture vkernel_arc of vkernel is
  type opcodes is (
    w_move,
    w_and,
    w_or,
    w_xor,
    w_not
  );
  -- CODE MEMORY
  type kinds is (reg,mem,bv_imm,int_imm,io);
  type vis_arg is record
    kind: kinds;
    bv_value: std_ulogic_vector(31 downto 0);
    int_value: integer;
  end record;
  type vis_instruction is record
    opcode: opcodes;
    dest: vis_arg;
    src: vis_arg;
  end record;
  type code_memory is array(0 to code_size-1)
    of vis_instruction;
  signal code: code_memory;
  -- DATA MEMORY
  type vis_variable is record
    value: std_ulogic_vector(31 downto 0);
    size: sizes;
  end record;
  type data_memory is array(0 to data_size-1)
    of vis_variable;
  signal data: data_memory;
  -- DATA REGISTERS
  type data_register is std_ulogic_vector(31
    downto 0);
  type data_bank is array(0 to DBANK_SIZE-1)
    of data_register;
  signal dbr: data_bank;
  -- CODE POINTERS
  -- current instruction pointer
  ip: integer range 0 to code_size-1;
  -- auxiliary pointer for indirect jump
  aux_ip: integer range 0 to code_size-1;
  -- TIMING TABLE
  type timing_table is array (0 to
    opcodes'SIZE-1) of integer;
  signal t_table: timing_table;
```

Figure 15. VHDL data structures for code/data segments and register bank.

```vhdl
architecture vkernel_arc of vkernel is
  ...
begin
  process
    variable i: vis_instruction;
  begin
    wait until clk='1' and clk'last_value =
      '0' and clk'event;
      i := code(ip);
      case i.opcode is
        when jump =>
          ip <= i.src.int_val;
          when ind_jump =>
          ip <= ip_aux;
          when w_move =>
          ...
          when w_and =>
          ...
        end case;
      end process;
    end;
```

Figure 16. Instruction fetch/decode VHDL template.

- the modeling of target-dependent instruction delays by means of a customizable table (t_table) mapping opcodes onto the corresponding number of clock cycles necessary to execute the instruction;

- the cooperation between the virtual kernel and the I/O manager in case of operands located in coprocessor memory-mapped registers.

Concerning the last issue, it should be noted that the kernel suspends itself until the I/O manager has completed its own task, by entering into an idle loop as long as a certain number of clock cycles (specified by the BUS_READ_DELAY parameter) is expired. The delay value related to bus write operations is not needed since it can be computed by subtracting BUS_READ_DELAY from the total instruction delay. For instructions not involving input/output, the delay is simply modeled by a waiting cycle activated after the (instantaneous) instruction execution.

5. Concluding Remarks

This paper has presented a suitable methodology to support hw/sw co-design. A prototype toolset covering co-specification, hw/sw architectural exploration, co-synthesis and co-simulation activities has been developed. The system achieves a good integration with the existing commercial design environments through the VHDL description of the hardware part, the assembly level synthesis of the software modules (and of the operating system support) and the import of design models defined via different design environments (e.g. speedCHART). The focus of this paper have been mainly the co-synthesis and co-simulation steps.

Software synthesis is performed by translating the software-bound architecture units into a Virtual Assembly code which satisfies all real-time constraints by means of an optimal static schedule. The Virtual Assembly is then translated into the actual microprocessor assembly chosen for the system. This solution allows an higher degree of control of the software execution and a greater flexibility in evaluating alternative microprocessor cores. Moreover, the fine granularity evaluation of the software characteristics improves the reliability of its cost estimation during the partitioning process with respect to a C-level analysis of the software parts.

The hardware modules are generated as VHDL code together with the interfaces which are, at this time, fixed. Different paradigms of communication will be made available in future versions of the framework.

Finally, co-simulation is achieved by completely modeling the hardware and software parts in a common VHDL-based environment.

Evaluation of these strategies have been performed on a number of medium size examples, allowing the identification of optimal solution in a reduced time. We are currently developing a large telecom example to test all features of the proposed approach.

Figure 17. VHDL implementation of a VIS instruction.

References

1. M. Altmae, P. Gibson, L. Taxen, and K. Torkelsson. Verification of systems containing hardware and software. In *Proc. of EURO-VHDL '91*, Stockholm, September 1991.
2. S. Antoniazzi, A. Balboni, W. Fornaciari, and D. Sciuto. HW/SW co-design for embedded telecom systems. In *Proc. of ICCD'94 IEEE Int. Conf. on Computer Design*, pages 278–291, Cambridge, Massachusetts, October 10–12, 1994.
3. S. Antoniazzi, A. Balboni, W. Fornaciari, and D. Sciuto. The role of VHDL within the TOSCA co-design framework. In *Proc. of Euro-VHDL'94*, Grenoble, France, September 1994.
4. A. Balboni, W. Fornaciari, and D. Sciuto. TOSCA: a pragmatic approach to co-design automation of control dominated systems. *Hardware/Software Co-design, NATO ASI Series, Series E: Applied Sciences*, vol. 310, pp. 265–294. Kluwer Academic Publisher, 1996.
5. A. Balboni, W. Fornaciari, and D. Sciuto. System-level exploration for control-dominated embedded systems. In *Proc. of APCHDL'96*, Bangalore, India, January 1996.
6. T. Benner, R. Ernst, and J. Henkel. Hardware-software cosynthesis for microcontrollers. *IEEE Design & Test*, 10(4), December 1993.
7. J. Buck, S. Ha, A. Lee, and D. G. Messerschmitt. Ptolemy: a framework for simulating and prototyping heterogeneous systems. *Int. Journal of Computer Simulation*, 4:155–182, April 1994.
8. M. Chiodo, P. Giusto, A. Jurecska, L. Lavagno, H. Hsieh, and A. Sangiovanni-Vincentelli. Synthesis of mixed software-hardware implementations from CFSM specifications. In *Proc. of 2nd Workshop on HW/SW Co-Design*, Cambridge, Massachussetts, October 1993.
9. M. Chiodo, P. Giusto, A. Jurecska, H. C. Hsieh, A. Sangiovanni-Vincentelli, and L. Lavagno. Hardware-software codesign of embedded systems. *IEEE Micro*, 14(4):26–36, August 1994.
10. P. Chou, E. A. Wlakup, and G. Borriello. Scheduling for reactive real-time systems. *IEEE Micro*, 14(4):37–47, August 1994.
11. G. De Micheli et al. The Olympus synthesis system. *IEEE Design and Test of Computers*, 7(5):37–53, October 1990.
12. W. Fornaciari, A. Agostini, G. S. Sturniolo, N. Missere, M. Vincenzi, and S. Prodi. Hardware-software co-design within the TOSCA design environment. In *Proc. of IEEE-ICRAM95*, Istanbul, Turkey, August 1995.
13. D. Gajski, F. Vahid, and S. Narayan. A system-design methodology: executable-specification refinement. In *Proc. of EDAC'94*, Paris, France, February 1994.
14. S. Narayan and D. Gajski. Synthesis of system-level bus interfaces. In *Proc. of EDAC'94*, Paris, France, February 1994.
15. R. K. Gupta, C. Coelho, and G. De Micheli. Synthesis and simulation of digital systems containing interacting hardware and software components. In *Proc. of the 29th DAC*, June 1992.
16. R. K. Gupta and G. De Micheli. Hardware-software cosynthesis for digital systems. *IEEE Design & Test*, September 1993.
17. D. Harel. *Statecharts: A Visual Formalism for Complex Systems*, Science of Computer Programming. North-Holland, 1987.
18. D. Harel et al. STATEMATE: a working environment for the development of complex reactive systems. *IEEE Trans. on Software Engineering*, 16(4): April 1990.
19. C. A. R. Hoare. Communicating sequential processes. *Communications of the ACM*, 18(8):66–77. August 1978.
20. T. Ismail, K. O'Brien, and A. Jerraya. Interactive system-level partitioning with PARTIF. In *Proc. of EDAC'94*, Paris, France, February 1994.
21. H. Jifeng, I. Page e J. Bowen. Towards a Provably Correct Hardware Implementation of OCCAM. Technical Report, Oxford University Computing Laboratory, 1994.
22. A. K. Mok. The design of real-time programming systems based on process models. In *Proc. of IEEE Real-Time Systems Symposium*, pp. 5–17, December 1984.
23. U. Steinhausen, R. Camposano, H. Gunther, P. Ploger, M. Theibinger, H. Veit, H. T. Vierhaus, U. Westerholz, and J. Wilberg. System-synthesis using hardware/software co-design. In *Proc. of 2nd Workshop on HW/SW Co-Design*, Cambridge, Massachusetts, October 1993.
24. S. Sutarwala, P. Paulin, and Y. Kumar. Insulin: an instruction set simulation environment. In *Proc. of CHDL'93*, pages 355–362, Ottawa, Canada, April 1993.

Appendix 1

The annotated VIS code for the Hamming decoder of fig. 11 is here reported.

```
//PROC HammingEncoder (CHAN OF BYTE inChannel, CHAN OF [12]BIT outChannel)
  <ports>
    inChannel
    outChannel
  </ports>
//PAR
  <data>     <group>
  </data>    </group>
//b0 := c2 BITOR c4 BITOR c6 BITOR c8 BITOR c10
           <process><case R0>
  //BYTE datain:                move.b    @c2(BP),R0  <2 4>
  datain  defb  0               or.b      @c4(BP),R0  <2 4>
                                or.b      @c6(BP),R0  <2 4>
  //[12]BIT dataOut:             or.b      @c8(BP),R0  <2 4>
  dataOut  defw  0               move.b    @c10(BP),R0 <2 4>
                                          R0, @b0(BP) <2 4> <free R0>
                                </process 12 24 24>
  //BIT b0,b1,b3,b7:    ... similarly for b1 and b3 ....
  b0    defb  0
  b1    defb  0   //b7 := c8 BITOR c9 BITOR c10 BITOR c11
  b3    defb  0             <process><case R0>
  b7    defb  0                move.b    @c8(BP),R0   <2 4>
                               or.b      @c9(BP),R0   <2 4>
                               or.b      @c10(BP),R0  <2 4>
  //BIT c2,c4,c5,c6,c8,c9,c10,c11:  or.b  @c11(BP),R0 <2 4>
  c2   defb  0                 move.b    R0, @b7(BP) <2 4> <free R0>
  c4   defb  0                 </process 10 20 20>
  c5   defb  0             </group>
  c6   defb  0
  c8   defb  0   //dataOut := [b0,b1,c2,b3,c4,c5,b7,c8,c9,c10,c11]
  c9   defb  0             <process><case R0>
  c10  defb  0                move.b    @b0(BP),R0    <2 4>
  c11  defb  0                move.w    0001h,R1           <2 2 6>
                              and.w     R1,R0              <1 12>
  </data>                     <use R2>
                              move.b    @b1(BP),R2    <2 4>
  //code>                     shl.w     #1,R1              <1 12>
                              and.w     R1,R2              <1 12>
// inChannel ? dataIn          or.w      R2,R0              <1 12> <free R2>
                              <use R2>
  <process>
  <atomic><live none>  ... similarly for c2, b3, c4, c5, c6, b7, c8, c9, c10 ....
  move.l  inChannel,R1   <2 2 6>    //not necessary
  call    read_byte                 //result in R0
  move.b  R0,@dataIn(BP)  <2 4>     //save in R1
  </atomic 6 10 16>        //outChannel ! dataOut
  </process>                <process>
                            <atomic><live R0>    //in this case atomic it is not
  //PAR                        move.l   outChannel,R1  <2 2 6>  //actually necessary
                               call     write_int            <2 4 6>  //dataOut is yet in R0
  //c2 := dataIn[0]            </atomic 4 6 12>
  <process><case R0>        </process 59 84 12>
     move.b  @dataIn(BP),R0  <2 4>
     and.b   01h,R0          <1 2 4> //result in R0    ret
     move.b  R0,@c2(BP)      <2 4> <free R0>              <22 2><live none>
  </process 6 10 16>
                             </code>
  ... similarly for c4, c5, c6, c8, c9, c10 ....

  //c11 := dataIn[7]
  <process><case R0>
     move.b  @dataIn(BP),R0   <2 4>
     and.b   80h,R0           <1 2 4>
     move.b  R0,@c11(BP)      <2 4> <free R0>
  </process 5 10 12>
```

25. F. Vahid and D. Gajski. SLIF: a specification-level intermediate format for system design. In *Proc. ED & TC 95*, pages 185–188.
26. F. Vahid and D. D. Gajski. Specification and design of embedded hardware-software systems. *IEEE Design & Test of Computer*, pages 53–67, Spring 1995.
27. W. Wolf, A. Takach, C. Huang, and R. Manno. The Princeton University Behavioral Synthesis System. *29th DAC*, 1992.
28. W. H. Wolf. Hardware-software co-design of embedded systems. In *Proceedings of the IEEE*, 82(7), July 1994.

CoWare—A Design Environment for Heterogeneous Hardware/Software Systems

D. VERKEST, K. VAN ROMPAEY, I. BOLSENS
IMEC, Kapeldreef 75, B-3001 Leuven, Belgium

H. DE MAN
Katholieke Universiteit Leuven, Belgium

Received August 24, 1995; Accepted February 14, 1996

Abstract. This paper addresses CoWare: an environment for design of heterogeneous systems on chip. These systems are heterogeneous both in terms of specification and implementation. CoWare is based on a communicating processes data-model which supports encapsulation and refinement and makes a strict separation between functional and communication behaviour. Encapsulation enables the reuse of existing specification and design environments (languages, simulators, compilers). Refinement provides for a consistent and integrated path from specification to implementation. The design steps that will be addressed include: system specification, simulation at various abstraction levels, data path synthesis, communication refinement and hardware/software co-design. A spread-spectrum based pager system serves to illuminate the design process in the CoWare environment.

1. Introduction

The functional specification of a complex system involves various specification paradigms. Each of these paradigms has an associated specification language and environment. The signal processing parts of a complex system are best modelled by data-flow graphs with synchronous (SDF [8]) or dynamic (BDF [11]) semantics. These parts can be efficiently described by applicative programming languages such as SILAGE [6] or DFL [18]. The control oriented parts may best be modelled using (hierarchial) co-operating finite state machines which can be specified using, for example, StateCharts [5] or SpecCharts [10]. Other parts, such as the user interface, exhibit reactive semantics.

For each of these paradigms various specification languages and environments are available nowadays. However, to functionally specify a system requires an environment based on a data-model that allows to combine these different specification paradigms and their associated languages and environments. PTOLEMY [2] is a system that provides for such multi-paradigm specification and simulation.

The implementation of a complex system on silicon is also heterogeneous. It consists of a combination of different kind of components such as DSP cores, hardware accelerators, micro controllers, memory and communication blocks, etc. Depending on the required degree of programmability, these systems also contain software components that are implemented on the micro-controller or DSP core. DSP cores are used to perform low-rate signal processing. They can be programmed by making use of a C compiler that accompanies the processor but, due to the poor quality of the code generated by the compiler, are often programmed in assembly language. Hardware accelerators implement the high-rate signal processing. These components are synthesised from a high-level description (e.g. in Silage or DFL) by accelerator compilers such as CATHEDRAL-3 [11], PHIDEO [17], or HYPER [13]. Micro controllers are used for the implementation of the user interface and/or the control loops and are programmed in C. All these different components communicate with each other through a large number of communication blocks.

For most of the components in a complex system efficient implementation environments are available to date. However, to actually implement the complete system requires an environment that allows to link all the component implementations.

The above observations about the heterogeneous nature of system specifications and implementations have led to the development of the CoWare design environment. The starting point of this development is that both system specification and system implementation consist of an interconnection of heterogeneous components that have to communicate with each other. At the specification level a system consists of communicating *processes*. Each of these processes consists of a behavioral description in some existing specification language (C, VHDL, SILAGE, etc.) each of which has its own existing simulation environment. At the implementation level a system consists of a number of communicating *processors* each of which is generated by a specific existing design environment. In that respect, system simulation is no different from system implementation. For simulation each of the processes in the specification is implemented on a suitable simulator. The key characteristic of heterogeneous system implementations (both for simulation and on silicon) is that each of the components has a fixed interface that is determined by the compiler that generates it. In order to reuse existing specification, simulation, and implementation environments, on an "as is" basis, the design environment has to allow the incorporation of existing components with a fixed interface. In CoWare this *re-use* is achieved through the concept of *encapsulation*. The data-model on which the design environment is based, supports *refinement* which allows a consistent path from system specification to implementation. The design environment supports the refinement of the communication between the processes. The communication between the software components and the hardware components over the fixed hardware interface of a programmable processor is a particular important problem that is dealt with in this environment.

The CoWare environment and the data-model on which it is based are presented in section 2. In section 3 the design of a spread-spectrum based pager system in the CoWare environment is discussed.

2. CoWare: A Data-Model Supporting HW/SW Co-Design

Essential to the philosophy of CoWare is the strict separation between functional behaviour and communication. This allows the introduction of reusable (library) components in a system without a need to modify either the description of the reusable component or the description of the environment in which the component is introduced.

In CoWare, system components are modelled by means of *processes*. Communication between the processes takes place through a behavioral interface, which consists of *ports*. For two processes to be able to communicate, their ports must be connected with a *channel*. The data-model fixes the communication semantics needed when two processes exchange data and control information. The *communication semantics are built on the concept of the Remote Procedure Call (RPC)*, i.e. one process can trigger the execution of a thread in another process. The channel carries both the control and data information for/from the remote thread. For a motivation of RPC as basic communication mechanism we refer to section 2.1.

The data-model is hierarchically structured and allows to refine a *process*, a *channel*, and a *port* into lower level *processes*. Figure 1 shows the relations between the data-model objects. The semantics of the data-model objects are defined as follows:

- *Processes* are used to describe the behaviour of the system components. A *primitive process* is one whose behaviour is described in a host language, e.g. C, DFL, or VHDL. A *hierarchical process* is defined in terms of other processes and described in the CoWare language. Every process has a unique behavioural interface and at least one implementation. If a process has alternative implementations, then the behaviour of these implementations should be functionally equivalent.

  A primitive process consists of a context and a number of threads. The *context* contains code that is common to all threads in the process. It is used for declaring variables and defining functions that are shared by all threads. As such, the context provides for inter-thread (intra-process) communication.

- *Ports* are objects through which processes communicate. A port can be primitive or hierarchical. Hierarchical ports are used to describe protocol conversions and data formatting. A *primitive port* is used in all other cases; it consists of a *protocol* and a data type parameter.

  Each process has one special, implicit, *construct* port. This slave port is activated exactly once when the system is started.

- *Protocols* define the communication semantics of a port. Protocols can be primitive or hierarchical. A *primitive protocol* is one of *inmaster, outmaster, inoutmaster, inslave, outslave, inoutslave*. Each primitive protocol indicates another way of data transport. The *in, out* or *inout* prefix indicates the direction of the data. The *master, slave* postfix indicates whether the protocol activates an RPC (master) or services and RPC (slave). A primitive protocol does not imply any specific protocol implementation, i.e. it does not fix the timing diagram. For that purpose, one must use hierarchical protocols. Such a *hierarchical protocol* makes use of a number of *terminals* and further consists of a timing diagram that indicates how the logic values on the terminals evolve over time during data transport.

- A *thread* is a single flow of control within a process. A process can contain multiple threads. We distinguish between *slave threads* and *time-loop threads*.

  - *Slave threads* are uniquely associated to slave ports and their code is executed when the slave port is activated. There is one special slave thread which is associated to the *construct* port and can be used to initialise the process.
  - *Time-loop threads* are not associated to any port and their code is executed in an infinite time-loop.

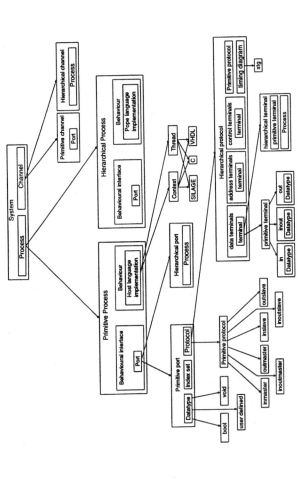

Figure 1. The CoWare data-model objects.

- A *terminal* is one of *in, out* or *inout*, indicating the data direction.

- A *channel* connects a master port to a slave port. Two ports that are connected by a channel can exchange data. A channel can be primitive or hierarchical. A *primitive channel* provides for unbuffered communications. A *hierarchical channel* is a process of which the behavioural interface is fixed by the ports that are connected by the channel. At the *conceptual level*, hierarchical channels can be used to model a communication channel, e.g. bandwidth limitations or noise sources interacting with a wireless communication channel. For *implementation*, a hierarchical channel is used to specify communication buffers, e.g. FIFOs, stacks.

The example in Figure 2 shows the refinement of a very simple system that consists of two processes that communicate over a single channel. At the most abstract level (top of Figure 2) the system is described by the two processes P1 and P2. Process P1 has a master port p1 which is connected by a channel to the slave port p2 process P2. The behaviour of process P1 is specified by a timeloop thread. The behaviour of process P2 is specified by a context and two slave threads connected to the slave ports of the process. Once the system is started, the timeloop thread in process P1 executes continuously. Every time the statement RPC(p1, data) is reached, a remote procedure is started over port p1. The timeloop thread in process P1 is halted, until the RPC is complete. The RPC is serviced by

A final refinement consists of replacing the ports of the format and FIFO process by hierarchical ports with a hierarchical protocol. In the example of Figure 2, these hierarchical ports implement an RS232 protocol. In the RS232 hierarchical port an RPC call issued in the format process is converted to manipulations of logical values on the terminals according to a timing diagram. When the behaviour of the RS232 hierarchical port is described in the C language, the terminals can be manipulated by the three functions Put, Sample, and Wait. When the behaviour is described in VHDL, the terminals can be manipulated directly.

By using primitive ports and primitive protocols, the designer can concentrate on the functionality of the system while abstracting from terminals, signals, and handshakes. As the design progresses, these abstract objects (ports and protocols) are refined by making them hierarchical: a hierarchical protocol or port describes in a more detailed way the behaviour of the primitive port or protocol. Hierarchical ports are used for protocol conversion (implementation) and data formatting (conceptual level). Hierarchical protocols allow to refine the specification of a protocol with a timing diagram and its associated terminals. Hierarchical channels allow the specification of complex communication behaviour both at the conceptual and implementation level. Hierarchical processes are used to split a complete system into manageable parts.

The example of Figure 2 also nicely illustrates the three communication mechanisms supported by the CoWare environment:

- intra-process (inter-thread) communication via shared variables in the context of the process;
- inter-process (inter-thread) communication with a primitive protocol of which the behaviour is based on RPC semantics;
- inter-process (inter-thread) communication with a hierarchical protocol of which the behaviour is completely determined by the protocol.

2.1. *RPC as a Basic Communication Mechanism*

The choice for RPC as basic communication mechanism is motivated by the following observations.

- **Abstract**: by using RPC, a designer concentrates on functionality without bothering about signals and handshakes. The signals and handshakes can be introduced later on in the design process by refining the primitive protocol in a hierarchical protocol.
- **Minimal**: other communication mechanisms can be modelled by making use of RPC.
- **Modular**: functional and communication behaviour of a process are separated.
- **Removable**: a slave thread servicing an RPC can be inlined in the calling process with zero overhead.

The above observations can be summarised in the following statement: *RPC supports design for re-use and re-use of designs*.

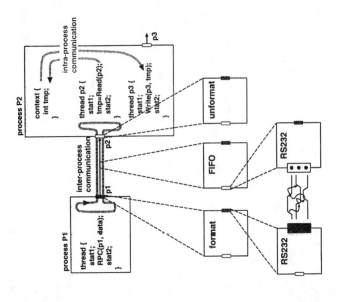

Figure 2. Illustration of the usage of the data-model objects.

slave thread p2 that is connected to port p1 via the channel. In the code of slave thread p2 the data is read from the associated slave port p2 and stored in the shared variable tmp that is declared in the context of process P2. After the last statement (which is not necessary the Read statement) of the slave thread is executed, the timeloop thread in process P1 resumes. Process P2 also contains a second slave thread that services an RPC over slave port p3 and writes the value of the shared variable tmp to some other process.

A first refinement consists of formatting the data that is transported over the channel. This is achieved by making the primitive ports, p1 and p2, hierarchical. A hierarchical port is a process that describes the behaviour that we want to implement in the primitive port. The format process that refines port p1 might for example, add a cyclic redundancy check (CRC) to the data that is transported. The unformat process that refines port p2 can then use this CRC to determine whether the received data is valid.

A second refinement consists of making the channel hierarchical by specifying its behaviour in a process. In the example the hierarchical channel has a FIFO behaviour. The FIFO process decouples the timeloop thread of process P1 and the slave thread p2 of process P2. The effect is that the rate at which process P1 can issue RPC calls is no longer determined by the rate at which process P2 can service the RPC calls. The FIFO process takes care of the necessary buffering of data.

Traditionally, the description of a component contains both functional and communication behaviour in an interleaved way. When such a component has to be re-used, in an environment other than it was intended for, the designer has to change those parts of the description of the component that have to do with communication. In CoWare, a component's behaviour is described by a process that makes use of RPC calls to communicate with the outside world. Such processes can be connected with each other without modifying their description (modularity). Further on in the design process, hierarchical channels, ports and protocols can be used to refine the inter-process communications behaviour. Again this is achieved without modifying the description of any of the processes involved. Because of this property it is feasible to construct libraries of functional building blocks and libraries of communication blocks that are re-usable: they can be plugged together without modifying their description. After blocks have been plugged together, any communication overhead (chains of remote procedure calls) can be removed by inlining the slave threads that serve the RPCs (see section 2.4). The result is a description of the component in which function and communication are interleaved seamlessly and which can be compiled into software or hardware as efficiently as a description in the traditional design process.

2.2. Simulation in the CoWare Environment

In this hardware/software co-design environment, system simulation is considered as a pure software implementation of the system on a UNIX work station. In Figure 3 the simulation script is shown taking into account the three host languages considered so far. For each host language a path to simulation is required.

In general, building a system simulation consists of the following steps:

1. The DFL processes[1] are converted to C processes using a DFL to C translator [16] (DFL2C in Figure 3). Next, the designer decides what processes to run on what simulator. Normally, all processes described in the same host language will run on a single simulator for that host language. However, distributed simulation is also possible by using more than one simulator for a host language (e.g. the two VHDL branches in Figure 3 are simulated on different VHDL simulators).

2. For efficiency, all processes assigned to the same simulator are merged by a tool called INLINER (see section 2.4). We now have a single, possibly multi-threaded, merged process per simulator.

3. The communication between the single merged C process and the merged VHDL process(es) corresponds to the initially specified communication. However, the VHDL simulator(s) and the multi-threaded C library [15] on which the VHDL process(es) and the C process have to run can not, as such, communicate with each other. To make them communicate, UNIX specific communication primitives must be used. This is achieved by making the ports of the merged C and VHDL process(es) hierarchical. The hierarchical ports are available from a library and describe how the VHDL simulator(s) and the multi-threaded C library can communicate using UNIX communication primi-

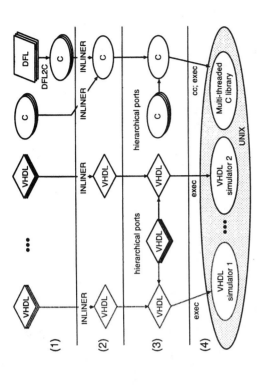

Figure 3. The compilation script for simulation.

tives. The VHDL and C port processes that are introduced are again merged into one VHDL and C process, respectively.

4. Finally, the merged VHDL process(es) are executed on the VHDL simulator(s) and the C code of the C process is compiled, linked with the multi-threaded C library and executed: the system simulation is running.

Input stimuli for the system simulation are generated by C processes that are added to the system description. These stimuli generators e.g. read input data from a file or contain functions that generate input data. In the same way the system outputs and internal signals can be observed by adding monitor processes to the system. These monitor processes e.g. dump data to a file or display them in a window on the work station. In the simulation script these generator and monitor processes are treated in exactly the same way as any other C process.

2.3. Principles of Hardware/Software Co-Design in CoWare

The hardware/software implementation script, shown in Figure 4, does not differ much from the simulation script. The main difference is in the implementation path for C processes, where hardware/software co-design is important, and in the final integration of the processors, where protocol conversion is important.

Before starting the compilation, the processes are merged into clusters each of which is assigned to a compatible processor.

416 CHAPTER 4: System-Level Partitioning, Synthesis, and Interfacing

The path for DFL and VHDL processes[2] is quite similar: all processes assigned to the same processor are merged by the INLINER and that single process is compiled by the appropriate compiler (CATHEDRAL-2/3 and Synopsys, respectively) resulting in a single VHDL process (a net list). To encapsulate the generated processors, the appropriate hierarchical ports are added. The INLINER is then called once more to merge these VHDL processes.

The path for C processes is more complicated. After inlining all C processes assigned to the same processor we would like to compile the result (C process (I) in Figure 4) directly onto the processor core. However, the interface of a processor core is fixed and, usually, does not correspond with the interface required for C process (I) that has to be executed on it. To remedy this a double action has to be taken.

1. A number of C processes (device drivers) need to be added at the software side. The resulting extra C processes are again inlined and the result (C process (II) in Figure 4) is compiled on the processor core. The result is a VHDL process (a ROM with the machine code of the program including the device drivers).

2. Some extra hardware components need to be added at the hardware side of the processor. These extra VHDL processes are then merged with the VHDL process representing the hardware view of the processor core to produce a single VHDL process.

The addition of the extra software and hardware processes is performed by the tools SHOCK and INTEGRAL that are discussed in sections 2.5.

The task remaining at this point is the integration of the VHDL processes. Because the ports that were introduced in the different implementation paths have hierarchical protocols (i.e. terminals and a timing diagram) that are not necessarily compatible, they cannot in general be connected straight away. Protocol conversion will be required in between every two interconnected ports that have an incompatible hierarchical protocol. The protocol conversion tool INTEGRAL [9] is used for this purpose.

After protocol conversion, the complete system consists of processors described in VHDL and all connected ports are compatible. A final call to the INLINER merges all these VHDL processes into a single system processor described in VHDL.

Both the compilation and the implementation path make use of only a small set of tools that will be discussed in the next sections.

2.4. INLINER: A Process Merger

The goal of the INLINER is to merge all processes described in the same host language and assigned to the same target processor.

In the process of merging, all remote procedure calls are inlined: each slave thread is inlined in the code of the master thread that calls it. This "inlining" transformation eliminates the overhead that accompanies the execution of (remote) procedure calls. It reduces the number of threads and therefore the overhead that accompanies the switching between threads. Finally, it allows compilers to optimise the merged process which allows optimisation over the boundaries of the original processes.

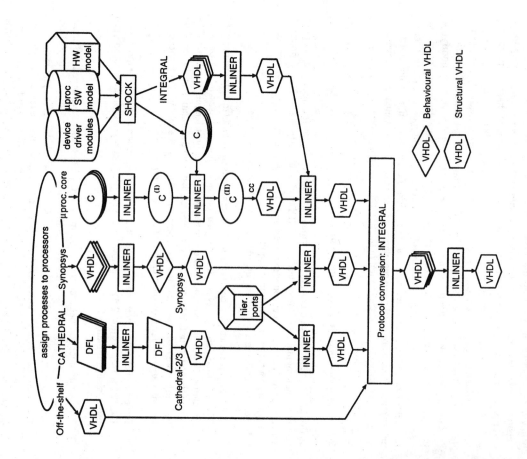

Figure 4. The script for hardware/software implementation.

The result of merging is a single process that

- contains a single context;
- contains a single construct thread;
- contains one or more time-loop threads;
- possibly contains multiple slave threads through which RPC requests from external processes (assigned to different processors) are serviced;
- possibly contains multiple RPC calls to slave threads in external processes (assigned to different processors).

An example of the INLINER at work is given in Figure 9 in section 3.3.1.

2.5. SHOCK: Software/Hardware Optimizing Co-Design Kit

In this section we discuss the tasks that need to be performed to implement a (software) process on a programmable processor and connect it with the (hardware) processes it communicates with. The environment that accomplishes this is called SHOCK and is schematically depicted in Figure 5. The task of SHOCK is to generate the I/O device drivers and the hardware interfaces. The I/O device drivers link the original C process (1) to the software interface (3) of the processor. The hardware interface makes the link between the hardware interface (2) of the processor and the processes external to the processor. The input to SHOCK consists of:

1. The primitive CoWare process described in C that must be mapped onto the programmable processor.

2. A hardware model of the programmable processor consisting of a CoWare process that formalises the information that is available in the hardware section of the data sheet of the programmable processor. For each programmable processor used in the design team, this hardware model has to be constructed. Once constructed, the hardware model is part of a a library from where it can be retrieved by SHOCK. In Figure 5 this hardware model is represented by the rectangle marked "processor HW model" and the ports at the outside of the rectangle's perimeter.
The hardware model CoWare process is characterised by

- A behavioural interface that is conforming with the hardware interface of the programmable processor. All ports have hierarchical protocols: they consist of terminals and a timing diagram (including timing constraints) as is shown in Figure 5 for one particular port.
- An optional[3] VHDL description
  - at net list level. This net list can be used for simulation and can also be included in the final description of the implementation.
  - at simulation level. Usually the exact net list of a processor is not available. Instead a simulation model is provided that behaves exactly as the net list in terms of timing, bit-true behaviour, ...

3. A software model of the programmable processor consisting of a CoWare process that formalises the information that is available in the software section of the data sheet of the programmable processor. For each programmable processor used in the design team, this software model has to be constructed. Once constructed, the software model is part of a a library from where it can be retrieved by SHOCK. In Figure 5 this software model is represented by the rectangle marked "processor SW model" and the ports at the inside of the rectangle's perimeter.
SHOCK is based on the observation that programmable processors have a number of common communication methods to get data in or out of the processor (memory mapped, via a co-processor port, etc). SHOCK is an interactive tool, that leaves the decision of which communication method to use to the user. Once the communication method is fixed, SHOCK generates the I/O device drivers for that communication method by combining a number of generic processes. These I/O device drivers are based on a model of the communication method that makes abstraction of the details of the method for the specific processor. The link between the abstracted model of a communication method and the actual implementation on a specific processor is made via the software model of the processor.
The software model is a CoWare process characterised by

- A behavioural interface that is conforming with the software interface of the programmable processor. All ports have primitive protocols (the software model is more abstract). The software model identifies, for example, what ports can be used as interrupt ports and what their characteristics are (priority of the interrupt, maskable interrupt or not, ...). Some ports that are present in the hardware model, are not found back in the software model. For example, the ARM6 processor has (hardware) ports that indicate the mode of the processor: normal processing, dealing with interrupt, etc. These ports are not directly accessible from the software side and hence do not feature in the software model of the processor.

- A behavioural description that allows to compile a C process into machine code. For example: functions to manage processor specific actions such as installing an interrupt vector, enabling/ disabling interrupts, etc. The compilation can be done by a target specific compiler or by a retargetable compiler (e.g. CHESS [7]). In the latter case an instruction level description of the processor should be available (e.g. in nML [3]). In the former case such a description is not needed; it is hard linked in the target specific compiler.

The output of SHOCK is a set of primitive CoWare processes described in C and VHDL.

- The C processes added by SHOCK are I/O device drivers.
- The VHDL processes are the hardware interfaces used by the I/O device drivers to cross the hardware/software boundary. The VHDL processes are synthesised

3. Co-Design of the Pager Application

In this section we discuss the application of the design trajectory outlined in section 2 to the pager system. We discuss how the functional specification of the pager in Figure 6.a is gradually refined into the mixed hardware/software implementation shown in Figure 6.b.

3.1. Specification of the Pager

Each block in Figure 6 corresponds to a process implementing a specific function of the pager. This functional decomposition determines the initial partitioning. *The finest granularity is determined by the functions in the system.* It does not make sense to have a finer grain partitioning: the communication inside each process is very intense, the communication with external processes is limited. Hence, the partitioning of the system is determined by the functional characteristics of the system.

The arrows in between the processes indicate communication via a Remote Procedure Call (RPC) mechanism. Figure 7 shows the RPC communication in detail for *part of* the pager design. The blocks in the figure correspond to the processes from Figure 6.a. The small rectangles on the perimeter of the processes are the ports. The shaded ports are master ports, the others are slave ports.

The Sample Clock Generator process contains a time-loop thread. This thread runs continuously. It performs an RPC over its input port ip to the Tracking & Acquisition process to obtain a new value for delta. The time-loop thread of the process adds the delta parameter to some internal variable until a threshold is exceeded. In this way it implements a sawtooth function. When the sawtooth exceeds the threshold an RPC call is issued to the A/D converter process.

The slave thread clock in the A/D converter process samples the analogue input, and sends the result to the Down-conversion process via an RPC call. This in turn will activate the Decimation process via an RPC call, etc.

The Correlator & Noise Estimator process contains a slave thread associated with port par to compute the correlation values. This slave thread is activated when the Phase Correction process writes data to the Correlator & Noise Estimator process (i.e. when the Phase Correction process performs an RPC to the ip port of the Correlator & Noise Estimator process). The slave thread reads in the data and then performs an RPC to the User Interface process to obtain a new value for the parameter par it requires for computing the correlation values. Finally, the new correlation results are sent to the Tracking & Acquisition process via an RPC call on its op port.

The slave thread in the Tracking & Acquisition process updates the delta value for the sawtooth function implemented by the Sample Clock Generator process. It puts the updated value in the context, where it is retrieved by the slave thread op which serves RPC requests from the Sample Clock Generator process. In this way the Tracking & Acquisition process influences the frequency of the clock generated by the Sample Clock Generator process. This example shows how the context is used for communication between threads inside the same process whereas the RPC mechanism is used for communication between threads in different processes. The locking and unlocking of the context is required to avoid concurrent

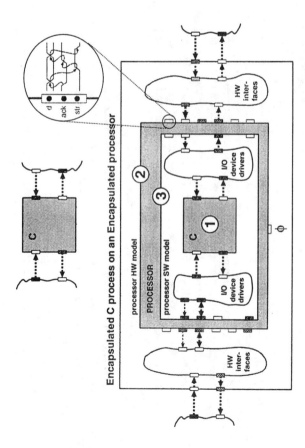

Figure 5. Mapping a C process to a programmable processor. The original C process is shown at the top. At the bottom, we see the result of SHOCK: an encapsulated process on an encapsulated processor. From outside to inside, one recognises: the HW interface to the processor, the processor HW model (marked 2), the actual processor, the processor SW model (marked 3), and finally the original C process (marked 1).

by INTEGRAL [9] starting from information provided by SHOCK. This information consists of the protocols of the processor ports, the protocols of the ports of the original C process, and a high-level behavioural description of the hardware interface.

The hardware/software model of the programmable processor is a representation of the hardware/software boundary that must be crossed to implement the behavioural C process onto a specific programmable processor. The channels which are present in the system specification (at the top of Figure 5) must cross the hardware/software boundary in some way or another. The extra hardware and software added by SHOCK and INTEGRAL achieves just this. The original C process is found back unmodified as the inner rectangle in Figure 5. The outermost rectangle has exactly the same behavioural interface as the original C process defined in the functional specification and, therefore, interfaces to the environment in exactly the same way as the original C process. One could say that INTEGRAL introduces hardware interfaces of which the functionality is exactly the inverse of the software I/O drivers introduced by SHOCK.

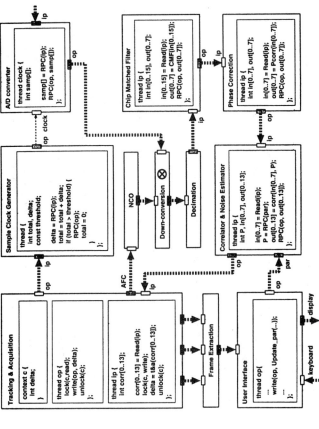

Figure 7. RPC as a basic communication mechanism between processes.

accesses to the variable delta. The lock in the slave thread op locks the context for read: other threads are still allowed to read from the context, but no other thread may write the context. The lock in the slave thread ip locks the context for write: no other thread is allowed to write or read to context until it is unlocked again.

Each process is described in the language that is best fit for the characteristics of the function it implements.[4] The data-flow blocks (NCO, Down-conversion, Decimation, Chip Matched Filter, Phase Correction, Correlator & Noise Estimator, and Sample Clock Generator) are described in Silage/DFL. The control oriented blocks (Tracking & Acquisition, Frame Extraction and User Interface) are described in C. The description of the DSP blocks consists of approximately 900 lines of Silage/DFL code. The description of the control oriented blocks consists of approximately 100 lines of C code.

At this moment it is not yet decided what process will be implemented on what kind of target processor nor is it defined how the RPC communication will be implemented. However, the choice of the specification language for each process restricts the choice of the component compiler and in that sense partly determines the target processor. Hence, studying possible alternative buildings of a process to a target processor may require the availability of a description of the process in more than one specification language or a clear guess of the best solution.

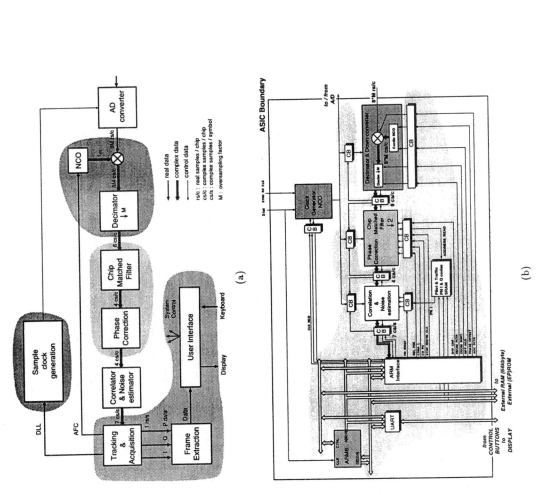

Figure 6. (a) Functional specification of a spread-spectrum pager, (b) a possible implementation using an ARM processor-accelerator-memory architecture.

3.3.1. Partitioning and Mapping

This step determines what processes will be implemented on what target processor. As explained in section 3.1 the initial specification shows the finest grain partitioning: a process in the initial specification will never be split over several processors. However, it may be opportune to combine a number of processes inside a single processor. This is achieved by merging these processes into a single process that can then be mapped on the selected target processor. Merging of processes is only allowed when the processes are described in the same specification language. Hence, studying possible alternative mergers may require that for a number of processes (e.g. Correlator & Noise Estimator process) a description is available in more than one specification language. After partitioning and binding, one obtains a partitioning of the initial specification such that there is a one-to-one binding of merged processes to processors.

In the pager example (Figure 6.a) the following merging and binding takes place:

- The NCO, Down-conversion, and Decimation processes are merged and mapped in hardware onto an application specific DSP CATHEDRAL processor because the sample rate of the merged processes is identical[5] which implies that they can be clocked at the same frequency. The advantage is that only one clock tree needs to be generated per merged process (i.s.o. one per original process). An additional advantage is that the scan-chains for the processes that are merged can be combined.

- The Chip Matched Filter, and Phase Correction processes are merged and mapped onto a CATHEDRAL processor because their sample rates are identical.[6]

- The Correlator & Noise Estimator process is mapped onto a CATHEDRAL processor. It is not merged with the Phase Correction process because it operates at a four times lower frequency.[7]

- The Sample clock generator is mapped onto a CATHEDRAL processor.

- Tracking & Acquisition, Frame Extraction, and User Interface are merged and mapped on a programmable processor. For this design an ARM6 processor is chosen. The Hardware/Software tradeoffs are based on the following observations. To obtain a maximal degree of flexibility as much of the functionality as possible is implemented in software on the ARM6. However, due to performance constraints of the ARM6 processor, there is a limit to what can be implemented in software. The two main factors that play a role in this problem are

  - The Tracking & Acquisition process has to be implemented in software because the algorithm used to perform tracking and acquisition may be modified depending on the application domain of the pager system.

  - The Correlator & Noise Estimator process is not included in software because the input rate for the Correlator & Noise Estimator is too high to realise a real-time communication between the ARM6 and the Phase Correction process. In addition an estimation of the number of cycles required to execute each function on the

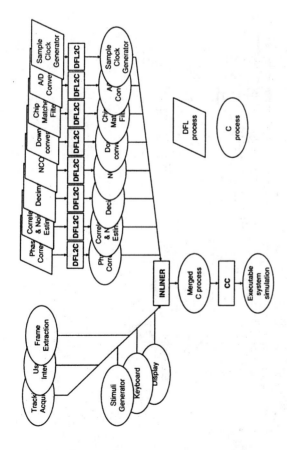

Figure 8. Simulation of the initial pager system specification. At the left-hand side, the C processes from the specification and the stimuli generator and monitor processes are shown. At the right-hand side, the DFL processes from the specification are shown.

3.2. Simulation of the Initial Specification

Simulation is a repeated activity during the design process. After every refinement step, simulation is used to verify the correctness of the refinement step. In section 2.2 the simulation script is explained. Figure 8 applies this script to the pager design of Figures 6.a and 7. All the DFL processes are translated to C processes by DFL2C. These C processes are then merged by the INLINER with the original C processes from the pager system specification and with the stimuli generator and monitor processes. In the pager system, input stimuli for the A/D Converter process are generated by a process that reads the data that we want to page from the keyboard, encodes the data using the algorithms that are implemented in the transmitter, and modifies the encoded data to simulate the distortion of the signal (noise, reflection, Doppler shift, ...) in a real transmission channel.

3.3. Design Process

After the initial specification of the system has been validated by simulation, the designer starts the refinement process.

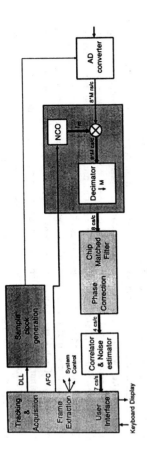
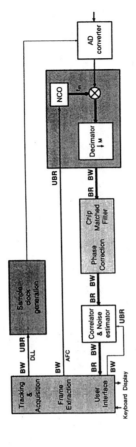

Figure 10. The pager design after merging of the partitions.

Figure 11. The pager design with Blocked/UnBlocked Read/Write communication.

3.3.2. Communication Mechanism Selection

After the partitioning of the system has been verified by simulation and before the actual implementation takes place, the designer may choose to refine the communication mechanism between the processors. This can be achieved by explicitising the behaviour of the channels between the processors.

In the running example, the processors can, in principle, operate concurrently because each processor has its own thread of control. By refining the RPC based communication scheme we can pipeline the processors: all processors operate concurrently and at I/O points they synchronise. This refined communication scheme is called *Blocked/UnBlocked Read/Write communication*. Figure 11 shows the pager with the refined communication mechanism. The input and outputs of the processors have been labelled with BW for Blocked Write, BR for Blocked Read, and UBR for UnBlocked Read.

BW-BR communication guarantees that no data is ever lost. When the writing process has data available, it will signal that to the reading process. If the reading process is at that moment not ready to receive the data (because it is still processing the previous data), the writing process will block until the reading process is ready to communicate. Alternatively, if the reading process needs new data, it will signal that to the writing process. If the

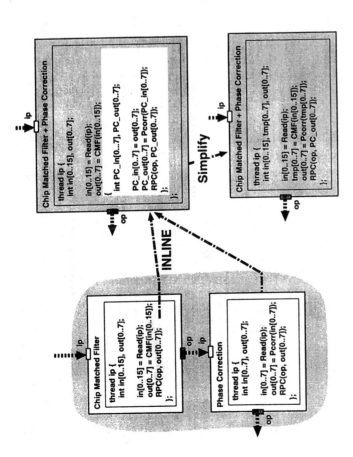

Figure 9. Merging of the Chip Matched Filter and Phase Correction processes.

Figure 9 shows the effect of merging the Chip Matched Filter process and the Phase Correction process. On the right-hand top side the RPC call in the Chip Matched Filter process has been replaced with the code of the slave thread in the Phase Correction process. After simplification one obtains the description of the merged process at the right-hand bottom side of Figure 9. The communication overhead associated with an RPC call has completely vanished. We refer to section 2.4 for details about the merging.

Similarly the other partitions are merged. The result is shown in Figure 10. Each of the merged processes can now be implemented on a separate target processor by the appropriate compiler. The communication between the merged processes is still done via the RPC mechanism. *At this point a simulation of the partitioned system could be done to verify that the merging step was carried out correctly.*

ARM6[8] shows that the implementation of Correlator & Noise Estimator process in software leaves insufficient time to perform tracking and acquisition in between two symbols.

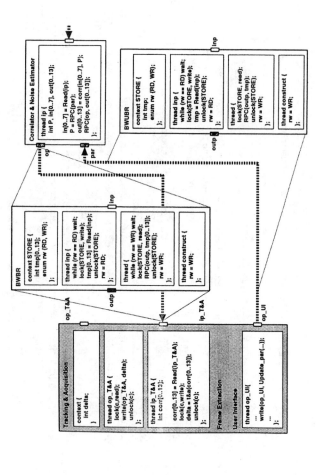

Figure 12. Introduction of Blocked Write–(Un)Blocked Read communication. The channel between ip_T&A and op is refined into the hierarchical BWBR channel. The channel between op_UI and par is refined into the hierarchical BWUBR channel.

writing process is at that moment not ready to send the data (because it is still computing the data), the reading process will block until the writing process is ready to communicate. The BW-BR scheme is used in the main signal path.

A BW-BR scheme, however, is not used for the parameter and mode setting for the main signal path. If an accelerator uses BR to read a parameter value it will be blocked until the parameter is provided. Since the parameter setting is done is software, this will slow down the computations in the main signal path considerably. Therefore parameter setting is done via a BW-UBR scheme. This makes sure that every parameter change is read by the accelerators, but it leaves it up to the accelerator to decide when to read the parameter.

In the CoWare design environment the refinement of the communication mechanism is performed by making use of a *hierarchical channel*. A hierarchical channel replaces a primitive channel by a process that describes *how* communication over that channel is carried out. The hierarchical channel contains more detail than the primitive channel and hence can be considered as a refinement of the primitive channel.

The introduction of BW-BR and BW-UBR communication is shown in detail for the Correlator & Noise Estimator and the Tracking & Acquisition process in Figure 12. The BWBR channel contains a time-loop thread and a slave thread that communicate with each other via the shared variable tmp[0..13] in the context. The slave thread is activated by an RPC from the Correlator & Noise Estimator process and it tries to update the context with new correlation values. The time-loop thread continuously tries to read the correlation values from the context and send them to the output port via an RPC, in this way activating the Tracking & Acquisition process that is attached to that output. The blocking character of the communication is taken care of by the use of a binary semaphore rw. This guarantees that the input thread will block until the previous data has been read by the time-loop thread (no data is overwritten before it has been read), and that the time-loop thread will block until new data is available (no data is read twice). When the input slave thread is blocked, the Correlator & Noise Estimator process that requested its service via an RPC is also blocked because the RPC will only return after the slave thread has completed. When the time-loop thread is blocked, there are no RPC requests to the Tracking & Acquisition process, so that process is blocked automatically.

In the case of Blocked Write, UnBlocked Read communication, the code for the time-loop thread is slightly modified. The thread always sends the value stored in the context, without checking whether it is updated. The same value can be sent more than once, but the thread will never be blocked. The input slave thread is identical to the BWBR case, and will block until the data has been read.

In both cases, locking and unlocking of the context is required to avoid concurrent accesses to the shared variable in the context and, as such, has nothing to do with the blocking character of the communication.

3.3.3. *Simulation of the Communication Mechanism*

The refinement of the system communication to a Blocked/UnBlocked Read/Write mechanism effectively pipelines the pager system. A simulation of the system at this moment, allows to verify that all processes run concurrently and synchronise when they want to perform I/O. Due to the introduction of the BWBR and BWUBR processes from Figure 12 the resulting C executable now contains a number of concurrent threads. In order to execute these threads concurrently, we use a multi-threaded C library [15].

Distributed simulation of the system is now[9] also an option. This requires that the user identifies which C processes to run on which work station. Per work station all the C processes are merged. Since the merged processes communicate with each other, the executables that eventually run on the work stations must also be able to communicate. This can be achieved via UNIX Inter-Process Communication between the executables on the work stations. To realise this in CoWare, the I/O ports of the merged processes are made hierarchical. Each hierarchical port, contains C code to communicate with a hierarchical port of another process. Once all the I/O ports are made hierarchical, these ports are merged with the previously merged processes. Each merged C process can then be compiled, linked with the multi-threaded C library and executed on the work stations.

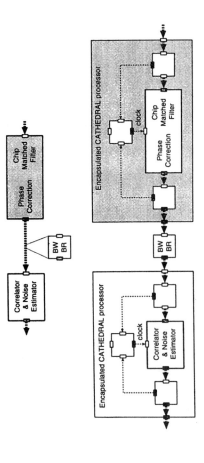
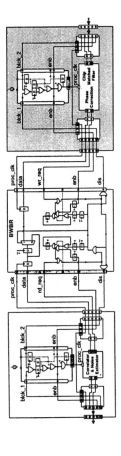

Figure 13. Implementation in hardware of the Correlation & Noise Estimator process and the merged Phase Correction and Chip Matched Filter process.

Figure 14. A typical communication buffer (CB) between two encapsulated accelerators. ϕ is the system clock.

3.4. *Implementation of the Pager*

After the newly introduced communication mechanism has been verified by simulation, each process has to be synthesised on its assigned target processor. In section 3.4.1 we discuss the implementation of processes in hardware. In section 3.4.2 we study the implementation of processes in software. In both cases the implementation involves a compilation and an encapsulation step. The compilation step consists of the actual implementation of the process in hardware or software. For this step we use existing compilers that generate processors with specific characteristics. These processors do not necessarily have a behavioural interface that is consistent with the original specification. Therefore an encapsulation step is required to encapsulate the generated processors in such a way that they are consistent with the original specifications. For processes that are implemented in hardware the encapsulation is rather straightforward. For processes that are implemented in software, such as the Tracking & Acquisition, the encapsulation is more complex. At the software side, it requires the introduction of I/O device drivers to link the software process to the physical processor on which it will run. At the hardware side, it requires the introduction of interfaces to link the physical processor to the hardware processors it has to communicate with.

3.4.1. *Implementation of a Process in Hardware*

Figure 13 illustrates the pure hardware implementation for the Correlator & Noise Estimator process and the merged Phase Correction and Chip Matched Filter process. This hardware implementation for the pager consists of three distinct steps:

- The (merged) DFL processes are synthesised by the CATHEDRAL silicon compiler. The compiler only generates processors of which all the inputs and outputs are of the master type. These processors are shown in Figure 13 as the inner rectangles.

- Each processor is encapsulated to make it consistent with the specification in which the DFL processes have slave inputs. In addition, the encapsulation includes clock gating circuitry to control the activity of the processor. The encapsulated processors are shown in Figure 13 as the big rectangles: they include the processor generated by CATHEDRAL and some encapsulation hardware. As can be observed the input ports of the encapsulated processors are now of the slave type. The encapsulation hardware is shown in detail in Figure 14.

- The BWBR process is implemented in hardware. In this case we obtain the gate-level implementation of this process from the library. This implementation is functionally equivalent to the original C-like description of these blocks in Figure 12. Figure 14 shows a detail of the implementation of the BWBR process that is used in the main signal path of the pager.

3.4.2. *Implementation of a Process in Software*

Figure 15 shows the implementation in software of the Tracking & Acquisition, Frame Extraction and User Interface processes. In the figure we recognise the original merged C processes at the left-hand side, followed by a software I/O device driver, the software/hardware interface of the processor, a hardware interface, and finally the hardware processor that implements the Correlator & Noise Estimator process, preceded by the BWBR channel. The BWUBR communication channel between the User Interface process and the Correlator & Noise Estimator process is not shown in Figure 15. The main tasks to realise this implementation are the generation of the software I/O device drivers and the hardware interface to the ARM processor.

Software I/O Device Drivers. In the specification, the transfer of the 14 correlation values to the input port of the Tracking & Acquisition process is done via a single RPC. To

424 CHAPTER 4: System-Level Partitioning, Synthesis, and Interfacing

cannot send these 14 correlation values over the memory port of the ARM as a single array. Hence, we need to refine the data master output port of the Polled process to retrieve the 14 correlation values one by one over the memory port and pack them into an array that can be sent to the Tracking & Acquisition process. This is achieved by the Pack process in which the single RPC call on the data port (from the Polled) process is translated into 14 RPC calls.

- The memory port of the ARM's software model contains the functions that describe how an actual memory access with a specific address is done in terms of ARM primitives. It is the ARM processor (hardware) itself that translates this into low-level protocol actions on the data bus, address bus and control terminals of the memory port.

- The original merged C process (Tracking & Acquisition, Frame Extraction and User Interface) and the processes of the I/O device driver (s2m, Polled, Pack and Mux) are now merged and compiled with an ARM-specific C compiler. The result is a VHDL process (a ROM with the machine code for the C processes including the device drivers).

Hardware Interface to the ARM Processor. The final step is to generate the hardware part of the interface with INTEGRAL [9]. Figure 16 shows all the inputs provided to INTEGRAL: the protocol of the memory port, the protocol of the BWBR channel, and the algorithmic description (provided by SHOCK) of the hardware interface performing the inverse function of the software I/O device driver. Starting from that information INTEGRAL will then automatically generate the hardware interface as shown in Figure 15.

The generic implementation script of Figure 4 also contains a final linking step to perform protocol conversion between possibly incompatible protocols. In the pager design, all protocols are compatible: the protocol of the BW(U)BR channels is tuned to the protocol of the CATHEDRAL processors to which they are connected and the protocol conversion for the ARM processor is taken care of by INTEGRAL during the hardware interface synthesis.

The single chip implementation of the pager [12] contains 340 K transistors occupying 47 mm^2 in a .6 μ technology and operates at a clock frequency of 40 Mhz.

4. Conclusions

Specification of complex systems requires various paradigms: SDF, DDF, hierarchical co-operating FSMs, etc. Specification languages, their simulators and synthesis tools are strongly linked to these paradigms. Hence the need for a *specification environment based on a data-model that allows the encapsulation of different host languages, simulation and synthesis paradigms.*

Complex systems are also heterogeneous at the architectural level. The implementation of a complex system consists of DSP processors, micro controllers, hardware accelerators, communication blocks, memory, etc.

The system design process must bridge the gap between the heterogeneous functional specification and the heterogeneous implementation of a complex system.

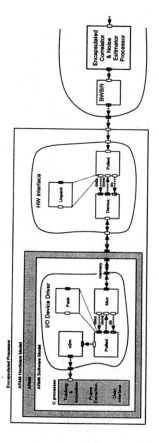

Figure 15. Implementation in software of the Tracking & Acquisition, Frame Extraction and User Interface processes.

implement this transfer, we have to choose one or more of the physical ports of the ARM. None of these ports is large enough to transfer the 14 correlation values simultaneously, so the transfer will have to be serialised. Also, since an RPC is not available as a primitive operation on the ARM, we have to implement an RPC in terms of ARM primitives on the physical ports of the ARM. The realisation of this software I/O device driver is done by SHOCK (see section 2.5) and consists of several steps.

* To transfer the correlation values a memory mapped I/O scheme is used via the memory port of the ARM. This port consists of a 32-bit address bus, a 32-bit data bus (which coincides with the 32-bit word length of each of the 14 correlation values) and a number of control terminals.

* Implementing the RPC in terms of ARM primitives on the memory port is done by the processes **s2m**, **Polled** and **Mux**. These processes are generic and are available from a library.

  - **s2m.** This process issues RPC calls to the Tracking & Acquisition process, transmitting data that it first retrieved from the Polled process (also via an RPC). The s2m process is the main thread in software. It initiates all other threads.

  - **Polled.** This process implements RPC in terms of ARM primitives by polling the memory port to see if there is data available. It does that by making use of three ports labelled **do**, **done**, and **data**. The process will wait until there are new data available. This is implemented by observing the **do** port. It will then retrieve that data (over the **data** port) and send it to the s2m process. Finally it will signal that it has received the data via the **done** port.

  - **Mux.** The ports **do**, **done** and **data** have to communicate with hardware that is external to the ARM via the memory port. Therefore, each of the ports, is mapped to a specific address. That address mapping is performed by the Mux process.

* The RPC from the Polled process to the Tracking & Acquisition process transmits all 14 correlation values in a single array via one RPC call. However, it is clear that we

tion languages, their simulators and design environments and forms the basis for system simulation and implementation.

The CoWare data-model is based on the concept of communicating processes and makes a strict separation between functional behaviour and communication. Processes can be described in their own host language to support specification heterogeneity. Host languages and their simulators can be reused through the concept of encapsulation. This allows for co-simulation and emulation on a UNIX work station. Constructs are provided to assign processes to components and existing component compilers can be reused through the concept of encapsulation. Finally, constructs are provided to describe and refine inter-process communication channels based on protocol libraries and component compiler encapsulation.

The design process for a spread-spectrum based pager system was described to show the feasibility of the CoWare data-model and the design flow implemented in the CoWare environment.

The implementation of the CoWare design environment is ongoing. Furthermore, some aspects that were neglected in this contribution require further investigation. The use of existing component compilers restricts the system specification. For example DFL/CATHEDRAL does not allow multiple threads inside a process. These compilers have to be extended to deal with multiple threads. Also, the verification of the functional and timing behaviour of complete complex systems is a problem.

Simulation as described in this contribution allows to verify the functional behaviour of the system at several abstraction levels. However, as the level at which simulation takes place is lowered, the required CPU time becomes excessive. Verification of the correct real-time behaviour of feedback loops such as the tracking and acquisition requires simulation of the complete system over tens of seconds (real-time). At the implementation level this corresponds to simulations that run for weeks. At higher abstraction levels the simulation times are less excessive. However, when the processes in the system run concurrently (e.g. after pipelining the pager system), the real-time behaviour of the system depends on the relative execution speeds of the concurrent processes. These are only known at the implementation level. At higher levels, no conclusions about the correct *real-time* behaviour of the system can be drawn.

When the communication mechanism of a complex system is refined, for example by pipelining the main DSP path in the pager design, the timing behaviour of the system may be radically altered. This might introduce deadlock or starvation of processes and hence analysis of the timing behaviour of systems to detect such malfunctions becomes an important issue.

Hence, there is a very hard need for bottom-up formal verification tools both for functionality and timing. Symbolic verification methods, such as signal flow graph tracing [4] and code transformation verification [14], have been shown to be very efficient for the DSP parts. However, a lot of effort is still required to extend these methods to deal with the non-DSP parts of a complex system.

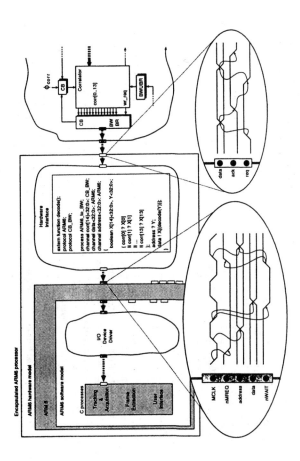

Figure 16. Interface synthesis between an ARM processor and the hardware correlator block. Given the protocol of the memory port, the protocol of the BWBR process, and an algorithmic description of the channel, INTEGRAL generates the implementation of the hardware interface.

Today's component compilers allow to synthesise and program all the components once the global system architecture is defined. What is needed are the models and tools to refine the functional specifications into the detailed architecture: the definition and allocation of the components and their communication and synchronisation. The allocation and binding step implies the hardware/software partitioning step.

The generation of the necessary hardware and software to make processors, accelerators, etc. and the environment communicate is the next problem. This involves

- Synthesis of communication hardware given the communication protocols and the behaviour of the channel.

- Synthesis of hardware and software for implementation of channels that connect software on programmable processors with hardware processors.

- Encapsulation of components so that they communicate with their neighbour components as specified in the functional specification.

CoWare is a system design environment which supports specification of heterogeneous systems and supports the systematic refinement of the specification to a heterogeneous implementation. The CoWare data-model allows for encapsulation of existing specifica-

Acknowledgements

The research reported in this contribution was partly sponsored by ESA under the SCADES-2 and SCADES-3 projects.

Obviously much of the work would have been impossible without the cooperation of many colleagues. The work on CoWare is supported by A. Demarée, S. Samel, E. Umans, B. Vanthournout, and S. Vercauteren. The UNIX IPC communication was implemented by S. De Troch and S. Samel. The pager chip was designed by J. Vanhoof, V. Derudddere, S. Vernalde, M. Wouters, L. Philips, X. Gao, B. Vanhoof, and B. Gyselinckx who was especially helpful and patient in explaining the details of the design.

Notes

1. For conciseness we usually write VHDL, DFL and C process instead of the more accurate "primitive CoWare process described in VHDL, DFL and C".
2. Please note that in this context "VHDL process" means a primitive CoWare process described in VHDL. This VHDL code can be at the behavioural level or at the structural level. Hence, "VHDL process" does not denote a process in VHDL terminology (see also footnote 1 on page 361).
3. To construct a description of the final implementation, a black box view of the processor is sufficient. Simulation of the implementation is in that case not possible.
4. The language used in Figure 7 is pseudo-code meant to illustrate the RPC concept; it does not correspond to any of the languages mentioned in this document.
5. The sample rate is 8 * M samples/chip where M is the oversampling rate. The input rate for the Decimation process is 8 * M complex samples/chip but since it processes the real and imaginary part of each sample concurrently, the Decimation effectively operates at 8 * M samples/chip.
6. The sample rate is 4 complex samples/chip. The input rate for the Chip Matched Filter process is 8 complex samples/chip but it processes even and odd samples concurrently which leaves 2 cycles available for the processing of each sample.
7. The sample rate is 1 complex sample/chip because the Correlator & Noise Estimator process selects only one of the 4 complex samples/chip at its input.
8. This implies the availability of a description in C for the Correlator & Noise Estimator process (possibly derived from the DFL description with DFL2C).
9. Distributed simulation makes no sense for the specification. Since all communication is RPC based, only one process is active at the same instant anyway.

References

1. J. Buck et al., "The token flow model," in *Proceedings of the Data Flow Workshop*, Hamilton Island, Australia, May 1992.
2. J. Buck et al., "PTOLEMY: A framework for simulating and prototyping heterogeneous systems." *International Journal on Computer Simulation*, January 1994.
3. A. Fauth, J. Van Praet, and M. Freericks, "Describing instruction set processors using nML," in *Proceedings of the European Design and Test Conference, ED&TC 1995*, Paris, France, March 1995, pp. 505–507.
4. M. Genoe, L. Claesen, E. Verlind, F. Proesmans, and H. De Man, "Illustration of the SFG-Tracing multi level behavioral verification methodology," in *Proceedings of the ICCD 91*, Cambridge, MA, October 1991, pp. 338–341.
5. D. Harel, "A visual formalism for complex systems." *Science of Computer Programming* (8), pp. 231–274, 1987.
6. P. N. Hilfinger, J. Rabaey, D. Genin, C. Scheers, and H. De Man, "DSP specification using the SILAGE language," in *Proceedings International Conference on Acoustics, Speech and Signal Processing*, Albuquerque, NM, April 1990, pp. 1057–1060.
7. D. Lanneer, J. Van Praet, K. Schoofs, W. Geurts, A. Kifli, F. Thoen, and G. Goossens, "CHESS, retargetable code generation for embedded processors," in *Code Generation for Embedded Processors*, P. Marwedel and G. Goossens, eds., Kluwer Academic Publishers, Boston, 1995.
8. E. A. Lee and D. G. Messerschmitt, "Synchronous data flow." *IEEE Proceedings*, September 1987.
9. B. Lin and S. Vercauteren, "Synthesis of concurrent system interface modules with automatic protocol conversion generation," in *Proceedings of the IEEE International Conference on Computer-Aided Design, ICCAD 94*, San José, CA, November 1994, pp. 101–108.
10. S. Narayan, F. Vahid, and D. D. Gajski, "System specification with the SpecCharts language." *IEEE Design & Test of Computers* pp. 6–13, December 1992.
11. S. Note, W. Geurts, F. Catthoor, and H. De Man, "Cathedral III: Architecture driven high-level synthesis for high throughput DSP applications," in *Proceedings of the 28th ACM/IEEE Design Automation Conference, DAC 91*, San Francisco, CA, June 1991, pp. 597–602.
12. L. Philips, J. Vanhoof, M. Wouters, B. Gyselinckx, I. Bolsens, and H. De Man, "A programmable spread spectrum modem for wireless communications," in *1996 On-Chip System Design Conference, Design Supercon 96*, Santa Clara, USA, Jan. 30–Feb. 1 1996, pp. 10.1–10.18.
13. J. Rabaey, C. Chu, P. Hoang, and M. Potkonjak, "Fast prototyping of datapath-intensive architectures." *IEEE Design & Test of Computers* 8(6), pp. 40–51, June 1991.
14. H. Samsom, F. Franssen, F. Catthoor, and H. De Man, "Verification of loop transformations for real time signal processing applications," in *VLSI Signal Processing VII*, J. Rabaey, P. Chau, and J. Eldon, eds., IEEE Press, New York, NY, 1994, pp. 208–217.
15. UNIX System Laboratories, Inc. *USL C++ Language System Release 3.0 Library Manual*, 1992.
16. M. Van Canneyt, "Specification, simulation and implementation of a GSM speech codec with DSP station." *DSP & Multimedia Technology* 3(5), pp. 6–15, May 1994.
17. J. van Meerbergen et al., "PHIDEO: High-level synthesis of high throughput applications." *Journal of VLSI Signal Processing* 9(1–2), pp. 89–104, January 1995.
18. P. Willekens et al., "Algorithm specification in DSP station using data flow language." *DSP Applications* 3(1), pp. 8–16, January 1994.

CHAPTER FIVE

Implementation Generation

Embedded Software in Real-Time Signal Processing Systems: Design Technologies 433
    G. Goossens, J. Van Praet, D. Lanneer, W. Geurts, A. Kifli, C. Liem, and P. G. Paulin

Generating Compact Code from Dataflow Specifications of Multirate
Signal Processing Algorithms 452
    S. S. Bhattacharyya, J. T. Buck, S. Ha, and E. A. Lee

Memory Management for Embedded Network Applications 465
    S. Wuytack, J. L. da Silva, Jr., F. Catthoor, G. de Jong, and C. Ykman-Couvreur

Lower Bound on Latency for VLIW ASIP Datapaths 477
    M. F. Jacome and G. de Veciana

Constraint Analysis for DSP Code Generation 485
    B. Mesman, A. H. Timmer, J. L. van Meerbergen, and J. A. G. Jess

Instruction Selection Using Binate Covering for Code Size Optimization 499
    S. Liao, S. Devadas, K. Keutzer, and S. Tijang

A Retargetable Compilation Methodology for Embedded Digital Signal Processors
Using a Machine-Dependent Code Optimization Library 506
    A. Sudarsanam, S. Malik, and M. Fujita

Incremental Hardware Estimation During Hardware/Software Functional Partitioning 516
    F. Vahid and D. D. Gajski

After the early stages of co-synthesis select an appropriate architecture, the details of the components—both hardware and software—must be fleshed out. Clearly, efficient implementation generation is important to ensuring a high-quality design. However, the techniques used to generate the implementation have implications elsewhere in the co-synthesis process. The models used to guide implementation generation can affect higher-level estimates of synthesis choices.

Researchers have studied implementation generation of both hardware and software components. However, many hardware implementation generation techniques are borrowed from high-level synthesis. Much of the work in this area has concentrated on efficient generation of real-time software implementations. A great deal of the work in software implementation has been devoted to efficient compilation for DSPs, since many popular DSPs use instructions that make difficult compilation targets.

SOFTWARE IMPLEMENTATION

Goosens et al. [Goo97] provide a thorough overview of embedded software for real-time signal processing. They examine the applications of signal processing, processors used for digital signal processing, and the requirements placed on embedded development tools.

Battacharyya et al. [Bha95] consider the synthesis of code from synchronous data-flow (SDF) representations. Because SDF descriptions include multi-rate behavior, the graphs often imply looping. Their algorithm schedules SDF systems on uniprocessors so as to extract compact loops that minimize the sizes of buffers required to store values being transferred between SDF nodes.

Wuytack et al. [Wuy99] describe a methodology of memory management for embedded network applications. Their methodology considers both the synthesis of a custom memory architecture and dynamic memory management during execution, as well as area and power. In their methodology, they first analyzes the application's abstract data types and selects concrete data structures to implement them. They next create a custom virtual memory manager to handle the allocation and deallocation tasks required by the selected data types. They then split virtual memory into basic groups to improve data accessability. Finally, they schedule memory accesses and allocates memories.

Jacome and de Veciana [Jac99] study performance estimation for VLIW processors. These processors often have distributed register files to support the large number of data paths in the CPU. As a result, it can take time to transfer the required data to the register file that needs it. They developed an accurate technique for estimating the latency of a data-flow graph while taking into account data transfer delays.

Mesman et al. [Mes99] present an algorithm for combined instruction scheduling and register allocation in DSPs. Their algorithm considers both data dependencies and dependencies introduced by the DSP architecture.

Liao et al. [Lia95] describe techniques for generating code for DSPs with non-orthogonal instruction sets caused by irregular data paths. They show how to schedule instructions to minimize mode changes, such as those required to support different arithmetic modes. They also consider the interactions between scheduling and register allocation for machines with a small number of registers; for example the TI TMS320C25 has only one accumulator for data operations.

Sudarsanam, Malik, and Fujita [Sud99] describe a methodology for retargetable DSP compilation. They consider parameterized algorithms that can be retargeted by a compiler developer to a class of processors that share common characteristics. They describe their experience developing compilers for three DSPs: the TMS320C25, the Motorola DSP56000, and the Fujitsu Elixir.

HARDWARE IMPLEMENTATION

Vahid and Gajski [Vah95] describe a fast algorithm for hardware size estimation. Their algorithm is based on a data structure that can quickly update a cost estimate given incremental changes to the design. Their algorithm uses a control unit/data path model. They estimate the number of function units and storage size in the hardware unit based on parameters such as the number of states, data path elements, and so forth.

ADDITIONAL READINGS IN IMPLEMENTATION GENERATION

[Son00] L. Song, K. K. Parhi, I. Kuroda, T. Nishitani, "Hardware/software codesign of finite field data-path for low-energy Reed-Solomon codecs," *IEEE Transactions on VLSI Systems* 8, no. 2 (April 2000): 160–72. *Uses co-design techniques to design a programmable data path for Reed-Solomon coding, using a heterogeneous digit-serial architecture.*

[Che00] S. Chen and A. Postula, "Synthesis of custom interleaved memory systems," *IEEE Transactions on VLSI Systems* 8, no. 1 (Feb. 2000): 74–83. *Synthesizes an interleaved memory system by analyzing periodicies in memory accesses.*

[Lek00] H. Lekatsas, J. Henkel, and W. Wolf, "Code compression for low power embedded system design," in *Proceedings, 37th Design Automation Conference*, ACM Press, New York, 2000, 294–99. *Describes how code compression can be used to reduce power consumption by reducing cache miss rates.*

[Ben00] L. Benini, A. Macii, E. Macii, and M. Poncino, "Synthesis of application-specific memories for power optimization in embedded systems," in *Proceedings, 37th Design Automation Conference*, ACM Press, New York, 2000, 300–03. *Synthesizes a custom memory and maps heavily accessed locations to lower-power units in the memory system.*

[Kan00] M. Kandemir, N. Vijaykrishnan, M. J. Irwin, and W. Ye, "Influence of compiler optimizations on system power," in *Proceedings, 37th Design Automation Conference*, ACM Press, New York, 2000, 304–07. *Considers the effects of performance-oriented compiler optimizations on software power requirements using a complete system model.*

[Gru00] P. Grun, N. Dutt, and A. Nicolau, "Memory aware compilation through accurate timing extraction," in *Proceedings, 37th Design Automation Conference*, ACM Press, New York, 2000, 316–21. *Uses accurate models of memory system performance to improve instruction scheduling.*

[Gha00] N. Ghazal, R. Newton, and J. Rabaey, "Predicting performance potential of modern DSPs," in *Proceedings, 37th Design Automation*

Conference, ACM Press, New York, 2000, 332–35. *Describes the use of static analysis and profiling to accurately estimate the maximum achievable performance of a program.*

[Edw00] S. A. Edwards, "Compiling Esterel into sequential code," in *Proceedings, 37th Design Automation Conference*, ACM Press, New York, 2000, 322–27. *Presents techniques for generating implementations of the Esterel reactive systems language.*

[Chi00] D. Chiou, P. Jain, L. Rudolph, and S. Devadas, "Application-specific memory management for embedded systems using software-controlled caches," in *Proceedings, 37th Design Automation Conference*, ACM Press, New York, 2000, 416–19. *Proposes using column-configurable caches to allow software control of on-chip memory.*

[Pan99] P. R. Panda and N. D. Dutt, "Low-power memory mapping through reducing address bus activity," *IEEE Transactions on VLSI Systems* 7, no. 3 (Sept. 1999): 309–20. *Analyzes regularity and spatial locality to reduce memory bus activity.*

[Kir99] D. Kirovski, C. Lee, M. Potkonjak, and W. H. Mangione-Smith, "Application-driven synthesis of memory-intensive systems-on-chip," *IEEE Transactions on CAD of Integrated Circuits and Systems* 18, no. 9 (Sept. 1999): 1316–26. *Optimizes code to reorganize basic blocks so as to minimize cache misses.*

[Knu99] P. V. Knudsen and J. Madsen, "Integrating communication protocol selection with hardware/software codesign," *IEEE Transactions on CAD of Integrated Circuits and Systems* 18, no. 8 (Aug. 1999): 1077–95. *Models communication protocols for estimation of communication effects during co-synthesis.*

[Geb99] C. H. Gebotys, "A minimum-cost circulation approach to DSP address-code generation," *IEEE Transactions on CAD of Integrated Circuits and Systems* 18, no. 6 (June 1999): 726–41. *Analyzes program control flow to make efficient use of address generation logic.*

[Bal99] F. Balarin, M. Chiodo, P. Giusto, H. Hsieh, A. Jurecska, L. Lavagno, A. Sangiovanni-Vincentelli, E. M. Sentovicy, and K. Suzuki, "Synthesis of software programs for embedded control applications," *IEEE Transactions on CAD of Integrated Circuits and Systems* 18, no. 6 (June 1999): 834–49. *Describes the synthesis of optimized software from networks of CFSMs.*

[Wuy99] S. Wuytack, J. L. da Silva, Jr., F. Catthoor, G. de Jong, and C. Ykman-Couvreur, "Memory management for embedded network applications," *IEEE Transactions on CAD of Integrated Circuits and Systems* 18, no. 5 (May 1999): 533–44. *Describes techniques for virtual and physical memory management for networked applications.*

[Leu99] R. Leupers, "Exploiting conditional instructions in code generation for embedded VLIW processors," in *Proceedings, DATE 99*, IEEE Computer Society Press, Los Alamitos, 1999, 105–11. *Describes techniques for optimizing code using conditionally executed instructions such as those found in VLIW processors.*

[Ver99] S. Vercauteren, D. Verkest, and J. Van Der Steen, "Combining software synthesis and hardware/software interface generation to meet hard real-time constraints," in *Proceedings, DATE 99*, IEEE Computer Society Press, Los Alamitos, 1999, 556–61. *Presents techniques in the CoWare system that make use of preemptive scheduling methods and automatically generated interfaces to meet deadlines.*

[Ben99a] D. Benyamin and W. H. Mangione-Smith, "Function unit specialization through code analysis," in *Proceedings, ICCAD 99*, IEEE, New York, 1999, 257–60. *Uses modulo scheduling to choose the data-path function units required for an ASIP.*

[Ben99b] L. Benini, A. Macii, E. Macii, M. Poncio, and R. Scarsi, "Synthesis of low-overhead interfaces for power-efficient communication over wide busses," in *Proceedings, 36th Design Automation Conference*, ACM Press, New York, 1999, 128–33. *Describes a technique for bus encoding to minimize toggle-related power consumption.*

[Fis99] J. A. Fisher, "Customized instruction-sets for embedded processors," in *Proceedings, 36th Design Automation Conference*, ACM Press, New York, 1999, 253–57. *Surveys barriers to the development of custom instruction sets for embedded applications and ways in which those problems can be surmounted.*

[Lek99] H. Lekatsas and W. Wolf, "SAMC: a code compression algorithm for embedded processors," *IEEE Transactions on CAD of Integrated Circuits and Systems* 18, no. 12 (Dec. 1999): 1689–1701. *Uses arithmetic coding to compress program instructions.*

[Sud99] A. Sudarsanam, S. Liao, and S. Devadas, "Analysis and evaluation of address arithmetic capabilities in custom DSP architectures," *Design*

Automation for Embedded Systems 4, no. 1 (Jan. 1999): 5–22. *Describes code generation for DSP-style addressing mechanisms.*

[Des99] *Design Automation for Embedded Systems* 4, no. 2/3 (March 1999). *Special issue on code generation for embedded processors.*

[Hon99] I. Hong and M. Potkonjak, "Efficient block scheduling to minimize block scheduling time for programmable embedded processors," *Design Automation for Embedded Systems* 4, no. 4 (Oct. 1999): 310–28. *Uses process-level scheduling to minimize context switching.*

[Ver99] S. Vercauteren, D. Verkest, and J. U. Van Der Steen, "Combining software synthesis and hardware/software interface generation to meet hard real-time constraints," in *DATE Conference Proceedings*, IEEE Computer Society Press, Los Alamitos, 1999, 556–61. *Uses a combination of software synthesis and hardware/software interface generation to create interfaces that meet real-time constraints for communications systems.*

[Lia98] S. Y. Liao, S. Devadas, and K. Keutzer, "Code density optimization for embedded DSP processors using data compression techniques," *IEEE Transactions on CAD of Integrated Circuits and Systems* 17, no. 7 (July 1998): 601–08. *Uses set-covering methods to compress program binaries.*

[ONi99] M. O'Nils and A. Jantsch, "Operating system sensitive device driver synthesis from implemenetation independent protocol specification," in *DATE Conference Proceedings*, IEEE Computer Society Press, Los Alamitos, 1999, 562–67. *Uses a grammar to specify a hardware/software interface and libraries to capture processor and OS specifications.*

[Lin98] B. Lin, "Efficient compilation of process-based concurrent programs without run-time scheduling," in *Proceedings, DATE 98*, IEEE Computer Society Press, Los Alamitos, 1998, 211–17. *Uses Petri nets to generate an implementation of multiple software processes that does not require an operating system for scheduling.*

[Hon98] Y. Hong, P. A. Beerel, L. Lavagno, and E. M. Sentovich, "Don't care-based BDD minimization for embedded software," in *Proceedings, 35th Design Automation Conference*, ACM Press, New York, 1998, 506–09. *Uses binary decision diagrams (BDDs) to optimize FSM-oriented software.*

[Leu97] R. Leupers and P. Marwedel, "Time-constrained code compaction for DSP's," *IEEE Transactions on VLSI Systems* 5, no.1 (March 1997): 112–22. *Uses integer programming to model code compaction that exploits instruction-level parallelism.*

[Lee97] M. T.-C. Lee, V. Tiwari, S. Malik, and M. Fujita, "Power analysis and minimization techniques for embedded DSP software," *IEEE Transactions on VLSI Systems* 5, no. 1 (March 1997): 123–35. *Analyzes the power consumption of a Fujitsu DSP and then develops a power model for the processor and a code scheduling technique.*

[Han97] S. Hanono and S. Devadas, "Instruction selection, resource allocation, and scheduling in the AVIV retargetable code generator," in *Proceedings, 34th Design Automation Conference*, ACM Press, New York, 1997, 510–15. *Presents an integrated approach to several problems in code generation.*

[Ade97] M. Ade, R. Lauwereins, and J. A. Peterstraete, "Data memory minimization for synchronous data flow graphs emulated on DSP-FPGA targets," in *Proceedings, 34th Design Automation Conference*, ACM Press, New York, 1997, 64–69. *Describes an algorithm to determine near-minimal data buffer sizes for synchronous data-flow graph applications.*

[Sha97] B. Shackleford, M. Yasuda, E. Okushi, H. Koizumi, H. Tomiyama, and H. Yasuura, "Memory-CPU size optimization for embedded system designs," in *Proceedings, 34th Design Automation Conference*, ACM Press, New York, 1997, 246–51. *Optimizes CPU word size to maximize chip utilization for systems-on-chips.*

[Har97] M. R. Hartoog, J. A. Rowson, P. D. Reddy, S. Desai, D. D. Dunlop, E. A. Harcourt, and N. Khullar, "Generation of software tools from processor descriptions for hardware/software codesign," in *Proceedings, 34th Design Automation Conference*, ACM Press, New York, 1997, 303–06. *Describes a set of tools that can generate an instruction set simulator, assembler, and disassembler from a single description.*

[Ort98] R. B. Ortega and G. Borriello, "Communication synthesis for distributed embedded systems" in *Proceedings, ICCAD 98*, ACM Press, New York, 1998, 437–44. *Maps a high-level specification into bus protocols.*

[Gas98] M. Gasteier, M. Munich, and M. Glesner, "Generation of interconnect topologies for communication synthesis," in *Proceedings, DATE 98*, IEEE Computer Society Press, Los Alamitos, 1998, 36–42. *Clusters processes to map communication onto channels.*

[Geb97] C. Gebotys, "DSP address optimization using a minimum cost circulation technique," in *Proceedings, ICCAD 97*, IEEE, New York, 1997, 100–03. *Describes a technique for address generation in DSP code.*

Embedded Software in Real-Time Signal Processing Systems: Design Technologies

GERT GOOSSENS, MEMBER, IEEE, JOHAN VAN PRAET, MEMBER, IEEE,
DIRK LANNEER, MEMBER, IEEE, WERNER GEURTS, MEMBER, IEEE, AUGUSLI KIFLI,
CLIFFORD LIEM, AND PIERRE G. PAULIN, MEMBER, IEEE

Invited Paper

The increasing use of embedded software, often implemented on a core processor in a single-chip system, is a clear trend in the telecommunications, multimedia, and consumer electronics industries. A companion paper in this issue [1] presents a survey of application and architecture trends for embedded systems in these growth markets.

However, the lack of suitable design technology remains a significant obstacle in the development of such systems. One of the key requirements is more efficient software compilation technology. Especially in the case of fixed-point digital signal processor (DSP) cores, it is often cited that commercially available compilers are unable to take full advantage of the architectural features of the processor. Moreover, due to the shorter lifetimes and the architectural specialization of many processor cores, processor designers are often compelled to neglect the issue of compiler support.

This situation has resulted in an increased research activity in the area of design tool support for embedded processors. This paper discusses design technology issues for embedded systems using processor cores, with a focus on software compilation tools. Architectural characteristics of contemporary processor cores are reviewed and tool requirements are formulated. This is followed by a comprehensive survey of both existing and new software compilation techniques that are considered important in the context of embedded processors.

I. INTRODUCTION

Software is playing an increasingly important role in the design of embedded systems. This is especially true for personal telecommunications and multimedia systems, which form extremely competitive segments of the embedded systems market. In many cases the software runs on a processor core, integrated in a very large scale integrated (VLSI) chip. Recent studies indicate that up to 60% of the development time of an embedded system is spent in software coding [1]–[3]. While this figure is a confirmation of an ongoing paradigm shift from *hardware* to *software*, at the same time it is an indication that the software design phase is becoming a bottleneck in the system design process.

A. A Paradigm Shift from Hardware to Software

By increasing the amount of software in an embedded system, several important advantages can be obtained. First, it becomes possible to include late specification changes in the design cycle. Second, it becomes easier to differentiate an existing design, by adding new features to it. Finally, the use of software facilitates the reuse of previously designed functions, independently from the selected implementation platform. The latter requires that functions are described at a processor-independent abstraction level (e.g., C code).

There are different types of core processors used in embedded systems.

- *General-purpose processors*. Several vendors of off-the-shelf programmable processors are now offering existing processors as core components, available as a library element in their silicon foundry [4]. Both microcontroller cores and digital signal processor (DSP) cores are available. From a system designer's point of view, general-purpose processor cores offer a quick and reliable route to embedded software, that is especially amenable to low/medium production volumes.

- *Application-specific instruction-set processors*. For high-volume consumer products, many system companies prefer to design an in-house application-specific instruction-set processor (ASIP) [1], [3]. By customizing the core's architecture and instruction set, the system's cost and power dissipation can be reduced significantly. The latter is crucial for portable and network-powered equipment. Furthermore, in-house

---

Manuscript received February 1, 1996; revised December 2, 1996.

G. Goossens, J. Van Praet, D. Lanneer, and W. Geurts are with the Target Compiler Technologies and IMEC, B-3001 Leuven, Belgium (e-mail: goossens@imec.be; vanpraet@imec.be; lanneer@imec.be; guerts@imec.be).

A. Kifli is with IMEC, B-3001 Leuven, Belgium (e-mail: kifli@imec.be).

C. Liem is with TIMA Laboratories, INPG and SGS-Thomson Microelectronics, F-38031 Grenoble, France (e-mail: liem@verdon.imag.fr).

P. G. Paulin is with SGS-Thomson Microelectronics, F-38921 Crolles Cedex, France (e-mail: pierre.paulin@st.com).

Publisher Item Identifier S 0018-9219(97)02051-3.

processors eliminate the dependency from external processor vendors.
- *Parameterizable processors.* An intermediary between the previous two solutions is provided by both traditional and new "fabless" processor vendors [5]–[7] as well as by semiconductor departments within bigger system companies [8], [9]. These groups are offering processor cores with a given basic architecture, but that are available in several versions, e.g., with different register file sizes or bus widths, or with optional functional units. Designers can select the instance that best matches their application.

B. Software, a Bottleneck in System Design?

The increasing use of software in embedded systems results in an increased flexibility from a system designer's point of view. However, the different types of processor cores introduced above typically suffer from a lack of supporting tools, such as efficient software compilers or instruction-set simulators.

Most *general-purpose microcontroller* and *DSP cores* are supported with a compiler and a simulator, available via the processor vendor. However, in the case of fixed-point DSP processors, it is well known that the code quality produced by these compilers is often insufficient [1], [10]. In most cases these tools are based on standard software compiler techniques developed in the 1970's and 1980's, which are not well-suited for the peculiar architecture of DSP processors. In the case of ASIP's, compiler support is normally nonexisting. Both for parameterizable processors and ASIP's, the major problem in developing a compiler is that the target architecture is not fixed beforehand.

As a result, current day's design teams using general-purpose DSP or ASIP cores are forced to spend a large amount of time in handwriting of machine code (usually assembly code). This situation has some obvious economical drawbacks. Programming DSP's and ASIP's at such a low level of abstraction leads to a *low designer's productivity*. Moreover, it results in massive amounts of *legacy code* that cannot easily be transferred to new processors. This situation is clearly undesirable, in an era where the lifetime of a processor is becoming increasingly short and architectural innovation has become key to successful products. All the above factors act as a brake on the expected productivity gain of embedded software.

Fortunately, the research community is responding to this situation with a renewed interest in software compilation, focusing on embedded processors [11]. Two main aspects deserve special attention in these developments:

- *Architectural retargetability.* Compilation tools must be easily adaptable to different processor architectures. This is essential to cope with the large degree of architectural variation, seen in DSP's and ASIP's. Moreover, market pressure results in increasingly shorter lifetimes of processor architectures. For example, an ASIP will typically serve for one or two product generations only. In this context, retargetable compilation is the only solution to provide system designers with supporting tools.
- *Code quality.* The instruction and cycle count of the compiled machine code must be comparable to solutions designed manually by experienced assembly programmers. In other words, the compiled solution should exploit all the architectural features of the DSP or ASIP architecture. A low *cycle count* (or high execution speed) may be essential to cope with the real-time constraints imposed on embedded systems. A low *instruction count* (or high machine code density) is especially required when the machine code program is stored on the chip, in which case it contributes to a low silicon area and power dissipation. Note that although cycle count and instruction count are different parameters, compilers usually try to optimize both at the same time.

This paper is organized as follows. First an architectural classification of embedded processor cores is presented, in Section II. Section III introduces the problem of software compilation in an embedded context, and summarizes the main issues. Section IV then focuses on techniques for software compilation. Several traditional approaches are discussed, as well as newer research work in an embedded processor context. Section V fomulates conclusions and a future outlook.

II. A Compilation View of Processor Architectures

The availability of efficient supporting tools is becoming a prerequisite for the fast and correct design of embedded systems. A major requirement is the availability of *software compilation* tools. In Section IV, different techniques for software compilation in the context of embedded processors will be discussed. One of the issues that will be emphasized is architectural *retargetability*, i.e., the ability to quickly adapt the compiler to new processor architectures.

A *retargetable* compiler is normally based on an *architectural model*. The compiler can generate code (of sufficient code quality) for the class of processor architectures that fit its model. Both for users and for developers of software compilers, it is useful to indicate the class of architectures that can be addressed with a given method. In this section we will therefore introduce a *classification scheme* for programmable processors [12]. An overview of programmable DSP architectures has been presented in [13]. Compared to that paper our classification scheme is more specific, in that it emphasizes those aspects that are relevant for a software compiler. It can be used to:

- *characterize a given compiler* (or compiler method), in terms of the classes of architectures that it can handle successfully;
- *characterize a given processor*, so that one can quickly find out whether suitable compiler support can be found.

We classify a processor architecture based on the following parameters: arithmetic specialization, data type, code type, instruction format, memory structure, register structure, and control-flow capabilities. These parameters will be explained in the sequel, and typical parameter values will be given for existing embedded processors in telecom and consumer applications.

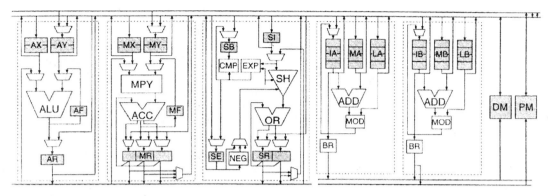

Fig. 1. Structure of the ADSP-21xx processor.

23	22	21	20	19	18	17	16	15	14	13	12	11	10	9	8	7	6	5	4	3	2	1	0
11: ALU/ MAC oper'n with DM/PM load				PM load destin. = 00:AY0 01:AY1 10:MY0 11:MY1				DM load destin. = 00:AX0 01:AX1 10:MX0 11:MX1				Arithmetic oper'n = 0: MAC oper'n			0000:nop Opcode = ... 0100:$X*Y_{ss}$ 0101:$X*Y_{su}$ 0110:$X*Y_{us}$ 0111:$X*Y_{uu}$ 1000:$MR+X*Y_{ss}$ 1001:$MR+X*Y_{su}$ ... 1111:$MR-X*Y_{uu}$				Y = 00:MY0 01:MY1 10:MF 11:zero			X = 000:MX0 001:MX1 010:AR 011:MR0 100:MR1 101:MR2 110:SR0 111:SR1		PM-AGU oper'n = Idx = 00:IB0 01:IB1 10:IB2 11:IB3		Mdf,Len = 00:MB0,LB0 01:MB1,LB1 10:MB2,LB2 11:MB3,LB3		Idx = 00:IA0 01:IA1 10:IA2 11:IA3	DM-AGU oper'n =			Mdf,Len = 00:MA0,LA0 01:MA1,LA1 10:MA2,LA2 11:MA3,LA3		
							1: ALU oper'n		Opcode = 0000:Y 0001:Y+1 0010:X+Y+C 0011:X+Y 0100:not X ... 1111:abs X				Y = 00:AY0 01:AY1 10:AF 11:zero			X = 000:AX0 001:AX1 010:AR 011:MR0 100:MR1 ... 111:SR1										

Fig. 2. Part of the instruction set of the ADSP-21xx processor. Columns show different instruction fields, encoded by the instruction bits listed at the top.

Throughout this section we will refer to an existing DSP processor by means of example: the ADSP-21xx fixed-point DSP of Analog Devices [14]. This processor is chosen because it has many features that are also encountered in ASIP's. The ADSP-21xx architecture is shown in Fig. 1. The instruction-set of this processor supports about 30 different formats, of which the most parallel one is depicted in Fig. 2: an arithmetic operation on the ALU or multiplier, together with two parallel memory loads and two address calculations.

A. Definitions

1) Arithmetic Specialization: Compared to other microprocessor architectures, a distinguishing feature of a DSP is the use by the latter of a parallel multiplier/accumulator unit. By virtue of this *arithmetic specialization*, the execution of correlation-like algorithms (digital filters, auto, and cross correlation, etc.) can be speeded up significantly.

In ASIP's, the idea of *arithmetic specialization* is even carried further. More specialized arithmetic units are introduced, controlled from the processor's instruction set, in such a way that the critical sections of the target algorithms (e.g., deeply nested loop bodies) can be executed in a minimal number of machine cycles and without excessive storage of intermediate values. A typical example is the hardware support for a butterfly function in Viterbi decoding, encountered in ASIP's for wireless telecom [7], [15].

2) Data Type: Embedded processor cores for consumer and telecom applications normally support *fixed-point arithmetic* only. The reason is that floating-point units (as occurring, e.g., in many general-purpose microprocessors) require additional silicon area and dissipate more power. Floating-point arithmetic can however be avoided relatively easily in the VLSI implementation of consumer and telecom systems, without sacrificing numerical accuracy, by including the appropriate scaling operations in software or in hardware.

In a general-purpose DSP, different fixed-point data types are typically encountered. A distinct case is the ADSP-21xx architecture (Fig. 1), of which the most important data types are: a 16-bit type for ALU and multiplier operands, a 32-bit type for multiplier or shifter results, a 40-bit accumulator type, an 8-bit type for shift factors, and a 14-bit address type. Conversions between data types may be provided in the processor hardware. Consider the ADSP's accumulator register MR, which is 40-bits wide. In this case one 8-bit

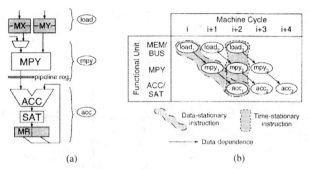

Fig. 3. Different code types, illustrated for a multiply-accumulate instruction (b), on a pipelined datapath (a).

and two 16-bit subwords of MR (called MR2, MR1, and MR0, respectively) are separately addressable, as the source operand of different arithmetic operations.

A comparable variety of data types can typically be found in ASIP's, where the bit-widths of functional units, busses and memories are chosen in function of the application. A good example is the ASIP for a private local telephone switch developed by Northern Telecom [1].

3) Code Type: Processors with instruction-level parallelism are often able to execute sequences of operations in a *data pipeline*. Fig. 3(a) shows an example of a multiplier-accumulator that can implement a three-stage data pipeline. In parallel with the *current* multiplication ("mpy"), this architecture can execute the accumulation with the *previous* multiplication result ("acc") and the load of the *next* multiplication operand from memory ("load").[1]

To control the operations in the data pipeline, two different mechanisms are commonly used in computer architecture: *data-stationary* and *time-stationary* coding [16].

- In the case of *data-stationary* coding, every instruction that is part of the processor's instruction-set controls a complete sequence of operations that have to be executed *on a specific data item*, as it traverses the data pipeline. Once the instruction has been fetched from program memory and decoded, the processor controller hardware will make sure that the composing operations are executed in the correct machine cycle.
- In the case of *time-stationary* coding, every instruction that is part of the processor's instruction-set controls a complete set of operations that have to be executed *in a single machine cycle*. These operations may be processing several different data items traversing the data pipeline. In this case it is the responsibility of the programmer or compiler to set up and maintain the data pipeline. The resulting pipeline schedule is fully visible in the machine code program.

Both code types are illustrated in Fig. 3(b). According to the authors' observations, time-stationary coding is used more often in *ASIP cores*, whereas *general-purpose processors* can use either type.

In addition to the operations in the data pipeline described above, a processor also has to fetch instructions from the program memory and decode them in an instruction decoder. This is done in one or more *instruction pipeline* stages, preceding the *data pipeline* stages. In processors with a *data-stationary* code type, instruction fetch and instruction decode are normally done in two separate instruction pipeline stages. For example, the data-stationary processor of Fig. 3(b) would typically have an overall pipeline depth of five cycles (fetch, decode, load, multiply, and accumulate). In processors with a *time-stationary* code type, instruction fetch and instruction decode are usually done in either a single or in two separate instruction pipeline stages, preceding the single execution cycle.

Processors with a time-stationary code type and a single fetch/decode cycle are often called *microcoded* processors. They have been studied intensively since the 1960's by the "microprogramming community." In contrast, processors with multiple instruction pipeline stages, whether of time or data-stationary code type, are referred to as *macrocoded* processors [17].[2]

Macrocoded processors may exhibit pipeline hazards [17]. Depending on the processor, pipeline hazards may have to be resolved in the machine code program (statically) or by means of interlocking in the processor controller (dynamically). Macrocoded processors with interlocking are relatively easy to program, although it may be more difficult for a designer to predict their exact cycle time behavior.

4) Instruction Format: A distinction is made between orthogonal and encoded instruction formats.

- An *orthogonal format* consists of fixed control fields that can be set independently from each other. For example, very long instruction word (VLIW) processors [18] have an orthogonal instruction format. Note that the instruction bits within every control field may additionally have been encoded to reduce the field's width.
- In the case of an *encoded format*, the interpretation of the instruction bits as control fields may be different from instruction to instruction. The correct interpretation can be deduced from the value of designated bits in the instruction word (e.g., special format bits, like instruction bits 23 and 22 in Fig. 2, or specific opcode bits).

The processor's instruction decoder will translate instruction bits into control signals steering the different units in the processor.

When the processor is used as an *embedded core*, the application program will most often reside on-chip. In this case, processor designers aim at restricting the instruction word's width, in order to reduce the chip area and especially the power dissipation relating to program memory accesses. Should the chip be *field programmable*, it is convenient to choose an instruction width equal to the width of the chip's parallel data port (so that the instructions can be loaded via

---

[1] Since the multiplication result is kept in the accumulator register MR, there is no need for a fourth stage to store the result in memory. Furthermore, we did not consider any address calculations for the operand loads; the latter could be put in an additional pipeline stage as well.

[2] Note that the term *microcode* was originally introduced to refer to a lower level of control inside a processor controller, to decode and execute macrocoded instructions.

this port) and/or equal to the width of standard memory components (used for program memory).

For these reasons, many general-purpose DSP's have a 16-, 24-, or 32-bit wide instruction format. In contrast, many ASIP's have more uncommon instruction widths. In both cases, the instruction format is typically *encoded*.

Encoding in general restricts the *instruction-level parallelism* offered by the processor. A challenging task in the design of an ASIP is to determine an instruction set that can be encoded using a restricted number of instruction bits, while still offering a sufficient degree of parallelism for critical functions in the target application. Speed requirements for typical *telecom* and *consumer* applications make it possible to design efficient ASIP's that have a relatively high degree of instruction encoding. In contrast, *image processing* and *multimedia* applications may require a higher amount of instruction-level parallelism to meet their speed requirements. Most current ASIP's for these application domains therefore have orthogonal instruction formats [19]–[21].

5) Memory Structure: Many DSP and ASIP cores have *efficient memory and register structures*, which ensure a high communication bandwidth between the different datapath units, and between datapath and memory. In this section we will discuss memory structures; register structures will be treated in the next section.

 a) Memory access: Memory structures are often classified on the basis of accessibility of data and program memory:
- *Von Neumann architecture*. These processors have a single memory space that is used to store both *data* and *program*. This was always the case in older microprocessor architectures of the CISC type.
- *Harvard architecture*. This term refers to the case where data and program are *accessible through separate hardware*. When applied to general-purpose RISC processors, this means that the data and program busses are separated. When applied to DSP processors, it means that the data and program memory spaces are separated. In many cases even *two* data memory spaces are provided, each with their own address generator. This is the case for the ADSP-21xx of Fig. 1.

In the remainder of this paper we will always assume that the processor has a Harvard architecture, with separate data and program memory spaces. This is the case for most current DSP's and ASIP's.

From a software compiler point of view, the choices of *addressing modes* and *operand location* are important issues. These will be discussed next.

 b) Addressing modes: Processors usually support *multiple addressing modes* for data memories, such as *immediate*, *direct*, and *indirect* addressing. In the case of DSP's and ASIP's, indirected addressing is typically implemented on one or more address generation units. Often these units support specialized address operations, such as modulo counting to implement circular buffers for filter applications, counting with reversed carry propagation for FFT applications, and address post-modify instructions which allow to compute the "next" memory address simultaneously with the current memory access. It is essential that these features are supported by the compiler.

 c) Operand location: With respect to *operand location*, the following classification of memory structures is most relevant [17]:
- *Load-store architecture* (also called *register-register architecture*). In a load-store architecture, all arithmetic operations get their operands from, and produce results in *addressable registers*. Communication between memories and registers requires separate "load" and "store" operations, which may be scheduled in parallel with arithmetic operations if permitted by the instruction set. The load-store concept is one of the basic ideas behind RISC architectures.

  An example is the ADSP-21xx processor, of which one instruction format is shown in Fig. 2. As can be seen, all arithmetic operations belonging to this format operate on registers (addressed by instruction bits 12–8). Multiplication results are always written to register MR, while ALU results are written to AR. In parallel with the arithmetic operation, two load operations are executed to prepare the arithmetic operands for the next instruction cycle (in the registers addressed by instruction bits 21–18).
- *Memory-memory* and *memory-register architecture*. In this case, arithmetic instructions can be specified with *data memory* locations as operands. An example is the TMS320C5x DSP processor, which can execute a multiplication on two operands, respectively residing in a memory and in a register (and eventually store the result in an accumulator register).

Processor cores encountered in embedded systems can be of any of the above types. Note that in the case of a core processor, data and program memories are often placed on-chip to reduce board cost, access time (allowing for single-cycle access) and power dissipation.

6) Register Structure: Any processor will contain a *register set* for temporary storage of intermediate data values. Before discussing register structures in more detail, the following terms are introduced.
- *Homogeneous register set*. This is a register set in which all registers are interchangeable. If an instruction reads an operand from or writes a result to the register set, the programmer (or compiler) is allowed to select *any* element of the set.
- *Heterogeneous register set*. This type of register set consists of special-purpose registers. In this case, a register can only serve as an operand or result register of *specific* instructions. Likewise, an instruction can only read its operands from or write its results to *specific* elements of the register set.

Consider again the example of the ADSP-21xx processor. For the arithmetic operations belonging to the format of Fig. 2, the left and right operands are *restricted* to the registers indicated in the fields of instruction bits 10 to 8, and 12 to 11, respectively. Results can *only* be stored in MR (for multiplications), and AR (for ALU operations).

Table 1 Scope of Retargetability of the Chess Compiler Using the Classification Scheme

Parameter	Supported values
Data type	Fixed and floating point
Code type	Standard and user-defined data types
	Time-stationary
Instruction format	Harvard, multiple data memories
	Load Store
	Addressing modes with post-modification
Register structure	Heterogeneous and homogeneous
Control flow	Zero overhead loops
	Residual control ...

The homogeneous case is an extreme point in the solution space: practical register sets are always more or less heterogeneous. In other words, the processor can be positioned anywhere on the axis from homogeneous to heterogeneous.

The register set of a processor can be partitioned into different *register classes*. A register class is a *subset* of the processor's register set, that can be viewed as homogeneous from the point of view of a certain instruction's operand or result. For example, {MY0,MY1,MF} constitutes a register class in the ADSP-21xx processor, since all elements of this set can serve as the right operand register of a multiplication in the format of Fig. 2. Note that register classes can be contained in each other or overlap with each other. The total number of register classes in a processor can now be considered as a measure for its heterogeneity.

The following is a rough classification of existing processor types.

- General-purpose *microprocessors* usually have a relatively *homogeneous* register set. In the case of fixed-point processors, the register set is normally divided in two register classes: the data-register class and the address-register class. In the case of floating-point architectures, the floating-point registers constitute a third class.
- General-purpose *DSP's* typically have a parallel multiplier. Compared to their microprocessor counterparts, this introduces at least one additional register class to store multiplication results. When the instruction format is encoded, some restrictions may exist on the choice of source and destination registers, which results in additional register classes.
- *ASIP's* typically have a strongly *heterogeneous* register set. The reasons are twofold. First, ASIP's may support many different data types, which often result in different register classes. Secondly, ASIP designers aim at a high degree of instruction encoding without significantly compromising the available instruction-level parallelism for the target application. This can be done by reducing the number of instruction bits for register addressing, in favor of the instruction bits for arithmetic or memory access operations. In this way a larger number of arithmetic and/or memory access operations can be executed in parallel, but the register structure becomes heterogeneous.

From the above discussion, it becomes clear that the optimization of the register structure is an important task in the design of an ASIP architecture. However, the design of machine code that exploits such a heterogeneous register structure in an efficient way is nontrivial as well. As a matter of fact, the inefficient use of heterogeneous register structures is one of the prime reasons for the reported low code quality in the case of commercially available compilers for fixed-point DSP's (see Section I).

7) Control Flow: Many DSP's and ASIP's support standard control-flow instructions, like conditional branching based on bit values in the condition code register. However, several additional measures are usually taken to guarantee good performance in the presence of control flow. The following examples are typical.

- First, branch penalties are usually small, i.e., zero or one cycles. The branch penalty is the delay incurred in executing a branch due to the instruction pipeline.
- Furthermore, many DSP's and ASIP's have *zero-overhead loop* instructions. This allows to execute the body of a repetitive algorithm without spending separate cycles for loop control. This feature is essential for many time-critical applications.
- Several arithmetic or move instructions are *conditionally executable*. In many specific cases, this avoids the overhead of conditionally loading the program counter.
- Some arithmetic operations can be *residually controlled*. In this case the behavior of the operation depends on specific bit-values in a residual control register, which can be written by other operations. Typical examples are saturation modes for ALU or accumulate operations.
- The interrupt controller sometimes supports specialized context saving mechanisms like register shadowing, to minimize context switch times.

B. Use of the Classification Scheme

The classification scheme introduced above can be used for different purposes. First of all, it can be used to characterize a given (retargetable) compiler, and indicate its "scope of retargetability." As an example, Table 1 indicates the scope of retargetability of the current version of the Chess compiler [22].

Second, the classification scheme can be used to characterize a given processor and quickly identify the issues related to compiler development. In this case, the model gives an indication of how easily a compiler can be built for the processor, and which existing compilers might be suited. For example, Table 2 shows the classification of a number of existing DSP and ASIP architectures.

III. ISSUES IN SOFTWARE COMPILATION

Software compilation has been addressed since the 1950's. The aspect of architectural retargetability has been taken into consideration since the early 1970's. Due to the continuous evolution of processor architectures, software compilation has never lost its importance, both from a researcher's and from a practical user's point of view (see Fig. 4). The software compiler community has

Table 2 Classification of Existing DSP-ASIP's Based on Six Parameters of Classification Scheme

Parameter	EPICS10 [8]	TMS320C54x [15]	LODE [7]	TCEC MPEG [19]
Arithmetic specialization	Plug-in applic.-spec. unit	Viterbi ALU	Dual multipl.-accumulator	
Data type	Fixed point	Fixed point	Fixed point	Fixed point
Code type	Time-stationarity	Data-stationarity	Data-stationarity	Time-stationarity
Instruction format	Encoded	Encoded	Encoded	Orthogonal
Memory structure	Harvard with two data memories Load-store Address. modes with post-modification	Harvard with two data memories Memory-reg. Address. modes with post-modification	Harvard with two data memories Memory-reg. Address. modes with post-modification	Harvard with four data memories Load-store Address. modes with post-modification
Register structure	Heterogenous	Heterogenous	Heterogenous	Heterogenous

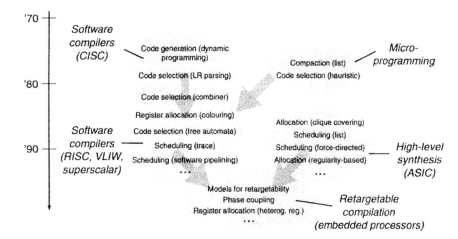

Fig. 4. Evolution of retargetable compiler research in the past decades.

been focusing mostly on general-purpose microprocessors, which evolved from traditional CISC architectures, over RISC's, to more parallel VLIW and superscalar architectures. Until recently, DSP processors—and obviously ASIP's—received relatively little attention.

Most processor vendors offer *C* compilers with their processors. In several cases these compilers are ports of *GCC*, a compiler framework distributed by the Free Software Foundation [23]. *GCC* combines a number of techniques developed by the compiler community, primarily for general-purpose microprocessors. With the free distribution of its *C* source code, *GCC* has been ported to countless processors and has been retargeted to even more. Examples of existing DSP's for which commercial retargets of *GCC* are available include: Analog Devices 2101, AT&T 1610, Motorola 56001, and SGS-Thomson D950. It has become the *de facto*, pragmatic approach to develop compilers from a freely available environment. For processors close to the intent of *GCC* this can be fairly quick.

Nonetheless, as mentioned in Section I and in the companion paper [1], the code generated by the available compilers for fixed-point DSP's is too often of unacceptable quality for industrial use, so that design teams have to resort to manual assembly coding.

Fortunately, the emerging market of embedded processors has initiated a revival of software compilation research for DSP's and ASIP's, since the early 1990's [11] (Fig. 4).

In Section IV a survey will be presented of some traditional software compilation techniques that are relevant

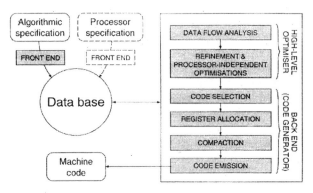

Fig. 5. Anatomy of a software compiler.

in the context of embedded processors. In addition, an outline be will presented of recent developments in software compilation for embedded processor architectures.

Fig. 5 shows the typical anatomy of a software compiler. The starting point of the compilation process is an application program in an *algorithmic specification language*. Most compilers for embedded processors use *C* as the algorithmic specification language. A drawback of standard *C* is its restricted support for different data types. DSP's and ASIP's often accommodate a wide variety of (fixed-point) data types. For these cases, the *C* language is sometimes augmented to support user-definable data types [24].

The algorithmic specification is translated into an *intermediate representation*, by means of a language-dependent front-end. The intermediate representation, which is kept in the compiler's data base, is accessible by the subsequent compilation phases. Well-known intermediate representations for representing the algorithm include the *static single assignment form* (SSA form) [25], and the *control/dataflow graph* (CDFG) [26], [27].

In addition to the algorithmic specification, a *retargetable* compiler will also use a processor specification, that must be available in an internal model in the compiler's data base. This model may be generated automatically, starting from a *processor specification language*. Examples of specification languages and internal compiler models for representing processors will be discussed in Section IV-A–B. A *compiler generator*[3] is a tool that automatically builds a processor-specific compiler, with its internal model, from a description in a processor specification language.

The software compilation process is traditionally divided into high-level optimization and back-end compilation. In the *high-level optimizer*, a data-flow analysis [28] is carried out to determine all required data dependencies in the algorithm, needed to build the SSA form or CDFG. Processor-independent optimizations are carried out, to reduce the number of operations or the sequentiality of the description. The set of optimizations is quite standard, and includes common subexpression elimination, dead code removal, constant propagation and folding, etc. [28]. The *back-end* performs the actual *code generation*, whereby the intermediate representation is mapped on the instruction set of the target processor. In this code generation process, different *phases* can be distinguished:

- *Code selection:* The operations in the algorithmic model are bound to the *partial instructions*, supported by the target processor's instruction set. Multiple operations can be combined in the same partial instruction. This is determined by *covering* the operations in the model with (complex) patterns, each representing a partial instruction.
- *Register allocation:* Intermediate computation values are bound to *registers* or *memories*. If necessary, additional data move operations are added.
- *Scheduling:* In this phase the code generator attempts to exploit the remaining *instruction-level parallelism* that is available in the processor architecture. Partial instructions that can execute in parallel are *grouped* into complete instructions, and assigned to *machine cycles*. Whereas the set of partial instructions after code selection and register allocation is usually called *vertical code*, the final instructions after scheduling are referred to as *horizontal code* [29]. The transformation from vertical to horizontal code is sometimes also called *code compaction*.

It is important to note that in many compilers, a partial ordering of operations is already determined during the earlier phases of code selection and register allocation. As a matter of fact, determining a vertical ordering of partial instructions is a critical issue in several code selection and register allocation algorithms, that affects the eventual code quality.

The above described code generation phases are encountered in software compilers for general-purpose microprocessors as well as in more recent compilers for embedded processors. In traditional compilers for *CISC* processors, code selection was the most important code generation phase. In this case, local register allocation was included in the code selection phase. In current compilers for *RISC* processors, code selection and (global) register allocation are typically done in separate phases.[4] Furthermore, instruction ordering has become an important issue in these compilers, due to the possible occurrence of pipeline hazards. With the advent of *VLIW* and *superscalar* processors, more emphasis is being put on efficient scheduling, to cope with the larger amount of instruction-level parallelism in these architectures [30].

In today's context of *embedded processors*, the following new aspects are added to the problem: *architectural retargetability* and the requirement of *high code quality* for irregular architectures (see Section I). The latter requirement has a dual impact on the compilation methodology:

- Because of instruction-level parallelism and the occurrence of heterogeneous register structures, the different compilation phases become strongly interdependent. In order to generate high quality code, each code generation phase should take the impact on other phases into account. This is called *phase coupling* [31].
- In order to generate high quality code, more specialized compiler algorithms may be required, that explicitly take into account aspects like heterogeneous register structures. Examples will be given in Sections IV-C–F. An important point is that larger compilation times can be tolerated in the case of embedded processors, compared to general-purpose microprocessors.

In order to tackle these new challenges, several compiler researchers are investigating synergies between *software compilation* techniques for *general-purpose* processors and techniques for *high-level synthesis* of *application-specific hardware* [11]. This approach is motivated by the fact that several high-level synthesis tools are targeting irregular architectures with instruction-level parallelism.

IV. A Survey of Compilation Techniques

Following the discussion of processor architectures and of general compiler issues, next a survey is provided of existing techniques for processor modeling and software compilation.

A. Processor Specification Languages

The use of efficient and powerful models to represent all required characteristics of a processor is a key aspect in making the software compilation process retargetable. Although many compilers use *separate, specialized models* for each of the compilation phases, attempts have been made to use a *single processor model* for retargetable compilation, supported with a user-friendly *processor specification language*. In this section, processor specification

---

[3] Also termed a *compiler compiler* or (when restricted to the compiler's back end) a *code-generator generator*.

[4] The terms *local* and *global* register allocation will be defined more precisely in Section IV-C.

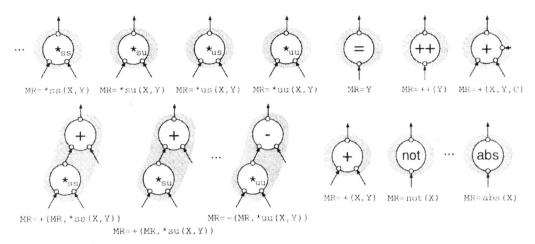

Fig. 6. Part of a tree pattern base, derived for the ADSP-21xx instruction format of Fig. 2. Below each tree the corresponding grammar representation is shown. In this example, source operand registers are not modeled in the pattern base.

languages are discussed. Processor models for compilers are treated separately in Section IV-B.

1) Netlist-Based Languages: A first type of processor specification languages describe the processor as a *netlist of hardware building blocks*, including datapath, memories, instruction decoder, and controller. This approach is followed in the MSSQ compiler, which accepts a processor specification in the *Mimola* language [32]. The advantage of these languages is their completeness. However, a netlist may not always be available to the compiler designer. Furthermore, this approach requires that the architectural design is completed, which precludes building compilers *during* the architecture exploration phase in ASIP design.

2) High-Level Languages: As an alternative to netlist-based formalisms, several high-level processor description languages have been proposed. The idea behind these languages is to capture the information that is available in a *programmer's manual* of a processor. Usually such a description contains a structural skeleton of the processor (essentially a declaration of storage elements and data types), and a description of the actual instruction set. A first example is the *ISP* language [33], with its descendant *ISPS* [34]. In *ISP* the instruction set is captured by specifying the behavior that corresponds to specific sets of instruction bits. For the latter, a procedural formalism is used. More recently, the *nML* language was proposed [35]. *nML* uses an attributed grammar. The grammar's production rules define the composition of the instruction set, in a compact hierarchical way. The semantics of the instructions (e.g., their register-transfer behavior and their assembly and binary encoding) are captured by attributes. *nML* is used by the CBC [36] and Chess [22] compilers.

B. Processor Models for Compilation

1) Template Pattern Bases: A first approach, used by traditional compilers for general-purpose CISC and RISC processors [28], [37], is to represent the target processor by means of a *template pattern base*, that essentially enumerates the different partial instructions available in the instruction set. Each partial instruction is represented as a pattern, expressed by means of the algorithm intermediate representation. Fig. 6 shows an example of a pattern base, where a graphical representation is used in the form of CDFG patterns. Often the patterns are expressed using a *grammar*.

As will be explained in Section IV-C, several code generators restrict the allowed template patterns to *tree structures*. This is the case in Fig. 6, where each pattern computes a result value from one or more operand values. The corresponding grammar model is a "regular tree grammar," in which each production rule describes a partial instruction as a pattern in (usually prefix) linearized form. Terminal grammar symbols correspond to operations executed by an instruction, while nonterminal symbols may correspond to possible storage locations. To reduce the number of grammar rules, common subpatterns can be factored out; the rule describing a subpattern is then connected to the remaining rules via additional nonterminals.

Examples of code-selector generators using regular tree grammars include *Twig* [38], *Burg* [39], *Iburg* [40], and the *Graham-Glanville* code generators[5] [41]. Several recent compilers for embedded processors have adopted *Iburg* for the code selection phase, such as *CBC* [36], *Record* [42], and the *Spam* project compiler [43]. In the *CBC* compiler the regular tree grammar, that serves as the input to *Iburg*, is derived automatically from an *nML* specification of the target processor [36]. Similarly, in *Record* this grammar is derived from a *Mimola* specification [44]. In *Spam* a regular tree grammar is specified by the user, in the format supported by the *Olive* code-selector generator which is similar to *Iburg*. Other compilers for embedded processors using a pattern base include *CodeSyn* [45].

Although a template pattern base in the first place describes the processor's *instruction set*, it is often also extended with additional *structural* information to reflect the processor's register structure. For example, additional patterns, called *chain rules*, may be inserted to describe

---

[5] As will be discussed in Section IV-C, Graham–Glanville code generators actually use *string* grammars, which have the same textual representation as regular tree grammars.

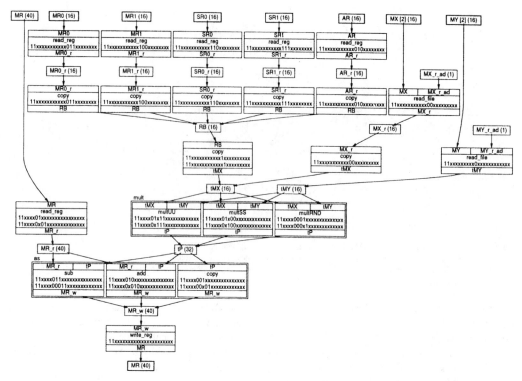

Fig. 7. Part of the *ISG* representation of the ADSP-21xx processor.

possible moves between storage elements. The grouping of registers into register classes can be modeled. In [46], a more specialized processor model is proposed, based on *Trellis diagrams*, which in essence combine tree patterns with structural information.

2) Graph Models: An alternative approach, mainly used in compilers for embedded processors, is to represent the processor by means of a *graph model*. Such a model has the advantage that it can more readily represent structural information, which makes it possible to describe several of the peculiarities of ASIP architectures.

The *MSSQ* compiler [47] uses a "connection-operation graph" that is derived from a detailed processor netlist. In the *RL compiler* [48] a "place-time graph" is used, i.e., a graph that captures all legal data moves in the processor. The *Chess* compiler is built around an "instruction-set graph" (ISG) [49], which is used by all code generation phases. Fig. 7 shows the *ISG* representation of a part of the ADSP-21xx processor, introduced in Fig. 1. The *ISG* captures both *behavioral* (instruction set) and *structural* (register structure, pipeline behavior, and structural hazards) information. The *ISG* is a bipartite graph, with vertices representing *structural elements* (small boxes in the figure representing registers, memories, or connections) and *microoperations* (large boxes), respectively. These objects are annotated with their enabling condition, to indicate the binary instruction format(s) to which they belong. Edges indicate the legal *dataflow* between the structural elements.

C. Code Selection

The phase of code selection has received a lot of attention in the software compiler community. In early compilers for CISC architectures, code selection was the main code generation phase. In these compilers, code selection also determines local register allocation as a by-product. This is possible because CISC's always have a memory-register or a memory-memory structure, so that the number of available registers is restricted.

Later on, the same techniques have been applied to RISC compilers as well. In these compilers, register allocation is normally deferred to a separate code generation phase. However, the issue of phase coupling between code selection and register allocation has received renewed interest in recent compilers for DSP's and ASIP's, due to the occurrence of heterogeneous register structures.

It has been shown that code generation is an NP-complete problem, for intermediate representations that take the form of a directed acyclic graph (DAG) [50], [51]. However, *optimal vertical code* (i.e., without instruction-level parallelism) can be generated in polynomial time, when the following conditions are satisfied [37], [52]:

1) the intermediate representation is an *expression tree* (hereafter called the *subject tree*);
2) the template pattern base is restricted to contain only *tree patterns* (as in Fig. 6), i.e., it can be represented as a *regular tree grammar* (see Section IV-B);
3) the processor has a *homogeneous register structure*.

Different code generation algorithms have been developed to solve this canonical problem. However, since the above conditions are often not satisfied in practice, code generators often incorporate *extensions* of those basic algorithms. Some of these basic algorithms, as well as various practical extensions, are surveyed below. The discussion in this

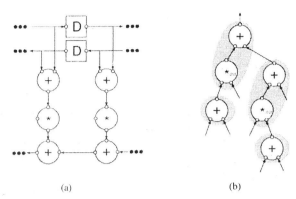

Fig. 8. Code selection for a symmetrical filter, using the tree pattern base of Fig. 6: (a) CDFG of the application and (b) tree-structured intermediate representation with a possible cover.

section will be restricted to the *code selection* phase of code generation, including those approaches that incorporate *local register allocation* in the code selection process. In this context, "local" means that register allocation is done for values *within the subject tree* only. Techniques for global register allocation, as a *separate* code generation phase, are discussed in Section IV-D.

1) Dynamic Programming: Several code-selector generators are based on a stepwise partitioning of the code selection problem, using *dynamic programming*. It is assumed here that conditions 1) and 2) of the canonical problem above are satisfied. Two phases are distinguished in the code selection problem:

- *tree pattern matching*, i.e., locating parts of the subject tree that correspond to available tree patterns in the pattern base.
- *tree covering*, i.e., finding a complete cover of the subject tree with available patterns (see Fig. 8).

The use of dynamic programming was first proposed by Aho and Johnson [37], assuming a *homogeneous* register structure [see condition 3)]. *Tree pattern matching* is done in a straightforward way, in a bottom-up traversal of the subject tree (i.e., from the leaves to the root). For each tree node, the method computes the minimal *cost* to cover the subtrees rooted at that node. Cost calculations are done using the principle of dynamic programming. The cost takes into account both the register utilization of the subtrees and the different possible orderings of these subtrees. In this way, both local register allocation and scheduling (within the expression tree under consideration) are included in the algorithm. During a top-down traversal of the subject tree, the *tree cover* is finally found, by determining the minimal cost at the tree's root node. In [37] it is proven that the program, resulting from the application of dynamic programming, is a *strong normal form* program. This is a program that consists of sequences of vertical code which are strongly contiguous, meaning that for each node it is guaranteed that one subtree of the node is completely executed before the next of its subtrees is executed. [37] also proves that these strong normal forms are optimal for the canonical problem introduced above.

Dynamic programming is also used in more recent code selection approaches for processors with a *heterogeneous register structure*, such as the code selectors generated by *Twig* [38], *Beg* [53], and *Iburg* [40]. Again, dynamic programming is used for cost calculation. However, this time a *separate cost* is calculated *per register class*, at each of the nodes in the subject tree. To keep the problem tractable, a number of simplifications are made. First of all, it is assumed that every register class has an *infinite number of registers*. Secondly, the costs that are calculated do not reflect any local register allocation nor operation ordering. These issues are delayed to the subsequent code generation phases. Yet the technique will insert data *move* operations between different register classes of the processor, when appropriate.

The implementations of *Twig*, *Beg*, and *Iburg* use a *tree automaton* to traverse the subject tree in the tree pattern matching step. An improvement of tree automaton based code selection is provided by the "bottom-up rewrite system" (BURS) theory [54]. Whereas the original methods calculate the intermediate costs *during* the actual code selection, BURS theory allows to shift these calculations to the *generation phase* of the code selector. This results in much faster code selection. However, a drawback of BURS theory is that the cost function is restricted to a constant additive model. *Burg* [39], [55] is a code-selector generator based on BURS theory. A formal treatment of tree-automaton based code selection can be found in [56].

Several recent compilers for embedded processors are using adaptations of one of the dynamic programming methods described above. The following adaptations can be mentioned.

- In practice, intermediate representations are often *graphs* rather than trees. The traditional method to partition a DAG representation into different expression trees is to cut the DAG at each edge representing a value that is used multiple times. This is illustrated in Fig. 8 by the derivation of the tree (b) from the graph (a). Dynamic programming based techniques are then applied to the individual trees, and afterwards the results are combined by allocating registers for the values that are shared among trees. Based on this extension, dynamic programming has been adopted among others by the following compilers: *CodeSyn* (using straightforward pattern matching) [57], *CBC* [36], *Record* [44], and *Spam* [43] (all three using *Iburg* or variations of it).

- As mentioned in Section II, many DSP's and ASIP's have a *heterogeneous* register structure. While dynamic programming based code selection has been extended to heterogeneous structures (see above), these methods suffer from a rather weak phase coupling with *register allocation*. For example, they do not consider optimizations like spilling of data values to memory, or the constraint that the register capacity (i.e., the number of registers) in a register class is restricted. Both issues are then deferred to a separate register allocation step. An alternative approach is provided in [46], presenting a combined method for code selection and register allocation for heterogeneous structures. Spilling is considered, as are register capacity constraints. The covering problem is reformulated as a path search problem in *Trellis trees*, which produces strong normal form programs. For heterogeneous register structures, these programs cannot be guaranteed to be optimal. In the *Spam* project a different approach is followed: in [43] a subclass of architectures with a heterogeneous register structure is identified for which *optimal* vertical code can be produced using a dynamic programming based code selector. These architectures do not necessitate spilling. In this approach strong normal form programs are produced. The method includes register allocation and ordering. In practice, this formulation is applicable to the TMS320C25 architecture.

2) LR Parsing: When the processor model is a *regular tree grammar* (see Section IV-B), code selection can be viewed as a problem of *parsing* the subject tree using the specified grammar. As a matter of fact, the tree-automaton based methods described above (see dynamic programming) are parsing methods for regular tree grammars. For most practical processors, the regular tree grammar is highly ambiguous: several derivations may be obtained for the same expression, which represent the optimization space for the code selector. The dynamic programming method allows to find an optimized solution within this space.

Parsing approaches to code selection were however known long before the introduction of tree-automaton based methods. Graham–Glanville code generators [41], [58], developed in the 1970's, use the same type of grammar but interpret it as a *string* grammar. Subject trees are linearized expression trees, which are then parsed with a *left-right (LR) parsing technique*. Because of the linearization of patterns, Graham–Glanville code selectors perform tree pattern matching in a left-operand biased fashion, i.e., when generating code for a subtree, the code for the left operand of the root node is selected without considering the right operand. This may produce inferior results, compared to the dynamic programming based methods.

Other recent parsing approaches to code selection have been described in [59], [60].

3) Graph Matching: As explained above, dynamic programming-based approaches to code selection suffer from the restriction that the pattern base and the intermediate representation must consist of tree structures. Some authors therefore proposed pattern matching algorithms that directly support DAG structures. In [51] a code selection algorithm was presented that can generate optimal vertical code for DAG's, on a processor with only a single register. In [61] this algorithm has been further refined to support commutative operations and multiregister architectures similar to the TMS320C25 processor.

4) Bundling: The code selection techniques described hitherto rely on the availability of a template pattern base, possibly in the form of a regular tree grammar, which essentially enumerates *all* legal partial instructions *in advance*.

An alternative approach to code selection is to use a *bundling* algorithm, in which *only the required patterns are constructed* on the fly during a traversal of the intermediate representation. Whether or not such a pattern (also called a *bundle*) is legal, can be derived from the processor model, which in this case is given in the form of a graph model (see Section IV-B).

An early example of a bundling approach to code selection is the *combiner* algorithm [62], a variation of the peephole optimization technique presented in [63] and used in the *GCC* compiler. More recently, bundling algorithms have been developed for compilers for embedded processors, such as *MSSQ* [47], *MSSV* [64], and *Chess* [22].

An advantage of these bundling algorithms is that they support intermediate representations and partial instructions that are graphs rather than trees. These features are useful in a DSP and ASIP context. A disadvantage is the increased algorithmic complexity, compared to dynamic programming or parsing methods. Note that the bundling algorithms in *MSSQ* and *MSSV* include local register allocation. In *Chess*, register allocation is however deferred to a separate compiler phase. Phase coupling is supported though, primarily through the principle of late binding: when several legal bundles exist for the same group of operations in the intermediate representation, the choice will be deferred to the register allocation or even the scheduling phase.

The approach is illustrated in Fig. 9 for the example of Fig. 8, assuming that the processor is specified using the *ISG* graph model. First all possible mappings of individual CDFG operations to partial instructions are determined [Fig. 9(b)]. Next the CDFG is traversed to find combinations of operations that correspond to more complex partial instructions, while taking into account that their operands and results can be read from, resp. written to, available storage elements [Fig. 9(c)].

5) Rule-Driven Code Selection: Rule-driven approaches to code generation have been explored, e.g., in [65], and have more recently been used in the *FlexCC* compiler [66]. These approaches combine a progressive set of refinement phases to produce machine code. At *each phase* of compilation, a *set of rules* is provided in a well-structured programming environment which guides each transformation.

The critical phase of the process is code selection, where the compiler developer defines a *virtual machine* which resembles as closely as possible the instruction-set of the real machine, but is sequential in operation. This virtual machine does not support any instruction-level parallelism. The issue of parallelism is deferred to the code compaction phase. Using the definition of the available register sets and addressing modes of the architecture, the developer specifies a set of rules which map operation patterns onto instructions of the virtual machine (Fig. 10). Although there is no fundamental restriction, practical implementations assume *tree* structured patterns.

To produce the rule base, the developer has at his disposal a set of primitives to manipulate the standard set of tree patterns onto the virtual machine instructions, the available register sets, and the addressing modes.

Operands of operation trees are allocated to register sets based on matchings to the *C* data types (char, int, ptr, float, long, etc.) which are declared in the specification.

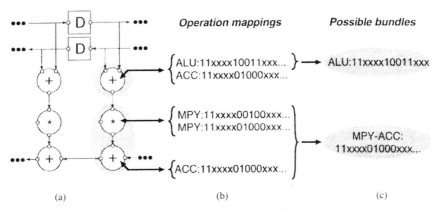

Fig. 9. Code selection using a bundling approach: (a) CDFG, to be mapped on the *ISG* of Fig. 7, (b) initial mappings of CDFG on *ISG* vertices, and (c) construction of bundles.

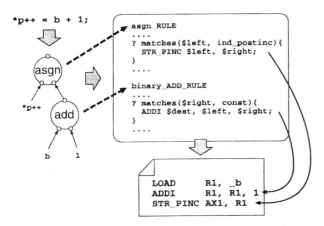

Fig. 10. Virtual code selection.

Optionally this allocation may be constrained to specific registers or register sets of the virtual machine instructions within the rules for selection. This flexibility is important for the support of the specialization of register functions in embedded processors. Register assignment within each register set is performed independently of the code selection process.

After mapping operation patterns onto the virtual machine, user-supplied transformation rules are used to optimize the description and generate instructions for the actual processor.

While rule-driven compilation provides a fast way to compiler generation, the quality of the compiler is directly dependent on the skills of the user to write adequate transformation rules. Furthermore, as illustrated in [66], to generate high quality code the user may have to rewrite the source code program to a level close to the target instruction set. For example, pointer referencing may have to be used for array variables, and the register allocation may have to be predetermined partly by the user.

D. Register Allocation

In the register allocation phase, the compiler assigns intermediate computation values to storage locations in the processor. In Section IV-C several techniques have already been discussed that essentially perform *code selection*, but are able to carry out local register allocation decisions on the fly. In this section, techniques will be reviewed that essentially perform *global register allocation*, as a separate code generation phase. However, it will be shown that several of these techniques are also able to perform remaining code selection decisions on the fly. This illustrates that the exact partitioning of the code generation process in different phases is nontrivial, and has to be decided by compiler developers based on the architectural context.

1) Graph Coloring: A standard formulation of the register allocation problem, on which several practical implementations are based, is in terms of *graph coloring* on an interference graph [67]. To explain the basic graph coloring formalism, we make the following initial assumptions:

1) the processor has a *homogeneous* register structure;
2) the register set's capacity (i.e., number of registers) is *restricted* to a predefined value, say N;
3) *code selection* has been accomplished in a preceding phase;
4) an *execution ordering* of the different instructions has been determined (e.g., in the code selection phase).

The execution order determines a *live range* for every intermediate computation value. Based on these live ranges, an interference graph is constructed. This is an undirected graph of which the vertices correspond to live ranges of values, and edges connect the vertices of interfering (i.e., overlapping) live ranges. Register allocation then is equivalent to finding an acceptable vertex coloring of the interference graph, using at most N colors. Heuristic graph coloring algorithms are used.

Fig. 11 shows the interference graph constructed for a set of values with given live ranges. In this example the vertices of the interference graph can be colored using at most three colors, each resulting in a different register. If the interference graph cannot be colored with N colors, the register capacity is exceeded. In this case, a standard solution is to temporarily *spill values to memory*. Alternatively, values that serve as an operand of multiple operations, can be recomputed prior to every use. This transformation is called *rematerialization*. Chaitin proposed a number of heuristics for spilling and rematerialization,

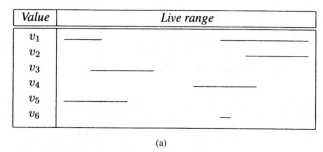
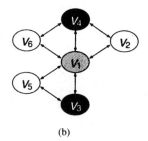

Fig. 11. Register allocation based on graph coloring: (a) live ranges displayed on a time axis and (b) interference graph.

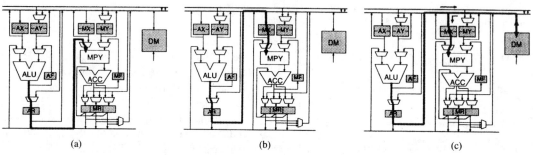

Fig. 12. Three alternative register allocations for the multiplication operand in the symmetrical FIR filter. The route followed is indicated in bold: (a) storage in AR, (b) storage in AR followed by MX, and (c) spilling to data memory DM. The last two alternatives require the insertion of extra register transfers.

in which the graph coloring procedure is called iteratively [67]. Further improvements of these principles have been described [68]–[70].

In practice, several of the assumptions made above may not be satisfied. First of all, most practical processors have a *heterogeneous* register structure. Extensions of the technique have been proposed, to take register classes into account during graph coloring [68], [70]. Furthermore, the graph coloring approach assumes that the live range of each value is known *beforehand*. Recent papers investigate the interaction between register allocation and scheduling [71], [72].

2) Data Routing: The above mentioned extension of graph coloring toward heterogeneous register structures has been applied to general-purpose processors, which typically have *a few* register classes (e.g., floating-point registers, fixed-point registers, and address registers). DSP and ASIP architectures often have a strongly heterogeneous register structure with *many* special-purpose registers.

In this context, more specialized register allocation techniques have been developed, often referred to as *data routing* techniques. To transfer data between functional units via intermediate registers, specific routes may have to be followed. The selection of the most appropriate route is nontrivial. In some cases indirect routes may have to be followed, requiring the insertion of extra register-transfer operations. Therefore an efficient mechanism for phase coupling between *register allocation* and *scheduling* becomes essential [73].

As an illustration, Fig. 12 shows a number of alternative solutions for the multiplication operand of the symmetrical FIR filter application, implemented on the ADSP-21xx processor (see Fig. 8).

Several techniques have been presented for data routing in compilers for embedded processors. A first approach is to determine the required data routes *during the execution of the scheduling algorithm*. This approach was first applied in the *Bulldog* compiler for VLIW machines [18], and subsequently adapted in compilers for embedded processors like the *RL compiler* [48] and CBC [74]. In order to prevent a combinational explosion of the problem, these methods only incorporate local, greedy search techniques to determine data routes. The approach typically lacks the power to identify good candidate values for *spilling* to memory.

A global data routing technique has been proposed in the *Chess* compiler [75]. This method supports many different schemes to route values between functional units. It starts from an unordered description, but may introduce a partial ordering of operations to reduce the number of overlapping live ranges. The algorithm is based on branch-and-bound searches to insert new data moves, to introduce partial orderings, and to select candidate values for spilling. Phase coupling with scheduling is supported, by the use of probabilistic scheduling estimators during the register allocation process.

E. Memory Allocation and Address Generation

A problem related to register allocation is the allocation of data memory locations for (scalar) data values in the intermediate representation. This is important, e.g., when memory spills have been introduced in the register allocation phase, or for passing argument values in the case of function calls. Often these values will be stored in a stack frame in data memory. The memory assignment for array data values, e.g., [97], is beyond the scope of this paper.

In [76], an approach was described for memory allocation, using a graph coloring technique comparable to the register allocation method described previously.

An important issue is the addressing of values in a stack frame in memory. Typically a pointer is maintained to the stack frame. In conventional architectures, updating the pointer for the next access may require several instructions. However, as discussed in Section II, DSP processors and ASIP's typically have specialized address generation units which support address modifications in parallel with normal arithmetic operations. Often this is implemented by means of *postmodification*, i.e., the next address can be calculated by adding a modifier value to the current address while the current memory access is taking place. In this way the address pointer can updated without an instruction cycle penalty. In some cases the modifier value is restricted to $+1$ or -1.

When pointer modification is supported, it is advantageous to allocate memory locations in such a way that consecutively ordered memory accesses use adjacent memory locations—or locations that are close enough to each other to permit the use of pointer modification. This optimization, which is typical for DSP processors, was first described by Bartley [77] in the context of the TMS320C2X processor which supports post-increment and post-decrement instructions. In Bartley's formalism, an undirected graph is used with vertices corresponding to data values and edges reflecting the preferences for using neighboring storage locations for value pairs. A solution with a maximal number of post-increments and -decrements is obtained by finding a Hamiltonian path in the graph. Since this is an NP-complete problem, heuristic algorithms are proposed. Bartley's approach has been refined by other authors [78], [79].

F. Scheduling

As already explained in the previous sections, compilers for CISC processors typically integrate code selection, local register allocation and instruction ordering in a single phase. Due to the lack of instruction level parallelism, no additional scheduling (or code compaction) phase is required.

The scheduling task is essential however for architectures that exhibit *pipeline hazards* or *instruction-level parallelism*. The former is the case in many RISC architectures. In VLIW and superscalar architectures, both features are found. Therefore the scheduling task has gained importance in software compilation, with the introduction of these architectural paradigms.

DSP processors and ASIP's can have a moderate to high degree of instruction-level parallelism. For example, these processors typically allow several data moves in parallel with arithmetic instructions (see the example of Fig. 2). Even when the parallelism is restricted, scheduling is a crucial task for these targets, because of the requirement of *high code quality*, which implies that the scarce architectural resources should be used as efficiently as possible, including the possibilities for data pipelining. This is especially true for deeply nested blocks in the algorithmic specification.

1) Local Versus Global Scheduling: A *local scheduler* is a scheduler that operates at the level of basic blocks (i.e., linear sequences of code without branching) in the intermediate representation. A well-known local scheduling technique is *list scheduling* [80]. More recently, in the context of embedded processors, integer-programming based scheduling formalisms have been described [81]–[83].

When the architecture has only a restricted amount of instruction-level parallelism, a local scheduling approach may already produce efficient results. Note however that this assumes that the scheduler has access to a detailed conflict model for partial instructions, describing precisely all structural and instruction encoding conflicts.

However, in the case of more parallel architectures, including most DSP's and ASIP's, there may be a mismatch between the *architectural* parallelism offered by the processor and the *algorithmic* parallelism within individual basic blocks. To use the processor's resources effectively, a *global scheduling* approach is required, whereby partial instructions can be moved across basic block boundaries. These moves are also termed *code motions*. Code motions may only be applied when they do not change the semantics of the overall program.

Fig. 13 illustrates several important types of code motions, in the presence of *conditional branches* [84]. A *useful* code motion moves instructions across a complete conditional branch. *Speculative execution* implies that a conditional instruction will be executed unconditionally. Special care is required to assure that the result has no effect when the branch in which the instruction resided originally is not taken. *Copy up* and *copy down* motions result in code duplication into conditional blocks. *Code hoisting* means that identical instructions in mutually exclusive conditional branches are merged and executed unconditionally.

Another important class of code motions relates to *iterators* in the program, as illustrated in Fig. 14. *Loop unrolling* is a standard transformation whereby consecutive iterations of a loop are scheduled as a large basic block. *Software pipelining* is a transformation that restructures the loop, by moving operations from one loop iteration to another. Both transformations result an a larger amount of parallelism in the eventual loop body. Due to the frequent occurrence of iterators in signal processing applications, these transformations are of crucial importance in compilers for DSP's and ASIP's.

2) Global Scheduling Techniques for Conditional Branches: Global scheduling has been given a lot of attention in the context of VLIW architectures. Several of these techniques can be reused in the case of embedded processors like DSP's and ASIP's.

Trace scheduling is a global scheduling technique developed for VLIW's [85]. Based on execution probabilities of conditional branches, traces (i.e., linear sequences of

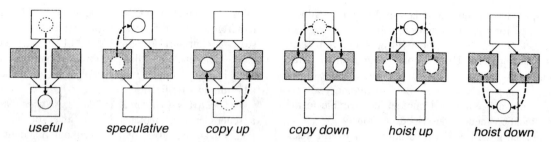

Fig. 13. Different types of code motions in a global scheduler. White and gray boxes represent unconditional and conditional basic blocks, respectively. Dotted and solid circles represent partial instruction before and after code motion, respectively. Dotted arrows symbolize code motion.

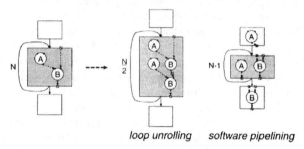

Fig. 14. Loop transformations in a global scheduler. Gray boxes represent a loop body, the number of iterations of which is indicated to its left. White boxes represent the loop's pre- and post-amble.

basic blocks) are identified. Each trace is scheduled as if it were a big basic block. Hence, operations in a trace can move beyond the original basic block boundaries. When this happens, a bookkeeping mechanism inserts the necessary compensation code in the other (less critical) traces to guarantee that semantical correctness is preserved. Improvements of the bookkeeping mechanism have been presented in [86].

A related technique is *superblock scheduling* [87]. A superblock is a linear sequence of basic blocks that has a single entry point only. A trace structure can be transformed into a superblock structure by a process called tail duplication. Superblocks are then scheduled in a way similar to traces. Compared to trace scheduling, the advantage is that the bookkeeping mechanism can be simplified considerably.

Percolation based scheduling is based on a complete set of semantics preserving transformations to move instructions between basic blocks [88]. Instruction are moved repeatedly in the upward direction, between *adjacent* basic blocks. A drawback of this strategy is that longer moves (e.g., the useful code motion of Fig. 13) are only possible if the incremental moves between adjacent blocks that compose the long move are all beneficial.

In [89] a global code motion technique is proposed, in which only those types of motions are supported that do not require any code duplication. In [90] a technique is proposed based on the concept of *region scheduling*. In [84] a global code motion tool is presented for DSP and ASIP architectures, that makes use of fast probabilistic estimators for schedule length and register occupation, in order to trade different possible code motions. The actual scheduling is done afterwards, in a separate phase. This has the advantage that the code motion tool can also be invoked at earlier stages in code generation, e.g., before register allocation.

3) Software Pipelining: Techniques for software pipelining can be divided in two categories: those that iteratively call a local scheduler to evaluate the effect of certain moves, and those that incorporate software pipelining in a single global scheduling algorithm.

Modulo scheduling, presented in [91], first converts conditional branches in the loop into straight line code and subsequently applies a local scheduling algorithm that pipelines the loop. *Loop folding* [92] is an iterative approach to software pipelining. In every step of the algorithm, a local list schedule is computed for the loop body. Based on this schedule, partial instructions are selected and moved between loop iterations. A similar strategy has been added to the global code motion tool of [84] (mentioned previously). As a result, code motions across conditional branch boundaries and software pipelining can be incorporated in the same algorithm.

Examples of global scheduling algorithms that perform software pipelining include *enhanced pipeline scheduling* [93] and *GURPR* [94]. The latter of these methods is based on partial loop unrolling, after which a parallel schedule is composed for the unrolled loop, followed by a rerolling step.

Finally, note that some VLIW architectures have special hardware support to facilitate the implementation of software pipelining [95], [96]. Typically special register sets are dedicated to data communication between loop iterations.

V. Conclusion

As motivated in Section I and in the companion paper on application and architectural trends [1], embedded processor cores represent a key component in contemporary and future systems for telecommunication and multimedia. Core processor technology has created a new role for general-purpose DSP's. In addition, there is a clear and important use of ASIP's. For products manufactured in large volumes, ASIP's are clearly more cost efficient, while power dissipation can be reduced significantly. These advantages are obtained without giving up the flexibility of a programmable solution.

The lack of suitable design technologies to support the phases of processor development and of application programming however remains a significant obstacle for system design teams. One of the goals of this paper was to motivate an increased research effort in the area of CAD for embedded system design.

In this paper we have focused primarily on the issue of software compilation technologies for embedded processors. Our starting point was the observation that many commercially available C compilers, especially for fixed-point DSP's, are unable to take full advantage of the architectural features of the processor. In the case of ASIP's, compiler support is nonexisting due to the lack of retargeting capabilities of the existing tools.

Many of these compilers are employing traditional code generation techniques, developed in the 1970's and 1980's in the software compiler community. These techniques were primarily developed for general-purpose microprocessors, which have highly regular architectures with homogeneous register structures, without many of the architectural peculiarities that are typical of fixed-point DSP's.

In the past five years, however, new research efforts emerged in the area of software compilation, focusing on embedded DSP's and ASIP's. Many of these research teams are operating on the frontier of software compilation and high-level VLSI synthesis. The synergy between both disciplines has already resulted in a number of new techniques for modeling of (irregular) instruction-set architectures and for higher quality code generation. Besides code quality, the issue of architectural retargetability is gaining a lot of attention. Retargetability is an essential feature of a software compilation environment in the context of embedded processors, due to the increasingly shorter lifetime of a processor and due to the requirement to use ASIP's.

In this paper we have outlined the main architectural features of contemporary DSP's and ASIP's, that are relevant from a software compilation point of view. A classification of architectures has been presented, based on a number of elementary characteristics. Proper understanding of processor architectures is a prerequisite for successful compiler development. In addition, a survey has been presented of existing software compilation techniques that are considered relevant in the context of DSP's and ASIP's for telecom, multimedia, and consumer applications. This survey also covered recent research in retargetable software compilation for embedded processors.

In addition to retargetable software compilation, there are several other important design technology issues, that have not been discussed in this paper. The authors believe the following will become increasingly important in the future.

- System level algorithmic optimizations. Many specifications of systems are produced without a precise knowledge of the implications on hardware and software cost. Important savings are possible by carrying out system level optimizations, such as control-flow transformations to optimize the memory and power cost of data memories.
- System partitioning and interface synthesis. Whereas the problems of hardware synthesis and software compilation are reasonably well understood, the design of the glue between these components is still done manually, and therefore error-prone.
- Synthesis of real-time kernels. A kernel takes care of run-time scheduling of tasks, taking into account the interaction with the system's environment. In some cases, general-purpose operating systems are used. However, these solutions are expensive in terms of execution speed and code size. Recent research is therefore focusing on the automatic synthesis of lightweight, application-specific kernels that obey user-specified timing constraints.

REFERENCES

[1] P. G. Paulin, C. Liem, M. Cornero, F. Naçabal, and G. Goossens, "Embedded software in real-time signal processing systems: Application and architecture trends," *Proc. IEEE*, this issue, pp. 419–435.

[2] J. Morse and S. Hargrave, "The increasing importance of software," *Electronic Design*, vol. 44, no. 1, Jan. 1996.

[3] P. G. Paulin et al., "Trends in embedded systems technology: An industrial perspective," in *Hardware/Software Co-Design*, G. De Micheli and M. Sami, Eds. Boston: Kluwer, 1996.

[4] D. Bursky, "Tuned RISC devices deliver top performance," *Electronic Design*, pp. 77–100, Mar. 18, 1996.

[5] A. van Someren and C. Atack, *The ARM RISC Chip, a Programmer's Guide*. Reading, MA: Addison-Wesley, 1994.

[6] S. Berger, "An application specific DSP for personal communications applications," in *Proc. DSPx Expos. and Symp.*, June 1994.

[7] A. Bindra, "Two 'Lode' up on TCSI's new DSP core," *EE Times*, Jan. 16, 1995.

[8] R. A. M. Beltman et al., "EPICS10: Development platform for next generation EPICS DSP products," in *Proc. 6th Int. Conf. on Signal Proc. Applic. and Technol.*, Oct. 1995.

[9] *D950-Core Specification*, doc. no. 2509, SGS-Thomson Microelectron., Grenoble, France, Jan. 1995.

[10] V. Živojnović et al., "DSPstone: A DSP-oriented benchmarking methodology," in *Proc. Int. Conf. on Signal Proc. Applic. and Technol.*, Oct. 1994.

[11] P. Marwedel and G. Goossens, *Code Generation for Embedded Processors*. Boston: Kluwer, 1995.

[12] G. Goossens et al., "Programmable chips in consumer electronics and telecommunications: Architectures and design technology," in *Hardware/Software Co-Design*, G. De Micheli and M. Sami, Eds. Boston: Kluwer, 1996.

[13] E. A. Lee, "Programmable DSP architectures: Part I & Part II," *IEEE ASSP Mag.*, Dec. 1988 and Jan. 1989.

[14] "ADSP-2100 user's manual," Norwood: Analog devices, 1989.

[15] *TMS320C54x, TMS320LC54x, TMS320VC54x Fixed-Point Digital Signal Processors*, Houston: Texas Instrum., 1996.

[16] P. M. Kogge, *The Architecture of Pipelined Computers*. New York: McGraw-Hill, 1981.

[17] J. L. Hennessy and D. A. Patterson, *Computer Architecture: A Quantitative Approach*. San Mateo, CA: Morgan Kaufmann, 1990.

[18] J. R. Ellis, *Bulldog: A Compiler for VLIW Architectures*. Cambridge, MA: MIT Press, 1986.

[19] L. Bergher et al., "MPEG audio decoder for consumer applications," in *Proc. IEEE Custom Integr. Circ. Conf.*, May 1995.

[20] G. Essink, "Architecture and programming of a VLIW style programmable video signal processor," in *Proc. 24th ACM/IEEE Int. Symp. on Microarchitecture*, Nov. 1991.

[21] P. Clarke and R. Wilson, "Philips preps VLIW DSP for multimedia," *EE Times*, p. 1, Nov. 14, 1994.

[22] D. Lanneer et al., "Chess: Retargetable code generation for embedded DSP processors," in *Code Generation for Embedded Processors*, P. Marwedel and G. Goossens, Eds. Boston: Kluwer, 1995.

[23] R. M. Stallman, *Using and Porting GNU CC*, Free Software Foundation, June 1993.

[24] J. Van Praet et al., "Modeling hardware-specific data-types for simulation and compilation in HW/SW co-design," in *Proc. 6th Workshop on Synth. and Syst. Integr. of Mixed Technol.*, Nov. 1996.

[25] R. Cytron et al., "Efficiently computing static single assignment form and the control dependence graph," *ACM Trans. Prog. Lang. and Syst.*, vol. 13, no. 4, pp. 451–490, Oct. 1991.

[26] M. C. McFarland, A. C. Parker, and R. Camposano, "The high level synthesis of digital systems," in *Proc. IEEE*, vol. 78, pp. 301–318. Feb. 1990.

[27] J. T. J. van Eijndhoven and L. Stok, "A data flow graph exchange standard," in *Proc. Europe. Design Autom. Conf.*, Mar. 1992, pp. 193–199.

[28] A. V. Aho et al., *Compilers—Principles, Techniques, and Tools.* Reading, MA: Addison-Wesley, 1986.

[29] D. Landskov et al., "Local microcode compaction techniques," *ACM Comp. Surveys*, vol. 12, no. 3, pp. 261–294, Sept. 1980.

[30] M. Johnson, *Superscalar Microprocessor Design.* Englewood Cliffs, NJ: Prentice-Hall, 1991.

[31] S. R. Vegdahl, "Phase coupling and constant generation in an optimizing microcode compiler," in *Proc. 15th Micro*, 1982, pp. 125–133.

[32] S. Bashford et al., *The Mimola Language*, vers. 4.1, Techn. Rep., Univ. Dortmund, Sept. 1994.

[33] C. G. Bell and A. Newell, *Computer Structures: Readings and Examples.* New York: McGraw-Hill, 1991.

[34] M. R. Barbacci, "Instruction set processor specifications (ISPS): The notation and its applications," *IEEE Trans. Computer*, Jan. 1981.

[35] A. Fauth et al., "Describing instruction set processors using nML," in *Proc. Europe. Design and Test Conf.*, Mar. 1995.

[36] A. Fauth, "Beyond tool-specific machine descriptions," in *Code Generation for Embedded Processors*, P. Marwedel and G. Goossens, Eds. Boston: Kluwer, 1995.

[37] A. V. Aho and S. C. Johnson, "Optimal code generation for expression trees," *J. ACM*, vol.23, no.3, pp.488–501, July 1976.

[38] A. V. Aho et al., "Code generation using tree matching and dynamic programming," *ACM Trans. Prog. Lang. and Syst.*, vol. 11, no. 4, pp. 491–516, Oct. 1989.

[39] C. W. Fraser et al., "Burg—Fast optimal instruction selection and tree parsing," *ACM Sigplan Notices*, vol. 27, no. 4, pp. 68–76, Apr. 1992.

[40] ——, "Engineering a simple, efficient code-generator generator," *ACM Lett. on Prog. Lang. and Syst.*, vol. 1, no. 3, pp. 213–226, Sept. 1993.

[41] R. S. Glanville and S. L. Graham, "A new method for compiler code generation," in *Proc. 5th ACM Ann. Symp. on Principles of Prog. Lang.*, 1978.

[42] R. Leupers and P. Marwedel, "Instruction selection for embedded DSP's with complex instructions," in *Proc. Europe. Design Autom. Conf.*, Sept. 1996.

[43] G. Araujo and S. Malik, "Optimal code generation for embedded memory nonhomogeneous register architectures," in *Proc. 8th Int. Symp. on Syst. Synthesis*, Sept. 1995.

[44] R. Leupers and P. Marwedel, "A BDD-based frontend for retargetable compilers," in *Proc. Europe. Design and Test Conf.*, Mar. 1996, pp. 239–243.

[45] P. G. Paulin et al., "Flexware: A flexible firmware development environment for embedded systems," in *Code Generation for Embedded Processors*, P. Marwedel and G. Goossens, Eds. Boston: Kluwer, pp. 67–84, 1995.

[46] B. Wess, "Code generation based on trellis diagrams," in *Code Generation for Embedded Processors*, P. Marwedel and G. Goossens, Eds. Boston: Kluwer, 1995, pp. 188–202.

[47] L. Nowak and P. Marwedel, "Verification of hardware descriptions by retargetable code generation," in *Proc. 26th ACM/IEEE Design Autom. Conf.*, June 1989, pp. 441–447.

[48] K. Rimey and P. N. Hilfinger, "A compiler for application-specific signal processors," in *VLSI Signal Processing*, vol. 3. New York: IEEE Press, 1988, pp. 341–351.

[49] J. Van Praet et al., "A graph based processor model for retargetable code generation," in *Proc. Europe. Design and Test Conf.*, Mar. 1996.

[50] J. Bruno and R. Sethi, "Code generation for a one-register machine," *J. ACM*, vol. 23, no. 3, pp. 502–510, July 1976.

[51] A. V. Aho et al., "Code generation for expressions with common subexpressions," *J. ACM*, vol. 24, no. 1, pp. 146–160, Jan. 1977.

[52] R. Sethi and J. D. Ullman, "The generation of optimal code for arithmetic expressions," *J. ACM*, vol. 17, no. 4, pp. 715–728, Oct. 1970.

[53] H. Emmelmann et al., "Beg—A generator for efficient back ends," in *Proc. ACM SIGPLAN Conf. Prog. Lang. Design and Implem.*, 1989, pp. 227–237.

[54] E. Pelegri–Llopart, "Optimal code generation for expression trees: An application of BURS theory," in *Proc. 15th ACM Symp. Principles of Prog. Lang.*, 1988, pp. 294–308.

[55] T. A. Proebsting, "Simple and efficient BURS table generation," in *Proc. SIGPLAN Conf. Prog. Lang. Design and Implem.*, 1992.

[56] R. Wilhelm and D. Maurer, *Compiler Design.* Reading, MA: Addison-Wesley, 1995.

[57] C. Liem et al., "Instruction-set matching and selection for DSP and ASIP code generation," in *Proc. Europe. Design and Test Conf.*, Feb. 1994.

[58] S. L. Graham et al., "An experiment in table driven code generation," in *Proc. SIGPLAN Symp. Compiler Construction*, 1982, pp. 32–43.

[59] M. Ganapathi and C. N. Fisher, "Affix grammar driven code generation," *ACM Tr. Prog. Lang. and Syst.*, vol. 7, no. 4, pp. 347–364, Apr. 1984.

[60] M. Mahmood et al., "A formal language model of microcode synthesis," in *Formal VLSI Specification and Synthesis*, L. Claesen, Ed. Amsterdam: North Holland, 1990, pp. 23–41.

[61] S. Liao, "Code generation and optimization for embedded digital signal processors," Ph.D. dissertation, MIT, June 1996.

[62] J. W. Davidson and C. W. Fraser, "Code selection through object code optimization," *ACM Trans. Prog. Lang. and Syst.*, Oct. 1984.

[63] ——, "The design and application of a retargetable peephole optimizer," *ACM Trans. Prog. Lang. and Syst.*, vol. 2, no. 2, pp. 191–202, Apr. 1980.

[64] P. Marwedel, "Tree-based mapping of algorithms to predefined structures," in *Proc. IEEE Int. Conf. Computer-Aided Design*, Nov. 1993, pp. 586–593.

[65] R. P. Gurd, "Experience developing microcode using a high-level language," in *Proc. 16th Annu. Microprog. Workshop*, Oct. 1983.

[66] C. Liem et al., "Industrial experience using rule-driven retargetable code generation for multimedia applications," in *Proc. IEEE/ACM Int. Symp. on Syst. Synthesis*, Sept. 1995.

[67] G. J. Chaitin, "Register allocation and spilling via graph coloring," *ACM SIGPLAN Notices*, vol.17, no.6, pp.98–105, June 1982.

[68] F. C. Chow and J. L. Hennessy, "The priority-based coloring approach to register allocation," *ACM Trans. Prog. Lang. and Syst.*, Oct. 1990.

[69] D. Callahan and B. Koblenz, "Register allocation via hierarchical graph coloring," *ACM SIGPLAN Notices*, June 1991.

[70] P. Briggs, "Register allocation via graph coloring," Ph.D. dissertation, Rice Univ., Houston, Apr. 1992.

[71] S. Pinter, "Register allocation with instruction scheduling: A new approach," *SIGPLAN Notices*, June 1993.

[72] W. Ambrosch et al., "Dependence conscious global register allocation," in *Programming Language and System Architecture*, J. Gutknecht, Ed. Berlin: Springer, 1994.

[73] S. Freudenberg and J. Ruttenberg, "Phase-ordering of register allocation and instruction scheduling," in *Code Generation—Concepts, Tools, Techniques*, R. Giegerich and S. Graham, Eds. Berlin: Springer, 1991.

[74] R. Hartmann, "Combined scheduling and data routing for programmable ASIC systems," in *Proc. Europe. Conf. on Design Autom.*, Mar. 1992, pp. 486–490.

[75] D. Lanneer et al., "Data routing: a paradigm for efficient data-path synthesis and code generation," in *Proc. 7th ACM/IEEE Int. Symp. on High-Level Synth.*, May 1994, pp. 17–22.

[76] A. Sudarsanam and S. Malik, "Memory bank and register allocation in software synthesis for ASIP's," in *Proc. IEEE Int. Conf. Computer-Aided Design*, Nov. 1995, pp. 388–392.

[77] D. H. Bartley, "Optimizing stack frame accesses for processors with restricted addressing modes," *Software-Practice and Experience*, vol. 22, no. 2, pp. 101–110, Feb. 1992.

[78] S. Liao et al., "Storage assignment to decrease code size," *ACM SIGPLAN Notices*, vol. 30, no. 7, pp. 186–195, June 1995.

[79] R. Leupers and P. Marwedel, "Algorithms for address assignment in DSP code generation," in *Proc. IEEE Int. Conf. Computer Aided Design*, Nov. 1996.

[80] S. Davidson et al., "Some experiments in local microcode compaction for horizontal machines," *IEEE Trans. Computers*, vol. C-30, no. 7, pp. 460–477, July 1981.

[81] T. Wilson et al., "An integrated approach to retargetable code generation," in *Proc. 7th ACM/IEEE Int. Symp. High-Level Synthesis*, May 1994, pp. 70–75.

[82] R. Leupers and P. Marwedel, "Time-constrained code compaction for DSP's," in *Proc. 8th Int. Symp. Syst. Synthesis*, Sept. 1995, pp. 239–243.

[83] F. Depuydt, "Register optimization and scheduling for real-time digital signal processing architectures," Ph.D. dissertation, Kath. Univ. Leuven, Belgium, Nov. 1993.

[84] A. Kifli, "Global scheduling in high-level synthesis and code generation for embedded processors," Ph.D. dissertation, Kath. Univ. Leuven, Belgium, Nov. 1996.

[85] J. A. Fisher, "Trace scheduling: A technique for global microcode compaction," *IEEE Trans. Computers*, vol. C-30, pp. 478–490, July 1981.

[86] T. Gross and M. Ward, "The suppression of compensation code," *ACM Trans. Prog. Lang. and Systems*, Oct. 1991.

[87] W. M. Hwu et al., "The superblock: An effective technique for VLIW and superscalar compilation," *J. Supercomputing*, 1993.

[88] A. Nicolau, "Percolation scheduling: A parallel compilation technique," Tech. Rep. TR85-678, Cornell Univ., May 1985.

[89] D. Bernstein et al., "Code duplication: An assist for global instruction scheduling," in *Proc. ACM Micro-24*, 1991, pp. 103–113.

[90] V. H. Allan et al., "Enhanced region scheduling on a program dependence graph," in *Proc. ACM Micro-25*, 1992, pp. 72–80.

[91] M. Lam, "Software pipelining: An effective scheduling technique for VLIW machines," in *Proc. ACM SIGPLAN Conf. Prog. Lang. Design and Implement.*, 1988, pp. 318–328.

[92] G. Goossens et al., "Loop optimization in register-transfer scheduling for DSP-systems," in *Proc. 26th IEEE/ACM Design Autom. Conf.*, June 1989.

[93] K. Ebcioglu and T. Nakatani, "A new compilation technique for parallelizing loops with unpredictable branches on a VLIW architecture," *2nd Workshop Lang. and Compil. for Paral. Comp.*, Aug. 1989, pp. 213–229.

[94] B. Su et al., "GURPR: A method for global software pipelining," in *Proc. ACM MICRO-20*, 1987.

[95] B. R. Rau et al., "Efficient code generation for horizontal architectures: Compiler techniques and architectural support," in *Proc. 9th Annu. Symp. Comp. Archit.*, Apr. 1982, pp. 131–139.

[96] B. Su et al., "A software pipelining based VLIW architecture and optimizing compiler," in *Proc. MICRO-23*, 1990, pp. 17–27.

[97] C. Liem et al., "Address calculation for retargetable compilation and exploration of instruction-set archetectures," in *Proc. 33rd ACM/IEEE Design Autom. Conf.*, June 1996.

Gert Goossens (Member, IEEE), for a photograph and biography, see this issue, pp. 435.

Johan Van Praet (Member, IEEE) received a degree in electrical engineering from the Katholieke Universiteit Leuven, Belgium, in 1990. Since 1991 he has been working toward the Ph.D. degree on retargetable software compilation technology at the same university.

In 1996, he co-founded Target Compiler Technologies, Leuven, Belgium, where he is responsible for product development. From 1991 to 1996 he was with IMEC as a Research Assistant. In 1990 he worked on the design of a chip architecture for a GSM mobile phone, in a joint project of the Interuniversity Micro-Electronics Centre (IMEC) and Alcatel Bell Telephone in Belgium.

Dirk Lanneer (Member, IEEE) received a degree in electrical engineering and the Ph.D. degree in applied sciences from the Katholieke Universiteit Leuven, Belgium, in 1986 and 1993, respectively.

In 1996, he co-founded Target Compiler Technologies, Leuven, Belgium, where he is responsible for research and development. From 1986 to 1996 was a Technical Staff Member at the Interuniversity Micro-Electronics Centre (IMEC), Leuven, Belgium, where he started as a Research Assistant of high-level synthesis projects, and co-initiated work on the "Chess" retargetable software compilation project.

Werner Geurts (Member, IEEE) received degrees in electrical engineering from the Industriële Hogeschool, Antwerp, Belgium, and from the Katholieke Universiteit Leuven, Belgium, in 1985 and 1988, respectively. He received the Ph.D. degree in electrical engineering from the Katholieke Universiteit Leuven in 1995.

In 1996, he co-founded Target Compiler Technologies, where he is responsible for product development. From 1989 to 1996 he was with the VLSI Design Methodologies Division of the Interuniversity Micro-Electronics Centre (IMEC), Leuven, Belgium, where he worked on high-level synthesis techniques for high throughput applications, and on retargetable software compilation for application-specific DSP cores.

Augusli Kifli received the B.Sc. degree in electrical engineering from the National Taiwan University, Taiwan, in 1987, and the M.Sc. and Ph.D. degrees in applied sciences from the Katholieke Universiteit Leuven, Belgium, in 1990 and 1996, respectively.

From 1993 to 1996 he was a member of Interuniversity Micro-Electronics Centre's (IMEC) retargetable software compilation group. From 1990 to 1993 was a Research Assistant at IMEC, initially working in the area of high-level synthesis.

Clifford Liem, for a photograph and biography, see this issue, pp. 435.

Pierre G. Paulin (Member, IEEE), for a photograph and biography, see this issue, pp. 434.

Generating Compact Code from Dataflow Specifications of Multirate Signal Processing Algorithms

Shuvra S. Bhattacharyya, *Member, IEEE*, Joseph T. Buck, Soonhoi Ha, *Member, IEEE*, and Edward A. Lee, *Fellow, IEEE*

Abstract— Synchronous dataflow (SDF) semantics are well-suited to representing and compiling multirate signal processing algorithms. A key to this match is the ability to cleanly express iteration without overspecifying the execution order of computations, thereby allowing efficient schedules to be constructed. Due to limited program memory, it is often desirable to translate the iteration in an SDF graph into groups of repetitive firing patterns so that loops can be constructed in the target code. This paper establishes fundamental topological relationships between iteration and looping in SDF graphs, and presents a scheduling framework that provably synthesizes the most compact looping structures for a large class of practical SDF graphs. By modularizing different components of the scheduling framework, and establishing their independence, we show how other scheduling objectives, such as minimizing data buffering requirements or increasing the number of data transfers that occur in registers, can be incorporated in a manner that does not conflict with the goal of code compactness.

I. INTRODUCTION

IN THE dataflow model of computation, pioneered by Dennis [6], a program is represented as a directed graph in which the nodes represent computations and the arcs specify the passage of data. Synchronous dataflow (SDF) [15] is a restricted form of dataflow in which the nodes, called *actors*, consume a fixed number of data items, called *tokens* or *samples*, per invocation and produce a fixed number of output samples per invocation. SDF and related models have been

Manuscript received May 25, 1993; revised December 1, 1994. This work was part of the Ptolemy project, supported by the Advanced Research Projects Agency and U. S. Air Force (RASSP program, Contract F33615-93-C-1317), Semiconductor Research Corporation (Project 94-DC-008), National Science Foundation (MIP-9201605), Office of Naval Technology (Naval Research Laboratories), State of California MICRO program, and the following companies: Bell Northern Research, Cadence, Dolby, Hitachi, Mentor Graphics, Mitsubishi, NEC, Pacific Bell, Philips, Rockwell, Sony, and Synopsys. This paper was recommended by Associate Editor D. Mlynski.

S. S. Bhattacharyya was with the Department of Electrical Engineering and Computer Sciences, University of California, Berkeley, CA 94720 USA. He is now with the Semiconductor Research Laboratory, Hitachi America, Ltd., San Jose, CA 95134 USA.

J. T. Buck was with the Department of Electrical Engineering and Computer Sciences, University of California, Berkeley, CA 94720 USA. He is now with Synopsys, Inc., Mountain View, CA 94043 USA.

S. Ha was with the Department of Electrical Engineering and Computer Sciences, University of California, Berkeley, CA 94720 USA. He is now with the Department of Computer Engineering, Seoul National University, Sinlim-Dong, Gwanak-Ku, Seoul 151-742 Korea.

E. A. Lee is with the Department of Electrical Engineering and Computer Sciences, University of California, Berkeley, CA 94720 USA.

IEEE Log Number 9409315.

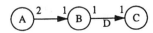

Fig. 1. A simple SDF graph.

studied extensively in the context of synthesizing assembly code for signal processing applications, for example [8]–[11], [17], [19]–[21].

Fig. 1 shows a simple SDF graph with three actors, labeled A, B and C. Each arc is annotated with the number of samples produced by its source and the number of samples consumed by its sink. Thus, actor A produces two samples on its output arc each time it is invoked and B consumes one sample from its input arc. The "D" on the arc directed from B to C designates a unit delay, which we implement as an initial token on the arc.

In SDF, *iteration* is induced whenever the number of samples produced on an arc (per invocation of the source actor) does not match the number of samples consumed (per sink invocation) [13]. For example, in Fig. 1, actor B must be invoked two times for every invocation of actor A. Multirate applications often involve a large amount of iteration and thus subroutine calls must be used extensively, code must be replicated, or loops must be organized in the target program. The use of subroutine calls to implement repetition may reduce throughput significantly however, particularly for graphs involving small granularity. On the other hand, we have found that code duplication can quickly exhaust on-chip program memory [12]. Thus, it may be essential that we arrange loops in the target code. In this paper we develop topological relationships between iteration and looping in SDF graphs.

We emphasize that in this paper, we view dataflow as a programming model, not as a form of computer architecture [2]. Several programming languages used for DSP, such as Lucid [25], SISAL [16], and Silage [10] are based on, or include dataflow semantics. The developments in this paper are applicable to this class of languages. Compilers for such languages can easily construct a representation of the input program as a hierarchy of dataflow graphs. It is important for a compiler to recognize SDF components of this hierarchy, since in DSP applications, usually a large fraction of the computation can be expressed with SDF semantics. For example, in [7] Dennis shows how to convert recursive stream functions in SISAL-2 into SDF graphs.

In [12] How showed that we can often greatly improve looping by clustering subgraphs that operate at the same repetition rate, and scheduling such subgraphs as a single unit. Fig. 1 shows how this technique can improve looping. A naive scheduler might schedule this SDF graph as CABCB, which offers no looping possibility within the schedule period. However, if we first group the subgraph $\{B, C\}$ into a hierarchical "supernode" Ω, a scheduler will generate the schedule $A\Omega\Omega$. To highlight the repetition in a schedule, we let the notation $(nX_1X_2\cdots X_m)$ designate n successive repetitions of the firing sequence $X_1X_2\cdots X_m$. We refer to a schedule expressed with this notation as a **looped schedule**. Using this notation, and substituting each occurrence of Ω with a subschedule for the corresponding subgraph, our clustering of the uniform-rate set $\{B, C\}$ leads to either $A(2BC)$ or $A(2CB)$, both of which expose the full potential for looping in the SDF graph of Fig. 1.

We explored the looping problem further in [5]. First, we generalized How's scheme to exploit looping opportunities that occur across sample-rate changes. Our approach involved constructing the subgraph hierarchy in a pairwise fashion by clustering exactly two nodes at each step. Our subgraph selection was based on frequency of occurrence—we selected the pair of adjacent nodes whose associated subgraph had the largest repetition count. The "repetition count" of a subgraph can be viewed as the number of times that a minimal schedule for the subgraph is repeated in a minimal schedule for the overall graph. We will define this concept precisely in the next section.

By not discriminating against sample-rate boundaries, our approach exposed looping more thoroughly than How's scheme. Furthermore, by selecting subgraphs based on repetition count, we reduced data memory requirements, an aspect that How's scheme did not address.

Clustering a subgraph must be done with care since certain groupings cause deadlock. Thus, for each candidate subgraph, we must first verify that its consolidation does not result in an unschedulable graph. One way to perform this check is to attempt to schedule the new SDF graph [14], but this approach is extremely time consuming if a large number of clustering candidates must be considered. In [5], we employed a computationally more efficient method in which we maintained the subgraph hierarchy on the acyclic precedence graph rather than the SDF graph. Thus we could verify whether or not a grouping introduced deadlock by checking whether or not it introduced a cycle in the precedence graph. Furthermore, we showed that this check can be performed quickly by applying a *reachability matrix*, which indicates for any two precedence graph nodes (invocations) P_1 and P_2, whether there is a precedence path from P_1 to P_2.

Two limitations surfaced in the approach of [5]. First, the storage cost of the reachability matrix proved prohibitive for multirate applications involving very large sample rate changes. Observe that this cost is quadratic in the number of distinct actor *invocations* (precedence graph nodes). For example, a rasterization actor that decomposes an image into component pixels may involve a sample-rate change on the order of 250 000 to 1. If the rasterization output is connected to a homogenous block (for example, a gamma level correction), this block alone will produce on the order of $(250\,000)^2 = 6.25 \times 10^{10}$ entries in the reachability matrix! Thus very large rate changes preclude straightforward application of the reachability matrix; this is unfortunate because looping is most important precisely for such cases. The second limitation in [5] is its failure to process cyclic paths in the graph optimally. Since cyclic paths limit looping, first priority should be given to preserving the full amount of looping available within the strongly connected components [1] of the graph. As Fig. 2 illustrates, clustering subgraphs based on repetition count alone does not fully carry out this goal.

In this paper, we develop a class of uniprocessor scheduling algorithms that extract the most compact looping structure from the cyclic paths in the SDF graph. This scheduling *framework* is based on a topological quality that we call "tight interdependence." We show that for SDF graphs that contain no tightly interdependent subgraphs, our framework always synthesizes the most compact looping structures. Interestingly and fortunately, a large majority of practical SDF graphs seem to fall into this category. Furthermore, for this class of graphs, our technique does not require use of the reachability matrix, the precedence graph, or any other unreasonably large data structure. For graphs that contain tightly interdependent subgraphs, we show that our scheduling framework naturally isolates the minimal subgraphs that require special care. Only when analyzing these "tightly interdependent components," do we need to apply reachability matrix-based analysis, or some other explicit deadlock-detection scheme.

An important aspect of our scheduling framework is its flexibility. By modularizing the framework into "sub-algorithms," we allow other scheduling objectives to be integrated in a manner that does not conflict with code compactness objectives. Also, we show how decisions that a scheduler makes about grouping, or "clustering," computations together can be formally evaluated in terms of their effects on program compactness. As an example, we demonstrate a very efficient clustering technique for increasing the amount of buffering that is done in machine registers, as opposed to memory, and we prove that this clustering strategy preserves codes space compactness for a large class of SDF graphs.

II. BACKGROUND

An SDF program is normally translated into a loop, where each iteration of the loop executes one cycle of a periodic schedule for the graph. In this section we summarize important properties of such periodic schedules. Most of the terminology introduced in this and subsequent sections is summarized in the glossary at the end of the paper.

For an SDF graph G, we denote the set of nodes in G by $N(G)$ and the set of arcs in G by $A(G)$. For an SDF arc α, we let $source(\alpha)$ and $sink(\alpha)$ denote the nodes at the source and the sink of α; we let $p(\alpha)$ denote the number of samples produced by $source(\alpha)$, $c(\alpha)$ denote the number of samples consumed by $sink(\alpha)$, and we denote the delay on α by $delay(\alpha)$. We define a **subgraph** of G to be that SDF graph formed by any $Z \subseteq N(G)$ together with the set of arcs

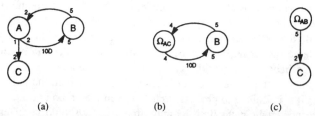

Fig. 2. This example illustrates how clustering based on repetition count alone can conceal looping opportunities within cyclic paths. Part (a) depicts a multirate SDF graph. Two pairwise clusterings lead to graphs that have schedules—{A, B}, having repetition count 2, and {A, C}, having repetition count 5 (clustering B and C results in deadlock). Clustering the subgraph with the highest repetition count yields the hierarchical topology in (b), for which the most compact schedule is $(2B)(2\Omega_{AC})B\Omega_{AC}B(2\Omega_{AC}) \Rightarrow (2B)(2(2A)C)B(2A)CB(2(2A)C)$. Clustering the subgraph {A, B} of lower repetition count, as depicted in part (c), yields the more compact schedule $(2\Omega_{AB})(5C) \Rightarrow (2(2B)(5A))(5C)$.

$\{\alpha \in A(G) | source(\alpha), sink(\alpha) \in Z\}$. We denote the subgraph associated with the subset of nodes Z by $subgraph(Z, G)$; if G is understood, we may simply write $subgraph(Z)$. If N_1 and N_2 are two nodes in an SDF graph, we say that N_1 is a *successor* of N_2 if there is an arc directed from N_2 to N_1; we say that N_1 is a *predecessor* of N_2 if N_2 is a successor of N_1; and we say that N_1 and N_2 are *adjacent* if N_1 is a predecessor or successor of N_2. A sequence of nodes $(N_1, N_2, \cdots, N_k)$ is a *path* from N_1 to N_k if N_{i+1} is a successor of N_i for $i = 1, 2, \cdots, (k-1)$. A sequence of nodes $(N_1, N_2, \cdots, N_k)$ is a *chain* that joins N_1 and N_k if N_{i+1} is adjacent to N_i for $i = 1, 2, \cdots, (k-1)$.

We can think of each arc in G as having a FIFO queue that buffers the tokens that pass through the arc. Each FIFO contains an initial number of samples equal to the delay on the associated arc. Firing a node in G corresponds to removing $c(\alpha)$ tokens from the head of the FIFO for each input arc α, and appending $p(\beta)$ tokens to the FIFO for each output arc β. After a sequence of 0 or more firings, we say that a node is *fireable* if there are enough tokens on each input FIFO to fire the node. An *admissable sequential schedule* ("sequential" is used to distinguish this type of schedule from a parallel schedule) for G is a finite sequence $S = S_1 S_2 \cdots S_N$ of nodes in G such that each S_i is fireable immediately after $S_1, S_2, \cdots, S_{i-1}$ have fired in succession.

We say that a sequential schedule S is a *periodic schedule* if it invokes each node at least once and produces no net change in the number of tokens on any arc's FIFO—for each arc α, (the number of times $source(\alpha)$ is fired in S) $\times p(\alpha) =$ (the number of times $sink(\alpha)$ is fired in S) $\times c(\alpha)$. A *periodic admissable sequential schedule* (PASS) is a schedule that is both periodic and admissable. We will use the term *valid schedule* to describe a schedule that is a PASS, and the term *consistent* to describe an SDF graph that has a PASS. Except where otherwise stated, we deal only with consistent SDF graphs in this paper.

In [14], it is shown that for each connected SDF graph G, there is a unique minimum number of times that each node needs to be invoked in a periodic schedule. We specify these minimum numbers of firings by a vector of positive integers $\mathbf{q}_G$, which is indexed by the nodes in G, and we denote the component of $\mathbf{q}_G$ corresponding to a node N by $\mathbf{q}_G(N)$. Every PASS for G invokes each node N a multiple of $\mathbf{q}_G(N)$ times, and corresponding to each PASS S, there is a positive integer $J(S)$ called the *blocking factor* of S, such that S invokes each $N \in N(G)$ exactly $J\mathbf{q}_G(N)$ times. We call $\mathbf{q}_G$ the *repetitions vector* of G. For example in Fig. 2(a), $\mathbf{q}_G(A) = 10, \mathbf{q}_G(B) = 4$, and $\mathbf{q}_G(C) = 5$. The following properties of repetitions vectors are established in [14]:

Fact 1: The components of a repetitions vector are collectively coprime.

Fact 2: The *balance equation* $\mathbf{q}_G(source(\alpha)) \times p(\alpha) = \mathbf{q}_G(sink(\alpha)) \times c(\alpha)$ is satisfied for each arc α in G.

Given a subset Z of nodes in a connected SDF graph G, we define $q_G(Z) = gcd(\{\mathbf{q}_G(N) | N \in Z\})$, where gcd denotes the greatest common divisor. We can interpret $q_G(Z)$ as the number of times that G invokes the "subsystem" Z. We will use the following property of connected subsystems which is derived in [4].

Fact 3: If G is a connected SDF graph, and Z is a connected subset of $N(G)$, then for each $N \in Z$, $\mathbf{q}_G(N) = q_G(Z) \mathbf{q}_{subgraph(Z)}(N)$.

For our hierarchical scheduling approach, we will apply the concept of *clustering* a subgraph. This process is illustrated in Fig. 2. Here $subgraph(\{A, C\})$ of (a) is clustered into the hierarchical node Ω_{AC}, and the resulting SDF graph is shown in (b). Similarly, clustering $subgraph(\{A, B\})$ results in the graph of (c). Each input arc α to a clustered subgraph P is replaced by an arc α' having $p(\alpha') = p(\alpha)$, and $c(\alpha') = c(\alpha) \times \mathbf{q}_G(sink(\alpha))/q_G(N(P))$, the number of samples consumed from α in one *invocation of subgraph* P. Similarly we replace each output arc β with β' such that $c(\beta') = c(\beta)$, and

$$p(\beta') = p(\beta) \times \mathbf{q}_G(source(\alpha))/q_G(N(P)).$$

The following properties of clustered subgraphs are proven in [4].

Fact 4: Suppose G is a connected SDF graph, Z is a subset of nodes in G, G' is the SDF graph that results from clustering $subgraph(Z)$ into the hierarchical node Ω, and S' is a PASS for G'. Suppose that S_Z is a PASS for $subgraph(Z)$ such that for each $N \in Z, S_Z$ invokes N $(\mathbf{q}_G(N)/q_G(Z))$ times. Let S^* denote the schedule that results from replacing each appearance of Ω in S with S_Z. Then S^* is a PASS for G.

Fact 5: Suppose G is a connected SDF graph, Z is a subset of nodes in G, and G' is the SDF graph that results from clustering $subgraph(Z)$ into the node Ω. Then $\mathbf{q}_{G'}(\Omega) = q_G(Z)$; and for any node N in G' other that $\Omega, \mathbf{q}_{G'}(N) = \mathbf{q}_G(N)$.

Given a directed graph G, we say that G is **strongly connected** if for any pair of distinct nodes A, B in G, there is a path from A to B and a path from B to A. We say that a strongly connected graph is *nontrivial* if it contains more than one node. Finally, a *strongly connected component* of G is a subset of nodes Z such that $subgraph(Z, G)$ is strongly connected, and there is no strongly connected subset of $N(G)$ that properly contains Z. For example {A, B} and {C} are the strongly connected components of Fig. 2(a).

Similarly, we define a *connected component* of a directed graph G to be a maximal subset of nodes Z such that for any

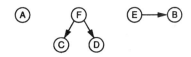

Fig. 3. A directed graph that has three connected components.

pair of distinct members A, B of Z, there is a chain that joins A and B. For example in Fig. 3, the connected components are {A}, {C, D, F}, and {B, E}.

Given a connected SDF graph G, and an arc α in G, we define *total_consumed*(α, G) to be the total number of samples consumed from α in a minimal schedule period for G. Thus *total_consumed*(α, G) = $q_G(sink(\alpha))c(\alpha)$. Finally, given an SDF graph G, a looped schedule S for G and a node N in G, we define *appearances*(N, S) to be the number of times that N appears in S, and we say that S is a **single appearance schedule** if for each $N \in N(G)$, *appearances*(N, S) = 1. For example, consider the two schedules S_1 = CA(2B)C and S_2 = A(2B)(2C) for Fig. 1. We have *appearances*(C, S_1) = 2; *appearances*(C, S_2) = 1; S_1 is not a single appearance schedule because C appears more than once; and S_2 is a single appearance schedule. Single appearance schedules form the class of schedules that allow in line code generation without any code space or subroutine penalty.

III. Subindependence

Our scheduling framework for synthesizing compact nested loop structures is based on a form of precedence independence, which we call *subindependence*.

Definition 1: Suppose that G is a connected SDF graph. If Z_1 and Z_2 are disjoint, nonempty subsets of $N(G)$ we say that "Z_1 is **subindependent** of Z_2 in G" if for every arc α in G such that $source(\alpha) \in Z_2$ and $sink(\alpha) \in Z_1$, we have $delay(\alpha) \geq total\_consumed(\alpha, G)$. We occasionally drop the "in G" qualification if G is understood from context. If (Z_1 is subindependent of Z_2) and ($Z_1 \cup Z_2 = N(G)$), then we write ($Z_1|GZ_2$), and we say that Z_1 *is subindependent* in G.

Thus Z_1 is subindependent of Z_2 if no samples produced from Z_2 are consumed by Z_1 in the same schedule period that they are produced; and $Z_1|GZ_2$ if Z_1 is subindependent of Z_2, and Z_1 and Z_2 form a partition of the nodes in G. For example, consider Fig. 2(a). Here $q_G(A, B, C) = (10, 4, 5)$, and the complete set of subindependence relationships is (1) {A} is subindependent of {C}; (2) {B} is subindependent of {C}; (3) {A, B} |G {C}; and {C} is subindependent of {B}.

The following property of subindependence follows immediately from definition 1.

Fact 6: If G is a strongly connected SDF graph and X, Y, and Z are disjoint subsets of $N(G)$, then (a) (X is subindependent of Z) and (Y is subindependent of Z) $\Rightarrow$ (X $\cup$ Y) is subindependent of Z. (b) (X is subindependent of Y) and (X is subindependent of Z) $\Rightarrow$ X is subindependent of (Y $\cup$ Z).

Our scheduling framework is based on the following condition for the existence of a single appearance schedule, which is developed in [4].

Fact 7: An SDF graph has a valid single appearance schedule iff for each nontrivial strongly connected component Z,

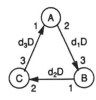

Fig. 4. An illustration of loose and tight interdependence. Here d_1, d_2, and d_3 represent the number of delays on the associated arcs. This SDF graph is tightly interdependent if and only if ($d_1 < 6$), ($d_2 < 2$), and ($d_3 < 3$).

there exists a partition X, Y of Z such that X |*subgraph*(Z) Y, and *subgraph*(X) and *subgraph*(Y) each have single appearance schedules.

A related condition was developed independently by Ritz *et al.* in [22], which discusses single appearance schedules in the context of *minimum activation schedules*. For example, the schedule A(2CB) for Fig. 1 results in 5 activations since invocations of C and B are interleaved. In contrast, the schedule A(2B)(2C) requires only one activation per actor, for a total of 3 activations. In the objectives of [22], the latter schedule is preferable because in that code generation framework there is a large overhead associated with each activation. However such overhead can often be avoided with careful instruction scheduling and register allocation, as [19] demonstrates. We prefer the former schedule, which has less looping overhead and requires less memory for buffering.

Fact 7 implies that for an SDF graph to have a single appearance schedule, we must be able to decompose each nontrivial strongly connected component into two subsets in such a way that one subset is subindependent of the other. Another implication of fact 7 is that every acyclic SDF graph has a single appearance schedule. We can easily construct a single appearance schedule for an acyclic SDF graph. We simply pick a root node N_1; schedule all of its invocations in succession; remove N_1 from the graph and pick a root node N_2 of the remaining graph; schedule all of N_2's invocations in succession; and so on until we have scheduled all of the nodes. By this procedure, we get a cascade of loops $(q_G(N_1)N_1)(q_G(N_2)N_2) \cdots (q_G(N_k)N_k)$, which gives us a single appearance schedule.

Definition 2: Suppose that G is a nontrivial strongly connected SDF graph. Then we say that G is **loosely interdependent** if $N(G)$ can be partitioned into Z_1 and Z_2 such that $Z_1|GZ_2$. We say that G is **tightly interdependent** if it is not loosely interdependent.

For example, consider the strongly connected SDF graph in Fig. 4. The repetitions vector for this graph is $q_G(A, B, C) = (3, 2, 1)$. Thus the graph is loosely interdependent if and only if ($d_1 \geq 6$) or ($d_2 \geq 2$) or ($d_3 \geq 3$).

In this section we have introduced topological properties of SDF graphs that are related to the existence of single appearance schedules. In the following section we use these properties to develop our scheduling framework and to demonstrate some of its useful qualities.

IV. The Class of Loose Interdependence Algorithms

The properties of loose/tight interdependence are important for organizing loops because, as we will show, the existence of a single appearance schedule is equivalent to the absence of tightly interdependent subgraphs. However, these properties are useful even when tightly interdependent subgraphs are present. The following definition specifies how to use loose interdependence to guide the looping process.

Definition 3: Let A_1 be any algorithm that takes as input a nontrivial strongly connected SDF graph G, determines whether G is loosely interdependent, and if so, finds a subindependent subset of $N(G)$. Let A_2 be any algorithm that finds the strongly connected components of a directed graph. Let A_3 be any algorithm that takes an acyclic SDF graph and generates a valid single appearance schedule. Finally, let A_4 be any algorithm that takes a tightly interdependent SDF graph, and generates a valid looped schedule of blocking factor 1. We define the algorithm $L(A_1, A_2, A_3, A_4)$ as follows:

Input: a connected SDF graph G.
Output: a valid unit-blocking-factor looped schedule $S_L(G)$ for G.
Step 1: Use A_2 to determine the nontrivial strongly connected components $Z_1, Z_2, \cdots, Z_s$ of G.
Step 2: Cluster $Z_1, Z_2, \cdots, Z_s$ into nodes $\Omega_1, \Omega_2, \cdots, \Omega_s$ respectively, and call the resulting graph G'. This is an acyclic SDF graph.
Step 3: Apply A_3 to G': denote the resulting schedule $S'(G)$.
Step 4: (Shown at the bottom of the page.)

The *for*-loop replaces each "Ω_i" in $S'(G)$ with a valid looped schedule for $subgraph(Z_i)$. From repeated application of fact 4, we know that these replacements yield a valid looped schedule S_L for G. We output S_L. ∎

Remark 1: Observe that step 4 does not insert or delete appearances of actors that are not contained in a nontrivial strongly connected component Z_i. Since A_3 generates a single appearance schedule for G', we have that for every node N that is not contained in a nontrivial strongly connected component of G, $appearances(N, S_L(G)) = 1$.

Remark 2: If C is a nontrivial strongly connected component of G and $N \in C$, then since $S_L(G)$ is derived from $S'(G)$ by replacing the single appearance of each Ω_i, we have $appearances(N, S_L(G)) = appearances(N, S_L(subgraph(C)))$.

Remark 3: For each strongly connected component Z_k whose subgraph is loosely interdependent, L partitions Z_k into X and Y such that $X|subgraph(Z_k)Y$, and replaces the single appearance of Ω_k in $S'(G)$ with $S_x S_y$. If N is a member of the connected component X_i, then $N \neq Y$, so $appearances(N, S_x S_y) = appearances(N, S_L(subgraph(X_i)))$. Also since N cannot be in any other strongly connected component besides Z_k, and since $S'(G)$ contains only one appearance of Ω_k, we have $appearances(N, S_L(G)) = appearances(N, S_x S_y)$. Thus, for $i = 1, 2, \cdots, v, N \in X_i \Rightarrow appearances(N, S_L(G)) = appearances(N, S_L(subgraph(X_i)))$. By the same argument, we can show that for $i = 1, 2, \cdots, w, N \in Y_i \Rightarrow appearances(N, S_L(G)) = appearances(N, S_L(subgraph(Y_i)))$.

$L(\bullet, \bullet, \bullet, \bullet)$ defines a family of algorithms, which we call **loose interdependence algorithms** because they exploit loose interdependence to decompose the input SDF graph. Since nested recursive calls decompose a graph into finer and finer strongly connected components, it is easy to verify that any loose interdependence algorithm always terminates. Each loose interdependence algorithm $\lambda = L(A_1, A_2, A_3, A_4)$ involves the "sub-algorithms" A_1, A_2, A_3, and A_4, which we call, respectively, the *subindependence partitioning algorithm of* λ, the *strongly connected components algorithm of* λ, the *acyclic scheduling algorithm of* λ, and the *tight scheduling algorithm of* λ.

We will apply a loose interdependence algorithm to derive a *nonrecursive* necessary and sufficient condition for the existence of a single appearance schedule. First, we introduce two lemmas.

Lemma 1: Suppose G is a connected SDF graph; N is a node in G that is not contained in any tightly interdependent subgraph of G; and λ is a loose interdependence algorithm. Then N appears only once in $S_\lambda(G)$, the schedule generated by λ.

Step 4:
for $i = 1, 2, \cdots, s$
    Let SZ denote $subgraph(Z_i)$.
    Apply A_1 to SZ.
    if $X, Y \subseteq Z_i$ are found such that $X|SZ\,Y$,
    then
        • Determine the connected components $X_1, X_2, \cdots, X_v$ of $subgraph(X)$, and the connected components $Y_1, Y_2, \cdots, Y_w$ of $subgraph(Y)$.
        • Recursively apply algorithm L to construct the schedules
$S_x = (q_{SZ}(X_1) S_L(subgraph(X_1))) \cdots (q_{SZ}(X_v) S_L(subgraph(X_v)))$,
$S_y = (q_{SZ}(Y_1) S_L(subgraph(Y_1))) \cdots (q_{SZ}(Y_w) S_L(subgraph(Y_w)))$.
        • Replace the (single) appearance of Ω_i in $S'(G)$ with $S_x S_y$.
    else (SZ is tightly interdependent)
        • Apply A_4 to obtain a valid schedule S_i for SZ.
        • Replace the single appearance of Ω_i in $S'(G)$ with S_i.
    end − if
end − for

The proof of lemma 1 can be found in the appendix.

Lemma 2: Suppose that G is a strongly connected SDF graph, $P \subseteq N(G)$ is subindependent in G, and C is a strongly connected subset of $N(G)$ such that $C \cap P \neq C$ and $C \cap P \neq \emptyset$. Then $C \cap P$ is subindependent in *subgraph*(C).

Proof: Suppose that α is an arc directed from a member of $(C - (C \cap P))$ to a member of $(C \cap P)$. By the subindependence of P in G, $delay(\alpha) \geq c(\alpha) \times q_G(sink(\alpha))$, and by fact 3, $q_G(sink(\alpha)) \geq q_{subgraph(C)}(sink(\alpha))$. Thus, $delay(\alpha) \geq c(\alpha) \times q_{subgraph(C)}(sink(\alpha))$. Since this holds for any α directed from $(C - (C \cap P))$ to $(C \cap P)$, we conclude that $(C \cap P)$ is subindependent in C. QED

Corollary 1: Suppose that G is a strongly connected SDF graph, Z_1 and Z_2 are subsets of $N(G)$ such that $Z_1|GZ_2$, and T is a tightly interdependent subgraph of G. Then $N(T) \subseteq Z_1$ or $N(T) \subseteq Z_2$.

Proof: (By contraposition.) If $N(T)$ has nonempty intersection with both Z_1 and Z_2, then from lemma 2, $N(T) \cap Z_1$ is subindependent in T, so T is loosely interdependent. QED

Theorem 1: Suppose that G is a strongly connected SDF graph. Then G has a single appearance schedule iff every nontrivial strongly connected subgraph of G is loosely interdependent.

Proof: $\Leftarrow$ Suppose every nontrivial strongly connected subgraph of G is loosely interdependent, and let λ be any loose interdependence algorithm. Since no node in G is contained in a tightly interdependent subgraph, lemma 1 guarantees that $S_\lambda(G)$ is a single appearance schedule for G.

$\Rightarrow$ Suppose that G has a single appearance schedule and that C is a strongly connected subset of $N(G)$. Set $Z_0 = G$. From fact 7, there exist $X_0, Y_0 \subseteq Z_0$ such that $X_0|subgraph(Z_0)Y_0$, and $subgraph(X_0)$ and $subgraph(Y_0)$ both have single appearance schedules. If X_0 and Y_0 do not both intersect C then C is completely contained in some strongly connected component Z_1 of $subgraph(X_0)$ or $subgraph(Y_0)$. We can then apply fact 7 to partition Z_1 into X_1, Y_1, and continue recursively in this manner until we obtain a strongly connected $Z_k \subseteq N(G)$, with the following properties: Z_k can be partitioned into X_k and Y_k such that $X_k|subgraph(Z_k)Y_k; C \subseteq Z_k$; and $(X_k \cap C)$ and $(Y_k \cap C)$ are both nonempty. From lemma 2, $(X_k \cap C)$ is subindependent in $subgraph(C)$, so C must be loosely interdependent. QED

Corollary 2: Given a connected SDF graph G, any loose interdependence algorithm will obtain a single appearance schedule if one exists.

Proof: If a single appearance schedule for G exists, then from theorem 1, G contains no tightly interdependent subgraphs. In other words, no node in G is contained in a tightly interdependent subgraph of G. From lemma 1, the schedule resulting from any loose interdependence algorithm contains only one appearance for each actor in G. QED

Thus, a loose interdependence algorithm always obtains an optimally compact solution when a single appearance schedule exists. When a single appearance schedule does not exist, strongly connected graphs are repeatedly decomposed until tightly interdependent subgraphs are found. In general, however, there may be more than one way to decompose $N(G)$ into two parts so that one of the parts is subindependent of the other. Thus, it is natural to ask the following question: Given two distinct partitions $\{Z_1, Z_2\}$ and $\{Z'_1, Z'_2\}$ such that $Z_1|GZ_2$ and $Z'_1|GZ'_2$, is it possible that one of these partitions leads to a more compact schedule than the other? Fortunately, as we will show in the remainder of this section, the answer to this question is "No". In other words, any two loose interdependence algorithms that use the same tight scheduling algorithm always lead to equally compact schedules. The key reason is that tight interdependence is an additive property.

Lemma 3: Suppose that G is a connected SDF graph, Y and Z are subsets of $N(G)$ such that $(Y \cap Z) \neq \emptyset$, and $subgraph(Y)$ and $subgraph(Z)$ are both tightly interdependent. Then $subgraph(Y \cup Z)$ is tightly interdependent.

Proof: (By contraposition.) Let $H = Y \cup Z$, and suppose that $subgraph(H)$ is loosely interdependent. Then there exist H_1 and H_2 such that $H = H_1 \cup H_2$ and $H_1|subgraph(H)H_2$. From $H_1 \cup H_2 = Y \cup Z$, and $Y \cap Z \neq \emptyset$, it is easily seen that H_1 and H_2 both have a nonempty intersection with Y, or they both have a nonempty intersection with Z. Without loss of generality, assume that $H_1 \cap Y \neq \emptyset$ and $H_2 \cap Y \neq \emptyset$. From lemma 2, $(H_1 \cap Y)$ is subindependent in $subgraph(Y)$, and thus $subgraph(Y)$ is not tightly interdependent. QED

Lemma 3 implies that each SDF graph G has a *unique* set $\{C_1, C_2, \cdots, C_n\}$ of maximal tightly interdependent subgraphs such that $i \neq j \Rightarrow N(C_i) \cap N(C_j) = \emptyset$, and every tightly interdependent subgraph in G is contained in some C_i. We call each $N(C_i)$ a *tightly interdependent component* of G. It follows from theorem 1 that G has a single appearance schedule iff G has no tightly interdependent components. Furthermore, since the tightly interdependent components are unique, the performance of a loose interdependence algorithm, with regards to schedule compactness, is not dependent on the particular subindependence partitioning algorithm, the sub-algorithm used to partition the loosely interdependent components. The following theorem develops this result.

Theorem 2: Suppose G is an SDF graph that has a PASS, N is a node in G, and λ is a loose interdependence algorithm. If N is not contained in a tightly interdependent component of G, then N appears only once in $S_\lambda(G)$. On the other hand, if N is contained in a tightly interdependent component T then $appearances(N, S_\lambda(G)) = appearances(N, S_\lambda(subgraph(T)))$—the number of appearances of N is determined entirely by the tight scheduling algorithm of λ.

Proof: If N is not contained in a tightly interdependent component of G, then N is not contained in any tightly interdependent subgraph. Then from lemma 1, $appearances(N, S_\lambda(G)) = 1$.

Now suppose that N is contained in some tightly interdependent component T of G. If $T = N(G)$ we are done. Otherwise we set $M_0 = N(G)$, and thus $T \neq M_0$; by definition, tightly interdependent graphs are strongly connected, so T is contained in some strongly connected component C of $subgraph(M_0)$.

If T is a proper subset of C, then $subgraph(C)$ must be loosely interdependent, since otherwise $subgraph(T)$ would not be a maximal tightly interdependent subgraph.

Thus, λ partitions *subgraph*(C) into X and Y such that X |*subgraph*(C) Y. We set M_1 to be that connected component of *subgraph*(X) or *subgraph*(Y) that contains N. Since X, Y partition C, M_1 is a proper subset of M_o. Also, from remark 3, $appearances(N, S_\lambda(subgraph(M_0))) = appearances(N, S_\lambda(subgraph(M_1)))$, and from corollary 1, $N(T) \subseteq M_1$.

On the other hand, if $T = C$, then we set $M_1 = T$. Since $T \neq M_0$, M_1 is a proper subset of M_0; from remark 2, $appearances(N, S_\lambda(subgraph(M_0))) = appearances(N, S_\lambda(subgraph(M_1)))$; and trivially, $T \subseteq M_1$.

If $T \neq M_1$, then we can repeat the above procedure to obtain a proper subset M_2 of M_1 such that $appearances(N, S_\lambda(subgraph(M_1))) = appearances(N, S_\lambda(subgraph(M_2)))$, and $N(T) \subseteq M_2$. Continuing this process, we get a sequence $M_1, M_2, \ldots$. Since each M_i is a proper subset of its predecessor, we cannot repeat this process indefinitely—eventually, for some $k \geq 0$, we will have $N(T) = M_k$. But, by construction, $appearances(N, S_\lambda(G)) = appearances(N, S_\lambda(subgraph(M_0))) = appearances(N, S_\lambda(subgraph(M_1))) = \cdots = appearances(N, S_\lambda(subgraph(M_k)))$; and thus $appearances(N, S_\lambda(G)) = appearances(N, S_\lambda(subgraph(T)))$. QED

Theorem 2 states that the tight scheduling algorithm is independent of the subindependence partitioning algorithm, and vice-versa. Any subindependence partitioning algorithm makes sure that there is only one appearance for each actor outside the tightly interdependent components, and the tight scheduling algorithm completely determines the number of appearances for actors inside the tightly interdependent components. For example, if we develop a new subindependence partitioning algorithm that is more efficient in some way (e.g., it is faster or minimizes data memory requirements), we can replace it for any existing subindependence partitioning algorithm without changing the "compactness" of the resulting schedules—we don't need to analyze its interaction with the rest of the loose interdependence algorithm. Similarly, if we develop a new tight scheduling algorithm that schedules any tightly interdependent graph more compactly than the existing tight scheduling algorithm, we are guaranteed that using the new algorithm instead of the old one will lead to more compact schedules *overall*.

V. Computational Efficiency

The complexity of a loose interdependence algorithm λ depends on its subindependence partitioning algorithm λ_{sp}, strongly connected components algorithm λ_{sc}, acyclic scheduling algorithm λ_{as}, and tight scheduling algorithm λ_{ts}. From the proof of theorem 2, we see that λ_{ts} is applied exactly once for each tightly interdependent component. For example, the simplest solution for a tight scheduling algorithm would be to apply an algorithm from the family of class-S scheduling algorithms that are defined in [14]; class-S algorithms exist whose complexity is linear in the number of actor firings (assuming that the number of input and output edges for a given actor is bounded) [3]. Alternatively, a more elaborate technique such as that presented in [5] can be employed.

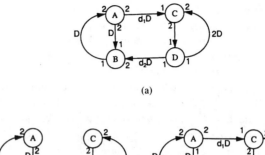

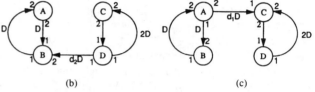

Fig. 5. An illustration of Theorem 3.

As mentioned earlier, one drawback of the technique of [5] is that it requires a reachability matrix, which has a storage cost that is quadratic in the number of actor firings. However, we greatly reduce this drawback by restricting application of the algorithm to only the tightly interdependent components. We are currently investigating other alternatives to scheduling tightly interdependent SDF graphs.

The other subalgorithms, λ_{sc}, λ_{as}, and λ_{sp}, are successively applied to decompose an SDF graph, and the process is repeated until all tightly interdependent components are found. In the worst case, each decomposition step isolates a single node from the current n-node subgraph, and the decomposition must be recursively applied to the remaining $(n-1)$—node subgraph. Thus, if the original program has n nodes, n decomposition steps are required in the worst case. Tarjan [24] first showed that the strongly connected components of a graph can be found in $O(m)$ time, where $m = max$(number of nodes, number of arcs). Hence λ_{sc} can be chosen to be linear, and since at most $n \leq m$ decomposition steps are required, the total time that such a λ_{sc} accounts for in λ is $O(m^2)$. In Section III we presented a simple linear-time algorithm that constructs a single appearance schedule for an acyclic SDF graph. Thus λ_{as} can be chosen such that its total time is also $O(m^2)$.

The following theorem presents a simple topological condition for loose interdependence that leads to a linear subindependence partitioning algorithm λ_{sp}.

Theorem 3: Suppose that G is a nontrivial strongly connected SDF graph. From G, remove all arcs α for which $delay(\alpha) \geq c(\alpha) \times \mathbf{q}_G(sink(\alpha))$, and call the resulting SDF graph G'. Then G is tightly interdependent if and only if G' is strongly connected.

For example, suppose that G is the strongly connected SDF graph in Fig. 5(a). The repetitions vector for G is $\mathbf{q}_G(A, B, C, D) = (1, 2, 2, 4)$. This graph is loosely interdependent if $d_1 \geq 2$, which corresponds to $\{C, D\}|G\{A, B\}$, or if $d_2 \geq 4$, which corresponds to $\{A, B\}|G\{C, D\}$. The corresponding G''s are depicted at the bottom of Fig. 5: Fig. 5(b) shows G' when $d_1 \geq 2$ and $d_2 < 4$, and Fig. 5(c) shows G' when $d_2 \geq 4$ and $d_1 < 2$. Observe that in both of these cases, G' is not strongly connected.

Proof: We prove both directions by contraposition.

⇒ Suppose that G′ is not strongly connected. Then $N(G′)$ can be partitioned into Z_1 and Z_2 such that there is no arc directed from a member of Z_2 to a member of Z_1 in G′. Since no nodes were removed in constructing G′, Z_1 and Z_2 partition $N(G)$. Also, none of the arcs directed from Z_2 to Z_1 in G occur in G′. Thus, by the construction of G′, for each arc α in G directed from a member of Z_2 to a member of Z_1, we have $delay(\alpha) \geq c(\alpha) \times \mathbf{q}_G(sink(\alpha))$. It follows that $Z_1|_G Z_2$, so G is loosely interdependent.

⇐ Suppose that G is loosely interdependent. Then $N(G)$ can be partitioned into Z_1 and Z_2 such that $Z_1|_G Z_2$. By construction of G′, there are no arcs in G′ directed from a member of Z_2 to a member of Z_1, so G′ is not strongly connected. QED

Thus, λ_{sp} can be constructed as follows: (1) Determine $\mathbf{q}_G(N)$ for each node N; (2) Remove each arc α whose delay is at least $c(\alpha) \times \mathbf{q}_G(sink(\alpha))$; (3) Determine the strongly connected components of the resulting graph; (4) If the entire graph is the only strongly connected component, then G is tightly interdependent; otherwise (5) cluster the strongly connected components—the resulting graph is acyclic and has at least two nodes. The strongly connected component corresponding to any root node of this graph is subindependent of the rest of the graph. An algorithm (first used in the Gabriel system [11]) that performs (1) in time $O(m)$ is described in [3]; it is obvious that (2) is $O(m)$; Tarjan's algorithm allows $O(m)$ for (3); and the checks in (4) and (5) are clearly $O(m)$ as well. Thus, we have a linear λ_{sp}, and the total time that λ spends in λ_{sp} is $O(m^2)$.

We have specified λ_{sp}, λ_{sc}, λ_{as}, and λ_{ts} such that the time complexity of the corresponding loose interdependence algorithm is $O(m^2 + f)$, where m is *max*(number of nodes, number of arcs), and f is the number of actor firings. Note that our worst case estimate is conservative—in practice only a few decomposition steps are required to fully schedule a strongly connected subgraph, while our estimate assumes n steps, where n is the number of nodes in the input graph.

VI. CLUSTERING TO MAKE DATA TRANSFERS MORE EFFICIENT

In this section, we present a useful clustering technique for increasing the frequency of data transfers that occur through machine registers rather than memory, and we prove that this technique does not interfere with the code compactness potential of a loose interdependence algorithm—this clustering preserves the properties of loose interdependence algorithms discussed in Section IV.

Fig. 6 illustrates two ways in which arbitrary clustering decisions can conflict with code compactness objectives. Observe that Fig. 6(a) is an acyclic graph so it must have a single appearance schedule. Fig. 6(b) is the hierarchical SDF graph that results from clustering A and B in Fig. 6(a). It is easy to verify that this is a tightly interdependent graph. In fact, the only minimal periodic schedule for Fig. 6(a) that we can derive from this clustering is $C\Omega C \Rightarrow CABC$. Thus, the

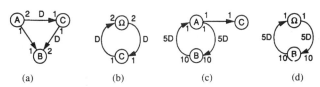

Fig. 6. Examples of how clustering can conflict with the goal of code compactness.

clustering of A and B in Fig. 6(a) cancels the existence of a single appearance schedule.

In Fig. 6(c), {A, B} forms a tightly interdependent component and C is not contained in any tightly interdependent subgraph. From theorem 2, we know that any loose interdependence algorithm will schedule Fig. 6(c) in such a way that C appears only once. Now observe that the graph that results from clustering A and C, shown in Fig. 6(d), is tightly interdependent. It can be verified that the most compact minimal periodic schedule for this graph is $(5\Omega)B(5\Omega)$, which leads to the schedule (5 AC)B(5 AC) for Fig. 6(c). By increasing the "extent" of the tightly interdependent component {A, B} to subsume C, this clustering decision increases the minimum number of appearances of C in the final schedule.

Thus we see that a clustering decision can conflict with optimal code compactness if it introduces a new tightly interdependent component or extends an existing tightly interdependent component. In this section we present a clustering technique of great practical use and prove that it neither extends nor introduces tight interdependence. Our clustering technique and its compatibility with loose interdependence algorithms is summarized by the following claim: *Clustering two adjacent nodes A and B in an SDF graph does not introduce or extend a tightly interdependent component if (a) Neither A nor B is contained in a tightly interdependent component; (b) At least one arc directed from A to B has zero delay; (c) A and B are invoked the same number of times in a periodic schedule; and (d) B has no predecessors other than A or B.* The remainder of this section is devoted to proving this claim and explaining the corresponding clustering technique.

We motivate our clustering technique with the example shown in Fig. 7. One possible single appearance schedule for Fig. 7(a) is (10 X)(10 Y)ZV(10 W). This is the *minimum activation* schedule preferred by Ritz *et al.* [22]; however, it is inefficient with respect to buffering. Due to the loop that specifies ten successive invocations of X, the data transfers between X and Y cannot take place in machine registers and 10 words of data-memory are required to implement the arc connecting X and Y. However, observe that conditions (a)–(d) of our above claim all hold for the adjacent pairs {X, Y} and {Z, V}. Thus, we can cluster these pairs without cancelling the existence of a single appearance schedule. The hierarchical graph that results from this clustering is shown in Fig. 7(d); this graph leads to the single appearance schedule $(10\Omega_2)\Omega_1(10W) \Rightarrow$ (10 XY)ZV(10 W). In this second schedule, each sample produced by X is consumed by Y in the same loop iteration, so all of the transfers between X and Y can occur through a single machine register. Thus, the clustering of X and Y saves 10 words of buffer space for the

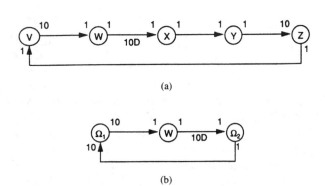

Fig. 7. An example of clustering to increase the amount of buffering that occurs through registers.

data transfers between X and Y, and it allows these transfers to be performed through registers rather than memory, which will usually result in faster code.

We will use the following additional notation in the development of this section.

Notation: Let G be an SDF graph and suppose that we cluster a subset W of nodes in G. We will refer to the resulting hierarchical graph as G', and we will refer to the node in G' into which W has been clustered as Ω. For each arc α in G that is not contained in $subgraph(W)$, we denote the corresponding arc in G' by α'. Finally, if $X \subseteq N(G)$, we refer to the "corresponding" subset of $N(G')$ as X'. That is, X' consists of all members of X that are not in W; and if X contains a member of W, then X' also contains Ω.

For example, if G is the SDF graph in Fig. 6(a), $W = \{A, B\}$, and α and β respectively denote the arc directed from A to C and the arc directed from C to B, then we denote the graph in Fig. 6(b) by G', and in G' we denote the arc directed from Ω to C by α' and the arc denoted from C to Ω by β'. Also, If $X = \{A, C\}$, then $X' = \{\Omega, C\}$.

Lemma 4: Suppose that G is a strongly connected SDF graph and X_1, X_2 partition $N(G)$ such that $X_1 | G X_2$. Also suppose that A, B are nodes in G such that $A, B \in X_1$ or $A, B \in X_2$. If we cluster $W = \{A, B\}$ then the resulting SDF graph G' is loosely interdependent.[1]

The proof of lemma 4 can be found in the appendix.

Definition 4: We say that two SDF graphs G_1 and G_2 are *isomorphic* if there exist bijective mappings $f_1: N(G_1) \rightarrow N(G_2)$ and $f_2: A(G_1) \rightarrow A(G_2)$ such that for each $\alpha \in A(G_1), source(f_2(\alpha)) = f_1(source(\alpha)), sink(f_2(\alpha)) = f_1(sink(\alpha)), delay(f_2(\alpha)) = delay(\alpha), p(f_2(\alpha)) = p(\alpha),$ and $c(f_2(\alpha)) = c(\alpha)$. Intuitively, two SDF graphs are isomorphic if they differ only by a relabeling of the nodes. For example, the SDF graph in Fig. 6(d) is isomorphic to $subgraph(\{A, B\})$ in Fig. 6(c).

We will use the following obvious fact about isomorphic SDF graphs.

Fact 8: If G_1 and G_2 are two isomorphic SDF graphs and G_1 is loosely interdependent then G_2 is loosely interdependent.

[1] However, G' may be deadlocked even if G is not. This will not be a problem in our application of lemma 4.

Lemma 5: Suppose that G is an SDF graph, $M \subseteq N(G)$, $A_1 \in M$, and A_2 is an SDF node that is contained in $N(G)$ but not in M such that

1) A_2 is not adjacent to any member of $(M - \{A_1\})$, and
2) for some positive integer k, $q(A_2) = kq(A_1)$.

Then if we cluster $W = \{A_1, A_2\}$ in G, then $subgraph(M - \{A_1\} + \{\Omega\}, G')$ is isomorphic to $subgraph(M, G)$.

As a simple illustration, consider again the clustering example of Fig. 6(c) and (d). Let G and G' respectively denote the graphs of Fig. 6(c) and (d), and in Fig. 6(c), let $M = \{A, B\}$, $A_1 = A$, and $A_2 = C$. Then $(M - \{A_1\} + \{\Omega\}) = \{B, \Omega\}$, and clearly, $subgraph(\{B, \Omega\}, G')$ is isomorphic to $subgraph(\{A, B\}, G)$. The proof of lemma 5 can be found in the appendix.

Lemma 6: Suppose that G is a strongly connected SDF graph, and Z is a strongly connected subset of nodes in G such that $q_G(Z) = 1$. Suppose Z_1 and Z_2 are disjoint subsets of Z such that Z_1 is subindependent of Z_2 in $subgraph(Z)$. Then Z_1 is subindependent of Z_2 in G.

Proof: For each arc α directed from a member of Z_2 to a member of Z_1, we have $delay(\alpha) \geq total\_consumed(\alpha, subgraph(Z))$. From fact 3, $q_{subgraph(Z)}(N) = q_G(N)$ for all $N \in Z$. Thus, for all arcs α in $subgraph(Z), total\_consumed(\alpha, subgraph(Z)) = total\_consumed(\alpha, G)$, and we conclude that Z_1 is subindependent of Z_2 in G. QED

Lemma 7: Suppose G is a strongly connected SDF graph, A and B are distinct nodes in G, and $W = \{A, B\}$ forms a proper subset of $N(G)$. Suppose also that the following conditions all hold:

1) Neither A nor B is contained in a tightly interdependent subgraph of G.
2) There is at least one arc directed from A to B that has no delay.
3) B has no predecessors other than A or B.
4) $q_G(B) = kq_G(C)$ for some $C \in N(G), C \neq B$.

Then the SDF graph G' that results from clustering W is loosely interdependent.

Proof: From (1) G must be loosely interdependent, so there exist subsets X_1, X_2 of $N(G)$ such that $X_1 | G X_2$. If $A, B \in X_1$ or $A, B \in X_2$, then from lemma 4, we are done. Now condition (2) precludes the scenario $(B \in X_1, A \in X_2)$, so the only remaining possibility is $(A \in X_1, B \in X_2)$. There are two cases to consider here:

i) B is not the only member of X_2. Then from (3), $(X_1 + \{B\}) | G(X_2 - \{B\})$. But $A, B \in (X_1 + \{B\})$, so lemma 4 again guarantees that G' is loosely interdependent.

ii) A is not the only member of X_1 and $X_2 = \{B\}$. Thus we have $X_1 | G\{B\}$, so

$$\forall \alpha \in A(G), (source(\alpha) = B) \Rightarrow delay(\alpha) \geq total\_consumed(\alpha, G). \tag{1}$$

Also, since $C \in X_1$ we have from (4) that $q_G(X_1) = gcd(\{q_G(N) | N \in X_1\}) = gcd(\{q_G(N) | N \in X_1\} \cup \{kq_G(C)\}) = gcd(\{q_G(N) | N \in X_1\} \cup \{q_G(B)\}) =$

$gcd(\{q_G(N)|N \in N(G)\}) = 1$. That is,

$$q_G(X_1) = 1. \qquad (2)$$

Now if X_1 is not strongly connected, then it has a proper subset Z such that there are no arcs directed from a member of $(X_1 - Z)$ to a member of Z. Furthermore, from condition (3), $A \notin Z$. This is true because if Z contained A, then no member of $(X_1 - Z)$ would have a path to B, and thus G would not be strongly connected. Thus $A \in (X_1 - Z)$, and there are no arcs directed from $(X_1 - Z)$ to Z. So all arcs directed from $(X_1 - Z + \{B\})$ to Z have node B as their source. From (1) it follows that $Z|G(X_1 - Z + \{B\})$. Now $A, B \in (X_1 - Z + \{B\})$, so applying lemma 4 we conclude that G' is loosely interdependent.

If X_1 is strongly connected, we know from condition (1) that there exist Y_1, Y_2 such that $Y_1|subgraph(X_1)Y_2$. From (2) and lemma 6, Y_1 is subindependent of Y_2 in G. Now if $A \in Y_1$, then from condition (3), B is subindependent of Y_2 in G, so from fact 6(a), $(Y_1 \cup \{B\})|GY_2$. Applying lemma 4, we see that G' is loosely interdependent. On the other hand, suppose that $A \in Y_2$. From (1), we know that Y_1 is subindependent of $\{B\}$ in G. From fact 6(b), it follows that Y_1 is subindependent of $(Y_2 \cup \{B\})$, so again we can apply lemma 4 to conclude that G' is loosely interdependent. QED

Theorem 4: Suppose G is a connected SDF graph, A and B are distinct nodes in G such that B is a successor of A, and $W = \{A, B\}$ is a proper subset of $N(G)$. If we cluster W in G then the tightly interdependent components of G' are the same as the tightly interdependent components of G if the following conditions all hold:

1) Neither A nor B is contained in a tightly interdependent component of G.
2) At least one arc directed from A to B has zero delay.
3) $q_G(B) = kq_G(A)$ for some positive integer k.
4) B has no predecessors other than A and B.

Proof: It suffices to show that all strongly connected subgraphs in G' that contain Ω are loosely interdependent. So we suppose that Z' is a strongly connected subset of $N(G')$ that contains Ω, and we let Z denote the "corresponding" subset in G; that is, $Z = Z' - \{\Omega\} + \{A, B\}$. Now in Z', suppose that there is a directed circuit $(C \to \Omega \to D \to C)$ containing the node Ω. From condition (4), this implies that there is a directed circuit in G containing A, C, D, and possibly B. The two possible ways in which a directed circuit in G introduces a directed circuit involving Ω in G' are illustrated in Fig. 8(a) and (b); the situation in (c) cannot arise because of condition (4).

Now in Z', if one or more of the circuits involving Ω corresponds to Fig. 8(a), then Z must be strongly connected. Otherwise, all of the circuits involving Ω correspond to Fig. 8(b), so $(Z - \{B\})$ is strongly connected, and from condition (4), no member of $(Z - \{A, B\})$ is adjacent to B. In the former case, lemma 7 yields the loose interdependence of Z'.

In the latter case, lemma 5 guarantees that $(Z - \{B\})$ is isomorphic to Z'. Since $A \in (Z-\{B\})$, and since from condition (1), A is not contained in any tightly interdependent subgraph of G, it follows that Z' is loosely interdependent. QED

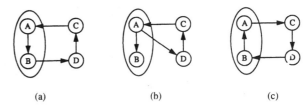

Fig. 8. An illustration of how a directed circuit involving Ω originates in G' for Theorem 4. The two possible scenarios are shown in (a) and (b); (c) will not occur due to condition (4). SDF parameters on the arcs have not been assigned because they are irrelevant to the introduction of directed cycles.

If we assume that the input SDF graph has a single appearance schedule then we can ignore condition (1). From our observations, this is a valid assumption for the vast majority of practical SDF graphs. Also, condition (3) can be verified by examining any single arc directed from A to B; if α is directed from A to B then condition (3) is equivalent to $p(\alpha) = kc(\alpha)$. In our current implementation, we consider only the case $k = 1$ for condition (3) because in practice, this corresponds to most of the opportunities for efficiently using registers.

We see that the clustering process defined by theorem 4—under the assumption that the original graph has a single appearance schedule—requires only *local* dataflow information, and thus it can be implemented very efficiently. If our assumption that a single appearance schedule exists is wrong, then we can always undo our clustering decisions. Since the assumption is frequently valid, and since it leads to a very efficient algorithm, this is the form in which we have implemented theorem 4. Finally, in addition to making data transfers more efficient, our clustering process provides a fast way to reduce the size of the graph without canceling the existence the existence of a single appearance schedule. When used as a preprocessing technique, this can sharply reduce the execution time of a loose interdependence algorithm.

VII. CONCLUSIONS

This paper has presented fundamental topological relationships between iteration and looping in SDF graphs, and we have shown how to exploit these relationships to synthesize the most compact looping structures for a large class of applications. Furthermore, we have extended the developments of [5] by showing how to isolate the minimal subgraphs that require explicit deadlock detection schemes, such as the reachability matrix, when organizing hierarchy.

This paper also defines a framework for evaluating different scheduling schemes having different objectives, with regard to their effect on schedule compactness. The developments of this paper apply to any scheduling algorithm that imposes hierarchy on the SDF graph. For example, by successively repeating the same block of code, we can reduce "context-switch" overhead [22]. We can identify subgraphs that use as much of the available hardware resources as possible, and these can be clustered, as the computations to be repeatedly invoked. However, the hierarchy imposed by such a scheme must be evaluated against its impact on program compactness.

For example, if a cluster introduces tight interdependence, then it may be impossible to fit the resulting program on chip, even though the original graph had a sufficiently compact schedule.

The techniques developed in this paper have been successfully incorporated into a block-diagram software synthesis environment for DSP [18]. We are currently investigating how to systematically incorporate these techniques into other scheduling objectives—for example, how to balance parallelization objectives with program compactness constraints.

APPENDIX

This appendix contains proofs of some the lemmas that were stated and used in Sections IV–VI.

Proof of Lemma 1:

From remark 1, if N is not contained in a nontrivial strongly connected component of G, the result is obvious, so we assume, without loss of generality, that N is in some nontrivial strongly connected component H_1 of G. From our assumptions, $subgraph(H_1)$ must be loosely interdependent, so λ partitions H_1 into X and Y, where $X|subgraph(H_1)Y$. Let H_1' denote that connected component of $subgraph(X)$ or $subgraph(Y)$ that contains N. From remark 3, $appearances(N, S_\lambda(G)) = appearances(N, S_\lambda(subgraph(H_1')))$.

From our assumptions, all nontrivial strongly connected subgraphs of H_1' that contain N are loosely interdependent. Thus, if N is contained in a nontrivial strongly connected component H_2 of H_1', then λ will partition H_2, and we will obtain a proper subset H_2' of H_1' such that $appearances(N, S_\lambda(subgraph(H_1'))) = appearances(N, S_\lambda(subgraph(H_2')))$. Continuing in this manner, we get a sequence $H_1', H_2', \ldots$ of subsets of $N(G)$ such that each H_i' is a proper subset of H_{i-1}', N is contained in each H_i', and $appearances(N, S_\lambda(G)) = appearances(N, S_\lambda(subgraph(H_1'))) = appearances(N, S_\lambda(subgraph(H_2'))) = \ldots$. Since each H_i' is a strict subset of its predecessor, we can continue this process only a finite number, say m, of times. Then $N \in H_m', N$ is not contained in a nontrivial strongly connected component of $subgraph(H_m')$, and $appearances(N, S_\lambda(G)) = appearances(N, S_\lambda(subgraph(H_m')))$. But from remark 1, $S_\lambda(subgraph(H_m'))$ contains only one appearance of N. QED

Proof of Lemma 4:

Let Φ denote the set of arcs directed from a node in X_2 to a node in X_1, and let Φ' denote the set of arcs directed from a node in X_2' to a node in X_1'. Since $subgraph(\{A,B\})$ does not contain any arcs in Φ, it follows that $\Phi' = \{\alpha'|\alpha \in \Phi\}$. From fact 5, it can easily be verified that for all $\alpha', total\_consumed(\alpha', G') = total\_consumed(\alpha, G)$. Now since $X_1|GX_2$, we have $\forall \alpha \in \Phi, delay(\alpha') \geq total\_consumed(\alpha, G)$. It follows that $\forall \alpha' \in \Phi', delay(\alpha') \geq total\_consumed(\alpha', G')$. We conclude that X_1' is subindependent of X_2' in G'. QED

Proof of Lemma 5:

Let $C = subgraph(M - \{A_1\} + \{\Omega\}, G')$, let Φ denote the set of arcs in $subgraph(M, G)$, and let Φ' denote the set of arcs in C. From (1), every arc in C has a corresponding arc in $subgraph(M, G)$ and vice-versa, and thus $\Phi' = \{\alpha'|\alpha \in \Phi\}$. Now from the definition of clustering a subgraph, we know that $p(\alpha') = p(\alpha)$ for any arc $\alpha \in \Phi$ such that $source(\alpha) \neq A_1$. If $source(\alpha) = A_1$, then α is replaced by α' with $source(\alpha') = \Omega$, and $p(\alpha') = p(\alpha)q(A_1)/gcd(q(A_1), q(A_2))$. But $gcd(q(A_1), q(A_2)) = gcd(q(A_1), kq(A_1)) = q(A_1)$, so $p(\alpha') = p(\alpha)$. Thus $p(\alpha') = p(\alpha)$ for all $\alpha \in \Phi$. Similarly, we can show that $c(\alpha') = c(\alpha)$ for all $\alpha \in \Phi$. Thus, the mappings $f_1: M \to N(C)$ and $f_2: \Phi \to \Phi'$ defined by

$$f_1(N) = N \text{ if } N \neq A_1,$$
$$f_1(A_1) = \Omega; \quad \text{and} \quad f_2(\alpha) = \alpha'$$

demonstrate that $subgraph(M, G)$ is isomorphic to C. QED

GLOSSARY

$Z_1|GZ_2$: If G is an SDF graph and Z_1 and Z_2 form a partition of the nodes in G such that Z_1 is subindependent of Z_2 in G, then we write $Z_1|GZ_2$.

$A(G)$: The set of arcs in the SDF graph G.

appearances(N, S): The number of times that actor N appears in the looped schedule S.

admissable schedule: A schedule $S_1 S_2 \cdots S_k$ such that each S_i has sufficient input data to fire immediately after its antecedents $S_1 S_2 \cdots S_{i-1}$ have fired.

$c(\alpha)$: The number of samples consumed from SDF arc α by one invocation of $sink(\alpha)$.

delay(α): The number of delays on SDF arc α.

gcd: Greatest common divisor.

$N(G)$: The set of nodes in the SDF graph G.

PASS: A periodic admissable sequential schedule.

$p(\alpha)$: The number of samples produced onto SDF arc α by one invocation of $source(\alpha)$.

periodic schedule: A schedule that invokes each node at least once and produces no net change in the number of samples buffered on any arc.

predecessor: Given two nodes A and B in an SDF graph, A is a predecessor of B if there is at least one arc directed from A to B.

q_G: The *repetitions vector* q_G of the SDF graph G is a vector that is indexed by the nodes in G. q_G has the property that every *PASS* for G invokes each node N a multiple of $q_G(N)$ times.

single appearance schedule: A schedule that contains only one appearance of each actor in the associated SDF graph.

$sink(\alpha)$: The actor at the sink of SDF arc α.

$source(\alpha)$: The actor at the source of SDF arc α.

subgraph: A *subgraph* of an SDF graph G is the graph formed by any subset Z of nodes in G together with all arcs α in G

for which $source(\alpha), sink(\alpha) \in Z$. We denote the subgraph corresponding to the subset of nodes Z by $subgraph(Z, G)$, or simply by $subgraph(Z)$ if G is understood from context.

subindependent: Given an SDF graph G, and two disjoint subsets Z_1, Z_2 of nodes in G, we say that Z_1 is subindependent of Z_2 in G if for every arc α in G with $source(\alpha) \in Z_2$ and $sink(\alpha) \in Z_1$, we have $delay(\alpha) \geq total\_consumed(\alpha, G)$. We say that Z_1 is subindependent in G if Z_1 is subindependent of $(N(G) - Z_1)$ in G.

successor: Given two nodes A and B in an SDF graph, A is a *successor* of B if there is at least one arc directed from B to A.

total_consumed(α, G): The total number of samples consumed from arc α in a minimal schedule period of the SDF graph G; that is, $total\_consumed(\alpha, G) = q_G(sink(\alpha))c(\alpha)$.

valid schedule: A schedule that is a *PASS*.

REFERENCES

[1] A. V. Aho, J. E. Hopcroft, and J. D. Ullman, "The design and analysis of computer algorithms." Reading, MA: Addison-Wesley, 1974.
[2] Arvind, L. Bic, and T. Ungerer, "Evolution of data-flow computers," in *Advanced Topics In Data-Flow Computing*, J. L. Gaudiot and L. Bic, Eds. Englewood Cliffs, NJ: Prentice-Hall, 1991.
[3] S. S. Bhattacharyya, "Compiling dataflow programs for digital signal processing," Memo. No. UCB/ERL M94/52, Electronics Research Lab., College of Engineering, Univ. of California, Berkeley, CA, July 1994.
[4] S. S. Bhattacharyya and E. A. Lee, "Looped schedules for dataflow descriptions of multirate DSP algorithms," Memo. No. UCB/ERL M93/36, Electronics Research Lab., College of Engineering, Univ. of California, Berkeley CA, May 1993.
[5] ———, "Scheduling synchronous dataflow graphs for efficient looping," *J. VLSI Signal Process.*, vol. 6, no. 3, pp. 271–288, Dec. 1993.
[6] J. B. Dennis, "First version of a dataflow procedure language," MIT/LCS/TM-61, MIT, Lab. for Computer Science, Cambridge, MA, 1975.
[7] ———, "Stream data types for signal processing," unpublished memorandum, Sept. 28, 1992.
[8] G. R. Gao, R. Govindarajan, and P. Panangaden, "Well-behaved programs for DSP computation," in *ICASSP*, San Francisco, CA, Mar. 1992.
[9] D. Genin, J. De Moortel, D. Desmet, and E. Van de Velde, "System design, optimization, and intelligent code generation for standard digital signal processors," in *ISCAS*, Portland, OR, May 1989.
[10] P. N. Hilfinger, "Silage reference manual, draft release 2.0," Computer Science Division, EECS Dept., Univ. of California, Berkeley, July 1989.
[11] W. H. Ho, E. A. Lee, and D. G. Messerschmitt, "High level dataflow programming for digital signal processing," in *VLSI Signal Processing III*. Piscataway, NJ: IEEE Press, 1988.
[12] S. How, "Code generation for multirate DSP systems in Gabriel," Memo. No. UCB/ERL M94/82, Electronics Research Lab., College of Engineering, Univ. of California, Berkeley, CA, Oct. 1994.
[13] E. A. Lee, "Static scheduling of dataflow programs for DSP," in *Advanced Topics in Dataflow Computing*, J. L. Gaudiot and L. Bic, Eds. Englewood Cliffs, NJ: Prentice-Hall, 1991.
[14] E. A. Lee and D. G. Messerschmitt, "Static scheduling of synchronous dataflow programs for digital signal processing," *IEEE Trans. Comput.*, vol. C-36, no. 1, pp. 24–35, Jan. 1987.
[15] E. A. Lee and D. G. Messerschmitt, "Synchronous dataflow," *Proc. IEEE*, vol. 75, no. 9, pp. 1235–1245, Sept. 1987.
[16] J. R. McGraw, S. K. Skedzielewski, S. Allan, D. Grit, R. Oldehoft, J. Glauert, I. Dobes, and P. Hohensee, "SISAL: Streams and iteration in a single assignment language," Language Reference Manual, Version 1.1., Lawrence Livermore National Laboratory, Livermore, CA, July 1983.
[17] D. R. O'Hallaron, "The ASSIGN parallel program generator," Memo. No. CMU-CS-91-141, School of Computer Science, Carnegie Mellon Univ., Pittsburgh, PA, May 1991.
[18] J. L. Pino, S. Ha, E. A. Lee, and J. T. Buck, "Software synthesis for DSP using ptolemy," to be published in *J. VLSI Signal Process.*, vol. 9, no. 1, pp. 7–21, Jan. 1995.
[19] D. B. Powell, E. A. Lee, and W. C. Newmann, "Direct synthesis of optimized DSP assembly code from signal flow block diagrams," in *ICASSP*, San Francisco, CA, Mar. 1992, pp. 553–556.
[20] H. Printz, "Automatic mapping of large signal processing systems to a parallel machine," Memo. No. CMU-CS-91-101, School of Computer Science, Carnegie-Mellon Univ., Pittsburgh, PA, May 1991.
[21] S. Ritz, M. Pankert, and H. Meyr, "High level software synthesis for signal processing systems," in *Proc. Int. Conf. Applicat. Specific Array Processors*, Berkeley, CA, Aug. 1992, pp. 679–693.
[22] S. Ritz, M. Pankert, and H. Meyr, "Optimum vectorization of scalable synchronous dataflow graphs," in *Proc. Int. Conf. Applicat. Specific Array Processors*, Venice, Oct. 1993, pp. 285–296.
[23] G. Sih, "Multiprocessor scheduling to account for interprocessor communication," Memo. No. UCB/ERL M91/29, Electronics Research Lab., Univ. of California, Berkeley, Apr. 1991.
[24] R. E. Tarjan, "Depth first search and linear graph algorithms," *SIAM J. Computing*, vol. 1, no. 2, pp. 146–160, June 1972.
[25] W. W. Wadge and E. A. Ashcroft, *Lucid, the Dataflow Language*. New York: Academic, 1985.

Shuvra S. Bhattacharyya (S'92–M'93) received the B.S. degree in electrical and computer engineering from the University of Wisconsin, Madison, in 1987, and the M.S. and Ph.D. degrees from the University of California, Berkeley, in 1991 and 1994, respectively.

From 1991 to 1992, he was employed by Kuck and Associates, Champaign, Illinois, where he designed and implemented optimizing program transformations for C and Fortran compilers. Since July 1994, he has been a researcher in the Semiconductor Research Laboratory at Hitachi America, Ltd., San Jose, CA. His current research interests include software, architectures, and rapid prototyping for digital signal processing; VLSI signal processing; and parallel computation.

Dr. Bhattacharyya has published several papers, and he is a member of the Association for Computing Machinery (ACM).

Joseph T. Buck received the B.E.E. degree from Catholic University of America in 1978, and the M.S. in computer science from George Washington University in 1981. He received the Ph.D. in 1993 from the University of California, Berkeley, where he was one of the main designers for Ptolemy, a design, simulation, and prototyping environment for heterogenous systems.

From 1979 to 1984 he participated in research in speech coding and recognition at the Naval Research Laboratory. From 1984 to 1989 he worked at Entropic Speech, Inc. on real-time implementations of speech compression algorithms for telephony applications. Presently, he is a staff research engineer in the Advanced Technology Group of Synopsys, Inc. His research interests include techniques for producing efficient hardware, software, and mixed implementations from dataflow graphs and other high-level representations of algorithms.

Soonhoi Ha (S'87–M'92) received the B.S. and M.S. degrees in electronics from Seoul National University, Seoul, Korea, in 1985 and 1987, respectively. He received the Ph.D. degree in the Electrical Engineering and Computer Science Department at the University of California, Berkeley, in 1992.

Currently, he is a full-time lecturer in the Computer Engineering Department at Seoul National University, Seoul, Korea. His research interests include architecture and scheduling techniques for parallel processing and design methodology for digital systems.

Dr. Ha is a member of the Association for Computing Machinery (ACM) and the IEEE Computer Society.

Edward A. Lee (S'80–M'86–SM'93–F'94) received the B.S. from Yale University in 1979, the M.S. from the Massachusetts Institute of Technology in 1981, and the Ph.D. from the University of California, Berkeley, in 1986.

From 1979 to 1982, he was a member of technical staff at Bell Telephone Laboratories in Holmdel, NJ, in the Advanced Data Communications Laboratory. At present, he is a Professor in the Electrical Engineering and Computer Science Department at the University of California, Berkeley. His research activities include real-time software, parallel computation, architecture and software techniques for signal processing, and design methodology for heterogeneous systems. He is Director of the Ptolemy project at UC Berkeley, and previously directed the Gabriel project. He is a founder of Berkeley Design Technology, Inc. and has consulted for a number of other companies. He is co-author of *Digital Communication* (Kluwer Academic Press, 1988 first ed., 1994 second ed.), and co-author of *Digital Signal Processing Experiments* (Prentice-Hall, 1989), as well as numerous technical papers.

Dr. Lee was recently Chairman of the VLSI Technical Committee of the Signal Processing Society, and Co-Program Chair of the 1992 Application Specific Array Processor Conference. He is an Associate Editor of *Design Automation for Embedded Systems* and is on the editorial board of the *Journal on VLSI Signal Processing*. As a Fellow of the IEEE, he has received the citation "For contributions to design methodologies and programming techniques for real-time digital signal processing systems." He was a recipient of a 1987 NSF Presidential Young Investigator award, an IBM faculty development award, the 1986 Sakrison Prize at U.C. Berkeley, and a paper award from the IEEE Signal Processing Society.

Memory Management for Embedded Network Applications

Sven Wuytack, Julio L. da Silva, Jr., Francky Catthoor, *Member, IEEE,* Gjalt de Jong, and Chantal Ykman-Couvreur

Abstract— In embedded network applications, typically a very large part of the area cost is due to memory units. Also the power for such applications is heavily dominated by the storage and transfers. Given its importance, we have developed a systematic memory management methodology in which the storage related issues are optimized as a first step. In this paper, we present our methodology for embedded network applications. It includes both a dynamic memory management stage, where the data types and virtual memory managers are defined, and a physical memory management stage, where the custom memory architecture is defined. As demonstrated on an industrial example, the application of the methodology results in a heavily power and/or area optimized custom memory architecture for a given application.

Index Terms— Communication systems, design automation, low-power design, memory management, virtual memories.

I. INTRODUCTION

THE COMPLEXITY of modern telecommunication systems is rapidly increasing. A wide variety of services has to be transported and elaborate network management is needed. Such complex systems require a combination of hardware and embedded software components in order to deliver the required functionalities at the desired performance level.

For applications in this domain, the desired behavior is often characterized by complex algorithms that operate on large dynamically allocated stored data structures [e.g., linked list, trees, dynamic first-in–first-out buffers (FIFO's)]. This includes especially the transport layer in asynchronous transfer mode (ATM) networks and LAN/WAN technology. Ideally, the specification should reflect the "conceptual" partitioning of the problem, which typically corresponds to the definition of abstract data types (ADT's) along with services provided on them, and algorithms for the different processing tasks. As these conceptual entities can be readily specified in an object-oriented programming model, using data abstraction and class inheritance features, one can use the C++ programming language for the behavioral algorithmic specification as motivated in our global MATISSE approach [4].

In embedded network applications, typically a very large part of the area is due to memory units. Also the power for data-dominated applications is heavily dominated by the storage and transfers, as demonstrated by recent work at Inter-University Micro-Electronics Center (IMEC) (Leuven, Belgium) [2], at Princeton University (Princeton, NJ) [18], at Stanford University (Stanford, CA) [12], and in the IRAM project [9] (Berkeley, CA). Hence, we believe that a dominating factor in the system level design is provided by the organization of the data storage and the way data is managed. This aspect is not sufficiently addressed in a systematic way in current design practice. Moreover, it is practically infeasible to fully integrate this exploration in the existing compilation and hardware synthesis methodologies.

For these reasons, we have proposed a systematic design methodology in which the storage related issues are optimized as a first step, *before* doing the detailed compilation on an embedded processor or the scheduling and data-path and controller synthesis in case of a custom hardware mapping. This preprocessing includes both a dynamic memory management and a physical memory management stage.

If we compare our work with the state of the art in the literature, we see that virtual memory management (VMM) is usually restricted to large programmable processors. While in our case, instead of a single virtual memory space, custom hardware implementations such as dedicated distributed memory structures may be employed. This requires new techniques for the memory management, though. Likewise, if we compare our work with software implementations, we see that currently the programmer or the operating system takes care of the ADT and VMM refinements in a more-or-less default way and that performance is usually the only cost factor [1], [20]. While in our application domain, power and area are more dominant cost factors, and performance is a hard constraint that has to be met. This heavily changes the required design methodology for the dynamic memory management stage.

Comparing our work in the context of hardware implementations, we see that behavioral synthesis has been an active field of research [6] and that commercial behavioral synthesis tools are available [e.g., Synopsys' Behavioral Compiler (BC) and Mentor Graphics' Monet]. However, support for complex data structures and memory synthesis related problems is generally limited. Also in research, most emphasis in physical memory management has been on register allocation for scalar data [16]. An exception to this is the video and image

---

Manuscript received July 16, 1998; revised October 29, 1998. This work was supported by the Flemish IWT and Alcatel under the HASTEC Project, in part by the Esprit Project 21929 (MEDIA), and in part by a Brazilian Government Scholarship—CAPES. This paper was recommended by Associate Editor G. Borriello.

S. Wuytack is with the DESICS Division, Inter-University Micro-Electronics Center (IMEC), B-3001 Leuven, Belgium (e-mail: wuytack@imec.be).

J. L. da Silva, Jr. is with Pontifica Universidade Catolica do Rio Grande do Sul (PUCRS), Brasil.

F. Catthoor and C. Ykman-Couvreur are with the DESICS Division, Inter-University Micro-Electronics Center (IMEC), B-3001 Leuven, Belgium.

G. de Jong is with Alcatel Telecom, B-2018 Antwerp, Belgium.

Publisher Item Identifier S 0278-0070(99)02962-0.

processing area [2], [11], [14]. The latter is however restricted to statically allocated arrays and records. The data structures in the network and communication protocol domain are however different, as they heavily use *dynamically allocated* data. Hence, modified physical memory management methodologies and design tool support are required. Note that, in contrast with most other approaches, our techniques work on groups of scalars instead of scalars, thereby allowing for tractable optimizations for real-life applications.

In this paper, we propose a top-down methodology for the memory management of network applications. Application studies and detailed problem and sensitivity analysis have guided the definition and ordering of the individual phases in the flow. Several steps in our methodology are supported by prototype tools which are not elaborated in this paper however (see [3], [4], [15], and [22]). This paper only deals with the dynamic memory management and physical memory management in network applications. The synthesis aspects to a final hardware realization are not addressed either. Such information can be found, e.g., in [4] and [15] and their references.

The target architecture can be both embedded software or custom hardware. In the former case, the memory organization will be partly limited due to predefined memory sizes and bus structures. These constraints can however be relatively easily incorporated in the methodology discussed below.

The extensive design exploration, which is feasible by applying our methodology, and its heavy impact on embedded processor cost issues will be illustrated based on a representative module of an industrial ATM application provided by Alcatel, namely the segment protocol processor (SPP) [17].

The rest of the paper is organized as follows. Section II presents the test vehicle used to demonstrate our methodology. Section III summarizes the power models we have used for estimating the power consumption of the memory architecture. Section IV gives an overview of our global design flow for embedded network applications. Section V describes the ADT refinement step. Section VI describes the VMM step. Section VII describes the physical memory management step. And Section VIII concludes the paper.

II. CASE STUDY: SPP

ATM networks are characterized by a connection-oriented mode of operation. The Alcatel Connectionless Transport Server (ACTS) [17] is a user transparent connectionless router developed by Alcatel. It provides the necessary functions for the direct provision and support of data communication between geographically distributed computers or between LAN's over an ATM-based broadband network. This is depicted in Fig. 1.

In its current implementation, the ACTS consists of several boards, each one consisting of several processors and coprocessors (PHP, PCC, and SPP), implemented as custom ASIC's, and a programmable supervising microprocessor for executive control. A concrete example of one of those ASIC's, named segment protocol processor (SPP) [17], is used to illustrate the characteristics of our target domain.

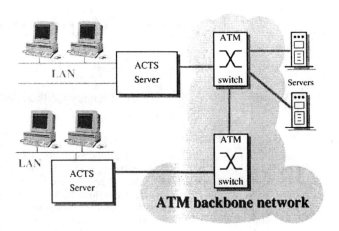

Fig. 1. ACTS environment.

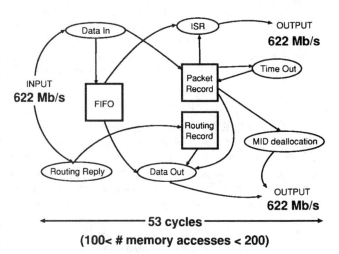

Fig. 2. SPP task level diagram.

The SPP implements the ATM adaptation layer 3/4 of the ACTS. The SPP has to store and forward user cells, to perform a number of checks by itself, to issue requests to other coprocessors to perform other checks, to issue a request for routing, and to process routing replies.

The SPP can be described as a set of concurrent tasks that cooperate with each other through shared data types, as shown in Fig. 2. The tasks are represented by ellipses and the shared data types are represented by squares. The tasks have to be performed for each incoming frame, consisting of four ATM cells of 53 bytes each, at a frame rate of 622 Mbit/s. These tasks are combined, in order to satisfy design constraints such as memory bandwidth.

The algorithms, implementing the SPP functionality, make use of ADT's. One particular implementation of the ADT's is shown in Fig. 3. The right side of the figure shows a queue, where incoming user cells are buffered. Packet records are accessed through two keys: the local identifiers (LID) and multiplexing identifiers (MID). A packet record (IPI) contains various fields, such as the number of cells received so far,

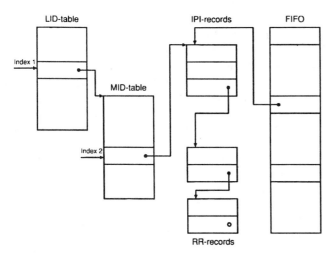

Fig. 3. Concrete data types of the segment protocol processor.

TABLE I
SPP DATA TYPES

	Area (%)	Width (bits)	Size (no. of blocks)
Cell	62	448	11 200
IPI	16	384	3350
RR	22	128	13 400

the time the first cell was received and a pointer to a list of routing records (RR).

In the SPP, the total memory size is targeted to be 128 K words (of 64 bits) for the main off-chip memory. In Table I, the three data types in the SPP that correspond to the largest amount of data in the main off-chip memory are presented. The area distribution for these three data types is shown in the first column of Table I. The width of each data type is shown in the second column. The approximate maximum number of blocks used for each data type is shown in the third column.

Other ASIC's used in the ACTS, such as the packet handler processor (PHP) and the preventive congestion control (PCC) processor, and other network components can be described in a similar way, by means of a set of cooperative tasks operating on shared data types.

In summary, the SPP has the following seven main characteristics, that are also present in a number of other network applications.

1) *Large Amount of Dynamically Allocated Data:* Storage space for such data contributes to a major part of the area. Data is (de)allocated at run-time and may be shared among a set of concurrent tasks. Examples include cell queue, packet records, and routing records that correspond to approximately 5 Mbyte in the SPP (Fig. 3).
2) *Intensive Data Transfer Required to Background Storage:* The large amount of data transfers to large storage units contributes to a major part of the power. Examples include transfers to cell queue, MID/LID tables, packet records, and routing records that correspond to approx-imately 200 memory accesses per 53 cycles in the SPP (Fig. 3).
3) *Concurrently Operating Set of Tasks:* Tasks define the coarse grain concurrency (Fig. 4). Constructs, such as *if-then-else, for,* and *while loops* are essential for capturing the algorithmic behavior of each task.
4) *Mix of Global and Local Control:* Each task has its own control flow. However, next to this there is a global control for all tasks on the task control flow layer. Examples include the different flow of execution for each type of cell, for instance in the SPP (Fig. 2), for a Begin Of Message cell, tasks Data_IN, ISR, and Data_Out have to be executed, while for a End Of Message cell tasks Data_IN, MID_deallocation, and Data_Out have to be executed.
5) *Little Data Processing:* As a result, the data processing part contributes to a small part of the area and power. In the SPP final implementation, it contributes to less than 5% of the total area.
6) *Real-Time Requirements:* These applications operate under stringent real-time requirements, for instance, the cell rate of 622 Mbit/s in the SPP.
7) *Embedded Hardware/Software Realization:* Due to area, power, performance, and flexibility constraints, these applications are partly realized as embedded hardware/software. In embedded applications, power and area must be optimized because they are crucial cost factors. For instance, the ACTS (Fig. 1) has been implemented as a set of custom processors (SPP, PHP, PCC) and an instruction set processor. In the future, this functionality will be integrated in a single chip solution, following the same trend as wireless applications [7].

III. POWER MODELS

We measure the effect of our optimizations by means of a cost function that is the weighted sum of area and power of the memory architecture. In this paper we have focused on power optimizations and, hence, only need to estimate the power consumption of the different parts of a memory architecture.

For the on-chip memories, the energy consumption of one memory access increases with the memory size, i.e., bitwidth and number of words. The dependency is between linear and logarithmic depending on the memory library used. For our experiments we have used a proprietary memory library of TI, for which we can only publish relative values. Given the size of the memory, we can calculate the energy per access using a tool. This value has to be multiplied by the number of memory accesses per time unit to get the power value.

The power of the internal interconnect and of the address calculation is small (less than 20%) compared to that of the internal memories and can be neglected in the high-level power estimations.

For the off-chip memories, the energy consumption can be considered more or less independent from the memory size for various reasons. We have used a value of 260 mW for an static random access memory (SRAM) operating at 100 MHz. If the SRAM is accessed at a lower frequency, this value has to be scaled accordingly.

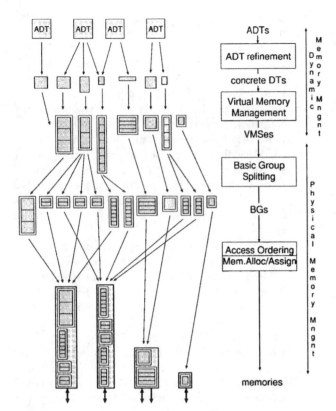

Fig. 4. Global memory management design flow.

The power of the external interconnect is large compared to that of the external memories. Luckily it does not vary very much because a large part of the capacitance is determined by the pins of the ASIC and the memory chip. We have used a value of 20 pF per bus line. For a 27-bit-wide bus, operating at 100 MHz and 5 V and an activity factor of 0.5, this results in a power consumption of 675 mW. If the bus is accessed at a lower frequency this value has to be scaled accordingly.

Hence, power can be saved by reducing the number of accesses to large memories, or by assigning the data to smaller memories.

IV. GLOBAL DESIGN FLOW ISSUES

Fig. 4 gives an overview of the proposed memory management design flow, which is the result from detailed application and solution strategy studies. Each of the steps will be detailed in the following sections.

At the highest level, the application is specified in terms of ADT's. The *ADT refinement step* refines these ADT's into a combination of concrete data structures, such as linked lists or pointer arrays with one or more access keys. The *virtual memory management step*, defines a number of *virtual memory segments* and their corresponding custom memory managers. Each virtual memory segment reserves an amount of memory to store all instances of one or more concrete data types. To this end, the virtual memory segment is divided into a number of slots, each capable of storing a single instance of the data type. The VMM step determines, via analysis or simulation of a number of scenarios, the amount of slots that is required to store all instances of that data type.

For dynamically allocated data types, the VMM step also determines a custom memory manager for the corresponding virtual memory segment, implementing the allocation and deallocation functions. The ADT and VMM refinement are combined in the dynamic memory management stage.

During the physical memory management stage, the virtual memory segments will be assigned to a number of allocated memories. However, to increase the mapping freedom and the simultaneous accessibility of the data, the virtual memory segments are first split into so called *basic groups* according to some specific rules.

Next, the background memory accesses are ordered to optimize the required storage bandwidth. Finally, the memory allocation and assignment step allocates a number of memories and assigns the basic groups to them. This determines the size of the memories in terms of bitwidth and word depth as well as the number and type (read, write, or read/write) of ports on each memory. The result is a heavily power and/or area optimized custom memory architecture for the given application.

V. ADT REFINEMENT

In an implementation independent specification, complex data structures are typically specified by means of ADT's that represent a certain functionality without imposing implementation decisions. A set of records that are identified by a unique integer number called a key value, is a typical and important example of an ADT that frequently occurs in network applications. The ADT provides a number of services (e.g., inserting, locating, and removing a record from a set) to the application. These services can be used without knowing the actual implementation of the ADT, allowing the designer to specify the functionality of an application without imposing unnecessary implementation decisions. ADT refinement determines the optimal implementation for all ADT's in the application.

A set of records accessible through one or more keys can be implemented by many different concrete data types. All of these have different characteristics in terms of memory occupation, number of memory accesses to locate a certain record, power dissipation, and the like. To allow the designer to make a motivated choice, all possible data structures have to be represented in a formalized model such that the best solutions for a given application can be searched for. The following subsections illustrate the ADT refinement for the *set-of-records* ADT.

A. A Hierarchical Model for Set-of-Records

In our model there are four primitive data structures (linked lists, tree structures, arrays, and pointer arrays) that can be combined to create more complex data structures. These are the typical choices in set data base applications.

Fig. 5 shows a tree representing a complex data structure composed of primitive data structures. With every key corresponds a layer in the tree. The bottom layer is the record

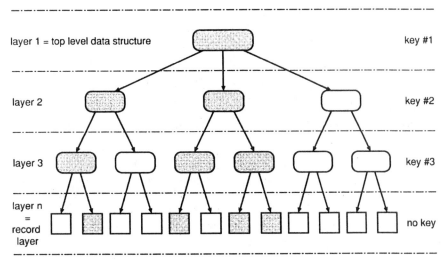

Fig. 5. Hierarchical data structure model.

layer which has no key associated with it. The top layer data structure (i.e., the root of the tree) represents the whole set of records. Each layer below represents a partitioning of the whole set into a number of subsets. Specifying a value for the key corresponding to the top layer, selects the subset of records for which the first key has the specified value. Additionally specifying a value for the key corresponding to the second layer selects a subset of this subset. This process can be continued until all keys have been specified. At this time a single record has been selected.

Each node in the tree has to associate values of the key corresponding to its layer with a node on the next layer in the tree, except for the records on the bottom layer. This functionality can be implemented using one of the primitive data structures presented above.

B. Key Management

Instead of having one key per layer, keys can also be split into *subkeys*, or several keys can be combined into one *super key*. This may heavily impact the implementation cost. Similarly, the order in which the keys are used to access the set heavily impacts the required memory size, the average number of memory accesses to locate a record, and the power cost. Therefore, it is important to find the optimal key ordering for the given application as well as the optimal number of layers with subkeys.

C. Key Transformation

If the keys are not uniformly distributed, key transformation can be used to improve the results by applying a permutation function to any key or combination of keys. Note that key transformation can be combined with any of the primitive data structures, thereby providing an orthogonal axis of freedom in the search space. Key transformation is especially useful in combination with key splitting, because it allows to reduce the average size of the primitive data structures associated with the subkeys after splitting. This is the case when the values of the subkeys after splitting are somehow correlated.

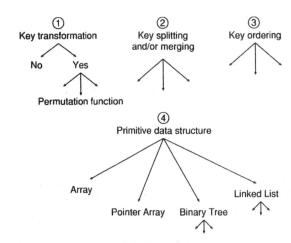

Fig. 6. ADT search space and decision ordering.

Transforming the combined key before splitting can reduce this correlation and, hence, reduce the average size of the primitive data structures by spreading their elements over more primitive data structures. This is only useful when these data structures have a variable size, i.e., are linked lists or binary trees. For fixed-size data structures, i.e., arrays and pointer arrays, the permutation function can better be tuned to concentrate correlated key values in as few primitive data structures as possible. Depending on the primitive data structures involved, either one or the other can lead to improved results.

D. Optimization Methodology

There are many possible data structures within the model that realize a given set of records. Each of these can be seen as a combination of different major options which are orthogonal relative to each other (Fig. 6). Within each option, more detailed choices can still be made.

Finding the best combination for a given application is not so trivial, since it depends on the parameters in the model, e.g., average number of records, size of the records, average number of accesses to the records, ratio of insert/locate/delete

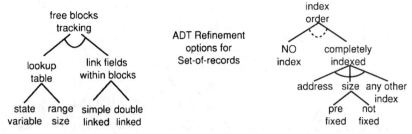

Fig. 7. Decision trees for keeping track of free blocks.

operations, etc. Moreover, the full search space is too large to be scanned exhaustively. To determine the optimal data structure we have to find the optimal number of layers in the hierarchy, the optimal key ordering, the optimal permutation function for each key or combination of keys, and the optimal primitive data structure for every layer in the hierarchy. Our experiments showed that all of these optimizations influence each other, so it is not possible to optimize each aspect fully independently to obtain the global optimum. In practice, however, some decisions are much more important than others, and a heuristic decision ordering, indicated in Fig. 6, can be proposed, which leads to near optimal solutions without exhaustively exploring all combinations. For a detailed description of the full optimization methodology, we refer to [21].

Results on SPP: The set-of-records ADT for the IPI records in Fig. 2 was optimized with a power function for two realistic scenarios. The first one assumed a realistic number of records to be stored in a memory built with 1 Mbit SRAM's. The second one did the same for a memory built with 4-Mbit SRAM's (the next generation). This resulted in about 8000 records for the first scenario and 60 000 for the second scenario. The original specification already contained two keys, LID and MID, which had good characteristics. So no key splitting or key transformation was used for this application. The two scenarios have resulted in two different optimal data structures for the set. Both of them are two layer structures, using the two keys in the same order, and a pointer array accessed with the LID key for the first layer. Only the primitive data structure on the second layer is different: a pointer array for the small number of records, and an array for the large number of records. The solution for the first scenario is shown in Fig. 3. For a full description on how we arrived at this solution in a systematic way, we refer to [21].

Applying the optimal data structure for one set of parameters in the context for which the other data structure was optimized, results in a power consumption that is more than 2.5 times above that of the optimal data structure. Moreover, the entire search space spans a power range of four orders of magnitude, clearly substantiating the importance of a very optimized exploration decision.

VI. VIRTUAL MEMORY MANAGEMENT

The VMM step [5] reserves storage space for each concrete data type obtained during the ADT refinement step. First, the virtual memory segments for all ADT's are defined and sized (VMM sizing substep). Subsequently, it determines custom virtual memory managers for those data types that are dynamically allocated in the application (VMM refinement substep). As the data needed for the operation of these managers can also be an ADT on their own, they need to be stored in memory too which leads to additional virtual memory segments (see Fig. 4).

VMM consists of allocation, recycling and mapping. Allocation is the mechanism that searches the pool of free blocks and returns a free block large enough in order to satisfy a request of a given application. Recycling is the mechanism that returns a block which is not used anymore to the pool of free blocks enabling its reuse. Mapping is the mechanism that translates virtual memory addresses into physical memory addresses.

Nowadays, the programmer either uses the default allocation mechanism provided in a library or implements an allocation mechanism that satisfies his performance needs, such as speed or memory usage. An alternative is to run the application with different allocators and then choose the most convenient one. Yet another possibility, not explored up to now, is to use a methodology, manually or automatically steered, that evaluates characteristics of the application and provides the best allocator for that application.

Much literature is available about possible implementation choices [1], [20] but none of the earlier work provides a complete search space useful for a systematic exploration. In order to derive a methodology it is essential to understand all the relevant possibilities for implementing allocation mechanisms. Similar to the ADT refinement problem, this is only feasible in practice by identifying the orthogonal decision trees in the available search space[1] from which all allocation schemes can then be derived by combination.

In the following subsections we present the decision trees for allocation and recycling mechanisms. In Figs. 7–11, a solid arc between two or more choices represents that all possible combinations between these leaves of the decision tree are feasible. A dashed arc between two choices represents a set of possibilities that can vary from one extreme to another in the decision tree over an enumerated axis. In principle, any combination of leafs in each choice tree represents a valid allocation mechanism.

A. Keeping Track of Free Blocks

The allocator keeps track of free blocks using either link fields within free blocks or lookup tables. The free blocks may be indexed by size, address, etc. Free blocks may be

---

[1] We do not consider implicit recycling mechanisms, known as garbage collectors, in our search space.

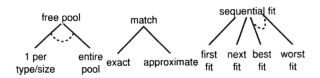

Fig. 8. Decision trees for choosing a free block.

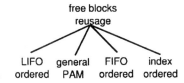

Fig. 9. Decision tree for freeing used blocks.

organized in linked lists, trees, pointer arrays, or arrays. Those decision trees are depicted in Fig. 7. The decision trees for ADT refinement of these free blocks involve several aspects (see Section V).

Using link fields within free blocks avoids overhead in terms of memory usage as long as a minimum block size is respected, while lookup tables always incur an overhead in terms of memory usage.

B. Choosing a Free Block

The possibilities for choosing a block from the free blocks pool, in order to satisfy a given request, are depicted in Fig. 8. Free blocks may be either in an entire pool or grouped in sectors. These sectors may group blocks per size or type. The sectors may use an exact or approximate match policy. For instance, a sector could group blocks of a specific size or a set of sizes.

In a sequential way the allocator tries to satisfy a given request by finding either the first free block large enough (*first fit*) or the closest fit (*best fit*). A variation of first fit (*next fit*) keeps a pointer to the free block after the previous allocated block. This pointer is used as a starting point for searching the next free block.

When the sizes or types to be allocated are known at compile time, keeping a segregated storage policy [20] improves the allocation speed and eliminates internal fragmentation but may increase external fragmentation.

C. Freeing Used Blocks

The possibilities for returning a recently freed block to the pool of free blocks are depicted in Fig. 9. The indexed ordered option is usually slower than the FIFO and LIFO ordered options because it returns a block to the pool of free blocks respecting an index order instead of simply returning it to the top or bottom of the pool. However, it may avoid wasted memory when combined with merging and splitting techniques. The performance of an indexed ordered scheme may be improved by using hashing, but it does not work well for all ADT choices.

D. Splitting Blocks

When the free block chosen to satisfy a request is larger than needed, a policy for splitting the block being allocated should be implemented (Fig. 10).

The splitting of a block may be done: never, sometimes, or always. The splitting may be done only if the block is larger than a minimum size. Which part of the free block is used first should also be chosen. The splitting may have to respect some index, such as size. The remainder of the split should return to the pool of free blocks obeying a decision tree equivalent to the one presented in Section VI-C.

E. Merging Free Blocks

When address adjacent blocks are free they may be merged following one of the possibilities depicted in Fig. 11. For instance, for already large blocks it may be uninteresting to merge them, because the result will be an even larger block.

In general it is interesting to defer the merging decision in order to avoid subsequent splitting operations. Deferred merging may be implemented in different ways: wait for a fixed or variable amount of allocation requests before merging or wait for an unsatisfied allocation request before merging.

The amount of blocks to be merged should be chosen from merging all mergeable blocks to merging only enough blocks to satisfy the last request. When the free blocks are kept in an indexed ordered way, the merging mechanism must also respect the index used.

F. Optimization Methodology

The decisions that should be taken in the decision trees when selecting a VMM mechanism are not totally independent. A decision taken in one tree may affect the cost characteristics of other decision trees. A systematic exploration methodology consists of: identifying how much each decision influences a given cost parameter and identifying the dependencies among the decisions.

In a memory oriented power model, the access count (number of accesses to memory) has the major (linear) influence on power, because the memory size only has a sublinear effect [8]. For a given record, the access count is the sum of the number of accesses during its allocation plus the accesses during its lifetime plus the ones during deallocation. Hence, when the number of accesses during allocation and deallocation of a block is dominant over the number of accesses during its lifetime, the power exploration can be based on the access oriented exploration methodology briefly presented in the rest of this section. However, for some data types, the number of accesses during lifetime of a block is dominant over the number of accesses during allocation and deallocation. In this case, it does make sense to try to minimize memory size which still influences power in a less direct way. Moreover, also the area cost is heavily decreased this way. A memory size exploration methodology is not presented in this paper.

The most important decision tree involves selecting between using one subpool per data type or using an entire pool for all data types because this has a global effect. This decision affects

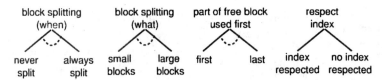

Fig. 10. Decision trees for splitting blocks.

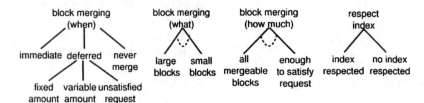

Fig. 11. Decision trees for merging free blocks.

all data types and all the other decisions. All other choices are done for each subpool independently.

The second decision that has influence on several other decision trees is about the use of an index to order the free blocks. The impact is now per subpool, according to the first decision. However, the use of an index still heavily influences the number of accesses during (de)allocation.

The third decision that has interdependencies is about the merging/splitting choices. The decisions taken for the merging policy should be compatible with the decisions taken for the splitting policy. For instance, it only makes sense to use a merging technique if its splitting counterpart is also used.

Apart from these major interdependencies, the other decisions are independent in terms of influence on the number of accesses. Thus, the leaf that minimizes the number of accesses locally in each decision tree can be selected. The description of the local effect on power for each decision tree is not given here, but this is done by comparing the impact of each leaf of these trees on the number of accesses.

Results on SPP—VMM Sizing Substep: Five virtual memory segments were defined and sized for the SPP: one for each concrete data type (LID-table, MID-tables, IPI-records, FIFO, and RR-records). The critical path went down from 26 cycles for one common memory implementation, to 15 cycles for the implementation with virtual memory segments. All cycles in this paper are memory cycles: one memory access can occur per cycle and per memory port.

Results on SPP—VMM Refinement Substep: The total memory size is targeted to be 128 K words for the main off-chip memory. In the SPP, the largest block size equals seven words, and the smallest one two words. Using a systematic methodology we can traverse the search space of Figs. 7–11 for the best solutions in terms of access count, power, or area. For the five virtual memory segments with the best choices of independent allocation mechanisms, each allocation/deallocation takes only 15 memory accesses in the worst case, which is an enormous difference with most other cases. For instance, collapsing all virtual memory segments into one and using a single allocation mechanism, each allocation/deallocation can take up to 500 K accesses in the worst case.

VII. Physical Memory Management

The physical memory management step determines an optimized memory architecture for the application. To satisfy the strict timing constraints of network applications, this is done in three steps: first a *basic group splitting step,* followed by a *storage-bandwidth optimization step,* and a *memory allocation and assignment step.* For a hierarchical memory organization involving caches, also cache related optimizations can be incorporated at the end [10].

A. Basic Group Splitting

The basic group splitting step splits virtual memory segments into smaller groups of data, called basic groups, to increase the mapping freedom and the parallel accessibility of the data. This leads to improved results in the rest of the physical memory management step.

Most data in an optimized memory architecture is stored in one-port memories, because multiport memories are much more expensive both in terms of area and power. Therefore, if a virtual memory segment is assigned as a whole to a single one-port memory, its data can only be accessed sequentially. If, on the other hand, a virtual memory segment is split into basic groups and these basic groups are assigned to different memories, data that belongs to different basic groups can be accessed simultaneously. Since network applications have strict timing constraints (e.g., a cycle budget), increasing the parallel accessibility of data, helps a lot to improve the implementation. An added benefit of splitting virtual memory segments is that it increases the assignment freedom for the next step. Experiments have shown that splitting virtual memory segments into basic groups leads to much better results.

To be useful, the basic group splitting must be done according to some strict rules. Listing them falls outside the scope of this paper. The most important rule, however, is that each read and write operation in the code should access data of *exactly one* basic group. Due to data dependent indexing and dynamic allocation of data, this rule puts a lower bound on the size of the basic groups.

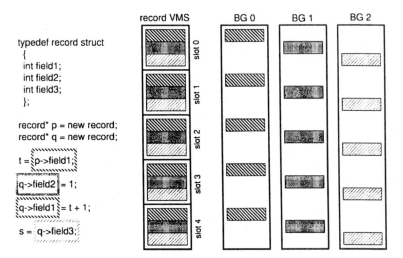

Fig. 12. Basic group splitting.

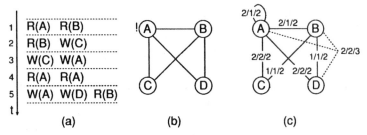

Fig. 13. Storage-bandwidth optimization: (a) ordering, (b) conflict graph, and (c) extended conflict graph.

As an example of basic group splitting consider a virtual memory segment for storing a number of dynamically allocated records (Fig. 12). Let p be a pointer to such a record. The data access operation $p \rightarrow field1$ can access a field in each slot of the virtual memory segment because the slot p points to is run-time dependent. Hence, according to the above mentioned rule, all $field1$'s of the virtual memory segment belong to the same basic group. Since all read/write operations accessing the records in the virtual memory segment specify the field being accessed, the virtual memory segment can be split according to the fields: with every field of the record corresponds a single basic group. The first basic group is an array containing the $field1$'s of all records in the virtual memory segment. The second basic group contains all $field2$'s, and so on.

Results on SPP: The five virtual memory segments of the SPP can be split in 14 basic groups. This reduces the critical path further from 15 to nine cycles.

B. Storage-Bandwidth Optimization

The storage-bandwidth optimization step determines *which* basic groups should be made simultaneously accessible in the memory architecture such that the imposed timing constraints can be met with minimal memory cost.

The storage-bandwidth optimization step orders data accesses within a given cycle budget [Fig. 13(a)]. Whenever two accesses to two basic groups occur in the same cycle, we say there is an access conflict between these basic groups because they cannot share the same memory port. All access conflicts are collected in a conflict graph, where the nodes represent basic groups, and the edges indicate access conflicts between the corresponding basic groups [Fig. 13(b)]. These conflicts have to be resolved during the subsequent memory allocation and assignment step. This can be done by assigning conflicting basic groups either to different memories or to a multiport memory such that they are simultaneously accessible. When all conflicts in the conflict graph are resolved during the memory allocation and assignment step, it is guaranteed that a valid schedule exists for the obtained memory architecture.

When multiport memories are allowed in the memory architecture, more information is needed than present in a simple conflict graph. Therefore, we have defined an extended conflict graph. In an extended conflict graph, every conflict is annotated with three numbers [indicated in the form R/W/RW in Fig. 13(c)]: the maximal number of simultaneous read accesses (R), the maximal number of simultaneous write accesses (W), and the maximal number of simultaneous memory accesses, i.e., read or write, (RW) that can occur between the conflicting basic groups during the execution of the algorithm. Also conflicts between more than two basic groups have to be taken into account, because several conflicting basic groups can be stored in a single multiport memory as long as the number of simultaneous memory accesses is not exceeding the access capabilities of the memory. This results in the inclusion of hyper edges in the extended conflict graph, indicating the conflicts between more than two basic groups. When multiport memories are available in the memory library, basic groups can be allowed to be in conflict with themselves, leading to self edges in the conflict graph. Such self conflicts are very costly because they force the allocation of expensive multiport memories.

We have defined a cost function for extended conflict graphs, such that more costly extended conflict graphs are likely to lead to more costly memory architectures [15]. The cost function includes three weighted terms:

1) a term to minimize the number of self conflicts;
2) a measure for the required number of memories;
3) the number of conflicts (importance weighted).

The idea of storage-bandwidth optimization is then to derive a partial ordering of the data accesses that leads to an extended conflict graph with minimal cost. All accessibility constraints that have to be respected in the subsequent memory allocation and assignment step are expressed in the extended conflict graph. Therefore, the partial ordering information can be thrown away after storage-bandwidth optimization. Indeed, the memory allocation and assignment step decides which basic groups are simultaneously accessible in the *optimized* memory architecture. Therefore, it is the memory allocation and assignment step, and not the storage-bandwidth optimization step, that determines the constraints for the detailed scheduling step that comes after physical memory management in our global design flow. The ordering of the memory accesses in the final schedule can be completely different from the partial ordering obtained during storage-bandwidth optimization.

Our current storage-bandwidth optimization prototype tool uses an iterative search strategy to order the memory accesses similar to improved force directed scheduling of [19] but with a totally different cost function. More details are given in [15] and [22].

Results on SPP: We have compared our storage-bandwidth optimization methodology with a conventional approach without storage-bandwidth optimization using Synopsys' BC for the SPP and a cycle budget of 17 cycles. The extended conflict graph derived from BC's schedule, contained 25 conflicts and required at least six one-port memories in the memory architecture. The extended conflict graph obtained with our storage-bandwidth optimization methodology, contained only 13 conflicts and required only three one-port memories. The required storage-bandwidth is reduced by a factor two using our methodology.

C. Memory Allocation and Assignment

The memory allocation and assignment step determines the number and type of the memories, the number and type of their ports, and an assignment of basic groups on the allocated memories in a power and/or area optimized memory architecture (Fig. 14). The accessibility constraints, expressed in the form of an extended conflict graph, restrict its search space to memory architectures that provide enough memory bandwidth to meet the timing constraints.

The memory allocation and assignment is done in two phases. The *memory allocation phase* determines the memory configuration, i.e., the number of memories in the memory

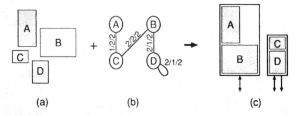

Fig. 14. Memory allocation and assignment: (a) characterization of basic groups, (b) extended conflict graph, and (c) resulting memory architecture.

architecture and the number of ports on each memory. A minimal memory configuration can easily be extracted from the extended conflict graph. This minimal memory configuration is not necessarily the optimal one. For instance, adding more memories is usually good for power as more memories means smaller and, hence, less power consuming memories. If the basic groups have different bitwidths, allocating more memories allows to reduce the amount of bits wasted by storing basic groups with different bitwidth in the same memory. Allocating too many memories is not good because of the increased design complexity, interconnect overhead, and increased interface count for off-chip memories. It is important to find the right tradeoff here. The *memory assignment phase* assigns the basic groups to the allocated memories such that the memory architecture cost is minimized and all accessibility constraints expressed in the extended conflict graph are satisfied. The assignment determines the size of the memories as well as the type of ports on each memory. The bitwidth of a memory is simply the maximum bitwidth of all basic groups assigned to it. If the data are permanent—which is common in network applications—and do not exhibit partially exclusive lifetimes, the memory space cannot be partially shared. So the word depth is simply the sum of the number of words of all basic groups assigned to it. The type of the ports on a memory can easily be extracted from the R/W/RW numbers in the extended conflict graph and the list of basic groups assigned to it. Given the characteristics of all memories the total area and power consumption of the memory architecture can be calculated.

In our current memory allocation and assignment prototype tool, the allocation is decided by the designer and the assignment is done automatically by means of a customized branch-and-bound type algorithm [15].

Results on SPP: We have examined the effect of allocation on the power consumption of the SPP. The values presented are relative figures after optimal assignment: six memories $\rightarrow$ 1.00, three memories $\rightarrow$ 1.98, one memory $\rightarrow$ 6.85. Clearly, allocating more memories allows to reduce the memory power consumption a lot. To get an idea of the influence of assignment on the power consumption, we have calculated some figures for the extended conflict graph obtained for 24 cycles and an allocation of three one-port memories. The average power consumption of a random assignment within the extended conflict graph constraints is about 20% above that of the optimal assignment found by our memory allocation and assignment tool. The worst possible assignment results in a power consumption that is about 75% above the optimal.

VIII. Conclusions

In this paper we have presented our systematic memory exploration methodology for embedded network applications. We have shown, through an industrial example, that our methodology can achieve a heavily power and/or area optimized custom memory architecture for a given application, still meeting given timing constraints. The methodology is also successfully applied to other industrial applications than the SPP, e.g., the STORM application of Alcatel [15].

Acknowledgment

The authors gratefully acknowledge the discussions with their colleagues at IMEC and Alcatel and especially the contributions of M. Miranda, A. Vandecappelle, P. Slock, K. Croes, M. Genoe, C. Verdonck, B. Lin, D. Verkest, and P. Six.

References

[1] G. Attardi and T. Flagea, "A customisable memory management framework," in *Proc. USENIX C++ Conf.,* Cambridge, MA, 1994.
[2] F. Catthoor, F. Franssen, S. Wuytack, L. Nachtergaele, and H. De Man, "Global communication and memory optimizing transformations for low power signal processing systems," in *Proc. IEEE Workshop on VLSI Signal Processing,* La Jolla CA, Oct. 1994; in *VLSI Signal Processing VII,* J. Rabaey, P. Chau, J. Eldon, Eds. Piscataway, NJ: IEEE Press, 1994, pp. 178–187.
[3] J. L. da Silva Jr., C. Ykman, and G. de Jong, "MATISSE: A concurrent and object-oriented system specification language," presented at *Int. Conf VLSI (IFIP),* Aug. 1997.
[4] J. L. da Silva, Jr., C. Ykman-Couvreur, M. Miranda, K. Croes, S. Wuytack, G. de Jong, F. Catthoor, D. Verkest, P. Six, and H. De Man, "Efficient system exploration and synthesis of applications with dynamic data storage and intensive data transfer," presented at *35th ACM/IEEE Design Automation Conf.,* San Francisco, CA, June 1998.
[5] J. L. da Silva Jr., F. Catthoor, D. Verkest, and H. De Man, "Power exploration for dynamic data types through virtual memory management refinement," in *Proc. Int. Symp. Low-Power Design,* Monterey, CA, Aug. 1998, pp. 311–316.
[6] D. Gajski, N. Dutt, and A. Wu, *High-Level Synthesis: Introduction to Chip and System Design.* Boston, MA: Kluwer Academic, 1992.
[7] B. Gyselinckx, L. Rijnders, M. Engels, and I. Bolsens, "A 4*2. 5Mchip/s direct sequence spread spectrum receiver ASIC with digital IF and integrated ARM6 core," in *Proc. IEEE Custom Integrated Circuits Conf.,* Santa Clara, CA, May 1997, pp. 461–464.
[8] K. Itoh, K. Sasaki, and Y. Nakagome, "Trends in low-power RAM circuit technologies," *Low Power Electronics, Proc. IEEE,* special issue, Apr. 1995, vol. 83, pp. 524–543, Apr. 1995.
[9] C. Kozyrakis, S. Perissakis, D. A. Patterson, T. Anderson, K. Adanovic, N. Cardwell, R. Fromm, J. Golbus, B. Gribstad, K. Keeton, R. Thomas, N. Treuhaft, and K. Yelick, "Scalable processors in the billion-transistor era: IRAM," *IEEE Comput., Mag.,* vol. 30, no. 9, pp. 75–78, Sept. 1997.
[10] C. Kulkarni, F. Catthoor, and H. De Man, "Cache Optimization for multimedia compilation on embedded processors for low power," presented at *Int. Parallel Proc. Symp. (IPPS),* Orlanda FL, Apr. 1998.
[11] P. Lippens, J. van Meerbergen, W. Verhaegh, and A. van der Werf, "Allocation of multiport memories for hierarchical data streams," presented at *IEEE Int. Conf. Computer-Aided Design,* Santa Clara, CA, Nov. 1993.
[12] T. H. Meng, B. Gordon, E. Tsern, and A. Hung, "Portable video-on-demand in wireless communication," *Proc. IEEE, special issue on Low Power Electronics,* vol. 83, pp. 659–680, Apr. 1995.
[13] M. Miranda, F. Catthoor, M. Janssen, and H. De Man, "High-level address optimization and synthesis techniques for data-transfer intensive applications," *IEEE Trans. VLSI Syst.,* vol. 6, Dec. 1998, to be published.
[14] L. Ramachandran, D. Gajski, and V. Chaiyakul, "An algorithm for array variable clustering," in *Proc. 5th ACM/IEEE Eur. Design and Test Conf.,* Paris, France, Feb. 1994, pp. 262–266.
[15] P. Slock, S. Wuytack, F. Catthoor, and G. de Jong, "Fast and extensive system-level memory exploration for ATM applications," in *Proc. 10th ACM/IEEE Int. Symp. System-Level Synthesis,* Antwerp, Belgium, Sept. 1997, pp. 74–81.
[16] L. Stok and J. Jess, "Foreground memory management in data path synthesis," *Int. J. Circuit Theory, Applicat.,* vol. 20, pp. 235–255, 1992.
[17] Y. Therasse, G. Petit, and M. Delvaux, "VLSI architecture of a SDMS/ATM router," *Annales des Telecommunications,* vol. 48, 1993.
[18] V. Tiwari, S. Malik, A. Wolfe, and M. Lee, "Instruction-level power analysis and optimization of software," in *Journal of VLSI Signal Processing.,* no. 13. Boston, MA: Kluwer, 1996, pp. 223–238.
[19] W. Verhaegh, P. Lippens, E. Aarts, J. Korst, J. van Meerbergen, and A. van der Werf, "Improved force-directed scheduling in high-throughput digital signal processing," *IEEE Trans. Computer-Aided Design Syst,* vol. 14, Aug. 1995.
[20] P. R. Wilson, M. Johnstone, M. Neely, and D. Boles, "Dynamic storage allocation: A survey and critical review," presented at *Int. Workshop Memory Management,* Kinross, Scotland, Sept. 1995.
[21] S. Wuytack, F. Catthoor, and H. De Man, "Transforming set data types to power optimal data structures," *IEEE Trans. Computer-Aided Design,* vol. 15, pp. 619–629, June 1996.
[22] S. Wuytack, F. Catthoor, G. De Jong, B. Lin, and H. De Man, "Flow graph balancing for minimizing the required memory bandwidth," in *Proc. 9th ACM/IEEE Int. Symp. System-Level Synthesis,* La Jolla, CA, Nov. 1996, pp. 127–132.

Sven Wuytack received the engineering degree and the Ph.D. degree in electrical engineering from the Katholieke Universiteit Leuven, Belgium, in 1993 and 1998, respectively.

Since 1993, he has been a Researcher at the Inter-university Micro-Electronics Center (IMEC), Heverlee, Belgium. His research interests include system and architecture-level power optimization, mainly oriented toward memory organization, and memory management in general. The major target application domains where this research is relevant are data structure dominated modules in telecom networks and real-time signal and data processing algorithms in image, video, and end-user telecom applications.

Julio L. da Silva, Jr. was born in Porto Alegre, Brazil, in 1965. He received the electrical engineering degree from the Federal University of Rio Grande do Sul, Brazil, in 1986. He received the masters degree in 1990 from the same University. He has been a Ph.D. degree candidate at the Inter-university Micro-Electronics Center (IMEC), Belgium, since 1994.

His research interests include system power optimization, mainly oriented toward memory management. The major target application domains where this research is relevant are data structure dominated modules in telecom networks applications.

Francky Catthoor (S'86–M'87) received the engineering degree and the Ph.D. degree in electrical engineering from the Katholieke Universiteit Leuven, Belgium, in 1982 and 1987, respectively.

Since 1987, he has headed several research domains in the area of high-level and system synthesis techniques and architectural methodologies, all within the Design Technology for Integrated Information and Telecom Systems (DESICS—formerly VSDM) division at the Inter-university Micro-Electronics Center (IMEC), Heverlee, Belgium. He has been an Assistant Professor at the EE Department of the K.U. Leuven since 1989. Since 1996, he has been an Associate Editor of the *Journal of VLSI Signal Processing*. He was the Program Chair of the 1997 International Symposium on System Synthesis (ISSS) and is the General Chair for the 1998 ISSS.

In 1986, Dr. Catthoor received the Young Scientist Award from the Marconi International Fellowship Council. Since 1995, he has been an Associate Editor for the IEEE Transactions on Very Large Scale Integrated Circuits and Systems.

Gjalt de Jong received the M.Sc.E.E. and Ph.D. degrees from Eindhoven University of Technology, Eidhoven, The Netherlands, in 1987 and 1993, respectively.

In 1996, he joined the Staff Research Group of Alcatel, Antwerp, responsible for future hardware design methodologies in Alcatel. Currently, his main activities are in the area of system level and hardware/software codesign. Prior to joining Alcatel, he was a Researcher at the Inter-university Micro-Electronics Center (IMEC) Research Institute in Leuven, Belgium. His prime research interests are in the fields of formal specification and verification. He has authored or coauthored more than 20 papers, of which several have been nominated for best paper awards in the prime EDA conferences.

Chantal Ykman-Couvreur is a mathematician. She first worked at Philips Research Laboratory of Belgium, from November 1979 until June 1991. Her main activities were concentrated on information theory and coding, cryptography (publi-key cryptosystems, authentication methods and digital signatures, factorization methods and discrete logarithms, fast generation of large prime numbers for cryptographic applications, scrambling-unscrambling methods for pay-TV systems), multilevel logic synthesis for VLSI circuits (research and development of a new multilevel logical optimization system, called PHIFACT, and based on factorization of Boolean functions). She joined Inter-university Micro-Electronics Center (IMEC) in September 1991, to develop techniques and implement new tools in the ASSASSIN compiler for both specifications and synthesis of asynchronous control circuits. She is currently working on hardware/software codesign of systems at the chip level.

Lower Bound on Latency for VLIW ASIP Datapaths *

Margarida F. Jacome and Gustavo de Veciana
Department of Electrical and Computer Engineering
University of Texas, Austin, TX 78712
Tel: (512) 471-2051   Fax: (512) 471-5532
{jacome,gustavo}@ece.utexas.edu

Abstract

Traditional lower bound estimates on latency for dataflow graphs assume no data transfer delays. While such approaches can generate tight lower bounds for datapaths with a centralized register file, the results may be uninformative for datapaths with distributed register file structures that are characteristic of VLIW ASIPs. In this paper we propose a latency bound that accounts for such data transfer delays. The novelty of our approach lies in constructing the "window dependency graph" and bounds associated with the problem which capture delay penalties due to operation serialization and/or data moves among distributed register files. Through a set of benchmark examples, we show that the bound is competitive with state-of-the-art approaches. Moreover, our experiments show that the approach can aid an iterative improvement algorithm in determining good functional unit assignments — a key step in code generation for VLIW ASIPs.

1 Introduction

Lower bound estimates on latency for Data Flow Graphs (DFGs) executing on datapaths have been extensively investigated, see e.g., [11, 6, 10]. High-level synthesis tools have traditionally used these lower bound estimates to identify and prune inferior designs during design space exploration. While some of the bounding approaches give tight bounds when applied to datapaths with a *centralized register file*, they may be uninformative when applied to datapaths with *distributed* register file structures, see e.g., Fig.1. Since the datapaths of Very Large Instruction Word (VLIW) Application-Specific Instruction-Set Processors (ASIPs) typically exhibit such distributed storage structures [8, 7], there is a need to develop bounds that can be informative in this context. These bounds can in turn provide guidance during code generation for this important class of embedded processors — in particular, as discussed in the sequel, during the functional unit binding (assignment) phase of code generation.

In this paper, we propose an approach to lower bounding the execution latency of a DFG, for a *given* binding of the DFG to a datapath, which considers the impact of distributed register file structures on latency. In particular, we will focus on DFGs corresponding to *single basic blocks* within a loop body, since these are typically the time critical segments for the embedded applications and are likely to benefit the most from using VLIW ASIPs [8, 7].

In our DFG examples, we will use the convention of naming activities that require multiplication operations by m, ALU operations by a and a bus use by b, see e.g., Figs.1 and 2. The key issue underlying our work is as follows: when two activities *share* a data object, as $m1$ and $a1$ share $r1[i]$ in Fig.1, it is of interest to bind them to functional resources that *share* common register files – e.g., multiplier M1 and ALU A1 share register file RF1. By doing so, one can in principle avoid delays incurred in moving the result of $m1$ to a new register file before $a1$ can execute. The primary contribution of this paper is the development of a latency bound which directly accounts for such data transfer delays. Since for datapaths with distributed register files the delays associated with such transfers can be significant, the availability of tight lower bounds is critical in the context of VLIW ASIPs.

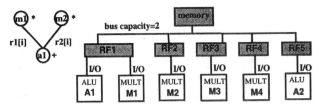

Figure 1: Segment of DFG and VLIW ASIP datapath.

In order to avoid delays due to data transfers, one might seek a binding of DFG activities to datapath functional resources, in which *shared* (result/operand) data objects reside in the same register files. However, in doing so, one may bind two activities, that could have been executed concurrently, to the same resource resulting in a *serialization* of the operations. For example, to avoid data moves between register files, one may bind both $m1$ and $m2$ to M1, so that their results are placed in RF1 from which $a1$ draws its inputs. By doing so, a serialization penalty will be incurred since $m1$ and $m2$ can no longer be executed concurrently. Thus, one can view the binding task as a tradeoff between 1) delays incurred from having to move data objects across distributed register files, and 2) delays incurred from needlessly serializing operations. Fig.2 exhibits two bindings for our example – on the left a binding attempting to avoid moves and, on the right, a binding avoiding serialization. Note that, in this simple example, both bindings lead to the same latency, but in general this will not be the case.

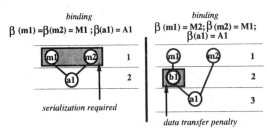

Figure 2: Serialization versus data transfers.

A second contribution of this paper is to develop a model, the *window dependency graph*, capable of capturing chains of increased execution delays caused by such operation serializations. This model proves to be useful in assisting incremental changes to bindings which tradeoff the delays resulting from data moves and opera-

---

*This work is supported by a National Science Foundation NSF CAREER Award MIP-9624321 and by Grant ATP-003658-088 of the Texas Higher Education Coordinating Board.

tion serialization. We argue that the proposed window dependency graph can be of use during code generation for VLIW ASIPs.

The paper is structured as follows. Section 2 formally defines the problem to be addressed. Section 3 presents the proposed lower-bound on execution latency. Section 4 discusses how the information provided by the proposed lower bounding method may be used in exploring tradeoffs during code generation. Section 5 discusses related work and presents benchmark examples. Conclusions are given in §6.

2 Dataflow graphs, datapaths and bindings

A DFG will be modeled by a DAG, $G(A, E)$, where the nodes A represent *activities*, i.e., operations to be carried out on datapath resources, e.g., adds and moves, and the edges $E \subset A \times A$ represent *data objects* that are "produced" and "consumed" by activities during the flow of execution. Without loss of generality, we assume that an activity can consume at most two data objects, i.e., the in-degree of any node is at most 2. We focus on code segments corresponding to a single basic block within a *loop body*, thus the DFG shown in Fig.1 includes data object labels with iteration indices, e.g., $r1[i], r2[i]$. As discussed below, the DFG model will also include move (i.e., data transfer) activities, required for a given binding of functional activities to datapath resources.

Let R denote the set of datapath resources. These may include ALUs, multipliers and other functional units, as well as buses. For each resource $r \in R$, we let $c(r) \in Z^+$ denote the capacity of that resource, e.g., an ALU would have a capacity of 1, signifying that it can perform 1 operation per step, whereas a bus resource might have a capacity 2, signifying that it can perform 2 concurrent data transfers.[1] For simplicity we will assume that all activities take a unit step to execute, but the approach can be extended to multicycle and/or pipelined functional units. The datapath is also specified in terms of its (distributed) register files, their connectivity to functional resources and, for simplicity, a shared bus with a given capacity, see e.g., Fig.1.

We assume that functional activities of the DFG have been bound to datapath resources, that is, each activity $a \in A$ is bound to a resource $\beta(a) \in R$ which is capable of carrying out that activity. Given such a binding and the register file connectivity, we identify data object moves that will need to take place between operations, and explicitly include nodes in the DFG corresponding to such moves. Move operations are bound to the datapath's bus. For example, if $\beta(m1) = M1$ and $\beta(m2) = M2$ then an additional node would be inserted between $m2$ and $a2$ to capture the delay to move the result of $m2$ in register file RF2 to register file RF1, see Figs.1 and 2.

3 Lower bound on latency

Recall that our first goal is to determine a *lower bound* on the execution latency for a *given* binding of a DFG to a datapath. The second goal is to generate information that can assist tradeoff exploration during functional unit assignment (binding). We will do this by first determining a *global lower bound*, L, on the latency and then, generating a *window dependency graph*, that will permit assessing the additional delays on activities that are incurred due to resource and/or precedence constraints.

---
[1]In general, one might consider binding activities to *clusters* of functional units sharing a common register file. In this case, one would define the capacity of a cluster to perform a particular type of operation, which would depend on the number of functional units capable of executing the operation in the cluster. This is in fact the manner in which the binding is specified but, to simplify notation, in this paper we will specify bindings directly to resources.

3.1 Global lower bound L

Various methods are available to determine global lower bounds on latency of the schedule, e.g., [11]. For concreteness, we will use the maximum of two simple bounds, however more sophisticated approaches can be used. We first perform an, as soon as possible, ASAP scheduling of the DFG to determine the minimum number of steps that would be required. Next we sum the total number of moves that were explicitly introduced between activities in the DFG with the total number of primary inputs/outputs that are required, and divide by the bus capacity to find the minimum number of steps that would be required to perform the required data transfers. The global lower bound L is given by the maximum of these two numbers.

3.2 Windows

We shall construct three types of *windows* associated with the problem at hand, *individual*, *basic*, and *aggregated* windows. A window, indexed by i, is specified by a four-tuple

$$w(i) = (s(i), f(i), r(i), A_i)$$

where $s(i)$ and $f(i)$ are the start and finish steps for the window, $r(i)$ is a datapath resource associated with the window, and A_i is a set of activities bound to $r(i)$ which ideally would be executed within the scheduling range $[s(i), f(i)]$.

To establish approximate scheduling ranges in which activities might be scheduled we use an ASAP scheduling of the DFG and, given the global lower bound L, perform an as late as possible (ALAP) scheduling of the DFG. Let the activities A be indexed $k = 1, 2, \ldots |A|$, where $|A|$ denotes the cardinality of set A. For each activity $a_k \in A$, we define an *individual window* $w^I(k) = (s^I(k), f^I(k), \beta(a_k), \{a_k\})$ where $s^I(k), f^I(k)$ denote the earliest and latest possible steps at which the activity could be executed, based on the ASAP and ALAP schedules, and $\beta(a_k)$ is the resource to which a_k is bound. Note that since the scheduling ranges associated with these windows were derived based on ASAP/ALAP schedules that disregard resource constraints, a schedule in with each activity lies within its individual scheduling range may not be feasible.

Individual windows provide an activity-centric point of view on scheduling constraints. However, there may be multiple activities bound to the *same* resource which share the *same* scheduling range. Given the set of individual windows, we shall construct a reduced set of $j = 1, \ldots n^B$ basic windows denoted by $w^B(j) = (s^B(j), f^B(j), r^B(j), A^B_j)$ where A^B_j is the *largest* set of activities bound to $r^B(j)$ with the same individual scheduling range $[s^B(j), f^B(j)]$. A basic window thus groups activities sharing a common resource and the same scheduling range.

Given the collection of basic windows, we then generate a collection of $i = 1, \ldots n^A$ aggregated windows, denoted by $w(i) = (s(i), f(i), r(i), A_i)$.[2] The set of aggregated windows includes all the basic windows as well as *mergings* of one or more basic windows, associated with activities bound to the *same* datapath resource. Only windows with scheduling ranges that abut or overlap with each other can be merged and only those with a maximal number of activities for the given scheduling range are kept. Thus each aggregate window corresponds to a maximal number of activities associated with a given scheduling range to be executed on a common resource. Aggregated windows, provide a resource/scheduling range centric view on the problem, by collectively capturing the aggregate resource demands on various ranges of steps.

Fig.3 exhibits a DFG including only additions and multiplications, and the various types of windows that would be generated.

---
[2]Note that to keep the notation simple we suppress the superscript A that would indicate that these are aggregate windows versus individual I or basic B windows.

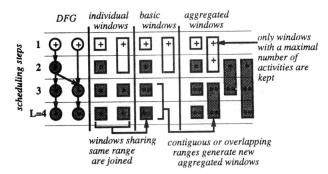

Figure 3: Example of individual, basic and aggregated window construction.

For simplicity we have not labeled windows and activities. Note for example, that one of the addition activities can be scheduled at the earliest on the first step or at the latest on the second step, thus has an individual window with a scheduling range of two steps. Also note that the multiplication activities on the last two steps have the same individual ranges, and hence are collapsed into single basic windows associated with two activities. This better captures the resource demands on these last two steps. Finally, windows that abut or overlap with each other generate new merged aggregate windows. Thus the basic window associated with the activity having a range of two steps is merged with the smaller fully overlapping individual window of the same type. Also various larger windows containing only multiplication activities are generated, capturing the high resource requirements over larger ranges of scheduling steps. A complexity analysis for the window generation process can be found in §3.7.

3.3 Local delays - Resource constrained scheduling

Each aggregated window i corresponds to a set of activities A_i to be executed on resource $r(i)$ within a range of scheduling steps $[s(i), f(i)]$. In the best case, if there are no constraints on the activities in a window, they can be executed in only 1 step, e.g., step $s(i)$. However, usually, due to resource/precedence constraints, the activities associated with the window require several steps to execute, and in some cases might even exceed the upper limit $f(i)$ on their scheduling range. To capture this effect we shall compute a lower bound on the *additional* number of steps, i.e., beyond the 1 step case considered above, that any feasible resource constrained schedule will require to execute the activities in A_i. We later define this bound as the *local delay*, $\lambda(i)$, of the window. The bound is obtained by considering the activities A_i in *isolation* i.e., only considering direct precedence constraints among them and the capacity of the resource to which they are bound.

We develop our bound for an arbitrary set of activities, $A' \subset A$ in the graph $G(A, E)$ which are to be executed on the *same* resource r - windows are thus a special case. Let $G(A', E')$ denote the subgraph of $G(A, E)$ which includes the activities A' and all edges $E' \subset E$ between activities in A'. This induced graph captures only direct precedence constraints among activities in A', optimistically dropping all others. Next perform an ASAP scheduling for the activities in the subgraph. Let $l = 1, \ldots m$ denote the steps of this schedule, n_l denote the number of activities scheduled on step l, and m be the last non-empty step. Based on the above ASAP schedule, at best, the activities in A' can be completed in m steps. However, since these activities are to be executed on resource r with capacity $c(r)$, no more than $c(r)$ activities may be scheduled per step, i.e., $n_l \leq c(r)$. The bound is based on the following observation: a feasible resource constrained schedule may not execute any activity prior to its execution step in the ASAP schedule for the subgraph and may schedule at most $c(r)$ activities per step. Alternatively, we make the *optimistic* assumption that once an activity on step l of the subgraph's ASAP schedule *completes* execution, *any* activity on step $l+1$ can be scheduled for execution. By relaxing constraints among the activities in A' and dropping constraints among A' and the rest of the DAG we can obtain the following local bound on the relative number of steps needed to execute the activities in A'.

Lemma 3.1 *Suppose $A' \subset A$ is a nonempty set of activities bound to a resource r with capacity $c(r)$ and let n_l denote the number of activities in the steps $l = 1, \ldots, m$ of the ASAP schedule for the subgraph $G(A', E')$ defined above. Define* $\mathrm{bound}(A', r)$ *by*

$$x_0 = 0,$$
$$x_{l+1} = \max\{n_l + x_l - c(r), 0\}, \quad l = 1, \ldots m,$$
$$\mathrm{bound}(A', r) = \lceil \frac{x_{m+1}}{c(r)} \rceil + m - 1.$$

Then $\mathrm{bound}(A', r)$ *is a lower bound on the number of steps, beyond the first one, that any feasible resource constrained schedule would require to complete execution of the activities in A'.*

The proof of this lemma is straightforward and included in the appendix. The iteration which defines the bound corresponds to greedily packing activities, consistent with not beginning execution prior to their associated subgraph ASAP step, and not exceeding the resource's capacity.

With this result in hand we define the *local delay* for window i by $\lambda(i) = \mathrm{bound}(A_i, r(i))$. Thus the last activity in window i must be executed on or after step $s(i) + \lambda(i)$. This must be the case since no activity in A_i can begin execution prior to $s(i)$ and according to Lemma 3.1 at least $\lambda(i)$ additional steps are required. If this exceeds $f(i)$ then the precedence/resource constraints will force activities to be executed outside the window's scheduling range, i.e., incur excess delays, providing valuable localized information on where a particular binding may be leading to scheduling delays.

3.4 Propagated delays - Key Lemma

Local delays capture delays incurred due to precedence/resource constraints within a given window. Due to dependencies among activities in different windows, additional delays may be propagated from one window to another. Without loss of generality consider two aggregate windows, indexed by 1 and 2. We shall define dependencies among windows as follows.

Definition 3.1 *We say that Window 2* **depends** *on Window 1 if among Window 2's activities, A_2, there are activities with direct data dependencies from activities A_1 in Window 1. More specifically let $P_{1,2} \times C_{1,2} := (A_1 \times A_2) \cap E$ be the set of edges on the DFG from activities in Window 1 to activities in Window 2, thus Window 2 depends on Window 1 if $P_{1,2} \times C_{1,2} \neq \emptyset$.*

We call $P_{1,2}$ and $C_{1,2}$ the set of *producer* and *consumer* activities associated with this dependency relation. Note that dependency is a directed relationship, i.e., in the above definition, Window 2 depends on Window 1. In the sequel we will use the following notation $P_a := \{b \in A_1 | (b, a) \in E\}$ to denote producers in Window 1 for an activity a and $C_b := \{a \in A_2 | (b, a) \in E\}$ to denote consumers in Window 2 for activity b. Also we define L_2 as the set of activities on first step of ASAP schedule for subgraph $G(A_2, E')$ induced by the activities in Window 2.

We let $\delta(i)$ denote a *lower bound* on the additional delay propagated to an aggregate window $w(i)$ from other windows. Thus, for a given $\delta(i)$, we can guarantee that any feasible schedule for the DFG will have an activity in A_i scheduled on or after step $s(i) + \lambda(i) + \delta(i)$, i.e., after the first scheduling step for the window plus its local and propagated delays. Our goal is to systematically find such incremental bounds, showing where combinations of resource and precedence constraints are likely to lead to propagation of delays across windows, which in turn will increase the latency of the schedule. The algorithm proposed below is based on recognizing two ways in which the activities in Window 1 can further delay the last activity in Window 2. The first is that there is a non-empty set of activities in Window 2 that can only be scheduled after completion of the last activity in $P_{1,2}$. The second is that depending on the minimum number of producers required by the activities in L_2 of Window 2, the start time for execution of the activities A_2 may need to be delayed. For a detailed discussion of the proposed algorithm see the proof of Lemma 3.2 in the appendix. Below we present a concrete example and discussion that should clarify the general idea.

propagated-delay$(1, 2)$
initialize $P_{1,2}, P_a, C_b$ and L_2
if ($P_{1,2} = A_1$)   /* compute bound on last producer step */
    last-producer-step $= s(1) + \lambda(1) + \delta(1)$;
else start-step $= \min_{a_k}\{s^I(k)|a_k \in P_{1,2}\}$;
    last-producer-step $=$ start-step $+$bound$(P_{1,2}, r(1))$;
    /* compute bound on last consumer step */
if $(c(r(1)) = 1$ and $\forall a \in L_2, |P_a| = 2)$
    last-consumer-step $= \max\{s(1) + 2, s(2)\} + \lambda(2)$;
else last-consumer-step $= s(2) + \lambda(2) + \delta(2)$;
    /* take the worst of the two */
num-consumers-for-last-producer $= \min_b\{|C_b| \mid b \in P_{1,2}\}$;
delay $= \lceil$num-consumers-for-last-producer$/c(r(2))\rceil$;
last-consumer-step $=$
    $\max\{$last-producer-step $+$ delay, last-consumer-step$\}$;
    /* compute pairwise propagated delay for Window 2 from 1 */
$\Delta(1,2) =$ last-consumer-step $- [s(2) + \lambda(2)]$;
    /* update worst case propagated delay for Window 2 */
$\delta(2) = \max\{\delta(2), \Delta(1,2)\}$;

Lemma 3.2 *Given two aggregate windows, Windows 1 and 2, with associated local and current worst case propagated delays $\lambda(1), \delta(1)$ and $\lambda(2), \delta(2)$ respectively, such that Window 2 depends on Window 1, then the algorithm* **propagated-delay** *above computes a (possibly tighter) updated worst case propagated delay $\delta(2)$ for Window 2, and a pairwise propagated delay $\Delta(1,2)$, i.e., the propagated delay resulting from Window 1.*

Fig.4 shows two windows, 1 and 2, such that Window 2 depends on Window 1. For this example, the dependency between two windows can be shown to further delay the execution of activities in Window 2 and thus increases the lower bound, $\delta(2)$, on the number of additional steps required to execute the activities A_2 in Window 2. Based on their local and current worst case propagated delays, our algorithm computes a new propagated delay $\delta(2)$ for Window 2.[3] The example in the Fig.4 captures one of the cases considered in our algorithm. In particular, that in which all of the activities in A_2 that could have been scheduled on step $s(2)$ (i.e., activity a_4), according to the ASAP schedule, depend on two producers in Window 1. Since the capacity $c(1)$ of the resource associated with Window 1 is only 1, this delays the beginning of execution for activities in Window 2, causing its last consumer to be scheduled on Step 4. Now, since this exceeds $s(1) + \lambda(1) = 3$, the dependency of Window 2 on Window 1 causes the worst case propagated delay for Window 2 to become 1.

We note that it is possible to obtain more aggressive estimates for propagated delays, however we have found the above to be adequate so far.

[3]As discussed in the sequel, we will initially set all worst case propagated delays to 0.

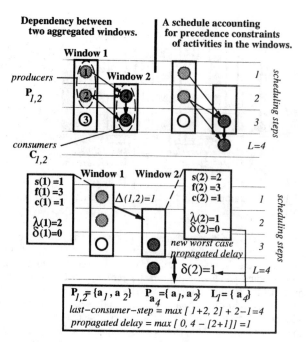

Figure 4: Window dependencies and propagated delays.

3.5 Construction of the Window Dependency Graph

Let $W = \{1, \ldots n^A\}$ be an index set for the aggregated windows associated with the problem. We define a *window dependency graph* (WDG), $G(W, D)$, with n^A nodes representing aggregated windows, and including directed arc's $D \subset W \times W$ between nodes (aggregate windows) that depend on one another. That is, $(i, j) \in D$ if window j depends on window i. However, to avoid cycles, not all dependencies, i.e., arcs, are included in the graph. The following rule is used to prune edges.

Pruning Rule: Prune $(i, j) \in D$ if no producer activity can be executed on the first step $s(i)$ and/or last step of window i or if no consumer activity can be executed on the first step $s(j)$ of window j. That is, either $s(i) < \min_{a_k}\{s^I(k)|a_k \in P_{i,j}\}$ and/or $f(i) > \max_{a_k}\{f^I(k)|a_k \in P_{i,j}\}$ and/or $s(j) < \min_{a_k}\{s^I(k)|a_k \in C_{i,j}\}$, where $s^I(k)$ is the scheduling step for activity $a_k \in A$ in the ASAP schedule.

The intuition underlying this rule is that the dependency (arc (i, j)) should only be retained if, among all aggregate windows containing the same set of producer activities $P_{i,j}$, window i has the largest lower limit on its scheduling range, i.e., $s(i)$. Indeed, dependencies from aggregate windows starting earlier can be easily shown to result in the same or smaller worst case propagated delays, thus removing such dependencies will not compromise our lower bound on latency. Note, however, that our rule may actually remove more dependencies than those associated with aggregate windows including activities $P_{i,j}$ but starting the latest. Indeed, in some cases an aggregate window including a specific set of producer activities $P_{i,j}$ may not include a producer activity that can be executed on the first step of the window. A similar intuition accompanies the case in looking at consumers in the dependent window j. While in some cases this pruning may weaken the resulting bounds, it allows us to easily establish that the pruned WDG is acyclic, see the appendix for a proof. This in turn significantly reduces the complexity of our proposed algorithm.

Theorem 3.1 *A window dependency graph $G(W, D)$ pruned according to the above rule is acyclic.*

3.6 Algorithm to compute propagated delays

Given an acyclic window dependency graph $G(W, D)$, we next discuss how to compute the worst case propagated delay for all windows in the graph. We first set $\delta(j) = 0$ for all $j \in W$. Then, starting from the source nodes (aggregated windows) in the window dependency graph, we iteratively determine the worst case propagated delay of each node j, $\delta(j)$, not yet considered, but whose parent nodes' worst case propagated delays are known, via

$$\forall i \text{ s.t. } (i,j) \in D \; : \; \textbf{propagated-delay}(i,j).$$

The propagated delay for each source node is assumed to be 0 upon initialization.

Theorem 3.2 *This iterative algorithm returns a set of propagation delays $\{\delta(i) | i \in W\}$ for windows in the graph.*

The proof of this theorem follows directly from Lemma 3.2.

The final lower bound, L^*, on the execution latency of the DFG, is given by the worst case lower bound over all windows in the WDG, i.e.,

$$L^* = \max_i \{s(i) + \lambda(i) + \delta(i) | i \in W\}.$$

The complexity analysis of the algorithm for computing propagated delays and L^* can be found in the next section.

3.7 Complexity analysis

In what follows we briefly discuss the asymptotic time complexity of the algorithms for creating the WDG and computing L^* for the WDG. The set of individual windows is created using ASAP and ALAP scheduling algorithms, and thus takes $O(|A| + |E|)$. Since the maximum number of edges incident on each activity (i.e., number of operands) is two, $|E| \leq 2 * |A|$, and thus the generation of individual windows takes $O(|A|)$.

Next we discuss the generation of aggregate windows.[4] Note that the maximum number of aggregate windows per resource is given by $\sum_{i=0}^{L-1}(L-i)(i+1) \approx L^3$. Indeed for each resource, one can have at most L windows of size 1, $L-1$ windows of size 2, down to 1 window of size L. The simple algorithm currently used to create the aggregate windows is as follows. For each resource, we create a list of L^3 empty candidate aggregated windows, with corresponding ranges, ordered by start time. Each candidate aggregate window has a set of steps, from start step s to finish step f. Each such step is initialized as unused, and a window's local counter of unused steps is initialized to the number of steps contained in its range. In the first phase of the algorithm, for each individual window, we search for all candidate aggregate windows (defined for the corresponding resource) that contain its scheduling range. Whenever one is found, the individual window's activity is inserted in the aggregate window, and all steps that the individual window shares with the candidate aggregate window that are currently unused are marked as used. The counter of unused layers for the candidate aggregate window is then updated. This first phase takes $O(|A|L^4)$, since each of the $O(|A|)$ individual windows needs to iterate though the $O(L^3)$ candidate aggregate windows of its corresponding resource, and update unused layers at a cost of $O(L)$. In the second phase of the algorithm, each resulting candidate aggregate window is validated, by checking if its counter of unused layers is zero. If not, the candidate aggregate window is invalid, and is deleted from the ordered list of aggregate windows for the resource. If the candidate aggregate window is valid, we perform the ASAP schedule for the induced subgraph associated with the activities in the window, and compute the local delay $\lambda(i)$ of the window - the complexity of this step is $O(|A|)$. The second phase of the algorithm has a complexity of $O(|R|L^3|A|)$ since $O(|R|L^3)$ tentative aggregate windows must be considered.[5] The final number of aggregate windows is $O(|R|L^3)$.

Next we consider the algorithm for creating the pruned WDG's edges, and simultaneously computing the propagated delays between all aggregate windows. The worst case propagated delays for each window are first set to 0. We then sequentially consider the aggregate windows of all resources, ordered by start time. Suppose aggregate window j is selected for consideration, we shall call it the pivot. Next we select a candidate producer window for the pivot. (Due to the pruning rule, only aggregate windows whose start time is less than that of the pivot can be selected.) Next one verifies if the pruning condition holds (which takes $O(|A|^2)$) in which case the edge is not constructed between the aggregated windows and the next candidate producer window is considered. Otherwise, an edge (i,j) is created, and the algorithm for computing the pairwise propagated delay $\Delta(i,j)$ described in §3.4, is executed, and the value is associated with edge (i,j).[6] If the new pairwise propagated delay is greater than the current worst case propagated delay $\delta(j)$ of the pivot window, the value is updated. The algorithm to update worst case propagated delay of the pivot for a given candidate producer takes $O(|A|^2)$. Thus the computation of the bound (and simultaneous generation of the edges in the WDG), is done by applying the previous step to pairs of aggregate windows, and takes $O(|R|^2L^6|A|^2)$. In summary, the generation of the WDG and the computation of L^* have an asymptotic complexity of $O(|R|^2L^6|A|^2)$.

For VLIW datapaths with multiple functional units (intended to explore parallelism in the DFG), L is typically much smaller than $|A|$. Moreover, the number of aggregated windows that needs to be considered in the various steps of the algorithm has in practice been (and is expected to be) much smaller than $|R|L^3$.[7] Thus, we expect the above theoretical asymptotic complexity to be very pessimistic for the class of problems of interest. For all the DSP benchmarks considered in §5, the total execution time has never exceeded 0.5 sec on an UltraSparc 1.

4 Window dependency graph and tradeoff exploration

In this section we discuss a simple binding heuristic which takes advantage of the window dependency graph (WDG) to explore tradeoffs between 1) reducing data transfers and 2) avoiding operation serialization, see §1. The experimental results in §5 exhibit the effectiveness of this heuristic based on the WDG, which in turn could be used by an iterative improvement binding algorithm.

As a starting point in the generation of our examples, we considered an initial binding that reduced moves between operations on the longest paths of the DFG. The idea is to bind activities on those paths such that their shared data objects remain on register files shared by the assigned functional units. The remaining binding of operations to functional units was performed to minimize serialization of concurrent operations. This process was done manually.

---

[4] For most practical cases, we expect that the intermediate step of generating basic windows will pay off, i.e., improve the overall efficiency of the algorithm, since it may significantly reduce the number of windows that need to be individually considered in the expensive merging step that follows. However, for the purpose of determining asymptotic complexity since one would still need to consider $|A|$ basic windows, the basic window generation step will be omitted in this analysis.

[5] Note that this second step of the generation of aggregate windows can (and should) be actually integrated in the final phase of the algorithm, but for clarity of the explanation, we consider it here independently.

[6] Note that the computation of $\Delta(i,j)$ for the WDG edges is truly not required for computing L^*. However, these values are informative if one wants to reason about binding modifications likely to improve latency (see discussion on §4 and §5).

[7] In practice, it has been consistently sub-quadratic in L.

Next, based on the window dependency graph, we determined our lower bound L^* on latency. If $L^* = L$, and L is in fact equal to the last step of the ASAP schedule for $G(A,E)$ (see §3), then the current binding is optimal[8]. Otherwise it may be desirable to *modify* the functional unit assignment to try to lower execution latency. Recall that each aggregate window i has a scheduling range $[s(i), f(i)]$, a local delay $\lambda(i)$, and a worst case propagated delay $\delta(i)$ such that $s(i) + \lambda(i) + \delta(i)$ is a lower bound on the last step activities in the window will be scheduled. We shall refer to the difference between this bound and $f(i)$ as the window's *excess delay*. The key insight in selecting which activity bindings to modify is to 1) find windows with *high positive* excess delays that 2) lie on "critical paths" of the WDG. Recall that a window represents a set of activities bound to a common resource that have to be (serially) executed over a given scheduling range. A window with a large positive excess delay is one for which serialization due to resource constraints and/or pairwise propagated delays from parent windows, Δ, lead to delays beyond this scheduling range. Thus, in order to reduce latency it may be worthwhile to reconsider the binding of activities in such windows. Note, however, that not all such windows are problematic. Indeed, only windows on the "critical paths" of the WDG, i.e., those leading to an increased overall latency, either directly or through a sequence of pairwise propagated delays, need to be considered. We identify "critical paths" on the WDG by backtracking from sink nodes (windows) in the WDG whose *final lower bound* on execution exceeds the global lower bound L, and traverse the graph up to parent windows with non-zero excess delays.

Still, not all windows with positive excess delay, and lying on the WDG's critical paths, would be candidates for iterative improvement on binding. Two simple rules can be used to determine windows for which a given binding is likely to be optimal. First, a window with no additional delays propagated from its producer windows and with an excess delay ≤ 1 need not have the binding of its activities reconsidered. Indeed, as shown in the example in Fig.2, the benefits of removing serialization in such cases will be canceled by the additional delay incurred by required move operations. Similarly, a window with a non-zero propagated delay from its producer windows and an excess delay ≤ 2 need not have the binding of its activities reconsidered. It follows that a WDG that only contains such windows is unlikely to have its latency improved by further modifying the binding. These simple heuristic rules proved to be effective when applied to the benchmarks in §5.

This concludes our brief qualitative discussion. As mentioned above, the purpose of this section is not to propose an algorithm to perform this complex trade-off exploration, but rather to show that the information contained in the WDG can be helpful to such an exploration process.

5 Related work and benchmark examples

In the context of distributed register files, if one wants to consider the deleterious effect of required data object moves on the latency of a schedule, one must explicitly consider a binding of the dataflow nodes to the functional units in the datapath. The basic problem formulated and addressed in this paper is thus different from those considered in [6, 11], for they assume no data transfer delays. However, one can apply these techniques to the dataflow after a binding function has been determined. Indeed, by making each functional unit a distinct resource type with capacity 1, and the bus a resource type with a specific capacity, these methods can also be made binding specific. Given this, one can compare the absolute quality of our lower bound with that reported in [6, 11]. With few exceptions [11] performs better than [6], thus we shall compare our work with an implementation of the algorithm in [11].

Table 1 summarizes our results. Several benchmark dataflows were bound to the datapath shown in Fig.1. Initial and improved bindings were obtained manually based on the simple heuristics discussed in §4. Columns 2 and 4 of the table show the minimum achievable latency for centralized and for distributed register file structures, respectively. Differences between these indicate the crudeness of assuming a centralized register file structure when it is in fact distributed. Starred entries are known to be optimal latencies over all possible bindings, thus the improvement heuristic was effective.

Our lower bound on latency L^*, shown in column 5, was consistently tight and for seven of the ten benchmarks outperformed [11].

DFG	Central. RF	Binding	Distrib. RFs	Lower Bds Our L^*	[11]
FFT Butterfly [3]	4	initial	8	8	6
		imprvd.	5*	5	4
4th order Avenhous Filter [5]	7	initial	10	10	9
		imprvd.	9*	9	9
4th order IIR Filter retimed [3]	4	initial	9	9	8
		imprvd.	6*	6	5
Beamforming Filter (3 beams) [9]	4	initial	8	8	7
		imprvd.	6*	6	5
AR Filter [2]	8	initial	15	13	14
		imprvd	13	13	13

Table 1: Experimental results.

In addition, note that [6, 11] only generate bounds on the earliest possible execution time of *individual* nodes in the DFG, so, the information on serialization (for FUs and buses) that we capture via the WDG is not available. Since the latency of a schedule can *vary significantly* for different bindings, particularly for datapaths with distributed register files, our approach has a significant added value, in that it can provide guidance on how to modify binding functions to achieve lower latencies.

Code generation for VLIW ASIPs has been addressed extensively in the literature, see e.g., [8, 7]. Although discussing this work is beyond the scope of this paper, to further illustrate the relevance of the trade-off information captured by the WDG, we will briefly discuss the AVIV code generator[4]. This work specifically considers the same trade-offs, while deriving a functional unit binding/assignment for a given expression tree.

As discussed below, AVIV greedily prunes binding alternatives based on a *local* cost function. Given an expression tree, an ASAP schedule of the expression tree is performed, and nodes (operations) on the resulting levels are sequentially considered (in any order) from the lowest to the highest level. As the operations are considered, a search tree is constructed, representing possible binding alternatives. Heuristically inferior alternatives are immediately pruned - based on a *local* cost function. The cost associated with binding an operation to a functional unit is the sum of 1) the number of required data transfers given the bindings made for the ancestor nodes of that particular path of the decision tree, and 2) the number of operations at the current level that are assigned to the same functional unit, again considering the bindings for the ancestor nodes. While this greedy policy would execute faster than our lower bound algorithm, it makes decisions strictly based on local information. Thus, for example, it does not discriminate among operations that have different mobility (i.e., scheduling windows), which can compromise the overall quality of the binding. An iterative improvement algorithm using the WDG can instead create binding alternatives based on a more "global" view of such trade-offs, at the expense of an increase in runtime. This concludes our

---
[8]Optimal at our level of abstraction, i.e., disregarding register files sizes and port assignments.

discussion of the relevance to code generation of the tradeoffs explicitly modeled in our approach.

6 Conclusion

We have proposed an approach to generating lower bounds on execution latency for DFGs on datapaths typical of VLIW ASIPs for a given functional unit binding/assignment. While the bound was found to be competitive with state-of-the-art approaches, its key advantage lies in capturing delay penalties due to operation serialization and/or data moves among distributed register files. In order to estimate such delays, the scheduling problem is relaxed (decomposed) into a number of simpler scheduling sub-problems, jointly represented using the window dependency graph model. Our results show that the relaxed, less computationally expensive, version of the scheduling problem results in tight bounds. Moreover, it can provide valuable information/guidance to heuristic binding algorithms for "clustered" VLIW ASIP datapaths. Functional unit assignment/binding is a key step of the difficult code generation problem for VLIW ASIPs. We are currently working on developing binding algorithms, supported by the window dependency graph mode, to address this problem.

References

[1] G. de Micheli. *Synthesis and Optimization of Digital Ciruits*. McGraw-Hill, Inc, 1994.

[2] R. Jain et. al. Experience with the Adam synthesis system. In *Proc. of DAC*, pages 56–62, 1989.

[3] V. Zivojnovic et. al. DSPstone: A DSP oriented benchmarking methodology. In *Proc. of ICSPAT'94*, Oct. 1994.

[4] S. Hanno and S. Devadas. Instruction selection, resource allocation and scheduling in the AVIV retargetable code generator. In *Proc. of the 35th DAC*, pages 510–15, June 1998.

[5] E. Ifeachor and B. Jervis. *Digital signal processing: A practical approach*. Addison-Wesley, 1993.

[6] M. Langevin and E. Cerny. A recursive technique for computing lower-bound performance of schedules. *ACM Trans. on Design Automation of Electronic Systems*, 1(4):443–56, 1996.

[7] C. Liem. *Retargetable compilers for embedded core processors*. Kluwer Academic Publishers, 1997.

[8] P. Marwedel and Gert Goossens, editors. *Code Generation for Embedded Processors*. Kluwer Academic Publishers, 1995.

[9] R. Mucci. A comparison of efficient beamforming algorithms. *IEEE Trans. on Signal Processing*, 32(3):548–58, 1984.

[10] M. Rim and R. Jain. Lower bound performance estimation for the high-level synthesis scheduling problem. *IEEE Trans. on CAD of ICs and Systems*, 13(4):451–58, 1994.

[11] G. Tiruvuri and M. Chung. Estimation of lower bounds in scheduling algorithms for high-level synthesis. *ACM Trans. on DAES (TODAES)*, 3(2):162–80, 1998.

A Proof of Lemma 3.1

The main idea underlying this lemma is that any relaxation of constraints, e.g., precedence or resource constraints, on the original resource constrained scheduling problem can only reduce the starting time of an activity in the corresponding optimal schedule. Hence, consider the subgraph $G(A', E')$ induced by the set of activities A', i.e., including only arcs in the original graph that are between activities in A'. This subgraph corresponds to a relaxation of all precedence constraints external to the set of activities A'. Next we perform an ASAP scheduling for the DFG $G(A', E')$ and let $l = 1, \ldots m$ denote the steps in this schedule, and n_l denote the number of activities scheduled on step l. Since these activities are to be executed on a resource r with capacity $c(r)$ the above ASAP schedule may not be feasible. To obtain a lower bound on necessary delay penalties due to the resource constraints we consider a new hypothetical resource constrained scheduling problem which further relaxes internal precedence constraints among the activities in A'. We assume that once an activity on step l of the subgraph's ASAP schedule is executed all n_{l+1} activities on step $l+1$ can be scheduled on the subsequent step.

This new hypothetical problem can be solved directly using a greedy algorithm that schedules activities as soon as possible. Let x_l denote the number of activities that are eligible for execution prior to step l but, due to capacity constraints, will need to be scheduled on step l or later. Thus on step l the total number of activities eligible for execution is $n_l + x_l$, however only $c(r)$ can be scheduled, thus x_{l+1} (see Eq. 1) activities will be postponed to the next step. Naturally since the schedule starts on step 1, $x_0 = 0$. Note that which activities are are actually scheduled on a given step is irrelevant, since we can always assume that at least one actually belongs to step l of the ASAP schedule, and thus all activities on the next step will become eligible for execution. The iterative computation in (1) finishes on step m where x_{m+1} corresponds to the number of activities that had to be postponed, if any, beyond the last step m of the ASAP schedule due to resource constraints.

$$x_{l+1} = \max\{n_l + x_l - c(r), 0\}, \quad l = 1, \ldots m, \quad (1)$$
$$\text{bound}(A', r) = \lceil \frac{x_{m+1}}{c(r)} \rceil + m - 1. \quad (2)$$

From there on we can compute the additional number scheduling steps required to execute the postponed activities, if any, i.e., $\lceil \frac{x_{m+1}}{c(r)} \rceil$ Finally, to obtain our bound we subtract 1 since the bound is on the number of *additional* steps beyond the first one, that are required to execute the activities.

B Proof of Lemma 3.2

The goal of **propagated-delay** is to find a lower bound on the last step on which activities in Window 2 will be executed.

We first consider lower bounds on the time the last producer activity in Window 1 is scheduled. If $A_1^a = P_{1,2}$ then, by definition of the local delay and worst case propagated delay of Window 1, the last activity must be scheduled on or after step

$$\text{last-producer-step} = f(1) + \lambda(1) + \delta(1).$$

If $A_1^a \neq P_{1,2}$ then, using the result in Lemma 3.1, the last producer must be scheduled on or after step

$$\text{last-producer-step} = \text{start-step} + \text{bound}(P_{1,2}, r(1))$$

where start-step $= \min_{a_k} \{s^I(k) | a_k \in P_{1,2}\}$ corresponds to the earliest possible step on which an activity in $P_{1,2}$ may be scheduled. Now, since at least one consumer activity in Window 2 depends on the last producer activity, the last consumer step must strictly exceed the last-producer-step computed above. In fact there are at least

$$\text{num-consumers-for-last-producer} = \min_{b}\{|C_b| \mid b \in P_{1,2}\}$$

consumers depending on the last producer. Thus we set the "delay" variable equal to

$$\text{delay} = \lceil \text{num-consumers-for-last-producer}/c(r(2)) \rceil,$$

so the last consumer step must exceed the last-producer-step + delay.

Next we find a lower bound for the last step on which an activity in the dependent Window 2 will be executed. Let $G(A_2, E')$ be the subgraph of $G(A,E)$ which includes the activities A_2 and all the edges $E' \subset E$ among these activities. Suppose we perform an ASAP schedule for this subgraph, and let L_2 denote the set of activities on the first step of that schedule. Also for any activity $a \in A_2$, let P_a denote its producer activities in Window 1, i.e., $P_a = \{b \in A_1 | (b,a) \in E\}$.

We consider two cases. We first test if $c(r(1)) = 1$ and $\forall a \in L_2, |P_a| = 2$. Since every activity in L_2 depends on two producer activities in Window 1 and the capacity of the resource associated with the producer window is 1, no activity in the dependent Window 2 can begin execution prior to step $s(1)+2$ or, of course, its own starting step $s(2)$. Thus the following lower bound follows immediately from Lemma 3.1:

$$\text{last-consumer-step} = \max\{s(1)+2, s(2)\} + \lambda(2).$$

Note that due to the pruning rule discussed in §3.5, $s(1)+1 \leq s(2)$ thus when $\forall a \in L_2, |P_a| \geq 1$ the analogous bound to the above would degenerate to $s(2) + \lambda(2)$, i.e., would leave the current propagated delay of the window unchanged.

If the condition for the previous case is untrue then we make the optimistic assumption that activities in Window 2 can begin execution on the first step of the window $s(2)$, even though there may be dependencies on Window 1. This gives the following bound

$$\text{last-consumer-step} = s(2) + \lambda(2) + \delta(2).$$

Thus we have two lower bounds for the step on which the last activity in the dependent window is executed.

Finally, we take the maximum of these two bounds, i.e.,

last-consumer-step =
$$= \max\{\text{last-producer-step} + \text{delay}, \text{last-consumer-step}\}.$$

The pairwise propagated delay associated with Window 2's dependency on Window 1 is then given by

$$\Delta(1,2) = \text{last-consumer-step} - [s(2) + \lambda(2)].$$

The worst case propagated delay associated with Window 2, $\delta(2)$, is then updated by taking the worst of the old propagated delay, and the just computed pairwise propagated delay

$$\delta(2) = \max\{\delta(2), \Delta(1,2)\}.$$

C Proof of Theorem 3.1

We shall prove the theorem by contradiction. Suppose there exists a cycle in the pruned window dependency graph $G(W,D)$. Without loss of generality suppose the cycle visits nodes (windows) $1,2,3,..j$ and then back to 1. Given our pruning rule, aggregate Window 1 must have a producer activity, say $a_1 \in P_{1,2}$, that can execute on the last step $f(1)$ of the window's scheduling range. Thus $f(1)$ would correspond to position (step) of a_1 in the ALAP schedule used to define that activity's individual window. Since Window 2 contains at least one activity b_2 that depends on a_1, in the same ALAP schedule b_2 must be scheduled on a step beyond $f(1)$. Thus the final step $f(2)$ in the scheduling range of Window 2 must satisfy $f(2) \geq f(1) + 1$. Using this same argument until we reach Window j we can show that $f(j) \geq f(1) + j - 1$. Since Window 1 also depends on Window j, the pruning rule guarantees that at least one producer activity $a_j \in P_{j,1}$ in Window j can execute on step $f(j)$. Now, since there exists an activity in Window 1 that depends on a_j, Window 1's last step $f(1)$ must be at least $f(j) + 1$. Clearly this is a contradiction since this would imply that $f(1) \geq f(j) + 1 \geq f(1) + j$.

Constraint Analysis for DSP Code Generation

Bart Mesman, Adwin H. Timmer, Jef L. van Meerbergen, and Jochen A. G. Jess

Abstract— Code generation methods for digital signal-processing (DSP) applications are hampered by the combination of tight timing constraints imposed by the performance requirements of DSP algorithms and resource constraints imposed by a hardware architecture. In this paper, we present a method for register binding and instruction scheduling based on the exploitation and analysis of the combination of resource and timing constraints. The analysis identifies implicit sequencing relations between operations in addition to the preceding constraints. Without the explicit modeling of these sequencing constraints, a scheduler is often not capable of finding a solution that satisfies the timing and resource constraints. The presented approach results in an efficient method to obtain high-quality instruction schedules with low register requirements.

Index Terms—Code generation, register binding, scheduling.

I. INTRODUCTION

DIGITAL signal-processing (DSP) design groups and embedded processor users indicate the increasing use of application-domain-specific instruction-set processors (ASIP's) [1] as a significant trend [2]. ASIP's are tuned toward specific application domains and have become popular due to their advantageous tradeoff between flexibility and cost. This tradeoff is present neither in application-specific integrated circuit (ASIC) design, where emphasis is placed on cost, nor in the design of general-purpose DSP's, where emphasis is placed on flexibility. Because of the importance of time-to-market, software for these ASIP's is preferably written in a high-level programming language, thus requiring the use of a compiler. In this paper, we will address some of the compiler issues that have not been addressed thoroughly yet: the problems of register binding and scheduling under timing constraints. Note that we do not consider resource binding. Although resource binding can have a major effect on the quality of the code, much work has been done on this subject [3]. Furthermore, ASIP's mostly have such irregular architectures that there is often little choice for mapping an operation. For example, addresses are calculated on a dedicated unit complying with the desired bit width, there is usually only one functional unit performing barrel shifting, etc. Because we consider distributed register-file architectures where a register file usually provides input for only one functional unit, the resource binding induces a binding of values to register files. In our experiments (Section IX), resource binding has been done by the Mistral2 toolset [4] for a very long instruction word (VLIW) architecture.

The reason that register binding and scheduling under timing constraints have not yet been addressed thoroughly is that most of the currently available software compiling techniques were originally developed for general-purpose processors (GPP's), which have characteristics different from those of ASIP's.

- GPP's most often have a single large register file, accessible from all functional units, thus providing a lot of freedom for both scheduling and register binding. ASIP's usually have a distributed register-file architecture (for a large access bandwidth) accompanied by special-purpose registers. Automated register binding is severely hampered by this type of architecture.
- ASIP's are mostly used for implementing DSP functionality that enforces strict real-time constraints on the schedule. GPP compilers use timing as an optimization criterion but do not take timing constraints as a guideline during scheduling.
- Designing a compiler comprises a tradeoff between compile time and code quality. Typically, GPP software should compile quickly, and code quality is less important. For embedded software (that is, for an ASIP), however, code quality is of utmost importance, which may require intensive user interaction and longer compile times.

As a result of these characteristics, compiling techniques originating from the GPP world are less suitable for the mapping problems of ASIP architectures. The field of high-level synthesis [5], concerned with generating application-specific hardware, has also been engaged in the scheduling and register-binding problem. Because the resource-constrained scheduling problem was proven NP-complete [6], most solution approaches from this field have chosen to maintain the following two characteristics.

- Decomposition in a scheduling and register allocation phase. Because these phases have to be ordered, the result of the first phase is a constraint for the second phase. A decision in the first phase may lead to an infeasible constraint set for the second phase.
- The use of heuristics in both phases.

Heuristics for register binding and operation scheduling are runtime efficient. When used in an ASIP compiler, however, they are unable to cope with the interactions of timing, resource, and register constraints. The user often has to provide

---

Manuscript received April 1, 1998; revised August 27, 1998. This paper was recommended by Associate Editor G. Borriello.

B. Mesman and J. L. van Meerbergen are with Philips Research Laboratories, Eindhoven 5656 AA The Netherlands and the Department of Electrical Engineering, Eindhoven University of Technology, Eindhoven, The Netherlands.

A. H. Timmer is with Philips Research Laboratories, Eindhoven 5656 AA The Netherlands.

J. A. G. Jess is with the Department of Electrical Engineering, Eindhoven University of Technology, Eindhoven, The Netherlands.

Publisher Item Identifier S 0278-0070(99)00810-6.

pragmas (compiler hints) to help the scheduler in satisfying the constraints. Furthermore, in order to obtain higher utilization rates for the resources and to satisfy the timing constraints, software pipelining [7], also called loop pipelining or loop folding, is required. In Section III, we will show that a heuristic-like list scheduling is already unable to satisfy the timing and resource constraints on a very simple pipeline example.

We discuss related work in Section II. In Section III, the dataflow graph (DFG) model is introduced with some definitions. An example of a tightly constrained schedule problem will demonstrate why traditional heuristics are not suitable to cope with the combination of different types of tight constraints. In Section IV, the problem statement is given and a global solution strategy is proposed. Sections V–VII focus on analysis. In Section VIII, complexity issues are discussed. Section IX shows some experimental results.

II. Related Work

Code generation for embedded processors has become a major trend in the CAD community. Most active in this area are the group of Paulin with the FlexWare environment [8], Marwedel's group [9], IMEC with the Chess environment [10], and Philips [11]. Because of the pressure for small instructions, mostly irregular processor architectures are used. A structural processor model for these irregular architectures, combined with the demand for *retargetability*, caused a great emphasis on code selection [12]. Compilers for these platforms have produced rather disappointing results when compared to manually written program code. Therefore, we choose to model the instruction-set irregularities procedural as hardware conflicts during the scheduling phase. This reduces the dependencies between the different code-generation phases and enables the expression of all different constraints (instruction-set irregularities, resource constraints, timing and throughput constraints, precedence, register binding, etc.) as much as possible in a single model.

Software pipelining has been the subject of many research projects. The modulo scheduling scheme by Rau [13] has inspired many researchers. His approach is essentially a list-scheduling heuristic. Backtracking is used when an operation cannot be scheduled.

Many more approaches are based on the list-scheduling heuristic, notably the work of Goossens [7] and Lam [14].

The group of Nicolau [15] devised a heuristic that often finds an efficient schedule with respect to timing. It does not take constraints on the timing into account, however, and the latency and initiation interval are difficult to control. Because implicit unrolling is performed until a steady state has been reached, code duplication occurs frequently, resulting in possibly large code sizes. These are intolerable for embedded processors with on-chip instruction memory, especially for VLIW architectures.

Integer linear programming (ILP) approaches to finding pipelined schedules started with the work of Hwang [16]. A considerable amount of constraints caused most formal methods to generate intolerable runtimes for DFG's containing more than about 20 operations.

Rau *et al.* [17] successfully performed register binding tuned to pipelined loops. They mention that for better code quality, "concurrent scheduling and register allocation is preferable," but for reasons of runtime efficiency they solve the problem of scheduling and register binding in separate phases.

Some approaches have been reported that perform scheduling (with loop pipelining) and register binding simultaneously. Eichenberger *et al.* [18] solve some of the shortcomings of the approach used by Govindarajan *et al.* [19], but both try to solve the entire problem using an ILP approach, which is computationally too expensive for practical instances of the problem depicted above. Following is a summary of these points.

- On one hand, the combination of timing, resource, and register constraints does not describe a search space that can be suitably traversed by simple heuristics.
- On the other hand, practical instances of the total problem are too large to be efficiently solved with ILP-based methods.

Therefore, we will try a different approach based on the analysis of the constraints without exhaustively exploring the search space. Timmer *et al.* [20] successfully performed constraint analysis on a schedule problem using bipartite matching, but this work is difficult to extend to register constraints.

III. Definitions

In this section, we will introduce the general high-level synthesis scheduling problem. The difficulty of solving this problem when the constraints are tight is illustrated with a simple example. A perspective is introduced to understand the reasons why this is a difficult problem to solve for traditional methods.

A. High-Level Synthesis Scheduling

A DSP application can be expressed using a DFG [21].

Definition 1—DFG: A DFG is a five-tuple $(V, E_d \cup E_s, Y, val, w)$, where:

- V is the set of vertices (operations);
- $E_s \subseteq V \times V$ is the set of sequence precedence edges;
- $E_d \subseteq V \times V$ is the set of data precedence edges;
- Y is a set of values;
- $val: E_d \to Y$ is a function describing which value is communicated over a data precedence edge;
- $w: E_s \cup E_d \to \mathbb{Z}$ is a function describing the timing delay associated with a precedence edge.

In Fig. 13(a), for example, the set of operations $V =$ source, a, b, c, d, e, sink. The set of sequence precedence edges E_s = {(source, a), (b, c), (d, e), (e, sink)}, and the set of data precedence edges E_d = {(a, b), (c, d)}. The set of values $Y = \{v, w\}$. Furthermore $val\,(a, b) = v$, and $val\,(c, d) = w$. Every edge $(v_i, v_j) \in E$ has $w(v_i, v_j) = 1$ except $w(\text{source, a}) = 0$.

Two (dummy) operations are always (implicitly) part of the DFG: the source and the sink. They have no execution delay, but they do have a start time. The source operation is the "first" operation, and the sink operation is the "last" one.

A DFG describes the primitive actions performed in a DSP algorithm and the dependencies between those actions. A *schedule* defines when these actions are performed.

Definition 2: A schedule $s: V \to \mathbb{Z}$ describes the start times of operations.

For $v \in V$, $s(v)$ denotes the start time of operation v. We also consider *pipelined* schedules: in a loop construction, the *loop body* is executed a number of times. In a traditional schedule, iteration $i+1$ of the loop body is executed strictly after the execution of the ith iteration. Goossens [7] demonstrates a practical way to overlap the executions of different loop-body iterations, thus obtaining potentially much more efficient schedules. The pipelined schedule is executed periodically.

Definition 3—Initiation Interval (II): An II is the period between the start times of the execution of two successive loop-body iterations.

A schedule has to satisfy the following constraints. The *precedence constraints*, specified by the precedence edges, state that

$$\forall (v_i, v_j) \in E: s(v_j) \geq s(v_i) + w(v_i, v_j).$$

Furthermore, the source and sink operations have an implicit precedence relation with the other operations

$$\forall v_i \in V: s(v_i) \geq s(\text{source}).$$

When a DFG is mapped on a hardware platform, we encounter several resource limitations. These *resource constraints* are given by the function $rsc(v_i, v_j): V \times V \to \{0, 1\}$, defined by

$$rsc(v_i, v_j) = \begin{cases} 0, & \text{if } v_i \text{ and } v_j \text{ have a conflict} \\ 1, & \text{otherwise.} \end{cases}$$

A conflict can be anything that prevents the operations v_i and v_j from executing simultaneously. For example, they are executed on the same functional unit, transport the result of the computation over the same bus, or there is no instruction for the parallel execution of v_i and v_j [20]. A resource constraint $rsc(v_i, v_j)$ thus states that

$$rsc(v_i, v_j) = 1 \Rightarrow s(v_i) \neq s(v_j).$$

For loop-pipelined schedules, the implication of a resource constraint is

$$rsc(v_i, v_j) = 1 \Rightarrow s(v_i) \neq s(v_j) \bmod \text{II}.$$

For reasons of simplicity, we assume that all operations have an execution delay of one clock cycle. In Section V-A, we will show how pipelined or multicycle operations are modeled using precedence constraints. The general high-level synthesis scheduling problem (HLSSP) is formulated as follows.

Problem Definition 1—HLSSP: Given are a DFG, a set of resource constraints $rsc(v_i, v_j)$, an II, and a constraint on the latency l (completion time). Find a schedule s that satisfies the precedence constraints $E_d \cup E_s$, the resource constraints, and the timing constraints II and l.

In Section V-A, we will introduce some additional constraints that characterize our specific problem. We note that HLSSP is NP-hard [6].

B. Schedule Freedom

In the previous subsection, we introduced the high-level synthesis scheduling problem. In order to solve this problem (and the extended scheduling problem from Section IV), it is convenient to describe the set of possible solutions: the *solution space*. In this subsection, we will describe the solution space as a range of possible start times for each operation. Because this set of feasible start times is as difficult to find as it is to find a schedule, we will approximate it by the "as soon as possible/as late as possible" (ASAP–ALAP; Definitions 8 and 9) interval, the construction of which is solely based on the precedence constraints $E_d \cup E_s$. By generating additional precedence constraints that are implied by the combination of all constraints, the ASAP–ALAP interval provides an increasingly more accurate estimate of the set of feasible start times.

We start with a description of the solution space.

Definition 4: The set of feasible schedules S is the set of schedules such that each schedule $s \in S$ satisfies the precedence constraints, the resource constraints, and the timing constraints.

An operation thus has a range of feasible start times, each corresponding to a different schedule.

Definition 5: The actual schedule freedom of a DFG is the average size of the set of feasible start times minus one

$$\frac{1}{|V|} \sum_{v_i \in V} (|T(v_i)| - 1).$$

The actual schedule freedom quantifies the amount of choice for making schedule decisions. For traditional schedule heuristics, a large actual schedule freedom is advantageous because it gives the scheduler more room for optimization. The actual schedule freedom is defined by the application (the DFG and the timing constraints) and the available hardware platform. A large actual schedule freedom is not guaranteed, and we have to deal with a tightly constrained scheduling problem.

Because of the complexity of finding the set of feasible start times, a conservative ASAP–ALAP estimate is more practical. For the definition of the ASAP–ALAP interval, we need the notion of immediate predecessors and successors.

Definition 6: The immediate predecessors, successors

$$\forall (v \in V): \begin{array}{l} pred(v) = \{u \in V | (u, v) \in E\} \\ succ(v) = \{u \in V | (v, u) \in E\}. \end{array}$$

The ASAP value is recursively defined as follows.
Definition 7—ASAP Value:

$$\text{ASAP}(v) = \begin{cases} 0, & \text{if } pred(v) = \emptyset \\ \max_{u \in pred(v)} \cdot (\text{ASAP}(u) + w(u, v)), & \text{otherwise.} \end{cases}$$

The latest possible start time is called the ALAP value. Let l denote the latency constraint. Then $\text{ALAP}(\text{sink}) = l$, and for all other operations, the following holds.

Definition 8—ALAP Value:

$$\text{ALAP}(v) = \begin{cases} l - w(v, \text{sink}), & \text{if } succ(v) = \emptyset \\ \min_{u \in succ(v)} \cdot \text{ALAP}(u) - w(v, u), & \text{otherwise}. \end{cases}$$

The start time of each operation must lie in between the ASAP and ALAP values, inclusively

$$\forall (v \in V): \text{ASAP}(v) \leq s(v) \leq \text{ALAP}(v).$$

Therefore, the ASAP–ALAP interval is a conservative estimate of (contains) the set of feasible start times.

In this paper, we will extract sequencing constraints that are necessarily implied by the combination of all constraints. These sequencing constraints are then explicitly added to the DFG as precedence constraints. Because the ASAP–ALAP interval is based solely on the precedence constraints, it provides an increasingly more accurate estimate of the set of feasible start times. For most scheduling methods, either the ASAP–ALAP intervals or the precedence constraints are an extremely important guideline: these methods take the precedence or the ASAP–ALAP interval explicitly as a basis. Schedule choices are made with respect to the available resources. When the ASAP–ALAP interval does not reflect the actual schedule freedom very accurately, there will often come a point in the schedule process where there are no available resources for an operation, and the operation cannot be scheduled. In this way, the precedence constraints and the resulting ASAP–ALAP interval implicitly represent the "search scope" of the scheduler. Therefore, we also define the "apparent freedom," also called mobility or slack.

Definition 9—Apparent Schedule Freedom (Mobility, Slack): The apparent schedule freedom is the average size of the set of ASAP–ALAP intervals

$$\frac{1}{|V|} \sum_{v_i \in V} \text{ALAP}(v_i) - \text{ASAP}(v_i).$$

Because the precedence and the ASAP–ALAP interval form the basis for making schedule decisions, the performance of a scheduler depends largely on the accuracy of the interval. When the ASAP–ALAP interval is an accurate estimate of the set of feasible start times $T(v_i)$, the mobility is an accurate estimate of the actual schedule freedom and vice versa. Therefore, we will use the mobility before and after the constraint analysis as a performance measure of the analysis.

C. A Small Example

Often a schedule heuristic is "deceived" by the apparent schedule freedom and is unable to generate a feasible schedule. A combination of several types of constraints is responsible for the fact that the actual schedule freedom is smaller than the apparent freedom. A small example illustrates the difficulty of handling the combination of different types of constraints.

In Fig. 1, a precedence graph of five operations is given (the arrows indicate a precedence relation). The [ASAP, ALAP] interval is printed directly left of the corresponding operation. In order to meet the constraint of three clock cycles on an

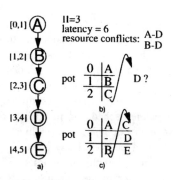

Fig. 1. Example with loop folding: (a) precedence graph, (b) list-schedule, and (c) only feasible schedule in six clock cycles.

II, loop folding has to be applied [indicated by the arrow in Fig. 1(b) and (c)]. Because folding introduces extra code, we do not want to fold more than once, which constrains the latency to six clock cycles. In Fig. 1(b), the result of a list scheduler is shown. The left column contains the *time potential* (schedule time modulo II). The list scheduler greedily schedules A, B, and C as soon as possible (ASAP), and concludes that D cannot be scheduled. In Fig. 1(c), a feasible schedule is given. The key to obtaining this schedule is to postpone B one clock cycle relative to its ASAP value. In Fig. 1, the apparent freedom or mobility equals one clock cycle per operation. The reader can verify that the combination of precedence, resource, latency, and throughput constraints leaves no actual schedule freedom at all: the schedule in Fig. 1(c) is the only possible schedule in six clock cycles. The [ASAP, ALAP] estimate of the schedule interval was not accurate enough, and the other constraints should have been considered as well. In Section V-B, we will show how the analysis of the combination of all constraints provides the most accurate ASAP–ALAP intervals (equal to the actual schedule freedom) for the schedule problem of Fig. 1.

IV. Problem Statement and Global Approach

In the previous section, we introduced the general HLSSP. In this section, we define our characteristic scheduling problem and combine it with the problem of finding a register binding. We will decompose the problem and construct a block diagram of the global approach. Our characteristic problem statement for finding a feasible schedule and register assignment is as follows.

Problem Definition 2—Register Binding and Operation Scheduling Problem: Given a cyclic DFG, the resource constraints $rsc(v_i, v_j)$, a binding of values to register files, an II, and a constraint on the latency l, find an assignment of values to registers and a schedule s that satisfies the precedence constraints $E_d \cup E_s$, the resource constraints, and the timing constraints II and l.

Because it is difficult to make a register binding and a schedule simultaneously, we decompose the problem in separate phases, as depicted in Fig. 2. First, an initial register binding (discussed in Section VII-A) is constructed in a simple manner. The II for each hierarchical level is also fixed prior to the analysis. Most often, it is set by the designer. Otherwise, we start with a lower bound based on loop-carried dependen-

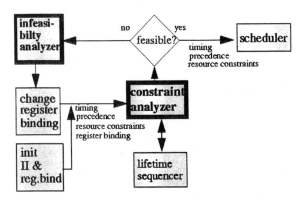

Fig. 2. Global approach.

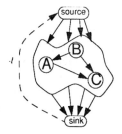

Fig. 3. Modeling the latency.

cies [22] and available resources. When this II is not feasible, it is incremented by one clock cycle. Profiling suggests that the optimal II is usually only one or two clock cycles away from the lower bound.

The central part, the constraint analyzer (discussed in Sections V and VI), generates additional precedence constraints that are implied by the combination of all constraints, including the given register binding. These additional precedence refine the ASAP–ALAP intervals, thus providing a much more accurate estimate of the set of feasible start times. They will guide the scheduler and often prevent it from making schedule decisions leading to infeasibility.

The new precedence constraints are such that the register binding is guaranteed: all lifetimes between values residing in the same register have been sequentialized. The constraint analyzer (and the lifetime sequencer) thus replaces the register-binding constraints completely by precedence constraints. When the constraint set leaves some room for different lifetime sequentializations, the *lifetime sequencer*, discussed in Section VI-C, chooses between several alternatives. When the constraint set is tight, as is the case in most of the benchmarks of Section IX, only one or two choices are made by the lifetime sequencer. A branch and bound algorithm is therefore runtime-efficient enough for the lifetime sequencer.

The added precedence may cause violation of the constraint set (including the register binding). An *infeasibility analysis* (discussed in Section VII-B) uses the administrative bookkeeping done by the constraint analyzer to find the bottleneck in the constraint set and the register binding. The "change register binding" block in Fig. 2 tries to solve this bottleneck by rebinding a value to a different register. This scheme is iterated until the constraint set and the register binding are feasible. Last, the precedence generated by the constraint analyzer is fed to a simple external schedule heuristic.

An advantage of this new approach is that in practice, a simple off-the-shelf scheduler can be used to complete the schedule. Although the existence of a schedule is not strictly guaranteed after the constraint analyzer, a schedule was found for all problem instances. As the scheduler and its heuristics are not critical in this approach, we will not focus on them in this paper.

Note that a main characteristic of our approach is that we perform register binding prior to schedule analysis. The primary reason for this is our goal to obtain an efficient register binding given the timing and resource constraints. Therefore, we first want to fix the register binding, and constrain the schedule accordingly without violating the other constraints. The additional precedence constraints will guide the scheduler more accurately toward a feasible solution.

When violation of the constraint set does occur, the infeasibility analyzer should be able to find the bottleneck.

A. Problem Statement for the Constraint Analyzer and the Infeasibility Analyzer

It is necessary that the constraint analyzer does some administrative bookkeeping, such that the infeasibility analysis is able to indicate a bottleneck in the register binding. The problem statement for the constraint analyzer and the infeasibility analyzer is therefore as follows.

Problem Definition 3—Operation Ordering and Bottleneck Identification Problem (OOBIP): Given a cyclic DFG, a register binding, a set of resource constraints $rsc(v_i, v_j)$, an II, and a constraint on the latency l, find either a partial order of operations satisfying the register binding (if the constraint set is feasible) or a smallest infeasible subset of value conflicts.

B. Effect of the Scheduler

The question rises as to whether or not the scheduler is always able to find a solution when the constraint set passes the infeasibility check. We distinguish two situations: pipelined and nonpipelined schedules.

For nonpipelined schedules, the scheduler is always able to find a solution that complies with the register binding. Experience shows, however, that the latency constraint may not always be satisfied in the final schedule.

A pipelined schedule is more difficult to obtain; sometimes a decision is made that inevitably violates the constraint set. It is therefore wise to alternate between scheduler and constraint analyzer; first the scheduler makes a schedule decision. The decision is then modeled in terms of precedence relations (Section V-A), and the constraint analyzer computes the effect of this decision on the mobility of the other operations. In this way, the search space of the scheduler is reduced according to decisions previously made in the schedule process. Although there is still no absolute guarantee that a solution is found in this way, a solution was found on all problem instances tried so far. If the scheduler fails after all, the infeasibility analyzer will indicate which value conflicts, resource conflicts, and schedule decisions are responsible for this failure. The designer himself will then have to enforce a different schedule decision or partial rebinding.

The following sections comprise a solution to OOBIP. Section V is concerned with the analysis of resource conflicts, precedence, and timing constraints. Section VI extends the analysis to a given register binding. In Section VII-B, we will demonstrate the infeasibility analyzer based on the results of Sections V and VI.

V. RESOURCE-CONSTRAINED ANALYSIS

In the previous section, we introduced a block diagram of our global approach. This section will focus on part of the constraint analyzer [23]. Section V-A models the different constraints as much as possible in terms of precedence. Section V-B analyzes the resource constraints, and generates precedence as well, so that most of the constraint set is expressed in a unified model (the DFG). The analysis is illustrated on the example from Section III-C. In Section VI, the analysis is extended to handle *value conflicts* that result from a given register binding.

A. Modeling the Constraints

We start this section by showing how some of the constraints can be represented in the DFG model introduced in Section III.

- *Latency:* A constraint l on the latency is translated to an arc (sink, source) with $w = -l$, as illustrated in Fig. 3. This is interpreted as $s(\text{source}) \geq s(\text{sink}) - l$, which is equivalent to $s(\text{sink}) \leq s(\text{source}) + l$, meaning the last operation may not be executed more than l clock cycles after the start of the first operation.

- *Microcoded controller and loop folding:* We assume that the architecture contains a microcoded controller. As a consequence, the same code is executed every loop iteration. This implies that a communicated value is written in the same register each iteration. When loop iterations overlap, we have to ensure that a value is consumed before it is overwritten by the next production. Since subsequent productions are exactly II clock cycles apart, a value cannot be alive longer than II clock cycles. So the operation C that consumes a value must execute within II clock cycles after the operation P that produces the value. Just like the latency constraint, a necessary and sufficient translation to the precedence model is that for each data dependency (P, C), there is an arc (C, P) with $w = -\text{II}$. Lemma 8 gives conditions when this timing constraint can be tightened.

- *Pipelined executions and multicycle operations:* Pipelined executions and multicycle operations can be modeled by introducing an operation for each stage of the execution. Subsequent stages are linked in time using two sequence edges, as indicated in Fig. 4. For multicycle operations, A and B occupy the same resource.

- *Scheduling decisions:* When schedule decisions are taken during the process, the schedule intervals of other operations are affected. Therefore, it is desirable to be able to

Fig. 4. Modeling pipelined and multicycle operations.

Fig. 5. Modeling a schedule decision.

express a schedule decision in the DFG so that its effect can be analyzed in the context of the other constraints. Scheduling decisions may take different forms. A timing relation between two operations can be directly translated to a sequence edge. When an operation v is fixed at a certain clock cycle c, we need two sequence edges, as indicated in Fig. 5.

- *Resource conflicts and instruction-set conflicts:* We use method [20] to model instruction set conflicts as resource conflicts $rsc(v_i, v_j)$, introduced in Section III-A.

B. Resource-Constraint Analysis

We now come to the point of explaining the analysis process. By observing a combination of constraints, we can reduce the search space. This reduction is made explicit by adding precedence constraints (sequence edges). In this section, a lemma will be given that observes the interaction between resource conflicts, precedence, and timing constraints. The next section demonstrates lemmas to incorporate register conflicts. All the lemmas used in our approach rely on the concept of a path between operations.

Definition 10—Path: A path of length d from operation v_i to operation v_j is a chain of precedence $v_i \rightarrow v_k \rightarrow \cdots v_l \rightarrow v_j$ that implies $s(v_j) \geq s(v_i) + d$.

Definition 11—Distance: The distance $d(v_i, v_j)$ from operation v_i to v_j is the length of the longest path from v_i to v_j.

A path in the graph thus represents a minimum timing delay. For example, in Fig. 1, the path A $\rightarrow$ B $\rightarrow$ C indicates a minimum timing delay of two clock cycles between the start times of A and C. The first lemma presented below affects the timing relation between conflicting operations. It is based on the fact that two operations with a resource conflict cannot be scheduled at the same potential. The *time potential* associated to a time t is t mod II. So if the distance between these operations would cause them to be scheduled at the same potential, the distance has to be increased by at least one clock cycle.

Lemma 1: If $d(v_i, v_j) \bmod \text{II} = 0$ and $rsc(v_i, v_j) = 1$, we can add a sequence precedence edge (v_i, v_j) with weight $d(v_i, v_j) + 1$ without excluding any feasible schedules.

This lemma will help us to solve the schedule problem in Fig. 1. Remember that the key decision to obtaining a feasible

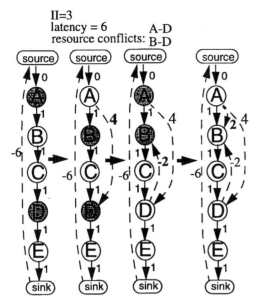

Fig. 6. Derivation of a schedule for Fig. 1.

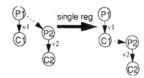

Fig. 7. Lemma 2 for sequentialized value lifetimes.

schedule is to put a gap of one clock cycle between A and B. So our goal is to derive that $d(A, B) = 2$. This derivation is given in Fig. 6. Fig. 6(a) represents the DFG model of Fig. 1(a). In Fig. 6(a), we see a path $A \rightarrow B \rightarrow C \rightarrow D$ of length 3 mod II = 0 from A to D. According to Lemma 1, we can add a sequence edge $A \rightarrow D$ of weight $3 + 1 = 4$ because A and D have a resource conflict. This edge is drawn in Fig. 6(b). Next, there is a path $D \rightarrow E \rightarrow$ sink $\rightarrow$ source $\rightarrow A \rightarrow B$ of length $1 + 1 - 6 + 0 + 1 = -3$ clock cycles. Because of the resource conflict D–B, this length has to be increased by one clock cycle. This gives a sequence edge $D \rightarrow B$ of weight -2, as given in Fig. 6(c). We conclude by finding a path of length $4 - 2 = 2$ clock cycles. In Fig. 6(d), the associated sequence edge (A, B) of weight two is explicitly drawn. The precedence relations now completely fix the schedule. The reader can verify that the [ASAP, ALAP] intervals based on the extended DFG of Fig. 6(d) all contain just one clock cycle, and the estimated schedule freedom equals zero.

VI. REGISTER-CONSTRAINT ANALYSIS

The previous section introduced the methodology used in the constraint analyzer of Fig. 2. In this section, we will extend the techniques to analyze value conflicts that result from a given register binding [24]. This will be done by introducing lemmas similar to Lemma 1 in the previous section. These lemmas provide necessary conditions (in terms of precedence relations) to guarantee a given register binding. Section VI-A is restricted to nonfolded schedules in order to explain the concept more clearly. The lemmas will be generalized in Section VI-B for register conflicts that cross loop boundaries, which occur when folded schedules are considered.

A. Nonfolded Schedules

In this subsection, two lemmas observe the combination of a given register binding, precedence, and timing constraints for nonfolded schedules. Their use is demonstrated with a small example. In all given examples, a path is indicated using a dashed arc labeled with the length of the path. Sequence edges are dotted. Standard delay (if not labeled) for a sequence edge is zero clock cycle; for a data dependence, it is one clock cycle.

Lemma 2: Let value $v1$, produced by operation P1 and consumed by C1, and value $v2$, produced by operation P2 and consumed by C2, reside in the same register. If $d(P1, P2) \geq 0$, we can add a sequence precedence edge (C1, P2) with weight zero without excluding any feasible schedules.

Lemma 2 is illustrated in Fig. 7. The values $v1$ and $v2$ are bound to the same register. If there is a path of positive length from P1 to P2, then the whole lifetime of value $v1$ has to precede the lifetime of $v2$. This is made explicit by adding a sequence edge from the consumer C1 to the producer P2. A similar lemma is valid when there is a path between the consumers of the values.

Lemma 3: Let value $v1$, produced by operation P1 and consumed by C1, and value $v2$, produced by operation P2 and consumed by C2, reside in the same register. If $d(C1, C2) \geq 0$, we can add a sequence precedence edge (C1, P2) with weight zero without excluding any feasible schedules.

When there is a path between the producer of one value and the consumer of the other, we can only exclude a possibility if the delay of the path is strictly greater than zero. Otherwise, the alternative sequentializations, $C2 \rightarrow P1$, could still yield a feasible schedule when P1 and C2 are scheduled in the same clock cycle.

Lemma 4: Let value $v1$, produced by operation P1 and consumed by C1, and value $v2$, produced by operation P2 and consumed by C2, reside in the same register. If $d(P1, C2) \geq 1$, we can add a sequence precedence edge (C1, P2) with weight zero without excluding any feasible schedules.

Lemma 4 is illustrated in Fig. 8. The overall method of analysis is demonstrated in Fig. 9. In this figure, values $v1$ and $v2$ reside in the same register, as do values $w1$ and $w2$. Because operation 1 consumes value $v1$ and operation 7 consumes value $v2$, the lifetime of $v1$ has to precede the lifetime of $v2$ as a result of the precedence $1 \rightarrow 7$ (Lemma 3 applies). Therefore, the sequence edge $1 \rightarrow 8$ is added. Now there is a path $2 \rightarrow 1 \rightarrow 8$ from the consumer of $w1$ to the consumer of $w2$, and Lemma 3 applies again. The sequence edge $2 \rightarrow 9$ is added as a result. Any schedule heuristic can now find a schedule without violating the register binding, which is not the case if the sequence edges were not added.

B. Folded Schedules

In this section, we extend the lemmas from Section VI-A for sequentialized value lifetimes to handle pipelined loop schedules. An example demonstrates the use of the extended lemmas.

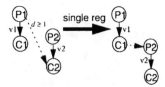

Fig. 8. Lemma 4 for sequentialized value lifetimes.

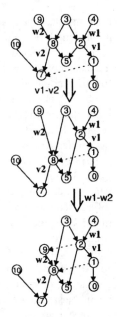

Fig. 9. Example demonstrating the use of Lemma 3.

Fig. 10. Timing perspective of serializing alternatives.

When schedules are not folded, it is relatively simple to avoid overlapping lifetimes of values residing in the same register. Only two alternatives have to be considered, as depicted in Fig. 10, where the solid lines indicate the occupation of the register. When loop iterations overlap in time, we also have to take care that the ith lifetime of value $v2$ does not overlap with the $i + 1$st (and the $i - 1$st) lifetime of value $v1$, as depicted in Fig. 11. Applying the lemmas in this section will eliminate some alternatives, but it is not guaranteed that only one alternative remains. In this case, the lifetime sequencer in Fig. 2 will have to make a decision in order to avoid overlapping lifetimes. This is the subject of Section VI-C.

Sequentialized value lifetimes that belong to different loop iterations pose a problem for the graph model because it makes no difference between operation A_i and A_{i+1} (where A_i denotes the ith execution of A). This suggests that a timing relation between A_i and B_{i+1} has to be translated to a timing relation between A_i and B_i. This translation is straightforward: $s(B_{i+1}) = s(B_i) + \mathrm{II}$, so that the relation $s(A_i) \geq s(B_{i+1}) + d$ is translated to the relation $s(A_i) \geq s(B_i) + \mathrm{II} + d$, which

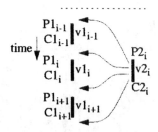

Fig. 11. Serializing alternatives when folding once.

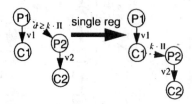

Fig. 12. Lemma 5 for sequentialized value lifetimes.

is equivalent to a sequence edge B → A with delay $\mathrm{II} + d$. Lemmas 2 and 3 are now easily generalized to Lemmas 5 and 6.

Lemma 5: Let value $v1$, produced by operation P1 and consumed by C1, and value $v2$, produced by operation P2 and consumed by C2, reside in the same register. If $d(\mathrm{P1}, \mathrm{P2}) \geq k \times \mathrm{II}$, we can add a sequence precedence edge (C1, P2) with weight $k \times \mathrm{II}$ without excluding any feasible schedules.

Lemma 6: Let value $v1$, produced by operation P1 and consumed by C1, and value $v2$, produced by operation P2 and consumed by C2, reside in the same register. If $d(\mathrm{C1}, \mathrm{C2}) \geq k \times \mathrm{II}$, we can add a sequence precedence edge (C1, P2) with weight $k \times \mathrm{II}$ without excluding any feasible schedules.

Lemma 5 is illustrated in Fig. 12. Lemma 4 is generalized to Lemma 7.

Lemma 7: Let value $v1$, produced by operation P1 and consumed by C1, and value $v2$, produced by operation P2 and consumed by C2, reside in the same register. If $d(\mathrm{P1}, \mathrm{C2}) \geq k \times \mathrm{II} + 1$, we can add a sequence precedence edge (C1, P2) with weight $k \times \mathrm{II}$ without excluding any feasible schedules.

The last lemma we introduce with respect to folded schedules does not serialize lifetimes like the previous lemmas but restricts the lifetime of a value when there exist other values assigned to the same register.

Lemma 8: Let W be the set of values that reside in a register r, and let $\mathrm{minlt}(v)$ denote the minimal lifetime of value v (the distance from the producer of v to the last consumer of v). Then each value $u \in W$ has a maximum lifetime equal to

$$\mathrm{II} - \sum_{v \in W/u} \mathrm{minlt}(v).$$

Initially, all values have a minimum lifetime of one clock cycle. The lifetime expression in Lemma 8 is then simplified to $\mathrm{II} - (k-1)$, where k equals the number of values assigned to register r. When, for example, $\mathrm{II} = 4$, and there are two values in register r, each of these values has a maximum lifetime of $4 - (2 - 1) = 3$ clock cycles. When three values reside in r, the maximum lifetime becomes two clock cycles. This

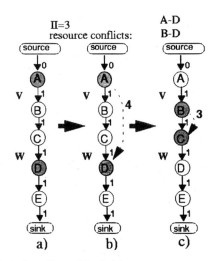

Fig. 13. Derivation of a partial schedule.

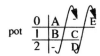

Fig. 14. Folded ASAP schedule for Fig. 13.

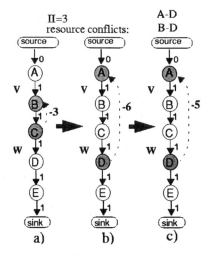

Fig. 15. Derivation of Fig. 13 continued.

maximum lifetime is modeled as a sequence edge with weight-maxlt from the consumer to the producer of the value, similar to modeling the latency.

We illustrate the use of these lemmas with the example in Fig. 13. It is similar to the example of Fig. 1, but it is extended with a register binding. Value v, communicated from operation A to B, and value w, communicated from operation C to D, are bound to the same register. The same resource conflicts and the same initiation interval are used, but there is no constraint on the latency. The first step from (a) to (b) is the same as the first step in Fig. 6.

From Fig. 13(b) to (c), the value v is produced by A and consumed by B. Value w is produced by C and consumed by D. Because of Lemma 7 and $d(A, D) \geq 4 = 1 \times II + 1$, we can add a sequence edge (B, C) with weight $1 \times II = 3$ without excluding any feasible schedules.

In Fig. 14, a folded ASAP schedule is given that satisfies the newly added precedence constraints, and thus also the resource constraints and the register binding. In Fig. 14, the leftmost column indicates the time potential (schedule time modulo II), so operation C is scheduled in clock cycle 4, D in clock cycle 5, etc. Notice that the constraints have forced a gap of two clock cycles between operations B and C. A greedy scheduling approach does not put gaps between operations and would never have found a schedule that satisfies all constraints.

In Fig. 15, it is proven that operations A, B, C, and D are actually fixed at their schedule times given in Fig. 14. Fig. 15(a) shows a sequence edge (C, B) with weight $-II = -3$ as a result of modeling the loop-folding constraint as given in Section V-A. It is also a special case of Lemma 8, where r contains only one value.

From Fig. 15(a) to (b), the sequence edge generates a path from C (producer of value w) to B (consumer of value v) with distance $-3 \geq -2 \times II + 1 = -5$. Because of Lemma 7, we can now add a sequence edge from D (consumer of value w) to A (producer of value v) of weight $-2 \times II = -6$.

From Fig. 15(b) to (c), there is now a path from D to A of distance $-6 = -2 \times II$. Because A and D have a resource conflict, Lemma 1 states that the distance is increased by one clock cycle. Accordingly, a sequence edge (D, A) with weight -5 is added.

As a result of this last sequence constraint, operation D cannot be scheduled further than five clock cycles from operation A, which is also the minimum distance because of the sequence edge from B to C of weight three. The intermediate operations (B and C) are also fixed in this way. Only operation E can be scheduled at clock cycle 6, 7, or 8.

We have now covered the basic techniques used in the constraint analyzer of Fig. 2. Note that these techniques do not guarantee that every conflict is solved (that all lifetimes of values in the same register are serialized); especially when the schedule is not pipelined, the constraints are often not sufficient to eliminate every conflict. In such a case, a schedule decision has to be made to serialize two value lifetimes, which is the subject of the next section.

C. Lifetime Sequencing

Suppose we have a value conflict between value $v1$, produced by operation P1 and consumed by C1, and value $v2$, produced by operation P2 and consumed by C2. We distinguish two situations:

- nonpipelined schedules;
- pipelined schedules.

In the first situation, the lifetime sequencer has to solve a value conflict by choosing either C2 $\rightarrow$ P1 or C1 $\rightarrow$ P2. In the pipelined situation, the iteration index must be considered as well: the alternatives are C2$_i$ $\rightarrow$ P1$_{i+k}$ and C1$_{i+k}$ $\rightarrow$ P2$_i$ for possibly more than one value of k. This is illustrated in Fig. 11 for $k \in \{-1, 0, 1\}$.

Nonpipelined blocks are sometimes large (>1000 operations), and constraints are not tight. This has two effects:

- many decisions have to be made;
- a lot of schedule freedom is available.

An actual branch and bound approach does not seem appropriate in this case: the number of decisions are too large to guarantee reasonable runtimes, and because of all the available schedule freedom, a heuristic approach suffices. Although it is not guaranteed that a feasible schedule is found in this way (in this case the values are simply separated), we have not yet encountered infeasibility in practice. Therefore, we choose one of the sequentializations by reusing the schedule procedures applied in the actual scheduler (in Fig. 2) so that our approach is maximally tuned to the existing design flow. Since our approach is being integrated in the Mistral2 [4] compiler, the ASAP values of P1 and P2 determine the highest priority. In Section IX, we included an experiment showing the effects of sequencing lifetimes for a nonpipelined schedule.

For pipelined schedules, the reverse is true: pipelined loops consist of relatively few operations (typically <200), and the constraints are much more tight (all lifetimes are restricted to II, resource constraints and value conflicts cross the loop iteration boundaries, etc.). As a result, only a few actual schedule decisions have to be made (typically <10). The pipelined benchmarks in Section IX required at most two decisions. In this case, a branch and bound approach is runtime efficient. Such an approach is also required because in the context of different types of very tight constraints, the effects of a schedule decision are very difficult to anticipate, and we are likely to make a "wrong" decision. For the same reason, we do not want to reuse the schedule procedures of the actual scheduler in Fig. 2: the constraints are simply too tight to take any optimization criteria into account. Instead, our first choice is determined by the alternative ($C2_i \rightarrow P1_{i+k}$ or $C1_{i+k} \rightarrow P2_i$ for some k) that reduces the mobility of P1, C1, P2, and C2 the least. Note that there is no actual "cost function" involved in this branch and bound approach: the detection of infeasibility (violation of the constraints) determines when to backtrack.

The infeasibility analysis is able to assist in selecting the decision to backtrack: in Section VII-B, it is explained in detail that infeasibility is detected as a positive delay cycle in the precedence graph. A decision is backtracked *only* when it is part of such a cycle, because only then may it be inconsistent with the constraints or previously made decisions.

VII. Register Binding

In this section, we cover two blocks from our global approach of Fig. 2 that are related to the register binding. The first is the initial binding, addressed in Section VII-A, and the second is the infeasibility analyzer, addressed in Section VII-B.

A. Initial Binding

It is clear from Fig. 16 that an initial register binding has to be made to start the iteration of the constraint analyzer, given the binding of values to register files. We choose the binding such that each register file holds one register. In this way, all values bound to a registrable r need to have their lifetimes sequentialized. This choice is made for two reasons. First, it produces the least hardware when ASIC's are concerned, and

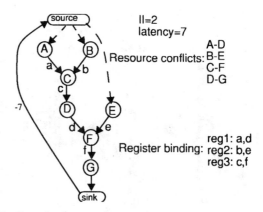

Fig. 16. Example of a precedence graph.

Fig. 17. v and w cannot be in the same register.

provides useful user feedback when programmable platforms are concerned. Second, when the constraints are more tight, the constraint analyzer generates more precedence constraints, so it is better able to guide the scheduler toward a feasible solution.

Starting from this minimum binding, some changes can be made trivially based on the hierarchy of basic blocks. For example, if value v is produced before loop l and consumed after loop l, it occupies a register during the entire execution of loop l. During the analysis of loop l, a register is therefore reserved for value v. Another trivial decision is based on dataflow. For example, in the precedence graph in Fig. 17, values v and w cannot reside in the same register because the value lifetimes cannot be sequentialized.

B. Infeasibility Analysis

The schedule analysis is often capable of detecting that the register binding together with the constraint set yields an infeasible result. In order to make a sensible change in the register binding, we want the infeasibility analyzer to identify the bottleneck in the register binding. More precisely, we want the analyzer to give a *smallest infeasible subset of value conflicts,* that is, a subset of value conflicts (two values residing in the same register) that together cause infeasibility. Identifying such a subset of decisions is tightly related to detecting infeasibility. The constraint analyzer detects infeasibility based on longest path information in the following way: when the longest path algorithm finds a path from an operation v to itself (a cycle in the precedence graph) and this path has a positive length, the operation v is forced to execute strictly before its own start time, which is clearly not possible. So a precedence cycle of strictly positive length indicates infeasibility.

The bottleneck lies directly in the way that the positive length cycle came into existence. For example, if in Fig. 13 the latency was constrained to six clock cycles, there was a sequence edge from the sink to the source with a delay of

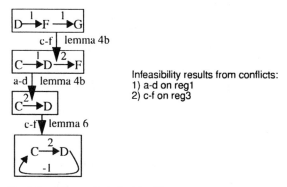

Fig. 18. Infeasibility analysis for Fig. 16.

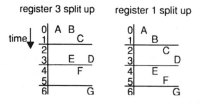

Fig. 19. The only two feasible schedules for Fig. 16 with changes in the register binding.

−6 clock cycles. In Fig. 13(c), that would yield a positive delay cycle. Most edges in the precedence cycle involve data precedence, one involves the latency, and one involves a register conflict. The sequence edge B → C is a result of two components: 1) the register conflict $v - w$ and 2) a path of length four from A to D. The path from A to D consists of one sequence edge that is added as a result of the resource conflict A–D and a path A → D of length three that consists entirely of data precedence. We can thus conclude that infeasibility is caused as a result of the following combination of factors:

1) a register conflict $v - w$;
2) a resource conflict A–D;
3) the latency constraint;
4) data precedence.

When all constraints are fixed except for the register binding, we conclude that the decision to put the values v and w together in a single register is the cause of infeasibility.

Another example is the graph depicted in Fig. 16. The constraint set is infeasible with the register binding, which is derived as follows. The infeasibility analysis is graphically depicted in Fig. 18. Each block represents a path, and each downward arrow represents an inference. The derivation is top down. The path D → G of length two (= II) and register conflict $c - f$ lead to the sequence edge D → F of weight II = 2 as a consequence of Lemma 6 (where $k = 1$). The downward arrows show that this sequence edge is part in the path underneath. The second block from the top indicates a path C → F of length three. Together with the register conflict $a - d$, this yields a sequence edge C → D of weight two as a result of Lemma 6. In the block at the bottom of Fig. 18, the sequence edge D → C of weight −1 is generated as a result of Lemma 8. (value c and f in the same register limits their lifetimes to II−(2 − 1) = 2 − 1 = 1 clock cycles). The same block shows that this sequence edge causes a positive precedence cycle C → D → C with a delay of $2 + (-1) = 1$ clock cycle. As a result of this positive precedence cycle, we conclude that the register binding is infeasible.

The infeasibility analysis is done in bottom-up fashion to identify exactly those sequence edges and conflicts that have contributed to the positive precedence cycle. The combination of register conflicts that yield infeasibility is identified as:

1) $a - d$ on register 1;
2) $c - f$ on register 3.

Note that the conflict $b - e$ on register 2 did not contribute to the infeasibility, and thus it is useless to put the values b and e in separate registers. Instead, we have to choose to split either register 1 or register 3. Both decisions yield a feasible schedule, as depicted in Fig. 19.

C. Rebinding

The infeasibility analysis generates a list of value conflicts. A conflict arises between two values. The list of value conflicts is ordered on a number of criteria.

- The number of times the conflict appears in the conflict list. When a conflict occurs more often in the list, the conflict contributes more extensively to the bottleneck.

For ASIC's, it is ordered on the following.

- The type of the values; we prefer allocating an additional 6-bit register to an additional 28-bit register.
- Addressability; when a register file contains four registers, allocating an additional register requires an additional addressing bit in the instruction word. We prefer to extend a register file with three or five to seven registers.

For ASIP's, it is ordered on the following.

- Availability of registers; we prefer to move values within a register file that contains more spare registers.

After the conflict list is ordered, only the top conflict is chosen. One of the two conflicting values is then allocated to the next register. In this way, convergence is guaranteed. The disadvantage is that the same value conflicts may arise in subsequent iterations of the scheme in Fig. 2. Because this has not proven to be a problem on our problem instances, no work has been done to overcome the disadvantage.

VIII. COMPLEXITY

In this section, we analyze the runtime complexity and memory requirements of our approach. The two major contributions to runtime are:

- finding the longest paths and updating the paths as a result of applying the lemmas from Sections V and VI;
- infeasibility analysis and changing the register binding.

A. Finding and Updating the Longest Paths

We will first consider the complexity of the former contribution. In our implementation, the longest path between each pair of operations is administrated. The memory requirements thus have order $O(V^2)$.

If a new edge is added, the impact on the current longest paths has to be calculated. Therefore, the complexity of adding a sequence edge is the dominant factor in runtime. This complexity is essentially determined by the number of paths that need to be updated as a result of the new sequence edge. Because we are only interested in the longest paths found so far, the number of updates equals V^2 in the worst case. In most cases, the addition of a sequence edge will affect a few paths. In cases where many paths need to be updated, the estimates of schedule intervals will also be improved substantially.

An upper bound on the number of path updates (as a result of adding a sequence edge) can be derived as follows. A path can have a length between $-l$ and $+l$, where l is the constraint on the latency. Because a path is updated only if its length is increased (by at least one clock cycle), the number of times a path can be updated is at most $2l$. Since the maximum number of paths we keep track of equals V^2, the number of path updates can be at most $2l \cdot V^2$. A single path update takes constant time, so the runtime of the constraint analysis is polynomially bounded.

B. Infeasibility Analysis and Rebinding

As the reader may have noticed in the examples, the infeasibility analysis requires a lot of administrative bookkeeping. Almost every path constructed during the longest path analysis has to be kept in memory for reference. A feasible implementation requiring a limited amount of memory to run an implementation of our method is only guaranteed if the storage of a path has a memory cost of $O(1)$. This is possible with the use of an *adjacency matrix* [25], which is based on the following fact of longest paths: if the longest path from A to C travels through B, then the part B to C is the longest path from B to C. As a result, the only administration necessary for the path from A (row of the matrix) to C (column of the matrix) is the first node on the path after A. To facilitate the infeasibility analysis, we also administrate the first edge traversed on the path A to C. Each sequence edge on its turn has a pointer to a register conflict (if there is one) and the matrix entry representing the path that gave rise to the edge. The complexity of the infeasibility analysis is thus bounded by $O(E \cdot \log E)$. We assume, however, that the longest paths have already been calculated in the constraint analyzer.

The complexity of rebinding is determined by the procedure of ordering the conflict list as explained in Section VII-C. Because a value conflict gives rise to a sequence edge, the number of conflicts in the list cannot exceed the number of edges in the precedence graph. Therefore, the complexity of rebinding is bounded by $O(E \cdot \log E)$.

We conclude that the complexity of one iteration of the scheme in Fig. 2 equals $O(2l \cdot V^2 + E \cdot \log E)$. In the worst case, the number of iterations is bounded by $|Y|$, the number of values in the dataflow graph. In the results section, we will also depict the iteration count for the different applications.

IX. RESULTS

Our implementation on an HP 9000/735 has been tested on the inner loops from four different real-life industrial

TABLE I
RESULTS OF EXPERIMENTS

experiment	$|V|$	II	#iterations	run time	mobility before analysis	mobility after analysis
IIR	23	6	3	0.2 s	2.70	0.13
FFTa	40	4	11	17 s	4.46	0.46
FFTb	60	8	20	25 s	6.85	0.52
Rad4	81	4	1	0.8 s	4.93	1.38

examples that have been mapped on a VLIW architecture with distributed register files. The results are shown in Table I. The fourth column represents the number of iterations over the constraint analyzer (see Fig. 2) before a feasible solution was found. The last two columns indicate the mobility of the operations in terms of average number of clock cycles per operation (Definition 10). The sixth column indicates the mobility before the analysis; the last column, after analysis (what is left for the scheduler to fill in). With respect to the numbers in Table I, no comparison could be made to other approaches because the register allocator and the schedulers available to us (several list schedulers) are unable to find any solution for the given constraints.

The first experiment concerns an infinite impulse response (IIR) filter of 23 operations, including fetching the coefficients and data from memory. The minimum latency is ten clock cycles, which equals the latency constraint. The other experiments concern fast Fourier transform (FFT) applications, the largest of which holds 81 operations. Note in Table I that the runtimes are mainly determined by the number of iterations over the constraint analyzer. The number of iterations is a measure of the difficulty of finding a register binding because it reflects the number of changes made to the original binding in order to get a feasible schedule. In these experiments, the schedule generated by our method provided a more efficient register binding than a handmade schedule. Analyses of the minimal value lifetimes suggested that little or no improvement could be made on the generated register binding.

The mobility is decreased by a factor ranging from 3.6 (Rad4) to 13.2 (FFTb) as a result of the schedule analysis. Because this decrease of mobility is due to the constraints, it is a measure for the analyzers' capability of directing the scheduler and preventing it from making schedule decisions that violate the constraints.

We have included one more experiment to test the performance of our method on a problem instance that was not constrained with respect to timing. It is a preliminary test executed by Frontier Design, who are integrating our method within the Mistral2 toolset. The benchmark, Par2, contains 91 operations. The original schedule, generated by the Mistral2 toolset, counts 61 clock cycles. As a result of the available parallelism and the number of memory accesses, the register binder required six registers at the address-generation unit. The schedule generated by our method counts only 56 clock cycles and requires only one register at the address-generation unit. Because of the schedule freedom, a total of 111 schedule decisions had to be made by the lifetime sequencer. Runtime was less than a second. The efficient register binding of the new schedule was expected (it was enforced), unlike the reduction in the number of clock cycles. This reduction is explained as follows: because of the serialization of the address lifetimes, the precedence graph became more regular. It is a well-known fact that heuristics such as the list scheduling are able to find more efficient schedules when the precedence graph contains more regularity.

X. CONCLUSIONS AND FURTHER RESEARCH

In this paper, we presented an approach for register binding and scheduling in the context of loop pipelining, based on the analysis of precedence, timing, and resource constraints. By expressing as much of the constraints as possible in a graph model and calculating the longest paths, we are able to see the interaction between the different constraints and compute the effect on the mobility available to a scheduler. When the combination of constraints and the register binding is infeasible, an efficient infeasibility analyzer is able to indicate a change in the binding that is necessary to obtain a feasible schedule. The results in Section IX show that our method is able to find a register binding and a pipelined schedule in short runtimes for industrially relevant designs. We also showed that the obtained reduction in mobility really prevents a greedy scheduler from making a wrong decision. When constraints are not very tight, we are still able to find more efficient schedules than heuristics. We conclude that analysis tools such as our implementation are needed in order to obtain a feasible schedule when facing resource constraints, register constraints, and tight timing constraints. Our method is being integrated in the Mistral2 toolset by Frontier Design.

Further research will focus on the analysis of other register-file models, such as first-in, first-out and stacks.

ACKNOWLEDGMENT

The authors would like to thank M. Strik, K. van Eijk, and P. Lippens for their support and constructive discussions.

REFERENCES

[1] R. Leupers, W. Schenk, and P. Marwedel, "Microcode generation for flexible parallel architectures," in *Proc. Working Conf. Parallel Architectures and Compiler Technology*, 1994.
[2] P. G. Paulin, C. Liem, T. C. May, and S. Sutarwala, "DSP design tool requirements for embedded systems: A telecommunications industrial perspective," *J. VLSI Signal Process.*, vol. 9, no. 1, 1995.
[3] P. Marwedel and G. Goossens, Eds., *Code Generation for Embedded Processors*. Boston, MA: Academic, 1995.
[4] M. T. J. Strik, "Efficient code generation for application domain specific processors," Eindhoven University of Technology, The Netherlands, Tech. Rep. 90-5282-390-1, 1994.
[5] M. C. McFarland, A. C. Parker, and R. Camposano, "Tutorial on high-level synthesis," in *Proceedings of the 25th ACM/IEEE Design Automation Conference*. Anaheim, CA: ACM and IEEE Computer Society, 1988, pp. 330–336.
[6] M. R. Garey and D. S. Johnson, *Computers and Intractability: A Guide to the Theory of NP-Completeness*. San Francisco, CA: Freeman, 1979.
[7] G. Goossens, J. Vandewalle, and H. De Man, "Loop optimization in register-transfer scheduling for DSP-systems," in *Proceedings of the 26th ACM/IEEE Design Automation Conference*. Las Vegas, NV: ACM and IEEE Computer Society, 1989, pp. 826–831.
[8] P. G. Paulin, C. Liem, T. C. May, and S. Sutarwala, "FlexWare: A flexible firmware development environment for embedded systems," in P. Marwedel and G. Goossens, Eds., *Code Generation for Embedded Processors*. Boston, MA: Academic, 1995.
[9] R. Leupers and P. Marwedel, "Retargetable code generation based on structural processor descriptions," *Design Automation Embedded Syst.*, vol. 3, no. 1, 1998.
[10] D. Lanneer, J. van Praet, A. Kifli, K. Schoofs, W. Geurts, F. Thoen, and G. Goossens, "Chess: Retargetable code generation for embedded DSP processors," in P. Marwedel and G. Goossens, Eds., *Code Generation for Embedded Processors*. Boston, MA: Academic, 1995.
[11] M. T. J. Strik, J. L. van Meerbergen, A. H. Timmer, and J. A. G. Jess, "Efficient code generation for in-house DSP-cores," in *Proceedings of the European Design and Test Conference*. Paris, France: IEEE Computer Society Press, 1995, pp. 244–249.
[12] C. Liem, T. May, and P. Paulin, "Instruction-set matching and selection for DSP and ASIP code generation," in *Proceedings the European Design and Test Conference*. Paris, France: IEEE Computer Society Press, 1997, pp. 31–37.
[13] B. R. Rau and C. D. Glaeser, "Some scheduling techniques and an easily schedulable horizontal architecture for high performance scientific computing," in *Proc. Ann. Workshop Microprogramming*, Oct. 1981, pp. 183–198.
[14] M. Lam, "Software pipelining: An effective scheduling technique for VLIW machines," in *Proc. SIGPLAN Conf. Programming Language Design and Implementation*, June 1988, p. 328.
[15] A. Aiken, A. Nicolau, and S. Novack, "Resource-constrained software pipelining," *IEEE Trans. Parallel Distrib. Syst.*, vol. 6, pp. 1248–1270, Dec. 1995.
[16] C. T. Hwang, Y. C. Hsu, and Y. L. Lin, "A formal approach to the scheduling problem in high level synthesis," *IEEE Trans. Computer-Aided Design*, vol. 10, pp. 464–475, Apr. 1991.
[17] B. R. Rau, M. Lee, P. P. Tirumalai, and M. S. Schlansker, "Register allocation for software pipelined loops," in *Proc. SIGPLAN Conf. Programming Language Design and Implementation*, June 1992, pp. 283–299.
[18] A. E. Eichenberger, E. S. Davidson, and S. G. Abraham, "Optimum modulo schedules for minimum register requirements," in *Proc. Int. Conf. Supercomputing*, Barcelona, Spain, July 1995, pp. 31–40.
[19] R. Govindarajan, E. R. Altman, and G. R. Gao, "Minimizing register requirements under resource-constrained rate-optimal software pipelining," in *Proc. Symp. Microarchitecture*, Nov. 1994, pp. 85–94.
[20] A. H. Timmer, M. T. J. Strik, J. L. van Meerbergen, and J. A. G. Jess, "Conflict modeling and instruction scheduling in code generation for in-house DSP cores," in *Proceedings of the 32nd ACM/IEEE Design Automation Conference*. San Francisco, CA: ACM and IEEE Computer Society, 1995.
[21] D. C. Ku and G. De Micheli, Eds., *High Level Synthesis of ASIC's Under Timing and Synchronization Constraints*. Norwell, MA: Kluwer Academic, 1992.
[22] R. Reiter, "Scheduling parallel computation," *J. ACM*, vol. 15, pp. 590–599, 1968.
[23] B. Mesman, M. T. J. Strik, A. H. Timmer, J. L. van Meerbergen, and J. A. G. Jess, "Constraint analysis for DSP code generation," in *Proc. Int. Symp. System Synthesis*, Antwerp, Sept. 1997.
[24] ———, "A constraint driven approach to loop pipelining and register binding," in *Proceeding of the Design Automation and Test in Europe*. Paris, France: IEEE Computer Society Press, 1998.
[25] T. H. Cormen, C. E. Leiserson, and R. L. Rivest, *Introduction to Algorithms*. Cambridge, MA: MIT Press, 1990.

Bart Mesman received the Electrical Engineering degree (with honors) from the Eindhoven University of Technology, Eindhoven, The Netherlands, in 1995, where he currently is pursuing the Ph.D. degree.

His doctoral work is on the subject of scheduling for embedded DSP processor architectures with the explicit goal of codesigning processor architectures and a code-generation methodology based on constraint analysis. Since 1995, he has been a Member of both the Digital VLSI Group at Philips Research, Eindhoven, and the Information and Communication Systems Group of the Electrical Engineering Department at the University of Technology, Eindhoven. His research interests include high-level synthesis, ASIP architectures, and code generation for embedded DSP's.

Adwin H. Timmer received the Electrical Engineering and Ph.D. degrees from the Eindhoven University of Technology, Eindhoven, The Netherlands, in 1990 and 1996, respectively.

In 1995, he joined Philips Research Laboratories, Eindhoven. In 1998, he was a Visiting IC Architect with the Philips Semiconductors WSG business line, Mountain View, CA. His current interests are in IC architectures for high-performance signal-processing applications, system-level design methods, hardware/software codesign, and compilation techniques for embedded DSP's.

Jef L. van Meerbergen received the Electrical Engineering and Ph.D. degrees from the Katholieke Universiteit Leuven, Belgium, in 1975 and 1980, respectively.

In 1979, he joined Philips Research Laboratories in Eindhoven, The Netherlands. He was engaged in the design of MOS digital circuits, domain-specific processors, and general-purpose digital signal processors. In 1985, he began working on application-driven high-level synthesis. Initially, this work was targeted toward audio and telecom DSP applications. Later, the application domain shifted toward high-throughput applications (Phideo). His current interests are in system-level design methods, heterogeneous multiprocessor systems, and reconfigurable architectures. He is a Philips Research Fellow and, since 1998, a Professor at the Eindhoven University of Technology. He is an Associate Editor of *Design Automation for Embedded Systems*.

Dr. van Meerbergen received the Best Paper Award at the 1997 ED&TC conference.

Jochen A. G. Jess received the master's and Ph.D. degrees from Aken University of Technology, Germany, in 1961 and 1963, respectively.

He became a Full Professor of electrical engineering at the Eindhoven University of Technology, Eindhoven, The Netherlands, in 1971. For a number of years, he had various research and teaching appointments at Karlsruhe University of Technology, where he was one of the founders of the Computer Science Department. During 1968–1969, he spent a sabbatical year at the University of Maryland, College Park. In Eindhoven, he was involved in founding and running the Design Automation Section. This task implied devising a long-term research program in the area of VLSI design automation and complementing it with the necessary curricular components. His is a coauthor of about 125 papers. He guided 31 Ph.D. students to graduation. In 1985, he joined IBM T. J. Watson Laboratories, Yorktown Heights, NY, for a short period to contribute to a silicon compilation path for the 801 RISC pipeline in a project guided by R. K. Brayton and R. Otten. Recently, his interest has focused on hardware platforms for multimedia systems and the problems of compilation for performance when mapping high-performance, real-time tasks onto those platforms. He is member of the board of the European Design Automation Association and has been its Chairman for a number of years. He is a Cofounder of the Design Automation and Test in Europe conference. He was Program Chair and General Chair, respectively, of ICCAD-93 and ICCAD-94.

Instruction Selection Using Binate Covering for Code Size Optimization

Stan Liao Srinivas Devadas
Department of EECS
Massachusetts Institute of Technology
{syliao,devadas}@rle-vlsi.mit.edu

Kurt Keutzer Steve Tjiang
Advanced Technology Group
Synopsys, Inc.
{keutzer,tjiang}@synopsys.com

http://rle-vlsi.mit.edu/spam

Abstract—We address the problem of instruction selection in code generation for embedded DSP microprocessors. Such processors have highly irregular data-paths, and conventional code generation methods typically result in inefficient code.

Instruction selection can be formulated as directed acyclic graph (DAG) covering. Conventional methods for instruction selection use heuristics that break up the DAG into a forest of trees and then cover them independently. This breakup can result in suboptimal solutions for the original DAG. Alternatively, the DAG covering problem can be formulated as a binate covering problem, and solved exactly or heuristically using branch-and-bound methods.

We show that optimal instruction selection on a DAG in the case of accumulator-based architectures requires a partial scheduling of nodes in the DAG, and we augment the binate covering formulation to minimize spills and reloads. We show how the irregular data transfer costs of typical DSP data-paths can be modeled in the binate covering formulation.

Keywords—code generation, instruction selection, digital signal processors

I. INTRODUCTION

An increasingly common micro-architecture for embedded systems is to integrate a microprocessor or microcontroller, a ROM and an ASIC all on a single IC. Such a micro-architecture can currently be found in many diverse embedded systems, e.g., FAX modems, laser printers, and cellular telephones.

The programmable component in embedded systems can be an application-specific instruction processor (ASIP), a general-purpose microprocessor such as the SPARC, a microcontroller such as Intel 8051, or a digital signal processor such as TMS320C25. This paper focuses on the DSP application domain, where embedded systems are increasingly used. Many of these systems use processors from the TMS320C2x, DSP5600x or ADSP families, all fixed-point DSP microprocessors with irregular data-paths.

Code size matters a great deal in embedded systems since program code resides in on-chip ROM, the size of which directly translates into silicon area and cost. Designers often devote a significant amount of time to reduce code size so that the code will fit into available ROM; exceeding on-chip ROM size could require expensive redesign of the entire IC [7]. As a result, a compiler that automatically generates small, dense code will result in a significant productivity gain as well.

We believe that generating the best code for embedded processors will require not only traditional optimization techniques, but also new techniques that take advantage of special architectural features that decrease code size. This paper presents one of our efforts at developing such techniques. We address the problem of *instruction selection* in code generation for embedded DSP microprocessors. We emphasize decreasing code size, although our techniques can also increase execution speed.

Instruction selection can be formulated as directed acyclic graph (DAG) covering. Conventional methods for instruction selection use heuristics that break up the DAG into a forest of trees, which are then covered optimally but independently [1] [3]. Independent covering of the trees may result in a suboptimal solution for the original DAG. Trees, as a *heuristic formulation*, inherently preclude the use of complex instructions in cases where internal nodes are shared. Alternatively, the DAG covering problem can be formulated as a binate covering problem [11], and solved exactly or heuristically using branch-and-bound methods. We present the basic binate covering formulation of instruction selection in Section III. Unlike the heuristic formulation of trees, a good *heuristic procedure* for solving the covering problem is likely to elude the difficulties faced by trees.

The formulation of Section III ignores data transfer costs between nodes in the DAG. This formulation is used to obtain a preliminary instruction selection where pattern DAGs that cover more than two nodes in the given binary DAG are selected. The binary DAG is transformed into a general DAG and a second step of instruction selection taking into account data transfer costs is performed.

In Section IV, we generalize the work of Aho et al. [2] and give a binate covering formulation for optimal code generation for a one-register machine, which takes into account spill and reload costs. Next we provide a formulation in Section V which takes into account irregular data transfer costs under a more general machine model.

II. MOTIVATING EXAMPLE

Fig. 1 shows a simplified model of the data-path of Texas Instruments' popular TMS320C25 architecture. The TMS320C25 is an accumulator-based machine. In addition to the usual ALU, there is a separate multiplier which takes input from the T register and memory and places the result in the P register. Note that there are no general-purpose registers other than the accumulator.

An important feature in this architecture and other DSP architectures is that certain instructions assume their operands are in specific locations (registers or memory) and deposit their results in specific registers. For example, the MPY instruction assumes that the multiplier and multiplicand come from memory and the T register and writes the result into the P register. Another example is the ADDT instruction, which adds an operand from the memory, shifted by the amount specified in the T register, to the accumulator.

It is also not unusual to find complex instructions in DSPs. Typical examples include *add-with-shift* (e.g., TMS320C25 ADD and ADDT) and *multiply-accumulate* (e.g., DSP56000 MAC). Utilizing these instructions is essential to generating compact and efficient code. The conventional heuristic of breaking up a DAG into trees prohibits the use of these complex instructions in the case where internal nodes are shared. In addition, this heuristic may introduce unnecessary stores of intermediate values.

Consider the subject DAG and pattern DAGs shown in Fig. 2. Conventional tree-covering will first break up the DAG at node n_3, thereby prohibiting the use of pattern (d). Fig. 3(a) shows the result-

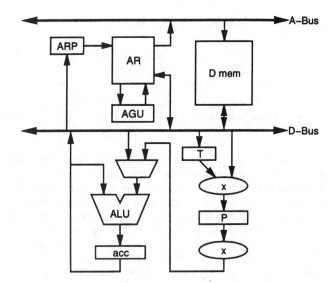

Fig. 1. TMS320C25 data-path (simplified model)

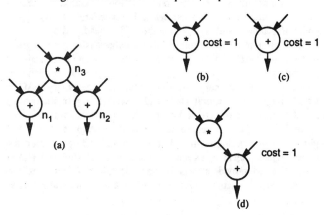

Fig. 2. (a) Subject DAG and (b)-(d) Pattern DAGs

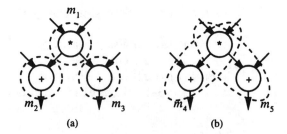

Fig. 3. Two coverings of subject DAG

	m_1	m_2	m_3	m_4	m_5
$m_2 + m_4$	2	1	2	1	2
$m_3 + m_5$	2	2	1	2	1
$\overline{m_2} + m_1$	1	0	2	2	2
$\overline{m_3} + m_1$	1	2	0	2	2

Fig. 4. Covering Matrix

There are three steps associated with DAG covering.
1. All matches of the pattern graphs in the subject graph are generated.
2. A covering matrix is created which expresses the conditions which lead to a legal cover.
3. A cover with minimum cost is obtained using a branch-and-bound algorithm. Alternatively, heuristic methods can be used to find covers with low cost.

Step 1 is a relatively straightforward pattern matching step. A Boolean variable, call it m_i, corresponds to each successful match of a pattern graph in the subject graph G. Let the nodes in the subject graph be n_j, $1 \leq j \leq N$. Each node $n_j \in G$ can be covered by a set of matches $m_{j_1}, m_{j_2}, \cdots, m_{j_P}$. All possible matches m_1 through m_5 for the example subject DAG are marked in Fig. 3.

Step 2 generates a covering matrix in which each column corresponds to a distinct match m_i. Let there be M columns, m_i, $1 \leq i \leq M$. The rows correspond to disjunctive clauses over the m_i's, and represent covering constraints. In the basic DAG covering formulation, there are two different sets of rows, i.e., disjunctive clauses.

- Rows in the first set represent the different ways that any particular node $n_j \in G$ can be covered using the different matches. For the subject graph of Fig. 2(a) the covering matrix is shown in Fig. 4. The first row in the matrix ($m_2 + m_4$) corresponds to node n_1 and indicates that node n_1 can be covered either by match m_2 or match m_4, as indicated in Fig. 3. Therefore, we put 1's in the entry corresponding to column m_2 and column m_4 and 2's in other columns. Similarly, the next row indicates that either m_3 or m_5 needs to be selected to cover node n_2.
Note that in this first set of rows we only need clauses that cover the *root* nodes, because the selection of a particular match will necessitate the selection of matches that cover nodes connected to inputs (see below).
- Matches are allowed to have nodes internal to the match feed nodes not in the match. This results in a second set of rows. For each match m_i, we have to ensure that the non-leaf inputs to the match are the outputs of other matches. By *non-leaf inputs* we mean *internal nodes* (in contrast to primary inputs) in the DAG that serve as inputs to other nodes. Let the non-leaf inputs to match m_i be $s_{i_1}, s_{i_2}, \cdots, s_{i_T}$. For each i_k, let W_{i_k} be the set of matches that have s_{i_k} as an output node. W_{i_k} can be viewed as a disjunctive expression over the Boolean variables corresponding to each match.

ing tree-cover, and Fig. 3(b) shows the optimal DAG cover. Even if the pattern (d) is not used, tree-covering may still result in inefficient code. For instance, using tree-covering we might first evaluate node n_3, store it into memory, and then evaluate nodes n_1 and n_2. However, with the data-path in Fig. 1, it is possible to let the intermediate result remain in the P register and evaluate n_1 and n_2 using the instruction APAC, which adds the contents of the P register to the accumulator without destroying the former.

In the sequel we will show how to solve both the problem of selecting complex instructions and the problem of data transfers using a binate-covering formulation of instruction selection. The first problem is easily taken into account in the basic DAG covering formulation (Section III). The second problem is tackled in Section IV and Section V.

III. BASIC FORMULATION

The formulation in this section assumes that the target machine is such that data transfers between registers or between registers and memory have zero cost.

A subject DAG corresponds to a basic block in the given program [3]. This subject DAG is covered using pattern DAGs that correspond to individual machine instructions. Each pattern DAG has an associated cost. The DAG covering problem is to cover the subject DAG with a set of pattern DAGs with minimum cost.

Selecting match m_i implies that we have to satisfy each of the W_{i_k}. We can write the expression

$$m_i \Rightarrow W_{i_k}, 1 \leq k \leq T$$

which translates to the clauses

$$(\overline{m_i} + W_{i_1}) \cdot (\overline{m_i} + W_{i_2}) \cdots (\overline{m_i} + W_{i_T}).$$

Each of these clauses corresponds to a distinct row in the covering matrix. Each match m_i generates T additional rows if it has T non-leaf inputs.

In the covering matrix of Fig. 4, the second set of rows correspond to these additional clauses. For match m_2, we have to implement the non-leaf node n_3 as the output of another match. This can be done using match m_1 alone. Therefore, we generate the clause $(\overline{m_2} + m_1)$, corresponding to the third row. Since m_2 is complemented in the clause we put a 0 in the entry corresponding to column m_2. We put a 1 in the entry corresponding to column m_1 and 2's in other columns. The fourth row is generated for match m_3, which if selected would require the selection of m_1.

The cost of a match $cost(m_i)$ is simply the cost of its associated pattern DAG. In Step 3, we select a set of columns from the covering matrix such that the cumulative cost of the columns is minimum, and such that every row either has a 1 in the entry corresponding to a selected column, or has a 0 in the entry corresponding to an unselected column. In our example, we will end up selecting m_4 and m_5 with a minimum total cost of $1 + 1 = 2$; this corresponds to the covering of Fig. 3(b). The reader can verify that selecting m_4 and m_5 satisfies all the disjunctive clauses of Fig. 4.

As an aside note that tree covering methods would not be able to discover the optimal solution of Fig. 3(b) since the subject DAG would be broken up into three trees, which when covered independently would result in the covering of Fig. 3(a) that has a cost of $1 + 1 + 1 = 3$.

This problem is called the binate covering problem because the variables m_i are present in their true and complemented forms. This problem is NP-complete, and has received considerable attention. Exact solutions are given in [5], [9]. These techniques have been improved recently in [6] without compromising optimality. Heuristic methods have been given in [8], [9].

We first solve the binate covering problem with zero data transfer costs and determine matches that use pattern DAGs with more than one operator, e.g., the pattern DAG of Fig. 2(b). The original DAG is modified to reflect the use of complex operators. Thus, the new DAG can have nodes with more than two inputs. A second step of binate covering is performed on the new DAG that accurately models spill and data transfer costs. This step is described in the next two sections.

IV. Data Transfer Costs in One-Register Machines

We focus on one-register machines, or accumulator-based architectures. In such architectures, accumulator spills to memory and reloads from memory can account for a large fraction of the instructions. The binate covering formulation must take this cost into account in order to find an optimal instruction selection.

The major complication in modeling memory spills is that the spilling of values depends on the chosen instruction schedule [10]. However, since we are performing instruction selection we do not as yet know the schedule. We therefore have to both choose the instructions and determine a (partial) schedule of these instructions in binate covering. The partial schedule is determined by adding Boolean variables corresponding to adjacency constraints over pairs of nodes in the DAG that are connected by an edge.

A. Previous Work

In [2] Aho et al. presented optimal code generation algorithms (on DAGs) for two different models of one-register machines:
- Non-commutative machines, in which available operations are:
1. $a \leftarrow a$ **op** m
2. $a \leftarrow m$ (load)
3. $m \leftarrow a$ (store)

where a denotes the accumulator and m denotes memory.
- Commutative machines, in which available operations are:
1. $a \leftarrow a$ **op** m
2. $a \leftarrow m$ **op** a
3. $a \leftarrow m$ (load)
4. $m \leftarrow a$ (store)

We find the models above inadequate for the following reasons. First, in our application the given DAG can have ternary or higher-arity operators depending on the complex patterns chosen in the first step of binate covering. Second, the non-commutative model of [2] does not take commutative operators into account. For example, in evaluating the expression $(b + c)$, the value of b must be first loaded to the accumulator and then added with c. However, if b and c are themselves expressions, the accumulator may already contain c immediately before the evaluation of $(b + c)$. Since addition is commutative, adding the accumulator with b is perfectly acceptable. The commutative model, on the other hand, assumes that the first operand of *any* operation can be in memory. In general, machines will have both commutative and non-commutative operators.

We believe the best way to handle commutativity is to treat each operation independently, using a separate pattern for the commutative forms of the operations wherever necessary, rather than assuming commutativity in the machine model.

We present a compact binate-covering formulation for the optimal code generation for the non-commutative one-register machine taking into account the commutativity of individual operators in the following sections. The operators can be binary, ternary or higher-arity operators. For ease of exposition we will concentrate on binary operators; however, the techniques generalize to higher-arity operators.

B. Definitions

Let H be a directed graph. A *u-cycle* in H is a set of edges that would form a cycle if the edges were considered undirected. If H contains a u-cycle, it is said to be *u-cyclic*; otherwise, it is *u-acyclic*. We use the terms *d-acyclic*, *d-cyclic*, and *d-cycle* for the case where the directions of the edges are considered.

A *worm* is a directed path in a DAG D such the nodes in the path will appear *consecutively* in the schedule [2]. A *worm-partition* of D is a set of disjoint worms. An edge is said to be *selected* with respect to a worm-partition if it belongs to some worm in the partition. Associated with a worm-partition is a directed graph G. Each node of G corresponds to a worm in D, and there is an edge between nodes w_1 and w_2 of G whenever there is an edge in D between some node of worm w_1 and some node of worm w_2. We can think of deriving G from D (given a worm-partition) by successively merging the nodes that are connected by selected edges (*imploding* the edge).

A worm-partition is said to be *legal* if a valid schedule can be derived from G such that the nodes of each worm appear consecutively in the schedule. Henceforth we shall denote by D the original expression DAG, and by G the induced graph of a worm-partition of D. A sufficient condition for a worm-partition to be legal is that G is d-acyclic [2]. (This condition, however, is not always necessary. See Theorem 4.)

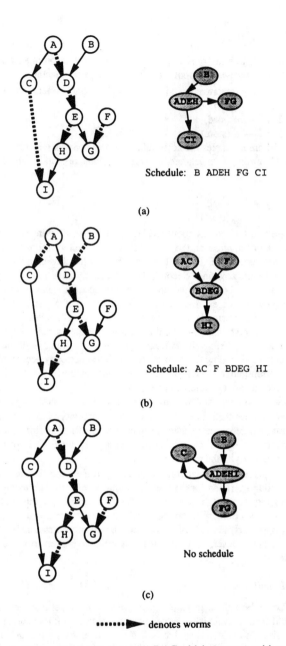

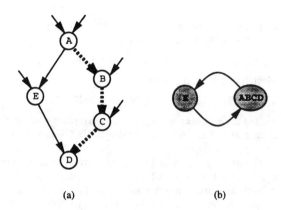

Fig. 6. (a) Reconvergence in a DAG with a worm (b) A cycle in G due to the worm

satisfied.

If a node has multiple fanouts, then at most one of the fanout edges may be selected. If a node has multiple fanins, then at most one the fanin edges may be selected.

Clearly the fundamental clauses are necessary for a worm-partition to be legal in any DAG. (Simply stated, in any schedule each node may have at most one immediate predecessor and at most one immediate successor.) Let e_i be a Boolean variable which takes the value of 1 if edge i is selected, and 0 otherwise. The fundamental clauses are, for each node n,

$$\overline{e_i} + \overline{e_j} \tag{1}$$

for every pair of fanout edges i and j of n, and for every pair of fanin edges i and j of n. We have to satisfy each clause generated above. The cost of all the e_k's is equal to zero. However, not choosing an e_k will imply spilling and reloading and associated costs, as described in Section IV-E.

The following theorem shows that these fundamental clauses are sufficient for u-acyclic DAGs.

Theorem 1: If the subject DAG D is u-acyclic, then the fundamental clauses are sufficient. In other words, any worm-partition that satisfies the fundamental clauses is legal.

Proof: If D is u-acyclic, then selecting an edge and merging the head- and tail-nodes of the edge results in a DAG that remains u-acyclic. By repeating this process we cannot possibly create a u-cycle. Therefore, by merging the nodes according to the selected edges of the worm-partition, no u-cycle (much less a d-cycle) will appear in G. This implies that the worm-partition is legal. ∎

If there are u-cycles in D the fundamental clauses become insufficient. A good example is one of reconvergent paths (Fig. 6). Note, on the other hand, that selecting an edge that is not part of any u-cycle in D will not create a d-cycle in G. Thus we only need to focus on writing additional clauses for u-cycles.

D. Clauses for U-Cycles

Since u-cycles in D may lead to d-cycles in G, we need to add clauses that prevent this from happening. Let C be a u-cycle of D, and arbitrarily choose a direction of traversal on C as the forward direction, and label the edges as forward and backward accordingly.

Theorem 2: If all forward edges (or all backward edges) in a u-cycle are selected, then imploding the selected edges will result in a d-cycle. Conversely, if at least one forward edge and at least one backward edge are not selected, then the u-cycle remains d-acyclic after implosion.

Proof: ⇒: If all forward edges in a u-cycle are selected, then in the imploded u-cycle only the backward edges remain. Since

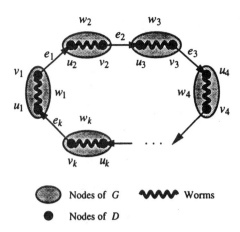

Fig. 7. From a d-cycle of G we can always find a u-cycle in D that produced it

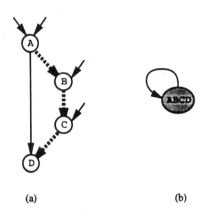

Fig. 8. (a) A portion of a DAG D with a selected worm (b) The induced self-loop in G

all the edges of the imploded u-cycle are in the same direction, the imploded u-cycle is also a d-cycle.

$\Leftarrow$: If at least one forward edge and at least one backward edge are not selected, then the imploded u-cycle have at least two edges pointing to the opposite directions; hence, the imploded u-cycle remains d-acyclic. ∎

Therefore, it is necessary that for each cycle we do not select all edges of the same orientation. Is it possible that, even if the selected edges satisfy this condition for every cycle (including the composite cycles), there is still a d-cycle in G? That is, is it possible that a d-cycle in G arises from another cause than u-cycles in D? The following theorem shows that this is impossible, thereby establishing the sufficiency of this condition.

Theorem 3: If G is d-cyclic, then there exists a u-cycle in D of which all the forward edges (or all backward edges) are selected. Therefore, if the clauses derived from Theorem 2 are satisfied for every u-cycle in D, then G is d-acyclic.

Proof: Let $w_1, w_2, \ldots, w_k$ be the nodes of a d-cycle in G, which also denote the corresponding worms in D. By the definition of G, there exist nodes $v_1 \in w_1$ and $u_2 \in w_2$ such that an edge $e_1 = (v_1, u_2)$ exists between them. Similarly, there exist edges $e_i = (v_i, u_{i+1})$ for $i = 2, \ldots, k-1$, and $e_k = (v_k, u_1)$ (Fig. 7). Since v_i and u_i are nodes in a worm, there is a path between them (in one direction or the other). Denote by P_i the path between v_i and u_i. Now $(P_1, e_1, P_2, e_2, \ldots, P_k, e_k)$ form a u-cycle in D. Furthermore, regardless of the orientations of the paths P_i's, in this u-cycle every edge in the direction opposite to the e_i's is selected (recall all edges of P_i are selected edges). ∎

It turns out that we can compactly write clauses to require that at least one forward edge and one backward edge are selected, as follows. Let $f_1, f_2, \ldots, f_k$ be the Boolean variables for the forward edges of a u-cycle in D. The clause

$$\overline{f_1} + \overline{f_2} + \cdots + \overline{f_k} \quad (2)$$

will ensure that not all of these edges are selected. A similar clause is written for the backward edges. Hence, two clauses for each u-cycle suffice. No new variables are introduced into the formulation merely additional clauses.

One important exception needs to be made regarding self-loops in G (which was not addressed in [2]). Consider the portion of a DAG shown in Fig. 8. If we choose the path A→B→C→D (which are all of the forward edges in this u-cycle), then a d-cycle results in G (in accordance with Theorem 2). However, this d-cycle is a *self-loop*. It can be easily verified that the worm thus chosen is actually legal: the schedule ABCD, in which the nodes of the worm (namely, A–D) appear consecutively, is admissible. This example shows that self-loops do not make the worm-partition illegal. The lemma and the theorem that follow state this formally.

Lemma 1: Let C be a self-loop of G. The corresponding u-cycle in D must consist of two reconvergent paths. Furthermore, if u and v are the end-points of the reconvergent paths, one of these paths must be an edge from u to v.

Proof: The loop-edge of C corresponds to a single edge from some node u of the worm to some other node v of the worm. Other than the edge (u, v), there is another path P from u to v (the worm). With respect to D, u must be a predecessor of v (otherwise the DAG would not be d-acyclic). Thus we have the two reconvergent paths: the edge (u, v) and the path P. ∎

Theorem 4: If all d-cycles of a worm-partition G are self-loops, then G is legal. Conversely, if a d-cycle of G contains more than one node, then G is illegal.

Proof: Self-loops arise solely from the kind of reconvergent paths described in Lemma 1, with the long path being part of a worm. Thus when we schedule these nodes consecutively, the precedence relation required by the edge (u, v) is not violated. On the other hand, if there are more than one node in a d-cycle of G, scheduling the nodes of one worm consecutively will be unsuccessful because some node of the current worm depends on some node of another worm, which in turn depend on the current worm. ∎

In light of Theorem 4, Clauses (2) are not required for self-loops. Instead, a clause consisting of a single variable requiring the edge (u, v) *not* to be selected is prescribed—clearly, choosing the edge (u, v) would lead to a non-trivial d-cycle in G. If, on the other hand, the reconvergent path is itself a single edge (e.g., when an operator takes both operands from the same node), then neither the cycle- nor the reconvergence-clauses is necessary—the fundamental clauses described in Section IV-C ensure that at most one of these edges is selected.

E. Clauses for Reloads and Spills

Depending on where an operation takes its operands from and which edges are selected, spills and reloads may be required between computations. We now describe precisely how to write clauses to activate spills and reloads.

Fig. 9(a) shows a fragment of a DAG. Consider the edge (C,B), whose corresponding Boolean variable is e_2. There are four cases to consider for this edge:

1. Match m_1 is used and $e_2 = 1$. Since m_1 requires its left-operand from the accumulator, and B is immediately after C,

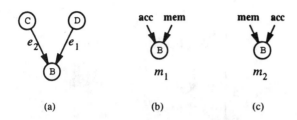

(a)   (b)   (c)

Fig. 9. Spilling and reloading according to adjacency of nodes

no spill on C or reload on the edge (C,B) is necessary.
2. Match m_1 is used and $e_2 = 0$. In this case, a spill on C is required, because a node other than B immediately follows C and destroys the contents of the accumulator, but this value is needed by B later. Also, a reload is necessary immediately before B is scheduled, because m_1 takes its left-operand from the accumulator.
3. Match m_2 is used and $e_2 = 1$. Even though B immediately follows C, a spill is still required because m_2 takes its left-operand from the memory. No reload is necessary.
4. Match m_2 is used and $e_2 = 0$. As in the previous case, only a spill is required.

Let **spill**(C) denote the match that transfers the value of C from the accumulator to the memory immediately after C is computed, and **reload**(C,B) denote the match that loads the value of C from the memory to the accumulator immediately before B is scheduled. We can then express the above conditions by the following clauses:

$$\overline{m_1} + e_2 + \textbf{spill}(C) \qquad (3)$$

$$\overline{m_1} + e_2 + \textbf{reload}(C,B) \qquad (4)$$

$$\overline{m_2} + \textbf{spill}(C) \qquad (5)$$

Similar clauses are prescribed for edge e_1, as well as every other node and all possible matches on it.

Given the DAG with the complex patterns selected, the fundamental clauses, u-cycle clauses and the clauses for reloads and spills are added to the clauses for the node matches. The clauses for the node matches are very simple for a one-register machine, since the only choices for a node are where the inputs come from, as shown in Fig. 9.

V. Data Transfer Costs in Multiple-Register Machines

A. Target Architecture

We will now assume that the target architecture can be modeled conveniently with the $[1, \infty]$ model [4]. In the $[1, \infty]$ model each resource class is assumed to have either one element or an infinite number of elements. For resource classes that have more than one element, we will perform a separate pass of storage allocation at or after scheduling, as in [12].

As shown in Section II, the typical fixed point DSP has irregular data-paths, and certain registers have specialized uses. Consequently, at completion of an operation its results may not be available for use by another operation that takes operands from other registers. For example, the MPY operator requires one of its operands to come from the treg register and the other from the memory. Thus a *data transfer* is necessary to move the operands to the desired register(s). Tree-covering methodology models the cost of this transfer is modeled by associating a cost with a *unit production*, a production with a non-terminal in each of the left- and right-sides. In this section, we show how to incorporate data transfers into the binate covering formulation.

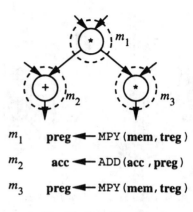

$m_1 \quad \textbf{preg} \leftarrow \textbf{MPY}(\textbf{mem}, \textbf{treg})$

$m_2 \quad \textbf{acc} \leftarrow \textbf{ADD}(\textbf{acc}, \textbf{preg})$

$m_3 \quad \textbf{preg} \leftarrow \textbf{MPY}(\textbf{mem}, \textbf{treg})$

Fig. 10. Data Transfers

B. Example

Consider a fragment of an expression DAG in Fig. 10. The operation covered by match m_3 requires that its left operand come from the memory and its right operand come from the **treg** register. However, the match m_1 produces its result in the **preg** register. A match m_4 that transfers the contents of the **preg** register to memory is required. Hence, we write:

$$\overline{m_3} + \overline{m_1} + m_4 \qquad (6)$$

to require the selection of match m_4 in the event that both m_1 and m_3 are selected. Similar clauses are also prescribed for other matches on node 1.

C. Constructing the Clauses

Based on the example in Section V-B, we now describe a general procedure for constructing the clauses necessary for data transfers. We add these clauses to all the clauses summarized at the end of Section IV. For every pair of nodes n_1 and n_2 in the given DAG connected by an edge, for each possible match m_i on n_1 and each possible match m_j on n_2, we will write

$$\overline{m_i} + \overline{m_j} + q_{ij} \qquad (7)$$

where matching q_{ij} indicates a transfer of the result of match m_i to the location required by m_j. If m_i results in writing an operand into memory, and m_j requires reading from register **preg**, then q_{ij} will correspond to a match that moves data from memory to **preg**. Similarly, for other moves across different register classes. If m_i writes into a register **acc** and m_j reads from the same register **acc**, q_{ij} is the disjunction of an adjacency constraint between the output node of m_i and the input node of m_j, and a spill/reload match (cf. Section IV-E).

We assume that this adjacency constraint has to be satisfied in the schedule to guarantee a correct data transfer without a spill/reload. Satisfying the adjacency constraint is not necessary for correct data transfer in multiple-register machines; in-between instructions can exist but should write registers other than **acc**. However, relaxing this assumption would require a life-time analysis of registers and a very large number of clauses. After instruction selection and partial scheduling using binate covering an optimized complete schedule can be generated which exploits life-time analysis.

In some cases, due to data-path constraints, it is not possible to move the contents of one location to another location via a single move. For example, suppose there is no direct path from the **preg** register to the memory, and the only way to accomplish the move from **preg** to memory is through the accumulator. In this case, two moves will be required, and q_{ij} will represent the conjunction of the two corresponding matches.

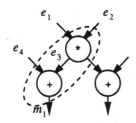

Fig. 11. Matches altering fundamental clauses

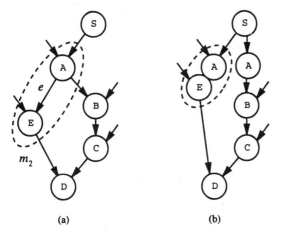

Fig. 12. (a) A u-cycle in a DAG (b) Modified u-cycle

VII. SUMMARY AND ONGOING WORK

We have presented a formulation of the instruction selection problem as that of binate covering. This formulation captures data transfer and memory spill costs commonly associated with DSP processors.

Our preliminary experiments indicate that exact binate covering can be applied to small-to-moderate sized basic blocks for the TMS320C25 processor. These optimal solutions are better than those produced by the tree covering heuristic in many cases. For large basic blocks or entire procedures, however, computationally efficient heuristic strategies are required. Two avenues are being explored. First, large basic blocks will be broken into simpler blocks which can be covered using the exact binate covering algorithm. Second, heuristics which restrict the number of matches and therefore clauses in the covering matrix will be investigated.

VIII. ACKNOWLEDGEMENTS

We thank Richard Rudell and Olivier Coudert for help with the binate covering formulation. This research was supported in part by the Advanced Research Projects Agency under contract DABT63-94-C-0053, and in part by a NSF Young Investigator Award with matching funds from Mitsubishi Corporation.

REFERENCES

[1] A. Aho and S. Johnson. Optimal code generation for expression trees. *Journal of the ACM*, 23:488–501, July 1976.

[2] A. Aho, S. Johnson, and J. Ullman. Code generation for expressions with common subexpressions. *Journal of the ACM*, pages 146–160, January 1977.

[3] A. Aho, R. Sethi, and J. Ullman. *Compilers: Principles, Techniques and Tools*. Addison-Wesley, 1986.

[4] G. Araujo and S. Malik. Optimal Code Generation for Embedded Memory Non-Homogeneous Register Architectures. In *Proceedings of 1995 International Symposium on System Synthesis*, 1995.

[5] R. K. Brayton and F. Somenzi. Boolean Relations and the Incomplete Specification of Logic Networks. In *Proceedings of the Int'l Conference on Computer-Aided Design*, pages 316–319, November 1989.

[6] O. Coudert and J-C. Madre. New Ideas for Solving Covering Problems. In *Proceedings of the 32nd Design Automation Conference*, pages 641–646, June 1995.

[7] J. G. Ganssle. *The Art of Programming Embedded Systems*. San Diego, CA: Academic Press, Inc., 1992.

[8] J. Gimpel. The Minimization of TANT Networks. *IEEE Transactions on Electronic Computers*, EC-16(1):18–38, February 1967.

[9] A. Grasselli and F. Luccio. A Method for Minimizing the Number of Internal States in Incompletely Specified Machines. *IEEE Transactions on Electronic Computers*, EC-14(3):350–359, June 1965.

[10] S. Liao, S. Devadas, K. Keutzer, S. Tjiang, and A. Wang. Code Optimization Techniques in Embedded DSP Microprocessors. In *Proceedings of the 32nd Design Automation Conference*, pages 599–604, June 1995.

[11] R. Rudell. Logic Synthesis for VLSI Design. In *U. C. Berkeley, ERL Memo 89/49*, April 1989.

[12] A. Sudarsanam and S. Malik. Memory Bank and Register Allocation in Software Synthesis for ASIPs. In *Proceedings of the International Conference on Computer-Aided Design*, 1995 (this volume).

VI. DISCUSSION

We presented a two-pass strategy. The first step selects complex operators, and the second step selects matches that minimize data transfer costs on a transformed DAG. Can both these steps be performed simultaneously by solving a single binate covering problem?

The answer is yes, but the number of clauses in binate covering can become very large. The reason is that the selection of complex operators affects the fundamental adjacency clauses and the clauses for u-cycles.

The fundamental clauses corresponding to the marked edges of the DAG of Fig. 11 are $\overline{e_1} + \overline{e_2}$, and $\overline{e_3} + \overline{e_4}$. However, if match m_1 is selected, then the fundamental clauses should become $\overline{e_1} + \overline{e_2}$, $\overline{e_1} + \overline{e_4}$, and $\overline{e_2} + \overline{e_4}$. This can be incorporated by writing the following clauses: $\overline{e_1} + \overline{e_2}$, $\overline{e_3} + \overline{e_4} + m_1$, $\overline{e_1} + \overline{e_4} + \overline{m_1}$, and $\overline{e_2} + \overline{e_4} + \overline{m_1}$. This has to be done for *each* match which corresponds to a complex pattern that covers any edge of the DAG, in the manner that m_1 covers e_3 in our example above.

If the DAG is u-acyclic the fundamental clauses are sufficient, and the above modification will be enough. However, u-cycle clauses have be modified in the general case. This modification can result in a very large number of clauses, since choosing a complex pattern can change the u-cycles of a DAG. To understand this consider Fig. 12. If match m_2 is selected in Fig. 12(a), then in effect, the DAG is modified to the one shown in Fig. 12(b). There is a new u-cycle beginning from the node S! This means that we have to write clauses corresponding to this new u-cycle when match m_2 is selected, and when it is not. Note that if all u-cycles begin from level 1 nodes in the DAG, i.e., nodes whose inputs are leaves, then no new u-cycles will be introduced due to complex operators. Even if a new u-cycle is not generated, we still have to modify the original u-cycle clauses since edge e is covered by m_2, as in the fundamental clause case.

A Retargetable Compilation Methodology for Embedded Digital Signal Processors Using a Machine-Dependent Code Optimization Library

ASHOK SUDARSANAM ashok@ee.princeton.edu
SHARAD MALIK sharad@ee.princeton.edu
Department of Electrical Engineering, Princeton University, Princeton, NJ USA

MASAHIRO FUJITA fujita@fla.fujitsu.com
Fujitsu Laboratories of America, Santa Clara, CA USA

Abstract. We address the problem of code generation for embedded DSP systems. Such systems devote a limited quantity of silicon to program memory, so the embedded software must be sufficiently dense. Additionally, this software must be written so as to meet various high-performance constraints. Unfortunately, current compiler technology is unable to generate dense, high-performance code for DSPs, due to the fact that it does not provide adequate support for the specialized architectural features of DSPs via *machine-dependent code optimizations*. Thus, designers often produce the embedded software in assembly, a very time-consuming task. In order to increase productivity, compilers must be developed that are capable of generating high-quality code for DSPs. The compilation process must also be made *retargetable*, so that a variety of DSPs may be efficiently evaluated for potential use in an embedded system.

We present a retargetable compilation methodology that enables high-quality code to be generated for a wide range of DSPs. Previous work in retargetable DSP compilation has focused on complete automation, and this desire for automation has limited the number of machine-dependent optimizations that can be supported. In our efforts, we have given code quality higher priority over complete automation. We demonstrate how by using a library of machine-dependent optimization routines accessible via a programming interface, it is possible to support a wide range of machine-dependent optimizations, albeit at some cost to automation. Experimental results demonstrate the effectiveness of our methodology, which has been used to build good-quality compilers for three fixed-point DSPs.

Keywords: Digital signal processor, code generation, code optimization, retargetability

1. Introduction

We address the problem of code generation for embedded DSP systems. An emerging trend in the implementation of these systems is the integration of one or more *digital signal processors* (DSPs), program memory, and ASIC circuitry onto a single IC. An immediate consequence of this microarchitectural design is the limited quantity of silicon that is dedicated to program memory, whose purpose is to store the embedded software that executes on the DSP(s). Thus, system designers must ensure that the embedded software is sufficiently dense so as to fit within the allocated area. Additionally, since embedded DSP systems operate in real-time environments, the embedded software must be written so as to meet various high-performance constraints, which may include *hard* real-time constraints.

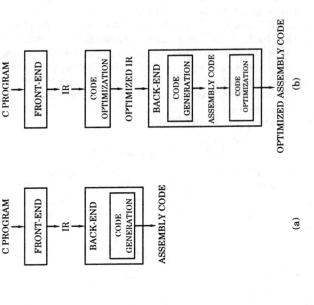

Figure 1. Structure of a C compiler (a) unoptimizing compiler (b) optimizing compiler

1.1. Basic Compiler Review

In this section, we provide a brief overview of compilers. Although this overview consists of generally standard material, we provide it in order to sharply point out the limitations of existing DSP compilation efforts. A *compiler* is a computer program that translates a program written in a high-level language (HLL), such as C, into an equivalent assembly language program [2]. A basic compiler consists of the following components (see Figure 1(a)):

- the *front-end* takes as input an HLL program and generates an *intermediate representation* (IR) of this program that is independent of the target machine.

- the *back-end* translates this IR into target machine assembly code. In particular, the back-end performs the phases of *instruction selection*, *instruction scheduling*, and *register allocation*, which are collectively known as *code generation*.

An *optimizing compiler* features two sets of code optimization modules, in addition to the components that were described above (see Figure 1(b)):

- *machine-independent* optimizations apply various optimizing transformations to the front-end-generated IR.

- *machine-dependent* or *post-pass* optimizations apply various optimizing transformations to the generated assembly code.

Unfortunately, existing compilers for embedded DSPs are generally unable to generate assembly code that is sufficiently dense. There are two reasons for this:

- first, most existing embedded DSP compilers make use of traditional machine-independent optimization techniques [2], in which the primary metric is performance, rather than code density. Although some optimizations improve the performance and density of the embedded software (e.g. *common-subexpression elimination* and *dead-code elimination*), many optimizations result in a speed-size tradeoff. For example, *loop unrolling* and *procedure inlining* significantly increase performance, but also increase code size.

- second, current DSP compilers fail to provide adequate support for the specialized architectural features of DSPs via post-pass optimizations. These features not only allow for the fast execution of common DSP operations, but also allow for the generation of dense assembly code that specifies these operations.

In order to guarantee that all density and performance requirements are safely met, designers usually hand-program the embedded software in assembly, which is a very time-consuming task. In order to increase productivity, optimizing compilers must be developed that are capable of generating high-quality code for DSPs.

1.2. Need for Retargetable Compilation

During the design phase of an embedded DSP system, the designer may wish to evaluate a wide variety of DSPs in order to determine the most appropriate processor for the system. These DSPs may come from a predefined set (these are referred to as *off-the-shelf processors*) or they may be specially designed for the intended application (these are referred to as *application-specific instruction set processors*, or *ASIPs*). Optimizing compilers for the off-the-shelf DSPs under evaluation may already be available; however, such compilers are generally unavailable for ASIPs. If a compiler is unavailable for the DSP currently under evaluation, then the design process must include the construction of such a compiler.

Clearly, the design process will be very time-consuming if an optimizing compiler must be constructed from scratch for each ASIP architecture under evaluation. In order to allow the designer to efficiently evaluate a wide variety of off-the-shelf and ASIP DSPs, the compilation process must be made *retargetable*, i.e. with minor modifications, an optimizing DSP compiler must be able to generate good-quality code for a new DSP architecture.

In this paper, we present a retargetable compilation methodology that enables high-quality code to be generated for a wide range of DSPs. The focus of previous work in retargetable DSP compilation has been on complete automation. Starting with some machine-readable description of the architecture and microarchitecture, the goal is to develop a high-quality compiler automatically. While significant research efforts have been devoted to this task, the goal of achieving high quality has not been achieved simultaneously with automation. The primary reason for this is the difficulty in inferring specialized properties of the architecture and microarchitecture, and then exploiting them via post-pass optimization algorithms. Thus, the desire for automation has limited the number of machine-dependent optimizations that can be supported.

In our efforts, we have given code quality higher priority over complete automation. Rather than automate the process of inferring the specific architectural/microarchitectural features, we choose to focus on the post-pass code optimizations and the ability to use a library of such functions across multiple compilers. Some developer effort is needed in using such a library, but the additional effort pays off in terms of the high quality of code obtained. We believe this methodology is an interesting balance between quality and automation in a domain where code quality is very critical, and traditionally has taken priority over productivity enhancement via automation. Also, we believe that this is an important intermediate step in our quest towards high-quality fully-automatic retargetable code generation. We demonstrate the results of this tradeoff between complete automation and quality of results by providing quantitative results for three compilers, for three different fixed-point DSPs, that were constructed using this methodology.

This paper is organized as follows: Section 2 outlines related work that has been done in the area of compilation for DSPs; Section 3 describes our retargetable compilation methodology; Section 4 provides an overview of the *SPAM* compiler infrastructure, which is our retargetable compilation framework for embedded DSPs; Section 5 presents case studies that detail how our compilation framework has been retargeted to three fixed-point DSPs; Section 6 provides quantitative results pertaining to the retargeting process; finally, we conclude in Section 7.

2. Related Work in Compilation for DSPs

The discussion of related work in this section is divided into two parts. First, we discuss related work that has been done in the area of code-density optimization for DSPs. Thereafter, we discuss related work that has been done in the area of retargetable compilation for DSPs.

2.1. Related Work in Code-Density Optimization

Several works in code-density optimization for DSPs have specifically focused on expression computation. Assembly code is traditionally generated on a per-*basic block* basis, where a basic block is a straight-line code sequence that has a single entry and exit point. In [3], a linear-time algorithm is presented that performs optimal instruction selection, register allocation, and instruction scheduling for a certain class of DSP architectures, provided that each basic block is represented by a sequence of *expression trees*.

Other approaches to expression tree code generation have been proposed by Wess. For instance, in [25], an algorithm is described that uses a *trellis diagram* description of the target processor to perform optimal instruction selection for expression trees. A different approach to expression computation is presented in [15]. The proposed algorithm generates optimal code directly from the more general *expression DAG* representation of a basic block by means of a *binate covering* formulation.

- a description of the target processor which consists of a description of the ISA, a *structural graph* that specifies all possible data movements in the processor, and a classification of all resources in this graph.

CODESYN subsequently uses the description of the target processor to generate code from the CDFG representation of the source program.

3. Developer-Retargetable Compilation

In order for an optimizing DSP compiler to be truly retargetable, it must meet the following requirements: first, it must be possible to construct a code generator for the target machine in a retargetable manner; second, it must be possible to exploit various post-pass code optimizations in a retargetable manner.

As was mentioned in the previous section, techniques exist that allow for the retargetable construction of code generators that perform optimal instruction selection. However, no prior compilation methodology exists that allows for the retargetable utilization of a wide range of post-pass code optimizations. We now present such a methodology. This methodology assumes the existence of a basic compilation framework that must be constructed by compiler designers as follows:

- first, examine a range of architectures that are considered to be representative of contemporary DSPs, and determine a set of problems that typically occur in post-pass code optimization for these architectures.

- next, develop a *parameterized* solution for each of these problems and implement it in the framework. A parameterized solution to a code optimization problem yields a *procedural interface* to the optimization. Each procedure in an interface requires various target-specific parameters – some of these parameters may be simple constant values (e.g. the total number of registers in the architecture), while more complex parameters may be *pointers to procedures* that perform a sequence of machine-dependent actions (e.g. such a procedure may construct and return a pointer to a large machine-specific data structure).

Define a *developer* to be a person who has had experience in compiler design. One method that enables post-pass optimizations to be utilized in a retargetable manner is to permit the developer to *tailor* the compiler to the target machine – we refer to this compilation methodology as *developer-retargetable* compilation. In particular, given a compilation framework featuring a *library* of post-pass optimization algorithms, the developer may construct an optimizing compiler for some DSP by performing the following sequence of steps:

- first, the developer determines all post-pass code optimizations that are applicable to the target machine by thoroughly studying the architectural and microarchitectural characteristics of this machine.

- second, for each applicable post-pass code optimization O, the developer determines whether or not a parameterized solution to O exists in the compilation framework. If such a

A significant number of research efforts in DSP code-density optimization have focused on address generation. In particular, many algorithms have been presented that exploit the *auto-increment* capability of specialized *address registers* in order to generate efficient code for register-indirect memory accesses [16], [13], [26], [8]. In [4], an algorithm is described that exploits auto-increment arithmetic in order to generate efficient code for a sequence of array accesses that occurs within a loop. This algorithm is based on finding a *minimum-cardinality disjoint path covering* of an acyclic *indexing graph*, which conveys the distance between each pair of array indices in the loop. Another approach to array index allocation is presented in [12] – this approach proposes a branch-and-bound solution to the allocation problem.

A number of research efforts in DSP compilation have been directed towards the development of code optimization techniques that exploit available *instruction-level parallelism* (ILP) in DSP architectures. In [21], an algorithm is presented that exploits the ILP that is offered by the dual data memory bank architecture of the *Motorola DSP56000* DSP [18]. Specifically, this algorithm uses simulated annealing to perform the phases of memory bank and register allocation simultaneously. The work of Saghir et al. [20] also provides support for dual data memory banks; however, rather than focusing on a particular commercial DSP, this work targets a synthetic DSP architecture that features a large general-purpose register file.

Meanwhile, the local compaction algorithm of [14] uses a two-phase technique to exploit the limited ILP that exists between the multiplier and accumulator in the *Texas Instruments TMS320C25* DSP architecture [23].

2.2. Related Work in Retargetable Compilation

Previous work in retargetable compilation for DSPs (e.g. [17], [19], [6], [11], [10]) has focused on a level of retargetability known as *user retargetability*. In this scenario, a description of the target processor is provided to a *compiler-compiler*, which first determines the set of all built-in optimizations that are applicable to this processor, then automatically constructs an optimizing compiler for it. User retargetability has been successfully incorporated into the code generation phase of compilation: the *Twig* [1] and *lburg* [7] code generator-generators take as input a description of the target machine *instruction set architecture* (ISA), then automatically construct code generators that perform, in linear time, optimal instruction selection for expression trees. The primary disadvantage of this level of retargetability is that it supports a very limited number of machine-dependent optimizations. In particular, there does not exist a machine-description format that enables a user-retargetable compiler to automatically infer the set of all post-pass code optimizations that are applicable to the target DSP architecture – these optimizations must be performed in order for code of the highest quality to be generated.

The CODESYN system [19] is an example of a compiler that exhibits user retargetability. The input to CODESYN consists of two items:

- an HLL description of the application, which is converted by a source-level parser into a hierarchy of *control-data flow graphs* (CDFGs).

solution exists, then the developer simply provides the procedural interface with the necessary machine-specific parameters; otherwise, the developer *implements* a parameterized solution to O, adds this solution to the library of parameterized solutions in the compilation framework, and then provides the procedural interface with the appropriate parameters.

- finally, the developer invokes all applicable interfaces in the most effective order.

The effectiveness of developer retargetability is measured by the amount of *code reuse* that occurs during the retargetting process. Specifically, a compiler is said to exhibit sufficient retargetability if the developer is able to make use of a significant quantity of source code that already exists in the compiler. In this scenario, reusable source code encompasses all parameterized optimization algorithms, as well as any other source code modules that are built into the compilation framework and provided to the developer.

Although developer-retargetable compilation generally requires more user intervention than user-retargetable compilation, we believe that the former is currently the only level of retargetability that can support the wide range of post-pass optimizations that are needed to generate high-quality code for embedded DSPs. Ultimately, the most benefit will be provided by a user-retargetable compilation framework that can support a wide range of post-pass optimizations. We believe, however, that a complete study of developer-retargetable compilation is the appropriate first step towards understanding all that is involved in constructing such a user-retargetable environment.

4. The SPAM Compiler Infrastructure

The work presented in this paper is part of a project known as the *SPAM Project*. The goal of this project is to develop a retargetable optimizing compiler for embedded DSPs. This project has led to the development of the *SPAM compiler infrastructure* [22], which is a *developer-retargetable* compiler for embedded fixed-point DSPs. In particular, the optimization algorithms in the SPAM compiler are currently restricted to embedded fixed-point DSPs with limited parallelism. However, we are in the process of augmenting the infrastructure with a new suite of algorithms that will enable it to support additional classes of embedded DSPs, such as floating-point and VLIW DSPs. The structure of the SPAM compiler, which is publicly available on the internet, is shown in Figure 2 and outlined below:

- the *Stanford University Intermediate Format* (SUIF) compiler [27] implements the front-end of the SPAM compiler. SUIF takes as input a source program written in C, and generates an unoptimized IR.

- a series of machine-independent *scalar optimizations* apply various code density-improving transformations to this IR.

- the back-end of SPAM, which is known as *TWIF*, consists of two components. The first component is a library of *data structures* that encapsulate the various source program intermediate representations. The second component is a library of *algorithms* that perform code generation and post-pass code optimization by analyzing and manipulating

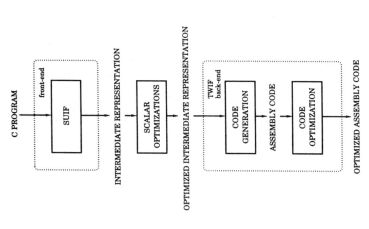

Figure 2. Structure of the SPAM compiler infrastructure

these data structures. In order to provide for developer retargetability, each post-pass optimization algorithm has been implemented in a parameterized manner.

SUIF was incorporated into the SPAM framework for two reasons. First, the object-oriented design style of SUIF provides well-defined interfaces to all front-end data structures. These interfaces considerably reduce the amount of effort required to implement new machine-independent optimizations. Second, SUIF propagates to the IR various *abstract* data structures corresponding to high-level constructs that were utilized in the source program – these high-level constructs include *for loops* and *array accesses*. Since many fixed-point DSPs include specialized architectural features that support the efficient execution of these constructs, the propagation of these abstract data structures to the IR enables the optimization algorithms in TWIF to easily recognize potential opportunities to exploit these features.

Included in the code generation algorithms is the *Olive* code generator-generator, which is based on the *Twig* and *Iburg* code-generator generators. Olive enables a code generator to be constructed for a particular target machine in a *user-retargetable* manner. It takes as input a grammar-based description of the ISA that maps IR tree patterns onto target machine

```
class ZeroOverheadLoopClass {
public:
    ZeroOverheadLoopClass( CFGFor* );
    ~ZeroOverheadLoopClass() { }

    virtual boolean CanPerformRepeatLoop( CFGFor* ) = 0;
    virtual boolean CanPerformDoLoop( CFGFor* ) = 0;
    virtual CompactedInstructionList* GenerateRepeatOperations( CFGFor* ) = 0;
    virtual CompactedInstructionList* GenerateDoOperations( CFGFor*, label_sym* ) = 0;
    virtual void UndoLoopOptimizations( CFGFor* ) = 0;

    void Optimize();
};
```

Figure 3. Procedural interface for zero-overhead looping optimization

assembly code, and then constructs a code generator that performs, in linear time, optimal instruction selection for expression trees. The basis of the instruction selection algorithm is a combination of efficient pattern-matching and dynamic programming techniques.

In the following section, we describe how developer retargetability has been incorporated into the SPAM compiler. We first discuss the implementation style that was chosen for the post-pass code optimizations; we then present an example of a post-pass code optimization that is applicable to many fixed-point DSPs, as well as the procedural interface that was developed for this optimization.

4.1. Developer Retargetability in the SPAM Compiler

4.1.1. Procedural Interface Implementation

As was previously described, a procedural interface may require some of its more complex machine-specific parameters to perform a sequence of machine-dependent actions. For instance, a parameter may be required to perform a series of modifications to a certain data structure – the developer may implement such a parameter by passing to the interface a *pointer* to a procedure that performs the necessary actions.

We have incorporated into the SPAM compiler a cleaner variant of this implementation technique, which does not require the developer to explicitly pass function pointers as parameters. Specifically, we have used the fact that TWIF is written in C++ to exploit the *abstract class* capability that is offered by C++ – although this topic is standard material for C++ users, we briefly describe it here in order to point out its usefulness in our context. In this scenario, each post-pass code optimization is implemented by a *class* (hence, the *public methods* in the class declaration constitute the procedural interface to the optimization) and all machine-specific procedures that must be written by the developer are declared to be *pure virtual functions*. The presence of a pure virtual function in a class renders that class to be *abstract* – in order to utilize an optimization that has been implemented by an abstract class A, the developer must perform the following tasks: first, a class B must be *derived* from A; second, in the class definition of B, a definition must be provided for each pure virtual function of A.

A key advantage of the abstract class implementation of an optimization is that a compile-time error will occur if the developer attempts to make use of a procedural interface without providing definitions for all pure virtual functions in the interface.

4.1.2. Generic Assembly Representation

In order to improve the retargetability of the SPAM compiler, we have also developed a generic representation of an *assembly instruction*. This representation, which is implemented by the *CompactedInstruction* class, forms the basis of all post-pass optimizations in the SPAM compiler. A CompactedInstruction object is simply a container of *assembly operations*, which are implemented by the *AsmOperation* class. An AsmOperation object consists of an integer opcode, plus a sequence of assembly operands. Each CompactedInstruction object specifies that the encapsulated assembly operations are to execute in parallel during a given cycle.

We chose this generic representation so that both *horizontally* and *vertically*-encoded DSP architectures could be supported by the SPAM framework. In particular, each Compac-tedInstruction object in a horizontally-encoded architecture will encapsulate one or more AsmOperation objects, while each CompactedInstruction in a vertically-encoded architecture will encapsulate *exactly one* AsmOperation.

4.1.3. Procedural Interface Example

In this section, we discuss a typical post-pass code optimization for fixed-point DSPs, namely the use of *zero-overhead looping hardware*. We subsequently describe the structure of a procedural interface that enables this optimization to be utilized in a retargetable manner.

Many DSP architectures feature zero-overhead looping hardware, which is specialized hardware that supports the efficient execution of loops and also allows for the generation of dense assembly code that specifies looping constructs. Zero-overhead looping hardware consists of specialized logic that repeatedly executes one or more instructions without incurring the index-variable-update and conditional-branch overhead that is generally associated with software loops. There exist two configurations of this hardware:

- the *single-instruction* configuration supports the repeated execution of *one* instruction only. This instruction, which is stored in a one-word *repeat buffer*, must be fetched from program memory during the first loop iteration only – during subsequent iterations, this instruction is fetched from the buffer.

- the *multi-instruction* configuration supports the repeated execution of multiple instructions. In general, every instruction in the loop body must be fetched from program memory during each iteration.

Included in TWIF is a post-pass code optimization, implemented by the *ZeroOverheadLoopClass* class, that provides support for zero-overhead looping hardware. The procedural interface for this optimization is shown in Figure 3. In this figure, the "=0" notation specifies that *f* is a pure virtual function. Additionally, the *CFGFor* class is the TWIF representation of a well-structured for loop that occurred in the source program. Embedded in a CFGFor object are various loop parameters (e.g. loop

sented that describe the amount of effort that was involved in retargeting the SPAM compiler to two commercial fixed-point DSPs – the *TMS320C25* and *DSP56000* – and one proprietary fixed-point DSP – the *Fujitsu Elixir*.

In the SPAM compiler, reusable source code encompasses the built-in optimization algorithms and data structures in TWIF. Now, TWIF was originally developed with a library of parameterized optimization algorithms that provide support for various specialized architectural features of the TMS320C25 and DSP56000 (these DSPs will henceforth be referred to as the *C25* and *56K*, respectively). Consequently, many of the built-in algorithms in TWIF were utilized during the retargetting of the SPAM compiler to the C25 and 56K. In order to keep our experimental results as fair as possible, however, we will *not* consider the use of these algorithms in the C25 and 56K compilers to be automatic instances of code reuse; instead, we will consider the use of built-in source code to be an instance of code reuse only if this source code is utilized in *more than one* compiler. TWIF was developed with this particular suite of algorithms because the specialized features of the C25 and 56K are very typical of those that exist in contemporary DSP architectures. Therefore, we expect that many of the built-in algorithms in TWIF will be utilized during the retargetting of the SPAM framework to other DSPs.

In the following sections, we briefly describe some of the post-pass code optimizations that we found to be applicable to each of the three DSPs. Thereafter, we discuss the manner in which each of these optimizations was implemented, i.e. whether a built-in procedural interface was utilized or a parameterized algorithm was implemented. In these case studies, it should be noted that the retargeting process was performed by a *single* developer.

5.1. Code Optimizations for the TMS320C25

The C25 DSP, whose architecture is shown in Figure 4(a), features a single accumulator and a single data memory bank. Additionally, a very limited amount of ILP exists in the datapath between the multiplier and accumulator. The optimizations that were incorporated into the C25 compiler include the following:

- the C25 features a file of address registers that can be incremented or decremented by one at no extra cost. A procedural interface in TWIF was utilized that exploits this *auto-increment* capability in order to generate efficient code for pointer variable accesses in the source program.

- an interface in TWIF was utilized that exploits this auto-increment capability in order to generate efficient code for array accesses in the source program [4].

- after code generation, the code may contain instructions that overwrite certain *mode variables* with their current value. Global data-flow analysis techniques [2] may be used to identify and eliminate such instructions. Interfaces in TWIF for various data-flow analysis algorithms were utilized for this purpose.

- the automatic variables of each non-recursive procedure in the program are *statically* allocated by the C25 compiler. This allocation technique, which exploits the fact that DSP programs tend to be non-recursive in nature, obviates the need for instructions that

bounds) and the assembly code that implements the loop body. We briefly describe each method in this interface, with the exception of the constructor and destructor:

- **CanPerformRepeatLoop**: this pure virtual function takes as input a pointer to a CFGFor object, and returns TRUE if it is permissible to implement the associated for loop on the *single-instruction* zero-overhead looping hardware.

- **CanPerformDoLoop**: this pure virtual function takes as input a pointer to a CFGFor object, and returns TRUE if it is permissible to implement the associated for loop on the *multi-instruction* hardware. It is necessary for the developer to define this method and implement the previous method, since DSP architectures differ in the restrictions that they impose on the use of zero-overhead looping hardware. For instance, some DSPs do not allow zero-overhead looping hardware to be utilized if the given looping construct contains a nested loop that already makes use of the hardware; meanwhile, other DSPs impose no such restrictions.

- **GenerateRepeatOperations**: given a pointer to a CFGFor object which represents a for loop that can be implemented on the *single-instruction* looping hardware, this pure virtual function returns a pointer to a list of instructions that control this hardware configuration – this list, which will typically consist of a single *REPEAT* instruction that specifies the loop iteration count, is inserted immediately before the loop body and is the sole code overhead.

- **GenerateDoOperations**: given a pointer to a CFGFor object which represents a for loop that can be implemented on the *multi-instruction* hardware, and a pointer to a label that signifies the address *following* the last loop body instruction, this pure virtual function returns a pointer to a list of instructions that control this hardware configuration – this list, which will typically consist of a single *DO* instruction that specifies the loop iteration count and this end-of-loop label, is inserted immediately before the loop body. If the target ISA dictates that the label must specify the address of the last loop body instruction, instead of the address following this instruction, then it is the developer's responsibility to insert an appropriate instruction (e.g. a *NOP*) at this address.

- **UndoLoopOptimizations**: given a pointer to a CFGFor object which represents a for loop that can *not* be implemented on zero-overhead looping hardware, this pure virtual function generates conventional looping code for the looping construct (i.e. assembly code that implements the index variable initialization, initial test, index variable update, and final test) and inserts it at the appropriate location(s). This method is required since SUIF does not generate the IR form of this code whenever loops are represented by abstract structures.

- **Optimize**: optimizes the for loop that was provided to the constructor by invoking the various pure virtual functions.

5. Case Studies

In this section, the effectiveness of the SPAM compiler infrastructure as a developer-retargetable compilation framework is evaluated. Specifically, three case studies are pre-

- the automatic variables of each non-recursive procedure in the program are statically allocated by the 56K compiler, since DSP programs tend to be non-recursive in nature. Procedural interfaces in TWIF to the live-variable analysis algorithm and Briggs' graph coloring algorithm were utilized in order to reduce the data memory requirements due to static allocation.

- a procedural interface in TWIF to the *list scheduling* local compaction algorithm was utilized in order to exploit available ILP within basic block boundaries.

- the code generator generates preliminary assembly code in which all variable and register references are *symbolic*. A procedural interface in TWIF was utilized that attempts to assign memory banks and physical data registers to the symbolic variables and registers, respectively, such that the maximum number of memory accesses can be performed in parallel. This interface performs the phases of memory bank and register allocation *simultaneously* [21], since these two phases are highly *dependent* on one another with respect to the 56K ISA.

5.3. Code Optimizations for the Elixir

The Fujitsu Elixir, whose architecture is shown in Figure 4(c), is a proprietary DSP that is primarily used in cellular phones. It features two accumulators (*CX* and *DX*), four general-purpose data registers (*A0, A1, B0,* and *B1*), and two data memory banks (*A* and *B*), which enable two data memory accesses to occur in parallel provided that the associated variables and registers have been allocated accordingly. Based on Figure 4(c), it is apparent that the basic architectures of the Elixir and 56K are very similar. Consequently, many post-pass optimizations that were applicable to the 56K were also applicable to the Elixir. However, several major differences exist between these two DSPs, due to significant variations in their microarchitectures. For instance, in contrast to the 56K ISA, the Elixir ISA only permits a limited number of ALU operations to execute in parallel with data memory accesses. Furthermore, the Elixir ISA imposes fewer memory bank and register allocation constraints on parallel memory access specifications. The optimizations that were incorporated into the Elixir compiler include the following:

- the Elixir features both configurations of zero-overhead looping hardware. The procedural interface in TWIF (see Figure 3) that exploits this specialized hardware was utilized in the SPAM-based Elixir compiler.

- the Elixir features two files of address registers that can be auto-incremented at no extra cost. This capability was used to generate efficient code for pointer variable and array accesses by means of the procedural interfaces in TWIF that were previously mentioned.

- since DSP programs tend to be non-recursive, the Elixir compiler statically allocates the automatic variables of each non-recursive procedure. Interfaces in TWIF to the live-variable analysis algorithm and Briggs' algorithm were utilized in order to reduce the data memory requirements due to static allocation.

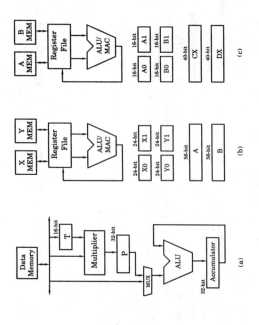

Figure 4. Architectural overviews (a) TMS320C25 (b) DSP56000 (c) Elixir

allocate and deallocate a stack-frame on procedure entry and exit, respectively. The data memory requirements due to static allocation may be subsequently reduced by allowing those automatic variables with non-overlapping life-times to share the same storage location. Procedural interfaces in TWIF to the live-variable analysis algorithm and Briggs' *graph coloring* algorithm [5] were utilized in order to implement this sharing of storage.

5.2. Code Optimizations for the DSP56000

The 56K DSP, whose architecture is shown in Figure 4(b), features two accumulators (*A* and *B*) and four general-purpose data registers (*X0, X1, Y0,* and *Y1*). This DSP also features two data memory banks (*X* and *Y*), which permit two data memory accesses to occur in parallel provided that the referenced variables and registers have been allocated appropriately. A significant amount of ILP exists in the 56K architecture, specifically between the ALU and data memory banks. The optimizations that were incorporated into the 56K compiler include the following:

- the 56K features both configurations of zero-overhead looping hardware. The procedural interface in TWIF (see Figure 3) that exploits this specialized hardware was utilized in the SPAM-based 56K compiler.

- the 56K features two files of address registers that can be auto-incremented at no extra cost. The procedural interfaces in TWIF were utilized that exploit this auto-increment capability in order to generate efficient code for pointer variable and array accesses in the source program.

attributed to two factors. First, the entire library of data structures in TWIF was utilized in each compiler. Not only were these data structures utilized by the built-in algorithms, but more importantly, they were also utilized by the machine-specific source code that was developed for each compiler. This observation leads to the conclusion that TWIF provides a comprehensive library of data structures for the development of machine-specific source code.

Second, many of the algorithms in TWIF were utilized in more than one compiler. For instance, as is described in the three case studies, all three compilers make use of the procedural interface for Briggs' graph coloring algorithm, the post-pass live variable analysis interface, and the interfaces which exploit the auto-increment capability of address registers in order to generate efficient code for pointer variable and array accesses in the source program. Furthermore, both the 56K and Elixir compilers make use of the list scheduling interface.

Now, an important point that should be made about developer-retargetable compilation is that the amount of code reuse that occurs during the retargeting process can be expected to *increase* as more and more compilers are incorporated into the SPAM framework. This is because as the SPAM compiler is retargetted to more and more DSPs, the probability increases that a piece of reusable source code in a particular compiler will be utilized in at least one other compiler.

6.1.1. Overall Development Time

Another metric that quantifies the amount of developer effort involved during the retargeting process is overall development time – on average, approximately 80 hours were spent developing each compiler. It is our view, however, that overall development time is an inappropriate metric: since many developers will initially have very little familiarity with the SPAM software package, it is highly probable that these developers will initially require considerably more than 80 hours to develop a compiler. We believe that overall code reuse is a much more appropriate metric for developer effort, since it is independent of the developer's familiarity with the SPAM package.

6.2. Quality of Optimizing Compilers

In this section, experimental results are presented that pertain to the quality of code that is generated by the SPAM-based Elixir, C25, and 56K compilers, respectively. The quality of the Elixir optimizing compiler is first discussed.

6.2.1. Quality of the Elixir Compiler

Due to the absence of a compiler for the Elixir, Fujitsu designers have to resort to hand-writing all Elixir applications in assembly. Although a *naive* compiler for the Elixir could have easily been constructed, Fujitsu's experience with naive compilers for other DSPs has shown that it is not uncommon for such compilers to generate code whose size is *ten* times greater than the size of the corresponding hand-written code. In order to determine the quality of the SPAM-based Elixir compiler, we obtained four hand-written assembly-coded benchmarks that form part of a large Fujitsu cellular telephone application. Associated with each benchmark was an algorithmic description of the benchmark, which we subsequently translated into a semantically-equivalent C program.

- available ILP within basic block boundaries was exploited by means of the list scheduling procedural interface in TWIF.

- the code generator generates preliminary assembly code in which all variable and register references are symbolic. Due to the nature of the Elixir microarchitecture, the phases of memory bank and register allocation are *independent* of one another and hence, may be performed *separately*. The problem of determining an optimal memory bank allocation of the program variables may be formulated as the problem of determining a *maximum-weighted cut* (MAX-CUT) of a graph that specifies all possible variable accesses that may be performed in parallel. A procedural interface for MAX-CUT was not available in TWIF. However, an implementation of a MAX-CUT heuristic [9] was obtained and subsequently added to the library of parameterized algorithms in TWIF.

6. Experimental Results

6.1. Quantitative Measurements of Code Reuse

Quantitative measurements are presented in Table 1 that pertain to the amount of code reuse that occurred during the construction of the three optimizing compilers. This table is organized as follows: the three DSPs are listed in the first column; the second column specifies the total size (in lines of code) of the source code that implements the corresponding compiler – these numbers only include code that forms part of TWIF, as well as machine-specific code that has been written by the developer; the third column specifies the total size (in lines of code) of all source code in the compiler that was reused (i.e. code that was used in at least one other compiler); the next two columns specify the total size (in lines of code) of the reused code that represents built-in algorithms and data structures, respectively; the final column specifies the percentage of source code in the compiler that was reused.

Before these results are discussed, it should be noted that prior to the retargeting process, TWIF contained approximately 20,700 lines of source code: 11,500 lines of code implemented the algorithms component, and 9,200 lines of code implemented the structures component. It should also be noted that in our measurements of code reuse, we disregard the order in which the compilers have been constructed. Specifically, suppose that during the construction of some compiler X, the developer has implemented a parameterized algorithm O due to the unavailability of a procedural interface for O. Now, suppose that some compiler Y constructed after X makes use of O. In this scenario, we say that O is reused in both X and Y.

Based on Table 1, it can be seen that a significant amount of code reuse occurred during the retargeting of the SPAM framework to all three DSPs – the average percentage of compiler source code that was reused was *61.5%*. This high rate of code reuse may be

Table 1. Code reuse measurements

Fixed-Point DSP	Code Size (lines of code)				Reuse Rate
	Total	Reused	Algorithms	Structures	
TMS320C25	24,100	14,800	5,600	9,200	61.4%
DSP56000	27,400	17,400	8,200	9,200	63.5%
Elixir	29,150	17,400	8,200	9,200	59.7%

514 CHAPTER 5: Implementation Generation

Table 2. Comparison of Elixir compiled code with hand-written code

Benchmark	Code Size (Hand-Written)	Code Size (Compiled)	Compiled Code Overhead
hup	17	20	17.6%
yhaten	28	36	28.6%
kncal	36	38	5.6%
dt_pow	148	176	18.9%

Experimental results are presented in Table 2 that compare the quality of the Elixir compiled code with that of the hand-written code: the four benchmarks – *hup*, *yhaten*, *kncal*, and *dt_pow* – are listed in the first column; the size of the corresponding hand-written code (in instruction words) is specified in the second column; the third column specifies the size of the code (in instruction words) that the compiler generated for the equivalent C program; the final column specifies the percentage code size overhead of the compiled code over the hand-written code.

These results demonstrate that the average code size overhead of the compiled code over the corresponding hand-written code was *17.7%*, which is significantly less than the overhead that is typically associated with naive DSP compilers. A close analysis of the compiler-generated and hand-written code revealed that there were two primary reasons for the compiled code overhead. First, the Elixir compiler was unable to perform code compaction within loops as efficiently as the assembly programmer. Second, the compiled code contained more *address arithmetic* instructions than the hand-written code. Now, if an address register does not point to the current variable that is to be indirectly addressed, then address arithmetic instructions must be generated that cause an available address register to point to the desired memory location. The goal of the *Offset Assignment* (OA) algorithm [16] is to order the variables in memory so as to minimize the number of required address arithmetic instructions. A close study of the hand-written code revealed that the assembly programmer manually performed *optimal* OA. Since OA is an NP-complete problem, however, the OA implementation in TWIF uses various heuristics that determine a good, though not always optimal, variable ordering.

6.2.2. Quality of the C25 and 56K Compilers

In Table 3, experimental results are presented that compare the quality of the C25 and 56K compiled code with that of hand-written code. This table is organized as follows: C-coded benchmarks from the DSPstone benchmark suite [24] are listed in the first column – these benchmarks are small kernels that represent typical DSP algorithms; the size of the corresponding C25 (56K) reference hand-written code (in instruction words) is specified in the second (fifth) column; the third (sixth) column specifies the size of the assembly code (in instruction words) that was generated by the SPAM-based C25 (56K) compiler; the fourth (seventh) column specifies the percentage code size overhead of the C25 (56K) compiled code over the hand-written code.

These results demonstrate that the average compiled code overhead associated with the C25 and 56K compilers was 24.9% and 20.9%, respectively. With respect to the *convolution*, *dot_product*, *fir*, and *least_mean_square* benchmarks, which make extensive use of looping constructs,

Table 3. Comparison of C25 and 56K compiled code with hand-written code

Benchmark	TMS320C25			DSP56000		
	Size (Hand)	Size (Comp)	Over-head	Size (Hand)	Size (Comp)	Over-head
complex_multiply	21	13	-38.1%	15	11	-26.7%
convolution	12	19	58.3%	10	16	60.0%
dot_product	15	18	20.0%	10	16	60.0%
fir	12	21	75.0%	14	17	21.4%
iir_biquad_one_section	23	19	-17.4%	22	20	-9.1%
least_mean_square	35	53	51.4%	40	48	20.0%

may primarily be attributed to the fact that the compilers were unable to perform code compaction within loops as effectively as the assembly programmer.

Table 3 demonstrates that the quality of the C25 and 56K compiled code for the *complex_multiply* and *iir_biquad_one_section* benchmarks was superior to the quality of the corresponding hand-written code. With respect to the C25, this result may be attributed to the fact that the C25 ISA allows for very efficient use of the absolute addressing mode [22], and the C25 compiler was able to absolutely address all local variables of these benchmarks (neither of which makes use of looping constructs) with essentially no overhead. However, in the hand-written code, all local variables were indirectly addressed through multiple address registers – the additional assembly instructions in the hand-written code that initialized these address registers were the cause of the code size overhead.

With respect to the 56K, the number of address registers that were utilized in the hand-written code to indirectly address the local variables was greater than the number of address registers that were utilized in the compiled code – the additional address register initialization instructions in the hand-written code were the cause of the code size overhead.

7. Conclusions

In order to enable a system designer to efficiently evaluate a wide variety of DSPs for potential use in an embedded DSP system, a DSP compiler must feature some degree of retargetability. Although existing retargetable compilation frameworks for DSPs are able to completely automate the compiler-construction process, they are unable to generate dense, high-performance code for embedded DSPs.

In this paper, we have presented a compilation methodology that enables a wide range of post-pass optimizations to be supported in a retargetable manner. The basis of this methodology is the existence of a compilation framework that features a library of reusable machine-dependent code optimization algorithms – a developer may retarget this framework to a particular DSP by tailoring all applicable algorithms to this DSP. Although the developer may be required to write a sizable quantity of source code during the retargeting process, we believe that such developer effort is necessary in order for high-quality code to be generated. We have described the SPAM compiler infrastructure, which is a developer-retargetable compiler for embedded DSPs. Case studies were presented that detailed the retargeting of this compiler to three fixed-point DSPs, as well as provided results on the quality of the resultant code that is generated by these optimizing compilers. These studies demonstrated that many optimization algorithms in the infrastructure were reused in these compilers. Furthermore, we expect the amount of code reuse to increase as more and more compilers are incorporated into the SPAM framework. We strongly believe that the quality of code that is generated by these compilers is high enough to be accepted as a substitute for hand-coding by designers.

8. Acknowledgements

This research was supported by DARPA grant DABT63-97-1-0002, NSF grant MIP9457396, and grants from Fujitsu Laboratories of America, Rockwell Semiconductor Systems, and the NJ Center for Multimedia Research.

References

1. A. Aho, M. Ganapathi, and S. Tjiang. Code Generation Using Tree Matching and Dynamic Programming. *ACM Transactions on Programming Languages and Systems*, 11(4):491–516, October 1989.
2. A. Aho, R. Sethi, and J. Ullman. *Compilers Principles, Techniques and Tools*. Addison-Wesley, 1986.
3. G. Araujo and S. Malik. Optimal Code Generation for Embedded Memory Non-Homogeneous Register Architectures. In *Proceedings of 8th International Symposium on System Synthesis*, pages 36–41, 1995.
4. G. Araujo, A. Sudarsanam, and S. Malik. Instruction Set Design and Optimization for Address Computation in DSP Architectures. In *Proceedings of 9th International Symposium on System Synthesis*, pages 102–107, 1996.
5. P. Briggs, K.D. Cooper, and L. Torczon. Improvements to Graph Coloring Register Allocation. *ACM Transactions on Programming Languages and Systems*, 16(3):428–455, May 1994.
6. A. Fauth. Beyond Tool-Specific Machine Descriptions. In P. Marwedel and G. Goossens, editors, *Code Generation for Embedded Processors*, chapter 8, pages 138–152. Kluwer Academic Publishers, 1995. ISBN 0-7923-9577-8.
7. C.W. Fraser, D.R. Hanson, and T.A. Proebsting. Engineering a Simple, Efficient Code-Generator Generator. *ACM Letters of Programming Languages and Systems*, 1(3):213–226, September 1992.
8. C. Gebotys. DSP Address Optimization Using a Minimum Cost Circulation Technique. In *Proceedings of the International Conference on Computer-Aided Design*, pages 100–103, November 1997.
9. M.X. Goemans and D.P. Williamson. Improved approximation algorithms for maximum cut and satisfiability problems using semidefinite programming. *Journal of the ACM*, 42:1115–1145, 1995.
10. S. Hadjiyiannis, S. Hanono, and S. Devadas. ISDL: An Instruction Set Description Language for Retargetability. In *Proceedings of the 34th Design Automation Conference*, pages 299–302, June 1997.
11. D. Lanneer, J. Van Praet, A. Kifli, K. Schoofs, W. Geurts, F. Thoen, and G. Goossens. CHESS: Retargetable Code Generation for Embedded DSP Processors. In P. Marwedel and G. Goossens, editors, *Code Generation for Embedded Processors*, chapter 5, pages 85–102. Kluwer Academic Publishers, 1995. ISBN 0-7923-9577-8.
12. R. Leupers, A. Basu, and P. Marwedel. Optimized Array Index Computation in DSP Programs. In *Proceedings of the Asia-Pacific Design Automation Conference*, pages 87–92, February 1998.
13. R. Leupers and P. Marwedel. Algorithms for Address Assignment in DSP Code Generation. In *Proceedings of the International Conference on Computer-Aided Design*, pages 109–112, 1996.
14. R. Leupers and P. Marwedel. Instruction Selection for Embedded DSPs with Complex Instructions. In *Proceedings of the European Design Automation Conference*, pages 200–205, 1996.
15. S. Liao, S. Devadas, K. Keutzer, and S. Tjiang. Instruction Selection Using Binate Covering for Code Size Optimization. In *Proceedings of the International Conference on Computer-Aided Design*, pages 393–399, 1995.
16. S. Liao, S. Devadas, K. Keutzer, S. Tjiang, and A. Wang. Storage Assignment to Decrease Code Size. In *ACM Transactions on Programming Languages and Systems*, volume 18, pages 235–253, May 1996.
17. P. Marwedel. The MIMOLA Design System: Tools for the Design of Digital Processors. In *Proceedings of the 21st Design Automation Conference*, pages 587–593, 1997.
18. Motorola. *DSP56000/DSP56001 Digital Signal Processor User's Manual*, 1990.
19. P.G. Paulin, C. Liem, T.C. May, and S. Sutarwala. CodeSyn: A Retargetable Code Synthesis System. In *Proceedings of the 7th International Symposium on High-Level Synthesis*, page 94, April 1994.
20. M.A.R. Saghir, P. Chow, and C.G. Lee. Exploiting Dual Data-Memory Banks in Digital Signal Processors. In *Proceedings of the ACM SIGARCH Conference on Architectural Support for Programming Languages and Operating Systems*, pages 234–243, 1996.
21. A. Sudarsanam and S. Malik. Memory Bank and Register Allocation in Software Synthesis for ASIPs. In *Proceedings of the International Conference on Computer-Aided Design*, pages 388–392, 1995.
22. Ashok Sudarsanam. *Code Optimization Libraries for Retargetable Compilation for Embedded Digital Signal Processors*. PhD thesis, Princeton University, November 1998.
23. Texas Instruments. *TMS320C2x User's Guide*. January 1993. Revision C.
24. V. Živojnović, J. Martinez Velarde, and C. Schläger. DSPstone: A DSP-oriented Benchmarking Methodology. Technical report, Aachen University of Technology, August 1994.
25. B. Wess. Automatic Instruction Code Generation Based on Trellis Diagrams. In *Proceedings of the International Symposium on Circuits and Systems*, pages 645–648, 1992.
26. B. Wess and M. Gotschlich. Constructing Memory Layouts for Address Generation Units Supporting Offset 2 Access. In *Proceedings of the International Conference on Acoustics, Speech, and Signal Processing*, pages 683–686, 1997.
27. R. Wilson, R. French, C. Wilson, S. Amarasinghe, J. Anderson, S. Tjiang, S.-W. Liao, C.-W. Tseng, M. Hall, M. Lam, and J. Hennessy. SUIF: A Parallelizing and Optimizing Research Compiler. Technical report, CSL-TR-94-620, Stanford University, May 1994.

Incremental Hardware Estimation During Hardware/Software Functional Partitioning

Frank Vahid and Daniel D. Gajski

Abstract—To aid in the functional partitioning of a system into interacting hardware and software components, fast yet accurate estimations of hardware size are necessary. We introduce a technique for obtaining such estimates in two orders of magnitude less time than previous approaches without sacrificing substantial accuracy, by incrementally updating a design model for a changed partition rather than re-estimating entirely.

Index Terms— Constant-time complexity, estimation, hardware size, hardware-software co-design, incremental design, interactive design, system design, system partitioning.

I. Introduction

The designer of an embedded system is often faced with the challenge of partitioning the system functionality for implementation among hardware and software components, such as among ASIC's and processors. New approaches for such partitioning start with a simulatable specification of system functionality, and then explore numerous possible partitions of that specification's functions among the hardware and software components [1]. We therefore need a method to determine, among other things, the hardware size of a set of functions, to see if that set will meet constraints.

Manuscript received April 19, 1994; revised September 19, 1994. This work was supported by the National Science Foundation under Grant MIP-8922851 and by the Semiconductor Research Corporation under Grant 92-DJ-146.

F. Vahid is with the Department of Computer Science, University of California, Riverside, CA 92521 USA.

D. D. Gajski is with the Department of Information and Computer Science, University of California, Irvine, CA 92717 USA.

IEEE Log Number 9413466.

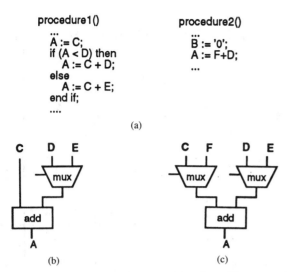

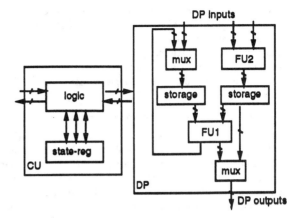

Fig. 1. Example of incremental change resulting from object move: (a) functional objects, (b) partial datapath for Procedure1, and (c) partial datapath for both procedures.

Fig. 2. CU/DP area model.

There are several possible methods. The most accurate would be to synthesize a design for the set of functions, but such an approach requires too much time if we wish to examine more than a few possible partitions, as is usually the case. To overcome this limitation, several research efforts incorporate a hardware size estimator [2]–[5]. In essence, those estimators roughly synthesize a design for the given functions, while omitting the time-consuming synthesis tasks such as logic optimization, so they require only a few seconds to obtain a fairly accurate estimate. Such estimators based on a *design model* have the advantage of obtaining accurate estimates in just a few seconds. At times, though, we wish to examine hundreds or thousands of partitions using an iterative-improvement partitioning heuristic such as simulated annealing, thus requiring faster estimators. Approaches that use iterative-improvement heuristics have until now used abstract-weight-based estimators, in which an abstract weight is assigned to each function, and then a hardware "cost" for a given partition is obtained quickly just by adding all the weights of functions in hardware [6]–[8]. Alternatively, they assume an already scheduled input and estimate hardware size as the size of required functional units [9]. These approaches have the advantage of obtaining very rapid estimations.

In developing our system that partitions an unscheduled specification among hardware and software components, we desired to use an estimator based on a design-model in order to obtain accuracy, but we also wanted to use iterative-improvement algorithms to explore many possibilities. Since previous estimation methods had not addressed both goals, we needed to develop a new method. Toward this end, we observed that iterative-improvement algorithms make only a few changes between iterations, so the change between one partition's design and the next one is incremental. For example, Fig. 1(a) shows two functions and Fig. 1(b) shows a partial datapath for one of those functions. When we add the other function, the datapath only requires one additional multiplexer, as shown in Fig. 1(c).

We took advantage of this incremental change by developing a data structure (representing an incrementally modifiable design model) and an algorithm that can quickly provide the basic design parameters needed by a hardware-size estimator. As we shall see, we were able to do this by assuming that the granularity at which we partition the specification is at the procedural level (sometimes called the process or task level), as is the case in many new functional partitioning techniques [7], [8], [10]–[15]. Our contribution is the development of this incremental hardware-size estimation method, consisting of a new data structure and algorithm, that achieves the advantages of both classes of previous approaches, namely accuracy and speed.

This paper is organized as follows. In Section II, we describe the design-model that we use for hardware-size estimation, a model adopted from previous design-based estimators. In Section III, we describe a new data structure that captures not only the design model, but also the contribution of each function to the design. In Section IV, we detail an algorithm for updating, in constant time, this data structure when a function is moved. In Section V, we summarize our results that show the speed of our method.

II. ESTIMATION DESIGN MODEL

The design model we use to obtain hardware-size estimates for a set of functions is a control-unit/datapath (CU/DP) model [2], [16], as shown in Fig. 2. The size for the model can be computed as the sum of the following: *functional-unit and storage-unit size* (including registers, register files and memories), *multiplexer size*, *state-register size*, *control-logic size*, and *wiring size*. Each is a function of one or more of the following basic *design parameters*:

1) *states*   number of possible controller states,
2) *size_list*   a list of datapath units, where each unit has an associated size,
3) *srcs_list*   a list of datapath units, where the number of sources (i.e., outputs of other units or datapath inputs) that must at some time be input to each unit is specified,
4) *ctrl*   the number of control lines between the controller and the datapath,
5) *active_list*   a list of all control lines, where the number of states for which a control line must be asserted is associated with each control line,
6) *units*   the number of units in the datapath, regardless of their types,
7) *wires*   the number of wires in the datapath.

For example, the *functional-unit and storage-unit size* may be a function of all $size\_list$ values, the *multiplexer size* may be a function of $srcs\_list$, the *state-register size* may be a function of *states*, the *control-logic size* may be a function of *states*, *ctrl*, and $active\_list$, and the *wiring size* may be a function of *units*, $size\_list$, and *wires*. The details of these functions are beyond the scope of this paper; any function that uses the above design parameters could be used in conjunction with our method, and more than one form of each function may exist to support estimation for various technologies. To avoid going into specific details of those functions, in this article we assume that a function $HwSize$ exists, which uses the above parameters and which returns a hardware size with the appropriate units for the particular hardware technology, such as square microns, transistors, gates, or combinational logic blocks.

III. INCREMENTALLY UPDATABLE DATA STRUCTURE

We now describe the data structure that allows us to represent a roughly synthesized design using the above model, while at the same time allowing us to incrementally modify that design in *constant time* when a functional object is added or deleted. We assume that the specification consists of a single process with hundreds or thousands of sequential statements, including loops, branches, and procedure calls. We later describe a simple extension for multiple processes. We shall hereon refer to the specification pieces to be distributed among hardware and software components as functional objects.

A. Preprocessed Information

Our first task is create a hardware design that implements the entire set of functional objects, and to determine the contribution that each functional object makes to that design (in order to support incremental change). Since this information can be obtained before creating a partition, we call it *preprocessed information*.

To obtain the hardware design, we must allocate a set of functional units (FU's) and storage units (SU's), bind operations and data values to FU's and SU's, and schedule operations into control steps (not necessarily in the given order). The heuristics that we use to do these tasks should match the heuristics that will be used to synthesize the final hardware, in order to obtain the highest accuracy; if the algorithms are not known, then we can use default heuristics instead.

To determine the contribution of each functional object to the design, we first consider the datapath. We create a list of FU's for each functional object. For example, if a functional object uses two adder units, then we append two adder units to that object's FU list. We create a similar list of SU's for each functional object. Turning to multiplexers, we note that the size of a multiplexer in front of an FU, SU, or datapath output is determined by how many possible *sources* (i.e., SU or FU outputs, or datapath inputs) may need to be input to that FU, SU, or datapath output. Thus for each functional object, we associate a list of sources contributed by that object to each FU, SU, and datapath output. Turning our attention to the control unit, we record the number of possible states for each functional object, and the number of states that each FU, SU, and datapath output is active.

At this point, an assumption that we wish to make explicit is that a functional object represents a coarse-grained computation, such as a process, procedure, or a large basic block, as also assumed in many new functional partitioning techniques (see Section I). The larger the number of statements in each object, the more accurate the estimations will be, since inter-object synthesis optimizations would then play a smaller role in the overall design. The reason is that we assume that the tasks of scheduling, allocation and binding for two functional objects will be roughly the same whether we consider each object independently or together, because in our approach, we perform those tasks on each functional object independently. On the other hand, lower levels of granularity, such as small basic blocks, would result in less accurate estimates since current synthesis techniques (such as path-based scheduling and percolation scheduling) optimize across basic block boundaries.

Fig. 3 shows the preprocessed information created for each procedure of the example in Fig. 1(a). Note that this example is trivially small, but that it sufficiently demonstrates our technique.

Functional object	States	Destination	Sources	Active states
Procedure1	5	A	C	3
			adder1	
		comparator1	A	1
			D	
		adder1	C	2
			D	
			E	
		storage1	comparator1	1
Procedure2	2	A	adder1	1
		adder1	F	1
			D	
		B	'0'	1

Fig. 3. Preprocessed information for functional objects O.

More formally, the data structure of preprocessed information, or PP, is a four-tuple $\langle O, DPI, DPO, U \rangle$. DPI is a set of datapath inputs $\{dpi_1, dpi_2, \cdots\}$, and DPO is a set of datapath outputs $\{dpo_1, dpo_2, \cdots\}$. U is a set of available functional and storage units $\{u_1, u_2, \cdots\}$. Each unit u_i is a pair $= \langle size, ctrl \rangle$, where $size$ is a natural number representing the size of the unit (in transistors, gates, or whatever type is assumed by the estimation functions), and $ctrl$ is a natural number representing the number of control lines on that unit.

O is a set of functional objects $\{o_1, o_2, \cdots, o_n\}$. Each functional object o_i is a pair $\langle states, dsts \rangle$. $states$ is a natural number representing the number of possible control states for the functional object. $dsts$ is a set of destinations, $\{dst_1, dst_2, \cdots\}$, written to by the object. A destination dst_i is a three-tuple $\langle id, srcs, active \rangle$. The destination identifier id is the particular FU, SU, or DP-output that dst represents, so $id \in DPO \bigcup U$. $active$ is a natural number representing the number of states for which the destination is active for this object. $srcs$ is a set of sources, $\{src_1, src_2, \cdots\}$, that the object assigns to this destination. Each src_i is either a datapath input or a unit, so $src_i \in DPI \bigcup U$.

B. Design Information

Given the preprocessed information PP, we can focus on creating a design for the subset of functional objects that have been mapped to hardware. We need to assemble the datapath and controller. Specifically, the datapath FU's required to implement the hardware objects are determined as the union of the FU's needed by each object. For example, if one object requires units *u1* and *u2*, and another requires units *u1* and *u3*, then the datapath FU's will be *u1*, *u2*, and *u3*. The datapath SU's are determined similarly. The multiplexer sizes are determined for each destination by taking the union of the sources contributed to that destination by each object. The number of states in the controller is simply the sum of the number of states of the functional objects (remember that this is the number of *possible* states, rather than a measure of the start-to-finish performance), and the number of states that each datapath control line is active is the sum of those contributed by each object. We store the information in a table. For example, Fig. 4 shows this information for the case when *Procedure1* from Fig. 1(a) is the only functional object mapped to hardware.

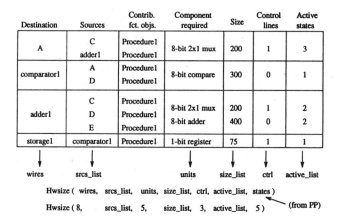

Fig. 4. Hardware design information for procedure1.

From the above discussion, we see that values for the basic parameters for the hardware size functions have been determined, so the size can now be computed by calling $HwSize$, as shown in Fig. 4.

We will now define our data structure that maintains the design information in an incrementally updatable manner. The design information data structure D is a five-tuple $\langle usize, units, ctrl, wires, dsts \rangle$. The first four items are natural numbers. $usize$ represents the total size of all the FU's, SU's, and multiplexers. $units$ represents the total number of all FU's, SU's, and multiplexers. $ctrl$ represents the total number of control lines between the controller and the datapath. $wires$ represents the number of wires in the datapath.

The fifth item, $dsts$, is a set of all destinations in the design, $\{dst_1, dst_2, \cdots\}$. Each destination dst_i is a three-tuple $\langle id, src\_cons, active \rangle$. The identifier id indicates the unit or DP output that this destination represents, so $id \in DPO \bigcup U$. $active$ is a natural number that indicates the total number of states that this destination is active. src_cons is a set $\{src\_con_1, src\_con_2, \cdots\}$, where each src_con_i is a pair $\langle src, con \rangle$. src is a source, from the preprocessed information PP, that must be input to the destination dst_i. con is a set of functional objects (i.e., $con \subset PP.O$), where each functional object requires a path from the source to the destination. In other words, the objects are the contributors of the source to the destination.

Relative to the number n of functional objects, the complexity of building PP and D is $O(n)$. For the industry examples that we have examined, n has ranged from 15 to 120. The complexity is usually dominated by the scheduling algorithm, whose complexity may range from $O[c^2 \log(c)]$ to $O(c^3)$, where there are c nodes in the functional object's dataflow graph.

IV. CONSTANT-TIME UPDATE ALGORITHM

We now turn our attention to the movement of functional objects between the hardware and software components, or more specifically, to the addition or deletion of a functional object to or from hardware. We define an algorithm to update the design information D for an addition of a functional object o to hardware. The algorithm uses a procedure *SeekDesignDst* which returns the design destination that refers to the same unit as the given object destination. A procedure *NewDesignDst* creates a new design destination for the given object destination. Procedures *Size* and *Ctrl* return the size and number of control lines, respectively, for the given object destination's unit, returning 0 if the destination corresponds to a datapath output. A procedure *SeekSrc_con* returns the design's source/contributors item that corresponds to the given source. A procedure $NewSrc\_con$ creates a new source/contributors item for the given source. A procedure *GetMuxSize* determines the size of the multiplexor(s) needed in front of a particular destination for the given sources. The size is dependent on the number of sources and on whether there are one or two inputs on the destination (e.g., an adder has two inputs so no multiplexer is needed for two sources, whereas an incrementer with two sources does need a multiplexer since it has only one input). If there is more than one input on the destination, we assume the sources are uniformly distributed among those inputs.

Algorithm 4.1 $UpdateDesignInfoForObjectAdd(D, o)$:

for each $dst_o \in o.dsts$ **loop**
  —Add destination to design if it doesn't yet exist
  $dst_d = SeekDesignDst(D, dst_o.id)$
  if $dst_d = NULL$ **then**
    $dst_d = NewDesignDst(dst_o)$
    $D.dsts = D.dsts \bigcup dst_d$
    $D.usize = D.usize + Size(dst_o)$
    $D.ctrl = D.ctrl + Ctrl(dst_o)$
    if $dst_o.id \in FU \bigcup SU$ **then**
      $D.units = D.units + 1$
    end if
  end if
  —Update mux sources and sizes
  $muxsize\_bef = GetMuxSize(src\_cons, dst_o.id)$
  for each $src \in dst_o.srcs$ **loop**
    $src\_con = SeekSrc\_con(dst_d.src\_cons, src)$
    if $src\_con = NULL$ **then**
      $src\_con = NewSrc\_con(src)$
      $dst_d.src\_cons = dst_d.src\_cons \bigcup src\_con$
      $D.wires = D.wires + 1$
    end if
    $src\_con.contribs = src\_con.contribs \bigcup o$
  end loop
  $muxsize\_aft = GetMuxSize(src\_cons, dst_o.id)$
  $D.usize = D.usize - muxsize\_bef + muxsize\_aft$
  if $muxsize\_bef = 0$ **and** $muxsize\_aft > 0$ **then**
    $D.units = D.units + 1$
  end if
  —Update control line active states for this dst
  $dst_d.active = dst_d.active + dst_o.active$
end loop
—Update controller states
$D.states = D.states + o.states$
return

The algorithm performs the following for each destination written in o. First, it adds that destination to the design if it doesn't already exist. Such an addition requires updating the number and size of DP units, and the number of control lines between the CU and DP. Second, it unions the sources of that destination with the corresponding design destination's sources. If such a union adds sources, then we must update the number of DP wires and the size of the destination's multiplexer. If previously no multiplexer was needed, but after adding a source a multiplexer is needed, then the number of DP units is incremented. Third, the algorithm increases the number of states for which the destination must be asserted by the number of states for which o asserts that destination. After repeating the above three steps for all destinations, the algorithm updates the number of possible controller states by the number of states for o. The algorithm for deleting a functional object is complementary to that for adding an object; we have omitted it for brevity.

Destination	Sources	Contrib. fct. objs.	Component required	Size	Control lines	Active states
A	C, adder1	Procedure1, Procedure1, Procedure2	8-bit 2x1 mux	200	1	4
comparator1	A, D	Procedure1, Procedure1	8-bit compare	300	0	1
adder1	C, D, E, F	Procedure1, Procedure1, Procedure1, Procedure2	8-bit 2x1 mux, 8-bit 2x1 mux, 8-bit adder	200, 200, 400	1, 1, 0	2, 2, 2
storage1	comparator1	Procedure1	1-bit register	75	1	1
B	'0'	Procedure2	--			1

↓ wires ↓ srcs_list ↓ units ↓ size_list ↓ ctrl ↓ active_list

Hwsize(wires, srcs_list, units, size_list, ctrl, active_list, states)
Hwsize(10, srcs_list, 6, size_list, 4, active_list, 7)   (from PP)

Fig. 5. Hardware design information after procedure2 is added.

example	# fct. objects	# lines code	time for preproc.	# moves examined	final size of ASIC1	avg. time per move	est time	prev est time	speedup
mwt	28	603	33.2	639	9231	.007	4.5	1917	426
ans	61	726	63.5	19564	14918	.006	117.4	58692	500
draco	15	302	12.6	1855	6241	.006	11.1	5565	501
ether	64	967	26.0	24251	42095	.004	96.3	72753	755

Fig. 6. Results show the method's speed and constant-time computation.

Fig. 5 illustrates several changes we make to the design information when adding *Procedure2* to the hardware. First, we create a new destination B. Second, we increase the adder's active states from 3 to 4. Third, we associate a new source with the adder, resulting in the need for another multiplexer. We then update the parameters to the $HwSize$ function accordingly.

The algorithm executes in constant time, if we assume that the number of destinations per object is roughly constant for a given example. This assumption holds unless each functional object accesses every data item and external port. However, since functional objects (such as procedures) serve to modularize a specification, such a situation is highly unlikely. Instead, each object will likely access a small (constant) number of data items and ports.

Multiple processes can be handled with a straightforward extension. Since we assume each process will use its own controller and datapath, then we simply keep separate design information for each process, and we then add the sizes of all CU/DP's in hardware. The additional processes therefore do not affect the constant-time characteristics of the estimation. We could also handle partitioning among multiple hardware components (such as among ASIC's or among blocks on an ASIC) simply by maintaining separate design information for each ASIC.

V. RESULTS

We have implemented a design-based incremental hardware-size estimator using the previously described data structure and algorithm, and have incorporated it into a functional partitioning tool. The input is a VHDL behavioral description, and the output a refined description containing partition detail. The implementation consists of approximately 16 000 lines of C code. The functional partitioning tool has been released to over 20 companies as part of the SpecSyn system-design environment, and has been used in an industry design (a fuzzy-logic controller) involving five ASIC's, and tested on numerous other industry examples including an interactive TV processor and a missile-detection system. The tool is presently being applied to several industry examples in various companies.

The speed of our incremental estimation data structure and algorithm on several examples is illustrated in Fig. 6. Examples include a microwave-transmitter controller (mwt), a telephone answering machine (ans), the DRACO peripheral interface (draco), and an Ethernet coprocessor (ether). To provide a notion for the size of each example, we indicate the number of functional objects to be partitioned, the number of specification lines, and the final size of one hardware ASIC (in gates) after partitioning, as estimated by our $HwSize$ function. Incidentally, the first three examples consisted of one process, while the Ethernet coprocessor example contained 14 processes. For each example, we first measured the time to build the preprocessed information. We then applied the group migration heuristic [17], using the cost function specified in [10]. Shown in the table are the number of moves that the heuristic examined, and the CPU time (in seconds on a Sparc1) required to update the estimation information and obtain a new hardware size estimate for each move. Note that the time-per-move is roughly the same across all four examples, demonstrating that computation is indeed done in constant time. More importantly, note the extremely fast time-per-move shown. The last two columns demonstrate the increased speed compared with a previous design-based estimator [16]. That estimator requires roughly 3 s for a given partition, which is the same magnitude of time required by several other design-based estimators [2], [3]. Multiplying by the number of moves yields a predicted estimation time; note the unacceptably long times for the large number of moves examined. The last column shows the speedup of our estimator over those previous ones, ranging from 426 to 755; such speedup is obtained while using the same design model.

We also conducted experiments to determine the effect of performing scheduling and allocation on each behavior individually, rather than considering all behaviors at the same time as in previous, slower design-based estimators. For the *ether* and *ans* examples, we inlined all subroutines; for the *mwt* example, such inlining generated an enormous output due to the many nested levels of subroutine calls, so we instead considered a subset of the specification consisting of four subroutines. We then applied the same scheduling and allocation tool to those inlined versions. Results of estimating all-hardware implementations are summarized in Fig. 7; since we are considering all behaviors, the numbers are likely the worst case. Note that the number of states *States*, the number of control lines *Ctrl*, and the functional unit and multiplexor component areas *Comparea* are quite close, and the total sizes computed by the $Hwsize$ function have an average error of only 7%. We also compared these estimates with what would have been obtained using previous weight-based techniques: we performed scheduling and allocation for each behavior, computed the size of each behavior, and then summed those sizes over the entire design. Note that the weight-based estimates are extremely inaccurate, with an average error of 80%. Those estimates greatly underestimate the control and routing area, while overestimating the total component area. Weight-based techniques assume that the behaviors combine in a linear manner, but the behaviors in fact share many components, and the PLA and routing sizes grow nonlinearly (hence, there is no simple factor by which we can multiply the weights to improve the accuracy over all cases).

It is difficult to compare our estimates with implementation values. The reason is that there are many possible implementations for a given set of functions that trade off speed and size, so choosing the implementation to compare with is hard. A second difficulty is that because we are dealing with large, industry examples, obtaining a

	Weight based	Incremental design-based				Standard design-based			
Example	Total	States	Ctrl	Comparea	Total	States	Ctrl	Comparea	Total
ether	30029	208	218	15060	176680	220	232	19186	198445
mwt	7562	54	41	3465	11260	54	49	3665	12090
ans	14895	124	122	8061	64813	106	104	7035	62088

Fig. 7. Comparison with weight-based and standard estimates.

real implementation takes many months. A third difficulty lies in the fact that there are many possible $HwSize$ functions that can be used in conjunction with our design parameters. Nonetheless, we compared our size estimations for part of the answering machine example with an implementation. The implementation was developed by a designer who hand-designed the datapath and hand-specified the controlling state-machine; the state-machine was then implemented with the KISS synthesis tool. We estimated 7804 gates, while the implementation consisted of 5372 gates. A second rough comparison can be made with an industry design of a fuzzy-logic controller. We estimated 129 000 gates, whereas the actual implementation consisted of five 20 000 gate FPGA's. We hope to obtain more comparisons as the tool is used in more designs.

VI. CONCLUSIONS

We have introduced a method to rapidly estimate hardware size during functional partitioning. The method includes a data structure representing a design model, and an algorithm that incrementally updates that data structure during functional partitioning, thus yielding rapidly computed design parameters that can be input to any number of hardware estimation functions. The method is the first to achieve both advantages of being based on a design model, and of computing estimates in constant time; previous approaches achieved one advantage or the other, but not both. The method therefore enhances the usefulness of hardware as well as hardware/software functional partitioning tools in real design environments. The general method of developing an incrementally updatable design model for estimation purposes may be applicable to many other estimation problems, such as estimation of hardware or software power consumption, hardware or software execution time, and bus bitrates. Thus, the method may become increasingly significant as design effort shifts toward system-level design exploration.

ACKNOWLEDGMENT

The authors would like to thank S. Narayan for his development of the estimation tools on which this work is based.

REFERENCES

[1] W. Wolf, "Hardware-software co-design of embedded systems," *Proc. IEEE*, vol. 82, pp. 967–989, 1994.
[2] E. Lagnese and D. Thomas, "Architectural partitioning for system level synthesis of integrated circuits," *IEEE Trans. Computer-Aided Design*, pp. 847–860, July 1991.
[3] K. Kucukcakar and A. Parker, "CHOP: A constraint-driven system-level partitioner," in *Proc. Design Automat. Conf.*, 1991, pp. 514–519.
[4] S. Antoniazzi, A. Balboni, W. Fornaciari, and D. Sciuto, "A methodology for control-dominated systems codesign," in *Int. Workshop Hardware-Software Co-Design*, 1994, pp. 2–9.
[5] X. Xiong, E. Barros, and W. Rosentiel, "A method for partitioning UNITY language in hardware and software," in *Proc. Europ. Design Automat. Conf. (EuroDAC)*, 1994.
[6] R. Ernst, J. Henkel, and T. Benner, "Hardware-software cosynthesis for microcontrollers," *IEEE Design Test Comput.*, pp. 64–75, Dec. 1994.
[7] R. Gupta and G. DeMicheli, "Hardware-software cosynthesis for digital systems," *IEEE Design Test Comput.*, pp. 29–41, Oct. 1993.
[8] A. Kalavade and E. Lee, "A global criticality/local phase driven algorithm for the constrained hardware/software partitioning problem," in *Int. Workshop Hardware-Software Co-Design*, 1994, pp. 42–48.
[9] Y. Chen, Y. Hsu, and C. King, "MULTIPAR: Behavioral partition for synthesizing multiprocessor architectures," *IEEE Trans. Very Large Scale Integr. Syst.*, vol. 2, pp. 21–32, Mar. 1994.
[10] F. Vahid and D. Gajski, "Specification partitioning for system design," in *Proc. Design Automat. Conf.*, 1992, pp. 219–224.
[11] D. Thomas, J. Adams, and H. Schmit, "A model and methodology for hardware/software codesign," *IEEE Design Test Comput.*, pp. 6–15, 1993.
[12] P. Gupta, C. Chen, J. DeSouza-Batista, and A. Parker, "Experience with image compression chip design using unified system construction tools," in *Proc. Design Automat. Conf.*, 1994, pp. 250–256.
[13] T. Ismail, M. Abid, and A. Jerraya, "COSMOS: A codesign approach for communicating systems," in *Int. Workshop on Hardware-Software Co-Design,*, 1994, pp. 17–24.
[14] J. D'Ambrosio and X. Hu, "Configuration-level hardware/software partitioning for real-time embedded systems," in *Int. Workshop Hardware-Software Co-Design*, 1994, pp. 34–41.
[15] P. Eles, Z. Peng, and A. Doboli, "VHDL system-level specification and partitioning in a hardware/software co-synthesis environment," in *Int. Workshop on Hardware-Software Co-Design*, 1992, pp. 49–55.
[16] D. Gajski, F. Vahid, S. Narayan, and J. Gong, *Specification and Design of Embedded Systems*. Englewood Cliffs, NJ: Prentice–Hall, 1994.

Chapter Six

Co-simulation and Emulation

Ptolemy: A Framework for Simulating and Prototyping Heterogeneous Systems 527
    J. Buck, S. Ha, E. A. Lee, and D. G. Messerschmitt

Synthesis and Simulation of Digital Systems Containing Interacting
Hardware and Software Components 544
    R. K. Gupta, C. N. Coelho, Jr., and G. De Micheli

An Engineering Environment for Hardware/Software Co-simulation 550
    D. Becker, R. K. Singh, and S. G. Tell

A Hardware-Software Codesign Methodology for DSP Applications 556
    A. Kalavade and E. A. Lee

A Hardware-Software Co-simulator for Embedded System Design and Debugging 569
    A. Ghosh, M. Bershteyn, R. Casley, C. Chien, A. Jain, M. Lipsie,
    D. Tarrodaychik, and O. Yamamoto

A Unified Model for Co-simulation and Co-synthesis of Mixed Hardware/Software Systems 579
    C. A. Valderrama, A. Changuel, P. V. Raghavan, M. Abid, T. Ben Ismail, and A. A. Jerraya

Compiled HW/SW Co-simulation 584
    V. Živojnović and H. Meyr

Hardware-Software Prototyping from LOTOS 590
    L. Sánchez Fernández, Gernot Koch, N. Martínez Madrid, M. L. Lopéz Vallejo,
    C. Delgado Kloos, and W. Rosenstiel

CO-SIMULATION

Hardware-software co-simulation combines the simulation of software running on a programmable processor hardware with the simulation of weakly programmable or fixed-function hardware components or subsystems. Because a detailed processor simulation (at the register-transfer or gate levels) is too time consuming when simulating larger software programs, abstract processor models are needed. For that purpose, processors are modeled at a higher level of abstraction than the other hardware components. The co-simulation problem is to couple models at different levels of abstraction such that the overall simulation results are sufficiently precise. Often, several abstract models are used in different contexts. A *bus functional model* abstracts from program execution and describes the processor bus interface function and timing only. It can be used to validate the processor bus and memory interfaces. A *cycle-accurate model* executes the program instructions with the accurate number of processor clock cycles but without detailed interface timing. Such a model allows the designer to analyze the system timing and to validate the cooperation of hardware components and processors. The *instruction set simulator model* executes the program instructions preserving the program function but completely abstracts from timing. Main applications are program validation and debugging.

Cycle-accurate and instruction set simulator models

are well suited to compiled simulation. This technique is well established in hardware simulation. Rather than interpreting the execution of a simulation model as described in the hardware modeling language (*e.g.*, VHDL or Verilog), compiled simulation translates a model to a sequential software process (*e.g.*, in the C language), which is then compiled to object code of the host workstation or PC that runs the simulator. This object code is then used as a simulation primitive. The approach is particularly efficient if hardware timing is to a large extent input data independent such that the hardware operations can be statically scheduled for simulation. In the paper by Živojnović and Meyr [Živ96] it is demonstrated that compiled simulation of processors is very time efficient.

In co-simulation, interaction with hardware components requiring sharing of buses and memories constrains the use of compiled processor models. To increase co-simulation efficiency, abstraction can be adapted to the system activity. If, for example, a processor accesses the internal cache or there is no access conflict to external memory, processor and cache or memory can be combined in a single model that abstracts from interface details between processor and memory. If conflicts can occur, memory and bus accesses require cycle true modeling. A commercial example for this approach is the Mentor Graphics Seamless CVS co-simulator. Ghosh *et al.* [Gho95] provide a comprehensive introduction to co-simulation techniques for implementation validation and debugging.

Abstract models are not only simpler and therefore faster to execute, but abstraction can also be used in early phases of a design where implementation details are still open. When the specification of a system can already be simulated, then this is called an executable specification. These specifications typically consist of a set of communicating processes. Communication and concurrency of these processes and the data they communicate can be very different. The semantics of communication and concurrency define the model of computation that underlies an abstract system description. Examples are communicating FSMs, data-flow graphs, Petri nets, and continuous time systems such as those needed to model analog signals. Because different parts of a system function may be described in different languages and models of computations, combining these models is an essential task.

The Ptolemy system [Buc94] was an important step forward in that it provided a framework that supported the combined simulation of different models of computation. It is based on an object-oriented approach that regards each model of computation together with its simulation environment as an object, a so-called domain. Objects in one domain are simulated in an encapsulated environment. Different domains communicate via discrete events across an *event horizon*, which adapts the different timing models using a time stamp mechanism. Domains can be arranged in a hierarchy, where one domain may contain encapsulated objects of other domains. In effect, Ptolemy provides an easily extendable integration framework for several discrete event simulators, rather than a simulator that supports different models of computation.

Modeling of process communication remains a key task throughout system implementation. Kalavade and Lee [Kal93] show how to create a co-design system based on Ptolemy including manual hardware/software partitioning, code generation and hardware synthesis. Their paper explains how the event horizon functionality must be substituted by insertion of communication statements in the processes. For fixed and simple architectures, this substitution can be done automatically, as demonstrated for the processor-coprocessor architecture of the Vulcan system [Gup93].

To simplify the implementation of process communication, standard process communication protocols for processes have been introduced. The process communication protocol is already used in co-simulation. One approach is to use operating system primitives, such as UNIX pipes, for communication between the different tasks. This way, compiled C code can communicate with simulation models running, for example, under a VHDL or Verilog simulator. Even interrupts can be modeled using the signal mechanism in UNIX. Debugging and monitoring tools are easily integrated. The engineering environment described by Becker *et al.* [Bec92] is an example for this simulation technique.

UNIX system primitives, however, cannot, in general, be mapped efficiently to arbitrary hardware/software systems because the standard UNIX primitives assume a memory-coupled single processor system. Other protocols have been proposed, mostly message passing, such as remote procedure calls [Val95] or client-server protocols [Bol97] or send-receive commands [Gaj00]. These protocols map efficiently to bus-based hardware/software systems. For co-simulation, these communication procedures are mapped to communication primitives of a simulator backplane. This method allows designers to easily combine models at different levels of abstraction in a single simulation run.

EMULATION

While co-simulation uses abstract models to form a virtual prototype, co-emulation provides a real prototype (rapid prototype) by function implementation in hardware. This prototype can be used to accelerate co-simulation, but it can also be installed in the real environment ("hardware-in-the-loop") to investigate the system function under real conditions. The availability of large field programmable gate arrays (FPGAs) drastically cuts the time needed to develop a rapid prototype such that co-emulation has become a practical validation technique in system design. A highly automated co-emulation approach is described by Fernández et al. [Fer98].

ADDITIONAL READINGS IN CO-SIMULATION, AND EMULATION

[Sta00] J. Staunstrup, H. R. Andersen, H. Hulgaard, J. Lind-Nielsen, K. G. Larsen, G. B. K. Kristoffersen, A. Skou, H. Leerberg, and N. B. Theilgaard, "Practical verification of embedded software," *IEEE Computer* 33, no. 5 (May 2000): 68–75. *Introduces the compositional backward technique algorithm for efficiently evaluating system models.*

[Jan99] A. Jantsch and J. Notbauer, "Functional validation of mixed hardware/software systems based on specification, partitioning, and simulation of test cases," *Design Automation for Embedded Systems* 5, no. 1 (Feb. 1999): 5–28. *Describes a methodology for test-case development for large embedded systems.*

[Tab99] B. Tabbara, M. Sgroi, A. Sangiovanni-Vincentelli, E. Filippi, and L. Lavagno, "Fast hardware-software co-simulation using VHDL models," in *Proceedings, DATE 99*, IEEE Computer Society Press, Los Alamitos, 1999, 309–15. *Uses behavioral VHDL to model software constructs, providing an almost cycle-accurate, uniform simulation environment.*

[Hsi99] H. Hsieh, F. Balarin, A. Sangiovanni-Vincentelli, and L. Lavagno, "Synchronous equivalence for embedded systems: A tool for design exploration," in *Proceedings, ICCAD 99*, IEEE, New York, 1999, 505–09. *Defines an equivalence criterion for embedded systems and efficient algorithms for testing equivalence.*

[Zhu99] J. Zhu and D. Gajski, "A retargetable, ultra-fast instruction set simulator," in *DATE Conference Proceedings*, IEEE Computer Society Press, Los Alamitos, 1999, 298–302. *Presents improved methods for efficient instruction set architecture simulation.*

[Och99] K. Ochiai, H. Iwasaki, J. Naganuma, M. Endo, and T. Ogura, "High-speed software-based platform for embedded software of a single-chip MPEG-2 video encoder LSI with HDTV scalability," in *DATE Conference Proceedings*, IEEE Computer Society Press, Los Alamitos, 1999, 303–08. *Describes a C/C++–based simulation platform, used to design an MPEG-2 encoder.*

[Hin97] K. Hines and G. Borriello, "Dynamic communication models in embedded system *co-simulation,*" in *Proceedings, 34th Design Automation Conference*, ACM Press, New York, 1997, 395–400. *Represents communication at multiple levels of detail to improve co-simulation performance.*

August 31, 1992

Ptolemy: A Framework for Simulating and Prototyping Heterogeneous Systems

Joseph Buck
Soonhoi Ha
Edward A. Lee
David G. Messerschmitt

Department of Electrical Engineering
and Computer Science
University of California
Berkeley, California 94720

1.0 ABSTRACT

Ptolemy is an environment for simulation and prototyping of heterogeneous systems. It uses modern object-oriented software technology (C++) to model each subsystem in a natural and efficient manner, and to integrate these subsystems into a whole. Ptolemy encompasses practically all aspects of designing signal processing and communications systems, ranging from algorithms and communication strategies, simulation, hardware and software design, parallel computing, and generating real-time prototypes. To accommodate this breadth, Ptolemy must support a plethora of widely-differing design styles. The core of Ptolemy is a set of object-oriented class definitions that makes few assumptions about the system to be modeled; rather, standard interfaces are provided for generic objects and more specialized, application-specific objects are derived from these. A basic abstraction in Ptolemy is the Domain, which realizes a computational model appropriate for a particular type of subsystem. Current examples of domains include synchronous and dynamic dataflow, discrete-event, and others appropriate for control software and embedded microcontrollers. Domains can be mixed as appropriate to realize an overall system simulation. Some current applications of Ptolemy include networking and transport, call-processing and signaling software, embedded microcontrollers, signal processing (including implementation in real-time real-time), scheduling of parallel digital signal processors, board-level hardware timing simulation, and combinations of these.

Key words: Heterogeneity, mixed-mode, simulation, prototyping, object-oriented programming

Invited paper in the *International Journal of Computer Simulation* special issue on "Simulation Software Development".

2.0 INTRODUCTION

Ptolemy is a simulation and rapid prototyping framework for heterogeneous systems. It is ideal for applications in which heterogeneity is a key characteristic, such as:

- Design of multimedia networks;
- Real-time embedded software;
- Hardware/Software codesign;
- Control and call-processing in telecommunications networks;
- Rapid prototyping of new telecommunications services;
- Mixed-mode hardware simulation;
- Mapping applications onto heterogeneous multiprocessor systems; and
- Mixed signal processing and real-time control.

For example, in the design of multimedia networks, we are interested in studying the interaction between transport, compression or compositing signal processing, and control software in voice or video services over cell-relay networks. In telecommunication systems we are interested in studying the interaction between call-processing software and hardware switch elements. To develop new telecommunication services, we must jointly design control software, signal processing, transport, and hardware elements.

In hardware design we are interested in modeling components with varying detail, such as behavioral, logic, timing, and circuit. In system-level design, we may wish to jointly design the communications infrastructure and the processing elements. We may also wish to synthesize (in combination) microcode for specialized processors, C code for generic processors, routing tables for field-programmable gate arrays, and custom VLSI. We may wish to automate mappings onto parallel processors by mixing specialized schedulers, such as those that target systolic arrays [11], or those that address only applications with predictable control flow [28].

INTRODUCTION

Simulation and system specification environments that support heterogeneity have been developed before. For example, mixed-mode circuit simulation is now the standard way to deal with complex VLSI circuits. At a higher level, the STATEMATE system by i-Logix [11] combines activity charts, which describe dataflow, with statecharts [10], which describe control. A very different flavor of heterogeneous system is a *coordination language*, like Granular Lucid [14], which combines standard procedural languages with an "indexical model" (a sort of multidimensional declarative model). Another example of a coordination language is Linda [5]. All of these heterogeneous systems, however, assume a small number of pre-defined sets of semantics that prove central to the system design. We avoid pre-defining the semantics we can accommodate.

An alternative to heterogeneity is generality. For example, VHDL is a relatively large language with considerable semantic richness, so that it can accommodate different styles of system description [13]. Petri nets can model parallelism and timing relationships in a huge variety of applications [26]. In addition, specialized models can be combined into more general models with unified semantics. For example, dataflow and discrete-event semantics have been combined for hardware design [33] and graphical programming [31]. However, such generality has a price. Analysis of systems using such general descriptions is difficult, and efficient compilers are difficult to implement. In the case of VHDL, for example, all effective VLSI synthesis tools restrict their domain to a subset of the language. Unfortunately, each tool chooses a different subset, nullifying the benefits of a standardized language. Similarly, effective parallel schedulers restrict their domain to special cases of Petri nets. Furthermore, the complexity and diversity in system-level design is only going to increase. Although any Turing-equivalent model can, in principle, handle any computational design, clearly there are benefits from specializing the specification language. We believe we cannot anticipate all the languages and models of computation that will prove effective. Our approach, therefore, is to embrace heterogeneity by allowing the user to mix different subsystem modeling descriptions, without restricting those descriptions.

The key innovation in Ptolemy is a *non-dogmatic* kernel that does not presuppose a dataflow or functional model, finite-state machines, statecharts, communicating sequential processes, or Petri nets. Rather, Ptolemy can accommodate all of these. Most importantly, the objective is to combine descriptions so that complex systems can be designed *heterogeneously*. Ptolemy can be viewed as a coordination language, but since it is not a language in any conventional sense, we prefer to describe it as a *coordination framework*.

Of course, our limited resources have made it impossible to explore combinations of all the models of computation described above. Hence, we cannot yet claim to have fully proven our concept. Furthermore, our experience indicates that combining highly dissimilar models of computation is not trivial. Our hope is that by providing an open architecture with well-defined interfaces, a community of users with very different design approaches can test our ideas.

A typical large system is structured as shown in Figure 1. It consists of heterogenous subsystems (some implemented in hardware, some in software) together with a software control subsystem and a communications infrastructure. Ptolemy models such systems well. Consider for example a portion of a multimedia connection through a broadband packet network as shown in Figure 2. In this heterogenous system, the video compression (signal processing), transport (networking) and control (software) subsystems are most conveniently modeled in much different ways, and yet there is a desire to study the interaction of these subsystems. Another example that requires similar heterogeneity is shown in Figure 3. A computing resource (perhaps a futuristic workstation) consists of a familiar UNIX[1] processor, a separate processor running a specialized real-time operating system, a third processor for hard-real-time signal processing (running no operating system), and programmable hardware for truly intensive tasks (such as protocol implementations and I/O interfaces to custom devices). A unified environment for programming such a

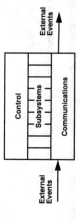

Figure 1. Typical structure of a large system.

---

1. UNIX is a trademark of AT&T.

INTRODUCTION

heterogeneous combination of computing resources must support the different design styles that would be used for each resource.

Ptolemy uses object-oriented software principles to achieve the following goals:

- *Agility*: Support distinct computational models, so that each subsystem can be simulated and prototyped in a manner that is appropriate and natural to that subsystem.
- *Heterogeneity*: Allow distinct computational models to coexist seamlessly for the purpose of studying interactions among subsystems.

INTRODUCTION

- *Extensibility*: Support seamless integration of new computational models and allow them to interoperate with existing models with no changes to Ptolemy or to existing models.
- *Friendliness*: Use a modern graphical interface with a hierarchical block-diagram style of representation.

In Figure 4, we show a simplified but complete example that combines signal processing with network simulation, and hence demonstrates the heterogeneity in Ptolemy. In this example, the lower block diagram models a highly simplified packet-switched communication network, in which packets randomly traverse one of two paths. The upper path has no delay, while the lower

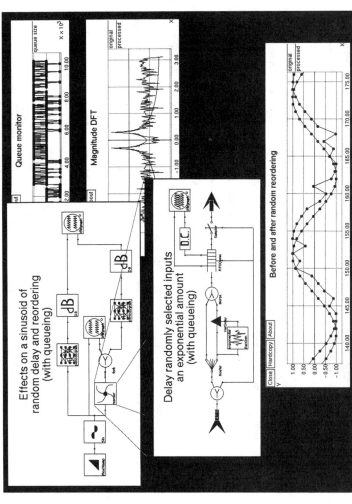

Figure 4. Simulation of the effect of a very simple model of a packet switched network on a sinusoid, illustrating a mixture of signal processing and networking in one simulation.

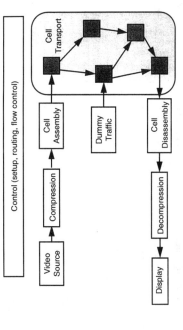

Figure 2. A packet video connection through an ATM broadband packet network.

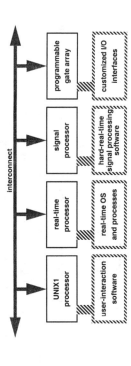

Figure 3. A heterogeneous hardware and software platform.

path has random delay. At the receiving end, a queue stores incoming packets until they are needed by the destination. In the upper left window is a highly simplified signal processing system making use of the network. A sinusoid is generated and packetized, one sample per packet, and launched into the network. At the receiving end, packets are used to reconstruct the sinusoid at the same sample rate. The packets are used in the order of arrival, so the samples of the sinusoid get randomly scrambled, as shown in the lower plot. Real-time constraints are modeled, so if packets do not arrive in time, earlier packets are re-used. The effect on the spectrum is shown in the middle plot, and the size of the queue is monitored in the upper plot.

In practical applications with similar structure, both the network model and the signal processing will be much more elaborate. For instance, Ptolemy is currently being used to evaluate video encoding algorithms for transmission over ATM (asynchronous transfer mode) networks.

3.0 Internal Structure of Ptolemy

Ptolemy relies heavily on the methodology of object-oriented programming (OOP). In this section we describe the essentials of the class hierarchy that defines the Ptolemy kernel.

3.1 Blocks and Particles

The basic unit of modularity in Ptolemy is the Block[1], illustrated in Figure 5. A Block contains a module of code (the "go()" method) that is invoked at run-time, typically examining data present at its input Portholes and generating data on its output Portholes. Depending on the model of computation, however, the functionality of the go() method can be very different; it may spawn processes, for example, or synthesize assembly code for a target processor. Its invocation is directed by a Scheduler (another modular object). A Scheduler determines the operational semantics of a network of Blocks. Blocks and Schedulers can be designed by end users, lending generality while encouraging modularity. The hope is that Blocks will be well documented and stored in standard libraries, rendering them modular, reusable software components.

PortHoles provide the standard interface through which Blocks communicate. Some of the key PortHole methods are shown in Figure 5, such as "grabData()" and "sendData()," which can be invoked within the "go" method. A Scheduler interacts with Blocks through a standard set of polymorphic[1] methods such as "start()" to initialize the state of the Block, "go()" for runtime execution, and "wrapup()" to conclude the execution. Ptolemy also defines methods for building and editing a network of Blocks, such as the "clone()" for creating another instance of the Block.

The user-interface view of the system is an interconnected block diagram. Blocks can communicate using streams of Particles. A Particle is a base type for all messages. Simple examples of classes derived from Particle are FloatSample, FixSample, and ComplexSample, all used in stream-oriented domains such as dataflow and discrete-event. A user can derive other message types from the Particle, such as one-dimensional and two-dimensional data structures, data packets, and control tokens, invisibly to Ptolemy. This use of OOP inheritance[2] allows Ptolemy to deal transparently with many system modeling problems, such as speech, video, and packet data net-

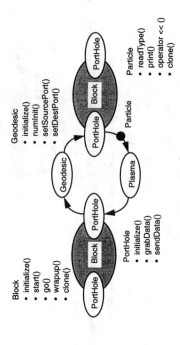

Figure 5. Block objects in Ptolemy send and receive data encapsulated in Particles to the outside world through Portholes. Buffering and transport is handled by the Geodesic and garbage collection by the Plasma.

---

1. Polymorphic methods is a term from object-oriented programming that refers to methods applied uniformly across a group of similar objects. Each object substitutes the correct functionality for that object. Polymorphism is a powerful abstraction tool used extensively in Ptolemy.

2. In object-oriented programming, inheritance refers to the derivation of a new, more functional and specialized, object type by including an existing inherited type and adding or replacing states and methods.

---

1. When we capitalize a modular element, then it represents an object type. In object-oriented programming, objects encapsulate both data, the state of the object, and functions operating on that state, called methods.

works. The Geodesic class establishes the connection between PortHoles. The Plasma class manages the reclamation of the used Particles so that elaborate garbage collection is not required.

Type conversions are performed automatically for the basic types provided with Ptolemy, so that a block that produces integers can be connected with a block that expects real values, for example. Type conversions may also be defined for user-defined Particles. Blocks can also be defined to accept ANYTYPE; such blocks can route or duplicate Particles without regard to their types. These Blocks manipulate Particles using only methods defined in the base class.

3.2 Stars, Galaxies, and the Universe

A conventional way to manage the complexity of a large system is to introduce a hierarchy in the description, as shown in Figure 6. The lowest level (atomic) objects in Ptolemy are of type Star, derived from Block. A Star that performs some computation belongs to a *domain*, as explained below. The Stars in domain named "XXX" are of type XXXStar, derived from Star. A Galaxy, also derived from Block, contains other Blocks internally. A Galaxy may contain internally both Galaxies and Stars. A Galaxy may exist only as a descriptive tool, in that a Scheduler may ignore the hierarchy, viewing the entire network of blocks as flat. All our dataflow schedulers do this to maximize the visible concurrency, getting the effect of non-strict function invocation. Alternatively, a Scheduler may make use of the hierarchy to minimize scheduling complexity or

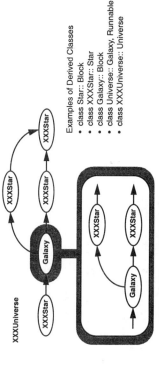

Figure 6. A complete Ptolemy application (a Universe) consists of a network of Blocks. Blocks may be Stars (atomic) or Galaxies (composite). The "XXX" prefix symbolizes a particular domain (or model of computation).

to structure synthesized code in a readable way. A Universe, which contains a complete Ptolemy application, is a type of Galaxy. It is multiply derived from Galaxy and class Runnable. The latter class contains methods for execution of simulation or synthesis of code.

3.3 Targets and Schedulers

A Target, also derived from Block, controls the execution of an application. In a simulation-oriented application, it will typically invoke a Scheduler to manage the order in which Star methods are invoked. For a synthesis-oriented application, it can do much more. It can, for example, synthesize assembly code for a programmable DSP, invoke an assembler, download the code into attached hardware, execute the code, and manage the communication between the host and the attached processor. It can also partition a heterogeneous application among subtargets (by invoking a Scheduler) and then invoke Schedulers in the subtargets to handle the detailed synthesis. This is illustrated in Figure 7, where some of the representative methods and members of the Target class are shown. Targets can have parameters that may be set by the end user.

The top-level Universe object contains a pointer to a dynamically allocated Target. For most simulation applications, the default Target simply passes its messages on to a Scheduler appropriate for the model of computation being used.

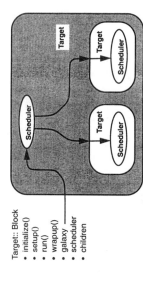

Figure 7. A Target, derived from Block, manages a simulation or synthesis execution. It can invoke it's own Scheduler on a Galaxy, which can in turn invoke Schedulers in sub-Targets.

532 CHAPTER 6: Co-Simulation and Emulation

3.4 Heterogeneity: The Domain

A Domain in Ptolemy consists of a set of Blocks, Targets, and associated Schedulers that conform to a common computational model. By "computational model" we mean the operational semantics governing how Blocks interact with one another. A Scheduler will exploit knowledge of these semantics to order the execution of the Blocks. Two domains are shown within each domain. The inner Domain (designated YYY) in Figure 8 is an illustration of a *sub-Domain*, which implements a more specialized model of computation than the outer Domain (XXX). Hence all its Stars and Targets can also be used with the outer Domain. Schedulers can be associated with more than one Domain, but a Scheduler for a sub-Domain is not necessarily valid within the outer Domain. The Domain and the mechanism for co-existence of Domains are the primary abstractions that distinguished Ptolemy from otherwise comparable systems.

Some examples of Domains that are currently available or being designed are listed below:

- Dynamic dataflow (DDF) is a data-driven model of computation originally proposed by Dennis [7]. Although frequently applied to design parallel architectures, it is also suitable as a programming model [6], and is particularly well-suited to signal processing that includes asynchronous operations. An equivalent model is embodied in the predecessor system Blosim [23][24]. In DDF, Stars are enabled by data at their input PortHoles. That data may or may not be consumed by the Star when it fires, and the Star may or may not produce data on its outputs. More than one Star may be fired at one time if the Target supports this parallelism. We have used this domain to experiment with static scheduling of programs with run-time dynamics [9]. The DDF Domain does not attempt to model the relative timing relationship of Block invocations.

- Synchronous dataflow (SDF) [17][18] is a sub-Domain of DDF. SDF Stars consume and generate a static and known number of data tokens on each invocation. Since this is clearly a special case of DDF, any Star or Target that works under the SDF model will also work under the DDF model. However, an SDF Scheduler can take advantage of this static information to construct a schedule that can be used repeatedly. Such a Scheduler will not always work with DDF Stars. SDF is an appropriate model for multirate signal processing systems with rationally-related sampling rates throughout [3], and is the model used exclusively in Ptolemy's predecessor system Gabriel [19][2]. The advantages of SDF are ease of programming (since the availability of data tokens is static and doesn't need to be checked), a greater degree of setup-time syntax checking (since sample-rate inconsistencies are easily detected by the system), run-time efficiency (since the ordering of Block invocation is statically determined at setup-time rather dynamically at run-time), and automatic parallel scheduling [29][30][20].

- Boolean dataflow (BDF) is a model intermediate between SDF and DDF, in which a limited but practically important set of asynchronous operations (analogous to the if-then-else or case statement in C) is supported, with many if not most of the advantages of SDF [4][21]. This is an experimental domain currently being developed, and will be described in detail in a future paper.

- Discrete event (DE) is a model in which only changes in system state (called events) are modeled. This is an asynchronous model like DDF, but unlike DDF incorporates the concept of global time in the system and orders Block invocations properly in time. A completely general simulation system could be developed in the DE domain, at the expense of run-time efficiency and ease and naturalness of programming for many applications like signal processing.

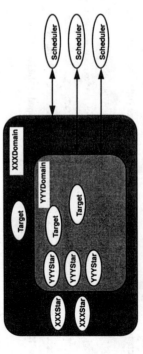

Figure 8. A Domain (XXX) consists of a set of Stars, Targets and Schedulers that support a particular model of computation. A sub-Domain (YYY) may support a more specialized model of computation.

- Message queue (MQ) is a model similar to DDF but with many more capabilities for dynamically creating and destroying Blocks. The MQ domain is another experimental domain under development targeted at software control applications, such as telephone switching call-processing software. An interesting distinction between MQ and many other domains is that graphical representations of the applications is probably neither reasonable nor appropriate.

In addition to these domains, it is possible to create domains out of previously-existing simulation systems, as has been demonstrated with the Capsim [8] domain (incorporating the Capsim signal processing system that is based on Blosim) and the Thor domain (incorporating the Thor hardware timing simulator [32]). We are also beginning to design a domain with finite-state-machine semantics.

The Domain class by itself makes Ptolemy agile (enabling modeling of different types of systems in a natural and efficient manner), but we need to be able to mix those descriptions at the system level). To accomplish this, Ptolemy allows different Domains to co-exist at different levels of the hierarchy. Within a domain, it is permissible to have Blocks containing foreign domains.

At the user interface, a foreign Domain appears to be a property of an internal Galaxy. However, at runtime it is a much different entity. A Galaxy does not have a Scheduler, and may be destroyed by flattening prior to runtime, while a foreign Domain does have a Scheduler and must not be flattened (its internal structure does not conform to the external model of computation). A given simulation can therefore contain a number of Schedulers, which must be coordinated.

3.5 The Wormhole

The manner in which different domains coexist is a critical design element of Ptolemy, and will therefore be further elaborated. As illustrated in Figure 9, the top-level view of a simulation consists of a Universe. This Universe has an associated domain, say XXX, and is a Block of type XXXUniverse (as shown in Figure 6). Internal to that Block is an XXXScheduler and a set of XXXStars. (The description of the Universe may also include Galaxies, but we omit them because they may be destroyed by flattening at runtime.) The introduction of a subsystem from a foreign domain, say domain YYY, is illustrated in Figure 10. This is accomplished by adding a Block which appears in the XXXDomain to be an XXXStar, but which is actually a much differ-

ent object internally because it contains a YYYScheduler and a set of YYYStars. We call this special object an XXXWormhole. One way to think of a Wormhole is as a Block which appears externally to be a Star (it obeys the operational semantics of the external domain and appears to be atomic to the external domain), but internally consists of an entire foreign Universe (Scheduler for a foreign domain and Stars for that domain). A Wormhole can be introduced into the XXX domain without any need for the XXXScheduler or other XXXStars to have knowledge of the semantics of domain YYY.

It should be clarified that although most existing domains in Ptolemy have the internal structure of Scheduler plus Stars, and are viewed at the user interface as an interconnected block

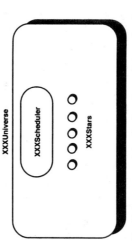

Figure 9. The Universe consists of a domain, and at runtime internal Stars which conform to the operational semantics of that domain's Scheduler.

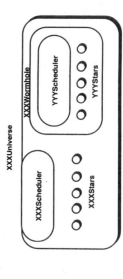

Figure 10. A new domain YYY is introduced by adding a Wormhole to the Universe.

diagram, this assumption is not built into Ptolemy. For purposes of interoperability, the only relevant view of a domain is the external interface of a Wormhole, and as long as it conforms to this external view it can have any internal structure whatsoever (just as a Star can have any internal code). For example, one could have domains where every object talks to every other object, and an interconnected block diagram makes no sense.

Wormhole objects also contain Target pointers; the Target by default may be the same as that for the parent Universe, but can be different. This facility can be used to execute part of a simulation on a workstation, while running another part of the simulation on a DSP board with code generated and downloaded by Ptolemy. In this case, the Target object in the Wormhole knows how to download and execute code on the DSP board.

3.6 The EventHorizon

The key to the support of heterogeneity in Ptolemy is the interoperability of different domains at runtime. In turn, the key to this interoperability is the interface between the internal structure of a Wormhole and its external environment. This interface is called the EventHorizon, and is illustrated in Figure 11. A "universal" EventHorizon is shared by all domains, so that each domain only needs to provide an interface to this EventHorizon. Hence we avoid having N^2 interfaces for N Domains.

There are two types of interactions that occur at the EventHorizon as illustrated in Figure 11. The first is the conversion of Particles passing through the EventHorizon. For example, in some domains each Particle has an associated timestamp, and in other domains it does not, and hence there is the function of adding or deleting timestamps. The second interaction is the coordination of the Schedulers associated with the inside and outside domains. We will now describe both interactions in more detail.

3.6.1 Particle Conversion at the EventHorizon

Conversion between domain-specific representations of a Particle is accomplished by objects of class ToEventHorizon and FromEventHorizon, derived from EventHorizon, derived in turn from Porthole. For each specific Domain XXX, we define XXXtoUniversal and XXXfromUniversal. Since these are ultimately derived from class XXXPorthole, the XXXWormhole looks just like a XXXStar to XXX Domain. Particles are read from the XXXtoUniversal, transferred to the YYYfromUniversal, and sent to the inside YYY domain.

Some Domains have a notion of simulated time, and some do not. In order for the event horizon to work with both, when a Particle passes through the EventHorizon, it is always associated with a time stamp. A domain therefore need not know with which domain it is interacting. See the next subsection for the detailed discussion of timing relationship between domains.

EventHorizons may have other domain-specific responsibilities. One example can be found in SDFfromUniversal class. Suppose that the inner domain is SDF, the outer domain is DE, and the DEWormhole has more than one input. The DEWormhole is executed when any input has new data (an event). However, the inner SDF domain requires that all input data be available before execution. To resolve this conflict, the DEWormhole checks all SDFfromUniversal EventHorizons to see if they have enough data before turning control over to the inner SDFScheduler. Thus, the SDFfromUniversal synchronizes the input data, enforcing the model of computation assumed in the inside domain.

In some domains, Particle types are very restricted. For example, the Thor domain (used for timing simulations of hardware) allows only bits. Particle type conversion, however, is not the task of the EventHorizon. The Particle type of an EventHorizon is inherited from that of the Port-

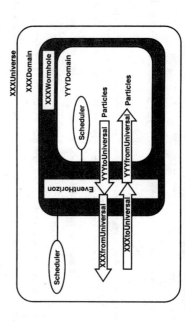

Figure 11. The universal EventHorizon provides an interface between the external and internal domains.

Internal Structure of Ptolemy

Hole connected to it. Particle type conversion between two different types of Particles is performed automatically by the type conversion methods defined in the Particle class if both are built-in types such as integer, float, and complex. Otherwise, the type conversion should be managed explicitly by inserting special Stars (Packetize star, IntToBits Star, etc.).

3.6.2 Scheduler Coordination Across the EventHorizon

Viewed from the EventHorizon, every Wormhole contains a Target which in turn contains a Scheduler, and every Scheduler has a set of polymorphic methods for the purposes of execution of the domain and the coordination of Schedulers on both sides of an EventHorizon. Some of these methods are illustrated in Figure 12. For purposes of executing a domain, the setup() method does whatever is appropriate before execution of Blocks in the domain, for example the static scheduling of Blocks in the SDF domain based on the interconnection topology and relative sampling rates. The run() method then executes the Blocks by calling their run() methods in turn.

For purposes of coordinating two or more Schedulers, each Ptolemy Scheduler has an additional concept of a StopTime. That is, run() is allowed to execute the Blocks in the domain only up to the StopTime. One method of a Scheduler, setStopTime(), allows the StopTime to be set externally.

Using these methods, multiple Schedulers can be made to behave logically as a single Scheduler. Coordination of multiple DE Schedulers has been addressed in the area of distributed simulation of discrete event systems, for example in *conservative scheduling* [25][28], but may introduce artificial deadlocks because a notion of global time is not available to all processors. In Ptolemy, Schedulers are hierarchically nested, making it easy to maintain a global time. Multiple Schedulers behave logically as a single Scheduler and there is no artificial deadlock. To see how this is achieved, assume for the moment that both the inside and outside Schedulers are (possibly

Scheduler: setup()
run()
setStopTime()
resetStopTime()

Figure 12. An illustration of some of the polymorphic messages of type Scheduler that support the coordination of two Schedulers.

Internal Structure of Ptolemy

different) DE Schedulers. The basic structure of a DE Scheduler is shown in Figure 13. It incorporates the concept of a CurrentTime, and is parameterized by a StopTime, which is the maximum allowed value of CurrentTime before execution is suspended. The EventQueue stores the un-processed events, each corresponding to an action (typically arrival of a particular Particle at a particular PortHole of a particular Block) with a TimeStamp specifying the time of that action. The EventQueue sorts the set of events by TimeStamp. In this and subsequent figures we assume that the earliest event is on the left and the latest event is on the right.

The coordination of Schedulers across the EventHorizon is illustrated in Figure 14. Suppose the oldest (earliest) event in the EventQueue of the outer domain is an event at a Wormhole EventHorizon. The outer-domain Scheduler calls the go() method of the WormHole (it treats it like an ordinary star). The WormHole obtains the CurrentTime of the outer domain (which is available to any Star) and sets the StopTime of its Scheduler to equal that time. It then invokes the run() method of its Target, which in turn invokes the run() method of its Scheduler. By setting the inner StopTime equal to the outer CurrentTime, the WormHole ensures that the inner domain cannot get ahead of the outer domain in time. The CurrentTime of the outer domain can safely get ahead of the CurrentTime of the inner domain, because the outer domain supplies all events to the inner domain.

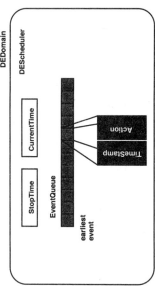

Figure 13. A discrete-event style of Scheduler keeps a sorted EventQueue and is parameterized by a StopTime.

Internal Structure of Ptolemy

Typically, the inner-domain Scheduler suspends execution at the StopTime, leaving unprocessed the next event on its EventQueue. To ensure that it has an opportunity to execute that event at the proper time, before it returns control to the outer-domain Scheduler, the inner-domain adds an event to the outer-domain EventQueue. Again, this is an action available to any Star. This "self-scheduling event" asks the outer domain to invoke the go() method of the Wormhole at the specified future time, and is the critical feature distinguishing Ptolemy from conservative scheduling.

The above interaction works for any pair of DE Schedulers that are based on event queues. Distinct DE Schedulers are of interest in Ptolemy. For one thing, we want to import pre-existing simulation environments to Ptolemy as domains without the need to replace their Schedulers. For another, different specializations of DE scheduling are of interest; for example, those that associate delay with blocks (enabling data dependency) and those that associate delay with arcs (a simpler model appropriate for hardware timing simulation). In addition, many Ptolemy Schedulers are not recognizable as DE, although they are required to present the same interface at the Event-Horizon. Generally we can divide Schedulers into two categories: timed and untimed. Timed Schedulers keep track of time for each action in the domain, either explicitly (as in the DE exam-

ple) or implicitly (as in the SDF Scheduler, where Particles do not have associated TimeStamps, but nevertheless the Scheduler can associate a time with each new Particle implicitly because it has the sampling rates or equivalent information). Untimed Schedulers do not keep track of time. A Wormhole encapsulating an untimed domain must still model time from an external perspective in case the external domain is timed. However, such a Wormhole is considered to be instantaneous; that is, it executes in zero time by associating the same TimeStamp with each outgoing Particle as the TimeStamp of the most recent input. If this is too coarse a model for any particular subsystem, then a timed-domain model can be substituted.

3.6.3 Inheritance Structure of Blocks

We are now in a position to understand the internal design of Blocks in Ptolemy. A multiple inheritance diagram[1] is shown in Figure 15.

A Block is a base class that includes the data structures of all Blocks, such as a list of States (data structure elements observable from outside a Block) and PortHoles. It also has three key methods invoked by the Scheduler: initialize(), start(), and wrapup(), invoked before executing the Block, at the start of an execution, and at the end of an execution. Runnable is a class that contains a Target, which in turn contains a Scheduler and provides an interface to that Scheduler such as run() and setStopTime().

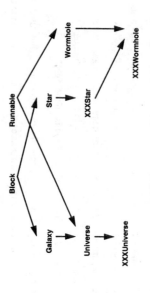

Figure 15. Inheritance diagram for Blocks within domain XXX.

---
1. Multiple inheritance simply means that a class assumes the characteristics of two or more base classes.

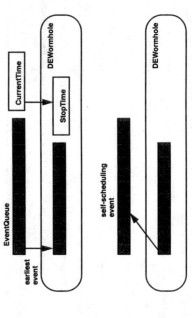

Figure 14. An illustration of conservative scheduling for coordinating two discrete-event Schedulers.

Internal Structure of Ptolemy

From these base types, we define the particular types of Blocks. A Galaxy does not include a Scheduler, but simply includes a list of internal Blocks with both internal and external connections to those Block's PortHoles. A Star is a Block that includes the additional method go() (execute the internal code). A Universe is a Block that has all the characteristics of a Galaxy (internally composed of interconnected Blocks) but also includes a Target and hence is a Runnable. A Wormhole is simply a Runnable (has an internal Target) that includes an internal Galaxy as well (in this sense it is very similar to a Universe)[1].

For a specific domain XXX, there is an XXXUniverse which is a Universe with a compatible Target that contains an XXXScheduler. An XXXStar is a Star that obeys the particular operational semantics of domain XXX; that is, it obeys specific rules on how it generates and consumes Particles at its PortHoles. Finally, the domain has an XXXWormhole derived from XXXStar. Thus the XXXWormhole provides all the methods of an XXXStar, but internally it is has a Galaxy and a Scheduler, unlike XXXStars). Any type of Scheduler and Blocks can be inside the Wormhole. Neither the XXX domain nor the implementation of the XXXWormhole needs to know about the inner domain.

An XXXWormhole is externally indistinguishable from an XXXStar, and hence can be inserted into any XXX domain. How this exploits polymorphism is shown in Figure 16. The Figure shows two methods, start(), which is characteristic of all Blocks (including Stars), and go(),

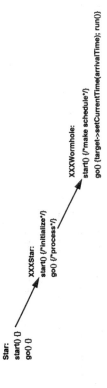

Figure 16. An illustration of how polymorphism allows the XXXStar and XXXWormhole to have the same external interface, even though they are implemented quite differently internally.

which is characteristic of all Stars. The method start() is called each time a simulation is started or restarted, and in the case of an XXXStar this method typically initializes the internal data structures of the XXXStar (as defined by the programmer of that XXXStar). In the case of an XXX-Wormhole, this method does something quite different; namely, it calls a polymorphic Scheduler method that initializes the schedule. Similarly, the method go() executes user-provided code in the case of any XXXStar, but for an XXXWormhole calls the run() method provided by any Runnable, which executes the schedule and in turn executes the Stars inside the Wormhole in the proper order (through their respective go() methods).

In this manner, polymorphism allows us to achieve extensibility. Any new domain can be added without any modifications to existing domains or to the kernel of Ptolemy itself, and that new domain will be interoperable with the old domains.

3.7 Code Generation

The basic idea of code generation in Ptolemy is simple. The go() method of a code generation Star adds ASCII text to a data structure in the Target. The Scheduler, therefore, controls the sequence of generated code. The Target collects the code and supervises the compilation and execution, if any. Any generic optimization capabilities can be put into the base class of the Target or the code generation stars.

While a domain is specific to the computational model used, for code synthesis it is also specific to the type of language generated. Hence, a C code generation domain following SDF semantics is different from an assembly code generation domain following SDF semantics. This is because the libraries of Stars and Targets for the two are quite distinct. The Target is specific to the hardware that will run the code. A given language, particularly a generic language such as C, may run on many targets; code generation functions are therefore cleanly divided between the Domain and the Target.

---

1. The XXXWormhole is not derived from Galaxy, but rather contains a Galaxy because it does not have the external interface of a Galaxy while it does have the external interface of an XXXStar.

4.0 Practical Details

Ptolemy has been coded in C++, and successfully compiled using both commercial (Cfront-based) and freely re-distributable (GNU) compilers. The development used Sun-3 and Sun-4 (Sparc) platforms, and Ptolemy has been ported to the DECstation. Efforts are underway to port it to an HP platform as well. The documentation for Ptolemy is extensive [1].

4.1 The Graphical User Interface

The Ptolemy interactive graphical interface (pigi) is a design editor based on tools from the Berkeley CAD framework: the Oct database and the Vem graphical editor [12]. Using pigi, Ptolemy applications are constructed graphically, by interconnecting icons. A special Ptolemy class, InterpGalaxy (a derived type of Galaxy), is used to dynamically construct simulations based on commands from the graphical interface. Incremental linking is supported, permitting additional stars to be defined, linked into the running pigi executable, and instantiated in the simulation.

The graphical interface runs as two processes: one process is the Vem graphic editor; the second, called pigiRpc, contains the Ptolemy kernel and the portion of the graphical interface that knows about Ptolemy. The Unix RPC protocol is used for communication between the two processes.

The graphical interface is by no means integral to Ptolemy. Indeed, we do not believe that any single, homogeneous graphical interface will manage all Domains. Two separate textual interfaces, one with a Lisp-like syntax, and a second based on an embedded interpreter, Tcl [26], have been developed. As with the graphical interface, the text-based interfaces also communicate with the InterpGalaxy class to build and run simulations.

4.2 States

Ptolemy provides a State class, together with type-specific subclasses (IntState, FloatState, StringState, IntArrayState, etc.) for use as parameters, observable variables, and as memory for code generation applications. Because State objects are visible from the user interface, they can be used to monitor and control the simulation, or to collect statistics.

Every State type has an initial-value string, which may be an expression that refers to other states defined at higher levels (initializers for states in a star may refer to states in the parent galaxy). Initial values of states are referred to as parameters by the user interface. The hierarchical nature of states, and the fairly general expressions permitted, make it easy to define parameterizable Galaxy objects.

4.3 Star Preprocessor Language

The Ptolemy preprocessor (a "schema compiler") has been developed to make it easier to write and document Star and Galaxy class definitions for use with Ptolemy. Instead of writing all the initialization code required for a Ptolemy star (which contains quite a bit of "standard boilerplate"), the user can concentrate on writing the action code for a star and let the preprocessor generate the standard initialization code for PortHoles, States, etc. The preprocessor also generates documentation in a standard format for inclusion in the manual.

5.0 Some Representative Applications

Several applications of Ptolemy that have been pursued will now be described. One purpose of this will be to illustrate how the heterogenous aspect of Ptolemy manifests itself to the user, and another purpose will be to illustrate how the use of OOP at the user-modeling level can result in much more flexible models.

5.1 Broadband Networking

In the introduction, the use of Ptolemy for simulation of a broadband packet network with associated signal processing is mentioned. Here we give a bit more detail. A block diagram of such a simulation is shown in Figure 17. At the top (Universe) level, the cell-relay network connects a set of terminals. The DE domain is used to model only non-empty cells travelling between terminal and network, each cell marked with a TimeStamp. Internally the terminals have a com-

Some Representative Applications

plicated structure (control, signal processing for video compression, etc.), but let us concentrate on the network. Internally it consists of a signalling entity (programmed in the MQ domain) and a set of interconnected ATM switches. The internal simulation of each ATM switch is in the SDF domain (so that all cells are modelled, including empty cells) because the most convenient model is as a synchronous digital machine (especially if we anticipate moving down to logic and timing hardware-modeling levels). Within the switch there is another call-processing entity (in the MQ domain) for control of this switch, and a shuffle-exchange type of interconnected 2x2 switches. Finally, those switches consist of a 2x2 switching matrix plus associated routing tables.

Most interesting is the interconnection of foreign domains. Internal to Ptolemy this is handled by the Wormhole, but it is also an issue at the level of user modeling. For example, cells that arrive from the DE domain at a switch must be augmented with empty cells internal to the switch to fill out an isochronous (constant rate) stream of cells, because the switch is modeled in the SDF domain. This requires a cell interpolator driven by an isochronous clock at the interfaces to the switch within the DE domain, so that cells passing the EventHorizon into the SDF domain have uniformly spaced TimeStamps. Similarly, the communication between the call-processing in the MQ domain within the switch and the routing tables within the switch in the SDF domain requires an interpolator. In this case the MQ domain is untimed, and operates instantaneously from a timed domain's perspective. When a messages arrives from the network-level call processing, it passes through the DE domain and therefore has appended TimeStamps. The switch-level call processing then generates messages in response to update the routing tables, and these messages have the same TimeStamp (since the MQ domain is untimed, the call-processing operates instantaneously). Before these messages can be sent, however, they must be interpolated to an isochronous message stream, because the routine tables are in the SDF domain.

This example illustrates that Ptolemy does not automatically solve all problems related to interconnecting domains; rather, there is often work to be done at the user modeling level. Often, however, this work is not an artifact of the modeling technique, but is a functional requirement in the system being simulated. For example, the interpolation of messages from the call processing arriving at the routing tables, a synchronous digital system, is a functional requirement of the system being modeled.

5.2 Signal Processing

A wide variety of signal processing applications have been developed using Ptolemy, including several adaptive filtering applications, power spectrum estimation, several parametric and waveform coding techniques based on linear prediction, communication channel modeling, digital communication receivers, beamforming, digital filter design, chaos simulations, phase-locked loops, image coding, and music synthesis. Many of these applications are distributed with the Ptolemy code as demonstrations.

Most signal processing *algorithms* are conveniently defined within the synchronous data-flow model of computation. Hence, for algorithm development and simulation, there is little need for heterogeneity. However, turning an algorithm into a product involves both real-time prototyp-

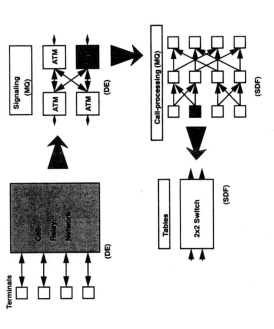

Figure 17. An ATM cell-relay simulation in Ptolemy, illustrating the hierarchical description and mixture of domains. In each case the shaded block is shown in internal detail.

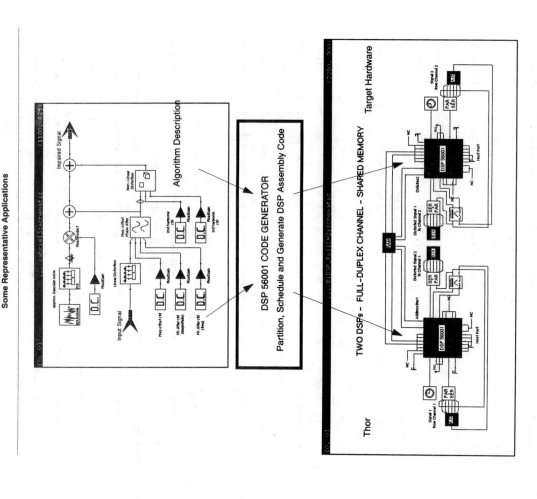

Figure 18. A hardware design (bottom) containing programmable DSPs can be developed together with the software (top) that will run on the DSPs. This Figure shows the top level only of a telephone channel simulation algorithm (top window) being mapped onto a board design with two Motorola DSP56001 DSPs.

ing and real-time control. For the former, we have been concentrating on synthesis of code for parallel programmable DSP processors.

Ptolemy is capable of automatically partitioning, scheduling, and generating DSP assembly language for a multi-processor DSP system [29][30]. Currently, it is required that the problem fit the synchronous dataflow model; a future version will exploit heterogeneity to remove that restriction by mixing Schedulers that operate at code-generation time with Schedulers that synthesize run-time code [9]. For real-time control, using the Wormhole concept, part of an application can be run on a DSP board while the remainder of an application is executed on a host microprocessor.

At present, Ptolemy can generate C code, Motorola 56000 and 96000 assembly code, and assembly code for the Sproc multiprocessor DSP from Star Semiconductor. Code generation for other processors is planned.

5.3 Hardware-Software Co-design

Most electronic systems mix custom circuit designs with programmable commodity parts. Ptolemy supports such designs as a unit, since using the various domains described above, all parts of the system can be modeled. For example, the Thor domain can be combined with a code generation domain to design boards that mix custom hardware with programmable DSPs. Since the hardware and software are both modeled within the same software framework, a designer can easily explore tradeoffs between hardware and software implementations of various functions.

An example of such a design is shown in Figure 18 [15]. The top window shows the top level of an algorithm that simulates the impairments of a telephone channel. This algorithm is fairly complicated, including linear and non-linear distortion, frequency offset, phase jitter, and additive Gaussian noise. The design is built in a code generation domain compatible with the SDF model of computation. The bottom window shows a hardware design in the Thor domain containing two programmable DSPs communicating through a dual ported shared memory. This hardware might be used to implement the telephone channel simulator for production-line testing of voiceband data modems.

Some Representative Applications

The design shown in Figure 18 is one of many that could accomplish the stated objectives. Using Ptolemy, the entire design, ranging from algorithm development to circuit design, can be carried out within a unified environment. This enables exploration of many design alternatives before resources are committed to hardware prototyping.

The hardware-software co-design problem is becoming increasingly important in large (and even small) system design. One of the key advantages of Ptolemy is the ability to freely mix behavioral, hardware, and software entities, modeling each in a natural way. In fact, in many instances the actual production software can be developed in an appropriate Ptolemy domain, and functionally tested in combination with its associated hardware subsystems.

5.4 Source and Link Modeling

A final example will illustrate the value of OOP abstractions in obtaining flexible models in Ptolemy, using the simple example of the modeling of sources and links in the communications network. Consider the simple situation modeled in Figure 19. We would like to be able to freely intermix source and link models, regardless of the nature of the source or link. For example, the source could generate data packets or speech samples or video frames, and the link could consist of a simple bit-error model or a full physical-layer simulation. Using polymorphism in the Particle can achieve this goal by defining in the Particle class methods convertToBits() and convertFromBits() which generate a bit-string representation of any Particle. The link model then accepts Particles, and employs convertToBits() to generate a bit string, apply the link model to that bit string, and use Particle convertFromBits() to convert back to Particles at the output. There are a number of issues in actually implementing this, but this oversimplification does illustrate the value of OOP at the user-modeling level.

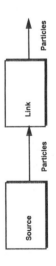

Figure 19. A simple network modeling problem.

6.0 CONCLUSIONS

Ptolemy has been used internally in Berkeley for approximately two years for a growing number of simulation efforts, such as signal processing, electric power network simulation, and wireless and broadband network simulation. It has also been used successfully for instructional purposes in one graduate and one undergraduate course. It has been distributed externally for about one year, and is now used in a growing community of academic and industrial organizations. Aside from the usual problems of installation and environment compatibility, these efforts can generally be characterized as very successful. The ability of Ptolemy to simulate, and to a lesser extent rapidly prototype heterogeneous systems has been demonstrated by a number of applications.

In terms of useful user models (Stars and Galaxies), the most fully-developed domain is SDF, with many models for signal processing and data communications. Currently a similar set of models is being developed in the DE domain for networking (packet, multiple access, and wireless) simulations. New domains are also under development. For example, a high-level circuit synthesis domain based on synthesis work at Berkeley is planned.

There are also recognized deficiencies in the kernel of Ptolemy, and enhancements are planned. One deficiency is the relatively simplistic manner in which a simulation is controlled from the GUI at runtime. Another deficiency is the GUI itself, which unlike the remainder of Ptolemy is not object-oriented. An OOP GUI design would encapsulate the interface to each domain within that domain itself, allowing graphical interfaces to be customized for a domain.

Some of the extended capabilities of Ptolemy can be achieved in other ways, and it is useful to compare them. For example, the generality of Ptolemy could be achieved by a single discrete-event domain, which is itself completely general as a modelling tool. There are two disadvantages:

- The discrete-event modeling of certain subsystems is unnatural, and will likely be resisted by designers. Examples include multirate signal processing (where associating a time stamp with each sample is unnecessary and awkward) and control software domains (where not only is it unnatural, but could not be considered for production software).

- Discrete-event modeling is significantly less efficient at runtime for some subsystems (the aforementioned included). This needs, however, to be balanced by the additional overhead of EventHorizon conversion in Ptolemy.

CAD frameworks allow design databases to be transferred from one tool to another. Unlike Ptolemy they are focused on applying different toolkits (simulation, routing, logic minimization, etc.) to a common design. Such frameworks do not address the heterogeneous subsystem problem directly (for example do not address control software). Further, frameworks typically work through interprocess communication or file formats, whereas Ptolemy performs the simulation in a common virtual address space (advantageous for efficiency in large simulations). With respect to CAD frameworks, Ptolemy can be considered to be one tool.

The appropriate use of Ptolemy is as a basic framework for simulations (as well as prototyping tools). It can be used is a diversity of design groups focused on different aspects of a large system design, where each group can tailor a domain or small set of domains to their need and liking. The major advantage is that the efforts of the different groups can readily be merged for the purpose of checking interoperability. Also, different details of modeling can be used for each subsystem (another form of heterogeneity): a high level (and rapidly executing) model for routine use in simulation of other subsystems, down to a very detailed model of every subsystem (and very slow execution) for final verification of the design. This is typically not done today.

With the increasing complexity of systems, the goal should be a design that is "right from the start". Ptolemy is a tool that can support that rigorous design style.

7.0 ACKNOWLEDGEMENTS

While this paper emphasizes the internal design of the Ptolemy kernel, a number of our colleagues have contributed to Ptolemy and to the modeling in Ptolemy. The broader Ptolemy project currently includes more than twenty students and three full-time-equivalent staff members. Many of these people have made significant contributions to the ideas described in this paper. Ichiro Kuroda contributed extensively to the early design of the State processor and interpreter. Edwin Goei is the principle architect of the GUI, with Wan-Teh Chang contributing some refinements. The OCT/VEM group at Berkeley has been most cooperative in responding to our requests for enhancements to that system.

The applications mentioned here have been pursued by other colleagues. Alan Lao, Wan-Teh Chang, John Loh, and Philip Bitar have worked on networking models. Asawaree Kalavade is working on hardware/software co-design and Tom Parks is working on embedded microcontrollers. Jose Pino is working on assembly code generation. A number of other colleagues are working on other applications.

The Ptolemy project has been supported by the Defense Advanced Projects Research Agency, the Semiconductor Research Corporation through its Berkeley Center of Excellence in CAD/IC (Grant 92-DC-008), the National Science Foundation, the State of California MICRO program, Bell Northern Research, Comdisco Systems, Dolby Labs, Hitachi, Hughes Network Systems, Motorola, NEC, Philips, Rockwell, Sony, Star Semiconductor, and US West.

8.0 REFERENCES

[1] *The Almagest: Manual for Ptolemy Version 0.3.1*, Department of EECS, University of California, Berkeley, CA 94720, USA, January, 1992.

[2] J. Bier, E. Goei, W. Ho, P. Lapsley, M. O'Reilly, G. Sih and E.A. Lee, "Gabriel: A Design Environment for DSP," *IEEE Micro Magazine*, October 1990, Vol. 10, No. 5, pp. 28-45.

[3] J. Buck, S. Ha, E. A. Lee, and D. G. Messerschmitt, "Multirate Signal Processing in Ptolemy", *Proc. of the Int. Conf. on Acoustics, Speech, and Signal Processing*, Toronto, Canada, April, 1991.

[4] J. Buck and E. A. Lee, "The Token Flow Model," presented at *Data Flow Workshop*, Hamilton Island, Australia, May, 1992.

[5] N. Carriero and D. Gelernter, "Linda in Context," *Comm. of the ACM*, Vol. 32, No. 4, pp. 444-458, April 1989.

[6] A. L. Davis and R. M. Keller, "Data Flow Program Graphs," *IEEE Computer*, Vol 15, No. 2, February 1982.

[7] J. B. Dennis, "Data Flow Supercomputers," *IEEE Computer*, Vol 13, No. 11, November, 1980.

[8] L. James Faber, "Capsim", ECE Dept. North Carolina State University, Raleigh, NC 27695

[9] Soonhoi Ha and E.A. Lee, "Compile-Time Scheduling and Assignment of Dataflow Program Graphs with Data-Dependent Iteration," *IEEE Transactions on Computers*, November, 1991.

REFERENCES

[10] D. Harel, "Statecharts: A Visual Formalism for Complex Systems," *Sci. Comput. Program.*, vol 8, pp. 231-274, 1987.

[11] D. Harel, H. Lachover, A. Naamad, A. Pnueli, M. Politi, R. Sherman, A. Shtull-Trauring, M. Trakhtenbrot, "STATEMATE: A Working Environment for the Development of Complex Reactive Systems," *IEEE Tr. on Software Engineering*, Vol. 16, No. 4, April 1990.

[12] D. S. Harrison, P. Moore, R. Spickelmier, A. R. Newton, "Data Management and Graphics Editing in the Berkeley Design Environment," *Proc. of the IEEE Int. Conf. on Computer-Aided Design*, November 1986.

[13] *IEEE Standard VHDL Language Reference Manual*, IEEE STD 1076-1987, The IEEE, Inc., 345 East 47th St., New York, NY, USA, 1987.

[14] R. Jagannathan and A.A. Faustini, "The GLU Programming Language," Technical Report SRI-CSL-90-11, Computer Science Laboratory, SRI International, Menlo Park, California 94025, USA, November, 1990.

[15] A. Kalavade, "Hardware/Software Co-design Using Ptolemy", MS Report, Electronics Research Laboratory, University of California, Berkeley, CA 94720, December, 1991.

[16] S. Y. Kung, *VLSI Array Processors*, Prentice-Hall, Englewood Cliffs, New Jersey, 1988.

[17] E. A. Lee and D. G. Messerschmitt, "Static Scheduling of Synchronous Data Flow Programs for Digital Signal Processing," *IEEE Transactions on Computers*, January, 1987.

[18] E. A. Lee and D. G. Messerschmitt, "Synchronous Data Flow," *IEEE Proceedings*, September, 1987.

[19] E. A. Lee, W.-H. Ho, E. Goei, J. Bier, and S. Bhattacharyya, "Gabriel: A Design Environment for DSP", *IEEE Trans. on ASSP*, November, 1989.

[20] E. A. Lee and J. C. Bier, "Architectures for Statically Scheduled Dataflow", reprinted in *Parallel Algorithms and Architectures for DSP Applications*, ed. M. A. Bayoumi, Kluwer Academic Pub., 1991.

[21] E. A. Lee, "Consistency in Dataflow Graphs", *IEEE Transactions on Parallel and Distributed Systems*, Vol. 2, No. 2, April 1991.

[22] E. A. Lee, "A Design Lab for Statistical Signal Processing," *Proceedings of ICASSP*, San Francisco, March, 1992.

[23] D. G. Messerschmitt, "A Tool for Structured Functional Simulation," *IEEE J. on Selected Areas in Communications*, Vol. SAC-2, No. 1, January 1984.

[24] D. G. Messerschmitt, "Structured Interconnection of Signal Processing Programs," *Proc. of Globecom*, Atlanta, Georgia, 1984.

[25] J.Misra, "Distributed Discrete-Event Simulation", *Computing Surveys*, Vol. 18, No. 1, Nov. 1985.

[26] J. K. Ousterhout, "Tcl: An Embeddable Command Language", 1990 Winter USENIX Proceedings, 1990.

[27] J. L. Peterson, *Petri Net Theory and the Modeling of Systems*, Prentice-Hall, Englewood Cliffs, New Jersey, 1981.

[28] R. Righter, J. C. Walrand, "Distributed Simulation of Discrete Event Systems," *IEEE Proceedings*, Vol. 77, No. 1, pp. 99-113, January 1989.

[29] G.C. Sih, E.A. Lee, "A Compile-Time Scheduling Heuristic for Interconnection-Constrained Heterogeneous Processor Architectures", to appear, *IEEE Trans. on Parallel and Distributed Systems*, 1992.

[30] G. C. Sih and E. A. Lee, "Declustering: A New Multiprocessor Scheduling Technique," to appear in *IEEE Trans. on Parallel and Distributed Systems*, 1992.

[31] P. D. Stotts, "The PFG Language: Visual Programming for Concurrent Computing," *Proc. Int. Conf. on Parallel Programming*, Vol. 2, pp. 72-79, 1988.

[32] *Thor Tutorial*, VLSI/CAD Group, Stanford University, 1986.

[33] G. S. Whitcomb and A. R. Newton, "Data-Flow/Event Graphs," Memorandum No. UCB/ERL M92/24, Electronics Research Lab, University of California, Berkeley, CA 94720, USA, March 4, 1992.

Synthesis and Simulation of Digital Systems Containing Interacting Hardware and Software Components

Rajesh K. Gupta   Claudionor Nunes Coelho, Jr.   Giovanni De Micheli

Center for Integrated Systems
Stanford University, Stanford, CA94305.

Abstract

Synthesis of systems containing application-specific as well as reprogrammable components, such as off-the-shelf microprocessors, provides a promising approach to realization of complex systems using a minimal amount of application-specific hardware while still meeting the required performance constraints. We describe an approach to synthesis of such hardware-software systems starting from a behavioral description as input. The input system model is partitioned into hardware and software components based on imposed performance constraints. Synchronization between various elements of a mixed system design is one of the key issues that any synthesis system must address. In this paper, we consider software and interface synchronization schemes that facilitate communication between system components.

We present tools to perform synthesis and simulation of a system description into hardware and software components. In particular, we describe a program, Poseidon, *that performs concurrent event-driven simulation of multiple functional modules implemented either as a program or as behavioral or structural hardware models. Input to* Poseidon *consists of description of interacting functional models with their respective clock cycle times and the interface synchronization scheme chosen by the partitioner. The resulting software component is assumed to be implemented for the DLX machine, a load/store microprocessor. We present simulation examples and design of a graphics controller demonstrate the feasibility of mixed system synthesis.*

1 Introduction

In this paper we consider an approach to extend the high-level synthesis techniques to synthesize system designs using application-specific and reprogrammable components. We refer to the application-specific component as the *hardware* component, while the program running on the reprogrammable component as the *software* component. Our approach to system synthesis using hardware and software components is inspired by the fact that in practice most systems used in embedded control and telecommunication applications consist of application-specific hardware components as well as reprogrammable components. While most digital functions can be implemented by software programs, a major reason for building dedicated ASIC hardware is satisfaction of performance constraints. The performance constraints can be on the overall time (latency) to perform a given task or on the input/output data rates. Typically, the pure software implementations of a system design are often too slow to meet the imposed performance constraints. Therefore, specialized hardware chips are often needed to complement or assist the reprogrammable component on certain performance-critical tasks. Further, *mixed* system designs reduce the size of the synthesis task by reducing the number of application-specific chips required while at the same time achieving the flexibility of software reprogramming to alter system behavior. Such a flexibility is also important in achieving rapid prototyping of complex system designs where non performance-critical and unconstrained operations are shifted into a program running on an off-the-shelf microprocessor.

Whereas the focus of high-level synthesis techniques thus far has been to generate a purely hardware implementation of a system design either as a single chip or as an interconnection of multiple chips, each of which is individually synthesized [1] [2] [3] [4], attempts at system synthesis using both hardware and software components have been rare and limited to developing frameworks for facilitating the design process [5].

The problem of synthesis of mixed systems is fairly complex. There are many subproblems that must be solved before an effective synthesis system can be developed. Among the important issues are the problems of modeling of system functionality and constraints, determination of the boundary between hardware and software components in the system model, specification and synthesis of the hardware-software interface, and implementation of hardware and software components. In this paper, we summarize a systematic approach to automatic synthesis of mixed systems and focus on the issue of interface design and the synchronization mechanisms that are used to facilitate communication between system models and ensure correctness of system functionality.

Figure 1 shows organization of the CAD design system used for synthesis of mixed system designs. The input to our synthesis system is an algorithmic description of system functionality. We model system behavior using the *HardwareC* [6] language that has a C-like syntax and supports timing and resource constraints. *HardwareC* supports specification of unknown delay operations that can arise from data dependent decisions and external synchronizations. The *HardwareC* description is compiled into a **system graph model** based on data-flow graphs[6]. The system graph model consists of vertices representing operations, and edges which represent either a data dependency or a control dependency. Overall the system graph model is composed of concurrent data-flow sections which are ordered by the system control flow. The data-flow sections simplify the tasks of identification of concurrency in the system model, while use of control constructs such

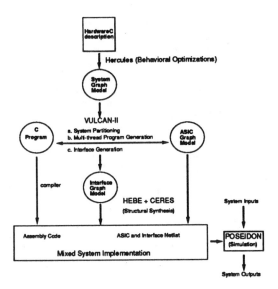

Figure 1: *System Synthesis Procedure*

as conditionals and loops obviate the need for a separate description of control flow. Associated with input/output statements, we specify corresponding constraints on input/output data rates. The input (output) rate constraints refer to the rates at which the data is required to be consumed (produced). The system graph model is input to *Vulcan-II* which partitions the system graph model into portions to be implemented either as dedicated hardware modules or as a sequence of instructions on a reprogrammable processor based on feasibility of satisfaction of externally imposed data-rate constraints. System partitioning constitutes an important phase of the system synthesis process. However, it is not the intent of this paper to delve into the partitioning issues. For an approach to system partitioning the reader is referred to [7]. Hardware synthesis of the models identified by *Vulcan-II* is performed by program *Hebe* [6]. For synthesis of the software component, we generate a corresponding C-description after generating a total order of operations in accordance with the partial order imposed by the graph model. The C-code is then compiled into assembly code for the target processor using existing software compilers. The interface synthesis is performed by *Vulcan-II* under timing constraints imposed on the system model. At the present time, *Vulcan-II* is a framework to carry out various synthesis tasks, and it is not yet an automated tool.

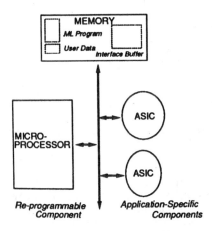

Figure 2: *Target System Architecture*

Target System Architecture

Figure 2 illustrates the *broad* features of the system architecture that is the target of our system synthesis approach. The target architecture consists of a general-purpose processor assisted by application-specific hardware components. The memory used for program and data-storage may be on-board the processor. However, the interface buffer memory needs to be accessible to the hardware modules directly. Because of the complexities associated with modeling hierarchical memory design, in this paper we consider the case where all memory accesses are to a single level memory, i.e., outside the reprogrammable component. The hardware modules are connected to the system address and data busses. Thus all the communication between the processor and different hardware modules takes place over a shared medium. Further, the mechanisms of data transfer between processor and application-specific components are constrained to those supported by the processor.

Concurrently executing hardware modules generate data that is consumed by the program(s) running on the processor. Due to the inherent serialization of operations implemented on the processor, any implementation must ensure that the data transfer across components takes place in an efficient manner that reduces the associated area and time overheads. The data transfer between the program(s) and the hardware modules is facilitated by the hardware and software synchronization mechanisms used. The choice of a data transfer scheme is determined by the individual execution rates of different models and control model used for scheduling various components. For example, a blocking transfer protocol may ensure correctness of the data-transfer but it may impose undue overheads on speed of execution of hardware modules. Whereas a non-blocking transfer may starve or overrun the interface buffers.

In the following sections, we outline our approach to system synthesis, and discuss different synchronization mechanisms used for synthesis for software and hardware components. The issue of synchronization between operations in a system model is closely related to the issue of communication between operations. For this reason, a choice for synchronization scheme is influenced by the selection of the communication scheme between system components. We first present the communication model supported in our synthesis system and then describe the synchronization schemes in context. We then address issues related to design of the hardware-software interface.

2 System Synthesis

Synthesis of application-specific hardware components under timing and resource constraints requires generation of a schedule of operations which satisfies the imposed timing constraints, an allocation of hardware resources that satisfies the resource constraints and finally the construction of a suitable control to facilitate hardware execution. Our model of hardware supports specification of data-dependent operations. Since data-dependent operations may offer unbounded delays it becomes necessary to schedule these operations dynamically. Therefore, we refer to data-dependent delay operations as points of synchronization in the system model. Our approach to synthesis of hardware under relative scheduling formulation has been described in detail elsewhere [6]. Briefly, the relative scheduling formulation makes it possible to achieve a data-driven dynamic schedule of operations with respect to a set of synchronization points (also referred to as *anchors* in [6]).

Here we focus on the problem of synthesis of the software component of the target system design. The software component is implemented as a program running on the onboard processor, i.e., the reprogrammable component. We assume that this program is small enough that it can be mapped to real memory, so that the issues related to virtual memory management can be ignored. As indicated in Figure 1, we start with a partition of the system graph model. System partitioning into hardware and software components is performed under the constraint that specified system input/output data rates can be supported by the final system implementation. One such partitioning approach relies on identifying and partitioning unbounded delay operations [7]. As a result of system partitioning we essentially have a set of concurrently executing hardware and software models. The software component consists of a set of concurrently executing routines, called *threads*. All threads begin with a point of synchronization and as such these are scheduled dynamically. However, within each thread of execution all the operations are statically scheduled. Therefore, for a given reprogrammable component the latency of each thread is known statically. As an example, data-dependent loops in software are implemented as a single thread with a data-dependent repeat count.

The problem of concurrent multi-thread implementation is well known [8]. In general, the program threads may be implemented either as a subroutines to a global task scheduler or as coroutines. However, in the context of mixed system designs where the processor is completely dedicated to the implementation of the system model and all software tasks are known statically, it is possible to use simpler and more relevant schemes to implement the software component. In the following, we present two schemes for implementation of the software component.

Software Implementation as Coroutines

Coroutines provide an attractive means of achieving concurrency between various program threads by reducing the cost of switching execution from one thread to another [9]. In this scheme, the reprogrammable component runs a task scheduler based on a priority assigned to various routines which are maintained in a co-operative, rather than hierarchical, relationship to each other. Each coroutine maintains a local state and *willingly* relinquishes control of the execution machine at points of synchronization. Coroutines provide a limited form of message passing via following two primitive operations: *resume* and *detach*. A coroutine switch consists in saving the current machine status and restoring the machine status of the next process to be executed. In the most general case, where any interruptions or exceptions may cause a context switch, all machine registers and flags should be saved. In case of an R/M processor, that is a processor that provides instructions with a register and memory operands such as 8086, the code for a coroutine based scheduler amounts to 34 instructions taking about 100 bytes. The coroutine switch takes 364 cycles when implemented for 8086 processor. By contrast, implementation of a global task scheduler using subroutines takes 728 clock cycles for the 8086 processor [10].

It is possible to reduce the overhead due to context switch if all the coroutine switches are explicit and known at the compile time. By making sure that during code optimization, variable lifetimes do not cross the coroutine boundaries, then the only register that needs to be saved is the *program counter* of the current coroutine and also only register that should be restored is the *program counter* of the next coroutine to be executed. The code for a such a scheduler on 8086 processor takes 103 cycles for each context switch. By comparison, on an load/store (L/S) machine, such as DLX [11], the code for task scheduler is reduced to 17 instructions (19 machine cycles), as opposed to the general case when all 64 registers would have to be saved requiring 192 instructions.

Software Implementation using Case Descriptions

In this approach, we merge different routines and describe all operations in a single routine using a method of description by cases [12]. This scheme is simpler than the coroutine scheme presented above. Here we construct a single program which has a unique case assignment for each point of synchronization. Thus each thread now corresponds to a case description of a rather large conditional in the final program. A global state register is used to store the state of execution of a thread. This method is restrictive since it precludes use of nested routines and requires description as a single switch statement, which in cases of particularly large software descriptions, may be too cumbersome. Overhead due to state save and restore amounts to 85 clock cycles for every point of synchronization when implemented on a 8086 processor. Consequently this scheme entails smaller overheads when compared to the general coroutine scheme described earlier. Corresponding overheads for the DLX processor amounts to 35 clock cycles for every point of synchronization.

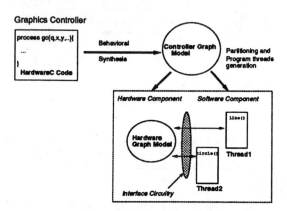

Figure 3: *System Synthesis Example*

In order to illustrate our system synthesis approach we consider synthesis of a graphics controller that provides for drawing of lines and circles given the end coordinates (and radius in case of a circle). Figure 3 illustrates some of the steps in synthesis of the graphics controller. The *HardwareC* description consisting of 457 lines of code is input to the behavioral synthesis phase. The resulting system graph model is input to *Vulcan-II*. As a result of system partitioning and program threads generation in *Vulcan-II*, the system design at this stage consists of interacting hardware modules modeled by the hardware graph models and a software component modeled by program threads. Next step is to synthesize the interface circuitry that would facilitate synchronization and communication between heterogeneous system components. Synthesis of interface circuitry is driven by the requirements imposed by system synchronization. We shall revisit this example in Section 4 to show how multiple program threads are synchronized with the concurrently operating hardware portions.

3 System Synchronization

A system design consists of various components which carry out operations in response to input data. An event refers to the execution of a data input/output operation. Synchronization in a system design refers to constraints on system design that ensure the partial ordering of events and operation executions imposed by the system model must be observed in *any* execution trace of the system model. Some synchronization constraints are needed to ensure correctness of the execution model, for example, all the data generated within the system model must be consumed in the time order in which it was generated. Typically this is guaranteed by appropriate choice of the execution semantics for the system model. Additional constraints may be needed to ensure correctness of a set of concurrently executing models. Further, some synchronization conditions may be externally imposed. For example, a certain *precedence* or *simultaneity* condition between execution of two operations imposed by the system control flow.

Communication Model

In the system graph model, communication between two operations is indicated by presence of an edge between respective operation vertices. When considering hardware synthesis, an edge between two operations may translate into either a physical wire connection, or it may be buffered and/or blocked to facilitate asynchronous communication. Final selection of data-transfer mechanism is made based on the data transfer requirement and how individual communicating models are implemented. However, note that in a mixed system implementation, due to inherently different rates of computation between hardware and software modules, it is necessary to allow multiple executions of individual models in order to achieve high system throughput. However, in presence of variation in rates of communication across different models appropriate buffering and handshake mechanisms may be required.

3.1 Software Synchronization

Our model of software component relies on the sequential execution of different threads of execution. Due to this serialization of the input system model, software synchronization is needed to ensure correct ordering of operations within the program threads and between different threads. A thread of execution already maintains an order of execution of its instructions, so a schedule of the operations is implicit to the sequential execution model of the instructions in a reprogrammable component. This solves the problem when a single thread of execution can be found for an entire description or among operations implemented in software belonging to the same thread - synchronization is only needed in points of synchronization and where the control is transferred between software and hardware. When data-dependent loops, and asynchronous message passing are present in the code, it may not always be possible to find a static schedule of the operations. If the order of execution can still be found, a single thread of execution could be determined that preserves the order in which the operations are executed. In case no such thread of execution can be determined, multiple threads of execution are required. In presence of multiple threads of executions (whether implemented as multiple programs or a single program using case descriptions described before) software synchronization consists of a mechanism to transfer control from one thread to another. In case of small number of threads, such a transfer can be done based on a statically defined priority of threads. For example, in case of two threads, control would simply switch from one thread to the other. In the general case, however, due to unbounded delay operations, we look for a *dynamic* scheduling of different threads of execution. Such a scheduling is done based on availability of data. Suppose we were to time stamp each data generated and also for each data request. Then the next thread of execution to be scheduled would be the one with the smallest request time stamp. Further, in order to maintain the correct order of data production and consumption, at any time the data being consumed is the one with the smallest time stamp. Such an scheme is implemented using a control FIFO that contains pointer to the next thread to be scheduled for execution [7]. Data transfer between two threads of execution can be implemented with shared memory or message passing. Shared memory can be facilitated by maintaining read and write pointers on each data-transfer. Such an scheme would add the overhead of maintaining and updating the read and write pointer for each data transfer across the program threads. Non-register based data-transfers (or data transfers which could culminate in control transfer) are well suited to be implemented as a queue connected with the control FIFO. On the other hand, register based transfers have the characteristic that once something

is written, the data may be read many times. It is possible to use processor registers to transfer information between threads. However, such a scheme requires global register assignments which are not available for reassignment by the compiler. A limited form of message passing can be achieved by using co-routine model of implementation described before.

3.2 Hardware-Software Synchronization

Synchronization between hardware and software components is determined by the data transfer requirements between the sender and the receiver. A data transfer between two models can be either blocking or non-blocking. A blocking transfer protocol requires the sender(receiver) to block transfer until the corresponding receiver(sender) is ready to receive(send) data. Blocking can also be made conditional so as to reduce the associated timing penalties due to blocking [13]. With respect to their overheads, a non-blocking transfer consumes the system bus bandwidth, whereas a blocking transfer costs not only system bus bandwidth but also additional control lines that are needed to implement the required handshake. Therefore, for lower system costs, it is necessary to implement blocking only when absolutely necessary. A blocking transfer protocol can be thought of as a non-blocking transfer with an infinitely deep queue buffer. The queue size may be bounded by addition of handshake signals that treat queue as the sender or receiver of data. Alternatively, in presence of specific constraints on rates of data transfer, the queues can be sized algorithmically [14].

For a given data-transfer edge in the system graph model, we first attempt to determine the rates of data production and consumption associated with the sender and receiver models. Such a rate determination requires specification of data rates for external inputs and outputs. In case of unknown or varying data rates, a blocking protocol for both sending and receiving ends is selected. Either sender or receiver end of a transfer can be made non-blocking if it can be determined that the corresponding operations are always slower. In case of perfectly matched data-rates a synchronous non-blocking protocol is selected. After selecting transfer protocols for different data-transfers across the hardware and software models, the interface circuitry can be synthesized using asynchronous and synchronous logic synthesis techniques [15] [16]. For a description of the interface architecture the reader is referred to [7].

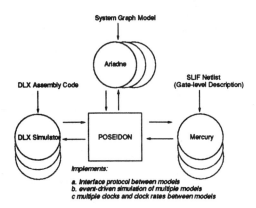

Figure 4: *Event-driven simulation of a mixed system design*

4 Simulation of Hardware-Software Systems

We have developed an event-driven simulator, named *Poseidon*, that performs concurrent simulation of multiple functional models

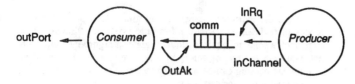

Figure 5: *Simulation Example 1*

implemented either as a program or as application-specific hardware. The software component is compiled into the assembly code of the target microprocessor. *Poseidon* currently supports simulation of assembly code for the DLX microprocessor, a RISC oriented load/store processor [11]. The hardware component of system design can be simulated either before or after the structural synthesis phase. The graph model before structural synthesis is simulated using program *Ariadne*. A gate-level description of the hardware component of system design is generated using structural synthesis techniques in program *Hebe* and simulated using program *Mercury*. Thus, *Poseidon* supports simulation of partially synthesized hardware modules along with the software component of the system design. *Poseidon* maintains an *event queue* which stores all simulation models sorted by their activation times. After simulating an event, the event is enqueued in the event queue. A system specification in *Poseidon* consists of following parts:

1. **Model declarations:** consists of declarations of the concurrently executing simulation models. Models can be either software or hardware models. Each model has an associated clock signal and clock cycle-time used for its simulation. It is assumed that the clock cycle-times are a rational multiple of each other. Further it is assumed that different models supply (latch) data at the interface using flip-flops at the interface edge-triggered by their respective clock signals.
2. **Model interconnections:** The interface between different system components is specified by *connections* among models. A connection between two models may be either a direct connection through a wire, or a port connection through a register or a queue. Queues can have multiple fanins and fanouts. Signal assignments indicate direct connections between respective models. For connections such as queues that require existence of additional control signals for synchronization, it is possible to group signals having identical synchronization requirements together for a given set of synchronization signals.
3. **Communication protocols:** Interface protocol for data-transfer is specified via *guarded* commands [17]. A guarded command is executed only when some precondition is true. Each precondition is specified as a logic equation of signal values and transitions. There are four commands recognized by the connection types. *Enqueue* and *dequeue* are used for queues port connections and *load* and *store* are used for register port connections.
4. **System outputs:** Outputs to be observed during simulation runs may be indicated by direct connections to the internal signals in the system model.

For illustration purposes, we consider a simple example of two models, Producer and Consumer connected by means of a finitely sized queue as shown in Figure 5. We consider two cases: one in which the producer model is implemented in software and consumer in hardware and the other in which producer, consumer implementations are reversed. Example 1 shows system specification for this example for the first case. The three first lines of the specification declare the models to be simulated. Model io models the external system inputs and outputs. The following parameter specifies the clock period of the clock signal associated with the respective model. A value of 3.0 for the consumer model

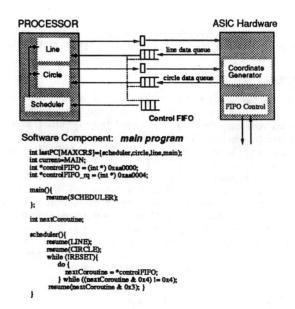

Figure 6: *Example 2: Graphics Controller Design*

indicates that consumer is implemented in an ASIC technology that uses a clock signal that is three times slower than the clock used by the reprogrammable component, which is usually a custom designed component. The system input/outputs are sampled here at the same rate as the consumer. The last two parameters specify the directory location where the model description can be found and the model name. The queue statement declares a queue named, comm, which is 4 bits wide and 3 words deep. We use rq and ak signals to implement a blocking communication protocol as indicated by the guarded commands. A '+' suffix indicates rising edge transition of the corresponding signal. A '-' suffix indicates falling edge transition. Symbols '&' and '!' indicate the boolean *and* and *not* operations.

Example 1: Specification of a producer-consumer pair (Figure 5).

```
# Models
model IO io 1.0 /local/ioDir IO;
model P dlx 1.0 /local/ProducerDir Producer;
model C mercury 3.0 /local/ConsumerDir Consumer;

# Connections
queue [4] comm[3];
C.RESET = IO.RESET;
C.r[0:0] = IO.r[0:0];

# Communication protocol
P.0xff004[0:0] = !comm.full;
C.b_rq = !comm.empty;
when (P.0xff000 wr+ & ! comm.full) do comm[0:3] enqueue P.0xff000[0:
when (C.b_ak+ & ! comm.empty) do comm[0:3] dequeue C.b[0:3];

# Outputs
IO.inChannel[0:3] = P.0xff000[0:3];
IO.outPort[0:3] = C.c[0:3];
IO.InRq = P.0xff000_wr;
IO.OutAk = C.b_ak;
```

In order to illustrate the effect of software and hardware-software synchronization mechanisms we now consider the design of the graphics controller introduced in Figure 3. Figure 6 shows the final implementation of the system design. The design consists of application-specific portions containing initial coordinate generators and control logic for controlFIFO and a software portion implemented on the DLX processor. The software component consists two threads of execution corresponding to the line and circle drawing routines. Both program threads generate coordinates that are used by the dedicated hardware. Input to *Poseidon* consists of gate-level description of the ASIC hardware, assembly code of the coroutines, and a description of the interface. Example 2 shows the *Poseidon* interface specification of the graphics controller design.

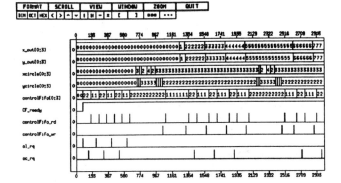

Figure 7: *Example 2: Simulation of Graphics Controller*

Example 2: Specification of the graphics controller interface (Figure 6).

```
model gc       io      1.0 DIR GraphicsController;
model ccoord   mercury 5.0 DIR gcircle;
model lcoord   mercury 5.0 DIR gline;
model mp       dlx     1.0 DIR main;
model CF       mercury 1.0 DIR control;

queue [1] lqueue[16], cqueue[16];
queue [3] controlFifo[2];

CF.r[0:0]    = lcoord.run[0:0] = ccoord.run[0:0] = gc.run[0:0];
CF.RESET     = lcoord.RESET = ccoord.RESET = gc.RESET;
CF.lrq[0:0]  = !lqueue.empty;
CF.lak[0:0]  = mp.0xff004_rd;
CF.crq[0:0]  = !cqueue.empty;
CF.cak[0:0]  = mp.0xee004_rd;
mp.0xee004[0:0] = !cqueue.empty;
mp.0xff004[0:0] = !lqueue.empty;

# Lqueue
when (lcoord.queue_rq+ & !lqueue.full) do lqueue[15:0] enqueue
     lcoord.queue[15:0];
lcoord.queue_ak = !lqueue.full;

when (mp.0xff000_rd+ & !lqueue.empty) do lqueue[15:0] dequeue
     mp.0xff000[15:0];
mp.0xff000[16:16] = !lqueue.empty;
...

# ControlFifo
when (CF.outline_rq+ & !controlFifo.full) do controlFifo[1:0] enqueue
     outline[1:0];
CF.outline_ak = !controlFifo.full;
...

# Output specification
gc.x_out[7:0]       = mp.0xff100[7:0];
gc.y_out[7:0]       = mp.0xff104[7:0];
gc.controlFifo[1:0] = controlFifo[1:0];
gc.CF_ready         = !controlFifo.empty;
...
```

Figure 7 shows some results of *Poseidon* simulations of the graphics controller. The hardware-software synchronization specified in Example 2 follows the scheme described in Section 3.2. The data-driven dynamic scheduling of program threads is achieved through the use of a 3-deep controlFIFO. In Figure 7, the circle and line drawing program threads are identified by id numbers 1 and 2 respectively. The program threads are implemented using the coroutine scheme described in Section 2. Signal `ol_rq` and `oc_rq` in Figure 7 indicate when the line and circle thread id's are being enqueued on data request from the software component. Variable time distance between `oc_rq` requests is due to data-dependent delay offered by the circle drawing routine in software. `controlFifo_wr` represents when a thread of execution enqueues its thread id in the control FIFO and then yields the execution to another thread. `x_out` and `y_out` are the coordinates generated by the line routine and `xcircle` and `ycircle` are the coordinates generated by the circle routine. `CF_ready` signals when the control FIFO is not empty and `controlFifo_rd` shows when the scheduler checks to see if the control FIFO is not empty (and eventually read it).

5 Conclusions

Synthesis using application-specific as well as reprogrammable components provides a promising extension of high-level synthesis approaches to realize complex system designs without corresponding increase in the magnitude of the synthesis tasks. Use of a reprogrammable component, however, poses interesting problems due to inherently serial nature of program execution that must interact with concurrently operating hardware portions. Thus synchronization between various components constitutes one of the most important issues in system synthesis.

We have presented an approach to synthesis of systems containing both application-specific and reprogrammable components and synchronization schemes that are used to facilitate data-transfer across concurrently executing system models. The resulting hardware and software components are simulated using an event-driven simulator, *Poseidon* which provides cycle-by-cycle simulation results. Since the selection of a synchronization scheme is driven by requirements of data-transfer rates, automatic selection of interface protocol can be made based on the data-rate constraints imposed on the system model. Work is underway to develop an automated tool to generate *Poseidon* interface specification and to synthesize appropriate interface circuitry once such a selection is made of all data transfers.

6 Acknowledgments

This research was sponsored by NSF-ARPA, under grant No. MIP 8719546 and, by DEC jointly with NSF, under a PYI Award program, and by a fellowship provided by Philips/Signetics. We acknowledge also support from ARPA, under contract No. J-FBI-89-101. The second author was partially supported by CNPq-Brazil under contract 200212/90.7.

References

[1] G. D. Micheli, D. C. Ku, F. Mailhot, and T. Truong, "The Olympus Synthesis System for Digital Design," *IEEE Design and Test Magazine*, pp. 37–53, Oct. 1990.

[2] J. Rabaey, H. D. Man, and *et. al.*, "Cathedral II: A Synthesis System for Multiprocessor DSP Systems", in *Silicon Compilation*, editor: D. Gajski , pp. 311–360. Addison Wesley, 1988.

[3] D. Thomas, E. Lagnese, R. Walker, J. Nestor, J. Rajan, and R. Blackburn, *Algorithmic and Register-Transfer Level: The System Architect's Workbench*. Kluwer Academic Publishers, 1990.

[4] R. Camposano and W. Rosenstiel, "Synthesizing Circuits from Behavioral Descriptions," *IEEE Transactions on CAD/ICAS*, vol. 8, no. 2, pp. 171–180, Feb. 1989.

[5] M. B. Srivastava and R. W. Broderson, "Rapid-Prototyping of Hardware and Software in a Unified Framework," in *Proceedings of the International Conference on Computer-Aided Design*, (Santa Clara), pp. 152–155, 1991.

[6] D. C. Ku and G. D. Micheli, "Synthesis of ASICs with Hercules and Hebe", in *High-level VLSI Synthesis*, editors: Raul Camposano, Wayne Wolf, pp. 177–203. Kluwer Academic Publishers, 1991.

[7] R. K. Gupta and G. D. Micheli, "System-level Synthesis Using Re-programmable Components," in *Proceedings of the European Design Automation Conference*, Mar. 1992.

[8] G. R. Andrews and F. Schneider, "Concepts and Notations for Concurrent Programming," *ACM Computing Surveys*, vol. 15, no. 1, pp. 3–44, Mar. 1983.

[9] M. E. Conway, "Design of a Separate Transition-Diagram Compiler," *Comm. of the ACM*, vol. 6, pp. 396–408, 1963.

[10] R. K. Gupta and G. D. Micheli, "System Synthesis via Hardware-Software Co-design," CSL Technical Report CSL-TR, Stanford University, 1992.

[11] J. L. Hennessey and D. A. Patterson, *Computer Architecture: A Quantitative Approach*, ch. 3. Morgan-Kaufmann, 1990.

[12] P. J. H. King, "Decision Tables," *The Computer Journal*, vol. 10, no. 2, Aug. 1967.

[13] I. C. Wand and A. J. Wellings, *Distributed Computing*, F. B. Chambers et. al. editors, ch. 14: Programming Languages, pp. 201–215. Academic Press, 1984.

[14] T. Amon and G. Borriello, "Sizing Synchronization Queues: A Case Study in Higher Level Synthesis," in *Proceedings of the 28th Design Automation Conference*, June 1991.

[15] T. H. Meng, *Synchronization Design for Digital Systems*, ch. Synthesis of Self-Timed Circuits, pp. 23–63. Kluwer Academic Publishers, 1991.

[16] G. Borriello and R. Katz, "Synthesis and Optimization of Interface Transducer Logic," in *Proceedings of the IEEE Transactions on CAD/ICAS*, Nov. 1987.

[17] E. W. Dijkstra, "Guarded Commands, Nondeterminacy, and Formal Derivation of Programs," *CACM*, vol. 18, no. 8, pp. 453–457, Aug. 1975.

An Engineering Environment for Hardware/Software Co-Simulation

David Becker, Raj K. Singh, Stephen G. Tell

Department of Computer Science
University of North Carolina at Chapel Hill

Abstract

We describe an environment supporting concurrent hardware and software engineering for high performance systems. In place of a conventional bread-boarded prototype, we used distributed communicating processes to allow software and simulated hardware to interact. We extended the Cadence Verilog-XL simulator to enable software debugging and testing using hardware simulation. The environment was proven during a successful system design.

1 Introduction

Many applications demand system designs with high performance packed in a small space. Prototyping practices such as wire-wrapping or bread-boarding cannot handle the speed and density of these high performance systems. Even the first prototype must be a printed circuit board. Debugging an assembled board is time consuming and difficult. Modifications are often impossible without building a new board. Hardware simulation handles these challenges with tools that analyze the design at speed and account for the effects of physical layout on signal integrity. A designer can expect the resulting system to be as good as the simulation of that system.

An accurate simulation cannot ignore the software components of a system. A design may require firmware for an embedded microprocessor or might interact with software on existing systems. Thorough hardware simulation needs the developing software to exercise all parts of the design and, ideally, the system software should be developed in parallel with the hardware. Developing software using a hardware prototype fails on both counts so a method is needed to exercise the simulated hardware with the real software.

We created a co-simulation engineering environment that links the software components of a system to the simulation of the hardware components. Using Unix networking facilities and the Verilog-XL simulator from Cadence Design Systems, the software components can control and react to events within the hardware simulation. This facility was applied to development of software for a high-speed custom communication interface, called a Network Interface Unit (NIU)[1].

The hardware and software components of the NIU were developed concurrently. The NIU hardware design was simulated with a Verilog model and exercised by the evolving software components, which in turn were tested by running them on the simulated hardware. The resulting circuit board worked at its initial power-up and the software performed as expected.

Before describing the simulation interface, a brief description of the NIU system is presented in section 2. The concurrent engineering environment is discussed in section 3 and two implementations are discussed in section 4. We conclude with the results of our effort and discuss possible directions for future work.

2 NIU system overview

The NIU is a custom high speed intelligent communication interface for a gigabit B-ISDN network[2]. The system interfaces a 800 Mbit/s HIPPI[3] link to the backplane ring network of the Pixel Planes 5 (PXPL5) heterogeneous graphics multicomputer[4]. The ring backplane is connected to the NIU and other boards through a "ring board" providing two 640 Mbit/s message-passing ports. A Cypress CY7C611 SPARC integer processing unit supervises the inbound and outbound hardware data pipelines and handles all protocol processing for the HIPPI packets.

Figure 1 shows the NIU software components and how they fit into the hardware design. The processor firmware responds to interrupts from the data pipelines and supervises the data flow with control and status registers. Monitor software, executing on the PXPL5 host workstation, communicates with the NIU processor by passing messages over the ring backplane.

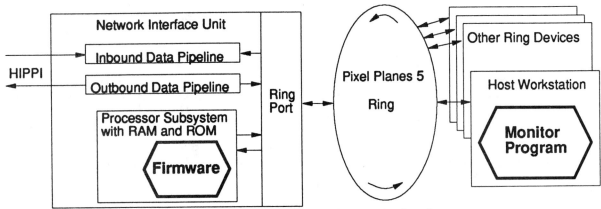

Figure 1. The NIU software components and their relation to the hardware.

The completed NIU circuit board consists of 619 parts on a 10-layer board connected by 1351 signals. The hardware model was written in 4000 lines of Verilog code. An additional 6000 lines of Verilog code modeled the logic devices including 60 PLDs. The two software components totalled 2000 lines of C++ code.

3 Simulation architecture

The goals we had for co-simulation were to be able to write the majority of the NIU software, minimize the changes needed when the real hardware arrived and use a minimum of project resources. The first solution considered was integrating our software into the simulator as user extensions to the Verilog simulator. Preventing the software components and the simulator proper from interfering with each other would have been very difficult. Another approach considered was purchasing or writing a complete model of the SPARC processor for the hardware simulation. Verilog could then simulate all the firmware but such models are expensive. This solution would not address development of the host monitoring code.

Our solution implements the software components as separate programs that use Unix interprocess communication (IPC) mechanisms to interact with the hardware simulation. The co-simulation environment is a layer of software below the system's software and hardware simulation components that encapsulates the interprocess communication links among the components. This solution does not accurately simulate the relative speeds of the hardware and software components, but we deemed this limitation acceptable in our application.

One key to creating a link between a software component and the hardware is selecting the appropriate level of abstraction for the interprocess communication. Our environment places no constraint on IPC message formats, but we find it best to model them after low-level software/hardware interaction, e.g. "put value A in register X." A hardware level model with messages like "signals x1, x3, x4 are asserted this clock cycle," would require significant simulation-specific software. Similarly, a higher level of abstraction with messages like "shut down pipeline", would increase the amount of software changes needed to switch to real hardware.

This link between the software component and hardware component has three parts. First, the *hardware interface functions* of the software component are rewritten to communicate with the simulation. Second, a *simulation module* must be modified to handle the communications with its corresponding software component. These first two parts are the end points of a link and must be customized for each link. The final part are the *simulator extensions* which connect the end points of the link. These extensions allow simulator modules to communicate over a TCP connection to software components.

The NIU co-simulation contains two instances of this technique: one link for the firmware and another for the host monitor software components. Figure 2 illustrates our environment as applied to the NIU co-simulation. The next section will describes how all parts of the software/hardware links were implemented in the NIU co-simulation.

4 Interface implementation

The NIU host monitor link has simple examples of the two parts of the co-simulation environment specific to each link: the hardware interface functions and the simulation module. The NIU processor firmware is a more complex example. The next two subsections will describe these two co-simulation links and examine the considerations in designing both the communication model and the interface at each endpoint.

Later, we describe the implementation of the IPC simulator extensions, which are largely independent of the interface issues handled in the other two components. Our original implementation of this environment required an IPC extension customized for each co-simulation link. The

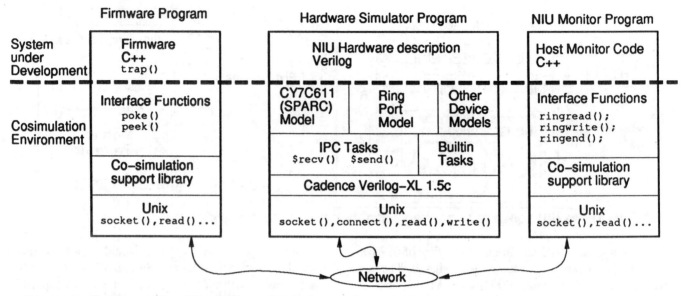

Figure 2. Components of the NIU co-simulation environment.

current environment employs a general-purpose simulator extension that is reused for all co-simulation links.

4.1 NIU host monitor code

The NIU and the other boards in Pixel Planes 5 send messages to each over a high speed ring. The ring packets are of unlimited length, sent a word at a time with a data valid signal and completed by an end of message signal. The IPC message format used by the host monitor co-simulation link reflects how the real ring packets function. Messages to the simulator are "put X in the write register and assert data-valid" and "assert end of message signal". Return messages are "X was written to the read register" and "end of message".

The format for a host monitor message is two words long where the first word is the message type identifier and the second is a data word. A simulated ring packet is sent by successively sending messages of type WRITEDATA for each data word in the ring packet. The hardware interface function that writes these data words to a register is replaced with a function that sends WRITEDATA messages to the simulation followed by a WRITEEND message. When the host expects a ring packet from the NIU, it waits for READDATA messages followed by a READEND message from the simulator that together form the simulated ring packet.

IPC messages are sent and received by a Verilog simulation module that represents the ring board connector in the hardware description. This module checks each clock cycle for an incoming IPC message and when one arrives, it asserts the appropriate signals on the simulated NIU ring connector pins. If the module sees outgoing data on the connector, it sends a message containing that data back to the host monitor program. The Verilog module is responsible for the correct signal timing on its input and output wires.

```
module ringconnector (/*...*/);
reg [31:0] ringserv_fd, msg_type, msg_data;
initial $makeserver(ringserv_fd, 7000);
always @(posedge CLOCK) begin
   $recv(ringserv_fd, msg_type, msg_data);
   if (msg_type==WRITEDATA)
     /* put signals for msg_data on connec-
     tor wires */
   else if (msg_type == WRITEEND)
     /*raise end of packet connector wire*/
   else if (msg_type == 0)
     /* no message; set connector write
     wires accordingly */
   if /* outgoing dataword valid */
     $send(ringserv_fd,READDATA,dataword)
   else if /* outgoing end wire raised */
     $send(ringserv_fd, READEND);
end
```

Figure 3. Ring connector module managing IPC messages

The host monitor software component of the NIU system was written using this co-simulation interface to exchange messages with simulated hardware. When the real hardware arrived, the functions to read and write words of a ring packet were rewritten to use the real hardware registers rather than send IPC messages. The rest of the code remained the same and ran correctly since it had already be tested.

4.2 NIU processor firmware

The processor firmware controls the NIU data pipelines through several control, status, and data registers mapped into the processor address space. Also, several data pipeline events interrupt the processor. In co-simulation, the firmware sends messages to the simulator of the form "poke X into address A", "peek what is in address A" or "trap handler done". The simulator sends messages of the form "address A holds X" or "interrupt X has occurred".

The firmware program uses the hardware interface functions `poke()` and `peek()` for all operations on memory-mapped I/O registers. These two functions are written to send IPC messages during co-simulation and are replaced with simple macros when using real hardware. The processor firmware has a function called `trap()` for trap handling, where the traps of interest are the hardware interrupts. In the real system, `trap()` is called from assembly language via the trap vector table. In co-simulation, an interface function checks for incoming messages and calls `trap()` asynchronously.

The simulator module of this link is a behavioral model of the SPARC processor's internal pipeline which generates accurate control signals for testing the memory and I/O devices on our board. Our model normally fetches instructions from memory, but treats all instructions as no-operation (NOP) instead of decoding fetched instructions. The decode stage of the pipeline checks for IPC messages from the firmware. If a POKE or PEEK message is received, a store or load cycle is executed instead of NOP. When a load cycle completes, a PEEKREPLY message with the result of the load is sent back to the firmware program. When external hardware asserts the interrupt lines of the processor model, an INTERRUPT message is sent to the program indicating which interrupt occurred. When the firmware returns a TRAPDONE message, a return from trap cycle is simulated.

An INTERRUPT message needs to interrupt the firmware asynchronously to allow trap handling to be realistically simulated. We used the Unix signal mechanism to duplicate this asynchronous behavior. The co-simulation support library linked with the firmware program requests Unix to send a signal when a message arrives from the simulator. This signal interrupts the firmware program and moves execution to a signal handling function which is part of the support code. This handler reads an INTERRUPT message and calls the firmware's trap handling function. If a PEEK is in progress, the signal handler waits for the PEEKREPLY before calling `trap()` because PEEK and PEEKREPLY comprise a single indivisible instruction. When the trap handler completes, a TRAPDONE message is sent to the simulator and Unix moves firmware execution back to where it was interrupted.

The most complex part of the firmware co-simulation was writing the processor pipeline model. The pipeline model, however, would also have to be written for other simulation strategies and only a small part of it is concerned with sending and receiving IPC messages. The bootstrap code and assembly language parts of trap handling were written after the board arrived. The firmware was linked to this assembly and ran on the new hardware just as it did on the simulation, only a bit faster.

4.3 Communication through the Verilog simulator

The Verilog hardware description language does not incorporate any interprocess communication facilities. It does have a Programming Language Interface (PLI) that allows user written C or C++ code to be called from within the simulation[5]. We used this PLI facility to add extensions to the simulator so the remote software programs could make a TCP connection to the simulator program and communicate with modules within the simulation. The first strategy we used involved specialized extensions for each co-simulation link. From that experience, we devised a general mechanism that we feel is much easier to use and describe.

The Verilog PLI facility associates a user written subroutine with a Verilog task name. Invoking a user written task in a Verilog program will cause the simulation to call the C++ function associated with that task name. These functions are called under several circumstances. One possible configuration is to have the C++ function called whenever an argument to the Verilog task changes during simulation. Our first communication mechanism is based on this form of user function.

Two tasks were added to Verilog in the original solution: `$sparc()` and `$ring()`. In the processor module, the pipeline executes NOP instructions unless the `$sparc()` task signals through one of its arguments that the firmware requests execution of an LD, ST or RETT instruction. The Verilog module and `$sparc()` communicate through a small set of arguments, shown in Figure 4.

```
initial begin
    // start up the SPARC interface task
$sparc(data, address, read_inst,
    write_inst, rett_inst, ResetL,
    cycle_done, PSR, traptype, Clock);
end
```

Figure 4. Parameters passed to `$sparc()` by the `cy7c611()` module.

Since the clock signal is an argument, the C++ code associated with `$sparc()` is called every clock cycle.

During each cycle the C++ code can read and write the signal lines connected to it. On the initial cycle, it connects to the firmware process. When the reset signal is negated, a RESET message is sent to the firmware process. On subsequent cycles, $sparc() checks for messages from the firmware process. The C++ code sets the $sparc() parameters to the instruction, address and data as needed for that cycle. When the cycle completes, $sparc() is signalled with the results so the C++ code can send a message back to the firmware process. With the exception of the clock, these arguments do not represent any actual electrical signals, but are only a communication mechanism between the simulation module and C++ code.

The ring port simulation module functions in a similar fashion, associating $ring() with its C++ code. When $ring() is initially called, it creates a socket to which the monitoring program can connect. Thereafter, on every clock cycle $ring() checks to see if the command program has connected. Once connected, $ring() relays messages between the simulated hardware port and the monitor program. When a WRITE message is received, it begins clocking the message into the port one word per cycle. When the hardware sends data to the port, $ring() stores it until the end of message signal is asserted. At the end of the message, a READ message is sent over the socket to the monitoring process.

A custom addition to the Verilog simulator for each link had several problems. One was writing a third piece of custom code for each link and another was the difficulty of modifying the simulator program. Further, the original C++ code performed some link-specific operations on the messages which were easily moved into Verilog or deemed unnecessary. Verilog is more suited for checking signals each clock cycle and sending acknowledgment signals. C++ is suited for making the networking system calls, so our new implementation extends Verilog with tasks only for generalized interprocess communication (IPC). The form of task/user function association used with these tasks arranges for the C++ function to be called every time its task is invoked during simulation.

The IPC facility added to Verilog allows modules to create TCP connections to remote Unix programs during the simulation. The $makeserver() task creates a Unix socket at the specified TCP port on the machine running the simulation. The software component of the co-simulation can connect to the simulation by using the IP address of the computer running Verilog and the TCP port number being served.

The $send() and $recv() tasks communicate with programs that connect to the TCP ports set up by $makeserver(). The send task takes a variable number of arguments, all of which are put into a packet and sent to the remote program. If the server is not connected to a remote program, the $send() call is ignored. Each call of the $recv() task checks for an arriving message. If a message has arrived, the arguments to $recv() are filled with the message data. When no remote program is connected or no incoming data is waiting, $recv() sets its first data parameter, conventionally used for a message type identifier, to zero and ignores the other parameters.

Some software components need to know the state of the simulation when they connect. The $connect() task returns true if the associated server is connected to a remote program. Start-up messages can be sent when the connection is established. The $disconnect() task terminates the current connection of the server and can be preceded by shutdown messages. Only one remote program can connect to a server at a time. After a server disconnects, a new connection can be polled for with the connect call. This mechanism is used by our processor co-simulation to start the firmware process when the processor reset signal is negated.

The software developed for the co-simulation environment includes Verilog simulator extensions, Verilog simulation modules and modified versions of the hardware interface functions. The Verilog modules for the processor and ring port were moderately complex, requiring about 700 lines of commented code for behavioral simulation. Only a small portion of this code is concerned with interprocess communications; the rest would have to be written for other simulation strategies as well. The IPC tasks added to the interpreter were written in about 200 lines of commented C++ code and the simulation interface functions for the software components required 300 lines of commented C++ code.

5 Conclusions and future work

We have developed an environment for the concurrent design and implementation of software controlled hardware systems. Independent processes executing the controlling software use interface function to connect to Verilog models of the hardware via custom code linked into the simulator. With this connection, the Verilog models of the software controlled devices can exhibit their high level behavior during simulation. Concurrent development allowed hardware and software division of labor to happen on the fly as the trade-offs became apparent. This should be especially useful for developing systems with embedded software components.

This environment was an important factor in the successful development of a high speed network interface circuit board, its processor firmware, and the command software running on a host computer. The final simulations of the hardware design were driven by completed software components. To prepare for the actual hardware, the software interface functions were recast from simulated form to hardware form. After these had been debugged with the delivered hardware, the entire system performed as expected.

Other models of communication may prove useful. Perhaps all the signal changes on the interface could be sent over the network for handling by other types of programs or other Verilog interpreters. Another potential direction is to add a thread package to the simulator and run the software processes as separate threads in the same process instead of running them as independent processes. This could simplify the communication and make the communication timing more predictable. It may also be possible to direct unmodified hardware interface functions to unmapped memory and handle the resulting page faults by emulating the I/O instruction with co-simulation messages. Another suitable application of the co-simulation would be to link a software microprocessor emulation to the board level Verilog simulation.

Acknowledgments

We would like to acknowledge the support of Cadence Design Systems, Inc. for providing us with the Verilog-XL software under their university program. The work reported in this paper is supported, in part, by the National Science Foundation and the Defense Advanced Research Projects Agency under cooperative agreement NCR 8919038 with the Corporation for National Research Initiatives. Support is also provided by Bell South and GTE Corp.

References

1. Raj K. Singh, S.G. Tell, and D. Becker, "VISTAnet Network Interface Unit: Prototype System Specifications," TR91-017, Department of Computer Science, University of North Carolina at Chapel Hill, 1991.

2. B. E. Basch, "VISTAnet: A B-ISDN Field Trial," *IEEE-LTS*, pp. 22-30, Aug 1991.

3. H. Fuchs, "Pixel Planes 5: A Heterogeneous Multiprocessor Graphics System Using Processor Enhanced Memories," *Computer Graphics*, vol. 23, no. 3, pp. 79-88, 1989.

4. X3T9.3 Task Group, "HIPPI Framing Protocol Specification (HIPPI-FP)," Revision 2.8, American National Standard for Information Systems, 24 June 1991.

5. Verilog-XL Version 1.5c, *Reference Manual*, Cadence Design Systems, June 1990.

A Hardware-Software Codesign Methodology for DSP Applications

ASAWAREE KALAVADE
EDWARD A. LEE
University of California,
Berkeley

The authors describe a systematic, heterogeneous design methodology using the Ptolemy framework for simulation, prototyping, and software synthesis of systems containing a mixture of hardware and software components. They focus on signal-processing systems, where the hardware typically consists of custom data paths, FSMs, glue logic, and programmable processors, and the software is one or more embedded programs running on the programmable components.

APPLICATION-SPECIFIC SYSTEMS are often the solution whenever general-purpose systems cannot meet portability, compactness, cost, or performance requirements. Important applications include communications, multimedia systems, consumer products, robotics, and control systems.

Although the term *application-specific* often summons the companion term *integrated circuit*, ASIC design is no longer the research challenge it once was. Concerted effort in design automation has resulted in sophisticated and widely used tools for routinely designing large special-purpose chips. Although continued improvement of such tools is valuable, much research is refocusing on the system-level design problem.

Two opposing philosophies for system-level design are emerging. One is the *unified* approach, which seeks a consistent semantics for specification of the complete system. The other is the *heterogeneous* approach, which seeks to systematically combine disjoint semantics. Although the intellectual appeal of the unified approach is compelling, we have adopted the heterogeneous approach. We believe that the diversity of today's design styles precludes a unified solution in the foreseeable future. Combining hardware and software in a single system implementation is but one manifestation of this diversity.

Even without good design tools, application-specific systems routinely mix diverse design styles. The component subsystems commonly found in these systems include the following:

- *Software or firmware.* An application-specific system with no software is rare. At the very least, a low-cost microprocessor or microcontroller manages the user interface. But it is also common to implement some of the core functions in software, often using somewhat specialized programmable processors such as programmable DSPs (digital signal processors). Occasionally, an application-specific system is implemented entirely in software. In that case, it is application-specific only if reprogramming by the user is not possible.
- *ASICs.* ASIC design has been the focus of synthesis tools, even so-called high-level synthesis tools,[1] for over a

decade. The tools have developed to the point that they can synthesize certain systems fairly quickly. However, this design approach is not always suitable. Complex, low-speed control functions are often better implemented in software. Moreover, many applications inherently require programmability—for example, to customize the user interface. ASICs also cannot accommodate late design changes, and iterations of the design are expensive. Thus, ASICs may not be suitable for implementation of immature applications. Increasingly, designers use one or more ASICs for an application's better-understood and more performance-intensive portions, combined with programmable processors to implement the rest.

- *Domain-specific programmable processors.* Design reuse can drive down development time and system cost. For this reason, introducing enough programmability into a circuit to broaden its base of applications is often advisable. Suitable applications range from a half dozen different algorithms to an entire domain such as signal processing. One can design the processor itself by jointly optimizing the architecture, the instruction set, and the programs for the applications. A major drawback of this approach is that it often requires a support infrastructure in the form of software and development systems to make reuse feasible.
- *Core-based ASICs.* This emerging design style combines programmable processor cores with custom data paths within a single die. Manufacturers of programmable processors are making the cores of their processors available as megacells that designers can use in such designs.[2] Alternatively, one can use the core of an in-house processor.[3] Core-based designs offer numerous advantages: performance improvement (because critical components are implemented in custom data paths and internal communication between hardware and software is faster), field and mask programmability (due to the programmable core), and area and power reduction (due to integration of hardware and software within a single core). These designs are especially attractive for portable applications, such as applications in digital cellular telephony.[4] Designing such systems requires partitioning the application into hardware and software and exploring trade-offs in different implementations. Design tools currently do not support this technique well.
- *Application-specific multiprocessors.* Some intensive applications have high enough complexity and speed requirements to justify development of an application-specific multiprocessor system. In these systems, the interconnections can be customized, along with the software and the selection of processors. Examples of design approaches for such systems range from homogeneous interconnections of off-the-shelf programmable components to heterogeneous interconnections of arbitrary custom or commodity processors.[5]

Other possible components include analog circuits and field-programmable gate arrays (FPGAs). Often, components are mixed within a single system design—for example, multiple programmable processors along with custom ASICs. Furthermore, processors need not be of the same kind.

The design issues for such systems include hardware-software partitioning of the algorithm, selection of the type and number of processors, selection of the interconnection network, software synthesis (partitioning, scheduling, and code generation), and custom-hardware synthesis. Tools that synthesize either complete software or complete hardware solutions are common, but tools that support a mixture are rare.

What is codesign?

We refer to the simultaneous design of the hardware and software components of these multifarious systems as hardware-software codesign. In a traditional design strategy, designers make the hardware and software partitioning decisions at an early stage in the development cycle and develop the hardware and software designs independently from then on. There is little interaction between the two designs because of the lack of a unified representation, simulation, and synthesis framework.

The new systems demand a more flexible design strategy, in which hardware and software designs proceed in parallel, with feedback and interaction between the two. The designer can then make the final hardware-software split after evaluating alternative structures with respect to performance, programmability, area, power, nonrecurring (development) costs, recurring (manufacturing) costs, reliability, maintenance, and design evolution. This strategy demands tools that support unified hardware-software representation, heterogeneous simulation at different levels of abstraction, and hardware-software synthesis.

DSP applications. We are developing a codesign methodology applicable to digital signal-processing and communications systems. DSP applications have the desirable feature of moderately simple algorithms, yet they demand high performance and throughput. Furthermore, exploring the cost and performance trade-offs between different implementations is critical for consumer products and portable applications, where DSP is being widely used.

We are focusing on the design of the hardware and software for such systems,

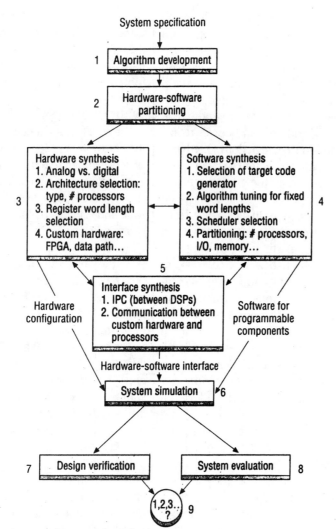

Figure 1. A generic codesign methodology.

in which the hardware typically comprises custom data paths, FSMs, glue logic, and programmable signal processors, and the software is the program running on the programmable components. A variety of commercial DSP microprocessors are suitable for most of the sophisticated signal processing required in these applications; one can synthesize custom hardware for some of the computation-intensive components.

A generic codesign methodology

Figure 1 diagrams a methodology for designing heterogeneous hardware-software systems. It is a general codesign scheme that does not apply to any framework in particular. The numbers in parentheses in the following discussion correspond to the stages shown in Figure 1.

The codesign task is to produce an optimal hardware-software design that meets the given specifications, within a set of design constraints (real-time requirements, performance, speed, area, code size, memory requirements, power consumption, and programmability).

Given a system specification, the designer develops an algorithm, using high-level functional simulations (1), without any assumptions about implementation (such as available instruction set or register precision). For instance, in the design of a modem, the designer would experiment with different algorithms for timing recovery at this stage.

The designer then partitions the algorithm into hardware and software (2), guided by speed, complexity, and flexibility requirements. Components that need field programmability or that are inherently better accomplished in software are assigned to software implementations. For instance, in the design of a transceiver, a software realization of the coder/decoder would allow changing the constellation easily, enabling the support of multiple modem standards. Operations with critical execution speed are allocated to hardware. Phase detectors, for example, can be implemented with the CORDIC (coordinate rotation digital computer) algorithm,[3] which is suitable for compact VLSI designs. Of course, to explore the design space, the designer would iterate the partitioning process.

Partitioning is followed by hardware (3), software (4), and interface (5) synthesis. The three are closely linked; changing one has immediate effects on the others. Hardware design decisions include selection of the programmable processor (directly affecting selection of the code generator) and determination of the number of processors and their connectivity (influencing code partitioning and software-hardware interface synthesis). In custom-hardware synthesis, the choices range from generating custom data paths to generating masks for FPGAs. In designing custom data paths, the designer must choose the register word lengths. Some hardware structures (filter realizations, for instance) may meet performance requirements with smaller register widths than those estimated for other structures.

On the software front, in the case of fixed-point processors, some algorithmic modifications might be necessary to minimize the effects of finite precision (such as limit cycles and quantization errors). Software synthesis involves partitioning and scheduling the code on multiple processors and synthesizing the code for interprocessor communication. These decisions depend on the architecture selected. The designer partitions among different processors by optimizing cost functions such as communication cost, memory bandwidth, and local and global memory sizes.

Interface synthesis involves adding latches, FIFOs, or address decoders in hardware and inserting code for I/O operations and semaphore synchronization in software. The typical way of solving this cyclic problem is to start with a design and work on it iteratively to explore different options.

Once the hardware and software components are synthesized, the next step is a heterogeneous simulation (6). In particular, the simulated hardware must run the generated software. This involves interaction of a number of different simulators if various specification languages are used.

The designer then uses the simulation results to verify (7) that the design meets the specifications. Having performed the hardware and software synthesis for a particular design choice, the designer can estimate area, power, critical path, component and bus utilization, and other factors. After using these estimates to evaluate the design (8), the designer may repartition the system to try out different options (9). Thus, the entire process is iterative.

The Ptolemy framework

The generic codesign methodology we have described requires a unified framework that allows the hardware and software components to be integrated from the specification through the synthesis, simulation, and evaluation phases. The Ptolemy design environment[6,9] is such a framework.

Ptolemy is a software environment for simulation and prototyping of heterogeneous systems. It uses object-oriented software technology to model each sub-

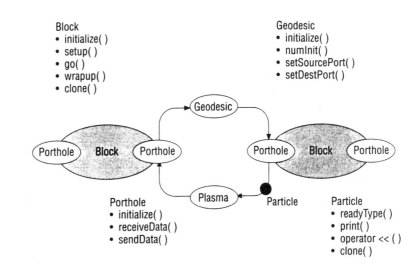

Figure 2. Block objects in Ptolemy send and receive data encapsulated in particles to and from the outside world through portholes. The geodesic class handles buffering and transport, and the plasma class handles garbage collection.

system in the most natural and efficient manner, and it has mechanisms to integrate heterogeneous subsystems into a whole.

Internal structure of Ptolemy. Figure 2 shows the structural components of Ptolemy. The basic unit of modularity in Ptolemy is the block. Portholes provide the standard interface through which blocks communicate. A block contains a module of code (the "go()" method) that is invoked at runtime, typically examining data present at its input portholes and generating data at its output portholes. The invocation of go() methods is directed by a scheduler that determines the operational semantics of a network of blocks. Blocks communicate using streams of particles, which form the base type for all messages passed. The geodesic class establishes the connection between portholes. The plasma class manages the reclamation of used particles.

The lowest level (atomic) objects in Ptolemy are of the type star, derived from block. A galaxy, also derived from block, contains other blocks. A galaxy may contain both galaxies and stars. A target, also derived from block, controls the execution of an application. In a simulation-oriented application, it will typically invoke a scheduler to manage the order in which star methods are invoked. For a synthesis-oriented application, it can synthesize assembly code for a programmable DSP, invoke the assembler, and run a simulation. A universe, which contains a complete Ptolemy application, is a type of galaxy.

Heterogeneous simulation. Ptolemy accomplishes multiparadigm simulation by supporting a number of different design styles encapsulated in objects called domains. A domain realizes a computational model appropriate for a particular type of subsystem. A domain in Ptolemy consists of a set of blocks, targets, and associated schedulers that conform to a common computational model—the operational semantics that govern how blocks interact. The domain and the mechanism of domain coexistence are the primary features that distinguish Ptolemy from otherwise comparable systems such as Comdisco's SPW and Bones, Mentor Graphic's DSPstation, and the University

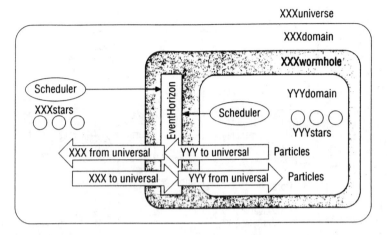

Figure 3. *The universal EventHorizon provides an interface between the external and internal domains.*

of New Mexico's Khoros System.[10] Some of the simulation domains that Ptolemy supports are synchronous dataflow (SDF),[11] dynamic dataflow (DDF), discrete event (DE), and digital-hardware modeling (Thor).[12]

The domain class by itself gives Ptolemy the ability to model subsystems differently, using a model appropriate for each subsystem. It also supports mixing models at the system level to develop a heterogeneous system with different levels of abstraction. The mixture is hierarchical. Any computation model can be used at the top level of the hierarchy. Within each level, blocks can contain foreign domains. Ptolemy uses the object-oriented principles of polymorphism and information hiding to achieve modular interoperability. This hierarchical heterogeneity is quite different from the simulation backplane concept, implemented in Viewlogic's SimBus system, for example. A simulation backplane imposes a top-level computation model through which all subsystems interact.

Figure 3 shows the top view of a universe associated with a domain called "XXX," associated with which are XXXstars and an XXXscheduler. A foreign subsystem that belongs to the YYYdomain and has its own set of YYYstars and a YYYscheduler is embedded in this XXXdomain universe. This foreign subsystem is contained entirely within an object called an XXXwormhole. An XXXwormhole is a type of XXXstar, so at its external interface it obeys the operational semantics of the external domain, but internally it consists of an entire foreign subsystem. A wormhole can be introduced into the XXXdomain without any need for the XXXscheduler to know of the existence of the YYYdomain.

The key to this interoperability is the interface between the internal structure of a wormhole and its external environment. This interface, called the EventHorizon, is a minimal interface that supports exchange of data and permits rudimentary, standardized interaction of schedulers. Each domain provides an interface to the EventHorizon, and thus gains an interface to any other domain. Additional details on the operation of the EventHorizon and a complete description of the Ptolemy kernel are available in other works.[6,9]

A second mechanism in Ptolemy supports heterogeneity in a different way. A synthesis or simulation operation is managed by an object called a target. For example, if we are synthesizing a software implementation, the target is responsible for generating the code, compiling or assembling it, possibly downloading it into attached hardware for execution, and managing the execution. Instead of attached hardware, however, the target can consist of simulated hardware implemented in another Ptolemy domain. The target, therefore, is the executive manager of a cosimulation.

We now describe the SDF and Thor simulation domains, used in our co-design methodology, in further detail.

Synchronous dataflow domain. SDF is a data-driven, statically scheduled domain. *Data-driven* means that the availability of particles on the inputs of a star enables the star for execution. Stars with no inputs are always enabled. *Statically scheduled* implies that the firing order of the stars is determined only once during the start-up phase, and this schedule is periodic. The SDF domain supports simulation of algorithms and also allows functional modeling of components such as filters and signal generators.[13]

Thor domain. Implementing the Thor simulator, a functional simulator for digital hardware, the Thor domain simulates circuits from the gate level to the behavioral level. Thor thus gives Ptolemy the ability to simulate digital components ranging in complexity from simple logic gates to programmable DSP chips.[14] It is essentially equivalent to many event-driven, register-transfer-level circuit simulators available commercially. We use Thor in preference to a commercial system only because, in our experimental framework, we require access to the source code, and we wish to freely distribute our software to disseminate the ideas embodied in it.

We have developed a Thor model in Ptolemy for the Motorola DSP56000. The setup() method of the DSP star under Thor simply establishes a socket connection with Sim56000, Motorola's stand-alone simulator for the DSP56000. Sim56000 is different from most other processor simulators. It is a complete behavioral simulator for the processor, not just an instruction set simulator or a bus functional model. Thus, it accurately models the behavior of each of the processor's signal pins, while executing the code. Instruction set simulators do not support this feature of modeling the pin-level behavior. Bus functional models just emulate a given pattern of the bus activity; they do not execute any code.

During its go() method, this star translates the logic values present at the processor's pins into values meaningful to the simulator, transfers them to Sim56000, and commands the simulator to advance the simulation by one step. It waits for the simulator to transmit the new logic values back to the processor pins and continues with the rest of the simulation. By interrupting the simulator window, we can halt the simulation at any time to examine intermediate register contents. Figure 4 illustrates this behavior.

Besides processors and digital logic, we must also model analog components such as A/D and D/A converters and filters that operate in conjunction with the digital hardware. We can most conveniently represent these analog components by their functional models, using the SDF domain. Often, abstract functional modeling of components such as filters is sufficient—detailed behavioral modeling is not needed—particularly if the final implementation will use an off-the-shelf component with well-understood behavior. We use the wormhole mechanism discussed earlier to mix the data-driven, statically scheduled SDF models of analog components with event-driven, logic-valued Thor models of digital components in a single simulation. Thus, Ptolemy makes analog and digital hardware modeling at different levels of abstraction possible.

Retargetable code generation. Given a block diagram description of an algorithm, *code generation* refers to the synthesis of software corresponding to

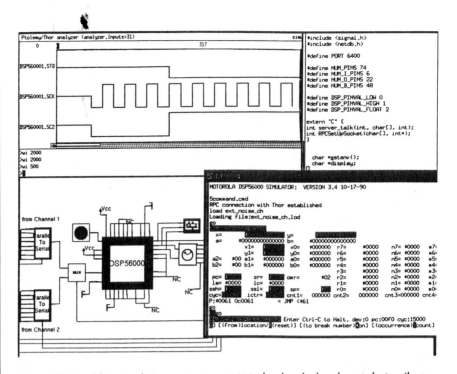

Figure 4. The Ptolemy simulation environment. We develop the hardware design (bottom left), containing a programmable DSP, using the Thor and SDF domains. Running the DSP star invokes the Motorola DSP56000 simulator (bottom right), which executes the code. For timing verification, a Thor logic analyzer (top left) monitors the output on the serial port of the DSP. The Ptolemy C++ code for the DSP block is shown at top right.

the algorithm. This software can be synthesized for a variety of target processors. Our research group has implemented assembly code generators for the Motorola DSP56001 (a 24-bit fixed-point processor) and DSP96002 (a floating-point processor); our group has also implemented C and C++ code generators suitable for a wider variety of processors.[7] The target processors can take a range of configurations: uniprocessor systems, shared-memory parallel architectures, shared-bus parallel architectures, and message-passing architectures. The target object encapsulates any code generation capabilities peculiar to a particular target architecture, such as the interprocessor communication mechanism. Thus, it is possible to synthesize software for the new configuration just by specifying a new target.

In Ptolemy, code generation domains are subdivided according to the language synthesized. Hence, an SDF domain synthesizing C code is called CGC (code generation in C), and a domain synthesizing assembly code for the DSP56000 family is called CG56. Each such domain has a simple default target that defines how the code generated for individual stars is collected, specifies and allocates resources such as memory, defines code necessary for initialization of the platform, and optionally compiles or assembles it. More elaborate targets can be derived from the simple targets. The more elaborate targets generate and run code on specific hardware platforms or on simulated hardware.

Code generation for programmable processors (software synthesis). One can use the CG56 and CG96 domains to synthesize assembly code for architectures (specified by the target) consisting of one or more programmable DSPs (the

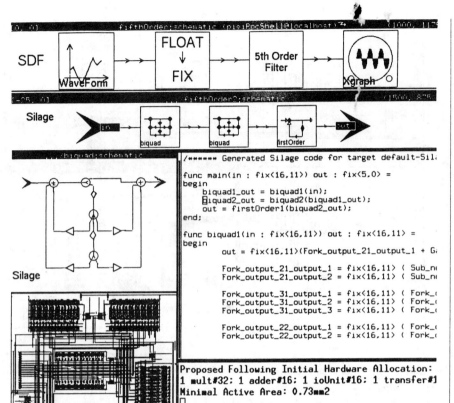

Figure 5. The top window shows the SDF universe with a Silage galaxy for a fifth-order filter. The filter is implemented in the Silage domain (second window from top) as a cascade of two biquad sections and a first-order filter. Each biquad (mid-left) is implemented with discrete components. The Silage code generated by Ptolemy appears on the right, the layout at the bottom left, and hardware estimates for the custom data path for the biquad section (generated by Hyper) at the bottom right.

a functional or applicative language; each operation can be thought of as applying a function on a set of inputs and generating a set of outputs. One can specify the numerical precision for the inputs and outputs of these functions, as well as the precision for internal computations. In addition, one can specify multirate computations such as down-sampling and up-sampling. These properties make Silage an attractive language for high-level specification of DSP applications. Furthermore, a number of high-level synthesis systems that use Silage for specification of their inputs are available.[3,17] As a result, the Silage code generated by Ptolemy provides a link to these synthesis tools, thereby permitting custom-hardware synthesis. Thus, the function of the Silage domain is twofold: custom-hardware synthesis and bit-true modeling of synthesized custom hardware.

When a Silage galaxy is nested in an SDF universe, the blocks in the SDF domain send data to the Silage galaxy. On processing this data, the Silage galaxy generates outputs that can be further processed in the SDF domain. Thus, Silage galaxies in the SDF domain represent function application. Such an SDF-Silage system runs as follows:

1. The setup() phase generates Silage code. The designer then feeds this code to high-level synthesis tools such as Hyper[17] to synthesize a custom data path. The designer obtains estimates of the critical path, power consumption, and area. A single Silage star (generated by compiling the Silage code and dynamically linking it into the running simulation) automatically replaces the Silage galaxy. The portholes of this Silage star are of type "fix." The designer can specify the precision of the data along these portholes, as well as the precision of intermediate results. This capability makes it possible to run bit-true simulations for experimenting with different

Motorola 56000 and 96000 respectively). Alternatively, one can use the C code generation domain to synthesize C code, which can be compiled to the desired target processor. We have also implemented multiprocessor code generation in Ptolemy: a suite of schedulers that use properties of the SDF computation model to partition the code onto multiple processors, schedule code execution, and insert code for interprocessor communication.

For example, MultiSim56000 is a multiprocessor target that controls code generation for a multiprocessor system in a shared-memory configuration (Figure 7 on p. 25). The designer provides the number of processors and the shared-memory address to this target. The target then invokes the appropriate parallel scheduler, which partitions and schedules the code onto the processors, inserts semaphore synchronization code, and generates assembly code for each processor. An example we present later in the article illustrates this target in further detail.

We are working on the design of heterogeneous multiprocessor targets, in which more than one type of programmable processor can be used. Sih has developed parallel schedulers that use different cost functions for partitioning and scheduling the code on heterogeneous programmable components.[15]

Code generation for hardware synthesis. We have developed a Silage[16] code generation domain for Ptolemy. Silage is

word lengths.
2. The go() phase simulates the complete system. The new Silage star (corresponding to the Silage galaxy) models the functionality of the physical hardware. If Silage is nested within a timed domain (such as Thor), the designer uses critical-path estimates obtained from the synthesis tools to model the hardware execution delay.

The Silage domain thus permits: 1) high-level simulation (for functional verification), 2) bit-true simulation (for analysis of finite-precision effects, fine-tuning of the algorithm for finite word lengths, and determination of optimal word lengths), and 3) synthesis of custom data paths for parts of the algorithm committed to hardware implementation. Figure 5 illustrates these capabilities.

Ptolemy and hardware-software codesign

This section describes how we apply the components of Ptolemy to the generic hardware-software codesign methodology outlined earlier. Figure 1 is redrawn in Figure 6 to show how the Ptolemy domains support the phases of the codesign process.

We carry out high-level simulations and algorithm development (1) in the SDF domain. We perform hardware-software partitioning (2) manually, specifying whether a block is to be implemented in hardware or software. This information generates wormholes for each of the two types of implementation: The algorithm components to be implemented in custom hardware are grouped in a Silage wormhole; the parts to be implemented as software running on programmable processors are clustered into a CG wormhole corresponding to the target processor (CG56, CG96, and so on).

We then make a preliminary hardware design decision (3) regarding the number of processors to be used. (Fur-

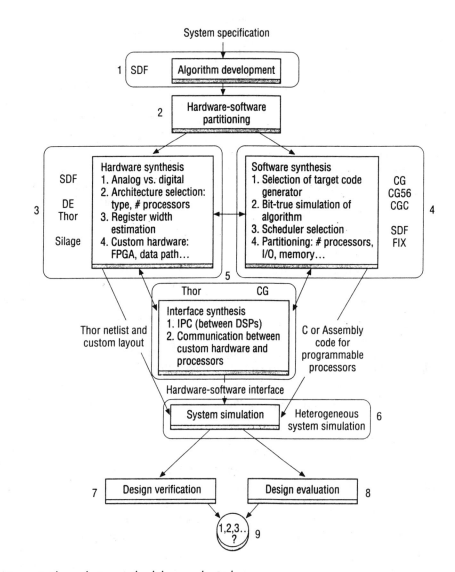

Figure 6. The codesign methodology under Ptolemy.

ther simulations may prove that this was not a good choice, and we can make changes iteratively.) In the case of multiprocessor systems, we then select the system configuration, thus determining the interface (5) between DSPs (such as a shared multiported memory, a shared bus, or serial communication). Next, we construct a Thor simulation model for this architecture, using Thor models for the DSP chips and glue logic. Functional models for analog components such as A/D converters and analog front ends are developed in SDF and added to the Thor model as wormholes. We carry out bit-true simulations for the components allocated to custom hardware in the Silage domain. These simulations give an estimate of the optimal word lengths. Finally, we feed the generated Silage code to synthesis tools to estimate the critical path, power, and area. The Silage blocks are added to the system simulation model to represent the custom hardware.

On the software (4) side, selection of the programmable processor determines the code generation domain. We then select the hardware-software interface (5). For instance, the DSP can communicate with external hardware either through one of its serial ports or through memory-mapped I/O. Based on the hardware-software interface and the interprocessor interface, we select an appropriate code generation target and generate the assembly code. We insert interface and synchronization code in the program, at the same time adding hardware components for the interface. For example, serial I/O requires a serial-to-parallel register and appropriate clocking circuitry. Similarly, for memory-mapped I/O, we insert address decoders and latches.

We then analyze the code size to determine whether the program fits in the on-chip program memory. If not, an external memory is required, and we add a corresponding Thor memory model to the hardware model. Alternatively, we can try different schedulers (to replace multiple instances of the code by efficient loops, for example), or we can repartition to reduce the software load by shifting some components to hardware. To identify computation-intensive components, we determine the number of cycles necessary to execute the critical sections of code. To make sure real-time requirements are met, we compare the time available between consecutive samples to the number of cycles required to process one sample. If the requirements have not been met, we can either repartition the system or select alternative configurations.

Next, we run a mixed-domain simulation (6), using the components synthesized so far. The processors and glue logic are simulated in the Thor domain, custom-synthesized hardware is modeled via a bit-true Silage galaxy (with execution delay equal to the critical path), and analog components are represented by their functional models in SDF. The DSPs run the programs synthesized by the code generator.

We manually examine the simulation results to check whether performance constraints are satisfied (7 and 8). We can explore other design choices by repeating the procedure (9), making a final selection on the basis of the user's requirements.

At present, the infrastructure for these phases of the design process is available in Ptolemy. Work is under way toward automating some of these stages. We are developing a tool called the Design Assistant, which will automatically create the wormholes for the hardware and the software blocks and insert the interfaces. It will also assist in analysis and verification (currently done manually) and enable easy exploration of the design space. The Design Assistant will formalize and partially automate the design process, building upon the basic facilities that already exist in Ptolemy.

Hardware-software codesign examples

Two examples demonstrate the codesign methodology under Ptolemy. The first illustrates a methodology for multiprocessor-system design; the second, an ASIC design based on a programmable-DSP core.

Multiprocessor-system design methodology. To meet real-time constraints, many signal-processing applications require multiple processors. We have selected a demonstration application that requires scarcely more than one processor for a fully functional implementation. As the technology improves, one processor will eventually be more than adequate for this application. Nonetheless, it has just enough complexity to illustrate our methodology.

Consider the design of a full-duplex telephone channel simulator.[8,13,18] It models the behavior of a physical telephone channel by introducing impairments such as linear distortion, frequency offset, phase jitter, nonlinear distortion, and noise. Voice-band data modem designers use it to test modem performance under a variety of channel responses. Satisfactory performance under these impairment conditions provides robust assurance of modem performance on most telephone lines in the public switched telephone network.

The goal in our example is to design an implementation for this bidirectional channel simulator. Figure 7a shows the algorithm for one direction of the full-duplex channel simulator (in SDF). Similar processing would be performed on the signal coming in the opposite direction.

To test the modems under different channel conditions, we must be able to change the degree of various impairments. Thus, we want to incorporate as much functionality in software as possible. As a first cut, we partition the algorithm so that it is implemented entirely in software. We select the DSP56001 as the target processor. As a conservative choice, we design the telephone channel simulator around two DSPs, each handling one direction of impairments. The hardware thus consists of two DSPs, A/D and D/A converters, and other glue logic. The software is the program running on the two processors.

A simple design is to have the two processors run identical code, each impairing the signal in one direction. The algorithm is provided to a single-processor code generator (CG56). The code generator synthesizes code for one processor, and the same code runs on the other processor. However, analysis of the generated code shows that the code size is more than the capacity of the DSP's on-chip program memory. Two alternatives are possible: use an external program memory for the two processors, or partition the code onto the processors so that each implements a part of the algorithm (thereby requiring less code space).

The second option seems more cost effective, so we explore it next. In this case, the first processor creates some distortion in the signal received from the sending modem and passes the partially impaired signal to the other processor. The second processor then adds the remaining distortion components and sends the impaired signal to the receiving modem.

The next design decision is the selection of the interface between the two processors. Again, two options are available: communication over the serial port or use of a shared memory. Selecting the latter, we build a hardware model for the system. We present the algorithm to the code generator again, with the new target (MultiSim56000): a two-processor system, with the processors communicating via a dual-ported shared memory.

Figure 7 illustrates this design flow. We provide the algorithm description (Figure 7a) to the DSP56001 code generator (Figure 7b). MultiSim56000 is the code generation target. Figure 7b shows some of the parameters used by this target. The code generator partitions the algorithm and generates code for the two processors. In the resultant code, the first DSP performs linear distortion and phase shift operations, and the second adds Gaussian noise and second and third harmonic distortions.

We develop the hardware description of the system in the SDF and Thor domains. The top-level design, consisting of two processors and a shared memory, is developed in the Thor domain (Figure 7c). To accommodate signals from both directions, a multiplexer-demultiplexer combination is added at the input and output of the first and the second processor respectively. The analog components (A/D and D/A) are modeled in SDF (Figures 7d-7f) and added to the Thor universe as wormholes.

When we run the Thor universe (Figure 7c), the two DSPs run the code generated by the code generator (code0.asm and code1.asm). We observe the transmitted and received (impaired) signals at both ends of the channel and verify the design.

We can repeat this process for different interprocessor communication mechanisms or different hardware-software partitions. Author Kalavade's de-

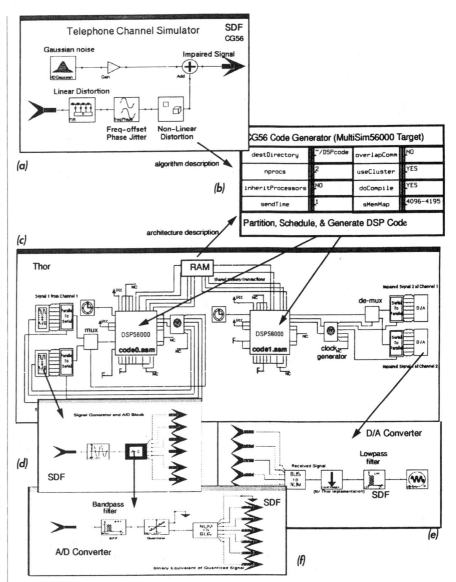

Figure 7. Telephone channel simulator: algorithm specification (a); code generator (b); digital (c) and analog (d-f) hardware components.

tailed presentation of this case study describes and evaluates multiprocessor as well as system-level design options.[8]

Programmable-DSP core-based ASIC design. Figure 8 (next page) shows the transmitter and receiver for a modem. We shall concentrate on the design of the receiver rather than the transmitter—the receiver is usually the more challenging of the two. Channel equalization, carrier recovery, timing re-

covery, and symbol decoding are the critical components of the receiver.

In the design of a modem to be embedded in a portable multimedia terminal, size, speed, and power are important considerations. Also, some programmability is necessary to allow changes in the signal constellation and fine tuning of the algorithm. In addition, the DSP used in the modem might also be used for other tasks in the terminal, such as front-end audio processing, fax,

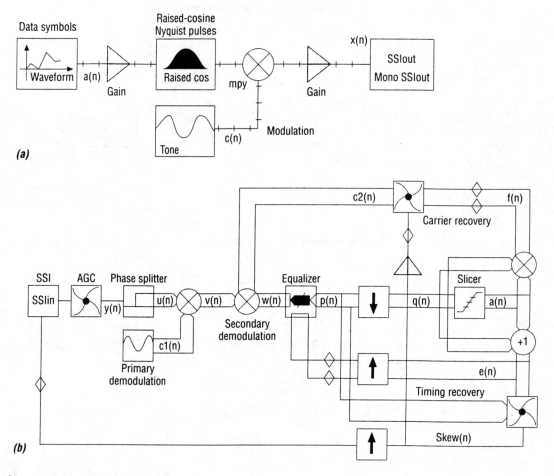

Figure 8. Modem transmitter (a) and receiver (b).

or voice mail. Thus, the design calls for high performance as well as programmability. The programmable-DSP core-based ASIC approach seems to be suitable for such a design.

Figure 9a shows a system consisting of two modems communicating over a channel. Our goal is to generate an implementation for the receiver section of one modem. The algorithm for the receiver section is shown in Figure 8b. As a first cut in the design of the receiver section, we map the entire algorithm to software, and thus input it to a single-processor code generator (Sim56). On analyzing the generated code, we find that it does not meet real-time requirements (the number of cycles between samples is less than the number required to process one sample). We then partition the algorithm so as to implement part of it in custom hardware.

Next, we model the part of the algorithm to be implemented in hardware (say the AGC block) in the Silage domain and the part to be implemented as software in CG56. When the Silage model is run, Silage code corresponding to that part of the algorithm is generated. This Silage code is passed to the Hyper synthesis tools, which generate the layout and give estimates of the area and execution time. When the CG56 model is run, DSP56001 assembly code is generated for the software part of the algorithm.

Next, we develop a hardware model for the receiver. The top-level description is in Thor (Figure 9b). The channel signal is passed to an A/D interface (modeled in SDF). The digitized signal is passed to a Silage galaxy representing custom hardware. Figure 9c shows the internal structure of the Silage galaxy. The "delay" block models the hardware execution delay (computed by the synthesis tools earlier). The signal from the custom hardware is transmitted to the DSP's serial port.

We implement the rest of the algorithm as software running on the DSP. Figure 9d shows the code generated by the CG56 target (Sim56). The DSP and glue logic are implemented in Thor. The receiver can thus be implemented partly in software (as the program running on a programmable DSP) and partly in custom hardware (as a custom data path). We can simulate the system model to verify functionality.

Using the DSP-core technology, we can synthesize this receiver as a single chip, with the custom data path, DSP core, hardware-software interface circuitry, and glue logic integrated in a single die. This integration of heterogeneous hardware-software structures improves performance and reduces system size and power consumption, while still meeting programmability requirements.

Of course, under Ptolemy we can similarly construct other options with different hardware-software partitions and explore the design space.

ALTHOUGH THERE IS NOTHING NEW about designing systems containing both hardware and software, what really distinguishes our hardware-software codesign methodology from traditional methodologies is its integration of two heterogeneous methodologies within a single framework. Its unified representation of hardware and software facilitates migration of functions between the two implementations. Our emphasis has not been on automating the process, but rather on providing the designer with advanced interoperable tools that enable creative exploration of the design space.

The design of the telephone channel simulator illustrates how different multiprocessor system configurations and hardware-software partitions can be explored quickly and easily. The second example demonstrates the mechanism for combining synthesis of custom hardware with synthesis of assembly code for programmable components. The custom hardware and the programmable processor are integrated in a single simulation for the mixed hardware-software system.

Now that we have a functional infrastructure for hardware-software codesign, we are working on higher level tools that support this methodology. The Design Assistant, for example, will take the user through the steps of the design, providing advice and feedback at every stage. The Design Assistant is a special target that coordinates operations of the individual targets in the hardware and software domains. We are currently focusing on the design of systems (either at the board level, or as a DSP core ASIC) containing a single processor and custom hardware. Next, we will extend the methodology to the design of heterogeneous systems containing multiple, diverse processing elements.

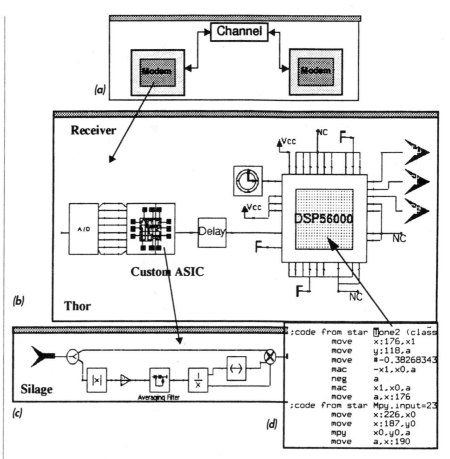

Figure 9. Modem design: two modems communicating over a channel (a); receiver configuration (b); components implemented in custom hardware (c); DSP code (d).

Acknowledgments

We gratefully acknowledge the Semiconductor Research Corporation for supporting this work through its Berkeley Center of Excellence in CAD/IC (contract 93-DC-008). DARPA, AT&T Bell Labs, the Office of Naval Research, Bell Northern Research, Motorola, and Rockwell have sponsored related work on the Ptolemy project.

Numerous individuals have contributed (and are contributing) to the development of the Ptolemy environment, and we gratefully acknowledge them: Shuvra Bhattacharyya, Joseph Buck, Wan-Teh Chang, Soonhoi Ha, Alan Kamas, Seungjun Lee, David G. Messerschmitt, Praveen Murthy, Thomas M. Parks, Jose Pino, and Kennard White. (White developed the algorithm for the 2PSK passband modem used as an example in the article.)

References

1. R. Camposano, "From Behavior to Structure: High-Level Synthesis," *IEEE Design*

1. ..., *& Test of Computers*, Vol. 7, No. 5, Oct. 1990, pp. 8-19.
2. J. Bier, P. Lapsley, and E.A. Lee, "Tools and Methodologies for the Design of DSP Systems," tech. report, Berkeley Design Technology, Inc., 38842 Helen Way, Fremont, CA 94536, 1993.
3. G. Goosens et al., "Integration of Medium-Throughput Signal Processing Algorithms on Flexible Instruction-Set Architectures," to be published in *J. VLSI Signal Processing*, special issue on Synthesis for DSP, 1993.
4. L. Mary, "DSP Based Technology for European Mobile Radio," *Signal Processing V: Theory and Applications, Proc. EUSIPCO-90*, Elsevier, Amsterdam, 1990, pp. 1495-1498.
5. Y.S. Wu and L.J. Wu, "An Architectural Framework for Signal Flow," *Proc. Int'l Conf. Digital Signal Processing*, North-Holland, Amsterdam, 1984, pp. 222–227.
6. J. Buck et al., "Ptolemy: A Framework for Simulating and Prototyping Heterogeneous Systems," to be published in *Int'l J. Computer Simulation*, special issue on Simulation Software Development, Jan. 1994.
7. J. Pino et al., "Software Synthesis for DSP Using Ptolemy," to be published in *J. VLSI Signal Processing*, special issue on Synthesis for DSP, 1993.
8. A. Kalavade, *Hardware/Software Codesign Using Ptolemy: A Case Study*, master's report, EECS Dept., Univ. of California, Berkeley, Dec. 1991.
9. J.T. Buck, *The Ptolemy Kernel*, Memorandum UCB/ERL M93/8, Univ. of California, Berkeley, Jan. 1993.
10. J. Rasure and C. Williams, "An Integrated Visual Language and Software Development Environment," *J. Visual Languages and Computing*, Vol. 2, No. 3, Sept. 1991, pp. 217-246.
11. E.A. Lee and D.G. Messerschmitt, "Synchronous Data Flow," *Proc. IEEE*, Vol. 75, No. 9, 1987, pp. 35-45.
12. *Thor Tutorial*, VLSI/CAD Group, Stanford Univ., Stanford, Calif., 1986.
13. A. Kalavade and E.A. Lee, "Hardware/Software Codesign Using Ptolemy: A Case Study," to be published in *Proc. First IFIP Int'l Workshop Hardware/Software Codesign*, IEEE Press, 1993.
14. J. Bier and E.A. Lee, "Frigg: A Simulation Environment for Multiprocessor DSP System Development," *Proc. Int'l Conf. Computer Design*, IEEE Computer Society Press, Los Alamitos, Calif., 1989, pp. 280-283.
15. G.C. Sih, *Multiprocessor Scheduling to Account for Interprocessor Communication*, PhD thesis, Electronic Research Laboratory, Univ. of California, Berkeley, Apr. 1991.
16. P. Hilfinger, "A High-Level Language and Silicon Compiler for Digital Signal Processing," *Proc. Custom Integrated Circuits Conf.*, IEEE Computer Society Press, Los Alamitos, Calif., 1985, pp. 213-216.
17. J. Rabaey et al., "Fast Prototyping of Datapath-Intensive Architectures," *IEEE Design & Test of Computers*, Vol. 8, No. 2, June 1991, pp. 40-51.
18. E.A. Lee and D.G. Messerschmitt, *Digital Communications*, Kluwer Academic, Boston, pp. 128-135.

Asawaree Kalavade is a PhD candidate in the Electrical Engineering and Computer Sciences Department at the University of California, Berkeley. Her research interests include system-level design methodologies, VLSI design, and signal processing. In collaboration with the Microprocessor Application Engineering Program in India, she developed a PC-based image-processing system now in commercial use. Kalavade received her BE in electronics and telecommunications from the University of Poona, India, where she also received the Best Student Award for academic excellence. She received her MS in electrical engineering from the University of California, Berkeley. She is a student member of the IEEE and the IEEE Computer Society.

Edward A. Lee is an associate professor in the Electrical Engineering and Computer Sciences Department at the University of California, Berkeley. His research interests include parallel computation, architecture and software techniques for programmable DSPs, design environments for development of real-time software and hardware, and digital communication. Earlier, he was a member of the technical staff at Bell Telephone Laboratories, where he worked on early programmable DSPs, voice-band data modem techniques, and simultaneous voice and data transmission. He received a BS from Yale University, an MS from MIT, and a PhD from UC Berkeley. Lee has served as chair of the Signal Processing Society's VLSI Technical Committee and program co-chair of the 1992 Application-Specific Array Processor Conference. He is a senior member of the IEEE and a member of the editorial board of the *Journal on VLSI Signal Processing*.

Send questions and comments about this article to Asawaree Kalavade, UC Berkeley, Department of Electrical Engineering and Computer Sciences, Berkeley, CA 94720; kalavade@eecs.berkeley.edu.

A Hardware-Software Co-simulator for Embedded System Design and Debugging

A. Ghosh, M. Bershteyn, R. Casley, C. Chien, A. Jain, M. Lipsie, D. Tarrodaychik, O. Yamamoto

Mitsubishi Electric Research Laboratories, Inc.

Sunnyvale, CA 94086

Abstract

One of the interesting problems in hardware-software co-design is that of debugging embedded software in conjunction with hardware. Currently, most software designers wait until a working hardware prototype is available before debugging software. Bugs discovered in hardware during the software debugging phase require re-design and re-fabrication, thereby not only delaying the project but also increasing cost. It also puts software debugging on hold until a new hardware prototype is available.

In this paper we describe a hardware-software co-simulator that can be used in the design, debugging and verification of embedded systems. This tool contains simulators for different parts of the system and a backplane which is used to integrate the simulators. This enables us to simulate hardware, software and their interaction efficiently. We also address the problem of simulation speed. Currently, the more accurate (in terms of timing) the models used, the longer it takes to simulate a system. Our main contribution is a set of techniques to speed up simulation of processors and peripherals without significant loss in timing accuracy.

Finally, we describe applications used to test the co-simulator and our experience in using it.

1 INTRODUCTION

Design of embedded systems containing both hardware and software requires solving several unique and difficult problems [4] [5] [12]. One of the interesting problems is that of debugging embedded software in conjunction with hardware. The traditional co-design process, where the software is debugged after hardware is fabricated, produces large design delays due to late discovery of errors in the hardware and in the interface between hardware and software. Integration on a chip will make this problem worse because currently used tools like In-Circuit Emulators (ICE) cannot be used and signals on a chip cannot be easily observed. There is an obvious need for a change in the co-design methodology whereby software and hardware can be jointly debugged earlier in the design cycle. However, this change in methodology can only happen when appropriate design tools are available.

There are two approaches to debugging hardware and software without building the actual hardware. The first one is based on emulation of hardware using, for example, Field Programmable Gate Arrays (FPGA) and using a separate board for the processor and memory. A designer can generate a prototype relatively quickly and debug software and interfaces on the prototype. After bugs are detected, the entire system can be recompiled within a relatively short time. In most cases, hardware emulators run only an order of magnitude slower than the actual system, allowing the designer to test the system with a large number of test cases. However, due to its high cost, this technique is economically feasible only in certain cases. It also cannot be used to model timing constraints accurately and in many cases designs have to be modified to suit emulation. Moreover, re-compiling hardware takes more time than compiling software or a HDL (Hardware Description Language) model for simulation. Finally, it is not always possible to observe the internal state of the circuit, both in the FPGA and in the processor, making debugging complicated and slow.

A complementary approach is to build software models for all the components of the system and use simulation to analyze behavior. There are many advantages of this approach. First, software can be combined with behavioral-level hardware descriptions to detect bugs as early as possible in the design phase. Hardware, software and interface routines can be designed and debugged in parallel. Second, timing constraints can be accurately modeled. Third, re-compilation of either hardware or software is quick. Detailed debugging, where internal states of all components can be accessed and altered at all time points can be easily supported. Finally, this approach is not as expensive as emulation.

Simulators have been mostly used for the design of hardware and there are few tools for co-simulation. In this paper, we describe a hardware-software co-simulator that can be used in the design, debugging and verification of embedded systems. This tool contains a simulation backplane which can be used to integrate processor, hardware (HDL) and dedicated simulators for peripherals, forming a co-simulator capable of efficiently simulating hardware, software and their interaction. Each simulator implements debugging functions like setting breakpoints, examining and altering internal states, single stepping, *etc*. In order to feed stimulus to the system and to observe its response a set of virtual instruments have been created. The co-simulator and the virtual instruments can be used to create a virtual laboratory that will provide users with a platform for rapid virtual prototyping. Performance metrics (like clock cycles needed to execute software) can be easily evaluated, allowing the user to explore different algorithms, hardware and software implementations and hardware-software trade-offs.

The main drawback of simulation is its speed. In many cases, simulation runs orders of magnitude slower than the actual system. Simulation time depends on the (timing) accuracy of the models, with time increasing with increased accuracy.

Therefore, reducing simulation time without sacrificing timing accuracy becomes a very important problem. Our main contribution is a set of techniques to speed up simulation of processors and peripherals without significant loss in timing accuracy. Processor simulation speed is improved by accurately (in terms of timing) simulating only those cycles where there is interaction with peripherals and by caching results of instruction decoding. Suppression of periodic signals and other techniques to be described speed up simulation of peripherals. Simulation overhead is kept low by managing time more efficiently.

We expect this tool to be used at any point after the initial architecture is determined. Software designers may use behavioral hardware models for initial debugging, evaluation and exploration of algorithms and implementations. System architects may use the tool to determine hardware-software trade-offs. Hardware designers can use prototype software to evaluate, test and debug their hardware. Finally, when hardware and software are ready, designers can work on testing and debugging the entire system.

The rest of this paper is organized as follows. Previous work is described in Section 2 followed by a description of the co-simulation framework in Section 3. Simulator coordination is the topic of Section 4. Simulation of processor is described in Section 5 followed by simulation of custom hardware in Section 6. Simulation of standard peripherals is described in Section 7. Interface to other simulators is described in Section 8. Example applications used to test the co-simulator are described in Section 9. Conclusions and directions for future work are presented in Section 10.

2 PREVIOUS WORK

In [7], a debugging tool for embedded system software is presented. The software is cross-compiled for the embedded processor and then executed on a model of the system. The system is modeled completely in hardware and simulated using a hardware simulator. During simulation, which may take several days, all interaction between the processor model and the surrounding hardware is logged. After simulation, the designer switches to a software debugging environment on a host workstation where the code is compiled for the host and re-linked to pseudo hardware drivers that interact with the logged information. The primary advantage of this approach is that during debugging, software can run at the host computer speed. However, when a bug is fixed, the entire system may have to be re-simulated, thereby increasing the debugging time. Further, during debugging, there is no way of interactively affecting system behavior by feeding the system a different set of inputs. In our opinion, such a debugger has limited usefulness.

An interesting approach presented in [1] is based on distributed communicating processes modeling hardware and software. Software is run on a host workstation and all interactions with hardware are replaced by remote procedure calls to a hardware simulator process. The main drawback of this approach is that there is no notion of timing accuracy as neither the software execution speed nor the interface between hardware and software are accurately modeled.

The Poseidon co-simulator is described in [4]. An event driven simulator is used to co-ordinate the execution of a hardware and a software simulator. The processor simulator is tied closely to the DLX microprocessor [4] model. There is no special handling of standard peripherals and little information regarding the debugging environment, simulation speed and accuracy is available.

In [6] the use of Ptolemy [2] in hardware-software co-design for a digital signal processing (DSP) application is described. The emphasis in [6] is on the use of the capabilities of Ptolemy for heterogeneous simulation and code synthesis for single and multiple processors. After code generation and hardware synthesis, co-simulation is performed using the hardware simulator *Thor* [13] and a simulator for the digital signal processor DSP56000. It is our belief that though what is described here in terms of the backplane and what is provided by Ptolemy may be similar in principal, Ptolemy does not address the efficiency issues related to hardware-software co-simulation, especially the simulation of processors and peripherals. From [6], few details are available regarding speed of simulation, accuracy, the way standard peripherals are handled and about the debugging environment.

The use of virtual instruments was introduced in [3] in the context of simulation of hardware systems. Currently, the tool described in [3] does not have any capabilities for hardware-software co-simulation. Use of a simulation backplane in mixed mode simulation is described in [10] and similar backplanes for the integration of hardware simulators are commercially available.

3 CO-SIMULATION FRAMEWORK

In designing the co-simulator the main goals were:

- to provide fast and timing-accurate simulation;
- to provide an extensible and flexible simulator-independent framework where new simulators can be easily integrated;
- to provide adequate debugging capability for both hardware and software;
- to provide virtual prototyping capability through the use of virtual instruments;
- to provide means for evaluation of performance metrics.

The architecture of the co-simulator is shown in Figure 1. We believe that different parts of an embedded system will be simulated using different simulators and therefore we need to allow for heterogeneity in the simulation environment. To

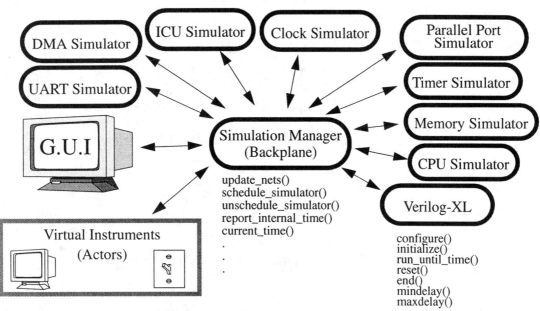

FIGURE 1. Architecture of the co-simulator

allow different simulators to interact with one another, a simulation backplane is used. This backplane, also called the simulation manager, is the main component of the tool. It manages simulation and debugging as well as communication with virtual instruments. A well-designed Graphical User Interface (GUI) makes the use of the co-simulator easy and natural for both software and hardware debugging. At the time of writing, only one processor simulator for an M16 microprocessor [8] and several dedicated simulators for standard peripherals have been integrated. A commercial simulator, Verilog-XL [14], is used for the simulation of hardware described in Verilog HDL.

The system to be simulated can be broadly divided into electrical and mechanical components (or even chemical components). The electrical components could be either hardware or software. The hardware could further be digital or analog. For example, to simulate a motor control system, we need to simulate the controller (electrical) as well as the motor (mechanical). Simulators for standard components are provided. It is our assumption that for special components like motors, engines, *etc.*, the user will be supplying their own models and/or simulators.

The input to the co-simulator is a description of the system to be simulated. It consists of the following items: a list of blocks and their simulators; a list of nets connecting the blocks; a list of virtual instruments and their connections; and a list of source/object files used by the software debugger and source/library files used by the hardware simulator. The simulation manager reads the system description, allocates necessary data structures and initializes all the simulators that would be needed to simulate the system. Once the system is loaded, the user may interact with any simulator, setting breakpoints, examining registers, *etc.* During simulation, virtual instruments are used for human interaction. When a breakpoint in any simulator is reached, simulation is stopped and the user is prompted for commands. Whenever a prompt is displayed, the user can issue commands for any simulator. Batch mode simulation can also be selected when no interactive input is required.

The co-simulator is implemented as a multithreaded program to allow easy integration of stand alone simulators. The simulation manager and some dedicated simulators constitute the main thread. Verilog-XL and the simulator for M16 are separate threads.

3.1 SIMULATION MANAGER

The simulation manager, hereafter SM, is the backbone of the co-simulator. It performs the following important functions.

- It manages the simulation and debugging session. All user commands are relayed by the GUI to the SM. It understands commands for loading the system to be simulated, for running simulation as well as for debugging (*e.g.* setting breakpoints at certain times). The SM also directs commands to simulators.

- It manages communication between the co-simulator and virtual instruments.

- Simulation of a system involves coordinating the activities of simulators, each of which is responsible for simulating a part of the system. The SM controls when a simulator is invoked, what events are passed to it, *etc*. This is the most important function of the SM and is discussed in Section 4.

3.2 GRAPHICAL USER INTERFACE

The graphical user interface, built using *Tcl/Tk* [9], allows the

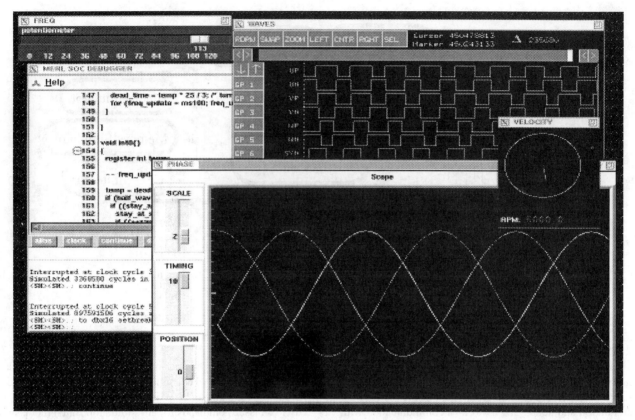

FIGURE 2. The graphical user interface, virtual instruments, and waveform display window

user to interact with the SM and the simulators easily and effectively. A snapshot of this interface is shown in Figure 2. The GUI consists of a source display window where source (for both software and hardware) and assembly-level code is displayed. There is also a command window for entering commands and a configurable button panel for frequently used commands. The source display window is used to display breakpoints, the current line where execution has stopped, and other relevant information found in most software debuggers. Additional windows are used to display variables, waveforms, *etc*.

3.3 VIRTUAL INSTRUMENTS

Virtual instruments, also called *actors*, are used primarily for human interaction with the system being simulated. They are used to provide stimulus as well as to observe response. As such they model parts of the environment with which the system interacts and enables the user to use the co-simulator as a virtual laboratory. They are implemented using *Tcl/Tk* [9]. Each virtual instrument is a separate process that communicates only with the SM using Unix sockets. The SM manages the socket traffic as well as the starting and termination of each actor. The virtual instruments that have been implemented include a variable voltage/current source, a switch, a simple LED probe, a meter, an oscilloscope, a video monitor, an electric motor and an automobile engine. The voltage source, electric motor and oscilloscope actors are used for a virtual prototype of a 3-phase motor control system shown in Figure 2. The voltage source actor (FREQ) has a slider that can be pulled to change the value of the voltage generated. Waveforms are viewed on the oscilloscope actor (PHASE). The motor actor (VELOCITY) shows the current motor r.p.m. Using virtual instruments, users can get both a quantitative measure as well as a qualitative feel for the system. In the example of Figure 2, the user can see the actual waveforms that would be generated by the system without building hardware and using an oscilloscope.

3.4 Simulators

It is possible to represent an entire system, including processor, memory, peripherals and custom circuitry in a HDL like Verilog and simulate it using a simulator like Verilog-XL. Using the right models, simulation can be accurate but will be very slow [7]. Our approach to speed up simulation is to create dedicated simulators for standard components like processors and peripherals and integrate them into a co-simulator using the simulation backplane.

The simulator for M16 is also a software debugger with sophisticated debugging capabilities. It allows both source-level as well as assembly-level debugging. It can also evaluate performance metrics like the number of clock cycles needed to execute a piece of code. Verilog-XL is a hardware debugger with capabilities that include display of waveforms (as shown in the WAVES window in Figure 2), monitoring of signal values, determination of set-up and hold time violations at latches, *etc.* Simulators for peripherals allow very primitive debugging like examining and setting internal registers. The debugging capabilities of simulators combined with those of the SM provide a powerful debugging and verification environment for embedded systems. It should be emphasized that a natural debugging environment is provided for both software and hardware, so neither the software nor the hardware designer is at a disadvantage.

4 SIMULATOR COORDINATION

The interface between the SM and a simulator consists of a set of functions, some implemented in the simulator and some in the SM (shown in Figure 1). A simulator simulates one or more blocks of the same type, with each block having a set of input and output pins. From a simulator's point of view, it is given a set of events at a particular time, which indicate a change in signal value on the input pins, and asked to simulate until some time in the future. During simulation, if the signal value at one of the output pins of a block changes, the simulator reports to the SM the new value and the time this event happened and stops simulating further. The SM sees the system as a set of blocks connected by nets. Whenever there is an event on a net, simulators for the blocks affected by the event are invoked. Simulator coordination includes determining which simulators to invoke, what events to pass to them and the simulation time when a simulator should stop simulating and return control to the SM. Simulator coordination overhead can be reduced by decreasing the number of events, allowing simulators to run uninterrupted for as long as possible, and managing time efficiently.

To manage time efficiently, the SM counts time in units of a fixed time called the *simulation period* and also bounds the size of the timing wheel. This has several important consequences. Since events can be produced only at certain times and a limited time into the future, the number of unique times to manage is smaller. It allows us to statically allocate the timing wheel before simulation begins. This reduces the run-time overhead in managing time and the timing wheel. Discretization of time allows us to take advantage of the cycle accuracy of processor and peripheral simulators which produce events only at discrete times. However, when timing accurate simulators (like circuit simulators) are used, events can be produced at any time. The interface routines round event times to the nearest discrete time value, thereby introducing errors in simulation. A small enough *simulation period* can reduce this error, but may offset the benefit obtained from using discrete time.

Simulator coordination and synchronization can be understood by following a co-simulation session. After the system description is read, the SM determines the simulators that need to be run and calls the **configure()** routine to let the simulators know that their services would be needed. Subsequently, for each block, the SM calls the **initialize()** routine with a pointer to the block, the pins of the block and the nets connected to the pins. This allows simulators to initialize their internal data structures and their interface routines. After this, the SM allocates and initializes the timing wheel. Each simulator is asked to report the minimum and maximum delay of each block it is going to simulate through the **mindelay()** and **maxdelay()** functions. The minimum and maximum delays are the minimum and maximum time required, respectively, for any event at an input to propagate to an output. Simulators that can ascertain the value of minimum and maximum delay may report it and the rest (like a circuit simulator) report a negative value, indicating unknown delays. The *simulation period* is decided on the basis of the timing accuracy required for simulation and is usually chosen to be the time between successive clock transitions of the processor/bus clock. The maximum of the maximum delays is used to guide the selection of the size of the timing wheel. This size is advertised to all simulators which can then use it during self-scheduling (to be described shortly).

During simulation, the SM first determines events at a particular time and the simulators that need to be run. If there is only one simulator to run, the SM determines the time for the next event on the timing wheel (if there is no event on the timing wheel, this time is considered to be infinity). It then calls the **run_until_time()** function in the simulator with an event list and a variable *stop time* set to the time of the next event on the wheel. If there are more than one simulator to run, the SM determines the minimum of the minimum delays of the simulators. This minimum delay is added to the current time to determine the *stop time*. This ensures that no simulator simulates beyond a time where an external event for it may be produced, thereby obviating the need to roll back simulation time. This is called running in lock step.

Each simulator, during **run_until_time()** transfers all external events to its internal event queue and simulates until the *stop time*. If an event on an external net is produced at or before the stop time is reached, the simulator suspends itself and reports the event to the SM by calling **update_nets()**. It reports the time at which it has stopped by calling **report_internal_time()** and then passes control back to the SM. When a simulator stops, if there are events to be processed in its internal queue, the simulator requests that it be called again at a specific time in the future (as determined by the time of the earliest internal event) by calling **schedule_simulator()**. This procedure, called self-scheduling, allows simulators to stop before exhausting all internal events. A simulator can schedule itself at any (discrete) time in the future provided it does not exceed the current time by the advertised maximum size of the timing wheel. Simulators that schedule themselves in the future but are invoked before that time by events at their inputs can remove their self-scheduling events by calling **unschedule_simulator()**. Note that when a simulator returns control to the SM, it is required to save its internal state so that simulation can be continued from where it was stopped. For simulators that run as separate threads, state is automatically saved on a thread switch. Other simulators have to implement this feature explicitly.

Apart from coordinating simulators, the SM controls the trade-off between simulation accuracy and speed. As will be explained in Section 5, the simulator for M16 has the capability to choose the appropriate level of speed and accuracy when the processor is trying to read from or write to a certain address. When the address is in the range of memory, no signals are produced on the bus, but when the address is outside the range, phase-accurate bus signals are produced. This is adequate for the simulation of most peripherals. However, there are certain peripherals, like a DMA controller, that 'listen' to the bus in order to detect vacant bus cycles and perform cycle-stealing DMA. For such situations, even when the processor is accessing memory, signals on the bus have to be produced. Therefore, each simulator like the DMA is marked as a bus listener. Whenever a bus listener has to be run in lock step with a processor simulator, the SM sets a special flag indicating to the processor simulator that bus signals should be produced. This ensures correct simulation of systems with DMA controllers and other bus listeners.

Another important function of the SM is the mapping of internal values of simulators to a uniform representation and back to allow mixed-level (*e.g.* gate and transistor) and mixed-mode (*e.g.* analog and digital) simulation. It should be noted that standard templates are provided for the interface functions that make the job of integrating simulators easier.

5 PROCESSOR SIMULATOR

Processor simulators can be divided into three categories depending on accuracy and speed of simulation.

- Instruction Set Simulator (ISS) simulates the instruction set and values in memory and registers accurately. Signals at the pins of the processor can be produced only at the boundaries of instructions. It does not model superscalar ordering effects, delayed branch, pipeline stalls, wait states, and cache access. Therefore accurate clock cycle count for code execution cannot be determined. However, it is the fastest processor simulator and can be used for pure software simulation and debugging.

- Cycle-Accurate Simulator (CAS) can simulate the instruction set, the pipeline and the local cache of a processor and can provide the signals at the pins of the CPU at each clock transition and also provide accurate clock cycle counts. Superscalar ordering effects, pipeline stalls and wait states can be simulated accurately. However, it can be more than an order of magnitude slower than an instruction set simulator. In addition to software simulation, it can be used to model interaction with hardware components, though there might be inaccuracies in timing. A variation of a cycle-accurate simulator is a phase-accurate simulator (PAS) where the behavior of the processor in each clock phase is accurately simulated.

- Timing Accurate Simulator (TAS) can simulate the complete functionality of a processor with full timing accuracy. Because each pin can change at potentially unique times and the detailed timing behavior of the CPU together with the instruction set and the pipeline has to be simulated, this is the slowest of all simulators.

For M16, which is a scalar processor without a local cache, assuming that all memory accesses take the same amount of time, an ISS can be used to simulate the processor with little loss in accuracy. This is also based on the assumption that the interaction between processor and memory does not have to be debugged. However, an ISS cannot be used to simulate interaction with peripherals.

The choice between CAS/PAS or TAS depends on the level of accuracy required. Since a CAS/PAS produces signals at pins only at discrete times, the internal model for a CAS/PAS can be simpler and can run faster. The extra accuracy gained by using a TAS is that the signals can be produced in between clock cycles at the exact time they would be produced by the processor. Since the price for this increase in accuracy is steep, it is worthwhile investigating when full timing accuracy is required and when a CAS/PAS is adequate.

To determine whether a CAS/PAS is adequate, the first question to be answered is whether it is possible that certain signal transitions may not be generated or caught by a CAS/PAS. The M16 processor uses a synchronous bus protocol for the transfer of data to and from memory and peripherals. Address and data are latched by the processor and peripherals only at certain clock edges. The few fully asynchronous pins (like Data-Complete, Interrupt, Hold) are internally synchronized and therefore have to be active for at least one clock cycle. In other words, two events on the same net or that affect one another never happen without a clock edge in between. Our initial study of other processors indicates that this is true for the Intel i960 processor family and the Motorola MC68030 processors. Therefore, for these processors, a CAS/PAS that produces and samples bus signals only at each clock transition is equivalent to a TAS except for timing accuracy.

When the user is interested in determining if set-up and hold times are being violated, or when he/she is debugging an ASIC with tight timing constraints, the exact time when inputs arrive and when outputs are produced are important and there is no alternative to using a TAS. Therefore, a CAS/PAS can be sufficient only when the system has been designed so that set-up and hold times are not violated and all custom circuitry and peripherals meet their timing constraints. The M16 processor ensures that set-up and hold times are not violated in its peripherals by producing signals on the bus well in advance of the clock edge where they would be latched. Users manual also require that peripherals produce data a certain time before the clock edge where it will be latched by the processor. If a system is carefully designed and conservative design rules are followed, there may be few set-up and hold time violations. These violations can be detected using bus functional models and timing accurate simulation. Therefore, with an appropriate design methodology, the use of CAS/PAS may be sufficient for hardware-software co-simulation. We are conducting further study to validate this assertion.

The simulator for M16 is an integrated ISS and a PAS. Each processor clock cycle is divided into six periods and the PAS produces bus signals at the boundary of each period, while the ISS does not produce any bus signals. During execution of a program, depending on the instruction and operand address, the simulator automatically switches from ISS to PAS and *vice versa*. The ISS is used to simulate program execution when nothing but memory is accessed. Whenever the processor tries to access some region that is outside the address range allocated to memory or when the SM sets a flag that indicates that signals on the bus have to produced, the PAS is used. Note that switching between ISS and PAS requires that the ISS maintain some information about the state of the pipeline during execution. The PAS consists of a pipeline simulator and a bus interface module. The pipeline simulator simulates the pipeline of the CPU accurately while the bus interface generates the appropriate signals. Using the less accurate but fast ISS when only memory is accessed and switching to the more accurate but slower PAS only when required cuts down on the number of events too and speeds up simulation by more than an order of magnitude in most cases.

Most ISS can simulate anywhere between 2000 and 20,000 instructions per second [11]. In order to speed up the ISS and PAS for M16, we exploited the locality of reference in the program memory. Many embedded programs execute a group of instructions over and over (as in a loop). Each instruction, which includes opcode and operand(s), is decoded and the result is stored in a cache. Before decoding, a new instruction, it is looked up in the cache. For a cache hit, the decoded form is used directly, thereby avoiding the simulation of the complicated and time consuming decoding phase. This can increase the execution speed of the ISS and PAS by about a factor of 2. Currently, the M16 ISS can simulate about 50,000 instructions per second for typical programs on a Sun Sparcstation 10. The PAS can simulate about 4,000 instructions per second. The PAS does not simulate the instruction fetch cycle, assuming that no events for peripherals can be produced during this time and that instruction memory can only introduce a fixed number of wait states.

6 SIMULATION OF HARDWARE

Custom hardware represented using Verilog HDL is simulated using a commercial simulator, Verilog-XL [14]. Since a commercial simulator is designed to be a stand alone tool and does not implement the interface functions required by the SM, its integration poses certain problems. For Verilog-XL, the interface functions were implemented using the Programming Language Interface (PLI) for the simulator [14]. The PLI allows user defined functions (written in C) to be called from Verilog-XL during simulation. It also allows these functions to call certain functions for simulation control in Verilog-XL. The details of the implementation are skipped for the sake of brevity.

In our implementation, the user is required to call the function **$codebug** in an **initial** block of the top level module in the custom circuit description. There are some requirements on the way input, output and bi-directional lines are represented. There is no other restriction, and hardware can be represented at any level of abstraction allowed in Verilog. Verilog-XL is currently the only timing accurate simulator in our framework. Since other simulators are only phase-accurate, the interface functions for Verilog-XL may introduce errors during rounding of event times if proper care is not exerted in describing the hardware.

7 SIMULATION OF STANDARD PERIPHERALS

Embedded processors are often used in conjunction with a set of standard peripherals. Instead of describing them in some HDL and using a hardware simulator, we use dedicated simulators to simulate each type of peripheral. Each simulator consists of a behavioral model written in C and a bus interface. The behavioral model simulates the phase-accurate behavior of the peripheral and the bus interface generates the appropriate signals at every clock transition.

There are several advantages of using dedicated simulators. First, multiple instances of the same standard peripheral can be simulated more efficiently. Consider, for example, a system that has several parallel ports. When the processor writes to one of them, events are generated for each parallel port which then decode the address to determine the recipient. In most cases, only one parallel port will respond to the write while others will ignore it. Therefore, for all but one parallel port, decoding of the address is a useless operation that cannot be prevented if a hardware simulator is used. Using a dedicated simulator, all parallel ports can be simulated together so that when a processor writes an address on the bus, only one set of events is created for all the parallel ports and given to the simulator. The simulator decodes the address only once to determine which one of the parallel ports the CPU is talking to. Therefore, not only is the number of events reduced, but useless decode operations are avoided.

The second advantage of dedicated simulators is better handling of periodic signals. Such signals impair simulation efficiency by increasing simulation overhead. In [15], it was shown that suppression of periodic signals during concurrent fault simulation can produce significant savings in simulation time. We adopt a similar approach here. Each clock generator advertises its clock signal as a triple, describing the period, the rise time and the fall time. The use of this information is illustrated by the timer simulator. A timer is a counter that is initialized with a value corresponding to the number of clock pulses to be counted. On receipt of a start signal, the timer

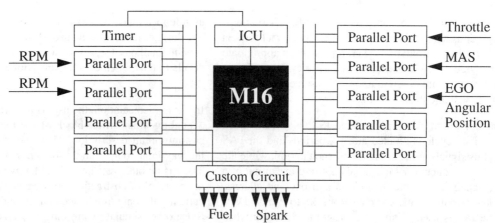

FIGURE 3. Architecture of an Engine Control Unit

starts to decrement the value of the counter at each positive/negative edge of the clock. If simulated using a hardware simulator, clock events have to be fed to the counter periodically. However, a dedicated timer simulator can use the advertised clock signal and the value of the counter to determine at what time the counter is going to expire. It can then schedule itself at the right time in the future to produce the appropriate event. This decreases the number of events generated, the number of simulators invoked to handle each event, and the time spent in simulating the timer. For the motor control application to be described in Section 9.2, this can reduce the number of events per revolution of the motor from 129,640 to 840. The other advantage of this method is that other simulators, like the processor simulator can run uninterrupted during the time the timer is counting, thereby reducing synchronization overhead further. Note that it is not possible to avoid the generation of the clock signal at all times, *e.g.* when the clock is an input to custom circuitry. In such situations, we use a local clock generator which uses the advertised clock signal to generate a clock only for the module that needs it. Once again, this reduces simulation overhead because periodic signals are produced locally where they are needed.

The third advantage of dedicated simulators can be illustrated using an Interrupt Control Unit (ICU). The algorithm for interrupt priority resolution requires complicated and deeply pipelined hardware. Simulation of this hardware takes more time than executing the algorithm directly in the simulator. The advertized clock signal is used to determine the state of the pipeline and how long it takes to generate an interrupt signal. For an example application, replacing the dedicated ICU simulator with a RTL Verilog model slowed down simulation by two orders of magnitude. Though a part of this slowdown can be attributed to Verilog-XL and its interface to the backplane, this result is still significant. Also, this technique is fairly representative of the techniques that can be used to speed up simulation.

It is obvious from the discussion above that dedicated phase-accurate simulators for standard peripherals may be able to speed up simulation in ways that HDL simulators cannot. However, there are certain drawbacks. For every new peripheral a new simulator has to be written and integrated into the backplane. Also, it is not always possible to implement the kind of techniques mentioned above for all standard peripherals. We are working on a tool that will solve the first problem by providing the standard boiler-plate needed for a simulator. For the second problem, we rely on the ingenuity of the simulator developer.

8 OTHER SIMULATORS

We have developed an interface between the co-simulator described in this paper and the Tsutsuji hardware simulation system [3]. The Tsutsuji system is capable of efficiently modeling and simulating signal processing functions. Systems that have both control and signal processing functions, like motion detectors, can be easily simulated. We are also in the process of developing an interface to the Ptolemy simulator to allow us to use the heterogeneous simulation environment of Ptolemy.

In addition, a simulator for a three-phase electric motor and for a rudimentary automobile engine has been developed for the design and debugging of motor and engine control systems. It is our hope that as this system finds more and more use, a large library of simulators for diverse application areas will develop and will increase the usefulness of this tool.

9 EXAMPLE APPLICATIONS

Several applications were used to test the capabilities of the co-simulator. They include an engine control unit, a three-phase motor control unit, a real-time operating system for the M16 microprocessor, a motion detector and a computer modem. The first three applications and our experience in using the co-simulator are described briefly in this section.

9.1 ENGINE CONTROL UNIT

The operation of an engine is controlled by varying the airflow, the duration for which fuel is injected into each cylinder and the spark time. The engine control unit receives inputs from the mass air flow sensor (MAS), the RPM sensor, the

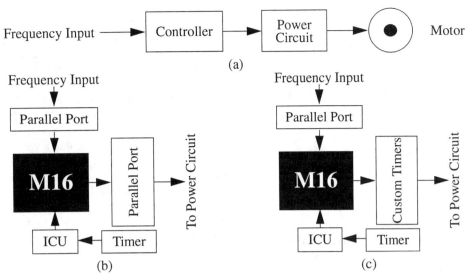

FIGURE 4. 3-phase motor controller (a) block diagram (b) first and (c) second implementation

exhaust gas oxygen sensor (EGO), the throttle position sensor and the crankshaft angular position sensor. The controller controls the idle valve (not shown in the figure), the throttle-body fuel injectors, and the spark plugs.

An architecture of a simplified engine control unit is shown in Figure 3. It consists of an M16 processor, a timer, an ICU, nine parallel ports and some custom circuitry. The custom circuitry can be implemented in approximately 2000 gates. The C source code for the engine controller is about 1000 lines long.

The software for the controller and the RTL description of the custom circuit were developed and debugged solely using the co-simulator. 1500 CPU cycles (approximately 300 machine instructions) could be simulated per second on a Sun Sparcstation 10. At this speed, it takes 40 minutes to simulate the behavior of the engine and the controller as it goes from 0 to 7000 r.p.m. This represents a slowdown of about a factor of 400 over real time operation, an adequate speed for debugging. Note that the emissions from the engine were not modeled and a simplified dynamic control algorithms was used for the controller.

9.2 THREE-PHASE MOTOR CONTROL

A three-phase motor controller, shown in Figure 4(a), takes as an input the desired frequency of rotation and produces pulse width modulated signals which are demodulated by the power circuit, producing three sinusoidal signals at the required frequency but phase shifted 120 degrees with respect to one another.

An implementation of this controller using a microprocessor and standard peripherals is shown in Figure 4(b). All computation required to produce the pulse width modulated signals is performed in the microprocessor. At high frequencies, the demodulated waveforms show a mean square error of 8% from an ideal sine wave because the processor cannot keep up with the required rate of calculation. An alternative architecture is shown in Figure 4(c) where some custom circuitry is used in conjunction with the microprocessor. The calculation for pulse width modulation are still performed in the processor but the actual generation of the signals is moved to custom hardware. The demodulated waveforms now show a mean square error of less than 1% from an ideal sine wave at all frequencies. The amount of ROM required to store the program and the tables is also smaller. This is a good example of how the co-simulator may be used to determine hardware-software trade-offs at the implementation level.

The controller of Figure 4(b), can be implemented in 600 lines of C code and simulation runs about a factor of 3200 slower than the actual system. The controller of Figure 4(c) can be implemented with only 200 lines of C code while the custom circuit is represented using 100 lines of behavioral-level Verilog. Simulation runs about 7400 times slower than the actual system for the second implementation, showing the effect of Verilog-XL on simulation time. It has been our experience that use of custom hardware significantly slows down simulation. Note that the power circuit and the motor is simulated using a special simulator. A screen image of this simulation is shown in Figure 2.

9.3 RTOS AND DEVICE DRIVER DEBUGGING

Traditionally, operating systems and device drivers have been debugged using working hardware. A part of the real-time operating system kernel and device drivers for a microcontroller based on the M16 processor has been debugged using the co-simulator. The hardware used for this purpose consists of an M16 CPU, an ICU, three timers and two parallel ports. Interrupts are fed to the system from two external buttons and are also generated by the timers.

The software running on this system consists of six tasks and the real-time OS. Task1 is invoked when there is an interrupt from any timer and counts the number of timer interrupts. Task 2 is invoked when there is an interrupt from the first button and counts the number of button interrupts. Task 3 is invoked when there is an interrupt from the second button and resets the count kept by task 2. The rest of the tasks, numbered 4 to 6 are scheduled in round robin fashion. The task number being executed is displayed through one parallel port and the number of button interrupts is displayed through the other one.

Simulation of the RTOS can be performed at a speed of 23,000 instructions per second. This represents a slowdown of 1500 compared to the RTOS running on an M16. This speed is adequate for the debugging of the RTOS. The debugging environment is natural for a software developer and the greater observability of the internal state of the processor during simulation also helps debugging.

Our experience so far suggests that a PAS is adequate for debugging the interface between hardware and software. However, we recommend the use of more accurate timing simulation using bus functional models in conjunction with co-simulation.

10 CONCLUSIONS AND FUTURE WORK

We have presented a hardware-software co-simulator for embedded system design and debugging. This tool provides a natural environment for joint debugging of software and hardware and is also useful for evaluating system performance, selection of algorithms and implementations and also for exploring hardware-software trade-offs. We have addressed the problem of simulation speed and have outlined various methods to speed up simulation. The improved speed of the co-simulator comes from various sources. First, our co-simulator is targeted towards phase-accurate simulation. Switching between ISS and PAS during simulation, caching of decoded instructions and not simulating instruction fetch cycles all contribute to the increased speed of simulation of processors. Use of dedicated simulators, suppression of periodic signals and associated events, and specific short cuts reduce the time required for simulation of peripherals. Making time discrete and using a statically allocated timing wheel helps keep coordination overhead low. We have demonstrated the use of the tool in three design examples and have shown that the simulation speed is adequate.

The usefulness of this tool will depend on several factors. First amongst these is the availability of simulators for standard components. Second, is the adequacy of cycle-accurate simulation in system verification. We are continuing our research in this area. We feel a co-design methodology with conservative design rules, use of bus functional models to ensure compliance and an overall design style to aid simulation may be required.

Apart from the items mentioned before, in the future we are looking at incorporating other processor and hardware simulators into our framework. We believe that the next major increase in simulation speed will come from compiled simulation and we are investigating promising techniques in this area, especially in the simulation of processors. We are also investigating the use of a network of workstations to speed up simulation. There is ongoing work on a better user interface that includes system schematic capture, dynamic attachment of virtual instruments, *etc.* so that a virtual laboratory can be created on the desktop. Improving the efficiency of the simulation backplane is another area of ongoing work. The actor library is being enhanced to include commonly used components in embedded system design. We are also developing links to compilers and hardware design tools so that the co-simulator can be easily integrated into a design methodology.

References

[1] D. Becker, R. K. Singh and S. G. Tell, "An Engineering Environment for Hardware/Software Co-simulation", *Proceedings of the 29th Design Automation Conference*, Anaheim, CA, 1992.

[2] J. Buck, S. Ha, E. A. Lee and D. G. Messerschmitt, "Ptolemy: a Framework for Simulating and Prototyping Heterogeneous Systems", *International Journal of Computer Simulation*, special issue on "Simulation Software Development," January, 1994.

[3] W. B. Culbertson, T. Osame, Y. Ohtsuru, J. B. Shackleford and M. Tanaka, "The HP Tsutsuji Logic Synthesis System", Hewlett-Packard Journal, August 1993.

[4] R. K. Gupta, C. N. Coelho Jr. and G. De Michel, "Synthesis and Simulation of Digital Systems Containing Interacting Hardware and Software Components", *Proceedings of the 29th Design Automation Conference*, Anaheim, CA, 1992.

[5] IEEE Design and Test Magazine Roundtable, "Hardware/Software Codesign", IEEE Design and Test Magazine, March 1993.

[6] A. Kalavade and E. A. Lee, "A Hardware/Software Codesign Methodology for DSP Applications", *IEEE Design and Test*, September, 1993.

[7] Y. Kra, "A Cross-Debugging Method for Hardware/Software Co-design Environments", *Proceedings of the 30th Design Automation Conference*, Dallas, TX, 1993.

[8] The M31000S2FP Users Manual, Mitsubishi Electric Corporation, Japan.

[9] J. K. Ousterhout, *An Introduction to Tcl and Tk*, Addison-Wesley Publishing Company, 1994.

[10] H. El Tahawy, D. Rodriguez, S. Garcia-Sabiro and J-J. Mayol, "VHDeLDO: A New Mixed Mode Simulation", *Proceedings of the European Design Automation Conference*, CCH Hamburg, 1993.

[11] J. A. Rawson, "Hardware/Software Co-simulation", *Proceedings of the 31st Design Automation Conference*, San Diego, CA, 1994.

[12] D. E. Thomas, J. K. Adams and H. Schmit, "A Model and Methodology for Hardware-Software Codesign", IEEE Design and Test of Computers, September, 1993.

[13] *Thor Tutorial*, VLSI/CAD Group, Stanford University, 1986.

[14] *Verilog-XL Reference and Programming Language Interface Manuals*, Cadence Design Systems, 1992.

[15] T. Weber and F. Somenzi, "Periodic Signal Suppression in a Concurrent Fault Simulator", *Proceedings of the European Conference on Design Automation*, Amsterdam, 1991.

A Unified Model for Co-simulation and Co-synthesis of Mixed Hardware/Software Systems

C. A. Valderrama [1] A. Changuel P.V. Raghavan M. Abid[2] T. Ben Ismail A. A. Jerraya

TIMA / INPG, System-Level Synthesis Group
46 avenue Félix Viallet 38031 Grenoble CEDEX, FRANCE

Abstract

This paper presents a methodology for a unified co-simulation and co-synthesis of hardware-software systems. This approach addresses the modeling of communication between the hardware and software modules at different abstraction levels and for different design tools. The main contribution is the use of a multi-view library concept in order to hide specific hardware/software implementation details and communication schemes. A system is viewed as a set of communicating hardware(VHDL) and software(C) sub-systems. The same C, VHDL descriptions can be used for both co-simulation and hardware-software co-synthesis. This approach is ilustrated by an example.

1. Introduction

The goal of this work is to develop a methodology for the design of highly modular and flexible electronic systems including both software and hardware. In this paper, a system stands for the composition of a set of distributed modules communicating through a network. The general model is composed of three kinds of modules: (1) Software (SW) modules, (2) Hardware (HW) modules, and (3) Communication components.

This paper deal with the co-simulation and co-synthesis of such heterogeneous system starting from a mixed C,VHDL description. During this stage of the Co-Design process, we assume that hardware software partitioning is already made. The remaining steps include co-simulation (joint simulation of the hardware and the software) and co-synthesis (mapping of the model onto an architecture including hardware blocks and software blocks).

The definition of a joint environment co-synthesis and co-simulation poses the following challenges:
- communication between the HW and SW modules,
- coherence between the results of co-simulation and co-synthesis and
- support for multiple platforms aimed at co-simulation and co-synthesis.

The first issue is essentially caused due to three reasons: Mismatch in the HW/SW execution speeds, communication influenced by data dependencies and support for different protocols [2].

The second issue is coming from the fact that different environments are used for simulation and synthesis. In order to evaluate the HW, the co-simulation environment generally uses a co-simulation library that provides means for communication between the HW and the SW. On the other hand, the co-synthesis produces code and/or HW that will execute on a real architecture. If enough care is not taken, this could result in two different descriptions for co-simulation and co-synthesis.

The third issue is imposed by the target architecture. In general, the co-design is mapping a system specification onto a HW-SW platform that includes a processor to execute the SW and a set of ASICs to realize the HW. In such a platform (Example: a standard PC with an extended FPGA card), the communication model is generally fixed. Of course, the goal is to be able to support as many different platforms as possible.

This paper presents a flexible modeling strategy allowing to deal with the three above mentioned problems. The general model allows to separate the behaviour of the modules (hardware and software) and the communication units. Inter-modules interaction is abstracted using communication primitives that hide the implementation details of the communication units.

In the following section, we give a brief overview of the existing co-design solutions. In section 3, we describe the models used for co-synthesis and co-simulation, followed by a real example (section 4). Finally, in section 5, we conclude with perspectives and directions for the future work.

2. Previous work

Several researchers have described frameworks and methodologies for HW/SW Codesign [1]6][7][9][12]. Moreover, different methodologies have been apppplied to the co-simulation of heterogeneous HW/SW systems [2][3][4][8][9][10][11].

Most of the previous works have been targetted towards

1: On leave from the Federal University of Rio deJaneiro, under grant suported by CAPES/COFECUB, BRAZIL.
2: On leave from University of Monastir, Tunisia.

either co-simulation or co-synthesis. Very few of them tried to combine both [8][9][10]. However, they do not address all the 3 problems mentioned in the previous section, especially that of supporting multiple platforms. Generally, they use a fixed communication scheme provided by the chosen platform (Example: a PC-FPGA platform) in which case, the first two problems addressed are easily handled [5][7][8][12].

The goal of this work is to combine the co-simulation and co-synthesis into a unified environment. The modeling approach hides specific HW/SW implementation details and communication schemes, thus, allowing the co-synthesis and co-simulation to start from the same description.

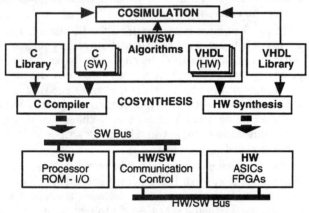

Figure 1: Modeling methodology

Figure 1 shows a global view of the proposed methodology. It starts from a modular description composed of three parts: a set of HW components described in VHDL, a set of SW components as C programs, and a set of communication component(s) to connect the above two parts. The latter, namely the communication components, corresponds to a library of components, which helps to hide the possibly complex behavior of an existing platform. The first step is to validate the above description using a HW/SW co-simulation. In this paper, we assume a VHDL-based co-simulation environment.

To be precise, a VHDL entity is used to connect a HW module with that of SW. The same description will be used for co-synthesis as well. Each module can be synthesized using the corresponding tool. Hardware(VHDL) components are treated by high-level synthesis tools, while software(C) components are handled by available software compilers. The communication units are placed into a

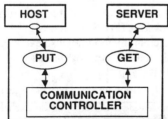

Figure 2: The Communication Unit concept

library of components and are not synthesized. System-level interaction is abstracted using communication primitives that hide the underlying communication protocol. Therefore, each sub-system can be treated independently of the communication scheme. This methodology enables the user to profit from a wide range of communication schemes. This will be introduced in the following section.

3. Communication Modeling

Communication between sub-systems is performed using communication units [14]. A communication unit is an entity able to execute a communication scheme invoked through a procedure call mechanism. Access to the communication unit is achieved by a fixed set of procedures, known as *methods* or *services*. In order to communicate, a system needs to access at least one procedure by means of procedure call(s). The communication unit can include a controller which guards its current state as well as conflict-resolution functions. The complexity of the *controller* may range from a simple handshake protocol to as complex as a layered protocol. The procedures interact with the controller which in turn modifies the unit's global state and synchronizes the communication. By using this mechanism, it is possible to model most system-level communication properties such as message passing, shared resources and other more complex protocols.

Figure 2 shows an abstract view of a communication unit linking two processes (*Host-Server*) and offering two services (procedures *get* and *put*). Each process can be designed independently of one another.

In this conceptual view, the communication unit is an object that can execute one or several procedures (*get* and *put*) that may share some common resource(s) (*communication controller*). A communication unit may correspond to either an existing communication platform, or a design produced by external tools, or to a subsystem resulting from an early design session. This concept is similar to the concept of system function library in programming languages.

The use of procedures allows to hide the details related to the communication unit. All access to the interface of the communication unit is made through these procedures.

The procedures fix the protocol of exchanging parameters between the sub-systems and the communication unit. Communication abstraction in this manner, enables modular specification [16]. This kind of model is very common in the field of telecommunication.

In order to allow the use of a communication unit by different modules, that may be either HW or SW, we need to describe its communication procedures into different views. The number and type of these views for each procedure depend on the co-simulation and co-synthesis environments.

Figure 3 gives three different views for the procedure *put*, of which two are software views and one hardware view. The two SW views are needed for co-simulation and co-synthesis respectively. The SW simulation view hides the simulation environment. The SW synthesis view hides the VHDL, which is common to both co-simulation and co-compilation environment. The HW view is given in synthesis. In the case where we use different synthesis systems supporting different abstraction levels (e.g. a behavioral synthesis and an RTL synthesis), we may need different views for the communication procedures.

The software synthesis view will depend upon the choice of a target architecture. That is the reason why we observe a stack of multiple SW Synthesis views in Figure

a) SW synthesis views

```
/*IBM/PC software synthesis view*/
typedef enum { INIT, . . ., IDLE } STATETABLE;
STATETABLE NEXTSTATE = INIT;
int PUT(REQUEST) INTEGER REQUEST;
{ switch(NEXTSTATE)
  { case INIT:
    { if(ToBIT(inport(map(B_FULL))) == BIT_1)
      { NEXTSTATE := WAIT_B_FULL; break; }
      outport(map(DATAIN),FromINTEGER(REQUEST));
      NEXTSTATE := DATA_RDY; break; }
    case WAIT_B_FULL:
    { if(ToBIT(inport(map(B_FULL))) == BIT_0)
      { NEXTSTATE := INIT; break; }}
      /*other "case" clauses*/
      default :{ NEXTSTATE = INIT; break; } }
  if (NEXTSTATE == IDLE)  DONE = 0;
  else {NEXTSTATE == INIT; DONE = 1; }
  return DONE; }
```

b) SW simulation view

```
typedef enum { INIT, . . ., IDLE } STATETABLE;
STATETABLE NEXTSTATE = INIT;
int PUT(REQUEST) INTEGER REQUEST;
{ switch(NEXTSTATE)
  { case INIT:
    { if(ToBIT(cliGetPortValue(map(B_FULL))) == BIT_1)
      { NEXTSTATE = WAIT_B_FULL; break; }
      cliOutput(map(DATAIN),FromINTEGER(REQUEST));
      NEXTSTATE = DATA_RDY; break; }
    case WAIT_B_FULL :
    { if(ToBIT(cliGetPortValue(map(B_FULL))) == BIT_0)
      { NEXTSTATE = INIT; break; }}
      /*other "case" clauses*/
      default: { NEXTSTATE = INIT; break; } }
  if (NEXTSTATE == IDLE)  DONE = 0;
  else {NEXTSTATE = INIT; DONE = 1; }
  return DONE; }
```

c) HW view

```
procedure PUT(REQUEST: in INTEGER) is
begin
  case NEXT_STATE is
    when INIT =>
      if B_FULL = '1' then NEXT_STATE := WAIT_B_FULL;
      end if;
      DATAIN <= REQUEST; NEXT_STATE := DATA_RDY;
    when WAIT_B_FULL =>
      if B_FULL = '0' then  NEXT_STATE := INIT;  end if;
    --other "when" clauses
    when OTHERS => NEXTSTATE := INIT;
  end case;
  if NEXTSTATE = IDLE then DONE := '0';
  else NEXTSTATE = INIT; DONE := '1'; end if;
end procedure;
```

Figure 3 : Different views of a communication procedure

3. If the communication is entirely a software executing on a given operating system, communication procedure calls are expanded into system calls, making use of existing communication mechanisms available within the system (for example, Inter Process Communication of UNIX®). If the communication is to be executed on a standard processor, the call becomes an access to a bus routine written as an assembler code. The communication can also be executed as an embedded software on a hardware datapath controlled by a micro-coded controller, in which case, our communication procedure call will become a call to a standard micro-code routine. To summarize, we have one HW view given in VHDL, one SW simulation view given in C, and a SW synthesis view specific to each target architecture.

4. An example

Our approach has been successfully used for modelling an Adaptative Motor Controller system. The Adaptative Motor Controller adjusts the position and speed parameters of a motor to avoid discontinuous operation problems. For example, the control in a 2-D space needs one motor for each axis (X and Y) and an associated control system for a continuous movement. As shown in figure 4, the Adaptative Motor Controller is composed of two sub-systems communicating via a channel of communication.

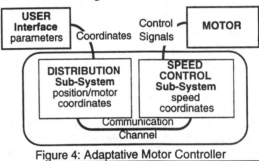

Figure 4: Adaptative Motor Controller

The *Distribution* sub-system provides the traveling distance to the *Speed Control* sub-system. With the specified final position and the current state of a motor, the Speed Control sub-system computes the number of speed control pulses and translates them into motor control signals. The system is partitioned into communicating HW/SW sub-systems and its associated communication units (figure 5). The communication between software and hardware is described using a SW/HW communication unit composed of two groups of access procedures (*Distribution_Interface* and *Control_Interface*). The communication between the Speed Control sub-system and the motor is achieved by a HW/HW communication unit (accesed by a collection of procedures called *Motor_Interface*). The use of the above communication units enables the description of the sub-systems independent of the architectural platform that may be chosen.

The Distribution sub-system is a software model. Figure 6a shows its main computation steps and the main

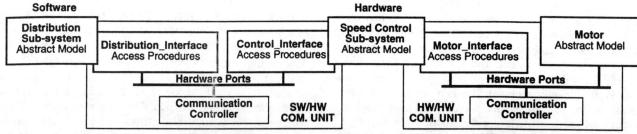

Figure 5: The Adaptative Motor Controller: HW/SW communicating sub-systems

communication primitives used by this subsystem. It activates the Speed Control sub-system of the motor by specifying the maximum position value and the maximum number of speed-pulses.

The total translation distance of the motor is divided into segments and is sent to the Speed Control sub-system as bundles of data. The initialization data, motor selection and position coordinates are transmitted to the Speed Control sub-system by the Distribution_Interface access procedures (*SetupControl*, *MotorPosition*, and *ReadMotorState*) which communicate through the I/O interface (SW/HW ports).

Figure 6b shows an extract of the C code corresponding to the Distribution Sub-system. The code is organized as a finite state machine composed of states and transitions. During simulation, each time a software component is activated, all the code is executed. In our case, only one transition is executed. This model allows for a precise synchronization between software and hardware.

The Speed Control sub-system is a hardware model described in VHDL (figure 7). This sub-system uses communication procedures, which are described in VHDL. The sub-system is composed of three parallel units, named: *Position*, *Core* and *Timer*. The *Position* unit communicates with the Distribution sub-system using the Control_Interface access procedures by sending the actual motor state (via *ReturnMotorState* access procedure) and waiting for the new coordinates and motor constraint parameters (*ReadMotorConstraints* and *ReadMotorPosition* access procedures). The *Core* unit computes the residual position and the next operation conditions. It communicates with the two other units using simple VHDL signals. The *Timer* unit sends a set of control pulses to the motor and reads the motor coordinates using the Motor_Interface access procedures (*SendMotorPulses* and *ReadSampledData*).

As stated above we use a VHDL based simulator. The cosimulation step allows for a functional validation of the specification. Once the co-simulation step is achieved, co-synthesis may start. In this case we used an architecture composed of a PC-AT communicationg with an FPGA based board via the extension bus of the PC. During co-synthesis, the communication primitives selected correspond to the target architectures. The software primitives correspond to C programs that makes use of specific system calls (I/O routines) requiring some physical addresses. The communication primitives used by the hardware side are written in order to respect the timing and the protocol considerations required by the PC and the motor signals. As shown in figure 8, the Distribution sub-system (a C program) was compiled on a 386-based PC-AT which communicates with a development board (the Speed Control sub-system) via a 16-bit parallel bus (synchronous communication, 10 Mhz, address 300h). The Speed Control sub-system was synthesized onto a Xilinx 4000-series FPGA, associated with memories (EPROMs) and a microcomputer interface. An analysis of the prototype system indicates that this solution correctly implements the system functionality while meeting the real-time constraints.

In order to map this application onto another target architecture, we need to have the corresponding

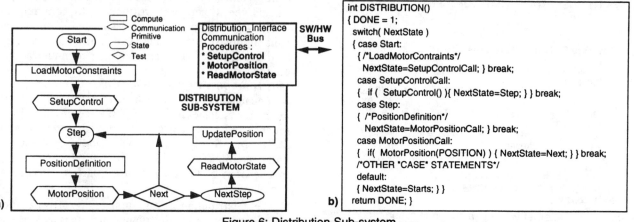

Figure 6: Distribution Sub-system

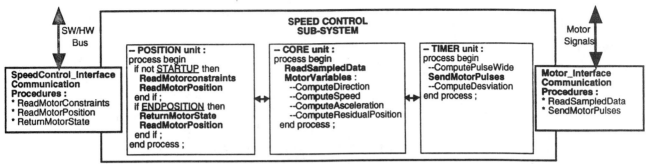

Figure 7: Speed Control System(VHDL)

communication primitives. One can note that the target architecture may be a complex multiprocessor architecture.

5. Conclusion

This paper presented an environment for hardware-software co-design based on mixed C, VHDL specifications. A unified co-synthesis and co-simulation methodology is ensured by the utilization of the same descriptions for both steps. It also allows to accomodate several architectural models through the use of a library of communication models enabling the abstraction of existing communication schemes. In other words, the same module descriptions are usable with different architectures in terms of their underlying communication protocols. Future work consists of developing tools for evaluation and back-annotation with the results of co-synthesis tools.

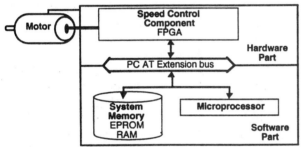

Figure 8: The Adaptative Motor Controller System Prototype

References

[1] T.Ben Ismail, M.Abid, K.O'Brien, A.A.Jerraya, "An Approach for Hardware-Software Codesign", RSP'94, Grenoble, France, June 1994.

[2] K.Ten Hagen, H.Meyer, "Timed and Untimed Hardware/ Software Cosimulation: Application and Efficient Implementation", International Workshop on Hardware-Software Codesign,Cambridge,October 1993.

[3] W.M.Loucks,B.J.Doray,D.G.Agnew,"Experiences In Real Time Hardware-Software Cosimulation",Proc VHDL Int. Users Forum (VIUF),Otawa,Canada,pp.47-57,April 1993.

[4] B.K.Fross, "Modeling Techniques Using VHDL/C-language Interfacing", March 30,1993.

[5] R.K.Gupta,G.De Micheli,"System-level Synthesis using Re-programmable Components",Proc.Third European Conf. Design Automation, IEEE CS Press,pp.2-7,1992.

[6] A.Kalavade,E.A.Lee,"A Hardware-Software Codesign Methodology for DSP Applications",IEEE Design and Test of Computers,pp.16-28,September 1993.

[7] J.K.Adams, H.Schmit, D.E.Thomas, "A Model and Methodology for Hardware-Software Codesign", International Workshop on Hardware-Software Codesign, Cambridge, October 1993.

[8] S.Lee,J.M.Rabaey,"A Hardware Software Cosimulation Environment",International Workshop on Hardware-Software Codesign,Cambridge,October 1993.

[9] H.Fleukers,J.A.Jess,"ESCAPE: A Flexible Design and Simulation Environment", Proc. of The Synthesis and Simulation Meeting and International Interchange, SASIMI'93,pp.277-288,Oct.1993.

[10] N.L. Rethman, P.A.Wilsey, "RAPID: A Tool For Hardware/ Software Tradeoff Analysis", Proc. CHDL'93, Otawa,Canada,April 1993.

[11] P.Camurati, F.Corno, P.Prinetto, C.Bayol, B.Soulas, "System-Level Modeling and Verification: a Comprehensive Design Methodology", Proc. of EDAC-ETC-EuroASIC'94,Paris,February 1994.

[12] E.A.Walkup,G.Boriello,"Automatic Synthesis of Device Drivers for Hardware/Software Co-design", International Workshop on Hardware-Software Codesign, Cambridge, October 1993.

[13] A.A.Jerraya,K.O'Brien, "SOLAR: An Intermediate Format for System-level Modeling and Synthesis", "Computer Aided Software/Hardware Engineering", J.Rozenblit, K.Buchenrieder(eds),IEEE Press,1994.

[14] K.O'Brien,T.Ben Ismail,A.A.Jerraya,"A Flexible Communication Modelling Paradigm for System-level Synthesis",International Workshop on Hardware-Software Codesign,Cambridge,October 1993.

[15] "Synopsys VHDL System Simulator Interfaces Manual: C-language Interface",Synopsys Inc.,Version 3.0b,June 1993.

[16] D.Ungar, R.B.Smith, C.Chambers, U.Holzle, "Object, Message, and Perfomance: How They Coexist in Self", IEEE Computer, October1992.

COMPILED HW/SW CO-SIMULATION

Vojin Živojnović and Heinrich Meyr

Integrated Systems for Signal Processing
Aachen University of Technology
Templergraben 55, 52056-Aachen, Germany
zivojnov[meyr]@ert.rwth-aachen.de

ABSTRACT

This paper presents a technique for simulating processors and attached hardware using the principle of compiled simulation. Unlike existing, in-house and off-the-shelf hardware/software co-simulators, which use interpretive processor simulation, the proposed technique performs instruction decoding and simulation scheduling at compile time. The technique offers up to three orders of magnitude faster simulation. The high speed allows the user to explore algorithms and hardware/software trade-offs before any hardware implementation. In this paper, the sources of the speedup and the limitations of the technique are analyzed and the realization of the simulation compiler is presented.

I. Introduction

Simultaneous design of hardware and software can take place at different abstraction levels. At the *HLL-level* compiler and processor are designed jointly in order to obtain optimum performance on selected high-level language constructs. At the *application-level* the on- and off-chip hardware have a role of a processing accelerator, or external interface, and are optimized to deliver optimum results for a specific application or a class of them. The goal of *instruction-level* HW/SW co-design is to make frequently used instructions fast by appropriate design of the instruction set architecture of the processor. All three levels correspond to *software-based* HW/SW co-design, where the realization in software is the starting point, and hardware alternatives are introduced in order to speedup execution. Independently of the abstraction level, the co-design cycle has to be closed by intensive verification of hardware and software.

Debugging and verification can be done using hardware or software models, i.e. emulators or simulators, respectively. The main advantage of hardware models, like emulators is their speed, which is mostly only an order of magnitude slower than the speed of the final system. However, emulators are costly, offer low visibility of the internal state of the device, possess low flexibility, deliver inaccurate timing, and the design has to be specially adapted in order to be run on an emulation platform. Also, with emulators the boundary between hardware and software is mostly a priori fixed. This contradicts directly the main philosophy of HW/SW co-design — to take advantage of a flexible boundary between hardware and software, and to position it in an optimum way.

All these drawbacks are easily circumvented using a software model. The price paid is the significantly reduced speed. Although selecting the appropriate simulation accuracy can deliver faster simulation, there are still up to four orders of magnitude difference in speed between emulators and simulators.

In this paper we describe a new technique for HW/SW co-simulation. It relies on the principle of compiled simulation for simulation of both hardware and software. Whereas compiled simulation is a well known approach to hardware simulation, its use for simulation of software is new. All reported HW/SW co-simulation environments rely on the classical interpretive processor simulation technique. We show that compiled simulation is able to deliver bit-true, clock-true simulation of the instruction set architecture of the processor with a speedup of up to three orders of magnitude compared to the classical interpretive technique. The new simulation technique can be applied equally well to verification of *HLL-*, *application-*, or *instruction-level* HW/SW co-designs.

According to Amdahl's law, even a significant speedup in software simulation can be of minor value for HW/SW co-simulation if hardware simulation is the bottleneck. However, if the cycle-based behavioral or RTL model of the hardware is appropriate, the amount of co-simulated hardware is limited, or if the interaction between software and hardware is localized to specific code fragments or initiated only by events which happen less frequently than the clock edge of the processor, the increased software simulation speed can influence the overall HW/SW co-simulation speed significantly. Our experience shows that in a great deal of embedded systems with DSP functionality both of these conditions are met.

Additional advantage of the compiled approach is comfortable HW/SW debugging with a single source level debugger for hardware and software. If the C code is selected as the intermediate format for software simulation, and the behavioral model of the hardware is written in C, the standard source level debugger of the host can be used to debug hardware and software. Thereby, the HW/SW debugger has all the program-control and state-observation features of standard instruction level debuggers, and at the same time permits cycle-based hardware debugging.

Compiled simulation achieves the high speed by additional compile-time preprocessing which influences the overall turnaround time. The increased preprocessing time is the price which has to be paid for improved runtime performance and presents the main drawback of the technique. However, using incremental compilation only the redesigned parts of the code can be preprocessed and thereby the overall preprocessing time reduced.

The paper is organized as follows. After the introduction in Section II the motivation guiding this work is explained. Section III discusses previous work which is related to those presented in the paper. The principle of compiled simulation for programmable architectures is presented in Section IV. The realization of the simulation compiler for three off-the-shelf DSP processors with different architectures is reported in Section V. Section VI provides a detailed discussion about HW/SW co-simulation and debugging using the compiled technique. Finally, in Section VII the conclusions are given.

II. Motivation

The main motivation for the work presented in this paper was the low speed of the instruction-level simulators found in HW/SW co-simulation environments. The following example arises from the development of the ADPCM G.721 and G.726 speech transcoders for the Digital European Cordless Telecommunications (DECT) and Digital Circuit Multiplication Equipment (DCME).

First, we used an off-the-shelf DSP processor. Off-line verification of the hand-written software implementation ($\sim$93 millions instructions) on the standard set of CCITT-ITU test sequences (13 seconds of speech signals) on the target hardware took 7 seconds. The same verification using the instruction set simulator (4K insns/s) provided by the DSP chip vendor took approximately 6.4 hours on an 86 MIPS machine (Sparc-10).

Next, we wanted to explore ways to speedup execution of the transcoder introducing changes in the architecture. It is well known that the FMULT procedure of the G.726 algorithm is the time-critical part of the algorithm. We extended the processor model with a simple hardware accelerator executing the normalization operation of the FMULT procedure. The additional clock-accurate behavioral model of the accelerator had almost no impact on the verification speed. Multiple instructions have been replaced by a single I/O write/read function, so that the simulation speed was decreased only modestly, However, we needed additional 7 hours of simulation to validate correctness and performance of the new design. Experimentation with finite-word length issues could not be done with this simulator.

If the same algorithm is expressed in C, and compiled using the C compiler provided by the chip-vendor, off-line verification of the resulting code ($\sim$750 millions instructions) on the simulator would last for 2 days and 3 hours. Obviously, the turnaround time has to be measured in days and any experimentation with application-oriented compiler and processor adaptations is impossible.

We observed that for the kind of HW/SW co-designs we are interested in, the software simulator is the bottleneck. It is well known that in most cases the clock-accurate model of the attached hardware consumes more simulation time than the simulation of a single clock-cycle of the processor. However, in *software-based* HW/SW co-designs the interaction with the hardware is mostly localized to specific code fragments of the software. In this case the hardware can be modeled using a less accurate model during periods of no interaction, and a more accurate when the interaction with the software takes place. As a consequence, the overall simulation speed of the hardware is significantly higher than the speed of the software simulator, and the software simulator becomes a limiting factor.

III. Previous Work

Processor simulators such as instruction set simulators are almost always supplied with off-the-shelf or in-house DSP processor. They enable comfortable debugging and verification through controlled program execution and provide visibility of processor resources necessary for code development. All currently available instruction set simulators use the interpretive simulation technique. Their main disadvantages are the low simulation speed (2K-20K insns/s [1]) and their inability to be extended by the user.

Instruction set simulators are standard components of HW/SW co-design environments [2,3]. The speed of these simulators ranges from 300 insns/s to 20K insns/s depending on the character of the processor model, the simulation technique applied or the accuracy level provided.

The compiled simulation technique we use for our simulator is well known in simulation of hardware circuits, e.g. [4]. We follow the same general idea, but apply it to the simulation of the instruction set architecture. Our approach resembles binary translation used for migrating executables from one machine to another [5], or collecting run-time statistics [6]. However, clock/bit-true translation and debugging are not objectives of binary translation.

IV. Compiled Simulation of Programmable Architectures

Interpretive simulators process instructions using a software model of the target processor. A virtual processor is built using a data structure representing the state of the processor, and a program which changes the processor state according to the stimuli — either a new instruction pointed to by the program sequencer or some external events, such as interrupts. In general, interpretive simulators can be summarized as a loop in which instructions are fetched, decoded, and executed using a "big switch" statement, such as the one below:

```
       while(run) {
           next = fetch(PC);
           insn = decode(next);
           switch (insn) {
               ...
   add:        exe_add(); break;
               ...
           }
       }
```

Our approach translates each target instruction directly to one or more host instructions. For example, if the following three target instructions

```
           add r1,r2;
           mov r2,mem(0x175);
           mul r2,r3;
```

are interpreted, the above simulation loop iterates once for each instruction. The compiled simulation approach translates the target instructions into the following host instructions, represented here as macros:

```
ADD(_R1,_R2); SAT(_R2); ADJ_FL(_R2); PC();
MOV(_R2,MEM(0x175)); ADJ_FL(); PC();
MUL(_R2,_R3); SAT(_R3); ADJ_FL(_R3); PC();
```

where `SAT()`, `ADJ_FL()`, and `PC()` model the saturation logic, adjustment of the flags, and the change of the program counter, respectively. The translation completely eliminates the fetch and decode steps, and loop overheads of interpretation, resulting in a faster simulation. For target processors with complex instruction encoding, the decode step can account for a significant amount of time. Additional speedup is created because the compiled-simulation generates code tailored to the required accuracy level, while an interpreter provides a fixed level of accuracy. For example, if interrupts are not required, compiled-simulation suppresses the simulation of the interrupt logic already at compile-time, and no run-time penalty is payed.

For large programs, the speed of compiled simulation could be degraded by low locality of reference if the generated simulation code is much larger than the available cache. In this situation, an interpreter would perform better. DSP programs, however, typically exhibit high locality; as a result, the generated simulation program does also. Moreover, the program memory of DSP processors, especially fixed-point ones, is small compared to typical host-machine cache sizes. Our measurements show no difference in simulation speed between small and large DSP programs. However, a detailed analysis still has to be done.

However, compiled-simulation assumes that the code does not change during run-time. Therefore self-modifying programs will force us to use a hybrid interpretive/compiled scheme. Fortunately, self-modifying programs are rare. The isolated cases we encountered so far are limited to programs that change the target address in branch instructions. This type of self-modifying code, however, can be easily handled without interpreting.

The binary-to-binary translation process can be organized in two ways. The direct approach translates target binary to host binary directly (Fig. 1a). It guarantees fast translation and simulation times, but the translator is more complex and less portable between hosts. To simplify the translator and improve its portability, we split the translation process into two parts — compile the target code to a program written in a high-level language such as C (front-end processing), and then compile the program into host code (back-end processing) (Fig. 1b). In this way we take advantage of existing compilers on the host and we reduce the realization of the simulation compiler to building the front-end. Portability is greatly improved but with a possible loss in simulation speed.

Some features of machine code are difficult to represent in a high-level language like C. For example, in the absence of very sophisticated analysis, compiled simulation must assume that every instruction can be a target of an indirect branch statement. Therefore, every

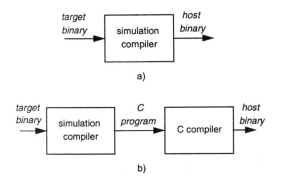

Figure 1: Two Approaches to Binary-To-Binary Translation.

compiled instruction must have a label, and computed `goto` or `switch` statements are used to simulate indirect branching. These labels reduce the effectiveness of many compiler optimizations. If indirect branching is not used in the code, and this is reported to the simulation compiler by an appropriate flag, the generated intermediate code is more amenable to compiler optimizations.

V. Realization of the Simulation Compiler

The simulation environment *SuperSim* SS-21xx has been implemented for the Analog Devices ADSP-21xx family of DSP processors. It consists of the simulation compiler (`ssc`), host C compiler (`gcc`), and C source level debugger (`dbx`). This enables cycle- and bit-true behavioral simulation of the processor in a comfortable debugging environment.

The `ssc` simulation compiler has a form of a two-pass translator with a translation speed of about 1500 target insns/s (Sun-10/64MB). Translating the whole program memory (16 Kinsns) of the ADSP-2105 into intermediate C representation takes less than 11 seconds. To enable additional trade-off between recompilation and execution speed, the simulation compiler can translate target instructions into intermediate C code using macros or function calls.

Compiling the intermediate C code to the host executable takes most of the overall translation time. For the version with function-calls the compilation speed of the `gcc-2.5.8` compiler with optimization -O1 was about 240 target insns/s (120 target insns/s for -O3). For all 16 Kinsns the compilation with -O1 takes less than 2 minutes. Using macros the compilation speed slows down almost 5 times compared to the function-call version. In the same time the speedup in execution time is only about 30%. Our current work is concentrating on speeding up the compilation by recompiling only those parts of the target binary which have been changed.

Table 1 presents some real-life examples of SS-21xx performance. Simulation speed measured in insns/s depends on the complexity of instructions found in the target code. The FIR filter example is generated by the C compiler of the target that generates compound instructions rarely. However, the ADPCM example is hand-coded optimally and uses complex compound instructions frequently. The results from Table 1 show that our simulator outperforms the standard simulator by almost three orders of magnitude on the FIR example and by about 200 times on the ADPCM example. The same verification which took 6.4 hours with the standard ADSP-21xx simulator is reduced to less than 2 minutes using *SuperSim*.

The speed improvement we obtained has two main sources. One source is the compile-time decoding and scheduling of the instructions. The other source is that the final simulation program does not include any debugging-related code, but still offers complete debugging support. All the necessary debugging information is inserted by the compiler of the host, and the host-specific debugger. The existing interpretive simulators are designed to support host-independent debugging, and are forced to insert debugging-related operations (e.g. breakpoint checking) at the source level. This introduces an additional, significant slowdown of the simulation.

The ADSP-21xx does not have a visible pipeline. In order to prove our concepts on architectures with pipeline effects, we have written compiled simulation examples for the TI's TMS320C50 and NEC's μPD77016 processors. Despite overhead introduced for pipeline modeling, results from Table 1 show that our approach still achieves significant speedup. Our analysis has shown that the compiled simulation technique fails if indirect delayed branches have to be simulated. In this case the simulator has to switch to the interpretive simulation. More details about compiled simulation of pipelines can be found in [7].

VI. HW/SW Co-Simulation

Designers frequently, during an early stage of the design process, create a software prototype of the design. At this stage, designers can explore implementation options in which some of the functions are shifted into hardware. *SuperSim* supports this exploration because it attaches easily to behavioral models of the hardware. Later, the behavioral models can serve as a starting point in hardware design. Co-simulation becomes useful again, once the behavioral models have been refined into hardware, perhaps rendered using a hardware description language (HDL such as VHDL or Verilog) or as a net list. One can verify such hardware components by attaching either a HDL simulator or a logic simulator to *SuperSim*.

example	simulator	optimization	insns/s	speedup
FIR filter	ADSP-21xx	-	3.9K	1
	SS-21xx	-O3	2.5M	640
	"	-O2	2.0M	510
	"	-O1	1.6M	420
	TI-C50	-	2.4K	1
	SS-C50[†]	-O3	0.4M	160
	SS-77016[†]	-O3	0.4M	-
ADPCM	ADSP-21xx	-	4.0K	1
	SS-21xx	-O3	0.8M	200
	"	-O2	0.6M	150
	"	-O1	0.4M	100

host: Sun-10/64MB; SS-21xx flags: -f; compiler: gcc 2.5.8; †-preliminary;

Table 1: Simulation Examples - Performance Results.

We coupled our compiled simulator to a block-diagram editor, a C library of clock-accurate behavioral models of hardware components, and a C code generator. The resulting HW/SW co-simulation environment is able to deliver fast, clock-accurate simulation.

Figure 2 presents an example of an A/D converter with glue logic attached to a DSP processor. Commu-

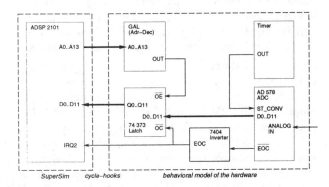

Figure 2: HW/SW Co-Simulation Using SuperSim.

nication between software and hardware is mediated by cycle hooks. The hooks pass control to the hardware model which is written in C. The hooks also accept data from the hardware models. We can insert different cycle hooks executing different hardware models depending on the type of instruction which is executed in the current cycle, or in the cycles before or after. In this way we are able to control the accuracy of the hardware simulator and thereby the speed. Obviously, the same procedure could be applied to interpretive simulators. However, in the case of compiled simulators the selection can be done already at compile-time, and no run-time overhead for selecting the appropriate hardware model is introduced.

Table 2 presents some simulation results. The example is taken from the front-end of a speech processing device. It consists of an FIR filter executing on a DSP processor, and external acquisition hardware. If the state of the hardware is updated at each clock tick using the same hardware model hook, the resulting speed of the compiled HW/SW co-simulator is 89.0K insns/s. Using the ADSP-21xx interpretive simulator delivering 4.0K insns/s the resulting HW/SW co-simulation speed would be only 3.8K insns/s. Attaching different hardware model hooks to different instruction instantiations, the simulation speed was raised to 1.1M insns/s with the SS-21xx compiled simulator, and to only 4.2K insns/s with the interpretive one.

When the hardware models are written in C, the hooks are simple calls. However, when the models are written in HDL, the hooks are more complicated. They must synchronize *SuperSim* to the HDL simulator and also convert data values before and after communicating with the HDL simulator.

Our simulator offers full debugging support using the standard C level debugger (e.g. `dbx` or `gdb`). It offers breakpoint setting and watching of registers, memory, flags, stack and pins. This is a large advantage compared to standard interpretive debuggers which are highly target dependent. Figure 3 shows an example of the graphical user interface of the `dbxtool` debugger which was adapted to execute C code of the simulator, and in the same time display assembly instructions of the target or the C code of the simulator. As soon as the simulation program reaches the clock-cycle hook, the same debugger which was used for software debugging switches to the code describing the behavioral model of the attached hardware.

Debugging of software and hardware with a standard source-level debugger is one of the main advantages of the compiled technique over the standard interpretive approach. If behavioral models of the hardware are expressed in C, and if the C language is used for the intermediate representation of the software model, compiled simulation seems to be the optimum solution for comfortable debugging of HW/SW co-designs.

simulator	model	insns(cycles)/s
SW only (ADSP-21xx)	interpretive ISA	4.0 K
SW only (SS-21xx)	compiled ISA	2.5 M
HW only	behavioral C	93.0 M
HW/SW (ADSP-21xx)	code-independent HW model	3.8 K
HW/SW (SS-21xx)	"	89.0 K
HW/SW (ADSP-21xx)	code-dependent HW model	4.2 K
HW/SW (SS-21xx)	"	1.1M
host: Sun-10/64MB; SS-21xx flags: -f; compiler: gcc 2.5.8; optimization -O3		

Table 2: HW/SW Co-Simulation - FIR Filter with Acquisition Hardware.

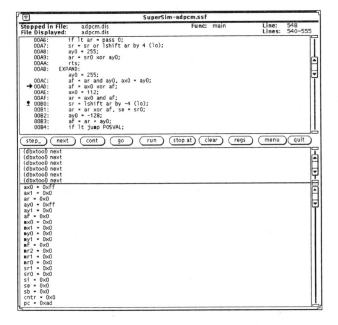

Figure 3: Debugging with *SuperSim*.

VII. Conclusions and Further Research

Compiled simulation provides very fast and accurate instruction set simulation. The presented simulation environment generates bit-, cycle-, and pin-accurate HW/SW co-simulation engines that are two to three orders of magnitude faster than interpretive simulators. Moreover, standard source level debuggers offer a comfortable debugging environment and the intermediate representation in C is open for extensions by the designer. The presented compiled simulator is easily interfaced to behavioral hardware models. In addition to fast simulation, it offers a comfortable debugging environment in which hardware and software are debugged using the same debugger.

Currently, recompilations (with *SuperSim*) after design changes are relatively slow. Though recompilation will always take additional time relative to interpretation, we believe that we can reduce the time by limiting recompilation only to code that has changed. Moreover, a *SuperSim*-interpreter hybrid, in addition to alleviating the problems of indirect delayed branches, can provide fast simulation speed, as well as fast turn-around time on design changes.

We are also investigating two key problem areas in interfacing *SuperSim* to hardware simulators: how accurate do we need to model the processor pin interface. With behavioral models, we have idealized the processor interface to a small set of pins: the data, the address, and interrupt request lines, but not detailed handshaking signals. With more detailed hardware models, however, it may be advantageous to use a detailed processor interface that simulates all pins accurately. We are investigating the attachment of commercially-available processor-interface models to *SuperSim*.

VIII. References

[1] J. Rowson, "Hardware/Software co-simulation," in *31st ACM/IEEE Design Automation Conference*, 1994.

[2] A. Kalavade and E. Lee, "A hardware-software codesign methodology for DSP applications," *IEEE Design & Test of Computers*, pp. 16–28, Sept. 1993.

[3] S. Sutarwala, P. Paulin, and Y. Kumar, "Insulin: An instruction set simulation environment," in *Proc. of CHDL-93, Ottawa, Canada*, pp. 355–362, 1993.

[4] Z. Barzilai, *et al.*, "HSS - A high speed simulator," *IEEE Trans. on CAD*, vol. CAD-6, pp. 601–616, July 1987. 1987.

[5] R. Sites, *et al.*, "Binary translation," *Comm. of the ACM*, vol. 36, pp. 69–81, Feb. 1993.

[6] J. Davidson and D. Whalley, "A design environment for addressing architecture and compiler interactions," *Microprocessors and Microsystems*, vol. 15, pp. 459–472, Nov. 1991.

[7] V. Živojnović, S. Tjiang, and H. Meyr, "Compiled simulation of programmable DSP architectures," in *Proc. of 1995 IEEE Workshop on VLSI in Signal Processing, Osaka, Japan*, Oct. 1995.

Hardware-Software Prototyping from LOTOS

LUIS SÁNCHEZ FERNÁNDEZ
Dep. Tecnologías Comunicaciones, Univ. Carlos III Madrid, E-28911 Leganés/Madrid, Spain

GERNOT KOCH
Forschungszentrum Informatik (FZI), Haid-und-Neu-Straße 10-14, D-76131 Karlsruhe, Germany

NATIVIDAD MARTÍNEZ MADRID
Dep. Tecnologías Comunicaciones, Univ. Carlos III Madrid, E-28911 Leganés/Madrid, Spain

MARÍA LUISA LÓPEZ VALLEJO
Dep. Ing. Electrónica (DIE), ETSIT, Univ. Polit. Madrid, E-28040 Madrid, Spain

CARLOS DELGADO KLOOS
Dep. Tecnologías Comunicaciones, Univ. Carlos III Madrid, E-28911 Leganés/Madrid, Spain

WOLFGANG ROSENSTIEL
FZI and University of Tübingen, Sand 13, D-72076 Tübingen, Germany

Abstract. In this paper we present an extension to the co-design approach based on LOTOS presented in Fourth International Workshop on Hardware-Software Co-Design, 1996. In this new version we add a prototyping stage to our design flow, that allows to validate the design at the implementation level. We present the complete approach, stressing the prototyping stage after partitioning. An example of an Ethernet bridge serves us to illustrate our approach and present some results.

Keywords: LOTOS, system-level design, co-design, prototyping

1. Introduction

Over the last few years, the level of abstraction applied to the description and design of hardware systems has risen. Initially, descriptions were based at the circuit level. Since then, description styles have moved to gate, register transfer (RTL) and behavioural level. We will follow the convention that, at the higher levels of abstraction, the word *specification* will be used instead of *description*. A specification denotes an abstraction. It represents what the system should do, not how it should do.

This move to higher levels of abstraction is a consequence of a number of factors. A higher level of abstraction allows the designer to reduce the time spent in specification because he/she does not need to take care of low-level implementation details. In high-level specifications the functionality of the system is clearer, allowing for a more extensive exploration of the design space. The improved ability to detect (and correct) design errors in early phases of the design process—testing the design takes less time because the number of objects in the specification is lowered by an order of magnitude—is also a significant factor. Also, this early testing reduces the number of errors to be detected at the implementation level and thus the effort to be spent there.

There is a growing awareness of high-level specification languages in system-level hardware design. The interested reader is referred to [2] for details of some of the different formalisms currently being explored. The software design world experienced an analogous phenomenon in the recent past, but the process is still ongoing in the hardware design field.

Hardware-software co-design is a new design technique that aim at an integrated design of hardware and software components of embedded systems. Which is the best specification style for co-design is still an open issue. The co-design approaches presently available make use of a broad set of specification styles. Some of them start with implementation oriented languages in the style of C or VHDL [7, 9, 27]. Others use state-oriented specification languages [8].

Some other approaches also use high-level specification languages provided with a well-founded formal semantics [1, 3, 4, 12, 24]. Apart from the points mentioned above, a high-level specification language for co-design has the advantage of allowing for a fair assignment of components, without being biased towards software or hardware realizations—as in the case of C or VHDL-like languages. In the work described in [1], UNITY is used as specification language. This work concentrates on the partitioning aspects of co-design. The specification of hardware, software and interface components described in [24], is based on FOCUS. FOCUS is a framework for the specification and development of systems based on streams. Neither [1] nor [24] provide a complete co-design flow from specification to prototyping. Two other approaches [4, 12] offer co-design systems that accept high-level specification languages as input (ESTEREL and SDL, respectively).

A co-design methodology based on the formal description technique LOTOS [11] has been developed in the ESPRIT project COBRA. In this paper the design flow presented in [3] is extended with a prototyping stage. A worked example is used to illustrate the extended design flow and present some results.

The layout for the rest of the paper is as follows. Section 2 is devoted to introduce the LOTOS language and Section 3 to show why LOTOS is better specification language than commonly used languages for many applications. Section 4 presents the LOTOS design flow. Section 5 presents the prototyping environment developed in the COBRA project. Section 6 describes the process of deriving a prototype from the partitioning obtained. Section 7 presents the worked example. We conclude with a discussion of the results obtained.

2. LOTOS

LOTOS (ISO standard IS-8807) is a system-level specification language that supports concurrency, synchronisation, composition of processes and nondeterminism. The language supports a wide range of abstraction levels, from algebraic specifications to algorithmic-style versions. The standard also includes a formal semantics, and therefore formal refinement

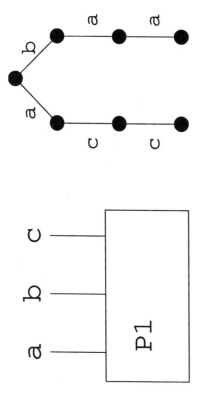

Figure 1. A LOTOS process and its behaviour tree.

and verification of LOTOS specifications are possible. LOTOS was originally designed for the specification of computer protocols, but it can also model any concurrent system; it is especially well suited to control-oriented applications. Translators from LOTOS to C [17] (TOPO) and to synthesisable VHDL [6] (HARPO) are currently available. In the rest of this section we will survey the LOTOS language. More information about LOTOS can be found in [6, 25].

System behaviour in LOTOS is defined by giving the possible sequences of interactions between the system and its environment. In contrast with other languages (for instance, C), where the behaviour of the system is defined by an algorithm that describes the internal computations that are performed in the system, in LOTOS we see the system as a black box, and we only define the behaviour of the system as seen by an external observer.

A system and its components are represented in LOTOS by *processes*. A process interacts with its environment via *gates*. A gate models a logical or physical attachment point between a system and its environment. The external observer can try to interact with a system described in LOTOS through one of its gates. This interaction can be accepted or not accepted by the system. A LOTOS description defines which are the possible sequences of interaction accepted by the system. In the case that a LOTOS process is a component of the global system, its environment is formed by the other LOTOS processes that interact with it plus the external observer.

The units of interaction between any LOTOS process and its environment are called *events* or *actions*. Events are atomic in the sense that they occur instantaneously, without consuming time. An event is an abstraction of a communication that takes place between two or more entities. An entity may be either a LOTOS process or the external observer. An event can represent different communication mechanisms, ranging from simple read/write operations through complex communication protocols depending on the abstraction level of the specification. The communication is symmetric in the sense that all the entities involved in an event (including the external observer if the event is externally observable) must agree on performing it. When several LOTOS processes agree to communicate through a common gate (i.e., to perform an event), we say that these processes *synchronise* at that gate. During an event, data can be exchanged between the entities that take part in it.

The usual graphical representation of the behaviour of a LOTOS process is a tree that defines the possible sequences of events accepted by the LOTOS process (as the traces through the tree from the root).

Figure 1 represents a LOTOS process named P1 (left side) and a graphical representation of its behaviour as a tree of accepted events (right side). This process has three gates, labelled a, b and c. At the beginning the process accepts a communication with its environment through gate a (that is, accepts an event at gate a) or gate b. If the process and its environment agree to communicate through gate a, then the process will next accept two communications through gate c (accept two consecutive events in gate c) and then will not accept any further communication with its environment. If the process and its environment agree to communicate through gate b, then the process will next accept two communications through gate a and then will not accept any further communication with its environment. Remember that each event represents an atomic communication (at the specified abstraction level) between the process and its environment. In the example in figure 1 the behaviour of the LOTOS process is finite. Later we will see how to define infinite LOTOS behaviours.

Also, in this example no data is exchanged between the process and its environment. The process and its environment only interact in order to synchronise each other. How data can be exchanged between a process and its environment will also be explained later.

LOTOS processes are defined by giving its name, the gates that define the interface between the description of the behaviour of a LOTOS process, and a behaviour expression. A behaviour expression is given below. This LOTOS process implements the behaviour of the process presented in figure 1.

```
PROCESS P1 [a, b, c] : noexit:=
    (a; b; c; stop)
    []
    (b; a; a; stop)
ENDPROC
```

The first line declares the name of the process (P1) and its gates (a, b, c). The noexit keyword is used to indicate that this process will not successfully terminate, but this is not important for the LOTOS overview we are going to give here. The next three lines form the behaviour expression that defines the behaviour of process P1. The last line indicates that the definition of the process has finished.

Let us take another look at figure 1. As we have already said, in its initial state process P1 accepts an event at gate a or an event at gate b. What does that mean exactly? First, it is not possible that both events happen. In the semantics of LOTOS it is forbidden that two events happen simultaneously. That is, in LOTOS events are temporally ordered one after the other (in fact, LOTOS stands for Language Of Temporal Ordering Specification). Therefore, if one of them happens the other branch of the behaviour tree is deleted and can no longer be executed. How can it be known which of the events would be executed? This depends on the environment. The environment of the process can accept one of the events, none or both of them. In the first case, the event accepted by the environment is the one executed. In the second case, no event can be executed. This situation (no further event can be executed) is named deadlock. In the third case one of the possible events will be nondeterministically chosen.

We have already introduced the concepts of event, synchronisation, nondeterminism and deadlock. In the rest of this section we present the main elements of the LOTOS language.

2.1. Basic LOTOS

Basic LOTOS is a subset of LOTOS in which events do not carry data. They are used just to synchronise the processes with their environment. The first element of the LOTOS language that we are going to present is the completely inactive process. It is named stop. and it cannot accept any event from its environment.

A number of operators are available in LOTOS to combine LOTOS behaviour expressions into new ones. Using these operators complex behaviour expressions can be built up. The first operator that we are going to present is the action prefix. An action prefix allows to prepend an action to a behaviour expression. Given a behaviour expression B and a gate g, the behaviour expression g ; B is equivalent to first an event in gate g and then the behaviour defined by B. It is possible to prepend an internal event also (an event that cannot be seen from the process environment). This is done by using the reserved word i instead of a gate name (i.e., i ; B).

A second operator is nondeterministic choice. This operator allows to combine two behaviour expressions to get a new one that is equivalent either to the behaviour defined by the first behaviour expression or the behaviour defined by the second one. It is represented by $B1$ [] $B2$, where $B1$ and $B2$ are the two LOTOS behaviour expressions that are being nondeterministically composed.

With the basic process stop and the two operators we have just presented we are ready to understand the LOTOS behaviour expression that describe the behaviour of the system (in figure 1), that we have already seen.

We see an example of another LOTOS behaviour expression and its corresponding event tree in figure 2.

This behaviour expression in figure 2 initially can accept an event on gate b or can decide to execute an internal event. Suppose that the environment can accept an event on gate b. What would happen? Remember that in Section 2 we said that when two events were possible in a process one of them is nondeterministically chosen. It may happen that even if the environment accepts an event on gate b the process decides to execute the internal event. Therefore, an external observer would find that sometimes this process starts accepting an event on gate b and sometimes does not. This kind of behaviour expressions can be used to model for instance timeouts (the timeout is represented by the internal event).

Another group of LOTOS operators are those that are used to model two entities that synchronise with each other. The most general LOTOS synchronisation operator is of the form $B1$ |[$g1, \ldots, gn$]| $B2$, where $g1, \ldots, gn$ is the set of gates in which the behaviour expressions $B1$ and $B2$ are synchronised. Let S be the set of gates $g1, \ldots, gn$. The events

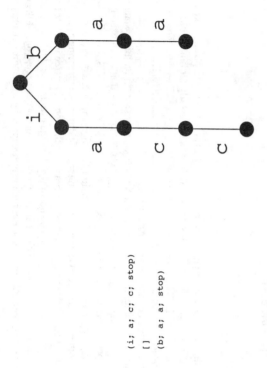

```
(i; a; c; c; stop)
[]
(b; a; a; stop)
```

Figure 2. A behaviour expression with internal events.

accepted by this LOTOS behaviour expression are:

- If an event is accepted in $B1$ at a gate that is not in S then this event would also be accepted in $B1$ |[$g1, \ldots, gn$]| $B2$.
- If an event is accepted in $B2$ at a gate that is not in S then this event would also be accepted in $B1$ |[$g1, \ldots, gn$]| $B2$.
- If an event is accepted in $B1$ and in $B2$ at a gate that is in S then this event would also be accepted in $B1$ |[$g1, \ldots, gn$]| $B2$.

If none of the above, then the event would not take place. An example of a LOTOS behaviour expression with the synchronisation operator can be found in figure 3.

There are two additional synchronisation operators that are particular cases of the one we have just presented. The full synchronisation operator (represented with ||) is used when the processes synchronise on all gates. The interleaving operator (represented with |||) is used when the processes do not synchronise on any gate.

When defining the behaviour of a system it happens quite often that we need to represent internal channels that cannot be accessed from outside the system. We do this in LOTOS with the hiding operator. The hiding operator hides the events that take place in the selected gates from the environment of a LOTOS behaviour expression, and therefore the events at these gates become internal events from the point of view of an external observer. An example can be found in figure 4.

There are other two LOTOS operators in basic LOTOS. One operator (enabling) is used to model a process that is executed after the successful termination of another. The other operator (disabling) is used to model a LOTOS process that is interrupted by another.

It is possible to define in LOTOS recursive and mutually recursive processes. A recursive process in LOTOS is built by instantiating itself in its behaviour expression. Recursion is the means in LOTOS of defining infinite behaviours. An example of an infinite behaviour defined with a recursive process is presented below.

```
PROCESS Prec [a, b]: noexit :=
        a; b; Prec [a, b]
    ENDPROC
```

This LOTOS process represents a system that is able to perform the following sequence of events: a, b, a, b, a, b, ….

2.2. Full LOTOS

In this section we present the complete LOTOS language including data aspects and events that carry data values. Section 2.2.1 is devoted to present LOTOS data types. Then we will present the main features of full LOTOS in Section 2.2.2.

2.2.1. LOTOS Data Types.
The representation of values and expressions in LOTOS is by means of abstract data types. Abstract data types do not represent how data values are manipulated and stored in memory. Instead, a data type is defined by giving a set of properties that the data and its operations should meet. The definition of a data type has three parts:

- Declaration of the *data carriers* (sets of data). Examples of data carriers are boolean, integer, etc. The names of the data carriers are referred to as sorts.
- Declaration of the *operations* over the data carriers. For each operation the following are defined: its domain (zero or more sorts) and its range (which consists of exactly one sort). An operation whose domain has zero sorts is a constant.
- Definition of *equations* that describe the properties of the operations. Sorts and operations are just definition of the syntax of the data type elements. The equations define their semantics.

An example of the definition of a data type in LOTOS is presented in figure 5. This example is a definition of a two-valued logic. We define one sort (bit) and five operations: the constants 0 and 1 and the logic operations and, or and not. Then we use the equations to define the semantics of the data type. The semantics of the and and the not operations is given by case. Then we can define the semantics of the or operation based on the two previously defined operations.

Although abstract data types are adequate for formal reasoning and formal verification, they cannot be easily and efficiently implemented. Therefore, when translating from LOTOS to C or VHDL we will not translate the data types but use predefined libraries.

2.2.2. Full LOTOS Features.
In this section we present the LOTOS features that make use of data types. The main use of data types is to specify events that carry data values.

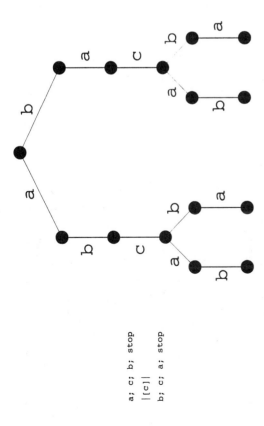

```
a; c; b; stop
|[c]|
b; c; a; stop
```

Figure 3. Example of synchronisation operator.

```
hide d in
    (a; d; stop
    |[d]|
    b; d; stop)
    |[d]|
    c; d; stop
```

Figure 4. Example with hiding.

It is possible to refer to a previously defined LOTOS process in a behaviour expression. This is called *process instantiation*. An example of process instantiation is presented below.

```
P1 [a, b, c]
|[b]|
P1 [b, a, c]
```

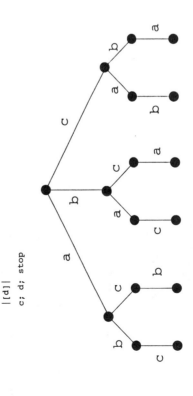

An action prefix with a selection predicate has the form g ?x: sort [P]; where P is the predicate that should be met. An example is b ?x: integer [x gt 0];.

When a process reads a value in a variable declaration we might also want to make the behaviour of the process depend on the value read. This can be done by means of guards. A guard means that a behaviour expression can only be executed when the predicate inside the guard is satisfied. Guards are of the form [P] -> B where P is the predicate of the guard and B is the protected behaviour expression. As an example, the following LOTOS behaviour expression can be used to compute the absolute value of an integer:

```
a ?x: integer;
    (([x ge 0] -> b !x; stop)
    []
    ([x lt 0] -> b !-x; stop))
```

In the example above ge is the *greater than or equal* relational operator and lt is the *less than* relational operator.

We can also have processes with parameters. In this case the value of the parameters is defined when the process is instantiated. This is useful, for instance, when we have a recursive process and we want to maintain some values between one instantiation of the process and another. The following example is a LOTOS process that outputs the natural numbers (supposing that it is initially instantiated with its parameter set to 0.

```
PROCESS naturals [a] (n: integer): noexit:=
    a !n; naturals [a] (n+1)
ENDPROC
```

2.3. LOTOS Subsets Supported by TOPO and HARPO

At this point we have completed the discussion of the LOTOS language as it is defined in the standard. The specification of systems to be implemented partly in software and partly in hardware has to take into account some restrictions and features of the translators from LOTOS to C and VHDL (specially). In this section we are going to present these features. TOPO (the translator from LOTOS to C we are using) supports almost all the LOTOS language. It has a few limitations. Specifications that may generate an unbounded number of processes may cause a run-time error. If the data types are translated automatically, the equations must be interpretable as a rewrite system: the left-hand sides of the equations are names for patterns that can be substituted in the right-hand sides. Nevertheless, automatically generated data types are very inefficient, so we use hand-coded libraries, which are also supported by TOPO.

With respect to the performance of the C generated by TOPO, it should be taken into account that the parallel operators (although fully supported) are not as efficiently implemented as the action prefix and choice operators. This should not be surprising for a software implementation. As a consequence, before implementing the software part of our system we collapse all the processes into one to get better performance results.

```
TYPE Bit_op IS

SORTS bit

OPNS
    0   : -> bit
    1   : -> bit
    and : bit,bit -> bit
    or  : bit,bit -> bit
    not : bit -> bit

EQNS forall b1,b2,b3: bit ofsort bit
    and(1,1) = 1;
    and(0,1) = 0;
    and(1,0) = 0;
    and(0,0) = 0;
    not(1) = 0;
    not(0) = 1;
    or(b1,b2) = not(and(not(b1),not(b2)));
ENDTYPE
```

Figure 5. Example of a data type definition in LOTOS.

LOTOS gates are not typed, and therefore we can have an event at a LOTOS gate carrying a boolean and later another event at the same LOTOS gate carrying an integer. Nevertheless, in practice events at a gate usually are always of the same type (in particular, this is required in the subset of LOTOS that is supported by HARPO). An event can only take place if all the LOTOS processes involved in the event (and the environment if the gate is not hidden) agree on the sort and value of the data carried by the event.

The action prefix presented in Section 2.1 will now be extended so that actions are allowed to carry data information. There are two possibilities: *value declaration* and *variable declaration*. The first case is of the form g !e;. g is the name of the gate where the event is taking place as we did in Section 2.1. e is an expression which defines the value (and therefore the sort) that is imposed and that should be carried by the event. An example of action prefix with value declaration is b !1;. In the case of variable declaration the action prefix is of the form g ?x: sort;. x is the name of a variable of sort *sort*. In this case, the process is able to accept an event that carries a data of sort *sort* in gate g whatever the data is. If the event takes place the value of the data being carried is stored in the variable. This value can be later used by the LOTOS process. An example of variable declaration is b ?x: bit;.

There can be from 0 to N processes involved in a LOTOS event performing an action declaration. The same can be said with respect to actions of kind variable declaration. Of course, at least one process should be present. If no process forces a value in the event (no action of kind value declaration is present), the value exchanged is nondeterministically chosen. If several processes try to impose a value, all of them must offer the same value. Otherwise the event will not be performed.

It may be the case that we do not want to impose a single value on an event but a range of values. This can be done by means of selection predicates. A selection predicate is a condition that is attached to a variable declaration and that should be met by the event.

HARPO supports a smaller subset of LOTOS:

- LOTOS allows dynamic creation of processes. This is not supported by HARPO. HARPO needs to identify a static architecture of processes to be able to translate the LOTOS specification to VHDL. Recursive process instantiation is supported, providing that the static architecture is not changed.
- LOTOS gates must be typed (the data carried through a LOTOS gate must be always of the same sort). All the actions at a gate in a process should be of the same kind (value declaration or variable declaration). Synchronisation is restricted to 1 to N (1 action of kind value declaration and N of kind variable declaration).
- The data types must be implemented in a VHDL library by hand.

3. Why LOTOS?

We have already mentioned some of the features of LOTOS that make it suitable as system-level specification language adequate for co-design: its high degree of abstraction and powerful description features, it is not biased towards software or hardware and it possesses a standard formal semantics.

As LOTOS descriptions are based on the interaction between a system and its environment, it is especially well suited to specifying systems that implement telecommunication protocols (in fact, LOTOS was designed to describe them). Nevertheless, there are many other embedded systems that are suitable for specification in LOTOS. It happens quite often that complex systems are composed of a set of subsystems that communicate among themselves by means of one or several complex protocols. This kind of systems can be very well described in LOTOS, because the description of the behaviour of communicating subsystems is much more simpler in LOTOS than in conventional system description languages such as VHDL. As an example, the following code (taken from [5]) is a VHDL process that communicates with its environment by means of a handshaking protocol:

```
process
begin
  BUSY <= F0;
  wait until START = F1;
  BUSY <= F1;
  C := A + B;
  D <= C * E;
  wait until START = F0;
end process;
```

The same behaviour can be represented in LOTOS as follows:

```
PROCESS Example [gate_a, gate_b, gate_d, gate_e]: noexit :=
  gate_a ?a: integer;
  gate_b ?b: integer;
  gate_e ?e: integer;
  gate_d !(a + b) * e;
  Example [gate_a, gate_b, gate_d, gate_e]
ENDPROC
```

We can get rid of BUSY, START and the wait statements, in charge of synchronising the process with its environment, because the synchronisation mechanism is abstracted in LOTOS.

When specifying a system that is going to be co-designed it is necessary to split its behaviour into several communicating subsystems. This is another aspect that make LOTOS suitable as specification language for co-design.

4. LOTOS Co-Design Flow

The LOTOS design flow is illustrated in figure 6. Three different design stages are considered, corresponding to three abstraction levels: system specification and refinement, hardware and software specification and hardware-software prototyping. In the remainder of this section we will sketch the design flow corresponding to the first two design stages. In Section 5 we present the prototyping environment and architecture we have used. We devote a separate section to the prototyping design stage (Section 6).

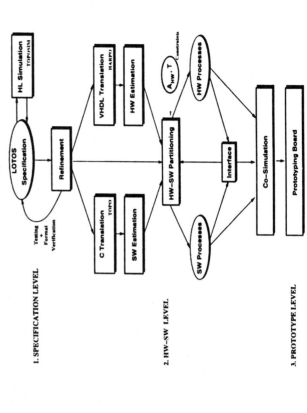

Figure 6. LOTOS design flow.

4.1. System Specification

The high level of abstraction of LOTOS as a specification language allows us to avoid making assumptions about the implementation at early stages of the design process. In the specification phase, systems are not described by means of algorithms, but as a set of properties or axioms. This allows us to concentrate on *what* is to be designed rather than on *how* it is going to be achieved. Algebraic specification techniques are well-known and form a standard part of languages such as LOTOS. They are used for the algebraic specification of data; we will use them in the initial stage of the specification of whole systems.

The transition from the specification to the design involves the definition of an algorithm that satisfies the desired properties, or in other words, one has to find a model for the algebraic specification. Please note that the algebraic specification needs not specify a unique model (up to isomorphism); there might be several (non-isomorphic) models. The only requirement is that it is not inconsistent (i.e., has no contradictory axioms), which would imply that there is no model.

Therefore, the transition is a highly creative process, since it involves the definition of an initial algorithm. The axioms, nevertheless, create a reference for checking it against. Some specifications can be very concrete and interpreted directly as algorithms, e.g., the inversion of a list:

$$inv : list \rightarrow list$$
$$inv(emptylist) = emptylist$$
$$inv(a \,\&\, l) = inv(l) \,\&\, a$$

But some might be very abstract, and require in addition strategies to make them run, e.g., the inversion of a matrix:

$$inv : matrix \rightarrow matrix$$
$$inv(a) \times a = I$$
$$a \times inv(a) = I$$

The first version of an algorithm might be easy to understand, but not efficiently implementable. Several refinements of the initial algorithm can be tried. Only the run-time properties of the implementation change from trial to trial and the abstract specification is satisfied in each case.

In general, there are two ways to check the correctness of an algorithm: testing via simulation and formal proof. Both of them are available in LOTOS. There is currently available a tool, named LOLA [20], that allows the simulation of LOTOS specifications. In addition, the fact that LOTOS has been provided with a standard formal semantics allows us to construct formal proofs using LOTOS specifications. LOLA can also be used for this (some formally correct transformations of specifications are supported).

LOTOS allows the designer to specify the behaviour of a system, but not non-functional information such as throughput, cost, etc. We have extended LOTOS with annotations [21, 22] that allow the designer to specify the non-functional requirements together with the estimates and measures that will be obtained along the design process. After specification and refinement of a system, the next step is to enter into the LOTOS specification the desired non-functional requirements.

4.2. Hardware-Software Specification

Once the system has been completely specified, both in its functional and non-functional aspects, the next step is to assign each process in the specification to software or to hardware in such a way that the final implementation will meet its non-functional requirements. At the end of this process we obtain two specifications, one for the part to be implemented in software and another for the part to be implemented in hardware.

In order to begin the partitioning process, some information is needed. Several parameters of the design will be used as inputs to the partitioning strategy. These parameters can be estimated either by a static or a dynamic analysis of the LOTOS code. By static analysis, we mean estimates obtained by means of a non-standard interpretation of the LOTOS code. By dynamic analysis, we mean the measures obtained by repeated execution of the implementation or simulation of the specification.

The main parameters to be statically estimated are the area and the clock period of the hardware implementations for each LOTOS process. The parameters that will be calculated dynamically are: number of clock cycles spent in each component (obtained via RTL VHDL simulation), software execution time (obtained by profiling) and communication cost (explained below).

For the hardware implementation, every LOTOS process is translated into a VHDL entity. This entity is composed of a finite state machine and a set of pre-synthesised library components. Area estimation is only needed for the finite state machine. The estimation is obtained from the state transition table.

The communication cost is obtained by means of a tool, called TOPOSIM [18]. TOPOSIM performs repeated simulations of the system behaviour against a stochastic model of inputs. Processes determine the "grain size" of the partitioning algorithm. They are atomically assigned to either hardware or software. In general, this implies a rather coarse granularity, although the designer is free to choose how big a process is. This approach has been chosen for the following reasons:

- granularity, fixed at the level of processes, is suitable for the translation procedure used by TOPO and HARPO;
- it is reasonable to maintain the processes as defined by the designer in the system-level specification;
- the complexity of the problem is reduced because the search space is smaller;
- designer interaction is allowed and, therefore, manual changes are supported.

Hardware-software partitioning is performed in two steps: first, a constructive algorithm is employed to build the initial partition (a classical clustering algorithm [13]). Second, the output obtained is refined by means of an iterative procedure.

The clustering algorithm is guided by a closeness function which takes into account the estimates given as inputs. Initially, objects are assumed to be implemented in software. The closeness function groups those objects that have the best improvement on time when moved to hardware. Consequently, the most important parameters that weight this function are the communication rates between processes. Those processes that communicate frequently with each other are grouped together to prevent introducing a high communication overhead in the interface between hardware and software. The processes that belong to the final cluster constitute the initial hardware block, whereas the rest are considered to be implemented in software.

Every time a process is added to the main cluster, the system constraints (hardware area, memory size and global latency) are checked. The clustering process stops when it reaches any of the following states:

1. The time constraints are satisfied (with the hardware area within acceptable bounds).
2. The hardware area exceeds the maximum allowed (with the time constraint still not satisfied).

If the clustering process stops because the system timing requirement (latency) is met (state 1), the global algorithm finishes. The resulting partition can be considered as solution because the hardware area restriction has not been violated. Otherwise, the hardware area requirement is the criterion that stops the clustering process (state 2). In this case, a second phase is necessary in order to refine the partition represented by the cluster tree. Refinement is performed by a group migration algorithm [14] that shuffles the last objects added to the hardware cluster. It ends when the time requirement is satisfied.

For more details about the partitioning process see [3, 16]. This is a general partitioning procedure developed in the COBRA project following the methodology proposed in [3]. This procedure can be applied to many different LOTOS specifications annotated with all the parameters previously described. Although the example that we are going to present here has a reduced number of processes, and could be partitioned by hand, in more complex applications the number of processes in the specification would make manual partitioning infeasible. This justifies the need of automatic partitioning.

Up to this point, we have split the global specification into processes according to its functionality. This has served us the basis to the partitioning process. Once the partition is decided, the software performance can be further improved by collapsing all processes assigned to the same CPU into one.

5. Prototyping Environment

This section aims at describing the prototyping architecture we have used to build a prototype from a LOTOS specification and the associated design environment.

5.1. Hardware Modules

For prototyping we used the WEAVER environment designed by FZI Karlsruhe. This environment is designed especially for prototyping of entire hardware/software systems [15].

It is a modular and extensible system which can cope with high gate complexity. The different types of modules allow both the integration of standard or predefined components and adaptation to the needs of the application.

WEAVER uses a hardwired regular interconnection scheme. Thus, fewer signals have to be routed through programmable devices, which results in better performance. Nevertheless it will not always be possible to avoid routing signals through the FPGAs. Bus modules are provided for the interconnection of modules. These offer 88-bit wide buses.

The basic module carries four Xilinx FPGAs for the configurable logic. On each side of the quadratic base module a connector with 96 pins is located. Each FPGA is connected to one of these connectors. Also, every FPGA has a 75-bit link to two of its neighbours. A Control Unit is located on the basic module. It handles the programming and readback of particular FPGAs. A separate bus leads to the control unit of each base module in the system, which is programmed serially via this separate bus. The programming data is annotated with address information for the basic module and the particular FPGA on the basic module. In that way the control unit determines if the programming data on the bus is relevant to its own basic module. If so, it forwards the programming data to the FPGA for which it is intended. Readback of configuration data and shadow registers is done in the same way.

A RAM module with 4 MB static RAM can be added in order to provide for the storage of global or local data. It can be plugged into a bus module, so several modules may have access to it, or it can be connected directly to a base module. Then this module has exclusive access to the memory. The requests from other modules must be routed through the FPGAs of the directly connected base module. This is time consuming. The bus module makes it possible to plug modules together in a bus-oriented way. With a bus on each side of the base module this architecture can be used to build multiprocessing systems with arbitrary structure.

To be able to integrate standard processors, these must be located on their own modules which must meet the connection conventions of the other modules. For the work described in this paper, we used an evaluation board for the Hyperstone E1 32-bit processor [10]. A board carrying a PowerPC processor is also available.

Using these modules, arbitrary structures can be built. The structure depends on the application which is to be prototyped. Thus, a running system contains all modules needed, but not more. That is important in order to reduce overhead and to keep the price low. The basic module and a more complex structure is depicted in figure 7. This picture shows an architecture in top view and in side view. The architecture is built in three dimensions and consists of four basic modules, a RAM module and an I/O module. On the right-hand side is a tower of three basic modules which are connected via three bus modules. On the left hand-side is another basic module with a local RAM module and an I/O module. The gross number of gates in this example is about 400K, which corresponds to approx. 120K usable gates. Thus, it is an example which would be sufficient for many applications.

5.2. Supporting Software

The supporting software can be split into synthesis software and software, which supports the handling of the environment. For hardware synthesis, we rely on commercial software

describe these primitives. These connect the code generated by TOPO and HARPO with its environment.

6.1. Interfacing Mechanisms of TOPO and HARPO

6.1.1. TOPO. In order to indicate how communications with the environment are to be carried out by the software side of the interface, the designer annotates the LOTOS code. These annotations are in fact user-defined C functions. The annotations are special LOTOS comments that begin with (*| and end with |*). The TOPO tool then converts the annotated specification to C. We use four annotations to build the software part of the interface:

- (*| C *C_statements* |*): The annotation keyword C means *code* and applies to actions. The C statements are executed just after the action is involved in a successful event.

```
g2b: bool
(*| C
printf ("g");
|*) ;
```

- (*| wait *C_expression* |*): One of the most important annotations is the wait annotation. This can be attached to a LOTOS action. During the execution, if the action can take place, then the expression in the wait annotation is evaluated at each execution step until it returns true. Then the action can be performed. Busy wait on a wait does not preclude other actions, from occurring.

```
(*| wait prot_in() |*) req !1;
```

- (*| use *C_expression* |*): This applies to actions of type variable declaration. *C_expression* value is imposed as the value attached to the event. It is equivalent to a value declaration with value *C_expression*.

```
get ?d (*| use get_input() |*) : nat;
```

- (*| priority *C_expression* |*): This *C_expression* evaluates to a number and expresses the priority of the action that comes after it. The default priority is 0. The priority can be greater or lower than 0. If nothing else makes a difference, that is, if several events can take place at a given execution point, priorities affect fairness of the behaviour, forcing a selection. The action with the highest priority is selected. Thus, a positive priority value implies a preference, while a negative value labels an undesired event.

6.1.2. HARPO. LOTOS communications imply synchronising, exchanging of data and agreeing on the data among the parties. This scheme can be translated to VHDL by means of a protocol that has been implemented in the HARPO tool. The protocol is implemented in a library of components.

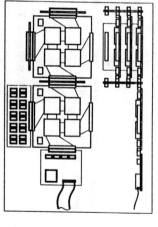

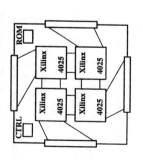

Figure 7. The Weaver hardware.

like Synopsys or any other tool for hardware synthesis, and the Xilinx tool suite. For large circuits, a netlist partitioning software was developed. This tool allows for the partitioning of a large netlist onto a given device interconnection structure [28].

Software development is done in the particular software development environments provided by the processor vendors. In the case of the Hyperstone processor, software development is done with PC-based cross development tools including a source level debugger which allows for the debugging of programs running on the target processor.

The WEAVER environment includes a tool which provides a user interface to the accessible functionality: selection of particular boards and FPGAs on the architecture and programming, and readback of selected devices. The user has control over the circuit clock, which can be interrupted and chosen from a set of different sources including clock divisors. The user can also set, enable and disable the RESET signal by software means.

6. LOTOS Prototyping

Two kind of inputs are needed in order to construct a prototype: the hardware and software LOTOS specifications obtained after the partitioning process (see Section 4.2) and the target architecture (as defined in Section 5). Previous to the construction of the prototype, it is necessary to build an interface that connects the software and the hardware components. The resulting code (C and VHDL derived from the LOTOS specifications and also the interface code) is then co-simulated in order to test the functionality of the whole system. Finally, the hardware part is mapped onto the FPGA board and the software part to the Hyperstone board. Then the whole system is run. At this step some low-level details related to the interface still have to be debugged. The final result is a working prototype.

As we have already explained in Section 2, a system described using LOTOS communicates with its environment by means of events. When translating a LOTOS specification to an implementation language it is necessary to describe how the environment communicates with the system to perform an event using implementation language primitives, such as functions and variables in the case of C or signals in VHDL. From these primitives we build the hardware-software interface is constructed. Before explaining how the interface is built we

indicating that some of the receivers did not accept the value, it sets gate_r to 11, which implies that the synchronisation has not occurred and the data is not valid.

Synch_Val can set gate_r to 11 even if it had received a 10, and is basically due to the existence of several possible synchronisations to commit, and the necessity of discarding all but one. It is important to note that following this protocol the writer is the one who decides finally if a synchronisation takes place or not once the reader has accepted it. We will take advantage of this when we build the interface.

6.2. Interface Construction

Currently the interface is still being constructed by hand. Nevertheless, the process could be automated, at least for a fixed target architecture. Some guidelines for the construction of interfaces between hardware and software components which have been obtained from LOTOS specifications can be found in [23]. In the following we explain the basis of the process we have considered, although communication schemes different to the one presented here could be implemented.

The interface is composed of two parts: one for the software side and one for the hardware side.

6.2.1. Software Interface.
The hardware part of the co-designed system is translated from LOTOS to VHDL by means of HARPO. The VHDL processes generated communicate with each other following the handshake protocol we just described. Handshaking also takes place between the hardware and software parts using the same protocol. Thus, the software part of the interface has to support the protocol. This is achieved through the appropriate use of the wait annotation. Before each action on a gate in the interface we place a wait annotation.

When a LOTOS process in the software part wants to read a value from the hardware part (the LOTOS process in the software part wants to perform an action of kind variable declaration) the wait annotation performs the required protocol on its behalf (using the C function prot_in) and returns true if the synchronisation succeeds. These LOTOS actions have the highest priority, because we need to guarantee that if the wait annotation succeeds the software will execute that action. If more than one read can occur at a time we use semaphores (in the example below the semaphore is the C variable in_sw_smph) to resolve the potential conflicts:

```
(*| wait ((in_sw_smph == 0) && prot_in()) |*)
(*| priority 1 |*)
(* prot_in makes the whole protocol, that's why it has
   highest priority *)
ans? outp (*| use NATdatum(registers_map[3][LOW]) |*): nat;
(* store value read in outp *)
```

When a LOTOS process in the software part wants to write a value to the hardware part (the LOTOS process in the software part wants to perform an action of kind value declaration),

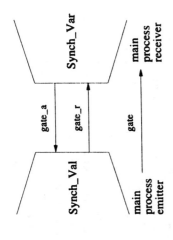

Figure 8. Implementation of a gate interface in HARPO.

A LOTOS process is translated to a VHDL entity which contains one main process and several instantiations (one for each gate) of the library components. The mentioned components are controlled by the main processes and perform the synchronisations when required. Another benefit is the possibility for parallelising several synchronisations, as different instantiations of these components can be triggered in parallel. The components are two: Synch_Val for sending and Synch_Var for receiving (see figure 8). We use three signals in VHDL for each LOTOS gate. gate_r and gate_a are used to perform the handshaking protocol and gate is used to carry the data value send from the emitter to the receiver. The protocol that links the library components Synch_Val and Synch_Var is one of the possible implementations of the LOTOS synchronisation mechanism between two processes willing to perform an action on a common gate. Let us study a simple synchronisation between two LOTOS processes, one offering a variable and the other offering a value. For the interaction to take place, three requirements are necessary:

1. The two processes must be ready to interact, i.e., they wait for each other.
2. The value must be of the same sort of the variable.
3. Both of them will continue their behaviour after the synchronisation simultaneously.

The second condition is warranted in this approach by imposing on LOTOS gates a given direction and type.

Let us describe the protocol used by HARPO. There are four stages in order:

1. Synch_Val sets gate_r to 01 and waits for a 01 at gate_a.
2. Synch_Var waits for a 01 at gate_r and then it sets gate_a to 01. This step indicates that both processes are willing to synchronise on this gate.
3. Data is exchanged. When valid data is already at gate, Synch_Val sets gate_r to 00 and waits for a 10 or a 11 in gate_a. Synch_Var waits for a 00 in gate_r and it sets gate_a to 10 if the data is accepted, or to 11 otherwise.
4. Processes continue their execution. If Synch_Val received a 10 it sets gate_r to 10, meaning that the synchronisation has finished successfully: if the value received was 11,

the wait annotation performs the protocol by means of the C function prot_out until the point where it has to decide if the synchronisation takes place or not, and returns true if the hardware agrees to receive the value on the requested gate. If the execution of the event then takes place, the protocol finishes successfully with the C function end_prot. After each step, all the pending protocols are terminated with failure (remember that the last choice was on the writer's side). In this case no priorities or semaphores are needed. Below there is an example.

```
(*| wait prot_out(0) |*)
(* This starts the protocol. If the HW refuses it,
   it finishes. If it accepts, it is added to the list of
   pending protocols *)
req!Table_info(Get_source(Get_frame(brinf)),
               Get_dest(Get_frame(brinf)),
               Get_port(brinf)) (*| C end_prot(0); |*);
```

As this protocol is designed to be independent of the target architecture, so the C functions that implement it are also largely architecture-independent. The only part where the interface is architecture-dependent is where the hardware is directly accessed—that is, the actual reading and writing of data from and to the hardware. This encapsulation makes relatively easy to port the interface to another target architecture. In Appendix we present the C routines prot_in, prot_out and end_prot.

6.2.2. Hardware Interface. The hardware interface is a layer between the VHDL generated by HARPO and the environment expected by the target architecture. It is in charge of the following tasks:

- Setting the input ports of the LOTOS processes on the hardware side to the values assigned from the software side. This may require some registers in which to store the values.
- Informing the software about the values held at the output ports of the LOTOS processes on the hardware side.
- Synchronising the read/write operations with the timing imposed by the processor.

In other co-design approaches [9, 26], the interface also includes a handshake protocol which passes values between the software and the hardware sides. This is not the case in our approach because, the VHDL generated by HARPO includes that protocol.

In the target architecture (see figure 9) the software accesses the hardware using a message-passing schema. The hardware side is seen by the software side as a set of special addresses in the address space. The hardware interface is accessed by the software by means of a data bus, an address bus and two control lines, one for reading operations (iord) and the other for writing operations (iowr). Each of the ports offered by the VHDL generated by HARPO has an associated address that can be accessed from the software side. When the software reads a value, the interface fetches the value from the corresponding hardware output, and puts it on the data bus. When the software writes a value, it is stored in a register whose output is connected to the desired hardware input port.

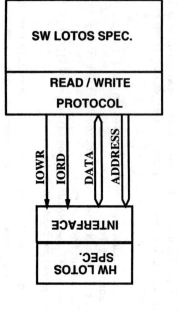

Figure 9. Interface model.

6.3. Co-Simulation

Once the construction of the interface has been finished, it is necessary to check whether the software and hardware parts (together with their interfaces) work correctly together. To do this we execute the software part and simulate (using a VHDL simulator) the hardware part on a SUN workstation. The two parts communicate with each other via files. In the software part the functions that perform reading and writing through the FPGA board are replaced by functions that read and write into files. In the hardware part we add an extra VHDL component to the interface. It is a wrapper for a set of C functions that perform reading and writing operations on files. This strategy allows us to test nearly the same code that will be implemented on the prototyping board. It allows us to detect at least some of the errors that must not appear in the interface construction.

Figure 10 shows the validation steps that have been introduced into the co-design methodology. We provide for three main checkpoints in the design flow. The first checkpoint is a validation performed at specification level. It incorporates both testing and formal verification. The second checkpoint is provided by co-simulation of the output of the partitioning. We distinguish two validation sub-steps here: RTL co-simulation and gate level (post-synthesis) co-simulation. The third checkpoint is the prototype. The construction of tests for the validation of LOTOS specifications is a well researched topic [19]. As the figure shows we can use the same test bench in all the validation points. Therefore, we can use this knowledge to validate the functionality of the system at all the checkpoints. In validation via co-simulation this is enabled via translation to C (or VHDL) of a LOTOS description of the testbench.

7. An Example

As a working example we have chosen to specify, design and implement an Ethernet bridge. Bridges are used to extend LANs, providing increased length, number of stations, performance and reliability. An Ethernet bridge connects two or more Ethernet LANs

to the appropriate port, if it is different from the one at which it was received. If both ports are the same, (i.e., the destination is located in the original segment) the frame is not redirected.

The source address is inserted in the database if it was not already present. The identifier of the port and a time-stamp are attached to each address. If the address is already in the database, then the port identifier is updated with the current value, and the time-stamp is refreshed. Data is removed from the database when the time-stamp indicates that a station has been silent for a long time. The removal time, usually a few minutes, is given as a parameter to the specification.

7.1. Specification and Partitioning

Three successive refinements of the initial specification have been completed. The initial specification handled two Ethernet segments, and defined an algebraic data type for the database and the operations to be performed upon it. The first refinement left the database as an algebraic data type and introduced more structure in the ports and control blocks. We designed three port managers, with input and output queues of frames. The second refinement addressed the database specification. The functionality of the database was reallocated to a LOTOS behaviour from a LOTOS data type. The new database behaves like a hash table.

Figure 11 shows the architecture of the refined LOTOS specification. It connects three segments of LANs, which suffices to exercise the different functionalities of the forwarding algorithm. Each Ethernet card connection to the bridge is an instantiation of process P_Port. It provides additional buffering.

The ports are connected to a single multiplexor process, P_Mux, that sends requests on to the controller. It colours each incoming frame with the identifier of the entry port.

The controller process P_Control takes the entry from the multiplexor and queries the database. The reply to the query should be the port to which the destination address is connected.

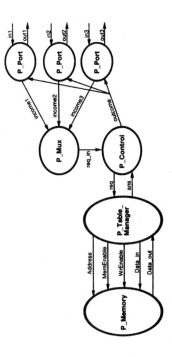

Figure 11. LOTOS specification of an Ethernet bridge.

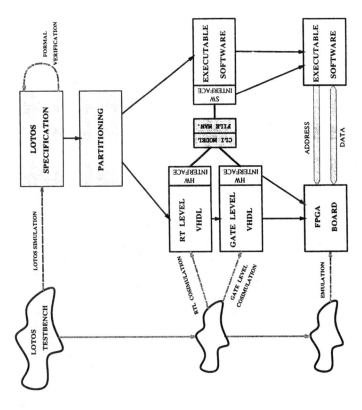

Figure 10. Validation in the design flow.

operating under the CSMA/CD access method. Bridges (defined by the IEEE 802.1 media access control (MAC) bridge standard) connect two or more segments of LANs in a transparent way. They automatically initialise, configure themselves and run with no intervention from the network manager.

The basic functions performed by bridges are:

- frame forwarding,
- learning station addresses,
- resolving loops in the topology using a spanning tree algorithm (this function is not considered in the present study).

The bridge maintains port connections to different segments of LANs. It also contains a forwarding database which is dynamically updated with the segments to which each station is attached.

When a new frame is received on a port, its destination address is compared to those contained in the forwarding database. If it is not there, the frame is sent to the rest of the ports ("flooding"). If the destination address is in the database, the frame is redirected

Table 1. Area and CPU estimates.

Process	Area	CPU (%)
P_Port	5570	4.99
P_Mux	1570	1.68
P_Control	1340	3.16
P_Table_Manager	1910	46.22
P_Memory	2160	33.97

Table 2. Communication estimates.

Gate	Processes involved	Average
income1	P_Port 1, P_Mux	0.33
income2	P_Port 2, P_Mux	0.33
income3	P_Port 3, P_Mux	0.33
outcome	P_Port (1,2,3), P_Control	0.82
req_in	P_Mux, P_Control	1.0
req	P_Control, P_Table_Manager	1.0
ans	P_Control, P_Table_Manager	1.0
Address	P_Table_Manager, P_Memory	13.37
MemoryEnable	P_Table_Manager, P_Memory	13.37
WriteEnable	P_Table_Manager, P_Memory	13.37
DataIn	P_Table_Manager, P_Memory	0.53
DataOut	P_Table_Manager, P_Memory	12.84

The process that manages the database and performs the hash table behaviour is P_Table_Manager. P_Memory is taken from a library of components, and it models a RAM. When the LOTOS specification is translated to VHDL with HARPO, this component is linked with an existing VHDL RAM description.

Tables 1 and 2 show some estimates obtained for the LOTOS specification of the Ethernet bridge. In Table 1 the area and CPU consumption (on a SUN Sparc workstation) estimates that have been obtained (in equivalent gates and percentage, respectively) are displayed. In Table 2 we show the average number of data exchanges in each channel per input data for communication considerations.

We have applied our partitioning method to the Ethernet bridge example with the aim of achieving a performance goal of 3000 frames/s. This is a value in the range of what can be found in existing commercial bridges. In this example, only the clustering step proved necessary. This was due to the early verification of the timing requirements after grouping the first pair of processes. These processes are P_Table_Manager and P_Memory, which are clustered because their closeness value is much greater than that of the rest. This high proximity between both processes is a consequence of the large communication factor between them and the big improvement obtained by assigning them to hardware.

Table 3. CPU profiling results of refined version.

Process	Software part	P_Table_Manager	P_Memory
CPU consumed	3.70%	56.76%	39.54%

Thus, the final partition of the Ethernet bridge consists of a hardware part containing the processes P_Table_Manager and P_Memory. The remaining blocks of the specification are assigned to the software part. After the decision has been made on which processes go to hardware and which to software, a further refinement step of the LOTOS specification takes place. In this refinement we collapse all the processes in the software into one process in order to increase performance. The CPU profiling information obtained is displayed in Table 3.

7.2. Prototyping

Several different implementations have been mapped to the prototyping environment. These range from a pure software implementation to testbench versions which allowed for better design space exploration and different debugging levels. The C and VHDL code for software and hardware were mainly automatically generated from the specification. Manual changes were made in the process or tailoring the C code for the Hyperstone processor used in the prototype. Manual additions were necessary to implement the communication interfaces for hardware/software-communication. These additions were made in the software and in the hardware. This kind of manual work is expected to be required for each new target architecture, since every migration to another target architecture involves slight changes of the communication scheme and a different software development environment, which imposes different constraints on the software.

A major advantage of prototyping derives from the existence of such manually coded parts. These parts are typically very difficult to simulate, since they mostly refer to interfacing, be it hardware/software interfaces or interfaces to the world. A prototype allows for much deeper validation by running under realistic conditions and by running in real-time and thus covering system times of hours, while simulation can only cover system times of a few seconds. This was also true in the case of the example presented in this paper.

The Ethernet bridge was implemented by a processor-coprocessor architecture. The communication between processor and coprocessor is done directly via the 32-bit wide processor bus. The coprocessor appears as a set of I/O addresses to the processor and the software. For the presented application, five addresses were used, two for reading from the hardware and three for writing to the hardware. The communication is synchronised via the transferred data, not via a status register. The whole address decoding and bus protocol handling is done by the hardware on the FPGAs, which represents the coprocessor. The RAM needed by the coprocessor is implemented as on-chip SRAM directly on the FPGAs.

7.3. Results

Physical prototyping can of course only be used for validation, since the mapping effort is too high to use prototyping for design space exploration. Therefore, it was only applied to two

an initial abstract specification written in LOTOS. A worked example, the Ethernet bridge served to illustrate the proposed design flow. The speedup and performance results that we have presented prove the feasibility of the proposed approach.

Our design flow is composed of three different phases corresponding to three abstraction levels (high-level specification, hardware and software specification, prototyping). The design flow is validated at the high-level specification level (by means of simulation and formal verification) and at the prototype level (by means of cosimulation and by running the obtained prototype on the prototype board). The techniques used at high-level specification (abstract specification, formal verification and refinement, testing) and at the prototype level (co-simulation and hardware-software prototyping from VHDL and C code obtained from the specification and the interface) are not new. Our aim was to develop a coherent path from this high-level specification formalisms to prototyping. This makes it possible to apply the features available in high-level specification languages for the development of real designs.

Appendix

Functions Used in the Ethernet Bridge Interface

We present here the C code used in the implementation of the Ethernet bridge interface, together with a short explanation of how the functions work.

We use two variables called registers_map and in_reg to store the values that are read and written in the hardware part. For the data carried through gate req we need three elements of registers_map (req1, req2 and req3).

```
/* registers_map[0][HIGH] = req_r  */
/* registers_map[0][LOW]  = ans_a  */
/* registers_map[1][HIGH] = req1   */
/* registers_map[1][LOW]  = req2   */
/* registers_map[2][HIGH] = req3   */
/* registers_map[2][LOW]  = ---    */
/* registers_map[3][HIGH] = ---    */
/* registers_map[3][LOW]  = ans    */
/* in_reg[HIGH] -- req_a  */
/* in_reg[LOW]  -- ans_r  */
```

prot_in implements the protocol that reads a value from the hardware. It follows the protocol described in Section 6.1.2. If it succeeds it returns 1 else it returns 0. The functions write_register and read_register are used to write to and read data from the hardware. The function valid decides if the value offered by the hardware is to be accepted.

```
int
prot_in()
```

Table 4. Implementation alternatives.

Processor	Hardware	Frame processing rate (frames/s)
Hyperstone	No HW	26
Hyperstone	Table manager	624
Sparc	No HW	135
Sparc	Table manager	3100

different design alternatives. The first is a pure software implementation, which is required to learn about the speedup, and the second is the mixed hardware/software-implementation suggested by hardware/software-partitioning.

The C code representing the software part of the application has a size of 8732 lines of code, which resulted in an executable of approximately 120 K. The specification of the hardware part consists of 1340 lines of code which corresponds to approximately 5000 gates.

Since the Hyperstone processor uses a synchronous bus interface and runs at a clock frequency of 25 MHz, the hardware had to run at least with a clock frequency of 3.3 MHz to meet the requirements of the synchronous processor bus. Otherwise data dropouts could happen. In our implementation on the board, the hardware ran with a 10 MHz clock. Thus, these constraints were easily met.

Table 4 gives an overview of some different implementation alternatives and their performance. A speedup factor of approx. 24 was achieved for the Hyperstone processor through partitioning the design and implementing a crucial part in hardware. We used this speedup factor to estimate the performance of a Sparc—coprocessor combination based on the pure software performance of the Sparc processor. This combination could not be measured, since there is no Sparc processor available in the WEAVER environment.

Through the use of emulation, we found two errors in the manually coded parts of the design. One was a hardware error in the VHDL specification of the hardware/software interface part. This error resulted in an data dropout under certain conditions. These conditions made the data dropout appear randomly and unpredictably. This error did not occur during co-simulation. It was corrected after identification and thorough examination of the responsible design parts.

The other error was a software error. There was a memory leak, which lead to a segmentation fault after several minutes runtime. With co-simulation, if detectable at all, this error would have occurred after several weeks of simulation time. Thus, for this example, the prototyping hardware has proven itself to be useful for both functional validation and performance validation.

8. Conclusions

In this paper, we have presented a complete design flow for hardware-software co-design based on LOTOS. The design flow allows us to build a hardware-software prototype from

```c
{
    DATA in_reg;

    read_register(4, in_reg);
    if (in_reg[LOW] != V_01)
        return 0;
    registers_map[0][LOW] = V_01; /* ans_r = "01" */
    write_register(0, registers_map[0]); /* ans_a = "01" */
    read_register(4, in_reg);
    while (in_reg[LOW] != V_00) /* wait until ans_r == "00" */
        read_register(4, in_reg);
    read_register(3, registers_map[3]); /* reads ans */
    if (valid(registers_map[3][LOW])) {
        registers_map[0][LOW] = V_10;
        write_register(0, registers_map[0]);
        read_register(4, in_reg);
        while (in_reg[LOW] == V_00) /* wait until ans_r != "00" */
            read_register(4, in_reg);
        if (in_reg[LOW] == V_10) /* if ans_r == "10" */
            return 1;
        else /* if ans_r == "11" */
            return 0;
    }
    else { /* invalid dat in ans */
        registers_map[0][LOW] = V_11;
        write_register(0, registers_map[0]);
        return 0;
    }
}
```

prot_out implements the protocol that writes a value in the hardware. It also follows the protocol described in Section 6.1.2. If it succeeds it returns 1 else it returns 0. If the hardware agrees to synchronise, it returns 1 and adds this to the list of pending protocols setting flags[id_port − 1] to 1. If the software decides to synchronise, this protocol will be terminated with success by end_prot else it will be terminated with failure after the current step is finished.

```c
int
prot_out(int id_port)
{
    DATA in_reg;

    registers_map[0][HIGH] = V_01; /* req_r = 01 */
    write_register(0, registers_map[0]);
    usleep(HW_RESPONSE_TIME); /* time for the HW to answer */
    read_register(4, in_reg);
    if (in_reg[HIGH] == V_01) {/* req_a = "01" */
        write_register(1, registers_map[1]);
        /* send req1,req2,req3 */
        write_register(2, registers_map[2]);
        registers_map[0][HIGH] = V_00; /* req_r = 00 */
        write_register(0, registers_map[0]);
        read_register(4, in_reg);
        while ((in_reg[HIGH] != V_10) && (in_reg[HIGH] != V_11))
            read_register(4, in_reg); /* req_a = 10 or req_a=11 */
        if (in_reg[HIGH] == V_11) {
            registers_map[0][HIGH] = V_11; /* req_r = 11 */
            write_register(0, registers_map[0]);
            return 0;
        }
        if (in_reg[HIGH] == V_10) {
            flags[id_port - 1] = 1;
            return 1;
        }
    }
    return 0;
}
```

Finally, end_prot completes a writing protocol that has succeeded.

```c
void
end_prot(int id_port)
{
    registers_map[0][HIGH] = V_10; /* req_r = 10 */
    write_register(0, registers_map[0]);
    flags[id_port - 1] = 0;
}
```

Acknowledgments

We would like to thank Juan Carlos López López and Carlos Carreras Vaquer for their fruitful collaboration in the development of the LOTOS design flow during the COBRA project. We would also want to thank the teams that developed the translators from LOTOS to C and VHDL for their support, especially Andrés Marín López. Helpful comments and suggestions made by Peter T. Breuer are gratefully acknowledged.

This work has been partially funded by ESPRIT project No. 8135 COBRA and CICYT project TIC94-0627-CE.

References

1. E. Barros, W. Rosenstiel, and X. Xiong, "Hardware/software partitioning with UNITY," *2nd International Workshop on Hardware-Software Co-Design*, Cambridge, MA, October 1993.
2. J. Bergé, O. Levia, and J. Rouillard, eds., *High-Level System Modeling: Specification Languages. Current Issues in Electronic Modeling*, Vol. 3, Kluwer Academic Publishers, September 1995.
3. C. Carreras, J.C. López, M.L. López, C. Delgado-Kloos, N. Martínez, and L. Sánchez, "A co-design methodology based on formal specification and high-level estimation," *4th International Workshop on Hardware-Software Co-Design*, Pittsburgh, IEEE Computer Society Press, March 1996.
4. M. Chiodo, P. Giusto, H. Hsieh, A. Jurecska, L. Lavagno, and A. Sangiovanni-Vincentelli, "Hardware-software codesign of embedded systems," *IEEE Micro*, 14(4): 26–36, August 1994.
5. R.A. Cottrell, "ASIC design using silicon 1076," in *VHDL for Simulation, Synthesis and Formal Proofs of Hardware*, J. Mermet, ed., Kluwer Academic Publishers, 1992.
6. C. Delgado Kloos, A. Marín López, T. de Miguel Moro, and T. Robles Valladares, "From LOTOS to VHDL," in *High-Level System Modeling: Specification Languages. Current Issues in Electronic Modeling*, J. Bergé, O. Levia, and J. Rouillard, eds., Vol. 3, Kluwer Academic Publishers, September 1995.
7. R. Ernst, J. Henkel, and T. Benner, "Hardware-software cosynthesis for microcontrollers," *IEEE Design & Test of Computers*, pp. 64–75, December 1993.
8. D. Gajski, F. Vahid, S. Narayan, and J. Gong, *Specification and Design of Embedded Systems*, Prentice Hall, New Jersey, 1994.
9. R. Gupta and G. DeMicheli, "Hardware-software cosynthesis for digital systems," *IEEE Design & Test of Computers*, pp. 29–41, September 1993.
10. Hyperstone Electronics, *Hyperstone E1 32-Bit-Microprocessor User's Manual*, 1990.
11. Information Processing Systems—Open Systems Interconnection—LOTOS: A Formal Description Technique Based on the Temporal Ordering of Observational Behaviour, IS-8807, International Standards Organization, 1989.
12. T. Ismail and A. Jerraya, "Synthesis steps and design models for co-design," *IEEE Computer*, 28(2): 44–52, February 1995.
13. S.C. Johnson, "Hierarchical clustering schemes," *Psychometrika*, 32: 241–254, September 1967.
14. B.W. Kernighan and S. Lin, "An efficient heuristic procedure for partitioning graphs," *Bell Syst. Tech. J.*, 4(2): 291–308, 1970.
15. G. Koch, U. Kebschull, and W. Rosenstiel, "A prototyping architecture for hardware/software codesign in the COBRA project," in *Proceedings of 3rd international Workshop on Hardware/Software Codesign Codes/CASHE'94*, Grenoble, 1994.
16. M.L. López Vallejo et al., "Coarse grain partitioning for hardware-software co-design," *22nd Euromicro Conference, EUROMICRO'96*, Prague, September 1996.
17. J.A. Mañas and T. de Miguel, "From LOTOS to C," in *Formal Description Techniques, I*, K.J. Turner, ed., pp. 79–84, Stirling, Scotland, UK, 1989. IFIP, North-Holland. *Proceedings FORTE'88*, September 1988.
18. C. Miguel, A. Fernández, J.M. Ortuño, and L. Vidaller, "A LOTOS based performance evaluation tool," special issue of *Computer Networks and ISDN Systems*, in *Tools for FDTs*, 25(7): 791–813, February 1993.
19. J. Quemada, A. Azcorra, and S. Pavón, "Development with LOTOS," in *Using Formal Description Techniques*, K.J. Turner, ed., John Wiley and Sons, Chichester, UK, 1993, pp. 345–373.
20. J. Quemada, S. Pavón, and A. Fernández, "State exploration by transformation with LOLA," *Workshop on Automatic Verification Methods for Finite State Systems*, Grenoble, June 1989.
21. L. Sánchez Fernández, "Contribución a la especificación de aspectos no funcionales de sistemas hardware-software," Ph.D. Thesis, Technical University of Madrid, July 1997.
22. L. Sánchez Fernández, N. Martínez Madrid, and C. Delgado Kloos, "Integrating non-functional aspects into LOTOS," *Current Issues in Electronic Modeling*, Vol. 4, Kluwer Academic Publishers, December 1995.
23. L. Sánchez Fernández, N. Martínez Madrid, and C. Delgado Kloos, "LOTOS-based system co-design," Technical Report of the ESPRIT COBRA (EP 8135) project, Madrid, April 1996.
24. K. Stølen and M. Fuchs, "A formal method for hardware/software co-design," Technical Report, Institut für Informatik, Technische Universität München, May 1995.
25. K.J. Turner, ed., *Using Formal Description Techniques*, John Wiley and Sons, Chichester, UK, 1993.
26. S. Vercauteren and B. Lin, "Hardware/software communication and system integration for embedded architectures," *Design Automation for Embedded Systems*, 2(3/4): 359–382, May 1997.
27. C. Weiler, U. Kebschull, and W. Rosenstiel, "C++ base classes for specification, simulation and partitioning of a hardware/software system," in *Proceedings of VLSI'95*, pp. 777–784, 1995.
28. U. Weinmann, "FPGA partitioning under timing constraints," *Int. Workshop on Field Programmable Logic and Applications*, Oxford, September 1993.

CHAPTER SEVEN

Reconfigurable Computing Platforms

Programmable Active Memories: Reconfigurable Systems Come of Age 611
    J. Vuillemin, P. Bertin, D. Roncin, M. Shand, H. H. Touati, and P. Boucard

Logic Emulation with Virtual Wires 625
    J. Babb, R. Tessier, M. Dahl, S. Zimi Hanono, D. M. Hoki, and A. Agarwal

Embryonics: A New Methodology for Designing Field-Programmable
Gate Arrays with Self-Repair and Self-Replicating Properties 643
    D. Mange, E. Sanchez, A. Stauffer, G. Tempesti, P. Marchal, and C. Piguet

INTRODUCTION

Reconfigurable systems exploit field-programmable gate array (FPGA) technology, so that they can be personalized after manufacturing to fit a specific application. The operation of reconfigurable systems can either involve a configuration phase followed by an execution phase or concurrent (partial) configuration and execution. In the latter case, the systems are called *evolvable*.

Reconfigurable systems have numerous applications in computational acceleration and prototyping. In both cases, the complete systems include a reconfigurable subsystem that speed up software or the hardware execution of both. Several of these applications have lead to successful commercial products.

Let us first consider the acceleration of software execution. Software programs often contain bottlenecks that limit their performance (*e.g.*, executing transcendental floating-point operations, or inner loops where sequences of operations are iterated). ASIC co-processors can reduce the software execution time, if they are dedicated to support specific operations (*e.g.*, floating-point or graphic co-processors) or if they implement the critical loops in hardware while exploiting the local parallelism. Whereas ASIC co-processors accelerate specific functions, co-processors based on reconfigurable hardware can be applied to the speed-up of arbitrary software programs with some distinctive characteristics (*e.g.*, programs with parallelizable bit-level operations).

PROGRAMMABLE ACTIVE MEMORIES

One of the first examples of programmable co-processors is provided by *programmable active memories* (PAMs), from Vuillemin *et al.* [Vui96]. The system consists of a board of FPGAs and local memory interfaced to a host computer. Two models of PAMs, named PeRLe-0 and PeRLe-1, were manufactured first. They differ in the number and type of FPGA used, as well as operating frequency. Later, the *Pamette* card was introduced that can be plugged into a personal computer.

To accelerate the execution of a program with a PAM, the performance-critical portion of the program is first extracted and compiled into the patterns that configure the programmable board. Then, the noncritical portion of the program is executed on the host, while the critical portions are emulated by the reconfigurable subsystem. Experimental results show a speed-up of one to two orders of magnitude, on selective benchmark programs, as compared to the execution time on the host.

The principal hardware/software co-design problems consist of identifying the critical segments of the software programs and compiling them efficiently to run on the programmable hardware. The former task is not automated for PAMs and is achieved by successive refinement, under constraints of communication bandwidth and load balancing between the host and the programmable hardware. The latter task is based on hardware synthesis algorithms, and it benefits from performance optimization techniques for hardware circuits.

COMPUTER-AIDED PROTOTYPING

A different application of reconfigurable systems is for *computer-aided prototyping*. In this application, we are interested in validating a target system yet to be manufactured by configuring and executing a prototype implemented with a reconfigurable medium.

Prototypes provide design engineers with more realistic data on correctness and performance than system-level simulation, thus reducing the likelihood of an expensive redesign of the target system.

Prototyping of complex digital systems including multiple hardware components and software programs is appealing to designers, because they can test software programs on hardware, while retaining the ability to change the hardware (and software) implementation concurrently. Once the hardware configuration has been finalized, it can be mapped onto a "hard" silicon implementation using synthesis systems that accept as inputs hardware models compatible with those used by the emulation systems (*e.g.*, VHDL and Verilog HDL models).

Prototyping systems based on logic emulation can be characterized in different ways, such as interconnect topology (*e.g.*, full crossbar and two-dimensional meshes), type of FPGAs (*e.g.*, gate and pin count), and supporting software. Most systems are inefficient because of FPGA pin limitations. Despite the use of complex and expensive interconnect topologies, they can use only a fraction of the possible bandwidth, because they dedicate each FPGA pin (physical wire) to a single emulated signal (logical wire). Babb's *virtual wire* approach [Bab97] overcomes pin limitation by intelligently multiplexing each physical wire among logical wires and by pipelining these connections at the maximum speed of the FPGA. The resulting increase in bandwidth allows us to use simpler interconnect topologies, leading to low-cost and effective logic emulation.

FAULT-TOLERANT AND EVOLVABLE SYSTEMS

Evolvable systems are digital systems where reconfiguration of one of its parts is concurrent with execution. One of the goals of evolvable systems is to adapt automatically to the environment. As an example, consider a network interface unit that receives and retransmits data with different formats. Upon sensing the protocol and format of the incoming data, such a unit configures itself to optimize data translation and transmission. Although such a unit could be implemented with non-evolvable technology, the ability to reconfigure the hardware would result in higher data rates.

Fault tolerance in evolvable systems can be obtained by detecting the malfunctioning unit and by reconfiguring a part of the system to regenerate a fault-free replacement of the faulty unit. This result can be achieved under several assumptions, some of which are typical of fault-tolerant system design, including that of having enough spare reconfigurable circuits to implement the faulty unit on-the-fly.

Evolvable systems are the subject of several research efforts. An interesting application of reconfigurable hardware for fault-tolerance applications is *embryonics* (embryological electronics) by Mange *et al.* [Man98], a discipline where biological models of organization are used for electronic system design. There are a few implementations of embryonic systems, relying on this general implementation strategy. The underlying hardware is a memory-based field-programmable circuit that uses a decision diagram structure. The hardware is organized as a rectangular matrix of cells, each one addressable by its coordinates and communicating with its neighbors. The overall system function is mapped onto the programmable cells. Circuit configuration is performed by feeding each cell with a compiled software program (bit stream) containing the functionality of the entire system. This process parallels the organization of multicellular living beings, where the genome of each cell is a repository of information of the entire being. The program is transmitted from an initial cell to the others. Then, each cell extracts the portion of the overall program pertinent to its operation (using the coordinate information) and configures itself in a process analogous to the synthesis of a living cell from the gene structure.

After a boot phase in which the information is transmitted to all cells and the cells self-configure, the system can start operating. Upon failure of a cell to provide the required function, the neighboring cells readapt their operations so that the faulty cell is replaced by a working clone, and the overall system function is preserved. This reconfiguration, called *cicatrization*, allows the system to recover from failures after a finite delay.

Interesting applications of embryological circuits include embedded system applications with high reliability requirements, such as control of unmanned spacecraft or of robots operating in hostile environments. Hardware/software co-design problems relate to how software programs are used to configure and program the underlying hardware circuit, as well as to how the reconfigurable circuit is organized.

ADDITIONAL READINGS IN RECONFIGURABLE COMPUTING PLATFORMS

[Li00] Y. Li, T. Callahan, E. Darnell, R. Harr, U. Kurkure, and J. Stockwood, "Hardware-software co-design of embedded reconfigurable architectures," in *Proceedings, 37th Design Automation Conference*, ACM Press, New York, 2000, 501–06. *Describes co-design methods for a platform consisting of a CPU and a reconfigurable data path.*

[Sin00] H. Singh. G. Lu, M.-H. Lee, F. Kurdahi, N. Bagherzadeh, E. Filho, and R. Maestre, "MorphoSys: Case study of a reconfigurable computing system targeting multimedia applications," in *Proceedings, 37th Design Automation Conference*, ACM Press, New York, 2000, 567–72. *Describes a platform based on a CPU, an attached reconfigurable array, and a high-performance memory interface.*

[Hau98] S. Hauck. G. Borriello, and C. Ebeling, "Mesh routing topologies for multi-FPGA systems," *IEEE Transactions on VLSI Systems* 6, no. 3 (Sept. 1998): 400–08. *Analyzes mesh interconnection schemes for emulators and other systems built from multiple FPGAs.*

Pleadies Group home page:
http://bwrc.eecs. berkeley.edu
The Pleadies project at UC Berkeley is developing reconfigurable architectures for low-power heterogeneous DSP.

Mojave Project home page:
http://www.icsl.ucla.edu/~atr
The Mojave project is developing reconfigurable computing approaches to application-specific systems.

Programmable Active Memories: Reconfigurable Systems Come of Age

Jean E. Vuillemin, Patrice Bertin, Didier Roncin, Mark Shand, Hervé H. Touati, and Philippe Boucard

Abstract—Programmable active memories (PAM) are a novel form of universal reconfigurable hardware coprocessor. Based on *field-programmable gate array* (FPGA) technology, a PAM is a *virtual* machine, controlled by a standard microprocessor, which can be dynamically and indefinitely reconfigured into a large number of application-specific circuits. PAM's offer a new mixture of hardware performance and software versatility. We review the important architectural features of PAM's, through the example of DECPeRLe-1, an experimental device built in 1992. PAM programming is presented, in contrast to classical gate-array and full custom circuit design. Our emphasis is on large, code-generated synchronous systems descriptions; no compromise is made with regard to the performance of the target circuits. We exhibit a dozen applications where PAM technology proves superior, both in performance *and* cost, to every other existing technology, including supercomputers, massively parallel machines, and conventional custom hardware. The fields covered include computer arithmetic, cryptography, error correction, image analysis, stereo vision, video compression, sound synthesis, neural networks, high-energy physics, thermodynamics, biology and astronomy. At comparable cost, the computing power virtually available in a PAM exceeds that of conventional processors by a factor 10 to 1000, depending on the specific application, in 1992. A technology shrink increases the performance gap between conventional processors and PAM's. By Noyce's law, we predict by how much the performance gap will widen with time.

*Index Terms—*Programmable active memory, PAM, reconfigurable system, field-programmable gate array, FPGA.

I. Introduction

THERE are two ways to implement a specific high-speed digital processing task.

- The simplest is to program some general-purpose computer to perform the processing. In this *software* approach, one effectively maps the algorithm of interest onto a *fixed* machine architecture. However, the structure of that machine will have been highly optimized to process arbitrary code. In many cases, it will be poorly suited to the specific algorithm, so performance will be short of the required speed.

- The alternative is to design ad hoc circuitry for the specific algorithm. In this *hardware* approach, the machine structure—processors, storage and interconnect—is tailored to the application. The result is more efficient, with less actual circuitry than general-purpose computers require.

The disadvantage of the hardware approach is that a specific architecture is usually limited to processing a small number of algorithms, often a single one. Meanwhile, the general-purpose computer can be programmed to process *every* computable function, as we have known since the days of Church and Turing.

Adding special-purpose hardware to a universal machine, say for video compression, speeds up the processor—when the system is actually compressing video. It contributes nothing when the system is required to perform some different task, say cryptography or stereo vision.

We present an alternative machine architecture that offers the best of both worlds: software versatility *and* hardware performance. The proposal is a standard high-performance microprocessor enhanced by a PAM coprocessor. The PAM can be configured as a wide class of specific hardware systems, one for each interesting application. PAM's merge together hardware and software.

This paper presents results from seven years of research, at INRIA, DEC-PRL and other places. It addresses the following topics:

How to build PAM's.
How to program PAM's.
What are the applications?

Section II introduces the principles of the underlying FPGA technology. Section III highlights the interesting features of PAM architecture. Section IV presents some of the methods used in programming *large* PAM designs.

Section V describes a dozen applications, chosen from a wide variety of scientific fields. For each, PAM outperforms all other existing technologies. A hypothetical machine equipped with a dozen different conventional co-processors would achieve the same level of performance—at a higher price. Through reconfiguration, a PAM is able to *time-share* its internal circuitry between our 12 (and more) applications; the hypothetical machine would require different custom circuits for each, that must be physically present at all times.

We assess, in Section VI, the computing power of PAM technology, today and in the future.

Manuscript received July 5, 1994; revised October 26, 1994. This work was done at Digital Equipment Corporation's Paris Research Laboratory (DEC-PRL, 92500 Rueil-Malmaison, France) from 1988 to 1994.

J. Vuillemin, D. Roncin, M. Shand, H. Touati, and P. Boucard were with the Digital Equipment Corporation, Paris Research Laboratory, DEC-PRL, 92500 Rueil-Malmaison, France.

P. Bertin was a visiting scientist from Institut National de Recherche en Informatique et en Automatique, INRIA, 78150 Rocquencourt, France.

Publisher Item Identifier S 1063-8210(96)02081-1.

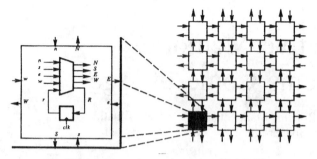

This PAB has 4 inputs $\langle n,s,e,w\rangle$, 4 outputs $\langle N,S,E,W\rangle$, one register (flip-flop) with input R and output r, and a combinational gate

$$g(n,s,e,w,r) = (N,S,E,W,R)$$

The truth table of g is specified by $160 = 5 \times 32$ bits.

Fig. 1. Field-programmable gate array.

II. VIRTUAL CIRCUITS

The first commercial FPGA was introduced in 1986 by Xilinx [1]. This revolutionary component has a large internal configuration memory, and two modes of operation: in *download* mode, the configuration memory can be written, as a whole, through some external device; once in *configured* mode a FPGA behaves like a regular *application-specific integrated circuit* (ASIC).

To realize a FPGA, one simply connects together in a regular mesh, $n \times m$ identical *programmmable active bits* (PAB's). Surprisingly enough, there are many ways to implement a PAB with the required universality. In particular, it can be built from either or both of the following primitives:

- a *configurable logic block* implements a boolean function with k inputs (typically $2 \leq k \leq 6$); its truth table is defined by 2^k (or less) configuration bits, stored in local registers;
- a *configurable routing block* implements a switchbox whose connectivity table is set by local configuration bits.

Such a FPGA implements a Von Neumann cellular automaton. What is more, the FPGA is a *universal* example of such a structure: any synchronous digital circuit can be emulated, through a suitable configuration, on a large enough FPGA, for a slow enough clock.

Some vendors, such as Xilinx [2] or AT&T [3], form their PAB's from both configurable routing and logic blocks. Other early ones, such as Algotronix [4] (now with Xilinx) or Concurrent Logic [5] (now with Atmel), combine routing and computing functions into a single primitive—this is the *fine grain* approach. An idealized implementation of this fine grain concept is given in Fig. 1. A third possibility is to build the PAB from a configurable routing box connected to a fixed (non configurable) universal gate such as a *nor* or a *multiplexor* [6].

Each FPGA implementation can emulate each of the others, granted enough PAB's. In order to make quantitative performance comparisons between the diverse significant implementations, let us, from now on, choose as our reference unit any active bit with one 4-input boolean function—configurable or not—and one internal bit of state (see Section VI and Vuillemin [7]). With its five 5-input functions, the PAB from Fig. 1 counts for 10 or so such units.

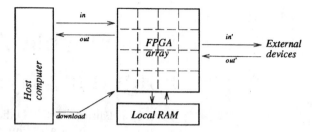

Fig. 2. Programmable active memory.

The FPGA is a *virtual circuit* which can behave like a number of different ASICs: all it takes to emulate a particular one is to feed the proper configuration bits. This means that prototypes can be made quickly, tested and corrected. The development cycle of circuits with FPGA technology is typically measured in weeks, as opposed to months for hardwired gate array techniques. But FPGA's are used not just for prototypes; they also get incorporated in many production units. In all branches of the electronics industry other than the mass market, the use of FPGA's is expanding, despite the fact that they still cost ten times as much as ASIC's in volume production. In 1992, FPGA's were the fastest growing part of the semi-conductor industry, increasing output by 40%, compared to 10% for chips overall.

As a consequence, FPGA's are on the leading edge of silicon chips. They grow bigger and faster at the rate of their enabling technology, namely that of the static RAM used for storing the internal configuration.

In the past 40 years, the feature size of silicon technology has been shrinking by a factor $1/\alpha \approx 1.25$ each year. This phenomenon is known as Moore's law; it was first observed in the early sixties. The implications of Moore's law for FPGA technology are analyzed by Vuillemin [7]. The prediction is that the leading edge FPGA, which has 400 PAB's operating at 25 MHz in 1992, will, by year 2001, contain 25k PAB's operating at 200 MHz.

III. PAM'S AS VIRTUAL MACHINES

The purpose of a PAM is to implement a *virtual machine* that can be dynamically configured as a large number of specific hardware devices.

The structure of a generic PAM is found in Fig. 2. It is connected—through the *in* and *out* links—to a host processor. A function of the host is to *download* configuration bitstreams into the PAM. After configuration, the PAM behaves, electrically and logically, like the ASIC defined by the specific bitstream. It may operate in stand-alone mode, hooked to some external system—through the in' and out' links. It may operate as a coprocessor under host control, specialized to speed-up some crucial computation. It may operate as both, and connect the host to some external system, like an audio or video device, or some other PAM.

To justify our choice of name, observe that a PAM is attached to some high-speed bus of the host computer, like any RAM memory module. The processor can write into, and read from the PAM. Unlike RAM however, a PAM processes data between write and read instructions—which makes it

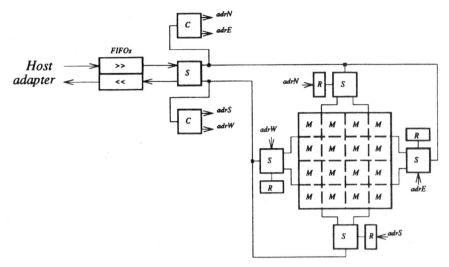

Fig. 3. DECPeRLe-1 architecture.

an "active" memory. The specific processing is determined by the contents of its configuration bitstream, which can be updated by the host in a matter of milliseconds—thus the "programmable" qualifier.

We now describe the architecture of a specific PAM: it is named DECPeRLe-1 and will be referred to as P_1. It was built at Digital's Paris Research Laboratory in 1992. A dozen copies operate at various scientific centers in the world; some are cited as we enumerate the operational applications in Section V.

The overall structure of P_1 is shown in Fig. 3. Each of the 23 squares denotes one Xilinx XC3090 FPGA [2]. Each of the 4 rectangles represents 1 MB of static RAM (letter R). Each line represents 32 wires, physically laid out on the printed circuit board (PCB) of P_1. A photo of the system is shown in Fig. 4.

The merit of this structure is to host, in a natural manner, the diverse networks of processing units presented in Section V. Depending upon the application, individual units are implemented within one to many FPGAs; they may also be implemented as *look-up tables* (LUT) through the local RAM; some slow processes are implemented by software running on the host. Connections between processing units are mapped, as part of the design configuration, either on PCB wires or on internal FPGA wires.

A. FPGA Matrix

The computational core of P_1 is a 4 × 4 matrix of XC3090—letter M in Fig. 3. Each FPGA has 16 *direct connections* to each of its four Manhattan neighbors. The four FPGA's in each row and each column share two common 16 b buses. There are thus four 64 b buses traversing the array, one per geographical direction N, S, E, W.

The purpose of this organization is to best extrapolate, at the PCB level, the internal structure of the FPGA. What we have is close to a large FPGA with 64 × 80 PAB's—except for a connection bottleneck every quarter of the array, as there are fewer wires on the PCB than inside the FPGA. By Noyce's thesis, P_1 implements, with 1992 technology, a leading edge FPGA that should become available on a single chip by 1998.

Fig. 4. DECPeRLe-1 and its TURBOchannel interface board.

B. Local RAM

Some applications, like RSA cryptography, are entirely implemented with FPGA logic; most others require some amount of RAM to buffer and re-order local data, or to implement specialized LUT's.

The size of this cache RAM is 4 MB for P_1, made up of four independent 32 b wide banks. The 18 b addresses and read/write signals for each RAM are generated within one of two *controller* FPGAs—letter C in Fig. 3. Data to and from each RAM goes to the corresponding *switch* FPGA—letter S.

All the presented applications that do use the RAM operate around 25 MHz. Many utilize the full RAM bandwidth available, namely 400 MB/s. Other applications, for which RAM access is not critical, operate at higher clock speeds, such as 40 MHz for RSA, and higher.

C. External Links

P_1 has four 32 b wide external connectors.

Three of these (not represented on Fig. 3) link edges of the FPGA matrix to external connectors. They are used for establishing *real-time* links, at up to 33 MHz, between P_1 and external devices: audio, video, physical detectors··· Their aggregated peak bandwidth exceeds 400 MB/s.

The fourth external connection links to the host interface of P_1: a 100 MB/s *TURBOchannel* adapter [8]. In order to avoid having to synchronize the host and PAM clocks, host data goes through two FIFO's, for input and output, respectively. To the PAM side of the FIFO's is another switch FPGA, which shares two 32 b buses with the other switches and controllers—see Fig. 3.

The host connection itself consists of a host-independent part implemented on the P_1 mother board and a host-dependent part implemented on a small option board specific to the host bus. A short cable links the two parts—see Fig. 4.

In addition to the above, P_1 features daughter-board connectors that can provide more than 1.2 GB/s of bandwidth to specialized hardware extensions.

D. Firmware

One extra FPGA on P_1 is not configurable by the user; call it POM, by analogy with ROM. Its function is to provide control over the state of the PAM, through software from the host.

The logical protocol of the host bus itself is *programmed* in POM configuration. Adapting from TURBOchannel to some other logical bus format, such as VME, HIPPI or PCI is just a matter of re-programming the POM and re-designing the small host-dependent interface board.

A function of the POM is to assist the host in downloading a PAM configuration—1.5 Mb for P_1. Thanks to this hardware assist, we are able to reconfigure P_1 up to fifty times per second, a crucial feature in some applications. One can regard P_1 as a *software silicon foundry*, with a 20 ms turn-around time.

We take advantage of an extra feature of the XC3090 component: it is possible to dynamically *read back* the contents of the internal state register of each PAB. Together with a *clock stepping* facility—stop the main clock and trigger clock cycles one at a time from the host—this provides a powerful debugging tool, where one takes a snapshot of the complete internal state of the system after each clock cycle. This feature drastically reduces the need for software simulation of our designs.

PAM designs are synchronous circuits: all registers are updated on each cycle of the same global clock. The maximum speed of a design is directly determined by its *critical combinational path*. This varies from one PAM design to another. It has thus been necessary to design a clock distribution system whose speed can be *programmed* as part of the design configuration. On P_1, the clock can be finely tuned, with increments on the order of 0.01%, for frequencies up to 100 MHz.

A typical P_1 design receives a logically uninterrupted flow of data, through the input FIFO. It performs some processing, and delivers its results, in the same manner, through the output FIFO. The host is responsible for filling-in and emptying-out the other side of both FIFO's. Our firmware supports a mode in which the application clock automatically *stops* when P_1 attempts to read an empty FIFO or write a full one, effectively providing fully automatic and transparent *flow-control*.

The full firmware functionality may be controlled through host software. Most of it is also available to the hardware design: all relevant wires are brought to the two controller FPGA's of P_1. This allows a design to synchronize itself, in the same manner, with some of the external links. Another unique possibility is the *dynamic tuning of the clock*. This feature is used in designs where a slow and infrequent operation—say changing the value of some global controls every 256 cycles—coexists with fast and frequent operations. The strategy is then to slow the clock down before the infrequent operation—every 256 cycles—and speed it up afterwards—for 255 cycles. Tricky, but doable.

E. Other Reconfigurable Systems

Besides our PAM's, which were built first at INRIA in 1987 up to Perle-0, whose architecture is described in some detail in an earlier report [9], then at DEC-PRL, other successful implementations of reconfigurable systems have been reported, in particular at the universities of Edinburgh [10] and Zurich [11], and at the Supercomputer Research Center in Maryland [12].

The ENABLE machine is a system, built from FPGA's and SRAM, specifically constructed at the university of Mannheim [13] for solving the TRT problem of Section V-G2). Many similar application-specific machines have been built in the recent years: their reconfigurable nature is exploited only while developing and debugging the application. Once complete, the final configuration is frozen, once and for all—until the next "hardware release."

Commercial products already exist: QuickTurn [14] sells large configurable systems, dedicated to hardware emulation. Compugen [15] sells a modular PAM-like hardware, together with several configurations focusing on genetic matching algorithms. More systems exist than just the ones mentioned here.

A thorough presentation of the issues involved in PAM design, with alternative implementation choices, is given by Bertin [16].

IV. PAM Programming

A PAM program consists of three parts:
- The *driving software*, which runs on the host and controls the PAM hardware.
- The logic equations describing the synchronous hardware implemented on the PAM board.
- The placement and routing directives that guide the implementation of the logic equations onto the PAM board.

The driving software is written in C or C++ and is linked to a runtime library encapsulating a device driver. The logic equations and the placement and routing directives are generated algorithmically by a C++ program. As a deliberate choice of methodology, all PAM design circuits are *digital* and *synchronous*. Asynchronous features—such as RAM write pulses, FIFO flags decoding or clock tuning—are pushed into the firmware (POM) where they get implemented once and for all.

A full P_1 design is a large piece of hardware: excluding the RAM, 23 XC3090 containing 15k PAB's are roughly the equivalent of 200 k gates. This amount of logic would barely fit in the largest gate arrays available in 1994.

The goal of a P_1 designer is to encode, through a 1.5 Mb bitstream, the logic equations, the placement and the routing of fifteen thousand PAB's in order to meet the performance requirements of a compute-intensive task. To achieve this goal with a reasonable degree of efficiency, a designer needs full control over the final logic implementation and layout. In 1992, no existing *computer-aided design* (CAD) tool was adapted to such needs.

Emerging synthesis tools were too wasteful in circuit area and delay. One has to keep in mind that we already pay a performance penalty by using SRAM-based FPGA's instead of raw silicon. Complex designs can be synthesized, placed and routed automatically only when they do not attempt to reach high device utilization; even then, the resulting circuitry is significantly slower than what can be achieved by careful hand placement.

Careful low-level circuit implementation has always been possible through a painful and laborious process: schematic capture. For PAM programming, schematic capture is not a viable alternative: it can provide the best performance, but it is too labor intensive for large designs.

Given these constraints, we have but one choice: a middle-ground approach where designs are described algorithmically at the structural level, and the structure can be annotated with geometry and routing information to help generate the final physical design.

```
template<int N>
struct RippleAdder: Block {
  RippleAdder(): Block("RippleAdder"){}
  void logic(Net<N>& a, Net<N>& b, Net<N>& c,
            Net<N>& sum, Net& carry) {
    input(a); input(b); input(c);
    output(sum); output(carry);
    for (int i = 0; i < N; i++){
      sum[i] = a[i] ^ b[i] ^ c[i];
      carry[i] = (a[i] & b[i])
               | (b[i] & c[i])
               | (c[i] & a[i]);
    }
  }
};
```

Fig. 5. Circuit description in C++.

```
void placement(Net<N>& sum, Net<N>& carry) {
  for (int i = 0; i < N; i++) {
    carry[i] <<= sum[i];
    sum[i+1] <<= sum[i] + OFFSET(0,1);
  }
}
```

Fig. 6. Circuit layout in C++.

A. Programming Tools

We first had to choose a programming language to describe circuits. Three choices were possible: a general-purpose programming language such as C++, a hardware description language such as VHDL, or our own language. We do not discuss the latter approach here; it is the subject of current research.

We decided to use C++ for reasons of economy and simplicity. VHDL is a complex, expensive language. C++ programming environments are considerably cheaper, and we are tapping a much wider market in terms of training, documentation and programming tools. Though we had to develop a generic software library to handle netlist generation and simulation, the amount of work remains limited. Moreover, we keep full control over the generated netlist, and we can include circuit geometry information as desired.

1) The Netlist Library: To describe synchronous circuits with our C++ library is straightforward. We introduce a new type Net, overload the boolean operators to describe combinational logic, and add a primitive for the synchronous register. From these, a C++ program can be written which *generates* a netlist representing any synchronous circuit. This type of low-level description is made convenient by the use of basic programming techniques such as arrays, for loops, procedures and data abstraction. Fig. 5 shows, for example, a piece of code representing a generic n-bit ripple-carry adder.

The execution of such a program builds a netlist in memory; this netlist can be analyzed and translated into an appropriate format (XNF or EDIF), or used directly for simulation. Linking a netlist description program with behavioral code yields mixed-mode simulation with no special effort.

Since we have direct access to the netlist at this level of description, we can easily annotate logic operators with placement directives. For example, to specify that our ripple-carry adder should be aligned vertically, with the paired carry and sum bits generated by the same logic block, we simply add the lines shown in Fig. 6 to the description of the adder.

Contrary to the silicon compilers from a decade ago [17], these placement annotations do not affect the logic behavior of the generated netlist. They do not specify contacts; they only specify the partitioning of logic into physical blocks and the absolute or relative placement of these blocks in a two-dimensional grid. A back-end tool analyzes these attributes and emulates the interface of a schematic capture software in order to guarantee that the placement and logic partitioning information is preserved by the FPGA vendor software.

2) The Runtime Library: At the system level, the programming environment provides two main functions: a device driver interface, and full simulation support of that interface. This simulation capability allows the designer to operate together the hardware and software parts from a PAM program. The device driver interface provides the mandatory controls to the application program: the usual UNIX I/O interface with open, close, synchronous and asynchronous read and write; download of the configuration bitstreams for the PAM FPGAs; readback of their state (i.e., the values of all PAB registers);

read and write of the PAM static RAMs; software control of the PAM board clock.

3) Lessons: The main lesson we draw from our experience with these programming tools is that PAM programming is much easier than ASIC development. Students with no electrical engineering background were able to use our tools after a few weeks of training. In particular, users can easily develop their own module generators in matters of days, while only highly skilled engineers are able to write module generators for custom VLSI. This capability is one of the main reasons why we were able to develop such complex applications spanning dozens of chips, with engineers and students not previously exposed to PAM, each in a matter of months.

B. Debugging and Optimization Tools

Debugging of a PAM design can be done entirely through software. Mixed-mode simulation at the block level allows designers to certify datapath components before using them in complex designs. Full-system simulation eliminates the need for generating special input patterns to test the hardware part of the program. Full-system simulation allows for *hardware/software codebug*: both application driver and hardware, working together.

After simple bugs have been removed, it becomes necessary to simulate the design on a large number of cycles. To do so, the most effective technique is to compile the design into a bitstream, download this bitstream into the board, and run the board in *trace* mode (single-step the clock, readback the board state at each cycle and collect these states for analysis; it is possible to run this mode at up to 100 Hz). In simple cases, this can be done with no modification to the runtime application source code. In complex cases, all necessary primitives are available to build application-specific code to generate and/or analyze the readback traces.

P_1's clock generator can also be operated in *double-step* mode. In that mode, the clock runs at full speed every second cycle. By comparing double-step traces taken at increasing clock frequencies with a previously recorded single-step trace, we can automatically locate the critical path of a design for a given execution. This method alleviates the need to rely on delay simulation as provided by the standard industrial simulation packages. It is necessary to perform that tedious task only once, when certifying the operating speed of the final design.

We developed a screen visualization tool called showRB to help analyze readback traces. It can display the state of every flip-flop in every FPGA of a PAM board, at the rate of tens of frames per second. In conjunction with the double-step mode, it can be used to detect critical paths along execution traces. Interestingly enough, such a tool also proved invaluable in *demonstrating* the structure of some hardware algorithms.

V. APPLICATIONS

Our applications were chosen to span a wide range of current leading-edge computational challenges. In each case, we provide a brief description of the design, a performance

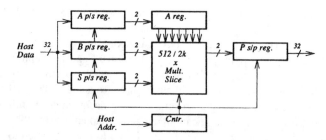

Fig. 7. Long multiplication.

comparison with similar reported work, and pointers to publications describing the work in more detail.

One paradigm was systematically applied:
cast the inner loop in PAM hardware; let software handle the rest!

In what follows, $a \div b$ denotes the quotient and $a \cdot | \cdot b$ the remainder in the euclidean integer division of a by b.

A. Long Integer Arithmetic

PAM's may be configured as long integer multipliers [18]. They compute the product

$$P = A \times B + S$$

where A is an n-bit long multiplier, and B, S are arbitrary size multiplicands and summands [19]; n may be up to 2 k for the P_1 implementation.

Our multipliers are interfaced with the public domain arbitrary-precision arithmetic package *BigNum* [20]: programs based on that software automatically benefit from the PAM, by simply linking with an appropriately modified BigNum library.

P_1 computes product bits at 66 Mb/s (using radix four operations at 33 MHz), which is faster than *all* previously published benchmarks. This is 16 times over the figures reported by Buell and Ward [21] for the Cray II and Cyber 170/750. P_1's multiplier can compute a 50 coefficient 16 b polynomial convolution (FIR filter) at 16 times *audio real time* (2×24 b samples at 48 kHz).

The first operational version of this multiplier was developed in less than a week. Two subsequent versions, which refined the design on the basis of actual performance measurements, were each developed in less than five man-days.

A more aggressive multiplier design is reported by Louie and Ercegovac [22]: using radix 16 and deep pipeline, this multiplier operates at 79 MHz, which is 2.5 faster than ours within 3 times the area. At that speed, this design is faster than conventional multipliers, even for short 32 b operands.

B. RSA Cryptography

To investigate further the tradeoffs in our hybrid hardware and software system, we have focused on the RSA cryptosystem [23]. Both encryption and decryption involve computing modular exponentials, which can be decomposed as sequences of long modular multiplications, with operand sizes ranging from 256 b to 1 kb.

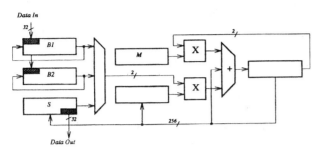

Fig. 8. RSA cryptography.

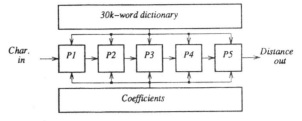

Fig. 9. String matching.

Fig. 10. Heat and Laplace equations.

TABLE I
RSA SPEEDUP TECHNIQUES

Algorithm	Speedup
Chinese remainders	4
Precompute powers	1.25
Hensel's division	1.5
Carry completion	≈ 2
Quotient pipelining	4

Starting from the general-purpose multiplier above, we have implemented a series of systems spanning two orders of magnitude in performance, over three years.

Our first system [18] uses three differently programmed Perle-0 boards, all operating in parallel with the host. At 200 kb/s decoding speed, this was faster than *all* existing 512 b RSA implementations, regardless of technology, in 1990. A survey by E. Brickell [24] grants the previous speed record for 512 b key RSA decryption to an ASIC from AT&T, at 19 kb/s.

Table I recalls the various original hardware algorithms used in our latest implementation of RSA, and quantifies each speedup achieved.

The resulting P_1 design for RSA cryptography combines all of the techniques above (see Shand and Vuillemin [25] for details). To fully exploit the available logic gates the P_1 design operates with 970 b keys. At this key length it delivers an RSA secret decryption rate of 185 kb/s. This is an order of magnitude faster than any previously reported running implementation. For 512 b keys the same datapath delivers a decryption rate in excess of 300 kb/s although it uses only half the logic resources in P_1.

PAM implementations of RSA rely on reconfigurability in many ways: we use a different PAM design for RSA encryption and decryption; we generate a different hardware modular multiplier for each different prime modulus with the coefficients of the binary representation of each modulus hardwired into the logic equations of the design.

C. Molecular Biology

Given an alphabet $\mathcal{A} = (a_1, \cdots, a_n)$, a probability $(S_{ij})_{i,j=1\cdots n}$ of substitution of a_i by a_j, and a probability $(I_i)_{i=1\cdots n}$ (respectively, $(D_i)_{i=1\cdots n}$) of insertion (respectively, deletion) of a_i, one can use a classical dynamic programming algorithm to compute the probability of transforming a word w_1 over $\mathcal{A}$ into another one w_2; this defines a *distance* between words in $\mathcal{A}$.

Applications include automated mail sorting through OCR scanners, on-the-fly keyboard spelling corrections, and DNA sequencing in biology.

D. Lavenier from IRISA (Rennes, France) has implemented this algorithm with a Perle-0 design which computes the distance between an input word and all 30 k words in a dictionary; it reports the k words found in the dictionary which are closest to the input. The system processes 200 k words/s which is faster than a solution previously implemented at CNET using 12 Transputers. It has only half of the performance obtained by a system previously developed at IRISA based on 28 custom VLSI chips and two printed-circuit boards.

The DNA matching algorithm [26] is one of the driving applications for the PAM developed at the Supercomputing Research Center in Maryland [12]: the reported performance is, here again, in excess of that obtained with existing supercomputers.

The *Compugen* commercial company [15] sells the *Bioccelerator*, a PAM which can be configured as a number of molecular biology search functions. This device is a coprocessor to a host server; it can be accessed through remote procedure call from any workstation on the network. It is interfaced with a widely used software package and its use is transparent, except for the speed-up advantages.

D. Heat and Laplace Equations

Solving the heat and Laplace equations has numerous applications in mechanics, integrated circuit technology, fluid dynamics, electrostatics, optics and finance [27].

The classical *finite difference method* [28] provides computational solutions to the heat and Laplace equations. Vuillemin [29] shows how to speed-up this computation with help from special-purpose hardware. A first implementation of the method on P_1, by Vuillemin and Rocheteau [29], operates with a pipeline depth of 128 operators. Each operator computes $(T + T')/2$ where T and T' are 24 b temperatures.

At 20 MHz, this first design processes 5 G operations—add and shift—per second. For such a smooth problem, one can easily show [29] that fixed-point yields the same results as floating-point operations. The performance achieved by this first 24 b P_1 design thus exceeds those reported by McBryan *et al.* [30], [31], for solving the same problems with the help

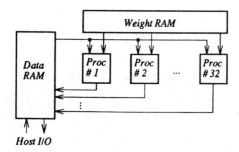

Fig. 11. Boltzmann machine.

of supercomputers. A sequential computer must execute 20 billion instructions per second in order to reproduce the same computation.

S. Hadinger and P. Raynaud-Richard further improved the implementation [32]. Refining the statistical analysis, they show that the datapath width can be reduced to 16 b provided that the rounding-off of the low-order bit is done *randomly*—with all deterministic round-off schemes, parasitic stable solutions exist which significantly perturb the result. Their implementation therefore uses a 64 b linear feedback shift-register to randomly set the rounding direction for each processing stage.

The width reduction in the datapath allows us to extend the pipeline length to 256, pushing the equivalent processing power up to 39 GIPS. Using P_1's fast DMA-based I/O capabilities and a large buffer of host memory, this design can accurately simulate the evolution of temperature over time in a 3-D volume, discretized on 512^3 points, with arbitrary power source distributions on the boundaries. It also supports the use of *multigrid* simulation, where one "zooms out" to coarser discretization grids in order to rapidly advance in simulated time, then "zooms back in" to full resolution, in order to accurately smooth out the desired final result.

E. Neural Networks

M. Skubiszewski [33], [34] has implemented a hardware emulator for binary neural networks, based on the *Boltzmann machine* model.

The Boltzmann machine is a probabilistic algorithm which minimizes quadratic forms over binary variables, i.e., expressions of the form

$$E(\vec{N}) = \sum_{i=0}^{n-1} \sum_{j=0}^{i} w_{i,j} N_i N_j$$

where $\vec{N} = (N_0, \cdots, N_{n-1})$ is a vector of binary variables and $(w_{i,j})_{0 \leq i,j < n}$ is a fixed matrix of *weights*. It is typically used to find approximate solutions to some $\mathcal{NP}$-hard problems, such as graph partitioning and circuit placement.

The latest P_1 realization solves problems with 1400 binary variables, using 16 b weights, for a total computing power of 500 *megasynapses per second*. (The megasynapse is the traditional unit used in this field; it amounts to one million additions and multiplications by small coefficients.)

F. Multistandard Video Compression

In view of the required input bandwidth (30 MB/s for standard TV color images) and the amount of computation required by current standards (respectively, 3, 4, and 8 Gop/s[1] for JPEG, DCT^{3-D} and MPEG), custom hardware is currently necessary for compressing video in real time.

Matters get complicated, as several different video compression standards are emerging. The following shows how a single configurable system such as P_1 can perform, through different designs, three (or more) of the current leading standards.

JPEG: The computation specified by the *Joint Photographic Expert Group* is performed in three stages, according to the following:

$$\text{Source Image} \mapsto \boxed{\mathcal{R}} \mapsto \boxed{\mathcal{DCT}^2} \mapsto \boxed{\mathcal{Q}} \mapsto \boxed{\mathcal{A}/\mathcal{HC}} \mapsto \text{Compressed Image}.$$

The initial RAM $\mathcal{R}$ is used to store 8 consecutive lines in the input image, with double buffering. It feeds the $\mathcal{DCT}^2$ module with 8×8 square subimages.

1) The two-dimensional $\mathcal{DCT}^2$ (discrete cosine transform) maps 8×8 squares from the space to the frequency domain.
2) Each frequency coefficient is divided by a number $Q = Q_{x,y}$. The choice of the *quantization* table Q provides a way to control the compromise between the compression factor and the quality of the decompressed image.
3) Runlength, and arithmetic or Huffman encodings $\mathcal{A}/\mathcal{HC}$ are performed on the quantized values.

MPEG: The *Motion Picture Expert Group* system does *motion compensation* ($\mathcal{MC}$) by computing a correlation between blocks within two time-consecutive images. The result is difference-coded, then goes through a processing similar to JPEG.

$$\text{Digital Video} \mapsto \boxed{\mathcal{R}} \mapsto \boxed{\mathcal{MC}} \mapsto \boxed{\Delta \, Code} \mapsto \text{Compressed Video}$$

MPEG-1 requires storage for only four images, after allowing for double buffering. The decoder is much simpler than the encoder, however, the MPEG decoder still requires about as much hardware as the following DCT^{3-D}.

A detailed FPGA mapping of the motion estimation algorithm—the core of the MPEG standard—is given by Furtek [35]. Mapping this fully laid-out design onto P_1 would be a straightforward task.[2]

Except for RAM, this method requires only half as much hardware as MPEG. It leads to an excellent compression factor, with an appropriate choice of the quantization table $Q = Q(x, y, t)$, a 512-entry cube. Early experiments indicate

---
[1] 10^9 16 b integer operations per second

[2] DCT^{3-D}. Vuillemin, D. Martineau, and J. Barraquand from PRL have used P_1 to experiment with DCT^{3-D}, a 3-D version of JPEG—the third dimension being time.

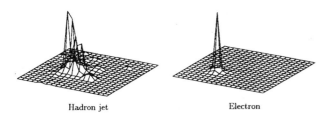

Fig. 12. Calorimeter typical input images.

that, for a given compression rate, the quality of the restituted video is (subjectively) better with DCT$^{3\text{-}D}$ than with MPEG.

The method performs the following sequence of computations:

$$\begin{array}{c}Digital\\ Video\end{array} \stackrel{30}{\mapsto} \boxed{\mathcal{R}} \stackrel{30}{\mapsto} \boxed{\mathcal{DCT}^3} \stackrel{60}{\mapsto} \boxed{\mathcal{A}/\mathcal{HC}} \stackrel{\approx 2}{\mapsto} \begin{array}{c}Compressed\\ Video.\end{array}$$

In this diagram, the numbers on the arrows indicate the transfer bandwidth, in MB/s.

- The algorithm needs a video buffer big enough to store 8 consecutive images (twice for double buffering). Thus, DCT$^{3\text{-}D}$ requires four times more RAM than MPEG.
- Past the initial video buffer, all the processing is performed in a straight pipeline operating on *video cubes* of size $8^3 \times 16b$, made of eight 8×8 squares consecutive in time.

This P_1 design computes 48 fixed-point operations (32 b outputs add, subtract, multiply and shift) at 25 MHz, for a total of 1.4 G operations per second. Based on our specification software, we rate this algorithm, which requires a lot of data movement, at 15 GIPS.

G. High-Energy Physics

1) Image Classification: The *calorimeter* is part of a series of benchmarks proposed by CERN[3] [36]. The goal is to measure the performance of various computer architectures, in order to build the electronics required for the *Large Hadron Collider* (LHC), before the turn of the millennium. The calorimeter is challenging, and well documented: CERN benchmarks seven different electronic boxes, including some of the fastest current computers, with architectures as different as DSP-based multiprocessors, systolic arrays, and massively parallel systems.

This problem is typical of high-energy physics data acquisition and filtering: $20 \times 20 \times 32$ b images are input every 10 μs from the particle detectors, and one must discriminate within a few μs whether the image is interesting or not. This is achieved by computing some simple statistics on it (maximum value, second-order moment, $\cdots$) and using them to decide whether or not a sharp peak is present (Fig. 12). What makes the problem difficult here are the high input bandwidth (160 MB/s) and the low latency constraint.

Vuillemin [7] analyzes in detail the possible implementations of the calorimeter, on both general-purpose computer architectures (single and multi processors, SIMD and MIMD) and special-purpose electronics (full-custom, gate-array, FPGA's). The conclusion provides an accurate quantitative analysis of the computing power required for this task: the PAM is the only structure found to meet this bound.

This algorithm was implemented by P. Boucard and J. Vuillemin on P_1 [37] [38]. Using the external I/O capabilities described in Section III-C, data is input from the detectors through two off-the-shelf HIPPI-to-TURBOchannel interface boards plugged directly onto P_1. The datapath itself uses about half of P_1's logic and RAM resources, for a virtual computing power of 39 GBOPS (Fig. 13).

2) Image Analysis: The *transition radiation tracker* (TRT) is another benchmark from CERN, analyzed in the same report [36]. The problem is to find straight lines (particle trajectories) in a noisy digital black and white image.

The algorithm used is based on the classical *Hough transform*: first compute the number of active ("on") pixels on each possible line crossing the image (here the physics of the problem limits the candidate lines to those having a small positive or negative slope), then select the line which has the maximum number of active pixels, or discard the image if no line has a sufficient number of active pixels. As above, the rate of the input data (160 MB/s) and the low latency requirement (≤ 2 images) preclude any implementation solution other than one using specialized hardware, as shown by CERN [36].

R. Männer and his team from University of Mannheim [13] have successfully built the specialized FPGA-based ENABLE machine for solving this problem, using the straightforward $O(N^3)$ implementation of the Hough transform. It computes the score for all lines of 16 different slopes crossing a 128×96 grid at the required 100 kHz rate, with a latency of two images (20 μs). It needs more than twice the computing power of P_1 to achieve this result.

J. Vuillemin [39] describes an $O(N^2 \log N)$ algorithm to compute the Hough transform, in a recursive way analogous to the Fast Fourier Transform (Fig. 14). The resulting gain in the processing power needed by the computation makes it just possible to fit it in one P_1 board.

This was implemented by L. Moll, P. Boucard, and J. Vuillemin [37], [38]. As above, data is directly input from the detectors through two HIPPI-to-TURBOchannel boards plugged in P_1's extension slots. The design computes 31 slopes at the required 100 kHz rate with a latency of 1 image (10 μs). A 64 b sequential processor would need to run at 1.2 GHz to achieve the same computation.

3) Cluster Detection: The NESTOR Neutrino Telescope under construction in the Mediterranean near Pylos, Greece, is an three-dimensional array of 168 photomultiplier tubes (PMT's) designed to detect Cherenkov radiation from fast muons created by neutrino interactions. Clustered detections from actual Cherenkov-generated photons are expected to happen at a maximum rate of a few per second, while the background noise originating from bioluminescence and radioactive potassium (^{40}K) causes random PMT firings at a rate of 100 kHz per PMT.

A P_1 board will be used to process the raw data and detect muon trajectories,[4] by looking for space- and time-correlation

---

[3] European Organization for Nuclear Research, Geneva, Switzerland

[4] In high-energy physics terminology, this is the *first level trigger*.

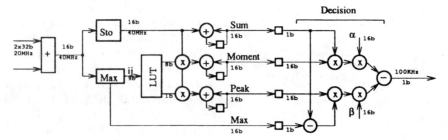

Fig. 13. Calorimeter datapath.

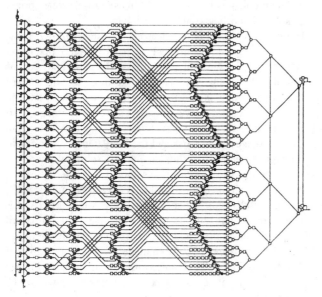

Fig. 14. Fast Hough transform.

among events. The peak and average data rates are 500 MB/s and 100 MB/s, respectively. Data enters directly through P_1's 256 b wide daughter-board connectors (see Section III-C). Provided the peak data rate can be accommodated—which is the case with the P_1 solution—subsequent processing is straightforward (see Katsanevas et al. [40] for details).

H. Image Acquisition

P_1's TURBOchannel adapter (see Section III-C), being built around a single XC3090, is a PAM in its own right—albeit a small one. M. Shand [41] describes a number of experiments based on this board, including an interface to a large frame CCD camera [42]. This camera delivers image data at 10 MB/s with no flow control. Conventionally an interface for such a camera would use a dedicated frame buffer. Our interface dispenses with this buffer by transfering the incoming image data directly into system memory, using direct memory access (DMA) over the TURBOchannel. In addition to the obvious cost savings of eliminating the frame buffer memory, use of system memory makes the captured image immediately available to software and allows the system to capture images continuously. These attributes prove essential to one use of this interface—the principal image acquisition system at the Swedish Vacuum Solar Telescope where the system has been in use since May 1993 [43].

The success of this small PAM (or *PAMette*) has lead us to develop a new PAM board, I/O-oriented and of small size, to explore these new kinds of application. M. Shand, in collaboration with G. Scharmer and Wang Wei of the Swedish Royal Observatory, is investigating the use of this board in an adaptive optics system combining image acquisition, image processing, and on-the-fly servo control.

I. Stereo Vision

Part of the research on stereo vision at INRIA[5] is focused on computing dense, accurate and reliable *range maps*, from simultaneous images obtained by two cameras. The selected stereo matching algorithm is presented by Faugeras et al. [44]: a recursive implementation of the score computation makes the method independent of the size of the correlation window, and the calibration method does not require the use of a calibration pattern.

Stereo matching is integrated in the navigation system of the INRIA cart, and used to correct for inertial and odometric navigation errors. Another application, jointly with CNES,[6] uses stereo to construct digital elevation maps for a future planetary rover.

A *software* implementation of the selected method computes the correlation between a pair of images in 59 s on a SPARC-Station II. A dedicated hardware implementation using four digital signal processors (DSP), developed jointly by INRIA and Matra MSII, performs the same task in 9.6 seconds. A P_1 implementation of the very same algorithm by L. Moll [45] runs over 30 times faster, in 0.28 s: a key step toward real-time stereo matching.

This design uses the full 100 MB/s bandwidth available between P_1 and its host. It also relies on fast reconfiguration, as the processing is a straight pipeline between three distinct PAM configurations, which are successively swapped in time for each image pair processed.

J. Sound Synthesis

In order to explore the digital signal processing domain, D. Roncin and P. Boucard implemented a real-time digital audio synthesizer on P_1, capable of producing up to 256 independant

[5] Institut de Recherche en Informatique et Automatique, Sophia-Antipolis, France.
[6] Centre National d'Etudes Spatiales, France.

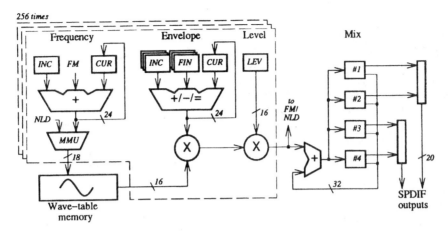

Fig. 15. Sound synthesizer.

voices at a sampling rate of 44.1 kHz. Primarily designed for the use of additive synthesis techniques based on lookup-tables, this implementation includes features which allow frequency-modulation synthesis and/or nonlinear distortion and can also be used as a sampling machine. This design contains 4 MB of wave-table memory, shared by the 256 voice generators, which can be partitioned into subtables of various sizes allowing the simultaneous use of up to 1 k different sound patterns. It also includes an output mixing section and global control.

Each of the 256 voices consists of the following.

- A phase computation section, which computes the index of a voice sample in the selected wave-table (using 24 b arithmetic). Using the output of another voice in this computation leads to frequency modulation and nonlinear distortion.
- An envelope generator and static level section, which computes the amplitude value for the current sample (also using 24 b arithmetic) and combines it with the output of the wave-table to produce the amplitude modulated sample. Dynamic amplitude envelopes are generated using linked linear segment techniques.
- A control section, which defines the operating mode of the voice: normal oscillator, carrier operator for frequency modulation, nonlinear transfer function operator, free-running or single shot, synchronous phase operation, wave-table size and location selection, output channel selection···.

The output mixing section contains four 32 b accumulators, which connect to two SPDIF[7] (stereo) digital audio output ports. Synthesizing this standard consumer audio format allows for the *direct* connection of P_1 to an off-the-shelf tape recorder or audio amplifier, through a mere cable.

All parameters and controls can be updated by the host at any time in parallel with the running synthesis. At 22 MHz, this design produces 11M samples per second, which amounts to about 22 M 16×16 b multiplications, 100 M ALU operations and 45 M load/store operations. A software implementation of this algorithm running on standard CPU's shows that the DECPeRLe-1 implementation is equivalent to a computing power of about 2 GIPS. A simpler version of this design has been ported on a standard DSP processor (27 MHz Motorola 56001). The DSP is capable of computing only 24 voices at the required sampling rate—less than one tenth the number computed by P_1.

K. Long Viterbi Decoder

In many of today's digital communications systems the signal-to-noise ratio (SNR) of the link has become the most severe limitation. Convolutional encoding with maximum likelihood (Viterbi) decoding provides a means to improve the SNR of a link without increasing the power budget, and has become an important technique in satellite and deep-space communications systems.[8]

The coding gain of a Viterbi system is primarily determined by the *constraint length* K of the code, while the complexity of the decoder increases exponentially with K. Today's VLSI implementations typically offer codes with $K = 7$ and $K = 8$. NASA's Galileo space probe is equipped with a constraint length 15 rate 1/4 encoder, for which a Viterbi decoder based on an array of 256 custom VLSI chips is being developed [46].

R. Keaney and D. Skellern from Macquarie University (Sydney, Australia), together with M. Shand and J. Vuillemin from PRL, have implemented a Viterbi decoder for the Galileo code on P_1 [47]. Using on-board RAM to trace through the 2^{14} possible states of the encoder, this design computes 4 states in parallel at each 40 ns clock cycle, for an overall decoding speed of 2 kb/s. The coding gain has been measured to be within 0.5 dB of the optimal gain for this particular code.

There is no analytical method to prove that a particular code provides the optimal coding gain for a given constraint length. Taking further advantage of PAM reconfigurability, this system will be used to perform a *code search* among constraint length 15 convolution codes, by recompiling a new P_1 configuration on-the-fly for each code.

---

[7] Sony/Philips Digital Audio Interface.

[8] The same techniques apply to high-density magnetic storage devices, for equivalent reasons.

VI. THE COMPUTING POWER OF PAM

Let us now *quantify* the computing power of a PAM processor. Following earlier reports [48], [7], we define the *virtual computing power* of a PAM with n PAB's which operate at f Hertz as the product $P = n \times f$. The resulting power P is expressed in *boolean operations per second* (BOPS). For $n = 800$ and $f = 25$ MHz, we find $P = 16$ GBOPS for a leading edge single FPGA in 1992, and 5000 GBOPS = 5 TBOPS in 2001. At 25 MHz, the PAM P_1 has a virtual computing power of 368 GBOPS—roughly equivalent to what we should get in a single FPGA near year 1996.

Our particular choice of unit for measuring computing power is based on the 4-input combinational function.[9] A *bit-serial binary adder*, which is composed of two functions of three inputs, also counts for one unit. The accounting rules that follow, for arithmetic and logic operations over n-bit wide inputs, are thus straightforward:

$\boxed{+}$ One $(n + n \mapsto n + 1)$-bit addition each nanosecond is worth n GBOPS. Subtraction, integer comparison and logical operations are bit-wise equivalent to addition.

$\boxed{-}$ One $(n \times m \mapsto n+m)$-bit multiplication each nanosecond is worth nm GBOPS. Division, integer shifts and transitive (see Vuillemin [49]) bit permutations are bit-wise equivalent to multiplication.

Due to the great variety of the operations required by each application, quantitative performance comparison between different computer architectures is a challenging art [50]. The *million of instructions per second* (MIPS) and *million of floating-point operations per second* (MFLOPS) are more traditional units for measuring computing power. By our definition, a 32 b standard microprocessor[10] operating at 100 MHz (100 MIPS) has a virtual computing power of 3.2 GBOPS, and a 200 MHz, 64 b processor features 12.8 GBOPS. A 100 MHz, 64 b floating-point multiplier delivering one operation per cycle (100 MFLOPS) would rate 281 GBOPS.

It follows from this accounting that P_1 has a virtual computing power which is higher than that of the fastest integer microprocessor existing in 1994.

VII. CONCLUSION

We have shown that it is now possible to build high-performance PAM's, with applications in a large number of domains. Table II updates what is feasible within 1994 technology. The technology curves for PAM cost/performance derive from those for FPGA and static RAM [51]; we can use them as a basis for extrapolation, from now into the future.

Let us compare the respective merits of three possible implementation technologies, for a given specific high-performance system. High-performance means here that the computational requirement far exceeds the possibilities of the fastest micro-processor. That leaves three implementation

TABLE II
VITAL FIGURES OF CURRENTLY FEASIBLE PAMS

	small	medium	large	
I/O bandwidth	200	400	1k	MB/s
Computing power	50	200	1k	GBOPS
FPGA area	1	4	20	kPAB's
RAM size	8	32	160	MB
Unit cost	800	3k	12k	$

possibilities: 1—program a parallel machine; 2—design a specific PAM configuration; 3—build a custom system. The first two involve only software; the third involves hardware as well. Let us review some of the comparative merits, for each technology.

1) Each reported PAM design was implemented and tested within one to three months, starting from the delivery of the specification software. This is roughly equivalent to the time it takes to implement a *highly optimized* software version of the same system on a supercomputer: both are technically challenging, yet both are orders of magnitude faster than what it takes to cast a system into custom ASIC's and printed-circuit boards.

2) For many specific high-speed computational problems, PAM technology has now proved superior, both in performance *and* cost, to all current forms of *general-purpose* processing systems: pipelined machines, massively parallel ones, networks of microprocessors, $\cdots$.
The cost of P_1 is comparable to that of a high-end workstation. This is *much* lower than the cost of a supercomputer. Based on figures from McBryan [30], the price (in dollars per operation per second) for solving the heat and Laplace equations is 100 times higher with supercomputers than with P_1.

3) PAM technology is currently best applied to low-level, massively repetitive tasks such as image or signal processing. Due to their software complexity, many current supercomputer applications still remain outside the possibilities of current PAM technology.

4) For many *real-time* problems, PAM's already have performance *and* cost equal to those of specific, custom systems: the lower the volume, the better for the PAM. By tuning a specific application for a PAM, we have shown that *very high performance* implementations are possible. For at least six of the cases presented in Section V, the performance achieved by our P_1 implementation exceeds, by at least one order of magnitude, those of any other implementation, including custom VLSI-based ones.

5) An important set of applications is accessible only through PAM technology: high-bandwidth interfaces to the external world, with a *fully programmable, real-time* capability. P_1 has 256 b wide connectors, capable of delivering up to 1.2 GB/s of external I/O bandwidth. It is then a "simple matter of hardware programming" to interface directly to any electrically-compatible external device, by programming its communication protocol into the PAM itself. Applications include high-bandwidth networks, audio and video input or output devices, and data acquisition.

---
[9]The particular choice of the unit function only affects our measure by a constant factor, provided we keep bounded fan-in.

[10]With no hardware multiplier.

References

[1] W. S. Carter, K. Duong, R. H. Freeman, H. C. Hsieh, J. Y. Ja, J. E. Mahoney, L. T. Ngo, and S. L. Sze, "A user programmable reconfigurable logic array," in *IEEE 1986 Custom Integr. Circuits Conf.*, 1986, pp. 233–235.

[2] Xilinx, Inc., *The Programmable Gate Array Data Book*, Xilinx, 2100 Logic Drive, San Jose, CA, 1993.

[3] D. D. Hill, B. K. Britton, B. Oswald, N. S. Woo, S. Singh, T. Poon, and B. Krambeck, "A new architecture for high-performance FPGAs," *Field Programmable Gate Arrays: Architecture and Tools for Rapid Prototyping*, in *Lecture Notes in Computer Science, Nr. 705*, H. Gruenbacher and R. W. Hartenstein, Eds. New York: Springer-Verlag, 1993.

[4] Algotronix Ltd., *The Configurable Logic Data Book*. Edinburgh, England: 1990.

[5] Concurrent Logic, Inc., *Cli6000 Series Field-Programmable Gate Arrays*, Concurrent Logic Inc., 1270 Oakmead Parkway, Sunnyvale, CA, 1992.

[6] GEC Plessey Semiconductors, *ERA60100 Electrically Reconfigurable Array Data Sheet*, GEC Plessey Semiconductors Ltd., Swindon, Wiltshire SN2 2QW, UK, 1991.

[7] J. E. Vuillemin, "On computing power," *Programming Languages and System Architectures*, in *Lecture Notes in Computer Science Nr. 782*, J. Gutknecht, Ed. Springer-Verlag, 1994, pp. 69–86.

[8] Digital Equipment Corp., *TURBOchannel Hardware Specification*, DEC document EK-369AA-OD-007B, 1991.

[9] P. Bertin, D. Roncin, and J. Vuillemin, "Introduction to programmable active memories," in *Systolic Array Processors*, J. McCanny, J. McWhirter, and E. Swartzlander, Jr., Eds. Englewood Cliffs, NJ: Prentice-Hall, 1989, pp. 301–309.

[10] T. Kean and I. Buchanan, "The use of FPGA's in a novel computing subsystem," *1st International ACM Workshop on Field-Programmable Gate Arrays*, pp. 60–66, Berkeley, CA, USA, 1992.

[11] B. Heeb and C. Pfister, "Chameleon, A workstation of a different color," *Field Programmable Gate Arrays: Architecture and Tools for Rapid Prototyping, Lecture Notes in Computer Science Nr. 705*, H. Gruenbacher and R. W. Hartenstein, Eds. New York: Springer-Verlag, 1993.

[12] J. Arnold, D. Buell, and E. Davis, "Splash II," in *4th ACM Symp. Parallel Algorithms and Architectures*, San Diego, CA, 1992, pp. 316–322.

[13] F. Klefenz, K. H. Noffz, R. Zoz, and R. Maenner, "ENABLE—A systolic 2nd-level trigger processor for track finding and e/pi discrimination for ATLAS/LHC," in *Proc. IEEE Nucl. Sci. Symp.*, San Francisco, CA, 1993, pp. 62–64.

[14] Quickturn Systems, Inc., *RPM Emulation System Data Sheet*, Quickturn Syst., Inc., Mountain View, CA 94043, USA, 1991.

[15] Compugen, *The Bioccelerator*, product brief, Compugen Ltd., Rosh-Ha'ayin, 40800 Israel, 1993.

[16] P. Bertin, *Mémoires actives programmables: conception, réalisation et programmation*, Thèse de Doctorat, Univ. Paris 7, Paris, France, 1993.

[17] D. D. Gajski, Ed., *Silicon Compilation*. Reading, MA: Addison-Wesley, 1988.

[18] M. Shand, P. Bertin and J. Vuillemin, "Hardware speedups in long integer multiplication," *Computer Architecture News*, vol. 19(1), pp. 106–114, 1991.

[19] R. F. Lyon, "Two's complement pipeline multipliers," *IEEE Trans. Commun.*, vol. COM-24, pp. 418–425, 1976.

[20] B. Serpette, J. Vuillemin, and J. C. Hervé, *BigNum: A Portable Efficient Package for Arbitrary-Precision Arithmetic*, Digital Equipment Corp., Paris Res. Lab., PRL Rep. 2, France, 1989.

[21] D. A. Buell and R. L. Ward, "A multiprecise integer arithmetic package," in *The Journal of Supercomputing*. Boston, MA: Kluwer-Academic, 1989, vol. 3, pp. 89–107.

[22] M. E. Louie and M. D. Ercegovac, "A variable precision multiplier for field-programmable gate arrays," in *2nd Int. ACM/SIGDA Workshop Field-Programmable Gate Arrays*, Berkeley, CA, Feb. 1994.

[23] R. L. Rivest, A. Shamir, and L. Adleman, "A method for obtaining digital signatures and public-key cryptosystems," *Commun. ACM*, vol. 21, no. 2, pp. 120–126, 1978.

[24] E. F. Brickell, "A survey of hardware implementations of RSA," in *Crypto '89*, also in *Lecture Notes in Computer Science Nr. 435*. New York: Springer-Verlag, 1990, pp. 368–370.

[25] M. Shand and J. Vuillemin, "Fast implementation of RSA cryptography," in *11th IEEE Symp. Comput. Arithmetic*, Windsor, Ontario, Canada, pp. 252–259, 1993.

[26] D. P. Lopresti, "P-NAC: a systolic array for comparing nucleic acid sequences," *Computer*, vol. 20(7), pp. 98–99, 1987.

[27] R. P. Feynman, R. B. Leighton, and M. Sands, *The Feynman Lectures on Physics*. Reading, PA: Addison-Wesley, 1963, 3 vols.

[28] R. Dautray and J. L. Lions, *Mathematical Analysis and Numerical Methods for Sciences and Technology*. New York: Springer-Verlag, 1990, 9 vols.

[29] J. E. Vuillemin, "Contribution à la résolution numérique des équations de Laplace et de la chaleur," in *Mathematical Modeling and Numerical Analysis*, AFCET Gauthier-Villars, RAIRO, vol. 27, no. 5, pp. 591–611, 1993.

[30] O. A. McBryan, "Connection Machine application performance," *Scientific Applications of the Connection Machine*, World Scientific, pp. 94–114, 1989.

[31] O. A. McBryan, P. O. Frederickson, J. Linden, A. Schüller, K. Solchenbach, K. Stüben, C-A. Thole, and U. Trottenberg, "Multigrid methods on parallel computers—a survey of recent developments," *Impact of Computing in Science and Engineering*. vol. 3, no. 1, pp. 1–75, 1991.

[32] S. Hadinger and P. Raynaud-Richard, *Résolution numérique des équations de Laplace et de la chaleur*, rapport d'option, Ecole Polytech., 91128 Palaiseau Cedex, France, 1993.

[33] M. Skubiszewski, "A hardware emulator for binary neural networks," in *1990 Int. Neural Network Conf.*, vol. 2, pp. 555–558, Paris, France, 1990.

[34] ——, "An exact hardware implementation of the Boltzmann machine," in *1992 Int. Conf. Application-Specific Array Processors*, Dallas, TX, 1992.

[35] F. Furtek, "A field-programmable gate array for systolic computing," in *1993 Symp. Integr. Syst.*, M.I.T., Cambridge, MA, 1993, pp. 183–200.

[36] J. Badier, R. K. Bock, Ph. Busson, S. Centro, C. Charlot, E. W. Davis, E. Denes, A. Gheorghe, F. Klefenz, W. Krischer, I. Legrand. W. Lourens, P. Malecki, R. Männer, Z. Natkaniec, P. Ni, K. H. Noffz, G. Odor, D. Pascoli, R. Zoz. A. Sobala, A. Taal, N. Tchamov, A. Thielmann, J. Vermeulen, and G. Vesztergombi, "Evaluating parallel architectures for two real-time applications with 100 kHz repetition rate," *IEEE Trans. Nucl. Sci.*, vol. 40, pp. 45–55, 1993.

[37] D. Belosloudtsev, P. Bertin, R. K. Bock, P. Boucard, V. Dörsing, P. Kammel, S. Khabarov, F. Klefenz, W. Krischer, A. Kugel, L. Lundheim, R. Männer, L. Moll, K. H. Noffz, A. Reinsch, M. Shand, J. Vuillemin, and R. Zoz, "Programmable active memories in real-time tasks: Implementing data-driven triggers for LHC experiments," *Journal of Nuclear Instruments and Methods for Physics Research*. New York: Elsevier, 1995.

[38] L. Moll, J. Vuillemin, and P. Boucard, "High-energy physics on DECPeRLe-1 programmable active memory," *ACM Int. Symp. FPGAs*, Monterey, CA, Feb. 1995.

[39] J. E. Vuillemin, "Fast linear Hough transform," in *1994 Int. Conf. Application-Specific Array Processors*, IEEE Computer Society, 1994, pp. 1–9.

[40] S. Katsanevas, M. Shand, and J. Vuillemin, "DECPeRLe-1 implementation of NESTOR's first level trigger," in *3rd NESTOR Int. Workshop*, Pylos, Greece, Oct. 1993.

[41] M. Shand, *Measuring System Performance with Reprogrammable Hardware*, Digital Equipment Corp., Paris Res. Lab., Cedex, France, PRL Rep. 19, Aug. 1992.

[42] Kodak Motion Analysis Systems, *Kodak Megaplus Camera, Model 1.4*, Eastman Kodak Company, Mar. 1992.

[43] G. W. Simon, P. N. Brandt, L. J. Nov., G. B. Scharmer, and R. A. Shine, "Large-scale photospheric motions: First results from an extraordinary eleven-hour granulation observation", *Solar Surface Magnetism*, R. J. Rutten and C. J. Schrijver, editors, NATO ASI Series C433, Kluwer, 1994.

[44] O. Faugeras, T. Viéville, E. Théron, J. Vuillemin, B. Hotz, Z. Zhang, L. Moll, P. Bertin, H. Mathieu, P. Fua, G. Berry, and C. Proy, *Real Time Correlation-Based Stereo: Algorithm, Implementations and Applications*, INRIA, 06902 Sophia-Antipolis, France, Res. Rep. 2013, 1993.

[45] L. Moll, *Implantation d'un algorithme de stéréovision par corrélation sur mémoire active programmable PeRLe-1*, rapport de stage, Ecole des Mines de Paris, Centre de Mathématiques Appliquées, 06904 Sophia-Antipolis, France, 1993.

[46] J. Statman, G. Zimmerman, F. Pollara, and O. Collins, "A long constraint length VLSI Viterbi decoder for the DSN," Jet Propulsion Lab., Pasadena, CA, TDA Progress Rep. 42-95, July-Sept. 1988.

[47] R. A. Keaney, L. H. C. Lee, D. J. Skellern, J. E. Vuillemin, and M. Shand, "Implementation of long constraint length Viterbi decoders using programmable active memories," in *11th Australian Microelectron.*, Surfers Paradise, QLD Australia, 1993.

[48] P. Bertin, D. Roncin, and J. Vuillemin, "Programmable Active Memories: A performance assessment," in *Symp. Integrated Syst.*, Seattle, WA, 1993.

[49] J. E. Vuillemin, "A combinatorial limit to the computing power of VLSI circuits," *IEEE Trans. Comput.*, Apr. 1983.
[50] J. L. Hennessy and D. A. Patterson, *Computer Architecture: A Quantitative Approach.* New York: Morgan Kaufmann, 1990.
[51] C. P. Thacker, *Computing in 2001*, Digital Equipment Corporation, Systems Res. Cen., Palo Alto, CA, 1993.

Jean E. Vuillemin is a graduate from Ecole Polytechnique. He received the Ph.D. degree from Stanford University in 1972, and one from Paris University in 1974.

He taught Computer Science at the University of California, Berkeley in 1975, and Université d'Orsay from 1976 to 1980. He was at INRIA from 1980 to 1987, and at DEC-PRL from 1988 to 1994. He is now professor at Faculté Léonard de Vinci. He has authored over 100 papers on program semantics, algorithm design and analysis, combinatorics and hardware structures. His current research interests concern programmable hardware, theory, implementations and applications.

Patrice Bertin received the Eng. degree from Ecole Polytechnique, Palaiseau, France, in 1984, and the Ph.D. degree in computer science degree from Université Paris 7, Paris, France, in 1993.

From 1988 to 1994, he worked on the PAM project at Digital Equipment Corporation's Paris Research Laboratory, as a visiting scientist from INRIA (Institut National de Recherches en Informatique et en Automatique, Rocquencourt, France). He is currently with the new Léonard-de-Vinci University in La Défense near Paris, France.

Didier Roncin received degrees in electrical engineering, computer science, musicology and computer music from Paris University. He worked at IRCAM, Paris, France, on research for acoustic and computer music from 1977 to 1984.

He joined Jean Vuillemin's team at INRIA from 1984 to 1987 where they started the PAM project in 1987. He went to Digital Equipment Corporation's Paris Research Laboratory from 1977 to 1994, where he worked principally on the PAM project's hardware architectures. He is currently at the Léonard-de-Vinci University in Paris, France, where he is investigating designs of generic PCI-based and low cost PAM's, as well as specific PAM architectures for digital audio and computer music applications.

Mark Shand attended the University of Sydney, where he received the B.S. degree in 1981 and the Ph.D. degree in 1987. His thesis was on VLSI CAD.

He spent 1987 and 1988 with the Australian Government's CSIRO continuing his VLSI CAD work. He was employed at Digital Equipment Corporation's Paris Research Laboratory from 1989 to 1994, where he worked principally on the programmable active memories project. He is currently at Digital Equipment Corporation's Systems Research Center in Palo Alto, CA.

Hervé H. Touati received the Ph.D. degree from University of California, Berkeley in 1990.

From 1991 to 1994 he was a research scientist at Digital Equipment Corporation's Paris Research Laboratory. He cofounded Xorix SARL.

Philippe Boucard received the Eng. degree from Ecole Nationale Supérieure des Télécommunications, Paris, France, in 1981.

From 1991 to 1994, he worked on the PAM project at Digital Equipment Corporation's Paris Research Laboratory. He is currently with Matra MHS, France, in the microcontroller design department.

Logic Emulation with Virtual Wires

Jonathan Babb, Russell Tessier, Matthew Dahl, Silvina Zimi Hanono, David M. Hoki, and Anant Agarwal

Abstract—Logic emulation enables designers to functionally verify complex integrated circuits prior to chip fabrication. However, traditional FPGA-based logic emulators have poor interchip communication bandwidth, commonly limiting gate utilization to less than 20%. Global routing contention mandates the use of expensive crossbar and PC-board technology in a system of otherwise low-cost commodity parts. Even with crossbar technology, current emulators only use a fraction of *potential* communication bandwidth because they dedicate each FPGA pin (physical wire) to a single emulated signal (logical wire). *Virtual wires* overcome pin limitations by intelligently multiplexing each physical wire among multiple logical wires, and pipelining these connections at the maximum clocking frequency of the FPGA. The resulting increase in bandwidth allows effective use of low-dimension direct interconnect. The size of the FPGA array can be decreased as well, resulting in low-cost logic emulation.

This paper covers major contributions of the MIT Virtual Wires project. In the context of a complete emulation system, we analyze phase-based static scheduling and routing algorithms, present virtual wires synthesis methodologies, and overview an operational prototype with 20K-gate boards. Results, including in-circuit emulation of a SPARC microprocessor, indicate that virtual wires eliminate the need for expensive crossbar technology while increasing FPGA utilization beyond 45%. Theoretical analysis predicts that virtual wires emulation scales with FPGA size and average routing distance, while traditional emulation does not.

I. Introduction

FIELD programmable gate array (FPGA)-based logic emulators are capable of emulating complex logic designs at clock speeds four–six orders of magnitude faster than software simulators. This performance is achieved by partitioning a logic design, described by a *netlist*, across an interconnected array of FPGA's. The netlist *partition* on each FPGA, configured directly into logic circuitry, is then executed at near hardware speeds.

Fig. 1 compares logic emulation to other prototyping methods, including simulation and accelerated simulation, as well as to final silicon. The y axis measures relative time for compiling or constructing a hypothetical design, while the x axis measures relative time for executing one set of test vectors on this design. As an example, consider final silicon which takes months to construct and runs a set of vectors in

Manuscript received March 20, 1995; revised April 26, 1996 and June 17, 1997. This work was supported by ARPA Contract N00014-91-J-1698 and NSF Grant MIP-9012773. This paper was recommended by Associate Editor C.-K. Cheng.
J. Babb, R. Tessier, S. Z. Hanono, and A. Agarwal are with the Laboratory for Computer Science, Massachusetts Institute of Technology, Cambridge, MA 02139 USA.
M. Dahl is with IKOS Systems, Inc., Cambridge, MA 02139 USA.
D. M. Hoki is with Charles Stark Draper Laboratory, Inc., Cambridge, MA 02139 USA.
Publisher Item Identifier S 0278-0070(97)07006-1.

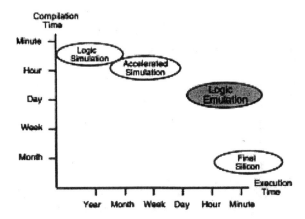

Fig. 1. Verification alternatives.

less than 1 min. The same design and vector set could be compiled for a logic simulator on the order of minutes, but would take years to execute. Logic emulation fills a wide gap between simulation and actual silicon. With both a moderately fast compile time and a fast execution time, emulation offers a compromise between the programmability of software and the fast execution speed of hardware.

Logic emulators are further characterized by interconnection topology, target FPGA, and supporting software. The interconnection topology describes the arrangement of FPGA devices and routing resources. Example interconnects include full crossbars and two-dimensional (2-D) meshes. Important target FPGA properties include gate count, pin count, and mapping efficiency. Supporting software is exptensive, combining netlist translators, logic optimizers, technology mappers, global and FPGA-specific partitioners, placers, and routers.

Traditional emulators are gate inefficient due to inherent pin limitations in the FPGA devices. To reduce pin limitations, these emulators supplement FPGA's with custom crossbar chips and expensive PC-board and backplane technology, further increasing the per-gate cost of emulation. This paper suggests an alternative solution to pin limitations based on multiplexing of FPGA resources.

A. Virtual Wires

In existing emulator architectures, both the logic configuration and the network connectivity remain fixed for the duration of the emulation. Every emulated partition of the input design, one per FPGA, consists of a set of gates and a set of signals communicating to other partitions. Each emulated gate is mapped to one or more FPGA equivalent gates, and each interpartition emulated signal is allocated to a pair of pins

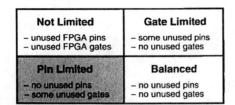

Fig. 2. Partition limitation scenarios.

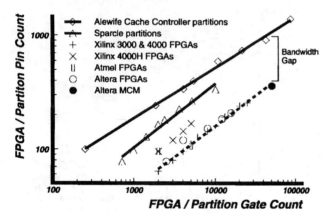

Fig. 3. Pin count as a function of FPGA partition size.

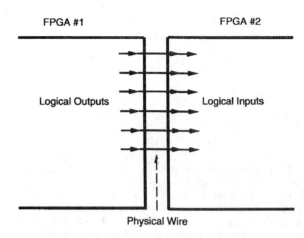

Fig. 4. Hard-wire interconnect.

between two FPGA's. Thus, for a partition to be feasible, the partition gate and pin requirements must be no greater that the available FPGA resources. These constraints yield four possible scenarios (Fig. 2).

When typical circuits are mapped onto available FPGA devices, partitions are predominantly pin limited. That is, all available FPGA gates cannot be utilized due to a lack of pin resources to support them. We demonstrate this resulting *bandwidth gap* with a set of partitionings of the Sparcle and CMMU benchmarks (see Section V-A) for various gate counts. Fig. 3 shows the resulting curves, plotted on a log–log scale. Partition gate count is scaled by a factor of 2 to get FPGA equivalent gates with an assumed mapping efficiency of 50%. On the same curve, we plot the pin and gate capacity of target FPGA's: the Xilinx 3000 and 4000 series [40], the Altera Flex 8000 series [3], and the Atmel 6000 series [5]. For equal average gate counts in the benchmark partitions and FPGA devices, the required average pin counts for partitions are much greater than the available pin capacity of the FPGA's.

Pin limits set a hard upper bound on the maximum usable gate count any FPGA gate count can provide. Low utilization of gate resources increases both the number of FPGA's needed for emulation and the time required to emulate a particular design. This discrepancy will only get worse as technology scales; current trends indicate that available gate counts are increasing faster than available pin counts. Future breakthroughs in area I/O [27] may partially address this problem for FPGA packaging, but will leave open the more difficult issues of interboard and system-level communication. Additionally, any new technology will be challenged to keep up as minimum feature size decreases faster than required bonding area.

Virtual wires eliminate the pin limitation problem of previous emulators by intelligently multiplexing each physical wire among multiple logical wires, and pipelining these connections at the maximum clocking frequency of the FPGA.[1] A virtual wire represents a simple connection between a logical output on one FPGA and a logical input on another FPGA. Established via a pipelined, statically routed communication network, these virtual wires increase available off-chip communication bandwidth by multiplexing the use of FPGA pin resources (physical wires) among multiple emulation signals (logical wires).

Without virtual wires, one-to-one allocation of logical wires to physical wires does not exploit available pin bandwidth because

- emulation clock frequencies are one or two orders of magnitude lower than the potential FPGA frequency;
- all logical wires are not active simultaneously.

However, by clocking physical wires at the maximum frequency of the FPGA technology, several logical connections can share the same physical resource. Fig. 4 shows an example of six logical wires allocated to six physical wires. Fig. 5 shows the same example with the six logical wires sharing a single physical wire. The physical wire is multiplexed between two pipelined *shift loops* (Section III). Each register in the pipeline carries a single bit of information from one logical output to the corresponding logical input in the neighboring FPGA.

Systems based on virtual wires exploit several properties of digital circuits to boost bandwidth from available pins. In a logic design, evaluation flows from system inputs to system outputs. In a synchronous design with no combinational loops, this flow can be represented as a directed acyclic graph. Thus, through analysis of the underlying logic circuit, logical values between circuit partitions only need to be transmitted once. Furthermore, since circuit communication is inherently static, communication patterns will repeat in a predictable fashion. By exploiting this predictability, communications can be scheduled to increase pin utilization.

---

[1] Although this paper focuses on logic emulation, virtual wires can be applied to any multichip system.

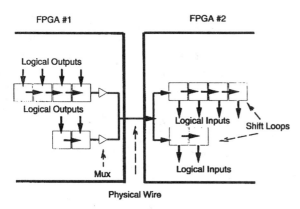

Fig. 5. Virtual wire interconnect.

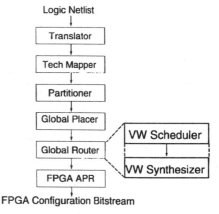

Fig. 6. Emulation software flow.

B. Emulation Software

Software for logic emulation with virtual wires roughly follows the standard emulation tool flow (Fig. 6). The input, a netlist of the logic design to be emulated, is transformed into a multi-FPGA configuration bit stream to be downloaded onto the emulator. Not shown are the technology libraries, target FPGA characteristics, and FPGA interconnect topology needed to make the correct transformations. We next describe the standard steps.

Translator: The input netlist to be emulated is typically generated with a hardware description language or a schematic capture program. The netlist must be syntactically translated into a format readable by the emulation software. Commercial and public domain tools are available for generic source-to-source translation. At MIT, we used both Verilog and LSI logic formats.

Tech Mapper: The translated netlist is still specified in terms of the source technology library—for example LSI Logic's LCA100K technology [26]. Before emulation, the netlist must be mapped to a target library of FPGA primitives. Although commercial and public domain tools are also available for mapping, our simple and fast technique is to create a mapping library which describes each source primitive in terms of primitives in the target library. The inefficiency of this mapping can be largely recovered with a following logic optimization pass.

Partitioner: After mapping the netlist to the target technology, the netlist is divided into partitions, each of which can fit into a single target FPGA. Without virtual wires, each partition must have both fewer gates and fewer pins than the target device. With virtual wires, the total gate count, including the overhead of virtual wires multiplexing logic, must be no greater than the target FPGA gate count. In the MIT implementation, we used the InCA Concept Silicon partitioner [19]. This partitioner performs K-way partitioning with min-cut and clustering techniques.

Global Placer: Individual circuit partitions must be placed into specific FPGA's. An ideal placement minimizes system communication, thus requiring fewer routing resources. We wrote a simple placer based on simulated annealing [21] to minimize total Manhattan wire length.

Global Router: In traditional emulation, inter-FPGA communication is established with a global routing phase. If crossbars are employed, this phase must also determine the routing configuration for each crossbar as well as pin assignments of partition I/O's to FPGA pins. For virtual wires emulation, there are no direct physical connections between partitions, and this phase is completely replaced with new virtualization software to be described in this paper.

FPGA APR: Once routing is complete, there is one netlist for each FPGA. Each netlist must be processed with FPGA-specific automated place-and-route (APR) software to produce configuration bit streams. We used the XACT [40] software for Xilinx FPGA's.

With virtual wires, we replace the global router of traditional software with modules created to specifically support automatic pin multiplexing: the virtual wires scheduler and the virtual wires synthesizer (Fig. 6). Together, we refer to the transformation performed by these two components as *virtualization*. Although each emulation step is an intriguing aspect of CAD research, this paper focuses on these novel virtualization components, described below.

Virtual Wires Scheduler: The resulting set of netlist partitions mapped to each FPGA, in conjunction with the routing resource constraints of the emulation system, is used to determine an appropriate schedule of logical wires onto physical wires. This schedule establishes a feasible time–space route for every logical wire, while guaranteeing that all multi-FPGA combinational paths are correctly ordered. Schedule optimizations include minimizing the total time needed to execute the circuit, as well as minimizing the virtual wires logic overhead. While this scheduling problem is similar to those encountered in high-level synthesis, it is complicated by inter-FPGA routing constraints and the need to account for multiplexing overheads. In Section II, we describe the phase-based scheduling algorithm implemented at MIT

Virtual Wires Synthesizer: This step implements the chosen routing schedule by synthesizing special multiplexers and registers that are added to the circuit partition in each FPGA. This logic is effectively a pipelined, statically routed network in the FPGA technology itself. For maximum efficiency, the synthesizer takes into account the underlying idiosyncrasies of the target FPGA technology. For example, FPGA pin assignment and allocation of internal tristate buses are carefully optimized. The resulting synthesized architectures provide

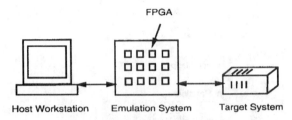

Fig. 7. Virtual wires emulation system.

insight into virtual wires implementation. Section III compares three different architectures for the Xilinx 4000 series.

C. Low-Cost Emulation System

Although virtualization can be used to map input designs to any FPGA-based logic emulator, the process is most valuable when enabling the use of inexpensive, direct interconnect and cheap, low pin count FPGA's. To demonstrate this advantage, we have constructed FPGA boards composed of 16 mesh-connected FPGA's and commodity SRAM's. These boards may themselves be mesh-connected, leading to straightforward software mapping and simplified system scalability. This system (Fig. 7), described in Section IV, has demonstrated the following functionality.

- *In-Circuit Emulation:* FPGA array mimics one or more components of the target system, and is pod-connected to the chip sockets of those missing components.
- *Simulation Acceleration:* FPGA array replaces a piece of a simulation model, and connects to the software simulation environment by remote calls through the host interface.
- *Hardware Subroutines:* FPGA array implements a Verilog version of a subroutine in a C program, and connects to the software by remote calls through the host interface [9].

Section V describes our results for both in-circuit emulation and simulation acceleration of the Sparcle benchmark on our system, including booting a multiprocessor operating system. We leave the exploration of hardware subroutines to future reports.

D. Scalable Technology

Not only can virtual wires be used to compose low-cost systems of gigantic numbers of FPGA's, but this technology also scales as FPGA sizes increase. To demonstrate this scalability, Section VI uses Rent's rule to derive theoretical models of emulation gate overheads for systems with and without virtual wires. This model accounts for the mismatch between circuit communication and FPGA communication in the hard-wired case, and includes a topological factor that explains why a mesh topology does not scale without virtual wires. With this model, we show how the derived virtual wire utilization scales with increasing FPGA device size and average routing distance, while hard-wired utilization may not.

E. Overview

The rest of this paper is organized as follows. Section II describes the virtual wires scheduling and routing algorithms.

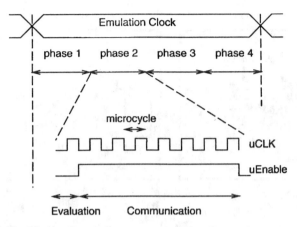

Fig. 8. Clocking framework.

Section III then compares three virtual wires synthesis architectures. After Section IV describes our demonstration hardware system, Section V then present results for both simulation acceleration and in-circuit emulation on this system. Section VI analyzes the overhead and scalability of virtual wires versus hard wires. Finally, Section VII describes related work in the field, and Section VIII makes concluding remarks.

II. SCHEDULING ALGORITHMS

Virtualization replaces the inter-FPGA routing steps of traditional emulation with software that synthesizes a routing network into the netlist partition on each FPGA. This network establishes global routes via statically scheduled bits rather than hard-wired interconnections. The first phase of this approach is a scheduling and routing algorithm. Our phase-based methodology suffices to prove the concept of virtual wires scheduling, and is within a factor of 2 of more optimal algorithms presented in recent literature [32]. Before describing the scheduling algorithms, let us first introduce the basic operating principles of virtual wires.

A. Phase-Based Operating Principles

The *emulation clock* period is the clock period of the logic design being emulated. To facilitate multiplexing, we break this period into a number of *microcycles* determined by a free-running μCLK (Fig. 8). In this scheme, a microcycle is the shortest distinguishable unit of time. All routing is scheduled in discrete microcycle increments. These microcycles are grouped into sequential *phases* to support combinational paths that extend across multiple chips. The advantage of this approach is a decoupling of logic execution speed from interchip communication speed, allowing high-speed communication cycles to coexist with a long-latency emulation clock period.

A μEnable signal divides each phase into an evaluation time span and a communication time span. Within a phase, a given number of microcycles are dedicated to the evaluation of the FPGA logic, followed by a set of cycles to communicate the results to other partitions in destination FPGA's. Evaluation takes place at the beginning of a phase, with logical inputs being propagated through each circuit partition to determine logical outputs for that phase. Not all inputs are available

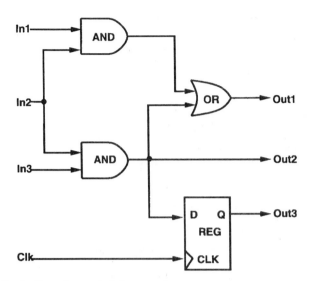

Fig. 9. Dependence calculation example.

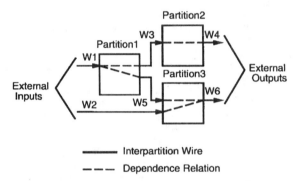

Fig. 10. Depth calculation example.

at the beginning of each phase, and not all outputs are produced. For inputs which are available, all logic is evaluated and subsequent outputs are produced. Each input and output transmission will be assigned to a single phase such that signal precedences are observed. At the end of the phase, the produced outputs are communicated to other circuit partitions at the microcycle clock rate. All necessary phases must be executed by the end of the emulation clock period.

For simplicity, we limited our approach to synchronous logic with a single global emulation clock. Any asynchronous signals cannot be statically routed, and therefore must be hard-wired to dedicated FPGA pins. Virtual wires can be extended to multiple clocks [32] and gated clocks, as well as certain types of asynchronous logic, such as multiple asynchronous clock domains.

B. Definition of Dependence and Depth

Two timing analysis computations, dependence and depth, aid in virtual wires scheduling. Both dependence and depth apply to interpartition wires.

To analyze input to output *dependence*, we scan the logic in each partition to determine the set of outputs to which a combinational path exists from each input. An output is said to be a dependent (or a child) of an input if a change in that input can combinationally change the output. The dependence relationships between inputs and outputs for a given partition are derived recursively from those of its constituent logic elements. In determining dependence, we assume that all outputs of a combinational library primitive are dependents of all of the inputs of that primitive. Similarly, no outputs are dependents of any of the inputs for sequential primitives.

Let Depend$[i]$ denote the set of outputs of a given partition that are dependents of an input of the same partition connected to an interpartition wire i. Similarly, let $D^{-1}[i]$ represent the set of inputs that are ancestors to an output driving an interpartition wire i. By our definition, inputs to storage elements and external outputs will have no dependents: Depend$[i] = \emptyset$, and outputs of storage elements as well as external inputs will have no ancestors: $D^{-1}[i] = \emptyset$.

Fig. 9 shows an example circuit partition containing four interconnected primitive logic elements with three inputs (not including the clock) and three outputs. The dependence relationships for this partition are as follows:

- Depend$[\text{In}_1] = \{\text{Out}_1\}$
- Depend$[\text{In}_2] = \{\text{Out}_1, \text{Out}_2\}$
- Depend$[\text{In}_3] = \{\text{Out}_1, \text{Out}_2\}$.

Likewise, the ancestors are as follows:

- $D^{-1}[\text{Out}_1] = \{\text{In}_1, \text{In}_2, \text{In}_3\}$
- $D^{-1}[\text{Out}_2] = \{\text{In}_2, \text{In}_3\}$
- $D^{-1}[\text{Out}_3] = \emptyset$ (REG is a storage element).

The *depth* calculations use the dependence relationships. The depth of interpartition wire i is the largest number of partitions in a forward combinational path starting at that wire. Depth is computed recursively from the wire dependence sets such that for each wire i:

$$\text{Depth}[i] = \begin{cases} 0 & \text{if Depend}[i] = \emptyset \\ 1 + \max_{j \in \text{Depend}[i]} \text{Depth}[j] & \text{otherwise.} \end{cases} \quad (1)$$

Fig. 10 shows an example design with three partitions and six interpartition wires. The dashed lines denote input–output dependence relationships. In this example, wires are at the following depths:

- depth 0: W_4, W_6
- depth 1: W_2, W_3, W_5
- depth 2: W_1.

Our phase assignment algorithm uses depth to prioritize routing of critical paths. During scheduling, although both W_1 and W_2 have no ancestors, W_1 has a greater depth and will be given priority.

C. Phase Assignment Algorithm

The goal of the phase assignment algorithm is to determine an appropriate schedule of logic wires between design partitions onto physical wires between FPGA's. The resulting schedule must establish a feasible time–space route for every logical wire, while observing FPGA routing resources constraints and guaranteeing that all multi-FPGA combinational paths are correctly ordered.

The core scheduling algorithm consists of a shortest path router inside a greedy phase assignment loop. Within the main loop of the phase assignment algorithm, Fig. 11, as many wires as possible are scheduled and routed. Once no more wires are available to schedule, the algorithm advances to the next phase. All unscheduled wires are thus pushed to the following phase when either their ancestors have not been scheduled, or there is no remaining routing path available in that phase. The phases are processed sequentially, and no attempt is made to go back and optimize previously scheduled phases. Given enough phases and at least one potential path between all pairs of FPGA's, any design can be scheduled. This is easier than hard-wired routing problems, in which various rip-up and retry strategies may be needed to find a feasible route.

The algorithm starts by first calculating the dependence and depth arrays for all wires as described in the previous section. An additional array, Done[i], is set to false to mark each wire i as unscheduled. The algorithm then initializes a DependCount[i] array from the dependence information of each wire. When this counter reaches zero, as the algorithm progresses, wire i will be ready to schedule. The algorithm proceeds by assigning wires to phases until all wires have been scheduled. Advancement to following phases occurs when no wires can be scheduled in the current phase. Within each phase, ready wires with the greatest depth are iterated first, guaranteeing that critical paths are given priority. The routing algorithm is successively called to route as many ready wires as possible.

Once a successful route is established from a source to destination FPGA, as many as ComCycles–distance additional ready wires between the same source and destination are formed into a shift group, where ComCycles is the number of communication cycles in a phase and distance is the number of FPGA crossings in the routing path. For example, if there are eight cycles per phase and the distance is 3, a total of five wires can be routed in the same shift group. The additional wires are also prioritized by depth. For each routed wire j in the shiftgroup, Done[j] is set, and the set of wires $k \in$ Depend[j] is iterated to decrement DependCount[k]. If DependCount[k] = 0, wire k can be scheduled in a following phase. Any ready signals that are not successfully routed in a phase are automatically delayed to following phases. As long as the delayed signals are not on the critical path, the total number of phases will not be affected.

The ComCycles parameter specifies the number of microcyles to spend in communication during each phase. This number must be greater than the routing diameter of the topology to guarantee that all signals can route. For the results in Section V, it turns out that eight communication cycles match the eight-way tristate busing of the Xilinx architecture.

D. Route Algorithm

The goal of the routing algorithm (Fig. 12) is to find a shortest available path, in terms of FPGA's, between the source and destination FPGA of a set of interpartition wires. The algorithm keeps track of the reserved and available physical connections between FPGA's in the emulator topology,

```
Given:
    I : set of inter-partition design wires
    ComCycles : communication cycles per phase
    c : total micro-cycles per phase

Produce:
    S : output schedule which assigns each wire i ∈ I
        to a shiftgroup in a particular phase

Procedure PhaseAssign
    call Depend ← CalcDependents(I)
    call Depth ← CalcDepth(Depend)
    initialize WaitCount array to zero
    initialize Done array to false

    for each wire i ∈ I
        for each dependent wire j ∈ Depend[i]
            DependCount[j] ← DependCount[j] + 1
        endfor
    endfor

    n ← 0 /*phase counter*/
    loop forever
        call RouteInit
        W ← wires with Done[i]=false and DependCount[i]=0
        if W is empty exit loop
        n ← n + 1
        sort W by Depth[i], greatest depth first
        for each wire i ∈ W
            src ← FPGA partition where source of i is placed
            dest ← FPGA partition where dest of i is placed
            path ← Route(src,dest)
            if path exists then
                distance = length(path) - 1
                maxSignals ← ComCycles - distance
                L ← i and up to maxSignals additional wires in
                    depth order from W with same src and dest as i
                for each j ∈ L
                    delete j from W
                    Done[j] ← true
                    for each k ∈ Depend[j]
                        DependCount[k] ← DependCount[k] - 1
                    endfor
                endfor
                shiftgroup ← { n, path, L }
                add shiftgroup to schedule S
            endif
        endfor
    endloop

    save n, c in schedule S /*final phase and cycle count*/
end Procedure
```

Fig. 11. Phase assignment algorithm.

and is repeatedly called from the inner loop of the phase assignment algorithm. Route uses shortest path analysis with a cost function based on channel availability. Shortest path routing minimizes both the number of microcycles needed per phase and intermediate hop logic overhead.

Before the beginning of each phase, a reservation matrix, Reserve[i, j], is initialized to the number of physical connections between FPGA's i and j in the emulator topology. Route applies Dijkstra's shortest path algorithm [34] to channel availability, Avail[i, j] = (Reserve[i, j] $\neq$ 0), to determine the

```
Given:
    T : emulator topology
    src : source FPGA in T
    dest : destination FPGA in T

Produce:
    path : list of FPGAs along shortest route from src to dest

Procedure RouteInit
    for each FPGA src ∈ T
        for each FPGA dest ∈ T
            Reserve[src,dest] ← connections in T from src to dest
            Avail[src,dest] ← (Reserve[src,dest] ≠ 0)
        endfor
    endfor
end Procedure

Procedure Route(src, dest)
    path ← ShortestPath(src,dest,Avail) /* Dijkstra's algorithm */
    if path exists then
        for each FPGA f ∈ path
            if f = src then /* first FPGA in path */
                src1 ← f
            else /* following FPGAs in path */
                dest1 ← f
                Reserve[src1,dest1] ← Reserve[src1,dest1]-1
                Avail[src1,dest1] ← (Reserve[src1,dest1] ≠ 0)
                src1 ← f
            endif
        endfor
        return path
    else
        return null path
    endif
end Procedure
```

Fig. 12. Routing algorithm.

```
Shiftgroup {
    phase number
    source FPGA, 2nd FPGA, 3rd FPGA, ..., dest. FPGA
    logical wire 1, logical wire 2, ..., logical wire N
}
```

Fig. 13. Shift group data structure.

shortest path between the source and destination FPGA's. If the shortest path exists, then the reservation matrix is updated by subtracting one from each element along that path and route returns with this path; else, route returns unsuccessfully.

After each successful route, PhaseAssign forms a new shiftgroup data structure (Fig. 13). This data structure includes the phase number, FPGA path, and set of logical wires in that group. This information is written to the schedule file, to be passed to the synthesis phase of virtualization.

E. Execution Speed Analysis

Before proceeding, let us compute the execution speed of virtual wires emulation. Based on our phased operating principles, the emulation clock cycle time will be determined by the total number of microcycles needed:

$$v = n \times c \qquad (2)$$

where n is the number of phases and c is the number of cycles per phase as previously defined. If c is the same across all phases, then we can immediately recognize that

$$n \geq L$$
$$c \geq D \qquad (3)$$

where D is the maximum distance of any shift group route (in the worst case, D is the network diameter of the FPGA topology), and L is the length of the critical path in the design netlist, equivalent to the maximum depth. That is, there must be enough cycles in each phase to route a signal across the diameter of the network, as well as enough total phases to schedule the longest combinational path between circuit partitions.

Additionally, we recognize that the total number of microcycles is also constrained by the maximum multiplexing performed at each FPGA:

$$v \geq \frac{P_C}{P_f} \qquad (4)$$

where P_C is the maximum circuit communication requirement, including partition pins and any additional pins required for through hops, and P_f is the pin count of each FPGA.[2] Combining these two observations and assuming that the number of microcycles per phase is constant across all phases, we get the following best-case speed result.

Best Case Microcycles: The cumulative microcycle count for all phases within a scheduled emulation clock period is bounded below by the following equation:

$$v \geq \max \left(\overbrace{L \times D}^{\text{latency bound}} , \overbrace{\frac{P_C}{P_f}}^{\text{bandwidth bound}} \right) \qquad (5)$$

where L is the critical path length, D is network diameter, P_C is the maximum circuit partition pin count including through hops, and P_f is the FPGA pin count.

In our practical experience, design emulation speed is determined predominantly by the latency bound.

F. Improvements

We proposed the preceding algorithms to demonstrate the feasibility of virtual wires and for ease of implementation of the synthesis structures described in the following section. These algorithms can be improved by scheduling at the granularity of a single microcycle and eliminating the phase barriers altogether. The advantages of such improvements [32] include the following.

- Possible initiation of computation and subsequent routing as early as one microcycle after a signal arrives at a destination rather than waiting for the following phase.

[2] Note that we have ignored pipeline startup overhead associated with each shift group.

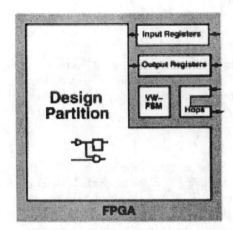

Fig. 14. Virtualized FPGA composition.

Fig. 15. 15 VW–FSM control logic.

- Potential overlapping of computation with communication in different parts of the system rather than execution in exclusive time spans.
- Support of different propagation delays for individual wires rather than observing a worst case delay for all computation in a phase.
- Flexible scheduling of wires at the microcycle granularity rather than scheduling of dedicating pipeline paths per phase. This scheduling also eliminates costly pipeline filling overhead at the beginning and end of each phase.

We continue by describing the synthesis architectures designed at MIT. These architectures implement the virtualized routing network produced by the phase assignment and routing procedures.

III. SYNTHESIS ARCHITECTURES

Although it would be possible to design an FPGA with multiplexed pins, we implemented virtual wires without custom hardware support. That is, the virtualization process synthesizes the required multiplexing components directly into the FPGA netlists, to be downloaded with the original design partitions. Thus, any existing FPGA-based logic emulation system can take advantage of virtual wires. After discussing the synthesis algorithms, this section proceeds to describe three of many possible synthesis architectures based on shift registers in Xilinx FPGA's.

A. Synthesis Algorithm

The virtual wires synthesizer flowchart component in Fig. 6 takes the following input:
- emulator topology
- external design I/O pin assignment

Given:
    T : emulator topology
    E : external I/O pin assignment
    S : routing schedule
    D : set of design partition netlists

Produce:
    X : set of virtualized FPGA netlists

Procedure Synthesize
    N ← number of phases in S
    C ← cycles per phase in S
    for each FPGA f ∈ T
        given (N,C) synthesize control logic vwFsm[f]
        virtualLogic[f] ← vwFsm[f]
    endfor

    for each phase P ∈ S
        for each shiftgroup G ∈ P
            R ← inter-FPGA routing path for G
            L ← number of logical wires ∈ shiftgroup G
            for each FPGA f ∈ R:
                if f is first FPGA in R **then**
                    logic ← synthesize output shifter of length L
                    assign each logical output in G to logic
                    assign physical FPGA output pin to logic
                else if f is an intermediate FPGA in R **then**
                    logic ← synthesize intermediate hop
                    assign physical FPGA I/O pins to logic
                else /* if f is last FPGA in R */
                    logic ← synthesize input shifter of length L
                    assign each logical input in G to logic
                    assign physical FPGA input pin to logic
                endif
                assign control nets for vwFsm[f] to logic
                virtualLogic[f] ← virtualLogic[f] + logic
        endfor
    endfor
for each external I/O e ∈ E
    assign e to its specified FPGA physical pin
endfor

for each FPGA f ∈ T
    partition[f] ← design partition in D placed on f
    X[f] ← virtualLogic[f] + partition[f]
endfor
end Procedure

Fig. 16. Synthesis algorithm.

- routing schedule
- design partition netlists

and produces
- one virtualized netlist for each FPGA.

As shown in Fig. 14, these new netlists contain the original design partition along with all necessary virtual wires communication logic. Synthesized logic includes input and output shift registers, through hops, and the VW–FSM finite-state machine control logic.

After reading in the appropriate inputs from previous compilation stages, the synthesizer algorithm (Fig. 16) proceeds to synthesize the VW–FSM control logic for each FPGA. For the most part, this logic is identical for each FPGA,

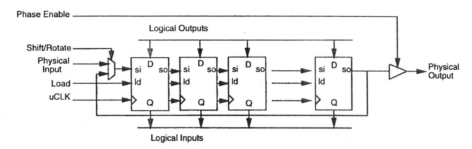

Fig. 17. Full shift register architecture.

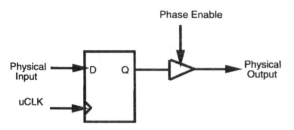

Fig. 18. Intermediate hop architecture.

determined solely by the number of phases and microcycles per phases in the schedule. The VW–FSM (Fig. 15) logic takes as input the μCLK and the μEnable signals, distributed to each FPGA, and generates the appropriate control signals during each microcycle. As described in Section II, the μCLK is the free-running pipeline clock, while the μEnable clock is synchronized to the emulation clock, and determines when to start the communication sequence for each emulation phase. The output control signals are responsible for strobing logical wires into the appropriate registers and controlling multiplexer selection.

The algorithm iterates through the shift groups in each phase to construct the input, intermediate hop, and output architectures. Each shift-group data structure contains the logical wires assigned to that group as well as the group's phase and FPGA path. As the architectures are synthesized, they are connected between the partition logical wires and FPGA physical wires, as well as to the appropriate control signals. Not shown in the algorithm, the synthesizer also makes low-level implementation decisions at this time to optimize the use of limited FPGA resources, including tristate buses and combinational logic blocks. In addition, we have added a simple pin permutation algorithm which minimizes the use of on-chip routing resources for hops.

The synthesizer lastly assigns any external connections to corresponding periphery FPGA pins. Some of these pins connect to external interface hardware for communication with a logic simulator or other control programs. Additional pins provide global clocks and sequencing signals. The remaining pins may be connected to external pods to support in-circuit emulation.

The accumulated logic synthesized for each FPGA is then merged with the original design partition for that FPGA, and a final virtualized netlist file is output in FPGA format (XNF for Xilinx). These files are input to the FPGA-specific place-and-route stage which creates the emulator bit stream.

B. Shift Register Architectures

We now compare three shift register architectures synthesizable to Xilinx 4000 FPGA's.

Full Shift Register: The full shift register architecture was originally proposed as a proof-of-concept virtual wires implementation [7]. This architecture consists of identical input and output *shift loops* (Fig. 17). In output mode, shift loops load emulated signal states at the beginning of each phase, and shift these states out serially onto a routed physical connection at the microcycle rate. For connections requiring multiple hops, a one-bit shift register is placed in each intermediate FPGA (Fig. 18), forming a shift register pipeline between source and destination. At the end of the pipeline, corresponding input mode shift loops demultiplex and latch the emulated signals, and drive them into the emulated logic. Note that the input shift loops must store their state so that all emulated logic inputs are available for subsequent evaluation. Output logic, however, can be reused for multiple groups of emulation signals in different phases. To support per-phase routing, each inter-FPGA I/O pad is preceded by a multiplexer that selects the appropriate shift loop output during its active phase. Pads are bidirectional with the pad driver enable signal asserted during phases in which that pad is an output. To minimize associated pad logic, the synthesizer groups inputs and outputs separately when possible.

Gated Shift Register: To reduce the virtual wires consumption of core FPGA resources, the synthesizer can utilize architecture-specific FPGA features. In low-cost, low-pin-count FPGA parts, many of the I/O pads are not connected to pins, and the synthesizer can concatenate their registers to form virtual wires shift registers (Fig. 19). Due to pad configuration constraints, these shift registers cannot be parallel-loaded, so they are not usable for output shift groups. However, the synthesizer can place input shift groups and intermediate hop shift registers here. Since input shift groups must hold the emulated signal state after receiving it, and these I/O registers do not have clock enables, the synthesizer generates and distributes a gated μCLK. During the portions of the virtual wires cycle in which the emulated logic is being evaluated, this clock is frozen. In addition, the length of the input shift groups is adjusted to divide evenly into the number of μCLK's between evaluation periods so that the state in these registers can recirculate without change. In the 84-pin PLCC Xilinx 4005, this approach recovered 102 input and hop shift register bits. However, clock gating and the slower timing of the I/O pad registers reduced the achievable μCLK rate.

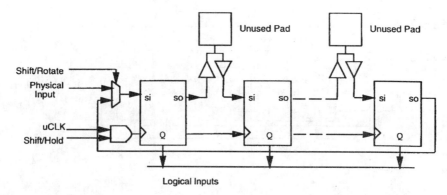

Fig. 19. Gated shift registers using pad registers.

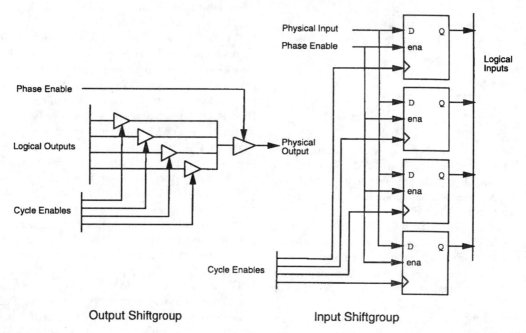

Fig. 20. Addressable shift loop architecture.

Addressable Shift Register: A further variation is to replace the output shift-group shift registers with tristate multiplexers available in the Xilinx architecture (Fig. 20). The synthesizer creates an additional set of global control signals, labeled cycle enables, to enable each bit of the multiplexer during the appropriate microclock tick of each virtual wires phase. The synthesizer also replaces the input shift registers with sets of individual register bits whose clock enables are controlled by the phase signal as before, but whose clocks are successive cycle enables. This architecture considerably reduces the cost of the virtual wires shift loops in terms of logic resources, but the additional control signals and the use of the tristate multiplexers add routing overhead. This overhead is reduced somewhat by placing many of the additional signals on global clock nets. Also, strategic use of the I/O pad registers for pipelining recovers speed. Finally, this architecture can support the more flexible virtual wires scheduling methods described in [32].

Comparisons: Table I compares each architecture in implementing the smallest benchmark circuit, Palindrome (see Section V-A), on the 16-FPGA demonstration hardware presented in Section V. Speed is measured in terms of the μCLK speed. We calculated overhead as a percentage of consumed resources taken up by virtual wires. This virtual wire resource consumption is computed by subtracting the emulation logic

TABLE I
ARCHITECTURAL COMPARISON

Resource	Design Logic	Total Logic (Virtual Overhead)		
		Fig	Fig	Fig
Packed CLBs (Total)	54	79 (32%)	80 (33%)	65 (17%)
Lookup Tables (Combinational)	115	165 (30%)	167 (31%)	131 (12%)
Registers (Sequential)	74	141 (48%)	102 (27%)	115 (36%)
Xilinx PIPs (Routing)	1009	1729 (42%)	1948 (48%)	1612 (37%)
		Average Resource Usage per FPGA		
μCLK Speed		33MHz	24MHz	25MHz
Emulation Speed		1.2MHz	.89MHz	.93MHz
		Maximum Clock Speed		

Fig. 21. Virtual wires emulation board.

resource consumption from total resource consumption. We measured emulation logic resource consumption by compiling unvirtualized partitions onto high-pin-count FPGA's. CLB refers to the basic Xilinx combinational logic block, which includes both combinational lookup tables and sequential registers. We list the programmable interconnect points (PIP's) as reported by the Xilinx router. Note that the reported numbers are for hardware emulation, and do not include any additional speed and resource overheads that may be attributed to simulation acceleration.

The full shift register implementation is relatively fast, but has significant overhead. The gated shift register architecture using the I/O pad registers is somewhat slower due to the reduced speed of these registers. This version does use fewer of the core registers, but routing overhead is higher because of the greater wiring distances covered between the pad registers and the core logic. Finally, the addressable scheme generally has lower logic and routing overhead while maintaining moderate speed. The results in the remainder of this paper are based on the basic full shift register scheme, although we believe the addressable scheme to be the best of the three schemes because it can support more sophisticated scheduling algorithms as described in [32].

IV. DEMONSTRATION HARDWARE SYSTEM

Our demonstration hardware building block is a scalable emulation board [36] which is inexpensive to manufacture and easy to build (Fig. 21). One or more boards are interfaced to a host workstation. Each board contains 16 Xilinx XC4005 FPGA's [40] interconnected in a 2-D nearest neighbor mesh. The board is six layers, uses only through-hole devices, and is 10 in^2 in size. System size is scaled by attaching additional boards on any of the four sides of the current system boards, without the need for crossbars or esoteric backplane technology. On-board SRAM supports the emulation of large design memories. At the present time, we use a SparcStation 10 as the host interface, although the emulation board may be reconfigured to interface to virtually any host computer. Any emulation board can communicate with this host workstation through either a serial or S-bus communication port. These interfaces are used to both observe in-circuit emulation status and to provide circuit inputs and outputs for simulation acceleration.

The following sections further detail the important features of the demonstration system.

A. FPGA Array

To emphasize the utility of virtual wires for interchip communication, we used no expensive crossbar chips and only low-pin-count FPGA's (84-pin PLCC's). These FPGA's may be clocked at speeds approaching 40 MHz, thus resulting in small interchip delays and high emulation throughput. Fig. 22 shows the board schematic. Each FPGA communicates with its four nearest neighbors (logically north, south, east, and west) through eight bidirectional I/O signals. To minimize multi-FPGA routing resources, these I/O signals are distributed along the chip package in an alternating pattern (Fig. 23). Thus, I/O port signals are physically allocated so that adjacent I/O pins are assigned to signals from differing ports. With this permutation a signal passing through the chip need only be routed the length of several pins rather than across the body of the entire chip. Two pin groups are located along each side of the package. This connection scheme is analyzed in detail in [18].

B. Scaling to Multiple-Board Systems

Each virtual wires prototype board can function as either a stand-alone system or as part of a larger group of boards.

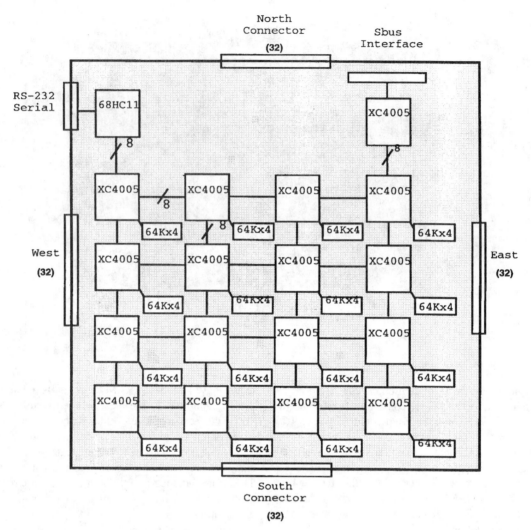

Fig. 22. Emulation board schematic.

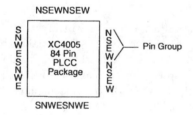

Fig. 23. FPGA pin permutation.

Multiple-board systems are constructed by connecting individual boards together to form a 2-D mesh (Fig. 24). A clock driver chip and remote leads for clock cables allow one board to serve as a single global source for the other boards. μCLK signals are fanned out to local logic at the destination boards using a clock distribution chip. Bidirectional FPGA I/O signals along the periphery of each board extend across connectors in each of the four directions. FPGA configuration information is transferred in a serial chain to all FPGA's in the system starting at the board connected to the download cable in the upper rightmost corner of the mesh. System size is currently constrained to a total of ten boards (160 chips) by the Xilinx-

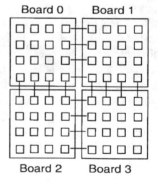

Fig. 24. Multiboard emulation system.

imposed limit on the configuration bit stream, although this limit may be overcome with multiple download cables.

C. Memory and Host Interfaces

Each FPGA in the mesh has 22 dedicated I/O lines which interface to a 64K × 4 SRAM chip. These chips can be used to emulate sections of on-chip memory, and are populated as needed. Virtual wires software is used to multiplex address, data, and control signals for the SRAM so that a number of individual memory accesses to the same SRAM chip may take place during each emulation clock cycle. The SRAM's used in the current prototype are 20 ns. SRAM interface signals have been allocated to dedicated FPGA pins to reduce capacitive loading on inter-FPGA signal lines and to simplify system software.

A low-bandwidth serial interface via an embedded microcontroller provides access to the array for data transfer, configuration, and FPGA state readback. Data signals from the controller interface directly to the north port of the FPGA in the upper left corner of the array. The embedded controller has the capability to download configuration information to the array, thus eliminating the need for an additional download cable from Xilinx.

To provide a higher bandwidth interface to the host, a seventeenth Xilinx XC4005 chip serves as an intermediary between an Sbus interface card located in the host SparcStation and the Xilinx array. This chip is capable of transferring words of data between the Sbus card [16] and the 8 bit north port of the Xilinx chip in the upper right position of the array.

D. Application

The prototype system allows the logical behavior of one circuit component to be *emulated* while the rest of the system is *simulated*. It contains a simulation interface to both the LSI Logic LSIM and Cadence Verilog simulators. At a given simulated clock edge, software drivers transfer data representing inputs to the host workstation which subsequently forwards these data to the emulation system via the serial or S-bus host interface. Once output results are generated, the drivers return them for display or further simulation.

As an alternative to simulation acceleration, a target system may be interfaced directly to the emulator with a prototyping pod. This pod plugs into the chip socket in the target system. After FPGA configuration, the emulation system exchanges data with the target system at each emulation clock while performing internal evaluation at FPGA device speeds.

In both modes of operation, simulation and emulation, the usability of the system is enhanced by our InnerView Hardware Debugger [17]. This tool consists of host software, embedded controller software, and FPGA circuitry which extracts the emulation state from all FPGA's and coordinates this state with the internal register names of the design under emulation. This tool takes advantage of the serial interface's capability to perform readback from FPGA's on a chip-by-chip basis. The controller can be programmed to trigger a readback bit stream from any FPGA in the system, and subsequently transfer the values back to the host workstation for evaluation.

V. RESULTS

We have successfully compiled designs up to 18K gates onto the demonstration system. In conjunction with the scheduling and synthesis algorithms described in this paper, we used the Synopsys Design Compiler [33] for translation and mapping, the InCA Concept Silicon partitioner [19] for partitioning, our simulated-annealing-based placer, and the standard Xilinx-

TABLE II
STATISTICS FOR BENCHMARK DESIGNS

Statistic	Palindrome	Sparcle	CMMU
LSI Gate Count	14,241	17,252	85,721
Element Count	4,623	4,802	37,871
Element Complexity	3.1	3.6	2.3
Memory Bit Count	0	4,352	na
Net Count	4,626	5,094	na

provided tools for FPGA-specific place and route. Compile time is roughly 3–4 h on a SparcStation 10, with 90% of this time consumed by the vendor-specific FPGA compile. This compilation can thus be accelerated by processing independent FPGA compiles in parallel. The following sections describe our benchmarks and report simulation and emulation results.

A. Emulation Benchmarks

Let us introduce relevant features of three benchmark designs for this paper (Table II). The first design, Palindrome, is a simple 15K gate systolic array used for debugging the system and calibrating the various virtual wires architectures. The remaining two designs are actual chips from the MIT Alewife Multiprocessor. Sparcle [2] is an 18K gate SPARC processor with some modifications to enhance its usefulness in a multiprocessor. The cache controller and memory management unit (CMMU) [22] is a complex 86K gate controller. For each design, our statistics include the LSI Logic LCA100K [26] gate count, the number of logic elements, the element complexity (gate count/element count), the number of on-chip memory bits, and the total number of nets connecting elements. Note that for CMMU measurements, the memory elements are not included.

B. Simulation Acceleration

We have collected results from the successful simulation acceleration of Sparcle and Palindrome (Table III). For simulation acceleration, speed refers to the evaluation rate of the emulation hardware rather than the actual simulation rate. The latter rate is currently limited by the speed of the simulator interface (2.1 kHz) or the bandwidth across the host interface (41 kHz for S-bus or 30 Hz for serial port). Fig. 25 shows the allocation of resources inside each FPGA for Sparcle. While there is a fixed overhead of roughly 12% of the CLB's for virtual wires, usable CLB's exceed 45%. Note that due to internal FPGA routing, total utilization approaching 100% is not achievable.

C. In-Circuit Emulation

We used the emulation system in place of a Sparcle chip in a testbed board developed for the Alewife multiprocessor project. The emulator plugs directly into the Sparcle chip PGA socket using a commercially built interface pod attached to the emulator board edge connectors. The emulator synchronizes automatically to the Sparcle system clock and control signals. Therefore, no modifications to the target system are needed other than slowing the system clock. The last column in Table III shows in-circuit emulation results for Sparcle.

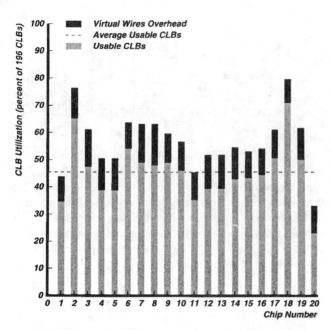

Fig. 25. FPGA resource allocation for sparcle.

TABLE III
SIMULATION, ACCELERATION, AND EMULATION RESULT

Results	Palindrome Simulation	Sparcle Simulation	Sparcle Emulation
FPGAs	16	20	24
Avg. partition Gates	890	868	714
Avg. partition I/O	45	126	119
Max. partition I/O	45	437	206
Emulation Speed (MHz)	1.00	0.12	0.18

Four additional FPGA chips are needed to support the pod interface for simulation acceleration. The emulated Sparcle has executed system test programs successfully, including booting the Alewife operating system at 180 kHz.

D. Comparison with Traditional Emulation

Table IV contrasts the required FPGA pin counts for Sparcle emulation on a hard-wired crossbar and mesh configurations with the actual virtual wires board pin counts. Note that the virtual wires pin count is not a fixed constraint like the hard-wired pin counts. By increasing the total number of microcyles, we can lower the virtual wires pin count to as low as two pins per FPGA. Hard-wired mesh pins were estimated by multiplying the required crossbar pins by the average route length. This estimate is actually an underestimate because some wires connect to multiple FPGA's. Shown beside the hard-wired I/O's is also the *pin multiplication factor* for each case. The PMF is simply the increase in pins needed if virtual wires are not employed. The table also compares emulation speed with estimated speeds for the hard-wired case. Virtual wires speed is computed by multiplying the number of phase and cycles-per-phase by the μCLK rate. Because our system does not have crossbars or FPGA's of the required pin count, we estimate potential hard-wired speeds. The estimate is based on the critical path length L and average route distance d in our circuit partitions. It also assumes 20 ns delays for FPGA-to-FPGA hops and FPGA-to-crossbar-to-FPGA delay, and 50 ns delay for internal FPGA logic partition paths. Thus, crossbar speed is $L \times 20\,\text{ns} + L \times 50\,\text{ns}$, while mesh speed is $L \times d \times 20\,\text{ns} + L \times 50\,\text{ns}$. Note that to achieve these speeds, FPGA's with the required pin counts must be used to maintain the same critical path and route lengths.

TABLE IV
COMPARISON WITH TRADITIONAL EMULATION

Results	Sparcle Simulation	Sparcle Emulation
FPGAs	20	24
Critical Path Length, L	10 partitions	11 partitions
Average Route Length, d	2.44 FPGAs	2.34 FPGAs
Maximum Route Length, D	7 FPGAs	6 FPGAs
Avg. VW-mesh I/O	25	29
Avg. HW-cross I/O (PMF)	126 (5.0)	119 (4.1)
Est. HW-mesh I/O (PMF)	294 (11.8)	293 (10.1)
VW-mesh μCLK Speed	12.0 MHz	18.0 MHz
VW-mesh phases $\times$ cycles	10 $\times$ 10	11 $\times$ 9
VW-cross phases $\times$ cycles	10 $\times$ 2	11 $\times$ 2
VW-mesh Emulation Speed	0.12 MHz	0.18 MHz
Est. VW-cross Emulation Speed	0.60 MHz	0.82 MHz
Est. HW-mesh Speed (ideal)	0.94 MHz	1.01 MHz
Est. HW-cross Speed (ideal)	1.30 MHz	1.43 MHz

It is beyond our partitioning capability to map Sparcle onto 32-pin mesh-connected FPGA's without virtual wires. However, in our earlier work [7], we did partition a version of Sparcle without memory or external I/O's onto 100-pin, 5000-gate FPGA's. We needed at least 31 FPGA's if they were fully connected, and greater than 100 FPGA's if they were connected in a torus. The FPGA explosion is correspondingly worse for the high-communication A-1000 benchmark.

As a final comparison, note that reported results for application of the TIERS virtual wires routing algorithm [32] to Sparcle claim microcycle counts as low as 40 for a mesh, and 16 for other direct-connected topologies. These results support potential Sparcle emulation in excess of 1 MHz.

VI. ANALYSIS

In this section, we derive theoretical gate utilization for logic emulation with and without virtual wires, and show that emulation with virtual wires scales with increasing FPGA device size.

A. Rent's Rule

We begin by reviewing an empirical observation made in 1960 by E. F. Rent of IBM. Rent prepared two internal memoranda containing the log plots of pins versus gates for portions of the IBM series 1400 computers [23]. The basic result is the following equation:

$$\text{Rent's rule:} \quad P = KG^B \qquad (6)$$

where P is the number of pins, G is the number of gates, K is Rent's constant, and B is Rent's exponent. As with most rules, it has limitations. Rent's rule can be used to measure the communication parameters of a given implementation technology as well as the parameters of a circuit. For a circuit, both its architecture and organization greatly affect the parameters. For example, pipelining a processor increases communication requirements due to dependencies between

TABLE V
RENT'S RULE PARAMETERS

Parameter	IBM	FPGAs	4000H	Sparcle	CMMU
K	2.5	0.84	0.93	1.3	8.4
B	0.6	0.57	0.60	0.62	0.45

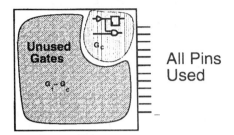

Fig. 26. Gate utilization without virtual wires.

pipeline stages. Table V shows the original reported IBM constants, as well as those we have measured for the FPGA technology and the Sparcle and CMMU benchmarks. Note that the 4000H FPGA's fall on a different curve due to their higher pin-to-gate ratio. For the other FPGA's, a B of 0.5 roughly corresponds to the area versus perimeter for the FPGA die. The lower B, the more locality there is within the circuit. Thus, the CMMU has more locality than Sparcle, although it has more total communication requirement K.

B. Hard-Wire Gate Utilization

For circuits that obey Rent's rule, we can determine the gate utilization for hard-wires, under pin-limited conditions (Fig. 26). Given pin limitations, the number of FPGA pins P_f dictates the number of circuit partition pins P_c available for the circuit:[3]

$$P_c = \frac{1}{d} P_f \quad (7)$$

where d is the average distance, in terms of FPGA boundary crossings, for each wire. This factor accounts for pins consumed by intermediate hop routing.[4] We next substitute Rent's equation for both sides of (7):

$$K_c G_c^{B_c} = \frac{1}{d} K_f G_f^{B_f}. \quad (8)$$

Solving for G_c yields the predicted number of mapped gates available to each circuit partition:

$$G_c = \left(\frac{1}{d} \frac{K_f}{K_c} G_f^{B_f} \right)^{1/B_c}. \quad (9)$$

In this analysis, *mapped gates* refers to the gate count in the circuit's native technology, not the much higher count, FPGA-equivalent gates, claimed by FPGA vendors.

We next define new parameters d_h, K_h, and B_h (Table VI) to simplify our work. Substitution of these newly defined parameters into (9) and dividing by G_f yields the average per-FPGA utilization with hard wires:

$$U_{hw} = \frac{1}{d_h} K_h G_f^{B_h}. \quad (10)$$

---

[3]For this analysis, we work with average partition pin and gate requirements. Pin limitation effects are worse when the circuit is nonuniform.

[4]For simplicity, we are ignoring the effect of global nets with multiple destinations.

TABLE VI
HARD-WIRED UTILIZATION PARAMETERS

$$d_h = d^{1/B_c}$$
$$K_h = \left(\frac{K_f}{K_c} \right)^{1/B_c}$$
$$B_h = \frac{B_f}{B_c} - 1$$

Note that if we combine the $1/d_h$ and K_h terms, this equation is very similar to the original Rent equation. Here, we leave these terms separate to provide insight into the factors which affect overall hard-wired utilization. Each parameter is significant as follows: B_h shows how utilization will scale with FPGA device size. If B_h is negative, utilization will decline with increasing size, with a slope of B_h on a log scale. On the other hand, utilization is directly proportional to K_h for a fixed device size, and inversely proportional to d_h. For a crossbar interconnect with $d_h = 1$, K_h determines the offset of the utilization curve. For nonideal interconnects and with B_c in the range of 0.5, the topological factor of d_h translates to a roughly quadratic decrease in hard-wired utilization as the average routing path length increases.

C. Virtual Wires Gate Utilization (Fig. 27)

Let us model per-FPGA virtual wires costs as $V_0 + V_1 \times dP_c$, where V_0 is the per-FPGA cost associated with the control circuitry and V_1 is the cost associated with each logic I/O. The total number of circuit pins is P_c, and d is the same distance factor used here to amortize the cost of intermediate hops for each virtual wire into the overall cost equation.

For mapping circuits which obey the Rent equation, we can substitute $P_c = K_c G_c^{B_c}$ to get the average virtual wires cost:

$$G_v = V_0 + V_1 d K_c G_c^{B_c}. \quad (11)$$

Furthermore, $d = 1$ for a crossbar, and a derived upper limit to the average wire length for a mesh as a function of the total number of FPGA's N, as reported by Bakoglu [8], is

$$d = \frac{2}{9} \left(7 \frac{N^{B_c - 0.5} - 1}{4^{B_c - 0.5} - 1} - \frac{1 - N^{B_c - 1.5}}{1 - 4^{B_c - 1.5}} \right) \frac{1 - 4^{B_c - 1}}{1 - N^{B_c - 1}}. \quad (12)$$

Thus, given Rent's parameters for a given design, the average virtual wires overhead can be expressed strictly in terms of circuit and FPGA gate counts. We can then relate the FPGA gate count to the circuit gate count and virtual wires overhead as

$$G_f = G_c + G_v. \quad (13)$$

Substituting (11) and rewriting yields

$$V_1 d K_c G_c^{B_c} + G_c - (G_f - V_0) = 0. \quad (14)$$

Solving (14) for G_c yields the optimal partition size for a particular FPGA device size and circuit Rent parameters. We can further rewrite (14) in terms of utilization $U_{vw} = G_c/G_f$ to get

$$V_1 d K_c G_f^{B_c} U_{vw}^{B_c} + (U_{vw} - 1) G_f + V_0 = 0. \quad (15)$$

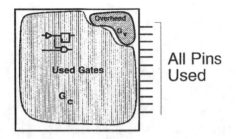

Fig. 27. Gate utilization with virtual wires.

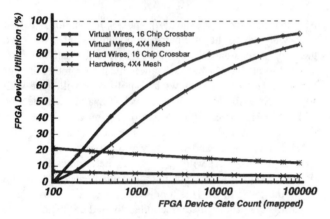

Fig. 28. Scalability with FPGA device size.

TABLE VII
PARAMETERS FOR SCALABILITY COMPARISON

Parameter	Value
B_c	0.60
B_f	0.55
K_c	2.0
K_f	1.0
$d_{crossbar}$	1 hop
d_{mesh}	2 hops
V_0	100 mapped gates
V_1	4 mapped gates

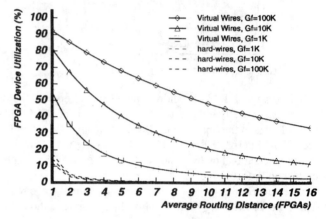

Fig. 29. Scalability with average routing distance.

Interestingly, (15), and the mathematical solution for U_{vw}, are not a function of P_f, the FPGA pin counts, or the FPGA Rent parameters. While lower pin counts may increase the pin multiplexing factor, and therefore emulation latency, utilization will not be affected. Finally, from (15), it is apparent that if $B_c < 1$, then as $G_f \to \infty$, virtual wire utilization will approach unity, $U_{vw} \to 1$, independent of other parameters. However, for small G_f, the gate utilization will be low due to the dominating V_0 factor. The following section compares these results to the hard-wired case for realistic design and FPGA parameters.

D. Scalability with FPGA Size

Using the results from the previous sections, we first compare achievable FPGA device utilization for both virtual wires and hard wires as FPGA size increases. Fig. 28 shows utilizations for a hypothetical design, characterized by Rent parameters, on both a 4×4 mesh and a 16-chip crossbar topology. These graphs are on a semilog scale, with the Y axis measuring percent of usable gates and the X axis logarithmically measuring FPGA device size. Table VII shows the assumed parameters for the design, the technology, and the virtual wires overhead. These assumptions roughly fall into the vicinity of our experimental measurements. Note that since the FPGA device size is increasing, with a constant number of devices, the circuit size is increasing as well. Also, the FPGA pin count is increasing with the gate count in accordance with the FPGA's Rent parameters.

The slope of both hard-wire curves is $B_h = B_f/B_c - 1$. In Fig. 28, B_h is negative, and thus the hardware curves slope downward. With a positive B_h, this curve would slope upward instead. As a general rule, this equation suggests that FPGA vendors should attempt to track $B_f = B_c$ for hard-wired FPGA systems. The log intercept is similarly K_h as earlier defined for the hard-wires crossbar. For the hardwired mesh, the offset is lower than the crossbar by $1/d_h$ in accordance with (10). For this example, the FPGA pin counts decrease with decreasing gate count such that FPGA's can never be fully utilized in the hard-wired case.

For virtual wires, the utilization is low for small gate count, partly due to the constant factor of V_0 control logic overhead. However, with increasing circuit size, this overhead is rapidly diluted: in both figures, the virtual wires gate utilization approaches 100% with increasing FPGA size. For a mesh topology, the utilization increases more slowly; however, it too asymptotically approaches unity. As a caveat to this comparison, note that for most FPGA devices, utilization will saturate at less than 100% due to internal routing restrictions.

E. Scalability with Routing Distance

As a final comparison, we consider the utilization effects of increasing the number of FPGA's, and therefore the average routing distance. To isolate topological effects, we show utilization as a function of the average routing distance (Fig. 29) for FPGA's of size 1, 10, and 100K mapped gates. As before, circuit size is assumed to increase as the FPGA array size increases. The same parameters as in Table VII are used with the exception of d, which is now a variable.

For the hard-wires curves, the utilizations for $d = 1$ and $d = 2$ match the same data points as in Fig. 28. As d increases, the utilization drops exponentially at the rate $d_h = d^{1/0.6}$ for all hard-wired cases. Additionally, note that the higher utilization curves correspond to lower gate count FPGA's G_f since B_h is negative. Here, we see that crossbars, with $d = 1$, are essential for emulation without virtual wires. After only a few average FPGA hops of through routing, hard-wired utilization is nearly zero.

For the virtual wires curves, the higher gate count FPGA's have a higher utilization, as demonstrated in Fig. 28. All curves asymptotically approach zero utilization as distance increases. However, for the larger gate count curves, a respectable utilization is maintained even for large values of d. For example, the $G_f = 100K$ curve has a utilization of 33% when $d = 16$. Thus, virtual wires enable emulation to scale to a gigantic number of FPGA's using simple direct-connected topologies.

VII. Related Work

IBM's Yorktown Simulation Engine [31] and the earlier Logic Simulation Engine [12], based on concepts of J. Cocke, used reconfiguring digital hardware to accelerate logic simulation. Actual logic emulation was first explored in cellular array research, such as F. Manning's 1975 thesis [29], even before FPGA's existed. His work explicitly shows how an "embedded machine" in programmable logic cells could be used in place of an actual machine. Since this work, FPGA-based logic emulation systems have been developed for design complexity ranging from several thousand to several million gates. Quickturn Design Systems, the pioneer of large FPGA-based emulators, first developed emulation systems that interconnect FPGA's in a 2-D mesh and later in a partial crossbar topology [38]. Their largest systems use a hierarchical approach to interconnection [37]. Thorough reviews of contemporary emulation systems are provided by Hauck [18] and Owen [30].

Multiplexing to overcome pin limitations was first proposed by Babb [6], [7] in 1993, and the first successful applications were discussed by Tessier [36], Dahl [13], [14], and Hanono [17]. Virtual wires technology has continued to evolve at Virtual Machine Works, Inc. [1], [32], where commercial emulators based on proprietary VirtualWires™ technology are now being produced.

Since the original application of multiplexing to FPGA systems, others have proposed several similar approaches. In [24], multiplexing is extended to field-programmable interconnect devices called dynamic FPID's. In [25], the resources inside the FPGA are multiplexed to reduce internal routing requirements. Recent time-multiplexed FPGA-like architectures include VEGA [20], Pegasus [28], DPGA [35], and Dharma [11]. Other related uses of static routing techniques include FPGA-based systolic arrays, such as Splash2 [4], and the very large simulation subsystem (VLSS) [39], a massively parallel simulation engine which uses time-division multiplexing to stagger logic evaluation. Finally, virtual wires are similar to virtual channels [15], which decouple resource allocation in dynamically routed networks, and to virtual circuits [10] found in a connection-oriented network.

VIII. Conclusions

We have illustrated the benefits of logic emulation with virtual wires as a verification alternative. Previous pin limitations encountered when mapping designs onto multi-FPGA systems are now overcome. We have described correct-by-construction virtualization software, including both phase-based scheduling and synthesis algorithms, which can automatically retime a synchronous input design to fit an arbitrary number and arrangement of FPGA's. We have demonstrated the success of virtual wires emulation on a low-cost system without crossbars, esoteric backplanes, or large pin-count FPGA devices. Finally, we have analyzed the overheads associated with virtual wires, and have found that FPGA utilization, over 45% in our emulation experiments, will asymptotically approach 100% in larger FPGA's if not limited by internal FPGA resource constraints.

Although this paper has focused on logic emulation, virtualization is a generic tool that may be applied to other multi-FPGA systems, enabling a collection of FPGA's to be treated as a single, gigantic FPGA. In the field of FPGA computing, more tools like virtual wires are needed to efficiently utilize increasing amounts of available FPGA gate capacity. A future direction is to speed up and potentially multiplex the place and route inside the FPGA. However, the current greatest deficiency for computing is in software compilation techniques to quickly map applications from a higher level language, such as C or Behavioral Verilog, into FPGA instructions.

References

[1] A. Agarwal, "VirtualWires: A technology for massive multi-FPGA systems," Virtual Machine Works, Inc., Tech. Rep., Dec. 1994; http://www.ikos.com/products/virtualwires.ps.
[2] A. Agarwal, J. Kubiatowicz, D. Kranz, B.-H. Lim, D. Yeung, G. D'Souza, and M. Parkin, "Sparcle: An evolutionary processor design for multiprocessors," *IEEE Micro*, vol. 13, pp. 48–61, June 1993.
[3] *Flex 8000 Handbook*. San Jose, CA: Altera Corporation, May 1994.
[4] J. M. Arnold, D. A. Buell, and E. G. Davis, "Splash 2," in *Proc. 4th Annu. ACM Symp. Parallel Algorithms and Architectures*, June 1992, pp. 316–324.
[5] Atmel Corp., *Atmel Configurable Logic Design and Application Book*, 1994.
[6] J. Babb, "Virtual Wires: Overcoming pin limitations in FPGA-based logic emulation," Master's thesis, Dept. Elect. Eng. Comput. Sci., Mass. Inst. Technol., Cambridge, Feb. 1994; also, MIT/LCS TR-586, Nov. 1993.
[7] J. Babb, R. Tessier, and A. Agarwal, "Virtual Wires: Overcoming pin limitations in FPGA-based logic emulators," in *Proc. IEEE Workshop on FPGA-Based Custom Computing Machines*, Napa, CA, Apr. 1993, pp. 142–151; also, MIT/LCS TM-491, Jan. 1993.
[8] H. B. Bakoglu, *Circuits, Interconnections, and Packaging for VLSI*. Reading, MA: Addison-Wesley, 1990.
[9] T. Bauer, "The design of an efficient hardware subroutine protocol for FPGA's," Master's thesis, Dept. Elect. Eng. Comput. Sci., Mass. Inst. Technol., Cambridge, May 1994.
[10] D. Bertsekas and R. Gallagher, Eds., *Data Networks*. Englewood Cliffs, NJ: Prentice-Hall, 1992.
[11] N. Bhat, "Novel techniques for high performance field programmable logic devices," Ph.D. dissertation, Electron. Res. Lab., Univ. California, Berkeley, Nov. 1993.
[12] J. Cocke and R. E. Miller, "Configurable computer system," IBM Tech. Disclosure Bull., Tech. Rep. 9, Feb. 1973.
[13] M. Dahl, "An implementation of the Virtual Wires interconnect scheme," Master's thesis, Master's thesis, Depart. Elect. Eng. Comput. Sci., Mass. Inst. Technol., Cambridge, Feb. 1994.
[14] M. Dahl, J. Babb, R. Tessier, S. Hanono, D. Hoki, and A. Agarwal, "Emulation of a SPARC microprocessor with the MIT Virtual Wires Emulation System," in *Proc. IEEE Workshop on FPGA-Based Custom Computing Machines*, IEEE, Napa, CA, Apr. 1994, pp. 14–22.
[15] W. J. Dally, "Virtual-channel flow control," *IEEE Trans. Parallel Distrib. Syst.*, vol. 3, no. 2, Mar. 1992.
[16] A. Dehon and S. Perentz, "Transit note no. 67: Transit Sbus interface," Artificial Intelligence Laboratory, Mass. Inst. Technol., Cambridge, Tech. Rep., June 1992.
[17] S. Hanono, "Innerview hardware debugger: A logic analysis tool for the Virtual Wires Emulation System," Master's thesis, Depart. Elect. Eng.

Comput. Sci., Mass. Inst. Technol., Cambridge, Feb. 1995.
[18] S. Hauck, "Multi-FPGA systems," Ph.D. dissertation, Depart. Comput. Sci. Eng., Univ. Washington, Seattle, June 1995.
[19] InCA Inc., *Concept Silicon Reference Manual*, version 1.1, Nov. 1992.
[20] D. Jones and D. Lewis, "A time-multiplexed FPGA architecture for logic emulation," in *Proc. 3rd Canadian Workshop on Field-Programmable Devices*, May 1995.
[21] S. Kirkpatrick, C. D. Gellatt, and M. P. Vecchi, "Simulated annealing," *Science*, 1983, p. 220.
[22] J. Kubiatowicz, "User's manual for the A-1000 communications and memory management unit," Lab. Comput. Sci., Mass. Inst. Tech., ALEWIFE Memo no. 19, Jan. 1991.
[23] B. Landman and R. Russo, "On a pin versus block relationship for partitions of logic graphs," *IEEE Trans. Comput.*, vol. C-20, no. 12, Dec. 1971.
[24] J. Li and C.-K. Cheng, "Routability improvement using dynamic interconnect architecture," in *Proc. IEEE Workshop on FPGA-Based Custom Computing Machines*, Napa, CA, Apr. 1995.
[25] C.-C. Lin, D. Chang, Y.-L. Wu, and M. Marek-Sadowska, "Time-multiplexed routing resources for FPGA design," in *Proc. 1996 ACM Int. Workshop on Field-Programmable Gate Arrays*, Monterey, CA, Feb. 1996.
[26] LSI Logic Corporation, *0.7-Micron Array-Based Products Databook*, Apr. 1990.
[27] V. MaheshWari, J. Darnauer, J. Ramireza, and W. W.-M. Dai, "Design of FPGA's with area I/O for field programmable MCM," in *FPGA'95*, Monterey, CA, Feb. 1995.
[28] L. Maliniak, "Hardware emulation draws speed from innovative 3D parallel processing based on custom IC's," *Electron. Design*, May 1994.
[29] F. P. Manning, "Automatic test, configuration, and repair of cellular arrays," Ph.D. dissertation, Dept. Elect. Eng. Comput. Sci., Mass. Instit. of Technol., June 1975.
[30] H. Owen, U. Khan, and J. Hughes, "FPGA-based ASIC hardware emulator architectures," in *Proc. International Workshop on Field Programmable Logic and Applications*, Oxford, U.K., Sept. 1993.
[31] G. F. Pfister, "The Yorktown simulation engine: Introduction," in *Proc. 19th Design Automation Conference*, IEEE Computer Society Press, 1982, pp. 51–54.
[32] C. Selvidge, A. Agarwal, M. Dahl, and J. Babb, "TIERS: Topology independent pipelined routing and scheduling for VirtualWire compilation," in *1995 ACM Int. Workshop on Field-Programmable Gate Arrays*, ACM, Berkeley, CA, Feb. 1995.
[33] Synopsys, Inc., *Command Reference Manual*, Version 3.0, Dec. 1992.
[34] R. R. T. Cormen and C. Leiserson, *Introduction to Algorithms*. Cambridge, MA: MIT Press, 1992.
[35] E. Tau, I. Eslick, D. Chen, J. Brown, and A. DeHon, "A first generation DPGA implementation," in *Proc. 3rd Canadian Workshop on Field-Programmable Devices*, May 1995.
[36] R. Tessier, J. Babb, M. Dahl, S. Hanono, and A. Agarwal, "The Virtual Wires Emulation System: A gate-efficient ASIC prototyping environment," in *1994 ACM International Workshop on Field-Programmable Gate Arrays*, ACM, Berkeley, CA, Feb. 1994.
[37] J. Varghese, M. Butts, and J. Batcheller, "An efficient logic emulation system," *IEEE Trans. VLSI Syst.*, vol. 1, no. 2, June 1993.
[38] S. Walters, "Computer-aided prototyping for ASIC-based systems," *IEEE Design and Test of Computers*, June 1992.
[39] Y.-C. Wei, C.-K. Cheng, and Z. Wurman, "Multiple-level partitioning: An application for the very large-scale hardware simulator," *IEEE J. Solid-State Circuits*, vol. 26, no. 5, May 1991.
[40] XILINX, Inc., 2100 Logic Drive, San Jose, CA 95214.
[41] *The Programmable Gate Array Data Book, The XC4000 Data Book*, Aug. 1992.

Jonathan Babb received the the B.S. degree in electrical engineering from the Georgia Institute of Technology, Atlanta, in 1991, the S.M. degree in electrical engineering from the Massachusetts Institute of Technology (MIT), Cambridge, in 1994 and is currently pursuing the Ph.D. degree as part of the RAW project at MIT.

He was a previously researcher in the Alewife multiprocessor and the Virtual Wires projects at MIT and was a founder of Virtual Machine Works, Inc.

Russell Tessier received the B.S. degree in computer engineering from Rensselaer Polytechnic Institute, Troy, NY, in 1989, and the S.M. degree in electrical engineering from the Massachusetts Institute of Technology (MIT), Cambridge, in 1992. He is currently pursuing the Ph.D. degree in computer science at the MIT Laboratory for Computer Science.

He is a founder of Virtual Machine Works, a commercial venture based on the concept of Virtual Wires. His research interests include computer architecture and CAD for field-programmable gate arrays.

Matthew Dahl is currently a Senior Staff Software Engineer at IKOS Systems, Inc., Cambridge, MA. He has previously been a member of the technical staff at the Laboratory for Computer Science, Massachusetts Institute of Technology, Cambridge, and a Senior Engineer at Digital Equipment Corp.

Silvina Zimi Hanono received the B.S. degree in electrical engineering from Cornell University, Ithaca, NY, in 1992, and the M.S. degree in electrical engineering and computer science from the Laboratory for Computer Science, Massachusetts Institute of Technology (MIT), Cambridge, in 1995. There she developed a hardware debugger for the Virtual Wires Logic Emulation system. She is currently pursuing the Ph.D. degree in the Research Laboratory of Electronics at MIT.

Under the direction of Prof. S. Devadas, she is developing a retargetable code generator for VLIW embedded processors. Her research interests include computer architecture and computer-aided design.

Ms. Hanono is a National Science Foundation Fellow and a member of the Eta Kappa Nu and Tau Beta Pi Engineering honor societies.

David M. Hoki received the B.S. degree in electrical and computer engineering from Brigham Young University (BYU), Provo, UT, in 1993.

He is currently a software engineer at Charles Stark Draper Laboratory, Inc., Cambridge, MA. He was a member of the research staff at the Laboratory for Computer Science, Massachusetts Institute of Technology, Cambridge, from 1993 to 1994. He was also a software developer at CADAM Inc. for three years while attending BYU. He was recently building a Global Positioning System (GPS) captive simulator, and is currently doing research in multi-project threaded planning and decision aids.

Anant Agarwal received the Ph.D. degree from Stanford University, Stanford, CA, in 1987 and the B.Tech. degree from the Indian Institute of Technology, Madras, India, in 1982.

He is with the Laboratory for Computer Science at the Massachusetts Institute of Technology (MIT), Cambridge, as an Associate Professor of Electrical Engineering and Computer Science. At Stanford, he participated in the MIPS and MIPS-X projects. He led the Alewife multiprocessor and the Virtual Wires projects at MIT. He was a founder of Virtual Machine Works, Inc., which was aimed at productizing the VirtualWires technology for logic emulation. He has recently initiated the RAW project, which is aimed at developing a configurable computer based on a new model of computation.

Embryonics: A New Methodology for Designing Field-Programmable Gate Arrays with Self-Repair and Self-Replicating Properties

Daniel Mange, *Member, IEEE,* Eduardo Sanchez, *Member, IEEE,* André Stauffer, *Member, IEEE,*
Gianluca Tempesti, *Member, IEEE,* Pierre Marchal, *Member, IEEE,* and Christian Piguet

Abstract—The growth and the operation of all living beings are directed through the interpretation, in each of their cells, of a chemical program, the DNA string or *genome*. This process is the source of inspiration for the Embryonics (embryonic electronics) project, whose final objective is the conception of very large scale integrated circuits endowed with properties usually associated with the living world: self-repair (cicatrization) and self-replication. We will begin by showing that any logic system can be represented by an ordered binary decision diagram (OBDD), and then embedded into a fine-grained field-programmable gate array (FPGA) whose basic cell is a multiplexer with programmable connections. The cellular array thus obtained is perfectly homogeneous: the function of each cell is defined by a configuration (or *gene*) and all the genes in the array, each associated with a pair of coordinates, make up the blueprint (or *genome*) of the artificial organism. In the second part of the project, we add to the basic cell a memory and an interpreter to, respectively, store and decode the complete genome. The interpreter extracts from the genome the gene of a particular cell as a function of its position in the array (its coordinates) and thus determines the exact configuration of the relative multiplexer. The considerable redundancy introduced by the presence of a genome in each cell has significant advantages: self-replication (the automatic production of one or more copies of the original organism) and self-repair (the automatic repair of one or more faulty cells) become relatively simple operations. The multiplexer-based FPGA cell and the interpreter are finally embedded into an electronic module; an array of such modules make it possible to demonstrate self-repair and self-replication.

Index Terms—Embryonic electronics, field-programmable gate arrays (FPGA's), multiplexer-based FPGA's, ordered binary decision diagrams, self-repairing FPGA's, self-replicating FPGA's.

I. INTRODUCTION

A. Toward Embryonics

A HUMAN being consists of approximately 60 trillion (60×10^{12}) cells. At each instant, in each of these 60 trillion cells, the *genome*, a ribbon of 2 billion characters,

Manuscript received October 18, 1995; revised May 18, 1998. This work was supported by the Swiss National Science Foundation under Grants 21-36'200.92 and 20-39'391.93.
D. Mange, E. Sanchez, A. Stauffer, and G. Tempesti are with the Logic Systems Laboratory, Swiss Federal Institute of Technolgy, Lausanne CH 1015 Switzerland.
P. Marchal and C. Piguet are with the Centre suisse d'électronique et de microtechnique SA, Neuchâtel CH 2007 Switzerland.
Publisher Item Identifier S 1063-8210(98)05984-8.

is decoded to produce the proteins needed for the survival of the organism. This genome contains the ensemble of the genetic inheritance of the individual and, at the same time, the instructions for both the construction and the operation of the organism. The parallel execution of 60 trillion genomes in as many cells occurs ceaselessly from the conception to the death of the individual. Faults are rare and, in the majority of cases, successfully detected and repaired. This process is remarkable for its complexity and its precision. Moreover, it relies on completely discrete processes: the chemical structure of DNA (the chemical substrate of the genome) is a sequence of four bases, usually designated with the letters A (adenine), C (cytosine), G (guanine), and T (thymine).

Our research is inspired by the basic processes of molecular biology [16]. By adopting certain features of cellular organization, and by transposing them to the two-dimensional (2-D) world of integrated circuits on silicon, we will show that properties unique to the living world, such as self-replication and self-repair, can also be applied to artificial objects (integrated circuits).

B. Objectives and Strategy

Our final objective is the development of very large scale integrated (VLSI) circuits capable of self-repair and self-replication. These two properties seem particularly desirable for complex artificial systems meant for hostile (nuclear plants) or inaccessible (space) environments. Self-replication allows the complete reconstruction of the original device in case of a major fault, while self-repair allows a partial reconstruction in case of a minor fault.

Section II introduces the fundamental features of the Embryonics project (for embryonic electronics), which is based on a general hypothesis, defining the silicon environment in which the quasi-biological development occurs, and on three features, which roughly mimic the process of cellular development: multicellular organization, cellular differentiation, and cellular division.

To represent and implement a given digital system on a FPGA we select, in Section III, an efficient and universal representation: the ordered binary decision diagram (OBDD). We will show that the use of such a representation greatly simplifies the realization of a new family of FPGA's, based on a fine-grained cell. This cell, called MUXTREE, contains essentially a multiplexer with one control variable and a nontrivial programmable connection network. Section IV describes in detail the MUXTREE cell, which in fact constitutes the application layer of the FPGA, and its 20 configuration bits. According to our biological approach, these 20 bits are the gene of the cell and all the genes of a given digital system are its genome.

Section V introduces the two configuration layers which will perform the computation of the gene of each cell. The first layer computes the coordinates of a given cell from the coordinates of its neighbors. The second layer determines, from the complete genome and from the local coordinates of the cell, its gene. This is the equivalent of the process of cellular differentiation, and is implemented through the use a very simple binary decision machine, which we call NANOPASCALINE, charged with the execution of the GENOME program. Finally, Section VI briefly describes the realization of the cellular division process, that is, the duplication of the genome of a mother cell into one or two neighboring daughter cells.

The final cell, made up of an application layer (MUXTREE) and two configuration layers (NANOPASCALINE), is finally embedded into a demonstration module: the BIODULE. Section VII shows that any given digital system implemented by an array of BIODULES is endowed with the properties of self-repair and self-replication. Section VIII illustrates the limitations of the current project and outlines the ongoing research, aimed at the development of an integrated circuit endowed with quasi-biological properties.

II. THE FOUNDATIONS OF EMBRYONICS

A. The General Hypothesis about the Environment

The general hypothesis describes the environment in which the quasi-biological development occurs. In the framework of electronics, it consists of a finite (but as large as desired) 2-D space of silicon, divided into rows and columns. The intersection of a row and a column defines a *cell*, and all cells have an identical structure, i.e., an identical network of connections and an identical set of logic operators. The physical space or *cellular array* is therefore *homogeneous*, that is, made up of absolutely identical cells: only the *state* of a cell can differentiate it from its neighbors.

B. First Feature: Multicellular Organization

The first feature is that of *multicellular organization*: the artificial organism is divided into a finite number of cells [Fig. 1(a)], where each cell realizes a unique function, determined by a number called the *gene* of the cell. Fig. 1(a) illustrates the example of a simple artificial organism, an *up–down counter*, realized with nine cells, each cell being defined by a different gene (a five-digit hexadecimal number). The calculation of these genes will be analyzed in detail later.

C. Second Feature: Cellular Differentiation

Let us call *genome* the set of all the genes of an artificial organism, where each gene is characterized by its value and

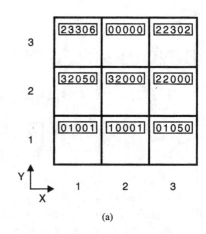

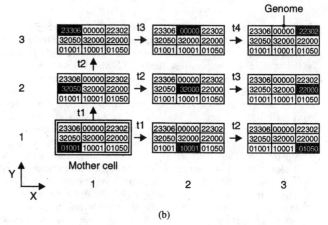

Fig. 1. The three features of embryonics applied to the example of an up–down counter. (a) Multicellular organization with a nine-gene genome. (b) Cellular differentiation with the complete genome in every cell and cellular division copying the genome of the mother cell into daughter cells ($t1 \cdots t4$: clock periods).

its position (its coordinates X, Y). Fig. 1(a) then shows the genome of the up–down counter, with the corresponding horizontal (X) and vertical (Y) coordinates. Let then each cell contain the entire genome [Fig. 1(b)]: depending on its position in the array, each cell interprets the genome and extracts the gene which configures it.

In summary, storing the whole genome in each cell makes this cell universal: it can realize any gene of the genome, given the proper coordinates.

D. Third Feature: Cellular Division

At startup, the mother cell [Fig. 1(b)], arbitrarily defined as having coordinates $X, Y = 1, 1$, holds the one and only copy of the genome. At time $t1$, the genome of the mother cell is copied into the two neighboring (daughter) cells to the north and to the east. The process then continues until the 2-D space is completely programmed. In our example, the furthest cell is programmed at time $t4$.

III. SYNTHESIS OF ORDERED BINARY DECISION DIAGRAMS (OBDD)

To fit our demands, we needed to find a method capable of generating, starting from a set of specifications, the configuration for a homogeneous network of cells, where each cell is defined by an identical architecture and a usually distinct function (gene).

To meet our requirements, we have selected a particular representation: the *ordered binary decision diagram* (OBDD). This representation, with its well-known intrinsic properties such as canonicity [2], [4], was chosen for two main reasons [see, for example, Fig. 2(c)]: on one hand, it is a graphical representation which exploits well the 2-D space and immediately suggests a physical realization on silicon; on the other hand, its structure leads us to a natural decomposition into cells realizing a logic test (a diamond), easily implemented by a multiplexer.

We will illustrate the handling of ordered binary decision diagrams through a simple example, an up–down counter. Our choice will lead us to define our new FPGA as a homogenous array where each cell contains a programmable multiplexer with one control variable, implementing precisely a logic test. Such an FPGA is said to be *fine-grained*.

A. Example of a Modulo-4 Up–Down Counter

As an example, let us consider the realization of the abovementioned modulo-4 up–down counter, defined by the following sequences:

$$\text{for } M = 0 : Q1, Q0 = 00 \rightarrow 01 \rightarrow 10 \rightarrow 11 \rightarrow 00$$
$$\text{(counting up)};$$
$$\text{for } M = 1 : Q1, Q0 = 00 \rightarrow 11 \rightarrow 10 \rightarrow 01 \rightarrow 00$$
$$\text{(counting down)}. \quad (1)$$

This definition is equivalent to the two state tables of Fig. 2(a), defining the future states $Q1+$ and $Q0+$.

B. Ordered Binary Decision Trees and Diagrams

We define a *complete* (or *canonical*) *binary decision tree* as a tree for n variables having 2^n branches corresponding to the 2^n possible input states; for the tree of Fig. 2(b), representing $Q1+$, we have $n = 3$ and $2^3 = 8$. Each test element of the tree is represented by a diamond and defined by a test variable: it has a single input, a "true" output (test variable equal to "1") and a "complemented" output (test variable equal to "0"), identified by a small circle. The leaf elements, represented as squares, define the output value of the given function ($Q1+$ in our example).

In our case, the use of Karnaugh maps for simplifying trees [8], [9] shows that no simplification of $Q1+$ is possible (Fig. 2(a): there is no block, i.e., no pattern formed by 2^m adjacent "0"'s or "1"'s). On the other hand, the Karnaugh map for $Q0+$ [Fig. 2(a)] reveals one block of four "0"'s and one block of four "1"'s, which gives us to the *minimal simplified tree* of Fig. 2(b), representing $Q0+$ and containing only two branches.

A more detailed analysis of the Karnaugh maps of Fig. 2(a) reveals two types of *blocks of blocks* (ST0 and ST1), representing subtrees of the tree of $Q1+$ [Fig. 2(b)]. It can be observed, moreover, that the function $Q0+$ is equal to the subtree $ST0 = Q0'$.

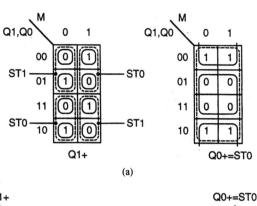

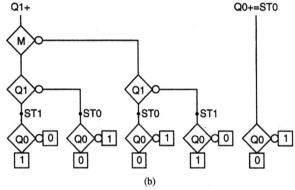

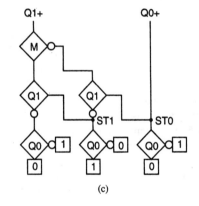

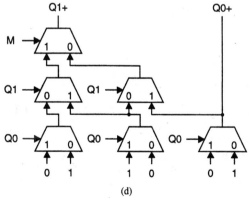

Fig. 2. Modulo-4 up–down counter. (a) State table (Karnaugh map). (b) Canonic ($Q1+$) and minimal ($Q0+$) binary decision trees. (c) Ordered binary decision diagrams for $Q1+$ and $Q0+$. (d) Multiplexer implementation of the OBDD's.

The sharing of identical subtrees implies the convergence of branches of the tree and its transformation into a new representation: the binary decision diagram (BDD). Finally, the sharing of a subtree (ST0) belonging to the two functions $Q1+$ and $Q0+$ and the permutation of the "0" and "1" outputs of certain diamonds lead us to the final diagram of Fig. 2(c), which represents a *forest of binary decision diagrams.*

In the above discussion, we have implied that the binary decision diagrams and trees were *ordered*, that is, characterized by a fixed position for the test variables: $Q0$ at the lower level, $Q1$ at the middle level, and M at the upper level. Using Bryant's notation [4], we will write

$$M < Q1 < Q0. \qquad (2)$$

It can be observed that all logic systems, combinational or sequential, of n variables will require a cellular network of n rows. On the other hand, the minimal number of columns will depend on the simplification method adopted to obtain the ordered binary decision diagrams from the original specifications. For problems of up to six variables, the Karnaugh map allows a relatively simple manual computation [8], [9]. Beyond six variables, more complex analytical methods require the use of a computer [4], [5].

C. Hardware Implementation

Our design decision has been to implement directly the ordered binary decision diagrams on silicon, and to build our fine-grained basic cell around a test element (a diamond). Such an implementation is possible if one replaces each test element with a 2-to-1 multiplexer, keeps the same interconnection diagram, and assigns the values of the leaf elements to the corresponding multiplexer inputs [8]. Fig. 2(d) shows the direct multiplexer implementation of the up–down counter. The two state functions $Q1+$ and $Q0+$ are available at the outputs of the top multiplexers: the ordered diagrams of Fig. 2(c) are read bottom-up in Fig. 2(d).

IV. A New Field-Programmable Gate Array Based on a Multiplexer Cell

A. General Remarks

A simple examination of Fig. 2(d) allows us to identify the main features of the programmable cell, henceforth referred to as MUXTREE (for multiplexer tree).

- Each of the two inputs of the multiplexer (labeled "0" and "1") will be programmable. The input will be either a logic constant ("0" or "1") or the output of the multiplexer of one of the neighboring cells to the south, southeast, or southwest.
- The output of the multiplexer will be, therefore, connected to the inputs of the multiplexers in the neighboring cells to the north, northeast, and northwest.
- The realization of sequential systems requires the presence, in each cell, of a synchronous memory element, a D-type flip-flop, which will allow, in our example, to obtain directly the values $Q1$ and $Q0$ (instead of $Q1+$ and $Q0+$) needed for the display and for the retroaction of the secondary variables.
- Long-distance connections are necessary to connect a cell to any other cell in the array. In our example, the variable $Q1$ (itself obtained at the output of the mentioned flip-flop) must be brought back to the inputs of the multiplexers of the middle row of cells. This type of connection demands a system of universal buses, running through the entire array.

In brief, the heart of the cell remains the 2-to-1 multiplexer, optionally followed by a flip-flop. Inputs and outputs are programmable and can be connected either to immediate neighbors, according to a topology proper to binary decision diagrams (where information flows from the bottom to the top), or to faraway cells through a network of perfectly symmetric universal buses.

To facilitate the detailed description of the MUXTREE cell, we will separate it into two levels: the *logic level*, that is, the basic multiplexer and its immediate connections, and the *connection level*, that is, the bus network for faraway connections.

B. Description of the Logic Level

The MUXTREE cell (Fig. 3) is based on a 2-to-1 multiplexer (in the lower part of the test block TB) and a D-type flip-flop (in the memory block MB) for clocked sequential behavior. Connections to the inputs of the main multiplexer are defined using the 8-to-1 multiplexers of the connection block CB. The 6 bits LEFT2:0 and RIGHT2:0 select one out of eight inputs for the left and right branches of the main multiplexer. The second 2-to-1 multiplexer of TB selects one of the east buses (EOBUS, EIBUS) to control the main multiplexer. The 2-to-1 multiplexer of the output block OB allows the connection of the output of the main multiplexer or the output of the flip-flop to the north output (NOUT). A switch block SB, described in Section IV-C, provides interconnections between the input buses (NIBUS, EIBUS, SIBUS, WIBUS), as well as the output NOUT, and the output buses (NOBUS, EOBUS, SOBUS, WOBUS). Finally, the field-program bit REG (Fig. 3) controls the combinational or sequential behavior of the cell, while the field-program bit PRESET determines if an action on the INIT signal implies an asynchronous set or reset of the flip-flop.

C. Description of the Bus Level and Global Representation

In order to implement long connections, the bus network includes one switch block SB per cell. Fig. 4(a) symbolizes the interconnection possibilities between the four input and four output oriented buses. All connections are possible, with the exception only of "U-turns." Fig. 4(b) shows the internal realization of the block. This realization, which also allows the north output (NOUT) to be connected to the four output buses, is realized using four 4-to-1 multiplexers. Each multiplexer is controlled by two field-program bits selecting one of the four possible inputs (the other directions input buses and the north output NOUT).

Fig. 11(b) summarizes the input and output signals of the MUXTREE cell. In order to facilitate the hexadecimal representation of its gene, the 17 field-program bits of the cell are organized as a 20-bit data GENE19:0 (Fig. 3).

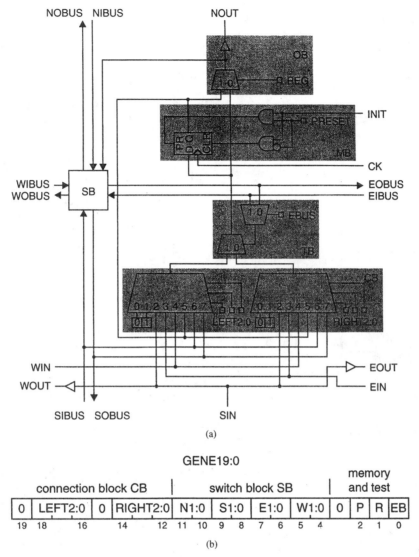

Fig. 3. MUXTREE cell. (a) Detailed architecture (the switch block SB is described in Fig. 4). (b) The 20-bit data GENE19:0 with P = PRESET, R = REG, and EB = EBUS.

D. Application: Modulo-4 Up–Down Counter

It can be immediately seen that the counter described by the ordered decision diagrams of Fig. 2(c) can be realized using an array of three lines and three columns (that is, by a total of nine MUXTREE cells).

Fig. 2(c) is modified and leads to the final diagram [Fig. 5(a)] where we have the following:

- the use of two D-type flip-flops, symbolized with a square around the corresponding diamonds, generates the variables $Q1$ and $Q0$ in place of $Q1+$ and $Q0+$;
- a cell is completely unused, while another cell is used exclusively as a direct connection (transmission of $Q0+$).

Using the bus level notation defined in a detailed description of the MUXTREE cell [11], we can then draw the connection layout of the counter [Fig. 5(b)].

Combining the information of Fig. 5(a) and (b) allows us to compute manually the 17 control bits of each gene, according to the format defined in Fig. 3, and finally produces the *genome* of Fig. 1(a). For all indifferent conditions (Φ-conditions), the corresponding bits were set to "0."

E. Conclusion

Thanks to the conception of the new family of field-programmable gate arrays (FPGA's) MUXTREE, we are currently able to realize any given logic system using a completely homogeneous cellular network. This realization is simplified by the direct mapping of the ordered binary decision diagrams onto the array. Thus, we have satisfied the general hypothesis on the environment described in Section II-A, as well as the first feature of the Embryonics project, that is, multicellular organization [Section II-B and Fig. 1(a)].

The manual computation of the genes can be very awkward. Two software tools (running on an Apple Macintosh) have been devised to overcome this problem. The first is a graphical editor, capable of determining the individual 20-bit genes for the MUXTREE implementation of any given function

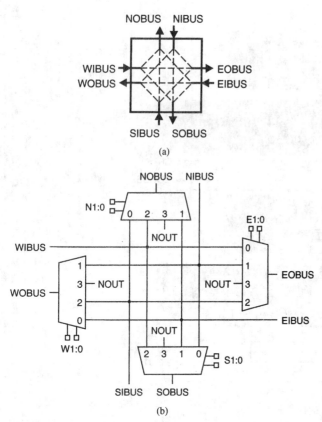

Fig. 4. The switch block SB. (a) Interconnection possibilities. (b) Detailed architecture.

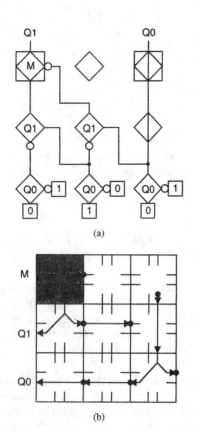

Fig. 5. Nine-cell implementation of the up–down counter. (a) Logic level and (b) bus level.

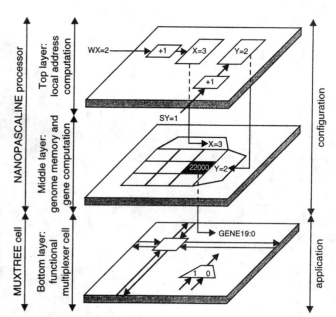

Fig. 6. Hierarchical overview of the three layers and the corresponding block schemes of the final embryonic cell.

represented by an OBDD. The second is a numerical simulator, allowing the functional verification of the implementation.

To this date, two physical realizations of arrays of MUX-TREE cells have been implemented. The first consists of 20 programmable ACTEL 1020A circuits, realizing a homogeneous surface of $15 \times 16 = 240$ cells. The second, realized in collaboration with the CMP-Grenoble (Circuits multi projets, Prof. B. Courtois), is an integrated circuit MUXCHIP consisting of $8 \times 8 = 64$ cells. The chip was fabricated at an SGS-Thomson Microelectronics facility [6].

V. CELLULAR DIFFERENTIATION: GENOME INTERPRETATION

A. A Hierarchical Overview

Rather than describing our final cell as a whole, we will, for the sake of simplicity, decompose it in three components or *layers* (Fig. 6) and describe each of these layers separately. The top layer is used to compute the local coordinates X, Y of the cell, usually by adding 1 to the coordinate WX of the western neighbor and to the coordinate SY of the southern neighbor. The middle layer contains a random access memory (RAM) and is used to store the entire genome: the memory stores a single gene per address, i.e., per pair of coordinates (X, Y). Finally, the selected gene controls the bottom layer, which contains the functional cell (i.e., the MUXTREE cell defined in the preceding section).

During normal operation, the top (address computation) and middle (genome) layers are fixed and the values they compute (X and Y coordinates, gene GENE19:0) are constant. We will say that these two layers, which are in fact *configuration layers*, are idle during operation. Modifications can only be effected at initialization (programming of the FPGA) or during the self-repair and self-replication processes.

On the other hand, the bottom layer is the operational part or *application layer*. Its values usually change with time.

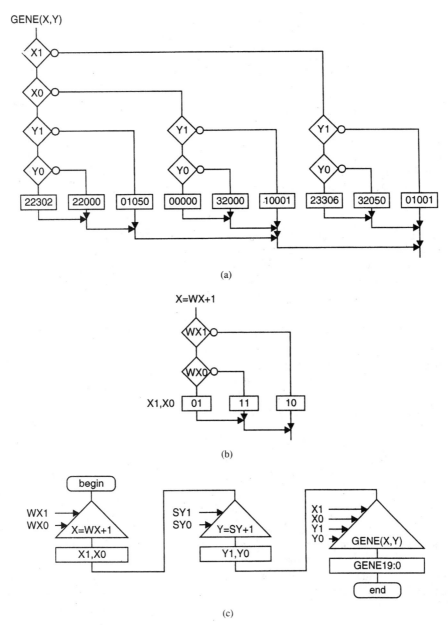

Fig. 7. Computation and genome representation. (a) Gene computation, (b) X coordinate computation, and (c) up–down counter genome.

B. Microprogrammed Realization

In all living beings, the genome is executed sequentially by a chemical processor, the *ribosome*. Drawing inspiration from this biological process, we will use a microprogram to compute the local coordinates X and Y and to extract from our artificial genome, as a function of the coordinates, the gene GENE19:0.

The artificial genome [for our example, that of the up–down counter of Fig. 1(a)] can be considered as a *truth table* (or *look-up table*) whose input states are the coordinates or addresses X and Y, and whose output states are the genes GENE19:0.

If we express the values of the coordinates X and Y in pure binary code, using the logic variables $X1$, $X0$, $Y1$ and $Y0$, we may apply the traditional simplification methods for binary decision trees [8], [9], and we finally obtain the structured subprogram GENE(X, Y) of Fig. 7(a), represented symbolically in the program of Fig. 7(c).

Assuming that the mother cell has coordinates $X, Y = 1, 1$, we observe the following (Fig. 6):

- each cell computes its horizontal coordinate X as a function of the horizontal coordinate WX of its western neighbor;
- each cell computes its vertical coordinate Y as a function of the vertical coordinate SY of its southern neighbor;
- the sequence of horizontal coordinates X is incremented and limited to a cycle $1 \to 2 \to 3 \to \cdots \to x$ by the width x of the cellular array;
- the sequence of vertical coordinates Y is incremented and limited to a cycle $1 \to 2 \to 3 \to \cdots \to y$ by the height y of the cellular array.

We can then write two subprograms realizing the expressions

$$X = (WX + 1) \bmod x \qquad (3)$$
$$Y = (SY + 1) \bmod y \qquad (4)$$

where $x = y = 3$ in the example of the up–down counter [Fig. 1(a)].

If we express the coordinates X and $WX \in \{1,2,3\}$ in pure binary code, using the logic variables $X1:0$ and $WX1:0$, the simplification of the binary decision tree generates the structured subprogram of Fig. 7(b). An identical computation can be performed on the $Y = Y1:0$ coordinate described by (4).

Merging the subprogram GENE(X,Y) [Fig. 7(a)] and the two subprograms which implement the increment of X as in (3) and of Y as in (4) generates the final structured microprogram or genome for the example of the up–down counter [Fig. 7(c)].

C. NANOPASCAL: A High-Level Language for Structured Microprogramming

We will now define a programming language particularly well suited for the description, the interpretation and the duplication of the genome. This language, called NANOPASCAL for historical reasons, consists in fact of an absolutely minimal subset of the MODULA-2 language [15].

The NANOPASCAL language is described by the *syntactic diagram* of Fig. 8(a), where we can count seven distinct terminal symbols (ovals), which make up the instructions of the language

$$\{\text{begin}, \text{end}, \text{NOP}, \text{do}\ldots, \text{if}\ldots, \text{else}, \text{endif}\}. \qquad (5)$$

The pseudo-instruction **begin** is in fact never executed, and simply indicates the start of the program. The instruction **end** forces an unconditional jump to address "0" (this is in fact the only jump implemented by the language). The **NOP** (*No operation*) instruction represents the execution of a neutral operation. The assignment **do**... realizes the synchronous transfer REG$j \leftarrow$ OUT of a constant OUT in a register REG of address j. Since no jumps are allowed by the language, all of the instructions making up the conditional construct **if** a **then** P **else** Q (where a is a test variable and P and Q are assignments) are read, and the execution of P or Q depends on the value of a signal EXEC (for EXECUTE) which, in turn, depends on the preceding values of the test variable a.

As an example, Fig. 8(b) shows the shape of the mnemonic program GENOME, realizing choosen parts of the final microprogram [Fig. 7(a) and (b)] in the syntax of the NANOPASCAL language.

Writing the microprogram for a relatively large genome can be a bothersome endeavor. Therefore, we have developed two software tools which successively allow the following:

- the compilation, starting from the truth table of the genome (Fig. 1(a), for example), of the complete NANOPASCAL mnemonic program, including the computation of the X and Y addresses [Fig. 8(b)];

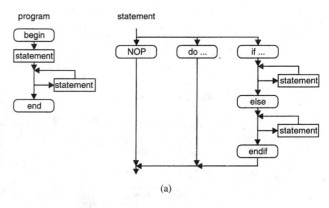

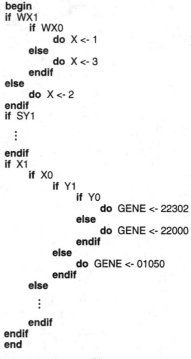

Fig. 8. NANOPASCAL language. (a) Syntactic diagram and (b) microprogram GENOME.

- the translation of the above-mentioned mnemonic program into a binary program directly executable by the interpreter (Section V-D).

D. NANOPASCALINE: An Interpreter for the NANOPASCAL Language

Fig. 9(a) suggests a possible format and operating code (OPC) for the six types of executable instructions of the NANOPASCAL language defined in (5). These six types of instruction are executed by a *binary decision machine* or *interpreter* of the NANOPASCAL language (NANOPASCALINE). It consists mainly of the following elements [Fig. 9(a)].

- A program memory RAM of 256 words of 8 bits.
- An address counter (CNT), whose output is the memory address ADR; ADR is incremented at each clock period (there are no jumps, with the exception of the instruction

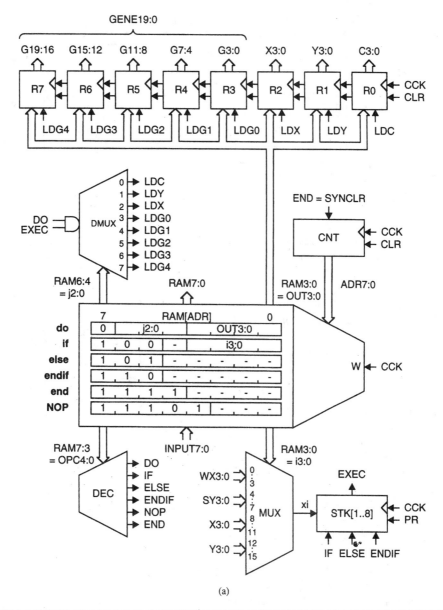

Fig. 9. NANOPASCALINE: NANOPASCAL interpreter. (a) Detailed architecture with format and operation code (OPC) for the six instructions of the language. (b) Stack operation table.

end which assures the jump to the address ADR = 0 through the signal SYNCLR = 1).

- Eight assignment registers of 4 bits each ($R7 \cdots R3$: GENE19:0; $R2$, $R1$: coordinates X, Y; $R0$: display). The selection of one register out of eight is made by a demultiplexer DMUX and will only be effective if both the following two conditions are met: 1) an instruction **do**... (signal DO=1) is being decoded and 2) the order of execution EXEC=1 is set. This last signal is crucial, and its value depends on the sequence of values of the test variable xi: the computation of the value of EXEC is performed by the stack STK described below.

- A stack STK of eight levels of 1 bit for the computation of the signal EXEC. If we call STK[1] the variable of the top level of the stack, and STK[2, $\cdots$, 8] the values of the levels below, then the table of Fig. 9(b) describes the global operation of the stack. The logic product

$$\begin{aligned}\text{EXEC} = &\,\text{STK}[1] \cdot \text{STK}[2] \cdot \text{STK}[3] \cdot \text{STK}[4] \cdot \text{STK}[5] \\ &\cdot \text{STK}[6] \cdot \text{STK}[7] \cdot \text{STK}[8] \end{aligned} \quad (6)$$

which controls the execution of the assignment instructions do REGj ←OUT depends therefore on the succession of values of the test variable xi.

- A multiplexer MUX which selects one out of 16 test variable xi.
- A decoder DEC, controlled by the five bits of the operating code OPC4:0, which will generate the signals controlling the address counter CNT (signal END), the demultiplexer DMUX (signal DO) and the STK (signals IF, ELSE, and ENDIF).

In conclusion, our NANOPASCALINE is limited to the computation of artificial organisms composed of at most $16 \times 16 = 256$ MUXTREE cells.

E. Conclusion

Our choice for the execution of the NANOPASCAL language is thus the following: the interpreter executes linearly all the instructions of the microprogram by incrementing the address ADR of the memory. The synchronous assignments REGj ←OUT are executed only if the signal EXEC, generated by the stack, is one. This choice provides two main advantages:

- the time of execution of the microprogram GENOME is constant and the same for all the cells;
- the duplication of the microprogram of a mother cell into an daughter cell can be executed in parallel with its interpretation (cellular division).

The time of execution of such a program is obviously greater than that of an equivalent program with jumps. This drawback is less important in our case, since the GENOME microprogram is active only during the configuration of the FPGA, and not during its operation.

VI. CELLULAR DIVISION: DUPLICATION OF THE GENOME

The duplication of the GENOME microprogram is accomplished automatically, in parallel with its interpretation. A register, controlled by the configuration clock CCK, is associated with the RAM in the NANOPASCALINE interpreter of each cell. At each rising edge of CCK, an instruction of the GENOME microprogram is copied into the cell through one of the SDATA or WDATA inputs selected by a physical jumper, manually set before start-up [Fig. 11(b)]. The copy of the instruction is then available on both of the NDATA and EDATA outputs.

The GENOME microprogram is thus duplicated in permanence, resulting in a great simplicity of wiring and an excellent reliability, since an eventual transient fault (copy error) during a cycle will be corrected in the next cycle.

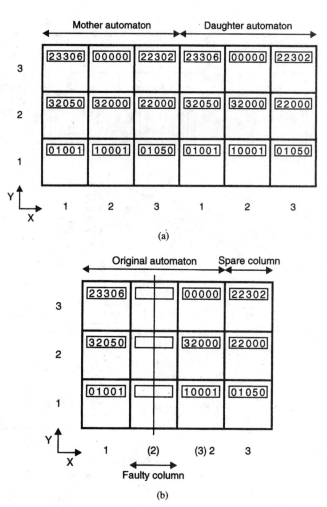

Fig. 10. Properties of the up–down counter. (a) Self-replication and (b) self-repair.

In the symbol of the NANOPASCALINE interpreter [Fig. 11(b)], KO = 1 characterizes a faulty cell.

VII. SELF-REPLICATION AND SELF-REPAIR PROPERTIES

A. Self-Replication

The self-replication of an artificial organism, for example the up–down counter of Fig. 1(a), rests on two hypotheses: 1) there exists a sufficient number of spare cells (unused cells at the right hand side of the array, at least three columns of three cells for our example) and 2) the calculation of the coordinates produces a cycle [$X = 1 \rightarrow 2 \rightarrow 3 \rightarrow 1$ in Fig. 7(b)].

As the same pattern of coordinates produces the same pattern of genes, self-replication can be easily accomplished if the microprogram GENOME, associated to the homogeneous network of cells, produces several occurrences of the basic pattern of coordinates [$X = 1 \rightarrow 2 \rightarrow 3$ and/or $Y = 1 \rightarrow 2 \rightarrow 3$ in Fig. 1(a)]. In our example, the repetition of the horizontal coordinate pattern, i.e., the production of the pattern $X = 1 \rightarrow 2 \rightarrow 3 \rightarrow 1 \rightarrow 2 \rightarrow 3$ [Fig. 10(a)], produces one copy, the *daughter automaton*, of the original or *mother automaton*. Given a sufficiently large space, the self-replication process can be repeated for any number of specimens, both

B. Self-Repair

Even if our long-term objective is the development of very large scale integrated circuits, we have started by realizing a demonstration system, based on *artificial digital cells* called BIODULES [Fig. 11(a)]. In this context, the existence of a fault is decided by the human user by pressing the KILL button of a cell. Therefore, fault detection and fault location, two features which will be indispensable in the final system, where they will be implemented using BIST (built-in self-test) techniques [1], [11]–[13], are not present in the BIODULES.

To implement self-repair, we have chosen, favoring simplicity, the following process [Figs. 10(b) and 11(a)]:

- pressing the KILL button identifies the faulty cell;
- the entire column to which the faulty cell belongs is considered faulty, and is deactivated (column $X = 2$ in Fig. 10(b) in the example of the up–down counter);
- all the functions of the application layer (MUXTREE) and of the configuration layers (NANOPASCALINE) of the column are shifted by one column to the right.

Obviously, this process requires as many spare columns, to the right of the array, as there are columns to repair [one spare column in the example of Fig. 10(b)]. It also implies some modifications to the application and configuration layers, so as to add the capability of jumping the faulty column and shifting to the right all or part of the original cellular array [Fig. 11(b)].

Finally, it should be mentioned that the final BIODULE [Fig. 11(a)] also realizes the series-parallel conversion of the data (DATA) and of the coordinates (X, Y) at the input, and the opposite conversion at the output. This conversion minimizes the number of connections between each BIODULE.

VIII. CONCLUSION

A. Results

The first result of our research is the development of a new family of FPGA's called MUXTREE and based on a fine-grained cell containing a multiplexer with one control variable. The original features of this FPGA are essentially the following:

- a completely homogenous organization of the cellular array;
- an integration of the routing into each cell, both for the short- and long-distance (bus) connections;
- a cell architecture allowing the direct mapping of binary decision diagrams onto the array.

The FPGA satisfies both the general hypothesis (Section II-A) and the first feature of the Embryonics project, that of multicellular organization (Section II-B). Two physical implementations have been realized: a prototype array of 240 cells, itself implemented using FPGA's of the ACTEL family, and a complementary metal–oxide–semiconductor (CMOS) integrated circuit containing 64 cells.

The second result is the realization of a quasi-biological cell based on an application layer (the MUXTREE cell) and two configuration layers computing, as a function of the local

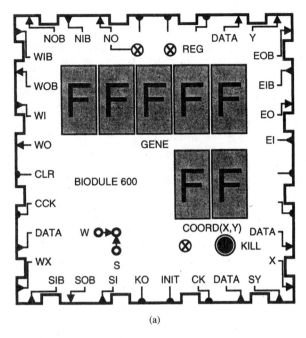

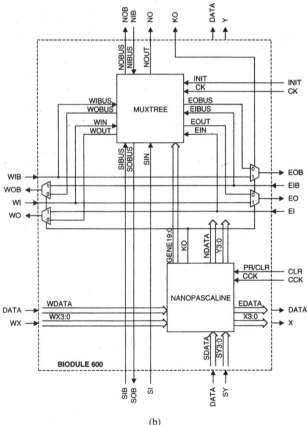

Fig. 11. BIODULE: demonstration artificial digital cell. (a) The front panel and (b) detailed architecture.

in the X and the Y axes. For a given cell, the dimensions of the artificial organism are limited in the first place by the coordinate space ($X = 0 \cdots 15$ and $Y = 0 \cdots 15$, that is, at most 256 cells in our implementation), and then by the dimensions of the RAM which will contain the GENOME microprogram (256 words of 8 bits in our case).

coordinates and of the genome, the specific gene controlling the application layer MUXTREE. The configuration layers are realized using a binary decision machine called NANOPASCALINE, which interprets the GENOME microprogram. The three layers of application and of configuration are finally embedded into a complete cell, implemented using an FPGA and a RAM, and then built as a demonstration module called BIODULE. We then show that an array of BIODULES satisfies the second and third features of the Embryonics project (Sections II-C and -D: cellular differentiation and division) and that it is endowed with the properties of self-replication and self-repair.

The interest of self-repair is immediately obvious, as this property allows the repair of isolated faults, for example, the fault of a single cell. The importance of self-replication is less evident, and can be justified by the following:

- the complete reconstruction of a device, in case of massive faults;
- the automatic realization of homogeneous 2-D cellular automata, by repetition of the same basic cell;
- the simplicity of moving a device in the cellular array by the simple alteration of the coordinates of the mother cell.

B. Future Perspectives

The main drawback of the BIODULE cell is the lack of balance between the application layer (MUXTREE), which realizes the universal function with a single variable, and the configuration layers (NANOPASCALINE), which store and interpret a rather complex microprogram. The development of a new coarse-grained FPGA cell will aim at correcting this imbalance [11]. The second drawback of the BIODULE, which is primarily a demonstration system, is the absence of a system for the detection and location of faults. While such a system could be implemented using relatively well-known techniques, we are trying to exploit the peculiar features of FPGA's (homogeneous cellular organization, possibility of reconfiguration) to obtain a BIST realization capable of being embodied into the integrated circuit which will finally have to possess all the computational power of an array of BIODULES [1], [11]–[13].

C. Historical and Theoretical Perspectives

The early history of the theory of self-replicating machines is basically the history of John von Neumann's thinking on the matter [7], [14]. Von Neumann's automaton is in accord with the general hypothesis outlined in Section II-A, as each of its elements is a finite state machine with 29 states. In his historic work [14], von Neumann successively showed that a possible configuration (a set of elements in a given state) of his automaton can implement a *universal constructor* endowed with the three following properties: constructional universality, self-replication of the universal constructor and self-replication of a universal calculator. In biology, the *cell* is the smallest part of a living being containing the complete blueprint of the being, the *genome*. On the basis of this definition, it can be shown that von Neumann's automaton is a *unicellular organism*, since it contains a single copy of the genome, i.e., the description of the universal constructor and computer [11]. Each element of the automaton is thus a part of the cell, or, in biological terms, a *molecule*. Von Neumann's automaton, therefore, is a *molecular automaton*, and universal construction and self-replication are complex processes, as they are caused by the interaction of thousands of elements, the molecules, each one realized by a finite state machine with 29 states.

Arbib [3] was the first to suggest a truly "cellular" automaton, in which every cell contains a complete copy of the genome, and a hierarchical organization, where each cell is itself decomposed into smaller and regular parts, the "molecules." Following this concept, the automaton we propose is a multicellular organism, as each of its elements contains a copy of the genome [nine copies in the case of the up–down counter of Fig. 1(a)]. Each element of our automaton is thus a *cell* in the biological sense, and our automaton is truly a *multicellular automaton*. Self-replication and self-repair are straightforward processes, as the BIODULE cell has been conceived especially to carry out globally the operations of cellular differentiation and division.

The property of *universal computation*, that is, the possibility of realizing, repairing, and replicating a universal Turing machine, can theoretically be verified with the BIODULE cell. But the implementation of such a machine will be strongly simplified by the creation of a second generation of cells, coarse-grained [10].

The property of *universal construction* poses problems of a different nature, since it requires (always according to von Neumann) that BIODULE cells be able to implement artificial organisms of any dimension. The finite dimensions of our cells (memories, registers, etc.) are, for the moment, preventing us from meeting this requirement, a challenge which remains one of our main concerns and which could be solved, according to Arbib's suggestion, by decomposing a cell into molecules.

REFERENCES

[1] M. Abramovici and C. Stroud, "No-overhead BIST for FPGA's," in *Proc. 1st IEEE Int. On-Line Testing Workshop*, July 1995, pp. 90–92.
[2] S. B. Akers, "Binary decision diagrams," *IEEE Trans. Comput.*, vol. C-27, pp. 509–516, June 1978.
[3] M. A. Arbib, *Theories of Abstract Automata*. Englewood Cliffs, NJ: Prentice Hall, 1969.
[4] R. E. Bryant, "Symbolic boolean manipulation with ordered binary-decision diagrams," *ACM Computing Surveys*, vol. 24, no. 3, pp. 293–318, 1992.
[5] M. Davio, J.-P. Deschamps, and A. Thayse, *Digital Systems with Algorithm Implementation*. New York: Wiley, 1983.
[6] S. Durand, "Muxchip," Logic Syst. Lab., Swiss Federal Inst. Technol., Lausanne, Switzerland, Tech. Rep., Oct. 1994.
[7] R. A. Freitas and W. P. Gilbreath, Eds., "Advanced automation for space missions," in *Proc. Nasa Conf.*, no. 2255, 1982.
[8] D. Mange, *Microprogrammed Systems: An Introduction to Firmware Theory*. London, U.K.: Chapman and Hall, 1992.
[9] D. Mange, "Teaching firmware as a bridge between hardware and software," *IEEE Trans. Educ.*, vol. 36, pp. 152–157, Mar. 1993.
[10] D. Mange, D. Madon, A. Stauffer, and G. Tempesti, "Von Neumann revisited: A turing machine with self-repair and self-replication properties," *Robot. Autonomous Syst.*, vol. 22, no. 1, pp. 35–58, 1997.
[11] D. Mange and M. Tomassini, Eds., *Bio-Inspired Computing Machines*. Lausanne, Switzerland: Polytechniques et Universitaires Romandes Press, 1998.
[12] E. J. McCluskey, *Logic Design Principles with Emphasis on Testable Semicustom Circuits*. Englewood Cliffs, NJ: Prentice Hall, 1986.

[13] G. Tempesti, D. Mange, and A. Stauffer, "A robust multiplexer-based FPGA inspired by biological systems," *J. Syst. Architecture*, vol. 43, no. 10, pp. 719–733, 1997.
[14] J. von Neumann, *Theory of Self-Reproducing Automata*. Urbana, IL: University of Illinois Press, 1966.
[15] N. Wirth, *Programming in MODULA-2, 2nd ed.* Berlin, Germany: Springer-Verlag, 1983.
[16] L. Wolpert, *The Triumph of the Embryo*. New York: Oxford University Press, 1991.

Daniel Mange (M'94) received the M.S. and Ph.D. degrees from the Swiss Federal Institute of Technology, Lausanne, Switzerland.

Since 1969, he has been a Professor at the Swiss Federal Institute of Technology. He held a position as Visiting Professor at the Center for Reliable Computing, Stanford University, Stanford, CA, in 1987. He is currently Director of the Logic Systems Laboratory, Swiss Federal Institute of Technology, and his chief interests include firmware theory (equivalence and transformation between hardwired systems and programs), cellular automata, artificial life, and embryonics (embryonic electronics).

Eduardo Sanchez (M'84) received the Diploma in electrical engineering from the Universidad del Valle, Cali, Colombia, and the Ph.D. degree from the Swiss Federal Institute of Technology, Lausanne, Switzerland.

He is Professor of Computer Science in the Logic Systems Laboratory, Swiss Federal Institute of Technology, where he is engaged in teaching and research. His chief interests include computer architecture, VLIW processors, reconfigurable logic, and evolvable hardware.

André Stauffer (S'68–M'69) received the Diploma in electrical engineering and the Ph.D. degree from the Swiss Federal Institute of Technology, Lausanne, Switzerland.

He spent one year as a Visiting Scientist at the IBM T. J. Watson Research Center, Yorktown Heights, NY, in 1986. He is a Senior Lecturer in the Department of Computer Science at the Swiss Federal Institute of Technology. In addition to digital design, his research interests include circuit reconfiguration and bio-inspired systems.

Gianluca Tempesti (M'95) received the B.S.E. degree in computer engineering from Princeton University, Princeton, NJ, in 1991 and the M.S.E. degree from the University of Michigan, Ann Arbor, in 1993.

Since 1994, he has been working as a Teaching and Research Assistant at the Logic Systems Laboratory in the Department of Computer Science, Swiss Federal Institute of Technology, Lausanne, Switzerland. His research interests include self-test and self-repair, programmable logic circuits, processor design, and parallel computer architecture.

Pierre Marchal (M'94) received the M.S. degree in computer science from the University of Grenoble, France, in 1980 and the Ph.D. degree in computer science from the Institut National Polytechnique, Grenoble, France, in 1983.

He joined the Microcomputing Laboratory of the Swiss Federal Institute of Technology, Lausanne, Switzerland, in 1987 and the Advanced Microelectronics Division of the CSEM Centre Suisse d'Electronique et de Microtechnique S.A., Neuchâtel, Switzerland, in 1991. He is presently involved in the design of low-power circuits, reconfigurable architectures, self-structuring circuits, and on-line arithmetics.

Christian Piguet received the M.S. and Ph.D. degrees in electrical engineering from the Swiss Federal Institute of Technology, Lausanne, Switzerland.

He is Head of the Ultra-Low-Power Sector at the CSEM Centre Suisse d'Electronique et de Microtechnique S.A., Neuchâtel, Switzerland. His main interests include the design of very low-power microprocessors, low-power standard cell libraries, gated-clock and low-power techniques, as well as asynchronous design.

CHAPTER EIGHT
Case Studies

Electronic and Firmware Design of the HP DesignJet Drafting Plotter 661
    A. H. Mebane IV, J. R. Schmedake, I.-S. Chen, and A. P. Kadonaga

Design and Implementation of a Robot Control System Using a Unified
Hardware-Software Rapid-Prototyping Framework 669
    M. B. Srivastava, T. I. Blumenau, and R. W. Brodersen

The Infopad Multimedia Terminal: A Portable Device for Wireless Information Access 673
    T. E. Truman, T. Pering, R. Doering, and R. W. Brodersen

A Processor-Coprocessor Architecture for High End Video Applications 688
    E. Maas, D. Hermann, R. Ernst, P. Rüffer, S. Hasenzahl, and M. Seitz

This chapter contains four practical case studies of industrial or academic designs that give insight into the problems of hardware/software design of embedded systems, into the engineering environment, and into design methodologies used.

The first case study, "Electronic and firmware design of the HP DesignJet drafting plotter," [Meb92] by Mebane *et al.*, is the oldest of the studies in this section, but the design process is in most aspects still up to date. The purpose of the HP DesignJet was to provide a fast monochrome output medium compatible with the family of HP pen plotters. The problem is divided into two parts, the vector-to-pixel conversion and the printer control. The vector-to-pixel conversion was necessary since the HP-GL language uses vectors to describe the lines that the pens have to draw. These lines must be converted to horizontal scans of an inkjet printer head. The printer control included print head and paper movements as well as the control of 50 ink nozzles, which had to be calibrated automatically.

The initial design decisions on the coarse architecture were based on a mixture of small experiments, expert knowledge, and intuitive estimations. The paper uses expressions like "The designer team felt..." to describe the decision process at this stage. The designers first selected the processor type based on the type of operations to be performed and on cost/performance estimations. Interestingly, they decided to include the vector-to-pixel translation problem in the printer specification—rather than executing it as PC software— because they expected that high computing performance for the printer control would be needed anyway. In other words, they modified the specification as a result of a design decision to add important features at low extra cost: a situation frequently found in embedded system design. It turned out, however, that the processor selection and the memory size were strongly influenced by the additional vector-to-pixel translation task when it came to implementation. A similar influence of design cost on specification is found in the printer interface design. The design team decided to remove some of the plotter interfaces from the specification. Instead, they adopted a technological feature from a successful laser printer design implementing only two widely used interfaces and an optional plug-in slot for less frequent interfaces. In total, this feature increased product flexibility. Another nonfunctional decision to improve design flexibility was the selection of a processor out of a family of processors that included pin-compatible higher performance processors—just in case it might have turned out that extra performance was necessary later. The memory design was completely driven by market and environment constraints.

When it came to printer control, the decision to use two microcontrollers was again based on architectural features, on availability, and on design time rather than on detailed analysis. This processor selection then laid the ground for the specifications of three ASICs. In summary, the architecture was developed in a stepwise approach, starting from the seemingly most important or obvious problem to the seemingly less critical parts of the architecture. Each of these decisions was based on experience and estimation, and each relied on the correctness of the previous one. This typical approach makes analysis and estimation critical tasks.

The designers used *virtual prototyping* to optically inspect the simulated printout. Such employment is a typical prototyping application. They also used prototyping for hardware design validation and software development by emulating the ASICs with programmable array logic (PAL) and field-programmable gate arrays (FPGAs). This process allowed the designer to debug the ASICs and to start software development before correct ASICs were available, thus reducing design time and risk.

The software architecture was based on an operating system in order to obtain better timing predictability (see Chapter 3, "Analysis and Estimation"). To improve software portability for future designs and to simplify debugging, the programming language C was used in most parts of the system. Mechanical engineers for the printer and printer head design and marketing people for the user interface design were involved in software development. They used their own languages and programming environments, another situation frequently found in hardware/software design of embedded systems.

The academic case study in "Design and implementation of a robot control system using a unified hardware-software rapid-prototyping framework" by Srivastava, Blumenau, and Brodersen [Sri92] is an early rapid-prototyping environment for a rather complex robotic control system. The application combines reactive tasks, (including the monitoring of numerous sensors for position, force, motor current, among others) and the control of the joint motor drivers, as well as transformative tasks such as the computation of optimized trajectories. The case study aimed at replacing the typical robot computing platform, which consisted of a homogeneous general-purpose multiprocessor and components off the shelf (COTS), with a dedicated hardware/software platform involving a much higher computing performance that supported more sophisticated control. The heterogeneous platform consists of four levels of hierarchy. The top-level UNIX workstation is connected to a second-level robot control CPU via Ethernet. The CPU is mounted on a single board and communicates with the robot control boards via the VME bus, a widely used standard bus for industrial control computers. The CPU runs VxWorks, a standard real-time operating system. The lower two levels contain custom VME boards, each consisting of a processor module (such as a digital signal processor [DSP] and hardware slave modules controlled by an on-board bus. The processor modules run a custom-operating system kernel. The slave modules consist of peripheral devices, analog-digital and digital-analog converters (ADC/DAC), and amplifiers and power electronics for sensors and actuators. Some of the modules contain FPGAs to implement hardware protocols and driver functions, such as pulse-width modulation (PWM). This quite heterogeneous hardware/software platform can be adapted at the board level by changing or adding VME bus boards.

The prototype design starts with a set of user-provided communicating processes, which describe the robot control system. The design environment includes compilers and software function libraries on the software side and several design tools for FPGA programming and VME board design on the hardware side. The input set of processes is manually mapped to a set of software processes, each running on one of the programmable processors of level 1, 2, or 3. Processes that shall be mapped to hardware modules are extended by a software "wrapper" process, which runs on a level 3 processor and communicates with the hardware module using a custom protocol. This way, all processes of the target architecture can use the same communication protocol, which greatly simplifies process remapping to a different hardware or software target architecture component. The authors report a very short design turn-around time of only two months.

"The InfoPad multimedia terminal: A portable device for wireless information access" [Tru98], by Truman *et al.*, presents different aspects of the InfoPad multimedia terminal designed at UC Berkeley. Several lightweight wireless terminals are connected to a fiber optic backbone network via a wireless base station. An important goal of the research project was to minimize power consumption of the wireless mobile terminal by appropriate design decisions at all levels, from function distribution between backbone network and wireless terminal to hardware/software architecture development, to logic design and power supply control. It pursues the idea of a very thin network client by moving as many computing and storage resources as possible from the wireless terminal to the compute and media servers on the backbone network. Because programmable processors typically have a significantly lower energy efficiency than custom hardware or even an FPGA when executing the same process, the designers decided to use programmable processors as little as possible. In the

InfoPad terminal, processors are mainly used for system control or for setup and to improve flexibility. A comparison to the previous case study shows that introducing a single constraint, namely limitation of power dissipation, resulted in a completely different architecture and design process.

The paper presents detailed power consumption data of the final design and discusses possible improvements of the architecture and the wireless communication protocol. This discussion combines "hard" data of the current design and other experiments with "soft" estimations in a spreadsheet type "what-if" analysis. As in the previous study, this discussion includes specification modification—this time the change of the wireless communication channel to a spread spectrum technique.

The fourth case study, "A processor-coprocessor architecture for high end video applications" [Maa97], by Maas *et al.*, presents an incremental design approach using an advanced hardware/software co-design system. Two video applications were implemented on a hardware platform consisting of a DSP multiprocessor, an FPGA, and several SRAM memory banks. Process specification, hardware/software partitioning, high-level transformations, and synthesis were executed iteratively to investigate to what extent video applications with high performance requirements can be implemented on such a platform. As in the previous papers, high-level estimation was needed, this time to guide manual code transformations aiming at memory access optimization.

The study showed that the DSP multiprocessor not only fell short on performance compared to the FPGA-based solution, but was even more difficult to use since program changes in the DSP multiprocessor required more manual code transformations than did the high-level synthesis tool used for FPGA configuration. Hence, from a designer's point of view, the FPGA provided more flexibility with regard to changes in specification than the DSP. This difference seriously affected design space exploration because it increased the design time on the software side, leading to a bias toward hardware implementation to cut iteration time. The result was a solution where most of the functionality was mapped to hardware, that is, the FPGA.

ADDITIONAL READINGS IN CASE STUDIES

[Hel99] R. Helaihel and K. Olukotun, "JMTP: An architecture for exploiting concurrency in embedded Java applications with real-time considerations," in *Proceedings, ICCAD 99*, IEEE, New York, 1999, 551–57. *Describes a multi-threaded processor designed to efficiently execute the Java Virtual Machine for real-time applications.*

[Jer99] T. Jeremiassen, "A DSP with caches—A study of the GSM-EFR codec on the TI C6211," in *Proceedings, ICCD 99*, IEEE Computer Society Press, Los Alamitos, 1999, 138–45. *Provides results of a series of experiments evaluating the effects of architectural features on the GSM-EFR speech codec.*

Electronic and Firmware Design of the HP DesignJet Drafting Plotter

High-performance vector-to-raster conversion and print engine control are provided by a RISC processor, two single-chip processors, and three custom integrated circuits. Development of the electronics and firmware made extensive use of emulation and simulation.

by Alfred Holt Mebane IV, James R. Schmedake, Iue-Shuenn Chen, and Anne P. Kadonaga

The HP DesignJet raster inkjet plotter project required contributions in the design of vector-to-raster conversion and print engine electronics. The project was constrained by cost and schedule, but the performance of the vector-to-raster converter and the inkjet print engine was considered of prime importance in meeting our user's needs. Our traditional approach to plotter electronics, while meeting cost and schedule goals, would have fallen short of the required performance goals. Existing electrostatic vector-to-raster converters, while meeting performance goals, were too expensive for our market. The approach we took was a fresh look at the requirements of both the vector-to-raster converter and the print engine.

Vector-to-Raster Converter
Two major tasks are performed by the vector-to-raster converter. The first is HP-GL/2 language parsing. The second is conversion of the parsed objects into the dot patterns printed on the page. In the DesignJet plotter, these two tasks are serial and do not occur simultaneously.

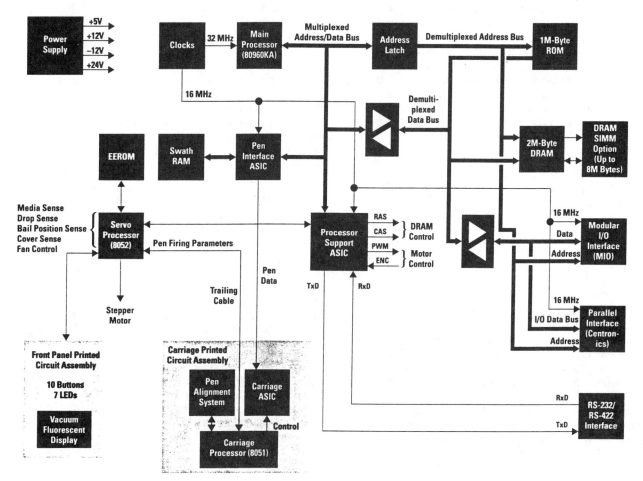

An early decision was made to include the vector-to-raster converter in the base machine electronics even though several low-cost competitive raster products omit this feature. The design team felt that a vector-to-raster converter could be integrated together with the print engine control logic at a reasonably low incremental cost. The major constraint placed upon this implementation was that it be of high enough performance to outpace the print engine in all but the most complex plots. It was acceptable to slow the print engine during very complex plots, but only for the affected carriage scans.

Initial investigations centered on the use of specialized graphics processors. These processors were more than adequate for the rasterization of lines, but were far too slow when parsing HP-GL/2. Next, an approach was investigated in which a general-purpose processor performed the parsing and print engine control while a graphics processor did only the raster conversion. The fundamental weakness of this approach is the cost of using two processors even though only one is required at any point in time.

The final design is based on a single, high-performance, RISC processor for both print engine control and the two vector-to-raster converter functions. The selection criteria were cost, a performance benchmark based on an existing HP-GL/2 parser, and an engineering estimation of potential raster conversion performance. The Intel 80960KA was selected from the available choices, which included both RISC and CISC microprocessors. Although they were not part of the original criteria, two other features of the 80960KA made it attractive in the DesignJet application. The first of these is the multiplexed address and data bus, which reduced the pin count on the application-specific integrated circuits (ASICs) that were being designed for the product (see "DesignJet ASIC Development" on page 18). The second is the existence of the 80960KB processor, which includes hardware floating-point capability. If at any time during the project the need for faster floating-point performance had arisen, the -KA version could have been replaced by the -KB version without any circuit board changes.

The remainder of the processor portion of the electronics consists of 2M bytes of DRAM, 1M byte of ROM, I/O, and DRAM memory expansion. A processor support ASIC in this section provides a DRAM controller, wait state timing for both RAM and ROM, interrupt control, and 80960 reset synchronization. This ASIC is described later in this article.

Fig. 1 is the electronic block diagram of the HP DesignJet plotter.

Input/Output
The DesignJet plotter was originally defined as a plotter solution for pen plotter users who require greater throughput on monochrome plots. This definition suggested incorporation of the three built-in I/O ports—RS-232-C, HP-IB (IEEE 488, IEC 625), and printer parallel—that are included in existing HP plotters. The DesignJet R&D team decided to pursue a more flexible approach. A strategy that had been adopted for the LaserJet IIISi printer was investigated in which there is no built-in I/O but instead a standardized, modular I/O slot (MIO) capable of accepting many different types of I/O options. After reviews with manufacturing and service representatives it was decided to keep the RS-232 and parallel interfaces built-in to allow the DesignJet plotter to leverage existing test and repair systems. The built-in HP-IB port has been replaced with an MIO slot to allow the DesignJet plotter to use some of the I/O options developed for the LaserJet IIISi. At introduction both the HP-IB and Novell Ethernet were available options.

Memory Expansion
One of the more difficult specifications to set for the DesignJet plotter was DRAM memory size. In a pen plotter, each vector is strobed out as it is received, so plotting can begin as soon as the first vector is parsed. The DesignJet plotter must parse and store all the incoming vectors before making the first carriage sweep. It is an inconvenient feature of vector languages that the last vector received may cross the portion of the page covered by the first carriage scan. This leads to a limitation on plot complexity based on the memory size available to store parsed vectors. The trade-off is the cost of memory versus the complexity of the possible plotted images. Hewlett-Packard electrostatic plotters solve this storage problem by means of magnetic disk storage. The drawbacks of a DesignJet implementation of a similar solution were cost and the difficulty of providing a mechanical mounting to allow a disk drive to survive the shipping and operating environments expected for the DesignJet plotter. The chosen solution is industry-standard, 72-pin single inline memory modules (SIMMs). This memory is added in the form of 1M-byte or 4M-byte SIMMs, which are available from HP for a variety of products in the personal computer and peripheral areas. Two sockets are available under a panel in the rear of the plotter. Addition of two 4M-byte SIMMs gives a user an additional 8M bytes of vector storage for complex plots. The use of SIMMs for memory expansion adds very little cost for users with needs fitting into the standard 2M-byte RAM and provides a relatively low-cost upgrade path for users requiring more.

Print Engine Control
Print engine control is a much less demanding task than vector-to-raster conversion. Print engine control includes two-axis servo motor control, front-panel control, keyboard scanning, front-panel display update, optical sensor scanning, and thermal inkjet pen service station control.

The servo motor control functions of position decoding and pulse width modulation of the motor voltage were added to the processor support ASIC. The other functions required mostly pins with very little logic, so alternatives were investigated that could implement them more efficiently. The result of this investigation is an approach that surprised most of the design team. A single-chip processor, the Intel 8052, was able to perform these functions with a lower production cost than an ASIC and for a fraction of the development cost. It also performs all of the real-time servo control, offloading this from the 80960KA.

The 8052 is designed into the architecture as a slave processor to the 80960KA. A bidirectional command and mailbox port is implemented in the processor support ASIC to allow processor-to-processor communication. Through this port the 8052 is able to return data to the 80960KA in response to commands or to generate one of several interrupts. Among these interrupts is the operating system time slice interrupt.

A vast portion of print engine control is the electronics required to support the thermal inkjet pens. The most difficult function performed in this area is the mapping from the image generated in memory by the vector-to-raster converter to the series of timing pulses sent to fire the pens. This task is made difficult by the fact that the DesignJet plotter uses two 50-nozzle pens that are not accurately aligned mechanically with each other. The mapping and alignment compensation are performed by two ASICs, one located on the main board and a companion part located on the circuit board that travels on the pen carriage. The two ASICs are connected by a serial link that runs through the trailing cable. The pen interface ASIC on the main board is initialized with the measured distances between the two pens and is able to select from image memory all the dot positions that are covered by pen nozzles at a given carriage position. As the carriage scans across the page, this ASIC sends groups of 100 bits up the serial link to the carriage ASIC at 1/300-inch intervals. The carriage ASIC buffers the 100 bits and creates the timing patterns used as inputs to the drivers that generate the firing waveforms for the thermal inkjet pens.

Pen Calibration

Offsets between the two pens are measured by another set of electronics located on the carriage board (see article, page 24). DesignJet pens are aligned by drawing a series of patterns on a page and then using an optical sensor to measure the relationship of patterns drawn with one pen to the patterns drawn by the other. These offsets are written to the thermal inkjet support ASICs as described in the paragraph above. The electronic components of the optical system are controlled by an 8051 microprocessor located on the carriage board. The decision to use the 8051 on the carriage is based on the same criteria used to select the 8052 for the main board—the 8051 can perform the sensor control functions at a lower part cost and a much lower development cost than a special-purpose ASIC. An added feature gained by using the 8051 is that it provides the serial communication path to the 8052 on the main board. This communication path is used both for the optical system and for sending pen firing constants to the ASIC on the carriage.

DesignJet ASIC Development

Often the custom IC design is in the critical path of electronic systems development. This was the case for the HP DesignJet plotter project. Three ASICs were needed to provide the necessary functionality and performance in the DesignJet plotter at a low cost.

The main challenges were clear right from the beginning. The team had to deliver three working ASICs on schedule. A turnaround in any of the ASICs would have meant a serious schedule slip, since the fully functional ASICs were needed to start much of the system-level testing. The team also had to provide the functionality of these ASICs before the first silicon became available to enable parallel development of the printer mechanisms and firmware. These needs had to be met with a limited number of engineers and a given budget to avoid adversely affecting other projects.

Processor Support ASIC

The processor support ASIC interfaces to both the main processor (80960KA) and the servo processor (8052) and performs various assist functions for each processor. The block diagram of the IC is shown in Fig. 2. The main processor side of the processor support ASIC consists of the 80960KA interface, the DRAM controller, the serial I/O interface, and the fire pulse controller. On the servo processor side, the IC contains the 8052 interface and the motion controller. The processor support ASIC also provides two modes of communication between the processors: a polled, bidirectional mailbox and an interrupt-driven, unidirectional block transfer buffer.

The 80960KA interface assists the processor during burst-mode ROM and DRAM accesses and handles the queueing and prioritizing of the incoming interrupts. The DRAM controller supports up to 20M bytes of memory of different sizes

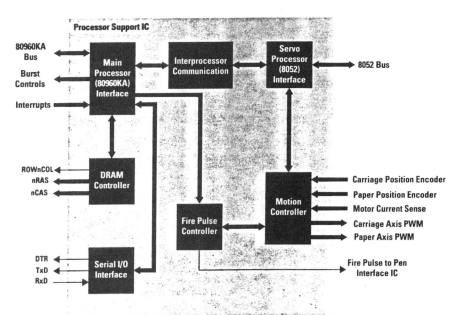

Fig. 2. Processor support ASIC block diagram.

and access times. The serial I/O interface consists of a baud rate generator and a UART (universal asynchronous receiver/transmitter). The fire pulse controller generates a synchronizing pulse for each column of pen data. The output is extrapolated from the carriage position encoder counts at one, two, or four times the frequency.

The motion controller decodes the position information for the carriage and paper axes. It also generates the PWM (pulse width modulation) signals for the dc motor drivers as needed for servo control of the carriage and paper axes. A watchdog timer monitors the servo loop and disables the PWM outputs in the event of a servo processor malfunction. A status register is also provided to log various motion control error conditions.

Pen Interface ASIC
A shuffler stage is needed to map the row-oriented image data into the column-oriented DeskJet pen nozzle data. In a departure from previous shuffler designs, the pen interface ASIC uses a dedicated external memory array to store its own copy of the image data and a programmable internal sequencer array to hold the shuffle pattern. The shuffling is done by copying an entire swath of image data from the system memory into its local memory and fetching the pixel data for each pen fire sequence according to the preloaded shuffle pattern. This approach offloads these tasks from the main processor bus and allows greater flexibility for supporting different pen nozzle configurations.

The pen interface ASIC contains three bus interfaces: the main processor (80960KA) bus, the swath memory interface, and the serial link to the carriage ASIC. The block diagram of the pen interface ASIC is shown in Fig. 3. In the copy mode, the data and address path from the main processor interface to the swath memory is enabled. The pixel counter counts the number of pixels to be printed, and its output is used to calculate the plot density and ink use. In the shuffle mode, the path from the swath memory to the serial interface is enabled. The serial data transmitter assembles the pixel data fetched from the swath memory for each fire sequence into a serial bit stream and sends it to the carriage ASIC. The pen interface ASIC and the carriage ASIC contain identical pixel checksum counters to check the integrity of the serial transmission.

The pixel address generator is the heart of the pen interface ASIC. It consists of an SRAM array for the programmable sequencer, a logical column counter, and an adder. The sequencer is preloaded with the pixel address offsets for each pen nozzle of a fire sequence. The offsets contain the column adjustment delays for pen alignment correction (see article, page 24). A mask pattern is tagged onto each entry to aid different print modes. The column counter is either incremented or decremented depending on the print direction, and its content is added to the pixel address offset from the sequencer to generate the physical DRAM address of each pixel's data.

Carriage ASIC
The carriage ASIC resides on the printed circuit board that is mounted on the moving pen carriage assembly. Its primary function is to generate the data and address signals for the pen driver ICs. The relative timing and the pulse widths of these signals are carefully controlled to adjust the pen-to-pen offsets, the bidirectional offsets, the pen-to-paper-axis deviation errors, and the pen turn-on energy variations.

The carriage ASIC contains three bus interfaces: the carriage processor (8052) bus, the serial link from the pen interface ASIC, and the pen driver IC interface. The block diagram of the IC is shown in Fig. 4. The processor bus is used to access the timing control registers. The serial data from the pen interface ASIC is shifted into a serial-to-parallel converter. A checksum counter monitors the serial input data to verify the integrity of the serial link. A parallel pipeline register follows the shift register to provide the double column buffering. The buffer outputs are divided into four delayed pipeline registers, each of which is delayed by the value in its corresponding delay time register. Each of the four data

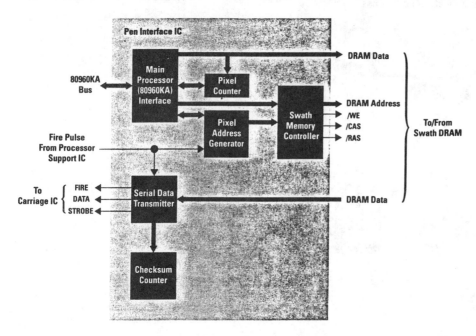

Fig. 3. Pen interface ASIC block diagram.

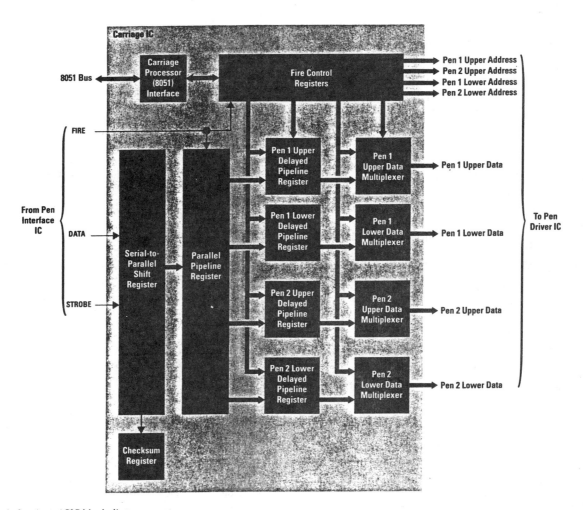

Fig. 4. Carriage ASIC block diagram.

multiplexers selects the data to be driven for one half of each pen.

Design Approach and Tools

Behavioral Simulation. The shuffler algorithm implemented in the pen interface ASIC and the carriage ASIC is a completely new design for any HP product. The shuffle path from the image data in the system memory to the pen outputs includes many hardware blocks and spans several different bus interfaces. The need to verify the correctness of the shuffler algorithm at a high level before any hardware design was apparent. A behavioral model of the algorithm was written in the C programming language. A graphics driver was added for both the input image data and the pen outputs. A complete graphical animation showed both the image data and the printed data as the pen swept across the screen. Any error in the shuffler algorithm was observable right on the display screen. This high-level verification approach turned out to be very valuable. The shuffler algorithm was completely debugged during the simulation phase before any hardware was designed.

Emulator Strategy. It was decided to build emulators for the three ASICs despite the substantial amount of additional resources required. As mentioned earlier, the functionalities of the ICs were needed before first silicon to enable parallel development of the printer mechanisms and the firmware. The emulators were able to meet this need. If there had been a major bug in the first silicon, the emulators could have continued to provide the necessary hardware platform at least for firmware development if not for further mechanical integration and system testing. Another important consideration was that in the absence of a system-level simulator, the emulators combined with the rest of the electronics supplemented the chip-level simulation in the overall functional verification effort. The emulators also proved very useful in isolating and diagnosing anomalies encountered while integrating the first silicon into the system.

The emulator for each IC presented a unique set of design requirements. The major problem for the processor support ASIC was the schedule because of its late start and complexity. To keep pace with the other two ASICs, much of the emulator and IC design was done in parallel. The emulators for both the processor support ASIC and the pen interface ASIC required fast, hence low-density, PAL (programmable array logic) parts to meet the 16-MHz clock frequency requirement. The processor support ASIC emulator consisted of fast PALs, standard logic parts, and a UART. The pen interface ASIC emulator used fast PALs for most of the logic and a high-speed SRAM for the pixel address sequencer. The swath DRAM parts, which reside outside of the IC, were also included in the emulator to avoid electrical problems related to board interconnects. The requirements of the carriage ASIC emulator were a large number of registers and a small board area. The slower clock frequency of 12 MHz allowed the use of high-density field-programmable gate arrays, which offered a large number of flip-flops per part.

Vendor Selection. After a preliminary screening of many ASIC suppliers, several vendors of both standard cell and gate array parts were closely evaluated. In addition to nonrecurring engineering charges, cost per part, and prototype lead time, also considered were the availability and cost of the hardware and software toolset, the quality of the technical support during development, and expected responsiveness after release to production. We decided that all three ASICs would use the same vendor and toolset for both technical and logistical reasons. We chose the CMOS34 standard-cell technology of the HP Circuit Technology Group, which offered the LogicArchitect ASIC development toolset, some of which is described below in more detail. The vendor also delivered the UART megacell for the processor support ASIC and the SRAM array for the pen interface ASIC.

Logic Synthesis. A logic synthesis tool was used extensively for transforming the control logic into the standard cells. The automation of this laborious task not only saved much time during the initial mapping of the logic into a combination of gates but also reduced the number of iterations through the compose-verify-correct loop. The synthesis tool was also used to generate the custom registers, decoders, and multiplexers. This approach was preferred over the use of TTL macro cells* because it made it possible to implement only the necessary functions using minimum-area cells. TTL macro cells were used for such blocks as counters, where they could be modified to provide only the necessary functions with the minimum-area cells.

The synthesis tool also offered area-versus-delay optimization capability, but this was of limited use for most blocks because the CMOS34 process is fast relative to the clock frequencies of 16 MHz and 12 MHz. In many cases, setting the area constraint at minimum sufficed. The exceptions were in control blocks where both the rising and falling edges of the clock were used, effectively doubling the frequency, and some critical timing path blocks. For these blocks, the delay constraint was set as needed with some margin. The worst path delay estimates included in the report files were useful in quickly verifying the timing margins at the block level.

Timing Analysis. Unlike a functional simulator, which requires a set of test vectors to exercise the circuit to verify the delay timing, a static timing analyzer calculates the delays through the specified paths based on the circuit structure alone. The static timing analyzer of the LogicArchitect toolset complemented the functional simulator by rapidly searching through the circuit delay paths before any test vectors were written. It was used to identify any unexpected critical timing paths and to verify the margins in the known critical timing paths. This tool was especially useful in determining the margins in input setup times and output delay times with respect to the clock edges.

Functional Simulation. As expected, the functional simulation took a major chunk of the total IC design time. A test vector generation interface in the LogicArchitect toolset saved a

---

* Most ASIC vendors offer macro cells for widely used off-the-shelf logic parts such as TTL parts. A macro cell is a collection of library standard cells and interconnections that performs the same function as the corresponding off-the-shelf logic part.

great deal of time by allowing the test vectors to be assembled from the subroutine functions and macros. Distributing the simulation jobs among various workstations also helped. Although the blocks were simulated at all levels in a bottoms-up order, the emphasis was different at each level. For example, once a comparator was verified at a low level with a semiexhaustive set of input combinations, it was not subjected to another input combinations test at a higher level. Instead, more time was spent exercising its interaction with the control logic. At the top level, special care was taken to set the correct input and output timing values and to choose the right types of load and delay models. A full set of top-level test vectors was repeated with the capacitance values extracted from the layout, and a special check of paths with potential skews was done.

Design for Testability. Three types of test support circuitry are designed into the DesignJet ASICs: scan paths for the automatic generation of the stuck-at fault test vectors, a boundary scan path in the carriage ASIC, and pad tristate control for the board testers. The HP CMOS34 standard cell methodology offers automatic test generation capability for stuck-at faults. The estimated hardware overhead for providing the necessary scan paths was about 10%. The designers of all three ASICs decided to support automatic test generation to achieve the highest possible fault coverage with the minimum of test vector generation effort. The scan paths were created by replacing each flip-flop with a scannable type and providing scan controls. Special controls were designed for the flip-flops clocked on the opposite edge of the clock, for bidirectional buses, and for asynchronous signals. A boundary scan path is implemented in the carriage ASIC to drive the output pads directly, bypassing the complicated internal configuration. The tristate control is provided for all pad drivers on each ASIC to allow the board tester to drive the IC pins directly.

ASIC Results

The DesignJet ASIC development team delivered the three fully functional ASICs on schedule. All three ASICs were released to manufacturing without any design changes. The processor support ASIC, packaged in an 84-pin PLCC (plastic leadless chip carrier), has the equivalent of 11,000 gates and a die area of 4.96 by 5.90 mm. (One equivalent gate represents four transistors needed to implement a two-input NAND gate.) The pen interface ASIC, also packaged in an 84-pin PLCC, came in at 4,000 gates and a die area of 4.87 by 5.56 mm, including the SRAM array. The carriage ASIC, packaged in a 68-pin PLCC, has a final gate count of 10,000 and a die area of 4.92 by 5.24 mm.

Each ASIC was successfully integrated into the system within a day of the arrival of the first silicon. This was possible partly because the system was already debugged using the ASIC emulators. With further code development later, a few corner-case problems that required minor firmware workarounds were uncovered. No other functional or electrical problems were found. This proved that our design approaches and the toolset were basically sound, but needed improvement in testing the corner cases. Even with the IC emulators, the corner-case testing was difficult because the code development continued well past the IC tape release. A collaborative effort by the ASIC and firmware designers involving their respective toolsets would help develop a better functional verification strategy. The design for testability allowed quick destaffing of the ASIC design team because no additional fault coverage test vectors were needed after the tape release.

DesignJet Firmware Development

The use of the Intel 80960KA processor in the DesignJet plotter created several development challenges for the firmware design team. First, hardware to exercise the code would not be available for several months after coding had begun. Second, the 80960 was a new processor to our division, so we needed to start almost from scratch on our development system. Third, we had extremely limited personnel resources and time to perform the necessary tasks. In the past, a main source of schedule investment was in the integration of independently developed code sections and the correction of timing problems between these independent sections of code. In addition, we generally spent much time tuning (if not totally redesigning) the user interface of the plotter once the code was integrated into the target. For the DesignJet project, we needed to minimize this largely nonproductive use of time. The solution was to build a development environment that was largely independent of the hardware, to leverage code and algorithm designs from outside groups, and to debug our code at the source level on both the target and host (simulator) systems. To ease integration and help with timing-related bugs, we chose to use an internally developed full-featured operating system.

Development Environment

The DesignJet development environment was different from any environment our division had used in the past. On past projects, almost all firmware engineers used a target-based emulator for all development work. Hardware was generally reused from past projects to run the emulators in an environment that closely matched the new system. Much of our past work had been done in assembly language. Therefore, the use of emulators was really a method of "source-level" debugging. On the DesignJet plotter project, our lack of hardware limited the use of emulators. In addition, there were no emulators available that interfaced with our HP 9000 Series 300 workstations, which were used for compiling and linking. These restrictions forced us to reconsider our past development methods. We decided that our code should run, as much as possible, on both our target system and our workstations. Since our coding was to be almost 100% in the C language, we maintained object modules compiled both for the target and workstation, or host, systems. Only where there were differences between the two systems was there any additional code to support the host system.

The main difference between the host and target systems was in the I/O and print engine subsystems. The I/O subsystem was easily modified to accommodate a host-based development system. The main input path was set up such that when running on the host, input was done from the host file system rather than a Centronics or RS-232 port. None of the code outside of one function "knew" where input was originating. The print engine that ran on the target was almost identical to the print engine on the host. The main difference was where to send data to print. On the target, hardware was the destination of completed bands, or swaths, of print engine data. On the host, a simulator was used. We obtained an X Window-based simulator that we were able to modify for our use on the DesignJet plotter. The simulator was passed an array of bitmap swaths, and when so instructed, opened an X Window on the workstation to display the data. The simulator had the ability to highlight individual swaths, scale the bitmap, and zoom in on specified areas of the bitmap. This allowed inspection of plotter output at the individual dot level, something that would have been next to impossible to do accurately on the target system. The simulator allowed all development of nontarget-specific code to be done on the host, especially debugging using cdb and xdb.

Large-format plotters require much interaction with the user, particularly in the areas of front-panel control and media loading. The front panel was developed with the aid of a front-panel simulator that ran on a PC. This important area of the user interface was then designed independently of the hardware and firmware of the plotter. The front-panel simulator was designed such that nonfirmware personnel, such as marketing and user interface experts, could design and finetune their own front panel. This freed a firmware engineer to work on other tasks.

The media-loading interaction was also subject to a great deal of modification. The basic loading algorithms were developed by mechanical engineers on simple breadboard mechanics. These generic motor controllers allow nonfirmware engineers to control motors precisely with simple HP-GL-like instructions from any computer. Typically, a mechanical engineer wrote BASIC programs on an HP 9000 Series 200 computer to develop media-loading sequences and algorithms. The generic motor controllers have general-purpose inputs and outputs, thus allowing the development engineers access to sensors and actuators as desired. Offloading these types of development activities allowed the firmware engineers to focus on software engineering problems. When algorithms were basically complete, the mechanical engineers documented their work graphically, allowing the firmware engineer to translate the algorithm into the DesignJet framework.

Code Reuse

A major portion of any printer or plotter is the language subsystem, in our case HP-GL/2. On the DesignJet plotter, we clearly did not have the resources to reinvent this wheel. We were able to use a language subsystem developed at our division that had been previously used on several products, including the LaserJet III printer. This proved to be extremely beneficial in several respects. Certainly, the time spent integrating this code was much less than would have been necessary to rewrite it. The most beneficial aspect, however, was that far less time was needed in testing because the code had already been thoroughly tested and debugged in previous products. This gave us the high-quality language subsystem that we wanted with a minimum of investment in time from our product team. A second area that was heavily leveraged was the vector-to-raster converter. The basic high-performance design that had been used in other raster products from HP was leveraged for the DesignJet plotter. While the original vector-to-raster converter was written in assembly language, we chose to rewrite the code in C. The previous products had used a different processor, so rewriting the code was necessary anyway. Using C, reuse in future products would be far easier no matter what processor might be chosen.

Debugger
The lack of emulators on the target system required the use of a new tool for our division: the retargetable remote debugger. We found that the GNU debugger, gdb960, worked very well on our system. gdb960 was developed by both The Free Software Foundation and Intel for use on the 80960. This source-level debugger uses a simple monitor on the target system while the main debugger runs on the host. Communication for debugging is via RS-232. We modified the monitor code so that we could download executable modules to the target system via our built-in Centronics interface. The monitor program, NINDY, was supplied by Intel and modified by us for our hardware. The modifications were minimal and were only in those areas of the code that dealt with serial I/O and downloading. The download capability was modified because the default method, RS-232, was too slow. With Centronics downloading, we were able to cut download times from about 10 minutes to about 10 seconds.

Using gdb960, we were able to resolve problems that appeared only on the target very quickly. The debugger functions much the same as the debugger cdb of the HP-UX* operating system. With our remote-reset and login capability, we were able to debug target-executing code from home on those nights when long hours were called for. The debugger is completely source-level; that is, breakpoints are set on C source lines, not particular addresses. Structures and arrays print as such; there is no need to examine memory addresses and reconstruct the data types of interest. If a bug manifested itself as a processor fault, the debugger showed us the entire stack frame and allowed us to move about within stack frames. This enabled us to find the real source of a problem, which was often several stack frames up from the fault itself. In short, debugging on the target was generally no more trouble than debugging on the host.

Operating System
At the outset of our design cycle, we determined that use of a formal operating system would be beneficial in two ways. First, it would provide a stable interface for interprocess communication. This would ease the process of integrating code that had been developed independently by several firmware engineers. Second, since the operating system we used was a preemptive operating system, timing problems typical of custom operating systems would be greatly reduced. Rather than invest in methods and hardware to debug complex timing problems, we decided to invest in an operating system that would prevent these problems. While sounding overly simplistic, this logic turned out to be quite accurate; we had very few timing-related problems. In addition, when hardware became available, code integration went very smoothly. There were very few problems with interface specifications changing because the operating system defined the interface.

The operating system was developed independently using a PC-based development board supplied by Intel. When hardware became available, the operating system was fully debugged and ready to install. The operating system is written in assembly language, translated from code that runs on the HP 9000 Series 300 workstations. This was another major subsystem for which we leveraged the design. The benefit of the operating system running on both the host and the target is obvious; the underlying code has no knowledge of its operating environment.

Firmware Summary
The development process of the DesignJet firmware was unlike any other project at the San Diego Division. Code was developed in a largely hardware-independent fashion. We strove to eliminate system timing problems through the use of a formal operating system. This had the additional benefit of defining a strict, stable interface between processes. The user interfaces of the plotter were developed by experts separate from the firmware design team. Debugging was accomplished using cdb on the host and gdb960 on the target. These debuggers provided source-level interfaces that greatly enhanced the engineers' productivity. The language subsystem consisted of a reusable code base, and the vector-to-raster converter subsystem we produced will be reused in future products. We believe that our development methodology was a key factor in meeting our project's goals.

Conclusion
The DesignJet plotter electronics provide a high-performance raster plotting system at a very aggressive price. The distribution and selection of ASICs and processors enabled us to design a robust, flexible, and cost-effective system. This design not only meets current customer needs, but contains the features necessary for leverage into future raster products.

Acknowledgments
We would like to acknowledge contributions by other members of the electronics and firmware teams: Curt Behrend, Craig Bosworth, Jack Cassidy, Keith Cobbs, George Corrigan, David Ellement, Diane Fisher, Milt Fisher, Dan Johnson, Tom Halpenny, Bob Haselby, Janet Mebane, Kent Takasuki, Teri Tracey and Irene Williams. In particular, we would like to thank the DesignJet firmware and language reuse group for being open to new development methodologies. We would also like to acknowledge our electronics project manager, Larry Hennessee, for providing the creative and productive environment, and our firmware manager, Jennie Hollis, for allowing us the freedom the explore new ideas. Our thanks also go to our ASIC partners at the HP Circuit Technology Group: Kwok Cheung, Bert Frescura, and others.

HP-UX is based on and is compatible with UNIX System Laboratories' UNIX* operating system. It also complies with X/Open's* XPG3, POSIX 1003.1 and SVID2 interface specifications.

UNIX is a registered trademark of UNIX System Laboratories Inc. in the U.S.A. and other countries.

X/Open is a trademark of X/Open Company Limited in the UK and other countries.

Design and Implementation of a Robot Control System Using a Unified Hardware-Software Rapid-Prototyping Framework

Mani B. Srivastava, Trevor I. Blumenau, and Robert W. Brodersen
EECS Department, University of California at Berkeley

Abstract

The increasing complexity of applications and the relative maturity of CAD tools for ASIC design have made design aids for the higher-level aspects of system design essential. We have developed a unified framework for the rapid-prototyping of hardware and software for application-specific systems. This framework is fully described in [1]. The application of the framework to the development of a real-time multi-sensory robot control system is described in this paper.

1.0 Introduction

The integration of heterogenous hardware, software, and electromechanical components to form a complete system presents a challenging design problem. Computer-aided design techniques are quite primitive at the system level when compared to those available at the chip level. Previous research in CAD has primarily concentrated on the design of individual application-specific ICs (ASICs) and has avoided taking a *systems* perspective of the design process.

Motivated by this we have been developing a CAD framework for the rapid-prototyping of application-specific systems that provides support for the design of not just chips, but boards and software as well. Details about the CAD framework can be found elsewhere [1].

In this paper we present the design of a real-time multi-sensory robot control system using our system rapid-prototyping framework. The key features of the computer-aided system design methodology offered by our framework are exemplified through this system. The system controls, in real-time, a six-degree of freedom articulated robot arm using position, force, and proximity sensing.

In addition to the novel system design methodology, another key aspect of the robot control system is the extensive use of special-purpose dedicated hardware, made feasible by our system-level rapid-prototyping framework. This provides much improved performance over commercial and other research robot control systems that are largely based around general-purpose computers.

2.0 Framework for rapid-prototyping of hardware and software

We have implemented a design framework [1] for dedicated board-level systems which uses a unified view for the hardware and software components that make up a system. As shown in Figure 1, and elaborated in the following subsections, a high-level specification of the system is implemented as a set of custom printed-circuit boards using a mix of software programmable and non-programmable hardware and ASICs, going through steps of architecture mapping, board-level hardware module and system software module generation.

2.1 System specification

The target system is viewed by the user as a parameterized, static, hierarchical network of sequential processes that operate concurrently, and interact using a well defined communication mechanism. Systems of interest to us, such as a robot controller or a speech recognizer, possess a large granularity parallelism, and are naturally expressed as a static set of processes communicating via message queues. This is also evident from the fact that the system software for such systems ends up looking like a custom distributed real-time OS. Communication is done using FIFO channels that connect input and output ports on the processes.

2.2 Architecture mapping

In architecture mapping each process in the original description is mapped either to a *software process* running on a programmable processor module, or to a *hardware process* running on a dedicated custom hardware module. A template mapping based approach is used in which the process network is partitioned to a parameterized architecture template. The template parameters and the partitioning are manually specified, although the h/w-s/w partitioning technique presented in [2] may be adaptable to automate part of this process.

The architecture template, shown in Figure 2, has a layered, distributed architecture with a hierarchical bus organization for increased bandwidth. There are four layers in the architecture. The bottom two layers of the hierarchy are spanned by custom boards. Each custom board has one or more programmable processor modules running a real-time OS kernel, and coordinating a number of application-specific slave modules with standard hardware and software interfaces. These slave modules form the lowest layer of the hierarchy, and can be either dedicated custom hardware modules or dedicated software programmable modules. The custom boards reside on a back-plane bus, and are slaves to another processor module running a real-time OS which forms the second layer of the hierarchy. The processing modules on the custom boards communicate and synchronize with the master layer 2 processing module using a standard hardware interface and software protocol. The topmost layer of the hierarchy is formed by a UNIX workstation that communicates with the layer 2 processor over a network using standard protocols. Computation power, the communication bandwidth, and the ability to meet real-time constraints increase as one goes down this layered architecture template.

2.3 Board-level hardware modules

The framework provides several board-level module generation aids to the user. We use the same database and design management tools as we use for ASICs, so that the various pre-existing ASIC generation tools are naturally available as special case board-level module generators. This includes a silicon assembler (LAGER [3]), a silicon compiler (C-to-Silicon [4]), and a behavioral-synthesis system (HYPER [5]).

A key component of our board-level hardware module generation strategy is a very extensive library of reusable parameterized board level sub-system modules. This includes a variety of complete processor modules, memory subsystems, data acquisition subsystems, bus interface modules, fiber optic communication modules, testing modules etc. For example, a TMS320C30 processor module in the library provides a complete microcomputer based around a powerful DSP whose configuration in terms of memory organization, I/O devices, and host interface is parameterized.

This library enables sub-system level reusability, and is essential in supporting the architecture template strategy described earlier. The system architecture template is essentially a parameterized network of library modules.

To facilitate the design of board level modules, a structural description language with lisp-based parameterization facilities, tools to do board level automatic/interactive/user-specified/tiling-based placement and routing, and a tool to map a behavioral description to a netlist of programmable devices, such as FPGAs, are also provided. An interface synthesis system ALOHA [6] has been integrated to provide the ability to synthesize interfaces between various modules such as a cpu-memory interface or a VME bus interface.

2.4 System software modules

Many processes in the original process network description of the system are implemented as software processes. Several of these software processes can map to a processor module.

To allow a uniform mapping of these software processes to the vari-

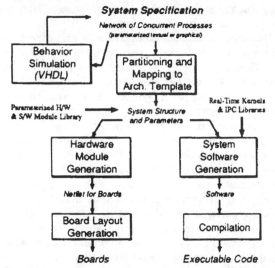

FIGURE 1: Overview of the CAD Framework for System-Level Design.

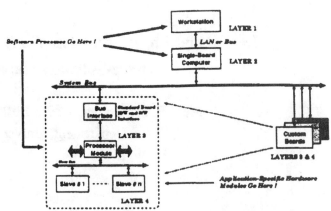

FIGURE 2: Layered Architecture Template.

ous programmable processor modules in the library, we have standardized on a set of efficient, real-time multi-tasking kernels for the processor modules. All software blocks in the system description are mapped as processes on one of these real-time kernels which also provide libraries implementing the channel based communication protocol. Each hardware process also has a wrapper software process running on the programmable processor to which it is attached. This results in a uniform interface to each process, whether it be hardware or software, and facilitates easy migration of functions between hardware and software.

Special software processes are run on the various processor modules to provide a consistent run-time environment for user-interface, file I/O, program loading etc. This is a trivial by-product of our use of multi-tasking kernels.

At present the framework supports processor modules based around TMS320C30, MC96002, DSP32C, MC68020 and SPARC, together with corresponding kernels. For example, we use SPOX real-time kernel for the TMS320C30 modules, and VDI [7], a simple home-grown kernel, for the DSP32C module.

3.0 Application to robot control system

In sharp contrast to architectures based around a general-purpose homogeneous shared-memory MIMD multi-processor with off-shelf I/O boards that are typical of most state-of-the-art robot control systems [8][9], our custom architecture approach offers much improved performance in a more compact package. The tasks in a robot control system not only have high real-time computation requirements, but also need extensive specialized I/O capabilities. This restricts the controllers based around general purpose machines with limited I/O capabilities to simple control mechanisms, or to non-real-time algorithm test benches at best.

Robotic control algorithms have become far more complicated than the simple PID joint controllers of the past. State of the art systems incorporate both force and position controllers (sometimes both running at the same time [10]). Position control is generally used when the robot does not touch anything. However, for tasks in which the robot touches an object, force control is almost a necessity [11]. For example, the robotic task of scraping paint from a surface cannot be easily performed using a position controller - any error in the system can be catastrophic. The ability to specify as a control input the desired force against the surface solves the problem.

We use a form of force control called impedance control [12], in which the force applied by the robot end-effector is proportional to the displacement from its goal position. This system is similar to a spring, where $F = K \cdot \Delta X$. This type of controller is well suited to tasks such as peg-in-hole insertions using a remote center of compliance as proposed by [13]. Figure 3 shows an extremely simplified process network view of the system.

Linearization of the robot control algorithm is based on the calculation of complicated inertial, Coriolis, and gravitational terms, and these terms have to be updated at a reasonably high frequency. There are also numerous frame transformations and unit conversions that must be performed inside the control loop. At a higher level, a trajectory control process continuously monitors the proximity sensor, and updates the controller inputs. Certainly, the hardware architecture must be designed to facilitate all these high bandwidth tasks.

3.1 Architecture of the system

The resulting architecture of the robot control system is shown in Figure 4. It is an instantiation of the layered architecture template described in section 2.2, and contains two custom robotic boards. The first is a controller board which in turn communicates with a custom peripheral board using a fiber-optic link. This peripheral board interfaces with the joint motors and current sensors in the robot arm. The controller board also communicates with force, position and other sensors.

3.1.1 Robot controller board

This is a custom board to which the processes related to the control law, position, velocity, force, and current sensing, and motor drive are mapped. It spans layers 3 and 4 of the architecture template discussed in section 2.2. There are two processor modules based around the 33 MHz TMS320C30, a powerful floating-point signal processor. The two TMS processing modules are distinguished by the kind of slave modules that they have. These slave modules reflect the specific requirements of the robot control tasks.

TMS processor module #1 has three slaves. First is a powerful programmable processor module based around a 50 MHz DSP32C which is dedicated to the trajectory calculation process. The second slave is a fiber-optic based communication link to connect the robot peripheral board at the other end, and serves as an interface to the robot motors. It is used to apply specific voltages or torques to the motor, to sense the motor currents, and to apply brakes to the robot. The ASIC that implements the protocol processing employs an asynchronous design methodology, and

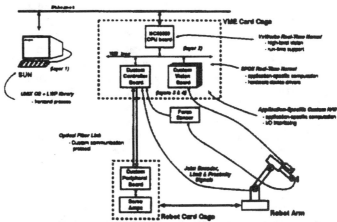

FIGURE 4: Implementation of the Robot Control System.

was synthesized using the interface synthesis tools. The third slave attached to TMS processor module #1 is a position-velocity sensing module. The ASICs for this module were automatically generated from a parameterized structural description.

The second processor module, TMS processor module #2, has three slaves. The first slave is a DSP32C based processor module, identical to the one attached to TMS processor module #1. This, however, is dedicated to the process calculating the Forward Kinematics and the Jacobian of the robot arm. The second slave is the force sensor module that interacts with a strain-gauge based force-torque sensing wrist. The third module is the position-velocity sensing module, which is in fact shared with the TMS processor module #1.

The board was fabricated as a 9U VME slave board, and is fully functional. Primarily as a result of the module-generators available, and the sub-system level library, this complex 500+ component 12" x 14" board had a design cycle of less than two months. Further, since it follows the architecture template, the system software was configured for it in very little time.

3.1.2 Robot peripheral board

This board is really part of the robot in that it provides interface to the robot joint motors and brakes. Its task is to receive voltage or current values from the controller board and apply them to the robot motors, to

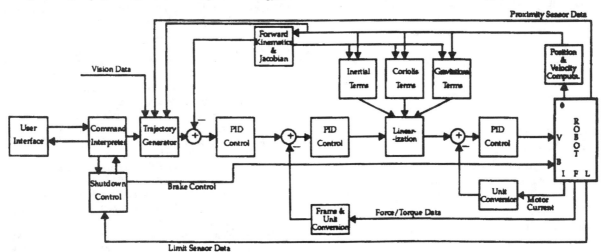

FIGURE 3: Simplified View of the Robot Control System

sense the motor current, and to apply the brakes in case of stalls or when commanded.

The board uses A/D, D/A, and optical communication modules from the sub-system module library. The protocol processors are synthesized using the ALOHA tool, while the digital pulse-width modulator is implemented with the FPGA module-generator. Only a small analog portion of the board (op-amp based filters) had to be custom designed for this board - the rest was either automatically generated or instantiated from the reusable parameterized subsystem library. As a result of this level of automation the entire development cycle from input description to the working board was again less than two months.

3.2 Organization of software processes

Due to the inherent large-grained parallelism present in the robot control system, it is easily decomposed into a network of processes. Some of these processes are *hardware processes* in that they run on their own dedicated hardware. Others however are implemented as *software processes*, and are mapped to one of the several software-programmable processors available in the top three layers of the architecture, where they run under the control of a kernel.

The SUN workstation in the top layer runs a user-interface process that provides an interactive environment based on top of a C interpreter. A library of robot specific C routines provides an interface to the lower-levels of the control system, and allow the user to switch between impedance control and position control modes, calibrate the robot, read sensor data, update the goal state of the robot (position, force, and gripper status), specify motion trajectory, etc.

The MC68020 based processor in the second layer is responsible for calculating position values from the data obtained from the vision board, as well as acting as a gateway between the SUN and the custom boards.

In the third layer, the TMS processor module #1 has the following software processes mapped to it:

- server process that interprets commands from the user-interface process on layer 1.

- process for computing the desired end-effector force to apply, by comparing the tool frame of the robot arm with the goal frame (F = K·ΔX).

- process adjusting the amount of voltage applied to the robot motors using the current sensor data obtained from the robot peripheral board.

The DSP32C slave module attached to this processor runs the trajectory calculation process.

The TMS processor module #2 has the following processes mapped to it:

- process to find the current tool-frame through forward kinematics.

- process to compute the error in applied force/torque using the data from the sensor.

- process to compute the desired output joint torque, the inertial, Coriolis, and gravitational terms, as well as the Jacobian transform.

The DSP32C slave module attached to this processor runs the Forward Kinematics and the Jacobian calculation process.

In addition to the user processes mentioned above, all the processing modules also run system processes in the background to provide run-time I/O services, and to handle data-routing.

4.0 Conclusions

We presented a case study of the design of a robot control system that employs extensive use of custom hardware at both chip and board levels to do simultaneous force and position control of a robot arm using data from a variety of sensors. In the design of a system of this complexity it is necessary that the chips, boards and software be *co-designed*, and this was made possible by our CAD framework. The heterogeneity inherent in such systems – both in terms of computation model and physical implementation – requires that a system-level CAD environment be much more than a mere scaling up of a chip level behavioral synthesis system to do hardware-software partitioning. Further, the flexibility and rapid-turnaround time offered by the CAD framework makes custom hardware attractive at all levels of the system. This is amply demonstrated when the architecture of our robot control system is contrasted with conventional controllers that have lower performance while using large general-purpose multi-processors.

Acknowledgments

This project was funded by DARPA. The second author was also partially funded by a NSF Graduate Fellowship.

References

[1] M. B. Srivastava, and R. W. Brodersen. *Rapid-Prototyping of Hardware and Software in a Unified Framework*. Proceedings of ICCAD, November 1991.

[2] R. K. Gupta and G. De Micheli. *System-level Synthesis using Re-programmable Components*. EDAC, March 1992.

[3] C. S. Shung, et al. *An Integrated CAD System for Algorithm-Specific IC Design*. IEEE Transactions on CAD of ICs and Systems, April 1991.

[4] L. Thon and R. W. Brodersen. *From C to Silicon*. Custom Integrated Circuit Conference, May 1992.

[5] C. M. Chu, M. Potkonjak, M. Thaler, and J. Rabaey. *HYPER: An Interactive Synthesis Environment for Real-Time Applications*. Proceedings of ICCD, October 1989.

[6] J. S. Sun and R. W. Brodersen. *System Module Interface Design in SIERA*. Under preparation.

[7] Manish Arya. *A Standard Software Platform for Shared Memory Multiprocessor Signal Processing Systems*. M. S. Report, EECS Department, U. C. Berkeley.

[8] J. B. Chen, et. al. *NYMPH: A Multiprocessor for Manipulator Applications*. IEEE International Conference on Robotics and Automation, April 1986.

[9] S. Narasimhan, D. Siegel, and J. M. Hollerbach. *Condor: A Revised Architecture for Controlling the Utah-MIT Hand*. IEEE International Conference on Robotics and Automation, April 1988.

[10] J. Craig and M. Raibert. *A Systematic Method for Hybrid Position/Force Control of a Manipulator*. IEEE Computer Software Application Conference, November 1979.

[11] D. E. Whitney. *Historical Perspective and State of the Art in Robot Force Control*. International Journal of Robotics Research, 6(1).

[12] N. Hogan. *Impedance Control: An Approach to Manipulation: Parts I, II & III*. ASME Journal of Dynamic Systems, Measurement and Control, vol 107:1-24.

[13] D. E. Whitney. *Quasi-Static Assembly of Compliant Supported Rigid Parts*. ASME Journal of Dynamic Systems, Measurement and Control, vol 104:65-77, 1982.

The InfoPad Multimedia Terminal: A Portable Device for Wireless Information Access

Thomas E. Truman, Trevor Pering, Roger Doering, *Member, IEEE*, and Robert W. Brodersen, *Fellow, IEEE*

Abstract—The architecture of a device that is optimized for wireless information access and display of multimedia data is substantially different than configurations designed for portable stand-alone operation. The requirements to reduce the weight and energy consumption are the same, but the availability of the wireless link, which is needed for the information access, allows utilization of remote resources. A limiting case is when the only computation that is provided in the portable terminal supports the wireless links or the I/O interfaces, and it is this extreme position that is explored in the InfoPad terminal design. The architecture of the InfoPad terminal, therefore, can be viewed as essentially a switch which connects multimedia data sources in the supporting wired network to appropriate InfoPad output devices (e.g., video display), and connects InfoPad input devices to remote processing (e.g., speech recognizer server) in the backbone network.

Index Terms—Mobile computing, wireless communication, low-power CMOS, system integration, design, specification.

―――――――――――――――― ♦ ――――――――――――――――

1 INTRODUCTION

THERE is presently a reexamination of the requirements of the system architecture and hardware needed for personal computing for the new and ever-growing class of users whose primary computing needs are to access network information and computing resources, as well as real-time interactive activities (chat rooms, games) and direct communications with other people. These applications, which are more communications-oriented than computation-oriented, require a "personal computer" that primarily has support for high bandwidth real-time communications, as well as multimedia I/O capabilities. User-accessible general purpose programmability and local high-performance computation are a secondary requirement, desirable only if the increased complexity and cost to support stand-alone operation, which is required for disconnected or poorly connected operation, can be justified.

As the dependence on network-accessible information storage and computation increases, the desire to ubiquitously access the network will require the terminal to have the portability of a paper notebook (1 lb, 8.5" x 11") while still being able to support real-time multimedia capabilities. These goals require a sophisticated wireless communications link that must provide connectivity even in the situation of large numbers of colocated users, such as in a classroom.

The InfoPad system design explores a highly optimized solution to the above goals, and critical to the design is the assumption that high bandwidth network connectivity is available (Fig. 1). The operating environment is divided into partially overlapping service areas ("picocells"), each with a coverage radius that is typically 10-30 meters, depending on the construction of the physical environment. Each picocell must provide service to approximately 50 users, and is expected to support a seamless handoff for roaming users.

These are the goals of the InfoPad system and, though not all of these specifications were met in the realization discussed here, the architecture that was developed would meet these goals with the application of even present state-of-the-art component technologies.

The primary aspect of the InfoPad system architecture that differentiates it from other portable computing systems is the role of the portable end-user device: *The InfoPad essentially functions as a remote I/O interface, instead of a computation and storage device.* Since portability and widespread consumer use was an important requirement, it was necessary to reduce the energy consumption, weight and cost of the end-user device as much as possible. For this reason, exploitation of the availability of the network connectivity and access to network servers was deeply built into the overall system architecture [2].

In our architecture, computing and storage resources are removed from the portable device and are placed on a shared, high-speed backbone network of servers that provide mass storage, general-purpose computation, and execution of system- and user-level applications [1], [3], [7]. No provision is made for local application execution and storage—laptops, palmtops, PDAs, and PIMs fundamentally differ from the InfoPad in this respect.

The user device, the InfoPad, consists of a radio modem, notebook-sized display, a pen pointing device, and video and audio input/output. The radio modem bandwidths are asymmetric, reflecting the importance of network information retrieval, with higher bandwidth (1-2 Mbits/sec per user) connectivity from the supporting backbone network

――――――――――――――――

- *T.E. Truman is with Lucent Tchnologies, 791 Holmdel-Keyport Rd., Room M-230A, Holmdel, NJ 07733. E-mail: ttruman@tesla.ho.lucent.com.*
- *T. Pering, R. Doering, and T.W. Brodersen are with the Department of Electrical Engineering and Computer Sciences, University of California, Berkeley, CA 94720.*
  E-mail: {pering, rogerd}@eecs.berkeley.edu.

Manuscript received 8 Apr. 1997.
For information on obtaining reprints of this article, please send e-mail to: tc@computer.org, and reference IEEECS Log Number 104806.

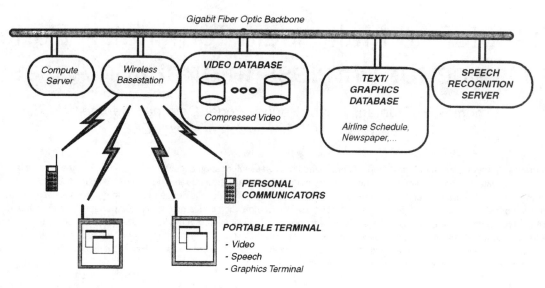

Fig. 1. Future infrastructure for information access.

to the terminal (downlink) and lower bandwidth connectivity (64-128 kbits/sec) in the reverse, uplink direction.

The InfoPad system architecture allows dramatic simplifications in both the actual hardware which is used, as well as the software and system management. A brief summary of some of the most important advantages are as follows:

- *Reduced cost, complexity, and energy consumption:* Moving the general purpose computing resources out of the portable device maximally reduces the cost, weight, and energy consumption by eliminating mass storage, high performance processors, and memories. Energy consumption for specific communication or I/O functions can be reduced by several orders of magnitude by replacing general-purpose computation with dedicated architectures.
- *Ease of use and remote system support:* The support for sophisticated applications and operating systems are provided by remote network managers. In this respect, the use model is closer to that provided by the telecommunications industry, in which the user I/O device, the telephone, has little complexity and the network providers perform system support and maintenance.
- *Appearance of unlimited storage and computational resources:* Since applications and server processes run on servers on the backbone network, it is possible to run sophisticated applications and computationally-intensive I/O algorithms—speech and handwriting recognition, for example—without the cost or energy consumption incurred in providing local high performance computation. Similarly, mass data storage is provided by storage and application servers rather than in local disks or flash memory.

This paper focuses on the architecture and implementation of the InfoPad: a portable information access device that supports real-time access to an infrastructure of multimedia information services via a high-bandwidth, low-latency wireless link.

The following section describes the hardware architecture of the InfoPad, which supports the above stated goals and associated internal protocols. This is followed by an evaluation on the critical characteristics along with directions for future developments.

2 Architectural Optimizations for Energy-Efficient Wireless Access to Multimedia Information

Externally, the InfoPad terminal provides a pen- and speech-based user interface to applications, along with a graphics and full-motion video display (Fig. 2). Since the link to the network is central to the operation of the device, a natural model for the portable device is that it is simply a multimedia-enabled extension of the backbone network. Several architectural features distinguish the InfoPad from desktop, notebook, and network computers, as well as from PDAs and PIMs. These features are outlined below.

2.1 Peripheral vs. Central Processing Unit

The InfoPad differs in a fundamental way from other portable computing platforms—including laptops and handheld personal information devices—in that *local execution of end-user applications is not supported*. The InfoPad system architecture embodies the logical extreme of thin-client computing.

Experience with an earlier prototype [3] indicated that the microprocessor subsystem, which was responsible for managing data transfers between the wireless modem and the I/O-processing chipset, consumed a significant fraction of the overall power budget and was also a primary performance bottleneck. The most delay-sensitive activities, such as moving the pen and expecting the cursor to track location in real-time, typically generate a large number of very small data transfers, so that the microprocessor spends the majority of its cycles entering and exiting interrupt service routines and setting up data transfers. Due to the delay-sensitivity and asynchronous nature of these transfers,

Fig. 2. The InfoPad portable multimedia terminal.

it is difficult to amortize the transfer setup overhead over more than one or two I/O packets.

Further, performing complex multimedia-data processing functions in dedicated hardware that is optimized for energy-efficient operation reduces the energy-per-operation by several orders of magnitude relative to software. Conventional general-purpose processors (e.g., Alpha, Pentium) focus entirely on instruction-per-second metrics, and typically require 100 milliwatts/MIP; energy-optimized, general-purpose processors such as the Strong Arm require 1-10 milliwatts/MIP. Fully dedicated, optimized hardware, on the other hand, typically requires less than 0.01 milliwatts/MIP.

Thus, for portable devices, there is a strong incentive to completely eliminate the microprocessor subsystem in favor of fully dedicated hardware. However, the disadvantage of dedicated hardware is the lack of flexibility and programmability and, for research purposes, it was desirable to have the ability to develop and test new algorithms and protocols.

The requirements outlined above lead to an optimization in which the user accessible central processing unit (CPU) is functionally removed from the architecture of the portable and networked based resources are used instead. Unlike a local CPU architecture, in which I/O peripherals enhance the functionality of the core processor, our goal was to design intelligent peripherals that are capable of processing I/O events and can manage data transfers without relying on a centralized processor.

The general-purpose processing unit is viewed as simply another peripheral subsystem that exists to complement the functionality of the I/O peripherals, thus the processor is more appropriately termed a *peripheral* processing unit (PPU). Our goal was to reduce the role of this PPU to be that of a simple controller that, in normal operation, initializes the system and handles complex protocol processing (e.g., handoff requests) that are most easily implemented in software.

2.2 Class-Based Communications Protocols

A second fundamental difference that separates the InfoPad from other mobile computing and information access devices is that it is primarily a *communications* device that is optimized for *energy-efficient* access to *multimedia* data in an indoor *wireless* environment. Thus, the algorithms, protocols, architecture, and components are all designed with a bias toward this specific context.

Throughout the InfoPad architecture, it was necessary to distinguish between classes of data, where each class has its own service needs, primarily because of the required support of interactive multimedia over a wireless network, where bandwidth is limited and reliability can vary dramatically. The heterogeneous mix of traffic supported over the wireless link requires that the link level protocol be aware of the delay and reliability requirements of a particular packet, and tailor the behavior of the protocol to meet the requirements of each class of traffic.

For example, in a vector-quantized image compression scheme, it is possible to differentiate the quantization codebook from the quantized image. Since the codebook is relatively small and will be used to decode many image frames, increasing the reliability of the codebook transmission (via forward error correction coding, retransmission, or a combination of both) has little impact on the overall bandwidth requirements but has a dramatic impact on the overall quality of the decompressed image. Data frames, which require more bandwidth and are more delay-sensitive, can be transmitted with little or no error correction: Corrupted image frames with bit-error rates of up to still provide the viewer with a good idea of the overall image composition [4].

2.3 Low-Overhead, Minimal-State Communications

Consistent with the goal of exploiting network resources, the amount of state maintained in the portable device is minimized and, for this reason, *explicit* support for end-to-end transport and internetworking protocols over the wireless link is avoided.

As we will discuss in detail in the following section, optimizing the portable device for energy-efficient operation presented a strong bias toward implementing the majority of the system in custom hardware and, to the extent possible, eliminating the role of the microprocessor as the central functional unit. Since the portable device was so heavily dependent upon the wireless link, a foremost priority was to eliminate the dependency on software-based protocol stacks. The resulting architecture of the portable device can be viewed as a packet-routing system that supports data transfer between I/O subsystems and the wireless link entirely in hardware (i.e., without microprocessor intervention). Thus, it was necessary to examine the merits of supporting fully general protocols, such as TCP and IP, in a hardware system.

Since applications execute on the backbone network and general-purpose network connections between applications exist entirely within the backbone infrastructure, the mobile is relieved from the task of handling "standard" protocols. Often, these protocols are designed for generality, and either require superfluous fields in the protocol data structures or exhibit behavior that is unsuitable

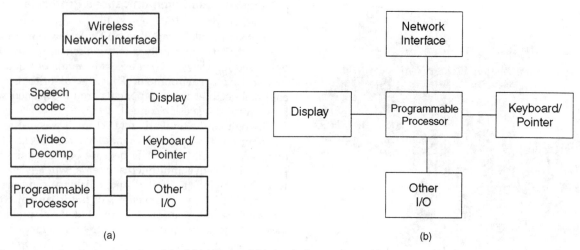

Fig. 3. Comparison of control organization of the (a) InfoPad and (b) classical computer architecture.

for use on error-prone wireless links. Terminating connection-oriented protocols at the basestation makes it possible to view the wireless link as a single-hop, point-to-point forwarding link.

Within the backbone network, a connection-oriented network that supports quality-of-service is assumed and, since the bandwidth requirements for the device are known in advance, it is possible to reserve the required network resources (bandwidth, server CPU cycles, etc.) at the time a connection is established. The InfoNet protocol suite [2] provides transport- and network-layer protocol services between the applications, servers, and basestations.

2.4 An Infrastructure for Mobile Multimedia Computing Research

An overarching design philosophy is that the InfoPad should be both a fully functional system and a research platform. In order to evaluate and test the computing model described above, it was necessary to design and build the entire system, from low-level, energy-efficient circuits to the infrastructure of network server and applications resources.

Thus, a primary goal of this work was to enable further research in the design of interactive applications, multimodal user interfaces, source/channel coding algorithms, network protocols, portable computing devices, and basestation architectures that are specifically targeted to wireless multimedia.

With this in mind, the remainder of the paper focuses on the architecture of the InfoPad multimedia terminal.

3 ARCHITECTURE OF THE INFOPAD MULTIMEDIA TERMINAL

Traditionally, personal computer systems are designed with a programmable processor at the core of the system (Fig. 3a). Since, in these systems, the primary system task is executing software applications, without the central processing unit the system would be useless. Peripheral I/O devices are added to support or enhance the functionality of the CPU core. When optimizing for the common case, system optimizations generally focus on increasing the fraction of time this central processing unit is able to give to applications.

Since the InfoPad system is designed to support a significantly different model of computing—one that is information access-centric—it is natural that the logical organization of the architecture is significantly different. The implementation of the InfoPad centers around the model of parallel I/O processing modules connected to a backbone network via a single-hop wireless link, rather than a central processing unit supported by peripheral I/O systems. With the long-term vision that the backbone network would exist within a virtual circuit-switched framework, our design philosophy was that the InfoPad should be an extension of the backbone network. Thus, the main function of the hardware is to support dataflow between the wireless link and multimedia sources or sinks.

Fig. 3b illustrates this organization. Foremost in the architecture is the wireless network interface, which supports full-duplex communications using both a 625 Kbit/s modem in the 2.4 GHz ISM band (downlink) and a 242 Kbit/s modem in the 920 MHz band (uplink). Other I/O subsystems are designed to autonomously interact with the network interface without support from the programmable processing unit. Data received on the downlink is transferred directly to the video, audio, and graphics subsystems without the assistance of the processor. Similarly, speech or pen input from the user is transferred directly to the uplink interface.

Conceptually, the architecture is analogous to an output-buffered, self-routing packet switch. At run-time, each data source is given a *type*-tag[1] which is used to identify the type of data generated (e.g., pen vs. speech) and, for each {*data source, type tag*} pair, a unique device destination address is assigned. When a source has data of a particular type available, it uses the *type* tag to dynamically determine the corresponding sink to which the data should be sent. Thus, once initialization is complete, data transfers between source and sink are autonomous, requiring no microprocessor intervention.

The *type* tag provides a mechanism to support lightweight protocols that provide data-specific transport services. For

---

1. The assignment of tags to a particular data class is globally shared with the backbone network software.

example, the transmitter interface module uses the tag to determine how the current packet is to be encapsulated, since optional fields such as packet length, forward error correction, or sequence number, may be omitted for certain types. Similarly, the receiver interface uses the *type* tag to decode a packet and to determine the destination of the incoming data (e.g., video frame buffer vs. audio codec interface). Using this mechanism, physical and link-level protocols can adaptively select what level of service a given packet requires by changing its *type*, or by changing the *type*-specific packetization options associated with that tag (to be discussed in Section 3.2). At a higher level, protocols supported by the InfoNet [2] gateway are able to utilize the *type* tag in making scheduling decisions.

3.1 Design Trade-Offs

Although the I/O devices were designed to operate autonomously, we chose not to eliminate the microprocessor from the design, primarily for the flexibility afforded by a general-purpose processor, for exploring these protocols is easiest in software. Since this does result in a less-than-optimal power budget, the system is designed to operate with the microprocessor providing only three support services: start-up initialization, packet scheduling for transmission over the wireless link, and support for link- and media-access protocols (including support for mobility).

A second power-related concession was made in the design of the wireless interface: The physical interface to the RF modems utilizes an commercially available FPGA to enable experimentation with both the wireless modem and the physical-layer protocols (e.g., FEC coding, clock recovery, etc.). Radio technology is rapidly advancing; and, while current radio technology is adequate for experimental designs, they do not provide the 2-10 Mbit/s envisioned for future devices. The FPGA design provides an interface which is easily changed to take advantage of new radios as they become available.

Overall, the primary technical challenge was to balance the low-power design against system flexibility (for use as a research tool) and system responsiveness (for actual use). In the following sections, as we discuss the specifics of the I/O subsystems, we will identify the design trade-offs and implementation choices that are driven by the architectural goals presented in Section 2.

3.2 IPbus Description

The core of the InfoPad hardware is a low-power bus, called the IPbus, dedicated to the movement of I/O data. Attached to this bus in a modular fashion are bus-mastering data sources and bus-slave sinks, as depicted in Fig. 4. Together, these I/O devices support two-way audio, pen input, monochrome graphics, and color video capabilities over a full-duplex wireless link; they are implemented as 10 full-custom ASICs in a 1.2-micron CMOS process. A microprocessor system is used to handle system initialization and higher-level protocol functions (e.g., collecting error statistics and signal strength measurements).

The IPbus is an 8-bus designed to run at a speed of 1MHz and a supply voltage of 1.2-1.5 Volts. This design provides a maximum throughput of 8 Mbit/s, well above

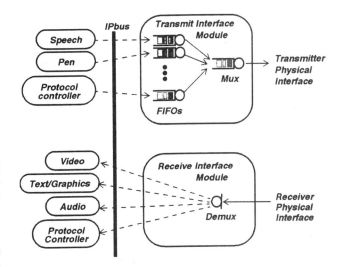

Fig. 4. Architectural organization of dataflow.

the 1 Mbit/s maximum supported by the radios, ensuring that the IPbus bandwidth is adequate for system dataflow. An 8-bit word size was chosen to minimize pin count, and hence package size, of the custom ASICs; a larger word size would not measurably improve system performance since the system throughput is constrained by the bandwidth of the radio channel.

The IPbus supports direct read/write transfers, as well as a packet-based transfer mechanism. Utilized only by the microprocessor subsystem, the direct read/write mechanism allows the processor to directly configure a device, query status, and respond to interrupt conditions. Packet-based transfers are used for interdevice communication: The source device indicates a new transfer by sending a start of packet (*SOP*) byte, followed by a variable number of data bytes, and terminates the transfer by sending an end of packet (*EOP*) byte to the sink device. Included in the *SOP* byte is the 6-bit *type* tag which identifies the data-type of the packet (e.g., pen, audio, etc.). The *EOP* byte contains additional (optional) status information which can be used to identify packets that are corrupted during transmission over the wireless link, for example.

Data transfers that are not required to be atomic: distinct data streams from different sources can be interleaved across the bus and simultaneous transfers to the same sink device by multiple sources are allowed. For example, it is possible for the audio, the pen, and the microprocessor to simultaneously transfer data to the transmitter interface. This removes the requirement for store-and-forward protocols in the I/O peripherals, decreasing the overall system delay, but requires that the sink devices be capable of demultiplexing the incoming data.

3.3 Wireless Interface Subsystem

In the early design phases (1992-1993), the dearth of high-speed wireless modems suitable for use in the InfoPad and the uncertainty that standard link-level protocols would provide adequate performance for multimedia over wireless, demanded reconfigurable wireless interface—one that was flexible in its ability to interface to a variety of wireless

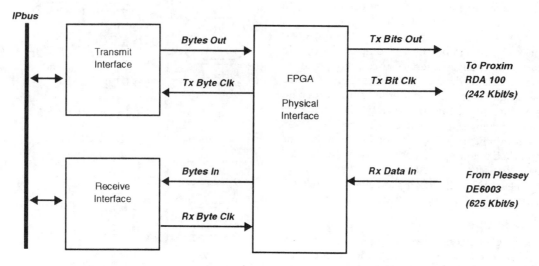

Fig. 5. Block diagram of wireless interface subsystem.

modems, as well as the ability to support experimentation with link and media access protocols. Our strategy was to partition the interface into three parts, shown in Fig. 5: a transmitter (TX) interface ASIC, a receiver (RX) interface ASIC, and a reconfigurable physical interface module, implemented in an FPGA. The TX and RX modules handle packet- and byte-oriented functions, while the FPGA provides bit-level manipulations, such as forward error correction (FEC) coding and the physical signalling interface to the wireless modems. This partitioning allows the underlying modem to change, requiring neither a change to byte- and packet-oriented operations nor an ASIC refabrication.

During the early design phases, the best commercially available radio modems suitable for use in the InfoPad terminal did not provide the 2-10 Mbits/sec envisioned for fully functional systems of the future. For this reason, to provide as much bandwidth as possible, separate uplink and downlink modems were utilized. The downlink modem, the Plessey DE6003, operates in the 2.4-2.5 GHz band and employs binary FSK modulation to provide a 625 Kbit/sec raw bit rate; this modem was designed for use in a slow frequency hopping system and has 100 available half-duplex frequency channels. The uplink modem, a Proxim RDA300, operates in the 902-926 MHz band and provides a 242 Kbit/sec raw data rate; four noninterfering, full rate and three noninterfering, half-rate (121 Kbits/sec) half-duplex channels are available.

Since the available bandwidth was below the ideal of 2-10 Mbits/sec, time-division multiplexing of the uplink and downlink channels was not considered for this prototype system. Instead, a simple frequency-division multiple access scheme was used within each picocell, where each cell is responsible for allocating a particular frequency band (i.e., channel) to each user in the system. Thus, the total number of InfoPads per cell in the prototype system was limited by the number of full-rate uplink channels to a maximum of four.

Several classes of data link protocols are supported in the InfoPad, corresponding to the level of reliability required. On the downlink, best-effort broadcast and multicast transmissions are supported, along with connection-oriented, variable-reliability service ranging from unacknowledged best-effort transmission to a Type I hybrid-ARQ [15] data transfer. With the exception of multicast transmission, the same data link protocols are supported on the uplink.

In the following subsections, we outline the salient features of the protocol support primitives.

3.3.1 Packet Structure

The basic packet structure supported over the wireless link is an extension of the IPbus packet format, shown in Fig. 6. The minimum overhead added by the wireless link is the single-byte pad alias, which is an address equivalent. Optionally, sequence number, packet length, and CRC fields may also be added. The inclusion of sequence numbers is a Pad-specific configuration parameter. The other optional fields are *type*-specific, giving a very fine granularity on how the link protocols treat particular classes of data, supporting our goal of providing lightweight, type-specific communications protocols.

3.3.2 Dynamic Network Addressing

Each InfoPad is assigned a unique identifier that is stored in nonvolatile memory and is presented to the backbone network to establish a connection. The backbone network uses this identifier to assigns a *pad alias*, which is a temporary, 1-byte, local network address used by both Pad and basestation indicate a radio packet's destination address. (Provision for multicast addressing is included and is discussed in Section 3.2).

3.3.3 Type-Specific Protocol Options

Many of the protocol primitives can be selectively enabled on a type-specific granularity. We outline these primitives below:

Variable error control: Multiple levels of error control and reliability effort are supported. At the lowest level of reliability, transmissions are unacknowledged and no error correction or error detection is employed; at the highest-level of reliability, a Type-1 Hybrid ARQ protocol is used.

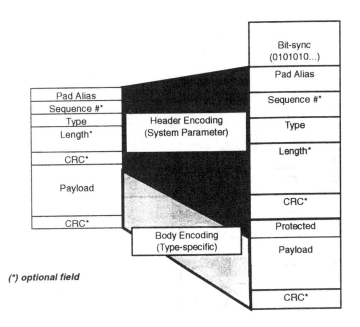

Fig. 6. Packet format.

Additionally, two different error correction codes[2] are available: a BCH (15, 5, 3) code, and a BCH (15, 11, 1) code. These variable-level encoding schemes allow bandwidth-intensive data (such as graphics or video) to be minimally encoded, while latency or content-critical data (such as video codebooks or pen packets) can be maximally encoded.

Differentiation of packet header and packet payload: An insight gained from experience with the earlier prototype is that, for many classes of data packets, there often are a few content-critical bytes which require higher reliability than the rest of the payload—a bitmap, for example, has an x- and y-coordinate followed by a series of pixel values, and displaying the bitmap at the correct location is far more critical than displaying every pixel value correctly.

For this reason, we chose to provide a mechanism that allows the link protocols to differentiate between packet header and packet payload: At a type-specific granularity, it is possible to encode the first 1-7 bytes of the payload with the same FEC coding as the packet header, while the remainder of the payload is encoded independently. An optional payload CRC field is available for data types that require correct transmission. In this way, it is possible to have the content-critical bytes maximally encoded, while the remainder of the payload is encoded at a completely different level. Interleaving is a standard mechanism for increasing the effectiveness of error correcting codes in the presence of burst errors [16].

Interleaving: The TX and RX subsystems provide a 15 × 16 interleaver/deinterleaver, which redistributes 240-bit blocks of FEC-encoded data into 16 15-byte blocks. In this configuration, we are able to correct a large number of burst errors of up to 48 bits in each 240-bit block.

In the remainder of this section, we outline the particular features of the wireless interface components.

---

2. An (n, k, t) error correcting block code uses n transmitted bits to send k information bits, and can correct up to t errors.

3.3.4 TX Interface

The TX subsystem is responsible for demultiplexing interleaved data streams (sent from different sources) and buffering them until they can be encapsulated and metered out to the FPGA interface. Data is encapsulated with the InfoPad radio packet format, which provides additional functionality such as error detection, length information, etc. Packet scheduling is accomplished in cooperation with the microprocessor subsystem.

The TX chip provides five distinct logical channels, each of which can handle one noninterleaved data stream. A single source per logical channel mapping is enforced in software. Associated with each logical channel is a ring buffer which provides storage for packets pending transmission (Fig. 7). Each ring buffer has a programmable number of entries—pointers to packets in an external memory—with up to 32 entries per ring. The number of buffers for each channel, as well as the size of each buffer, can be dynamically adjusted according to the type of traffic carried by the channel.

Since the link-level packet format is type-specific, the TX subsystem supports this functionality by optionally prepending *Pad alias*, *sequence number*, and *length* fields to each packet. At the start of each transmission, an internal lookup table—indexed by type—is consulted to determine which fields should be added to the current packet. In this way, the device provides a mechanism by which the link-level packet format can be dynamically adapted to the current transmission environment.

The architecture separates *packetization* from packet *scheduling*. For research purposes, the importance of this feature cannot be overstated, as it allows the processor to implement an arbitrary scheduling policy without requiring the processor to manage the transfers between peripheral I/O devices. Packet scheduling and link protocols are supervised by the microprocessor as follows:

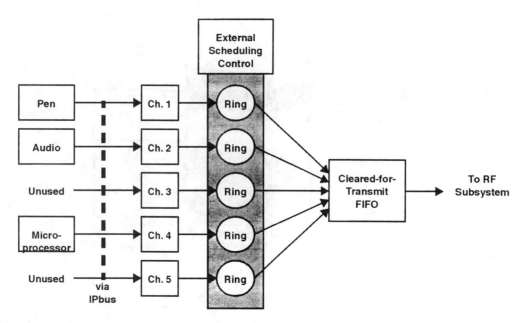

Fig. 7. Logical organization of TX buffering scheme.

Upon the receipt of a complete packet, the TX chip issues an interrupt to the processor subsystem. The processor reads the {ring number, buffer number, packet type, length} information from the device and records this information. At some time in the future, the processor may choose to queue this packet for transmission by pushing the {ring number, buffer number} to a "ready for transmit" FIFO in the TX module. At the completion of packet transmission, the TX chip again issues an interrupt, indicating that the packet represented by {ring number, buffer number} has completed transmission.

3.3.5 RX Interface

The RX subsystem is responsible for processing the incoming radio traffic. It processes the packet headers received from the FPGA and routes the data body to the appropriate destination. Packet headers can optionally be duplicated and forwarded to the local microprocessor for statistical monitoring, allowing the microprocessor to monitor the packet traffic, dropped packets, and passed/failed CRCs without processing or transporting body data.

The internal architecture of the device is a simple state machine that controls data flow to an internal FIFO. Packet destination is determined by a programmable lookup table based on the packet's *type* field which enables a variety of data flow scenarios. In normal operation, data is sent directly to the appropriate sink device, though for debugging, specific datatypes can be routed through the microprocessor, allowing monitoring, modifying, and rescheduling the packet before forwarding to its final destination.

The device performs only simple, pass-through routing: Once data is available in the receive FIFO, it is transferred out to the IPbus at the first opportunity. One disadvantage of this pipelined reception path is the inability of the receiver subsystem to drop incoming packets, since the payload CRC is not available until after the packet data has been forwarded on to the data sink. Therefore, data sinks that wish to discriminate between clean and corrupted data must buffer incoming bytes before processing can proceed.

In addition to supporting point-to-point addressing via the *pad alias*, the RX interface supports both multicast and broadcast addressing. A second alias, the *group alias*, is used to identify a particular multicast group; incoming packets with an Alias field matching either the *pad alias* register or the *group alias* register are accepted by the receiver module. With the exception of broadcast packets, all other packets are ignored.

3.3.6 FPGA Interface

The FPGA subsystem is the intermediary between the RX or TX subsystems and the physical radios. In addition to providing the error correction coding and CRC modules, the primary responsibilities are outlined below:

Signalling interface: Since there is no standard physical interface to wireless modems, supporting multiple physical interfaces is a task which is particularly well suited to programmable logic. Virtually all wireless modems support a common set of control signals, such as power up/down, channel selection, transmit/receive selection. The FPGA module provides an abstraction of the underlying mechanisms so that the RX, TX, and processor modules have a uniform view of the wireless modem primitives.

Timing and data recovery: On the downlink, the DE6003 modem interface presents only the raw received data signal—i.e., the analog output of a hard-limiting comparator (binary FSK modulation is used). This signal, which is has a nominal bit rate of 625 Kbits/sec, is oversampled by a factor of 16 (10 MHz), and is used to recover both the timing information and data sequence. At the start of a transmission, a sequence of 48 alternating 1s and 0s is sent, followed by a 32-bit framing character; once this is received, the tracking feedback loop is opened for the duration of the packet. Due to an implementation limitation of these modems, the maximum continuous transmission is 10 milliseconds, so that clock drift between transmitter and receiver during a packet time is small enough to ignore.[3]

Real-time interrupt: To support real-time protocol requirements (e.g., frequency hopping), a real-time interrupt is provided with up to a five resolution. For reservation-based media access, the guard interval between channel uses is inversely proportional to the accuracy of the reservation timer. Placing the timer block near the receive path provides a convenient mechanism for accurately (within a bit-time[4]) synchronizing the mobile with the basestation.

3.4 Microprocessor Subsystem

The microprocessor is responsible for system initialization and various high-level protocols. The system is based around an ARM60 microprocessor running at 10 MHz (i.e., 10 MIPs) with 512 KB of RAM, with 128 KB ROM for program storage. No cache or floating point unit is present in this microprocessor.

To maintain power efficiency, the microprocessor system is designed with hardware support for a software-initiated idle state. When the software determines that it has no more work to be done, i.e., when waiting for some external stimulus, it signals an external controller to initiate the idle state. This controller gates the system clock, freezing the processor in midcycle and driving its power consumption to a minimum. The processor interrupt line is monitored by the controller, and with the next interrupt (e.g., a timer event or incoming data), the controller reactivates the processor clock.

3.5 Microprocessor Interface Chip

The processor interface (ARMIF) device is the bridge between the microprocessor bus and the IPbus, and its main roles are buffering data, byte-to-word conversion, and performing miscellaneous control functions. In the active mode, the *Master* channel directs data from the processor to the peripheral I/O chips (video, text/graphics, audio, transmitter), while the *Slave* channel collects packets from the chipset (pen, speech, and radio transmitter). A third channel, the *Direct* read/write channel, provides an unbuffered read and write mechanism so that the processor is able to program the control registers and read back the status registers of the peripheral chips.

3.6 User Interface I/O Peripherals

3.6.1 Graphics Subsystem

The graphics subsystem is the primary output device for the InfoPad system. It consists of a low-power SRAM frame buffer (described fully in [7]), a controller module, and 640 × 480 monochrome LCD. Graphics operations (e.g., line drawing and text display) are performed in the backbone network in the *graphics server* [2], and the resulting bitmaps are sent directly over the wireless link and are rendered by the controller module.

Three shapes of bitmaps are supported: rectangular block, horizontal line, and vertical swath (32 bits wide, variable height.) Normally, received bitmaps are displayed regardless of the correctness of their content; if bit errors are incurred during wireless transmission, then the data is displayed with errors. This design choice was driven by the desire to maintain a responsive interactive user interface with bit error rates above .

A second mode, called protected mode, queues incoming bitmap data and displays it only if the packet payload passes CRC. This is used in conjunction with a technique known as asymptotically reliable transmission [4], [5]. To maintain the responsiveness of the user interface, an initial, possibly corrupted, version of a bitmap is rendered as quickly as possible; in the background, the graphics server follows the initial transmission with low-priority[4], protected-mode update packets that cyclically refresh the entire screen. In this scheme, corrupted packets that were previously displayed are eventually replaced by either a clean refresh image or an entirely new image (again, possibly corrupted). This approach provides a very responsive interactive feel while providing a means by which, asymptotically, the screen image can be rendered without errors.

3.6.2 Pen Subsystem

The pen interface utilizes a commercially available digitizer tablet, which is attached to the underside of the graphics LCD panel. This digitizer feeds pen coordinates and button status to a custom ASIC, which provides a buffered interface to the IPbus. With the first available byte of pen data, the ASIC initiates an IPBus transfer to the *Target Address*, followed by a programmable number of data bytes; this configuration allows the system software to fine-tune the buffer size in order to balance time-to-transmit delay against the overhead incurred by sending very short packets. (The time-to-transmit delay is approximately one millisecond per byte, and the target round-trip delay is 30 milliseconds or less. In the current implementation, the default pen packet size is five bytes).

3.6.3 Audio Subsystem

The audio subsystem performs bidirectional audio buffering and provides a physical interface to a commercial codec, amplifier, and speaker. The audio channel supports eight KHz 8-bit-law encoded audio, which presents the wireless link with 64 Kbit/s raw audio bandwidth. Downlink audio is buffered in a one Kbyte FIFO, smoothing the delay jitter in the incoming audio packets, and is metered out of this FIFO at the 64 Kbit/sec rate. Uplink audio is generated at the same 64 Kbit/sec rate and transferred to its destination (typically the TX interface) via the IPBus.

In the current implementation of the InfoNet and the InfoPad, the uplink audio and downlink audio streams are handled as separate entities; further, audio streams for separate users are handled as separate entities as well. Thus, applications that require synchronization between the uplink and downlink streams, or between multiple users, are not explicitly supported. However, extensions to the the audio server, along with specialized applications or servers, could in principle provide the support for these application.

---

3. The 20 MHz system clocks are accurate to ± 20 PPM

4. These packets can be transmitted at lowest priority utilizing otherwise unused transmission bandwidth.

3.6.4 Video Interface

The video subsystem supports full-motion color video. A custom ASIC implementation consisting of five decompression chips plus four custom, low-power frame buffer ASICs, drives the external add-on color display [7]. Ideally, the video display and graphics display would be combined, reducing system complexity; however, during the design phase, lightweight, thin, low-power, color LCDs were unavailable.

As detailed in [7], video data is transmitted using an adaptive vector quantization compression scheme which divides the compressed information into two distinct types—video *data* and video *codebooks*—each of which has differing transport demands. The compression scheme used can deliver up to 30 frames/second over the wireless link.

4 Evaluation and Measurements

Central to the InfoPad computing model is the premise that backbone network resources (e.g., computational power and network bandwidth) will become virtually unlimited due to technology improvements (Moore's Law). It is also assumed that the quality of a 1-2 Mbit/sec indoor link can be provided and maintained consistently throughout an indoor environment, freeing users to roam within a building. A third assumption is that the trend in computer use is toward real-time information access rather than heavy comptutation.

It is necessary to keep these three assumptions in mind as we evaluate the architecture and implementation of the InfoPad *terminal*. As with all large systems-building research projects, certain facets of the system are implemented with the sole purpose of demonstrating the larger system concept, and thus leave room for further work. For this reason, we focus on the evaluation of the multimedia terminal with the assumption that the our three key premises hold.

The implementation of the InfoPad terminal described in the proceeding section uses a combination of full-custom ASICs and commercially available components to provide the required functionality and demonstrate the viability of the architecture. In several places, providing this functionality with commercial components came at a significant increase in the power budget.

However, the lack of available components (or weaknesses in the underlying technology) has fueled further research efforts to close the gap. Energy efficient microprocessor design [11], low-power, energy-efficient DC-DC conversion [10], fully integrated, CDMA transmitter and receiver implemented in CMOS [9], and circuit design for energy-efficient reconfigurable logic devices are several of the complementary research projects which were spawned from the InfoPad project.

In this section, we evaluate the strengths and weaknesses of the design, making a distinction between architecture limitations and implementation-specific limitations. We begin with a power breakdown by subsystem.

4.1 Architectural Evaluation

As a preface to an architectural evaluation, we return to the fundamental assumption about the role of the terminal in the overall system: that the portable terminal is a remote interface to networked I/O servers where the interface devices generate data at a predetermined maximum rate. That is, the I/O subsystems on the portable terminal and the I/O servers on the backbone network collectively determine a throughput constraint[5] that the IPBus and the wireless link must support. Once this throughput constraint is met, there is no advantage to making the device "faster."

Hence, data throughput or computational performance alone is not a useful characterization of the system. Assuming that the backbone network has adequate computation resources, user-level application "performance" becomes a function of the latency inherent in the remote-I/O architecture. As described in [2], round-trip latencies within the backbone network (from basestation to servers and back to basestation) were typically between 10-15 milliseconds, with occasional latencies of 20 milliseconds.

In the following subsections, our evaluation instead focuses on how well the internal architecture supported the mobile computing paradigm of remote-I/O via a wireless link.

4.1.1 Processor Utilization

One of the primary goals was to push the model of thin-client computing to its logical extreme, in order to minimize—ideally eliminate—the role of the microprocessor subsystem in the overall design, in order to reduce power consumption. Thus, it is of interest to evaluate the dependence on the microprocessor.

While active, the processor spends the majority of its cycles servicing the TX module, which has only a one MHz read/write interface. Waiting for I/O peripherals while responding to *packet-ready* notifications, clearing packets for transmission, and responding to *transmission-complete* notifications dominate the time that the processor subsystem is not in sleep mode.

Fig. 8 illustrates that of the nonvideo power budget; the microprocessor subsystem accounts for 20 percent of the power consumption (approximately 1.4 Watts) in fully active operation (100 percent duty cycle). However, since the microprocessor subsystem is composed of fully-static CMOS components, gating the clock reduces the power consumption to approximately 0.25 Watts (power due to clock distribution only). During normal operation of the InfoPad, the measured duty cycle shows that the processor is active 7 percent of the time when running at 10 MHz; this yields an average power consumption of 0.33 Watts.

A new approach to microprocessor design that uses a technique called *dynamic voltage scaling* (DVS), [17] promises to reduce the power consumption of this subsystem even further. DVS takes advantage of the square-law reduction in power consumption that comes from reducing the supply voltage for a CMOS circuit.[6] Since decreasing the supply voltage reduces the switching speed of the circuit, it is necessary to simultaneously decrease the operating clock frequency.

---

5. Clearly, an upper bound on the throughput constraint is the raw available bandwidth of the wireless link
6. The energy per operation of a CMOS circuit is given by $E = CV^2$.

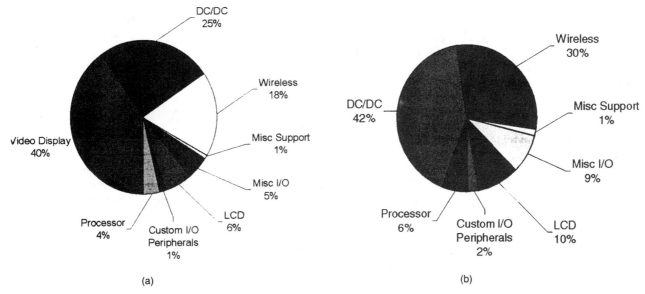

Fig. 8. Power breakdown by subsystem: (a) with color video display, (b) without color video display.

Scaling the processor clock with its supply voltage according to processor workload provides the opportunity to trade energy-efficiency against instantaneous MIPS. Further gains can be obtained by a tight integration of the processor subsystem components (e.g., DMA controllers, address decoding, etc.) onto the CPU core. Finally, by using optimized energy-efficient memories together with a low voltage-swing bus between the processor, it is expected that the entire processor subsystem will consume one to three milliwatts/MIP—an improvement of two orders of magnitude over the existing 250 milliwatts/MIP system [17].

4.1.2 Remote-I/O Processing Latency

A critical metric of the usefulness of the remote I/O architecture is the round-trip latency incurred as a packet moves through successive stages in the system. While the dominant source of latency is the network interfaces on the backbone network, early measurements ([2], [3], [8]) using standard workstations attached to a 10 Mbit/s Ethernet backbone demonstrate that a 30 millisecond round-trip latency was an achievable design constraint for a LAN-based backbone. This goal is based on the graphics refresh interval and gives the user an imperceptible difference between local- and remote-I/O processing for the pen-based user interface. Given this constraint, it is useful to evaluate the processing latency introduced by the interface between the IPbus peripherals and the wireless link. We break this latency into the following three components:

Packet generation: **3 microseconds**. This is defined to be the time elapsed from when the last byte of available uplink data until the packet is reported ready (i.e., a request for scheduling is generated). The bus-mastering architecture of the IPbus provides a direct path from each data source to the wireless network interface (via the TX chip buffers) without involving the processor. Thus, the packet generation latency is typically less than three IPbus clock cycles.

Scheduling: **160 microseconds**. This is the time required to process the scheduling request and clear the packet for transmission. To facilitate experimentation with a variety of scheduling algorithms and media-access protocols, packetization and scheduling are separated. Partitioning these functions into physically separate units increases the complexity of the packetizer by requiring it to support random access to available packets. This partitioning also increases intermodule communication by requiring the packetizer to interact with the scheduler several times for each packet, and each interaction requires several bus transactions.

The current implementation, with an idle transmitter and an empty transmit queue, has a worst case time on the order of 160 microseconds—50 microseconds to notify the processor, 10 microseconds for the processor to clear the packet for transmission, and 100 microseconds for the first bit of data (after 64 bits of synchronization preamble) to be transmitted over the wireless link.

Packet distribution: **1 microsecond**. This is defined as the time elapsed from the moment the first byte of available downlink data is ready until the first byte of the packet is sent to its destination device (e.g., pen, audio, etc.). Since the architecture employs direct, unbuffered routing from source to destination, the packet distribution latency is simply the time required to determine the hardware destination address for the given type, which can be accomplished in a single IPbus clock cycle.

The sum of these three components is 164 microseconds. This latency is insignificant compared to the latency incurred in the backbone network: 10-20 *milli*seconds on a standard 10 Mbit/sec LAN (well within the upper bound 30 millisecond round-trip). It is expected that state-of-the-art high-bandwidth networks that support QoS will be able to scale to support the 50 users per cell envisioned.

4.1.3 Communications Protocol Support

Because the InfoPad architecture supports type-specific link protocols, it is possible to experiment with a variety of protocols and, given the current transmission environment, to fine-tune the parameters of each protocol to best handle each type of data. By characterizing the typical traffic patterns for each data type—a characterization which may be performed either off-line or dynamically—it is possible to eliminate unused fields, and to optimize for the common case.

The data link protocol, which provides a unreliable point-to-point link over the wireless medium, relies on the 1-byte pad alias field to indicate the receive address, and on the type-tag field (one byte) to identify the data type of the current packet. Optionally, this layer includes any combination of the following: packet length (two bytes), sequence number (one byte), header CRC (one byte), and payload CRC (one byte). Relative to standard protocols for wireless transmissions, this 7-byte overhead is significantly less: On a 5-byte pen packet, for example, typically only the pad alias and two CRC fields are added, incurring a 37 percent overhead. For comparison, the IEEE 802.11 draft standard, which uses a 28-byte MAC frame header, requires 660 percent overhead.

4.2 Implementation Evaluation
4.2.1 Power Consumption

The totals for the power consumption, broken down by subsystem, are presented in Table 1 and are graphically summarized in Fig. 8. The figures indicates the maximum power consumption, which is measured when all subsystems are fully active (100 percent duty cycle). Complete with the video display module, the InfoPad consumes 9.6 Watts, an order of magnitude higher than the ideal power budget.

The external video display, however, was intended to demonstrate the feasibility of compressed full-motion video over a wireless link and to demonstrate the low-power decompression chipset. It is worthwhile to consider the system without the external color video display because it is such a large fraction of the power consumption (3.9 Watts) and since comparable color LCD panels that consume less than one Watt are now commercially available. In the discussion below, the we analyze the *nonvideo* power budget.

Without the video display, the inefficiencies of DC/DC conversion surprisingly dominates the total power dissipation. These standard, off-the-shelf converters typically operate at 60-70 percent efficiency, expending nearly 2.5 Watts (42 percent of the total power) in providing the required supply voltages. The need for efficient DC/DC conversion is clear: A 90 percent efficient voltage conversion, for example, reduces the 2.5 Watts currently dissipated to 0.9 Watts—a 25 percent reduction in the total InfoPad power budget (including add-on LCD screen).

To address this need, a new DC/DC conversion design methodology has been developed, and a proof-of-concept low-voltage prototype IC has been demonstrated which remedies many of the limitations of current-day solutions [10]. Smaller size and lower power systems are achieved through the highest levels of CMOS integration, together with higher operating frequencies and minimum-sized inductor selection. A synchronous rectifier, whose timing is controlled in a low-power DLL, enables nearly ideal soft-switching and efficient conduction, even at ultra-low output voltages. Typical converter efficiencies range from

TABLE 1
BREAKDOWN OF POWER CONSUMPTION BY SUBSYSTEM

Subsystem (TOTAL mW)	Component	Power (mW)
Radio (1700)	Downlink	550
	Uplink	525
	FPGA	600
	EEPROM	0
	A/D Converter	25
Processor Subsystem (1380 max. 330 typical with 7% duty cycle)	PAL	400
	512K SRAM	600
	Processor	120
	Clock Distribution	260
Custom I/O Peripherals (137)		137
Misc. I/O (Pen tablet, speaker, codec, etc.)		500
Text/Graphics Transflective LCD (550)		550
Video Display Module (optional add-on) (3850)	4" Color LCD	2580
	5DC -> 1000AC	425
	5DC -> -8DC	75
	9DC -> 5DC	770
DC/DC Conversion (2416)	9 -> 5	2350
	5 -> -5	30
	5 -> 1.5	36.7
Misc. Support Electronics		75
Debugging Aide (Serial Port UART, LEDS)		75
TOTAL:	w/o Video Display: 6.8 Watts	With Video Display: 9.6 Watts

above 90 percent at full load and 1.5 V and above, to 80 percent at minimum current load and voltages as low as 200 mV.

The second largest power consumer is the wireless link subsystem: including the FPGA interface module (0.6 Watts), the uplink, and downlink radios (0.55 and 0.53 Watts, respectively), and the A/D converter for measuring received signal strength (0.25 Watts). This accounts for 30 percent of the total power dissipation, and the desire to substantially reduce the power dissipation in this subsystem has fueled research both in low-power reconfigurable logic [12], and in low-power RF transceiver design [9].

In [9], a fully integrated, combined RF and baseband CDMA receiver implemented in 0.6 micron CMOS, was described, and the total power consumption was less than 30 milliwatts. It is believed that for an indoor pico-cellular environment, where the transmit power at the portable device can be reduced to 0 dBm, aggressive low-power optimizations and advanced CMOS technology would enable an uplink transmitter to be realized with a power budget of 100-200 milliwatts.

Finally, the I/O processing ASICs that perform the computationally intensive functionality consume only 137 milliwatts—2 percent of the system energy consumption (excluding the external color LCD display). Clearly, in light of the preceding discussion, further optimization of these components for energy-efficient operation will have an insignificant impact on the overall energy consumption.

Table 2 summarizes the projected power budget for an implementation that uses in due to application of new and emerging technologies. With the application of advanced wireless modem design, a dynamic voltage scaled processor subsystem, high-efficiency DC/DC conversion, and new LCD technologies, it is reasonable to expect that the InfoPad multimedia terminal could be implemented with a power budget of 1.3 milliwatts.

4.2.2 Form Factor

Including the battery pack, the InfoPad measures 11 inches by 12 inches, is 1.3 inches thick, and weighs 3.3 pounds (1.1 kg). An open-case view of the InfoPad is shown in Fig. 9. Fig. 10 graphically summarizes the contribution, by subsystem, to the weight and surface area of the device; the weight contributions are detailed in Table 3. The printed circuit board (PCB) required 12 layers to accomodate the required routing between ASICs.

Higher levels of integration is the most obvious way to improve the form factor. Preliminary estimates indicate that by using a 0.35-micron, three-metal CMOS process, it would be possible to combine all of the functions of the I/O-processing ASICs onto a single die, eliminating the 10 of the 11 ASICs. Reducing the number of high-pinout ASICs is beneficial in three ways:

1) Eliminates the weight of the chip packaging;
2) Reduces the surface area and, hence, weight of the PCB board;
3) Simplifies the PCB routing, and allows for a reduction in the number of layers in the board.

Together with the pinout and socket spacing, we estimate that at 30-40 percent of the existing surface area of the PCB, and 20-30 percent of the current weight. Pushing the higher integration between the analog and digital components is needed as well, given the large fraction of the overall board area that is utilized by discrete components.

TABLE 2
APPLICATION OF NEW TECHNOLOGY TO INFOPAD ARCHITECTURE

Subsystem	Current Power Consumption (mW)	New technology	After application of new technology (mW)
Radio subsystem	1700 mW	Eliminate FPGA Full-custom CDMA transceiver with multiuser detection	100 mW uplink (0 dBm output)
			50 mW downlink
10 MIP Processor + Main memory, I/O interfaces, main bus components	340 mW at 7% duty cycle, 5 Volts, 10 MHz (225 mW/MIP for entire subsystem)	Dynamic voltage scaling + energy-optimized ARM processor and subsystem 1.1 - 3.3 Volts 10 MHz, 1-3 mW/MIP	0.7 - 2.1 mW
DC/DC converters	2400 mW at 2.0 Volts 58% efficiency	High-efficiency, low-voltage DC/DC conversion at 1.1 Volts, 90% efficiency	200 mW
LCD panel	550 mW monochrome LCD	state-of-the-art 800x600 color LCD	800 mW
Misc I/O (standard RS-232, debugging ports, etc)	500 mW	fully-optimize & eliminate debugging circuits	10 mW
Custom I/O processing ASICs	150 mW at 2.0 Volts	1.1 Volt, single-chip implementation	50 mW
Approx. Total	5000 mW		1300 mW

5 Conclusion

Optimizing the system architecture and design of the future "personal computer" for mobile wireless access to network based services requires a new relationship between local computation and network access capability. The InfoPad explores a design point where the terminal functions as a remote I/O interface to user-accessible computing, information, and storage resources that are removed from the portable device and are placed on a shared, high-speed backbone network of servers. This optimization allows the minimal cost, weight, and energy consumption.

Results show that, by using an optimized architecture for communications, along with low-power design techniques, high real-time multimedia data can be manipulated while requiring only a small fraction of the overall system power. Future research should focus on the other power consuming components which includes displays, high-efficiency DC/DC conversion, energy-efficient microprocessor de-

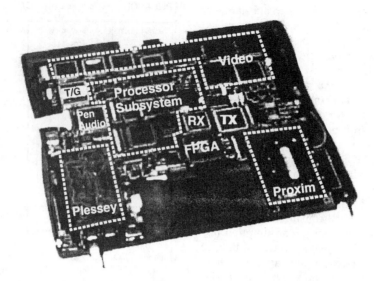

Fig. 9. Interior view of InfoPad terminal.

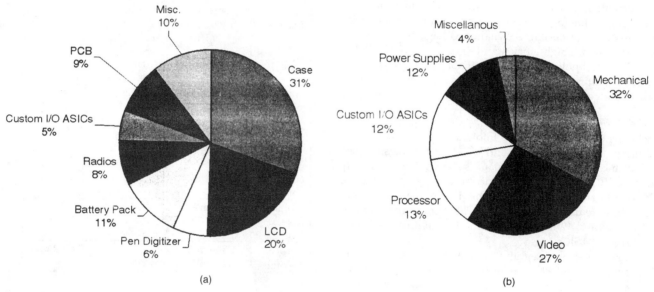

Fig. 10. Breakdown by subsystem of weight (a) and surface area utilization (b).

sign, fully integrated, low-power RF transceivers, and low-power programmable logic technologies.

ACKNOWLEDGMENTS

This work was supported by DARPA contract J-FBI-93-153.

REFERENCES

[1] S. Sheng, A. Chandrakasan, and R.W. Brodersen, "A Portable Multimedia Terminal," *IEEE Comm.*, vol. 30, no. 2, pp. 64-75, Dec. 1992.

[2] S. Narayanaswami et al., "Application and Network Support for InfoPad," *IEEE Personal Comm.*, vol. 3, no. 2, pp. 4-17, Apr. 1996.

[3] B. Barringer, T. Burd, F. Burghardt, A. Burstein, A. Chandrakasan, R. Doering, S. Narayanaswamy, T. Pering, B. Richards, T. Truman, J. Rabaey, and R. Brodersen, "InfoPad: A System Design for Portable Multimedia Access," *Proc. Calgary Wireless '94 Conf.*, July 1994.

[4] R. Han and D.G. Messerschmitt, "Asymptotically-Reliable Transport of Multimedia/Graphics Over Wireless Channels," *Proc. SPIE Multimedia Computing and Networking*, vol. 2,667, pp. 99-110, 1996.

[5] R. Han, "Progressive Delivery and Coding of Interactive Multimedia Over Wireless Channels," PhD dissertation, Univ. of California, Berkeley, ERL Memorandum #UCB/ERL M96/XX.

[6] A. Chandrakasan, "Low-Power Digital CMOS Design," PhD dissertation, Univ. of California, Berkeley, ERL Memorandum #UCB/ERL M94/65.

[7] A. Chandrakasan, A. Burstein, and R.W. Brodersen, "A Low-Power Chipset for a Portable Multimedia I/O Terminal," *IEEE J. Solid-State Circuits*, vol. 29, no. 12, pp. 1,415-1,428, Dec. 1994.

[8] M. Le, F. Burghart, S. Seshan, and J. Rabey, "InfoNet: The Networking Infrastructure for InfoPad," *Digest of Papers, IEEE COMPCON '95: Technologies for the Information Superhighway*, pp. 163-168, Mar. 1995.

[9] S. Sheng, L. Lynn, J. Peroulas, K. Stone, and R.W. Brodersen, "A Low-Power CMOS Chipset for Spread-Spectrum Communications," *Proc. Int'l Solid-State Circuits Conf.*, pp. 346-347, 471, San Francisco, 8-10 Feb. 1996.

TABLE 3
WEIGHT BREAKDOWN BY COMPONENTS

Component(s)	Weight (g)	% of Total	Comment
Battery	170	11%	5- 9V Batteries with connector strip
Case	482	30%	Injection-molded plastic
LCD Panel	326	20%	
Digitizer Board	99	6.2%	
Downlink radio	54	3.4%	Plessey DE6003
Uplink radio	71	4.4%	Proxim RDA 300
Custom I/O Processor ASICs	88	5.5%	15 ASICs, ceramic flat-pack casing
PCB	142	8.7%	12-layer board
Processor Subsystem	43	2.6%	ARM60, EEPROM, address decoder PAL, UART, RJ-45 serial port connector
Miscellaneous	125	7.8%	Connectors, sockets, discrete components, etc.

[10] A. Stratakos, S. Sanders, and R. Brodersen, "A Low-Voltage CMOS DC-DC Converter for a Portable Battery-Operated System," *Proc. 1994 Power Electronics Specialist Conf.*, vol. 1, pp. 619-626, Taipei, Taiwan, June 1994.

[11] T. Burd and R. Brodersen, "Processor Design for Portable Systems," *IEEE J. VLSI Signal Processing*, to appear 1997.

[12] A. Abnous and J. Rabey, "Ultra-Low-Power Domain-Specific Multimedia Processors," *Proc. IEEE VLSI Signal Processing Workshop*, San Francisco, Oct. 1996.

[13] H. Balakrishnan, V. Padmanabhan, S. Seshan, and R. Katz, "A Comparison of Mechanisms for Improving TCP Performance Over Wireless Links," *Computer Comm. Rev. (ACM SIGCOMM '96 Conf.*, vol. 26, no. 4, pp. 256-69, Oct. 1996.

[14] H. Zhang, "Service Disciplines for Guaranteed Performance Service in Packet-Switching Networks," *Proc. IEEE*, vol. 28, no. 10, pp. 1,374-1,396.

[15] S. Lin and D. Costello, *Error Control Coding*, chapter 6. Englewood Cliffs, N.J.: Prentice Hall, 1983.

[16] S. Lin and D. Costello, *Error Control Coding*, chapter 9. Englewood Cliffs, N.J.: Prentice Hall, 1983.

[17] T. Burd and R. Brodersen, "Processor Design for Portable Systems," *J. VLSI Signal Processing*, vol. 13, nos. 2/3, pp. 203-222, Aug./Sept. 1996.

Thomas E. Truman received the BS, MS, and PhD degrees from the University of California, Berkeley, in 1992, 1994, and 1998, respectively. From 1987-1992, he designed embedded systems software for automated test equipment for Pacific Western Systems in Mountain View, California. From 1997-1998, he was with Cadence Berkeley Labs and, since August 1998, he has been a member of the technical staff at Bell Labs in Holmdel, New Jersey. His research interests include hardware/software embedded systems, link- and MAC-layer protocols, formal protocol verification, and system-level design methodologies that span these fields.

Trevor Pering received the BS and MS degrees from the University of California, Berkeley, in 1993 and 1995, respectively. He is now a PhD candidate at UC Berkeley, where he is investigating energy efficient software, including operating systems for dynamic voltage scaled microprocessors.

Roger Doering received the BS degree from Case Western Reserve University in 1973, the MS degree from the University of California, Berkeley, in 1978, and is currently a doctoral candidate at UC Berkeley. His doctoral research involves the design and implementation of a single-chip, silicon micro-machined display ASIC for projection or mounting in a visor unit. He holds three U.S. Patents, with several others in progress. He co-authored the freshman-level text *Electrical Engineering Uncovered*. He is a member of the IEEE.

Robert Brodersen received the BS degree in electrical engineering and mathematics from California State Polytechnical University in 1966, the MS and Engineers degrees from Massachusetts Institute of Technology (MIT) in 1968, and the PhD degree in engineering from MIT in 1972. In 1972, he joined the Texas Instruments Central Research Lab. In 1976, he joined the faculty at the University of California, Berkeley, where he is currently a professor, holding the John R. Whinnery Chair in Electrical Engineering. He has received numerous best paper awards from conferences including ISSCC. He received the W.G. Baker Award for Best IEEE Publication in all areas in 1979. He became a fellow of the IEEE in 1982, received the IEEE Morris Liberman award for "Outstanding Contributions to an Emerging Technology" in 1983, and received Technical Achievement Awards from the IEEE Circuits and Systems Society in 1986 and from the IEEE Signal Processing Society in 1991. He became a member of the National Academy of Engineering in 1988.

A PROCESSOR-COPROCESSOR ARCHITECTURE FOR HIGH END VIDEO APPLICATIONS

Elmar Maas, Dirk Herrmann, Rolf Ernst, Peter Rüffer

Technische Universität Braunschweig, Germany
maas@ida.ing.tu-bs.de

Sieghard Hasenzahl, Martin Seitz

Philips BTS, ICC Weiterstadt, Germany
100726.1616@compuserve.com

ABSTRACT

High end video applications are still implemented in hardware consisting of many components. Integration of these components on one IC is difficult as they are typically low volume products and often customization is also required, e.g. in studio applications. This is easier on the board level than on an integrated system. Using hardware parameters for customization can partly overcome the flexibility problem with additional hardware costs. Low cost can be obtained by a change in the architecture paradigm to a processor-coprocessor system. This, however, requires careful design space exploration since the performance target is beyond current DSP processors while at the same time flexibility is required. The paper presents the application of high level synthesis [1] and novel Hardware-Software Co-Synthesis tools to design space exploration. It is shown that completely different algorithms can be mapped to the same target system at much a lower cost than the current approaches.

1. INTRODUCTION

As of now, *real-time* computing of high end studio video applications requires dedicated hardware. Developing dedicated hardware is a time consuming and thus an expensive task. Moreover a long development time increases the time to market. Once the hardware platform is implemented, it is difficult to make changes, but industrial experience in this low volume market shows that hardware adaptation to customer needs is required in almost every design. Thus, flexibility of the hardware platform is a major design issue. With our design approach we are targeting at both, reducing development time and cost, and improving hardware flexibility. This design approach was employed in an industrial cooperation project. In order to work on relevant examples, we chose two algorithms, each representing one of the two extremes in video signal processing, i.e. demand for computing power and memory bandwidth requirement. Starting with a specification of these algorithms in C-language, we used our Hardware-Software Co-Design environment COSYMA [2] for detailed design space exploration. In order to be able to use the COSYMA system, which was originally developed for designing embedded systems, we defined an architecture template (figure 1) consisting of a processor and a coprocessor which are synchronized with the environment by buffer memories. It is necessary to buffer the fixed rate video I/O to allow for non-trivial processor-coprocessor design solutions. COSYMA, along with its high level synthesis (HLS) system BSS[1] [3], allowed us not only to do useful code optimization but also to efficiently prune the design space to find an

---
[1] Braunschweig Synthesis System

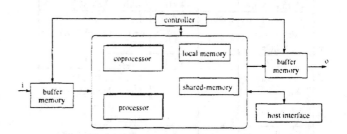

Figure 1: System Architecture Template

optimal architecture for the given signal processing tasks. In the following sections we describe

- our design flow, which is non-standard in the area of signal processing,
- the requirements that had to be met and
- the design space exploration and final system integration.

2. DEVELOPMENT ENVIRONMENT

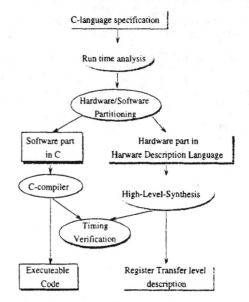

Figure 2: The COSYMA Approach to Hardware-Software Co-Design

Figure 2 shows the COSYMA approach to Hardware-Software Co-Design: A given C-specification with additional timing constraints is analyzed and automatically partitioned into software and hardware parts. For the software part, a C-program is generated which can be handled by standard compilers. The hardware part is translated into a hardware description language on behavioural level which is further processed by our HLS-system. BSS generates an RT-level description which is synthesizeable by commercial systems like the Synopsys Design-Compiler.

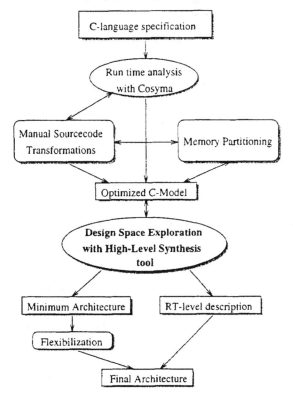

Figure 3: Design Flow in the Project

In this project we mainly used the tools from the hardware path highlighted in fig. 2 and shown in more detail in fig. 3. A signal processing algorithm in C, which was developed by the industrial partner, was evaluated with COSYMA. The requirements concerning run time and memory bandwidth, which will be discussed in detail in the next section, made manual source code transformations inevitable. These transformations were driven by the following goals:

- reducing the number of operations,
- reducing the number of memory accesses and
- increasing potential parallelism.

We executed loop merging for pairs of consecutive loops which performed computations on every pixel of the input image and thus ran over the same index range. This saved the evaluation of loop conditions, and since the results of the first loop could directly be used as an input for the corresponding iteration of the second loop, the memory traffic was reduced. As a side effect, potential parallelism for HLS was increased. This transformation is known from parallel compilers [4] [5]. Some functions, given as abstract behavioural descriptions, were rewritten to save operations: for example, a function for computing the median of five values, originally implemented by bubble-sorting, was replaced by a manually optimized solution which (in this function) reduced the number of comparisons by 56% and swap operations by 30%. Some source code transformations changed the number of memory accesses so that an existing memory partition had to be adapted. After changing the memory partition, restructuring of the source code often was required or considered advantageous. The effects of these transformations on system performance and cost were evaluated by the output of COSYMA's run time analysis as well as from the scheduler of its HLS tool. The optimization steps were iterated until the timing constraints were met and the number of external memories was minimized. The outcome of this iterative process was an optimized C-model, an RT-level description for the coprocessor and a minimum hardware architecture on board level. The latter was manually extended in order to allow special computation modes and to make the board reusable for other purposes.[2]

3. EXAMINING THE SOFTWARE

3.1. Some observations

We selected two applications which are highly relevant in practice: One is a chroma key (blue screen) algorithm which requires an extremely large number of computations and the other is a median noise reducer filter which is characterized by high memory bandwidth. In the beginning, there was little knowledge of the computational power and memory bandwidth requirements of these algorithms, as prior to this project, the complete knowledge of the applications was hidden in a large number of individually developed hardware modules. Therefore, the first step was to extract this knowledge and put it into a software specification. The result was a software description of the operations on the hardware platform which was by no means optimal for a DSP software implementation. It represents one design point and the aim was to prune the design space. An efficient small processor-coprocessor implementation required manual algorithmic transformations. The possible number of transformations is very large and the effect of these transformations on memory bandwidth and performance is not always easy to anticipate. Thus, design space exploration starting with a hardware solution is cumbersome.

To get a first impression, we started with a simplified algorithm to find a potentially useful set of transformations, a first memory architecture and a coarse estimation of the required performance. This first version of the chroma key algorithm was named qad (quick and dirty) since it was still functionally incomplete but from the viewpoint of the software designer it represented a coarse measure for the final version. This algorithm was gradually completed while the design architect started with the design space exploration. Figure 4 shows how the requirements of our two algorithms have changed over a few months. The data on which the diagrams are based has been created by COSYMA's RT-simulator for an LSI SPARC processor as a reference under the assumption that all data and programs were in first level cache. Compilation was done using the GNU gcc from the Free Software Foundation. Starting with the first version of the qad in December 1994, we could reduce the number of operations by almost one third simply by performing code transformations such as loop merging,

---
[2]It may be noted that reusability represents one aspect of flexibility.

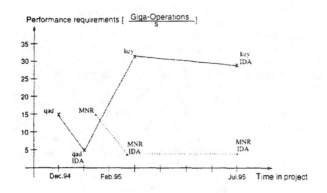

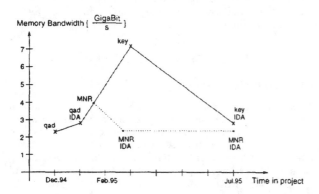

Figure 4: Requirements vs. Project Runtime

partial unrolling etc. The optimizations were done with respect to a processor-coprocessor system and a HLS system in mind, i.e. the original structure of the code was completely destroyed. Both the memory bandwidth and the performance requirements drastically increased when the algorithm was completed in the next quarter, the latter to more than 30 Giga-Operations/s (SPARC-instructions). One reason for this increase was the introduction of parameters for different standards[3] or to take care of potential customer requirements. The required computing effort was not anticipated which indicates that it can be difficult to estimate the performance of an algorithm implemented earlier on a completely different architecture. However, it is important to know the required computing effort to choose an appropriate computing platform.

3.2. Considering a DSP Design

In parallel to our Hardware-Software Co-Design approach we evaluated a software approach. In order to provide as much flexibility as possible, a solution with a programmable DSP would have been favorable at first glance. We decided to take one of the fastest DSPs on the market, the TMS320C80 (MVP) from Texas Instruments [6] [7]. With its four independent DSPs, a master RISC processor and 25 fast 2kByte memory banks on chip, it provides a peak performance of 2 GOPs per second. Unfortunately, the compiler support for the processor is rather poor so that C-code for this processor has to be rewritten in assembly language manually if it has to make use of the performance of the processor. In addition the memory traffic also has

---

[3] e.g. image size, background colour etc.

to be scheduled by hand Nevertheless, we mapped the median noise reducer algorithm to the MVP, which was smaller and easier to parallelize than the chroma key algorithm. Reimplementing the 166 lines of code for the MVP took almost one man month without taking the training period into consideration. Under the assumption of single cycle RAM accesses, data transfers were performed using the full bandwidth of the MVPs 64-bit bus. However, for the noise filter, the resulting optimized code was still 1.35 times slower than required for real-time, assuming a 50 MHz system. It might have been possible to achieve real-time requirements using two MVPs but this would have required repartitioning of the assembly code. In general, what-if analyses for an MVP system with different parameterization of the code as well as different hardware constellations prove to be very time consuming. In contrast, synthesis, which will be described in the next section, was considerably faster and allowed more efficient design space exploration.

4. DESIGNING WITH HLS

Our architecture template (figure 1) consists of a processor and coprocessor. COSYMA's partitioning goal is to place big parts of the algorithm onto the software side, which is executed by the processor, and only smaller and especially timing critical parts on the coprocessor. Assuming the processor is an LSI-SPARC, a speedup of 600(chroma key) or 300(median noise reducer) would be required by partitioning parts to the coprocessor. Taking a faster processor, particularly the MVP, could reduce the required speedups but communication and code generation cannot be done automatically with sufficient efficiency for such a kind of processor. Apart from that we also figured out from the synthesis results that moving relatively small parts of the algorithms to software would not significantly reduce hardware costs for the coprocessor but would increase the memory costs. Eventually the largest part of both algorithms was implemented in the coprocessor.

As a next step we used high level synthesis not only to optimize the mapping of the algorithms to the application specific coprocessor but also to do the design space exploration concerning the board level architecture. Thus, we had two parallel design goals: minimizing the number of computing units (i.e. ALUs, multipliers, etc.) on the chip and finding an optimal number of external memory ports. This optimization problem has been solved iteratively by evaluating the scheduling output of BSS. For example a certain number of ALUs is given to BSS and these ALUs turn out to be utilized concurrently in large parts of the schedule but on the other hand memory ports are idle, the number of ALUs was increased until the ALUs were no longer the bottleneck. Performing memory port optimization required a some more creativity: if the schedule revealed that the memory accesses were the bottleneck, we checked whether the arrays which were accessed could be partitioned to different memory banks.[4] If this was possible the introduction of a new memory port solved the problem. Iteratively applying algorithmic transformations and changing the parameters for HLS we were able to find an optimal board level architecture which suited both the algorithms and had an optimal number of computing units for the chip.

---

[4] Typically, this involved reformulation of the algorithm with loop splitting while loop merging was used for bandwidth reduction.

Category	mnr	key
Run-time [Mcycles]	1.66	1.87
Number of ALUs	9	30
Number of MULs	2	7
Input data stream [MByte/s]	19.77	39.56
Output data stream [MByte/s]	19.77	29.67
Potential I/O-Bandwidth [MByte/s]	416	349
Required on board memory [MByte]	7	6.25

Table 1: Final Results for the Coprocessor

The final results for the coprocessor are shown in table 1. The algorithms work on full PAL television images (720x576 pixels), so the coprocessor must consume less than 2 million clock cycles per image at 50 MHz clock rate if real-time computation has to be achieved:

$$\frac{40ms}{image} * \frac{50 \text{ M cycles}}{s} = 2 \text{ M cycles}$$

The table shows the minimum numbers of ALUs and multipliers, which BSS instantiated in the coprocessor, for real-time computation of the algorithms. Although the chroma key algorithm is computationally more intensive than the median noise reducer, the latter needs 20% more IO-bandwidth for computation. It is also quite interesting to observe that the algorithms need between 500% and 1000% more IO-bandwidth for computing purposes than for getting data on and off the board. The sum of the memory bandwidths for each algorithm in Table 1 is slightly above the values presented in figure 4 because the table shows the physically provided bandwidths whereas the figure is based on bandwidths obtained as a result of simulation. This reveals that the memory ports of our design are almost used to capacity.

5. OPTIMIZED BOARD ARCHITECTURE

As discussed in the last section, the major parts of the algorithms are implemented on the coprocessor, so we were rather free in the processor selection. Finally, we took the Texas Instruments MVP which potentially allows to perform simple algorithms in real-time. This permits the usage of the prototype board and the MVP programming knowledge for other applications – a matter of knowledge reuse. Apart from the main algorithmic features, the board was extended to allow special computation modes: a frame grab mode permits grabbing a frame out of the processed video stream and passing it on to the host processor via a PCI interface. The input buffer memory was implemented as a double buffer in order to allow MVP non real-time computation without input overflow. These extensions increased board flexibility but they almost doubled the number of pins and wires needed to connect the processors to the memories. Since the coprocessor would have to be connected to all memories anyway, the control logic and the switches were integrated onto it, thus, slightly increasing coprocessor cost but saving hundreds of pins and wires.

The final architecture is shown in figure 5. The prototype-board has a size of 185 mm x 311 mm. The total amount of memory on the prototype board sums up to 7 MBytes SRAM plus three 256k x 8 bit FIFO memories. On a commercial board, the SRAMs would be replaced by highly integrated fast SDRAMs which would reduce both board size and power consumption.

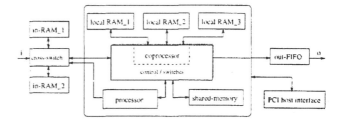

Figure 5: Final Board Architecture

6. CONCLUSIONS

We have shown that by using high level synthesis in the context of Hardware-Software Co-Design for fast design space exploration, a well suited hardware solution for several different applications can be found in a comparatively short period of time. Thus, development costs and time to market could be significantly reduced in future.

An important aspect was the role of flexibility. We found that the flexibility to be able to do "minor" (from the viewpoint of the software developer) changes within the specification could easily double system requirements (section 3.1). With respect to parameterization of the algorithms, which can also be regarded as flexibility, the studying of a competitive DSP solution (section 3.2) revealed that the software approach is not by definition flexible, as well as hardware is not completely inflexible. The implementation of the prototype brought up a third flavour of flexibility, that is the reuse of a design for other than the original purposes. All these manifestations of flexibility had certain impact on the design and eventually increased costs. Flexibility is a relevant factor in a system optimization process and will become more important with an increasing level of integration. It may be noted that designing for flexibility requires a more precise or even formal definition of what it actually is.

7. REFERENCES

[1] D. D. Gajski, N. D. Dutt, A. C-H Wu, and S. Y-L Lin. *High-Level Synthesis - Introduction to Chip and System Design*. Kluwer Academic Publishers, 1992.

[2] R. Ernst, J. Henkel, and Th. Benner. Hardware–software cosynthesis for microcontrollers. *IEEE Design & Test of Computers*, pages 64–75, December 1993.

[3] U. Holtmann and R. Ernst. Combining mbp-speculative computation and loop pipelining in high-level synthesis. In *ED&TC'95*, pages 550–555, 1995.

[4] U. Banerjee. *Loop Parallelization*. Kluwer Academic Publishers, 1994.

[5] D. E. Hudak and S. G. Abraham. *Compiling Parallel Loops for High Performance Computers*. Kluwer Academic Publishers, 1993.

[6] Texas Instruments, Inc. *TMS320C80(MVP) Online Documentation Reference Set*, 1994.

[7] Texas Instruments, Inc. *TMS320C8x System-Level Synopsys.*, 1995.

AUTHOR INDEX

Abid, M., 579
Agarwal, Anant, 625
Babb, Jonathan, 625
Balboni, Alessandro, 395
Battacharyya, Shuvra S., 452
Becker, David, 550
Benini, Luca, 231
Ben-Ismail, Tarek, 366, 579
Benner, T., 18
Benveniste, Albert, 147
Berry, Gérard, 147
Bershteyn, M., 569
Bertin, Patrice, 611
Blumenau, Trevor I., 669
Bogliolo, Alessandro, 231
Bolsens I., 412
Borriello, Gaetano, 350, 358
Boucard, Philippe, 611
Brewer, Forrest, 375
Brodersen, Robert W., 669, 673
Buck, Joseph T., 452, 527
Casley, R., 569
Catthoor, Francky, 278, 465
Changuel, A., 579
Chen, Iue-Shuenn, 661
Chien, C., 569
Chiodo, Massimiliano, 313
Chou, Pai, 350, 358
Coelho Jr., Claudionor N., 544
Corneu, Marco, 389
da Silva, Jr., Julio L., 465
Dahl, Matthew, 625
Danckaert, Koen, 278
Dasdan, Ali, 207
Daveau, Jean-Marc, 125, 366
de Jong, Gjalt, 465
De Man, Hugo, 278, 389, 412
De Micheli, Giovanni, 5, 30, 231, 544
de Veciana, Gustavo, 477
Devadas, Srinivas, 499
Doering, Roger, 673
Edwards, Stephen, 86

Ernst, Rolf, 18, 45, 283, 687
Fernández, Luis Sánchez, 590
Fornaciari, William, 249, 395
Fujita, Masahiro, 506
Gajski, Daniel D., 108, 516
Geurts, Werner, 433
Ghosh, A., 569
Giusto, Paolo, 313
Gong, Jie, 108
Goossen, Gert, 433, 389
Gubian, Paolo, 249
Gupta, Rajesh K., 5, 30, 207, 544
Ha, Soohoi, 452, 527
Hanono, Silvina Zimi, 625
Harel, David, 135
Hasenzahl, Seighard, 687
Henkel, Jörg, 18, 259, 283
Hermann, Dirk, 687
Hines, Ken, 350
Hoki, David M., 625
Hsieh, Harry C., 313
Jacome, Margarida F., 477
Jain, A., 569
Jerraya, Ahmed Amine, 125, 366, 579
Jess, Jochen A. G., 485
Jurecska, Attila, 313
Kadonaga, Anne P., 661
Kalavade, Asawaree, 293, 556
Keutzer, Kurt, 499
Kifli, Augusli, 433
Kloos, Carlos Delgado, 590
Koch, Gernot, 590
Lachover, Hagi, 135
Lanneer, Dirk, 433
Lavagno, Luciano, 86, 313
Layland, James W., 179
Lee, Edward A., 59, 86, 293, 452, 527, 556
Leim, Clifford, 433
Li, Yanbing, 259, 265
Li, Yau-Tsun Steven, 167
Liao, Stan, 499
Lipsie, M., 569

Liu, C. L., 179
Maas, Elmar, 687
Madrid, Natividad Martínez, 590
Malik, Sharad, 167, 222, 506
Mange, Daniel, 643
Marchal, Pierre, 643
Marchioro, Gilberto Fernandes, 125, 366
Mathur, Anmol, 207
Mebane IV, Alfred Holt, 661
Mesman, Bart, 485
Messerschmitt, David G., 527
Meyr, Heinrich, 584
Naamad, Amnon, 135
Narayan, Sanjiv, 108
Ortega, Ross B., 358
Parker, Alice C., 324
Parks, Thomas M., 59
Partridge, Kurt, 350
Paulin, Pierre G., 433
Pering, Trevor, 673
Piguet, Christian, 643
Pnueli, Amir, 135
Politi, Michal, 135
Prakash, Shiv, 324
Raghavan, P. V, 579
Roncin, Didier, 611
Rosenstiel Wolfgang, 590
Rüffer, Peter, 687
Sanchez, Eduardo, 643
Sangiovanni-Vincentelli, Alberto, 86, 313
Schmedake, James R., 661
Sciuto, Donatella, 249, 395
Seawright, Andrew, 375
Seitz, Marin, 687

Shand, Mark, 611
Sherman, Rivi, 135
Shtull-Trauring, Aharon, 135
Silvano, Cristina, 249
Singh, Raj K., 550
Srivastava, Mani B., 669
Stauffer, André, 643
Sudarsanam, Ashok, 506
Tarrodaychik, D., 569
Tell, Stephen G., 550
Tempesti, Gianluca, 643
Tessier, Russel, 625
Thoen, Filip, 389
Tijang, Steve, 499
Timmer, Adwin H., 485
Tiwari, Vivek, 222
Touati, Hervé H., 611
Trakhtenbrot, Mark, 135
Truman, Thomas E., 673
Vahid, Frank, 108, 516
Valderrama, Carlos Alberto, 125, 579
Vallejo, María Luisa López, 590
van Meerbergen, Jef L., 485
Van Praet, Johan, 433
Van Rompaey, K., 412
Verkest, D., 412
Vuillemin, Jean E., 611
Wolf, Wayne, 195, 265, 338
Wolfe, Andrew, 167, 222
Wuytack, Sven, 465
Yamamoto, O., 569
Yen, Ti-Yen, 195
Ykman-Couveur, Chantal, 465
Živojnović, Vojin, 584

SUBJECT INDEX

abstract control types, 350
address generation, 433
algorithms, 207
allocation, 338
analytical cache model for power, 259
application specific software synthesis, 395
application-specific instruction processor (ASIP), 30
architecture mapping, 669
architecture model, 338
ASIC, 661, 669
ASIP, 86, 477, 506
asynchronous machine, 147
automotive electronics, 313
avalanche, 259
average execution rate, 207

base energy cost, 222
behavior tree, 590
binary decision diagrams, 375
binary partitioning, 293

C programming language, 45, 412, 579
cache conflict graph, 167
CCS, 86
Cinderella, 167
clustering, 452
code generation, 135, 485, 499, 506
code optimiatization, 506
code selection, 433
co-design, 590
codesign finite state machine (CFSM), 313
communicating finite state machine, 86
communication synthesis, 45, 125, 366
communication systems, 465
compilation, 433
computing engine, 338
concurrency, communication, 86
concurrent processes, 59
concurrent system modeling, 207
constant-time complexity, 516
control dominated synthesis, 375, 395
Coroutines, 544
correct measurement, 222

co-simulation, 86, 412
COSSAP, 59
Cosyma, 18, 687
co-synthesis, 338
CoWare, 412
CSP, 86
Cx, 18

data flow graph, 477
dataflow process networks, 59, 86
deadline driven scheduling, 179
debugging, 661
decidability, 86
design, 207, 673
design automation, 465
design space exploration, 45, 259
device description, 358
digital signal processor, 499, 506
discrete-event system, 86
distributed embedded computing system, 338
distributed systems, 195
DSP, 506, 556, 687
dynamic power management, 231
dynamic scheduling, 59, 179

embedded computing systems, 338
embedded systems, 108, 195, 207, 249
embryonic electronics, 643
embryonics, 643
emulation, 625
energy, 222, 259
energy conservation, 231
energy management, 231
ES graph, 18
Esterel, 313
estimation, 45, 108, 516
executable specifications, 135
execution model, 59, 389
exploration, 108
extended partitioning, 293

field-programmable gate array (FPGA), 611, 625, 643
firing rule, 59
formal verification, 86
functional decomposition, 135
functional language, 59

global criticality/local phase (GCLP), 293

Hardware C, 544
hardware description languages, 375
hardware extraction loop, 18
hardware size, 516
hardware/software co-design, 108, 125, 249, 338, 366, 395, 516
hardware/software co-simulation, 395, 550, 569, 584
hardware/software co-synthesis, 265
hardware/software interface synthesis, 358
hardware/software partitioning, 5, 18, 30, 45, 86, 293, 412
HardwareC, 18
hardware-software synchronization, 544
heterogeneity, 527
heterogeneous simulation, 556
hierarchical modeling methodology, 108
high-level power estimation, 249
high-level synthesis, 375
HP Design Jet, 661

I/O port allocation, 358
incremental design, 516
instruction cache, 167
instruction format, 433
instruction selection, 499
instruction-level modeling, 222
Instruction-set architecture, 30
integer linear programming, 167, 293
interactive design, 516
interactive rate violation debugging, 207
interface generation, 366
inter-instruction effects, 222

Kahn process networks, 59

latency, 477
LOTOS, 590
low-power CMOS, 673
low-power design, 249, 465

mapping, 412
Markov model, 231

696 SUBJECT INDEX

MATLAB, nondeterminism, 59
memory hierarchy, 265
memory management, 465
memory-mapped I/O, 358
microarchitecture modeling, 167
Mixed integer linear programming, 324
mixed-mode, 527
mobile computing, 673
mode manager, 350
model processes, 350
Modeling, 45
modeling techniques, 207
multiplexer-based FPGA's, 643
multiprogram scheduling, 179

non-deterministic operation, 5

object-oriented programming, 527
optimization methods, 231
optimizations between modules, 278
ordered binary decision diagrams, 643

partitioning, 108, 313
path-based performance estimation, 283
performance, 207
performance analysis, 195
performance attributes, 207
performance estimation, 167
periodic tasks, 195
polymorphism, 59
port-width partitioining, 358
Poseidon, 544
power analysis, 222
power estimation, 249
power manageable components, 231
power-managed networks, 231
power-managed systems, 231
predictive shutdown, 231
priority assignment, 179
process specification languages, 433
processor utilization, 179
program path analysis, 167
programmable active memory (PAM), 611

protocol selection/allocation, 366
protocols, 412
prototyping, 135, 527, 590
Ptolemy, 59, 556

rate analysis, 207
rate constraints, 5, 207
reactive system, 86, 135, 147, 375
real-time, 265
real-time multiprogramming, 179
real-time process scheduling, 395
real-time systems, 195
reconfigurable system, 30, 611
recurrence, 59
recurrence equation, 147
refinement, 108
register allocation, 433
register binding, 485
remote procedure call, 412
resource-constrained scheduling, 477
retargetability, 506
retargetable code generation, 556
robot control system, 669
run-time scheduler, 389

safety, 147
scheduling, 30, 45, 179, 265, 338, 433, 485
SDL, 125
self-repairing FPGA's, 643
self-replicating FPGA's, 643
SHOCK, 412
simulation, 527
software transformations, 259
SOS, 324
SPAM, 506
specification, 108, 673
SpecSyn, 108
SPW, 59
state charts, 86
state encoding, 375
Statecharts, 135
STATEMATE, 135
stochastic control, 231
stream, 59

SUIF, 506
synchronous data flow (SDF), 86, 452
system design, 108, 516
system integration, 673
system level specification, 125
system model, 389
system partitioning, 516
system validation, 313
system-level design, 590
system-level energy optimization, 259, 278

tagged signal model, 86
tagged-token model, 59
target system architecture, 544
task graph, 324
technology description, 338
templates, 433
temporal correctness, 147
theory, 207
timing constraints, 5
TOSCA, 279
tree pattern matching, 433

verification, 45
Verilog, 30
very long instruction word (VLIW), 477
VHDL, 30, 45, 579
VHDL generation, 125
virtual instruments, 569
virtual memories, 465
virtual wires, 625
visual hierarcy, 59
Vulcan, 5

window dependency graph, 477
wireless communication, 673
worst-case execution time (WCET), 167

ABOUT THE AUTHORS

Giovanni De Micheli is professor of electrical engineering, and by courtesy, of computer science at Stanford University. Previously he was with the IBM T.J. Watson Research Center. He holds a degree in nuclear engineering from Politecnico di Milano in 1979 and an M.S. and a Ph.D. degree in Electrical Engineering and Computer Science from the University of California at Berkeley in 1980 and 1983, respectively. His research interests include several aspects of design technologies for integrated circuits and systems, with particular emphasis on synthesis, system-level design, hardware/software co-design and low-power design. He is author of *Synthesis and Optimization of Digital Circuits* and co-author and/or co-editor of four other books. Dr. De Micheli is a Fellow of ACM and IEEE. Currently, he is Editor in Chief of the IEEE Transactions on CAD/ICAS.

Rolf Ernst is professor of electrical engineering at the Technical University of Braunschweig, Germany. His research interests are VLSI CAD and digital circuit design. Previously, he was a member of the technical staff in the CAD and Test Laboratory of AT&T Bell Laboratories and a research assistant at the University of Erlangen, Germany. He holds a diploma in computer science and a Ph.D. in electrical engineering from the University of Erlangen. He is a member of the IEEE, the IEEE Computer Society, and the German GI (Society for Computer Science).

Wayne Wolf received the B.S., M.S., Ph.D. degrees in electrical engineering from Stanford University in 1980, 1981, and 1984, respectively. He was with AT&T Bell Laboratories from 1984 through 1989. He joined the Department of Electrical Engineering at Princeton University in 1989, where he is now a professor. His research interests include hardware/software co-design and embedded computing, multimedia computing systems, and video libraries. He is a fellow of the IEEE and a member of the ACM and SPIE. He is author of *Computers as Components: Principles of Embedded Computing System Design* and *Modern VLSI Design: A Systems Approach*. Also, he is co-series editor of the new Morgan Kaufmann Series in Systems on Silicon.